Strategic Management Process

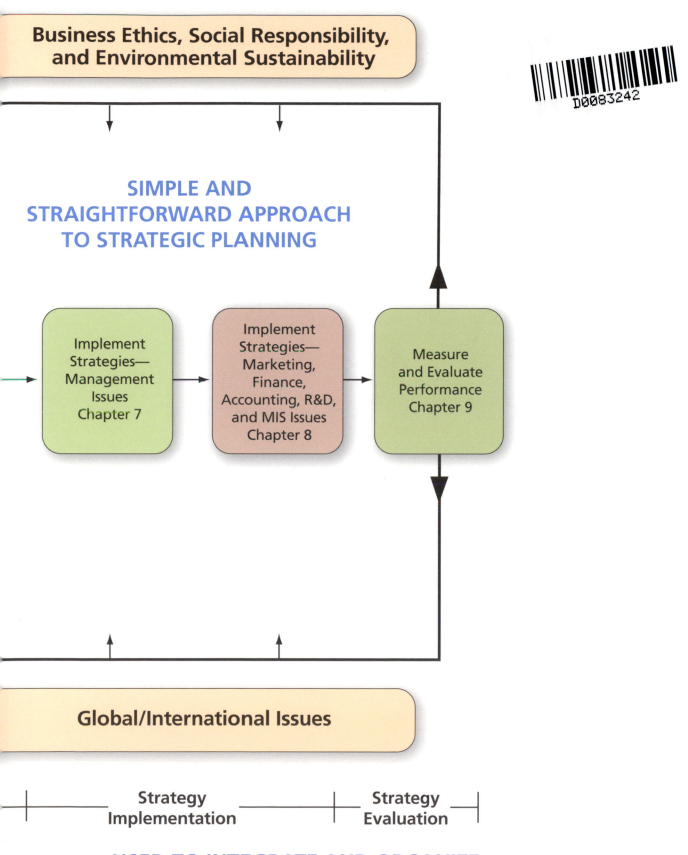

Business Ethics, Social Responsibility, and Environmental Sustainability

SIMPLE AND
STRAIGHTFORWARD APPROACH
TO STRATEGIC PLANNING

Implement Strategies— Management Issues Chapter 7

Implement Strategies— Marketing, Finance, Accounting, R&D, and MIS Issues Chapter 8

Measure and Evaluate Performance Chapter 9

Global/International Issues

Strategy Implementation

Strategy Evaluation

USED TO INTEGRATE AND ORGANIZE
ALL CHAPTERS IN THIS TEXT

Strategic Management
CONCEPTS AND CASES

THIRTEENTH EDITION

Strategic Management

CONCEPTS AND CASES

Fred R. David

Francis Marion University
Florence, South Carolina

Prentice Hall
Boston   Columbus   Indianapolis   New York   San Francisco   Upper Saddle River
Amsterdam   Cape Town   Dubai   London   Madrid   Milan   Munich   Paris   Montreal   Toronto
Delhi   Mexico City   Sao Paulo   Sydney   Hong Kong   Seoul   Singapore   Taipei   Tokyo

Editorial Director: Sally Yagan
Editor in Chief: Eric Svendsen
Acquisitions Editor: Kim Norbuta
Product Development Manager: Ashley Santora
Editorial Project Manager: Claudia Fernandes
Editorial Assistant: Meg O'Rourke
Director of Marketing: Patrice Lumumba Jones
Marketing Manager: Nikki Ayana Jones
Marketing Assistant: Ian Gold
Senior Managing Editor: Judy Leale
Associate Production Project Manager:
  Ana Jankowski
Operations Specialist: Ilene Kahn
Art Director: Steve Frim
Text and Cover Designer: Judy Allan

Manager, Visual Research: Beth Brenzel
Manager, Rights and Permissions: Zina Arabia
Image Permission Coordinator: Cynthia Vincenti
Manager, Cover Visual Research & Permissions:
  Karen Sanatar
Cover Art: Vetta TM Collection Dollar Bin:
  istockphoto
Editorial Media Project Manager: Ashley Lulling
Production Media Project Manager: Lisa Rinaldi
Full-Service Project Management: Thistle Hill
  Publishing Services, LLC
Composition: Integra Software Services, Ltd.
Printer/Binder: Courier/Kendallville
Cover Printer: Lehigh-Phoenix Color/Hagerstown
Text Font: 10/12 Times

Credits and acknowledgments borrowed from other sources and reproduced, with permission, in this textbook appear on appropriate page within text.

Many of the designations by manufacturers and seller to distinguish their products are claimed as trademarks. Where those designations appear in this book, and the publisher was aware of a trademark claim, the designations have been printed in initial caps or all caps.

Library of Congress Cataloging-in-Publication Data
David, Fred R.
  Strategic management: concepts and cases / Fred R. David.—13th ed.
    p. cm.
  Includes bibliographical references and index.
  ISBN-13: 978-0-13-612098-8 (casebound)
  ISBN-10: 0-13-612098-9 (casebound)
  1. Strategic planning.   2. Strategic planning—Case studies.   I. Title.
HD30.28.D385 2011
658.4'012—dc22

2009052036

10 9 8 7 6 5 4 3 2 1

Prentice Hall
is an imprint of

PEARSON

www.pearsonhighered.com

ISBN 10:   0-13-612098-9
ISBN 13: 978-0-13-612098-8

To Joy, Forest, Byron, and Meredith—
my wife and children—
for their encouragement and love.

Brief Contents

Contents

Part 3
Strategy Implementation 210

Cases

Preface

Why the Need for This New Edition?

The global economic recession has created a business world today that is quite different and more complex than it was just two years ago when the previous edition of this text was published. Thousands of businesses have vanished, and consumers have become extremely price sensitive and oftentimes reluctant purchasers of products and services. Very tight credit markets, high unemployment, and millions of new entrepreneurs have also changed the business landscape. Business firms that have survived the last three years of global economic turmoil are today leaner and meaner than ever before. Gaining and sustaining competitive advantage is harder than ever. Social networking and e-commerce have altered marketing to its core since the prior edition. This new edition reveals how to conduct effective strategic planning in this new world order.

Since the prior edition, thousands of liquidations, bankruptcies, divestitures, mergers, alliances, and partnerships captured the news. Corporate scandals highlighted the need for improved business ethics and corporate disclosure of financial transactions. Downsizing, rightsizing, and reengineering contributed to a permanently altered corporate landscape. Thousands of firms began doing business globally, and thousands more closed their global operations. Thousands prospered, and yet thousands failed in the last two years as the global recession spared few. Long-held competitive advantages have eroded as new ones formed. This new edition captures the complexity of this world business environment.

Both the challenges and opportunities facing organizations of all sizes today are greater than ever. There is less room than ever for error in the formulation and implementation of a strategic plan. This new edition provides a systematic effective approach for developing a clear strategic plan, even in the worst of times. Changes made in this edition are aimed squarely at illustrating the effect of new business concepts and techniques on strategic-management theory and practice.

Due to the magnitude of recent changes affecting companies, cultures, and countries, every page of this edition has been updated. The first edition of this text was published in 1986. Since then, this textbook has grown to be one of the most widely read strategic-management books, perhaps the most widely read, in the world. This text is now published in nine languages.

What Is New in This Edition?

This edition includes exciting new features, changes, and content designed to position this text as the clear leader and best choice for teaching strategic management. Here is a summary of what is new in this edition:

- A new Chapter 10, "Business Ethics/Social Responsibility/Environmental Sustainability"; there is extensive new coverage of ethics and sustainability because this text emphasizes that "good ethics is good business." Unique to strategic-management texts, the natural environment discussion is strengthened in this edition to promote and encourage firms to conduct operations in an environmentally sound manner. Respect for the natural environment has become an important concern for consumers, companies, society, and AACSB-International.
- A new Chapter 11, "Global/International Issues"; there is extensive new coverage of cultural and conceptual strategic-management differences across countries. Doing business globally has become a necessity, rather than a luxury in most industries because nearly all strategic decisions today are affected by global

issues and concerns. Every case company in this edition does business globally, providing students ample opportunity to evaluate and consider international aspects of doing business.

- A new boxed insert at the beginning of each chapter showcases a company that has done exceptionally well in the 2008–2010 global economic recession and reveals their strategy.
- Hundreds of new examples abound in every chapter.
- A new cohesion case on McDonald's Corporation (2010); this is one of the most successful, well-known, and best managed global companies in the world; students apply strategy concepts to McDonald's at the end of each chapter through new Assurance of Learning Exercises.
- Thirty-two new tables in the chapters to better capture key strategic-management concepts.
- A revised comprehensive strategic management model to reflect the new chapters.
- Extensive new narrative on strategic management theory and concepts in every chapter to illustrate the new business world order.
- On average, 15 new review questions at the end of each chapter.
- Forty-eight new Assurance of Learning Exercises at the end of chapters that apply chapter concepts; the exercises prepare students for strategic-management case analysis.
- Twenty-four new color photographs bring the edition to life and illustrate companies/concepts.
- All new current readings at the end of each chapter; new research and theories of seminal thinkers in strategy development, such as Ansoff, Chandler, Porter, Hamel, Prahalad, Mintzberg, and Barney are provided in the chapters; practical aspects of strategic management, however, are still center stage and the trademark of this text below.
- Twenty-nine new cases—grouped by industry; great mix of profit/nonprofit, large/small, and manufacturing/service organizations; all the cases have a 2009–2010 time setting; all the cases are "comprehensive" in the sense that each focuses on multiple business functions, rather than addressing one particular business problem or issue; all the cases are undisguised and feature real organizations in real industries using real names and real places (nothing is fictitious in any case); all the cases feature an organization "undergoing strategic change," thus offering students up-to-date issues to evaluate and consider; all the cases are written in a lively, concise writing style that captures the reader's interest and establishes a time setting, usually in the opening paragraph; all the cases provide excellent quantitative information such as numbers, ratios, percentages, dollar values, graphs, statistics, and maps so students can prepare a more specific, rational, and defensible strategic plan for the organization; all the cases provide excellent information about the industry and competitors.

This edition continues to offer many special time-tested features and content that have made this text so successful for over 20 years. Historical trademarks of this text that are strengthened in this edition are described below.

Chapters: Time-Tested Features

- This text meets AACSB-International guidelines that support a practitioner orientation rather than a theory/research approach. It offers a skills-oriented approach to developing a vision and mission statement; performing an external audit; conducting an internal assessment; and formulating, implementing, and evaluating strategies.
- The author's writing style is concise, conversational, interesting, logical, lively, and supported by numerous current examples throughout.

- A simple, integrative strategic-management model appears in all chapters and on the inside front cover of the text. This model is widely used for strategic planning among consultants and companies worldwide. One reviewer said, "One thing I have admired about David's text is that he follows the fundamental sequence of strategy formulation, implementation, and evaluation. There is a basic flow from mission/purposes to internal/external environmental scanning to strategy development, selection, implementation, and evaluation. This has been, and continues to be, a hallmark of the David text. Many other strategy texts are more disjointed in their presentation, and thus confusing to the student, especially at the undergraduate level."

- A Cohesion Case follows Chapter 1 and is revisited at the end of each chapter. This Cohesion Case allows students to apply strategic-management concepts and techniques to a real organization as chapter material is covered, which readies students for case analysis in the course.

- End-of-chapter Assurance of Learning Exercises effectively apply concepts and techniques in a challenging, meaningful, and enjoyable manner. Eighteen exercises apply text material to the Cohesion Case; 10 apply textual material to a college or university; another 10 exercises send students into the business world to explore important strategy topics. The exercises are relevant, interesting, and contemporary.

- There is excellent pedagogy in this text, including notable quotes and objectives to open each chapter, and key terms, current readings, discussion questions, and experiential exercises to close each chapter.

- There is excellent coverage of strategy formulation issues, such as business ethics, global versus domestic operations, vision/mission, matrix analysis, partnering, joint venturing, competitive analysis, governance, and guidelines for conducting an internal/external strategy assessment.

- There is excellent coverage of strategy implementation issues such as corporate culture, organizational structure, outsourcing, marketing concepts, financial analysis, and business ethics.

- A systematic, analytical approach is presented in Chapter 6, including matrices such as the SWOT, BCG, IE, GRAND, SPACE, and QSPM.

- The chapter material is again published in a four-color format.

- A chapters-only paperback version of the text is available.

- Custom-case publishing is available whereby an instructor can combine chapters from this text with cases from a variety of sources or select any number of cases desired from the 29 cases in the full text.

- For the chapter material, the outstanding ancillary package includes a comprehensive *Instructor's Manual,* computerized test bank, and PowerPoints.

*The comprehensive strategic-management model is displayed on the inside front cover of the text. At the start of each chapter, the section of the comprehensive strategy model covered in that chapter is highlighted and enlarged so students can see the focus of each chapter in the basic unifying comprehensive model.

*The Case Information Matrix and Case Description Matrix provided in the preface reveal (1) topical areas emphasized in each case and (2) contact and location information for each case company. These matrices provide suggestions on how the cases deal with concepts in the 11 chapters.

Cases: Time-Tested Features

- This edition contains the most current set of cases in any strategic-management text on the market. All cases include year-end 2009 financial data and information.

- The cases focus on well-known firms in the news making strategic changes. All cases are undisguised, and most are exclusively written for this text to reflect current strategic-management problems and practices. These are all "student-friendly" cases.

- Organized conveniently by industry (usually two competing firms per industry), the cases feature a great mix of small business, international, and not-for-profit firms.
- All cases have been class tested to ensure that they are interesting, challenging, and effective for illustrating strategic-management concepts.
- All the cases provide complete financial information about the firm, as well as an organizational chart and a vision and mission statement for the organization if those were available.
- Customized inclusion of cases to comprise a tailored text is available to meet the special needs of some professors.
- For the cases, the outstanding ancillary package includes an elaborate *Case Solutions Manual* and support from the www.strategyclub.com Web site.
- All of the cases are comprehensive in the sense that each provides a full description of the firm and its operations rather than focusing on one issue or problem such as a plant closing. Each case thus lends itself to students preparing a three-year strategic plan for the firm.

Special Note to Students

Welcome to strategic management. This is a challenging and exciting capstone course that will allow you to function as the owner or chief executive officer of different organizations. Your major task in this course will be to make strategic decisions and to justify those decisions through oral and written communication. Strategic decisions determine the future direction and competitive position of an enterprise for a long time. Decisions to expand geographically or to diversify are examples of strategic decisions.

Strategic decision-making occurs in all types and sizes of organizations, from Exxon and IBM to a small hardware store or small college. Many people's lives and jobs are affected by strategic decisions, so the stakes are very high. An organization's very survival is often at stake. The overall importance of strategic decisions makes this course especially exciting and challenging. You will be called upon in this course to demonstrate how your strategic decisions could be successfully implemented.

In this course, you can look forward to making strategic decisions both as an individual and as a member of a team. No matter how hard employees work, an organization is in real trouble if strategic decisions are not made effectively. Doing the right things (effectiveness) is more important than doing things right (efficiency). For example, many American newspapers are faltering as consumers increasingly switch to interactive media for news.

You will have the opportunity in this course to make actual strategic decisions, perhaps for the first time in your academic career. Do not hesitate to take a stand and defend specific strategies that you determine to be the best, based on tools and concepts in this textbook. The rationale for your strategic decisions will be more important than the actual decision, because no one knows for sure what the best strategy is for a particular organization at a given point in time. This fact accents the subjective, contingency nature of the strategic-management process.

Use the concepts and tools presented in this text, coupled with your own intuition, to recommend strategies that you can defend as being most appropriate for the organizations that you study. You will also need to integrate knowledge acquired in previous business courses. For this reason, strategic management is often called a capstone course; you may want to keep this book for your personal library.

A trademark of this text is its practitioner and applications orientation. This book presents techniques and content that will enable you to actually formulate, implement, and evaluate strategies in all kinds of profit and nonprofit organizations. The end-of-chapter Assurance of Learning Exercises allow you to apply what you've read in each chapter to the new McDonald's Cohesion Case and to your own university.

Definitely visit the Strategic Management Club Online at www.strategyclub.com. The templates and links there will save you time in performing analyses and will make your work look professional. Work hard in this course and have fun. Good luck!

Acknowledgments

Many persons have contributed time, energy, ideas, and suggestions for improving this text over 12 editions. The strength of this text is largely attributed to the collective wisdom, work, and experiences of strategic-management professors, researchers, students, and practitioners. Names of particular individuals whose published research is referenced in this edition of this text are listed alphabetically in the Name Index. To all individuals involved in making this text so popular and successful, I am indebted and thankful.

Many special persons and reviewers contributed valuable material and suggestions for this edition. I would like to thank my colleagues and friends at Auburn University, Mississippi State University, East Carolina University, and Francis Marion University. I have served on the management faculty at all these universities. Scores of students and professors at these schools helped shape the development of this text. Many thanks go to the following 15 reviewers of the prior edition whose comments shaped this thirteenth edition:

Moses Acquaah, The University of North Carolina at Greensboro

Charles M. Byles, Virginia Commonwealth University

Charles J. Capps III, Sam Houston State University

Neil Dworkin, Western Connecticut State University

John Frankenstein, Brooklyn College/City University of New York

Bill W. Godair, Landmark College, Community College of Vermont

Carol Jacobson, Purdue University

Susan M. Jensen, University of Nebraska at Kearney

Thomas E. Kulik, Washington University at St. Louis

Jerrold K. Leong, Oklahoma State University

Trina Lynch-Jackson, Indiana University NW, Purdue Calumet, Calumet College of St. Joseph, Indiana Wesleyan University

Raza Mir, William Paterson University

Thomas W. Sharkey, University of Toledo

Jill Lynn Vihtelic, Saint Mary's College

Michael W. Wakefield, Colorado State University–Pueblo

Individuals who develop cases for the North American Case Research Association Meeting, the Midwest Society for Case Research Meeting, the Eastern Case Writers Association Meeting, the European Case Research Association Meeting, and Harvard Case Services are vitally important for continued progress in the field of strategic management. From a research perspective, writing strategic management cases represents a valuable scholarly activity among faculty. Extensive research is required to structure business policy cases in a way that exposes strategic issues, decisions, and behavior. Pedagogically, strategic management cases are essential for students in learning how to apply concepts, evaluate situations, formulate a "game plan," and resolve implementation problems. Without a continuous stream of updated business policy cases, the strategic-management course and discipline would lose much of its energy and excitement.

Professors who teach this course supplement lecture with simulations, guest speakers, experiential exercises, class projects, and/or outside readings. Case analysis, however, is typically the backbone of the learning process in most strategic-management courses across the country. Case analysis is almost always an integral part of this course.

Analyzing strategic-management cases gives students the opportunity to work in teams to evaluate the internal operations and external issues facing various organizations and to craft strategies that can lead these firms to success. Working in teams gives students practical experience solving problems as part of a group. In the business world, important decisions are generally made within groups; strategic-management students learn to deal with overly aggressive group members and also timid, noncontributing group members. This experience is valuable as strategic-management students near graduation and soon enter the working world a full time.

Students can improve their oral and written communication skills as well as their analytical and interpersonal skills by proposing and defending particular courses of action for the case companies. Analyzing cases allows students to view a company, its competitors, and its industry concurrently, thus simulating the complex business world. Through case analysis, students learn how to apply concepts, evaluate situations, formulate strategies, and resolve implementation problems. Instructors typically ask students to prepare a three-year strategic plan for the firm. Analyzing a strategic-management case entails students applying concepts learned across their entire business curriculum. Students gain experience dealing with a wide range of organizational problems that impact all the business functions.

The following people wrote cases that were selected for inclusion in this thirteenth edition. These persons helped develop the most current compilation of cases ever assembled in a strategic-management text:

Dr. Alen Badal, The Union Institute

Dr. Mernoush Banton, Florida International University

Dr. Rochelle R. Brunson, Baylor University

Dr. John J. Burbridge, Elon University

Dr. Charles M. Byles, Virginia Commonwealth University

Dr. Donald Crooks, Wagner College

Forest R. David, MBA, Francis Marion University

Dr. James Harbin, Texas A&M University–Texarkana

Dr. Randall D. Harris, California State University–Stanislaus

Dr. Linda Herkenhoff, Saint Mary's College

Dr. Patricia Humphrey, Texas A&M University–Texarkana

Dr. Hamid H. Kazeroony, William Penn University

Dr. Joe W. Leonard, Miami University

Dr. Joanne Mack, Alverno College

Dr. Ellen Mansfield, La Salle University

Dr. Vijaya Narapareddy, University of Denver

Dr. Carol V. Pope, Alverno College

Dr. Lori Radulovich, Baldwin-Wallace College

Dr. John Ross III, Southwest Texas State University–San Marcos

Sherry Ross, Southwest Texas State University–San Marcos

Dr. Amit J. Shah, Frostburg State University

Dr. Greg Stone, Regent University

Dr. Sharynn M. Tomlin, Angelo State University

Mary Vradelis, Consultant in Berkeley, California

Dr. Anne M. Walsh, La Salle University

Scores of Prentice Hall employees and salespersons have worked diligently behind the scenes to make this text a leader in strategic management. I appreciate the continued hard work of all those professionals, such as Sally Yagan, Kim Norbuta, Claudia Fernandes, Ann Pulido, and Ana Jankowski.

I also want to thank you, the reader, for investing the time and effort to read and study this text. It will help you formulate, implement, and evaluate strategies for any organization with which you become associated. I hope you come to share my enthusiasm for the rich subject area of strategic management and for the systematic learning approach taken in this text.

Finally, I want to welcome and invite your suggestions, ideas, thoughts, comments, and questions regarding any part of this text or the ancillary materials. Please call me at 910-612-5343, fax me at 910-579-5132, e-mail me at freddavid9@gmail.com, or write me at the School of Business, Francis Marion University, Florence, SC 29501. I sincerely appreciate and need your input to continually improve this text in future editions. Your willingness to draw my attention to specific errors or deficiencies in coverage or exposition will especially be appreciated.

Thank you for using this text.

Fred R. David

About the Author

Dr. Fred R. David is the sole author of two mainstream strategic-management textbooks: (1) *Strategic Management: Concepts and Cases,* and (2) *Strategic-Management Concepts.* These texts have been on a two-year revision cycle since 1986 when the first edition was published. They are among the best if not the best-selling strategic-management textbooks in the world and have been used at more than 500 colleges and universities, including Harvard University, Duke University, Carnegie-Mellon University, Johns Hopkins University, the University of Maryland, University of North Carolina, University of Georgia, San Francisco State University, University of South Carolina, and Wake Forest University.

This textbook has been translated and published in Chinese, Japanese, Farsi, Spanish, Indonesian, Indian, Thai, and Arabic and is widely used across Asia and South America. It is the best-selling strategic-management textbook in Mexico, China, Peru, Chile, Japan, and number two in the United States. Approximately 90,000 students read Dr. David's textbook annually as well as thousands of businesspersons. The book has led the field of strategic management for more than a decade in providing an applications/practitioner approach to the discipline.

A native of Whiteville, North Carolina, Fred David received a BS degree in mathematics and an MBA from Wake Forest University before being employed as a bank manager with United Carolina Bank. He received a PhD in Business Administration from the University of South Carolina, where he majored in management. Currently the TranSouth Professor of Strategic Management at Francis Marion University (FMU) in Florence, South Carolina, Dr. David has also taught at Auburn University, Mississippi State University, East Carolina University, the University of South Carolina, and the University of North Carolina at Pembroke. He is the author of 152 referred publications, including 40 journal articles and 55 proceedings publications. David has articles published in such journals as *Academy of Management Review*, *Academy of Management Executive*, *Journal of Applied Psychology*, *Long Range Planning*, and *Advanced Management Journal*.

Dr. David received a Lifetime Honorary Professorship Award from the Universidad Ricardo Palma in Lima, Peru. He delivered the keynote speech at the twenty-first Annual Latin American Congress on Strategy hosted by the Centrum School of Business in Peru. Dr. David recently delivered an eight-hour Strategic Planning Workshop to the faculty at Pontificia Universidad Catolica Del in Lima, Peru, and an eight-hour Case Writing/ Analyzing Workshop to the faculty at Utah Valley State College in Orem, Utah. He has received numerous awards, including FMU's Board of Trustees Research Scholar Award, the university's Award for Excellence in Research given annually to the best faculty researcher on campus, and the Phil Carroll Advancement of Management Award, given annually by the Society for the Advancement of Management (SAM) to a management scholar for outstanding contributions in management research. He recently gave the graduation commencement speech at Troy University.

Case Information Matrix

Case Company	Stock Symbol	Headquarters	Web Site Address	#Employees	2008 Revenues in $millions
Cohesion Case					
McDonald's Corp.	MCD	Oak Brook, IL	www.mcdonalds.com	400,000	23,522
SERVICE FIRMS					
Hospitality/Entertainment					
1. Walt Disney Co.	DIS	Burbank, CA	www.disney.com	150,000	37,843
2. Merryland Amusement Park		Kansas City, MO		100	0.890
Airlines					
3. JetBlue Airways	JBLU	Forest Hills, NY	www.jetblue.com	10,047	3,388
4. AirTran Airways	AAI	Orlando, FL	www.airtran.com	7,850	2,552
Retail Stores					
5. Family Dollar Stores	FDO	Charlotte, NC	www.familydollar.com	25,000	6,983
6. Wal-Mart Stores	WMT	Bentonville, AR	www.walmartstores.com	2.1M	405,607
7. Whole Foods Market	WFMI	Austin, TX	www.wholefoodsmarket.com	46,800	7,953
8. Macy's	M	Cincinnati, Ohio	www.macysinc.com	167,000	24,892
Internet Based					
9. Yahoo	YHOO	Sunnyvale, CA	www.yahoo.com	13,600	7,208
10. eBay Inc.	EBAY	San Jose, CA	www.ebay.com	16,200	8,541
Financial					
11. Wells Fargo	WFC	San Francisco, CA	www.wellsfargo.com	272,800	52,389
Restaurants					
12. Krispy Kreme	KKD	Winston-Salem, NC	www.krispykreme.com	2,700	383
13. Starbucks Corporation	SBUX	Seattle, WA	www.starbucks.com	176,000	10,383
Nonprofit					
14. The United States Postal Service -		Washington, DC	www.usps.com	764,000	75,000
15. Amtrak (NRPC) -		Washington, DC	www.amtrak.com	19,000	2,400
16. Goodwill Industries		San Francisco, CA of San Francisco, San Mateo and Marin Counties	www.sfgoodwill.org/storeLocations2.aspx	500	28.1
MANUFACTURING					
Transportation					
17. Harley-Davidson	HOG	Milwaukee, WI	www.harlety-davidson.com	10,100	5,971
18. Ford Motor	FORD	Dearborn, MI	www.ford.com	213,000	146,277
Food					
19. Kraft Foods	KFT	Norfield, IL	www.kraft.com	98,000	42,201
20. Hershey Foods	HSY	Hershey, PA	www.hersheys.com	12,800	5,132

(continued)

Case Information Matrix   (continued)

Case Company	Stock Symbol	Headquarters	Web Site Address	#Employees	2008 Revenues in $millions
Personal Care					
21. Johnson & Johnson	JNJ	New Brunswick, NJ	www.jnj.com	118,700	63,747
22. Avon Products	AVP	New York, NY	www.avon.com	42,000	10,690
Beverage					
23. Molson Coors	TAP	Denver, CO	www.molsoncoors.com	14,000	4,774
Brewing					
24. PepsiCo	PEP	Purchase, NY	www.pepsico.com	198,000	43,251
Health Care					
25. Pfizer	PFE	New York, NY	www.pfizer.com	81,800	48,296
26. Merck	MRK	Whitehouse Station, NJ	www.merck.com	55,200	23,850
Sports					
27. Nike	NKE	Beaverton, OR	www.nike.com	32,500	18,627
28. Callaway Golf	ELY	Carlsbad, CA	www.callawaygolf.com	2,700	1,117
Energy					
29. Chevron	CVX	San Ramon, CA	www.chevron.com	67,000	273,005

Case Description Matrix

Topical Content Areas (Y = Yes and N = No)

	1	2	3	4	5	6	7	8	9	10	11	12	13	14
Cohesion Case – McDonald's Corp.	Y	Y	Y	Y	Y	Y	Y	Y	Y	N	N	Y	Y	N
Service Firms														
Hospitality/Entertainment														
1. Walt Disney Company	Y	Y	Y	Y	Y	Y	Y	Y	Y	N	N	Y	Y	N
2. Merryland Amusement Park	Y	Y	Y	Y	Y	Y	Y	Y	Y	Y	Y	Y	Y	N
Airlines														
3. JetBlue Airways	Y	N	Y	Y	Y	Y	Y	Y	Y	Y	Y	N	Y	N
4. AirTran Airways	Y	Y	Y	Y	Y	Y	Y	Y	Y	Y	Y	Y	Y	N
Retail Stores														
5. Family Dollar Stores	Y	Y	Y	N	Y	Y	Y	Y	Y	Y	N	N	Y	N
6. Wal-Mart Stores	Y	Y	Y	N	Y	Y	Y	Y	Y	Y	N	N	Y	N
7. Whole Foods Market	Y	Y	Y	N	Y	Y	Y	Y	Y	Y	N	N	Y	N
8. Macy's	Y	Y	Y	N	Y	Y	Y	Y	Y	Y	N	N	Y	N
Internet Based														
9. Yahoo	Y	Y	Y	N	Y	Y	Y	Y	Y	Y	Y	Y	Y	N
10. eBay Inc.	Y	Y	Y	Y	Y	Y	Y	Y	Y	Y	N	Y	Y	N
Financial														
11. Wells Fargo	Y	Y	Y	Y	Y	Y	Y	Y	Y	N	N	Y	Y	Y
Restaurants														
12. Krispy Kreme	Y	Y	N	Y	Y	Y	Y	Y	Y	Y	N	N	Y	N
13. Starbucks Corporation	Y	Y	Y	Y	Y	Y	Y	Y	Y	Y	Y	N	Y	Y
Nonprofit														
14. The United States Postal Service	Y	Y	N	N	Y	Y	Y	Y	Y	Y	N	Y	Y	N
15. Amtrak	Y	N	Y	Y	Y	Y	Y	Y	Y	Y	Y	Y	Y	N
16. Goodwill Industries of San Francisco, San Mateo and Marin Counties	Y	N	Y	Y	Y	Y	Y	Y	Y	Y	Y	Y	Y	N
Manufacturing Firms														
Transportation														
17. Harley-Davidson	Y	Y	Y	Y	Y	Y	Y	Y	Y	Y	N	N	Y	N
18. Ford Motor	Y	Y	Y	Y	Y	Y	Y	Y	Y	Y	N	Y	Y	N
Food														
19. Kraft Foods	Y	Y	Y	N	Y	Y	Y	Y	Y	Y	N	Y	Y	N
20. Hershey Foods	Y	Y	Y	Y	Y	Y	Y	Y	Y	Y	Y	Y	Y	N
Personal Care														
21. Johnson & Johnson	Y	Y	Y	N	Y	Y	Y	Y	Y	Y	Y	Y	Y	N
22. Avon Products	Y	Y	Y	N	Y	Y	Y	Y	Y	Y	N	N	Y	N
Beverage														
23. Molson Coors Brewing	Y	Y	Y	Y	Y	Y	Y	Y	Y	Y	Y	Y	Y	Y
24. PepsiCo	Y	N	Y	N	Y	Y	Y	Y	Y	N	N	Y	Y	N
Health Care														
25. Pfizer	Y	Y	Y	Y	Y	Y	Y	Y	Y	Y	N	N	Y	Y
26. Merck	Y	Y	Y	Y	Y	Y	Y	Y	Y	Y	N	Y	Y	N

(continued)

Case Description Matrix   (continued)

	1	2	3	4	5	6	7	8	9	10	11	12	13	14
Sports														
27. Nike	Y	N	Y	N	Y	Y	Y	Y	Y	N	Y	Y	Y	N
28. Callaway Golf Company	Y	Y	Y	Y	Y	Y	Y	Y	Y	N	N	Y	Y	N
Energy														
29. Chevron	Y	Y	Y	Y	Y	N	Y	Y	Y	Y	Y	Y	Y	N

1. Year-end 2006 Financial Statements Included?
2. Is Organizational Chart Included?
3. Does Company Do Business Outside the United States?
4. Is a Vision or Mission Statement Included?
5. E-Commerce Issues Included?
6. Natural Environment Issues Included?
7. Strategy Formulation Emphasis?
8. Strategy Implementation Included?
9. By-Segment Financial Data Included?
10. Firm Has Declining Revenues?
11. Firm Has Declining Net Income?
12. Discussion of Competitors is Provided?
13. Case Appears in Text for the First Time Ever?
14. Is Firm Headquartered Outside the United States?

Strategic Management

CONCEPTS AND CASES

CHAPTER 1
The Nature of Strategic Management

CHAPTER OBJECTIVES

After studying this chapter, you should be able to do the following:

1. Describe the strategic-management process.

2. Explain the need for integrating analysis and intuition in strategic management.

3. Define and give examples of key terms in strategic management.

4. Discuss the nature of strategy formulation, implementation, and evaluation activities.

5. Describe the benefits of good strategic management.

6. Discuss the relevance of Sun Tzu's *The Art of War* to strategic management.

7. Discuss how a firm may achieve sustained competitive advantage.

Assurance of Learning Exercises

Assurance of Learning Exercise 1A

Gathering Strategy Information

Assurance of Learning Exercise 1B

Strategic Planning for My University

Assurance of Learning Exercise 1C

Strategic Planning at a Local Company

Assurance of Learning Exercise 1D

Getting Familiar with SMCO

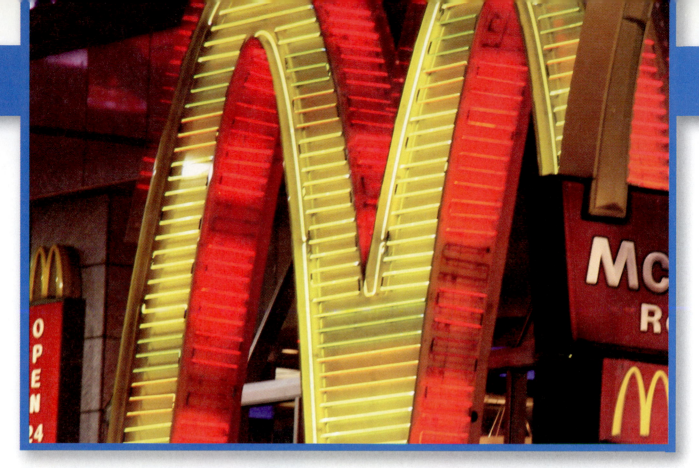

Source: Shutterstock/Photographer Jim Lopes

"Notable Quotes"

"If we know where we are and something about how we got there, we might see where we are trending—and if the outcomes which lie naturally in our course are unacceptable, to make timely change."

—Abraham Lincoln

"Without a strategy, an organization is like a ship without a rudder, going around in circles. It's like a tramp; it has no place to go."

—Joel Ross and Michael Kami

"Plans are less important than planning."

—Dale McConkey

"The formulation of strategy can develop competitive advantage only to the extent that the process can give meaning to workers in the trenches."

—David Hurst

"Most of us fear change. Even when our minds say change is normal, our stomachs quiver at the prospect. But for strategists and managers today, there is no choice but to change."

—Robert Waterman Jr.

"If a man takes no thought about what is distant, he will find sorrow near at hand. He who will not worry about what is far off will soon find something worse than worry."

—Confucius

When CEOs from the big three American automakers, Ford, General Motors (GM), and Chrysler, showed up without a clear strategic plan to ask congressional leaders for bailout monies, they were sent home with instructions to develop a clear strategic plan for the future. Austan Goolsbee, one of President Obama's top economic advisers, said, "Asking for a bailout without a convincing business plan was crazy." Goolsbee also said, "If the three auto CEOs need a bridge, it's got to be a bridge to somewhere, not a bridge to nowhere."[1] This textbook gives the instructions on how to develop a clear strategic plan—a bridge to somewhere rather than nowhere.

This chapter provides an overview of strategic management. It introduces a practical, integrative model of the strategic-management process; it defines basic activities and terms in strategic management.

This chapter also introduces the notion of boxed inserts. A boxed insert is provided in each chapter to examine how some firms are doing really well competing in a global economic recession. Some firms are strategically capitalizing on the harsh business climate and prospering as their rivals weaken. These firms are showcased in this edition to reveal how those companies achieved prosperity. Each boxed insert examines the strategies of firms doing great amid the worst recession in almost 30 years, the biggest stock market decline since 1937, high unemployment, record high and then record low oil prices, low consumer confidence, low interest rates, bankruptcies, liquidations, unavailability of credit, falling consumer demand for almost everything, and intense price competition as

Doing Great in a Weak Economy

McDonald's Corporation

When most firms were struggling in 2008, McDonald's increased its revenues from $22.7 billion in 2007 to $23.5 billion in 2008. Headquartered in Oak Brook, Illinois McDonald's net income nearly doubled during that time from $2.4 billion to $4.3 billion—quite impressive. *Fortune* magazine in 2009 rated McDonald's as their 16th "Most Admired Company in the World" in terms of their management and performance.

McDonald's added 650 new outlets in 2009 when many restaurants struggled to keep their doors open. McDonald's low prices and expanded menu items have attracted millions of new customers away from sit-down chains and independent eateries. Jim Skinner, CEO of McDonald's, says, "We do so well because our strategies have been so well planned out." McDonald's served about 60 million customers every day in 2009, 2 million more than in 2008. Nearly 80 percent of McDonald's are run by franchisees (or affiliates).

McDonald's in 2009 spent $2.1 billion to remodel many of its 32,000 restaurants and build new ones at a more rapid pace than in recent years. This is in stark contrast to most restaurant chains that are struggling to survive, laying off employees, closing restaurants, and reducing expansion plans. McDonald's restaurants are in 120 countries. Going out to eat is one of the first activities that customers cut in tough times. A rising U.S. dollar is another external factor that hurts McDonald's. An internal weakness of McDonald's is that the firm now offers upscale coffee drinks like lattes and cappuccinos in over 7,000 locations just as budget-conscious consumers are cutting back on such extravagances. About half of McDonald's 31,000 locations are outside the United States.

But McDonald's top management team says everything the firm does is for the long term. McDonald's for several years referred to their strategic plan as "Plan to Win." This strategy has been to increase sales at existing locations by improving the menu, remodeling dining rooms, extending hours, and adding snacks. The company has avoided deep price cuts on its menu items. McDonald's was only one of three large U.S. firms that saw its stock price rise in 2008.

The other two firms were Wal-Mart and Family Dollar Stores.

Other strategies being pursued currently by McDonald's include replacing gasoline-powered cars with energy-efficient cars, lowering advertising rates, halting building new outlets on street corners where nearby development shows signs of weakness, boosting the firm's coffee business, and improving the drive-through windows to increase sales and efficiency.

McDonald's receives nearly two thirds of its revenues from outside the United States. The company has 14,000 U.S. outlets and 18,000 outlets outside the United States. McDonald's feeds 58 million customers every day. The company operates Hamburger University in suburban Chicago. McDonald's reported that first quarter 2009 profits rose 4 percent and same-store sales rose 4.3 percent across the globe. Same-store sales in the second quarter of 2009 were up another 4.8 percent.

Source: Based on Janet Adamy, "McDonald's Seeks Way to Keep Sizzling," *Wall Street Journal* (March 10, 2009): A1, A11. Also, Geoff Colvin, "The World's Most Admired Companies," *Fortune* (March 16, 2009): 76–86.

consumers today purchase only what they need rather than what they want. Societies worldwide confront the most threatening economic conditions in nearly a century. The boxed insert in each chapter showcases excellent strategic management under harsh economic times.

The first company featured for excellent performance in the global recession is McDonald's Corporation, also showcased as the Cohesion Case in this 13th edition. McDonald's is featured as the Cohesion Case also because it is a well-known global firm undergoing strategic change and well managed. By working through McDonald's-related Assurance of Learning Exercises at the end of each chapter, you will be well prepared to develop an effective strategic plan for any company assigned to you this semester. The end-of-chapter exercises apply chapter tools and concepts.

What Is Strategic Management?

Once there were two company presidents who competed in the same industry. These two presidents decided to go on a camping trip to discuss a possible merger. They hiked deep into the woods. Suddenly, they came upon a grizzly bear that rose up on its hind legs and snarled. Instantly, the first president took off his knapsack and got out a pair of jogging shoes. The second president said, "Hey, you can't outrun that bear." The first president responded, "Maybe I can't outrun that bear, but I surely can outrun you!" This story captures the notion of strategic management, which is to achieve and maintain competitive advantage.

Defining Strategic Management

Strategic management can be defined as the art and science of formulating, implementing, and evaluating cross-functional decisions that enable an organization to achieve its objectives. As this definition implies, strategic management focuses on integrating management, marketing, finance/accounting, production/operations, research and development, and information systems to achieve organizational success. The term *strategic management* in this text is used synonymously with the term *strategic planning.* The latter term is more often used in the business world, whereas the former is often used in academia. Sometimes the term *strategic management* is used to refer to strategy formulation, implementation, and evaluation, with *strategic planning* referring only to strategy formulation. The purpose of strategic management is to exploit and create new and different opportunities for tomorrow; *long-range planning,* in contrast, tries to optimize for tomorrow the trends of today.

The term *strategic planning* originated in the 1950s and was very popular between the mid-1960s and the mid-1970s. During these years, strategic planning was widely believed to be the answer for all problems. At the time, much of corporate America was "obsessed" with strategic planning. Following that "boom," however, strategic planning was cast aside during the 1980s as various planning models did not yield higher returns. The 1990s, however, brought the revival of strategic planning, and the process is widely practiced today in the business world.

A strategic plan is, in essence, a company's game plan. Just as a football team needs a good game plan to have a chance for success, a company must have a good strategic plan to compete successfully. Profit margins among firms in most industries have been so reduced by the global economic recession that there is little room for error in the overall strategic plan. A strategic plan results from tough managerial choices among numerous good alternatives, and it signals commitment to specific markets, policies, procedures, and operations in lieu of other, "less desirable" courses of action.

The term *strategic management* is used at many colleges and universities as the subtitle for the capstone course in business administration. This course integrates material from all business courses. The Strategic Management Club Online at www.strategyclub.com offers many benefits for business policy and strategic management students. Professor Hansen at Stetson University provides a strategic management slide show for this entire text (www.stetson.edu/~rhansen/strategy).

Stages of Strategic Management

The *strategic-management process* consists of three stages: strategy formulation, strategy implementation, and strategy evaluation. *Strategy formulation* includes developing a vision and mission, identifying an organization's external opportunities and threats, determining internal strengths and weaknesses, establishing long-term objectives, generating alternative strategies, and choosing particular strategies to pursue. Strategy-formulation issues include deciding what new businesses to enter, what businesses to abandon, how to allocate resources, whether to expand operations or diversify, whether to enter international markets, whether to merge or form a joint venture, and how to avoid a hostile takeover.

Because no organization has unlimited resources, strategists must decide which alternative strategies will benefit the firm most. Strategy-formulation decisions commit an organization to specific products, markets, resources, and technologies over an extended period of time. Strategies determine long-term competitive advantages. For better or worse, strategic decisions have major multifunctional consequences and enduring effects on an organization. Top managers have the best perspective to understand fully the ramifications of strategy-formulation decisions; they have the authority to commit the resources necessary for implementation.

Strategy implementation requires a firm to establish annual objectives, devise policies, motivate employees, and allocate resources so that formulated strategies can be executed. Strategy implementation includes developing a strategy-supportive culture, creating an effective organizational structure, redirecting marketing efforts, preparing budgets, developing and utilizing information systems, and linking employee compensation to organizational performance.

Strategy implementation often is called the "action stage" of strategic management. Implementing strategy means mobilizing employees and managers to put formulated strategies into action. Often considered to be the most difficult stage in strategic management, strategy implementation requires personal discipline, commitment, and sacrifice. Successful strategy implementation hinges upon managers' ability to motivate employees, which is more an art than a science. Strategies formulated but not implemented serve no useful purpose.

Interpersonal skills are especially critical for successful strategy implementation. Strategy-implementation activities affect all employees and managers in an organization. Every division and department must decide on answers to questions, such as "What must we do to implement our part of the organization's strategy?" and "How best can we get the job done?" The challenge of implementation is to stimulate managers and employees throughout an organization to work with pride and enthusiasm toward achieving stated objectives.

Strategy evaluation is the final stage in strategic management. Managers desperately need to know when particular strategies are not working well; strategy evaluation is the primary means for obtaining this information. All strategies are subject to future modification because external and internal factors are constantly changing. Three fundamental strategy-evaluation activities are (1) reviewing external and internal factors that are the bases for current strategies, (2) measuring performance, and (3) taking corrective actions. Strategy evaluation is needed because success today is no guarantee of success tomorrow! Success always creates new and different problems; complacent organizations experience demise.

Strategy formulation, implementation, and evaluation activities occur at three hierarchical levels in a large organization: corporate, divisional or strategic business unit, and functional. By fostering communication and interaction among managers and employees across hierarchical levels, strategic management helps a firm function as a competitive team. Most small businesses and some large businesses do not have divisions or strategic business units; they have only the corporate and functional levels. Nevertheless, managers and employees at these two levels should be actively involved in strategic-management activities.

Peter Drucker says the prime task of strategic management is thinking through the overall mission of a business:

> . . . that is, of asking the question, "What is our business?" This leads to the setting of objectives, the development of strategies, and the making of today's decisions for tomorrow's results. This clearly must be done by a part of the organization that can see the entire business; that can balance objectives and the needs of today against the needs of tomorrow; and that can allocate resources of men and money to key results.[2]

Integrating Intuition and Analysis

Edward Deming once said, "In God we trust. All others bring data." The strategic-management process can be described as an objective, logical, systematic approach for making major decisions in an organization. It attempts to organize qualitative and quantitative information in a way that allows effective decisions to be made under conditions of uncertainty. Yet strategic management is not a pure science that lends itself to a nice, neat, one-two-three approach.

Based on past experiences, judgment, and feelings, most people recognize that *intuition* is essential to making good strategic decisions. Intuition is particularly useful for making decisions in situations of great uncertainty or little precedent. It is also helpful when highly interrelated variables exist or when it is necessary to choose from several plausible alternatives. Some managers and owners of businesses profess to have extraordinary abilities for using intuition alone in devising brilliant strategies. For example, Will Durant, who organized GM, was described by Alfred Sloan as "a man who would proceed on a course of action guided solely, as far as I could tell, by some intuitive flash of brilliance. He never felt obliged to make an engineering hunt for the facts. Yet at times, he was astoundingly correct in his judgment."[3] Albert Einstein acknowledged the importance of intuition when he said, "I believe in intuition and inspiration. At times I feel certain that I am right while not knowing the reason. Imagination is more important than knowledge, because knowledge is limited, whereas imagination embraces the entire world."[4]

Although some organizations today may survive and prosper because they have intuitive geniuses managing them, most are not so fortunate. Most organizations can benefit from strategic management, which is based upon integrating intuition and analysis in decision making. Choosing an intuitive or analytic approach to decision making is not an either–or proposition. Managers at all levels in an organization inject their intuition and judgment into strategic-management analyses. Analytical thinking and intuitive thinking complement each other.

Operating from the I've-already-made-up-my-mind-don't-bother-me-with-the-facts mode is not management by intuition; it is management by ignorance.[5] Drucker says, "I believe in intuition only if you discipline it. 'Hunch' artists, who make a diagnosis but don't check it out with the facts, are the ones in medicine who kill people, and in management kill businesses."[6] As Henderson notes:

> The accelerating rate of change today is producing a business world in which customary managerial habits in organizations are increasingly inadequate. Experience alone was an adequate guide when changes could be made in small increments. But intuitive and experience-based management philosophies are grossly inadequate when decisions are strategic and have major, irreversible consequences.[7]

In a sense, the strategic-management process is an attempt both to duplicate what goes on in the mind of a brilliant, intuitive person who knows the business and to couple it with analysis.

Adapting to Change

The strategic-management process is based on the belief that organizations should continually monitor internal and external events and trends so that timely changes can be made as needed. The rate and magnitude of changes that affect organizations are increasing dramatically as evidenced how the global economic recession has caught so many firms by surprise. Firms, like organisms, must be "adept at adapting" or they will not survive.

Corporate bankruptcies and defaults more than doubled in 2009 from an already bad 2008 year. All industries were hit hard, especially retail, chemicals, autos, and financial. As lenders tightened restrictions on borrowers, thousands of firms could not avoid bankruptcy. Even the economies of China, Japan, and South Korea stalled as demand for their goods from the United States and Europe dried up. China's annual growth slowed from 13 percent in 2007 to 9 percent in 2008 and then 5 percent for 2009. Consumer confidence indexes were falling all over the world as were housing prices.

Nine of 10 stocks in the S&P 1500 lost value in 2008. The Nasdaq composite index fell 40.5 percent in 2008, its worst year ever. S&P 500 stocks lost 38.5 percent of their value in 2008, the worst year since 1937. The Dow Jones Industrial Average lost 33.8 percent of its value in 2008, the worst loss since 1931 as shareholders lost $6.8 trillion in wealth. Only three S&P 500 stocks rose in 2008: Family Dollar up 38 percent, making it the best performer in the S&P 500; Wal-Mart Stores up 18 percent; and McDonald's up nearly 6 percent. The biggest decliner on the Dow in 2008 was GM, whose stock fell 87 percent. Citigroup lost 77 percent of its stock value in 2008. Even General Electric lost 56 percent of its value. Fannie Mae and Freddie Mac each slid 98 percent as did Fleetwood Enterprises, which makes recreational vehicles. And losses were also extensive worldwide. For example, Vanguard's Europe/Pacific Index, composed of stocks firms based on those continents, fell 43 percent in 2008.

To survive, all organizations must astutely identify and adapt to change. The strategic-management process is aimed at allowing organizations to adapt effectively to change over the long run. As Waterman has noted:

> In today's business environment, more than in any preceding era, the only constant is change. Successful organizations effectively manage change, continuously adapting their bureaucracies, strategies, systems, products, and cultures to survive the shocks and prosper from the forces that decimate the competition.[8]

E-commerce and globalization are external changes that are transforming business and society today. On a political map, the boundaries between countries may be clear, but on a competitive map showing the real flow of financial and industrial activity, the boundaries have largely disappeared. The speedy flow of information has eaten away at national boundaries so that people worldwide readily see for themselves how other people live and work. We have become a borderless world with global citizens, global competitors, global customers, global suppliers, and global distributors! U.S. firms are challenged by large rival companies in many industries. To say U.S. firms are being challenged in the automobile industry is an understatement. But this situation is true in many industries.

The need to adapt to change leads organizations to key strategic-management questions, such as "What kind of business should we become?" "Are we in the right field(s)?" "Should we reshape our business?" "What new competitors are entering our industry?" "What strategies should we pursue?" "How are our customers changing?" "Are new technologies being developed that could put us out of business?"

Key Terms in Strategic Management

Before we further discuss strategic management, we should define nine key terms: competitive advantage, strategists, vision and mission statements, external opportunities and threats, internal strengths and weaknesses, long-term objectives, strategies, annual objectives, and policies.

Competitive Advantage

Strategic management is all about gaining and maintaining *competitive advantage*. This term can be defined as "anything that a firm does especially well compared to rival firms." When a firm can do something that rival firms cannot do, or owns something that rival firms desire, that can represent a competitive advantage. For example, in a global economic recession, simply having ample cash on the firm's balance sheet can provide a major competitive advantage. Some cash-rich firms are buying distressed rivals. For example, BHP Billiton, the world's largest miner, is seeking to buy rival firms in Australia and South America. Freeport-McMoRan Copper & Gold Inc. also desires to expand its portfolio by acquiring distressed rival companies. French drug company SanofiAventis SA also is acquiring distressed rival firms to boost its drug development and diversification. Cash-rich Johnson & Johnson in the United States also is acquiring distressed rival firms. This can be an excellent strategy in a global economic recession.

Having less fixed assets than rival firms also can provide major competitive advantages in a global recession. For example, Apple has no manufacturing facilities of its own, and rival Sony has 57 electronics factories. Apple relies exclusively on contract manufacturers for production of all of its products, whereas Sony owns its own plants. Less fixed assets has enabled Apple to remain financially lean with virtually no long-term debt. Sony, in contrast, has built up massive debt on its balance sheet.

CEO Paco Underhill of Envirosell says, "Where it used to be a polite war, it's now a 21st-century bar fight, where everybody is competing with everyone else for the customers' money." Shoppers are "trading down," so Nordstrom is taking customers from Neiman Marcus and Saks Fifth Avenue, T.J. Maxx and Marshalls are taking customers from most other stores in the mall, and even Family Dollar is taking revenues from Wal-Mart.[9] Getting and keeping competitive advantage is essential for long-term success in an organization. The Industrial/Organizational (I/O) and the Resource-Based View (RBV) theories of organization (as discussed in Chapters 3 and 4, respectively) present different perspectives on how best to capture and keep competitive advantage—that is, how best to manage strategically. Pursuit of competitive advantage leads to organizational success or failure. Strategic management researchers and practitioners alike desire to better understand the nature and role of competitive advantage in various industries.

Normally, a firm can sustain a competitive advantage for only a certain period due to rival firms imitating and undermining that advantage. Thus it is not adequate to simply obtain competitive advantage. A firm must strive to achieve *sustained competitive advantage* by

(1) continually adapting to changes in external trends and events and internal capabilities, competencies, and resources; and by (2) effectively formulating, implementing, and evaluating strategies that capitalize upon those factors. For example, newspaper circulation in the United States is steadily declining. Most national newspapers are rapidly losing market share to the Internet, and other media that consumers use to stay informed. Daily newspaper circulation in the United States totals about 55 million copies annually, which is about the same as it was in 1954. Strategists ponder whether the newspaper circulation slide can be halted in the digital age. The six broadcast networks—ABC, CBS, Fox, NBC, UPN, and WB—are being assaulted by cable channels, video games, broadband, wireless technologies, satellite radio, high-definition TV, and digital video recorders. The three original broadcast networks captured about 90 percent of the prime-time audience in 1978, but today their combined market share is less than 50 percent.[10]

An increasing number of companies are gaining a competitive advantage by using the Internet for direct selling and for communication with suppliers, customers, creditors, partners, shareholders, clients, and competitors who may be dispersed globally. E-commerce allows firms to sell products, advertise, purchase supplies, bypass intermediaries, track inventory, eliminate paperwork, and share information. In total, e-commerce is minimizing the expense and cumbersomeness of time, distance, and space in doing business, thus yielding better customer service, greater efficiency, improved products, and higher profitability.

The Internet has changed the way we organize our lives; inhabit our homes; and relate to and interact with family, friends, neighbors, and even ourselves. The Internet promotes endless comparison shopping, which thus enables consumers worldwide to band together to demand discounts. The Internet has transferred power from businesses to individuals. Buyers used to face big obstacles when attempting to get the best price and service, such as limited time and data to compare, but now consumers can quickly scan hundreds of vendor offerings. Both the number of people shopping online and the average amount they spend is increasing dramatically. Digital communication has become the name of the game in marketing. Consumers today are flocking to blogs, short-post forums such as Twitter, video sites such as YouTube, and social networking sites such as Facebook, MySpace, and LinkedIn instead of television, radio, newspapers, and magazines. Facebook and MySpace recently unveiled features that further marry these social sites to the wider Internet. Users on these social sites now can log on to many business shopping sites with their IDs from their social site so their friends can see what items they have purchased on various shopping sites. Both of these social sites want their members to use their IDs to manage all their online identities. Most traditional retailers have learned that their online sales can boost in-store sales as they utilize their Web sites to promote in-store promotions.

Strategists

Strategists are the individuals who are most responsible for the success or failure of an organization. Strategists have various job titles, such as chief executive officer, president, owner, chair of the board, executive director, chancellor, dean, or entrepreneur. Jay Conger, professor of organizational behavior at the London Business School and author of *Building Leaders,* says, "All strategists have to be chief learning officers. We are in an extended period of change. If our leaders aren't highly adaptive and great models during this period, then our companies won't adapt either, because ultimately leadership is about being a role model."

Strategists help an organization gather, analyze, and organize information. They track industry and competitive trends, develop forecasting models and scenario analyses, evaluate corporate and divisional performance, spot emerging market opportunities, identify business threats, and develop creative action plans. Strategic planners usually serve in a support or staff role. Usually found in higher levels of management, they typically have considerable authority for decision making in the firm. The CEO is the most visible and critical strategic manager. Any manager who has responsibility for a unit or division, responsibility for profit and loss outcomes, or direct authority over a major piece of the business is a strategic manager (strategist). In the last five years, the position of chief strategy officer (CSO) has emerged as a new addition to the top management ranks of many organizations, including Sun Microsystems, Network Associates, Clarus, Lante, Marimba, Sapient, Commerce One,

BBDO, Cadbury Schweppes, General Motors, Ellie Mae, Cendant, Charles Schwab, Tyco, Campbell Soup, Morgan Stanley, and Reed-Elsevier. This new corporate officer title represents recognition of the growing importance of strategic planning in the business world.[11]

Strategists differ as much as organizations themselves, and these differences must be considered in the formulation, implementation, and evaluation of strategies. Some strategists will not consider some types of strategies because of their personal philosophies. Strategists differ in their attitudes, values, ethics, willingness to take risks, concern for social responsibility, concern for profitability, concern for short-run versus long-run aims, and management style. The founder of Hershey Foods, Milton Hershey, built the company to manage an orphanage. From corporate profits, Hershey Foods today cares for over a thousand boys and girls in its School for Orphans.

Vision and Mission Statements

Many organizations today develop a *vision statement* that answers the question "What do we want to become?" Developing a vision statement is often considered the first step in strategic planning, preceding even development of a mission statement. Many vision statements are a single sentence. For example, the vision statement of Stokes Eye Clinic in Florence, South Carolina, is "Our vision is to take care of your vision."

Mission statements are "enduring statements of purpose that distinguish one business from other similar firms. A mission statement identifies the scope of a firm's operations in product and market terms."[12] It addresses the basic question that faces all strategists: "What is our business?" A clear mission statement describes the values and priorities of an organization. Developing a mission statement compels strategists to think about the nature and scope of present operations and to assess the potential attractiveness of future markets and activities. A mission statement broadly charts the future direction of an organization. A mission statement is a constant reminder to its employees of why the organization exists and what the founders envisioned when they put their fame and fortune at risk to breathe life into their dreams. Here is an example of a mission statement for Barnes & Noble:

Our mission is to operate the best specialty retail business in America, regardless of the product we sell. Because the product we sell is books, our aspirations must be consistent with the promise and the ideals of the volumes which line our shelves. To say that our mission exists independent of the product we sell is to demean the importance and the distinction of being booksellers. As booksellers we are determined to be the very best in our business, regardless of the size, pedigree, or inclinations of our competitors. We will continue to bring our industry nuances of style and approaches to bookselling which are consistent with our evolving aspirations. Above all, we expect to be a credit to the communities we serve, a valuable resource to our customers, and a place where our dedicated booksellers can grow and prosper. Toward this end we will not only listen to our customers and booksellers but embrace the idea that the Company is at their service. (www.missionstatements.com)

External Opportunities and Threats

External opportunities and *external threats* refer to economic, social, cultural, demographic, environmental, political, legal, governmental, technological, and competitive trends and events that could significantly benefit or harm an organization in the future. Opportunities and threats are largely beyond the control of a single organization—thus the word *external*. In a global economic recession, a few opportunities and threats that face many firms are listed here:

- Availability of capital can no longer be taken for granted.
- Consumers expect green operations and products.
- Marketing has moving rapidly to the Internet.
- Consumers must see value in all that they consume.
- Global markets offer the highest growth in revenues.

- As the price of oil has collapsed, oil rich countries are focused on supporting their own economies, rather than seeking out investments in other countries.
- Too much debt can crush even the best firms.
- Layoffs are rampant among many firms as revenues and profits fall and credit sources dry up.
- The housing market is depressed.
- Demand for health services does not change much in a recession. For example, Almost Family Inc., a Louisville, Kentucky, provider of home nursing care, more than doubled its stock price in 2008 to $45.
- Dramatic slowdowns in consumer spending are apparent in virtually all sectors, except some discount retailers and restaurants.
- Emerging countries' economies could manage to grow 5 percent in 2009, but that is three full percentage points lower than in 2007.
- U.S. unemployment rates continue to rise to 10 percent on average.
- Borrowers are faced with much bigger collateral requirements than in years past.
- Equity lines of credit often now are not being extended.
- Firms that have cash or access to credit have a competitive advantage over debt-laden firms.
- Discretionary spending has fallen dramatically; consumers buy only essential items; this has crippled many luxury and recreational businesses such as boating and cycling.
- The stock market crash of 2008 left senior citizens with retirement worries, so millions of people cut back on spending to the bare essentials.
- The double whammy of falling demand and intense price competition is plaguing most firms, especially those with high fixed costs.
- The business world has moved from a credit-based economy to a cash-based economy.
- There is reduced capital spending in response to reduced consumer spending.

The types of changes mentioned above are creating a different type of consumer and consequently a need for different types of products, services, and strategies. Many companies in many industries face the severe external threat of online sales capturing increasing market share in their industry.

Other opportunities and threats may include the passage of a law, the introduction of a new product by a competitor, a national catastrophe, or the declining value of the dollar. A competitor's strength could be a threat. Unrest in the Middle East, rising energy costs, or the war against terrorism could represent an opportunity or a threat.

A basic tenet of strategic management is that firms need to formulate strategies to take advantage of external opportunities and to avoid or reduce the impact of external threats. For this reason, identifying, monitoring, and evaluating external opportunities and threats are essential for success. This process of conducting research and gathering and assimilating external information is sometimes called *environmental scanning* or industry analysis. Lobbying is one activity that some organizations utilize to influence external opportunities and threats.

Internal Strengths and Weaknesses

Internal strengths and *internal weaknesses* are an organization's controllable activities that are performed especially well or poorly. They arise in the management, marketing, finance/accounting, production/operations, research and development, and management information systems activities of a business. Identifying and evaluating organizational strengths and weaknesses in the functional areas of a business is an essential strategic-management activity. Organizations strive to pursue strategies that capitalize on internal strengths and eliminate internal weaknesses.

Strengths and weaknesses are determined relative to competitors. *Relative* deficiency or superiority is important information. Also, strengths and weaknesses can be determined by elements of being rather than performance. For example, a strength may involve ownership of natural resources or a historic reputation for quality. Strengths and weaknesses may be determined relative to a firm's own objectives. For example, high levels of inventory turnover may not be a strength to a firm that seeks never to stock-out.

Internal factors can be determined in a number of ways, including computing ratios, measuring performance, and comparing to past periods and industry averages. Various types of surveys also can be developed and administered to examine internal factors such as employee morale, production efficiency, advertising effectiveness, and customer loyalty.

Long-Term Objectives

Objectives can be defined as specific results that an organization seeks to achieve in pursuing its basic mission. *Long-term* means more than one year. Objectives are essential for organizational success because they state direction; aid in evaluation; create synergy; reveal priorities; focus coordination; and provide a basis for effective planning, organizing, motivating, and controlling activities. Objectives should be challenging, measurable, consistent, reasonable, and clear. In a multidimensional firm, objectives should be established for the overall company and for each division.

Strategies

Strategies are the means by which long-term objectives will be achieved. Business strategies may include geographic expansion, diversification, acquisition, product development, market penetration, retrenchment, divestiture, liquidation, and joint ventures. Strategies currently being pursued by some companies are described in Table 1-1.

Strategies are potential actions that require top management decisions and large amounts of the firm's resources. In addition, strategies affect an organization's long-term prosperity, typically for at least five years, and thus are future-oriented. Strategies have multifunctional or multidivisional consequences and require consideration of both the external and internal factors facing the firm.

Annual Objectives

Annual objectives are short-term milestones that organizations must achieve to reach long-term objectives. Like long-term objectives, annual objectives should be measurable, quantitative, challenging, realistic, consistent, and prioritized. They should be established at the

TABLE 1-1   Sample Strategies in Action in 2009

Best Buy

As soon as Best Buy Company became victorious over longtime archrival Circuit City Stores, Best Buy ran head on into a much larger, formidable competitor: Wal-Mart Stores. Based in Richfield, Minnesota, and having 3,900 stores worldwide, Best Buy reported a 20 percent decline in March 2009 earnings as its new rival Wal-Mart gained thousands of the old Circuit City customers. But Best Buy now meets Wal-Mart's prices on electronics items and provides great one-on-one customer service with its blue-shirted employees. Best Buy remains well ahead of Wal-Mart in U.S. electronics sales, but Wal-Mart is gaining strength.

Levi Strauss

San Francisco-based Levi Strauss added 30 new stores and acquired 72 others during the second quarter of 2009. Known worldwide for its jeans, Levi Strauss is expanding and entrenching worldwide while other retailers are faltering in the ailing economy. For that quarter, Levi's revenues in the Americas were up 8 percent to $518 million, although its Europe and Asia/Pacific revenues declined 17 percent and 13 percent respectively. Levi's CEO John Anderson says slim fit and skinny jeans are selling best; and the two most popular colors today are very dark and the distressed look.

New York Times Company

New York Times Company's CEO, Janet Robinson, says her company is selling off assets and investing heavily in Internet technology in order to convince advertisers that the newspaper is getting ahead of technological changes rapidly eroding the newspaper business. Ms. Robinson is considering plans to begin charging customers for access to the newspaper's online content, because online advertising revenues are not sufficient to support the business. The 160-year-old New York Times Company's advertising revenues fell 30 percent in the second quarter of 2009.

TABLE 1-2   Percentage of People Who Smoke in Selected Countries

Country	Percentage	
Greece	50	
Russia		High
Austria		
Spain		
U.K.		
France		
Germany		
Italy		
Belgium		
Switzerland		Low
USA	19	

Source: Based on Christina Passariello, "Smoking Culture Persists in Europe, Despite Bans," *Wall Street Journal* (January 2, 2009): A5.

corporate, divisional, and functional levels in a large organization. Annual objectives should be stated in terms of management, marketing, finance/accounting, production/operations, research and development, and management information systems (MIS) accomplishments. A set of annual objectives is needed for each long-term objective. Annual objectives are especially important in strategy implementation, whereas long-term objectives are particularly important in strategy formulation. Annual objectives represent the basis for allocating resources.

Policies

Policies are the means by which annual objectives will be achieved. Policies include guidelines, rules, and procedures established to support efforts to achieve stated objectives. Policies are guides to decision making and address repetitive or recurring situations.

Policies are most often stated in terms of management, marketing, finance/accounting, production/operations, research and development, and computer information systems activities. Policies can be established at the corporate level and apply to an entire organization at the divisional level and apply to a single division, or at the functional level and apply to particular operational activities or departments. Policies, like annual objectives, are especially important in strategy implementation because they outline an organization's expectations of its employees and managers. Policies allow consistency and coordination within and between organizational departments.

Substantial research suggests that a healthier workforce can more effectively and efficiently implement strategies. Smoking has become a heavy burden for Europe's state-run social welfare systems, with smoking-related diseases costing well over $100 billion a year. Smoking also is a huge burden on companies worldwide, so firms are continually implementing policies to curtail smoking. Table 1-2 gives a ranking of some countries by percentage of people who smoke.

The Strategic-Management Model

The strategic-management process can best be studied and applied using a model. Every model represents some kind of process. The framework illustrated in Figure 1-1 is a widely accepted, comprehensive model of the strategic-management process.[13] This model does not guarantee success, but it does represent a clear and practical approach for formulating, implementing, and evaluating strategies. Relationships among major components of the strategic-management process are shown in the model, which appears in all subsequent

FIGURE 1-1

A Comprehensive Strategic-Management Model

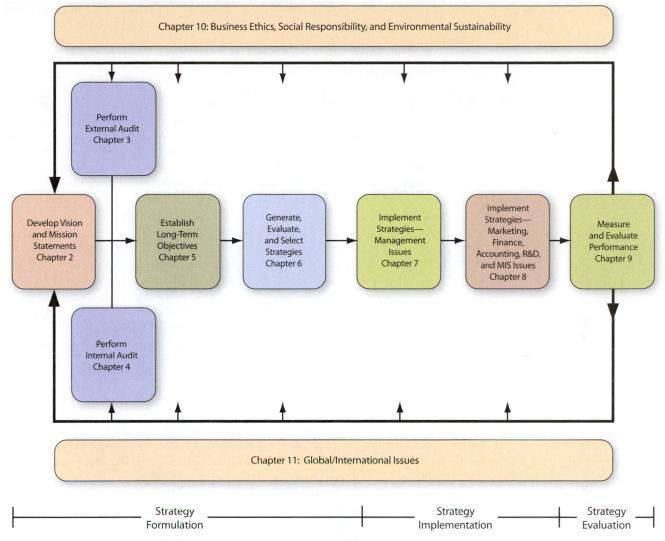

Source: Fred R. David, "How Companies Define Their Mission," *Long Range Planning* 22, no. 3 (June 1988): 40.

chapters with appropriate areas shaped to show the particular focus of each chapter. These are three important questions to answer in developing a strategic plan:

Where are we now?

Where do we want to go?

How are we going to get there?

Identifying an organization's existing vision, mission, objectives, and strategies is the logical starting point for strategic management because a firm's present situation and condition may preclude certain strategies and may even dictate a particular course of action. Every organization has a vision, mission, objectives, and strategy, even if these elements are not consciously designed, written, or communicated. The answer to where an organization is going can be determined largely by where the organization has been!

The strategic-management process is dynamic and continuous. A change in any one of the major components in the model can necessitate a change in any or all of the other components. For instance, a shift in the economy could represent a major opportunity and require a change in long-term objectives and strategies; a failure to accomplish annual objectives could require a change in policy; or a major competitor's change in strategy could require a change in the firm's mission. Therefore, strategy formulation, implementation, and evaluation activities should be performed on a continual basis, not just at the end of the year or semiannually. The strategic-management process never really ends.

Note in the strategic-management model that business ethics/social responsibility/ environmental sustainability issues impact all activities in the model as described in full in Chapter 10. Also, note in the model that global/international issues also impact virtually all strategic decisions today, even for small firms, as described in detail in Chapter 11. (Both Chapter 10 and Chapter 11 are new to this edition.)

The strategic-management process is not as cleanly divided and neatly performed in practice as the strategic-management model suggests. Strategists do not go through the process in lockstep fashion. Generally, there is give-and-take among hierarchical levels of an organization. Many organizations semiannually conduct formal meetings to discuss and update the firm's vision/mission, opportunities/threats, strengths/weaknesses, strategies, objectives, policies, and performance. These meetings are commonly held off-premises and are called *retreats*. The rationale for periodically conducting strategic-management meetings away from the work site is to encourage more creativity and candor from participants. Good communication and feedback are needed throughout the strategic-management process.

Application of the strategic-management process is typically more formal in larger and well-established organizations. Formality refers to the extent that participants, responsibilities, authority, duties, and approach are specified. Smaller businesses tend to be less formal. Firms that compete in complex, rapidly changing environments, such as technology companies, tend to be more formal in strategic planning. Firms that have many divisions, products, markets, and technologies also tend to be more formal in applying strategic-management concepts. Greater formality in applying the strategic-management process is usually positively associated with the cost, comprehensiveness, accuracy, and success of planning across all types and sizes of organizations.[14]

Benefits of Strategic Management

Strategic management allows an organization to be more proactive than reactive in shaping its own future; it allows an organization to initiate and influence (rather than just respond to) activities—and thus to exert control over its own destiny. Small business owners, chief executive officers, presidents, and managers of many for-profit and nonprofit organizations have recognized and realized the benefits of strategic management.

Historically, the principal benefit of strategic management has been to help organizations formulate better strategies through the use of a more systematic, logical, and rational approach to strategic choice. This certainly continues to be a major benefit of strategic management, but research studies now indicate that the process, rather than the decision or document, is the more important contribution of strategic management.[15] *Communication is a key to successful strategic management.* Through involvement in the process, in other words, through dialogue and participation, managers and employees become committed to supporting the organization. Figure 1-2 illustrates this intrinsic

FIGURE 1-2

Benefits to a Firm That Does Strategic Planning

Enhanced Communication	Deeper/Improved Understanding	Greater Commitment	THE RESULT
a. Dialogue b. Participation	a. Of others' views b. Of what the firm is doing/planning and why	a. To achieve objectives b. To implement strategies c. To work hard	All Managers and Employees on a Mission to Help the Firm Succeed

benefit of a firm engaging in strategic planning. Note that all firms need all employees on a mission to help the firm succeed.

The manner in which strategic management is carried out is thus exceptionally important. A major aim of the process is to achieve the understanding of and commitment from all managers and employees. Understanding may be the most important benefit of strategic management, followed by commitment. When managers and employees understand what the organization is doing and why, they often feel they are a part of the firm and become committed to assisting it. This is especially true when employees also understand linkages between their own compensation and organizational performance. Managers and employees become surprisingly creative and innovative when they understand and support the firm's mission, objectives, and strategies. A great benefit of strategic management, then, is the opportunity that the process provides to empower individuals. *Empowerment* is the act of strengthening employees' sense of effectiveness by encouraging them to participate in decision making and to exercise initiative and imagination, and rewarding them for doing so.

More and more organizations are decentralizing the strategic-management process, recognizing that planning must involve lower-level managers and employees. The notion of centralized staff planning is being replaced in organizations by decentralized line-manager planning. For example, Walt Disney Co. dismantled its strategic-planning department and gave those responsibilities back to the Disney business divisions. Former CEO Michael Eisner had favored the centralized strategic-planning approach, but CEO Robert Iger dissolved Disney's strategic-planning department within weeks of his taking over the top office at Disney.

The process is a learning, helping, educating, and supporting activity, not merely a paper-shuffling activity among top executives. Strategic-management dialogue is more important than a nicely bound strategic-management document.[16] The worst thing strategists can do is develop strategic plans themselves and then present them to operating managers to execute. Through involvement in the process, line managers become "owners" of the strategy. Ownership of strategies by the people who have to execute them is a key to success!

Although making good strategic decisions is the major responsibility of an organization's owner or chief executive officer, both managers and employees must also be involved in strategy formulation, implementation, and evaluation activities. Participation is a key to gaining commitment for needed changes.

An increasing number of corporations and institutions are using strategic management to make effective decisions. But strategic management is not a guarantee for success; it can be dysfunctional if conducted haphazardly.

Financial Benefits

Research indicates that organizations using strategic-management concepts are more profitable and successful than those that do not.[17] Businesses using strategic-management concepts show significant improvement in sales, profitability, and productivity compared to firms without systematic planning activities. High-performing firms tend to do systematic planning to prepare for future fluctuations in their external and internal environments. Firms with planning systems more closely resembling strategic-management theory generally exhibit superior long-term financial performance relative to their industry.

High-performing firms seem to make more informed decisions with good anticipation of both short- and long-term consequences. In contrast, firms that perform poorly often engage in activities that are shortsighted and do not reflect good forecasting of future conditions. Strategists of low-performing organizations are often preoccupied with solving internal problems and meeting paperwork deadlines. They typically underestimate their competitors' strengths and overestimate their own firm's strengths. They often attribute weak performance to uncontrollable factors such as a poor economy, technological change, or foreign competition.

More than 100,000 businesses in the United States fail annually. Business failures include bankruptcies, foreclosures, liquidations, and court-mandated receiverships. Although many factors besides a lack of effective strategic management can lead to business failure, the planning concepts and tools described in this text can yield substantial financial benefits for any organization. An excellent Web site for businesses engaged in strategic planning is www.checkmateplan.com.

Nonfinancial Benefits

Besides helping firms avoid financial demise, strategic management offers other tangible benefits, such as an enhanced awareness of external threats, an improved understanding of competitors' strategies, increased employee productivity, reduced resistance to change, and a clearer understanding of performance–reward relationships. Strategic management enhances the problem-prevention capabilities of organizations because it promotes interaction among managers at all divisional and functional levels. Firms that have nurtured their managers and employees, shared organizational objectives with them, empowered them to help improve the product or service, and recognized their contributions can turn to them for help in a pinch because of this interaction.

In addition to empowering managers and employees, strategic management often brings order and discipline to an otherwise floundering firm. It can be the beginning of an efficient and effective managerial system. Strategic management may renew confidence in the current business strategy or point to the need for corrective actions. The strategic-management process provides a basis for identifying and rationalizing the need for change to all managers and employees of a firm; it helps them view change as an opportunity rather than as a threat.

Greenley stated that strategic management offers the following benefits:

1. It allows for identification, prioritization, and exploitation of opportunities.
2. It provides an objective view of management problems.
3. It represents a framework for improved coordination and control of activities.
4. It minimizes the effects of adverse conditions and changes.
5. It allows major decisions to better support established objectives.
6. It allows more effective allocation of time and resources to identified opportunities.
7. It allows fewer resources and less time to be devoted to correcting erroneous or ad hoc decisions.
8. It creates a framework for internal communication among personnel.
9. It helps integrate the behavior of individuals into a total effort.
10. It provides a basis for clarifying individual responsibilities.
11. It encourages forward thinking.
12. It provides a cooperative, integrated, and enthusiastic approach to tackling problems and opportunities.
13. It encourages a favorable attitude toward change.
14. It gives a degree of discipline and formality to the management of a business.[18]

Why Some Firms Do No Strategic Planning

Some firms do not engage in strategic planning, and some firms do strategic planning but receive no support from managers and employees. Some reasons for poor or no strategic planning are as follows:

- *Lack of knowledge or experience in strategic planning*—No training in strategic planning.
- *Poor reward structures*—When an organization assumes success, it often fails to reward success. When failure occurs, then the firm may punish.
- *Firefighting*—An organization can be so deeply embroiled in resolving crises and firefighting that it reserves no time for planning.
- *Waste of time*—Some firms see planning as a waste of time because no marketable product is produced. Time spent on planning is an investment.
- *Too expensive*—Some organizations see planning as too expensive in time and money.
- *Laziness*—People may not want to put forth the effort needed to formulate a plan.

- *Content with success*—Particularly if a firm is successful, individuals may feel there is no need to plan because things are fine as they stand. But success today does not guarantee success tomorrow.
- *Fear of failure*—By not taking action, there is little risk of failure unless a problem is urgent and pressing. Whenever something worthwhile is attempted, there is some risk of failure.
- *Overconfidence*—As managers amass experience, they may rely less on formalized planning. Rarely, however, is this appropriate. Being overconfident or overestimating experience can bring demise. Forethought is rarely wasted and is often the mark of professionalism.
- *Prior bad experience*—People may have had a previous bad experience with planning, that is, cases in which plans have been long, cumbersome, impractical, or inflexible. Planning, like anything else, can be done badly.
- *Self-interest*—When someone has achieved status, privilege, or self-esteem through effectively using an old system, he or she often sees a new plan as a threat.
- *Fear of the unknown*—People may be uncertain of their abilities to learn new skills, of their aptitude with new systems, or of their ability to take on new roles.
- *Honest difference of opinion*—People may sincerely believe the plan is wrong. They may view the situation from a different viewpoint, or they may have aspirations for themselves or the organization that are different from the plan. Different people in different jobs have different perceptions of a situation.
- *Suspicion*—Employees may not trust management.[19]

Pitfalls in Strategic Planning

Strategic planning is an involved, intricate, and complex process that takes an organization into uncharted territory. It does not provide a ready-to-use prescription for success; instead, it takes the organization through a journey and offers a framework for addressing questions and solving problems. Being aware of potential pitfalls and being prepared to address them is essential to success.

Some pitfalls to watch for and avoid in strategic planning are these:

- Using strategic planning to gain control over decisions and resources
- Doing strategic planning only to satisfy accreditation or regulatory requirements
- Too hastily moving from mission development to strategy formulation
- Failing to communicate the plan to employees, who continue working in the dark
- Top managers making many intuitive decisions that conflict with the formal plan
- Top managers not actively supporting the strategic-planning process
- Failing to use plans as a standard for measuring performance
- Delegating planning to a "planner" rather than involving all managers
- Failing to involve key employees in all phases of planning
- Failing to create a collaborative climate supportive of change
- Viewing planning as unnecessary or unimportant
- Becoming so engrossed in current problems that insufficient or no planning is done
- Being so formal in planning that flexibility and creativity are stifled[20]

Guidelines for Effective Strategic Management

Failing to follow certain guidelines in conducting strategic management can foster criticisms of the process and create problems for the organization. Issues such as "Is strategic management in our firm a people process or a paper process?" should be addressed.

Even the most technically perfect strategic plan will serve little purpose if it is not implemented. Many organizations tend to spend an inordinate amount of time, money, and effort on developing the strategic plan, treating the means and circumstances under which it will be implemented as afterthoughts! Change comes through implementation and evaluation, not through the plan. A technically imperfect plan that is implemented well will achieve more than the perfect plan that never gets off the paper on which it is typed.[21]

Strategic management must not become a self-perpetuating bureaucratic mechanism. Rather, it must be a self-reflective learning process that familiarizes managers and employees in the organization with key strategic issues and feasible alternatives for resolving those issues. Strategic management must not become ritualistic, stilted, orchestrated, or too formal, predictable, and rigid. Words supported by numbers, rather than numbers supported by words, should represent the medium for explaining strategic issues and organizational responses. A key role of strategists is to facilitate continuous organizational learning and change.

R. T. Lenz offered some important guidelines for effective strategic management:

Keep the strategic-management process as simple and nonroutine as possible. Eliminate jargon and arcane planning language. Remember, strategic management is a process for fostering learning and action, not merely a formal system for control. To avoid routinized behavior, vary assignments, team membership, meeting formats, and the planning calendar. The process should not be totally predictable, and settings must be changed to stimulate creativity. Emphasize word-oriented plans with numbers as back-up material. If managers cannot express their strategy in a paragraph or so, they either do not have one or do not understand it. Stimulate thinking and action that challenge the assumptions underlying current corporate strategy. Welcome bad news. If strategy is not working, managers desperately need to know it. Further, no pertinent information should be classified as inadmissible merely because it cannot be quantified. Build a corporate culture in which the role of strategic management and its essential purposes are understood. Do not permit "technicians" to co-opt the process. It is ultimately a process for learning and action. Speak of it in these terms. Attend to psychological, social, and political dimensions, as well as the information infrastructure and administrative procedures supporting it.[22]

An important guideline for effective strategic management is open-mindedness. A willingness and eagerness to consider new information, new viewpoints, new ideas, and new possibilities is essential; all organizational members must share a spirit of inquiry and learning. Strategists such as chief executive officers, presidents, owners of small businesses, and heads of government agencies must commit themselves to listen to and understand managers' positions well enough to be able to restate those positions to the managers' satisfaction. In addition, managers and employees throughout the firm should be able to describe the strategists' positions to the satisfaction of the strategists. This degree of discipline will promote understanding and learning.

No organization has unlimited resources. No firm can take on an unlimited amount of debt or issue an unlimited amount of stock to raise capital. Therefore, no organization can pursue all the strategies that potentially could benefit the firm. Strategic decisions thus always have to be made to eliminate some courses of action and to allocate organizational resources among others. Most organizations can afford to pursue only a few corporate-level strategies at any given time. It is a critical mistake for managers to pursue too many strategies at the same time, thereby spreading the firm's resources so thin that all strategies are jeopardized. Joseph Charyk, CEO of the Communication Satellite Corporation (Comsat), said, "We have to face the cold fact that Comsat may not be able to do all it wants. We must make hard choices on which ventures to keep and which to fold."

Strategic decisions require trade-offs such as long-range versus short-range considerations or maximizing profits versus increasing shareholders' wealth. There are ethics issues too. Strategy trade-offs require subjective judgments and preferences. In many cases, a lack of objectivity in formulating strategy results in a loss of competitive posture and profitability. Most organizations today recognize that strategic-management concepts and techniques can enhance the effectiveness of decisions. Subjective factors such as attitudes toward risk, concern for social responsibility, and organizational culture will

TABLE 1-3   Seventeen Guidelines for the Strategic-Planning Process to Be Effective

1. It should be a people process more than a paper process.
2. It should be a learning process for all managers and employees.
3. It should be words supported by numbers rather than numbers supported by words.
4. It should be simple and nonroutine.
5. It should vary assignments, team memberships, meeting formats, and even the planning calendar.
6. It should challenge the assumptions underlying the current corporate strategy.
7. It should welcome bad news.
8. It should welcome open-mindness and a spirit of inquiry and learning.
9. It should not be a bureaucratic mechanism.
10. It should not become ritualistic, stilted, or orchestrated.
11. It should not be too formal, predictable, or rigid.
12. It should not contain jargon or arcane planning language.
13. It should not be a formal system for control.
14. It should not disregard qualitative information.
15. It should not be controlled by "technicians."
16. Do not pursue too many strategies at once.
17. Continually strengthen the "good ethics is good business" policy.

always affect strategy-formulation decisions, but organizations need to be as objective as possible in considering qualitative factors. Table 1-3 summarizes important guidelines for the strategic-planning process to be effective.

Comparing Business and Military Strategy

A strong military heritage underlies the study of strategic management. Terms such as *objectives, mission, strengths*, and *weaknesses* first were formulated to address problems on the battlefield. According to *Webster's New World Dictionary,* strategy is "the science of planning and directing large-scale military operations, of maneuvering forces into the most advantageous position prior to actual engagement with the enemy." The word *strategy* comes from the Greek *strategos*, which refers to a military general and combines *stratos* (the army) and *ago* (to lead). The history of strategic planning began in the military. A key aim of both business and military strategy is "to gain competitive advantage." In many respects, business strategy is like military strategy, and military strategists have learned much over the centuries that can benefit business strategists today. Both business and military organizations try to use their own strengths to exploit competitors' weaknesses. If an organization's overall strategy is wrong (ineffective), then all the efficiency in the world may not be enough to allow success. Business or military success is generally not the happy result of accidental strategies. Rather, success is the product of both continuous attention to changing external and internal conditions and the formulation and implementation of insightful adaptations to those conditions. The element of surprise provides great competitive advantages in both military and business strategy; information systems that provide data on opponents' or competitors' strategies and resources are also vitally important.

Of course, a fundamental difference between military and business strategy is that business strategy is formulated, implemented, and evaluated with an assumption of *competition,* whereas military strategy is based on an assumption of *conflict.* Nonetheless, military conflict and business competition are so similar that many strategic-management techniques apply equally to both. Business strategists have access to valuable insights that military thinkers have refined over time. Superior strategy formulation and implementation can overcome an opponent's superiority in numbers and resources.

Both business and military organizations must adapt to change and constantly improve to be successful. Too often, firms do not change their strategies when their environment and competitive conditions dictate the need to change. Gluck offered a classic military example of this:

> When Napoleon won, it was because his opponents were committed to the strategy, tactics, and organization of earlier wars. When he lost—against Wellington, the Russians, and the Spaniards—it was because he, in turn, used tried-and-true strategies against enemies who thought afresh, who were developing the strategies not of the last war but of the next.[23]

Similarities can be construed from Sun Tzu's writings to the practice of formulating and implementing strategies among businesses today. Table 1-4 provides narrative

TABLE 1-4   Excerpts from Sun Tzu's *The Art of War* Writings

- War is a matter of vital importance to the state: a matter of life or death, the road either to survival or ruin. Hence, it is imperative that it be studied thoroughly.
- Warfare is based on deception. When near the enemy, make it seem that you are far away; when far away, make it seem that you are near. Hold out baits to lure the enemy. Strike the enemy when he is in disorder. Avoid the enemy when he is stronger. If your opponent is of choleric temper, try to irritate him. If he is arrogant, try to encourage his egotism. If enemy troops are well prepared after reorganization, try to wear them down. If they are united, try to sow dissension among them. Attack the enemy where he is unprepared, and appear where you are not expected. These are the keys to victory for a strategist. It is not possible to formulate them in detail beforehand.
- A speedy victory is the main object in war. If this is long in coming, weapons are blunted and morale depressed. When the army engages in protracted campaigns, the resources of the state will fall short. Thus, while we have heard of stupid haste in war, we have not yet seen a clever operation that was prolonged.
- Generally, in war the best policy is to take a state intact; to ruin it is inferior to this. To capture the enemy's entire army is better than to destroy it; to take intact a regiment, a company, or a squad is better than to destroy it. For to win one hundred victories in one hundred battles is not the acme of skill. To subdue the enemy without fighting is the supreme excellence. Those skilled in war subdue the enemy's army without battle.
- The art of using troops is this: When ten to the enemy's one, surround him. When five times his strength, attack him. If double his strength, divide him. If equally matched, you may engage him with some good plan. If weaker, be capable of withdrawing. And if in all respects unequal, be capable of eluding him.
- Know your enemy and know yourself, and in a hundred battles you will never be defeated. When you are ignorant of the enemy but know yourself, your chances of winning or losing are equal. If ignorant both of your enemy and of yourself, you are sure to be defeated in every battle.
- He who occupies the field of battle first and awaits his enemy is at ease, and he who comes later to the scene and rushes into the fight is weary. And therefore, those skilled in war bring the enemy to the field of battle and are not brought there by him. Thus, when the enemy is at ease, be able to tire him; when well fed, be able to starve him; when at rest, be able to make him move.
- Analyze the enemy's plans so that you will know his shortcomings as well as his strong points. Agitate him to ascertain the pattern of his movement. Lure him out to reveal his dispositions and to ascertain his position. Launch a probing attack to learn where his strength is abundant and where deficient. It is according to the situation that plans are laid for victory, but the multitude does not comprehend this.
- An army may be likened to water, for just as flowing water avoids the heights and hastens to the lowlands, so an army should avoid strength and strike weakness. And as water shapes its flow in accordance with the ground, so an army manages its victory in accordance with the situation of the enemy. And as water has no constant form, there are in warfare no constant conditions. Thus, one able to win the victory by modifying his tactics in accordance with the enemy situation may be said to be divine.
- If you decide to go into battle, do not anounce your intentions or plans. Project "business as usual."
- Unskilled leaders work out their conflicts in courtrooms and battlefields. Brilliant strategists rarely go to battle or to court; they generally achieve their objectives through tactical positioning well in advance of any confrontation.
- When you do decide to challenge another company (or army), much calculating, estimating, analyzing, and positioning bring triumph. Little computation brings defeat.
- Skillful leaders do not let a strategy inhibit creative counter-movement. Nor should commands from those at a distance interfere with spontaneous maneuvering in the immediate situation.
- When a decisive advantage is gained over a rival, skillful leaders do not press on. They hold their position and give their rivals the opportunity to surrender or merge. They do not allow their forces to be damaged by those who have nothing to lose.
- Brilliant strategists forge ahead with illusion, obscuring the area(s) of major confrontation, so that opponents divide their forces in an attempt to defend many areas. Create the appearance of confusion, fear, or vulnerability so the opponent is helplessly drawn toward this illusion of advantage.

(Note: Substitute the words *strategy* or *strategic planning* for *war* or *warfare*)

Source: Based on *The Art of War* and from www.ccs.neu.edu/home/thigpen/html/art_of_war.html

excerpts from *The Art of War.* As you read through the table, consider which of the principles of war apply to business strategy as companies today compete aggressively to survive and grow.

Conclusion

All firms have a strategy, even if it is informal, unstructured, and sporadic. All organizations are heading somewhere, but unfortunately some organizations do not know where they are going. The old saying "If you do not know where you are going, then any road will lead you there!" accents the need for organizations to use strategic-management concepts and techniques. The strategic-management process is becoming more widely used by small firms, large companies, nonprofit institutions, governmental organizations, and multinational conglomerates alike. The process of empowering managers and employees has almost limitless benefits.

Organizations should take a proactive rather than a reactive approach in their industry, and they should strive to influence, anticipate, and initiate rather than just respond to events. The strategic-management process embodies this approach to decision making. It represents a logical, systematic, and objective approach for determining an enterprise's future direction. The stakes are generally too high for strategists to use intuition alone in choosing among alternative courses of action. Successful strategists take the time to think about their businesses, where they are with their businesses, and what they want to be as organizations—and then they implement programs and policies to get from where they are to where they want to be in a reasonable period of time.

It is a known and accepted fact that people and organizations that plan ahead are much more likely to become what they want to become than those that do not plan at all. A good strategist plans and controls his or her plans, whereas a bad strategist never plans and then tries to control people! This textbook is devoted to providing you with the tools necessary to be a good strategist.

We invite you to visit the David page on the Prentice Hall Companion Web site at http://www.pearsonhighered.com/david/ for this chapter's review quiz.

Key Terms and Concepts

Annual Objectives (p. 13)
Competitive Advantage (p. 9)
Empowerment (p. 17)
Environmental Scanning (p. 12)
External Opportunities (p. 11)
External Threats (p. 11)
Internal Strengths (p. 12)
Internal Weaknesses (p. 12)
Intuition (p. 7)
Long-Range Planning (p. 6)
Long-Term Objectives (p. 13)
Mission Statements (p. 11)
Policies (p. 14)

Retreats (p. 16)
Strategic Management (p. 6)
Strategic-Management Model (p. 14)
Strategic-Management Process (p. 6)
Strategic Planning (p. 6)
Strategies (p. 13)
Strategists (p. 10)
Strategy Evaluation (p. 7)
Strategy Formulation (p. 6)
Strategy Implementation (p. 6)
Sustained Competitive Advantage (p. 9)
Vision Statement (p. 11)

Issues for Review and Discussion

1. Distinguish between long-range planning and strategic planning.
2. Compare a company's strategic plan with a football team's game plan.
3. Describe the three activities that comprise strategy evaluation.

4. How important do you feel "being adept at adapting" is for business firms? Explain.
5. Compare the opossum and turtle to the woolly mammoth and saber-toothed tiger in terms of being adept at adapting. What can we learn from the opossum and turtle?
6. As cited in the chapter, Edward Deming, a famous businessman, once said, "In God we trust. All others bring data." What did Deming mean in terms of developing a strategic plan?
7. What strategies do you believe can save newspaper companies from extinction?
8. Distinguish between the concepts of vision and mission.
9. Your university has fierce competitors. List three external opportunities and three external threats that face your university.
10. List three internal strengths and three internal weaknesses that characterize your university.
11. List reasons why objectives are essential for organizational success.
12. List four strategies and a hypothetical example of each.
13. List six characteristics of annual objectives.
14. Why are policies especially important in strategy implementation?
15. What is a "retreat," and why do firms take the time and spend the money to have these?
16. Discuss the notion of strategic planning being more formal versus informal in an organization. On a 1 to 10 scale from formal to informal, what number best represents your view of the most effective approach? Why?
17. List 10 guidelines for making the strategic-planning process effective. Arrange your guidelines in prioritized order of importance in your opinion.
18. List what you feel are the five most important lessons for business that can be garnered from *The Art of War* book.
19. What is the fundamental difference between business strategy and military strategy in terms of basic assumptions?
20. Explain why the strategic management class is often called a "capstone course."
21. What aspect of strategy formulation do you think requires the most time? Why?
22. Why is strategy implementation often considered the most difficult stage in the strategic-management process?
23. Why is it so important to integrate intuition and analysis in strategic management?
24. Explain the importance of a vision and a mission statement.
25. Discuss relationships among objectives, strategies, and policies.
26. Why do you think some chief executive officers fail to use a strategic-management approach to decision making?
27. Discuss the importance of feedback in the strategic-management model.
28. How can strategists best ensure that strategies will be effectively implemented?
29. Give an example of a recent political development that changed the overall strategy of an organization.
30. Who are the major competitors of your college or university? What are their strengths and weaknesses? What are their strategies? How sucessful are these institutions compared to your college?
31. Would strategic-management concepts and techniques benefit foreign businesses as much as domestic firms? Justify your answer.
32. What do you believe are some potential pitfalls or risks in using a strategic-management approach to decision making?
33. In your opinion, what is the single major benefit of using a strategic-management approach to decision making? Justify your answer.
34. Compare business strategy and military strategy.
35. Why is it important for all business majors to study strategic management since most students will never become a chief executive officer nor even a top manager in a large company?
36. Describe the content available on the SMCO Web site at www.strategyclub.com
37. List four financial and four nonfinancial benefits of a firm engaging in strategic planning.
38. Why is it that a firm can normally sustain a competitive advantage for only a limited period of time?
39. Why it is not adequate to simply obtain competitive advantage?
40. How can a firm best achieve sustained competitive advantage?

Notes

1. Kathy Kiely, "Officials Say Auto CEOs Must Be Specific on Plans," *USA Today* (November 24, 2008): 3B.
2. Peter Drucker, *Management: Tasks, Responsibilities, and Practices* (New York: Harper & Row, 1974): 611.
3. Alfred Sloan, Jr., *Adventures of the White Collar Man* (New York: Doubleday, 1941): 104.
4. Quoted in Eugene Raudsepp, "Can You Trust Your Hunches?" *Management Review* 49, no. 4 (April 1960): 7.
5. Stephen Harper, "Intuition: What Separates Executives from Managers," *Business Horizons* 31, no. 5 (September–October 1988): 16.
6. Ron Nelson, "How to Be a Manager," *Success* (July–August 1985): 69.
7. Bruce Henderson, *Henderson on Corporate Strategy* (Boston: Abt Books, 1979): 6.
8. Robert Waterman, Jr., *The Renewal Factor: How the Best Get and Keep the Competitive Edge* (New York: Bantam, 1987). See also *BusinessWeek* (September 14, 1987): 100. Also, see *Academy of Management Executive* 3, no. 2 (May 1989): 115.
9. Jayne O'Donnell, "Shoppers Flock to Discount Stores," *USA Today* (February 25, 2009): B1.
10. Ethan Smith, "How Old Media Can Survive in a New World," *Wall Street Journal* (May 23, 2005): R4.
11. Daniel Delmar, "The Rise of the CSO," *Organization Design* (March–April 2003): 8–10.
12. John Pearce II and Fred David, "The Bottom Line on Corporate Mission Statements," *Academy of Management Executive* 1, no. 2 (May 1987): 109.
13. Fred R. David, "How Companies Define Their Mission," *Long Range Planning* 22, no. 1 (February 1989): 91.
14. Jack Pearce and Richard Robinson, *Strategic Management*, 7th ed. (New York: McGraw-Hill, 2000): 8.
15. Ann Langley, "The Roles of Formal Strategic Planning," *Long Range Planning* 21, no. 3 (June 1988): 40.
16. Bernard Reimann, "Getting Value from Strategic Planning," *Planning Review* 16, no. 3 (May–June 1988): 42.
17. G. L. Schwenk and K. Schrader, "Effects of Formal Strategic Planning in Financial Performance in Small Firms: A Meta-Analysis," *Entrepreneurship and Practice* 3, no. 17 (1993): 53–64. Also, C. C. Miller and L. B. Cardinal, "Strategic Planning and Firm Performance: A Synthesis of More Than Two Decades of Research," *Academy of Management Journal* 6, no. 27 (1994): 1649–1665; Michael Peel and John Bridge, "How Planning and Capital Budgeting Improve SME Performance," *Long Range Planning* 31, no. 6 (October 1998): 848–856; Julia Smith, "Strategies for Start-Ups," *Long Range Planning* 31, no. 6 (October 1998): 857–872.
18. Gordon Greenley, "Does Strategic Planning Improve Company Performance?" *Long Range Planning* 19, no. 2 (April 1986): 106.
19. Adapted from www.mindtools.com/plreschn.html.
20. Adapted from www.des.calstate.edu/limitations.html and www.entarga.com/stratplan/purposes.html
21. Dale McConkey, "Planning in a Changing Environment," *Business Horizons* (September–October 1988): 66.
22. R. T. Lenz, "Managing the Evolution of the Strategic Planning Process," *Business Horizons* 30, no. 1 (January–February 1987): 39.
23. Frederick Gluck, "Taking the Mystique out of Planning," *Across the Board* (July–August 1985): 59.

Current Readings

Adegbesan, J Adetunji. "On the Origins of Competitive Advantage: Strategic Factor Markets and Heterogeneous Resources Complementarity." *Academy of Management Review* (July 2009): 463–475.

Amabile, Teresa M., and Mukti Khaire. "Creativity and the Role of the Leader." *Harvard Business Review* (October 2008): 100.

Cailluet, Ludovic, and Richard Whittington. "The Crafts of Strategy: Special Issue Introduction by the Guest Editors." *Long Range Planning* 41, no. 3 (June 2008): 241.

Camilus, John C. "Strategy as a Wicked Problem." *Harvard Business Review* (May 2008): 98.

Carroll, Paul B., and Chunka Mui. "Seven Ways to Fail Big." *Harvard Business Review* (September 2008): 82.

Chen, Ming-Jer, and Donald C. Hambrick. "New Academic Fields as Admittance-Seeking Social Movements: The Case of Strategic Management." *The Academy of Management Review* 33, no. 1 (January 2008): 32.

Cummings, Stephen, and Urs Daellenback. "A Guide to the Future of Strategy? The History of Long Range Planning." *Long Range Planning* (April 2009): 234–263.

Davis, Alan, and Eric M. Olson. "Critical Competitive Strategy Issues Every Entrepreneur Should Consider Before Going into Business." *Business Horizons* 51, no. 3 (May–June 2008): 211.

Dominguez, Damian, Hagen Worch, Jachen Markard, Bernhard, Truffer, and Gujer Willi. "Closing the Capability Gap: Strategic Planning for the Infrastructure Sector." *California Management Review* (Winter 2009): 30–50.

Hansen, Morten T. "When Internal Collaboration Is Bad for Your Company." *Harvard Business Review* (April 2009): 82–89.

Joseph, John, and William Ocasio. "Rise and Fall or Transformation? The Evolution of Strategic Planning at the General Electric Company, 1940–2006." *Long Range Planning* 41, no. 3 (June 2008): 248.

Malhotra, Deepak, Gillian, Ku, and Keith J. Murnighan. "When Winning Is Everything." *Harvard Business Review* (May 2008): 78.

McCullough, David. "Timeless Leadership: A Conversation with David McCullough." *Harvard Business Review* (March 2008): 45.

Moldoveanu, Mihnea. "Thinking Strategically About Thinking Strategically: The Computational Structure and Dynamics of Managerial Problem Selection and Formulation." *Strategic Management Journal* (July 2009): 737–763.

Natarajan, Vivek, Sridhar P. Nerur, and Abdul A. Rasheed. "The Intellectual Structure of the Strategic Management Field: An Author Co-citation Analysis." *Strategic Management Journal* 29, no. 3 (March 2008): 319.

Newbert, Scott L. "Value, Rareness, Competitive Advantage, and Performance: A Conceptual-level Empirical Investigation of the Resource-Based View of the Firm." *Strategic Management Journal* 29, no. 7 (July 2008): 745.

Singer, John G. "What Strategy Is Not: Technology- or Platform-Driven Strategy Is a Fast Track to Commoditization." *MIT Sloan Management Review* 49, no. 2 (Winter 2008): 96.

THE COHESION CASE

McDonald's Corporation—2009

Vijaya Narapareddy

University of Denver
www.mcdonalds.com

On May 5, 2009, McDonald's Corporation (MCD, hereafter) and Starbucks went full force campaigning for the attention of coffee connoisseurs. Following its success with McCafés in Europe, MCD surprised Starbucks with its announcement to offer lattes and mochas in its McCafés in the United States. In an attempt to woo rival Starbucks' customers, MCD promised to offer premium taste at bargain prices. This announcement came at a time when Starbucks, hard hit by losses, was closing hundreds of stores in the United States. The MCD–Starbucks fight is everywhere on the tube, in print, and the airwaves. MCD even taunts Starbucks with ads on buses and billboards that read "4 bucks is dumb." Starbucks is retaliating by placing newspaper ads that read "Beware of a cheaper cup of coffee. It comes with a price."

In April 2009, MCD reported strong sales growth in the first quarter of 2009 in spite of recessionary conditions worldwide. MCD sales in the United States increased by 4.7 percent, in Europe by 3.2 percent, and in Asia/Pacific, Middle East, and Africa by 5.5 percent. But as the U.S. dollar gained strength against most currencies, especially the euro, British pound, Australian dollar, Canadian dollar, and the Russian ruble, MCD experienced $642 million in foreign currency translation losses in the first quarter of 2009, as indicated in Exhibit 1. Undeterred, however, MCD is forging ahead with a renewed commitment to allure coffee enthusiasts away from rivals, big and small.

History

MCD was launched in 1940 when brothers Dick and Mac McDonald opened a restaurant in San Bernadino, California. However, the credit of growing the corporation into a franchised, global operation is attributed to Ray Kroc, who acquired equity from the McDonald brothers and took the firm public in 1965. MCD has a really cool history timeline called "Travel in Time with Us" located at the http://www.aboutmcdonalds.com/mcd/our_company/mcd_history.html Web page. It reveals information such as the following:

1979	MCD introduced Happy Meals
1981	MCD opened stores in Spain, Denmark, and the Philippines
1983	MCD entered its 32nd country
1984	Ray Kroc passed away
1987	MCD introduced Fresh Salads
1990	MCD opened a store in Moscow, Russia
1992	MCD opened a store in Warsaw, Poland
1995	MCD's new ad was "Have You Had Your Break Today?"
1996	www.mcdonalds.com Web site introduced
1997	MCD's new ad was "Did Somebody Say McDonald's?"
2001	The Big N'Tasty sandwich introduced
2003	MCD introduced Premium Salads and its "Plan to Win" strategy
2006	MCD introduced Snack Wraps

EXHIBIT 1 Impact of Foreign Currency Translation ($ in millions, except per share data)

Quarter ended March 31	2009	2008	Currency Translation Profit/(Loss) in 2009
Revenues	$5,077.4	$5,614.8	(642.4)
Company-operated margins	564.2	659.2	(72.5)
Franchised margins	1,296.0	1,316.2	(109.0)
Selling, general, and administrative expenses	497.3	552.4	43.0
Operating income	1,400.4	1,462.8	(137.9)
Net income	979.5	946.1	(86.2)
Earnings per share—diluted	0.87	0.81	(0.08)

Source: SEC *10-Q,* May 5, 2009.

Today, MCD is the largest global food service retailer, with over 31,000 restaurants in 118 countries serving more than 58 million customers each day. Exhibit 2 shows MCD's global locations. The number of restaurants held and operated by MCD in 2008 and 2009 in each group indicates steady growth in every country of operation except for the United Kingdom, where the growth is flat.

EXHIBIT 2 MCD's Number of Restaurants Worldwide

As of March 31	2009	2008	Increase
U.S.	**13,898**	**13,871**	**27**
Europe			
Germany	1,337	1,301	36
United Kingdom	1,192	1,192	—
France	1,135	1,108	27
Spain	393	379	14
Italy	381	363	18
Other	2,212	2,142	70
Total Europe	**6,650**	**6,485**	**165**
APMEA (Asia/Pacific/Middle East/Asia)			
Japan	3,746	3,737	9
China	1,074	911	163
Australia	782	762	20
Taiwan	347	346	1
Other	2,378	2,216	162
Total APMEA	**8,327**	**7,972**	**355**
Other Countries and Corporate			
Canada	1,419	1,408	11
Brazil	563	553	10
Mexico	382	365	17
Other	821	785	36
Total Other Countries and Corporate	**3,185**	**3,111**	**74**
Systemwide restaurants	**32,060**	**31,439**	**621**
Total Countries	**118**	**118**	**—**

Source: SEC *10-K,* dated February 25, 2009.

Internal Issues

Organizational Structure

MCD's top leadership has seen some turnover recently. The position of controller stands vacant, and the McDonald's USA group currently includes new executives to head its East and West Divisions. Exhibit 3 provides a list of MCD's top leadership as well as the firm's organizational chart.

Note that MCD's operations are organized into a geographical structure with four key segments. These four segments are (1) McDonald's—USA, (2) McDonald's—Europe, (3) McDonald's—APMEA (Asia/Pacific, Middle East, and Africa), and (4) McDonald's—Other Countries and Corporate.

Finances

In addition to the steady growth in the number of restaurants, MCD exhibited strong financial performance by geographic segment between 2008 and 2009, even as the worldwide economic crisis negatively impacted MCD's key competitors. As shown in Exhibit 4, revenues and operating margins in the three key segments (United States, Europe, and APMEA) rose steadily in 2006 through 2008, offsetting declines in the "Other and Corporate" segment.

MCD delivers consistently good performance, making it a darling for investors. In April 2009, major industry analysts rated MCD as a "buy," suggesting low levels of risk for investors. MCD's

EXHIBIT 3   McDonald's Corporation: Executive Officers and Organizational Chart

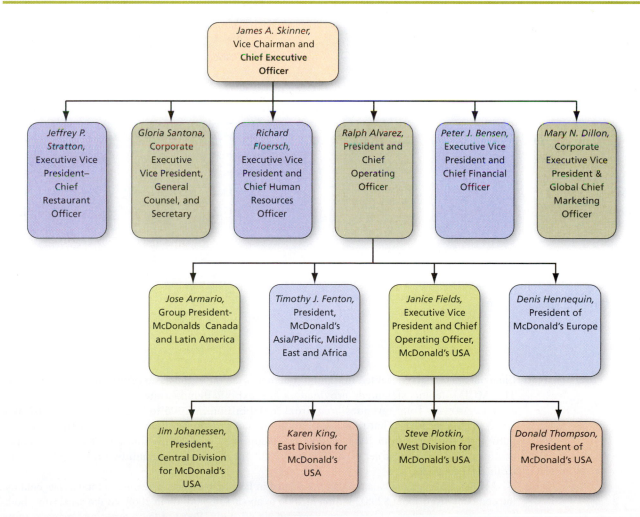

Source: http://www.aboutmcdonalds.com/mcd/our_company/bios.html

EXHIBIT 4   **Select Financial Data by Geographic Segment**

In millions	2008	2007	2006
U.S.	$ 8,078.3	$ 7,905.5	$ 7,464.1
Europe	9,922.9	8,926.2	7,637.7
APMEA (Asia/Pacific/Middle East/Africa)	4,230.8	3,598.9	3,053.5
Other Countries & Corporate	1,290.4	2,356.0	2,739.9
Total revenues	$23,522.4	$22,786.6	$20,895.2
U.S.	$ 3,059.7	$ 2,841.9	$ 2,657.0
Europe	2,608.0	2,125.4	1,610.2
APMEA	818.8	616.3	364.4
Other Countries & Corporate	(43.6)	(1,704.6)	(198.6)
Total operating income	$ 6,442.9	$ 3,879.0	$ 4,433.0
U.S.	$10,356.7	$10,031.8	$ 9,477.4
Europe	10,532.7	11,380.4	10,413.9
APMEA	4,074.6	4,145.3	3,727.6
Other Countries & Corporate	3,497.5	3,834.2	3,529.4
Businesses held for sale			1,631.5
Discontinued operations			194.7
Total assets	$28,461.5	$29,391.7	$28,974.5
U.S.	$ 837.4	$ 805.1	$ 774.3
Europe	864.1	687.4	504.9
APMEA	360.6	302.8	208.1
Other Countries & Corporate	73.6	97.3	85.4
		43.7	87.0
		10.3	82.2
Total capital expenditures	$ 2,135.7	$ 1,946.6	$ 1,741.9
U.S.	$ 400.9	$ 402.7	$ 390.5
Europe	506.3	473.3	436.4
APMEA	193.4	178.1	171.8
Other Countries & Corporate	107.2	112.6	110.4
		26.1	81.8
		21.3	59.0
	$ 1,207.8	$ 1,214.1	$ 1,249.9

Source: SEC *10-K,* February 25, 2009.

financial statements presented in Exhibit 5 demonstrate the enthusiasm of the analyst community. The MCD income statement provided in the exhibit demonstrates continuous and steady revenue growth. Total revenues grew from $20.9 billion in 2006 to $22.8 billion in 2007 and $23.5 billion in 2008. That translates into an annual growth of about 9.1 percent from 2006 to 2007 and 3.1 percent from 2007 to 2008. Net income shows a slightly different trend. Net income declined by 32.4 percent between 2006 and 2007 but regains momentum by growing 80 percent from 2007 to 2008.

MCD's consolidated balance sheet presented in Exhibit 6 depicts a decline in total assets held by the company from about $29.02 billion in 2006 to about $28.5 billion in 2008. At the same time, both long term debt and retained earnings increased significantly. Because the interest rate on short-term

EXHIBIT 5 McDonald's Consolidated Statement of Income

In millions, except per share data Years ended December 31	2008	2007	2006
REVENUES			
Sales by Company-operated restaurants	$16,560.9	$16,611.0	$15,402.4
Revenues from franchised restaurants	6,961.5	6,175.6	5,492.8
Total revenues	23,522.4	22,786.6	20,895.2
OPERATING COSTS AND EXPENSES			
Company-operated restaurant expenses			
Food & paper	5,586.1	5,487.4	5,111.8
Payroll & employee benefits	4,300.1	4,331.6	3,991.1
Occupancy & other operating expenses	3,766.7	3,922.7	3,802.2
Franchised restaurants–occupancy expenses	1,230.3	1,139.7	1,058.1
Selling, general & administrative expenses	2,355.5	2,367.0	2,295.7
Impairment and other charges, net	6.0	1,670.3	134.2
Other operating (income) expense, net	(165.2)	(11.1)	69.1
Total operating costs and expenses	17,079.5	18,907.6	16,462.2
Operating income	6,442.9	3,879.0	4,433.0
Interest expense–net of capitalized interest of $12.3, $6.9 and $5.4	522.6	410.1	401.9
Nonoperating (income) expense, net	(77.6)	(103.2)	(123.3)
Gain on sale of investment	(160.1)		
Income from continuing operations before provision for income taxes	6,158.0	3,572.1	4,154.4
Provision for income taxes	1,844.8	1,237.1	1,288.3
Income from continuing operations	4,313.2	2,335.0	2,866.1
Income from discontinued operations (net of taxes of $34.5 and $101.9)		60.1	678.1
Net income	$4,313.2	$2,395.1	$3,544.2
Per common share–basic:			
Continuing operations	$ 3.83	$ 1.96	$ 2.32
Discontinued operations		0.05	0.55
Net income	$ 3.83	$ 2.02	$ 2.87
Per common share–diluted:			
Continuing operations	$ 3.76	$ 1.93	$ 2.29
Discontinued operations		0.05	0.54
Net income	$ 3.76	$ 1.98	$ 2.83
Dividends declared per common share	$ 1.625	$ 1.50	$ 1.00
Weighted-average shares outstanding–basic	1,126.6	1,188.3	1,234.0
Weighted-average shares outstanding–diluted	1,146.0	1,211.8	1,251.7

Source: SEC *10-K,* February 25, 2009.

debt for MCD is less than 6 percent for both short- and long-term debt, an increase in MCD's borrowing should not be cause for concern.

Social Responsibility

MCD views its Plan to Win strategy, composed of the 5 P's (people, products, place, price, and promotion) as fundamental to its business success and to becoming better rather than just bigger. This plan aims at delivering exceptional customer experiences by undertaking several initiatives focused on each of the five P's grounded in a set of the corporate values shown in Exhibit 7.

EXHIBIT 6 MCD's Balance Sheet

PERIOD ENDING	31-Dec-08	31-Dec-07	31-Dec-06
Assets			
Current Assets			
Cash and Cash Equivalents	$2,063,400	$1,981,300	$2,136,400
Short Term Investments	—	—	—
Net Receivables	931,200	1,053,800	904,200
Inventory	111,500	125,300	149,000
Other Current Assets	411,500	421,500	435,700
Total Current Assets	**3,517,600**	**3,581,900**	**3,625,300**
Long Term Investments	1,222,300	1,156,400	1,036,200
Property Plant and Equipment	20,254,500	20,984,700	20,845,700
Goodwill	2,237,400	2,301,300	2,209,200
Intangible Assets	—	—	—
Accumulated Amortization	—	—	—
Other Assets	1,229,700	1,367,400	1,307,400
Deferred Long Term Asset Charges	—	—	—
Total Assets	**28,461,500**	**29,391,700**	**29,023,800**
Liabilities			
Current Liabilities			
Accounts Payable	2,506,100	3,634,000	2,739,000
Short/Current Long Term Debt	31,800	864,500	17,700
Other Current Liabilities	—	—	251,400
Total Current Liabilities	**2,537,900**	**4,498,500**	**3,008,100**
Long Term Debt	10,186,000	7,310,000	8,416,500
Other Liabilities	1,410,100	1,342,500	1,074,900
Deferred Long Term Liability Charges	944,900	960,900	1,066,000
Minority Interest	—	—	—
Negative Goodwill	—	—	—
Total Liabilities	**15,078,900**	**14,111,900**	**13,565,500**
Stockholders' Equity			
Misc. Stocks Options Warrants	—	—	—
Redeemable Preferred Stock	—	—	—
Preferred Stock	—	—	—
Common Stock	16,600	16,600	16,600
Retained Earnings	28,953,900	26,461,500	25,845,600
Treasury Stock	(20,289,400)	(16,762,400)	(13,552,200)
Capital Surplus	4,600,200	4,226,700	3,445,000
Other Stockholders' Equity	101,300	1,337,400	(296,700)
Total Stockholders' Equity	**13,382,600**	**15,279,800**	**15,458,300**
Total Liabilities and SE	**$28,461,500**	**$29,391,700**	**$29,023,800**

Source: http://finance.yahoo.com.

EXHIBIT 7 McDonald's Corporation's Values

We place the customer experience at the core of all we do

Our customers are the reason for our existence. We demonstrate our appreciation by providing them with high quality food and superior service, in a clean, welcoming environment, at a great value.

We are committed to our people

We provide opportunity, nurture talent, develop leaders and reward achievement. We believe that a team of well-trained individuals with diverse backgrounds and experiences, working together in an environment that fosters respect and drives high levels of engagement, is essential to our continued success.

We believe in the McDonald's system

McDonald's business model, depicted by the "three-legged stool" of owner/operators, suppliers, and company employees, is our foundation, and the balance of interests among the three groups is key.

We operate our business ethically

Sound ethics is good business. At McDonald's, we hold ourselves and conduct our business to high standards of fairness, honesty, and integrity. We are individually accountable and collectively responsible.

We give back to our communities

We take seriously the responsibilities that come with being a leader. We help our customers build better communities, support Ronald McDonald House Charities, and leverage our size, scope and resources to help make the world a better place.

We grow our business profitably

McDonald's is a publicly traded company. As such, we work to provide sustained profitable growth for our shareholders. This requires a continuing focus on our customers and the health of our system.

We strive continually to improve

We are a learning organization that aims to anticipate and respond to changing customer, employee and system needs through constant evolution and innovation.

Source: http://www.crmcdonalds.com.

MCD has made significant changes to become a socially and environmentally friendly company. It has been recognized for its efforts in inclusive excellence with respect to employing and creating opportunities for minorities. MCD has been listed among the "top 40 companies" by *Black Enterprise Magazine* for 2005 through 2007. It established its first Global Environmental Commitment in 1989. Since then it has been actively seeking to reduce its carbon footprint by using recycled packaging. Additionally, Ronald McDonald's Foundations raise millions of dollars each year for children-centered causes in the community.

According to Skinner, MCD's CEO, "Corporate responsibility means many things to many people. At McDonald's, being a responsible company means living our values to enable us to serve food responsibly, and work toward a sustainable future." (MCD either does not have a written mission statement nor vision statement or these documents are not publicly available because I could not locate either of these at the time this case was written.)

Competitors

The food service industry, also known as the restaurant industry, is large and lucrative with a market capitalization of $104 billion and a price-to-earnings (P/E) ratio of 80.2. Yet it is highly fragmented with over 550,000 restaurants ranging from small local eateries to global giants like MCD and Yum! Brands, Inc. MCD towers over its direct competitors in the industry with a market cap of $59.8 billion in May 2009. Yum! Brands, which has a market cap of only $16.3 billion, and Burger King Holdings, Inc., whose market cap is $2.46 billion, are second and third, respectively. Even though

Wendy's directly competes with MCD in this industry, Wendy's is currently owned by a private holding company, the Wendy's/Arby's Group. A brief summary of competitor financial highlights is provided in Exhibit 8.

Burger King (BKC)

Founded in Miami, Florida, in 1954 under the name "Insta Burger King" by James McLamore and David Edgerton, Burger King Corporation (BKC), a subsidiary of Burger King Holdings, Inc., owns or franchises about 11,500 restaurants in the United States and 70 foreign countries, including Canada, Europe, the Middle East, Africa, the Asia Pacific, and Latin America. Even though it is considered the second largest burger chain in the world, it ranks third in size in the food service industry. With a market capitalization of $2.46 billion, revenues of $2.55 billion, and 41,000 full-time employees, BKC trails behind McDonald's in several categories in the fast-food industry, including operating margins, earnings per share (EPS), and P/E ratio.

In addition to its famous "Whopper sandwich," BKC offers a variety of burgers, chicken sandwiches, breakfast items, and salads that compete directly with MCD. BKC, since the 1980s, has a long-standing contract with the Army and Air Force Exchange Service. As such, every major army and air force location worldwide has a Burger King restaurant on its premises.

Yum! Brands (YUM)

Yum! Brands, Inc., formerly known as TRICON Global Restaurants, Inc., was founded in 1997 and changed its name to Yum! Brands, Inc. in 2002. Yum! operates over 36,000 restaurants in 110 countries. Yum! owns prominent restaurant chains, such as Kentucky Fried Chicken (KFC), Pizza Hut, Taco Bell, Long John Silver's, and A&W. Headquartered in Louisville, Kentucky, it has a market cap of $15.56 billion, has 50,400 employees as of May 7, 2009, and is the closest competitor in size to McDonald's. Headquartered in Louisville, Kentucky, Yum! is considered the second largest in the global fast-food service industry. Offering more than one brand at a single location has helped Yum! increase traffic at a single real estate location. Each of its flagship brands also dominates the segment. For example, Taco Bell holds 60% of the Mexican fast-food segment, KFC holds a respectable 45% of the fast-food chicken business, and Pizza Hut leads the pizza business with a 15% market share in the pizza business segment. In addition to seeking growth through acquisition of prominent brands, since its restructuring in 2006, Yum! has been pursuing aggressive expansion overseas by expanding at the rate of 700 new locations for the seventh consecutive year since 1999. In China alone, it has more than 2,600 restaurants, accounting for 15% of its revenues.

EXHIBIT 8   McDonald's versus Rivals, Year-end 2008
(B = $billion; M = $million)

	MCD	YUM	BKC	(Fast) Food Service Industry	SBUX	Specialty Eateries Industry
Market Cap	61.17 B	15.57 B	2.45 B	161.69 M	10.1 B	1.64 B
Employees	400,000	50,400	41,000	5,700	176,000	2,140
Revenue	22.99 B	11.08 B	2.55 B	403.14 M	10.04 B	1.31 B
Gross Margin	37.09%	24.53%	33.13%	21.51%	54.24%	32.2%
Net Income	4.35 B	928 M	192 M	N/A	88 M	N/A
EPS	3.827	1.914	1.402	0.09	0.119	0.12
P/E	14.35	17.65	13.01	17.91	114.79	22.33

MCD = McDonald's Corporation

BKC = Burger King Holdings, Inc.

YUM = Yum! Brands, Inc.

SBUX = Starbucks

Source: Based on http://finance.yahoo.com.

Wendy's (WEN)

Founded in 1969, based in Dublin, Ohio, and operating over 6,600 restaurants, Wendy's International, Inc., owns 1,400 of the 6,600 restaurants. With 44,000 employees in 2007, Wendy's ranks fourth in the industry, behind McDonald's, Yum!, and Burger King. The company is well known for its unique square single, double, or triple made-to-order burgers and fries, and alternative menu items, such as baked potato, chili, and salads. Its new low-priced menus directly compete for market share with MCD. It holds a unique position in the industry as an old-fashioned eating place in the fast-food business and was recognized in 1986 as the most favorite quality brand by *QSR Magazine* for the second year in a row and earned first place for customer satisfaction in the "limited service restaurants" category in that year's American Customer Satisfaction Index survey. With revenues of $2,450 million in 2007, Wendy's currently operates as a subsidiary of the Wendy's/Arby's Group, a private company.

Starbucks Corporation (SBX)

Even though Starbucks is no direct competition for MCD's core business, MCD is now in the fighting ring with Starbucks for the specialty coffee niche. Therefore it is important to view Starbucks as a new direct competitor. Starbucks was founded in 1985 by Howard Schultz, who recently came out of retirement to serve as chairman, CEO, and president. The company is usually grouped with the high-priced, high-margins specialty eateries industry. Starbucks' annual revenues are $10.04 billion, less than half of MCD's. Starbuck's gross margins at 54.24 percent are 17 percent points higher than McDonald's. With 176,000 employees and strong brand recognition, Starbucks is seen as a leader in the specialty eateries industry.

External Threats

Because of its global reach and brand recognition, MCD continues to face significant threats to its aggressive growth strategy at home, one of which is the growing awareness among the medical and scientific community as well as the public of the direct relationship between diet and health. A joint research study recently conducted at the University of California, Berkeley, and Columbia University and published in March 2009 concluded that the presence of a fast-food restaurant within 500 feet of a school is associated with at least a 5.2 percent increase in the obesity rate in that school, suggesting significant health benefits of banning fast-food restaurants close to schools if communities are interested in fighting the growing epidemic of obesity among young adolescents in America.

MCD continues to encounter lawsuits brought about around the world by activists and irate parents of children less than 18 years of age. In 1990, in the McLibel Trial, also known as *McDonald's Restaurants v. Morris & Steel*, activists from a small group known as London Greenpeace with no affiliation with the Greenpeace organization printed and distributed information under the title, *"What's wrong with McDonald's?"* In that printed information that was widely circulated in London, they criticized MCD's environmental, health, and labor record. The corporation wrote to the group demanding them to retract and apologize, but when the two key activists refused to back down, MCD sued them for libel. It turned out to be not only one of the longest cases in British civil law, but it also turned out to be a public relations nightmare for MCD. A documentary film capturing this saga continues to been shown in several countries, including the United States.

MCD's premises continue to draw antiglobalization activists from around the world. In 1999, French activist José Bové vandalized a half-built McDonald's to protest against the introduction of fast food in the region. As recently as 2009, activists vandalized MCD's restaurants during the G-20 summit in protest of the poverty and income inequalities brought about by globalization.

The documentary film, *Super Size Me*, which argued that MCD's menu was contributing to the obesity epidemic and that the company provided no nutritional information about its products, caught MCD executive's attention quickly. Within six weeks after the film's debut, MCD eliminated the supersize option from its meal options.

In April 2006, the global activist organization Greenpeace alleged that MCD, as a client of the agricultural behemoth Cargill, was contributing to the destruction of the Amazon rain forest in Brazil and the invasion of the indigenous people's lands when it bought chickens fed with Brazilian soya. Furthermore, global activists argue that MCD's operations overburden scarce drinking water supply away from the poor local communities by diverting it to the frivolous production of supplies to support MCD.

Unfavorable changes on the sociopolitical, legal, and environmental fronts at home and overseas as well as currency rates may adversely affect MCD without prior notice. Cost of supplies may increase cutting into MCD's gross margins as is evident from its income statement (Exhibit 8). Total operating costs and expenses increased rose from about $16.5 billion in 2006 to $18.9 billion in 2007. Foreign currency translation losses displayed in Exhibit 1 show the extent of damage that global companies like MCD encounter due to the uncertainties in the global environment that no one has control over. In February 2009, MCD cut prices of its popular menu items in China by as much as 40 percent to reverse declining sales.

Conclusion

Success today is no guarantee for success tomorrow. However, McDonald's added 40 restaurants in India in 2008 and another 25 in 2009. Although people in India are predominantly Hindu and revere the cow, thus eating no beef, they love McDonald's, especially Chicken McNuggets, which were first introduced in India in May 2009. MCD's vegetable patties also are a big hit now in India.

For the second quarter, which ended June 30, 2009, MCD had positive global comparable sales in every area of the world, as well as higher revenues, operating income, and earnings per share compared with the prior year. "We're driving results by staying focused on our global business strategy, the Plan to Win," said Chief Executive Officer Jim Skinner. "As consumers find themselves more cash-strapped and time-challenged, they continue to count on McDonald's for value, convenience, and variety across our menu." MCD's second quarter 2009 results included global comparable sales up 4.8% with the United States up 3.5%, Europe up 6.9%, and Asia/Pacific, Middle East and Africa up 4.4% McDonald's Europe delivered strong second quarter comparable sales led by performance in the U.K., France, and Russia. In Asia/Pacific, Middle East, and Africa (APMEA), Australia led the segment's second quarter operating income increase of 34% in constant currencies.

Exhibit 9 provides mid-year 2009 MCD financials:

EXHIBIT 9   **MCD Financial Highlights, Second Quarter 2009 (dollars in millions, except per share data)**

	Quarter ended June 30		Six months ended June 30	
	2009	2008	2009	2008
Revenues	$5,647.2	$6,075.3	$10,724.6	$11,690.1
Operating income	1,681.5	1,654.2	3,081.9	3,117.0
Net income	1,093.7	1,190.5	2,073.2	2,136.6
Earnings per share	0.98	1.04	1.85	1.85

ASSURANCE OF LEARNING EXERCISES

Assurance of Learning Exercise 1A

Gathering Strategy Information

Purpose

The purpose of this exercise is to get you familiar with strategy terms introduced and defined in Chapter 1. Let's apply these terms to McDonald's Corporation (stock symbol = MCD).

Instructions

Step 1	Go to www.mcdonalds.com, which is McDonald's Web site. Click on the word Search. Then type in the words *Annual Report*. Then print the 2009 McDonald's *Annual Report*. This document may be 100 pages, so you may want to print it in your college library or order the report directly from McDonald's as indicated on the Web site. The *Annual Report* contains excellent information for developing a list of internal strengths and weaknesses for MCD.
Step 2	Go to your college library and make a copy of Standard & Poor's Industry Surveys for the restaurant industry. This document will contain excellent information for developing a list of external opportunities and threats facing MCD.
Step 3	Go to the www.finance.yahoo.com Web site. Enter MCD. Note the wealth of information on McDonald's that may be obtained by clicking any item along the left column. Click on Competitors down the left column. Then print out the resultant tables and information. Note that McDonald's two major competitors are Yum! Brands, Inc. and Burger King Holdings.
Step 4	Using the Cohesion Case, the www.finance.yahoo information, the *2009 Annual Report*, and the Industry Survey document, on a separate sheet of paper list what you consider to be MCD's three major strengths, three major weaknesses, three major opportunities, and three major threats. Each factor listed for this exercise must include a %, #, $, or ratio to reveal some quantified fact or trend. These factors provide the underlying basis for a strategic plan because a firm strives to take advantage of strengths, improve weaknesses, avoid threats, and capitalize on opportunities.
Step 5	Through class discussion, compare your lists of external and internal factors to those developed by other students and add to your lists of factors. Keep this information for use in later exercises at the end of other chapters.
Step 6	Be mindful that whatever case company is assigned to your team of students this semester, you can start to update the information on your company by following the steps just listed for any publicly-held firm.

Assurance of Learning Exercise 1B

Strategic Planning for My University

Purpose

External and internal factors are the underlying bases of strategies formulated and implemented by organizations. Your college or university faces numerous external opportunities/threats and has many internal strengths/weaknesses. The purpose of this exercise is to illustrate the process of identifying critical external and internal factors.

External influences include trends in the following areas: economic, social, cultural, demographic, environmental, technological, political, legal, governmental, and competitive. External factors could include declining numbers of high school graduates; population shifts; community relations; increased competitiveness among colleges and universities; rising numbers of adults returning to college; decreased support from local, state, and federal agencies; increasing numbers of foreign students attending U.S. colleges; and a rising number of Internet courses.

Internal factors of a college or university include faculty, students, staff, alumni, athletic programs, physical plant, grounds and maintenance, student housing, administration, fundraising, academic programs, food services, parking, placement, clubs, fraternities, sororities, and public relations.

Instructions

Step 1	On a separate sheet of paper, write four headings: External Opportunities, External Threats, Internal Strengths, and Internal Weaknesses.
Step 2	As related to your college or university, list five factors under each of the four headings.
Step 3	Discuss the factors as a class. Write the factors on the board.
Step 4	What new things did you learn about your university from the class discussion? How could this type of discussion benefit an organization?

Assurance of Learning Exercise 1C

Strategic Planning at a Local Company

Purpose

This activity is aimed at giving you practical knowledge about how organizations in your city or town are doing strategic planning. This exercise also will give you experience interacting on a professional basis with local business leaders.

Instructions

Step 1	Use the telephone to contact business owners or top managers. Find an organization that does strategic planning. Make an appointment to visit with the strategist (president, chief executive officer, or owner) of that business.
Step 2	Seek answers to the following questions during the interview:

- How does your firm formally conduct strategic planning? Who is involved in the process? Does the firm hold planning retreats? If yes, how often and where?
- Does your firm have a written mission statement? How was the statement developed? When was the statement last changed?
- What are the benefits of engaging in strategic planning?
- What are the major costs or problems in doing strategic planning in your business?
- Do you anticipate making any changes in the strategic-planning process at your company? If yes, please explain.

Step 3	Report your findings to the class.

Assurance of Learning Exercise 1D

Getting Familiar with SMCO

Purpose

This exercise is designed to get you familiar with the Strategic Management Club Online (SMCO), which offers many benefits for the strategy student. The SMCO site also offers templates for doing case analyses in this course.

Instructions

Step 1   Go to the www.strategyclub.com Web site. Review the various sections of this site.

Step 2   Select a section of the SMCO site that you feel will be most useful to you in this class. Write a one-page summary of that section and describe why you feel it will benefit you most.

CHAPTER 2
The Business Vision and Mission

CHAPTER OBJECTIVES

After studying this chapter, you should be able to do the following:

1. Describe the nature and role of vision and mission statements in strategic management.

2. Discuss why the process of developing a mission statement is as important as the resulting document.

3. Identify the components of mission statements.

4. Discuss how clear vision and mission statements can benefit other strategic-management activities.

5. Evaluate mission statements of different organizations.

6. Write good vision and mission statements.

Assurance of Learning Exercises

Assurance of Learning Exercise 2A
Evaluating Mission Statements

Assurance of Learning Exercise 2B
Writing a Vision and Mission Statement for McDonald's

Assurance of Learning Exercise 2C
Writing a Vision and Mission Statement for My University

Assurance of Learning Exercise 2D
Conducting Mission Statement Research

Source: Shutterstock/Photographer Dmitriy Shironosov

"Notable Quotes"

"A business is not defined by its name, statutes, or articles of incorporation. It is defined by the business mission. Only a clear definition of the mission and purpose of the organization makes possible clear and realistic business objectives."

—Peter Drucker

"A corporate vision can focus, direct, motivate, unify, and even excite a business into superior performance. The job of a strategist is to identify and project a clear vision."

—John Keane

"Where there is no vision, the people perish."

—Proverbs 29:18

"The last thing IBM needs right now is a vision. (July 1993) What IBM needs most right now is a vision. (March 1996)"

—Louis V. Gerstner Jr., CEO, IBM Corporation

"The best laid schemes of mice and men often go awry."

—Robert Burns (paraphrased)

"A strategist's job is to see the company not as it is ... but as it can become."

—John W. Teets, Chairman of Greyhound, Inc.

"That business mission is so rarely given adequate thought is perhaps the most important single cause of business frustration."

—Peter Drucker

"The very essence of leadership is that you have to have vision. You can't blow an uncertain trumpet."

—Theodore Hesburgh

This chapter focuses on the concepts and tools needed to evaluate and write business vision and mission statements. A practical framework for developing mission statements is provided. Actual mission statements from large and small organizations and for-profit and nonprofit enterprises are presented and critically examined. The process of creating a vision and mission statement is discussed. The global economic recession has resulted in many firms changing direction and thereby altering their entire vision and mission in order to survive. For example, in the Philippines, the largest food and beverage company, San Miguel Corp., recently diversified by purchasing Petron Corp., the country's largest oil refiner. San Miguel also purchased Meralco, formally named Manila Electric, thus broadening its mission to include energy-related businesses.

The boxed insert company examined in this chapter is Wal-Mart, which has a clear vision/mission and strategic plan. Wal-Mart is doing great in the global economic recession.

Doing Great in a Weak Economy

Wal-Mart

When most firms were struggling in 2008, Wal-Mart increased its revenues from $348 billion in 2007 to $378 billion in 2008. Wal-Mart's net income increased too, from $11.2 billion to $12.7 billion—quite impressive. *Fortune* magazine in 2009 rated Wal-Mart as their 11th "Most Admired Company in the World" in terms of their management and performance.

Wal-Mart Stores continues to expand internationally, particularly in emerging countries such as Brazil and India. From 2009 to 2013, Wal-Mart plans to devote 53 percent of its international spending to emerging markets, up from 33 percent in the prior five years. The company plans include remodeling U.S. stores rather than adding new stores and going to smaller stores. Wal-Mart's capital expenditures in the year ending January 2010 were $5.3 billion, up from $4.8 billion the prior year.

As electronics retailer Circuit City was declaring bankruptcy and liquidating in 2008, Wal-Mart was beefing up its electronics product line, directly attacking Best Buy. The two firms today are in a dogfight to obtain the millions of electronics products customers. Best Buy was *Fortune*'s 44th "Most Admired Company in the World" in 2009.

Wal-Mart recently revamped the electronics departments in its 3,500 U.S. stores to make them much more interactive and roomier. The company wants all the business that Circuit City's failure left and also wants all of Best Buy's and Amazon's business. Wal-Mart now carries sophisticated electronics products such as Research in Motion Ltd.'s Blackberry smart phones, Palm Inc.'s Pre smart phone, and Blu-ray disc players. Wal-Mart in June 2009 began selling Dell Inc.'s new Studio One 19 touch-screen computers.

Wal-Mart Stores is bigger than Europe's Carrefour, Tesco, and Metro AG combined. It is the world's number one retailer, with more than 7,870 stores, including about 890 discount stores, 2,970 combination discount and grocery stores (Wal-Mart Supercenters in the United States and ASDA in the United Kingdom), and 600 warehouse stores (Sam's Club). About 55 percent of its Wal-Mart stores are in the United States, but the company continues expanding internationally; it is the number-one retailer in Canada and Mexico and it has operations in Asia (where it owns a 95 percent stake in Japanese retailer SEIYU), Europe, and South America. Founder Sam Walton's heirs own about 40 percent of Wal-Mart.

Wal-Mart is a corporate leader in sustainability. The company in 2009 alone installed rooftop solar arrays on 20 stores and warehouses in California and Hawaii.

A Wal-Mart partner, BP Solar, installs, maintains, and owns these systems.

Perhaps more importantly, Wal-Mart in July 2009 unveiled a new environmental labeling program that requires all its vendors to calculate and disclose the full environmental costs of making their products. All vendors must soon distill that information into Wal-Mart's new labeling system, thus providing product environmental impact information to all Wal-Mart shoppers. This new Wal-Mart program may redefine the whole consumer products labeling process globally by the year 2012.

Source: Based on Geoff Colvin, "The World's Most Admired Companies," *Fortune* (March 16, 2009): 76–86; and Miguel Bustillo, "Wal-Mart Puts Green Movement Into Stores," *Wall Street Journal* (July 16, 2009): A1.

We can perhaps best understand vision and mission by focusing on a business when it is first started. In the beginning, a new business is simply a collection of ideas. Starting a new business rests on a set of beliefs that the new organization can offer some product or service to some customers, in some geographic area, using some type of technology, at a profitable price. A new business owner typically believes that the management philosophy of the new enterprise will result in a favorable public image and that this concept of the business can be communicated to, and will be adopted by, important constituencies. When the set of beliefs about a business at its inception is put into writing, the resulting document mirrors the same basic ideas that underlie the vision and mission statements. As a business grows, owners or managers find it necessary to revise the founding set of beliefs, but those original ideas usually are reflected in the revised statements of vision and mission.

Vision and mission statements often can be found in the front of annual reports. They often are displayed throughout a firm's premises and are distributed with company information sent to constituencies. The statements are part of numerous internal reports, such as loan requests, supplier agreements, labor relations contracts, business plans, and customer service agreements. In a recent study, researchers concluded that 90 percent of all companies have used a mission statement sometime in the previous five years.[1]

What Do We Want to Become?

It is especially important for managers and executives in any organization to agree on the basic vision that the firm strives to achieve in the long term. A vision statement should answer the basic question, "What do we want to become?" A clear vision provides the foundation for developing a comprehensive mission statement. Many organizations have both a vision and mission statement, but the vision statement should be established first and foremost. The vision statement should be short, preferably one sentence, and as many managers as possible should have input into developing the statement.

Several example vision statements are provided in Table 2-1.

What Is Our Business?

Current thought on mission statements is based largely on guidelines set forth in the mid-1970s by Peter Drucker, who is often called "the father of modern management" for his pioneering studies at General Motors Corporation and for his 22 books and hundreds of articles. *Harvard Business Review* has called Drucker "the preeminent management thinker of our time."

TABLE 2-1 Vision Statement Examples

Tyson Foods' vision is to be the world's first choice for protein solutions while maximizing shareholder value. (*Author comment: Good statement, unless Tyson provides nonprotein products*)

General Motors' vision is to be the world leader in transportation products and related services. (*Author comment: Good statement*)

PepsiCo's responsibility is to continually improve all aspects of the world in which we operate—environment, social, economic—creating a better tomorrow than today. (*Author comment: Statement is too vague; it should reveal beverage and food business*)

Dell's vision is to create a company culture where environmental excellence is second nature. (*Author comment: Statement is too vague; it should reveal computer business in some manner; the word* environmental *is generally used to refer to natural environment so is unclear in its use here*)

The vision of First Reliance Bank is to be recognized as the largest and most profitable bank in South Carolina. (*Author comment: This is a very small new bank headquartered in Florence, South Carolina, so this goal is not achievable in five years; the statement is too futuristic*)

Samsonite's vision is to provide innovative solutions for the traveling world. (*Author comment: Statement needs to be more specific, perhaps mention luggage; statement as is could refer to air carriers or cruise lines, which is not good*)

Royal Caribbean's vision is to empower and enable our employees to deliver the best vacation experience for our guests, thereby generating superior returns for our shareholders and enhancing the well-being of our communities. (*Author comment: Statement is good but could end after the word "guests"*)

Procter & Gamble's vision is to be, and be recognized as, the best consumer products company in the world. (*Author comment: Statement is too vague and readability is not that good*)

Drucker says that asking the question "What is our business?" is synonymous with asking the question "What is our mission?" An enduring statement of purpose that distinguishes one organization from other similar enterprises, the *mission statement* is a declaration of an organization's "reason for being." It answers the pivotal question "What is our business?" A clear mission statement is essential for effectively establishing objectives and formulating strategies.

Sometimes called a *creed statement*, a statement of purpose, a statement of philosophy, a statement of beliefs, a statement of business principles, or a statement "defining our business," a mission statement reveals what an organization wants to be and whom it wants to serve. All organizations have a reason for being, even if strategists have not consciously transformed this reason into writing. As illustrated in Figure 2-1, carefully prepared statements of vision and mission are widely recognized by both practitioners and academicians as the first step in strategic management.

Some example mission statements are provided in Table 2-2. Drucker has the following to say about mission statements:

A business mission is the foundation for priorities, strategies, plans, and work assignments. It is the starting point for the design of managerial jobs and, above all, for the design of managerial structures. Nothing may seem simpler or more obvious than to know what a company's business is. A steel mill makes steel, a railroad runs trains to carry freight and passengers, an insurance company underwrites fire risks, and a bank lends money. Actually, "What is our business?" is almost always a difficult question and the right answer is usually anything but obvious. The answer to this question is the first responsibility of strategists. Only strategists can make sure that this question receives the attention it deserves and that the answer makes sense and enables the business to plot its course and set its objectives.[2]

Some strategists spend almost every moment of every day on administrative and tactical concerns, and strategists who rush quickly to establish objectives and implement strategies often overlook the development of a vision and mission statement. This problem is widespread even among large organizations. Many corporations in America have not yet developed a formal vision or mission statement.[3] An increasing number of organizations are developing these statements.

Some companies develop mission statements simply because they feel it is fashionable, rather than out of any real commitment. However, as described in this chapter, firms that develop and systematically revisit their vision and mission statements, treat them as

FIGURE 2-1

A Comprehensive Strategic-Management Model

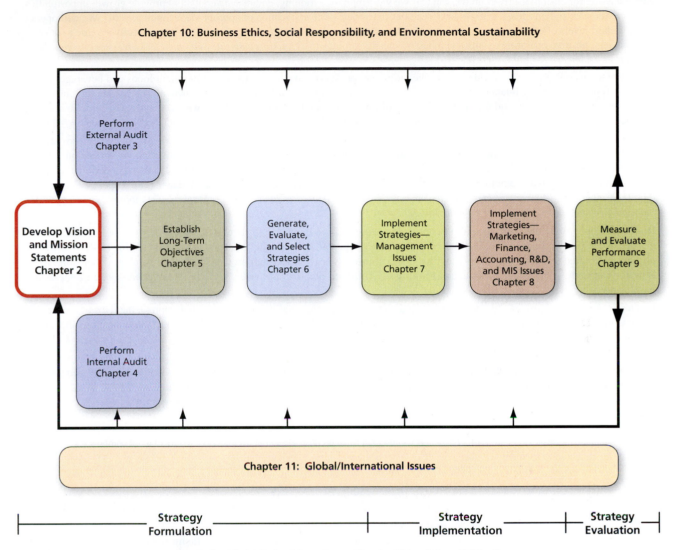

Source: Fred R. David, "How Companies Define Their Mission," *Long Range Planning* 22, no. 3 (June 1988): 40.

living documents, and consider them to be an integral part of the firm's culture realize great benefits. Johnson & Johnson (J&J) is an example firm. J&J managers meet regularly with employees to review, reword, and reaffirm the firm's vision and mission. The entire J&J workforce recognizes the value that top management places on this exercise, and these employees respond accordingly.

Vision versus Mission

Many organizations develop both a mission statement and a vision statement. Whereas the mission statement answers the question "What is our business?" the *vision statement* answers the question "What do we want to become?" Many organizations have both a mission and vision statement.

It can be argued that profit, not mission or vision, is the primary corporate motivator. But profit alone is not enough to motivate people.[4] Profit is perceived negatively by some employees in companies. Employees may see profit as something that they earn and management then uses and even gives away to shareholders. Although this perception is

TABLE 2-2 Example Mission Statements

Fleetwood Enterprises will lead the recreational vehicle and manufactured housing industries (2, 7) in providing quality products, with a passion for customer-driven innovation (1). We will emphasize training, embrace diversity and provide growth opportunities for our associates and our dealers (9). We will lead our industries in the application of appropriate technologies (4). We will operate at the highest levels of ethics and compliance with a focus on exemplary corporate governance (6). We will deliver value to our shareholders, positive operating results and industry-leading earnings (5). *(Author comment: Statement lacks two components: Markets and Concern for Public Image)*

We aspire to make PepsiCo the world's (3) premier consumer products company, focused on convenient foods and beverages (2). We seek to produce healthy financial rewards for investors (5) as we provide opportunities for growth and enrichment to our employees (9), our business partners and the communities (8) in which we operate. And in everything we do, we strive to act with honesty, openness, fairness and integrity (6). *(Author comment: Statement lacks three components: Customers, Technology, and Self-Concept)*

We are loyal to Royal Caribbean and Celebrity and strive for continuous improvement in everything we do. We always provide service with a friendly greeting and a smile (7). We anticipate the needs of our customers and make all efforts to exceed our customers' expectations (1). We take ownership of any problem that is brought to our attention. We engage in conduct that enhances our corporate reputation and employee morale (9). We are committed to act in the highest ethical manner and respect the rights and dignity of others (6). *(Author comment: Statement lacks five components: Products/Services, Markets, Technology, Concern for Survival/Growth/Profits, Concern for Public Image)*

Dell's mission is to be the most successful computer company (2) in the world (3) at delivering the best customer experience in markets we serve (1). In doing so, Dell will meet customer expectations of highest quality; leading technology (4); competitive pricing; individual and company accountability (6); best-in-class service and support (7); flexible customization capability (7); superior corporate citizenship (8); financial stability (5). *(Author comment: Statement lacks only one component: Concern for Employees)*

Procter & Gamble will provide branded products and services of superior quality and value (7) that improve the lives of the world's (3) consumers. As a result, consumers (1) will reward us with industry leadership in sales, profit (5), and value creation, allowing our people (9), our shareholders, and the communities (8) in which we live and work to prosper. *(Author comment: Statement lacks three components: Products/Services, Technology, and Philosophy)*

At L'Oreal, we believe that lasting business success is built upon ethical (6) standards which guide growth and on a genuine sense of responsibility to our employees (9), our consumers, our environment and to the communities in which we operate (8). *(Author comment: Statement lacks six components: Customers, Products/Services, Markets, Technology, Concern for Survival/Growth/Profits, Concern for Public Image)*

Note: The numbers in parentheses correspond to the nine components listed on page 51; author comment also refers to those components.

undesired and disturbing to management, it clearly indicates that both profit and vision are needed to motivate a workforce effectively.

When employees and managers together shape or fashion the vision and mission statements for a firm, the resultant documents can reflect the personal visions that managers and employees have in their hearts and minds about their own futures. Shared vision creates a commonality of interests that can lift workers out of the monotony of daily work and put them into a new world of opportunity and challenge.

The Process of Developing Vision and Mission Statements

As indicated in the strategic-management model, clear vision and mission statements are needed before alternative strategies can be formulated and implemented. As many managers as possible should be involved in the process of developing these statements because through involvement, people become committed to an organization.

A widely used approach to developing a vision and mission statement is first to select several articles about these statements and ask all managers to read these as background information. Then ask managers themselves to prepare a vision and mission statement for the organization. A facilitator, or committee of top managers, should then merge these statements into a single document and distribute the draft statements to all managers. A request for modifications, additions, and deletions is needed next, along with a meeting to revise the document. To the extent that all managers have input into and support the final documents, organizations can more easily obtain managers' support for other strategy formulation, implementation, and evaluation activities. Thus, the process of developing a vision and mission statement represents a great opportunity for strategists to obtain needed support from all managers in the firm.

During the process of developing vision and mission statements, some organizations use discussion groups of managers to develop and modify existing statements. Some organizations hire an outside consultant or facilitator to manage the process and help draft the language. Sometimes an outside person with expertise in developing such statements, who has unbiased views, can manage the process more effectively than an internal group or committee of managers. Decisions on how best to communicate the vision and mission to all managers, employees, and external constituencies of an organization are needed when the documents are in final form. Some organizations even develop a videotape to explain the statements, and how they were developed.

An article by Campbell and Yeung emphasizes that the process of developing a mission statement should create an "emotional bond" and "sense of mission" between the organization and its employees.[5] Commitment to a company's strategy and intellectual agreement on the strategies to be pursued do not necessarily translate into an emotional bond; hence, strategies that have been formulated may not be implemented. These researchers stress that an emotional bond comes when an individual personally identifies with the underlying values and behavior of a firm, thus turning intellectual agreement and commitment to strategy into a sense of mission. Campbell and Yeung also differentiate between the terms *vision* and *mission*, saying that vision is "a possible and desirable future state of an organization" that includes specific goals, whereas mission is more associated with behavior and the present.

Importance (Benefits) of Vision and Mission Statements

The importance (benefits) of vision and mission statements to effective strategic management is well documented in the literature, although research results are mixed. Rarick and Vitton found that firms with a formalized mission statement have twice the average return on shareholders' equity than those firms without a formalized mission statement have; Bart and Baetz found a positive relationship between mission statements and organizational performance; *BusinessWeek* reports that firms using mission statements have a 30 percent higher return on certain financial measures than those without such statements; however, some studies have found that having a mission statement does not directly contribute positively to financial performance.[6] The extent of manager and employee involvement in developing vision and mission statements can make a difference in business success. This chapter provides guidelines for developing these important documents. In actual practice, wide variations exist in the nature, composition, and use of both vision and mission statements. King and Cleland recommend that organizations carefully develop a written mission statement in order to reap the following benefits:

1. To ensure unanimity of purpose within the organization
2. To provide a basis, or standard, for allocating organizational resources
3. To establish a general tone or organizational climate
4. To serve as a focal point for individuals to identify with the organization's purpose and direction, and to deter those who cannot from participating further in the organization's activities
5. To facilitate the translation of objectives into a work structure involving the assignment of tasks to responsible elements within the organization
6. To specify organizational purposes and then to translate these purposes into objectives in such a way that cost, time, and performance parameters can be assessed and controlled.[7]

Reuben Mark, former CEO of Colgate, maintains that a clear mission increasingly must make sense internationally. Mark's thoughts on vision are as follows:

> When it comes to rallying everyone to the corporate banner, it's essential to push one vision globally rather than trying to drive home different messages in different cultures. The trick is to keep the vision simple but elevated: "We make the world's fastest computers" or "Telephone service for everyone." You're never going to get anyone to charge the machine guns only for financial objectives. It's got to be something that makes people feel better, feel a part of something.[8]

A Resolution of Divergent Views

Another benefit of developing a comprehensive mission statement is that divergent views among managers can be revealed and resolved through the process. The question "What is our business?" can create controversy. Raising the question often reveals differences among strategists in the organization. Individuals who have worked together for a long time and who think they know each other suddenly may realize that they are in fundamental disagreement. For example, in a college or university, divergent views regarding the relative importance of teaching, research, and service often are expressed during the mission statement development process. Negotiation, compromise, and eventual agreement on important issues are needed before people can focus on more specific strategy formulation activities.

> "What is our mission?" is a genuine decision; and a genuine decision must be based on divergent views to have a chance to be a right and effective decision. Developing a business mission is always a choice between alternatives, each of which rests on different assumptions regarding the reality of the business and its environment. It is always a high-risk decision. A change in mission always leads to changes in objectives, strategies, organization, and behavior. The mission decision is far too important to be made by acclamation. Developing a business mission is a big step toward management effectiveness. Hidden or half-understood disagreements on the definition of a business mission underlie many of the personality problems, communication problems, and irritations that tend to divide a top-management group. Establishing a mission should never be made on plausibility alone, should never be made fast, and should never be made painlessly.[9]

Considerable disagreement among an organization's strategists over vision and mission statements can cause trouble if not resolved. For example, unresolved disagreement over the business mission was one of the reasons for W. T. Grant's bankruptcy and eventual liquidation. As one executive reported:

> There was a lot of dissension within the company whether we should go the Kmart route or go after the Montgomery Ward and JCPenney position. Ed Staley and Lou Lustenberger (two top executives) were at loggerheads over the issue, with the upshot being we took a position between the two and that consequently stood for nothing.[10]

Too often, strategists develop vision and business mission statements only when the organization is in trouble. Of course, it is needed then. Developing and communicating a clear mission during troubled times indeed may have spectacular results and even may reverse decline. However, to wait until an organization is in trouble to develop a vision and mission statement is a gamble that characterizes irresponsible management. According to Drucker, the most important time to ask seriously, "What do we want to become?" and "What is our business?" is when a company has been successful:

> Success always obsoletes the very behavior that achieved it, always creates new realities, and always creates new and different problems. Only the fairy tale story ends, "They lived happily ever after." It is never popular to argue with success or to rock

the boat. The ancient Greeks knew that the penalty of success can be severe. The management that does not ask "What is our mission?" when the company is successful is, in effect, smug, lazy, and arrogant. It will not be long before success will turn into failure. Sooner or later, even the most successful answer to the question "What is our business?" becomes obsolete.[11]

In multidivisional organizations, strategists should ensure that divisional units perform strategic-management tasks, including the development of a statement of vision and mission. Each division should involve its own managers and employees in developing a vision and mission statement that is consistent with and supportive of the corporate mission.

An organization that fails to develop a vision statement as well as a comprehensive and inspiring mission statement loses the opportunity to present itself favorably to existing and potential stakeholders. All organizations need customers, employees, and managers, and most firms need creditors, suppliers, and distributors. The vision and mission statements are effective vehicles for communicating with important internal and external stakeholders. The principal benefit of these statements as tools of strategic management is derived from their specification of the ultimate aims of a firm:

They provide managers with a unity of direction that transcends individual, parochial, and transitory needs. They promote a sense of shared expectations among all levels and generations of employees. They consolidate values over time and across individuals and interest groups. They project a sense of worth and intent that can be identified and assimilated by company outsiders. Finally, they affirm the company's commitment to responsible action, which is symbiotic with its need to preserve and protect the essential claims of insiders for sustained survival, growth, and profitability of the firm.[12]

Characteristics of a Mission Statement

A Declaration of Attitude

A mission statement is more than a statement of specific details; it is a declaration of attitude and outlook. It usually is broad in scope for at least two major reasons. First, a good mission statement allows for the generation and consideration of a range of feasible alternative objectives and strategies without unduly stifling management creativity. Excess specificity would limit the potential of creative growth for the organization. However, an overly general statement that does not exclude any strategy alternatives could be dysfunctional. Apple Computer's mission statement, for example, should not open the possibility for diversification into pesticides—or Ford Motor Company's into food processing.

Second, a mission statement needs to be broad to reconcile differences effectively among, and appeal to, an organization's diverse *stakeholders*, the individuals and groups of individuals who have a special stake or claim on the company. Thus a mission statement should be *reconcilatory*. Stakeholders include employees, managers, stockholders, boards of directors, customers, suppliers, distributors, creditors, governments (local, state, federal, and foreign), unions, competitors, environmental groups, and the general public. Stakeholders affect and are affected by an organization's strategies, yet the claims and concerns of diverse constituencies vary and often conflict. For example, the general public is especially interested in social responsibility, whereas stockholders are more interested in profitability. Claims on any business literally may number in the thousands, and they often include clean air, jobs, taxes, investment opportunities, career opportunities, equal employment opportunities, employee benefits, salaries, wages, clean water, and community services. All stakeholders' claims on an organization cannot be pursued with equal emphasis. A good mission statement indicates the relative attention that an organization will devote to meeting the claims of various stakeholders.

The fine balance between specificity and generality is difficult to achieve, but it is well worth the effort. George Steiner offers the following insight on the need for a mission statement to be broad in scope:

> Most business statements of mission are expressed at high levels of abstraction. Vagueness nevertheless has its virtues. Mission statements are not designed to express concrete ends, but rather to provide motivation, general direction, an image, a tone, and a philosophy to guide the enterprise. An excess of detail could prove counterproductive since concrete specification could be the base for rallying opposition. Precision might stifle creativity in the formulation of an acceptable mission or purpose. Once an aim is cast in concrete, it creates a rigidity in an organization and resists change. Vagueness leaves room for other managers to fill in the details, perhaps even to modify general patterns. Vagueness permits more flexibility in adapting to changing environments and internal operations. It facilitates flexibility in implementation.[13]

As indicated in Table 2-3, in addition to being broad in scope, an effective mission statement should not be too lengthy; recommended length is less than 250 words. An effective mission statement should arouse positive feelings and emotions about an organization; it should be inspiring in the sense that it motivates readers to action. A mission statement should be enduring. All of these are desired characteristics of a statement. An effective mission statement generates the impression that a firm is successful, has direction, and is worthy of time, support, and investment—from all socioeconomic groups of people.

It reflects judgments about future growth directions and strategies that are based on forward-looking external and internal analyses. A business mission should provide useful criteria for selecting among alternative strategies. A clear mission statement provides a basis for generating and screening strategic options. The statement of mission should be dynamic in orientation, allowing judgments about the most promising growth directions and those considered less promising.

A Customer Orientation

A good mission statement describes an organization's purpose, customers, products or services, markets, philosophy, and basic technology. According to Vern McGinnis, a mission statement should (1) define what the organization is and what the organization aspires to be, (2) be limited enough to exclude some ventures and broad enough to allow for creative growth, (3) distinguish a given organization from all others, (4) serve as a framework for evaluating both current and prospective activities, and (5) be stated in terms sufficiently clear to be widely understood throughout the organization.[14]

A good mission statement reflects the anticipations of customers. Rather than developing a product and then trying to find a market, the operating philosophy of organizations should be to identify customers' needs and then provide a product or service to fulfill those needs.

TABLE 2-3   Ten Benefits of Having a Clear Mission and Vision

1. Achieve clarity of purpose among all managers and employees.
2. Provide a basis for all other strategic planning activities, including the internal and external assessment, establishing objectives, developing strategies, choosing among alternative strategies, devising policies, establishing organizational structure, allocating resources, and evaluating performance.
3. Provide direction.
4. Provide a focal point for all stakeholders of the firm.
5. Resolve divergent views among managers.
6. Promote a sense of shared expectations among all managers and employees.
7. Project a sense of worth and intent to all stakeholders.
8. Project an organized, motivated organization worthy of support.
9. Achieve higher organizational performance.
10. Achieve synergy among all managers and employees.

Good mission statements identify the utility of a firm's products to its customers. This is why AT&T's mission statement focuses on communication rather than on telephones; it is why ExxonMobil's mission statement focuses on energy rather than on oil and gas; it is why Union Pacific's mission statement focuses on transportation rather than on railroads; it is why Universal Studios' mission statement focuses on entertainment rather than on movies. The following utility statements are relevant in developing a mission statement:

Do not offer me things.

Do not offer me clothes. Offer me attractive looks.

Do not offer me shoes. Offer me comfort for my feet and the pleasure of walking.

Do not offer me a house. Offer me security, comfort, and a place that is clean and happy.

Do not offer me books. Offer me hours of pleasure and the benefit of knowledge.

Do not offer me CDs. Offer me leisure and the sound of music.

Do not offer me tools. Offer me the benefits and the pleasure that come from making beautiful things.

Do not offer me furniture. Offer me comfort and the quietness of a cozy place.

Do not offer me things. Offer me ideas, emotions, ambience, feelings, and benefits.

Please, do not offer me *things*.

A major reason for developing a business mission statement is to attract customers who give meaning to an organization. Hotel customers today want to use the Internet, so more and more hotels are providing Internet service. A classic description of the purpose of a business reveals the relative importance of customers in a statement of mission:

It is the customer who determines what a business is. It is the customer alone whose willingness to pay for a good or service converts economic resources into wealth and things into goods. What a business thinks it produces is not of first importance, especially not to the future of the business and to its success. What the customer thinks he/she is buying, what he/she considers value, is decisive—it determines what a business is, what it produces, and whether it will prosper. And what the customer buys and considers value is never a product. It is always utility, meaning what a product or service does for him or her. The customer is the foundation of a business and keeps it in existence.[15]

Mission Statement Components

Mission statements can and do vary in length, content, format, and specificity. Most practitioners and academicians of strategic management feel that an effective statement should include nine components. Because a mission statement is often the most visible and public part of the strategic-management process, it is important that it includes the nine characteristics as summarized in Table 2-4, as well as the following nine components:

1. *Customers*—Who are the firm's customers?
2. *Products or services*—What are the firm's major products or services?
3. *Markets*—Geographically, where does the firm compete?
4. *Technology*—Is the firm technologically current?
5. *Concern for survival, growth, and profitability*—Is the firm committed to growth and financial soundness?
6. *Philosophy*—What are the basic beliefs, values, aspirations, and ethical priorities of the firm?
7. *Self-concept*—What is the firm's distinctive competence or major competitive advantage?
8. *Concern for public image*—Is the firm responsive to social, community, and environmental concerns?
9. *Concern for employees*—Are employees a valuable asset of the firm?

Excerpts from the mission statements of different organizations are provided in Table 2-5 to exemplify the nine essential mission statement components.

TABLE 2-4 **Characteristics of a Mission Statement**

- Broad in scope; do not include monetary amounts, numbers, percentages, ratios, or objectives
- Less than 250 words in length
- Inspiring
- Identify the utility of a firm's products
- Reveal that the firm is socially responsible
- Reveal that the firm is environmentally responsible
- Include nine components
    customers, products or services, markets, technology, concern for survival/growth/
    profits, philosophy, self-concept, concern for public image, concern for employees
- Reconciliatory
- Enduring

TABLE 2-5 **Examples of the Nine Essential Components of a Mission Statement**

1. Customers

We believe our first responsibility is to the doctors, nurses, patients, mothers, and all others who use our products and services. (Johnson & Johnson)

To earn our customers' loyalty, we listen to them, anticipate their needs, and act to create value in their eyes. (Lexmark International)

2. Products or Services

AMAX's principal products are molybdenum, coal, iron ore, copper, lead, zinc, petroleum and natural gas, potash, phosphates, nickel, tungsten, silver, gold, and magnesium. (AMAX Engineering Company)

Standard Oil Company (Indiana) is in business to find and produce crude oil, natural gas, and natural gas liquids; to manufacture high-quality products useful to society from these raw materials; and to distribute and market those products and to provide dependable related services to the consuming public at reasonable prices. (Standard Oil Company)

3. Markets

We are dedicated to the total success of Corning Glass Works as a worldwide competitor. (Corning Glass Works)

Our emphasis is on North American markets, although global opportunities will be explored. (Blockway)

4. Technology

Control Data is in the business of applying micro-electronics and computer technology in two general areas: computer-related hardware; and computing-enhancing services, which include computation, information, education, and finance. (Control Data)

We will continually strive to meet the preferences of adult smokers by developing technologies that have the potential to reduce the health risks associated with smoking. (RJ Reynolds)

5. Concern for Survival, Growth, and Profitability

In this respect, the company will conduct its operations prudently and will provide the profits and growth which will assure Hoover's ultimate success. (Hoover Universal)

To serve the worldwide need for knowledge at a fair profit by adhering, evaluating, producing, and distributing valuable information in a way that benefits our customers, employees, other investors, and our society. (McGraw-Hill)

6. Philosophy

Our world-class leadership is dedicated to a management philosophy that holds people above profits. (Kellogg)

It's all part of the Mary Kay philosophy—a philosophy based on the golden rule. A spirit of sharing and caring where people give cheerfully of their time, knowledge, and experience. (Mary Kay Cosmetics)

7. Self-Concept

Crown Zellerbach is committed to leapfrogging ongoing competition within 1,000 days by unleashing the constructive and creative abilities and energies of each of its employees. (Crown Zellerbach)

8. Concern for Public Image

To share the world's obligation for the protection of the environment. (Dow Chemical)

To contribute to the economic strength of society and function as a good corporate citizen on a local, state, and national basis in all countries in which we do business. (Pfizer)

9. Concern for Employees

To recruit, develop, motivate, reward, and retain personnel of exceptional ability, character, and dedication by providing good working conditions, superior leadership, compensation on the basis of performance, an attractive benefit program, opportunity for growth, and a high degree of employment security. (The Wachovia Corporation)

To compensate its employees with remuneration and fringe benefits competitive with other employment opportunities in its geographical area and commensurate with their contributions toward efficient corporate operations. (Public Service Electric & Gas Company)

Writing and Evaluating Mission Statements

Perhaps the best way to develop a skill for writing and evaluating mission statements is to study actual company missions. Therefore, the mission statements presented on pages 44–46 are evaluated based on the nine desired components. Note earlier in Table 2-2 that numbers provided in each statement reveal what components are included in the respective documents. Among the statements in Table 2-2, note that the Dell mission statement is the best because it lacks only one component, whereas the L'Oreal statement is the worst, lacking six of the nine recommended components.

There is no one best mission statement for a particular organization, so good judgment is required in evaluating mission statements. Realize that some individuals are more demanding than others in assessing mission statements in this manner. For example, if a statement merely includes the word "customers" without specifying who the customers are, is that satisfactory? Ideally a statement would provide more than simply inclusion of a single word such as "products" or "employees" regarding a respective component. Why? Because the statement should be informative, inspiring, enduring, and serve to motivate stakeholders to action. Evaluation of a mission statement regarding inclusion of the nine components is just the beginning of the process to assess a statement's overall effectiveness.

Conclusion

Every organization has a unique purpose and reason for being. This uniqueness should be reflected in vision and mission statements. The nature of a business vision and mission can represent either a competitive advantage or disadvantage for the firm. An organization achieves a heightened sense of purpose when strategists, managers, and employees develop and communicate a clear business vision and mission. Drucker says that developing a clear business vision and mission is the "first responsibility of strategists."

A good mission statement reveals an organization's customers; products or services; markets; technology; concern for survival, growth, and profitability; philosophy; self-concept; concern for public image; and concern for employees. These nine basic components serve as a practical framework for evaluating and writing mission statements. As the first step in strategic management, the vision and mission statements provide direction for all planning activities.

Well-designed vision and mission statements are essential for formulating, implementing, and evaluating strategy. Developing and communicating a clear business vision and mission are the most commonly overlooked tasks in strategic management. Without clear statements of vision and mission, a firm's short-term actions can be counterproductive to long-term interests. Vision and mission statements always should be subject to revision, but, if carefully prepared, they will require infrequent major changes. Organizations usually reexamine their vision and mission statements annually. Effective mission statements stand the test of time.

Vision and mission statements are essential tools for strategists, a fact illustrated in a short story told by Porsche former CEO Peter Schultz:

> Three people were at work on a construction site. All were doing the same job, but when each was asked what his job was, the answers varied: "Breaking rocks," the first replied; "Earning a living," responded the second; "Helping to build a cathedral," said the third. Few of us can build cathedrals. But to the extent we can see the cathedral in whatever cause we are following, the job seems more worthwhile. Good strategists and a clear mission help us find those cathedrals in what otherwise could be dismal issues and empty causes.[16]

We invite you to visit the David page on the Prentice Hall Companion Web site at http://www.pearsonhighered.com/david/ for this chapter's review quiz.

Key Terms and Concepts

Concern for Employees (p. 51)
Concern for Public Image (p. 51)
Concern for Survival, Growth, and Profitability (p. 51)
Creed Statement (p. 44)
Customers (p. 51)
Markets (p. 51)
Mission Statement (p. 44)
Mission Statement Components (p. 51)

Philosophy (p. 51)
Products or Services (p. 51)
Reconciliatory (p. 52)
Self-Concept (p. 51)
Stakeholders (p. 49)
Technology (p. 51)
Vision Statement (p. 46)

Issues for Review and Discussion

1. What are some different names for "mission statement," and where will you likely find a firm's mission statement?
2. If your company does not have a vision or mission statement, describe a good process for developing these documents.
3. Explain how developing a mission statement can help resolve divergent views among managers in a firm.
4. Drucker says the most important time to seriously reexamine the firm's vision/mission is when the firm is very successful. Why is this?
5. Explain why a mission statement should not include monetary amounts, numbers, percentages, ratios, goals, or objectives.
6. Discuss the meaning of the following statement: "Good mission statements identify the utility of a firm's products to its customers."
7. Distinguish between the "self-concept" and the "philosophy" components in a mission statement. Give an example of each for your university.
8. When someone or some company is "on a mission" to achieve something, many times they cannot be stopped. List three things in prioritized order that you are "on a mission" to achieve in life.
9. Compare and contrast vision statements with mission statements in terms of composition and importance.
10. Do local service stations need to have written vision and mission statements? Why or why not?
11. Why do you think organizations that have a comprehensive mission tend to be high performers? Does having a comprehensive mission cause high performance?
12. Explain why a mission statement should not include strategies and objectives.
13. What is your college or university's self-concept? How would you state that in a mission statement?
14. Explain the principal value of a vision and a mission statement.
15. Why is it important for a mission statement to be reconciliatory?
16. In your opinion, what are the three most important components that should be included when writing a mission statement? Why?
17. How would the mission statements of a for-profit and a nonprofit organization differ?
18. Write a vision and mission statement for an organization of your choice.
19. Conduct a search on the Internet with the keywords *vision statement* and *mission statement*. Find various company vision and mission statements, and evaluate the documents. Write a one-page single-spaced report on your findings.
20. Who are the major stakeholders of the bank that you do business with locally? What are the major claims of those stakeholders?
21. List seven characteristics of a mission statement.
22. List eight benefits of having a clear mission statement.
23. How often do you think a firm's vision and mission statements should be changed?

Notes

1. Barbara Bartkus, Myron Glassman, and Bruce McAfee, "Mission Statements: Are They Smoke and Mirrors?" *Business Horizons* (November–December 2000): 23.

2. Peter Drucker, *Management: Tasks, Responsibilities, and Practices* (New York: Harper & Row, 1974): 61.

3. Fred David, "How Companies Define Their Mission," *Long Range Planning* 22, no. 1 (February 1989): 90–92; John Pearce II and Fred David, "Corporate Mission Statements: The Bottom Line," *Academy of Management Executive* 1, no. 2 (May 1987): 110.

4. Joseph Quigley, "Vision: How Leaders Develop It, Share It and Sustain It," *Business Horizons* (September–October 1994): 39.

5. Andrew Campbell and Sally Yeung, "Creating a Sense of Mission," *Long Range Planning* 24, no. 4 (August 1991): 17.

6. Charles Rarick and John Vitton, "Mission Statements Make Cents," *Journal of Business Strategy* 16 (1995): 11. Also, Christopher Bart and Mark Baetz, "The Relationship Between Mission Statements and Firm Performance: An Exploratory Study," *Journal of Management Studies* 35 (1998): 823; "Mission Possible," *Business Week* (August 1999): F12.

7. W. R. King and D. I. Cleland, *Strategic Planning and Policy* (New York: Van Nostrand Reinhold, 1979): 124.

8. Brian Dumaine, "What the Leaders of Tomorrow See," *Fortune* (July 3, 1989): 50.

9. Drucker, 78, 79.

10. "How W. T. Grant Lost $175 Million Last Year," *Business Week* (February 25, 1975): 75.

11. Drucker, 88.

12. John Pearce II, "The Company Mission as a Strategic Tool," *Sloan Management Review* 23, no. 3 (Spring 1982): 74.

13. George Steiner, *Strategic Planning: What Every Manager Must Know* (New York: The Free Press, 1979): 160.

14. Vern McGinnis, "The Mission Statement: A Key Step in Strategic Planning," *Business* 31, no. 6 (November–December 1981): 41.

15. Drucker, 61.

16. Robert Waterman Jr., *The Renewal Factor: How the Best Get and Keep the Competitive Edge* (New York: Bantam, 1987); *Business Week* (September 14, 1987): 120.

Current Readings

Baetz, Mark C., and Christopher K. Bart. "Developing Mission Statements Which Work." *Long Range Planning* 29, no. 4 (August 1996): 526–533.

Bartkus, Barbara, Myron Glassman, and R. Bruce McAfee. "Mission Statements: Are They Smoke and Mirrors?" *Business Horizons* 43, no. 6 (November–December 2000): 23.

Brabet, Julienne, and Mary Klemm. "Sharing the Vision: Company Mission Statements in Britain and France." *Long Range Planning* (February 1994): 84–94.

Collins, David J., and Michael G. Rukstad. "Can You Say What Your Strategy Is?" *Harvard Business Review* (April 2008): 82.

Collins, James C., and Jerry I. Porras. "Building a Visionary Company." *California Management Review* 37, no. 2 (Winter 1995): 80–100.

Collins, James C., and Jerry I. Porras. "Building Your Company's Vision." *Harvard Business Review* (September–October 1996): 65–78.

Conger, Jay A., and Douglas A. Ready. "Enabling Bold Visions." *MIT Sloan Management Review* 49, no. 2 (Winter 2008): 70.

Cummings, Stephen, and John Davies. "Brief Case—Mission, Vision, Fusion." *Long Range Planning* 27, no. 6 (December 1994): 147–150.

Davies, Stuart W., and Keith W. Glaister. "Business School Mission Statements—The Bland Leading the Bland?" *Long Range Planning* 30, no. 4 (August 1997): 594–604.

Day, George S., and Paul Schoemaker, "Peripheral Vision: Sensing and Acting on Weak Signals." *Long Range Planning* 37, no. 2 (April 2004): 117.

Gratton, Lynda. "Implementing a Strategic Vision—Key Factors for Success." *Long Range Planning* 29, no. 3 (June 1996): 290–303.

Ibarra, Herminia, and Otilia Obodaru. "Women and the Vision Thing." *Harvard Business Review* (January 2009): 62–71.

Larwood, Laurie, Cecilia M. Falbe, Mark P. Kriger, and Paul Miesing. "Structure and Meaning of Organizational Vision." *Academy of Management Journal* 38, no. 3 (June 1995): 740–769.

Lissak, Michael, and Johan Roos. "Be Coherent, Not Visionary." *Long Range Planning* 34, no. 1 (February 2001): 53.

McTavish, Ron. "One More Time: What Business Are You In?" *Long Range Planning* 28, no. 2 (April 1995): 49–60.

Newsom, Mi Kyong, David A. Collier, and Eric O. Olsen. "Using 'Biztainment' to Gain Competitive Advantage." *Business Horizons* (March–April 2009): 167–166.

ASSURANCE OF LEARNING EXERCISES

Assurance of Learning Exercise 2A

Evaluating Mission Statements

Purpose

A business mission statement is an integral part of strategic management. It provides direction for formulating, implementing, and evaluating strategic activities. This exercise will give you practice evaluating mission statements, a skill that is a prerequisite to writing a good mission statement.

Instructions

Step 1   On a clean sheet of paper, prepare a 9 × 3 matrix. Place the nine mission statement components down the left column and the following three companies across the top of your paper.

Step 2   Write *Yes* or *No* in each cell of your matrix to indicate whether you feel the particular mission statement includes the respective component.

Step 3   Turn your paper in to your instructor for a classwork grade.

Mission Statements

General Motors

Our mission is to be the world leader in transportation products and related services. We aim to maintain this position through enlightened customer enthusiasm and continuous improvement driven by integrity, teamwork, innovation and individual respect and responsibility of our employees.

North Carolina Zoo

Our mission is to encourage understanding of and commitment to the conservation of the world's wildlife and wild places through recognition of the interdependence of people and nature. We will do this by creating a sense of enjoyment, wonder and discovery throughout the Park and in our outreach programs.

Samsonite

Our mission is to be the leader in the travel industry. Samsonite's ambition is to provide unparalleled durability, security and dependability in all of its products, through leading edge functionality, features, innovation, technology, contemporary aesthetics and design. In order to fill every niche in the travel market, Samsonite will seek to create strategic alliances, combining our strengths with other partners in our brands.

Assurance of Learning Exercise 2B

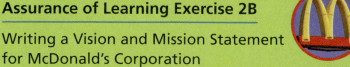

Writing a Vision and Mission Statement for McDonald's Corporation

Purpose

There is always room for improvement in regard to an existing vision and mission statement. Currently McDonald's does not have a vision statement or mission statement, so this exercise will ask you to develop one.

Instructions

Step 1	Refer back to page 33, the Cohesion Case, for McDonald's values statement.
Step 2	On a clean sheet of paper, write a one-sentence vision statement for McDonald's.
Step 3	On that same sheet of paper, write a mission statement for McDonald's.

Assurance of Learning Exercise 2C

Writing a Vision and Mission Statement for My University

Purpose

Most universities have a vision and mission statement. The purpose of this exercise is to give you practice writing a vision and mission statement for a nonprofit organization such as your own university.

Instructions

Step 1	Write a vision statement and a mission statement for your university. Your mission statement should include the nine characteristics summarized in Table 2-4.
Step 2	Read your vision and mission statement to the class.
Step 3	Determine whether your institution has a vision and/or mission statement. Look in the front of the college handbook. If your institution has a written statement, contact an appropriate administrator of the institution to inquire as to how and when the statement was prepared. Share this information with the class. Analyze your college's vision and mission statement in light of the concepts presented in this chapter.

Assurance of Learning Exercise 2D

Conducting Mission Statement Research

Purpose

This exercise gives you the opportunity to study the nature and role of vision and mission statements in strategic management.

Instructions

Step 1	Call various organizations in your city or county to identify firms that have developed a formal vision and/or mission statement. Contact nonprofit organizations and government agencies in addition to small and large businesses. Ask to speak with the director, owner, or chief executive officer of each organization. Explain that you are studying vision and mission statements in class and are conducting research as part of a class activity.
Step 2	Ask several executives the following four questions, and record their answers.
	1. When did your organization first develop its vision and/or mission statement? Who was primarily responsible for its development?
	2. How long have your current statements existed? When were they last modified? Why were they modified at that time?
	3. By what process are your firm's vision and mission statements altered?
	4. How are your vision and mission statements used in the firm?
Step 3	Provide an overview of your findings to the class.

CHAPTER 3
The External Assessment

CHAPTER OBJECTIVES

After studying this chapter, you should be able to do the following:

1. Describe how to conduct an external strategic-management audit.

2. Discuss 10 major external forces that affect organizations: economic, social, cultural, demographic, environmental, political, governmental, legal, technological, and competitive.

3. Describe key sources of external information, including the Internet.

4. Discuss important forecasting tools used in strategic management.

5. Discuss the importance of monitoring external trends and events.

6. Explain how to develop an EFE Matrix.

7. Explain how to develop a Competitive Profile Matrix.

8. Discuss the importance of gathering competitive intelligence.

9. Describe the trend toward cooperation among competitors.

10. Discuss market commonality and resource similarity in relation to competitive analysis.

Assurance of Learning Exercises

Assurance of Learning Exercise 3A

Developing an EFE Matrix for McDonald's Corporation

Assurance of Learning Exercise 3B

The External Assessment

Assurance of Learning Exercise 3C

Developing an EFE Matrix for My University

Assurance of Learning Exercise 3D

Developing a Competitive Profile Matrix for McDonald's Corporation

Source: Shutterstock/Photographer Emin Kuliyev

"Notable Quotes"

"If you're not faster than your competitor, you're in a tenuous position, and if you're only half as fast, you're terminal."

—George Salk

"The opportunities and threats existing in any situation always exceed the resources needed to exploit the opportunities or avoid the threats. Thus, strategy is essentially a problem of allocating resources. If strategy is to be successful, it must allocate superior resources against a decisive opportunity."

—William Cohen

"Organizations pursue strategies that will disrupt the normal course of industry events and forge new industry conditions to the disadvantage of competitors."

—Ian C. Macmillan

"If everyone is thinking alike, then somebody isn't thinking."

—George Patton

"It is not the strongest of the species that survive, nor the most intelligent, but the one most responsive to change."

—Charles Darwin

"Nothing focuses the mind better than the constant sight of a competitor who wants to wipe you off the map."

—Wayne Calloway

**Assurance of Learning
Exercise 3E**
**Developing a Competitive
Profile Matrix for My
University**

This chapter examines the tools and concepts needed to conduct an external strategic management audit (sometimes called *environmental scanning* or *industry analysis*). An *external audit* focuses on identifying and evaluating trends and events beyond the control of a single firm, such as increased foreign competition, population shifts to the Sunbelt, an aging society, consumer fear of traveling, and stock market volatility. An external audit reveals key opportunities and threats confronting an organization so that managers can formulate strategies to take advantage of the opportunities and avoid or reduce the impact of threats. This chapter presents a practical framework for gathering, assimilating, and analyzing external information. The Industrial Organization (I/O) view of strategic management is introduced.

The Chapter 3 boxed insert company pursuing excellent strategies in the midst of a global recession is Dunkin Brands, Inc.

Doing Great in a Weak Economy

Dunkin' Brands, Inc.

Dunkin' Donuts and Baskin-Robbins are under one umbrella company named Dunkin' Brands, Inc. Doughnuts and ice cream go hand-in-hand at this company, which has more than 13,000 locations in more than 40 countries. With more than 7,900 shops in 30 countries (5,800 of which are in North America), Dunkin' Donuts is the world's leading chain of donut shops. Baskin-Robbins is a leading seller of ice cream and frozen snacks with its nearly 6,000 outlets (about half are located in the United States). About 1,100 locations offer a combination of the company's brands. Dunkin' Brands is owned by a group of private investment firms including Bain Capital, The Carlyle Group, and Thomas H. Lee Partners.

Dunkin' Donuts in 2009 launched a $100 million advertising campaign around the theme "You Kin' Do It" that highlights everyday challenges, such as work and traffic. Dunkin' Donuts president Will Kussell says, "We're going to help you get through whatever you have to deal with every day." Dunkin' is also expanding its Dunkin' Deals, which bundles a bagel or sandwich for 99 cents with purchase of a coffee. Franchisee Jim Allen, who owns 18 stores, says, "Dunkin' Deals has been huge in this economy."

In June 2009, Dunkin' Donuts introduced its first 99 cent breakfast wrap. Called the Wake-Up Wrap and supported by the advertising phrase "America Saves at Dunkin'" Dunkin' launched fierce, frontal attacks on both McDonald's and Starbucks as those two firms battled each other over fancy coffee drinks. Dunkin' Donuts' brand marketing officer Frances Allen said: "Starbucks can't do food and McDonald's can't do coffee. We view breakfast as a 'value' meal as noted in our ad 'Breakfast, NOT Brokefast.'" Dunkin' is presently test marketing a six-item breakfast value menu, all priced at 99 cents with any beverage purchase.

Source: Based on Theresa Howard, "Dunkin' Donuts Expects a Solid 2009," USA Today (January 2, 2009): 5B.

The Nature of an External Audit

The purpose of an *external audit* is to develop a finite list of opportunities that could benefit a firm and threats that should be avoided. As the term *finite* suggests, the external audit is not aimed at developing an exhaustive list of every possible factor that could influence the business; rather, it is aimed at identifying key variables that offer actionable responses. Firms should be able to respond either offensively or defensively to the factors by formulating strategies that take advantage of external opportunities or that minimize the impact of potential threats. Figure 3-1 illustrates how the external audit fits into the strategic-management process.

Key External Forces

External forces can be divided into five broad categories: (1) economic forces; (2) social, cultural, demographic, and natural environment forces; (3) political, governmental, and legal forces; (4) technological forces; and (5) competitive forces. Relationships among these forces and an organization are depicted in Figure 3-2. External trends and events, such as the

FIGURE 3-1

A Comprehensive Strategic-Management Model

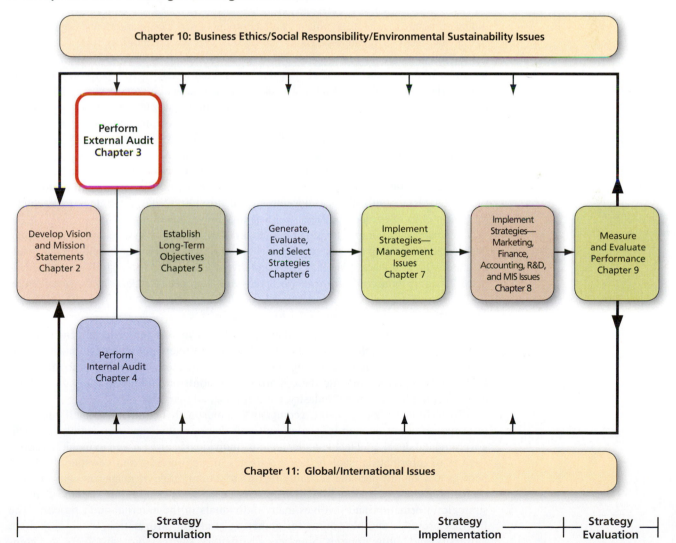

Source: Fred R. David, "How Companies Define Their Mission," *Long Range Planning* 22, no. 3 (June 1988): 40.

FIGURE 3-2

Relationships Between Key External Forces and an Organization

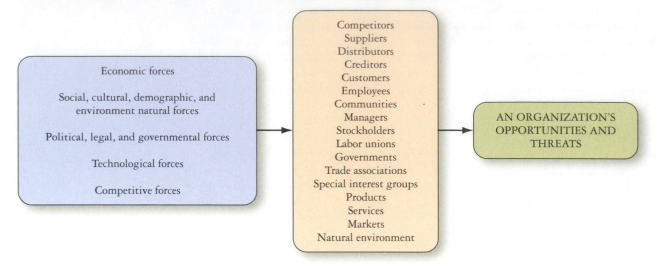

global economic recession, significantly affect products, services, markets, and organizations worldwide. The U.S. unemployment rate climbed to over 9 percent in July 2009 as more than 2.5 million jobs were lost in the United States in 2008—the most since 1945 when the country downsized from the war effort. The rate is expected to rise to 10.1 percent. All sectors witness rising unemployment rates, except for education, health-care services, and government employment. Many Americans are resorting to minimum wage jobs to make ends meet.

Changes in external forces translate into changes in consumer demand for both industrial and consumer products and services. External forces affect the types of products developed, the nature of positioning and market segmentation strategies, the type of services offered, and the choice of businesses to acquire or sell. External forces directly affect both suppliers and distributors. Identifying and evaluating external opportunities and threats enables organizations to develop a clear mission, to design strategies to achieve long-term objectives, and to develop policies to achieve annual objectives.

The increasing complexity of business today is evidenced by more countries developing the capacity and will to compete aggressively in world markets. Foreign businesses and countries are willing to learn, adapt, innovate, and invent to compete successfully in the marketplace. There are more competitive new technologies in Europe and Asia today than ever before.

The Process of Performing an External Audit

The process of performing an external audit must involve as many managers and employees as possible. As emphasized in earlier chapters, involvement in the strategic-management process can lead to understanding and commitment from organizational members. Individuals appreciate having the opportunity to contribute ideas and to gain a better understanding of their firms' industry, competitors, and markets.

To perform an external audit, a company first must gather competitive intelligence and information about economic, social, cultural, demographic, environmental, political, governmental, legal, and technological trends. Individuals can be asked to monitor various sources of information, such as key magazines, trade journals, and newspapers. These persons can submit periodic scanning reports to a committee of managers charged with performing the external audit. This approach provides a continuous stream of timely strategic information and involves many individuals in the external-audit process. The Internet provides another source for gathering strategic information, as do corporate, university, and public libraries. Suppliers, distributors, salespersons, customers, and competitors represent other sources of vital information.

Once information is gathered, it should be assimilated and evaluated. A meeting or series of meetings of managers is needed to collectively identify the most important opportunities and threats facing the firm. These key external factors should be listed on flip charts or a chalkboard. A prioritized list of these factors could be obtained by requesting that all managers rank the factors identified, from 1 for the most important opportunity/threat to 20 for the least important opportunity/threat. These key external factors can vary over time and by industry. Relationships with suppliers or distributors are often a critical success factor. Other variables commonly used include market share, breadth of competing products, world economies, foreign affiliates, proprietary and key account advantages, price competitiveness, technological advancements, population shifts, interest rates, and pollution abatement.

Freund emphasized that these key external factors should be (1) important to achieving long-term and annual objectives, (2) measurable, (3) applicable to all competing firms, and (4) hierarchical in the sense that some will pertain to the overall company and others will be more narrowly focused on functional or divisional areas.[1] A final list of the most important key external factors should be communicated and distributed widely in the organization. Both opportunities and threats can be key external factors.

The Industrial Organization (I/O) View

The *Industrial Organization (I/O)* approach to competitive advantage advocates that external (industry) factors are more important than internal factors in a firm achieving competitive advantage. Proponents of the I/O view, such as Michael Porter, contend that organizational performance will be primarily determined by industry forces. Porter's Five-Forces Model, presented later in this chapter, is an example of the I/O perspective, which focuses on analyzing external forces and industry variables as a basis for getting and keeping competitive advantage. Competitive advantage is determined largely by competitive positioning within an industry, according to I/O advocates. Managing strategically from the I/O perspective entails firms striving to compete in attractive industries, avoiding weak or faltering industries, and gaining a full understanding of key external factor relationships within that attractive industry. I/O research provides important contributions to our understanding of how to gain competitive advantage.

I/O theorists contend that external factors in general and the industry in which a firm chooses to compete has a stronger influence on the firm's performance than do the internal functional decisions managers make in marketing, finance, and the like. Firm performance, they contend, is primarily based more on industry properties, such as economies of scale, barriers to market entry, product differentiation, the economy, and level of competitiveness than on internal resources, capabilities, structure, and operations. The global economic recession's impact on both strong and weak firms has added credence of late to the notion that external forces are more important than internal. Many thousands of internally strong firms in 2006–2007 disappeared in 2008–2009.

The I/O view has enhanced our understanding of strategic management. However, it is not a question of whether external or internal factors are more important in gaining and maintaining competitive advantage. Effective integration and understanding of *both* external and internal factors is the key to securing and keeping a competitive advantage. In fact, as discussed in Chapter 6, matching key external opportunities/threats with key internal strengths/weaknesses provides the basis for successful strategy formulation.

Economic Forces

Increasing numbers of two-income households is an economic trend in the United States. Individuals place a premium on time. Improved customer service, immediate availability, trouble-free operation of products, and dependable maintenance and repair services are becoming more important. People today are more willing than ever to pay for good service if it limits inconvenience.

Economic factors have a direct impact on the potential attractiveness of various strategies. For example, when interest rates rise, funds needed for capital expansion become

TABLE 3-1 Key Economic Variables to Be Monitored

Shift to a service economy in the United States	Import/export factors
Availability of credit	Demand shifts for different categories of goods and services
Level of disposable income	Income differences by region and consumer groups
Propensity of people to spend	Price fluctuations
Interest rates	Export of labor and capital from the United States
Inflation rates	
Money market rates	Monetary policies
Federal government budget deficits	Fiscal policies
Gross domestic product trend	Tax rates
Consumption patterns	European Economic Community (EEC) policies
Unemployment trends	
Worker productivity levels	Organization of Petroleum Exporting Countries (OPEC) policies
Value of the dollar in world markets	
Stock market trends	Coalitions of Lesser Developed Countries (LDC) policies
Foreign countries' economic conditions	

more costly or unavailable. Also, when interest rates rise, discretionary income declines, and the demand for discretionary goods falls. When stock prices increase, the desirability of equity as a source of capital for market development increases. Also, when the market rises, consumer and business wealth expands. A summary of economic variables that often represent opportunities and threats for organizations is provided in Table 3-1.

An economic variable of significant importance in strategic planning is gross domestic product (GDP), especially across countries. Table 3-2 lists the GDP of various countries in Asia for all of 2009. Unlike most countries in Europe and the Americas, most Asian countries expect positive GDP growth in 2009.

Trends in the dollar's value have significant and unequal effects on companies in different industries and in different locations. For example, the pharmaceutical, tourism, entertainment, motor vehicle, aerospace, and forest products industries benefit greatly when the dollar falls against the yen and euro. Agricultural and petroleum industries are hurt by the dollar's rise against the currencies of Mexico, Brazil, Venezuela, and Australia. Generally, a strong or high dollar makes U.S. goods more expensive in overseas markets. This worsens the U.S. trade deficit. When the value of the dollar falls, tourism-oriented firms benefit because Americans do not travel abroad

TABLE 3-2 Expected GDP Growth in 2009 Among Countries in Asia

Country	Percent GDP Growth
China	High (7–8 percent)
India	High (7–8 percent)
Indonesia	Medium (3–4 percent)
Thailand	Medium (3–4 percent)
Philippines	Medium (3–4 percent)
Taiwan	Medium (3–4 percent)
Malaysia	Medium (3–4 percent)
South Korea	Low (1–2 percent)
Hong Kong	Low (1–2 percent)
Singapore	Low (1–2 percent)

Source: Based on Patrick Barta, "Sharp Downturn in Asia Nears," *Wall Street Journal* (October 27, 2008): A9.

as much when the value of the dollar is low; rather, foreigners visit and vacation more in the United States.

A low value of the dollar means lower imports and higher exports; it helps U.S. companies' competitiveness in world markets. The dollar has fallen to five-year lows against the euro and yen, which makes U.S. goods cheaper to foreign consumers and combats deflation by pushing up prices of imports. However, European firms such as Volkswagen AG, Nokia Corp., and Michelin complain that the strong euro hurts their financial performance. The low value of the dollar benefits the U.S. economy in many ways. First, it helps stave off the risks of deflation in the United States and also reduces the U.S. trade deficit. In addition, the low value of the dollar raises the foreign sales and profits of domestic firms, thanks to dollar-induced gains, and encourages foreign countries to lower interest rates and loosen fiscal policy, which stimulates worldwide economic expansion. Some sectors, such as consumer staples, energy, materials, technology, and health care, especially benefit from a low value of the dollar. Manufacturers in many domestic industries in fact benefit because of a weak dollar, which forces foreign rivals to raise prices and extinguish discounts. Domestic firms with big overseas sales, such as McDonald's, greatly benefit from a weak dollar.

Between March and June 2009, the U.S. dollar weakened 11.0 percent against the euro, due to the growing United States debt, which may soon exceed $12 trillion. Table 3-3 lists some advantages and disadvantages of a weak U.S. dollar for American firms.

Rising unemployment rates across the United States have touched off a race among states to attract businesses with tax breaks and financial incentives. New Jersey has promised to send a $3,000 check to every small business that hires a new employee. Minnesota is offering tax-free zones for companies that create "green jobs." Colorado has created a $5 million fund for banks that open credit lines for small businesses. To minimize risk in incentive deals, may states write in claw-back provisions that require companies to return funds if they fail to create the promised number of jobs.

The slumping economy worldwide and depressed prices of assets has dramatically slowed the migration of people from country to country and from the city to the suburbs. Because people are not moving nearly as much as in years past, there is lower and lower demand for new or used houses. Thus the housing market is expected to remain very sluggish well into 2010 and 2011.

TABLE 3-3 Advantages and Disadvantages of a Weak Dollar for Domestic Firms

Advantages	Disadvantages
1. Leads to more exports	1. Can lead to inflation
2. Leads to lower imports	2. Can cause rise in oil prices
3. Makes U.S. goods cheaper to foreign consumers	3. Can weaken U.S. government
4. Combats deflation by pushing up prices of imports	4. Makes it unattractive for Americans to travel globally
5. Can contribute to rise in stock prices in short run	5. Can contribute to fall in stock prices in long run
6. Stimulates worldwide economic recession	
7. Encourages foreign countries to lower interest rates	
8. Raises the revenues and profits of firms that do business outside the United States	
9. Stimulates worldwide economic expansion	
10. Forces foreign firms to raise prices	
11. Reduces the U.S. trade deficit	
12. Encourages firms to globalize	
13. Encourages foreigners to visit the United States	

Social, Cultural, Demographic, and Natural Environment Forces

Social, cultural, demographic, and environmental changes have a major impact on virtually all products, services, markets, and customers. Small, large, for-profit, and nonprofit organizations in all industries are being staggered and challenged by the opportunities and threats arising from changes in social, cultural, demographic, and environmental variables. In every way, the United States is much different today than it was yesterday, and tomorrow promises even greater changes.

The United States is getting older and less white. The oldest members of America's 76 million baby boomers plan to retire in 2011, and this has lawmakers and younger taxpayers deeply concerned about who will pay their Social Security, Medicare, and Medicaid. Individuals age 65 and older in the United States as a percentage of the population will rise to 18.5 percent by 2025. The five "oldest" states and five "youngest" states in 2007 are given in Table 3-4.

By 2075, the United States will have no racial or ethnic majority. This forecast is aggravating tensions over issues such as immigration and affirmative action. Hawaii, California, and New Mexico already have no majority race or ethnic group.

The population of the world surpassed 7.0 billion in 2010; the United States has just over 310 million people. That leaves billions of people outside the United States who may be interested in the products and services produced through domestic firms. Remaining solely domestic is an increasingly risky strategy, especially as the world population continues to grow to an estimated 8 billion in 2028 and 9 billion in 2054.

Social, cultural, demographic, and environmental trends are shaping the way Americans live, work, produce, and consume. New trends are creating a different type of consumer and, consequently, a need for different products, different services, and different strategies. There are now more American households with people living alone or with unrelated people than there are households consisting of married couples with children. American households are making more and more purchases online. Beer consumption in the United States is growing at only 0.5 percent per year, whereas wine consumption is growing 3.5 percent and distilled spirits consumption is growing at 2.0 percent.[2] Beer is still the most popular alcoholic beverage in the United States, but its market share has dropped from 59.5 percent in its peak year of 1995 to 56.7 percent today. For a wine company such as Gallo, this trend is an opportunity, whereas for a firm such as Adolph Coors Brewing, this trend is an external threat.

The trend toward an older America is good news for restaurants, hotels, airlines, cruise lines, tours, resorts, theme parks, luxury products and services, recreational vehicles, home builders, furniture producers, computer manufacturers, travel services, pharmaceutical firms, automakers, and funeral homes. Older Americans are especially interested in health care, financial services, travel, crime prevention, and leisure. The world's longest-living people are the Japanese, with Japanese women living to 86.3 years and men living to 80.1 years on average. By 2050, the Census Bureau projects that the number of Americans age 100 and older will increase to over 834,000 from just under 100,000 centenarians in the

TABLE 3-4   **The Oldest and Youngest States by Average Age of Residents**

Five Oldest States	Five Youngest States
Maine	Utah
Vermont	Texas
West Virginia	Alaska
Florida	Idaho
Pennsylvania	California

Source: Based on U.S. Census Bureau. Also, Ken Jackson, "State Population Changes by Race, Ethnicity," *USA Today* (May 17, 2007): 2A.

United States in 2000. Americans age 65 and over will increase from 12.6 percent of the U.S. population in 2000 to 20.0 percent by the year 2050.

The aging American population affects the strategic orientation of nearly all organizations. Apartment complexes for the elderly, with one meal a day, transportation, and utilities included in the rent, have increased nationwide. Called *lifecare facilities*, these complexes now exceed 2 million. Some well-known companies building these facilities include Avon, Marriott, and Hyatt. Individuals age 65 and older in the United States comprise 13 percent of the total population; Japan's elderly population ratio is 17 percent, and Germany's is 19 percent.

Americans were on the move in a population shift to the South and West (Sunbelt) and away from the Northeast and Midwest (Frostbelt), but the recession and housing bust nationwide has slowed migration throughout the United States. More Americans are staying in place rather than moving. New jobs are the primary reason people move across state lines, so with 3 million less jobs in the United States in 2008–2009 alone, there is less need to move. Falling home prices also have prompted people to avoid moving. The historical trend of people moving from the Northeast and Midwest to the Sunbelt and West has dramatically slowed. The worldwide recession is also reducing international immigration, down roughly 10 percent in both 2008 and 2009. Hard number data related to this information can represent key opportunities for many firms and thus can be essential for successful strategy formulation, including where to locate new plants and distribution centers and where to focus marketing efforts.

A summary of important social, cultural, demographic, and environmental variables that represent opportunities or threats for virtually all organizations is given in Table 3-5.

TABLE 3-5   Key Social, Cultural, Demographic, and Natural Environment Variables

Childbearing rates	Attitudes toward retirement
Number of special-interest groups	Attitudes toward leisure time
Number of marriages	Attitudes toward product quality
Number of divorces	Attitudes toward customer service
Number of births	Pollution control
Number of deaths	Attitudes toward foreign peoples
Immigration and emigration rates	Energy conservation
Social Security programs	Social programs
Life expectancy rates	Number of churches
Per capita income	Number of church members
Location of retailing, manufacturing, and service businesses	Social responsibility
Attitudes toward business	Attitudes toward careers
Lifestyles	Population changes by race, age, sex, and level of affluence
Traffic congestion	Attitudes toward authority
Inner-city environments	Population changes by city, county, state, region, and country
Average disposable income	Value placed on leisure time
Trust in government	Regional changes in tastes and preferences
Attitudes toward government	Number of women and minority workers
Attitudes toward work	Number of high school and college graduates by geographic area
Buying habits	Recycling
Ethical concerns	Waste management
Attitudes toward saving	Air pollution
Sex roles	Water pollution
Attitudes toward investing	Ozone depletion
Racial equality	Endangered species
Use of birth control	
Average level of education	
Government regulation	

Political, Governmental, and Legal Forces

Federal, state, local, and foreign governments are major regulators, deregulators, subsidizers, employers, and customers of organizations. Political, governmental, and legal factors, therefore, can represent key opportunities or threats for both small and large organizations.

For industries and firms that depend heavily on government contracts or subsidies, political forecasts can be the most important part of an external audit. Changes in patent laws, antitrust legislation, tax rates, and lobbying activities can affect firms significantly. The increasing global interdependence among economies, markets, governments, and organizations makes it imperative that firms consider the possible impact of political variables on the formulation and implementation of competitive strategies.

In the face of a deepening global recession, countries worldwide are resorting to protectionism to safeguard their own industries. European Union (EU) nations, for example, have tightened their own trade rules and resumed subsidies for various of their own industries while barring imports from certain other countries. The EU recently restricted imports of U.S. chicken and beef. India is increasing tariffs on foreign steel. Russia perhaps has instituted the most protectionist measures in recent months by raising tariffs on most imports and subsidizing its own exports. Russia even imposed a new toll on trucks from the EU, Switzerland, and Turkmenistan. Despite these measures taken by other countries, the United States has largely refrained from "Buy American" policies and protectionist measures, although there are increased tariffs on French cheese and Italian water. Many economists say the current rash of trade constraints will make it harder for global economic growth to recover from the global recession. Global trade is expected to decrease 2.1 percent in 2009 compared to an increase of 6.2 percent in 2008.[3] Russia has said that "protective tariffs are necessary to allow Russian companies to survive the recession." This view unfortunately is also the view at an increasing number of countries.

Governments are taking control of more and more companies as the global economic recession cripples firms considered vital to the nation's financial stability. For example, France in 2009 took a 2.35 percent equity stake in troubled car-parts maker Valeo SA. President Nicolas Sarkozy of France has created a $20 billion strategic fund to lend cash to banks and carmakers as many governments become more protectionist. The United States of course also is taking equity stakes in financial institutions and carmakers and is "bailing out" companies too.

The UK government in 2009 took a 95 percent stake in the banking giant Royal Bank of Scotland Group PLC in a dramatic move toward nationalization. The government gave the bank $37 billion and insured another $300 billion of the bank's assets. The UK government also recently increased its stake in Lloyds Banking Group PLC to 75 percent. Similarly, the U.S. government has taken over Fannie Mae and Freddie Mac and has raised its stake even in Citigroup to 40 percent.

As more and more companies around the world accept government bailouts, those companies are being forced to march to priorities set by political leaders. Even in the United States, the federal government is battling the recession with its deepest intervention in the economy since the Great Depression. The U.S. government now is a strategic manager in industries from banking to insurance to autos. Governments worldwide are under pressure to protect jobs at home and maintain the nation's industrial base. For example, in France, Renault SA's factory in Sandouville is one of the most unproductive auto factories in the world. However, Renault has taken $3.9 billion in low-interest loans from the French government, so the company cannot close any French factories for the duration of the loan or resort to mass layoffs in France for a year.

Political relations between Japan and China have thawed considerably in recent years, which is good for the world economy because China's low-cost manufactured goods have become essential for the functioning of most industrialized nations. Chinese premier Wen Jiabao addressed the Japanese parliament in 2007, something no Chinese leader has done for more than 20 years, and Japanese prime minister Shinzo Abe has visited Beijing. Japan's largest trading partner is China, and China's third-largest trading partner is Japan—after the European Union, number one, and the United States, number two.

TABLE 3-6 **Some Political, Governmental, and Legal Variables**

Government regulations or deregulations	Sino-American relationships
Changes in tax laws	Russian-American relationships
Special tariffs	European-American relationships
Political action committees	African-American relationships
Voter participation rates	Import–export regulations
Number, severity, and location of government protests	Government fiscal and monetary policy changes
Number of patents	Political conditions in foreign countries
Changes in patent laws	Special local, state, and federal laws
Environmental protection laws	Lobbying activities
Level of defense expenditures	Size of government budgets
Legislation on equal employment	World oil, currency, and labor markets
Level of government subsidies	Location and severity of terrorist activities
Antitrust legislation	Local, state, and national elections

Local, state, and federal laws; regulatory agencies; and special-interest groups can have a major impact on the strategies of small, large, for-profit, and nonprofit organizations. Many companies have altered or abandoned strategies in the past because of political or governmental actions. In the academic world, as state budgets have dropped in recent years, so too has state support for colleges and universities. Due to the decline in monies received from the state, many institutions of higher learning are doing more fundraising on their own—naming buildings and classrooms, for example, for donors. A summary of political, governmental, and legal variables that can represent key opportunities or threats to organizations is provided in Table 3-6.

Technological Forces

Revolutionary technological changes and discoveries are having a dramatic impact on organizations. CEO Chris DeWolfe of MySpace is using technology to expand the firm's 1,600-person workforce in 2009 even as the economic recession deepens. MySpace expects a 17 percent increase in revenue in 2009. Nearly half of the site's 130 million members worldwide are 35 and older, and 76 million of the members are from the United States. This compares to rival Facebook that has 150 million members worldwide but only 55 million in the United States. MySpace is continually redesigning the site and revamping the way its members can manage their profiles and categorize their friends, and enabling consumers to listen to free streaming audio and songs. Doug Morris, CEO of Universal Music Group, says, "There is a lot of conflict between technology and content, and Chris has successfully brought both together."[4]

The *Internet* has changed the very nature of opportunities and threats by altering the life cycles of products, increasing the speed of distribution, creating new products and services, erasing limitations of traditional geographic markets, and changing the historical trade-off between production standardization and flexibility. The Internet is altering economies of scale, changing entry barriers, and redefining the relationship between industries and various suppliers, creditors, customers, and competitors.

To effectively capitalize on e-commerce, a number of organizations are establishing two new positions in their firms: *chief information officer (CIO)* and *chief technology officer (CTO)*. This trend reflects the growing importance of *information technology (IT)* in strategic management. A CIO and CTO work together to ensure that information needed to formulate, implement, and evaluate strategies is available where and when it is needed. These individuals are responsible for developing, maintaining, and updating a company's information database. The CIO is more a manager, managing the firm's relationship with stakeholders; the CTO is more a technician, focusing on technical issues such as data acquisition, data processing, decision-support systems, and software and hardware acquisition.

Technological forces represent major opportunities and threats that must be considered in formulating strategies. Technological advancements can dramatically affect organizations' products, services, markets, suppliers, distributors, competitors, customers, manufacturing processes, marketing practices, and competitive position. Technological advancements can create new markets, result in a proliferation of new and improved products, change the relative competitive cost positions in an industry, and render existing products and services obsolete. Technological changes can reduce or eliminate cost barriers between businesses, create shorter production runs, create shortages in technical skills, and result in changing values and expectations of employees, managers, and customers. Technological advancements can create new competitive advantages that are more powerful than existing advantages. No company or industry today is insulated against emerging technological developments. In high-tech industries, identification and evaluation of key technological opportunities and threats can be the most important part of the external strategic-management audit.

Organizations that traditionally have limited technology expenditures to what they can fund after meeting marketing and financial requirements urgently need a reversal in thinking. The pace of technological change is increasing and literally wiping out businesses every day. An emerging consensus holds that technology management is one of the key responsibilities of strategists. Firms should pursue strategies that take advantage of technological opportunities to achieve sustainable, competitive advantages in the marketplace.

In practice, critical decisions about technology too often are delegated to lower organizational levels or are made without an understanding of their strategic implications. Many strategists spend countless hours determining market share, positioning products in terms of features and price, forecasting sales and market size, and monitoring distributors; yet too often, technology does not receive the same respect.

Not all sectors of the economy are affected equally by technological developments. The communications, electronics, aeronautics, and pharmaceutical industries are much more volatile than the textile, forestry, and metals industries. A recent article in the *Wall Street Journal* detailed how wireless technology will change 10 particular industries.[5] Table 3-7 provides a glimpse of this article.

TABLE 3-7 Examples of the Impact of Wireless Technology

Airlines—Many airlines now offer wireless technology in flight.

Automotive—Vehicles are becoming wireless.

Banking—Visa sends text message alerts after unusual transactions.

Education—Many secondary (and even college) students may use smart phones for math because research shows this to be greatly helpful.

Energy—Smart meters now provide power on demand in your home or business.

Health Care—Patients use mobile devices to monitor their own health, such as calories consumed.

Hotels—Days Inn sends daily specials and coupons to hotel guests via text messages.

Market Research—Cell phone respondents provide more honest answers, perhaps because they are away from eavesdropping ears.

Politics—President Obama won the election partly by mobilizing Facebook and MySpace users, revolutionizing political campaigns. Obama announced his vice presidential selection of Joe Biden by a text message.

Publishing—eBooks are increasingly available.

Source: Based on Joe Mullich, "10 Industries That Wireless Will Change," *Wall Street Journal* (April 1, 2009): A12.

Competitive Forces

The top U.S. competitors in four different industries are identified in Table 3-8. An important part of an external audit is identifying rival firms and determining their strengths, weaknesses, capabilities, opportunities, threats, objectives, and strategies.

Collecting and evaluating information on competitors is essential for successful strategy formulation. Identifying major competitors is not always easy because many firms have divisions that compete in different industries. Many multidivisional firms do not provide sales and profit information on a divisional basis for competitive reasons. Also, privately held firms do not publish any financial or marketing information. Addressing questions about competitors such as those presented in Table 3-9 is important in performing an external audit.

Competition in virtually all industries can be described as intense—and sometimes as cutthroat. For example, Walgreens and CVS pharmacies are located generally across the street from each other and battle each other every day on price and customer service. Most automobile dealerships also are located close to each other. Dollar General, based in Goodlettsville, Tennessee, and Family Dollar, based in Matthews, North Carolina, compete intensely on price to attract customers. Best Buy dropped prices wherever possible to finally put Circuit City totally out of business.

Seven characteristics describe the most competitive companies:

1. Market share matters; the 90th share point isn't as important as the 91st, and nothing is more dangerous than falling to 89.
2. Understand and remember precisely what business you are in.

TABLE 3-8 The Top U.S. Competitors in Four Different Industries

	2008 Sales (in millions)	% Change from 2007	2008 Profits (in millions)	% Change from 2007
Beverages				
Coca-Cola	$31,944	+11	$5,807	−3
Pepsi Bottling	13,796	+2	162	−70
Coca-Cola Enterprises	21,807	+4	(4,394)	−718
Molson Coors Brewing	4774	−23	388	−22
Pharmaceuticals				
Johnson & Johnson	63,747	+4	12,949	22
Pfizer	48,296	0	8,104	0
Merck	23,850	−1	7,808	138
Abbott Laboratories	29,528	+14	4,881	35
Wyeth	22,834	+2	4,418	−4
Construction and Farm Equipment				
Caterpillar	51,324	+14	3,557	0
Deere	28,438	+18	2,053	+13
Terek	9,890	+8	72	−88
Agco	8,425	+23	400	+62
Cummins	14,342	+10	755	+2
Computers				
Hewlett-Packard	118,364	+13	8,329	+15
Sun Microsystems	13,880	0	403	−15
Dell	61,101	0	2,478	−16
Xerox	17,608	+2	230	−80
Apple	32,479	+35	4,834	+38

Source: Based on *Fortune*, April 30, 2008, F50–F73.

TABLE 3-9   Key Questions About Competitors

1. What are the major competitors' strengths?
2. What are the major competitors' weaknesses?
3. What are the major competitors' objectives and strategies?
4. How will the major competitors most likely respond to current economic, social, cultural, demographic, environmental, political, governmental, legal, technological, and competitive trends affecting our industry?
5. How vulnerable are the major competitors to our alternative company strategies?
6. How vulnerable are our alternative strategies to successful counterattack by our major competitors?
7. How are our products or services positioned relative to major competitors?
8. To what extent are new firms entering and old firms leaving this industry?
9. What key factors have resulted in our present competitive position in this industry?
10. How have the sales and profit rankings of major competitors in the industry changed over recent years? Why have these rankings changed that way?
11. What is the nature of supplier and distributor relationships in this industry?
12. To what extent could substitute products or services be a threat to competitors in this industry?

3. Whether it's broke or not, fix it—make it better; not just products, but the whole company, if necessary.
4. Innovate or evaporate; particularly in technology-driven businesses, nothing quite recedes like success.
5. Acquisition is essential to growth; the most successful purchases are in niches that add a technology or a related market.
6. People make a difference; tired of hearing it? Too bad.
7. There is no substitute for quality and no greater threat than failing to be cost-competitive on a global basis.[6]

Competitive Intelligence Programs

What is competitive intelligence? *Competitive intelligence* (*CI*), as formally defined by the Society of Competitive Intelligence Professionals (SCIP), is a systematic and ethical process for gathering and analyzing information about the competition's activities and general business trends to further a business's own goals (SCIP Web site).

Good competitive intelligence in business, as in the military, is one of the keys to success. The more information and knowledge a firm can obtain about its competitors, the more likely it is that it can formulate and implement effective strategies. Major competitors' weaknesses can represent external opportunities; major competitors' strengths may represent key threats.

In April 2009, Starwood Hotels & Resorts Worldwide sued Hilton Hotels Corp. for allegedly stealing more than 100,000 confidential electronic and paper documents containing "Starwood's most competitively sensitive information." The complaint alleges that two Starwood executives, Ross Klein and Amar Lalvani, resigned from Starwood to join Hilton and took this information with them. The legal complaint says, "This is the clearest imaginable case of corporate espionage, theft of trade secrets, unfair competition and computer fraud." In addition to monetary awards, Starwood is seeking to force Hilton to cancel the rollout of the Denizen hotel chain. Hilton is owned by Blackstone Group.

Hiring top executives from rival firms is also a way companies obtain competitive intelligence. Just two days after Facebook's COO, Owen Van Natta, left the company in 2009, he accepted the CEO job at MySpace, replacing then CEO and cofounder Chris DeWolfe. Van Natta had previously also been Facebook's COO, chief revenue officer, and vice president of operations. The MySpace appointment now pits CEO Van Natta against his old boss at Facebook, CEO Mark Zuckerberg. Facebook passed MySpace in visitors worldwide in 2008 and is closing in on leadership in the United States. Both firms are fierce rivals in the Internet social-networking business.[7]

A recent article in the *Wall Street Journal* detailed how computer spies recently broke into the Pentagon's $300 billion Joint Strike fighter project, one of the costliest weapons programs ever.[8] This intrusion and similar episodes of late have confirmed that any information a firm has available to anyone within the firm online may be at risk of being copied and/or siphoned away by adversaries or rival firms. A recent Pentagon report says the Chinese military in particular has made "steady progress" in developing online-warfare techniques, but rival firms in many industries have expert computer engineers who may be capable of similar unethical/unlawful tactics.

Many U.S. executives grew up in times when U.S. firms dominated foreign competitors so much that gathering competitive intelligence did not seem worth the effort. Too many of these executives still cling to these attitudes—to the detriment of their organizations today. Even most MBA programs do not offer a course in competitive and business intelligence, thus reinforcing this attitude. As a consequence, three strong misperceptions about business intelligence prevail among U.S. executives today:

1. Running an intelligence program requires lots of people, computers, and other resources.
2. Collecting intelligence about competitors violates antitrust laws; business intelligence equals espionage.
3. Intelligence gathering is an unethical business practice.[9]

Any discussions with a competitor about price, market, or geography intentions could violate antitrust statutes. However, this fact must not lure a firm into underestimating the need for and benefits of systematically collecting information about competitors for Strategic Planning purposes. The Internet has become an excellent medium for gathering competitive intelligence. Information gathering from employees, managers, suppliers, distributors, customers, creditors, and consultants also can make the difference between having superior or just average intelligence and overall competitiveness.

Firms need an effective competitive intelligence (CI) program. The three basic objectives of a CI program are (1) to provide a general understanding of an industry and its competitors, (2) to identify areas in which competitors are vulnerable and to assess the impact strategic actions would have on competitors, and (3) to identify potential moves that a competitor might make that would endanger a firm's position in the market.[10] Competitive information is equally applicable for strategy formulation, implementation, and evaluation decisions. An effective CI program allows all areas of a firm to access consistent and verifiable information in making decisions. All members of an organization—from the chief executive officer to custodians—are valuable intelligence agents and should feel themselves to be a part of the CI process. Special characteristics of a successful CI program include flexibility, usefulness, timeliness, and cross-functional cooperation.

The increasing emphasis on *competitive analysis* in the United States is evidenced by corporations putting this function on their organizational charts under job titles such as Director of Competitive Analysis, Competitive Strategy Manager, Director of Information Services, or Associate Director of Competitive Assessment. The responsibilities of a *director of competitive analysis* include planning, collecting data, analyzing data, facilitating the process of gathering and analyzing data, disseminating intelligence on a timely basis, researching special issues, and recognizing what information is important and who needs to know. Competitive intelligence is not corporate espionage because 95 percent of the information a company needs to make strategic decisions is available and accessible to the public. Sources of competitive information include trade journals, want ads, newspaper articles, and government filings, as well as customers, suppliers, distributors, competitors themselves, and the Internet.

Unethical tactics such as bribery, wiretapping, and computer break-ins should never be used to obtain information. Marriott and Motorola—two U.S. companies that do a particularly good job of gathering competitive intelligence—agree that all the information you could wish for can be collected without resorting to unethical tactics. They keep their intelligence staffs small, usually under five people, and spend less than $200,000 per year on gathering competitive intelligence.

Unilever recently sued Procter & Gamble (P&G) over that company's corporate-espionage activities to obtain the secrets of its Unilever hair-care business. After spending $3 million to establish a team to find out about competitors in the domestic hair-care industry, P&G allegedly took roughly 80 documents from garbage bins outside Unilever's Chicago offices. P&G produces Pantene and Head & Shoulders shampoos; Unilever has hair-care brands such as ThermaSilk, Suave, Salon Selectives, and Finesse. Similarly, Oracle Corp. recently admitted that detectives it hired paid janitors to go through Microsoft Corp.'s garbage, looking for evidence to use in court.

Market Commonality and Resource Similarity

By definition, competitors are firms that offer similar products and services in the same market. Markets can be geographic or product areas or segments. For example, in the insurance industry the markets are broken down into commercial/consumer, health/life, or Europe/Asia. Researchers use the terms *market commonality* and *resource similarity* to study rivalry among competitors. *Market commonality* can be defined as the number and significance of markets that a firm competes in with rivals.[11] *Resource similarity* is the extent to which the type and amount of a firm's internal resources are comparable to a rival.[12] One way to analyze competitiveness between two or among several firms is to investigate market commonality and resource similarity issues while looking for areas of potential competitive advantage along each firm's value chain.

Competitive Analysis: Porter's Five-Forces Model

As illustrated in Figure 3-3, *Porter's Five-Forces Model* of competitive analysis is a widely used approach for developing strategies in many industries. The intensity of competition among firms varies widely across industries. Table 3-10 reveals the average profit margin and return on investment for firms in different industries. Note the substantial variation among industries. For example, the range in profit margin goes from 0 to 18 for food production to computer software, respectively. Intensity of competition is highest in lower-return industries. The collective impact of competitive forces is so brutal in some industries that the market is clearly "unattractive" from a profit-making standpoint. Rivalry among existing firms is severe, new rivals can enter the industry with relative ease, and both suppliers and customers can exercise considerable bargaining leverage. According to Porter, the nature of competitiveness in a given industry can be viewed as a composite of five forces:

1. Rivalry among competing firms
2. Potential entry of new competitors

FIGURE 3-3

The Five-Forces Model of Competition

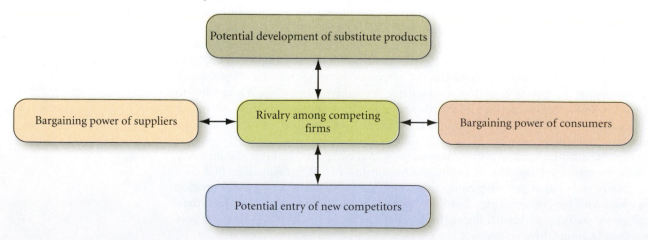

TABLE 3-10   Intensity of Competition Among Firms in Different
Industries (A through H industries only)

Industry	Year-End Profit Margin		Year-End Return on Investment	
	2006	2008	2006	2008
Aerospace and Defense	6	8	6	8
Airlines	2	−13	2	−14
Apparel	5	9	8	34
Automotive Retailing	1	−8	3	−10
Beverages	7	3	4	2
Chemicals	5	5	5	6
Commercial Banks	16	5	1.3	0.3
Computer Peripherals	8	10	7	12
Computer Software	18	32	8	20
Computers, Office Equipment	6	4	7	5
Diversified Financials	12	−1	1	0
Diversified Outsourcing Services	4	7	5	3
Electronics, Electrical Equipment	7	7	8	9
Energy	3	1	3	2
Engineering, Construction	2	3	4	5
Entertainment	10	−10	4	−3
Financial Data Services	10	12	6	2
Food and Drug Stores	2	2	5	4
Food Consumer Products	5	7	6	7
Food Production	0	1	1	1
Food Services	4	7	7	11
Forest and Paper Products	3	−10	4	−8
General Merchandisers	3	3	5	5
Health Care: Insurance	5	2	8	4
Health Care: Medical Facilities	4	2	4	3
Health Care: Pharmacy	3	3	9	7
Home Equipment/Furnishings	4	1	6	1
Homebuilders	6	−47	6	−43
Hotels, Casinos, Resorts	7	−5	3	0

Source: Based on John Moore, "Ranked Within Industries," *Fortune* (May 4, 2009): F-46–F-60.

3.   Potential development of substitute products
4.   Bargaining power of suppliers
5.   Bargaining power of consumers

The following three steps for using Porter's Five-Forces Model can indicate whether competition in a given industry is such that the firm can make an acceptable profit:

1.   Identify key aspects or elements of each competitive force that impact the firm.
2.   Evaluate how strong and important each element is for the firm.
3.   Decide whether the collective strength of the elements is worth the firm entering or staying in the industry.

Rivalry Among Competing Firms

Rivalry among competing firms is usually the most powerful of the five competitive forces. The strategies pursued by one firm can be successful only to the extent that they provide competitive advantage over the strategies pursued by rival firms. Changes in strategy by one firm may be met with retaliatory countermoves, such as lowering prices, enhancing quality, adding features, providing services, extending warranties, and increasing advertising.

Free-flowing information on the Internet is driving down prices and inflation worldwide. The Internet, coupled with the common currency in Europe, enables consumers to make price comparisons easily across countries. Just for a moment, consider the implications for car dealers who used to know everything about a new car's pricing, while you, the consumer, knew very little. You could bargain, but being in the dark, you rarely could win. Now you can shop online in a few hours at every dealership within 500 miles to find the best price and terms. So you, the consumer, can win. This is true in many, if not most, business-to-consumer and business-to-business sales transactions today.

The intensity of rivalry among competing firms tends to increase as the number of competitors increases, as competitors become more equal in size and capability, as demand for the industry's products declines, and as price cutting becomes common. Rivalry also increases when consumers can switch brands easily; when barriers to leaving the market are high; when fixed costs are high; when the product is perishable; when consumer demand is growing slowly or declines such that rivals have excess capacity and/or inventory; when the products being sold are commodities (not easily differentiated such as gasoline); when rival firms are diverse in strategies, origins, and culture; and when mergers and acquisitions are common in the industry. As rivalry among competing firms intensifies, industry profits decline, in some cases to the point where an industry becomes inherently unattractive. When rival firms sense weakness, typically they will intensify both marketing and production efforts to capitalize on the "opportunity." Table 3-11 summarizes conditions that cause high rivalry among competing firms.

Potential Entry of New Competitors

Whenever new firms can easily enter a particular industry, the intensity of competitiveness among firms increases. Barriers to entry, however, can include the need to gain economies of scale quickly, the need to gain technology and specialized know-how, the lack of experience, strong customer loyalty, strong brand preferences, large capital requirements, lack of adequate distribution channels, government regulatory policies, tariffs, lack of access to

TABLE 3-11 Conditions That Cause High Rivalry Among Competing Firms

1. High number of competing firms
2. Similar size of firms competing
3. Similar capability of firms competing
4. Falling demand for the industry's products
5. Falling product/service prices in the industry
6. When consumers can switch brands easily
7. When barriers to leaving the market are high
8. When barriers to entering the market are low
9. When fixed costs are high among firms competing
10. When the product is perishable
11. When rivals have excess capacity
12. When consumer demand is falling
13. When rivals have excess inventory
14. When rivals sell similar products/services
15. When mergers are common in the industry

raw materials, possession of patents, undesirable locations, counterattack by entrenched firms, and potential saturation of the market.

Despite numerous barriers to entry, new firms sometimes enter industries with higher-quality products, lower prices, and substantial marketing resources. The strategist's job, therefore, is to identify potential new firms entering the market, to monitor the new rival firms' strategies, to counterattack as needed, and to capitalize on existing strengths and opportunities. When the threat of new firms entering the market is strong, incumbent firms generally fortify their positions and take actions to deter new entrants, such as lowering prices, extending warranties, adding features, or offering financing specials.

Potential Development of Substitute Products

In many industries, firms are in close competition with producers of substitute products in other industries. Examples are plastic container producers competing with glass, paperboard, and aluminum can producers, and acetaminophen manufacturers competing with other manufacturers of pain and headache remedies. The presence of substitute products puts a ceiling on the price that can be charged before consumers will switch to the substitute product. Price ceilings equate to profit ceilings and more intense competition among rivals. Producers of eyeglasses and contact lenses, for example, face increasing competitive pressures from laser eye surgery. Producers of sugar face similar pressures from artificial sweeteners. Newspapers and magazines face substitute-product competitive pressures from the Internet and 24-hour cable television. The magnitude of competitive pressure derived from development of substitute products is generally evidenced by rivals' plans for expanding production capacity, as well as by their sales and profit growth numbers.

Competitive pressures arising from substitute products increase as the relative price of substitute products declines and as consumers' switching costs decrease. The competitive strength of substitute products is best measured by the inroads into the market share those products obtain, as well as those firms' plans for increased capacity and market penetration.

Bargaining Power of Suppliers

The bargaining power of suppliers affects the intensity of competition in an industry, especially when there is a large number of suppliers, when there are only a few good substitute raw materials, or when the cost of switching raw materials is especially costly. It is often in the best interest of both suppliers and producers to assist each other with reasonable prices, improved quality, development of new services, just-in-time deliveries, and reduced inventory costs, thus enhancing long-term profitability for all concerned.

Firms may pursue a backward integration strategy to gain control or ownership of suppliers. This strategy is especially effective when suppliers are unreliable, too costly, or not capable of meeting a firm's needs on a consistent basis. Firms generally can negotiate more favorable terms with suppliers when backward integration is a commonly used strategy among rival firms in an industry.

However, in many industries it is more economical to use outside suppliers of component parts than to self-manufacture the items. This is true, for example, in the outdoor power equipment industry where producers of lawn mowers, rotary tillers, leaf blowers, and edgers such as Murray generally obtain their small engines from outside manufacturers such as Briggs & Stratton who specialize in such engines and have huge economies of scale.

In more and more industries, sellers are forging strategic partnerships with select suppliers in efforts to (1) reduce inventory and logistics costs (e.g., through just-in-time deliveries); (2) speed the availability of next-generation components; (3) enhance the quality of the parts and components being supplied and reduce defect rates; and (4) squeeze out important cost savings for both themselves and their suppliers.[13]

Bargaining Power of Consumers

When customers are concentrated or large or buy in volume, their bargaining power represents a major force affecting the intensity of competition in an industry. Rival firms may offer extended warranties or special services to gain customer loyalty whenever the bargaining power of consumers is substantial. Bargaining power of consumers also is higher when the products being purchased are standard or undifferentiated. When this is the case, consumers often can negotiate selling price, warranty coverage, and accessory packages to a greater extent.

The bargaining power of consumers can be the most important force affecting competitive advantage. Consumers gain increasing bargaining power under the following circumstances:

1. If they can inexpensively switch to competing brands or substitutes
2. If they are particularly important to the seller
3. If sellers are struggling in the face of falling consumer demand
4. If they are informed about sellers' products, prices, and costs
5. If they have discretion in whether and when they purchase the product[14]

Sources of External Information

A wealth of strategic information is available to organizations from both published and unpublished sources. Unpublished sources include customer surveys, market research, speeches at professional and shareholders' meetings, television programs, interviews, and conversations with stakeholders. Published sources of strategic information include periodicals, journals, reports, government documents, abstracts, books, directories, newspapers, and manuals. The Internet has made it easier for firms to gather, assimilate, and evaluate information.

There are many excellent Web sites for gathering strategic information, but six that the author uses routinely are listed here:

1. http://marketwatch.multexinvestor.com
2. http://moneycentral.msn.com
3. http://finance.yahoo.com
4. www.clearstation.com
5. https://us.etrade.com/e/t/invest/markets
6. www.hoovers.com

Most college libraries subscribe to Standard & Poor's (S&P's) *Industry Surveys*. These documents are exceptionally up-to-date and give valuable information about many different industries. Each report is authored by a Standard & Poor's industry research analyst and includes the following sections:

1. Current Environment
2. Industry Trends
3. How the Industry Operates
4. Key Industry Ratios and Statistics
5. How to Analyze a Company
6. Glossary of Industry Terms
7. Additional Industry Information
8. References
9. Comparative Company Financial Analysis

Forecasting Tools and Techniques

Forecasts are educated assumptions about future trends and events. Forecasting is a complex activity because of factors such as technological innovation, cultural changes, new products, improved services, stronger competitors, shifts in government priorities, changing social values, unstable economic conditions, and unforeseen events. Managers often must rely on published forecasts to effectively identify key external opportunities and threats.

A sense of the future permeates all action and underlies every decision a person makes. People eat expecting to be satisfied and nourished in the future. People sleep assuming that in the future they will feel rested. They invest energy, money, and time because they believe their efforts will be rewarded in the future. They build highways assuming that automobiles and trucks will need them in the future. Parents educate children on the basis of forecasts that they will need certain skills, attitudes, and knowledge when they grow up. The truth is we all make implicit forecasts throughout our daily lives. The question, therefore, is not whether we should forecast but rather how we can best forecast to enable us to move beyond our ordinarily unarticulated assumptions about the future. Can we obtain information and then make educated assumptions (forecasts) to better guide our current decisions to achieve a more desirable future state of affairs? We should go into the future with our eyes and our minds open, rather than stumble into the future with our eyes closed.[15]

Many publications and sources on the Internet forecast external variables. Several published examples include *Industry Week's* "Trends and Forecasts," *BusinessWeek's* "Investment Outlook," and Standard & Poor's *Industry Survey.* The reputation and continued success of these publications depend partly on accurate forecasts, so published sources of information can offer excellent projections. An especially good Web site for industry forecasts is finance.yahoo.com. Just insert a firm's stock symbol and go from there.

Sometimes organizations must develop their own projections. Most organizations forecast (project) their own revenues and profits annually. Organizations sometimes forecast market share or customer loyalty in local areas. Because forecasting is so important in strategic management and because the ability to forecast (in contrast to the ability to use a forecast) is essential, selected forecasting tools are examined further here.

Forecasting tools can be broadly categorized into two groups: quantitative techniques and qualitative techniques. Quantitative forecasts are most appropriate when historical data are available and when the relationships among key variables are expected to remain the same in the future. *Linear regression*, for example, is based on the assumption that the future will be just like the past—which, of course, it never is. As historical relationships become less stable, quantitative forecasts become less accurate.

No forecast is perfect, and some forecasts are even wildly inaccurate. This fact accents the need for strategists to devote sufficient time and effort to study the underlying bases for published forecasts and to develop internal forecasts of their own. Key external opportunities and threats can be effectively identified only through good forecasts. Accurate forecasts can provide major competitive advantages for organizations. Forecasts are vital to the strategic-management process and to the success of organizations.

Making Assumptions

Planning would be impossible without assumptions. McConkey defines assumptions as the "best present estimates of the impact of major external factors, over which the manager has little if any control, but which may exert a significant impact on performance or the ability to achieve desired results."[16] Strategists are faced with countless variables and imponderables that can be neither controlled nor predicted with 100 percent accuracy. Wild guesses should never be made in formulating strategies, but reasonable assumptions based on available information must always be made.

By identifying future occurrences that could have a major effect on the firm and by making reasonable assumptions about those factors, strategists can carry the strategic-management process forward. Assumptions are needed only for future trends and events that are most likely to have a significant effect on the company's business. Based on the best information at the time, assumptions serve as checkpoints on the validity of strategies. If future occurrences deviate significantly from assumptions, strategists know that corrective actions may be needed. Without reasonable assumptions, the strategy-formulation process could not proceed effectively. Firms that have the best information generally make the most accurate assumptions, which can lead to major competitive advantages.

Industry Analysis: The External Factor Evaluation (EFE) Matrix

An *External Factor Evaluation (EFE)* Matrix allows strategists to summarize and evaluate economic, social, cultural, demographic, environmental, political, governmental, legal, technological, and competitive information. Illustrated in Table 3-12, the EFE Matrix can be developed in five steps:

1. List key external factors as identified in the external-audit process. Include a total of 15 to 20 factors, including both opportunities and threats, that affect the firm and its industry. List the opportunities first and then the threats. Be as specific as possible, using percentages, ratios, and comparative numbers whenever possible. Recall that Edward Deming said, "In God we trust. Everyone else bring data."
2. Assign to each factor a weight that ranges from 0.0 (not important) to 1.0 (very important). The weight indicates the relative importance of that factor to being successful in the firm's industry. Opportunities often receive higher weights than threats, but threats can receive high weights if they are especially severe or threatening. Appropriate weights can be determined by comparing successful with unsuccessful competitors or by discussing the factor and reaching a group consensus. The sum of all weights assigned to the factors must equal 1.0.
3. Assign a rating between 1 and 4 to each key external factor to indicate how effectively the firm's current strategies respond to the factor, where 4 = *the response is superior*, 3 = *the response is above average*, 2 = *the response is average*, and 1 = *the response is poor*. Ratings are based on effectiveness of the firm's strategies. Ratings are thus company-based, whereas the weights in Step 2 are industry-based. It is important to note that both threats and opportunities can receive a 1, 2, 3, or 4.
4. Multiply each factor's weight by its rating to determine a weighted score.
5. Sum the weighted scores for each variable to determine the total weighted score for the organization.

Regardless of the number of key opportunities and threats included in an EFE Matrix, the highest possible total weighted score for an organization is 4.0 and the lowest possible

TABLE 3-12 EFE Matrix for a Local Ten-Theatre Cinema Complex

Key External Factors	Weight	Rating	Weighted Score
Opportunities			
1. Rowan County is growing 8% annually in population	0.05	3	0.15
2. TDB University is expanding 6% annually	0.08	4	0.32
3. Major competitor across town recently ceased operations	0.08	3	0.24
4. Demand for going to cinema growing 10% annually	0.07	2	0.14
5. Two new neighborhoods being developed within 3 miles	0.09	1	0.09
6. Disposable income among citizens grew 5% in prior year	0.06	3	0.18
7. Unemployment rate in county declined to 3.1%	0.03	2	0.06
Threats			
8. Trend toward healthy eating eroding concession sales	0.12	4	0.48
9. Demand for online movies and DVDs growing 10% annually	0.06	2	0.12
10. Commercial property adjacent to cinemas for sale	0.06	3	0.18
11. TDB University installing an on-campus movie theatre	0.04	3	0.12
12. County and city property taxes increasing 25% this year	0.08	2	0.16
13. Local religious groups object to R-rated movies being shown	0.04	3	0.12
14. Movies rented from local Blockbuster store up 12%	0.08	2	0.16
15. Movies rented last quarter from Time Warner up 15%	0.06	1	0.06
Total	**1.00**		**2.58**

total weighted score is 1.0. The average total weighted score is 2.5. A total weighted score of 4.0 indicates that an organization is responding in an outstanding way to existing opportunities and threats in its industry. In other words, the firm's strategies effectively take advantage of existing opportunities and minimize the potential adverse effects of external threats. A total score of 1.0 indicates that the firm's strategies are not capitalizing on opportunities or avoiding external threats.

An example of an EFE Matrix is provided in Table 3-12 for a local ten-theatre cinema complex. Note that the most important factor to being successful in this business is "Trend toward healthy eating eroding concession sales" as indicated by the 0.12 weight. Also note that the local cinema is doing excellent in regard to handling two factors, "TDB University is expanding 6 percent annually" and "Trend toward healthy eating eroding concession sales." Perhaps the cinema is placing flyers on campus and also adding yogurt and healthy drinks to its concession menu. Note that you may have a 1, 2, 3, or 4 anywhere down the Rating column. Note also that the factors are stated in quantitative terms to the extent possible, rather than being stated in vague terms. Quantify the factors as much as possible in constructing an EFE Matrix. Finally, note that the total weighted score of 2.58 is above the average (midpoint) of 2.5, so this cinema business is doing pretty well, taking advantage of the external opportunities and avoiding the threats facing the firm. There is definitely room for improvement, though, because the highest total weighted score would be 4.0. As indicated by ratings of 1, this business needs to capitalize more on the "two new neighborhoods nearby" opportunity and the "movies rented from Time Warner" threat. Note also that there are many percentage-based factors among the group. Be quantitative to the extent possible! Note also that the ratings range from 1 to 4 on both the opportunities and threats.

The Competitive Profile Matrix (CPM)

The *Competitive Profile Matrix (CPM)* identifies a firm's major competitors and its particular strengths and weaknesses in relation to a sample firm's strategic position. The weights and total weighted scores in both a CPM and an EFE have the same meaning. However, *critical success* factors in a CPM include both internal and external issues; therefore, the ratings refer to strengths and weaknesses, where 4 = major strength, 3 = minor strength, 2 = minor weakness, and 1 = major weakness. The critical success factors in a CPM are not grouped into opportunities and threats as they are in an EFE. In a CPM, the ratings and total weighted scores for rival firms can be compared to the sample firm. This comparative analysis provides important internal strategic information.

A sample Competitive Profile Matrix is provided in Table 3-13. In this example, the two most important factors to being successful in the industry are "advertising" and

TABLE 3-13   An Example Competitive Profile Matrix

Critical Success Factors	Weight	Company 1 Rating	Company 1 Score	Company 2 Rating	Company 2 Score	Company 3 Rating	Company 3 Score
Advertising	0.20	1	0.20	4	0.80	3	0.60
Product Quality	0.10	4	0.40	3	0.30	2	0.20
Price Competitiveness	0.10	3	0.30	2	0.20	4	0.40
Management	0.10	4	0.40	3	0.20	3	0.30
Financial Position	0.15	4	0.60	2	0.30	3	0.45
Customer Loyalty	0.10	4	0.40	3	0.30	2	0.20
Global Expansion	0.20	4	0.80	1	0.20	2	0.40
Market Share	0.05	1	0.05	4	0.20	3	0.15
Total	**1.00**		**3.15**		**2.50**		**2.70**

Note: (1) The ratings values are as follows: 1 = major weakness, 2 = minor weakness, 3 = minor strength, 4 = major strength.
(2) As indicated by the total weighted score of 2.50, Competitor 2 is weakest. (3) Only eight critical success factors are included for simplicity; this is too few in actuality.

TABLE 3-14   Another Example Competitive Profile Matrix

Critical Success Factors	Weight	Company 1		Company 2		Company 3	
		Rating	Weighted Score	Rating	Weighted Score	Rating	Weighted Score
Market share	0.15	3	0.45	2	0.30	4	0.60
Inventory system	0.08	2	0.16	2	0.16	4	0.32
Financial position	0.10	2	0.20	3	0.30	4	0.40
Product quality	0.08	3	0.24	4	0.32	3	0.24
Consumer loyalty	0.02	3	0.06	3	0.06	4	0.08
Sales distribution	0.10	3	0.30	2	0.20	3	0.30
Global expansion	0.15	3	0.45	2	0.30	4	0.60
Organization structure	0.05	3	0.15	4	0.20	2	0.10
Production capacity	0.04	3	0.12	2	0.08	4	0.16
E-commerce	0.10	3	0.30	1	0.10	4	0.40
Customer service	0.10	3	0.30	2	0.20	4	0.40
Price competitive	0.02	4	0.08	1	0.02	3	0.06
Management experience	0.01	2	0.02	4	0.04	2	0.02
Total	**1.00**		**2.83**		**2.28**		**3.68**

"global expansion," as indicated by weights of 0.20. If there were no weight column in this analysis, note that each factor then would be equally important. Thus, having a weight column makes for a more robust analysis, because it enables the analyst to assign higher and lower numbers to capture perceived or actual levels of importance. Note in Table 3-13 that Company 1 is strongest on "product quality," as indicated by a rating of 4, whereas Company 2 is strongest on "advertising." Overall, Company 1 is strongest, as indicated by the total weighted score of 3.15.

Other than the critical success factors listed in the example CPM, factors often included in this analysis include breadth of product line, effectiveness of sales distribution, proprietary or patent advantages, location of facilities, production capacity and efficiency, experience, union relations, technological advantages, and e-commerce expertise.

A word on interpretation: Just because one firm receives a 3.2 rating and another receives a 2.80 rating in a Competitive Profile Matrix, it does not follow that the first firm is 20 percent better than the second. Numbers reveal the relative strengths of firms, but their implied precision is an illusion. Numbers are not magic. The aim is not to arrive at a single number, but rather to assimilate and evaluate information in a meaningful way that aids in decision making.

Another Competitive Profile Matrix is provided in Table 3-14. Note that Company 2 has the best product quality and management experience; Company 3 has the best market share and inventory system; and Company 1 has the best price as indicated by the ratings. Avoid assigning duplicate ratings on any row in a CPM.

Conclusion

Increasing turbulence in markets and industries around the world means the external audit has become an explicit and vital part of the strategic-management process. This chapter provides a framework for collecting and evaluating economic, social, cultural, demographic, environmental, political, governmental, legal, technological, and competitive information. Firms that do not mobilize and empower their managers and employees to identify, monitor, forecast, and evaluate key external forces may fail to anticipate emerging opportunities and threats and, consequently, may pursue ineffective strategies, miss opportunities, and invite organizational demise. Firms not taking advantage of the Internet are technologically falling behind.

A major responsibility of strategists is to ensure development of an effective external-audit system. This includes using information technology to devise a competitive intelligence system that works. The external-audit approach described in this chapter can be used effectively by any size or type of organization. Typically, the external-audit process is more informal in small firms, but the need to understand key trends and events is no less important for these firms. The EFE Matrix and Porter's Five-Forces Model can help strategists evaluate the market and industry, but these tools must be accompanied by good intuitive judgment. Multinational firms especially need a systematic and effective external-audit system because external forces among foreign countries vary so greatly.

We invite you to visit the David page on the Prentice Hall Companion Web site at http://www.pearsonhighered.com/david/ for this chapter's review quiz.

Key Terms and Concepts

Chief Information Officer (CIO) (p. 69)
Chief Technology Officer (CTO) (p. 69)
Competitive Analysis (p. 73)
Competitive Intelligence (CI) (p. 72)
Competitive Profile Matrix (CPM) (p. 81)
Director of Competitive Analysis (p. 73)
Environmental Scanning (p. 60)
External Audit (p. 61)
External Factor Evaluation (EFE) Matrix (p. 80)
External Forces (p. 61)

Industrial/Organization (I/O) (p. 63)
Industry Analysis (p. 60)
Information Technology (IT) (p. 69)
Internet (p. 69)
Lifecare Facilities (p. 67)
Linear Regression (p. 79)
Market Commonality (p. 74)
Porter's Five-Forces Model (p. 74)
Resource Similarity (p. 74)

Issues for Review and Discussion

1. Describe the "process of performing an external audit" in an organization doing strategic planning for the first time.
2. The global recession forced thousands of firms into bankruptcy. Does this fact alone confirm that "external factors are more important than internal factors" in strategic planning? Discuss.
3. Use a series of two-dimensional (two-variable) graphs to illustrate the historical relationship among the following variables: value of the dollar, oil prices, interest rates, and stock prices. Give one implication of each graph for strategic planning.
4. Do you feel the advantages of a low value of the dollar offset the disadvantages for (1) a firm that derives 60 percent of its revenues from foreign countries and (2) a firm that derives 10 percent of its revenues from foreign countries? Justify your opinion.
5. The lingering global recession has greatly slowed the migration of people from (1) region to region across the United States, from (2) city to suburb worldwide, and from (3) country to country across the globe. What are the strategic implications of these trends for companies?
6. Governments worldwide are turning to "nationalization of companies" to cope with economic recession. Examples in the United States include AIG, GM, and Citigroup. What are the strategic implications of this trend for firms that compete with these nationalized firms?
7. Governments worldwide are turning to "protectionism" to cope with economic recession, imposing tariffs and subsidies on foreign goods and restrictions/incentives on their own firms to keep jobs at home. What are the strategic implications of this trend for international commerce?
8. Compare and contrast the duties and responsibilities of a CIO with a CTO in a large firm.
9. What are the three basic objectives of a competitive intelligence program?
10. Distinguish between market commonality and resource similarity. Apply these concepts to two rival firms that you are familiar with.
11. Let's say you work for McDonald's and you applied Porter's Five-Forces Model to study the fast-food industry. Would information in your analysis provide factors more readily to an EFE Matrix, a CPM, or to neither matrix? Justify your answer.
12. Explain why it is appropriate for Ratings in an EFE Matrix to be 1, 2, 3, or 4 for any opportunity or threat.

13. Why is inclusion of about 20 factors recommended in the EFE Matrix rather than about 10 factors or about 40 factors?

14. In developing an EFE Matrix, would it be advantageous to arrange your opportunities according to the highest weight, and do likewise for your threats? Explain.

15. In developing an EFE Matrix, would it be best to have 10 opportunities and 10 threats, or would 17 opportunities (or threats) be fine with 3 of the other to achieve a total of 20 factors as desired?

16. Could/should critical success factors in a CPM include external factors? Explain.

17. Explain how to conduct an external strategic-management audit.

18. Identify a recent economic, social, political, or technological trend that significantly affects the local Pizza Hut.

19. Discuss the following statement: Major opportunities and threats usually result from an interaction among key environmental trends rather than from a single external event or factor.

20. Identify two industries experiencing rapid technological changes and three industries that are experiencing little technological change. How does the need for technological forecasting differ in these industries? Why?

21. Use Porter's Five-Forces Model to evaluate competitiveness within the U.S. banking industry.

22. What major forecasting techniques would you use to identify (1) economic opportunities and threats and (2) demographic opportunities and threats? Why are these techniques most appropriate?

23. How does the external audit affect other components of the strategic-management process?

24. As the owner of a small business, explain how you would organize a strategic-information scanning system. How would you organize such a system in a large organization?

25. Construct an EFE Matrix for an organization of your choice.

26. Make an appointment with a librarian at your university to learn how to use online databases. Report your findings in class.

27. Give some advantages and disadvantages of cooperative versus competitive strategies.

28. As strategist for a local bank, explain when you would use qualitative versus quantitative forecasts.

29. What is your forecast for interest rates and the stock market in the next several months? As the stock market moves up, do interest rates always move down? Why? What are the strategic implications of these trends?

30. Explain how information technology affects strategies of the organization where you worked most recently.

31. Let's say your boss develops an EFE Matrix that includes 62 factors. How would you suggest reducing the number of factors to 20?

32. Discuss the ethics of gathering competitive intelligence.

33. Discuss the ethics of cooperating with rival firms.

34. Visit the SEC Web site at www.sec.gov, and discuss the benefits of using information provided there.

35. Do you agree with I/O theorists that external factors are more important than internal factors to a firm's achieving competitive advantage? Explain both your and their position.

36. Define, compare, and contrast the weights versus ratings in an EFE Matrix.

37. Develop a Competitive Profile Matrix for your university. Include six factors.

38. List the 10 external areas that give rise to opportunities and threats.

Notes

1. York Freund, "Critical Success Factors," *Planning Review* 16, no. 4 (July–August 1988): 20.
2. S&P Industry Surveys, Beverage Industry, 2005.
3. John Miller, "Nations Rush to Establish New Barriers to Trade," *Wall Street Journal* (February 6, 2009): A1.
4. Jon Swartz, "MySpace Forges Ahead Despite Really Tough Times," *USA Today* (February 4, 2009): 3B.
5. Joe Mullich, "10 Industries That Wireless Will Change," *Wall Street Journal* (April 1, 2009): A12.
6. Bill Saporito, "Companies That Compete Best," *Fortune* (May 22, 1989): 36.
7. Jon Swartz, "Ex-Facebook COO Gets Top Job at MySpace," *USA Today* (April 27, 2009): 7B.
8. Evan Perez, "Computer Spies Breach Fighter-Jet Project," *Wall Street Journal* (April 21, 2009): A1.
9. Kenneth Sawka, "Demystifying Business Intelligence," *Management Review* (October 1996): 49.
10. John Prescott and Daniel Smith, "The Largest Survey of 'Leading-Edge' Competitor Intelligence Managers," *Planning Review* 17, no. 3 (May–June 1989): 6–13.

11. M. J. Chen, "Competitor Analysis and Interfirm Rivalry: Toward a Theoretical Integration," *Academy of Management Review* 21 (1996): 106.

12. S. Jayachandran, J. Gimeno, and P. R. Varadarajan, "Theory of Multimarket Competition: A Synthesis and Implications for Marketing Strategy," *Journal of Marketing* 63, 3 (1999): 59; and M. J. Chen. "Competitor Analysis and Interfirm Rivalry: Toward a Theoretical Integration," *Academy of Management Review* 21 (1996): 107–108.

13. Arthur Thompson, Jr., A. J. Strickland III, and John Gamble, *Crafting and Executing Strategy: Text and Readings* (New York: McGraw-Hill/Irwin, 2005): 63.

14. Michael E. Porter, *Competitive Strategy: Techniques for Analyzing Industries and Competitors* (New York: Free Press, 1980): 24–27.

15. horizon.unc.edu/projects/seminars/futuresresearch/rationale.asp.

16. Dale McConkey, "Planning in a Changing Environment," *Business Horizons* 31, no. 5 (September–October 1988): 67.

Current Readings

Capron, Laurence, and Olivier Chatain. "Competitors' Resource-Oriented Strategies: Acting on Competitors' Resources Through Interventions in Factor Markets and Political Markets." *The Academy of Management Review* 33, no. 1 (January 2008): 97.

Coyne, Kevin, and John Horn. "Predicting Your Competitor's Reaction." *Harvard Business Review* (April 2009): 90–110.

Delmas, Magali A., and Michael W. Toffel. "Organizational Responses to Environmental Demands: Opening the Black Box." *Strategic Management Journal* 29, no. 10 (October 2008): 1,027.

Hillman, Amy J., and Gerald D. Keim. "Political Environments and Business Strategy: Implications for Managers." *Business Horizons* 51, no. 1 (January–February 2008): 47.

Kachra, Ariff, and Roderick E. White. "Know-how Transfer: The Role of Social, Economic/Competitive, and Firm Boundary Factors." *Strategic Management Journal* 29, no. 4 (April 2008): 425.

Porter, Michael E. "The Five Competitive Forces That Shape Strategy." *Harvard Business Review* (January 2008): 78.

ASSURANCE OF LEARNING EXERCISES

Assurance of Learning Exercises 3A

Developing an EFE Matrix for McDonald's Corporation

Purpose

This exercise will give you practice developing an EFE Matrix. An EFE Matrix summarizes the results of an external audit. This is an important tool widely used by strategists.

Instructions

Step 1 Join with two other students in class, and jointly prepare an EFE Matrix for McDonald's Corporation. Refer back to the Cohesion Case and to Exercise 1A, if necessary, to identify external opportunities and threats. Use the information in the S&P Industry Surveys that you copied as part of Assurance of Learning Exercise 1A. Be sure not to include strategies as opportunities, but do include as many monetary amounts, percentages, numbers, and ratios as possible.

Step 2 All three-person teams participating in this exercise should record their EFE total weighted scores on the board. Put your initials after your score to identify it as your team's.

Step 3 Compare the total weighted scores. Which team's score came closest to the instructor's answer? Discuss reasons for variation in the scores reported on the board.

Assurance of Learning Exercise 3B

The External Assessment

Purpose

This exercise will help you become familiar with important sources of external information available in your college library. A key part of preparing an external audit is searching the Internet and examining published sources of information for relevant economic, social, cultural, demographic, environmental, political, governmental, legal, technological, and competitive trends and events. External opportunities and threats must be identified and evaluated before strategies can be formulated effectively.

Instructions

Step 1 Select a company or business where you currently or previously have worked. Conduct an external audit for this company. Find opportunities and threats in recent issues of newspapers and magazines. Search for information using the Internet. Use the following six Web sites:

> http://marketwatch.multexinvestor.com
> www.hoovers.com
> http://moneycentral.msn.com
> http://finance.yahoo.com
> www.clearstation.com
> https://us.etrade.com/e/t/invest/markets.

Step 2 On a separate sheet of paper, list 10 opportunities and 10 threats that face this company. Be specific in stating each factor.

Step 3 Include a bibliography to reveal where you found the information.

Step 4 Write a three-page summary of your findings, and submit it to your instructor.

Assurance of Learning Exercise 3C

Developing an EFE Matrix for My University

Purpose

More colleges and universities are embarking on the strategic-management process. Institutions are consciously and systematically identifying and evaluating external opportunities and threats facing higher education in your state, the nation, and the world.

Instructions

Step 1   Join with two other individuals in class and jointly prepare an EFE Matrix for your institution.

Step 2   Go to the board and record your total weighted score in a column that includes the scores of all three-person teams participating. Put your initials after your score to identify it as your team's.

Step 3   Which team viewed your college's strategies most positively? Which team viewed your college's strategies most negatively? Discuss the nature of the differences.

Assurance of Learning Exercise 3D

Developing a Competitive Profile Matrix for McDonald's Corporation

Purpose

Monitoring competitors' performance and strategies is a key aspect of an external audit. This exercise is designed to give you practice evaluating the competitive position of organizations in a given industry and assimilating that information in the form of a Competitive Profile Matrix.

Instructions

Step 1   Gather your information from Assurance of Learning Exercise 1A. Also, turn back to the Cohesion Case and review the section on competitors (pages 33–35).

Step 2   On a separate sheet of paper, prepare a Competitive Profile Matrix that includes McDonald's, Burger King Holdings, and Yum! Brands, Inc.

Step 3   Turn in your Competitive Profile Matrix for a classwork grade.

Assurance of Learning Exercise 3E

Developing a Competitive Profile Matrix for My University

Purpose

Your college or university competes with all other educational institutions in the world, especially those in your own state. State funds, students, faculty, staff, endowments, gifts, and federal funds are areas of competitiveness. Other areas include athletic programs, dorm life, academic reputation, location, and career services. The purpose of this exercise is to give you practice thinking competitively about the business of education in your state.

Instructions

Step 1   Identify two colleges or universities in your state that compete directly with your institution for students. Interview several persons, perhaps classmates, who are aware of particular strengths and weaknesses of those universities. Record information about the two competing universities.

Step 2   Prepare a Competitive Profile Matrix that includes your institution and the two competing institutions. Include at least the following ten factors in your analysis:
1. Tuition costs
2. Quality of faculty
3. Academic reputation
4. Average class size
5. Campus landscaping
6. Athletic programs
7. Quality of students
8. Graduate programs
9. Location of campus
10. Campus culture

Step 3   Submit your Competitive Profile Matrix to your instructor for evaluation.

CHAPTER 4
The Internal Assessment

CHAPTER OBJECTIVES

After studying this chapter, you should be able to do the following:

1. Describe how to perform an internal strategic-management audit.

2. Discuss the Resource-Based View (RBV) in strategic management.

3. Discuss key interrelationships among the functional areas of business.

4. Identify the basic functions or activities that make up management, marketing, finance/accounting, production/operations, research and development, and management information systems.

5. Explain how to determine and prioritize a firm's internal strengths and weaknesses.

6. Explain the importance of financial ratio analysis.

7. Discuss the nature and role of management information systems in strategic management.

8. Develop an Internal Factor Evaluation (IFE) Matrix.

9. Explain benchmarking as a strategic management tool.

Assurance of Learning Exercises

Assurance of Learning Exercise 4A
Performing a Financial Ratio Analysis for McDonald's Corporation

Assurance of Learning Exercise 4B
Constructing an IFE Matrix for McDonald's Corporation

Assurance of Learning Exercise 4C
Constructing an IFE Matrix for My University

Source: Shutterstock/Photographer Edyta Pawlowska

"Notable Quotes"

"Like a product or service, the planning process itself must be managed and shaped, if it is to serve executives as a vehicle for strategic decision-making."

—Robert Lenz

"The difference between now and five years ago is that information systems had limited function. You weren't betting your company on it. Now you are."

—William Gruber

"Weak leadership can wreck the soundest strategy."

—Sun Tzu

"A firm that continues to employ a previously successful strategy eventually and inevitably falls victim to a competitor."

—William Cohen

"Great spirits have always encountered violent opposition from mediocre minds."

—Albert Einstein

"The idea is to concentrate our strength against our competitor's relative weakness."

—Bruce Henderson

This chapter focuses on identifying and evaluating a firm's strengths and weaknesses in the functional areas of business, including management, marketing, finance/accounting, production/operations, research and development, and management information systems. Relationships among these areas of business are examined. Strategic implications of important functional area concepts are examined. The process of performing an internal audit is described. The Resource-Based View (RBV) of strategic management is introduced as is the Value Chain Analysis (VCA) concept.

Doing Great in a Weak Economy. How?

Amazon.com, Inc.

Based in Seattle, Washington, Amazon's sales grew 14 percent to $4.65 billion in the second quarter of 2009; the firm's worldwide electronics sales grew 35 percent. CEO Jeff Bezo's strategic plan for Amazon is to make the firm the "Wal-Mart of the Internet" through heavily discounted prices and expansion into more and more product offerings as well as free shipping. Amazon prides itself on offering the lowest prices anywhere on anything, and the firm is charging ahead as brick and mortar retailers falter, declare bankruptcy, and even liquidate. Amazon has no retail stores, just inventory warehouses. Therefore the firm has low fixed costs. Its primary online rival, E-bay, is incurring declining revenues and profits.

Amazon is the largest online bookseller in the United States and is making its Kindle e-books available for reading on Apple's iPhone and iPod Touch devices. E-books is a rapidly growing segment of the publishing business. Barnes & Noble recently acquired e-book firm Fictionwise for $15.7 million, and Google is getting heavily in the e-book business. Sony Electronics recently formed a partnership with Google to compete against Amazon in the growing digital books market. Amazon's Kindle electronic book reader is under attack from the partnership that enables readers to use the Sony Reader device to access more than half a million public domain books from Google's digital book library.

Amazon sold about 500,000 Kindles in 2008 and expects the Kindle could bring $3.7 billion in annual revenue by 2012. In July 2009, Amazon lowered the price of its Kindle product from $359 to $299 in an effort to make Kindle a blockbuster hit.

What started as the planet's biggest bookstore has rapidly become the planet's biggest anything store. The firm's main Web site offers millions of books, music, and movies (which still account for the majority of the firm's sales), not to mention auto parts, toys, electronics, home furnishings, apparel, health and beauty aids, prescription drugs, and groceries. Customers can also download books, games, MP3s, and films to their computers. In addition to Kindle, Amazon provides other products and services too, such as self-publishing, online advertising, and a Web store platform. The firm is capitalizing on a huge consumer shift toward online shopping during a recession.

Some states are strapped for cash and are forcing retailers to collect taxes on online sales. New York passed an Internet sales tax law in 2008. North Carolina, Hawaii, California, Maryland, Minnesota, and Tennessee are close to passing similar laws. Amazon is fighting these laws. Amazon collects sales tax only in the state of Washington, where it has offices and warehouses. In mid-2009, Amazon ended business relationships with marketing affiliates in North Carolina, Rhode Island, and Hawaii to avoid collecting sales tax in the state. A *marketing affiliate* can be defined as a business that gets a sales commission by featuring links to outside e-commerce sites on their own Web site. There are mounting tensions between online retailers and cash-strapped states across the country. Amazon contends that it is unconstitutional to require sellers with no physical presence in a state to collect sales tax on sales to buyers in that state.

Source: Based on Geoffrey Fowler, "Amazon's Sales Surge, Bucking Retail Slump," *Wall Street Journal* (January 30, 2009): B1; Yukari Iwatani Kane and Dan Gallagher, "Amazon Gets in Used-Game Business," *Wall Street Journal* (March 6, 2009): B5.

The Nature of an Internal Audit

All organizations have strengths and weaknesses in the functional areas of business. No enterprise is equally strong or weak in all areas. Maytag, for example, is known for excellent production and product design, whereas Procter & Gamble is known for superb marketing. Internal strengths/weaknesses, coupled with external opportunities/threats and a clear statement of mission, provide the basis for establishing objectives and strategies. Objectives and strategies are established with the intention of capitalizing upon internal strengths and overcoming weaknesses. The internal-audit part of the strategic-management process is illustrated in Figure 4-1.

Key Internal Forces

It is not possible in a strategic-management text to review in depth all the material presented in courses such as marketing, finance, accounting, management, management information systems, and production/operations; there are many subareas within these functions, such as customer service, warranties, advertising, packaging, and pricing under marketing.

For different types of organizations, such as hospitals, universities, and government agencies, the functional business areas, of course, differ. In a hospital, for example, functional areas may include cardiology, hematology, nursing, maintenance, physician support, and receivables. Functional areas of a university can include athletic programs, placement services, housing, fund-raising, academic research, counseling, and intramural programs. Within large organizations, each division has certain strengths and weaknesses.

A firm's strengths that cannot be easily matched or imitated by competitors are called *distinctive competencies.* Building competitive advantages involves taking advantage of distinctive competencies. For example, 3M exploits its distinctive competence in research and development by producing a wide range of innovative products. Strategies are designed in part to improve on a firm's weaknesses, turning them into strengths—and maybe even into distinctive competencies.

Figure 4-2 illustrates that all firms should continually strive to improve on their weaknesses, turning them into strengths, and ultimately developing distinctive competencies that can provide the firm with competitive advantages over rival firms.

The Process of Performing an Internal Audit

The process of performing an *internal audit* closely parallels the process of performing an external audit. Representative managers and employees from throughout the firm need to be involved in determining a firm's strengths and weaknesses. The internal audit requires gathering and assimilating information about the firm's management, marketing, finance/accounting, production/operations, research and development (R&D), and management information systems operations. Key factors should be prioritized as described in Chapter 3 so that the firm's most important strengths and weaknesses can be determined collectively.

Compared to the external audit, the process of performing an internal audit provides more opportunity for participants to understand how their jobs, departments, and divisions

FIGURE 4-1

A Comprehensive Strategic-Management Model

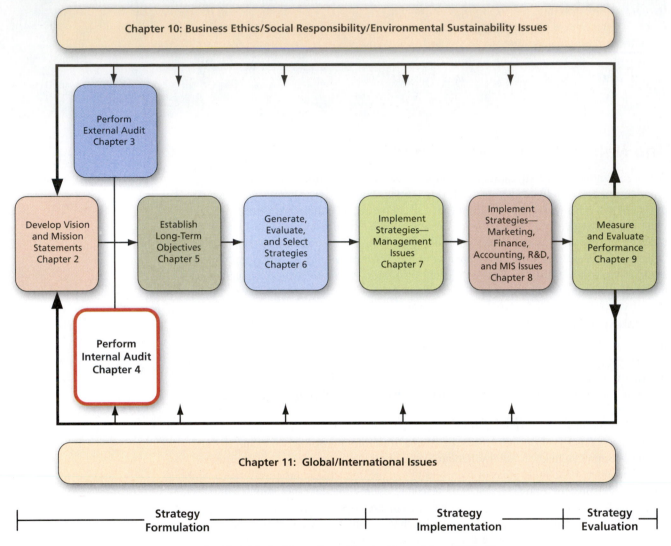

Source: Fred R. David, "How Companies Define Their Mission," *Long Range Planning* 22, no. 3 (June 1988): 40.

fit into the whole organization. This is a great benefit because managers and employees perform better when they understand how their work affects other areas and activities of the firm. For example, when marketing and manufacturing managers jointly discuss issues related to internal strengths and weaknesses, they gain a better appreciation of the issues, problems, concerns, and needs of all the functional areas. In organizations that do not use strategic management, marketing, finance, and manufacturing managers often do not interact with each other in significant ways. Performing an internal audit thus is an excellent vehicle or forum for improving the process of communication in the organization. *Communication* may be the most important word in management.

FIGURE 4-2

The Process of Gaining Competitive Advantage in a Firm

Weaknesses ⇒ Strengths ⇒ Distinctive Competencies ⇒ Competitive Advantage

Performing an internal audit requires gathering, assimilating, and evaluating information about the firm's operations. Critical success factors, consisting of both strengths and weaknesses, can be identified and prioritized in the manner discussed in Chapter 3. According to William King, a task force of managers from different units of the organization, supported by staff, should be charged with determining the 10 to 20 most important strengths and weaknesses that should influence the future of the organization. He says:

> The development of conclusions on the 10 to 20 most important organizational strengths and weaknesses can be, as any experienced manager knows, a difficult task, when it involves managers representing various organizational interests and points of view. Developing a 20-page list of strengths and weaknesses could be accomplished relatively easily, but a list of the 10 to 15 most important ones involves significant analysis and negotiation. This is true because of the judgments that are required and the impact which such a list will inevitably have as it is used in the formulation, implementation, and evaluation of strategies.[1]

Strategic management is a highly interactive process that requires effective coordination among management, marketing, finance/accounting, production/operations, R&D, and management information systems managers. Although the strategic-management process is overseen by strategists, success requires that managers and employees from all functional areas work together to provide ideas and information. Financial managers, for example, may need to restrict the number of feasible options available to operations managers, or R&D managers may develop products for which marketing managers need to set higher objectives. A key to organizational success is effective coordination and understanding among managers from all functional business areas. Through involvement in performing an internal strategic-management audit, managers from different departments and divisions of the firm come to understand the nature and effect of decisions in other functional business areas in their firm. Knowledge of these relationships is critical for effectively establishing objectives and strategies.

A failure to recognize and understand relationships among the functional areas of business can be detrimental to strategic management, and the number of those relationships that must be managed increases dramatically with a firm's size, diversity, geographic dispersion, and the number of products or services offered. Governmental and nonprofit enterprises traditionally have not placed sufficient emphasis on relationships among the business functions. Some firms place too great an emphasis on one function at the expense of others. Ansoff explained:

> During the first fifty years, successful firms focused their energies on optimizing the performance of one of the principal functions: production/operations, R&D, or marketing. Today, due to the growing complexity and dynamism of the environment, success increasingly depends on a judicious combination of several functional influences. This transition from a single function focus to a multifunction focus is essential for successful strategic management.[2]

Financial ratio analysis exemplifies the complexity of relationships among the functional areas of business. A declining return on investment or profit margin ratio could be the result of ineffective marketing, poor management policies, research and development errors, or a weak management information system. The effectiveness of strategy formulation, implementation, and evaluation activities hinges upon a clear understanding of how major business functions affect one another. For strategies to succeed, a coordinated effort among all the functional areas of business is needed. In the case of planning, George wrote:

> We may conceptually separate planning for the purpose of theoretical discussion and analysis, but in practice, neither is it a distinct entity nor is it capable of being separated. The planning function is mixed with all other business functions and, like ink once mixed with water, it cannot be set apart. It is spread throughout and is a part of the whole of managing an organization.[3]

The Resource-Based View (RBV)

Some researchers emphasize the importance of the internal audit part of the strategic-management process by comparing it to the external audit. Robert Grant concluded that the internal audit is more important, saying:

> In a world where customer preferences are volatile, the identity of customers is changing, and the technologies for serving customer requirements are continually evolving, an externally focused orientation does not provide a secure foundation for formulating long-term strategy. When the external environment is in a state of flux, the firm's own resources and capabilities may be a much more stable basis on which to define its identity. Hence, a definition of a business in terms of what it is capable of doing may offer a more durable basis for strategy than a definition based upon the needs which the business seeks to satisfy.[4]

The *Resource-Based View (RBV)* approach to competitive advantage contends that internal resources are more important for a firm than external factors in achieving and sustaining competitive advantage. In contrast to the I/O theory presented in the previous chapter, proponents of the RBV view contend that organizational performance will primarily be determined by internal resources that can be grouped into three all-encompassing categories: physical resources, human resources, and organizational resources.[5] Physical resources include all plant and equipment, location, technology, raw materials, machines; human resources include all employees, training, experience, intelligence, knowledge, skills, abilities; and organizational resources include firm structure, planning processes, information systems, patents, trademarks, copyrights, databases, and so on. RBV theory asserts that resources are actually what helps a firm exploit opportunities and neutralize threats.

The basic premise of the RBV is that the mix, type, amount, and nature of a firm's internal resources should be considered first and foremost in devising strategies that can lead to sustainable competitive advantage. Managing strategically according to the RBV involves developing and exploiting a firm's unique resources and capabilities, and continually maintaining and strengthening those resources. The theory asserts that it is advantageous for a firm to pursue a strategy that is not currently being implemented by any competing firm. When other firms are unable to duplicate a particular strategy, then the focal firm has a sustainable competitive advantage, according to RBV theorists.

For a resource to be valuable, it must be either (1) rare, (2) hard to imitate, or (3) not easily substitutable. Often called *empirical indicators*, these three characteristics of resources enable a firm to implement strategies that improve its efficiency and effectiveness and lead to a sustainable competitive advantage. The more a resource(s) is rare, nonimitable, and nonsubstitutable, the stronger a firm's competitive advantage will be and the longer it will last.

Rare resources are resources that other competing firms do not possess. If many firms have the same resource, then those firms will likely implement similar strategies, thus giving no one firm a sustainable competitive advantage. This is not to say that resources that are common are not valuable; they do indeed aid the firm in its chance for economic prosperity. However, to sustain a competitive advantage, it is more advantageous if the resource(s) is also rare.

It is also important that these same resources be difficult to imitate. If firms cannot easily gain the resources, say RBV theorists, then those resources will lead to a competitive advantage more so than resources easily imitable. Even if a firm employs resources that are rare, a sustainable competitive advantage may be achieved only if other firms cannot easily obtain these resources.

The third empirical indicator that can make resources a source of competitive advantage is substitutability. Borrowing from Porter's Five-Forces Model, to the degree that there are no viable substitutes, a firm will be able to sustain its competitive advantage. However, even if a competing firm cannot perfectly imitate a firm's resource, it can still obtain a sustainable competitive advantage of its own by obtaining resource substitutes.

The RBV has continued to grow in popularity and continues to seek a better under-standing of the relationship between resources and sustained competitive advantage in strategic management. However, as alluded to in Chapter 3, one cannot say with any degree of certainty that either external or internal factors will always or even consistently be more important in seeking competitive advantage. Understanding both external and internal factors, and more importantly, understanding the relationships among them, will be the key to effective strategy formulation (discussed in Chapter 6). Because both external and internal factors continually change, strategists seek to identify and take advantage of positive changes and buffer against negative changes in a continuing effort to gain and sustain a firm's competitive advantage. This is the essence and challenge of strategic man-agement, and oftentimes survival of the firm hinges on this work.

Integrating Strategy and Culture

Relationships among a firm's functional business activities perhaps can be exemplified best by focusing on organizational culture, an internal phenomenon that permeates all departments and divisions of an organization. *Organizational culture* can be defined as "a pattern of behavior that has been developed by an organization as it learns to cope with its problem of external adaptation and internal integration, and that has worked well enough to be considered valid and to be taught to new members as the correct way to perceive, think, and feel."[6] This definition emphasizes the importance of matching external with internal factors in making strategic decisions.

Organizational culture captures the subtle, elusive, and largely unconscious forces that shape a workplace. Remarkably resistant to change, culture can represent a major strength or weakness for the firm. It can be an underlying reason for strengths or weaknesses in any of the major business functions.

Defined in Table 4-1, *cultural products* include values, beliefs, rites, rituals, ceremonies, myths, stories, legends, sagas, language, metaphors, symbols, heroes, and heroines. These products or dimensions are levers that strategists can use to influence and direct strategy for-mulation, implementation, and evaluation activities. An organization's culture compares to an individual's personality in the sense that no two organizations have the same culture and no two individuals have the same personality. Both culture and personality are enduring and can be warm, aggressive, friendly, open, innovative, conservative, liberal, harsh, or likable.

At Google, the culture is very informal. Employees are encouraged to wander the halls on employee-sponsored scooters and brainstorm on public whiteboards provided everywhere.

TABLE 4-1   Example Cultural Products Defined

Rites	Planned sets of activities that consolidate various forms of cultural expressions into one event.
Ceremonial	Several rites connected together.
Ritual	A standardized set of behaviors used to manage anxieties.
Myth	A narrative of imagined events, usually not supported by facts.
Saga	A historical narrative describing the unique accomplishments of a group and its leaders.
Legend	A handed-down narrative of some wonderful event, usually not supported by facts.
Story	A narrative usually based on true events.
Folktale	A fictional story.
Symbol	Any object, act, event, quality, or relation used to convey meaning.
Language	The manner in which members of a group communicate.
Metaphors	Shorthand of words used to capture a vision or to reinforce old or new values
Values	Life-directing attitudes that serve as behavioral guidelines
Belief	An understanding of a particular phenomenon
Heroes/Heroines	Individuals greatly respected.

Source: Based on H. M. Trice and J. M. Beyer, "Studying Organizational Cultures through Rites and Ceremonials," *Academy of Management Review* 9, no. 4 (October 1984): 655.

In contrast, the culture at Procter & Gamble (P&G) is so rigid that employees jokingly call themselves "Proctoids." Despite this difference, the two companies are swapping employees and participating in each other's staff training sessions. Why? Because P&G spends more money on advertising than any other company and Google desires more of P&G's $8.7 billion annual advertising expenses; P&G has come to realize that the next generation of laundry-detergent, toilet-paper, and skin-cream customers now spend more time online than watching TV. Consumers age 18 to 27 say they use the Internet nearly 13 hours a week, compared to 10 hours of TV, according to market-data firm Forrester Research.[7]

Dimensions of organizational culture permeate all the functional areas of business. It is something of an art to uncover the basic values and beliefs that are deeply buried in an organization's rich collection of stories, language, heroes, and rituals, but cultural products can represent both important strengths and weaknesses. Culture is an aspect of an organization that can no longer be taken for granted in performing an internal strategic-management audit because culture and strategy must work together.

Table 4-2 provides some example (possible) aspects of an organization's culture. Note you could ask employees/managers to rate the degree that the dimension characterizes the firm. When one firm acquires another firm, integrating the two cultures can be important. For example, in Table 4-2, one firm may score mostly 1's and the other firm may score mostly 5's, which would present a challenging strategic problem.

The strategic-management process takes place largely within a particular organization's culture. Lorsch found that executives in successful companies are emotionally committed to the firm's culture, but he concluded that culture can inhibit strategic management in two basic ways. First, managers frequently miss the significance of changing external conditions because they are blinded by strongly held beliefs. Second, when a particular culture has been effective in the past, the natural response is to stick with it in the future, even during times of major strategic change.[8] An organization's culture must support the collective commitment of its people to a common purpose. It must foster competence and enthusiasm among managers and employees.

Organizational culture significantly affects business decisions and thus must be evaluated during an internal strategic-management audit. If strategies can capitalize on cultural strengths, such as a strong work ethic or highly ethical beliefs, then management often can swiftly and easily implement changes. However, if the firm's culture is not supportive, strategic changes may be ineffective or even counterproductive. A firm's culture can become antagonistic to new strategies, with the result being confusion and disorientation.

TABLE 4-2 **Fifteen Example (Possible) Aspects of an Organization's Culture**

Dimension	Degree				
1. Strong work ethic; arrive early and leave late	1	2	3	4	5
2. High ethical beliefs; clear code of business ethics followed	1	2	3	4	5
3. Formal dress; shirt and tie expected	1	2	3	4	5
4. Informal dress; many casual dress days	1	2	3	4	5
5. Socialize together outside of work	1	2	3	4	5
6. Do not question supervisor's decision	1	2	3	4	5
7. Encourage whistle-blowing	1	2	3	4	5
8. Be health conscious; have a wellness program	1	2	3	4	5
9. Allow substantial "working from home"	1	2	3	4	5
10. Encourage creativity/innovation/openmindness	1	2	3	4	5
11. Support women and minorities; no glass ceiling	1	2	3	4	5
12. Be highly socially responsible; be philanthropic	1	2	3	4	5
13. Have numerous meetings	1	2	3	4	5
14. Have a participative management style	1	2	3	4	5
15. Preserve the natural environment; have a sustainability program	1	2	3	4	5

An organization's culture should infuse individuals with enthusiasm for implementing strategies. Allarie and Firsirotu emphasized the need to understand culture:

> Culture provides an explanation for the insuperable difficulties a firm encounters when it attempts to shift its strategic direction. Not only has the "right" culture become the essence and foundation of corporate excellence, it is also claimed that success or failure of reforms hinges on management's sagacity and ability to change the firm's driving culture in time and in time with required changes in strategies.[9]

The potential value of organizational culture has not been realized fully in the study of strategic management. Ignoring the effect that culture can have on relationships among the functional areas of business can result in barriers to communication, lack of coordination, and an inability to adapt to changing conditions. Some tension between culture and a firm's strategy is inevitable, but the tension should be monitored so that it does not reach a point at which relationships are severed and the culture becomes antagonistic. The resulting disarray among members of the organization would disrupt strategy formulation, implementation, and evaluation. In contrast, a supportive organizational culture can make managing much easier.

Internal strengths and weaknesses associated with a firm's culture sometimes are overlooked because of the interfunctional nature of this phenomenon. It is important, therefore, for strategists to understand their firm as a sociocultural system. Success is often determined by linkages between a firm's culture and strategies. The challenge of strategic management today is to bring about the changes in organizational culture and individual mind-sets that are needed to support the formulation, implementation, and evaluation of strategies.

Management

The *functions of management* consist of five basic activities: planning, organizing, motivating, staffing, and controlling. An overview of these activities is provided in Table 4-3.

TABLE 4-3   The Basic Functions of Management

Function	Description	Stage of Strategic-Management Process When Most Important
Planning	Planning consists of all those managerial activities related to preparing for the future. Specific tasks include forecasting, establishing objectives, devising strategies, developing policies, and setting goals.	Strategy Formulation
Organizing	Organizing includes all those managerial activities that result in a structure of task and authority relationships. Specific areas include organizational design, job specialization, job descriptions, job specifications, span of control, unity of command, coordination, job design, and job analysis.	Strategy Implementation
Motivating	Motivating involves efforts directed toward shaping human behavior. Specific topics include leadership, communication, work groups, behavior modification, delegation of authority, job enrichment, job satisfaction, needs fulfillment, organizational change, employee morale, and managerial morale.	Strategy Implementation
Staffing	Staffing activities are centered on personnel or human resource management. Included are wage and salary administration, employee benefits, interviewing, hiring, firing, training, management development, employee safety, affirmative action, equal employment opportunity, union relations, career development, personnel research, discipline policies, grievance procedures, and public relations.	Strategy Implementation
Controlling	Controlling refers to all those managerial activities directed toward ensuring that actual results are consistent with planned results. Key areas of concern include quality control, financial control, sales control, inventory control, expense control, analysis of variances, rewards, and sanctions.	Strategy Evaluation

Planning

The only thing certain about the future of any organization is change, and *planning* is the essential bridge between the present and the future that increases the likelihood of achieving desired results. Planning is the process by which one determines whether to attempt a task, works out the most effective way of reaching desired objectives, and prepares to overcome unexpected difficulties with adequate resources. Planning is the start of the process by which an individual or business may turn empty dreams into achievements. Planning enables one to avoid the trap of working extremely hard but achieving little.

Planning is an up-front investment in success. Planning helps a firm achieve maximum effect from a given effort. Planning enables a firm to take into account relevant factors and focus on the critical ones. Planning helps ensure that the firm can be prepared for all reasonable eventualities and for all changes that will be needed. Planning enables a firm to gather the resources needed and carry out tasks in the most efficient way possible. Planning enables a firm to conserve its own resources, avoid wasting ecological resources, make a fair profit, and be seen as an effective, useful firm. Planning enables a firm to identify precisely what is to be achieved and to detail precisely the who, what, when, where, why, and how needed to achieve desired objectives. Planning enables a firm to assess whether the effort, costs, and implications associated with achieving desired objectives are warranted.[10] Planning is the cornerstone of effective strategy formulation. But even though it is considered the foundation of management, it is commonly the task that managers neglect most. Planning is essential for successful strategy implementation and strategy evaluation, largely because organizing, motivating, staffing, and controlling activities depend upon good planning.

The process of planning must involve managers and employees throughout an organization. The time horizon for planning decreases from two to five years for top-level to less than six months for lower-level managers. The important point is that all managers do planning and should involve subordinates in the process to facilitate employee understanding and commitment.

Planning can have a positive impact on organizational and individual performance. Planning allows an organization to identify and take advantage of external opportunities as well as minimize the impact of external threats. Planning is more than extrapolating from the past and present into the future. It also includes developing a mission, forecasting future events and trends, establishing objectives, and choosing strategies to pursue.

An organization can develop synergy through planning. *Synergy* exists when everyone pulls together as a team that knows what it wants to achieve; synergy is the $2 + 2 = 5$ effect. By establishing and communicating clear objectives, employees and managers can work together toward desired results. Synergy can result in powerful competitive advantages. The strategic-management process itself is aimed at creating synergy in an organization.

Planning allows a firm to adapt to changing markets and thus to shape its own destiny. Strategic management can be viewed as a formal planning process that allows an organization to pursue proactive rather than reactive strategies. Successful organizations strive to control their own futures rather than merely react to external forces and events as they occur. Historically, organisms and organizations that have not adapted to changing conditions have become extinct. Swift adaptation is needed today more than ever because changes in markets, economies, and competitors worldwide are accelerating. Many firms did not adapt to the global recession of late and went out of business.

Organizing

The purpose of *organizing* is to achieve coordinated effort by defining task and authority relationships. Organizing means determining who does what and who reports to whom. There are countless examples in history of well-organized enterprises successfully competing against—and in some cases defeating—much stronger but less-organized firms. A well-organized firm generally has motivated managers and employees who are committed to seeing the organization succeed. Resources are allocated more effectively and used more efficiently in a well-organized firm than in a disorganized firm.

The organizing function of management can be viewed as consisting of three sequential activities: breaking down tasks into jobs (work specialization), combining jobs to form departments (departmentalization), and delegating authority. Breaking down tasks into jobs requires the development of job descriptions and job specifications. These tools clarify for both managers and employees what particular jobs entail. In *The Wealth of Nations,* published in 1776, Adam Smith cited the advantages of work specialization in the manufacture of pins:

> One man draws the wire, another straightens it, a third cuts it, a fourth points it, a fifth grinds it at the top for receiving the head. Ten men working in this manner can produce 48,000 pins in a single day, but if they had all wrought separately and independently, each might at best produce twenty pins in a day.[11]

Combining jobs to form departments results in an organizational structure, span of control, and a chain of command. Changes in strategy often require changes in structure because positions may be created, deleted, or merged. Organizational structure dictates how resources are allocated and how objectives are established in a firm. Allocating resources and establishing objectives geographically, for example, is much different from doing so by product or customer.

The most common forms of departmentalization are functional, divisional, strategic business unit, and matrix. These types of structure are discussed further in Chapter 7.

Delegating authority is an important organizing activity, as evidenced in the old saying "You can tell how good a manager is by observing how his or her department functions when he or she isn't there." Employees today are more educated and more capable of participating in organizational decision making than ever before. In most cases, they expect to be delegated authority and responsibility and to be held accountable for results. Delegation of authority is embedded in the strategic-management process.

Motivating

Motivating can be defined as the process of influencing people to accomplish specific objectives.[12] Motivation explains why some people work hard and others do not. Objectives, strategies, and policies have little chance of succeeding if employees and managers are not motivated to implement strategies once they are formulated. The motivating function of management includes at least four major components: leadership, group dynamics, communication, and organizational change.

When managers and employees of a firm strive to achieve high levels of productivity, this indicates that the firm's strategists are good leaders. Good leaders establish rapport with subordinates, empathize with their needs and concerns, set a good example, and are trustworthy and fair. Leadership includes developing a vision of the firm's future and inspiring people to work hard to achieve that vision. Kirkpatrick and Locke reported that certain traits also characterize effective leaders: knowledge of the business, cognitive ability, self-confidence, honesty, integrity, and drive.[13]

Research suggests that democratic behavior on the part of leaders results in more positive attitudes toward change and higher productivity than does autocratic behavior. Drucker said:

> Leadership is not a magnetic personality. That can just as well be demagoguery. It is not "making friends and influencing people." That is flattery. Leadership is the lifting of a person's vision to higher sights, the raising of a person's performance to a higher standard, the building of a person's personality beyond its normal limitations.[14]

Group dynamics play a major role in employee morale and satisfaction. Informal groups or coalitions form in every organization. The norms of coalitions can range from being very positive to very negative toward management. It is important, therefore, that strategists identify the composition and nature of informal groups in an organization to facilitate strategy formulation, implementation, and evaluation. Leaders of informal groups are especially important in formulating and implementing strategy changes.

Communication, perhaps the most important word in management, is a major component in motivation. An organization's system of communication determines whether strategies can be implemented successfully. Good two-way communication is vital for gaining support for departmental and divisional objectives and policies. Top-down communication can encourage bottom-up communication. The strategic-management process becomes a lot easier when subordinates are encouraged to discuss their concerns, reveal their problems, provide recommendations, and give suggestions. A primary reason for instituting strategic management is to build and support effective communication networks throughout the firm.

> The manager of tomorrow must be able to get his people to commit themselves to the business, whether they are machine operators or junior vice-presidents. The key issue will be empowerment, a term whose strength suggests the need to get beyond merely sharing a little information and a bit of decision making.[15]

Staffing

The management function of *staffing,* also called *personnel management* or *human resource management,* includes activities such as recruiting, interviewing, testing, selecting, orienting, training, developing, caring for, evaluating, rewarding, disciplining, promoting, transferring, demoting, and dismissing employees, as well as managing union relations.

Staffing activities play a major role in strategy-implementation efforts, and for this reason, human resource managers are becoming more actively involved in the strategic-management process. It is important to identify strengths and weaknesses in the staffing area.

The complexity and importance of human resource activities have increased to such a degree that all but the smallest organizations now need a full-time human resource manager. Numerous court cases that directly affect staffing activities are decided each day. Organizations and individuals can be penalized severely for not following federal, state, and local laws and guidelines related to staffing. Line managers simply cannot stay abreast of all the legal developments and requirements regarding staffing. The human resources department coordinates staffing decisions in the firm so that an organization as a whole meets legal requirements. This department also provides needed consistency in administering company rules, wages, policies, and employee benefits as well as collective bargaining with unions.

Human resource management is particularly challenging for international companies. For example, the inability of spouses and children to adapt to new surroundings can be a staffing problem in overseas transfers. The problems include premature returns, job performance slumps, resignations, discharges, low morale, marital discord, and general discontent. Firms such as Ford Motor and ExxonMobil screen and interview spouses and children before assigning persons to overseas positions. 3M Corporation introduces children to peers in the target country and offers spouses educational benefits.

Controlling

The *controlling* function of management includes all of those activities undertaken to ensure that actual operations conform to planned operations. All managers in an organization have controlling responsibilities, such as conducting performance evaluations and taking necessary action to minimize inefficiencies. The controlling function of management is particularly important for effective strategy evaluation. Controlling consists of four basic steps:

1. Establishing performance standards
2. Measuring individual and organizational performance
3. Comparing actual performance to planned performance standards
4. Taking corrective actions

Measuring individual performance is often conducted ineffectively or not at all in organizations. Some reasons for this shortcoming are that evaluations can create confrontations that most managers prefer to avoid, can take more time than most managers are willing to give, and can require skills that many managers lack. No single approach to measuring individual performance is without limitations. For this reason, an organization should examine various methods, such as the graphic rating scale, the behaviorally anchored rating scale, and the critical incident method, and then develop or select a performance-appraisal approach that best suits the firm's needs. Increasingly, firms are striving to link organizational performance with managers' and employees' pay. This topic is discussed further in Chapter 7.

Management Audit Checklist of Questions

The following checklist of questions can help determine specific strengths and weaknesses in the functional area of business. An answer of *no* to any question could indicate a potential weakness, although the strategic significance and implications of negative answers, of course, will vary by organization, industry, and severity of the weakness. Positive or yes answers to the checklist questions suggest potential areas of strength.

1. Does the firm use strategic-management concepts?
2. Are company objectives and goals measurable and well communicated?
3. Do managers at all hierarchical levels plan effectively?
4. Do managers delegate authority well?
5. Is the organization's structure appropriate?
6. Are job descriptions and job specifications clear?
7. Is employee morale high?
8. Are employee turnover and absenteeism low?
9. Are organizational reward and control mechanisms effective?

Marketing

Marketing can be described as the process of defining, anticipating, creating, and fulfilling customers' needs and wants for products and services. There are seven basic *functions of marketing:* (1) customer analysis, (2) selling products/services, (3) product and service planning, (4) pricing, (5) distribution, (6) marketing research, and (7) opportunity analysis.[16] Understanding these functions helps strategists identify and evaluate marketing strengths and weaknesses.

Customer Analysis

Customer analysis—the examination and evaluation of consumer needs, desires, and wants—involves administering customer surveys, analyzing consumer information, evaluating market positioning strategies, developing customer profiles, and determining optimal market segmentation strategies. The information generated by customer analysis can be essential in developing an effective mission statement. Customer profiles can reveal the demographic characteristics of an organization's customers. Buyers, sellers, distributors, salespeople, managers, wholesalers, retailers, suppliers, and creditors can all participate in gathering information to successfully identify customers' needs and wants. Successful organizations continually monitor present and potential customers' buying patterns.

Selling Products/Services

Successful strategy implementation generally rests upon the ability of an organization to sell some product or service. *Selling* includes many marketing activities, such as advertising, sales promotion, publicity, personal selling, sales force management, customer relations, and dealer relations. These activities are especially critical when a firm pursues a market penetration strategy. The effectiveness of various selling tools for consumer and industrial products varies. Personal selling is most important for industrial goods companies, and advertising is most important for consumer goods companies.

U.S. advertising expenditures are expected to fall 6.2 percent in 2009 to $161.8 billion.[17] One aspect of ads in a recession is that they generally take more direct aim at competitors, and this marketing practice is holding true in our bad economic times. Nick Brien at Mediabrands says, "Ads have to get combative in bad times. It's a dog fight, and it's about getting leaner and meaner." Marketers in 2009 also say ads will be less lavish and glamorous

TABLE 4-4 Desirable Characteristics of Ads in a Global Economic Recession

1. Take direct aim at competitors, so leaner, meaner, and to the point.
2. Be less lavish and glamorous, requiring less production dollars to develop.
3. Be short and sweet, mostly 10- and 15-second ads rather than 30+ seconds.
4. "Make you feel good" or "put you in a good mood" because (a) ads can be more easily avoided than ever and (b) people are experiencing hard times and seek comfort.
5. Be more pervasive such as on buses, elevators, cell phones, and trucks.
6. Appear less on Web sites as banner ads become the new junk mail.
7. Red will overtake the color orange as the most popular ad color.
8. More than ever emphasize low price and value versus rivals.
9. More than ever emphasize how the product/service will make your life better.

Source: Based on Suzanne Vranica, "Ads to Go Leaner, Meaner in '09," *Wall Street Journal* (January 5, 2009): B8.

in a recession. Table 4-4 lists specific characteristics of ads forthcoming in late 2009 and 2010 in response to the economic hard times people nationwide and worldwide are facing. Total U.S. online advertising sending is expected to decline 0.3 percent to $36.9 billion in 2009, after growing 8.5 percent in 2008.

A 30-second advertisement on the Super Bowl in 2009 was $3 million. The NBC network airing the Super Bowl took in $206 million of ad revenue from the broadcast as just over 95 million people watched the Pittsburgh Steelers defeat the Arizona Cardinals in Super Bowl XLIII. The most watched television show in history was the 1983 season finale of *M*A*S*H*, which drew 106 million viewers.

Visa in 2009 launched a $140 million advertising campaign that includes print, TV, outdoor, and Internet ads designed to persuade consumers that debit cards "are more convenient, safer, and secure than cash or checks."

Pharmaceutical companies on average reduced their spending on consumer advertising of prescription drugs by 8 percent in 2008 to $4.4 billion. This was the first annual decrease since 1997 in their efforts to get patients to request a particular medicine from their doctor.

Determining organizational strengths and weaknesses in the selling function of marketing is an important part of performing an internal strategic-management audit. With regard to advertising products and services on the Internet, a new trend is to base advertising rates exclusively on sales rates. This new accountability contrasts sharply with traditional broadcast and print advertising, which bases rates on the number of persons expected to see a given advertisement. The new cost-per-sale online advertising rates are possible because any Web site can monitor which user clicks on which advertisement and then can record whether that consumer actually buys the product. If there are no sales, then the advertisement is free.

Product and Service Planning

Product and service planning includes activities such as test marketing; product and brand positioning; devising warranties; packaging; determining product options, features, style, and quality; deleting old products; and providing for customer service. Product and service planning is particularly important when a company is pursuing product development or diversification.

One of the most effective product and service planning techniques is *test marketing*. Test markets allow an organization to test alternative marketing plans and to forecast future sales of new products. In conducting a test market project, an organization must decide how many cities to include, which cities to include, how long to run the test, what information to collect during the test, and what action to take after the test has been completed. Test marketing is used more frequently by consumer goods companies than by industrial goods companies. Test marketing can allow an organization to avoid substantial losses by revealing weak products and ineffective marketing approaches before large-scale production begins. Starbucks is currently test marketing selling beer and wine in its stores to boost its "after 5 PM" sales.

Pricing

Five major stakeholders affect *pricing* decisions: consumers, governments, suppliers, distributors, and competitors. Sometimes an organization will pursue a forward integration strategy primarily to gain better control over prices charged to consumers. Governments can impose constraints on price fixing, price discrimination, minimum prices, unit pricing, price advertising, and price controls. For example, the Robinson-Patman Act prohibits manufacturers and wholesalers from discriminating in price among channel member purchasers (suppliers and distributors) if competition is injured.

Competing organizations must be careful not to coordinate discounts, credit terms, or condition of sale; not to discuss prices, markups, and costs at trade association meetings; and not to arrange to issue new price lists on the same date, to rotate low bids on contracts, or to uniformly restrict production to maintain high prices. Strategists should view price from both a short-run and a long-run perspective, because competitors can copy price changes with relative ease. Often a dominant firm will aggressively match all price cuts by competitors.

With regard to pricing, as the value of the dollar increases, U.S. multinational companies have a choice. They can raise prices in the local currency of a foreign country or risk losing sales and market share. Alternatively, multinational firms can keep prices steady and face reduced profit when their export revenue is reported in the United States in dollars.

Intense price competition, created by the global economic recession, coupled with Internet price-comparative shopping has reduced profit margins to bare minimum levels for most companies. For example, airline tickets, rental car prices, hotel room rates, and computer prices are lower today than they have been in many years.

In response to the economic recession, the family-dining chain Denny's did something that no family-dining chain had ever done before: give away breakfast from 6 AM until 2 PM on February 8, 2009, at all of its restaurants in the United States. More than 2 million people took advantage of the free breakfast at all but two of Denny's 1,550 restaurants nationwide. The entire promotion, including food, labor, and airing an ad on the Super Bowl the Sunday before, cost Denny's about $5 million. However, the firm reaped tons of positive public relations as well as $50 million of free news coverage nationwide and greatly increased customer loyalty. "People love free stuff when money's tight," says Dan Ariely, a business professor at Duke University. Other firms recently set a price of zero on their products, including McDonald's, Starbucks, Dunkin' Donuts, and Panera Bread. Denny's CEO Nelson Marchioli says that Denny's did better than break even on the free breakfast day, and it may do this promotion again.[18]

Distribution

Distribution includes warehousing, distribution channels, distribution coverage, retail site locations, sales territories, inventory levels and location, transportation carriers, wholesaling, and retailing. Most producers today do not sell their goods directly to consumers. Various marketing entities act as intermediaries; they bear a variety of names such as wholesalers, retailers, brokers, facilitators, agents, vendors—or simply distributors.

Distribution becomes especially important when a firm is striving to implement a market development or forward integration strategy. Some of the most complex and challenging decisions facing a firm concern product distribution. Intermediaries flourish in our economy because many producers lack the financial resources and expertise to carry out direct marketing. Manufacturers who could afford to sell directly to the public often can gain greater returns by expanding and improving their manufacturing operations.

Successful organizations identify and evaluate alternative ways to reach their ultimate market. Possible approaches vary from direct selling to using just one or many wholesalers and retailers. Strengths and weaknesses of each channel alternative should be determined according to economic, control, and adaptive criteria. Organizations should consider the costs and benefits of various wholesaling and retailing options. They must consider the need to motivate and control channel members and the need to adapt to changes in the future. Once a marketing channel is chosen, an organization usually must adhere to it for an extended period of time.

Marketing Research

Marketing research is the systematic gathering, recording, and analyzing of data about problems relating to the marketing of goods and services. Marketing research can uncover critical strengths and weaknesses, and marketing researchers employ numerous scales, instruments, procedures, concepts, and techniques to gather information. Marketing research activities support all of the major business functions of an organization. Organizations that possess excellent marketing research skills have a definite strength in pursuing generic strategies.

> The President of PepsiCo said, "Looking at the competition is the company's best form of market research. The majority of our strategic successes are ideas that we borrow from the marketplace, usually from a small regional or local competitor. In each case, we spot a promising new idea, improve on it, and then out-execute our competitor."[19]

Cost/Benefit Analysis

The seventh function of marketing is *cost/benefit analysis,* which involves assessing the costs, benefits, and risks associated with marketing decisions. Three steps are required to perform a cost/benefit analysis: (1) compute the total costs associated with a decision, (2) estimate the total benefits from the decision, and (3) compare the total costs with the total benefits. When expected benefits exceed total costs, an opportunity becomes more attractive. Sometimes the variables included in a cost/benefit analysis cannot be quantified or even measured, but usually reasonable estimates can be made to allow the analysis to be performed. One key factor to be considered is risk. Cost/benefit analysis should also be performed when a company is evaluating alternative ways to be socially responsible.

Marketing Audit Checklist of Questions

The following questions about marketing must be examined in strategic planning:

1. Are markets segmented effectively?
2. Is the organization positioned well among competitors?
3. Has the firm's market share been increasing?
4. Are present channels of distribution reliable and cost effective?
5. Does the firm have an effective sales organization?
6. Does the firm conduct market research?
7. Are product quality and customer service good?
8. Are the firm's products and services priced appropriately?
9. Does the firm have an effective promotion, advertising, and publicity strategy?
10. Are marketing, planning, and budgeting effective?
11. Do the firm's marketing managers have adequate experience and training?
12. Is the firm's Internet presence excellent as compared to rivals?

Finance/Accounting

Financial condition is often considered the single best measure of a firm's competitive position and overall attractiveness to investors. Determining an organization's financial strengths and weaknesses is essential to effectively formulating strategies. A firm's liquidity, leverage, working capital, profitability, asset utilization, cash flow, and equity can eliminate some strategies as being feasible alternatives. Financial factors often alter existing strategies and change implementation plans.

TABLE 4-5   Excellent Web Sites to Obtain Information on Companies, Including Financial Ratios

http://marketwatch.multexinvestor.com

http://moneycentral.msn.com

http://finance.yahoo.com

www.clearstation.com

https://us.etrade.com/e/t/invest/markets

www.hoovers.com

Especially good Web sites from which to obtain financial information about firms are provided in Table 4-5.

Finance/Accounting Functions

According to James Van Horne, the *functions of finance/accounting* comprise three decisions: the investment decision, the financing decision, and the dividend decision.[20] Financial ratio analysis is the most widely used method for determining an organization's strengths and weaknesses in the investment, financing, and dividend areas. Because the functional areas of business are so closely related, financial ratios can signal strengths or weaknesses in management, marketing, production, research and development, and management information systems activities. It is important to note here that financial ratios are equally applicable in for-profit and nonprofit organizations. Even though nonprofit organizations obviously would not have return-on-investment or earnings-per-share ratios, they would routinely monitor many other special ratios. For example, a church would monitor the ratio of dollar contributions to number of members, while a zoo would monitor dollar food sales to number of visitors. A university would monitor number of students divided by number of professors. Therefore, be creative when performing ratio analysis for nonprofit organizations because they strive to be financially sound just as for-profit firms do.

The *investment decision,* also called *capital budgeting,* is the allocation and reallocation of capital and resources to projects, products, assets, and divisions of an organization. Once strategies are formulated, capital budgeting decisions are required to successfully implement strategies. The *financing decision* determines the best capital structure for the firm and includes examining various methods by which the firm can raise capital (for example, by issuing stock, increasing debt, selling assets, or using a combination of these approaches). The financing decision must consider both short-term and long-term needs for working capital. Two key financial ratios that indicate whether a firm's financing decisions have been effective are the debt-to-equity ratio and the debt-to-total-assets ratio.

Dividend decisions concern issues such as the percentage of earnings paid to stockholders, the stability of dividends paid over time, and the repurchase or issuance of stock. Dividend decisions determine the amount of funds that are retained in a firm compared to the amount paid out to stockholders. Three financial ratios that are helpful in evaluating a firm's dividend decisions are the earnings-per-share ratio, the dividends-per-share ratio, and the price-earnings ratio. The benefits of paying dividends to investors must be balanced against the benefits of internally retaining funds, and there is no set formula on how to balance this trade-off. For the reasons listed here, dividends are sometimes paid out even when funds could be better reinvested in the business or when the firm has to obtain outside sources of capital:

1. Paying cash dividends is customary. Failure to do so could be thought of as a stigma. A dividend change is considered a signal about the future.
2. Dividends represent a sales point for investment bankers. Some institutional investors can buy only dividend-paying stocks.
3. Shareholders often demand dividends, even in companies with great opportunities for reinvesting all available funds.
4. A myth exists that paying dividends will result in a higher stock price.

More than 10 percent of S&P 500 companies cut their dividend payout in 2009. The record number of dividend cuts and dividend suspensions by companies continues. A total of 68 S&P 500 companies cut $40.61 billion in dividend payout money in 2008, but most of these cuts were among banks and brokerage firms. Stock prices for firms fell faster and farther in 2008 than did dividend payouts. Among all U.S. publicly held companies, about 225 increased their dividend payout in 2008.

Based in Stockholm, Sweden, telecom-equipment maker Ericsson recently cut its dividend to 1.85 kronor a share, down from 2.50 kronor the year before. The firm also laid off 5,000 employees in 2009 as its net income declined. Seagate Technology Inc. recently cut its quarterly dividend by 75 percent as part of a restructuring and strengthening of its balance sheet to cope with falling company demand. Seagate in 2009 laid off 2,950 employees and reduced the salaries of its top officers by as much as 25 percent.

Sherwin-Williams has a long-standing policy of paying dividends equal to 30 percent of the prior year's earnings. The firm followed through on this policy in 2008, paying $1.40 per share. The maker of paint and other coatings expects to maintain that policy again in 2009. Sherwin-Williams closed 80 of its 3,300 stores in 2008 and has a strong relationship with Wal-Mart Stores.

The world's largest steelmaker, ArcelorMittal, recently cut its 2009 dividend by 50 percent to 75 cents, reversing its pledge in 2008 to maintain a $1.50 dividend. Based in Luxembourg, ArcelorMittal has been incurring quarterly billion-dollar losses in earnings.

The New York Times Company's board of directors suspended the firm's dividend payments 100 percent in early 2009 to save about $34.5 million annually. The company is also trying to sell part of its 52-story headquarters building to raise cash. Times Company joins a growing list of media companies that have totally suspended their dividends, including E.W. Scripps Company, Media General Inc., and McClatchy Company.

In April 2009, IBM boosted its quarterly dividend 10 percent and added $3 billion to its stock-buyout program. This announcement came soon after IBM lost out to Oracle in its did to acquire Sun Microsystems Corp.

J.P. Morgan in 2009 cut its dividend by 87 percent to 5 cents per share, saving the firm $5 billion annually. Investors were surprised at the drastic cut because J.P. Morgan was regarded as one of the healthiest U.S. banks at the time. The firm's stock rose 6 percent on the news to $20.64 per share.

Wells Fargo in 2009 cut its dividend payout by 85 percent to 5 cents per share. This move came just two months after the firm purchased troubled rival Wachovia Corp. for $12.68 billion. Wells Fargo had paid the third largest dividend in the S&P 500 Index, behind AT&T and Exxon Mobil.

Oracle is doing great in the global economic recession. The company issued its first dividend ever in 2009 and posted a 2 percent revenue increase for its third quarter of fiscal 2009. Based in Redwood Shores, California, the business-software maker has $8.2 billion in cash and generates about $8 billion in cash a year.[21] Historically, tech companies have not issued dividends, and the few tech companies that do pay dividends, such as Microsoft and Intel, have not cut the payouts and continue to stockpile large reserves of cash.

Basic Types of Financial Ratios

Financial ratios are computed from an organization's income statement and balance sheet. Computing financial ratios is like taking a picture because the results reflect a situation at just one point in time. Comparing ratios over time and to industry averages is more likely to result in meaningful statistics that can be used to identify and evaluate strengths and weaknesses. Trend analysis, illustrated in Figure 4-3, is a useful technique that incorporates both the time and industry average dimensions of financial ratios. Note that the dotted lines reveal projected ratios. Some Web sites, such as those provided in Table 4-5, calculate financial ratios and provide data with charts.

Table 4-6 provides a summary of key financial ratios showing how each ratio is calculated and what each ratio measures. However, all the ratios are not significant for all industries and companies. For example, accounts receivable turnover and average collection

FIGURE 4-3

A Financial Ratio Trend Analysis

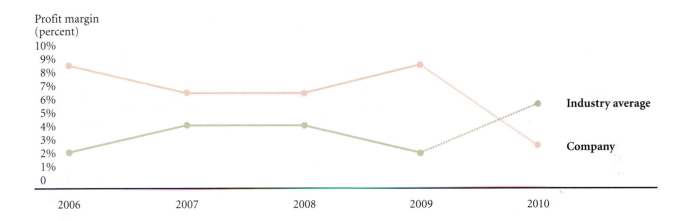

period are not very meaningful to a company that primarily does a cash receipts business. Key financial ratios can be classified into the following five types:

1. **Liquidity ratios** measure a firm's ability to meet maturing short-term obligations.
   Current ratio
   Quick (or acid-test) ratio

2. **Leverage ratios** measure the extent to which a firm has been financed by debt.
   Debt-to-total-assets ratio
   Debt-to-equity ratio
   Long-term debt-to-equity ratio
   Times-interest-earned (or coverage) ratio

3. **Activity ratios** measure how effectively a firm is using its resources.
   Inventory turnover
   Fixed assets turnover
   Total assets turnover
   Accounts receivable turnover
   Average collection period

4. **Profitability ratios** measure management's overall effectiveness as shown by the returns generated on sales and investment.
   Gross profit margin
   Operating profit margin
   Net profit margin
   Return on total assets (ROA)
   Return on stockholders' equity (ROE)
   Earnings per share (EPS)
   Price-earnings ratio

TABLE 4-6 A Summary of Key Financial Ratios

Ratio	How Calculated	What It Measures
Liquidity Ratios		
Current Ratio	$\dfrac{\text{Current assets}}{\text{Current liabilities}}$	The extent to which a firm can meet its short-term obligations
Quick Ratio	$\dfrac{\text{Current assets minus inventory}}{\text{Current liabilities}}$	The extent to which a firm can meet its short-term obligations without relying upon the sale of its inventories
Leverage Ratios		
Debt-to-Total-Assets Ratio	$\dfrac{\text{Total debt}}{\text{Total assets}}$	The percentage of total funds that are provided by creditors
Debt-to-Equity Ratio	$\dfrac{\text{Total debt}}{\text{Total stockholders' equity}}$	The percentage of total funds provided by creditors versus by owners
Long-Term Debt-to-Equity Ratio	$\dfrac{\text{Long-term debt}}{\text{Total stockholders' equity}}$	The balance between debt and equity in a firm's long-term capital structure
Times-Interest-Earned Ratio	$\dfrac{\text{Profits before interest and taxes}}{\text{Total interest charges}}$	The extent to which earnings can decline without the firm becoming unable to meet its annual interest costs
Activity Ratios		
Inventory Turnover	$\dfrac{\text{Sales}}{\text{Inventory of finished goods}}$	Whether a firm holds excessive stocks of inventories and whether a firm is slowly selling its inventories compared to the industry average
Fixed Assets Turnover	$\dfrac{\text{Sales}}{\text{Fixed assets}}$	Sales productivity and plant and equipment utilization
Total Assets Turnover	$\dfrac{\text{Sales}}{\text{Total assets}}$	Whether a firm is generating a sufficient volume of business for the size of its asset investment
Accounts Receivable Turnover	$\dfrac{\text{Annual credit sales}}{\text{Accounts receivable}}$	The average length of time it takes a firm to collect credit sales (in percentage terms)
Average Collection Period	$\dfrac{\text{Accounts receivable}}{\text{Total credit sales/365 days}}$	The average length of time it takes a firm to collect on credit sales (in days)
Profitability Ratios		
Gross Profit Margin	$\dfrac{\text{Sales minus cost of goods sold}}{\text{Sales}}$	The total margin available to cover operating expenses and yield a profit
Operating Profit Margin	$\dfrac{\text{Earnings before interest and taxes (EBIT)}}{\text{Sales}}$	Profitability without concern for taxes and interest
Net Profit Margin	$\dfrac{\text{Net income}}{\text{Sales}}$	After-tax profits per dollar of sales
Return on Total Assets (ROA)	$\dfrac{\text{Net income}}{\text{Total assets}}$	After-tax profits per dollar of assets; this ratio is also called return on investment (ROI)
Return on Stockholders' Equity (ROE)	$\dfrac{\text{Net income}}{\text{Total stockholders' equity}}$	After-tax profits per dollar of stockholders' investment in the firm

(continued)

TABLE 4-6   A Summary of Key Financial Ratios—continued

Ratio	How Calculated	What It Measures
Profitability Ratios		
Earnings Per Share (EPS)	$\dfrac{\text{Net income}}{\text{Number of shares of common stock outstanding}}$	Earnings available to the owners of common stock
Price-Earnings Ratio	$\dfrac{\text{Market price per share}}{\text{Earnings per share}}$	Attractiveness of firm on equity markets
Growth Ratios		
Sales	Annual percentage growth in total sales	Firm's growth rate in sales
Net Income	Annual percentage growth in profits	Firm's growth rate in profits
Earnings Per Share	Annual percentage growth in EPS	Firm's growth rate in EPS
Dividends Per Share	Annual percentage growth in dividends per share	Firm's growth rate in dividends per share

5.   *Growth ratios* measure the firm's ability to maintain its economic position in the growth of the economy and industry.
     Sales
     Net income
     Earnings per share
     Dividends per share

Financial ratio analysis must go beyond the actual calculation and interpretation of ratios. The analysis should be conducted on three separate fronts:

1.   *How has each ratio changed over time?* This information provides a means of evaluating historical trends. It is important to note whether each ratio has been historically increasing, decreasing, or nearly constant. For example, a 10 percent profit margin could be bad if the trend has been down 20 percent each of the last three years. But a 10 percent profit margin could be excellent if the trend has been up, up, up. Therefore, calculate the percentage change in each ratio from one year to the next to assess historical financial performance on that dimension. Identify and examine large percent changes in a financial ratio from one year to the next.

2.   *How does each ratio compare to industry norms?* A firm's inventory turnover ratio may appear impressive at first glance but may pale when compared to industry standards or norms. Industries can differ dramatically on certain ratios. For example grocery companies, such as Kroger, have a high inventory turnover whereas automobile dealerships have a lower turnover. Therefore, comparison of a firm's ratios within its particular industry can be essential in determining strength/weakness.

3.   *How does each ratio compare with key competitors?* Oftentimes competition is more intense between several competitors in a given industry or location than across all rival firms in the industry. When this is true, financial ratio analysis should include comparison to those key competitors. For example, if a firm's profitability ratio is trending up over time and compares favorably to the industry average, but it is trending down relative to its leading competitor, there may be reason for concern.

Financial ratio analysis is not without some limitations. First of all, financial ratios are based on accounting data, and firms differ in their treatment of such items as depreciation, inventory valuation, research and development expenditures, pension plan costs, mergers, and taxes. Also, seasonal factors can influence comparative ratios. Therefore, conformity to industry composite ratios does not establish with certainty that a firm is performing normally or that it is well managed. Likewise, departures from industry averages do not always indicate that a firm is doing especially well or badly. For example, a high inventory turnover ratio could indicate efficient inventory management and a strong working capital position, but it also could indicate a serious inventory shortage and a weak working capital position.

FIGURE 4-4

A Before and After Breakeven Chart When Prices Are Lowered

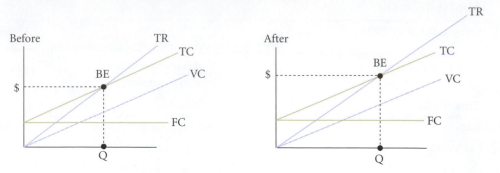

It is important to recognize that a firm's financial condition depends not only on the functions of finance, but also on many other factors that include (1) management, marketing, management production/operations, research and development, and management information systems decisions; (2) actions by competitors, suppliers, distributors, creditors, customers, and shareholders; and (3) economic, social, cultural, demographic, environmental, political, governmental, legal, and technological trends.

In a global economic recession when consumers are price sensitive, many firms are having to lower prices to compete. As a firm lowers prices, its *breakeven (BE) point* in terms of units sold increases, as illustrated in Figure 4-4. The breakeven point can be defined as the quantity of units that a firm must sell in order for its total revenues (TR) to equal its total costs (TC). Note that the before and after chart in Figure 4-4 reveals that the Total Revenue (TR) line rotates to the right with a decrease in Price, thus increasing the Quantity (Q) that must be sold just to break even. Increasing the breakeven point is thus a huge drawback of lowering prices. Of course when rivals are lowering prices, a firm may have to lower prices anyway to compete. However, the breakeven concept should be kept in mind because it is so important, especially in recessionary times.

Notice in Figure 4-5 that increasing Fixed Costs (FC) also raises a firm's breakeven quantity. Note the before and after chart in Figure 4-5 reveals that adding fixed costs such as more stores or more plants as part of a strategic plan raises the Total Cost (TC) line, which makes the intersection of the Total Cost (TC) and Total Revenue (TR) lines at a point farther down the Quantity axis. Increasing a firm's fixed costs (FC) thus significantly raises the quantity of goods that must be sold to break even. This is not just theory for the sake of theory. Firms with less fixed costs, such as Apple and Amazon.com, have lower breakeven points, which give them a decided advantage in harsh economic times. Figure 4-5 reveals that adding *fixed costs (FC)*, such as plant, equipment, stores, advertising, and land, may be detrimental whenever there is doubt that significantly more units can be sold to offset those expenditures.

FIGURE 4-5

A Before and After Breakeven Chart When Fixed Costs Are Increased

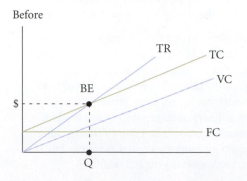
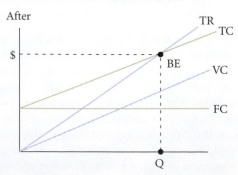

FIGURE 4-6

A Before and After Breakeven Chart When Prices Are Lowered and Fixed Costs Are Increased

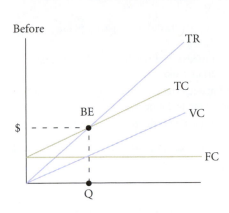
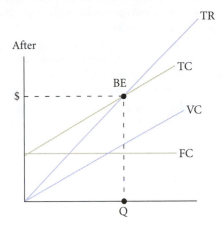

In a global economic recession especially, firms must be cognizant of the fact that lowering prices and adding fixed costs could be a catastrophic double whammy because the firm's breakeven quantity needed to be sold is increased dramatically. Figure 4-6 illustrates this double whammy. Note how far the breakeven point shifts with both a price decrease and an increase in fixed costs. If a firm does not break even, then it will of course incur losses, and losses are not good, especially sustained losses.

Finally, note in Figure 4-4, 4-5, and 4-6 that *Variable Costs (VC)* such as labor and materials when increased have the effect of raising the breakeven point too. Raising Variable Costs is reflected by the Variable Cost line shifting left or becoming steeper. When the Total Revenue (TR) line remains constant, the effect of increasing Variable Costs is to increase Total Costs, which increases the point at which Total Revenue = Total Costs (TC) = Breakeven (BE).

Suffice it to say here that various strategies can have dramatically beneficial or harmful effects on the firm's financial condition due to the concept of breakeven analysis.

Finance/Accounting Audit Checklist

The following finance/accounting questions, like the similar questions about marketing and management earlier, should be examined:

1. Where is the firm financially strong and weak as indicated by financial ratio analyses?
2. Can the firm raise needed short-term capital?
3. Can the firm raise needed long-term capital through debt and/or equity?
4. Does the firm have sufficient working capital?
5. Are capital budgeting procedures effective?
6. Are dividend payout policies reasonable?
7. Does the firm have good relations with its investors and stockholders?
8. Are the firm's financial managers experienced and well trained?
9. Is the firm's debt situation excellent?

Production/Operations

The *production/operations function* of a business consists of all those activities that transform inputs into goods and services. Production/operations management deals with inputs, transformations, and outputs that vary across industries and markets. A manufacturing operation transforms or converts inputs such as raw materials, labor, capital, machines, and facilities into finished goods and services. As indicated in Table 4-7, Roger Schroeder suggested that production/operations management comprises five functions or decision areas: process, capacity, inventory, workforce, and quality.

TABLE 4-7 The Basic Functions (Decisions) Within Production/Operations

Decision Areas	Example Decisions
1. Process	These decisions include choice of technology, facility layout, process flow analysis, facility location, line balancing, process control, and transportation analysis. Distances from raw materials to production sites to customers are a major consideration.
2. Capacity	These decisions include forecasting, facilities planning, aggregate planning, scheduling, capacity planning, and queuing analysis. Capacity utilization is a major consideration.
3. Inventory	These decisions involve managing the level of raw materials, work-in-process, and finished goods, especially considering what to order, when to order, how much to order, and materials handling.
4. Workforce	These decisions involve managing the skilled, unskilled, clerical, and managerial employees by caring for job design, work measurement, job enrichment, work standards, and motivation techniques.
5. Quality	These decisions are aimed at ensuring that high-quality goods and services are produced by caring for quality control, sampling, testing, quality assurance, and cost control.

Source: Adapted from R. Schroeder, *Operations Management* (New York: McGraw-Hill, 1981): 12.

Most automakers require a 30-day notice to build vehicles, but Toyota Motor fills a buyer's new car order in just 5 days. Honda Motor was considered the industry's fastest producer, filling orders in 15 days. Automakers have for years operated under just-in-time inventory systems, but Toyota's 360 suppliers are linked to the company via computers on a virtual assembly line. The new Toyota production system was developed in the company's Cambridge, Ontario, plant and now applies to its Solara, Camry, Corolla, and Tacoma vehicles.

Production/operations activities often represent the largest part of an organization's human and capital assets. In most industries, the major costs of producing a product or service are incurred within operations, so production/operations can have great value as a competitive weapon in a company's overall strategy. Strengths and weaknesses in the five functions of production can mean the success or failure of an enterprise.

Many production/operations managers are finding that cross-training of employees can help their firms respond faster to changing markets. Cross-training of workers can increase efficiency, quality, productivity, and job satisfaction. For example, at General Motors' Detroit gear and axle plant, costs related to product defects were reduced 400 percent in two years as a result of cross-training workers. A shortage of qualified labor in the United States is another reason cross-training is becoming a common management practice.

Singapore rivals Hong Kong as an attractive site for locating production facilities in Southeast Asia. Singapore is a city-state near Malaysia. An island nation of about 4 million, Singapore is changing from an economy built on trade and services to one built on information technology. A large-scale program in computer education for older (over age 26) residents is very popular. Singapore children receive outstanding computer training in schools. All government services are computerized nicely. Singapore lures multinational businesses with great tax breaks, world-class infrastructure, excellent courts that efficiently handle business disputes, exceptionally low tariffs, large land giveaways, impressive industrial parks, excellent port facilities, and a government very receptive to and cooperative with foreign businesses. Foreign firms now account for 70 percent of manufacturing output in Singapore.

In terms of ship container traffic processed annually, Singapore has the largest and busiest seaport in the world, followed by Hong Kong, Shanghai, Los Angeles, Busan (South Korea), Rotterdam, Hamburg, New York, and Tokyo. The Singapore seaport is five times the size of the New York City seaport.[22]

There is much reason for concern that many organizations have not taken sufficient account of the capabilities and limitations of the production/operations function in formulating strategies. Scholars contend that this neglect has had unfavorable consequences on corporate performance in America. As shown in Table 4-8, James Dilworth outlined implications of several types of strategic decisions that a company might make.

TABLE 4-8 **Implications of Various Strategies on Production/Operations**

Various Strategies	Implications
1. Low-cost provider	Creates high barriers to entry
	Creates larger market
	Requires longer production runs and fewer product changes
2. A high-quality provider	Requires more quality-assurance efforts
	Requires more expensive equipment
	Requires highly skilled workers and higher wages
3. Provide great customer service	Requires more service people, service parts, and equipment
	Requires rapid response to customer needs or changes in customer tastes
	Requires a higher inventory investment
4. Be the first to introduce new products	Has higher research and development costs
	Has high retraining and tooling costs
5. Become highly automated	Requires high capital investment
	Reduces flexibility
	May affect labor relations
	Makes maintenance more crucial
6. Minimize layoffs	Serves the security needs of employees and may develop employee loyalty
	Helps to attract and retain highly skilled employees

Source: Adapted from J. Dilworth, *Production and Operations Management: Manufacturing and Nonmanufacturing,* 2nd ed. Copyright © 1983 by Random House, Inc. Reprinted by permission of Random House, Inc.

Production/Operations Audit Checklist

Questions such as the following should be examined:

1.   Are supplies of raw materials, parts, and subassemblies reliable and reasonable?
2.   Are facilities, equipment, machinery, and offices in good condition?
3.   Are inventory-control policies and procedures effective?
4.   Are quality-control policies and procedures effective?
5.   Are facilities, resources, and markets strategically located?
6.   Does the firm have technological competencies?

Research and Development

The fifth major area of internal operations that should be examined for specific strengths and weaknesses is *research and development (R&D)*. Many firms today conduct no R&D, and yet many other companies depend on successful R&D activities for survival. Firms pursuing a product development strategy especially need to have a strong R&D orientation.

Organizations invest in R&D because they believe that such an investment will lead to a superior product or service and will give them competitive advantages. Research and development expenditures are directed at developing new products before competitors do, at improving product quality, or at improving manufacturing processes to reduce costs.

Effective management of the R&D function requires a strategic and operational partnership between R&D and the other vital business functions. A spirit of partnership and mutual trust between general and R&D managers is evident in the best-managed firms today. Managers in these firms jointly explore; assess; and decide the what, when, where, why, and how much of R&D. Priorities, costs, benefits, risks, and rewards associated with R&D activities are discussed openly and shared. The overall mission of R&D thus has become broad-based, including supporting existing businesses, helping launch new businesses, developing new products, improving product quality, improving manufacturing efficiency, and deepening or broadening the company's technological capabilities.[23]

The best-managed firms today seek to organize R&D activities in a way that breaks the isolation of R&D from the rest of the company and promotes a spirit of partnership between R&D managers and other managers in the firm. R&D decisions and plans must be integrated and coordinated across departments and divisions by having the departments share experiences and information. The strategic-management process facilitates this cross-functional approach to managing the R&D function.

Based in Sunnyvale, California, Juniper Networks spends about 20 percent of its revenues or $800 million annually on R&D. However, the company is struggling with falling demand for its products in a global recession. But rather than cutting R&D expenditures, the firm is cutting other expenses. About 70 percent of Juniper's revenues come from Internet routers for phone and cable companies. Juniper's annual R&D budget has not dropped since the company went public in 1999. Rival Cisco Systems spends 13 percent of its revenues on R&D. Motorola is slashing its R&D budget. Qualcomm Inc. is holding its R&D spending flat in 2009.

Although R&D is the lifeblood of pharmaceutical firms, Valeant Pharmaceuticals International recently cut its R&D budget by 50 percent to make acquisitions and buy back its own stock. Lead director Robert Ingram at Valeant says, "R&D is a high-risk bet, and the fact is we fail more often than we succeed." France's Sanofi-Aventis SA also recently cut its R&D spending, but for most pharmaceutical firms cutting such expenses is still taboo.

Internal and External R&D

Cost distributions among R&D activities vary by company and industry, but total R&D costs generally do not exceed manufacturing and marketing start-up costs. Four approaches to determining R&D budget allocations commonly are used: (1) financing as many project proposals as possible, (2) using a percentage-of-sales method, (3) budgeting about the same amount that competitors spend for R&D, or (4) deciding how many successful new products are needed and working backward to estimate the required R&D investment.

R&D in organizations can take two basic forms: (1) internal R&D, in which an organization operates its own R&D department, and/or (2) contract R&D, in which a firm hires independent researchers or independent agencies to develop specific products. Many companies use both approaches to develop new products. A widely used approach for obtaining outside R&D assistance is to pursue a joint venture with another firm. R&D strengths (capabilities) and weaknesses (limitations) play a major role in strategy formulation and strategy implementation.

Most firms have no choice but to continually develop new and improved products because of changing consumer needs and tastes, new technologies, shortened product life cycles, and increased domestic and foreign competition. A shortage of ideas for new products, increased global competition, increased market segmentation, strong special-interest groups, and increased government regulations are several factors making the successful development of new products more and more difficult, costly, and risky. In the pharmaceutical industry, for example, only one out of every few thousand drugs created in the laboratory ends up on pharmacists' shelves. Scarpello, Boulton, and Hofer emphasized that different strategies require different R&D capabilities:

> The focus of R&D efforts can vary greatly depending on a firm's competitive strategy. Some corporations attempt to be market leaders and innovators of new products, while others are satisfied to be market followers and developers of currently available products. The basic skills required to support these strategies will vary, depending on whether R&D becomes the driving force behind competitive strategy. In cases where new product introduction is the driving force for strategy, R&D activities must be extensive. The R&D unit must then be able to

TABLE 4-9   R&D Spending at Ten Sample Companies, 2008 Fourth Quarter ($Billion)

Company	Fourth Quarter R&D Spending
Microsoft	$2.29
Johnson & Johnson	2.11
IBM	1.53
Intel	1.28
Boeing	0.96
Google	0.73
Hewlett-Packard	0.73
Caterpillar	0.51
DuPont	0.34
Yahoo	0.28

Source: Based on Justin Scheck and Paul Glader, "R&D Spending Holds Steady in Slump," *Wall Street Journal* (April 6, 2009): A1; and Company *Form 10-K* Reports.

advance scientific and technological knowledge, exploit that knowledge, and manage the risks associated with ideas, products, services, and production requirements.[24]

Many U.S. companies are concerned about emerging from the recession with obsolete products, so their spending on R&D is holding steady even as their revenues fall. Intel, for example, is spending $5.4 billion on R&D in 2009, down slightly from 2008. 3M laid off 4,700 employees in 2008 and early 2009 and cut capital expenditures 30 percent in 2009, but its R&D spending increased slightly in 2009. Corning Inc. recently devised a strategy it called "rings of defense" against the economic downturn; R&D was placed in the innermost ring, making it among the last things to be cut. Then Corning soon cut its spending on marketing and administration by 31 percent, but R&D spending was unchanged. The company spent $627 million on R&D both in 2008 and in 2009.

Table 4-9 lists R&D spending at some U.S. companies in the fourth quarter of 2008 alone.

Research and Development Audit

Questions such as the following should be asked in performing an R&D audit:

1. Does the firm have R&D facilities? Are they adequate?
2. If outside R&D firms are used, are they cost-effective?
3. Are the organization's R&D personnel well qualified?
4. Are R&D resources allocated effectively?
5. Are management information and computer systems adequate?
6. Is communication between R&D and other organizational units effective?
7. Are present products technologically competitive?

Management Information Systems

Information ties all business functions together and provides the basis for all managerial decisions. It is the cornerstone of all organizations. Information represents a major source of competitive management advantage or disadvantage. Assessing a firm's internal strengths and weaknesses in information systems is a critical dimension of performing an internal audit. The company motto of Mitsui, a large Japanese trading company, is

"Information is the lifeblood of the company." A satellite network connects Mitsui's 200 worldwide offices.

A management information system's purpose is to improve the performance of an enterprise by improving the quality of managerial decisions. An effective information system thus collects, codes, stores, synthesizes, and presents information in such a manner that it answers important operating and strategic questions. The heart of an information system is a database containing the kinds of records and data important to managers.

A *management information system* receives raw material from both the external and internal evaluation of an organization. It gathers data about marketing, finance, production, and personnel matters internally, and social, cultural, demographic, environmental, economic, political, governmental, legal, technological, and competitive factors externally. Data are integrated in ways needed to support managerial decision making.

There is a logical flow of material in a computer information system, whereby data are input to the system and transformed into output. Outputs include computer printouts, written reports, tables, charts, graphs, checks, purchase orders, invoices, inventory records, payroll accounts, and a variety of other documents. Payoffs from alternative strategies can be calculated and estimated. *Data* become *information* only when they are evaluated, filtered, condensed, analyzed, and organized for a specific purpose, problem, individual, or time.

Because organizations are becoming more complex, decentralized, and globally dispersed, the function of information systems is growing in importance. Spurring this advance is the falling cost and increasing power of computers. There are costs and benefits associated with obtaining and evaluating information, just as with equipment and land. Like equipment, information can become obsolete and may need to be purged from the system. An effective information system is like a library, collecting, categorizing, and filing data for use by managers throughout the organization. Information systems are a major strategic resource, monitoring internal and external issues and trends, identifying competitive threats, and assisting in the implementation, evaluation, and control of strategy.

We are truly in an information age. Firms whose information-system skills are weak are at a competitive disadvantage. In contrast, strengths in information systems allow firms to establish distinctive competencies in other areas. Low-cost manufacturing and good customer service, for example, can depend on a good information system.

Strategic-Planning Software

Some strategic decision support systems, however, are too sophisticated, expensive, or restrictive to be used easily by managers in a firm. This is unfortunate because the strategic-management process must be a people process to be successful. People make the difference! Strategic-planning software should thus be simple and unsophisticated. Simplicity allows wide participation among managers in a firm and participation is essential for effective strategy implementation.

One strategic-planning software product that parallels this text and offers managers and executives a simple yet effective approach for developing organizational strategies is CheckMATE (www.checkmateplan.com). This personal computer software performs planning analyses and generates strategies a firm could pursue. CheckMATE incorporates the most modern strategic-planning techniques. No previous experience with computers or knowledge of strategic planning is required of the user. CheckMATE thus promotes communication, understanding, creativity, and forward thinking among users.

CheckMATE is not a spreadsheet program or database; it is an expert system that carries a firm through strategy formulation and implementation. A major strength of CheckMATE strategic-planning software is its simplicity and participative approach. The user is asked appropriate questions, responses are recorded, information is assimilated, and results are printed. Individuals can independently work through the software, and then the program will develop joint recommendations for the firm.

An individual license for CheckMATE costs $295. More information about CheckMATE can be obtained at www.checkmateplan.com or 910–579–5744 (phone).

The Web site www.strategyclub.com has become a leader in the world in providing strategic planning software, products, and services. This Web site provides the strategic Management Club Online as well as excellent economical software both for students and for business persons worldwide.

Management Information Systems Audit

Questions such as the following should be asked when conducting this audit:

1. Do all managers in the firm use the information system to make decisions?
2. Is there a chief information officer or director of information systems position in the firm?
3. Are data in the information system updated regularly?
4. Do managers from all functional areas of the firm contribute input to the information system?
5. Are there effective passwords for entry into the firm's information system?
6. Are strategists of the firm familiar with the information systems of rival firms?
7. Is the information system user-friendly?
8. Do all users of the information system understand the competitive advantages that information can provide firms?
9. Are computer training workshops provided for users of the information system?
10. Is the firm's information system continually being improved in content and user-friendliness?

Value Chain Analysis (VCA)

According to Porter, the business of a firm can best be described as a *value chain,* in which total revenues minus total costs of all activities undertaken to develop and market a product or service yields value. All firms in a given industry have a similar value chain, which includes activities such as obtaining raw materials, designing products, building manufacturing facilities, developing cooperative agreements, and providing customer service. A firm will be profitable as long as total revenues exceed the total costs incurred in creating and delivering the product or service. Firms should strive to understand not only their own value chain operations but also their competitors', suppliers', and distributors' value chains.

Value chain analysis (VCA) refers to the process whereby a firm determines the costs associated with organizational activities from purchasing raw materials to manufacturing product(s) to marketing those products. VCA aims to identify where low-cost advantages or disadvantages exist anywhere along the value chain from raw material to customer service activities. VCA can enable a firm to better identify its own strengths and weaknesses, especially as compared to competitors' value chain analyses and their own data examined over time.

Substantial judgment may be required in performing a VCA because different items along the value chain may impact other items positively or negatively, so there exist complex interrelationships. For example, exceptional customer service may be especially expensive yet may reduce the costs of returns and increase revenues. Cost and price differences among rival firms can have their origins in activities performed by suppliers, distributors, creditors, or even shareholders. Despite the complexity of VCA, the initial step in implementing this procedure is to divide a firm's operations into specific activities or business processes. Then the analyst attempts to attach a cost to each discrete activity, and the costs could be in terms of both time and money. Finally, the analyst converts the cost data into information by looking for competitive cost strengths and weaknesses that may yield competitive advantage or disadvantage. Conducting a VCA is supportive of the RBV's examination of a firm's assets and capabilities as sources of distinctive competence.

When a major competitor or new market entrant offers products or services at very low prices, this may be because that firm has substantially lower value chain costs or perhaps the rival firm is just waging a desperate attempt to gain sales or market share. Thus value chain analysis can be critically important for a firm in monitoring whether its prices and costs are competitive. An example value chain is illustrated in Figure 4-7. There can be more than a hundred particular value-creating activities associated with the business of producing and marketing a product or service, and each one of the activities can represent a competitive advantage or disadvantage for the firm. The combined costs of all the various activities in a company's value chain define the firm's cost of doing business. Firms should determine where cost advantages and disadvantages in their value chain occur *relative to the value chain of rival firms.*

Value chains differ immensely across industries and firms. Whereas a paper products company, such as Stone Container, would include on its value chain timber farming, logging, pulp mills, and papermaking, a computer company such as Hewlett-Packard would include programming, peripherals, software, hardware, and laptops. A motel would include food, housekeeping, check-in and check-out operations, Web site, reservations system, and so on. However all firms should use value chain analysis to develop and nurture a core competence and convert this competence into a distinctive competence. A *core competence* is a value chain activity that a firm performs especially well. When a core competence evolves into a major competitive advantage, then it is called a *distinctive competence.* Figure 4-8 illustrates this process.

More and more companies are using VCA to gain and sustain competitive advantage by being especially efficient and effective along various parts of the value chain. For example, Wal-Mart has built powerful value advantages by focusing on exceptionally tight inventory control, volume purchasing of products, and offering exemplary customer service. Computer companies in contrast compete aggressively along the distribution end of the value chain. Of course, price competitiveness is a key component of effectiveness among both mass retailers and computer firms.

Benchmarking

Benchmarking is an analytical tool used to determine whether a firm's value chain activities are competitive compared to rivals and thus conducive to winning in the marketplace. Benchmarking entails measuring costs of value chain activities across an industry to determine "best practices" among competing firms for the purpose of duplicating or improving upon those best practices. Benchmarking enables a firm to take action to improve its competitiveness by identifying (and improving upon) value chain activities where rival firms have comparative advantages in cost, service, reputation, or operation.

The hardest part of benchmarking can be gaining access to other firms' value chain activities with associated costs. Typical sources of benchmarking information, however, include published reports, trade publications, suppliers, distributors, customers, partners, creditors, shareholders, lobbyists, and willing rival firms. Some rival firms share benchmarking data. However, the International Benchmarking Clearinghouse provides guidelines to help ensure that restraint of trade, price fixing, bid rigging, bribery, and other improper business conduct do not arise between participating firms.

Due to the popularity of benchmarking today, numerous consulting firms such as Accenture, AT Kearney, Best Practices Benchmarking & Consulting, as well as the Strategic Planning Institute's Council on Benchmarking, gather benchmarking data, conduct benchmarking studies, and distribute benchmark information without identifying the sources.

FIGURE 4-7

An Example Value Chain for a Typical Manufacturing Firm

Supplier Costs
    Raw materials
    Fuel
    Energy
    Transportation
    Truck drivers
    Truck maintenance
    Component parts
    Inspection
    Storing
    Warehouse

Production Costs
    Inventory system
    Receiving
    Plant layout
    Maintenance
    Plant location
    Computer
    R&D
    Cost accounting

Distribution Costs
    Loading
    Shipping
    Budgeting
    Personnel
    Internet
    Trucking
    Railroads
    Fuel
    Maintenance

Sales and Marketing Costs
    Salespersons
    Web site
    Internet
    Publicity
    Promotion
    Advertising
    Transportation
    Food and lodging

Customer Service Costs
    Postage
    Phone
    Internet
    Warranty

Management Costs
    Human resources
    Administration
    Employee benefits
    Labor relations
    Managers
    Employees
    Finance and legal

FIGURE 4-8

Transforming Value Chain Activities into Sustained Competitive Advantage

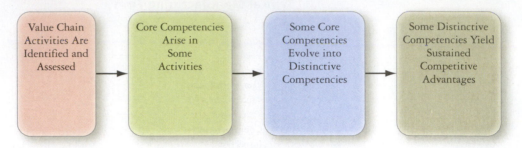

The Internal Factor Evaluation (IFE) Matrix

A summary step in conducting an internal strategic-management audit is to construct an *Internal Factor Evaluation (IFE) Matrix*. This strategy-formulation tool summarizes and evaluates the major strengths and weaknesses in the functional areas of a business, and it also provides a basis for identifying and evaluating relationships among those areas. Intuitive judgments are required in developing an IFE Matrix, so the appearance of a scientific approach should not be interpreted to mean this is an all-powerful technique. A thorough understanding of the factors included is more important than the actual numbers. Similar to the EFE Matrix and Competitive Profile Matrix described in Chapter 3, an IFE Matrix can be developed in five steps:

1. List key internal factors as identified in the internal-audit process. Use a total of from 10 to 20 internal factors, including both strengths and weaknesses. List strengths first and then weaknesses. Be as specific as possible, using percentages, ratios, and comparative numbers. Recall that Edward Deming said, "In God we trust. Everyone else bring data."

2. Assign a weight that ranges from 0.0 (not important) to 1.0 (all-important) to each factor. The weight assigned to a given factor indicates the relative importance of the factor to being successful in the firm's industry. Regardless of whether a key factor is an internal strength or weakness, factors considered to have the greatest effect on organizational performance should be assigned the highest weights. The sum of all weights must equal 1.0.

3. Assign a 1-to-4 rating to each factor to indicate whether that factor represents a major weakness (rating = 1), a minor weakness (rating = 2), a minor strength (rating = 3), or a major strength (rating = 4). Note that strengths must receive a 3 or 4 rating and weaknesses must receive a 1 or 2 rating. Ratings are thus company-based, whereas the weights in step 2 are industry-based.

4. Multiply each factor's weight by its rating to determine a weighted score for each variable.

5. Sum the weighted scores for each variable to determine the total weighted score for the organization.

Regardless of how many factors are included in an IFE Matrix, the total weighted score can range from a low of 1.0 to a high of 4.0, with the average score being 2.5. Total weighted scores well below 2.5 characterize organizations that are weak internally, whereas scores significantly above 2.5 indicate a strong internal position. Like the EFE Matrix, an IFE Matrix should include from 10 to 20 key factors. The number of factors has no effect upon the range of total weighted scores because the weights always sum to 1.0.

When a key internal factor is both a strength and a weakness, the factor should be included twice in the IFE Matrix, and a weight and rating should be assigned to each statement. For example, the Playboy logo both helps and hurts Playboy Enterprises; the logo

TABLE 4.10   A Sample Internal Factor Evaluation Matrix for a Retail Computer Store

Key Internal Factors	Weight	Rating	Weighted Score
Strengths			
1. Inventory turnover increased from 5.8 to 6.7	0.05	3	0.15
2. Average customer purchase increased from $97 to $128	0.07	4	0.28
3. Employee morale is excellent	0.10	3	0.30
4. In-store promotions resulted in 20 percent increase in sales	0.05	3	0.15
5. Newspaper advertising expenditures increased 10 percent	0.02	3	0.06
6. Revenues from repair/service segment of store up 16 percent	0.15	3	0.45
7. In-store technical support personnel have MIS college degrees	0.05	4	0.20
8. Store's debt-to-total assets ratio declined to 34 percent	0.03	3	0.09
9. Revenues per employee up 19 percent	0.02	3	0.06
Weaknesses			
1. Revenues from software segment of store down 12 percent	0.10	2	0.20
2. Location of store negatively impacted by new Highway 34	0.15	2	0.30
3. Carpet and paint in store somewhat in disrepair	0.02	1	0.02
4. Bathroom in store needs refurbishing	0.02	1	0.02
5. Revenues from businesses down 8 percent	0.04	1	0.04
6. Store has no Web site	0.05	2	0.10
7. Supplier on-time delivery increased to 2.4 days	0.03	1	0.03
8. Often customers have to wait to check out	0.05	1	0.05
Total	**1.00**		**2.50**

attracts customers to *Playboy* magazine, but it keeps the Playboy cable channel out of many markets. Be as quantitative as possible when stating factors. Use monetary amounts, percentages, numbers, and ratios to the extent possible.

An example of an IFE Matrix is provided in Table 4-10 for a retail computer store. Note that the two most important factors to be successful in the retail computer store business are "revenues from repair/service in the store" and "location of the store." Also note that the store is doing best on "average customer purchase amount" and "in-store technical support." The store is having major problems with its carpet, bathroom, paint, and checkout procedures. Note also that the matrix contains substantial quantitative data rather than vague statements; this is excellent. Overall, this store receives a 2.5 total weighted score, which on a 1-to-4 scale is exactly average/halfway, indicating there is definitely room for improvement in store operations, strategies, policies, and procedures.

The IFE Matrix provides important information for strategy formulation. For example, this retail computer store might want to hire another checkout person and repair its carpet, paint, and bathroom problems. Also, the store may want to increase advertising for its repair/services, because that is a really important (weight 0.15) factor to being successful in this business.

In multidivisional firms, each autonomous division or strategic business unit should construct an IFE Matrix. Divisional matrices then can be integrated to develop an overall corporate IFE Matrix.

Conclusion

Management, marketing, finance/accounting, production/operations, research and development, and management information systems represent the core operations of most businesses. A strategic-management audit of a firm's internal operations is vital to organizational health. Many companies still prefer to be judged solely on their bottom-line performance. However, an increasing number of successful organizations are using the internal audit to gain competitive advantages over rival firms.

Systematic methodologies for performing strength-weakness assessments are not well developed in the strategic-management literature, but it is clear that strategists must identify and evaluate internal strengths and weaknesses in order to effectively formulate and choose among alternative strategies. The EFE Matrix, Competitive Profile Matrix, IFE Matrix, and clear statements of vision and mission provide the basic information needed to successfully formulate competitive strategies. The process of performing an internal audit represents an opportunity for managers and employees throughout the organization to participate in determining the future of the firm. Involvement in the process can energize and mobilize managers and employees.

We invite you to visit the David page on the Prentice Hall Companion Web site at http://www.pearsonhighered.com/david/ for this chapter's review quiz.

Key Terms and Concepts

Activity Ratios (p. 109)
Benchmarking (p. 120)
Breakeven Point (p. 112)
Capital Budgeting (p. 107)
Communication (p. 94)
Controlling (p. 102)
Core Competence (p. 120)
Cost/Benefit Analysis (p. 106)
Cultural Products (p. 97)
Customer Analysis (p. 103)
Data (p. 118)
Distinctive Competencies (p. 93)
Distribution (p. 105)
Dividend Decisions (p. 107)
Empirical Indicators (p. 96)
Financial Ratio Analysis (p. 95)
Fixed Costs (p. 112)
Financing Decision (p. 107)
Functions of Finance/Accounting (p. 107)
Functions of Management (p. 99)
Functions of Marketing (p. 103)
Growth Ratios (p. 111)
Human Resource Management (p. 102)
Information (p. 118)
Internal Audit (p. 93)

Internal Factor Evaluation (IFE)
   Matrix (p. 122)
Investment Decision (p. 107)
Leverage Ratios (p. 109)
Liquidity Ratios (p. 109)
Management Information System (p. 118)
Marketing Affiliate (p. 93)
Marketing Research (p. 106)
Motivating (p. 101)
Organizational Culture (p. 97)
Organizing (p. 100)
Personnel Management (p. 102)
Planning (p. 100)
Pricing (p. 105)
Product and Service Planning (p. 104)
Production/Operations Function (p. 113)
Profitability Ratios (p. 109)
Research and Development (R&D) (p. 115)
Resource-Based View (RBV) (p. 96)
Selling (p. 103)
Staffing (p. 102)
Synergy (p. 100)
Test Marketing (p. 104)
Value Chain Analysis (VCA) (p. 119)
Variable Costs (p. 113)

Issues for Review and Discussion

1. List three firms you are familiar with and give a distinctive competence for each firm.
2. Give some key reasons why prioritizing strengths and weaknesses is essential.
3. Why may it be easier in performing an internal assessment to develop a list of 80 strengths/weaknesses than to decide on the top 20 to use in formulating strategies?
4. Think of an organization you are very familiar with. Lit three resources of that entity that are empirical indicators.
5. Think of an organization you are very familiar with. Rate that entity's organizational culture on the 15 example dimensions listed in Table 4-2.

6. If you and a partner were going to visit a foreign country where you have never been before, how much planning would you do ahead of time? What benefit would you expect that planning to provide?

7. Even though planning is considered the foundation of management, why do you think it is commonly the task that managers neglect most?

8. Are you more organized than the person sitting beside you in class? If not, what problems could that present in terms of your performance and rank in the class? How analogous is this situation to rival companies?

9. List the three ways that financial ratios should be compared/utilized. Which of the three comparisons do you feel is most important? Why?

10. Illustrate how value chain activities can become core competencies and eventually distinctive competencies. Give an example for an organization you are familiar with.

11. In an IFEM, would it be advantageous to list your strengths, and then your weaknesses, in order of increasing "weight"? Why?

12. In an IFEM, a critic may say there is no significant different between a "weight" of 0.08 and 0.06. How would you respond?

13. List six desirable characteristics of advertisements in recessionary times.

14. Why are so many firms cutting their dividend payout amounts?

15. When someone says dividends paid are double taxed, what are they referring to?

16. Draw a breakeven chart to illustrate a drop in labor costs.

17. Draw a breakeven chart to illustrate an increase in advertising expenses.

18. Draw a breakeven chart to illustrate closing stores.

19. Draw a breakeven chart to illustrate lowering price.

20. Explain why prioritizing the relative importance of strengths and weaknesses in an IFE Matrix is an important strategic-management activity.

21. How can delegation of authority contribute to effective strategic management?

22. Diagram a formal organizational chart that reflects the following positions: a president, 2 executive officers, 4 middle managers, and 18 lower-level managers. Now, diagram three overlapping and hypothetical informal group structures. How can this information be helpful to a strategist in formulating and implementing strategy?

23. Which of the three basic functions of finance/accounting do you feel is most important in a small electronics manufacturing concern? Justify your position.

24. Do you think aggregate R&D expenditures for U.S. firms will increase or decrease next year? Why?

25. Explain how you would motivate managers and employees to implement a major new strategy.

26. Why do you think production/operations managers often are not directly involved in strategy-formulation activities? Why can this be a major organizational weakness?

27. Give two examples of staffing strengths and two examples of staffing weaknesses of an organization with which you are familiar.

28. Would you ever pay out dividends when your firm's annual net profit is negative? Why? What effect could this have on a firm's strategies?

29. If a firm has zero debt in its capital structure, is that always an organizational strength? Why or why not?

30. Describe the production/operations system in a police department.

31. After conducting an internal audit, a firm discovers a total of 100 strengths and 100 weaknesses. What procedures then could be used to determine the most important of these? Why is it important to reduce the total number of key factors?

32. Why do you believe cultural products affect all the functions of business?

33. Do you think cultural products affect strategy formulation, implementation, or evaluation the most? Why?

34. Identify cultural products at your college or university. Do these products, viewed collectively or separately, represent a strength or weakness for the organization?

35. Describe the management information system at your college or university.

36. Explain the difference between data and information in terms of each being useful to strategists.

37. What are the most important characteristics of an effective management information system?

38. Do you agree or disagree with the RBV theorists that internal resources are more important for a firm than external factors in achieving and sustaining competitive advantage? Explain your and their position.

39. Define and discuss "empirical indicators."

40.   Define and discuss the "spam" problem in the United States.
41.   Define and explain value chain analysis (VCA).
42.   List five financial ratios that may be used by your university to monitor operations.
43.   Explain benchmarking.

Notes

1.   Reprinted by permission of the publisher from "Integrating Strength–Weakness Analysis into Strategic Planning," by William King, *Journal of Business Research* 2, no. 4: p. 481. Copyright 1983 by Elsevier Science Publishing Co., Inc.

2.   Igor Ansoff, "Strategic Management of Technology" *Journal of Business Strategy* 7, no. 3 (Winter 1987): 38.

3.   Claude George Jr., *The History of Management Thought*, 2nd ed. (Upper Saddle River, NJ: Prentice-Hall, 1972): 174.

4.   Robert Grant, "The Resource-Based Theory of Competitive Advantage: Implications for Strategy Formulation," *California Management Review* (Spring 1991): 116.

5.   J. B. Barney, "Firm Resources and Sustained Competitive Advantage," *Journal of Management* 17 (1991): 99–120; J. B. Barney, "The Resource-Based Theory of the Firm," *Organizational Science* 7 (1996): 469; J. B. Barney, "Is the Resource-Based 'View' a Useful Perspective for Strategic Management Research? Yes." *Academy of Management Review* 26, no. 1 (2001): 41–56.

6.   Edgar Schein, *Organizational Culture and Leadership* (San Francisco: Jossey-Bass, 1985): 9.

7.   Ellen Byron, "A New Odd Couple: Google, P&G Swap Workers to Spur Innovation," *Wall Street Journal* (November 19, 2008): A1.

8.   John Lorsch, "Managing Culture: The Invisible Barrier to Strategic Change," *California Management Review* 28, no. 2 (1986): 95–109.

9.   Y. Allarie and M. Firsirotu, "How to Implement Radical Strategies in Large Organizations," *Sloan Management Review* (Spring 1985): 19.

10.   www.mindtools.com/plfailpl.html.

11.   Adam Smith, *The Wealth of Nations* (New York: Modern Library, 1937): 3–4.

12.   Richard Daft, *Management*, 3rd ed. (Orlando, FL: Dryden Press, 1993): 512.

13.   Shelley Kirkpatrick and Edwin Locke, "Leadership: Do Traits Matter?" *Academy of Management Executive* 5, no. 2 (May 1991): 48.

14.   Peter Drucker, *Management Tasks, Responsibilities, and Practice* (New York: Harper & Row, 1973): 463.

15.   Brian Dumaine, "What the Leaders of Tomorrow See," *Fortune* (July 3, 1989): 51.

16.   J. Evans and B. Bergman, *Marketing* (New York: Macmillan, 1982): 17.

17.   Suzanne Vranica, "Ads to Go Leaner, Meaner in '09," *Wall Street Journal* (January 5, 2009): B8.

18.   Bruce Horowitz, "2 Million Enjoy Free Breakfast at Denny's," *USA Today* (February 4, 2009): 1B, 2B.

19.   Quoted in Robert Waterman, Jr., "The Renewal Factor," *BusinessWeek* (September 14, 1987): 108.

20.   J. Van Horne, *Financial Management and Policy* (Upper Saddle River, N.J.: Prentice-Hall, 1974): 10.

21.   Ben Worthen, "Oracle to Pay First Dividend," *Wall Street Journal* (March 19, 2009): B1.

22.   Kevin Klowden, "The Quiet Revolution in Transportation," *Wall Street Journal* (April 24, 2007): A14.

23.   Philip Rousebl, Kamal Saad, and Tamara Erickson, "The Evolution of Third Generation R&D," *Planning Review* 19, no. 2 (March–April 1991): 18–26.

24.   Vida Scarpello, William Boulton, and Charles Hofer, "Reintegrating R&D into Business Strategy," *Journal of Business Strategy* 6, no. 4 (Spring 1986): 50–51.

Current Readings

Aggarwal, Vikas, and David Hsu. "Modes of Cooperative R&D Commercialization by Start-Ups." *Strategic Management Journal* (August 2009): 835–864.

Amit, Raphael, and Christoph Zott. "The Fit Between Product Market Strategy and Business Model: Implications for Firm Performance." *Strategic Management Journal* 29, no. 1 (January 2008): 1.

Cannella, Albert A., Jr., Ho-Uk Lee, and Jong-Hun Park. "Top Management Team Functional Background Diversity and Firm Performance: Examining the Roles of Team Member Relocation and Environmental Uncertainty." *The Academy of Management Journal* 51, no. 4 (August 2008): 768.

Gandossy, Robert, and Robin Guarnieri. "Can You Measure Leadership?" *MIT Sloan Management Review* 50, no. 1 (Fall 2008): 65.

Favaro, Ken, Tim Romberger, and David Meer. "Five Rules for Retailing in a Recession." *Harvard Business Review* (April 2009): 64–73.

Fine, Leslie. "The Bottom Line: Marketing and Firm Performance." *Business Horizons* (May–June 2009): 209–214.

Garnier, Jean-Pierre. "Rebuilding the R&D Engine in Big Pharma." *Harvard Business Review* (May 2008): 68.

Montgomery, Cynthia A. "Putting Leadership Back into Strategy." *Harvard Business Review* (January 2008): 54.

Noble, Charles H., and Rajiv K. Sinha. "The Adoption of Radical Manufacturing Technologies and Firm Survival." *Strategic Management Journal* 29, no. 9 (September 2008): 943.

Sims, Henry Jr., Samer Faraj, and Seokhwa Yun. "When Should a Leader Be Directive or Empowering? How to Develop Your Own Situational Theory of Leadership." *Business Horizons* (March–April 2009): 105–108.

Quelch, John A., and Katherine E. Jocz. "How to Market in a Downturn." *Harvard Business Review* (April 2009): 52–63.

Wind, Yoram (Jerry). "A Plan to Invent the Marketing We Need Today." *MIT Sloan Management Review* 49, no. 4 (Summer 2008): 21.

ASSURANCE OF LEARNING EXERCISES

Assurance of Learning Exercise 4A

Performing a Financial Ratio Analysis for McDonald's Corporation (MCD)

Purpose

Financial ratio analysis is one of the best techniques for identifying and evaluating internal strengths and weaknesses. Potential investors and current shareholders look closely at firms' financial ratios, making detailed comparisons to industry averages and to previous periods of time. Financial ratio analyses provide vital input information for developing an IFE Matrix.

Instructions

Step 1   On a separate sheet of paper, number from 1 to 20. Referring to McDonald's income statement and balance sheet (pp. 31–32), calculate 20 financial ratios for 2008 for the company. Use Table 4-7 as a reference.

Step 2   In a second column, indicate whether you consider each ratio to be a strength, a weakness, or a neutral factor for McDonald's.

Step 3   Go to the Web sites in Table 4-6 that calculate McDonald's financial ratios, without your having to pay a subscription (fee) for the service. Make a copy of the ratio information provided and record the source. Report this research to your classmates and your professor.

Assurance of Learning Exercise 4B

Constructing an IFE Matrix for McDonald's Corporation

Purpose

This exercise will give you experience in developing an IFE Matrix. Identifying and prioritizing factors to include in an IFE Matrix fosters communication among functional and divisional managers. Preparing an IFE Matrix allows human resource, marketing, production/operations, finance/accounting, R&D, and management information systems managers to articulate their concerns and thoughts regarding the business condition of the firm. This results in an improved collective understanding of the business.

Instructions

Step 1   Join with two other individuals to form a three-person team. Develop a team IFE Matrix for McDonald's.

Step 2   Compare your team's IFE Matrix to other teams' IFE Matrices. Discuss any major differences.

Step 3   What strategies do you think would allow McDonald's to capitalize on its major strengths? What strategies would allow McDonald's to improve upon its major weaknesses?

Assurance of Learning Exercise 4C

Constructing an IFE Matrix for My University

Purpose

This exercise gives you the opportunity to evaluate your university's major strengths and weaknesses. As will become clearer in the next chapter, an organization's strategies are largely based upon striving to take advantage of strengths and improving upon weaknesses.

Instructions

Step 1   Join with two other individuals to form a three-person team. Develop a team IFE Matrix for your university. You may use the strengths/weaknesses determined in Assurance of Learning Exercise 1D.

Step 2   Go to the board and diagram your team's IFE Matrix.

Step 3   Compare your team's IFE Matrix to other teams' IFE Matrices. Discuss any major differences.

Step 4   What strategies do you think would allow your university to capitalize on its major strengths? What strategies would allow your university to improve upon its major weaknesses?

CHAPTER 5
Strategies in Action

CHAPTER OBJECTIVES

After studying this chapter, you should be able to do the following:

1. Discuss the value of establishing long-term objectives.

2. Identify 16 types of business strategies.

3. Identify numerous examples of organizations pursuing different types of strategies.

4. Discuss guidelines when particular strategies are most appropriate to pursue.

5. Discuss Porter's five generic strategies.

6. Describe strategic management in nonprofit, governmental, and small organizations.

7. Discuss joint ventures as a way to enter the Russian market.

8. Discuss the Balanced Scorecard.

9. Compare and contrast financial with strategic objectives.

10. Discuss the levels of strategies in large versus small firms.

11. Explain the First Mover Advantages concept.

12. Discuss recent trends in outsourcing.

13. Discuss strategies for competing in turbulent, high-velocity markets.

Assurance of Learning Exercises

Assurance of Learning Exercise 5A
What Strategies Should McDonald's Pursue in 2011–2013?

Assurance of Learning Exercise 5B
Examining Strategy Articles

Assurance of Learning Exercise 5C
Classifying Some Year 2009 Strategies

Assurance of Learning Exercise 5D
How Risky Are Various Alternative Strategies?

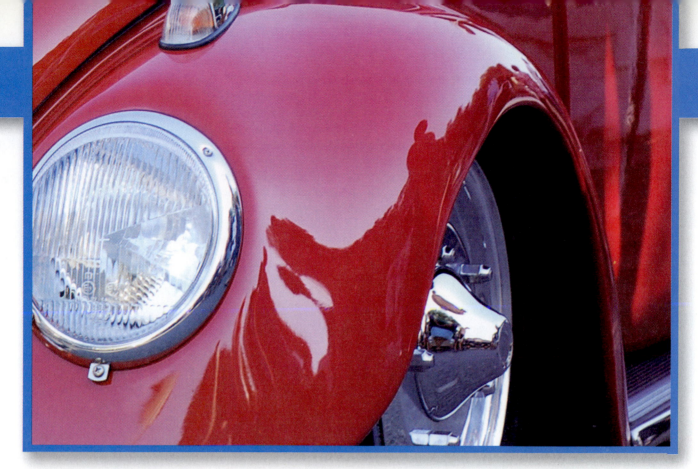

"Notable Quotes"

"Alice said, 'Would you please tell me which way to go from here?' The cat said, 'That depends on where you want to get to.'"

—Lewis Carroll

"Tomorrow always arrives. It is always different. And even the mightiest company is in trouble if it has not worked on the future. Being surprised by what happens is a risk that even the largest and richest company cannot afford, and even the smallest business need not run."

—Peter Drucker

"Planning. Doing things today to make us better tomorrow. Because the future belongs to those who make the hard decisions today."

—Eaton Corporation

"One big problem with American business is that when it gets into trouble, it redoubles its effort. It's like digging for gold. If you dig down twenty feet and haven't found it, one of the strategies you could use is to dig twice as deep. But if the gold is twenty feet to the side, you could dig a long time and not find it."

—Edward De Bono

"Even if you're on the right track, you'll get run over if you just sit there."

—Will Rogers

"Strategies for taking the hill won't necessarily hold it."

—Amar Bhide

"The early bird may get the worm, but the second mouse gets the cheese."

—Unknown

**Assurance of
Learning Exercise 5E**
Developing Alternative
Strategies for My University

**Assurance of Learning
Exercise 5F**
Lessons in Doing Business
Globally

Hundreds of companies today, including Sears, IBM, Searle, and Hewlett-Packard, have embraced strategic planning fully in their quest for higher revenues and profits. Kent Nelson, former chair of UPS, explains why his company has created a new strategic-planning department: "Because we're making bigger bets on investments in technology, we can't afford to spend a whole lot of money in one direction and then find out five years later it was the wrong direction."[1]

This chapter brings strategic management to life with many contemporary examples. Sixteen types of strategies are defined and exemplified, including Michael Porter's generic strategies: cost leadership, differentiation, and focus. Guidelines are presented for determining when it is most appropriate to pursue different types of strategies. An overview of strategic management in nonprofit organizations, governmental agencies, and small firms is provided.

Doing Great in a Weak Economy. How?

Volkswagen AG

While most automobile companies talk about bankruptcy, merger, collapse, and liquidation, Volkswagen AG is posting solid earnings. Based in Wolfsburg, Germany, and Europe's biggest automaker by sales, Volkswagen (VW) managed the global economic recession well by focusing on emerging markets such as China and Brazil and continually reducing costs. VW is the leading auto firm in China, not Toyota or Nissan. VW's market share in Western Europe rose to 20 percent in 2009 from 17.9 percent a year ago. While shrinking demand for new cars in major markets and high raw-material costs, and unfavorable exchange rates have reduced earnings of most European automakers, VW anticipated these conditions through excellent strategic planning and continues to take market share from rival firms worldwide.

The German truck maker and engineering company MAN AG is VW's largest single shareholder at 30 percent, and its business too has been good. MAN's third quarter of 2008 saw profit jump 34 percent, lifted by strong sales of trucks, diesel engines, and turbo machinery. VW is currently spending $1 billion to build a new plant in Chattanooga, Tennessee, for the production of a midsize sedan in 2011 with initial capacity of 150,000 cars annually. VW's plans for 2018 include increasing its U.S. market share from 2 percent to 6 percent by selling 800,000 vehicles annually in the United States. By 2018, VW also plans to export 125,000 vehicles from North America to Europe. VW's plans include large expansions at its Puebla, Mexico, plant.

While most auto companies are cutting expenses, VW is increasing is 2009 U.S. marketing budget by 15 percent in its Audi AG luxury division. The Audi ads even ran during the 2009 Super Bowl.

For all of 2008, VW's net profit rose 15 percent to 4.75 billion euros and revenues rose 4.5 percent to 114 billion. VW expects flat or even slight declines in 2009 but some of its competitors are incurring billion dollar losses.

VW has cars named for climate patterns, insects, and small mammals. Along with the New Beetle, VW's annual production of 6 million cars, trucks, and vans includes such models such as Passat (trade wind), Jetta (jet stream), Rabbit, and Fox. VW also owns several luxury carmakers, including AUDI, Lamborghini, Bentley, and Bugatti. Other VW makes include SEAT (family cars, Spain) and SKODA (family cars, the Czech Republic). VW operates plants in Africa, the Americas, Asia/Pacific, and Europe. VW holds 68 percent of the voting rights in Swedish truck maker Scania and about 30 percent of MAN AG. VW also offers consumer financing.

VW is acquiring Porsche Automobil Holding SE and merging their auto brands into VW. Based in Stuttgart, Germany, Porsche already owns 51 percent of VW but has weakened in 2009 after taking on $12 billion in new debt.

VW is in talks with China's BYD Co. to build hybrid and electric vehicles powered by lithium batteries. Based in Shenzhen, BYD will supply VW with the battery technology. This will be the first automotive partner for BYD, which is one of the world's largest suppliers of cell phone batteries.

VW is building a new assembly plant in Indonesia for $47 million about 1 hour east of Jakarta, the capital. This plant will assemble the Touran and employ about 3,000 persons. Toyota already has a manufacturing plant in Indonesia and dominates that market. Currently many VW vehicles are imported into Indonesia, thus being subject to a 200 percent tariff.

VW reported 2nd quarter 2009 earnings of $397 million; the Audi division was the biggest contributor to the gains.

Source: Based on Christoph Rauwald, "VW Earnings Buck Auto-Industry Trend," *Wall Street Journal* (October 31, 2008): B3; Christoph Rauwald, "Volkswagen to Raise Output by 2018," *Wall Street Journal* (April 28, 2009): B3.

Long-Term Objectives

Long-term objectives represent the results expected from pursuing certain strategies. Strategies represent the actions to be taken to accomplish long-term objectives. The time frame for objectives and strategies should be consistent, usually from two to five years.

The Nature of Long-Term Objectives

Objectives should be quantitative, measurable, realistic, understandable, challenging, hierarchical, obtainable, and congruent among organizational units. Each objective should also be associated with a timeline. Objectives are commonly stated in terms such as growth in assets, growth in sales, profitability, market share, degree and nature of diversification, degree and nature of vertical integration, earnings per share, and social responsibility. Clearly established objectives offer many benefits. They provide direction, allow synergy, aid in evaluation, establish priorities, reduce uncertainty, minimize conflicts, stimulate exertion, and aid in both the allocation of resources and the design of jobs. Objectives provide a basis for consistent decision making by managers whose values and attitudes differ. Objectives serve as standards by which individuals, groups, departments, divisions, and entire organizations can be evaluated.

Long-term objectives are needed at the corporate, divisional, and functional levels of an organization. They are an important measure of managerial performance. Many practitioners and academicians attribute a significant part of U.S. industry's competitive decline to the short-term, rather than long-term, strategy orientation of managers in the United States. Arthur D. Little argues that bonuses or merit pay for managers today must be based to a greater extent on long-term objectives and strategies. A general framework for relating objectives to performance evaluation is provided in Table 5-1. A particular organization could tailor these guidelines to meet its own needs, but incentives should be attached to both long-term and annual objectives.

Without long-term objectives, an organization would drift aimlessly toward some unknown end. It is hard to imagine an organization or individual being successful without clear objectives (see Tables 5-2 and 5-3). Success only rarely occurs by accident; rather, it is the result of hard work directed toward achieving certain objectives.

TABLE 5-1 Varying Performance Measures by Organizational Level

Organizational Level	Basis for Annual Bonus or Merit Pay
Corporate	75% based on long-term objectives
	25% based on annual objectives
Division	50% based on long-term objectives
	50% based on annual objectives
Function	25% based on long-term objectives
	75% based on annual objectives

TABLE 5-2 The Desired Characteristics of Objectives

1. Quantitative
2. Measurable
3. Realistic
4. Understandable
5. Challenging
6. Hierarchical
7. Obtainable
8. Congruent across departments

TABLE 5-3 The Benefits of Having Clear Objectives

1. Provide direction by revealing expectations
2. Allow synergy
3. Aid in evaluation by serving as standards
4. Establish priorities
5. Reduce uncertainty
6. Minimize conflicts
7. Stimulate exertion
8. Aid in allocation of resources
9. Aid in design of jobs
10. Provide basis for consistent decision making

Financial versus Strategic Objectives

Two types of objectives are especially common in organizations: financial and strategic objectives. Financial objectives include those associated with growth in revenues, growth in earnings, higher dividends, larger profit margins, greater return on investment, higher earnings per share, a rising stock price, improved cash flow, and so on; while strategic objectives include things such as a larger market share, quicker on-time delivery than rivals, shorter design-to-market times than rivals, lower costs than rivals, higher product quality than rivals, wider geographic coverage than rivals, achieving technological leadership, consistently getting new or improved products to market ahead of rivals, and so on.

Although financial objectives are especially important in firms, oftentimes there is a trade-off between financial and strategic objectives such that crucial decisions have to be made. For example, a firm can do certain things to maximize short-term financial objectives that would harm long-term strategic objectives. To improve financial position in the short run through higher prices may, for example, jeopardize long-term market share. The dangers associated with trading off long-term strategic objectives with near-term bottom-line performance are especially severe if competitors relentlessly pursue increased market share at the expense of short-term profitability. And there are other trade-offs between financial and strategic objectives, related to riskiness of actions, concern for business ethics, need to preserve the natural environment, and social responsibility issues. Both financial and strategic objectives should include both annual and long-term performance targets. Ultimately, the best way to sustain competitive advantage over the long run is to relentlessly pursue strategic objectives that strengthen a firm's business position over rivals. Financial objectives can best be met by focusing first and foremost on achievement of strategic objectives that improve a firm's competitiveness and market strength.

Not Managing by Objectives

An unidentified educator once said, "If you think education is expensive, try ignorance." The idea behind this saying also applies to establishing objectives. Strategists should avoid the following alternative ways to "not managing by objectives."

- *Managing by Extrapolation*—adheres to the principle "If it ain't broke, don't fix it." The idea is to keep on doing about the same things in the same ways because things are going well.
- *Managing by Crisis*—based on the belief that the true measure of a really good strategist is the ability to solve problems. Because there are plenty of crises and problems to go around for every person and every organization, strategists ought to bring their time and creative energy to bear on solving the most pressing problems of the day. Managing by crisis is actually a form of reacting rather than acting and of letting events dictate the what and when of management decisions.
- *Managing by Subjectives*—built on the idea that there is no general plan for which way to go and what to do; just do the best you can to accomplish what you think should be done. In short, "Do your own thing, the best way you know how" (sometimes referred to as *the mystery approach to decision making* because subordinates are left to figure out what is happening and why).
- *Managing by Hope*—based on the fact that the future is laden with great uncertainty and that if we try and do not succeed, then we hope our second (or third) attempt will succeed. Decisions are predicated on the hope that they will work and the good times are just around the corner, especially if luck and good fortune are on our side![2]

The Balanced Scorecard

Developed in 1993 by Harvard Business School professors Robert Kaplan and David Norton, and refined continually through today, the Balanced Scorecard is a strategy evaluation and control technique.[3] *Balanced Scorecard* derives its name from the perceived need of firms to "balance" financial measures that are oftentimes used exclusively in strategy evaluation and control with nonfinancial measures such as product quality and customer service. An effective Balanced Scorecard contains a carefully chosen combination of strategic and financial objectives tailored to the company's business. As a tool to manage and evaluate strategy, the Balanced Scorecard is currently in use at Sears, United Parcel Service, 3M Corporation, Heinz, and hundreds of other firms. For example, 3M Corporation has a financial objective to achieve annual growth in earnings per share of 10 percent or better, as well as a strategic objective to have at least 30 percent of sales come from products introduced in the past four years. The overall aim of the Balanced Scorecard is to "balance" shareholder objectives with customer and operational objectives. Obviously, these sets of objectives interrelate and many even conflict. For example, customers want low price and high service, which may conflict with shareholders' desire for a high return on their investment. The Balanced Scorecard concept is consistent with the notions of continuous improvement in management (CIM) and total quality management (TQM).

Although the Balanced Scorecard concept is covered in more detail in Chapter 9 as it relates to evaluating strategies, note here that firms should establish objectives and evaluate strategies on items other than financial measures. This is the basic tenet of the Balanced Scorecard. Financial measures and ratios are vitally important. However, of equal importance are factors such as customer service, employee morale, product quality, pollution abatement, business ethics, social responsibility, community involvement, and other such items. In conjunction with financial measures, these "softer" factors comprise an integral part of both the objective-setting process and the strategy-evaluation process. These factors can vary by organization, but such items, along with financial measures, comprise the essence of a Balanced Scorecard. A Balanced Scorecard for a firm is simply a listing of all key objectives to work toward, along with an associated time dimension of when each objective is to be accomplished, as well as a primary responsibility or contact person, department, or division for each objective.

Types of Strategies

The model illustrated in Figure 5-1 provides a conceptual basis for applying strategic management. Defined and exemplified in Table 5-4, alternative strategies that an enterprise could pursue can be categorized into 11 actions: forward integration, backward

FIGURE 5-1

A Comprehensive Strategic-Management Model

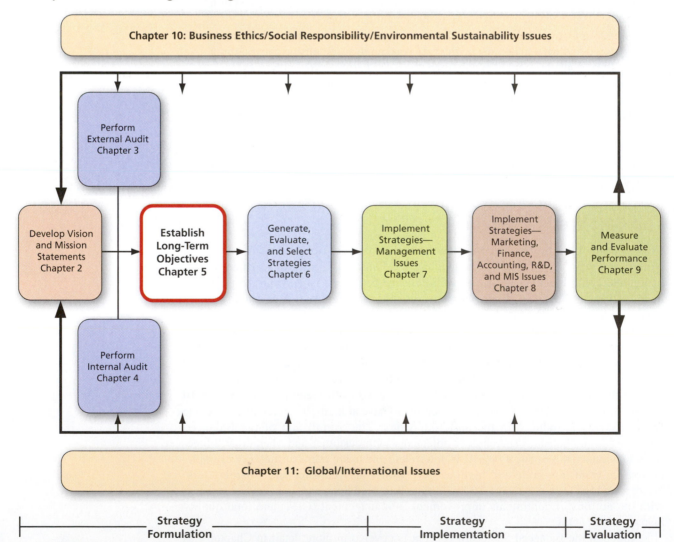

Source: Fred R. David, "How Companies Define Their Mission," *Long Range Planning* 22, no. 3 (June 1988): 40.

TABLE 5-4 Alternative Strategies Defined and Exemplified

Strategy	Definition	2009 Examples
Forward Integration	Gaining ownership or increased control over distributors or retailers	PepsiCo launched a hostile takeover of Pepsi Bottling Group after its $4.2 billion offer was rejected
Backward Integration	Seeking ownership or increased control of a firm's suppliers	Chinese carmaker Geely Automobile Holdings Ltd. purchased Australian car-parts maker Drivetrain Systems International Pty. Ltd.
Horizontal Integration	Seeking ownership or increased control over competitors	Pfizer acquires Wyeth; both are huge drug companies
Market Penetration	Seeking increased market share for present products or services in present markets through greater marketing efforts	Coke spending millions on its new slogan "Open Happiness"
Market Development	Introducing present products or services into new geographic area	Time Warner purchased 31 percent of Central European Media Enterprises Ltd. in order to expand into Romania, Czech Republic, Ukraine, and Bulgaria
Product Development	Seeking increased sales by improving present products or services or developing new ones	News Corp.'s book publisher HarperCollins began producing audio books for download, such as Jeff Jarvis's "What Would Google Do?"
Related Diversification	Adding new but related products or services	Sprint Nextel Corp. diversified from the cell phone business by partnering with Garmin Ltd. to deliver wireless Internet services into GPS machines
Unrelated Diversification	Adding new, unrelated products or services	Cisco Systems Inc. entered the camcorder business by acquiring Pure Digital Technology
Retrenchment	Regrouping through cost and asset reduction to reverse declining sales and profit	The world's largest steelmaker, ArcelorMittal, shut down half of its plants and laid off thousands of employees even amid worker protests worldwide
Divestiture	Selling a division or part of an organization	The British airport firm BAA Ltd. divested three UK airports
Liquidation	Selling all of a company's assets, in parts, for their tangible worth	Michigan newspapers such as the *Ann Arbor News*, *Detroit Free Press,* and *Detroit News* liquidated hard-copy operations

integration, horizontal integration, market penetration, market development, product development, related diversification, unrelated diversification, retrenchment, divestiture, and liquidation. Each alternative strategy has countless variations. For example, market penetration can include adding salespersons, increasing advertising expenditures, couponing, and using similar actions to increase market share in a given geographic area.

Many, if not most, organizations simultaneously pursue a combination of two or more strategies, but a *combination strategy* can be exceptionally risky if carried too far. No organization can afford to pursue all the strategies that might benefit the firm. Difficult decisions must be made. Priority must be established. Organizations, like individuals, have limited resources. Both organizations and individuals must choose among alternative strategies and avoid excessive indebtedness.

Hansen and Smith explain that strategic planning involves "choices that risk resources" and "trade-offs that sacrifice opportunity." In other words, if you have a strategy to go north, then you must buy snowshoes and warm jackets (spend resources) and forgo the opportunity of "faster population growth in southern states." You cannot have a strategy to go north and then take a step east, south, or west "just to be on the safe side." Firms spend resources and focus on a finite number of opportunities in pursuing strategies to achieve an uncertain outcome in the future. Strategic planning is much more than a roll of the dice; it is a wager based on predictions and hypotheses that are continually tested and refined by knowledge, research, experience, and learning. Survival of the firm itself may hinge on your strategic plan.[4]

Organizations cannot do too many things well because resources and talents get spread thin and competitors gain advantage. In large diversified companies, a combination strategy is commonly employed when different divisions pursue different strategies. Also, organizations struggling to survive may simultaneously employ a combination of several defensive strategies, such as divestiture, liquidation, and retrenchment.

Levels of Strategies

Strategy making is not just a task for top executives. As discussed in Chapter 1, middle- and lower-level managers too must be involved in the strategic-planning process to the extent possible. In large firms, there are actually four levels of strategies: corporate, divisional, functional, and operational—as illustrated in Figure 5-2. However, in small firms, there are actually three levels of strategies: company, functional, and operational.

In large firms, the persons primarily responsible for having effective strategies at the various levels include the CEO at the corporate level; the president or executive vice president at the divisional level; the respective chief finance officer (CFO), chief information officer (CIO), human resource manager (HRM), chief marketing officer (CMO), and so on, at the functional level; and the plant manager, regional sales manager, and so on, at the operational level. In small firms, the persons primarily responsible for having effective strategies at the various levels include the business owner or president at the company level and then the same range of persons at the lower two levels, as with a large firm.

It is important to note that all persons responsible for strategic planning at the various levels ideally participate and understand the strategies at the other organizational levels to help ensure coordination, facilitation, and commitment while avoiding inconsistency, inefficiency, and miscommunication. Plant managers, for example, need to understand and be supportive of the overall corporate strategic plan (game plan) while the president and the CEO need to be knowledgeable of strategies being employed in various sales territories and manufacturing plants.

FIGURE 5-2

Levels of Strategies with Persons Most Responsible

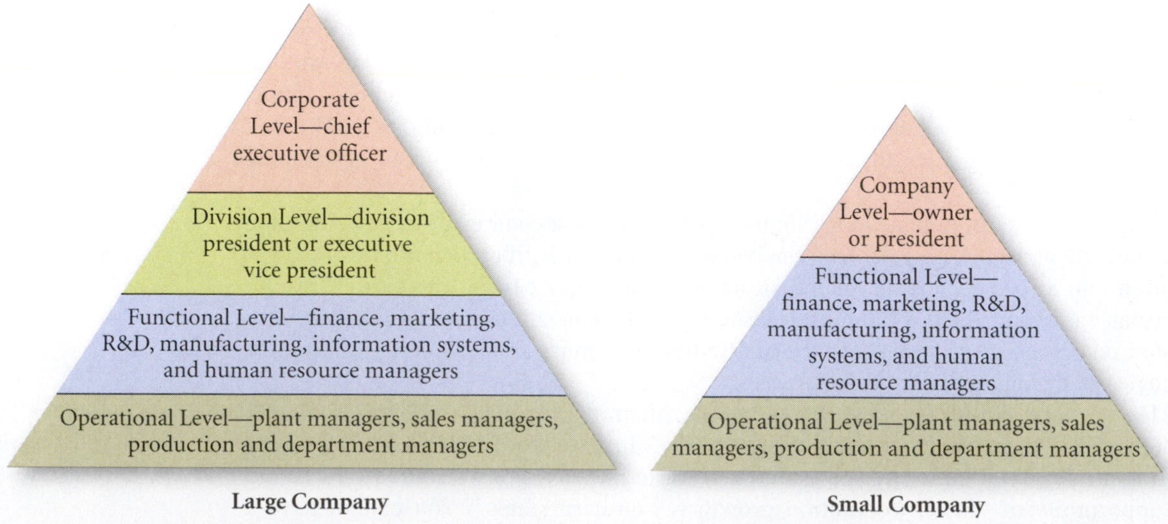

Corporate Level—chief executive officer

Division Level—division president or executive vice president

Functional Level—finance, marketing, R&D, manufacturing, information systems, and human resource managers

Operational Level—plant managers, sales managers, production and department managers

Large Company

Company Level—owner or president

Functional Level—finance, marketing, R&D, manufacturing, information systems, and human resource managers

Operational Level—plant managers, sales managers, production and department managers

Small Company

Integration Strategies

Forward integration, backward integration, and horizontal integration are sometimes collectively referred to as *vertical integration* strategies. Vertical integration strategies allow a firm to gain control over distributors, suppliers, and/or competitors.

Forward Integration

Forward integration involves gaining ownership or increased control over distributors or retailers. Increasing numbers of manufacturers (suppliers) today are pursuing a forward integration strategy by establishing Web sites to directly sell products to consumers. This strategy is causing turmoil in some industries. For example, Microsoft is opening its own retail stores, a forward integration strategy similar to rival Apple Inc., which currently has more than 200 stores around the world. Microsoft wants to learn firsthand about what consumers want and how they buy. CompUSA Inc. recently closed most of its retail stores, and neither Hewlett-Packard nor IBM have retail stores. Some Microsoft shareholders are concerned that the company's plans to open stores will irk existing retail partners such as Best Buy.

Automobile dealers have for many years pursued forward integration, perhaps too much. Ford has almost 4,000 dealers compared to Toyota, which has fewer than 2,000 U.S. dealers. That means the average Toyota dealer sold, for example, 1,628 vehicles in 2007 compared to 236 vehicles for Ford dealers. GM, Ford, and Chrysler are all reducing their number of dealers dramatically.

The Canadian company Research in Motion (RIM) opened its first online store for BlackBerry applications in April 2009. RIM is looking to tap a market for software made popular by Apple and its iPhone. BlackBerry users can download the new RIM storefront from the main RIM Web site, but then they need to buy applications using PayPal.

An effective means of implementing forward integration is *franchising*. Approximately 2,000 companies in about 50 different industries in the United States use franchising to distribute their products or services. Businesses can expand rapidly by franchising because costs and opportunities are spread among many individuals. Total sales by franchises in the United States are annually about $1 trillion.

In today's credit crunch reduced availability of financing, franchiser firms are more and more breaking tradition and helping franchisees out with liquidity needs. For example, RE/MAX International will finance 50 percent of its initial $25,000 franchise fee. Coverall Cleaning Concepts lends up to $6,800 of its initial franchise fee. Persons interested in becoming franchisees should go onto franchising blogs, such as Bleu MauMau, Franchise-Chat, Franchise Pundit, Rush On Business, Unhappy Franchisee, and WikidFranchise.org. These sites offer inside news, advice, and comments by people already owning franchise businesses.

However, a growing trend is for franchisees, who for example may operate 10 franchised restaurants, stores, or whatever, to buy out their part of the business from their franchiser (corporate owner). There is a growing rift between franchisees and franchisers as the segment often outperforms the parent. For example, McDonald's today owns less than 23 percent of its 32,000 restaurants, down from 26 percent in 2006. Restaurant chains are increasingly being pressured to own fewer of their locations. McDonald's sold 1,600 of its Latin America and Caribbean restaurants to Woods Staton, a former McDonald's executive. Companies such as McDonald's are using proceeds from the sale of company stores/restaurants to franchisees to buy back company stock, pay higher dividends, and make other investments to benefit shareholders.

These six guidelines indicate when forward integration may be an especially effective strategy:[5]

- When an organization's present distributors are especially expensive, or unreliable, or incapable of meeting the firm's distribution needs.
- When the availability of quality distributors is so limited as to offer a competitive advantage to those firms that integrate forward.
- When an organization competes in an industry that is growing and is expected to continue to grow markedly; this is a factor because forward integration reduces an organization's ability to diversify if its basic industry falters.

- When an organization has both the capital and human resources needed to manage the new business of distributing its own products.
- When the advantages of stable production are particularly high; this is a consideration because an organization can increase the predictability of the demand for its output through forward integration.
- When present distributors or retailers have high profit margins; this situation suggests that a company profitably could distribute its own products and price them more competitively by integrating forward.

Backward Integration

Both manufacturers and retailers purchase needed materials from suppliers. *Backward integration* is a strategy of seeking ownership or increased control of a firm's suppliers. This strategy can be especially appropriate when a firm's current suppliers are unreliable, too costly, or cannot meet the firm's needs.

When you buy a box of Pampers diapers at Wal-Mart, a scanner at the store's checkout counter instantly zaps an order to Procter & Gamble Company. In contrast, in most hospitals, reordering supplies is a logistical nightmare. Inefficiency caused by lack of control of suppliers in the health-care industry, however, is rapidly changing as many giant health-care purchasers, such as the U.S. Defense Department and Columbia/HCA Healthcare Corporation, move to require electronic bar codes on every supply item purchased. This allows instant tracking and recording without invoices and paperwork. Of the estimated $83 billion spent annually on hospital supplies, industry reports indicate that $11 billion can be eliminated through more effective backward integration.

In a major strategic shift to design its own computer chips, Apple Inc. in 2009 began a backward integration strategy to shield Apple technology from rival firms. Apple envisions soon to produce its own internally developed chips for its iPhone and iPod Touch devices. Online job postings from Apple describe dozens of chip-related positions. Apple's new strategy also is aimed at sharing fewer details about Apple technology plans with external chip suppliers. This new backward integration strategy marks a break from a long-term trend among most big electronics companies to outsource the development of chips and other components to external suppliers.

Some industries in the United States, such as the automotive and aluminum industries, are reducing their historical pursuit of backward integration. Instead of owning their suppliers, companies negotiate with several outside suppliers. Ford and Chrysler buy over half of their component parts from outside suppliers such as TRW, Eaton, General Electric, and Johnson Controls. *De-integration* makes sense in industries that have global sources of supply. Companies today shop around, play one seller against another, and go with the best deal. Global competition is also spurring firms to reduce their number of suppliers and to demand higher levels of service and quality from those they keep. Although traditionally relying on many suppliers to ensure uninterrupted supplies and low prices, American firms now are following the lead of Japanese firms, which have far fewer suppliers and closer, long-term relationships with those few. "Keeping track of so many suppliers is onerous," says Mark Shimelonis, formerly of Xerox.

Seven guidelines for when backward integration may be an especially effective strategy are:[6]

- When an organization's present suppliers are especially expensive, or unreliable, or incapable of meeting the firm's needs for parts, components, assemblies, or raw materials.
- When the number of suppliers is small and the number of competitors is large.
- When an organization competes in an industry that is growing rapidly; this is a factor because integrative-type strategies (forward, backward, and horizontal) reduce an organization's ability to diversify in a declining industry.
- When an organization has both capital and human resources to manage the new business of supplying its own raw materials.

- When the advantages of stable prices are particularly important; this is a factor because an organization can stabilize the cost of its raw materials and the associated price of its product(s) through backward integration.
- When present supplies have high profit margins, which suggests that the business of supplying products or services in the given industry is a worthwhile venture.
- When an organization needs to quickly acquire a needed resource.

Horizontal Integration

Horizontal integration refers to a strategy of seeking ownership of or increased control over a firm's competitors. One of the most significant trends in strategic management today is the increased use of horizontal integration as a growth strategy. Mergers, acquisitions, and takeovers among competitors allow for increased economies of scale and enhanced transfer of resources and competencies. Kenneth Davidson makes the following observation about horizontal integration:

> The trend towards horizontal integration seems to reflect strategists' misgivings about their ability to operate many unrelated businesses. Mergers between direct competitors are more likely to create efficiencies than mergers between unrelated businesses, both because there is a greater potential for eliminating duplicate facilities and because the management of the acquiring firm is more likely to understand the business of the target.[7]

These five guidelines indicate when horizontal integration may be an especially effective strategy:[8]

- When an organization can gain monopolistic characteristics in a particular area or region without being challenged by the federal government for "tending substantially" to reduce competition.
- When an organization competes in a growing industry.
- When increased economies of scale provide major competitive advantages.
- When an organization has both the capital and human talent needed to successfully manage an expanded organization.
- When competitors are faltering due to a lack of managerial expertise or a need for particular resources that an organization possesses; note that horizontal integration would not be appropriate if competitors are doing poorly, because in that case overall industry sales are declining.

Intensive Strategies

Market penetration, market development, and product development are sometimes referred to as *intensive strategies* because they require intensive efforts if a firm's competitive position with existing products is to improve.

Market Penetration

A *market penetration* strategy seeks to increase market share for present products or services in present markets through greater marketing efforts. This strategy is widely used alone and in combination with other strategies. Market penetration includes increasing the number of salespersons, increasing advertising expenditures, offering extensive sales promotion items, or increasing publicity efforts. As indicated in Table 5-4, Coke in 2009/2010 spent millions on its new advertising slogan, "Open Happiness," which replaced "The Coke Side of Life."

These five guidelines indicate when market penetration may be an especially effective strategy:[9]

- When current markets are not saturated with a particular product or service.
- When the usage rate of present customers could be increased significantly.

- When the market shares of major competitors have been declining while total industry sales have been increasing.
- When the correlation between dollar sales and dollar marketing expenditures historically has been high.
- When increased economies of scale provide major competitive advantages.

Market Development

Market development involves introducing present products or services into new geographic areas. For example, Retailers such as Wal-Mart Stores, Carrefour SA, and Tesco PLC are expanding further into China in 2009/2010 even in a world of slumping sales. Tesco is opening fewer stores in Britain to divert capital expenditures to China. French hypermarket chain Carrefour is opening 28 stores in China in 2009, up from 22 in 2008. Wal-Mart opened 30 stores in China in 2008 and plans to nearly double that number in 2009. Wal-Mart had roughly 250 stores in China at year-end 2009. Housing goods giant Ikea plans to build two more stores in China in 2009 to have eight stores total. All of these market development strategies come in the face of a slowing Chinese economy and faltering consumer confidence among Chinese consumers.

Delta Air Lines in 2009 began serving 15 new international destinations as part of a strategy by the Atlanta-based carrier to derive more traffic from international routes. This market development strategy is being implemented largely by deploying its recently acquired Northwest Airlines big jets from unprofitable domestic routes to global routes, especially into Asia, where Delta previously had only a few routes.

PepsiCo Inc. is spending $1 billion in China from 2009 to 2012 to build more plants, specifically in western and interior areas of China. Also in China, PepsiCo is developing products tailored to Chinese consumers, building a larger sales force, and expanding research and development efforts. China is Pepsi's second-largest beverage market by volume, behind the United States. Pepsi owns Lay's potato chips and in China sells the chips with Beijing duck flavor. Pepsi has 41 percent share of the potato chip market in China. Pepsi's new market development strategy is aimed primarily at rival Coke, which dominates Pepsi in the carbonated-soft-drink sector in China; Coke has a 51.9 percent share of the market to Pepsi's 32.6 percent.

Yum! Brands Inc., the parent company of Pizza Hut, KFC, and Taco Bell, recently said it would open 500 new KFC restaurants in China in 2009. In addition to these stores, Yum Brands is opening 900 other restaurants outside the United States in 2009. Yum Brands' most profitable brand has been Taco Bell, so the company plans to open these restaurants in both Spain and India in 2009. Taco Bell's target market is young consumers ages 16 to 24. The company's new strategic plan includes selling many if not most of its stores worldwide to existing franchisees or new investors.

These six guidelines indicate when market development may be an especially effective strategy:[10]

- When new channels of distribution are available that are reliable, inexpensive, and of good quality.
- When an organization is very successful at what it does.
- When new untapped or unsaturated markets exist.
- When an organization has the needed capital and human resources to manage expanded operations.
- When an organization has excess production capacity.
- When an organization's basic industry is rapidly becoming global in scope.

Product Development

Product development is a strategy that seeks increased sales by improving or modifying present products or services. Product development usually entails large research and development expenditures. Google's new Chrome OS operating system illuminates years of monies spent on product development. Google expects Chrome OS to overtake Microsoft Windows by 2015.

These five guidelines indicate when product development may be an especially effective strategy to pursue:[11]

- When an organization has successful products that are in the maturity stage of the product life cycle; the idea here is to attract satisfied customers to try new (improved) products as a result of their positive experience with the organization's present products or services.
- When an organization competes in an industry that is characterized by rapid technological developments.
- When major competitors offer better-quality products at comparable prices.
- When an organization competes in a high-growth industry.
- When an organization has especially strong research and development capabilities.

Diversification Strategies

There are two general types of *diversification strategies*: related and unrelated. Businesses are said to be *related* when their value chains posses competitively valuable cross-business strategic fits; businesses are said to be *unrelated* when their value chains are so dissimilar that no competitively valuable cross-business relationships exist.[12] Most companies favor related diversification strategies in order to capitalize on synergies as follows:

- Transferring competitively valuable expertise, technological know-how, or other capabilities from one business to another.
- Combining the related activities of separate businesses into a single operation to achieve lower costs.
- Exploiting common use of a well-known brand name.
- Cross-business collaboration to create competitively valuable resource strengths and capabilities.[13]

Diversification strategies are becoming less popular as organizations are finding it more difficult to manage diverse business activities. In the 1960s and 1970s, the trend was to diversify so as not to be dependent on any single industry, but the 1980s saw a general reversal of that thinking. Diversification is now on the retreat. Michael Porter, of the Harvard Business School, says, "Management found it couldn't manage the beast." Hence businesses are selling, or closing, less profitable divisions to focus on core businesses.

The greatest risk of being in a single industry is having all of the firm's eggs in one basket. Although many firms are successful operating in a single industry, new technologies, new products, or fast-shifting buyer preferences can decimate a particular business. For example, digital cameras are decimating the film and film processing industry, and cell phones have permanently altered the long-distance telephone calling industry.

Diversification must do more than simply spread business risk across different industries, however, because shareholders could accomplish this by simply purchasing equity in different firms across different industries or by investing in mutual funds. Diversification makes sense only to the extent the strategy adds more to shareholder value than what shareholders could accomplish acting individually. Thus, the chosen industry for diversification must be attractive enough to yield consistently high returns on investment and offer potential across the operating divisions for synergies greater than those entities could achieve alone.

A few companies today, however, pride themselves on being conglomerates, from small firms such as Pentair Inc., and Blount International to huge companies such as Textron, Allied Signal, Emerson Electric, General Electric, Viacom, and Samsung. Conglomerates prove that focus and diversity are not always mutually exclusive.

Many strategists contend that firms should "stick to the knitting" and not stray too far from the firms' basic areas of competence. However, diversification is still sometimes an appropriate strategy, especially when the company is competing in an unattractive industry. For example, United Technologies is diversifying away from its core aviation business due to the slumping airline industry. United Technologies now owns British electronic-security company Chubb PLC, as well as Otis Elevator Company and Carrier air conditioning to reduce its dependence on the volatile airline industry. United Technologies also owns UTC Fire & Security, Pratt & Whitney, Hamilton Sundstrand, and Sikorsky Black Hawk Helicopters. However, almost of all of the company's divisions expect a drop in sales in 2009, and so the firm is laying off thousands of employees. Only the Sikorsky division is expected to be profitable in 2009.

Hamish Maxwell, Philip Morris's former CEO, says, "We want to become a consumer-products company." Diversification makes sense for Philip Morris because cigarette consumption is declining, product liability suits are a risk, and some investors reject tobacco stocks on principle.

Related Diversification

Google's stated strategy is to organize all the world's information into searchable form, diversifying the firm beyond its roots as a Web search engine that sells advertising. The maker of jam, peanut butter, and Crisco oils, J. M. Smuckers Co. recently completed the acquisition of Procter & Gamble's Folger's coffee business for $2.65 billion, which nearly doubled Smuckers's annual sales. Smuckers continues to strive to acquire related food and consumer brand businesses as it pursues related diversification.

When Merck & Co. acquired rival Schering-Plough Corp for $41.1 billion in 2009, that acquisition brought to Merck three new, related businesses. The three new areas of business are biotech, consumer health, and animal health. In addition, the acquisition brought to Merck an expanded presence in Brazil, China, and other emerging markets.

Based in Baltimore, the sports apparel maker Under Armour pursued related diversification in 2009 when it introduced athletic "running" shoes for the first time. This strategy broadened Under Armour's appeal from boys and young men to women, older consumers, and more casual athletes. The athletic footwear business is dominated by Nike and Adidas, but Under Armour uses sophisticated design software, new manufacturing techniques, the latest in material engineering, and robust information technology systems to produce all its products. Under Armour's 2009 sales are expected to increase 20 percent to $900 million.

In a related diversification move in 2009, Tyson Foods entered the dog food business, selling refrigerated pet food targeted to consumers who give their pets everything from clothes and car seats to cemetery graves. Prior to this move by Tyson, meatpacking companies has been content to sell scraps such as chicken fat and by-products to makers of canned and dry pet food. Scott Morris of Freshpet Company in Secaucus, New Jersey, says this move by Tyson will change the fact that "pet food today looks the same as it did 30 years ago."

Six guidelines for when related diversification may be an effective strategy are as follows.[14]

- When an organization competes in a no-growth or a slow-growth industry.
- When adding new, but related, products would significantly enhance the sales of current products.
- When new, but related, products could be offered at highly competitive prices.
- When new, but related, products have seasonal sales levels that counterbalance an organization's existing peaks and valleys.
- When an organization's products are currently in the declining stage of the product's life cycle.
- When an organization has a strong management team.

Unrelated Diversification

An unrelated diversification strategy favors capitalizing on a portfolio of businesses that are capable of delivering excellent financial performance in their respective industries, rather than striving to capitalize on value chain strategic fits among the businesses. Firms that employ unrelated diversification continually search across different industries for companies that can be acquired for a deal and yet have potential to provide a high return on investment. Pursuing unrelated diversification entails being on the hunt to acquire companies whose assets are undervalued, or companies that are financially distressed, or companies that have high growth prospects but are short on investment capital. An obvious drawback of unrelated diversification is that the parent firm must have an excellent top management team that plans, organizes, motivates, delegates, and controls effectively. It is much more difficult to manage businesses in many industries than in a single industry. However, some firms are successful pursuing unrelated diversification, such as Walt Disney, which owns ABC, and General Electric, which owns NBC.

Many more firms have failed at unrelated diversification than have succeeded due to immense management challenges. However, unrelated diversification can be good, as it is for Cendant Corp., which owns the real-estate firm Century 21, the car-rental agency Avis, the travel-booking sites Orbitz and Flairview Travel, and the hotel brands Days Inn and Howard Johnson.

In what can be considered an unrelated diversification strategy, Dell Inc. recently began producing smart phones, which are similar to Apple's iPhone and Research in Motion's Web browsing phones. Dell has continued to lose market share with a 13.7 percent share of the personal computer, down from 14.6 percent.

San Diego–based Qualcomm Inc. recently diversified beyond cell phones into desktop hardware. The company's strategy is to bring Web access to places in the world that have cell phone networks but do not have Internet access because it is impractical or unafford-able. Qualcomm is test marketing its new device called Kayak. The company expects Intel to be its main competitor in this new product area.

IBM in 2009 entered the water management business with the creation of new desalination-membrane technology that removes arsenic and boron salts from contaminated groundwater. The company expects to license the technology rather than build desalination plants itself. But IBM has begun installing systems of water sensors and software to monitor water pipes, reservoirs, rivers, and harbors. It is all part of IBM's 2009 Big Green Innovations Initiative. The firm has always been known as Big Blue.

Cisco Systems diversified in 2009 by jumping into the fiercely competitive computer server market, placing it in direct competition for the first time with its longtime partners Hewlett-Packard and IBM. Before this strategic move, Cisco was primarily in the router and switch business, which directs Internet traffic. This new Cisco strategy highlights the fact that data centers are becoming a new battleground as large customers manage Internet traffic and energy costs escalate. Michael Corrado at IBM says it is not unusual for tech companies to be both partners and competitors. However, HP's Jim Ganthier says, "HP is delivering today what Cisco is promising tomorrow."[15]

French aerospace manufacturer Safran SA recently diversified further away from jet propulsion into maintenance and service operations by buying 81 percent of General Electric Company's Homeland Protection division for $580 million in cash. This new division of Safran focuses on explosive and narcotics detection. GE and Safran have worked together for more than 30 years, including a joint venture that produces the CFM commercial-jet engine.

Ten guidelines for when unrelated diversification may be an especially effective strategy are:[16]

- When revenues derived from an organization's current products or services would increase significantly by adding the new, unrelated products.
- When an organization competes in a highly competitive and/or a no-growth industry, as indicated by low industry profit margins and returns.
- When an organization's present channels of distribution can be used to market the new products to current customers.
- When the new products have countercyclical sales patterns compared to an organization's present products.
- When an organization's basic industry is experiencing declining annual sales and profits.
- When an organization has the capital and managerial talent needed to compete successfully in a new industry.
- When an organization has the opportunity to purchase an unrelated business that is an attractive investment opportunity.

- When there exists financial synergy between the acquired and acquiring firm. (Note that a key difference between related and unrelated diversification is that the former should be based on some commonality in markets, products, or technology, whereas the latter should be based more on profit considerations.)
- When existing markets for an organization's present products are saturated.
- When antitrust action could be charged against an organization that historically has concentrated on a single industry.

Defensive Strategies

In addition to integrative, intensive, and diversification strategies, organizations also could pursue retrenchment, divestiture, or liquidation.

Retrenchment

Retrenchment occurs when an organization regroups through cost and asset reduction to reverse declining sales and profits. Sometimes called a *turnaround* or *reorganizational strategy,* retrenchment is designed to fortify an organization's basic distinctive competence. During retrenchment, strategists work with limited resources and face pressure from shareholders, employees, and the media. Retrenchment can entail selling off land and buildings to raise needed cash, pruning product lines, closing marginal businesses, closing obsolete factories, automating processes, reducing the number of employees, and instituting expense control systems.

Smithfield Foods, the world's largest pork processor, is closing 6 of its 40 plants, laying off 1,800 employees, and cutting production by 10 percent in 2009 in efforts to stop the liquidity drain on the firm. The retrenchment moves are expected to save the firm $55 million in 2010 and $125 million in 2011. Pork is the world's most consumed meat by volume.[17]

Starbucks has launched a massive retrenchment strategy in efforts to save the company. CEO Howard Schultz says Starbucks will soon close 300 underperforming, company-operated stores worldwide, including 200 in the United States. These closing are on top of 600 recent Starbucks closings in the United States and 61 closings in Australia. However, the firm plans to open 140 stores in the United States in 2009 and open 170 stores outside the United States. Starbucks plans to cut 700 corporate and nonretail positions globally. In addition, as part of Starbucks's strategy to survive the global recession, the company will enter the value-meal race to combat McDonald's new McCafe coffee bars, which are spreading nationally and likely soon globally.

Pursing a heavy retrenchment strategy to survive, Citigroup recently announced that it is cutting 52,000 more jobs. This is the largest corporate layoff announcement since 1993, when IBM cut 60,000 jobs. Citigroup had already cut 23,000 jobs in 2008 as its stock price fell 70 percent in that year alone.

Tokyo-based Sony Corp. is cutting 8,000 jobs and closing 6 of its 57 factories by March 2010 as prices of televisions fall and consumer spending in general declines. Sony has also been hurt by falling demand for digital cameras and the sharp rise in the yen against major currencies, which has cut into profits by reducing its overseas revenue when converted back into the Japanese currency.

Most banks are pursuing retrenchment. A total of 25 banks failed in 2008, including 16 with less than $1 billion in assets. The three largest bank failures by size in 2008 were Washington Mutual in Seattle, Washington, IndyMac Bank in Pasadena, California, and Downey Savings and Loan Association in Newport Beach, California.

Macy's Inc. in 2009 eliminated 7,000 jobs among its 840 department stores and cut its dividend by 62 percent. The firm also ended merit pay increases for executives and slashed its 2009 capital-spending budget by $150 million to about $450 million, down from the planned amount of $1 billion. Also as part of its retrenchment strategy, Macy's bought back $950 million in debt. Macy's expects sales to be down about 8 percent on average per store in 2009. The company is merging its four divisions under one person and discounting its merchandise substantially.

The largest U.S. chemical company by revenue is Dow Chemical Company, and Dow is pursuing an aggressive retrenchment strategy. Dow recently closed 20 plants, put on idle 180 more plants, and laid off more than 5,000 employees.

In some cases, *bankruptcy* can be an effective type of retrenchment strategy. Bankruptcy can allow a firm to avoid major debt obligations and to void union contracts. There are five major types of bankruptcy: Chapter 7, Chapter 9, Chapter 11, Chapter 12, and Chapter 13.

Chapter 7 bankruptcy is a liquidation procedure used only when a corporation sees no hope of being able to operate successfully or to obtain the necessary creditor agreement. All the organization's assets are sold in parts for their tangible worth.

Chapter 9 bankruptcy applies to municipalities. A municipality that successfully declared bankruptcy is Camden, New Jersey, the state's poorest city and the fifth-poorest city in the United States. A crime-ridden city of 87,000, Camden received $62.5 million in state aid and has withdrawn its bankruptcy petition. Between 1980 and 2000, only 18 U.S. cities declared bankruptcy. Some states do not allow municipalities to declare bankruptcy.

Chapter 11 bankruptcy allows organizations to reorganize and come back after filing a petition for protection.

Chapter 12 bankruptcy was created by the Family Farmer Bankruptcy Act of 1986. This law became effective in 1987 and provides special relief to family farmers with debt equal to or less than $1.5 million.

Chapter 13 bankruptcy is a reorganization plan similar to Chapter 11, but it is available only to small businesses owned by individuals with unsecured debts of less than $100,000 and secured debts of less than $350,000. The Chapter 13 debtor is allowed to operate the business while a plan is being developed to provide for the successful operation of the business in the future.

More than 60 percent of Fortune 500 companies are incorporated in Wilmington, Delaware, so this city has recently become known as the "bankruptcy capital of the world." More than half of all large U.S. firms that declared bankruptcy in recent years have done so in Wilmington. Personal bankruptcy filings in the United States exceeded 1 million for the first time ever in 2008, coming on the heels of 822,590 and 617,660 filings in 2008 and 2007, respectively.

Telecom-equipment maker Nortel Networks filed for Chapter 11 bankruptcy in 2009 as its heavy debt load would not withstand falling demand. Rival firm Cisco Systems, Alcatel SA of France, Nokia Corp., and Avaya Inc. are sure to benefit from Nortel's demise. Nortel has been plagued by accounting restatements, price cutting, falling demand, and high interest payments.

Instead of emerging from bankruptcy, Nortel Networks is considering selling its two divisions: wireless equipment and telecom systems for offices. Potential buyers such as Avaya Inc. and Siemensw AG and Gores Group LLC and even Cisco Systems are in talks with Nortel.

Pilgrim's Pride, the largest chicken company in the United States, recently declared bankruptcy. Large debt, high feed costs, and lower prices for broilers have crushed the company's operations, especially in the United States. The company's Mexican operations were not included in the bankruptcy filing.

Tribune Company, which owns eight daily major newspapers, including the *Los Angeles Times* and *Chicago Tribune*, as well as the Chicago Cubs baseball team, recently declared bankruptcy. Tribune is the nation's second largest newspaper chain, but also owns quite a few television stations.

The year 2008 was especially tough for many financial firms, retailers, restaurants, and other companies. It was so rough that a record number of firms declared bankruptcy. Table 5-5 describes some well-known firms that recently declared Chapter 11 bankruptcy.

Five guidelines for when retrenchment may be an especially effective strategy to pursue are as follows:[18]

• When an organization has a clearly distinctive competence but has failed consistently to meet its objectives and goals over time.
• When an organization is one of the weaker competitors in a given industry.
• When an organization is plagued by inefficiency, low profitability, poor employee morale, and pressure from stockholders to improve performance.

TABLE 5-5 Companies That Recently Declared Chapter 11 Bankruptcy

Tribune Company—This media conglomerate that owns the *Chicago Tribune*, the *Los Angeles Times*, the Chicago Cubs, and Wrigley Field recently declared bankruptcy.

Advantage—This car rental company filed for bankruptcy in December 2008 as cash-strapped consumers do less traveling during a slumping economy. Advantage is closing about 40 percent of its U.S. retail locations.

Bally Total Fitness—For the second time in two years, this gym operator filed for bankruptcy protection in December 2008. The company operates nearly 350 facilities nationwide.

Pilgrim's Pride—U.S. meat makers' profits have shrunk in the wake of high feed prices and excessive debt. In December 2008, Pilgrim's Pride, the largest U.S. chicken producer, filed for Chapter 11 bankruptcy protection.

Hawaiian Telcom Communications Inc.—The largest telephone company on the Hawaiian Islands, this firm filed for Chapter 11 bankruptcy protection in December 2008. The company cited increased competition, economic volatility, and its failure to meet capital expenditure needs.

Circuit City—This electronics retailer recently closed 155 of its more than 700 stores and declared Chapter 11 bankruptcy.

Mattress Discounters—Following $2.9 million in losses in 2008 in the New England market, the firm closed 48 stores and filed for Chapter 11 protection.

Washington Mutual—This huge firm recently filed for bankruptcy protection after selling its banking operations to JPMorgan Chase. It was the biggest bank failure in U.S. history at the time.

Mrs. Fields Famous Brands LLC—The company was founded by housewife Debbi Fields in the late 1970s. Her famous homemade cookies quickly grew in popularity. The company filed for bankruptcy protection.

Tropicana Entertainment—The casino company declared Chapter 11 recently when its New Jersey casino license was revoked. The company has operated in the hotel/hospitality industry for more than 35 years.

Polaroid—Founded in 1937 by Edwin Land, the Massachusetts-based company was most famous for its instant film cameras. Polaroid ceased making cameras in 2007 and announced it will stop selling film in 2009. In December 2008, Polaroid filed for Chapter 11 bankruptcy protection.

- When an organization has failed to capitalize on external opportunities, minimize external threats, take advantage of internal strengths, and overcome internal weaknesses over time; that is, when the organization's strategic managers have failed (and possibly will be replaced by more competent individuals).
- When an organization has grown so large so quickly that major internal reorganization is needed.

Divestiture

Selling a division or part of an organization is called *divestiture*. Divestiture often is used to raise capital for further strategic acquisitions or investments. Divestiture can be part of an overall retrenchment strategy to rid an organization of businesses that are unprofitable, that require too much capital, or that do not fit well with the firm's other activities. Divestiture has also become a popular strategy for firms to focus on their core businesses and become less diversified. For example, to raise cash, Motorola in 2009 divested its Good Technology mobile e-mail division to Visto Corporation. Both Good Technology and Visto Corp. lag behind market leader Research in Motion Ltd. maker of BlackBerry devices. Motorola has fallen from being the number two maker of cell phones to number 5.

Ailing Lehman Brothers Holdings divested its venture-capital division in 2009 as the firm shed assets to raise cash and pay creditors. The acquiring firm, HarbourVEst Partners LLC, changed the name of the Lehman division to Tenaya Capital.

Cadbury PLC recently sold its Australian drinks business to Asahi Breweries Ltd. of Japan for $811.9 million. Asahi is Japan's largest beer brewer by market share. Just prior to this divestiture, Cadbury had divested its Dr Pepper Snapple business to a private-equity consortium. Table 5-6 gives a few more recent divestitures.

Historically firms have divested their unwanted or poorly performing divisions, but the global recession has witnessed firms simply closing such operations. For example, Home Depot is shutting down its Expo home-design stores; defense and aerospace manufacturer Textron Corp is closing groups that financed real estate deals; Pioneer Corp. will

leadership strategy successfully, a firm must ensure that its total costs across its overall value chain are lower than competitors' total costs. There are two ways to accomplish this:[21]

1. Perform value chain activities more efficiently than rivals and control the factors that drive the costs of value chain activities. Such activities could include altering the plant layout, mastering newly introduced technologies, using common parts or components in different products, simplifying product design, finding ways to operate close to full capacity year-round, and so on.
2. Revamp the firm's overall value chain to eliminate or bypass some cost-producing activities. Such activities could include securing new suppliers or distributors, selling products online, relocating manufacturing facilities, avoiding the use of union labor, and so on.

When employing a cost leadership strategy, a firm must be careful not to use such aggressive price cuts that their own profits are low or nonexistent. Constantly be mindful of cost-saving technological breakthroughs or any other value chain advancements that could erode or destroy the firm's competitive advantage. A Type 1 or Type 2 cost leadership strategy can be especially effective under the following conditions:[22]

1. When price competition among rival sellers is especially vigorous.
2. When the products of rival sellers are essentially identical and supplies are readily available from any of several eager sellers.
3. When there are few ways to achieve product differentiation that have value to buyers.
4. When most buyers use the product in the same ways.
5. When buyers incur low costs in switching their purchases from one seller to another.
6. When buyers are large and have significant power to bargain down prices.
7. When industry newcomers use introductory low prices to attract buyers and build a customer base.

A successful cost leadership strategy usually permeates the entire firm, as evidenced by high efficiency, low overhead, limited perks, intolerance of waste, intensive screening of budget requests, wide spans of control, rewards linked to cost containment, and broad employee participation in cost control efforts. Some risks of pursuing cost leadership are that competitors may imitate the strategy, thus driving overall industry profits down; that technological breakthroughs in the industry may make the strategy ineffective; or that buyer interest may swing to other differentiating features besides price. Several example firms that are well known for their low-cost leadership strategies are Wal-Mart, BIC, McDonald's, Black & Decker, Lincoln Electric, and Briggs & Stratton.

Differentiation Strategies (Type 3)

Different strategies offer different degrees of differentiation. Differentiation does not guarantee competitive advantage, especially if standard products sufficiently meet customer needs or if rapid imitation by competitors is possible. Durable products protected by barriers to quick copying by competitors are best. Successful differentiation can mean greater product flexibility, greater compatibility, lower costs, improved service, less maintenance, greater convenience, or more features. Product development is an example of a strategy that offers the advantages of differentiation.

A differentiation strategy should be pursued only after a careful study of buyers' needs and preferences to determine the feasibility of incorporating one or more differentiating features into a unique product that features the desired attributes. A successful differentiation strategy allows a firm to charge a higher price for its product and to gain customer loyalty because consumers may become strongly attached to the differentiation features. Special features that differentiate one's product can include superior service, spare parts availability, engineering design, product performance, useful life, gas mileage, or ease of use.

A risk of pursuing a differentiation strategy is that the unique product may not be valued highly enough by customers to justify the higher price. When this happens, a cost leadership strategy easily will defeat a differentiation strategy. Another risk of pursuing a differentiation strategy is that competitors may quickly develop ways to copy the differentiating features. Firms thus must find durable sources of uniqueness that cannot be imitated quickly or cheaply by rival firms.

Common organizational requirements for a successful differentiation strategy include strong coordination among the R&D and marketing functions and substantial amenities to attract scientists and creative people. Firms can pursue a differentiation (Type 3) strategy based on many different competitive aspects. For example, Mountain Dew and root beer have a unique taste; Lowe's, Home Depot, and Wal-Mart offer wide selection and one-stop shopping; Dell Computer and FedEx offer superior service; BMW and Porsche offer engineering design and performance; IBM and Hewlett-Packard offer a wide range of products; and E*Trade and Ameritrade offer Internet convenience. Differentiation opportunities exist or can potentially be developed anywhere along the firm's value chain, including supply chain activities, product R&D activities, production and technological activities, manufacturing activities, human resource management activities, distribution activities, or marketing activities.

The most effective differentiation bases are those that are hard or expensive for rivals to duplicate. Competitors are continually trying to imitate, duplicate, and outperform rivals along any differentiation variable that has yielded competitive advantage. For example, when U.S. Airways cut its prices, Delta quickly followed suit. When Caterpillar instituted its quick-delivery-of-spare-parts policy, John Deere soon followed suit. To the extent that differentiating attributes are tough for rivals to copy, a differentiation strategy will be especially effective, but the sources of uniqueness must be time-consuming, cost prohibitive, and simply too burdensome for rivals to match. A firm, therefore, must be careful when employing a differentiation (Type 3) strategy. Buyers will not pay the higher differentiation price unless their perceived value exceeds the price they are paying.[23] Based on such matters as attractive packaging, extensive advertising, quality of sales presentations, quality of Web site, list of customers, professionalism, size of the firm, and/or profitability of the company, perceived value may be more important to customers than actual value.

A Type 3 differentiation strategy can be especially effective under the following conditions:[24]

1. When there are many ways to differentiate the product or service and many buyers perceive these differences as having value.
2. When buyer needs and uses are diverse.
3. When few rival firms are following a similar differentiation approach.
4. When technological change is fast paced and competition revolves around rapidly evolving product features.

Focus Strategies (Type 4 and Type 5)

A successful focus strategy depends on an industry segment that is of sufficient size, has good growth potential, and is not crucial to the success of other major competitors. Strategies such as market penetration and market development offer substantial focusing advantages. Midsize and large firms can effectively pursue focus-based strategies only in conjunction with differentiation or cost leadership–based strategies. All firms in essence follow a differentiated strategy. Because only one firm can differentiate itself with the lowest cost, the remaining firms in the industry must find other ways to differentiate their products.

Focus strategies are most effective when consumers have distinctive preferences or requirements and when rival firms are not attempting to specialize in the same target segment. Sara Lee Corp. is pursuing a focus strategy as it is trying to divest of its European household and personal-care business so the firm can focus on its core food and beverage business. The company is asking about $2 billion for its household business. Sara Lee sells Jimmy Dean sausages and Ball Park Franks and a mix of coffee and baked goods. Possible bidders for its household business are Unilever PLC, Johnson & Johnson, and Colgate-Palmolive.

Risks of pursuing a focus strategy include the possibility that numerous competitors will recognize the successful focus strategy and copy it or that consumer preferences will drift toward the product attributes desired by the market as a whole. An organization using a focus strategy may concentrate on a particular group of customers, geographic markets, or on particular product-line segments to serve a well-defined but narrow market better than competitors who serve a broader market.

A low-cost (Type 4) or best-value (Type 5) focus strategy can be especially attractive under the following conditions:[25]

1. When the target market niche is large, profitable, and growing.
2. When industry leaders do not consider the niche to be crucial to their own success.
3. When industry leaders consider it too costly or difficult to meet the specialized needs of the target market niche while taking care of their mainstream customers.
4. When the industry has many different niches and segments, thereby allowing a focuser to pick a competitively attractive niche suited to its own resources.
5. When few, if any, other rivals are attempting to specialize in the same target segment.

Strategies for Competing in Turbulent, High-Velocity Markets

The world is changing more and more rapidly, and consequently industries and firms themselves are changing faster than ever. Some industries are changing so fast that researchers call them *turbulent, high-velocity markets,* such as telecommunications, medical, biotechnology, pharmaceuticals, computer hardware, software, and virtually all Internet-based industries. High-velocity change is clearly becoming more and more the rule rather than the exception, even in such industries as toys, phones, banking, defense, publishing, and communication.

Meeting the challenge of high-velocity change presents the firm with a choice of whether to react, anticipate, or lead the market in terms of its own strategies. To primarily react to changes in the industry would be a defensive strategy used to counter, for example, unexpected shifts in buyer tastes and technological breakthroughs. The react-to-change strategy would not be as effective as the anticipate-change strategy, which would entail devising and following through with plans for dealing with the expected changes. However, firms ideally strive to be in a position to lead the changes in high-velocity markets, whereby they pioneer new and better technologies and products and set industry standards. Being the leader or pioneer of change in a high-velocity market is an aggressive, offensive strategy that includes rushing next-generation products to market ahead of rivals and being continually proactive in shaping the market to one's own benefit. Although a lead-change strategy is best whenever the firm has the resources to pursue this approach, on occasion even the strongest firms in turbulent industries have to employ the react-to-the-market strategy and the anticipate-the-market strategy.

An example firm, Hewlett-Packard, pursued a lead-change strategy in 2009 in the computer industry, a turbulent, high-velocity market, when the firm introduced glossy, touch-sensitive screens, called TouchSmart desktops. HP is pushing these screens in commercial settings, such as their sale of 50 of these machines to Chicago's O'Hare International Airport.

Means for Achieving Strategies

Cooperation Among Competitors

Strategies that stress cooperation among competitors are being used more. For collaboration between competitors to succeed, both firms must contribute something distinctive, such as technology, distribution, basic research, or manufacturing capacity. But a major risk is that unintended transfers of important skills or technology may occur at organizational levels below where the deal was signed.[26] Information not covered in the formal agreement often gets traded in the day-to-day interactions and dealings of engineers, marketers, and product developers. Firms often give away too much information to rival firms when operating under cooperative agreements! Tighter formal agreements are needed.

Perhaps the best example of rival firms in an industry forming alliances to compete against each other is the airline industry. Today there are three major alliances. With the addition of Continental Airlines, the Star Alliance has 25 airlines such as Air Canada, Spanair, United, and Singapore Airlines; the OneWorld Alliance has 10 airlines such as American, British Air, and LanChile; and finally, SkyTeam Alliance has 15 airlines such as Air France, Delta, and Korean Air. Firms are moving to compete as groups within alliances more and more as it becomes increasingly difficult to survive alone in some industries.

The idea of joining forces with a competitor is not easily accepted by Americans, who often view cooperation and partnerships with skepticism and suspicion. Indeed, joint ventures and cooperative arrangements among competitors demand a certain amount of trust if companies are to combat paranoia about whether one firm will injure the other. However, multinational firms are becoming more globally cooperative, and increasing numbers of domestic firms are joining forces with competitive foreign firms to reap mutual benefits. Kathryn Harrigan at Columbia University says, "Within a decade, most companies will be members of teams that compete against each other." Once major rivals, Google's YouTube and Vivendi SA's Universal Music Group have formed a partnership called Vevo to provide a new music-video service. Google provides the technology and Universal Music provides the content, and both firms share the revenues. The two firms now operate the stand-alone site Vevo.com.

U.S. companies often enter alliances primarily to avoid investments, being more interested in reducing the costs and risks of entering new businesses or markets than in acquiring new skills. In contrast, *learning from the partner* is a major reason why Asian and European firms enter into cooperative agreements. U.S. firms, too, should place learning high on the list of reasons to be cooperative with competitors. U.S. companies often form alliances with Asian firms to gain an understanding of their manufacturing excellence, but Asian competence in this area is not easily transferable. Manufacturing excellence is a complex system that includes employee training and involvement, integration with suppliers, statistical process controls, value engineering, and design. In contrast, U.S. know-how in technology and related areas can be imitated more easily. U.S. firms thus need to be careful not to give away more intelligence than they receive in cooperative agreements with rival Asian firms.

Joint Venture/Partnering

Joint venture is a popular strategy that occurs when two or more companies form a temporary partnership or consortium for the purpose of capitalizing on some opportunity. Often, the two or more sponsoring firms form a separate organization and have shared equity ownership in the new entity. Other types of *cooperative arrangements* include research and development partnerships, cross-distribution agreements, cross-licensing agreements, cross-manufacturing agreements, and joint-bidding consortia. Once bitter rivals, Nokia Corp. and Qualcomm recently formed a cooperative agreement to develop next-generation cell phones for North America to hit the market in mid-2010. Based in Finland, Nokia has roughly 40 percent of the global cell phone market but has lagged behind in North America.

Nokia is also in discussion with Facebook Inc. to form a partnership that would embed parts of the social network into some Nokia phones. Contact information stored in Facebook, for example, could be integrated with the phone's address book. On the phone, when users look up a contact they can see whether their Facebook friends are logged on, send them messages, and post comments on their profile pages. Facebook is also in discussion with Palm Inc. and Motorola Inc. to form other partnerships to integrate Facebook features into cell phones. Facebook has fewer U.S. users than MySpace but has eclipsed MySpace in U.S. visitors from mobile phones. MySpace is owned by News Corporation, which also owns Dow Jones, publisher of the *Wall Street Journal*.

Microsoft, based in Redmond, Washington, and Yahoo, based in Sunnyvale, California, recently resumed talks about search and advertising partnerships as many firms are doing the same—shifting their focus from acquisitions to partnerships.

Joint ventures and cooperative arrangements are being used increasingly because they allow companies to improve communications and networking, to globalize operations, and to minimize risk. Joint ventures and partnerships are often used to pursue an opportunity that is too complex, uneconomical, or risky for a single firm to pursue alone. Such business creations also are used when achieving and sustaining competitive advantage when an industry requires a broader range of competencies and know-how than any one firm can marshal. Kathryn Rudie Harrigan, professor of strategic management at Columbia University, summarizes the trend toward increased joint venturing:

> In today's global business environment of scarce resources, rapid rates of technological change, and rising capital requirements, the important question is no longer "Shall we form a joint venture?" Now the question is "Which joint ventures and cooperative arrangements are most appropriate for our needs and expectations?" followed by "How do we manage these ventures most effectively?"[27]

In a global market tied together by the Internet, joint ventures, and partnerships, alliances are proving to be a more effective way to enhance corporate growth than mergers and acquisitions.[28] Strategic partnering takes many forms, including outsourcing, information sharing, joint marketing, and joint research and development. Many companies, such as Eli Lilly, now host partnership training classes for their managers and partners. There are today more than 10,000 joint ventures formed annually, more than all mergers and acquisitions. There are countless examples of successful strategic alliances, such as Internet coverage.

A major reason why firms are using partnering as a means to achieve strategies is globalization. Wal-Mart's successful joint venture with Mexico's Cifra is indicative of how a domestic firm can benefit immensely by partnering with a foreign company to gain substantial presence in that new country. Technology also is a major reason behind the need to form strategic alliances, with the Internet linking widely dispersed partners. The Internet paved the way and legitimized the need for alliances to serve as the primary means for corporate growth.

Evidence is mounting that firms should use partnering as a means for achieving strategies. However, the sad fact is that most U.S. firms in many industries—such as financial services, forest products, metals, and retailing—still operate in a merger or acquire mode to obtain growth. Partnering is not yet taught at most business schools and is often viewed within companies as a financial issue rather than a strategic issue. However, partnering has become a core competency, a strategic issue of such importance that top management involvement initially and throughout the life of an alliance is vital.[29]

Joint ventures among once rival firms are commonly being used to pursue strategies ranging from retrenchment to market development.

Although ventures and partnerships are preferred over mergers as a means for achieving strategies, certainly they are not all successful. The good news is that joint ventures and partnerships are less risky for companies than mergers, but the bad news is that many alliances fail. *Forbes* has reported that about 30 percent of all joint ventures and partnership alliances are outright failures, while another 17 percent have limited success and then dissipate due to problems.[30] There are countless examples of failed joint ventures. A few common problems that cause joint ventures to fail are as follows:

1. Managers who must collaborate daily in operating the venture are not involved in forming or shaping the venture.
2. The venture may benefit the partnering companies but may not benefit customers, who then complain about poorer service or criticize the companies in other ways.
3. The venture may not be supported equally by both partners. If supported unequally, problems arise.
4. The venture may begin to compete more with one of the partners than the other.[31]

Six guidelines for when a joint venture may be an especially effective means for pursuing strategies are:[32]

- When a privately owned organization is forming a joint venture with a publicly owned organization; there are some advantages to being privately held, such as closed ownership; there are some advantages of being publicly held, such as access to stock issuances as a source of capital. Sometimes, the unique advantages of being privately and publicly held can be synergistically combined in a joint venture.

- When a domestic organization is forming a joint venture with a foreign company; a joint venture can provide a domestic company with the opportunity for obtaining local management in a foreign country, thereby reducing risks such as expropriation and harassment by host country officials.
- When the distinct competencies of two or more firms complement each other especially well.
- When some project is potentially very profitable but requires overwhelming resources and risks.
- When two or more smaller firms have trouble competing with a large firm.
- When there exists a need to quickly introduce a new technology.

Merger/Acquisition

Merger and acquisition are two commonly used ways to pursue strategies. A *merger* occurs when two organizations of about equal size unite to form one enterprise. An *acquisition* occurs when a large organization purchases (acquires) a smaller firm, or vice versa. When a merger or acquisition is not desired by both parties, it can be called a *takeover* or *hostile takeover.* In contrast, if the acquisition is desired by both firms, it is termed a *friendly merger.* Most mergers are friendly.

There were numerous examples in 2009 of hostile takeover attempts. For example, Swiss drug company Roche Holding AG in 2009 launched an $86.50-a-share hostile takeover for the 44.2 percent of Genentech Inc. that it did not already own. Genentech's board of directors strongly urged shareholders not to accept the Roche Holding offer, saying that Roche's $40 billion offer was inadequate. Genentech's board said the firm was worth $112 per share at the time. A few weeks later, Roche increased its bid to $93 per share.

Headquartered near each other in California, Emulex Corp. in May 2009 rejected a hostile takeover bid from Broadcom Corp. even though the Broadcom offer represented a 40 percent premium over the Emulex current stock price. Emulex installed a "poison pill" in January 2009 as protection against hostile takeover offers. Both companies produce and sell networking equipment that connect servers in data centers.

As stock prices have plunged in many companies, their rivals with cash are eyeing them as takeover candidates. Fertilizer producer Agrium recently offered to buy rival Deerfield, Illinois–based CF Industries Holdings for $3.6 billion, which created a three-way hostile takeover battle because CF at the time had a hostile takeover offer on the table to acquire Terra Industries.

Private-equity-led buyouts, which accounted for 15 percent of all merger and acquisition in 2007, fell to 6 percent of the total in 2008. That smaller percentage is likely to remain in place in 2009 as big cross-border deals are unlikely in the near term. Private-equity investing in tech companies fell almost 80 percent in 2008 to $26.3 billion as sources of debt financing became scarce.

Private-equity firms such as Blackstone Group Inc. and Kohlberg Kravis Roberts & Co. that led the massive acquisition trend in 2006–2007 are still around, but they operate much more carefully now. Such firms are trying today to purchase the agricultural-sciences division (Agro Sciences) of Dow Chemical. Dow needs cash to complete its own acquisition of Rohm & Haas Co. Agro Sciences should be worth between $7 and $10 billion. A rival Swiss firm named Syngenta AG also is interested in acquiring Agro Sciences.

For all of 2008, global merger and acquisition volume fell 29 percent to $3.06 trillion, which was on par with 2005. Big deals in 2008 included Mars Inc.'s $23 billion acquisition of Wm. Wrigley Jr. Co., InBev NV's $52 billion purchase of Anheuser-Busch, and HP's $13.2 billion acquisition of EDS.

In a stock deal that created the nation's largest home builder, Pulte Homes recently acquired Centex Corp. for $1.3 billion. This merger signaled a bottom in the housing market, which had dropped so drastically in the United States in 2008 and early 2009.

Cross-border merger and acquisition (M&A) deals by companies in major nations fell 26 percent in the United States in 2008 versus 2007, as compared to a fall of 15 percent in France, and a fall of 67 percent in the United Kingdom.[33]

Firms with cash such as Marubeni and Itochu in Japan are on the hunt for super deals outside of Japan. Cross-border M&A deals in Japan grew 231 percent in 2008 and grew 101 percent in China. Japanese companies in total spent $77.8 billion in 2008 on acquisitions outside Japan, more than triple the amount spent in 2007. "Hard times often come hand in hand with opportunities," said Teruo Asada, president and chief executive of the 150-year-old Marubeni Corporation in Japan.

According to Strategas Research Partners, 168 of 419 nonfinancial firms in the S&P 500 have at least $1 billion in cash apiece, and 16 have more than $10 billion each.[34] Exxon/Mobil has $32 billion in cash, Cisco Systems has $29.5 billion, and Apple has $25.6 billion.

The largest business software firm in the world, Oracle Corp. is another cash-rich firm acquiring other firms, having completed 12 acquisition in the last 12 months. A few of the firms acquired by Oracle recently are mValent, Tacit Software, Primavera Systems, Advanced Visual Tech, ClearApp, Skywire Software, AdminServer, and Empirix. Many companies with high-quality products have turned into desperate sellers amid the worst recession in a generation. Oracle dominates the market for industrial-strength databases that companies rely on the organize everything from inventories to payrolls.

White knight is a term that refers to a firm that agrees to acquire another firm when that other firm is facing a hostile takeover by some company. For example, in 2009, Palo Alto, California–based CV Thereapeutics Inc., a heart-drug maker, was fighting a hostile takeover bid by Japan's Astellas Pharma. Then CVT struck a friendly deal to be acquired by Forest City, California–based Gilead Sciences at a higher price of $1.4 billion in cash. Gilead is known for its HIV drugs, so its move into the heart-drug business surprised many analysts.

Not all mergers are effective and successful. Pricewaterhouse Coopers LLP recently researched mergers and found that the average acquirer's stock was 3.7 percent lower than its industry peer group a year later. *BusinessWeek* and the *Wall Street Journal* studied mergers and concluded that about half produced negative returns to shareholders. Warren Buffett once said in a speech that "too-high purchase price for the stock of an excellent company can undo the effects of a subsequent decade of favorable business developments." Research suggests that perhaps 20 percent of all mergers and acquisitions are successful, approximately 60 percent produce disappointing results, and the last 20 percent are clear failures.[35] So a merger between two firms can yield great benefits, but the price and reasoning must be right. Some key reasons why many mergers and acquisitions fail are provided in Table 5-8.

Among mergers, acquisitions, and takeovers in recent years, same-industry combinations have predominated. A general market consolidation is occurring in many industries, especially banking, insurance, defense, and health care, but also in pharmaceuticals, food, airlines, accounting, publishing, computers, retailing, financial services, and biotechnology. For example, SXR Uranium One Inc. purchased rival uranium miner UrAsia Energy Ltd., creating the world's second-largest uranium company after Cameco

TABLE 5-8   Key Reasons Why Many Mergers and Acquisitions Fail

- Integration difficulties
- Inadequate evaluation of target
- Large or extraordinary debt
- Inability to achieve synergy
- Too much diversification
- Managers overly focused on acquisitions
- Too large an acquisition
- Difficult to integrate different organizational cultures
- Reduced employee morale due to layoffs and relocations

TABLE 5-9 Some Large Mergers Completed Globally in 2009

Acquiring Firm	Acquired Firm	Price (in $Billions)
InBev	Anheuser-Busch Cos.	52.000
Bank of America Corp.	Merrill Lynch & Co.	50.0
Wells Fargo & Co.	Wachovia Corp.	15.1
Delta Air Lines	Northwest Airlines Corp.	2.600
AT&T	Centennial Communications	0.937
Johnson & Johnson	Mentor Corp.	1.070
King Pharmaceuticals Inc.	Alpharma Inc.	1.600
CenturyTel	Embark	5.000

Corp. Similarly, Tenaris SA, based in Luxembourg and the world's biggest maker of steel tubes used in oil exploration and production, recently acquired rival Hydril Company, based in Houston, Texas.

Table 5-9 shows some mergers and acquisitions completed in 2009. There are many potential benefits of merging with or acquiring another firm, as indicated in Table 5-10.

Johnson & Johnson's (J&J) recent acquisition of Mentor for $1.07 billion was a hefty 92 percent premium over Mentor's closing price before the deal was announced, but was 23 percent below another widely used evaluation method that was number of shares outstanding times the target firm's 52-week stock price high. Many companies are being forced to sell under duress, so firms with a lot of cash such as J&J and Apple can pick up deals of a lifetime these days. J&J had $14 billion in cash on hand in 2009 when it purchased Omrix Pharmaceuticals for $438 million. Then the largest health-care company in the world, J&J purchased Mentor for $1.07 billion in cash. Bristol-Myers Squibb's CEO James Cornelius recently said that company is looking to do six or seven additional acquisitions or partnerships with the $9 billion in cash it has on hand to bolster its drug pipeline.

The volume of mergers completed annually worldwide is growing dramatically and exceeds $1 trillion. There are annually more than 10,000 mergers in the United States that total more than $700 billion. The proliferation of mergers is fueled by companies' drive for market share, efficiency, and pricing power, as well as by globalization, the need for greater economies of scale, reduced regulation and antitrust concerns, the Internet, and e-commerce.

A *leveraged buyout* (LBO) occurs when a corporation's shareholders are bought (hence *buyout*) by the company's management and other private investors using borrowed funds (hence *leverage*).[36] Besides trying to avoid a hostile takeover, other reasons for initiating an LBO are senior management decisions that particular divisions do not fit into an overall corporate strategy or must be sold to raise cash, or receipt of an attractive offering price. An LBO takes a corporation private.

TABLE 5-10 Potential Benefits of Merging with or Acquiring Another Firm

- To provide improved capacity utilization
- To make better use of the existing sales force
- To reduce managerial staff
- To gain economies of scale
- To smooth out seasonal trends in sales
- To gain access to new suppliers, distributors, customers, products, and creditors
- To gain new technology
- To reduce tax obligations

First Mover Advantages

First mover advantages refer to the benefits a firm may achieve by entering a new market or developing a new product or service prior to rival firms.[37] As indicated in Table 5-11, some advantages of being a first mover include securing access to rare resources, gaining new knowledge of key factors and issues, and carving out market share and a position that is easy to defend and costly for rival firms to overtake. First mover advantages are analogous to taking the high ground first, which puts one in an excellent strategic position to launch aggressive campaigns and to defend territory. Being the first mover can be especially wise when such actions (1) build a firm's image and reputation with buyers, (2) produce cost advantages over rivals in terms of new technologies, new components, new distribution channels, and so on, (3) create strongly loyal customers, and (4) make imitation or duplication by a rival hard or unlikely.[38]

To sustain the competitive advantage gained by being the first mover, such a firm also needs to be a fast learner. There would, however, be risks associated with being the first mover, such as unexpected and unanticipated problems and costs that occur from being the first firm doing business in the new market. Therefore, being a slow mover (also called *fast follower* or *late mover*) can be effective when a firm can easily copy or imitate the lead firm's products or services. If technology is advancing rapidly, slow movers can often leapfrog a first mover's products with improved second-generation products. However, slow movers often are relegated to relying on the first mover being a slow mover and making strategic and tactical mistakes. This situation does not occur often, so first mover advantages clearly offset the first mover disadvantages most of the time. Apple Inc. has always been a good example of a first mover firm.

Strategic-management research indicates that first mover advantages tend to be greatest when competitors are roughly the same size and possess similar resources. If competitors are not similar in size, then larger competitors can wait while others make initial investments and mistakes, and then respond with greater effectiveness and resources.

Outsourcing

Business-process outsourcing (BPO) is a rapidly growing new business that involves companies taking over the functional operations, such as human resources, information systems, payroll, accounting, customer service, and even marketing of other firms. Companies are choosing to outsource their functional operations more and more for several reasons: (1) it is less expensive, (2) it allows the firm to focus on its core businesses, and (3) it enables the firm to provide better services. Other advantages of outsourcing are that the strategy (1) allows the firm to align itself with "best-in-world" suppliers who focus on performing the special task, (2) provides the firm flexibility should customer needs shift unexpectedly, and (3) allows the firm to concentrate on other internal value chain activities critical to sustaining competitive advantage. BPO is a means for achieving strategies that are similar to partnering and joint venturing. The worldwide BPO market exceeds $173 billion.

Many firms, such as Dearborn, Michigan–based Visteon Corp. and J. P. Morgan Chase & Co., outsource their computer operations to IBM, which competes with firms such as Electronic Data Systems and Computer Sciences Corp. in the computer outsourcing

---

TABLE 5-11   Benefits of a Firm Being the First Mover

1. Secure access and commitments to rare resources
2. Gain new knowledge of critical success factors and issues
3. Gain market share and position in the best locations
4. Establish and secure long-term relationships with customers, suppliers, distributors, and investors
5. Gain customer loyalty and commitments

business. 3M Corp. is outsourcing all of its manufacturing operations to Flextronics International Ltd. of Singapore or Jabil Circuit in Florida. 3M is also outsourcing all design and manufacturing of low-end standardized volume products by building a new design center in Taiwan.

U.S. and European companies for more than a decade have been outsourcing their manufacturing, tech support, and back-office work, but most insisted on keeping research and development activities in-house. However, an ever-growing number of firms today are outsourcing their product design to Asian developers. China and India are becoming increasingly important suppliers of intellectual property. For companies that include Hewlett-Packard, PalmOne, Dell, Sony, Apple, Kodak, Motorola, Nokia, Ericsson, Lucent, Cisco, and Nortel, the design of personal computers and cameras is mostly outsourced to China and India.

Companies pay about $68 billion in outsourcing operations to other firms, but the details of what work to outsource, to whom, where, and for how much can challenge even the biggest, most sophisticated companies.[39] And some outsourcing deals do not work out, such as the J.P. Morgan Chase deal with IBM and Dow Chemical's deal with Electronic Data Systems. Both outsourcing deals were abandoned after several years. Lehman Brothers Holdings and Dell Inc. both recently reversed decisions to move customer call centers to India after a customer rebellion. India has become a booming place for outsourcing. Sprint Nextel Corp. in 2009 outsourced management of its cellular network to Swedish firm Telefon A.B. L.M. Ericsson, which transferred about 6,000 jobs from the United States to Sweden. Based in Overland Park, Kansas, Sprint sees network outsourcing as a way to free up resources to focus on areas like product development, marketing, and strategic partnerships. Ericsson, as well as Alcatel-Lucent SA and Nokia-Siemens Networks, have been aggressively courting service contracts to make up for declining prices of telecom equipment.

Strategic Management in Nonprofit and Governmental Organizations

The strategic-management process is being used effectively by countless nonprofit and governmental organizations, such as the Girl Scouts, Boy Scouts, the Red Cross, chambers of commerce, educational institutions, medical institutions, public utilities, libraries, government agencies, and churches. The nonprofit sector, surprisingly, is by far America's largest employer. Many nonprofit and governmental organizations outperform private firms and corporations on innovativeness, motivation, productivity, and strategic management. For many nonprofit examples of strategic planning in practice, click on Strategic Planning Links found at the www.strategyclub.com Web site.

Compared to for-profit firms, nonprofit and governmental organizations may be totally dependent on outside financing. Especially for these organizations, strategic management provides an excellent vehicle for developing and justifying requests for needed financial support.

Educational Institutions

Educational institutions are more frequently using strategic-management techniques and concepts. Richard Cyert, former president of Carnegie Mellon University, said, "I believe we do a far better job of strategic management than any company I know." Population shifts nationally from the Northeast and Midwest to the Southeast and West are but one factor causing trauma for educational institutions that have not planned for changing enrollments. Ivy League schools in the Northeast are recruiting more heavily in the Southeast and West. This trend represents a significant change in the competitive climate for attracting the best high school graduates each year.

Online college degrees are becoming common and represent a threat to traditional colleges and universities. "You can put the kids to bed and go to law school," says Andrew Rosen, chief operating officer of Kaplan Education Centers, a subsidiary of the Washington Post Company.

Medical Organizations

The $200 billion U.S. hospital industry is experiencing declining margins, excess capacity, bureaucratic overburdening, poorly planned and executed diversification strategies, soaring health care costs, reduced federal support, and high administrator turnover. The seriousness of this problem is accented by a 20 percent annual decline in use by inpatients nationwide. Declining occupancy rates, deregulation, and accelerating growth of health maintenance organizations, preferred provider organizations, urgent care centers, outpatient surgery centers, diagnostic centers, specialized clinics, and group practices are other major threats facing hospitals today. Many private and state-supported medical institutions are in financial trouble as a result of traditionally taking a reactive rather than a proactive approach in dealing with their industry.

Hospitals—originally intended to be warehouses for people dying of tuberculosis, smallpox, cancer, pneumonia, and infectious diseases—are creating new strategies today as advances in the diagnosis and treatment of chronic diseases are undercutting that earlier mission. Hospitals are beginning to bring services to the patient as much as bringing the patient to the hospital; health care is more and more being concentrated in the home and in the residential community, not on the hospital campus. Chronic care will require day-treatment facilities, electronic monitoring at home, user-friendly ambulatory services, decentralized service networks, and laboratory testing. A successful hospital strategy for the future will require renewed and deepened collaboration with physicians, who are central to hospitals' well-being, and a reallocation of resources from acute to chronic care in home and community settings.

Current strategies being pursued by many hospitals include creating home health services, establishing nursing homes, and forming rehabilitation centers. Backward integration strategies that some hospitals are pursuing include acquiring ambulance services, waste disposal services, and diagnostic services. Millions of persons annually research medical ailments online, which is causing a dramatic shift in the balance of power between doctor, patient, and hospitals. The number of persons using the Internet to obtain medical information is skyrocketing. A motivated patient using the Internet can gain knowledge on a particular subject far beyond his or her doctor's knowledge, because no person can keep up with the results and implications of billions of dollars' worth of medical research reported weekly. Patients today often walk into the doctor's office with a file folder of the latest articles detailing research and treatment options for their ailments.

Governmental Agencies and Departments

Federal, state, county, and municipal agencies and departments, such as police departments, chambers of commerce, forestry associations, and health departments, are responsible for formulating, implementing, and evaluating strategies that use taxpayers' dollars in the most cost-effective way to provide services and programs. Strategic-management concepts are generally required and thus widely used to enable governmental organizations to be more effective and efficient. For a list of government agency strategic plans, click on Strategic Planning Links found at the www.strategyclub.com Web site, and scroll down through the government sites.

Strategists in governmental organizations operate with less strategic autonomy than their counterparts in private firms. Public enterprises generally cannot diversify into unrelated businesses or merge with other firms. Governmental strategists usually enjoy little freedom in altering the organizations' missions or redirecting objectives. Legislators and politicians often have direct or indirect control over major decisions and resources. Strategic issues get discussed and debated in the media and legislatures. Issues become politicized, resulting in fewer strategic choice alternatives. There is now more predictability in the management of public sector enterprises.

Government agencies and departments are finding that their employees get excited about the opportunity to participate in the strategic-management process and thereby have an effect on the organization's mission, objectives, strategies, and policies. In addition, government agencies are using a strategic-management approach to develop and substantiate formal requests for additional funding.

Strategic Management in Small Firms

The reason why "becoming your own boss" has become a national obsession is that entrepreneurs are America's role models. Almost everyone wants to own a business—from teens and college students, who are signing up for entrepreneurial courses in record numbers, to those over age 65, who are forming more companies every year.

As hundreds of thousands of people have been laid off from work in the last two years, many of these individuals have started small businesses. The *Wall Street Journal* recently provided a 10-page article on how to be a successful entrepreneur.[40] Not only laid off employees but also college graduates are seeking more and more to open their own businesses. As of April 15, 2009, the Small Business Administration had approved more than $1.5 billion in Recovery Act loans and supported more than $2 billion in lending to small businesses. "I was not envisioning myself as an entrepreneur when I began the MBA program at Northwestern University, but this is part of the journey," said student Tiffany Urrechaga. "It's kind of a blessing that I didn't get a job because I was able to reshift my thinking."[41]

Strategic management is vital for large firms' success, but what about small firms? The strategic-management process is just as vital for small companies. From their inception, all organizations have a strategy, even if the strategy just evolves from day-to-day operations. Even if conducted informally or by a single owner/entrepreneur, the strategic-management process can significantly enhance small firms' growth and prosperity. Because an ever-increasing number of men and women in the United States are starting their own businesses, more individuals are becoming strategists. Widespread corporate layoffs have contributed to an explosion in small businesses and new ideas.

Numerous magazine and journal articles have focused on applying strategic-management concepts to small businesses. A major conclusion of these articles is that a lack of strategic-management knowledge is a serious obstacle for many small business owners. Other problems often encountered in applying strategic-management concepts to small businesses are a lack of both sufficient capital to exploit external opportunities and a day-to-day cognitive frame of reference. Research also indicates that strategic management in small firms is more informal than in large firms, but small firms that engage in strategic management outperform those that do not.

Conclusion

The main appeal of any managerial approach is the expectation that it will enhance organizational performance. This is especially true of strategic management. Through involvement in strategic-management activities, managers and employees achieve a better understanding of an organization's priorities and operations. Strategic management allows organizations to be efficient, but more important, it allows them to be effective. Although strategic management does not guarantee organizational success, the process allows proactive rather than reactive decision making. Strategic management may represent a radical change in philosophy for some organizations, so strategists must be trained to anticipate and constructively respond to questions and issues as they arise. The 16 strategies discussed in this chapter can represent a new beginning for many firms, especially if managers and employees in the organization understand and support the plan for action.

We invite you to visit the David page on the Prentice Hall Companion Web site at http://www.pearsonhighered.com/david/ for this chapter's review quiz.

Key Terms and Concepts

Acquisition (p. 158)

Backward Integration (p. 140)

Balanced Scorecard (p. 135)

Bankruptcy (p. 147)

Business-Processing Outsourcing (BPO) (p. 161)

Combination Strategy (p. 137)

Cooperative Arrangements (p. 156)

Cost Leadership (p. 151)

De-integration (p. 140)
Differentiation (p. 151)
Diversification Strategies (p. 143)
Divestiture (p. 148)
First Mover Advantages (p. 161)
Focus (p. 151)
Forward Integration (p. 139)
Franchising (p. 139)
Friendly Merger (p. 158)
Generic Strategies (p. 151)
Horizontal Integration (p. 141)
Hostile Takeover (p. 158)
Integration Strategies (p. 139)
Intensive Strategies (p. 141)
Joint Venture (p. 156)

Leveraged Buyout (p. 160)
Liquidation (p. 149)
Long-Term Objectives (p. 133)
Market Development (p. 142)
Market Penetration (p. 141)
Merger (p. 158)
Product Development (p. 142)
Related Diversification (p. 144)
Retrenchment (p. 146)
Takeover (p. 158)
Turbulent, High-Velocity Markets (p. 155)
Unrelated Diversification (p. 144)
Vertical Integration (p. 139)
White Knight (p. 159)

Issues for Review and Discussion

1. In order of importance, list six "characteristics of objectives."
2. In order of importance, list six "benefits of objectives."
3. Called de-integration, there appears to be a growing trend for firms to become less forward integrated. Discuss why.
4. Called de-integration, there appears to be a growing trend for firms to become less backward integrated. Discuss why.
5. If a company has $1 million to spend on a new strategy and is considering market development versus product development, what determining factors would be most important to consider?
6. What conditions, externally and internally, would be desired/necessary for a firm to diversify?
7. Discuss "nationalization versus bankruptcy" for large American icon firms such as General Motors, AIG, and Citigroup. Which strategy is best for (1) the company and (2) the U.S. economy? Discuss.
8. Could a firm simultaneously pursue focus, differentiation, and cost leadership? Should firms do that? Discuss.
9. There is a growing trend of increased collaboration among competitors. List the benefits and drawbacks of this practice.
10. List four major benefits of forming a joint venture to achieve desired objectives.
11. List six major benefits of acquiring another firm to achieve desired objectives.
12. List five reasons why many merger/acquisitions historically have failed.
13. Can you think of any reasons why not-for-profit firms would benefit less from doing strategic planning than for-profit companies?
14. Discuss how important it is for a college football or basketball team to have a good game plan for the big rival game this coming weekend. How much time and effort do you feel the coaching staff puts into developing that game plan? Why is such time and effort essential?
15. Why are more than 60 percent of Fortune 500 firms headquartered in Wilmington, Delaware?
16. Define and give a hypothetical example of a "white knight" in the fast-food industry.
17. How does strategy formulation differ for a small versus a large organization? How does it differ for a for-profit versus a nonprofit organization?
18. Give recent examples of market penetration, market development, and product development.
19. Give recent examples of forward integration, backward integration, and horizontal integration.
20. Give recent examples of related and unrelated diversification.
21. Give recent examples of joint venture, retrenchment, divestiture, and liquidation.
22. Do you think hostile takeovers are unethical? Why or why not?
23. What are the major advantages and disadvantages of diversification?
24. What are the major advantages and disadvantages of an integrative strategy?
25. How does strategic management differ in for-profit and nonprofit organizations?
26. Why is it not advisable to pursue too many strategies at once?

27. Consumers can purchase tennis shoes, food, cars, boats, and insurance on the Internet. Are there any products today than cannot be purchased online? What is the implication for traditional retailers?
28. What are the pros and cons of a firm merging with a rival firm?
29. Visit the CheckMATE strategic-planning software Web site at www.checkmateplan.com, and discuss the benefits offered.
30. Compare and contrast financial objectives with strategic objectives. Which type is more important in your opinion? Why?
31. Diagram a two-division organizational chart that includes a CEO, COO, CIO, CSO, CFO, CMO, HRM, R&D, and two division presidents. *Hint:* Division presidents report to the COO.
32. How do the levels of strategy differ in a large firm versus a small firm?
33. List 11 types of strategies. Give a hypothetical example of each strategy listed.
34. Discuss the nature of as well as the pros and cons of a "friendly merger" versus "hostile takeover" in acquiring another firm. Give an example of each.
35. Define and explain "first mover advantages."
36. Define and explain "outsourcing."
37. Discuss the business of offering a BBA or MBA degree online.
38. What strategies are best for turbulent, high-velocity markets?

Notes

1. John Byrne, "Strategic Planning—It's Back," *BusinessWeek* (August 26, 1996): 46.
2. Steven C. Brandt, *Strategic Planning in Emerging Companies* (Reading, MA: Addison-Wesley, 1981). Reprinted with permission of the publisher.
3. R. Kaplan and D. Norton, "Putting the Balanced Scorecard to Work," *Harvard Business Review* (September–October, 1993): 147.
4. F. Hansen and M. Smith, "Crisis in Corporate America: The Role of Strategy," *Business Horizons* (January–February 2003): 9.
5. Adapted from F. R. David, "How Do We Choose Among Alternative Growth Strategies?" *Managerial Planning* 33, no. 4 (January–February 1985): 14–17, 22.
6. Ibid.
7. Kenneth Davidson, "Do Megamergers Make Sense?" *Journal of Business Strategy* 7, no. 3 (Winter 1987): 45.
8. Op. cit., David.
9. Ibid.
10. Op. cit., David.
11. Ibid.
12. Arthur Thompson Jr., A. J. Strickland III, and John Gamble. *Crafting and Executing Strategy: Text and Readings* (New York: McGraw-Hill/Irwin, 2005): 241.
13. Michael E. Porter, *Competitive Strategy: Techniques for Analyzing Industries and Competitors* (New York: Free Press, 1980): 53–57, 318–319.
14. Sheila Muto, "Seeing a Boost, Hospitals Turn to Retail Stores," *Wall Street Journal* (November 7, 2001): B1, B8.
15. Jon Swartz, "Cisco Gets into Computer Server Market," *Wall Street Journal* (March 17, 2009): 4B.
16. Op. cit., David.
17. Doug Cameron, "Smithfield to Close Six Plants, Shed Jobs," *Wall Street Journal* (February 18, 2009): B3.
18. Op. cit., David.
19. Ibid.
20. Ibid.
21. Michael Porter, *Competitive Advantage* (New York: Free Press, 1985): 97. Also, Arthur Thompson Jr., A. J. Strickland III, and John Gamble, *Crafting and Executing Strategy: Text and Readings* (New York: McGraw-Hill/Irwin, 2005): 117.
22. Arthur Thompson Jr., A. J. Strickland III, and John Gamble, *Crafting and Executing Strategy: Text and Readings* (New York: McGraw-Hill/Irwin, 2005): 125–126.
23. Porter, *Competitive Advantage,* pp. 160–162.
24. Thompson, Strickland, and Gamble, pp. 129–130.
25. Ibid., 134.
26. Gary Hamel, Yves Doz, and C. K. Prahalad, "Collaborate with Your Competitors—and Win," *Harvard Business Review* 67, no. 1 (January–February 1989): 133.
27. Kathryn Rudie Harrigan, "Joint Ventures: Linking for a Leap Forward," *Planning Review* 14, no. 4 (July–August 1986): 10.
28. Matthew Schifrin, "Partner or Perish," *Forbes* (May 21, 2001): 26.
29. Ibid., p. 28.
30. Nikhil Hutheesing, "Marital Blisters," *Forbes* (May 21, 2001): 32.
31. Ibid., p. 32.
32. Steven Rattner, "Mergers: Windfalls or Pitfalls?" *Wall Street Journal* (October 11, 1999): A22; Nikhil Deogun, "Merger Wave Spurs More Stock Wipeouts," *Wall Street Journal* (November 29, 1999): C1.
33. Yuka Hayashi, "Japanese Firms, Flush with Cash, Step Up Deals," *Wall Street Journal* (January 6, 2009): B1.
34. Jason Zweig, "Corporate-Cash Umbrellas: Too Big for This Storm? *Wall Street Journal* (March 14–15, 2009): B1.
35. J. A. Schmidt, "Business Perspective on Mergers and Acquisitions," in J. A. Schmidt, ed., *Making Mergers Work,* Alexandria, VA: Society for Human Resource Management, (2002): 23–46.
36. Joel Millman, "Mexican Mergers/Acquisitions Triple from 2001," *Wall Street Journal* (December 27, 2002): A2.

37. Robert Davis, "Net Empowering Patients," *USA Today* (July 14, 1999): 1A.

38. M. J. Gannon, K. G. Smith, and C. Grimm, "An Organizational Information-Processing Profile of First Movers," *Journal of Business Research* 25 (1992): 231–241; M. B. Lieberman and D. B. Montgomery, "First Mover Advantages," *Strategic Management Journal* 9 (Summer 1988): 41–58.

39. Scott Thurm, "Behind Outsourcing: Promise and Pitfalls," *Wall Street Journal* (February 26, 2007): B3.

40. Kelly Spors, "So, You Want to Be an Entrepreneur," *Wall Street Journal* (February 28, 2009): R1.

41. Kim Thai and Laura Petrecca, "Today's MBA Graduates Create Their Own Jobs," *USA Today* (April 27, 2009): 7B.

Current Readings

Barkema, Harry G., and Mario Schijven. "How Do Firms Learn to Make Acquisitions? A Review of Past Research and an Agenda for the Future." *Journal of Management* 34, no. 3 (June 2008): 594.

Bowen, Harry P., and Margarethe Wiersema. "Corporate Diversification: The Impact of Foreign Competition, Industry Globalization, and Product Diversification." *Strategic Management Journal* 29, no. 2 (February 2008): 115.

Dalton, Catherine. "Strategic Alliances: There Are Battles and There Is the War." *Business Horizons* 52, no. 2 (March–April 2009): 105–108.

De Fontenay, Catherine C., and Joshua S. Gans. "A Bargaining Perspective on Strategic Outsourcing and Supply Competition." *Strategic Management Journal* 29, no. 8 (August 2008): 819.

Doving, Erik, and Paul N. Gooderham. "Dynamic Capabilities as Antecedents of the Scope of Related Diversification: The Case of Small Firm Accountancy Practices." *Strategic Management Journal* 29, no. 8 (August 2008): 841.

Dykes, Bernadine Johnson, Jerayr (John), Haleblian, and Gerry M. McNamara. "The Performance Implications of Participating in an Acquisition Wave: Early Mover Advantages, Bandwagon Effects, and in the Moderating Influence of Industry Characteristics and Acquirer Tactics." *The Academy of Management Journal* 51, no. 1 (February 2008): 113.

Garrette, Bernard, Xavier Castaner, and Pierre Dussauge. "Horizontal Alliances as an Alternative to Autonomous Production: Product Expansion Mode Choice in the Worldwide Aircraft Industry." *Strategic Management Journal* (August 2009): 885–894.

Hagiu, Andrei, and David B. Yoffie. "What's Your Google Strategy?" *Harvard Business Review* (April 2009): 74–83.

Haleblian, Jerayr, Cynthia Devers, Gerry McNamara, Mason Carpenter, and Robert Davison. "Taking Stock of What We Know About Mergers and Acquisitions: A Review and Research Agenda." *Journal of Management* (June 2009): 469–502.

Harding, David, Michael C. Mankins, and Rolf-Magnus Weddigen. "How the Best Divest." *Harvard Business Review* (October 2008): 92.

Hult, Tomas M., David J. Ketchen, David Meyer, and William Rebarick. "Best Value Supply Chains: A Key Competitive Weapon for the 21st Century." *Business Horizons* 51, no. 3 (May–June 2008): 235.

Kim, Jay, and Sydney Finkelstein. "The Effects of Strategic and Market Complementarity on Acquisition Performance: Evidence from the U.S. Commercial Banking Industry." *Strategic Management Journal* (June 2009): 617–646.

King, Brian L. "Strategizing at Leading Venture Capital Firms: Of Planning, Opportunism and Deliberate Emergence." *Long Range Planning* 41, no. 3 (June 2008): 345.

Kumar, Nirmalya. "How Emerging Giants Are Rewriting the Rules of M&A." *Harvard Business Review* (May 2009): 115–125.

Luo, Yadong. "Procedural Fairness and Interfirm Cooperation in Strategic Alliances." *Strategic Management Journal* 29, no. 1 (January 2008): 27.

Luo, Yadong. "Structuring Interorganizational Cooperation: The Role of Economic Integration in Strategic Alliances." *Strategic Management Journal* 29 (June 2008): 617.

Meyer, Christine Benedichte. "Value Leakages in Mergers and Acquisitions: Why They Occur and How They Can Be Addressed." *Long Range Planning* 41, no 2 (April 2008): 197.

Ozcan, Pinar, and Kathleen Eisenhardt. "Origin of Alliance Portfolios: Entrepreneurs, Network Strategies, and Firm Performance." *Academy of Management Journal* (April 2009): 246–279.

Pearce, John A., II, and Keith D. Robbins. "Strategic Transformation as the Essential Last Step in the Process of Business Turnaround." *Business Horizons* 51, no. 2 (March–April 2008): 121.

Shah, Reshma H., and Vanitha Swaminathan. "Factors Influencing Partner Selection in Strategic Alliances: The Moderating Role of Alliance Context." *Strategic Management Journal* 29, no. 5 (May 2008): 471.

Shanley, Mark, and Xiaoli Yin. "Industry Determinants of the 'Merger versus Alliance' Decision." *The Academy of Management Review* 33, no. 2 (April 2008): 473.

Slater, Stanley F., Robert A. Weigand, and Thomas J. Zwirlein. "The Business Case for Commitment to Diversity." *Business Horizons* 51, no. 3 (May–June 2008): 201.

ASSURANCE OF LEARNING EXERCISES

Assurance of Learning Exercise 5A

What Strategies Should McDonald's Pursue in 2011–2013?

Purpose

In performing strategic management case analysis, you can find information about the respective company's actual and planned strategies. Comparing what is planned versus *what you recommend* is an important part of case analysis. Do not recommend what the firm actually plans, unless in-depth analysis of the situation reveals those strategies to be best among all feasible alternatives. This exercise gives you experience conducting library and Internet research to determine what McDonald's should do in 2011–2013.

Instructions

Step 1   Look up McDonald's (MCD) and Burger King Holdings (BKC) using the Web sites provided in Table 4-5. Find some recent articles about firms in this industry. Scan Moody's, Dun & Bradstreet, and Standard & Poor's publications for information.

Step 2   Summarize your findings in a three-page report entitled "Strategies Being Pursued by McDonald's in 2010."

Assurance of Learning Exercise 5B

Examining Strategy Articles

Purpose

Strategy articles can be found weekly in journals, magazines, and newspapers. By reading and studying strategy articles, you can gain a better understanding of the strategic-management process. Several of the best journals in which to find corporate strategy articles are *Advanced Management Journal, Business Horizons, Long Range Planning, Journal of Business Strategy*, and *Strategic Management Journal*. These journals are devoted to reporting the results of empirical research in management. They apply strategic-management concepts to specific organizations and industries. They introduce new strategic-management techniques and provide short case studies on selected firms.

Other good journals in which to find strategic-management articles are *Harvard Business Review, Sloan Management Review, California Management Review, Academy of Management Review, Academy of Management Journal, Academy of Management Executive, Journal of Management*, and *Journal of Small Business Management*.

In addition to journals, many magazines regularly publish articles that focus on business strategies. Several of the best magazines in which to find applied strategy articles are *Dun's Business Month, Fortune, Forbes, BusinessWeek, Inc.,* and *Industry Week*. Newspapers such as *USA Today, Wall Street Journal, New York Times*, and *Barrons* cover strategy events when they occur—for example, a joint venture announcement, a bankruptcy declaration, a new advertising campaign start, acquisition of a company, divestiture of a division, a chief executive officer's hiring or firing, or a hostile takeover attempt.

In combination, journal, magazine, and newspaper articles can make the strategic-management course more exciting. They allow current strategies of for-profit and nonprofit organizations to be identified and studied.

Instructions

Step 1   Go to your college library and find a recent journal article that focuses on a strategic-management topic. Select your article from one of the journals listed previously, not from a magazine. Copy the article and bring it to class.

Step 2   Give a 3-minute oral report summarizing the most important information in your article. Include comments giving your personal reaction to the article. Pass your article around in class.

Assurance of Learning Exercise 5C

Classifying Some Year 2009 Strategies

Purpose

This exercise can improve your understanding of various strategies by giving you experience classifying strategies. This skill will help you use the strategy-formulation tools presented later. Consider the following 8 actual year-2009 strategies by various firms:

1. Microsoft developed a new videocamera for its Xbox 360 console that allowed players to control games with the movement of their bodies, rather than by holding a plastic wand in their hands, as required with Nintendo's popular Wii game console.
2. Wells Fargo and Bank of America began to "tweet"—post messages of 140 characters or less on Twitter.com, so customers could see product features. Banks are also putting marketing videos on YouTube.
3. The United Kingdom's huge telecom firm, BT Group PLC, cut 15,000 more jobs on top of the 15,000 the prior year.
4. Japanese electronics maker Panasonic Corp. acquired Osaka, Japan-based Sanyo Electric Company.
5. News Corp. sold off many of its television stations.
6. More than 1,000 Chrysler dealers closed their doors and ceased doing business.
7. Germany's Metro AG, the world's fourth-largest retailer after Wal-Mart, Carrefour SA, and Home Depot, is expanding aggressively into China.
8. Time Warner plans to spin off or sell all or part of AOL.

Instructions

Step 1   On a separate sheet of paper, number from 1 to 8. These numbers correspond to the strategies described.

Step 2   What type of strategy best describes the 8 actions cited? Indicate your answers.

Step 3   Exchange papers with a classmate, and grade each other's paper as your instructor gives the right answers.

Assurance of Learning Exercise 5D

How Risky Are Various Alternative Strategies?

Purpose

This exercise focuses on how risky various alternative strategies are for organizations to pursue. Different degrees of risk are based largely on varying degrees of *externality*, defined as movement away from present business into new markets and products. In general, the greater the degree of externality, the greater the probability of loss resulting from unexpected events. High-risk strategies generally are less attractive than low-risk strategies.

Instructions

Step 1   On a separate sheet of paper, number vertically from 1 to 10. Think of 1 as "most risky," 2 as "next most risky," and so forth to 10, "least risky."

Step 2   Write the following strategies beside the appropriate number to indicate how risky you believe the strategy is to pursue: horizontal integration, related diversification, liquidation, forward integration, backward integration, product development, market development, market penetration, retrenchment, and unrelated diversification.

Step 3   Grade your paper as your instructor gives you the right answers and supporting rationale. Each correct answer is worth 10 points.

Assurance of Learning Exercise 5E

Developing Alternative Strategies for My University

Purpose

It is important for representatives from all areas of a college or university to identify and discuss alternative strategies that could benefit faculty, students, alumni, staff, and other constituencies. As you complete this exercise, notice the learning and understanding that occurs as people express differences of opinion. Recall that *the process of planning is more important than the document.*

Instructions

Step 1   Recall or locate the external opportunity/threat and internal strength/weakness factors that you identified as part of Exercise 1B. If you did not do that exercise, discuss now as a class important external and internal factors facing your college or university.

Step 2   Identify and put on the chalkboard alternative strategies that you feel could benefit your college or university. Your proposed actions should allow the institution to capitalize on particular strengths, improve upon certain weaknesses, avoid external threats, and/or take advantage of particular external opportunities. List 10 possible strategies on the board. Number the strategies as they are written on the board.

Step 3   On a separate sheet of paper, number from 1 to 10. Everyone in class individually should rate the strategies identified, using a 1 to 3 scale, where 1 = *I do not support implementation*, 2 = *I am neutral about implementation*, and 3 = *I strongly support implementation*. In rating the strategies, recognize that your institution cannot do everything desired or potentially beneficial.

Step 4   Go to the board and record your ratings in a row beside the respective strategies. Everyone in class should do this, going to the board perhaps by rows in the class.

Step 5   Sum the ratings for each strategy so that a prioritized list of recommended strategies is obtained. This prioritized list reflects the collective wisdom of your class. Strategies with the highest score are deemed best.

Step 6   Discuss how this process could enable organizations to achieve understanding and commitment from individuals.

Step 7   Share your class results with a university administrator, and ask for comments regarding the process and top strategies recommended.

Assurance of Learning Exercise 5F

Lessons in Doing Business Globally

Purpose

The purpose of this exercise is to discover some important lessons learned by local businesses that do business internationally.

Instructions

Contact several local business leaders by phone. Find at least three firms that engage in international or export operations. Visit the owner or manager of each business in person. Ask the businessperson to give you several important lessons that his or her firm has learned in globally doing business. Record the lessons on paper, and report your findings to the class.

CHAPTER 6
Strategy Analysis and Choice

CHAPTER OBJECTIVES

After studying this chapter, you should be able to do the following:

1. Describe a three-stage framework for choosing among alternative strategies.

2. Explain how to develop a SWOT Matrix, SPACE Matrix, BCG Matrix, IE Matrix, and QSPM.

3. Identify important behavioral, political, ethical, and social responsibility considerations in strategy analysis and choice.

4. Discuss the role of intuition in strategic analysis and choice.

5. Discuss the role of organizational culture in strategic analysis and choice.

6. Discuss the role of a board of directors in choosing among alternative strategies.

Assurance of Learning Exercises

Assurance of Learning Exercise 6A
Developing a SWOT Matrix for McDonald's

Assurance of Learning Exercise 6B
Developing a SPACE Matrix for McDonald's

Assurance of Learning Exercise 6C
Developing a BCG Matrix for McDonald's

Assurance of Learning Exercise 6D
Developing a QSPM for McDonald's

Assurance of Learning Exercise 6E
Formulating Individual Strategies

Source: Shutterstock

"Notable Quotes"

"Strategic management is not a box of tricks or a bundle of techniques. It is analytical thinking and commitment of resources to action. But quantification alone is not planning. Some of the most important issues in strategic management cannot be quantified at all."

—Peter Drucker

"Objectives are not commands; they are commitments. They do not determine the future; they are the means to mobilize resources and energies of an organization for the making of the future."

—Peter Drucker

"Life is full of lousy options."

—General P. X. Kelley

"When a crisis forces choosing among alternatives, most people will choose the worst possible one."

—Rudin's Law

"Strategy isn't something you can nail together in slapdash fashion by sitting around a conference table."

—Terry Haller

"Planning is often doomed before it ever starts, either because too much is expected of it or because not enough is put into it."

—T. J. Cartwright

"Whether it's broke or not, fix it—make it better. Not just products, but the whole company if necessary."

—Bill Saporito

Assurance of Learning Exercise 6F
The Mach Test

Assurance of Learning Exercise 6G
Developing a BCG Matrix for My University

Assurance of Learning Exercise 6H
The Role of Boards of Directors

Assurance of Learning Exercise 6I
Locating Companies in a Grand Strategy Matrix

Strategy analysis and choice largely involve making subjective decisions based on objective information. This chapter introduces important concepts that can help strategists generate feasible alternatives, evaluate those alternatives, and choose a specific course of action. Behavioral aspects of strategy formulation are described, including politics, culture, ethics, and social responsibility considerations. Modern tools for formulating strategies are described, and the appropriate role of a board of directors is discussed.

Doing Great in a Weak Economy. How?

Apple

When most firms were struggling in 2008, Apple increased its revenues from $24.0 billion in 2007 to $32.4 billion in 2008. Apple's net income was $4.4 billion in 2008, up from $3.5 billion the prior year—wonderfully impressive in a global slump. *Fortune* magazine in 2009 rated Apple as their number-one "Most Admired Company in the World" in terms of their management and performance. That's right, number one out of millions of companies around the world.

In the global recession, technology purchases were deemed disposable or discretionary for most businesses and individuals. New orders for both business and consumer tech products plummeted, and technology firms shed workers rapidly. This led to massive layoffs in the computer industry and related industries. The meltdown permeated all the way down the supply chain to chip makers, hard drive makers, peripheral makers, software vendors, and other segments. Hewlett-Packard recently cut 24,600 employees and Dell laid off 8,900. Microsoft recently cut its travel budget 20 percent and laid off 5,000 employees.

Amid recession and faltering rivals, Apple is doing great. Brisk sales of iPods, iPhones, and laptops are yielding higher and higher revenues and profits every quarter. Legendary CEO Steve Jobs and his colleagues are implementing a great strategic plan. Apple has no manufacturing plants but does have retail stores. Apple continues to amaze the world with its new, innovative products, being one of the best examples of a "first mover" firm in developing new products. Apple has very loyal customers and has about $25.6

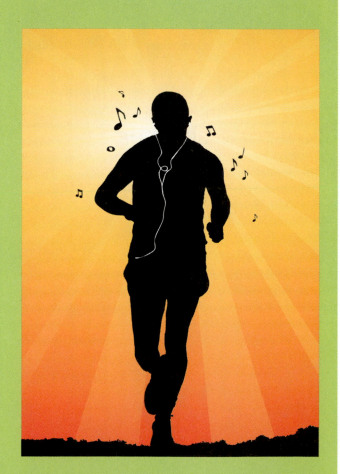

billion in cash on their balance sheet to go along with zero long-term debt.

Based in Cupertino, California, Apple has not cut prices of computers much at all during the recession, even as competitors have slashed prices dramatically.

On June 9, 2009, Apple did however lower the price of its entry-level iPhone by 50 percent to $99 and rolled out a next-generation model named iPhone 3GS which is faster than existing models and can capture videos. Apple by mid-2009 had sold over 20 million iPhones and reported in July 2009 that the company was unable to supply enough iPhones and Macintosh computers to meet demand. Apple sold 5.2 million iPhones in the quarter ending that month, more than 7 times what it sold the same quarter the prior year. Shipments of Macintosh computers that quarter were up 4 percent to 2.6 million. For the first 7 months of 2009, Apple's stock rose 80 percent compared to the Nasdaq Composite being up 25 percent.

Apple has aggressive new plans to design its own computer chips in order (1) obtain better chips for its unique products, and (2) share fewer details about its technology with external chip manufacturers.

Source: Based on Byron Acohido and Matt Krantz, "Even Tech Stalwarts Hit Hard," *USA Today* (January 23, 2009): B1, B2; Geoff Colvin, "The World's Most Admired Companies," *Fortune* (March 16, 2009): 76–86.

The Nature of Strategy Analysis and Choice

As indicated by Figure 6-1, this chapter focuses on generating and evaluating alternative strategies, as well as selecting strategies to pursue. Strategy analysis and choice seek to determine alternative courses of action that could best enable the firm to achieve its mission and objectives. The firm's present strategies, objectives, and mission, coupled with the external and internal audit information, provide a basis for generating and evaluating feasible alternative strategies.

Unless a desperate situation confronts the firm, alternative strategies will likely represent incremental steps that move the firm from its present position to a desired future position. Alternative strategies do not come out of the wild blue yonder; they are derived from the firm's vision, mission, objectives, external audit, and internal audit; they are consistent with, or build on, past strategies that have worked well.

The Process of Generating and Selecting Strategies

Strategists never consider all feasible alternatives that could benefit the firm because there are an infinite number of possible actions and an infinite number of ways to implement those actions. Therefore, a manageable set of the most attractive alternative strategies must be developed. The advantages, disadvantages, trade-offs, costs, and benefits of these strategies should be determined. This section discusses the process that many firms use to determine an appropriate set of alternative strategies.

Identifying and evaluating alternative strategies should involve many of the managers and employees who earlier assembled the organizational vision and mission statements, performed the external audit, and conducted the internal audit. Representatives from each department and division of the firm should be included in this process, as was the case in previous strategy-formulation activities. Recall that involvement provides the best opportunity for managers and employees to gain an understanding of what the firm is doing and why and to become committed to helping the firm accomplish its objectives.

All participants in the strategy analysis and choice activity should have the firm's external and internal audit information by their sides. This information, coupled with the firm's mission statement, will help participants crystallize in their own minds particular strategies that they believe could benefit the firm most. Creativity should be encouraged in this thought process.

Alternative strategies proposed by participants should be considered and discussed in a meeting or series of meetings. Proposed strategies should be listed in writing. When all feasible strategies identified by participants are given and understood, the strategies should be ranked in order of attractiveness by all participants, with 1 = should not be implemented, 2 = possibly should be implemented, 3 = probably should be implemented, and 4 = definitely should be implemented. This process will result in a prioritized list of best strategies that reflects the collective wisdom of the group.

FIGURE 6-1

A Comprehensive Strategic-Management Model

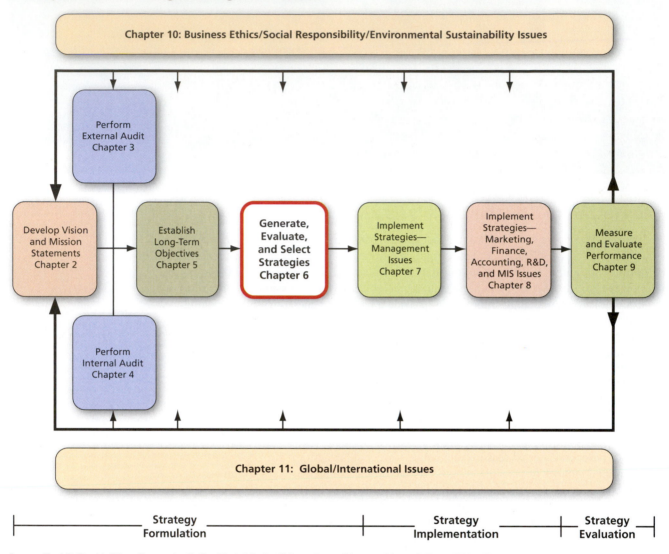

Source: Fred R. David, "How Companies Define Their Mission," *Long Range Planning* 22, no. 3 (June 1988): 40.

A Comprehensive Strategy-Formulation Framework

Important strategy-formulation techniques can be integrated into a three-stage decision-making framework, as shown in Figure 6-2. The tools presented in this framework are applicable to all sizes and types of organizations and can help strategists identify, evaluate, and select strategies.

Stage 1 of the formulation framework consists of the EFE Matrix, the IFE Matrix, and the Competitive Profile Matrix (CPM). Called the *Input Stage,* Stage 1 summarizes the basic input information needed to formulate strategies. Stage 2, called the *Matching Stage,* focuses upon generating feasible alternative strategies by aligning key external and internal factors. Stage 2 techniques include the Strengths-Weaknesses-Opportunities-Threats (SWOT) Matrix, the Strategic Position and Action Evaluation (SPACE) Matrix, the Boston Consulting Group (BCG) Matrix, the Internal-External (IE) Matrix, and the Grand Strategy Matrix. Stage 3, called the *Decision Stage,* involves a single technique, the Quantitative Strategic Planning Matrix (QSPM). A QSPM uses input information from Stage 1 to objectively evaluate feasible alternative strategies identified in Stage 2. A QSPM reveals the relative attractiveness of alternative strategies and thus provides objective basis for selecting specific strategies.

FIGURE 6-2

The Strategy-Formulation Analytical Framework

STAGE 1: THE INPUT STAGE		
External Factor Evaluation (EFE) Matrix	Competitive Profile Matrix (CPM)	Internal Factor Evaluation (IFE) Matrix

STAGE 2: THE MATCHING STAGE				
Strengths-Weaknesses-Opportunities-Threats (SWOT) Matrix	Strategic Position and Action Evaluation (SPACE) Matrix	Boston Consulting Group (BCG) Matrix	Internal-External (IE) Matrix	Grand Strategy Matrix

STAGE 3: THE DECISION STAGE
Quantitative Strategic Planning Matrix (QSPM)

All nine techniques included in the *strategy-formulation framework* require the integration of intuition and analysis. Autonomous divisions in an organization commonly use strategy-formulation techniques to develop strategies and objectives. Divisional analyses provide a basis for identifying, evaluating, and selecting among alternative corporate-level strategies.

Strategists themselves, not analytic tools, are always responsible and accountable for strategic decisions. Lenz emphasized that the shift from a words-oriented to a numbers-oriented planning process can give rise to a false sense of certainty; it can reduce dialogue, discussion, and argument as a means for exploring understandings, testing assumptions, and fostering organizational learning.[1] Strategists, therefore, must be wary of this possibility and use analytical tools to facilitate, rather than to diminish, communication. Without objective information and analysis, personal biases, politics, emotions, personalities, and *halo error* (the tendency to put too much weight on a single factor) unfortunately may play a dominant role in the strategy-formulation process.

The Input Stage

Procedures for developing an EFE Matrix, an IFE Matrix, and a CPM were presented in Chapters 3 and 4. The information derived from these three matrices provides basic input information for the matching and decision stage matrices described later in this chapter.

The input tools require strategists to quantify subjectivity during early stages of the strategy-formulation process. Making small decisions in the input matrices regarding the relative importance of external and internal factors allows strategists to more effectively generate and evaluate alternative strategies. Good intuitive judgment is always needed in determining appropriate weights and ratings.

The Matching Stage

Strategy is sometimes defined as the match an organization makes between its internal resources and skills and the opportunities and risks created by its external factors.[2] The matching stage of the strategy-formulation framework consists of five techniques that can be used in any sequence: the SWOT Matrix, the SPACE Matrix, the BCG Matrix, the IE Matrix, and the Grand Strategy Matrix. These tools rely upon information derived from the input stage to match external opportunities and threats with internal strengths and weaknesses. *Matching* external and internal critical success factors is the key to effectively generating feasible alternative strategies. For example, a firm with excess working capital (an internal strength) could take advantage of the cell phone industry's

TABLE 6-1   **Matching Key External and Internal Factors to Formulate Alternative Strategies**

Key Internal Factor	Key External Factor	Resultant Strategy
Excess working capital (an internal strength)	+ 20 percent annual growth in the cell phone industry (an external opportunity)	= Acquire Cellfone, Inc.
Insufficient capacity (an internal weakness)	+ Exit of two major foreign competitors from the industry (an external opportunity)	= Pursue horizontal integration by buying competitors' facilities
Strong R&D expertise (an internal strength)	+ Decreasing numbers of younger adults (an external threat)	= Develop new products for older adults
Poor employee morale (an internal weakness)	+ Rising healthcare costs (an external threat)	= Develop a new wellness program

20 percent annual growth rate (an external opportunity) by acquiring Cellfone, Inc., a firm in the cell phone industry. This example portrays simple one-to-one matching. In most situations, external and internal relationships are more complex, and the matching requires multiple alignments for each strategy generated. The basic concept of matching is illustrated in Table 6-1.

Any organization, whether military, product-oriented, service-oriented, governmental, or even athletic, must develop and execute good strategies to win. A good offense without a good defense, or vice versa, usually leads to defeat. Developing strategies that use strengths to capitalize on opportunities could be considered an offense, whereas strategies designed to improve upon weaknesses while avoiding threats could be termed defensive. Every organization has some external opportunities and threats and internal strengths and weaknesses that can be aligned to formulate feasible alternative strategies.

The Strengths-Weaknesses-Opportunities-Threats (SWOT) Matrix

The *Strengths-Weaknesses-Opportunities-Threats (SWOT) Matrix* is an important matching tool that helps managers develop four types of strategies: SO (strengths-opportunities) Strategies, WO (weaknesses-opportunities) Strategies, ST (strengths-threats) Strategies, and WT (weaknesses-threats) Strategies.[3] Matching key external and internal factors is the most difficult part of developing a SWOT Matrix and requires good judgment—and there is no one best set of matches. Note in Table 6-1 that the first, second, third, and fourth strategies are SO, WO, ST, and WT strategies, respectively.

SO Strategies use a firm's internal strengths to take advantage of external opportunities. All managers would like their organizations to be in a position in which internal strengths can be used to take advantage of external trends and events. Organizations generally will pursue WO, ST, or WT strategies to get into a situation in which they can apply SO Strategies. When a firm has major weaknesses, it will strive to overcome them and make them strengths. When an organization faces major threats, it will seek to avoid them to concentrate on opportunities.

WO Strategies aim at improving internal weaknesses by taking advantage of external opportunities. Sometimes key external opportunities exist, but a firm has internal weaknesses that prevent it from exploiting those opportunities. For example, there may be a high demand for electronic devices to control the amount and timing of fuel injection in automobile engines (opportunity), but a certain auto parts manufacturer may lack the technology required for producing these devices (weakness). One possible WO Strategy would be to acquire this technology by forming a joint venture with a firm having competency in this area. An alternative WO Strategy would be to hire and train people with the required technical capabilities.

ST Strategies use a firm's strengths to avoid or reduce the impact of external threats. This does not mean that a strong organization should always meet threats in the external environment head-on. An example of ST Strategy occurred when Texas Instruments used an excellent legal department (a strength) to collect nearly $700 million in damages and royalties from nine Japanese and Korean firms that infringed on patents for semiconductor memory chips (threat).

Rival firms that copy ideas, innovations, and patented products are a major threat in many industries. This is still a major problem for U.S. firms selling products in China.

WT Strategies are defensive tactics directed at reducing internal weakness and avoiding external threats. An organization faced with numerous external threats and internal weaknesses may indeed be in a precarious position. In fact, such a firm may have to fight for its survival, merge, retrench, declare bankruptcy, or choose liquidation.

A schematic representation of the SWOT Matrix is provided in Figure 6-3. Note that a SWOT Matrix is composed of nine cells. As shown, there are four key factor cells, four strategy cells, and one cell that is always left blank (the upper-left cell). The four strategy cells, labeled *SO, WO, ST,* and *WT,* are developed after completing four key factor cells, labeled *S, W, O,* and *T.* There are eight steps involved in constructing a SWOT Matrix:

1. List the firm's key external opportunities.
2. List the firm's key external threats.
3. List the firm's key internal strengths.
4. List the firm's key internal weaknesses.
5. Match internal strengths with external opportunities, and record the resultant SO Strategies in the appropriate cell.
6. Match internal weaknesses with external opportunities, and record the resultant WO Strategies.
7. Match internal strengths with external threats, and record the resultant ST Strategies.
8. Match internal weaknesses with external threats, and record the resultant WT Strategies.

Some important aspects of a SWOT Matrix are evidenced in Figure 6-3. For example, note that both the internal/external factors and the SO/ST/WO/WT Strategies are stated in quantitative terms to the extent possible. This is important. For example, regarding the second SO #2 and ST #1 strategies, if the analyst just said, "Add new repair/service persons," the reader might think that 20 new repair/service persons are needed. Actually only two are needed. Always *be specific* to the extent possible in stating factors and strategies.

It is also important to include the "S1, O2" type notation after each strategy in a SWOT Matrix. This notation reveals the rationale for each alternative strategy. Strategies do not rise out of the blue. Note in Figure 6-3 how this notation reveals the internal/external factors that were matched to formulate desirable strategies. For example, note that this retail computer store business may need to "purchase land to build new store" because a new Highway 34 will make its location less desirable. The notation (W2, O2) and (S8, T3) in Figure 6-3 exemplifies this matching process.

The purpose of each Stage 2 matching tool is to generate feasible alternative strategies, not to select or determine which strategies are best. Not all of the strategies developed in the SWOT Matrix, therefore, will be selected for implementation.

The strategy-formulation guidelines provided in Chapter 5 can enhance the process of matching key external and internal factors. For example, when an organization has both the capital and human resources needed to distribute its own products (internal strength) and distributors are unreliable, costly, or incapable of meeting the firm's needs (external threat), forward integration can be an attractive ST Strategy. When a firm has excess production capacity (internal weakness) and its basic industry is experiencing declining annual sales and profits (external threat), related diversification can be an effective WT Strategy.

Although the SWOT matrix is widely used in strategic planning, the analysis does have some limitations.[4] First, SWOT does not show how to achieve a competitive advantage, so it must not be an end in itself. The matrix should be the starting point for a discussion on how proposed strategies could be implemented as well as cost-benefit considerations that ultimately could lead to competitive advantage. Second, SWOT is a static assessment (or snapshot) in time. A SWOT matrix can be like studying a single frame of a motion picture where you see the lead characters and the setting but have no clue as to the plot. As circumstances, capabilities, threats, and strategies change, the dynamics of a competitive

FIGURE 6-3

A SWOT Matrix for a Retail Computer Store

	Strengths	Weaknesses
	1. Inventory turnover up 5.8 to 6.7	1. Software revenues in store down 12%
	2. Average customer purchase up $97 to $128	2. Location of store hurt by new Hwy 34
	3. Employee morale is excellent	3. Carpet and paint in store in disrepair
	4. In-store promotions = 20% increase in sales	4. Bathroom in store needs refurbishing
	5. Newspaper advertising expenditures down 10%	5. Total store revenues down 8%
	6. Revenues from repair/service in-store up 16%	6. Store has no Web site
	7. In-store technical support persons have MIS degrees	7. Supplier on-time-delivery up to 2.4 days
	8. Store's debt-to-total assets ratio down 34%	8. Customer checkout process too slow
		9. Revenues per employee up 19%

Opportunities	SO Strategies	WO Strategies
1. Population of city growing 10%	1. Add 4 new in-store promotions monthly (S4,O3)	1. Purchase land to build new store (W2, O2)
2. Rival computer store opening 1 mile away	2. Add 2 new repair/service persons (S6, O5)	2. Install new carpet/paint/bath (W3, W4, O1)
3. Vehicle traffic passing store up 12%	3. Send flyer to all seniors over age 55 (S5, O5)	3. Up Web site services by 50% (W6, O7, O8)
4. Vendors average six new products/yr		4. Launch mailout to all Realtors in city (W5, O7)
5. Senior citizen use of computers up 8%		
6. Small business growth in area up 10%		
7. Desire for Web sites up 18% by Realtors		
8. Desire for Web sites up 12% by small firms		

Threats	ST Strategies	WT Strategies
1. Best Buy opening new store in 1yr nearby	1. Hire two more repair persons and market these new services (S6, S7, T1)	1. Hire 2 new cashiers (W8, T1, T4)
2. Local university offers computer repair	2. Purchase land to build new store (S8, T3)	2. Install new carpet/paint/bath (W3, W4, T1)
3. New bypass Hwy 34 in 1 yr will divert traffic	3. Raise out-of-store service calls from $60 to $80 (S6, T5)	
4. New mall being built nearby		
5. Gas prices up 14%		
6. Vendors raising prices 8%		

environment may not be revealed in a single matrix. Third, SWOT analysis may lead the firm to overemphasize a single internal or external factor in formulating strategies. There are interrelationships among the key internal and external factors that SWOT does not reveal that may be important in devising strategies.

The Strategic Position and Action Evaluation (SPACE) Matrix

The *Strategic Position and Action Evaluation (SPACE) Matrix,* another important Stage 2 matching tool, is illustrated in Figure 6-4. Its four-quadrant framework indicates whether aggressive, conservative, defensive, or competitive strategies are most appropriate for a given organization. The axes of the SPACE Matrix represent two internal dimensions (*financial position [FP]* and *competitive position [CP]*) and two external dimensions (*stability position [SP]* and *industry position [IP]*). These four factors are perhaps the most important determinants of an organization's overall strategic position.[5]

Depending on the type of organization, numerous variables could make up each of the dimensions represented on the axes of the SPACE Matrix. Factors that were included earlier in the firm's EFE and IFE Matrices should be considered in developing a SPACE Matrix. Other variables commonly included are given in Table 6-2. For example, return on investment, leverage, liquidity, working capital, and cash flow are commonly considered to be determining factors of an organization's financial strength. Like the SWOT Matrix, the SPACE Matrix should be both tailored to the particular organization being studied and based on factual information as much as possible.

FIGURE 6-4

The SPACE Matrix

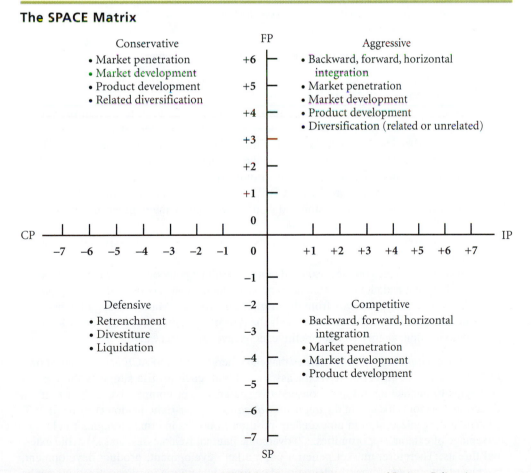

Source: Adapted from H. Rowe, R. Mason, and K. Dickel, *Strategic Management and Business Policy: A Methodological Approach* (Reading, MA: Addison-Wesley Publishing Co. Inc., © 1982): 155.

TABLE 6-2 Example Factors That Make Up the SPACE Matrix Axes

Internal Strategic Position	External Strategic Position
Financial Position (FP)	*Stability Position (SP)*
Return on investment	Technological changes
Leverage	Rate of inflation
Liquidity	Demand variability
Working capital	Price range of competing products
Cash flow	Barriers to entry into market
Inventory turnover	Competitive pressure
Earnings per share	Ease of exit from market
Price earnings ratio	Price elasticity of demand
	Risk involved in business
Competitive Position (CP)	*Industry Position (IP)*
Market share	Growth potential
Product quality	Profit potential
Product life cycle	Financial stability
Customer loyalty	Extent leveraged
Capacity utilization	Resource utilization
Technological know-how	Ease of entry into market
Control over suppliers and distributors	Productivity, capacity utilization

Source: Adapted from H. Rowe, R. Mason, and K. Dickel, *Strategic Management and Business Policy: A Methodological Approach* (Reading, MA: Addison-Wesley Publishing Co. Inc., © 1982): 155–156.

The steps required to develop a SPACE Matrix are as follows:

1. Select a set of variables to define financial position (FP), competitive position (CP), stability position (SP), and industry position (IP).
2. Assign a numerical value ranging from +1 (worst) to +7 (best) to each of the variables that make up the FP and IP dimensions. Assign a numerical value ranging from −1 (best) to −7 (worst) to each of the variables that make up the SP and CP dimensions. On the FP and CP axes, make comparison to competitors. On the IP and SP axes, make comparison to other industries.
3. Compute an average score for FP, CP, IP, and SP by summing the values given to the variables of each dimension and then by dividing by the number of variables included in the respective dimension.
4. Plot the average scores for FP, IP, SP, and CP on the appropriate axis in the SPACE Matrix.
5. Add the two scores on the *x*-axis and plot the resultant point on X. Add the two scores on the *y*-axis and plot the resultant point on Y. Plot the intersection of the new *xy* point.
6. Draw a *directional vector* from the origin of the SPACE Matrix through the new intersection point. This vector reveals the type of strategies recommended for the organization: aggressive, competitive, defensive, or conservative.

Some examples of strategy profiles that can emerge from a SPACE analysis are shown in Figure 6-5. The directional vector associated with each profile suggests the type of strategies to pursue: aggressive, conservative, defensive, or competitive. When a firm's directional vector is located in the *aggressive quadrant* (upper-right quadrant) of the SPACE Matrix, an organization is in an excellent position to use its internal strengths to (1) take advantage of external opportunities, (2) overcome internal weaknesses, and (3) avoid external threats. Therefore, market penetration, market development, product development, backward integration, forward integration, horizontal integration, or diversification, can be feasible, depending on the specific circumstances that face the firm.

FIGURE 6-5

Example Strategy Profiles

Aggressive Profiles

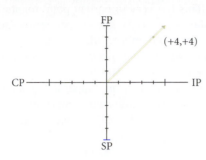

A financially strong firm that has achieved major competitive advantages in a growing and stable industry

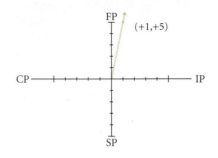

A firm whose financial strength is a dominating factor in the industry

Conservative Profiles

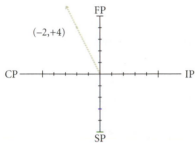

A firm that has achieved financial strength in a stable industry that is not growing; the firm has few competitive advantages

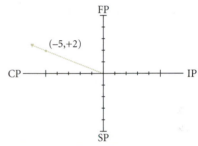

A firm that suffers from major competitive disadvantages in an industry that is technologically stable but declining in sales

Competitive Profiles

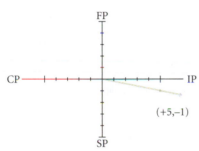

A firm with major competitive advantages in a high-growth industry

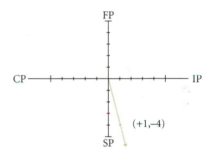

An organization that is competing fairly well in an unstable industry

Defensive Profiles

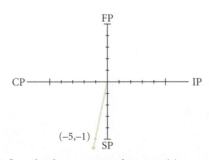

A firm that has a very weak competitive position in a negative growth, stable industry

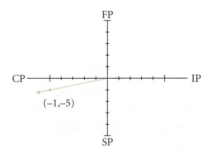

A financially troubled firm in a very unstable industry

Source: Adapted from H. Rowe, R. Mason, and K. Dickel, *Strategic Management and Business Policy: A Methodological Approach* (Reading, MA: Addison-Wesley Publishing Co. Inc., © 1982): 155.

When a particular company is known, the analyst must be much more specific in terms of implied strategies. For example, instead of saying market penetration is a recommended strategy when your vector goes in the Conservative quadrant, say that adding 34 new stores in India is a recommended strategy. This is a very important point for students doing case analyses because a particular company is generally known, and terms such as *market development* are too vague to use. That term could refer to adding a manufacturing plant in Thailand or Mexico or South Africa—*so students—Be specific to the extent possible regarding implications of all the matrices presented in Chapter 6.*

The directional vector may appear in the *conservative quadrant* (upper-left quadrant) of the SPACE Matrix, which implies staying close to the firm's basic competencies and not taking excessive risks. Conservative strategies most often include market penetration, market development, product development, and related diversification. The directional vector may be located in the lower-left or *defensive quadrant* of the SPACE Matrix, which suggests that the firm should focus on rectifying internal weaknesses and avoiding external threats. Defensive strategies include retrenchment, divestiture, liquidation, and related diversification. Finally, the directional vector may be located in the lower-right or *competitive quadrant* of the SPACE Matrix, indicating competitive strategies. Competitive strategies include backward, forward, and horizontal integration; market penetration; market development and product development.

A SPACE Matrix analysis for a bank is provided in Table 6-3. Note that competitive type strategies are recommended.

TABLE 6-3   A SPACE Matrix for a Bank

Financial Position (FP)	Ratings
The bank's primary capital ratio is 7.23 percent, which is 1.23 percentage points over the generally required ratio of 6 percent.	1.0
The bank's return on assets is negative 0.77, compared to a bank industry average ratio of positive 0.70.	1.0
The bank's net income was $183 million, down 9 percent from a year earlier.	3.0
The bank's revenues increased 7 percent to $3.46 billion.	4.0
	9.0

Industry Position (IP)	
Deregulation provides geographic and product freedom.	4.0
Deregulation increases competition in the banking industry.	2.0
Pennsylvania's interstate banking law allows the bank to acquire other banks in New Jersey, Ohio, Kentucky, the District of Columbia, and West Virginia.	4.0
	10.0

Stability Position (SP)	
Less-developed countries are experiencing high inflation and political instability.	−4.0
Headquartered in Pittsburgh, the bank historically has been heavily dependent on the steel, oil, and gas industries. These industries are depressed.	−5.0
Banking deregulation has created instability throughout the industry.	−4.0
	−13.0

Competitive Position (CP)	
The bank provides data processing services for more than 450 institutions in 38 states.	−2.0
Superregional banks, international banks, and nonbanks are becoming increasingly competitive.	−5.0
The bank has a large customer base.	−2.0
	−9.0

Conclusion

SP Average is −13.0 ÷ 3 = −4.33   IP Average is +10.0 ÷ 3 = 3.33

CP Average is −9.0 ÷ 3 = −3.00   FP Average is +9.0 ÷ 4 = 2.25

Directional Vector Coordinates: x-axis: −3.00 + (+3.33) = +0.33

y-axis: −4.33 + (+2.25) = −2.08

The bank should pursue Competitive Strategies.

The Boston Consulting Group (BCG) Matrix

Autonomous divisions (or profit centers) of an organization make up what is called a *business portfolio.* When a firm's divisions compete in different industries, a separate strategy often must be developed for each business. The *Boston Consulting Group (BCG) Matrix* and the *Internal-External (IE) Matrix* are designed specifically to enhance a multidivisional firm's efforts to formulate strategies. (BCG is a private management consulting firm based in Boston. BCG employs about 4,300 consultants worldwide.)

In a *Form 10K* or *Annual Report*, some companies do not disclose financial information by segment, so a BCG portfolio analysis is not possible by external entities. Reasons to disclose by-division financial information in the author's view, however, more than offset the reasons not to disclose, as indicated in Table 6-4.

The BCG Matrix graphically portrays differences among divisions in terms of relative market share position and industry growth rate. The BCG Matrix allows a multidivisional organization to manage its portfolio of businesses by examining the relative market share position and the industry growth rate of each division relative to all other divisions in the organization. *Relative market share position* is defined as the ratio of a division's own market share (or revenues) in a particular industry to the market share (or revenues) held by the largest rival firm in that industry. Note in Table 6-5 that other variables can be in this analysis besides revenues. Relative market share position for Heineken could also be determined by dividing Heineken's revenues by the leader Corona Extra's revenues.

Relative market share position is given on the *x*-axis of the BCG Matrix. The midpoint on the *x*-axis usually is set at .50, corresponding to a division that has half the market share of the leading firm in the industry. The *y*-axis represents the industry growth rate in sales, measured in percentage terms. The growth rate percentages on the *y*-axis could range from −20 to +20 percent, with 0.0 being the midpoint. The average annual increase in revenues for several leading firms in the industry would be a good estimate of the value. Also, various sources such as the S&P Industry Survey would provide this value. These numerical ranges on the *x*- and *y*-axes are often used, but other numerical values could be established as deemed appropriate for particular organizations, such as −10 to +10 percent.

The basic BCG Matrix appears in Figure 6-6. Each circle represents a separate division. The size of the circle corresponds to the proportion of corporate revenue generated by that business unit, and the pie slice indicates the proportion of corporate profits generated by that division. Divisions located in Quadrant I of the BCG Matrix are called "Question Marks," those located in Quadrant II are called "Stars," those located in Quadrant III are called "Cash Cows," and those divisions located in Quadrant IV are called "Dogs."

- *Question Marks*—Divisions in Quadrant I have a low relative market share position, yet they compete in a high-growth industry. Generally these firms' cash needs are

TABLE 6-4 Reasons to (or Not to) Disclose Financial Information by Segment (by Division)

Reasons to Disclose	Reasons Not to Disclose
1. Transparency is a good thing in today's world of Sarbanes-Oxley	1. Can become free competitive information for rival firms
2. Investors will better understand the firm, which can lead to greater support	2. Can hide performance failures
3. Managers/employees will better understand the firm, which should lead to greater commitment	3. Can reduce rivalry among segments
4. Disclosure enhances the communication process both within the firm and with outsiders	

TABLE 6-5 Market Share Data for Selected Industries in 2009

U.S. Top Five Airlines by Number of Passengers Boarded in 2008 (in millions; estimate)	
Southwest	7.5
American	5.0
Delta	4.5
United	4.0
US Airways	3.5

U.S. Top Five Imported Beers in 2008 (in millions of barrels imported)	
Corona Extra	8.0
Heineken	5.0
Modelo Especial	2.0
Tecate	1.5
Guinness	1.0

Source: Based on David Kesmodel, "U.S. Beer Imports Lose Their Fizz," *Wall Street Journal* (February 20, 2009): B5; S&P Industry Surveys and Company *Form 10-K* Reports.

high and their cash generation is low. These businesses are called *Question Marks* because the organization must decide whether to strengthen them by pursuing an intensive strategy (market penetration, market development, or product development) or to sell them.

- **Stars**—Quadrant II businesses (*Stars*) represent the organization's best long-run opportunities for growth and profitability. Divisions with a high relative market share and a high industry growth rate should receive substantial investment to maintain or strengthen their dominant positions. Forward, backward, and horizontal integration; market penetration; market development; and product development are appropriate strategies for these divisions to consider, as indicated in Figure 6-6.
- **Cash Cows**—Divisions positioned in Quadrant III have a high relative market share position but compete in a low-growth industry. Called *Cash Cows* because they generate cash in excess of their needs, they are often milked. Many of today's Cash

FIGURE 6-6

The BCG Matrix

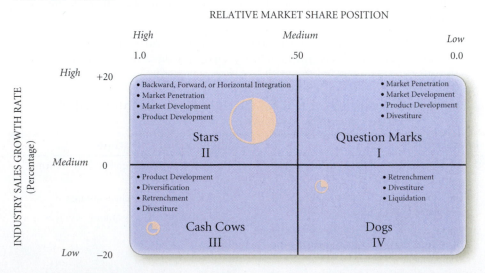

Source: Adapted from the BCG Portfolio Matrix from the Product Portfolio Matrix, © 1970, The Boston Consulting Group.

Cows were yesterday's Stars. Cash Cow divisions should be managed to maintain their strong position for as long as possible. Product development or diversification may be attractive strategies for strong Cash Cows. However, as a Cash Cow division becomes weak, retrenchment or divestiture can become more appropriate.

• **Dogs**—Quadrant IV divisions of the organization have a low relative market share position and compete in a slow- or no-market-growth industry; they are *Dogs* in the firm's portfolio. Because of their weak internal and external position, these businesses are often liquidated, divested, or trimmed down through retrenchment. When a division first becomes a Dog, retrenchment can be the best strategy to pursue because many Dogs have bounced back, after strenuous asset and cost reduction, to become viable, profitable divisions.

The major benefit of the BCG Matrix is that it draws attention to the cash flow, investment characteristics, and needs of an organization's various divisions. The divisions of many firms evolve over time: Dogs become Question Marks, Question Marks become Stars, Stars become Cash Cows, and Cash Cows become Dogs in an ongoing counterclockwise motion. Less frequently, Stars become Question Marks, Question Marks become Dogs, Dogs become Cash Cows, and Cash Cows become Stars (in a clockwise motion). In some organizations, no cyclical motion is apparent. Over time, organizations should strive to achieve a portfolio of divisions that are Stars.

An example BCG Matrix is provided in Figure 6-7, which illustrates an organization composed of five divisions with annual sales ranging from $5,000 to $60,000. Division 1 has the greatest sales volume, so the circle representing that division is the largest one in the matrix. The circle corresponding to Division 5 is the smallest because its sales volume ($5,000) is least among all the divisions. The pie slices within the circles reveal the percent of corporate profits contributed by each division. As shown, Division 1 contributes the highest profit percentage, 39 percent. Notice in the diagram that Division 1 is considered a Star, Division 2 is a Question Mark, Division 3 is also a Question Mark, Division 4 is a Cash Cow, and Division 5 is a Dog.

FIGURE 6-7

An Example BCG Matrix

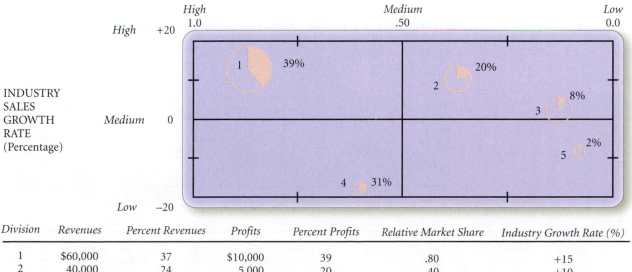

Division	Revenues	Percent Revenues	Profits	Percent Profits	Relative Market Share	Industry Growth Rate (%)
1	$60,000	37	$10,000	39	.80	+15
2	40,000	24	5,000	20	.40	+10
3	40,000	24	2,000	8	.10	+1
4	20,000	12	8,000	31	.60	−20
5	5,000	3	500	2	.05	−10
Total	$165,000	100	$25,500	100	—	—

The BCG Matrix, like all analytical techniques, has some limitations. For example, viewing every business as either a Star, Cash Cow, Dog, or Question Mark is an oversimplification; many businesses fall right in the middle of the BCG Matrix and thus are not easily classified. Furthermore, the BCG Matrix does not reflect whether or not various divisions or their industries are growing over time; that is, the matrix has no temporal qualities, but rather it is a snapshot of an organization at a given point in time. Finally, other variables besides relative market share position and industry growth rate in sales, such as size of the market and competitive advantages, are important in making strategic decisions about various divisions.

An example BCG Matrix is provided in Figure 6-8. Note in Figure 6-8 that Division 5 had an operating loss of $188 million. Take note how the percent profit column is still calculated because oftentimes a firm will have a division that incurs a loss for a year. In terms of the pie slice in circle 5 of the diagram, note that it is a *different color* from the positive profit segments in the other circles.

The Internal-External (IE) Matrix

The *Internal-External (IE) Matrix* positions an organization's various divisions in a nine-cell display, illustrated in Figure 6-9. The IE Matrix is similar to the BCG Matrix in that both tools involve plotting organization divisions in a schematic diagram; this is why they are both called "portfolio matrices." Also, the size of each circle represents the percentage sales contribution of each division, and pie slices reveal the percentage profit contribution of each division in both the BCG and IE Matrix.

But there are some important differences between the BCG Matrix and the IE Matrix. First, the axes are different. Also, the IE Matrix requires more information about the divisions than the BCG Matrix. Furthermore, the strategic implications of each matrix are different. For these reasons, strategists in multidivisional firms often develop both the BCG Matrix and the IE Matrix in formulating alternative strategies. A common practice is to develop a BCG Matrix and an IE Matrix for the present and then develop projected matrices to reflect expectations of the future. This before-and-after analysis forecasts the expected effect of strategic decisions on an organization's portfolio of divisions.

FIGURE 6-8

An Example BCG Matrix

RELATIVE MARKET SHARE POSITION (RMSP)

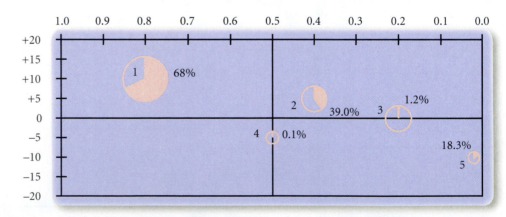

Division	$ Sales (millions)	% Sales	$ Profits (millions)	% Profits	RMSP	IG Rate %
1.	$5,139	51.5	$799	68.0	0.8	10
2.	2,556	25.6	400	39.0	0.4	05
3.	1,749	17.5	12	1.2	0.2	00
4.	493	4.9	4	0.1	0.5	−05
5.	42	0.5	−188	(18.3)	.02	−10
Total	$9,979	100.0	$1,027	100.0		

FIGURE 6-9

The Internal–External (IE) Matrix

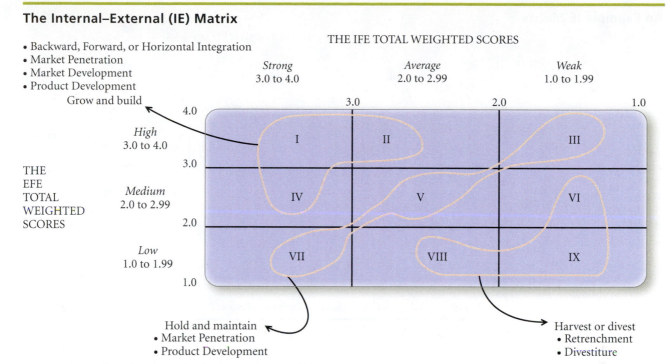

Source: Adapted. The IE Matrix was developed from the General Electric (GE) Business Screen Matrix. For a description of the GE Matrix see Michael Allen, "Diagramming GE's Planning for What's WATT," in R. Allio and M. Pennington, eds., *Corporate Planning: Techniques and Applications* (New York: AMACOM, 1979).

The IE Matrix is based on two key dimensions: the IFE total weighted scores on the *x*-axis and the EFE total weighted scores on the *y*-axis. Recall that each division of an organization should construct an IFE Matrix and an EFE Matrix for its part of the organization. The total weighted scores derived from the divisions allow construction of the corporate-level IE Matrix. On the *x*-axis of the IE Matrix, an IFE total weighted score of 1.0 to 1.99 represents a weak internal position; a score of 2.0 to 2.99 is considered average; and a score of 3.0 to 4.0 is strong. Similarly, on the *y*-axis, an EFE total weighted score of 1.0 to 1.99 is considered low; a score of 2.0 to 2.99 is medium; and a score of 3.0 to 4.0 is high.

The IE Matrix can be divided into three major regions that have different strategy implications. First, the prescription for divisions that fall into cells I, II, or IV can be described as *grow and build*. Intensive (market penetration, market development, and product development) or integrative (backward integration, forward integration, and horizontal integration) strategies can be most appropriate for these divisions. Second, divisions that fall into cells III, V, or VII can be managed best with *hold and maintain* strategies; market penetration and product development are two commonly employed strategies for these types of divisions. Third, a common prescription for divisions that fall into cells VI, VIII, or IX is *harvest or divest*. Successful organizations are able to achieve a portfolio of businesses positioned in or around cell I in the IE Matrix.

An example of a completed IE Matrix is given in Figure 6-10, which depicts an organization composed of four divisions. As indicated by the positioning of the circles, *grow and build* strategies are appropriate for Division 1, Division 2, and Division 3. Division 4 is a candidate for *harvest or divest*. Division 2 contributes the greatest percentage of company sales and thus is represented by the largest circle. Division 1 contributes the greatest proportion of total profits; it has the largest-percentage pie slice.

As indicated in Figure 6-11, the IE Matrix has five product segments. Note that Division #1 has the largest revenues (as indicated by the largest circle) and the largest profits (as indicated by the largest pie slice) in the matrix. It is common for organizations to

FIGURE 6-10

An Example IE Matrix

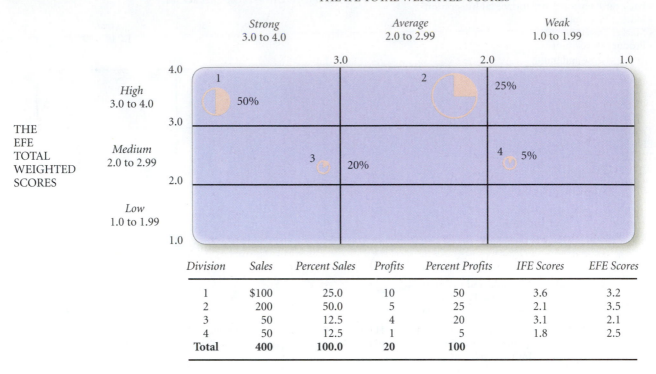

Division	Sales	Percent Sales	Profits	Percent Profits	IFE Scores	EFE Scores
1	$100	25.0	10	50	3.6	3.2
2	200	50.0	5	25	2.1	3.5
3	50	12.5	4	20	3.1	2.1
4	50	12.5	1	5	1.8	2.5
Total	**400**	**100.0**	**20**	**100**		

FIGURE 6-11

The IE Matrix

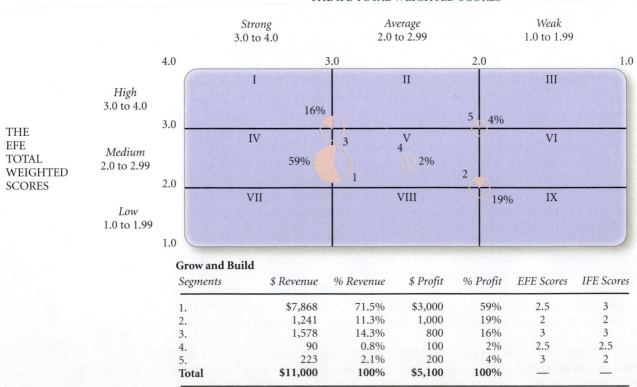

Grow and Build

Segments	$ Revenue	% Revenue	$ Profit	% Profit	EFE Scores	IFE Scores
1.	$7,868	71.5%	$3,000	59%	2.5	3
2.	1,241	11.3%	1,000	19%	2	2
3.	1,578	14.3%	800	16%	3	3
4.	90	0.8%	100	2%	2.5	2.5
5.	223	2.1%	200	4%	3	2
Total	**$11,000**	**100%**	**$5,100**	**100%**	**—**	**—**

develop both geographic and product-based IE Matrices to more effectively formulate strategies and allocate resources among divisions. In addition, firms often prepare an IE (or BCG) Matrix for competitors. Furthermore, firms will often prepare "before and after" IE (or BCG) Matrices to reveal the situation at present versus the expected situation after one year. This latter idea minimizes the limitation of these matrices being a "snapshot in time." In performing case analysis, feel free to estimate the IFE and EFE scores for the various divisions based upon your research into the company and industry—rather than preparing a separate IE Matrix for each division.

The Grand Strategy Matrix

In addition to the SWOT Matrix, SPACE Matrix, BCG Matrix, and IE Matrix, the *Grand Strategy Matrix* has become a popular tool for formulating alternative strategies. All organizations can be positioned in one of the Grand Strategy Matrix's four strategy quadrants. A firm's divisions likewise could be positioned. As illustrated in Figure 6-12, the Grand Strategy Matrix is based on two evaluative dimensions: competitive position and market (industry) growth. Any industry whose annual growth in sales exceeds 5 percent could be considered to have rapid growth. Appropriate strategies for an organization to consider are listed in sequential order of attractiveness in each quadrant of the matrix.

Firms located in Quadrant I of the Grand Strategy Matrix are in an excellent strategic position. For these firms, continued concentration on current markets (market penetration and market development) and products (product development) is an appropriate strategy. It is unwise for a Quadrant I firm to shift notably from its established competitive advantages. When a Quadrant I organization has excessive resources, then backward, forward, or horizontal integration may be effective strategies. When a Quadrant I firm is too heavily committed to a single product, then related diversification may reduce the risks associated with a narrow product line. Quadrant I firms can afford to take advantage of external opportunities in several areas. They can take risks aggressively when necessary.

FIGURE 6-12

The Grand Strategy Matrix

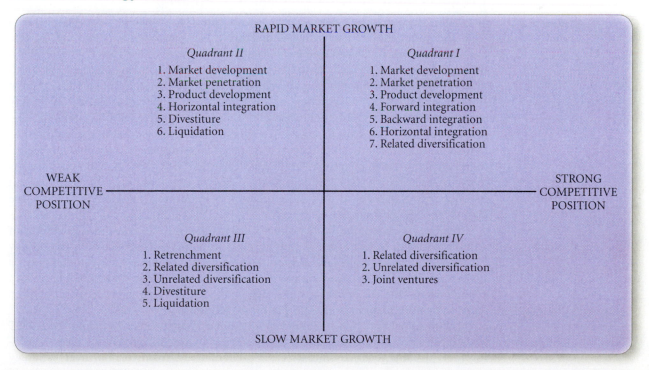

Source: Adapted from Roland Christensen, Norman Berg, and Malcolm Salter, *Policy Formulation and Administration* (Homewood, IL: Richard D. Irwin, 1976): 16–18.

Firms positioned in Quadrant II need to evaluate their present approach to the marketplace seriously. Although their industry is growing, they are unable to compete effectively, and they need to determine why the firm's current approach is ineffective and how the company can best change to improve its competitiveness. Because Quadrant II firms are in a rapid-market-growth industry, an intensive strategy (as opposed to integrative or diversification) is usually the first option that should be considered. However, if the firm is lacking a distinctive competence or competitive advantage, then horizontal integration is often a desirable alternative. As a last resort, divestiture or liquidation should be considered. Divestiture can provide funds needed to acquire other businesses or buy back shares of stock.

Quadrant III organizations compete in slow-growth industries and have weak competitive positions. These firms must make some drastic changes quickly to avoid further decline and possible liquidation. Extensive cost and asset reduction (retrenchment) should be pursued first. An alternative strategy is to shift resources away from the current business into different areas (diversify). If all else fails, the final options for Quadrant III businesses are divestiture or liquidation.

Finally, Quadrant IV businesses have a strong competitive position but are in a slow-growth industry. These firms have the strength to launch diversified programs into more promising growth areas: Quadrant IV firms have characteristically high cash-flow levels and limited internal growth needs and often can pursue related or unrelated diversification successfully. Quadrant IV firms also may pursue joint ventures.

The Decision Stage

Analysis and intuition provide a basis for making strategy-formulation decisions. The matching techniques just discussed reveal feasible alternative strategies. Many of these strategies will likely have been proposed by managers and employees participating in the strategy analysis and choice activity. Any additional strategies resulting from the matching analyses could be discussed and added to the list of feasible alternative options. As indicated earlier in this chapter, participants could rate these strategies on a 1 to 4 scale so that a prioritized list of the best strategies could be achieved.

The Quantitative Strategic Planning Matrix (QSPM)

Other than ranking strategies to achieve the prioritized list, there is only one analytical technique in the literature designed to determine the relative attractiveness of feasible alternative actions. This technique is the *Quantitative Strategic Planning Matrix (QSPM),* which comprises Stage 3 of the strategy-formulation analytical framework.[6] This technique objectively indicates which alternative strategies are best. The QSPM uses input from Stage 1 analyses and matching results from Stage 2 analyses to decide objectively among alternative strategies. That is, the EFE Matrix, IFE Matrix, and Competitive Profile Matrix that make up Stage 1, coupled with the SWOT Matrix, SPACE Matrix, BCG Matrix, IE Matrix, and Grand Strategy Matrix that make up Stage 2, provide the needed information for setting up the QSPM (Stage 3). The QSPM is a tool that allows strategists to evaluate alternative strategies objectively, based on previously identified external and internal critical success factors. Like other strategy-formulation analytical tools, the QSPM requires good intuitive judgment.

The basic format of the QSPM is illustrated in Table 6-6. Note that the left column of a QSPM consists of key external and internal factors (from Stage 1), and the top row consists of feasible alternative strategies (from Stage 2). Specifically, the left column of a QSPM consists of information obtained directly from the EFE Matrix and IFE Matrix. In a column adjacent to the critical success factors, the respective weights received by each factor in the EFE Matrix and the IFE Matrix are recorded.

The top row of a QSPM consists of alternative strategies derived from the SWOT Matrix, SPACE Matrix, BCG Matrix, IE Matrix, and Grand Strategy Matrix. These matching tools usually generate similar feasible alternatives. However, not every strategy suggested by the matching techniques has to be evaluated in a QSPM. Strategists should use good intuitive judgment in selecting strategies to include in a QSPM.

TABLE 6-6 **The Quantitative Strategic Planning Matrix—QSPM**

Key Factors	Weight	Strategic Alternatives		
		Strategy 1	Strategy 2	Strategy 3
Key External Factors				
Economy				
Political/Legal/Governmental				
Social/Cultural/Demographic/Environmental				
Technological				
Competitive				
Key Internal Factors				
Management				
Marketing				
Finance/Accounting				
Production/Operations				
Research and Development				
Management Information Systems				

Conceptually, the QSPM determines the relative attractiveness of various strategies based on the extent to which key external and internal critical success factors are capitalized upon or improved. The relative attractiveness of each strategy within a set of alternatives is computed by determining the cumulative impact of each external and internal critical success factor. Any number of sets of alternative strategies can be included in the QSPM, and any number of strategies can make up a given set, but only strategies within a given set are evaluated relative to each other. For example, one set of strategies may include diversification, whereas another set may include issuing stock and selling a division to raise needed capital. These two sets of strategies are totally different, and the QSPM evaluates strategies only within sets. Note in Table 6-6 that three strategies are included, and they make up just one set.

A QSPM for a retail computer store is provided in Table 6-7. This example illustrates all the components of the QSPM: Strategic Alternatives, Key Factors, Weights, Attractiveness Scores (AS), Total Attractiveness Scores (TAS), and the Sum Total Attractiveness Score. The three new terms just introduced—(1) Attractiveness Scores, (2) Total Attractiveness Scores, and (3) the Sum Total Attractiveness Score—are defined and explained as the six steps required to develop a QSPM are discussed:

Step 1 *Make a list of the firm's key external opportunities/threats and internal strengths/weaknesses in the left column of the QSPM.* This information should be taken directly from the EFE Matrix and IFE Matrix. A minimum of 10 external key success factors and 10 internal key success factors should be included in the QSPM.

Step 2 *Assign weights to each key external and internal factor.* These weights are identical to those in the EFE Matrix and the IFE Matrix. The weights are presented in a straight column just to the right of the external and internal critical success factors.

Step 3 *Examine the Stage 2 (matching) matrices, and identify alternative strategies that the organization should consider implementing.* Record these strategies in the top row of the QSPM. Group the strategies into mutually exclusive sets if possible.

Step 4 *Determine the Attractiveness Scores (AS)* defined as numerical values that indicate the relative attractiveness of each strategy in a given set of alternatives. *Attractiveness Scores (AS)* are determined by examining each key external or internal factor, one at a time, and asking the question "Does this factor affect the choice of strategies being made?" If the answer to this question is yes, then the strategies should be compared relative to that key factor. Specifically, Attractiveness Scores should be assigned to each strategy to indicate the relative attractiveness of one strategy over others, considering the particular factor. The range for Attractiveness Scores is 1 = not attractive, 2 = somewhat attractive, 3 = reasonably attractive, and

TABLE 6-7 A QSPM for a Retail Computer Store

Key Factors	Weight	Buy New Land and Build New Larger Store 1 AS	TAS	Fully Renovate Existing Store 2 AS	TAS
Opportunities					
1. Population of city growing 10%	0.10	4	0.40	2	0.20
2. Rival computer store opening 1 mile away	0.10	2	0.20	4	0.40
3. Vehicle traffic passing store up 12%	0.08	1	0.08	4	0.32
4. Vendors average six new products/year	0.05	—		—	
5. Senior citizen use of computers up 8%	0.05	—		—	
6. Small business growth in area up 10%	0.10	—		—	
7. Desire for Web sites up 18% by Realtors	0.06	—		—	
8. Desire for Web sites up 12% by small firms	0.06	—		—	
Threats					
1. Best Buy opening new store nearby in 1 year	0.15	4	0.60	3	0.45
2. Local university offers computer repair	0.08	—		—	
3. New bypass for Hwy 34 in 1 year will divert traffic	0.12	4	0.48	1	0.12
4. New mall being built nearby	0.08	2	0.16	4	0.32
5. Gas prices up 14%	0.04	—		—	
6. Vendors raising prices 8%	0.03	—		—	
	1.00				
Strengths					
1. Inventory turnover increased from 5.8 to 6.7	0.05	—		—	
2. Average customer purchase increased from $97 to $128	0.07	2	0.14	4	0.28
3. Employee morale is excellent	0.10	—		—	
4. In-store promotions resulted in 20% increase in sales	0.05	—		—	
5. Newspaper advertising expenditures increased 10%	0.02	—		—	
6. Revenues from repair/service segment of store up 16%	0.15	4	0.60	3	0.45
7. In-store technical support personnel have MIS college degrees	0.05	—		—	
8. Store's debt-to-total assets ratio declined to 34%	0.03	4	0.12	2	0.06
9. Revenues per employee up 19%	0.02	—		—	
Weaknesses					
1. Revenues from software segment of store down 12%	0.10	—		—	
2. Location of store negatively impacted by new Hwy 34	0.15	4	0.60	1	0.15
3. Carpet and paint in store somewhat in disrepair	0.02	1	0.02	4	0.08
4. Bathroom in store needs refurbishing	0.02	1	0.02	4	0.08
5. Revenues from businesses down 8%	0.04	3	0.12	4	0.16
6. Store has no Web site	0.05	—		—	
7. Supplier on-time delivery increased to 2.4 days	0.03	—		—	
8. Often customers have to wait to check out	0.05	2	0.10	4	0.20
Total	1.00		4.36		3.27

4 = highly attractive. By attractive, we mean the extent that one strategy, compared to others, enables the firm to either capitalize on the strength, improve on the weakness, exploit the opportunity, or avoid the threat. Work row by row in developing a QSPM. If the answer to the previous question is *no,* indicating that the respective key factor has no effect upon the specific choice being made, then do not assign Attractiveness Scores to the strategies in that set. Use a dash to indicate that the key factor does not affect the choice being made. *Note:* If you assign an AS score to one strategy, then assign AS score(s) to the other. In other words, if one strategy receives a dash, then all others must receive a dash in a given row.

Step 5   *Compute the Total Attractiveness Scores. Total Attractiveness Scores (TAS)* are defined as the product of multiplying the weights (Step 2) by the Attractiveness Scores (Step 4) in each row. The Total Attractiveness Scores indicate the relative attractiveness of each alternative strategy, considering only the impact of the adjacent external or internal critical success factor. The higher the Total Attractiveness Score, the more attractive the strategic alternative (considering only the adjacent critical success factor).

Step 6   *Compute the Sum Total Attractiveness Score.* Add Total Attractiveness Scores in each strategy column of the QSPM. The *Sum Total Attractiveness Scores (STAS)* reveal which strategy is most attractive in each set of alternatives. Higher scores indicate more attractive strategies, considering all the relevant external and internal factors that could affect the strategic decisions. The magnitude of the difference between the Sum Total Attractiveness Scores in a given set of strategic alternatives indicates the relative desirability of one strategy over another.

In Table 6-7, two alternative strategies—(1) buy new land and build new larger store and (2) fully renovate existing store—are being considered by a computer retail store. Note by sum total attractiveness scores of 4.63 versus 3.27 that the analysis indicates the business should buy new land and build a new larger store. Note the use of dashes to indicate which factors do not affect the strategy choice being considered. If a particular factor affects one strategy but not the other, it affects the choice being made, so attractiveness scores should be recorded for both strategies. Never rate one strategy and not the other. Note also in Table 6-7 that there are no double 1's, 2's, 3's, or 4's in a row. Never duplicate scores in a row. Never work column by column; always prepare a QSPM working row by row. If you have more than one strategy in the QSPM, then let the AS scores range from 1 to "the number of strategies being evaluated." This will enable you to have a different AS score for each strategy. These are all important guidelines to follow in developing a QSPM. In actual practice, the store did purchase the new land and build a new store; the business also did some minor refurbishing until the new store was operational.

There should be a rationale for each AS score assigned. Note in Table 6-7 in the first row that the "city population growing 10 percent annually" opportunity could be capitalized on best by strategy 1, "building the new, larger store," so an AS score of 4 was assigned to Strategy 1. AS scores, therefore, are not mere guesses; they should be rational, defensible, and reasonable.

Avoid giving each strategy the same AS score. Note in Table 6-7 that dashes are inserted all the way across the row when used. Also note that double 4's, or double 3's, or double 2's, or double 1's are never in a given row. Again work row by row, not column by column. These are important guidelines to follow in constructing a QSPM.

Positive Features and Limitations of the QSPM

A positive feature of the QSPM is that sets of strategies can be examined sequentially or simultaneously. For example, corporate-level strategies could be evaluated first, followed by division-level strategies, and then function-level strategies. There is no limit to the number of strategies that can be evaluated or the number of sets of strategies that can be examined at once using the QSPM.

Another positive feature of the QSPM is that it requires strategists to integrate pertinent external and internal factors into the decision process. Developing a QSPM makes it less likely that key factors will be overlooked or weighted inappropriately. A QSPM draws attention to important relationships that affect strategy decisions.

Although developing a QSPM requires a number of subjective decisions, making small decisions along the way enhances the probability that the final strategic decisions will be best for the organization. A QSPM can be adapted for use by small and large for-profit and nonprofit organizations so can be applied to virtually any type of organization. A QSPM can especially enhance strategic choice in multinational firms because many key factors and strategies can be considered at once. It also has been applied successfully by a number of small businesses.[7]

The QSPM is not without some limitations. First, it always requires intuitive judgments and educated assumptions. The ratings and attractiveness scores require judgmental decisions, even though they should be based on objective information. Discussion among strategists, managers, and employees throughout the strategy-formulation process, including development of a QSPM, is constructive and improves strategic decisions. Constructive discussion during strategy analysis and choice may arise because of genuine differences of interpretation of information and varying opinions. Another limitation of the QSPM is that it can be only as good as the prerequisite information and matching analyses upon which it is based.

Cultural Aspects of Strategy Choice

All organizations have a culture. *Culture* includes the set of shared values, beliefs, attitudes, customs, norms, personalities, heroes, and heroines that describe a firm. Culture is the unique way an organization does business. It is the human dimension that creates solidarity and meaning, and it inspires commitment and productivity in an organization when strategy changes are made. All human beings have a basic need to make sense of the world, to feel in control, and to make meaning. When events threaten meaning, individuals react defensively. Managers and employees may even sabotage new strategies in an effort to recapture the status quo.

It is beneficial to view strategic management from a cultural perspective because success often rests upon the degree of support that strategies receive from a firm's culture. If a firm's strategies are supported by cultural products such as values, beliefs, rites, rituals, ceremonies, stories, symbols, language, heroes, and heroines, then managers often can implement changes swiftly and easily. However, if a supportive culture does not exist and is not cultivated, then strategy changes may be ineffective or even counterproductive. A firm's culture can become antagonistic to new strategies, and the result of that antagonism may be confusion and disarray.

Strategies that require fewer cultural changes may be more attractive because extensive changes can take considerable time and effort. Whenever two firms merge, it becomes especially important to evaluate and consider culture-strategy linkages.

Culture provides an explanation for the difficulties a firm encounters when it attempts to shift its strategic direction, as the following statement explains:

> Not only has the "right" corporate culture become the essence and foundation of corporate excellence, but success or failure of needed corporate reforms hinges on management's sagacity and ability to change the firm's driving culture in time and in tune with required changes in strategies.[8]

The Politics of Strategy Choice

All organizations are political. Unless managed, political maneuvering consumes valuable time, subverts organizational objectives, diverts human energy, and results in the loss of some valuable employees. Sometimes political biases and personal preferences get unduly embedded in strategy choice decisions. Internal politics affect the choice of strategies in all organizations. The hierarchy of command in an organization, combined with the career aspirations of different people and the need to allocate scarce resources, guarantees the formation of coalitions of individuals who strive to take care of themselves first and the organization second, third, or fourth. Coalitions of individuals often form around key strategy issues that face an enterprise. A major responsibility of strategists is to guide the development of coalitions, to nurture an overall team concept, and to gain the support of key individuals and groups of individuals.

In the absence of objective analyses, strategy decisions too often are based on the politics of the moment. With development of improved strategy-formation tools, political factors become less important in making strategic decisions. In the absence of objectivity, political factors sometimes dictate strategies, and this is unfortunate. Managing political relationships is an integral part of building enthusiasm and esprit de corps in an organization.

A classic study of strategic management in nine large corporations examined the political tactics of successful and unsuccessful strategists.[9] Successful strategists were found to let weakly supported ideas and proposals die through inaction and to establish additional hurdles or tests for strongly supported ideas considered unacceptable but not openly opposed. Successful strategists kept a low political profile on unacceptable proposals and strived to let most negative decisions come from subordinates or a group consensus, thereby reserving their personal vetoes for big issues and crucial moments. Successful strategists did a lot of chatting and informal questioning to stay abreast of how things were progressing and to know when to intervene. They led strategy but did not dictate it. They gave few orders, announced few decisions, depended heavily on informal questioning, and sought to probe and clarify until a consensus emerged.

Successful strategists generously and visibly rewarded key thrusts that succeeded. They assigned responsibility for major new thrusts to *champions,* the individuals most strongly identified with the idea or product and whose futures were linked to its success. They stayed alert to the symbolic impact of their own actions and statements so as not to send false signals that could stimulate movements in unwanted directions.

Successful strategists ensured that all major power bases within an organization were represented in, or had access to, top management. They interjected new faces and new views into considerations of major changes. This is important because new employees and managers generally have more enthusiasm and drive than employees who have been with the firm a long time. New employees do not see the world the same old way; nor do they act as screens against changes. Successful strategists minimized their own political exposure on highly controversial issues and in circumstances in which major opposition from key power centers was likely. In combination, these findings provide a basis for managing political relationships in an organization.

Because strategies must be effective in the marketplace and capable of gaining internal commitment, the following tactics used by politicians for centuries can aid strategists:

- *Equifinality*—It is often possible to achieve similar results using different means or paths. Strategists should recognize that achieving a successful outcome is more important than imposing the method of achieving it. It may be possible to generate new alternatives that give equal results but with far greater potential for gaining commitment.
- *Satisfying*—Achieving satisfactory results with an acceptable strategy is far better than failing to achieve optimal results with an unpopular strategy.
- *Generalization*—Shifting focus from specific issues to more general ones may increase strategists' options for gaining organizational commitment.
- *Focus on Higher-Order Issues*—By raising an issue to a higher level, many short-term interests can be postponed in favor of long-term interests. For instance, by focusing on issues of survival, the airline and automotive industries were able to persuade unions to make concessions on wage increases.
- *Provide Political Access on Important Issues*—Strategy and policy decisions with significant negative consequences for middle managers will motivate intervention behavior from them. If middle managers do not have an opportunity to take a position on such decisions in appropriate political forums, they are capable of successfully resisting the decisions after they are made. Providing such political access provides strategists with information that otherwise might not be available and that could be useful in managing intervention behavior.[10]

Governance Issues

A "director," according to Webster's Dictionary, is "one of a group of persons entrusted with the overall direction of a corporate enterprise." A *board of directors* is a group of individuals who are elected by the ownership of a corporation to have oversight and guidance over management and who look out for shareholders' interests. The act of oversight and direction is referred to as *governance*. The National Association of Corporate Directors defines governance as "the characteristic of ensuring that long-term strategic objectives and plans are established and that the proper management structure is in place to achieve those objectives, while at the same time making sure that the structure functions to maintain the corporation's integrity, reputation, and responsibility to its various constituencies." This broad scope of responsibility for the board shows how boards are being held accountable for the entire performance of the firm. In the Worldcom, Tyco, and Enron bankruptcies and scandals, the firms' boards of directors were sued by shareholders for mismanaging their interests. New accounting rules in the United States and Europe now enhance corporate-governance codes and require much more extensive financial disclosure among publicly held firms. The roles and duties of a board of directors can be divided into four broad categories, as indicated in Table 6-8.

The recession and credit crunch of 2008–2009 prompted shareholders to become more wary of boards of directors. Shareholders of hundreds of firms are demanding that their boards do a better job of governing corporate America.[11] New compensation policies are needed as well as direct shareholder involvement in some director activities. For

TABLE 6-8   Board of Director Duties and Responsibilities

1. CONTROL AND OVERSIGHT OVER MANAGEMENT
   a. Select the Chief Executive Officer (CEO).
   b. Sanction the CEO's team.
   c. Provide the CEO with a forum.
   d. Ensure managerial competency.
   e. Evaluate management's performance.
   f. Set management's salary levels, including fringe benefits.
   g. Guarantee managerial integrity through continuous auditing.
   h. Chart the corporate course.
   i. Devise and revise policies to be implemented by management.

2. ADHERENCE TO LEGAL PRESCRIPTIONS
   a. Keep abreast of new laws.
   b. Ensure the entire organization fulfills legal prescriptions.
   c. Pass bylaws and related resolutions.
   d. Select new directors.
   e. Approve capital budgets.
   f. Authorize borrowing, new stock issues, bonds, and so on.

3. CONSIDERATION OF STAKEHOLDERS' INTERESTS
   a. Monitor product quality.
   b. Facilitate upward progression in employee quality of work life.
   c. Review labor policies and practices.
   d. Improve the customer climate.
   e. Keep community relations at the highest level.
   f. Use influence to better governmental, professional association, and educational contacts.
   g. Maintain good public image.

4. ADVANCEMENT OF STOCKHOLDERS' RIGHTS
   a. Preserve stockholders' equity.
   b. Stimulate corporate growth so that the firm will survive and flourish.
   c. Guard against equity dilution.
   d. Ensure equitable stockholder representation.
   e. Inform stockholders through letters, reports, and meetings.
   f. Declare proper dividends.
   g. Guarantee corporate survival.

example, boards could require CEOs to groom possible replacements from inside the firm because exorbitant compensation is most often paid to new CEOs coming from outside the firm.

Shareholders are also upset at boards for allowing CEOs to receive huge end-of-year bonuses when the firm's stock price drops drastically during the year.[12] For example, Chesapeake Energy Corp. and its board of directors are under fire from shareholders for paying Chairman and CEO Aubrey McClendon $112 million in 2008 as the firm's stock price plummeted. Investor Jeffrey Bronchick wrote in a letter to the Chesapeake board that the CEO's compensation was a "near perfect illustration of the complete collapse of appropriate corporate governance."

Until recently, boards of directors did most of their work sitting around polished wooden tables. However, Hewlett-Packard's directors, among many others, now log on to their own special board Web site twice a week and conduct business based on extensive confidential briefing information posted there by the firm's top management team. Then the board members meet face to face and fully informed every two months to discuss the biggest issues facing the firm. Even the decision of whether to locate operations in countries with low corporate tax rates would be reviewed by a board of directors.

Today, boards of directors are composed mostly of outsiders who are becoming more involved in organizations' strategic management. The trend in the United States is toward much greater board member accountability with smaller boards, now averaging 12 members rather than 18 as they did a few years ago. *BusinessWeek* recently evaluated the boards of most large U.S. companies and provided the following "principles of good governance":

1. No more than two directors are current or former company executives.
2. No directors do business with the company or accept consulting or legal fees from the firm.
3. The audit, compensation, and nominating committees are made up solely of outside directors.
4. Each director owns a large equity stake in the company, excluding stock options.
5. At least one outside director has extensive experience in the company's core business and at least one has been CEO of an equivalent-size company.
6. Fully employed directors sit on no more than four boards and retirees sit on no more than seven.
7. Each director attends at least 75 percent of all meetings.
8. The board meets regularly without management present and evaluates its own performance annually.
9. The audit committee meets at least four times a year.
10. The board is frugal on executive pay, diligent in CEO succession oversight responsibilities, and prompt to act when trouble arises.
11. The CEO is not also the chairperson of the board.
12. Shareholders have considerable power and information to choose and replace directors.
13. Stock options are considered a corporate expense.
14. There are no interlocking directorships (where a director or CEO sits on another director's board).[13]

Being a member of a board of directors today requires much more time, is much more difficult, and requires much more technical knowledge and financial commitment than in the past. Jeff Sonnerfeld, associate dean of the Yale School of Management, says, "Boards of directors are now rolling up their sleeves and becoming much more closely involved with management decision making." Since the Enron and Worldcom scandals, company CEOs and boards are required to personally certify financial statements; company loans to company executives and directors are illegal; and there is faster reporting of insider stock transactions.

Just as directors are beginning to place more emphasis on staying informed about an organization's health and operations, they are also taking a more active role in ensuring that publicly issued documents are accurate representations of a firm's status. It is becoming widely recognized that a board of directors has legal responsibilities to stockholders and society for all company activities, for corporate performance, and for ensuring that a firm has an effective strategy. Failure to accept responsibility for auditing or evaluating a firm's strategy is considered a serious breach of a director's duties. Stockholders, government agencies, and customers are filing legal suits against directors for fraud, omissions, inaccurate disclosures, lack of due diligence, and culpable ignorance about a firm's operations with increasing frequency. Liability insurance for directors has become exceptionally expensive and has caused numerous directors to resign.

The Sarbanes-Oxley Act resulted in scores of boardroom overhauls among publicly traded companies. The jobs of chief executive and chairman are now held by separate persons, and board audit committees must now have at least one financial expert as a member. Board audit committees now meet 10 or more times per year, rather than 3 or 4 times as they did prior to the act. The act put an end to the "country club" atmosphere of most boards and has shifted power from CEOs to directors. Although aimed at public companies, the act has also had a similar impact on privately owned companies.[14]

In Sweden, a new law has recently been passed requiring 25 percent female representation in boardrooms. The Norwegian government has passed a similar law that requires 40 percent of corporate director seats to go to women. In the United States, women currently hold about 13 percent of board seats at S&P 500 firms and 10 percent at S&P 1,500 firms. The Investor Responsibility Research Center in Washington, D.C. reports that minorities hold just 8.8 percent of board seats of S&P 1,500 companies. Progressive firms realize that women and minorities ask different questions and make different suggestions in boardrooms than white men, which is helpful because women and minorities comprise much of the consumer base everywhere.

A direct response of increased pressure on directors to stay informed and execute their responsibilities is that audit committees are becoming commonplace. A board of directors should conduct an annual strategy audit in much the same fashion that it reviews the annual financial audit. In performing such an audit, a board could work jointly with operating management and/or seek outside counsel. Boards should play a role beyond that of performing a strategic audit. They should provide greater input and advice in the strategy-formulation process to ensure that strategists are providing for the long-term needs of the firm. This is being done through the formation of three particular board committees: nominating committees to propose candidates for the board and senior officers of the firm; compensation committees to evaluate the performance of top executives and determine the terms and conditions of their employment; and audit committees to give board-level attention to company accounting and financial policies and performance.

Conclusion

The essence of strategy formulation is an assessment of whether an organization is doing the right things and how it can be more effective in what it does. Every organization should be wary of becoming a prisoner of its own strategy, because even the best strategies become obsolete sooner or later. Regular reappraisal of strategy helps management avoid complacency. Objectives and strategies should be consciously developed and coordinated and should not merely evolve out of day-to-day operating decisions.

An organization with no sense of direction and no coherent strategy precipitates its own demise. When an organization does not know where it wants to go, it usually ends up some place it does not want to be. Every organization needs to consciously establish and communicate clear objectives and strategies.

Modern strategy-formulation tools and concepts are described in this chapter and integrated into a practical three-stage framework. Tools such as the SWOT Matrix, SPACE Matrix, BCG Matrix, IE Matrix, and QSPM can significantly enhance the quality of strategic decisions, but they should never be used to dictate the choice of strategies. Behavioral, cultural, and political aspects of strategy generation and selection are always important to consider and manage. Because of increased legal pressure from outside groups, boards of directors are assuming a more active role in strategy analysis and choice. This is a positive trend for organizations.

We invite you to visit the David page on the Prentice Hall Companion Web site at http://www.pearsonhighered.com/david/ for this chapter's review quiz.

Key Terms and Concepts

Aggressive Quadrant (p. 182)
Attractiveness Scores (AS) (p. 193)
Board of Directors (p. 198)
Boston Consulting Group (BCG) Matrix (p. 184)
Business Portfolio (p. 184)
Cash Cows (p. 186)
Champions (p. 197)
Competitive Position (CP) (p. 181)
Competitive Quadrant (p. 184)
Conservative Quadrant (p. 184)
Culture (p. 196)
Decision Stage (p. 176)
Defensive Quadrant (p. 184)
Directional Vector (p. 182)
Dogs (p. 187)
Equifinality (p.197)
Financial Position (FP) (p. 181)
Governance (p. 198)
Grand Strategy Matrix (p. 191)
Halo Error (p. 177)
Industry Position (IP) (p. 181)

Input Stage (p. 176)
Internal-External (IE) Matrix (p. 184)
Matching (p. 177)
Matching Stage (p. 176)
Quantitative Strategic Planning Matrix (QSPM) (p. 192)
Question Marks (p. 186)
Relative Market Share Position (p. 184)
SO Strategies (p. 178)
Stability Position (SP) (p. 181)
Stars (p. 186)
Strategic Position and Action Evaluation (SPACE) Matrix (p. 181)
Strategy-Formulation Framework (p. 177)
Strengths-Weaknesses Opportunities-Threats (SWOT) Matrix (p. 178)
ST Strategies (p. 178)
Sum Total Attractiveness Scores (STAS) (p. 195)
Total Attractiveness Scores (TAS) (p. 195)
WO Strategies (p. 178)
WT Strategies (p. 179)

Issues for Review and Discussion

1. Many multidivisional firms do not report revenues or profits by division or segment in their *Form 10K* or *Annual Report*. What are the pros and cons of this management practice? Discuss.
2. Define halo error. How can halo error inhibit selecting the best strategies to pursue?
3. List six drawbacks of using only subjective information in formulating strategies.
4. For a firm that you know well, give an example SO Strategy, showing how an internal strength can be matched with an external opportunity to formulate a strategy.
5. For a firm that you know well, give an example WT Strategy, showing how an internal weakness can be matched with an external threat to formulate a strategy.
6. List three limitations of the SWOT matrix and analysis.
7. For the following three firms using the given factors, calculate a reasonable Stability Position (SP) coordinate to go on their SPACE Matrix axis, given what you know about the nature of those industries.

Factors	Winnebago	Apple	U.S. Postal Service
Barriers to entry into market			
Seasonal nature of business			
Technological changes			
SP Score			

8. Would the angle or degrees of the vector in a SPACE Matrix be important in generating alternative strategies? Explain.

9. On the Competitive Position (CP) axis of a SPACE Matrix, what level of capacity utilization would be necessary for you to give the firm a negative 1? Negative 7? Why?

10. If a firm has weak financial position and competes in an unstable industry, in which quadrant will the SPACE vector lie?

11. Describe a situation where the SPACE analysis would have no vector. In other words, describe a situation where the SPACE analysis coordinate would be (0,0). What should an analyst do in this situation?

12. Develop a BCG Matrix for your university. Because your college does not generate profits, what would be a good surrogate for the pie slice values? How many circles do you have and how large are they? Explain.

13. In a BCG Matrix, would the Question Mark quadrant or the Cash Cow quadrant be more desirable? Explain.

14. Would a BCG Matrix and analysis be worth performing if you do not know the profits of each segment? Why?

15. What major limitations of the BCG Matrix does the IE Matrix overcome?

16. In an IE Matrix, do you believe it is more advantageous for a division to be located in quadrant II or IV? Why?

17. Develop a $2 \times 2 \times 2$ QSPM for an organization of your choice (i.e., two strengths, two weaknesses, two opportunities, two threats, and two strategies). Follow all the QSPM guidelines presented in the chapter.

18. Give an example of "equifinality" as defined in the chapter.

19. Do you believe the reasons to disclose by-segment financial information offset the reasons not to disclose by-segment financial information? Explain why or why not.

20. How would application of the strategy-formulation framework differ from a small to a large organization?

21. What types of strategies would you recommend for an organization that achieves total weighted scores of 3.6 on the IFE and 1.2 on the EFE Matrix?

22. Given the following information, develop a SPACE Matrix for the XYZ Corporation: FP = +2; SP = −6; CP = −2; IP = +4.

23. Given the information in the following table, develop a BCG Matrix and an IE Matrix:

Divisions	1	2	3
Profits	$10	$15	$25
Sales	$100	$50	$100
Relative Market Share	0.2	0.5	0.8
Industry Growth Rate	+.20	+.10	−.10
IFE Total Weighted Scores	1.6	3.1	2.2
EFE Total Weighted Scores	2.5	1.8	3.3

24. Explain the steps involved in developing a QSPM.

25. How would you develop a set of objectives for your school or business?

26. What do you think is the appropriate role of a board of directors in strategic management? Why?

27. Discuss the limitations of various strategy-formulation analytical techniques.

28. Explain why cultural factors should be an important consideration in analyzing and choosing among alternative strategies.

29. How are the SWOT Matrix, SPACE Matrix, BCG Matrix, IE Matrix, and Grand Strategy Matrix similar? How are they different?

30. How would for-profit and nonprofit organizations differ in their applications of the strategy-formulation framework?

31. Develop a SPACE Matrix for a company that is weak financially and is a weak competitor. The industry for this company is pretty stable, but the industry's projected growth in revenues and profits is not good. Label all axes and quadrants.

32. List four limitations of a BCG Matrix.

33. Make up an example to show clearly and completely that you can develop an IE Matrix for a three-division company, where each division has $10, $20, and $40 in revenues and $2, $4, and $1 in profits. State other assumptions needed. Label axes and quadrants.

34. What procedures could be necessary if the SPACE vector falls right on the axis between the Competitive and Defensive quadrants?

35. In a BCG Matrix or the Grand Strategy Matrix, what would you consider to be a rapid market (or industry) growth rate?

36. What are the pros and cons of a company (and country) participating in a Sustainability Report?

37. How does the Sarbanes-Oxley Act of 2002 impact boards of directors?

38. Rank *BusinessWeek*'s "principles of good governance" from 1 to 14 (1 being most important and 14 least important) to reveal your assessment of these new rules.

39. Why is it important to work row by row instead of column by column in preparing a QSPM?

40. Why should one avoid putting double 4's in a row in preparing a QSPM?

41. Envision a QSPM with no weight column. Would that still be a useful analysis? Why or why not? What do you lose by deleting the weight column?

42. Prepare a BCG Matrix for a two-division firm with sales of $5 and $8 versus profits of $3 and $1, respectively. State assumptions for the RMSP and IGR axes to enable you to construct the diagram.

43. Consider developing a before-and-after BCG or IE Matrix to reveal the expected results of your proposed strategies. What limitation of the analysis would this procedure overcome somewhat?

44. If a firm has the leading market share in its industry, where on the BCG Matrix would the circle lie?

45. If a firm competes in a very unstable industry, such as telecommunications, where on the SP axis of the SPACE Matrix would you plot the appropriate point?

46. Why do you think the SWOT Matrix is the most widely used of all strategy matrices?

47. The strategy templates described at the www.strategyclub.com Web site have templates for all of the Chapter 6 matrices. How could those templates be useful in preparing an example BCG or IE Matrix?

Notes

1. R. T. Lenz, "Managing the Evolution of the Strategic Planning Process," *Business Horizons* 30, no. 1 (January–February 1987): 37.

2. Robert Grant, "The Resource-Based Theory of Competitive Advantage: Implications for Strategy Formulation," *California Management Review* (Spring 1991): 114.

3. Heinz Weihrich, "The TOWS Matrix: A Tool for Situational Analysis," *Long Range Planning* 15, no. 2 (April 1982): 61. Note: Although Dr. Weihrich first modified SWOT analysis to form the TOWS matrix, the acronym SWOT is much more widely used than TOWS in practice.

4. Greg, Dess, G. T. Lumpkin, and Alan Eisner, *Strategic Management: Text and Cases* (New York: McGraw-Hill/Irwin, 2006): 72.

5. Adapted from H. Rowe, R. Mason, and K. Dickel, *Strategic Management and Business Policy: A Methodological Approach* (Reading, MA: Addison-Wesley, 1982): 155–156.

6. Fred David, "The Strategic Planning Matrix—A Quantitative Approach," *Long Range Planning* 19, no. 5 (October 1986): 102; Andre Gib and Robert Margulies, "Making Competitive Intelligence Relevant to the User," *Planning Review* 19, no. 3 (May–June 1991): 21.

7. Fred David, "Computer-Assisted Strategic Planning in Small Businesses," *Journal of Systems Management* 36, no. 7 (July 1985): 24–34.

8. Y. Allarie and M. Firsirotu, "How to Implement Radical Strategies in Large Organizations," *Sloan Management Review* 26, no. 3 (Spring 1985): 19. Another excellent article is P. Shrivastava, "Integrating Strategy Formulation with Organizational Culture," *Journal of Business Strategy* 5, no. 3 (Winter 1985): 103–111.

9. James Brian Quinn, *Strategies for Changes: Logical Incrementalism* (Homewood, IL: Richard D. Irwin, 1980): 128–145. These political tactics are listed in A. Thompson and A. Strickland, *Strategic Management: Concepts and Cases* (Plano, TX: Business Publications, 1984): 261.

10. William Guth and Ian MacMillan, "Strategy Implementation Versus Middle Management Self-Interest," *Strategic Management Journal* 7, no. 4 (July–August 1986): 321.

11. Joann Lublin, "Corporate Directors' Group Gives Repair Plan to Boards," *Wall Street Journal* (March 24, 2009): B4.

12. Phred Dvorak, "Poor Year Doesn't Stop CEO Bonuses," *Wall Street Journal* (March 18, 2009): B1.

13. Louis Lavelle, "The Best and Worst Boards," *BusinessWeek* (October 7, 2002): 104–110.

14. Matt Murray, "Private Companies Also Feel Pressure to Clean Up Acts," *Wall Street Journal* (July 22, 2003): B1.

Current Readings

Angwin, Duncan, Sotirios, Paroutis, and Sarah Mitson. "Connecting Up Strategy: Are Senior Strategy Directors a Missing Link?" *California Management Review* (Spring 2009): 49–73.

Berdrow, Iris, Hsing-Er Lin, Edward F. McDonough, and Michael H. Zack. "The Threefold Path to Strategy: Adding Knowledge and Innovation Positions to the Mix." *MIT Sloan Management Review* 50, no. 1 (Fall 2008): 53.

Capron, Laurence, and Mauro Guillen. "National Corporate Governance Institutions and Post-Acquisition Target Reorganization." *Strategic Management Journal* (August 2008): 803–833.

Dahling, Jason, Brian Whitaker, and Paul Levy. "The Development and Validation of a New Machiavellianism Scale." *Journal of Management* (March 2009): 219–257.

Makadok, Richard, and Russell Coff. "Both Market and Hierarchy: An Incentive-System Theory of Hybrid Governance." *Academy of Management Review* (April 2009): 297–319.

Dalton, Catherine M. "From the Battlefield to the Boardroom." *Business Horizons* 51, no. 2 (March–April 2008): 79.

Dalton, Dan R., and Catherine M. Dalton. "Corporate Governance in the Post Sarbanes-Oxley Period: Compensation Disclosure and Analysis (CD&A)." *Business Horizons* 51, no. 2 (March–April 2008): 85.

Douglas, Thomas J., William Q. Judge, and Ali M. Kutan. "Institutional Antecedents of Corporate Governance Legitimacy." *Journal of Management* 34, no. 4 (August 2008): 765.

Graebner, Melissa E., Michael L. McDonald, and James D. Westphal, "What Do They Know? The Effects of Outside Director Acquisition Experience on Firm Acquisition. Performance." *Strategic Management Journal* 29, no. 11 (November 2008): 1155.

Khanna, Poonam, Michael L. McDonald, and James D. Westphal. "Getting Them to Think Outside the Circle: Corporate Governance, CEOs' External Advice Networks, and Firm Performance." *The Academy of Management Journal* 51, no. 3 (June 2008): 453.

Koka, Balaji R., and John E. Prescott. "Designing Alliance Networks: The Influence of Network Position, Environmental Change, and Strategy on Firm Performance." *Strategic Management Journal* 29, no. 6 (June 2008): 639.

Kroll, Mark, Bruce A. Walters, and Peter Wright. "Board Vigilance, Director Experience, and Corporate Outcomes." *Strategic Management Journal* 29, no. 4 (April 2008): 363.

MacMilan, Ian C., and Larry Selden. "The Incumbent's Advantage." *Harvard Business Review* (October 2008): 111.

Nayak, Ajit. "Enhancing the Innovation Performance of Firms by Balancing Cohesiveness and Bridging Ties." *Long Range Planning* 41, no. 4 (August 2008): 420.

Zhang, Yan, and Nandini Rajagopalan. "Corporate Governance Reforms in China and India: Challenges and Opportunities." *Business Horizons* 51, no. 1 (January–February 2008): 55.

ASSURANCE OF LEARNING EXERCISES

Assurance of Learning Exercise 6A

Developing a SWOT Matrix for McDonald's

Purpose

The most widely used strategy-formulation technique among U.S. firms is the SWOT Matrix. This exercise requires the development of a SWOT Matrix for McDonald's. Matching key external and internal factors in a SWOT Matrix requires good intuitive and conceptual skills. You will improve with practice in developing a SWOT Matrix.

Instructions

Recall from Experiential Exercise 1A that you already may have determined McDonald's external opportunities/threats and internal strengths/weaknesses. This information could be used to complete this exercise. Follow the steps outlined as follows:

Step 1	On a separate sheet of paper, construct a large nine-cell diagram that will represent your SWOT Matrix. Appropriately label the cells.
Step 2	Appropriately record McDonald's opportunities/threats and strengths/weaknesses in your diagram.
Step 3	Match external and internal factors to generate feasible alternative strategies for McDonald's. Record SO, WO, ST, and WT strategies in the appropriate cells of the SWOT Matrix. Use the proper notation to indicate the rationale for the strategies. You do not necessarily have to have strategies in all four strategy cells.
Step 4	Compare your SWOT Matrix to another student's SWOT Matrix. Discuss any major differences.

Assurance of Learning Exercise 6B

Developing a SPACE Matrix for McDonald's

Purpose

Should McDonald's pursue aggressive, conservative, competitive, or defensive strategies? Develop a SPACE Matrix for McDonald's to answer this question. Elaborate on the strategic implications of your directional vector. Be specific in terms of strategies that could benefit McDonald's.

Instructions

Step 1	Join with two other people in class and develop a joint SPACE Matrix for McDonald's.
Step 2	Diagram your SPACE Matrix on the board. Compare your matrix with other team's matrices.
Step 3	Discuss the implications of your SPACE Matrix.

Assurance of Learning Exercise 6C

Developing a BCG Matrix for McDonald's

Purpose

Portfolio matrices are widely used by multidivisional organizations to help identify and select strategies to pursue. A BCG analysis identifies particular divisions that should receive fewer resources than others. It may identify some divisions that need to be divested. This exercise can give you practice developing a BCG Matrix.

Instructions

Step 1	Place the following five column headings at the top of a separate sheet of paper: Divisions, Revenues, Profits, Relative Market Share Position, Industry Growth Rate. Down the far left of your page, list MCD's geographic divisions. Now turn back to the Cohesion Case and find information to fill in all the cells in your data table from page 30.
Step 2	Complete a BCG Matrix for McDonald's.
Step 3	Compare your BCG Matrix to other students' matrices. Discuss any major differences.

Assurance of Learning Exercise 6D

Developing a QSPM for McDonald's

Purpose

This exercise can give you practice developing a Quantitative Strategic Planning Matrix to determine the relative attractiveness of various strategic alternatives.

Instructions

Step 1	Join with two other students in class to develop a joint QSPM for McDonald's.
Step 2	Go to the blackboard and record your strategies and their Sum Total Attractiveness Score. Compare your team's strategies and Sum Total Attractiveness Score to those of other teams. Be sure not to assign the same AS score in a given row. Recall that dashes should be inserted all the way across a given row when used.
Step 3	Discuss any major differences.

Assurance of Learning Exercise 6E

Formulating Individual Strategies

Purpose

Individuals and organizations are alike in many ways. Each has competitors, and each should plan for the future. Every individual and organization faces some external opportunities and threats and has some internal strengths and weaknesses. Both individuals and organizations establish objectives and allocate resources. These and other similarities make it possible for individuals to use many strategic-management concepts and tools. This exercise is designed to demonstrate how the SWOT Matrix can be used by individuals to plan their futures. As one nears completion of a college degree and begins interviewing for jobs, planning can be particularly important.

Instructions

On a separate sheet of paper, construct a SWOT Matrix. Include what you consider to be your major external opportunities, your major external threats, your major strengths, and your major weaknesses. An internal weakness may be a low grade point average. An external opportunity may be that your university offers a graduate program that interests you. Match key external and internal factors by recording in the appropriate cell of the matrix alternative strategies or actions that would allow you to capitalize upon your strengths, overcome your weaknesses, take advantage of your external opportunities, and minimize the impact of external threats. Be sure to use the appropriate matching notation in the strategy cells of the matrix. Because every individual (and organization) is unique, there is no one right answer to this exercise.

Assurance of Learning Exercise 6F

The Mach Test

Purpose

The purpose of this exercise is to enhance your understanding and awareness of the impact that behavioral and political factors can have on strategy analysis and choice.

Instructions

Step 1   On a separate sheet of paper, number from 1 to 10. For each of the 10 statements given as follows, record a *1, 2, 3, 4,* or *5* to indicate your attitude,
where

1 = I disagree a lot.
2 = I disagree a little.
3 = My attitude is neutral.
4 = I agree a little.
5 = I agree a lot.

1. The best way to handle people is to tell them what they want to hear.
2. When you ask someone to do something for you, it is best to give the real reason for wanting it, rather than a reason that might carry more weight.
3. Anyone who completely trusts anyone else is asking for trouble.
4. It is hard to get ahead without cutting corners here and there.
5. It is safest to assume that all people have a vicious streak, and it will come out when they are given a chance.
6. One should take action only when it is morally right.
7. Most people are basically good and kind.
8. There is no excuse for lying to someone else.
9. Most people forget more easily the death of their father than the loss of their property.
10. Generally speaking, people won't work hard unless they're forced to do so.

Step 2   Add up the numbers you recorded beside statements 1, 3, 4, 5, 9, and 10. This sum is Subtotal One. For the other four statements, reverse the numbers you recorded, so a *5* becomes a *1, 4* becomes *2, 2* becomes *4, 1* becomes *5,* and *3* remains *3.* Then add those four numbers to get Subtotal Two. Finally, add Subtotal One and Subtotal Two to get your Final Score.

Your Final Score

Your Final Score is your Machiavellian Score. Machiavellian principles are defined in a dictionary as "manipulative, dishonest, deceiving, and favoring political expediency over morality." These tactics are not desirable, are not ethical, and are not recommended in the strategic-management process! You may, however, encounter some highly Machiavellian individuals in your career, so beware. It is important for strategists not to manipulate others in the pursuit of organizational objectives. Individuals today recognize and resent manipulative tactics more than ever before. J. R. Ewing (on *Dallas,* a television show in the 1980s) was a good example of someone who was a high Mach (score over 30). The National Opinion Research Center used this short quiz in a random sample of U.S. adults and found the national average Final Score to be 25.[1] The higher your score, the more Machiavellian (manipulative) you tend to be. The following scale is descriptive of individual scores on this test:

- Below 16: Never uses manipulation as a tool.
- 16 to 20: Rarely uses manipulation as a tool.
- 21 to 25: Sometimes uses manipulation as a tool.
- 26 to 30: Often uses manipulation as a tool.
- Over 30: Always uses manipulation as a tool.

Test Development

The Mach (Machiavellian) test was developed by Dr. Richard Christie, whose research suggests the following tendencies:

1. Men generally are more Machiavellian than women.
2. There is no significant difference between high Machs and low Machs on measures of intelligence or ability.
3. Although high Machs are detached from others, they are detached in a pathological sense.
4. Machiavellian scores are not statistically related to authoritarian values.
5. High Machs tend to be in professions that emphasize the control and manipulation of individuals— for example, law, psychiatry, and behavioral science.
6. Machiavellianism is not significantly related to major demographic characteristics such as educational level or marital status.
7. High Machs tend to come from a city or have urban backgrounds.
8. Older adults tend to have lower Mach scores than younger adults.[2]

A classic book on power relationships, *The Prince,* was written by Niccolo Machiavelli. Several excerpts from *The Prince* follow:

> Men must either be cajoled or crushed, for they will revenge themselves for slight wrongs, while for grave ones they cannot. The injury therefore that you do to a man should be such that you need not fear his revenge.
>
> We must bear in mind . . . that there is nothing more difficult and dangerous, or more doubtful of success, than an attempt to introduce a new order of things in any state. The innovator has for enemies all those who derived advantages from the old order of things, while those who expect to be benefitted by the new institution will be but lukewarm defenders.
>
> A wise prince, therefore, will steadily pursue such a course that the citizens of his state will always and under all circumstances feel the need for his authority, and will therefore always prove faithful to him.
>
> A prince should seem to be merciful, faithful, humane, religious, and upright, and should even be so in reality, but he should have his mind so trained that, when occasion requires it, he may know how to change to the opposite.[3]

Notes

1. Richard Christie and Florence Geis, *Studies in Machiavellianism* (Orlando, FL: Academic Press, 1970). Material in this exercise adapted with permission of the authors and the Academic Press.
2. Ibid., 82–83.
3. Niccolo Machiavelli, *The Prince* (New York: The Washington Press, 1963).

Assurance of Learning Exercise 6G

Developing a BCG Matrix for My University

Purpose

Developing a BCG Matrix for many nonprofit organizations, including colleges and universities, is a useful exercise. Of course, there are no profits for each division or department—and in some cases no revenues. However, you can be creative in performing a BCG Matrix. For example, the pie slice in the circles can represent the number of majors receiving jobs upon graduation, the number of faculty teaching in that area, or some other variable that you believe is important to consider. The size of the circles can represent the number of students majoring in particular departments or areas.

Instructions

Step 1   On a separate sheet of paper, develop a BCG Matrix for your university. Include all academic schools, departments, or colleges.

Step 2   Diagram your BCG Matrix on the blackboard.

Step 3   Discuss differences among the BCG Matrices on the board.

Assurance of Learning Exercise 6H

The Role of Boards of Directors

Purpose

This exercise will give you a better understanding of the role of boards of directors in formulating, implementing, and evaluating strategies.

Instructions

Identify a person in your community who serves on a board of directors. Make an appointment to interview that person, and seek answers to the following questions. Summarize your findings in a five-minute oral report to the class.

- On what board are you a member?
- How often does the board meet?
- How long have you served on the board?
- What role does the board play in this company?

- How has the role of the board changed in recent years?
- What changes would you like to see in the role of the board?
- To what extent do you prepare for the board meeting?
- To what extent are you involved in strategic management of the firm?

Assurance of Learning Exercise 6I

Locating Companies in a Grand Strategy Matrix

Purpose

The Grand Strategy Matrix is a popular tool for formulating alternative strategies. All organizations can be positioned in one of the Grand Strategy Matrix's four strategy quadrants. The divisions of a firm likewise could be positioned. The Grand Strategy Matrix is based on two evaluative dimensions: competitive position and market growth. Appropriate strategies for an organization to consider are listed in sequential order of attractiveness in each quadrant of the matrix. This exercise gives you experience using a Grand Strategy Matrix.

Instructions

Using the year-end 2008 financial information provided, prepare a Grand Strategy Matrix on a separate sheet of paper. Write the respective company names in the appropriate quadrant of the matrix. Based on this analysis, what strategies are recommended for each company?

Company	Company Sales/ Profit Growth (%)	Industry	Industry Sales/ Profit Growth (%)
Boeing	−8 / −34	Aerospace/defense	+7 / +13
DuPont	+4 / −33	Chemicals	+7 / −23
Wal-Mart	+7 / +5	General merchandise	−3 / −44
Sears Holdings	−8 / −94	General merchandise	−3 / −44
Black & Decker	−7 / −43	Home equipment	−9 / −111
TIAA-CREF	+7 / +7	Insurance	−1 / −178
Nucor	+43 / +24	Metals	−16 / −24
Allegheny	−3 / −24	Metals	−16 / −24

CHAPTER 7

Implementing Strategies: Management and Operations Issues

CHAPTER OBJECTIVES

After studying this chapter, you should be able to do the following:

1. Explain why strategy implementation is more difficult than strategy formulation.

2. Discuss the importance of annual objectives and policies in achieving organizational commitment for strategies to be implemented.

3. Explain why organizational structure is so important in strategy implementation.

4. Compare and contrast restructuring and reengineering.

5. Describe the relationships between production/operations and strategy implementation.

6. Explain how a firm can effectively link performance and pay to strategies.

7. Discuss employee stock ownership plans (ESOPs) as a strategic-management concept.

8. Describe how to modify an organizational culture to support new strategies.

9. Discuss the culture in Mexico and Japan.

10. Describe the glass ceiling in the United States.

Assurance of Learning Exercises

Assurance of Learning Exercise 7A
Revising McDonald's Organizational Chart

Assurance of Learning Exercise 7B
Do Organizations Really Establish Objectives?

Assurance of Learning Exercise 7C
Understanding My University's Culture

Source: Shutterstock, Photographer Feng Yu

"Notable Quotes"

"You want your people to run the business as if it were their own."

—William Fulmer

"Poor Ike; when he was a general, he gave an order and it was carried out. Now, he's going to sit in that office and give an order and not a damn thing is going to happen."

—Harry Truman

"Changing your pay plan is a big risk, but not changing it could be a bigger one."

—Nancy Perry

"Objectives can be compared to a compass bearing by which a ship navigates. A compass bearing is firm, but

"in actual navigation, a ship may veer off its course for many miles. Without a compass bearing, a ship would neither find its port nor be able to estimate the time required to get there."

—Peter Drucker

"The best game plan in the world never blocked or tackled anybody."

—Vince Lombardi

"Pretend that every single person you meet has a sign around his or her neck that says, 'Make me feel important.' "

—Mary Kay Ash

The strategic-management process does not end when the firm decides what strategy or strategies to pursue. There must be a translation of strategic thought into strategic action. This translation is much easier if managers and employees of the firm understand the business, feel a part of the company, and through involvement in strategy-formulation activities have become committed to helping the organization succeed. Without understanding and commitment, strategy-implementation efforts face major problems.

Implementing strategy affects an organization from top to bottom; it affects all the functional and divisional areas of a business. It is beyond the purpose and scope of this text to examine all of the business administration concepts and tools important in strategy implementation. This chapter focuses on management issues most central to implementing strategies in 2010–2011 and Chapter 8 focuses on marketing, finance/accounting, R&D, and management information systems issues.

Even the most technically perfect strategic plan will serve little purpose if it is not implemented. Many organizations tend to spend an inordinate amount of time, money, and effort on developing the strategic plan, treating the means and circumstances under which it will be implemented as afterthoughts! Change comes through implementation and evaluation, not through the plan. A technically imperfect plan that is implemented well will achieve more than the perfect plan that never gets off the paper on which it is typed.[1]

Doing Great in a Weak Economy. How?

Google

When most firms were struggling in 2008, Google increased its revenues and profits such that *Fortune* magazine in 2009 rated Google as their fourth "Most Admired Company in the World" in terms of their management and performance. Based in Mountain View, California, Google's first quarter of 2009 revenues grew 6.2 percent to $5.51 billion, followed by $5.52 billion the second quarter. These results widened Google's lead in overall searches and online advertising market share. Google owns both YouTube and DoubleClick.

Google in 2009 began selling books online. This related diversification strategy led Google to digitize close to 10 million books by year's end. Google cofounder Sergey Brin recently said, "Call me weird, but I think there are a lot of advantages to reading books online. Today's monitors have great resolution and you don't have to wait on the book to arrive once ordered."

Google does not charge people to use its search engine. Instead of charging what the market will bear as

most firms do, Google charges as little as they can bear. Thus Google obtains networks of people, millions of people, which strengthens its competitive position.

Google's founders, Larry Page and Sergey Brin, each have nearly 30 percent voting control of the firm and have established a golden rule that permeates Google's internal culture. The rule is to "Don't be evil," and this operating policy encourages all employees to challenge all managers on decisions—to make sure the decisions are true to the firm's mission. Another internal rule at Google is to "Give up control," which means giving up control to outsiders to reap the benefits of their input. This latter rule is done through beta launches of any new software, product, or service they do. Google's philosophy is that "Low prices are good, but free is better" because they want every customer they can get.

Google stock in July 2009 rose above $400 per share as the company prepares to launch its own operating system for computers, a direct assault on the business of software giant Microsoft. Google's strategic plan is to attack Microsoft in nearly all of its businesses, including browsers, where Google has 1.8 percent market share versus Microsoft's 66 percent, smartphone operating systems (Google 1.6% versus Microsoft 10%), office suites (Google 0.04% versus Microsoft 94%), and Web searches (Google 65% versus Microsoft 8%).

Google's Chrome OS operating system will require users to be connected to the Internet, unlike Microsoft's operating systems. CEO Eric Schmidt at Google has been on a mission for the last several years, according to analysts, to capture Microsoft's market share. The Google strategy is accelerating a shift in the personal computer (PC) industry to become more like the cell phone industry whereby customers pay monthly service fees for use of hardware and software.

Google's Chrome will be free to all computer makers such as Hewlett-Packard who historically have pre-installed Microsoft's operating system for a fee to consumers. Microsoft released its new Microsoft Windows 2010 in the fall 2009 and believes that the learning curve for any consumer to switch away to Google's operating system will not be worth the effort. Google.com is the most visited Web site in the world and even in 2009 offered its own online word processing, spreadsheet, and presentation programs free – called Google Docs. The Google strategy is a huge bet that online programs can eventually overtake and crush desktop software.

Due to its dominance in the Internet search and advertising business, Google is coming under increasing scrutiny from the U.S. Justice Department regarding possible antitrust infringement. The pending Microsoft/Yahoo merger may negate that Google vulnerability. Google obtains about 95 percent of its revenues from online advertising.

Source: Based on Jeff Jarvis, "How the Google Model Could Help Detroit," *Business Week* (February 9, 2009): 33–36; Geoff Colvin, "The World's Most Admired Companies," *Fortune* (March 16, 2009): 76–86.

The Nature of Strategy Implementation

The strategy-implementation stage of strategic management is revealed in Figure 7-1. Successful strategy formulation does not guarantee successful strategy implementation. It is always more difficult to do something (strategy implementation) than to say you are going to do it (strategy formulation)! Although inextricably linked, strategy implementation is fundamentally different from strategy formulation. Strategy formulation and implementation can be contrasted in the following ways:

- Strategy formulation is positioning forces before the action.
- Strategy implementation is managing forces during the action.
- Strategy formulation focuses on effectiveness.
- Strategy implementation focuses on efficiency.
- Strategy formulation is primarily an intellectual process.
- Strategy implementation is primarily an operational process.
- Strategy formulation requires good intuitive and analytical skills.
- Strategy implementation requires special motivation and leadership skills.
- Strategy formulation requires coordination among a few individuals.
- Strategy implementation requires coordination among many individuals.

Strategy-formulation concepts and tools do not differ greatly for small, large, for-profit, or nonprofit organizations. However, strategy implementation varies substantially among different types and sizes of organizations. Implementing strategies requires such actions as altering sales territories, adding new departments, closing facilities, hiring new employees, changing an organization's pricing strategy, developing financial budgets, developing new employee benefits, establishing cost-control procedures, changing advertising strategies, building new facilities, training new employees, transferring managers among

FIGURE 7-1

Comprehensive Strategic-Management Model

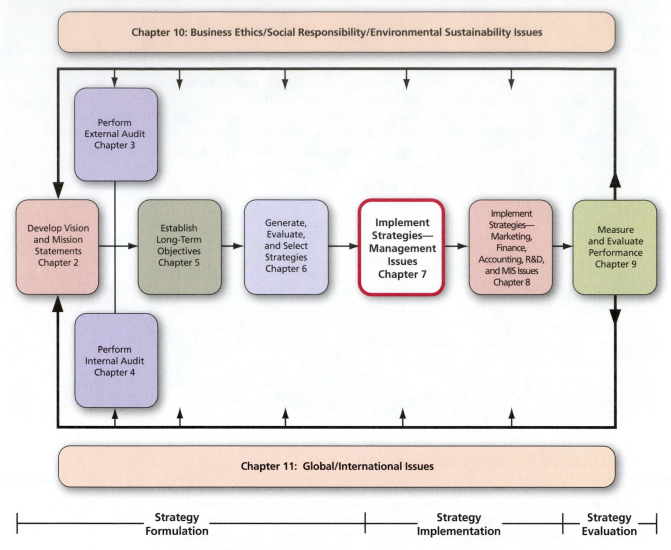

Source: Fred R. David, "How Companies Define Their Mission," *Long Range Planning* 22, no. 3 (June 1988): 40.

divisions, and building a better management information system. These types of activities obviously differ greatly between manufacturing, service, and governmental organizations.

Management Perspectives

In all but the smallest organizations, the transition from strategy formulation to strategy implementation requires a shift in responsibility from strategists to divisional and functional managers. Implementation problems can arise because of this shift in responsibility, especially if strategy-formulation decisions come as a surprise to middle- and lower-level managers. Managers and employees are motivated more by perceived self-interests than by organizational interests, unless the two coincide. Therefore, it is essential that divisional and functional managers be involved as much as possible in strategy-formulation activities. Of equal importance, strategists should be involved as much as possible in strategy-implementation activities.

As indicated in Table 7-1, management issues central to strategy implementation include establishing annual objectives, devising policies, allocating resources, altering an existing organizational structure, restructuring and reengineering, revising reward and incentive plans, minimizing resistance to change, matching managers with strategy, developing a strategy-supportive culture, adapting production/operations processes, developing an effective human

TABLE 7-1 Some Management Issues Central to Strategy Implementation

Establish annual objectives

Devise policies

Allocate resources

Alter an existing organizational structure

Restructure and reengineer

Revise reward and incentive plans

Minimize resistance to change

Match managers with strategy

Develop a strategy-supportive culture

Adapt production/operations processes

Develop an effective human resources function

Downsize and furlough as needed

Link performance and pay to strategies

resources function, and, if necessary, downsizing. Management changes are necessarily more extensive when strategies to be implemented move a firm in a major new direction.

Managers and employees throughout an organization should participate early and directly in strategy-implementation decisions. Their role in strategy implementation should build upon prior involvement in strategy-formulation activities. Strategists' genuine personal commitment to implementation is a necessary and powerful motivational force for managers and employees. Too often, strategists are too busy to actively support strategy-implementation efforts, and their lack of interest can be detrimental to organizational success. The rationale for objectives and strategies should be understood and clearly communicated throughout an organization. Major competitors' accomplishments, products, plans, actions, and performance should be apparent to all organizational members. Major external opportunities and threats should be clear, and managers' and employees' questions should be answered. Top-down flow of communication is essential for developing bottom-up support.

Firms need to develop a competitor focus at all hierarchical levels by gathering and widely distributing competitive intelligence; every employee should be able to benchmark her or his efforts against best-in-class competitors so that the challenge becomes personal. For example, Starbucks Corp. in 2009–2010 is instituting "lean production/operations" at its 11,000 U.S. stores. This system eliminates idle employee time and unnecessary employee motions, such as walking, reaching, and bending. Starbucks says 30 percent of employees' time is motion and the company wants to reduce that. They say "motion and work are two different things."

Annual Objectives

Establishing annual objectives is a decentralized activity that directly involves all managers in an organization. Active participation in establishing annual objectives can lead to acceptance and commitment. *Annual objectives* are essential for strategy implementation because they (1) represent the basis for allocating resources; (2) are a primary mechanism for evaluating managers; (3) are the major instrument for monitoring progress toward achieving long-term objectives; and (4) establish organizational, divisional, and departmental priorities. Considerable time and effort should be devoted to ensuring that annual objectives are well conceived, consistent with long-term objectives, and supportive of strategies to be implemented. Approving, revising, or rejecting annual objectives is much more than a rubber-stamp activity. The purpose of annual objectives can be summarized as follows:

Annual objectives serve as guidelines for action, directing and channeling efforts and activities of organization members. They provide a source of legitimacy in an enterprise by justifying activities to stakeholders. They serve as standards of performance.

They serve as an important source of employee motivation and identification. They give incentives for managers and employees to perform. They provide a basis for organizational design.[2]

Clearly stated and communicated objectives are critical to success in all types and sizes of firms. Annual objectives, stated in terms of profitability, growth, and market share by business segment, geographic area, customer groups, and product, are common in organizations. Figure 7-2 illustrates how the Stamus Company could establish annual objectives based on long-term objectives. Table 7-2 reveals associated revenue figures that correspond to the objectives outlined in Figure 7-2. Note that, according to plan, the

FIGURE 7-2

The Stamus Company's Hierarchy of Aims

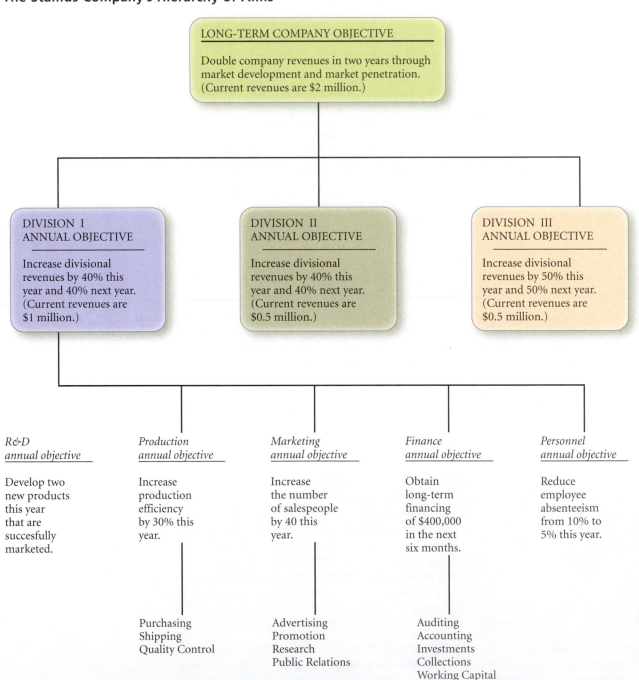

TABLE 7-2 The Stamus Company's Revenue Expectations (in $Millions)

	2010	2011	2012
Division I Revenues	1.0	1.400	1.960
Division II Revenues	0.5	0.700	0.980
Division III Revenues	0.5	0.750	1.125
Total Company Revenues	**2.0**	**2.850**	**4.065**

Stamus Company will slightly exceed its long-term objective of doubling company revenues between 2010 and 2012.

Figure 7-2 also reflects how a hierarchy of annual objectives can be established based on an organization's structure. Objectives should be consistent across hierarchical levels and form a network of supportive aims. *Horizontal consistency of objectives* is as important as *vertical consistency of objectives*. For instance, it would not be effective for manufacturing to achieve more than its annual objective of units produced if marketing could not sell the additional units.

Annual objectives should be measurable, consistent, reasonable, challenging, clear, communicated throughout the organization, characterized by an appropriate time dimension, and accompanied by commensurate rewards and sanctions. Too often, objectives are stated in generalities, with little operational usefulness. Annual objectives, such as "to improve communication" or "to improve performance," are not clear, specific, or measurable. Objectives should state quantity, quality, cost, and time—and also be verifiable. Terms and phrases such as *maximize, minimize, as soon as possible*, and *adequate* should be avoided.

Annual objectives should be compatible with employees' and managers' values and should be supported by clearly stated policies. More of something is not always better. Improved quality or reduced cost may, for example, be more important than quantity. It is important to tie rewards and sanctions to annual objectives so that employees and managers understand that achieving objectives is critical to successful strategy implementation. Clear annual objectives do not guarantee successful strategy implementation, but they do increase the likelihood that personal and organizational aims can be accomplished. Overemphasis on achieving objectives can result in undesirable conduct, such as faking the numbers, distorting the records, and letting objectives become ends in themselves. Managers must be alert to these potential problems.

Policies

Changes in a firm's strategic direction do not occur automatically. On a day-to-day basis, policies are needed to make a strategy work. Policies facilitate solving recurring problems and guide the implementation of strategy. Broadly defined, *policy* refers to specific guidelines, methods, procedures, rules, forms, and administrative practices established to support and encourage work toward stated goals. Policies are instruments for strategy implementation. Policies set boundaries, constraints, and limits on the kinds of administrative actions that can be taken to reward and sanction behavior; they clarify what can and cannot be done in pursuit of an organization's objectives. For example, Carnival's *Paradise* ship has a no smoking policy anywhere, anytime aboard ship. It is the first cruise ship to ban smoking comprehensively. Another example of corporate policy relates to surfing the Web while at work. About 40 percent of companies today do not have a formal policy preventing employees from surfing the Internet, but software is being marketed now that allows firms to monitor how, when, where, and how long various employees use the Internet at work.

Policies let both employees and managers know what is expected of them, thereby increasing the likelihood that strategies will be implemented successfully. They provide a basis for management control, allow coordination across organizational units, and reduce the amount of time managers spend making decisions. Policies also clarify what work is to be done and by whom. They promote delegation of decision making to appropriate managerial levels where various problems usually arise. Many organizations have a policy manual that serves to guide and direct behavior. Wal-Mart has a policy that it calls the "10 Foot" Rule, whereby customers can find assistance within 10 feet of anywhere in the store. This is a welcomed policy in Japan, where Wal-Mart is trying to gain a foothold; 58 percent of all retailers in Japan are mom-and-pop stores and consumers historically have had to pay "top yen" rather than "discounted prices" for merchandise.

Policies can apply to all divisions and departments (for example, "We are an equal opportunity employer"). Some policies apply to a single department ("Employees in this department must take at least one training and development course each year"). Whatever their scope and form, policies serve as a mechanism for implementing strategies and obtaining objectives. Policies should be stated in writing whenever possible. They represent the means for carrying out strategic decisions. Examples of policies that support a company strategy, a divisional objective, and a departmental objective are given in Table 7-3.

Some example issues that may require a management policy are provided in Table 7-4.

TABLE 7-3 A Hierarchy of Policies

Company Strategy

Acquire a chain of retail stores to meet our sales growth and profitability objectives.

Supporting Policies

1. "All stores will be open from 8 A.M. to 8 P.M. Monday through Saturday." (This policy could increase retail sales if stores currently are open only 40 hours a week.)

2. "All stores must submit a Monthly Control Data Report." (This policy could reduce expense-to-sales ratios.)

3. "All stores must support company advertising by contributing 5 percent of their total monthly revenues for this purpose." (This policy could allow the company to establish a national reputation.)

4. "All stores must adhere to the uniform pricing guidelines set forth in the Company Handbook." (This policy could help assure customers that the company offers a consistent product in terms of price and quality in all its stores.)

Divisional Objective

Increase the division's revenues from $10 million in 2009 to $15 million in 2010.

Supporting Policies

1. "Beginning in January 2010, each one of this division's salespersons must file a weekly activity report that includes the number of calls made, the number of miles traveled, the number of units sold, the dollar volume sold, and the number of new accounts opened." (This policy could ensure that salespersons do not place too great an emphasis in certain areas.)

2. "Beginning in January 2010, this division will return to its employees 5 percent of its gross revenues in the form of a Christmas bonus." (This policy could increase employee productivity.)

3. "Beginning in January 2010, inventory levels carried in warehouses will be decreased by 30 percent in accordance with a just-in-time (JIT) manufacturing approach." (This policy could reduce production expenses and thus free funds for increased marketing efforts.)

Production Department Objective

Increase production from 20,000 units in 2009 to 30,000 units in 2010.

Supporting Policies

1. "Beginning in January 2010, employees will have the option of working up to 20 hours of overtime per week." (This policy could minimize the need to hire additional employees.)

2. "Beginning in January 2010, perfect attendance awards in the amount of $100 will be given to all employees who do not miss a workday in a given year." (This policy could decrease absenteeism and increase productivity.)

3. "Beginning in January 2010, new equipment must be leased rather than purchased." (This policy could reduce tax liabilities and thus allow more funds to be invested in modernizing production processes.)

TABLE 7-4   Some Issues That May Require a Management Policy

- To offer extensive or limited management development workshops and seminars
- To centralize or decentralize employee-training activities
- To recruit through employment agencies, college campuses, and/or newspapers
- To promote from within or to hire from the outside
- To promote on the basis of merit or on the basis of seniority
- To tie executive compensation to long-term and/or annual objectives
- To offer numerous or few employee benefits
- To negotiate directly or indirectly with labor unions
- To delegate authority for large expenditures or to centrally retain this authority
- To allow much, some, or no overtime work
- To establish a high- or low-safety stock of inventory
- To use one or more suppliers
- To buy, lease, or rent new production equipment
- To greatly or somewhat stress quality control
- To establish many or only a few production standards
- To operate one, two, or three shifts
- To discourage using insider information for personal gain
- To discourage sexual harassment
- To discourage smoking at work
- To discourage insider trading
- To discourage moonlighting

Resource Allocation

Resource allocation is a central management activity that allows for strategy execution. In organizations that do not use a strategic-management approach to decision making, resource allocation is often based on political or personal factors. Strategic management enables resources to be allocated according to priorities established by annual objectives.

Nothing could be more detrimental to strategic management and to organizational success than for resources to be allocated in ways not consistent with priorities indicated by approved annual objectives.

All organizations have at least four types of resources that can be used to achieve desired objectives: financial resources, physical resources, human resources, and technological resources. Allocating resources to particular divisions and departments does not mean that strategies will be successfully implemented. A number of factors commonly prohibit effective resource allocation, including an overprotection of resources, too great an emphasis on short-run financial criteria, organizational politics, vague strategy targets, a reluctance to take risks, and a lack of sufficient knowledge.

Below the corporate level, there often exists an absence of systematic thinking about resources allocated and strategies of the firm. Yavitz and Newman explain why:

> Managers normally have many more tasks than they can do. Managers must allocate time and resources among these tasks. Pressure builds up. Expenses are too high. The CEO wants a good financial report for the third quarter. Strategy formulation and implementation activities often get deferred. Today's problems soak up available energies and resources. Scrambled accounts and budgets fail to reveal the shift in allocation away from strategic needs to currently squeaking wheels.[3]

The real value of any resource allocation program lies in the resulting accomplishment of an organization's objectives. Effective resource allocation does not guarantee successful strategy implementation because programs, personnel, controls, and commitment must breathe life into the resources provided. Strategic management itself is sometimes referred to as a "resource allocation process."

TABLE 7-5 Some Management Trade-Off Decisions Required in Strategy Implementation

To emphasize short-term profits or long-term growth

To emphasize profit margin or market share

To emphasize market development or market penetration

To lay off or furlough

To seek growth or stability

To take high risk or low risk

To be more socially responsible or more profitable

To outsource jobs or pay more to keep jobs at home

To acquire externally or to build internally

To restructure or reengineer

To use leverage or equity to raise funds

To use part-time or full-time employees

Managing Conflict

Interdependency of objectives and competition for limited resources often leads to conflict. *Conflict* can be defined as a disagreement between two or more parties on one or more issues. Establishing annual objectives can lead to conflict because individuals have different expectations and perceptions, schedules create pressure, personalities are incompatible, and misunderstandings between line managers (such as production supervisors) and staff managers (such as human resource specialists) occur. For example, a collection manager's objective of reducing bad debts by 50 percent in a given year may conflict with a divisional objective to increase sales by 20 percent.

Establishing objectives can lead to conflict because managers and strategists must make trade-offs, such as whether to emphasize short-term profits or long-term growth, profit margin or market share, market penetration or market development, growth or stability, high risk or low risk, and social responsiveness or profit maximization. Trade-offs are necessary because no firm has sufficient resources pursue all strategies to would benefit the firm. Table 7-5 reveals some important management trade-off decisions required in strategy implementation.

Conflict is unavoidable in organizations, so it is important that conflict be managed and resolved before dysfunctional consequences affect organizational performance. Conflict is not always bad. An absence of conflict can signal indifference and apathy. Conflict can serve to energize opposing groups into action and may help managers identify problems.

Various approaches for managing and resolving conflict can be classified into three categories: avoidance, defusion, and confrontation. *Avoidance* includes such actions as ignoring the problem in hopes that the conflict will resolve itself or physically separating the conflicting individuals (or groups). *Defusion* can include playing down differences between conflicting parties while accentuating similarities and common interests, compromising so that there is neither a clear winner nor loser, resorting to majority rule, appealing to a higher authority, or redesigning present positions. *Confrontation* is exemplified by exchanging members of conflicting parties so that each can gain an appreciation of the other's point of view or holding a meeting at which conflicting parties present their views and work through their differences.

Matching Structure with Strategy

Changes in strategy often require changes in the way an organization is structured for two major reasons. First, structure largely dictates how objectives and policies will be established. For example, objectives and policies established under a geographic organizational structure are couched in geographic terms. Objectives and policies are stated largely in terms of products in an organization whose structure is based on product groups. The structural format for developing objectives and policies can significantly impact all other strategy-implementation activities.

The second major reason why changes in strategy often require changes in structure is that structure dictates how resources will be allocated. If an organization's structure is based on customer groups, then resources will be allocated in that manner. Similarly, if an organization's structure is set up along functional business lines, then resources are allocated by functional areas. Unless new or revised strategies place emphasis in the same areas as old strategies, structural reorientation commonly becomes a part of strategy implementation.

Changes in strategy lead to changes in organizational structure. Structure should be designed to facilitate the strategic pursuit of a firm and, therefore, follow strategy. Without a strategy or reasons for being (mission), companies find it difficult to design an effective structure. Chandler found a particular structure sequence to be repeated often as organizations grow and change strategy over time; this sequence is depicted in Figure 7-3.

There is no one optimal organizational design or structure for a given strategy or type of organization. What is appropriate for one organization may not be appropriate for a similar firm, although successful firms in a given industry do tend to organize themselves in a similar way. For example, consumer goods companies tend to emulate the divisional structure-by-product form of organization. Small firms tend to be functionally structured (centralized). Medium-sized firms tend to be divisionally structured (decentralized). Large firms tend to use a strategic business unit (SBU) or matrix structure. As organizations grow, their structures generally change from simple to complex as a result of concatenation, or the linking together of several basic strategies.

Numerous external and internal forces affect an organization; no firm could change its structure in response to every one of these forces, because to do so would lead to chaos. However, when a firm changes its strategy, the existing organizational structure may become ineffective. As indicated in Table 7-6, symptoms of an ineffective organizational structure include too many levels of management, too many meetings attended by too many people, too much attention being directed toward solving interdepartmental conflicts, too large a span of control, and too many unachieved objectives. Changes in structure can facilitate strategy-implementation efforts, but changes in structure should not be expected to make a bad strategy good, to make bad managers good, or to make bad products sell.

Structure undeniably can and does influence strategy. Strategies formulated must be workable, so if a certain new strategy required massive structural changes it would not be an attractive choice. In this way, structure can shape the choice of strategies. But a more important concern is determining what types of structural changes are needed to implement new

FIGURE 7-3

Chandler's Strategy-Structure Relationship

Source: Adapted from Alfred Chandler, *Strategy and Structure* (Cambridge, MA: MIT Press, 1962).

TABLE 7-6 Symptoms of an Ineffective Organizational Structure

1. Too many levels of management
2. Too many meetings attended by too many people
3. Too much attention being directed toward solving interdepartmental conflicts
4. Too large a span of control
5. Too many unachieved objectives
6. Declining corporate or business performance
7. Losing ground to rival firms
8. Revenue and/or earnings divided by number of employees and/or number of managers is low compared to rival firms

strategies and how these changes can best be accomplished. We examine this issue by focusing on seven basic types of organizational structure: functional, divisional by geographic area, divisional by product, divisional by customer, divisional process, strategic business unit (SBU), and matrix.

The Functional Structure

The most widely used structure is the functional or centralized type because this structure is the simplest and least expensive of the seven alternatives. A *functional structure* groups tasks and activities by business function, such as production/operations, marketing, finance/accounting, research and development, and management information systems. A university may structure its activities by major functions that include academic affairs, student services, alumni relations, athletics, maintenance, and accounting. Besides being simple and inexpensive, a functional structure also promotes specialization of labor, encourages efficient use of managerial and technical talent, minimizes the need for an elaborate control system, and allows rapid decision making.

Some disadvantages of a functional structure are that it forces accountability to the top, minimizes career development opportunities, and is sometimes characterized by low employee morale, line/staff conflicts, poor delegation of authority, and inadequate planning for products and markets.

A functional structure often leads to short-term and narrow thinking that may undermine what is best for the firm as a whole. For example, the research and development department may strive to overdesign products and components to achieve technical elegance, while manufacturing may argue for low-frills products that can be mass produced more easily. Thus, communication is often not as good in a functional structure. Schein gives an example of a communication problem in a functional structure:

> The word "marketing" will mean product development to the engineer, studying customers through market research to the product manager, merchandising to the salesperson, and constant change in design to the manufacturing manager. Then when these managers try to work together, they often attribute disagreements to personalities and fail to notice the deeper, shared assumptions that vary and dictate how each function thinks.[4]

Most large companies have abandoned the functional structure in favor of decentralization and improved accountability. However, two large firms that still successfully use a functional structure are Nucor Steel, based in Charlotte, North Carolina, and Sharp, the $17 billion consumer electronics firm.

Table 7-7 summarizes the advantages and disadvantages of a functional organizational structure.

The Divisional Structure

The *divisional* or *decentralized structure* is the second most common type used by U.S. businesses. As a small organization grows, it has more difficulty managing different products and services in different markets. Some form of divisional structure generally

TABLE 7-7   Advantages and Disadvantages of a Functional Organizational Structure

Advantages	Disadvantages
1. Simple and inexpensive	1. Accountability forced to the top
2. Capitalizes on specialization of business activities such as marketing and finance	2. Delegation of authority and responsibility not encouraged
3. Minimizes need for elaborate control system	3. Minimizes career development
4. Allows for rapid decision making	4. Low employee/manager morale
	5. Inadequate planning for products and markets
	6. Leads to short-term, narrow thinking
	7. Leads to communication problems

becomes necessary to motivate employees, control operations, and compete successfully in diverse locations. The divisional structure can be organized in one of four ways: *by geographic area, by product* or *service, by customer,* or *by process.* With a divisional structure, functional activities are performed both centrally and in each separate division.

Cisco Systems recently discarded its divisional structure by customer and reorganized into a functional structure. CEO John Chambers replaced the three-customer structure based on big businesses, small businesses, and telecoms, and now the company has centralized its engineering and marketing units so that they focus on technologies such as wireless networks. Chambers says the goal was to eliminate duplication, but the change should not be viewed as a shift in strategy. Chambers's span of control in the new structure is reduced from 15 to 12 managers reporting directly to him. He continues to operate Cisco without a chief operating officer or a number-two executive.

Sun Microsystems recently reduced the number of its business units from seven to four. Kodak recently reduced its number of business units from seven by-customer divisions to five by-product divisions. As consumption patterns become increasingly similar worldwide, a by-product structure is becoming more effective than a by-customer or a by-geographic type divisional structure. In the restructuring, Kodak eliminated its global operations division and distributed those responsibilities across the new by-product divisions.

A divisional structure has some clear advantages. First and perhaps foremost, accountability is clear. That is, divisional managers can be held responsible for sales and profit levels. Because a divisional structure is based on extensive delegation of authority, managers and employees can easily see the results of their good or bad performances. As a result, employee morale is generally higher in a divisional structure than it is in a centralized structure. Other advantages of the divisional design are that it creates career development opportunities for managers, allows local control of situations, leads to a competitive climate within an organization, and allows new businesses and products to be added easily.

The divisional design is not without some limitations, however. Perhaps the most important limitation is that a divisional structure is costly, for a number of reasons. First, each division requires functional specialists who must be paid. Second, there exists some duplication of staff services, facilities, and personnel; for instance, functional specialists are also needed centrally (at headquarters) to coordinate divisional activities. Third, managers must be well qualified because the divisional design forces delegation of authority; better-qualified individuals require higher salaries. A divisional structure can also be costly because it requires an elaborate, headquarters-driven control system. Fourth, competition between divisions may become so intense that it is dysfunctional and leads to limited sharing of ideas and resources for the common good of the firm. Table 7-8 summarizes the advantages and disadvantages of divisional organizational structure.

TABLE 7-8 **Advantages and Disadvantages of a Divisional Organizational Structure**

Advantages	Disadvantages
1. Accountability is clear	1. Can be costly
2. Allows local control of local situations	2. Duplication of functional activities
3. Creates career development chances	3. Requires a skilled management force
4. Promotes delegation of authority	4. Requires an elaborate control system
5. Leads to competitive climate internally	5. Competition among divisions can become so intense as to be dysfunctional
6. Allows easy adding of new products or regions	6. Can lead to limited sharing of ideas and resources
7. Allows strict control and attention to products, customers, and/or regions	7. Some regions/products/customers may receive special treatment

Ghoshal and Bartlett, two leading scholars in strategic management, note the following:

As their label clearly warns, divisions divide. The divisional model fragments companies' resources; it creates vertical communication channels that insulate business units and prevents them from sharing their strengths with one another. Consequently, the whole of the corporation is often less than the sum of its parts. A final limitation of the divisional design is that certain regions, products, or customers may sometimes receive special treatment, and it may be difficult to maintain consistent, companywide practices. Nonetheless, for most large organizations and many small firms, the advantages of a divisional structure more than offset the potential limitations.[5]

A *divisional structure by geographic area* is appropriate for organizations whose strategies need to be tailored to fit the particular needs and characteristics of customers in different geographic areas. This type of structure can be most appropriate for organizations that have similar branch facilities located in widely dispersed areas. A divisional structure by geographic area allows local participation in decision making and improved coordination within a region. Hershey Foods is an example of a company organized using the divisional by geographic region type of structure. Hershey's divisions are United States, Canada, Mexico, Brazil, and Other. Analysts contend that this type of structure may not be best for Hershey because consumption patterns for candy are quite similar worldwide. An alternative—and perhaps better—type of structure for Hershey would be divisional by product because the company produces and sells three types of products worldwide: (1) chocolate, (2) nonchocolate, and (3) grocery.

The *divisional structure by product (or services)* is most effective for implementing strategies when specific products or services need special emphasis. Also, this type of structure is widely used when an organization offers only a few products or services or when an organization's products or services differ substantially. The divisional structure allows strict control over and attention to product lines, but it may also require a more skilled management force and reduced top management control. General Motors, DuPont, and Procter & Gamble use a divisional structure by product to implement strategies. Huffy, the largest bicycle company in the world, is another firm that is highly decentralized based on a divisional-by-product structure. Based in Ohio, Huffy's divisions are the Bicycle division, the Gerry Baby Products division, the Huffy Sports division, YLC Enterprises, and Washington Inventory Service. Harry Shaw, Huffy's chairman, believes decentralization is one of the keys to Huffy's success.

Eastman Chemical established a new by-product divisional organizational structure. The company's two new divisions, Eastman Company and Voridian Company, focus on chemicals and polymers, respectively. The Eastman division focuses on coatings, adhesives, inks, and plastics, whereas the Voridian division focuses on fibers, polyethylene, and other polymers. Microsoft recently reorganized the whole corporation into three large divisions-by-product. Headed by a president, the new divisions are (1) platform products and services, (2) business, and (3) entertainment and devices. The Swiss electrical-engineering company ABB Ltd. recently scrapped its two core divisions, (1) power technologies and (2) automation technologies, and replaced them with five new divisions: (1) power products, (2) power systems, (3) automation products, (4) process automation, and (5) robotics.

When a few major customers are of paramount importance and many different services are provided to these customers, then a *divisional structure by customer* can be the most effective way to implement strategies. This structure allows an organization to cater effectively to the requirements of clearly defined customer groups. For example, book publishing companies often organize their activities around customer groups, such as colleges, secondary schools, and private commercial schools. Some airline companies have two major customer divisions: passengers and freight or cargo services.

Merrill Lynch is organized into separate divisions that cater to different groups of customers, including wealthy individuals, institutional investors, and small corporations. Motorola's semiconductor chip division is also organized divisionally by customer, having three separate segments that sell to (1) the automotive and industrial market, (2) the mobile phone market, and (3) the data-networking market. The automotive and industrial segment is doing well, but the other two segments are faltering, which is a reason why Motorola is trying to divest its semiconductor operations.

A *divisional structure by process* is similar to a functional structure, because activities are organized according to the way work is actually performed. However, a key difference between these two designs is that functional departments are not accountable for profits or revenues, whereas divisional process departments are evaluated on these criteria. An example of a divisional structure by process is a manufacturing business organized into six divisions: electrical work, glass cutting, welding, grinding, painting, and foundry work. In this case, all operations related to these specific processes would be grouped under the separate divisions. Each process (division) would be responsible for generating revenues and profits. The divisional structure by process can be particularly effective in achieving objectives when distinct production processes represent the thrust of competitiveness in an industry.

The Strategic Business Unit (SBU) Structure

As the number, size, and diversity of divisions in an organization increase, controlling and evaluating divisional operations become increasingly difficult for strategists. Increases in sales often are not accompanied by similar increases in profitability. The span of control becomes too large at top levels of the firm. For example, in a large conglomerate organization composed of 90 divisions, such as ConAgra, the chief executive officer could have difficulty even remembering the first names of divisional presidents. In multidivisional organizations, an SBU structure can greatly facilitate strategy-implementation efforts. ConAgra has put its many divisions into three primary SBUs: (1) food service (restaurants), (2) retail (grocery stores), and (3) agricultural products.

The SBU structure groups similar divisions into strategic business units and delegates authority and responsibility for each unit to a senior executive who reports directly to the chief executive officer. This change in structure can facilitate strategy implementation by improving coordination between similar divisions and channeling accountability to distinct business units. In a 100-division conglomerate, the divisions could perhaps be regrouped into 10 SBUs according to certain common characteristics, such as competing in the same industry, being located in the same area, or having the same customers.

Two disadvantages of an SBU structure are that it requires an additional layer of management, which increases salary expenses. Also, the role of the group vice president is often ambiguous. However, these limitations often do not outweigh the advantages of improved coordination and accountability. Another advantage of the SBU structure is that it makes the tasks of planning and control by the corporate office more manageable.

Citigroup in 2009 reorganized the whole company into two SBUs: (1) Citigroup, which includes the retail bank, the corporate and investment bank, the private bank, and global transaction services; and (2) Citi Holdings, which includes Citi's asset management and consumer finance segments, CitiMortgage, CitiFinancial, and the joint brokerage operations with Morgan Stanley. Citigroup's CEO, Vikram Pandit, says the restructuring will allow the company to reduce operating costs and to divest (spin off) Citi Holdings.

The huge computer firm Dell Inc., reorganized in 2009 into two SBUs. One SBU is Consumer Products and the other is Commercial. As part of its reorganization, Dell deleted the geographic divisions within its Consumer Products segment. However within its Commercial segment, there are now three worldwide units: (1) large enterprise, (2) public sector, and (3) small and midsize businesses. Dell is also closing a manufacturing facility in Austin, Texas, and laying off more employees as the company struggles to compete. Computer prices and demand are falling as competition increases. Atlantic Richfield Fairchild Industries, and Honeywell International are examples of firms that successfully use an SBU-type structure.

As illustrated in Figure 7-4, Sonoco Products Corporation, based in Hartsville, South Carolina, utilizes an SBU organizational structure. Note that Sonoco's SBUs—Industrial Products and Consumer Products—each have four autonomous divisions that have their own sales, manufacturing, R&D, finance, HRM, and MIS functions.

The Matrix Structure

A *matrix structure* is the most complex of all designs because it depends upon both vertical and horizontal flows of authority and communication (hence the term *matrix*). In contrast, functional and divisional structures depend primarily on vertical flows of authority and communication. A matrix structure can result in higher overhead because it creates more management positions. Other disadvantages of a matrix structure that contribute to overall complexity include dual lines of budget authority (a violation of the unity-of-command principle), dual sources of reward and punishment, shared authority, dual reporting channels, and a need for an extensive and effective communication system.

Despite its complexity, the matrix structure is widely used in many industries, including construction, health care, research, and defense. As indicated in Table 7-9, some advantages of a matrix structure are that project objectives are clear, there are many channels of communication, workers can see the visible results of their work, and shutting down a project can be accomplished relatively easily. Another advantage of a matrix structure is that it facilitates the use of specialized personnel, equipment, and facilities. Functional resources are shared in a matrix structure, rather than duplicated as in a divisional structure. Individuals with a high degree of expertise can divide their time as needed among projects, and they in turn develop their own skills and competencies more than in other structures. Walt Disney Corp. relies on a matrix structure.

FIGURE 7-4

Sonoco Products' SBU Organizational Chart

TABLE 7-9 **Advantages and Disadvantages of a Matrix Structure**

Advantages	Disadvantages
1. Project objectives are clear	1. Requires excellent vertical and horizontal flows of communication
2. Employees can clearly see results of their work	2. Costly because creates more manager positions
3. Shutting down a project is easily accomplished	3. Violates unity of command principle
4. Facilitates uses of special equipment/ personnel/facilities	4. Creates dual lines of budget authority
5. Functional resources are shared instead of duplicated as in a divisional structure	5. Creates dual sources of reward/punishment
	6. Creates shared authority and reporting
	7. Requires mutual trust and understanding

A typical matrix structure is illustrated in Figure 7-5. Note that the letters (A through Z4) refer to managers. For example, if you were manager A, you would be responsible for financial aspects of Project 1, and you would have two bosses: the Project 1 Manager on site and the CFO off site.

For a matrix structure to be effective, organizations need participative planning, training, clear mutual understanding of roles and responsibilities, excellent internal communication, and mutual trust and confidence. The matrix structure is being used more

FIGURE 7-5

An Example Matrix Structure

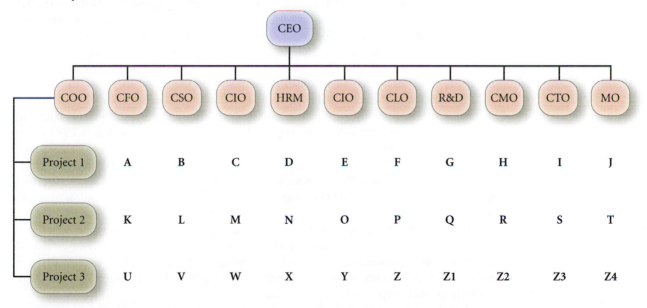

Notes: Titles spelled out as follows.

Chief Executive Officer (CEO)
Chief Finance Officer (CFO)
Chief Strategy Officer (CSO)
Chief Information Officer (CIO)
Human Resources Manager (HRM)
Chief Operating Officer (COO)
Chief Legal Officer (CLO)
Research & Development Officer (R&D)
Chief Marketing Officer (CMO)
Chief Technology Officer (CTO)
Competitive Intelligence Officer (CIO)
Maintenance Officer (MO)

frequently by U.S. businesses because firms are pursuing strategies that add new products, customer groups, and technology to their range of activities. Out of these changes are coming product managers, functional managers, and geographic-area managers, all of whom have important strategic responsibilities. When several variables, such as product, customer, technology, geography, functional area, and line of business, have roughly equal strategic priorities, a matrix organization can be an effective structural form.

Some Do's and Don'ts in Developing Organizational Charts

Students analyzing strategic management cases are often asked to revise and develop a firm's organizational structure. This section provides some basic guidelines for this endeavor. There are some basic do's and don'ts in regard to devising or constructing organizational charts, especially for midsize to large firms. First of all, reserve the title CEO for the top executive of the firm. Don't use the title "president" for the top person; use it for the division top managers if there are divisions within the firm. Also, do not use the title "president" for functional business executives. They should have the title "chief," or "vice president," or "manager," or "officer," such as "Chief Information Officer," or "VP of Human Resources." Further, do not recommend a dual title (such as "CEO and president") for just one executive. The chairman of the board and CEO of Bristol-Myers Squibb, Peter Dolan, recently gave up his title as chairman. However, Pfizer's CEO, Jeffrey Kindler, recently added chairman of the board to his title when he succeeded Hank McKinnell as chairman of Pfizer's board. And Comverse Technology recently named Andre Dahan as its president, chief executive officer, and board director. Actually, "chairperson" is much better than "chairman" for this title.

A significant movement began among corporate America in mid-2009 to split the chairperson of the board and the CEO positions in publicly held companies.[6] The movement includes asking the New York Stock Exchange and Nasdaq to adopt listing rules that would require separate positions. About 37 percent of companies in the S&P 500 stock index have separate positions, up from 22 percent in 2002, but this still leaves plenty of room for improvement. Among European and Asian companies, the split in these two positions is much more common. For example, 79 percent of British companies split the positions, and all German and Dutch companies split the position.

Directly below the CEO, it is best to have a COO (chief operating officer) with any division presidents reporting directly to the COO. On the same level as the COO and also reporting to the CEO, draw in your functional business executives, such as a CFO (chief financial officer), VP of human resources, a CSO (chief strategy officer), a CIO (chief information officer), a CMO (chief marketing Officer), a VP of R&D, a VP of legal affairs, an investment relations officer, maintenance officer, and so on. Note in Figure 7-6 that these positions are labeled and placed appropriately. Note that a controller and/or treasurer would normally report to the CFO.

In developing an organizational chart, avoid having a particular person reporting to more than one person above in the chain of command. This would violate the unity-of-command principle of management that "every employee should have just one boss." Also, do not have the CFO, CIO, CSO, human resource officer, or other functional positions report to the COO. All these positions report directly to the CEO.

A key consideration in devising an organizational structure concerns the divisions. Note whether the divisions (if any) of a firm presently are established based upon geography, customer, product, or process. If the firm's organizational chart is not available, you often can devise a chart based on the titles of executives. An important case analysis activity is for you to decide how the divisions of a firm should be organized for maximum effectiveness. Even if the firm presently has no divisions, determine whether the firm would operate better with divisions. In other words, which type of divisional breakdown do you (or your group or team) feel would be best for the firm in allocating resources, establishing objectives, and devising compensation incentives? This important strategic decision faces many midsize and large firms (and teams of students analyzing a strategic-management case). As consumption patterns become more and more similar worldwide, the divisional-by-product form of structure is increasingly the most effective. Be mindful that all firms

FIGURE 7-6

Typical Top Managers of a Large Firm

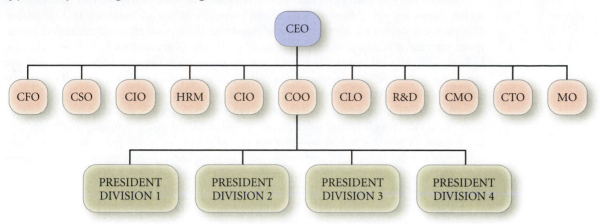

Notes: Titles spelled out as follows.

Chief Executive Officer (CEO)
Chief Finance Officer (CFO)
Chief Strategy Officer (CSO)
Chief Information Officer (CIO)
Human Resources Manager (HRM)
Chief Operating Officer (COO)
Chief Legal Officer (CLO)
Research & Development Officer (R&D)
Chief Marketing Officer (CMO)
Chief Technology Officer (CTO)
Competitive Intelligence Officer (CIO)
Maintenance Officer (MO)

have functional staff below their top executive and often readily provide this information, so be wary of concluding prematurely that a particular firm utilizes a functional structure. If you see the word "president" in the titles of executives, coupled with financial-reporting segments, such as by product or geographic region, then the firm is divisionally structured.

If the firm is large with numerous divisions, decide whether an SBU type of structure would be more appropriate to reduce the span of control reporting to the COO. Note in Figure 7-4 that the Sonoco Products' strategic business units (SBUs) are based on product groupings. An alternative SBU structure would have been to base the division groupings on location. One never knows for sure if a proposed or actual structure is indeed most effective for a particular firm. Note from Chandler's strategy-structure relationship (p. 221) illustrated previously in this chapter that declining financial performance signals a need for altering the structure.

Restructuring, Reengineering, and E-Engineering

Restructuring and reengineering are becoming commonplace on the corporate landscape across the United States and Europe. *Restructuring*—also called *downsizing, rightsizing,* or *delayering*—involves reducing the size of the firm in terms of number of employees, number of divisions or units, and number of hierarchical levels in the firm's organizational structure. This reduction in size is intended to improve both efficiency and effectiveness. Restructuring is concerned primarily with shareholder well-being rather than employee well-being.

Recessionary economic conditions have forced many European companies to downsize, laying off managers and employees. This was almost unheard of prior to the mid-1990s because European labor unions and laws required lengthy negotiations or huge severance checks before workers could be terminated. In contrast to the United States, labor union executives of large European firms sit on most boards of directors.

Job security in European companies is slowly moving toward a U.S. scenario, in which firms lay off almost at will. From banks in Milan to factories in Mannheim, European employers are starting to show people the door in an effort to streamline operations, increase efficiency, and compete against already slim and trim U.S. firms. Massive U.S.-style layoffs are still rare in Europe, but unemployment rates throughout the continent are rising quite rapidly. European firms still prefer to downsize by attrition and retirement rather than by blanket layoffs because of culture, laws, and unions.

In contrast, *reengineering* is concerned more with employee and customer well-being than shareholder well-being. Reengineering—also called process management, process innovation, or process redesign—involves reconfiguring or redesigning work, jobs, and processes for the purpose of improving cost, quality, service, and speed. Reengineering does not usually affect the organizational structure or chart, nor does it imply job loss or employee layoffs. Whereas restructuring is concerned with eliminating or establishing, shrinking or enlarging, and moving organizational departments and divisions, the focus of reengineering is changing the way work is actually carried out.

Reengineering is characterized by many tactical (short-term, business-function-specific) decisions, whereas restructuring is characterized by strategic (long-term, affecting all business functions) decisions. Developed by Motorola in 1986 and made famous by CEO Jack Welch at General Electric and more recently by Robert Nardelli, former CEO of Home Depot, *Six Sigma* is a quality-boosting process improvement technique that entails training several key persons in the firm in the techniques to monitor, measure, and improve processes and eliminate defects. Six Sigma has been widely applied across industries from retailing to financial services. CEO Dave Cote at Honeywell and CEO Jeff Immelt at General Electric spurred acceptance of Six Sigma, which aims to improve work processes and eliminate waste by training "select" employees who are given judo titles such as Master Black Belts, Black Belts, and Green Belts.

Six Sigma was criticized in a 2007 *Wall Street Journal* article that cited many example firms whose stock price fell for a number of years after adoption of Six Sigma. The technique's reliance on the special group of trained employees is problematic and its use within retail firms such as Home Depot has not been as successful as in manufacturing firms.[7]

Restructuring

Firms often employ restructuring when various ratios appear out of line with competitors as determined through benchmarking exercises. Recall that *benchmarking* simply involves comparing a firm against the best firms in the industry on a wide variety of performance-related criteria. Some benchmarking ratios commonly used in rationalizing the need for restructuring are headcount-to-sales-volume, or corporate-staff-to-operating-employees, or span-of-control figures.

The primary benefit sought from restructuring is cost reduction. For some highly bureaucratic firms, restructuring can actually rescue the firm from global competition and demise. But the downside of restructuring can be reduced employee commitment, creativity, and innovation that accompanies the uncertainty and trauma associated with pending and actual employee layoffs. In 2009, Walt Disney merged its ABC television network with its ABC Studios television production as part of a restructuring to cope with declining advertising and shrinking viewership. Disney also is laying off employees and offering buyouts to more than 600 executives. The Disney restructuring is paralleled by rival General Electric Company's merger of its NBC Network with its Universal Media Studios, which is also a bid to cut costs. Ad revenues at the four largest television networks in the United States fell 3 percent in 2009.

Another downside of restructuring is that many people today do not aspire to become managers, and many present-day managers are trying to get off the management track.[8] Sentiment against joining management ranks is higher today than ever. About 80 percent of employees say they want nothing to do with management, a major shift from just a decade ago when 60 to 70 percent hoped to become managers. Managing others historically led to enhanced career mobility, financial rewards, and executive perks; but in today's global, more competitive, restructured arena, managerial jobs demand more hours and headaches with fewer financial rewards. Managers today manage more people spread over different locations, travel more, manage diverse functions, and are change agents even when they have nothing to do with the creation of the plan or disagree with its approach. *Employers today are looking for people who can do things, not for people who make other people do things.* Restructuring in many firms has made a manager's job an invisible, thankless role. More workers today are self-managed, entrepreneurs, interpreneurs, or team-managed. Managers today need to be counselors, motivators, financial advisors, and psychologists. They also run the risk of becoming technologically behind in their areas of expertise. "Dilbert" cartoons commonly portray managers as enemies or as morons.

Reengineering

The argument for a firm engaging in reengineering usually goes as follows: Many companies historically have been organized vertically by business function. This arrangement has led over time to managers' and employees' mind-sets being defined by their particular functions rather than by overall customer service, product quality, or corporate performance. The logic is that all firms tend to bureaucratize over time. As routines become entrenched, turf becomes delineated and defended, and politics takes precedence over performance. Walls that exist in the physical workplace can be reflections of "mental" walls.

In reengineering, a firm uses information technology to break down functional barriers and create a work system based on business processes, products, or outputs rather than on functions or inputs. Cornerstones of reengineering are decentralization, reciprocal interdependence, and information sharing. A firm that exemplifies complete information sharing is Springfield Remanufacturing Corporation, which provides to all employees a weekly income statement of the firm, as well as extensive information on other companies' performances.

The *Wall Street Journal* noted that reengineering today must go beyond knocking down internal walls that keep parts of a company from cooperating effectively; it must also knock down the external walls that prohibit or discourage cooperation with other firms—even rival firms.[9] A maker of disposable diapers echoes this need differently when it says that to be successful "cooperation at the firm must stretch from stump to rump."

Hewlett-Packard is a good example of a company that has knocked down the external barriers to cooperation and practices modern reengineering. The HP of today shares its forecasts with all of its supply-chain partners and shares other critical information with its distributors and other stakeholders. HP does all the buying of resin for its many manufacturers, giving it a volume discount of up to 5 percent. HP has established many alliances and cooperative agreements of the kind discussed in Chapter 5.

A benefit of reengineering is that it offers employees the opportunity to see more clearly how their particular jobs affect the final product or service being marketed by the firm. However, reengineering can also raise manager and employee anxiety, which, unless calmed, can lead to corporate trauma.

Linking Performance and Pay to Strategies

Caterpillar Inc. is slashing its executive compensation by roughly 50 percent in 2009 and cutting pay for senior managers by up to 35 percent. Wages of other Caterpillar managers and employees are being lowered 15 percent. The company is cutting 20,000 more jobs amid a global slowdown in construction. Caterpillar's sales for 2009 are projected to be $40 billion, down sharply from $51.32 billion in 2008.

CEOs at Japanese companies with more than $10 billion in annual revenues are paid about $1.3 million annually, including bonuses and stock options.[10] This compares to an average CEO pay among European firms of $6 million and an average among U.S. firms of $12 million. As firms acquire other firms in other countries, these pay differences can cause resentment and even turmoil. Larger pay packages of American CEOs are socially less acceptable in many other countries. For example, in Japan, seniority rather than performance has been the key factor in determining pay, and harmony among managers is emphasized over individual excellence.

How can an organization's reward system be more closely linked to strategic performance? How can decisions on salary increases, promotions, merit pay, and bonuses be more closely aligned to support the long-term strategic objectives of the organization? There are no widely accepted answers to these questions, but a dual bonus system based on both annual objectives and long-term objectives is becoming common. The percentage of a manager's annual bonus attributable to short-term versus long-term results should vary by hierarchical level in the organization. A chief executive officer's annual bonus could, for example, be determined on a 75 percent short-term and 25 percent long-term basis. It is important that bonuses not be based solely on short-term results because such a system ignores long-term company strategies and objectives.

Wal-Mart Stores recently revamped its bonus program for hourly employees as the firm began paying bonuses based on sales, profit, and inventory performance at individual stores on a quarterly, rather than annual, basis. The average full-time employee at Wal-Mart in the United States is paid $10.51 per hour, but this is significantly below the $17.46 average paid to Costco Wholesale Corp. employees.[11]

One aspect of the deepening global recession is that companies are instituting policies to allow their shareholders to vote on executive compensation policies. A "say-on-pay" policy was installed at 14 large companies in 2008–2009. Aflac was the first U.S. corporation to voluntarily give shareholders an advisory vote on executive compensation. Aflac did this back in 2007. Apple did this in 2008, as did H&R Block. Several companies that instituted say-on-pay policies in 2009 were Ingersoll-Rand, Verizon, and Motorola. In 2010 and 2011, Occidental Petroleum and Hewlett-Packard are expected to institute such policies. These new policies underscore how the financial crisis and shareholder outrage about top executive pay has affected compensation practice. None of the shareholder votes are binding on the companies, however, at least not so far. The U.S. House of Representatives recently passed a bill to formalize this shareholder tactic, which is gaining steam across the country as a means to combat exorbitant executive pay.

In an effort to cut costs and increase productivity, more and more Japanese companies are switching from seniority-based pay to performance-based approaches. Toyota has switched to a full merit system for 20,000 of its 70,000 white-collar workers. Fujitsu, Sony, Matsushita Electric Industrial, and Kao also have switched to merit pay systems. This switching is hurting morale at some Japanese companies, which have trained workers for decades to cooperate rather than to compete and to work in groups rather than individually.

Richard Brown, CEO of Electronic Data Systems (EDS), once said,

> You have to start with an appraisal system that gives genuine feedback and differentiates performance. Some call it ranking people. That seems a little harsh. But you can't have a manager checking a box that says you're either stupendous, magnificent, very good, good, or average. Concise, constructive feedback is the fuel workers use to get better. A company that doesn't differentiate performance risks losing its best people.[12]

Profit sharing is another widely used form of incentive compensation. More than 30 percent of U.S. companies have profit sharing plans, but critics emphasize that too many factors affect profits for this to be a good criterion. Taxes, pricing, or an acquisition would wipe out profits, for example. Also, firms try to minimize profits in a sense to reduce taxes.

Still another criterion widely used to link performance and pay to strategies is gain sharing. *Gain sharing* requires employees or departments to establish performance targets; if actual results exceed objectives, all members get bonuses. More than 26 percent of U.S. companies use some form of gain sharing; about 75 percent of gain sharing plans have been adopted since 1980. Carrier, a subsidiary of United Technologies, has had excellent success with gain sharing in its six plants in Syracuse, New York; Firestone's tire plant in Wilson, North Carolina, has experienced similar success with gain sharing.

Criteria such as sales, profit, production efficiency, quality, and safety could also serve as bases for an effective *bonus system*. If an organization meets certain understood, agreed-upon profit objectives, every member of the enterprise should share in the harvest. A bonus system can be an effective tool for motivating individuals to support strategy-implementation efforts. BankAmerica, for example, recently overhauled its incentive system to link pay to sales of the bank's most profitable products and services. Branch managers receive a base salary plus a bonus based both on the number of new customers and on sales of bank products. Every employee in each branch is also eligible for a bonus if the branch exceeds its goals. Thomas Peterson, a top BankAmerica executive, says, "We want to make people responsible for meeting their goals, so we pay incentives on sales, not on controlling costs or on being sure the parking lot is swept."

Five tests are often used to determine whether a performance-pay plan will benefit an organization:

1. *Does the plan capture attention?* Are people talking more about their activities and taking pride in early successes under the plan?
2. *Do employees understand the plan?* Can participants explain how it works and what they need to do to earn the incentive?
3. *Is the plan improving communication?* Do employees know more than they used to about the company's mission, plans, and objectives?
4. *Does the plan pay out when it should?* Are incentives being paid for desired results—and being withheld when objectives are not met?
5. *Is the company or unit performing better?* Are profits up? Has market share grown? Have gains resulted in part from the incentives?[13]

In addition to a dual bonus system, a combination of reward strategy incentives, such as salary raises, stock options, fringe benefits, promotions, praise, recognition, criticism, fear, increased job autonomy, and awards, can be used to encourage managers and employees to push hard for successful strategic implementation. The range of options for getting people, departments, and divisions to actively support strategy-implementation activities in a particular organization is almost limitless. Merck, for example, recently gave each of its 37,000 employees a 10-year option to buy 100 shares of Merck stock at a set price of $127. Steven Darien, Merck's vice president of human resources, says, "We needed to find ways to get everyone in the workforce on board in terms of our goals and objectives. Company executives will begin meeting with all Merck workers to explore ways in which employees can contribute more."

Many countries worldwide are curbing executive pay in the wake of a global financial crisis. For example, the German cabinet recently imposed a $650,000 annual salary cap on banks that receive any government-backed capital injections. The German cabinet also imposed a ban on bank executive bonuses, stock options, and severance payments through 2012. Companies worldwide that participate in government bailouts or capital infusions are increasingly being constrained in executive compensation. The U.S. House of Representatives and Senate members severely criticized the CEOs of Ford, GM, and Chrysler for being paid so much in the face of failing companies.

There is rising public resentment over executive pay, and there are government restrictions on compensation. Based in Thousand Oaks, California, Amgen recently directed all shareholders to a 10-item questionnaire asking them what they think about the firm's compensation plan. Schering-Plough Corp. was going to use a similar survey just as it agreed to be acquired by Merck & Co. Home Depot now meets with shareholders regularly to hear their concerns. In April 2009, Royal Bank of Scotland Group PLC voted 9-to-1 against the bank's 2008 compensation package.

Executive pay declined slightly in 2008 and is expected to decrease somewhat substantially in 2009 as pressure for shareholders and government subsidy constraints lower payouts. The five CEOs who in 2008 received the highest compensation in a recent survey are Sanjay Jha at Motorola ($104 million), Ray Irani at Occidental Petroleum ($49.9 million), Robert Iger at Walt Disney ($49.7 million), Vikram Pandit at Citigroup ($38.2 million), and Louis Camilleri at Philip Morris ($36.4 million).[14]

Managing Resistance to Change

No organization or individual can escape change. But the thought of change raises anxieties because people fear economic loss, inconvenience, uncertainty, and a break in normal social patterns. Almost any change in structure, technology, people, or strategies has the potential to disrupt comfortable interaction patterns. For this reason, people resist change. The strategic-management process itself can impose major changes on individuals and processes. Reorienting an organization to get people to think and act strategically is not an easy task.

Resistance to change can be considered the single greatest threat to successful strategy implementation. Resistance regularly occurs in organizations in the form of sabotaging production machines, absenteeism, filing unfounded grievances, and an unwillingness to cooperate. People often resist strategy implementation because they do not understand what is happening or why changes are taking place. In that case, employees may simply need accurate information. Successful strategy implementation hinges upon managers' ability to develop an organizational climate conducive to change. Change must be viewed as an opportunity rather than as a threat by managers and employees.

Resistance to change can emerge at any stage or level of the strategy-implementation process. Although there are various approaches for implementing changes, three commonly used strategies are a force change strategy, an educative change strategy, and a rational or self-interest change strategy. A *force change strategy* involves giving orders and enforcing those orders; this strategy has the advantage of being fast, but it is plagued by low commitment and high resistance. The *educative change strategy* is one that presents information to convince people of the need for change; the disadvantage of an educative change strategy is that implementation becomes slow and difficult. However, this type of strategy evokes greater commitment and less resistance than does the force change strategy. Finally, a *rational* or *self-interest change strategy* is one that attempts to convince individuals that the change is to their personal advantage. When this appeal is successful, strategy implementation can be relatively easy. However, implementation changes are seldom to everyone's advantage.

The rational change strategy is the most desirable, so this approach is examined a bit further. Managers can improve the likelihood of successfully implementing change by carefully designing change efforts. Jack Duncan described a rational or self-interest change strategy as consisting of four steps. First, employees are invited to participate in the process of change and in the details of transition; participation allows everyone to give opinions, to feel a part of the change process, and to identify their own self-interests regarding the recommended change. Second, some motivation or incentive to change is required; self-interest can be the most important motivator. Third, communication is needed so that people can understand the purpose for the changes. Giving and receiving feedback is the fourth step: everyone enjoys knowing how things are going and how much progress is being made.[15]

Because of diverse external and internal forces, change is a fact of life in organizations. The rate, speed, magnitude, and direction of changes vary over time by industry and organization. Strategists should strive to create a work environment in which change is recognized as necessary and beneficial so that individuals can more easily adapt to change. Adopting a strategic-management approach to decision making can itself require major changes in the philosophy and operations of a firm.

Strategists can take a number of positive actions to minimize managers' and employees' resistance to change. For example, individuals who will be affected by a change should be involved in the decision to make the change and in decisions about how to implement the change. Strategists should anticipate changes and develop and offer training and development workshops so that managers and employees can adapt to those changes. They also need to effectively communicate the need for changes. The strategic-management process can be described as a process of managing change.

Organizational change should be viewed today as a continuous process rather than as a project or event. The most successful organizations today continuously adapt to changes in the competitive environment, which themselves continue to change at an accelerating rate. It is not sufficient today to simply react to change. Managers need to anticipate change and ideally be the creator of change. Viewing change as a continuous process is in stark contrast to an old management doctrine regarding change, which was to unfreeze behavior, change the behavior, and then refreeze the new behavior. The new "continuous organizational change" philosophy should mirror the popular "continuous quality improvement philosophy."

Creating a Strategy-Supportive Culture

Strategists should strive to preserve, emphasize, and build upon aspects of an existing *culture* that support proposed new strategies. Aspects of an existing culture that are antagonistic to a proposed strategy should be identified and changed. Substantial research indicates that new strategies are often market-driven and dictated by competitive forces. For this reason, changing a firm's culture to fit a new strategy is usually more effective than changing a strategy to fit an existing culture. As indicated in Table 7-10, numerous techniques are available to alter an organization's culture, including recruitment, training, transfer, promotion, restructure of an organization's design, role modeling, positive reinforcement, and mentoring.

Schein indicated that the following elements are most useful in linking culture to strategy:

1. Formal statements of organizational philosophy, charters, creeds, materials used for recruitment and selection, and socialization
2. Designing of physical spaces, facades, buildings
3. Deliberate role modeling, teaching, and coaching by leaders
4. Explicit reward and status system, promotion criteria
5. Stories, legends, myths, and parables about key people and events

TABLE 7-10   Ways and Means for Altering an Organization's Culture

1. Recruitment
2. Training
3. Transfer
4. Promotion
5. Restructuring
6. Reengineering
7. Role modeling
8. Positive reinforcement
9. Mentoring
10. Revising vision and/or mission
11. Redesigning physical spaces/facades
12. Altering reward system
13. Altering organizational policies/procedures/practices

6. What leaders pay attention to, measure, and control
7. Leader reactions to critical incidents and organizational crises
8. How the organization is designed and structured
9. Organizational systems and procedures
10. Criteria used for recruitment, selection, promotion, leveling off, retirement, and "excommunication" of people[16]

In the personal and religious side of life, the impact of loss and change is easy to see.[17] Memories of loss and change often haunt individuals and organizations for years. Ibsen wrote, "Rob the average man of his life illusion and you rob him of his happiness at the same stroke."[18] When attachments to a culture are severed in an organization's attempt to change direction, employees and managers often experience deep feelings of grief. This phenomenon commonly occurs when external conditions dictate the need for a new strategy. Managers and employees often struggle to find meaning in a situation that changed many years before. Some people find comfort in memories; others find solace in the present. Weak linkages between strategic management and organizational culture can jeopardize performance and success. Deal and Kennedy emphasized that making strategic changes in an organization always threatens a culture:

> People form strong attachments to heroes, legends, the rituals of daily life, the hoopla of extravaganza and ceremonies, and all the symbols of the workplace. Change strips relationships and leaves employees confused, insecure, and often angry. Unless something can be done to provide support for transitions from old to new, the force of a culture can neutralize and emasculate strategy changes.[19]

Production/Operations Concerns When Implementing Strategies

Production/operations capabilities, limitations, and policies can significantly enhance or inhibit the attainment of objectives. Production processes typically constitute more than 70 percent of a firm's total assets. A major part of the strategy-implementation process takes place at the production site. Production-related decisions on plant size, plant location, product design, choice of equipment, kind of tooling, size of inventory, inventory control, quality control, cost control, use of standards, job specialization, employee training, equipment and resource utilization, shipping and packaging, and technological innovation can have a dramatic impact on the success or failure of strategy-implementation efforts.

Examples of adjustments in production systems that could be required to implement various strategies are provided in Table 7-11 for both for-profit and nonprofit organizations. For instance, note that when a bank formulates and selects a strategy to add 10 new branches, a production-related implementation concern is site location. The largest bicycle company in the United States, Huffy, recently ended its own production of bikes and now contracts out those services to Asian and Mexican manufacturers. Huffy focuses instead on

TABLE 7-11 Production Management and Strategy Implementation

Type of Organization	Strategy Being Implemented	Production System Adjustments
Hospital	Adding a cancer center (Product Development)	Purchase specialized equipment and add specialized people.
Bank	Adding 10 new branches (Market Development)	Perform site location analysis.
Beer brewery	Purchasing a barley farm operation (Backward Integration)	Revise the inventory control system.
Steel manufacturer	Acquiring a fast-food chain (Unrelated Diversification)	Improve the quality control system.
Computer company	Purchasing a retail distribution chain (Forward Integration)	Alter the shipping, packaging, and transportation systems.

the design, marketing, and distribution of bikes, but it no longer produces bikes itself. The Dayton, Ohio, company closed its plants in Ohio, Missouri, and Mississippi.

Just-in-time (JIT) production approaches have withstood the test of time. JIT significantly reduces the costs of implementing strategies. With JIT, parts and materials are delivered to a production site just as they are needed, rather than being stockpiled as a hedge against later deliveries. Harley-Davidson reports that at one plant alone, JIT freed $22 million previously tied up in inventory and greatly reduced reorder lead time.

Factors that should be studied before locating production facilities include the availability of major resources, the prevailing wage rates in the area, transportation costs related to shipping and receiving, the location of major markets, political risks in the area or country, and the availability of trainable employees.

For high-technology companies, production costs may not be as important as production flexibility because major product changes can be needed often. Industries such as biogenetics and plastics rely on production systems that must be flexible enough to allow frequent changes and the rapid introduction of new products. An article in the *Harvard Business Review* explained why some organizations get into trouble:

> They too slowly realize that a change in product strategy alters the tasks of a production system. These tasks, which can be stated in terms of requirements for cost, product flexibility, volume flexibility, product performance, and product consistency, determine which manufacturing policies are appropriate. As strategies shift over time, so must production policies covering the location and scale of manufacturing facilities, the choice of manufacturing process, the degree of vertical integration of each manufacturing facility, the use of R&D units, the control of the production system, and the licensing of technology.[20]

A common management practice, cross-training of employees, can facilitate strategy implementation and can yield many benefits. Employees gain a better understanding of the whole business and can contribute better ideas in planning sessions. Cross-training employees can, however, thrust managers into roles that emphasize counseling and coaching over directing and enforcing and can necessitate substantial investments in training and incentives.

Human Resource Concerns When Implementing Strategies

More and more companies are instituting furloughs to cut costs as an alternative to laying off employees. *Furloughs* are temporary layoffs and even white-collar managers are being given furloughs, once confined to blue-collar workers. A few organizations furloughing professional workers in 2009 included Gulfstream Aerospace, Media General, Gannett, the University of Maryland, Clemson University, and Spansion. Recent research shows that 11 percent of larger U.S. companies implemented furloughs during the global economic recession.[21] Winnebago Industries, for example, required all salaried employees to take a week-long furlough, which saved the company $850,000. The Port of Seattle saved $2.9 million by furloughing all of its 800 nonunion workers, mostly professionals, for two weeks. Table 7-12 lists ways that companies today are reducing labor costs to stay financially sound.

The job of human resource manager is changing rapidly as companies continue to downsize and reorganize. Strategic responsibilities of the human resource manager include assessing the staffing needs and costs for alternative strategies proposed during strategy formulation and developing a staffing plan for effectively implementing strategies. This plan must consider how best to manage spiraling health care insurance costs. Employers' health coverage expenses consume an average 26 percent of firms' net profits, even though most companies now require employees to pay part of their health insurance premiums. The plan must also include how to motivate employees and managers during a time when layoffs are common and workloads are high.

TABLE 7-12   Labor Cost-Saving Tactics

Salary freeze

Hiring freeze

Salary reductions

Reduce employee benefits

Raise employee contribution to health-care premiums

Reduce employee 401(k)/403(b) match

Reduce employee workweek

Mandatory furlough

Voluntary furlough

Hire temporary instead of full-time employees

Hire contract employees instead of full-time employees

Volunteer buyouts (Walt Disney is doing this)

Halt production for 3 days a week (Toyota Motor is doing this)

Layoffs

Early retirement

Reducing/eliminating bonuses

Source: Based on Dana Mattioli, "Employers Make Cuts Despite Belief Upturn Is Near," *Wall Street Journal* (April 23, 2009): B4.

The human resource department must develop performance incentives that clearly link performance and pay to strategies. The process of empowering managers and employees through their involvement in strategic-management activities yields the greatest benefits when all organizational members understand clearly how they will benefit personally if the firm does well. Linking company and personal benefits is a major new strategic responsibility of human resource managers. Other new responsibilities for human resource managers may include establishing and administering an *employee stock ownership plan (ESOP)*, instituting an effective child-care policy, and providing leadership for managers and employees in a way that allows them to balance work and family.

A well-designed strategic-management system can fail if insufficient attention is given to the human resource dimension. Human resource problems that arise when businesses implement strategies can usually be traced to one of three causes: (1) disruption of social and political structures, (2) failure to match individuals' aptitudes with implementation tasks, and (3) inadequate top management support for implementation activities.[22]

Strategy implementation poses a threat to many managers and employees in an organization. New power and status relationships are anticipated and realized. New formal and informal groups' values, beliefs, and priorities may be largely unknown. Managers and employees may become engaged in resistance behavior as their roles, prerogatives, and power in the firm change. Disruption of social and political structures that accompany strategy execution must be anticipated and considered during strategy formulation and managed during strategy implementation.

A concern in matching managers with strategy is that jobs have specific and relatively static responsibilities, although people are dynamic in their personal development. Commonly used methods that match managers with strategies to be implemented include transferring managers, developing leadership workshops, offering career development activities, promotions, job enlargement, and job enrichment.

A number of other guidelines can help ensure that human relationships facilitate rather than disrupt strategy-implementation efforts. Specifically, managers should do a lot of chatting and informal questioning to stay abreast of how things are progressing and to know when to intervene. Managers can build support for strategy-implementation efforts by giving few orders, announcing few decisions, depending heavily on informal questioning, and seeking to probe and clarify until a consensus emerges. Key thrusts that succeed should be rewarded generously and visibly.

It is surprising that so often during strategy formulation, individual values, skills, and abilities needed for successful strategy implementation are not considered. It is rare that a firm selecting new strategies or significantly altering existing strategies possesses the right line and staff personnel in the right positions for successful strategy implementation. The need to match individual aptitudes with strategy-implementation tasks should be considered in strategy choice.

Inadequate support from strategists for implementation activities often undermines organizational success. Chief executive officers, small business owners, and government agency heads must be personally committed to strategy implementation and express this commitment in highly visible ways. Strategists' formal statements about the importance of strategic management must be consistent with actual support and rewards given for activities completed and objectives reached. Otherwise, stress created by inconsistency can cause uncertainty among managers and employees at all levels.

Perhaps the best method for preventing and overcoming human resource problems in strategic management is to actively involve as many managers and employees as possible in the process. Although time consuming, this approach builds understanding, trust, commitment, and ownership and reduces resentment and hostility. The true potential of strategy formulation and implementation resides in people.

Employee Stock Ownership Plans (ESOPs)

An *ESOP* is a tax-qualified, defined-contribution, employee-benefit plan whereby employees purchase stock of the company through borrowed money or cash contributions. ESOPs empower employees to work as owners; this is a primary reason why the number of ESOPs have grown dramatically to more than 10,000 firms covering more than 10 million employees. ESOPs now control more than $600 billion in corporate stock in the United States.

Besides reducing worker alienation and stimulating productivity, ESOPs allow firms other benefits, such as substantial tax savings. Principal, interest, and dividend payments on ESOP-funded debt are tax deductible. Banks lend money to ESOPs at interest rates below prime. This money can be repaid in pretax dollars, lowering the debt service as much as 30 percent in some cases. "The ownership culture really makes a difference, when management is a facilitator, not a dictator," says Corey Rosen, executive director of the National Center for Employee Ownership. Fifteen employee-owned companies are listed in Table 7-13.

TABLE 7-13   Fifteen Example ESOP Firms

Firm	Headquarters Location
Publix Supermarkets	Florida
Science Applications	California
Lifetouch	Minnesota
John Lewis Partnership	United Kingdom
Mondragon Cooperative	Spain
Houchens Industries	Kentucky
Amsted Industries	Illinois
Mast General Store	North Carolina
HDR, Inc.	Nebraska
Yoke's Fresh Market	Washington
SPARTA, Inc.	California
Hy-Vee	Iowa
Bi-Mart	Washington
Ferrellgas Partners	Kansas

Source: Based on Edward Iwata, "ESOPs Can Offer Both Upsides, Drawbacks," *USA Today* (April 3, 2007): 2B.

If an ESOP owns more than 50 percent of the firm, those who lend money to the ESOP are taxed on only 50 percent of the income received on the loans. ESOPs are not for every firm, however, because the initial legal, accounting, actuarial, and appraisal fees to set up an ESOP are about $50,000 for a small or midsized firm, with annual administration expenses of about $15,000. Analysts say ESOPs also do not work well in firms that have fluctuating payrolls and profits. Human resource managers in many firms conduct preliminary research to determine the desirability of an ESOP, and then they facilitate its establishment and administration if benefits outweigh the costs.

Wyatt Cafeterias, a southwestern United States operator of 120 cafeterias, also adopted the ESOP concept to prevent a hostile takeover. Employee productivity at Wyatt greatly increased since the ESOP began, as illustrated in the following quote:

> The key employee in our entire organization is the person serving the customer on the cafeteria line. In the past, because of high employee turnover and entry-level wages for many line jobs, these employees received far less attention and recognition than managers. We now tell the tea cart server, "You own the place. Don't wait for the manager to tell you how to do your job better or how to provide better service. You take care of it." Sure, we're looking for productivity increases, but since we began pushing decisions down to the level of people who deal directly with customers, we've discovered an awesome side effect— suddenly the work crews have this "happy to be here" attitude that the customers really love.[23]

Balancing Work Life and Home Life

Work/family strategies have become so popular among companies today that the strategies now represent a competitive advantage for those firms that offer such benefits as elder care assistance, flexible scheduling, job sharing, adoption benefits, an on-site summer camp, employee help lines, pet care, and even lawn service referrals. New corporate titles such as work/life coordinator and director of diversity are becoming common.

Working Mother magazine annually published its listing of "The 100 Best Companies for Working Mothers" (www.workingmother.com). Three especially important variables used in the ranking were availability of flextime, advancement opportunities, and equitable distribution of benefits among companies. Other important criteria are compressed weeks, telecommuting, job sharing, childcare facilities, maternity leave for both parents, mentoring, career development, and promotion for women. *Working Mother's* top eight best companies for working women in 2009 are provided in Table 7-14. *Working Mother* also conducts extensive research to determine the best U.S. firms for women of color.

Human resource managers need to foster a more effective balancing of professional and private lives because nearly 60 million people in the United States are now part of two-career families. A corporate objective to become more lean and mean must today

---

TABLE 7-14 A Few Excellent Workplaces for Women

1. Abbott—An elaborate child care center at headquarters serves 670 infants, toddlers, and pre-schoolers; employees can visit their children during the day.

2. Allstate Insurance—Child care centers are abundant: all employees have access to discounted child care.

3. American Express—Flex scheduling and tuition reimbursement enable most employees to continue their education.

4. Citi—Telecommuting for employees makes caring for family a priority.

5. Fannie Mae—Reimburses tuition-related expenses up to $10,000 per child; provides four weeks of paid maternity leave.

6. IBM—Work/life balance is an integral part of the IBM culture.

7. Johnson & Johnson—Nearly all employees say you never have to choose between family and work at J&J.

8. Merck & Company—Flextime and tuition reimbursement are available to nearly all Merck employees.

Source: Based on 2009 Web site, http://www.workingmother.com/web?service=direct/1/ViewArticlePage/dlinkFullArticle&sp=1780&sp=94.

include consideration for the fact that a good home life contributes immensely to a good work life.

The work/family issue is no longer just a women's issue. Some specific measures that firms are taking to address this issue are providing spouse relocation assistance as an employee benefit; providing company resources for family recreational and educational use; establishing employee country clubs, such as those at IBM and Bethlehem Steel; and creating family/work interaction opportunities. A study by Joseph Pleck of Wheaton College found that in companies that do not offer paternity leave for fathers as a benefit, most men take short, informal paternity leaves anyway by combining vacation time and sick days.

Some organizations have developed family days, when family members are invited into the workplace, taken on plant or office tours, dined by management, and given a chance to see exactly what other family members do each day. Family days are inexpensive and increase the employee's pride in working for the organization. Flexible working hours during the week are another human resource response to the need for individuals to balance work life and home life. The work/family topic is being made part of the agenda at meetings and thus is being discussed in many organizations.

Only 2.6 percent of Fortune 500 firms have a woman CEO. However, recent studies have found that companies with more female executives and directors outperform other firms.[24] Judy Rosener at the University of California, Irvine, says, "Brain scans prove that men and women think differently, so companies with a mix of male and female executives will outperform competitors that rely on leadership of a single sex." It is not that women are better than men, Rosener says. It is the mix of thinking styles that is key to management effectiveness.

During the first week of 2009, Ellen Kullman replaced Chad Holliday as CEO of DuPont, which brought to 13 the number of female CEOs running the 500 largest public firms in the United States. Thirteen is a record number, but only one more than the total for the prior year. Lynn Elsenhans became CEO of Sunoco in 2008. In 2008, two Fortune 500 women CEOs departed: Meg Whitman at eBay and Paula Reynolds at Safeco.

USA Today tracks the performance of women CEOs versus male CEOs, and their research shows virtually no difference in the two groups.[25] The year 2008 saw the S&P 500 stocks fall 38.5 percent, its worst year since 1937. The stock of firms that year with women CEOs fell 42.7 percent, but some firms run by women CEOs did much better, such as Kraft Foods, down only 18 percent under Irene Rosenfeld. Two firms doing great under woman CEOs are Avon under Andrea Jung and Reynolds American under Susan Ivey. Those stocks are up 65.4 percent and 20.8 percent, respectively, since those women became CEO. Table 7-15 gives the 13 Fortune 500 Women CEOs in 2009.

TABLE 7-15 Fortune 500 Women CEOs in 2009

CEO	Company	Fortune 500 Rank
Angela Braly	WellPoint	33
Patricia Woertz	Archer Daniels Midland	52
Lynn Elsenhans	Sunoco	56
Indra Nooyi	PepsiCo	59
Irene Rosenfeld	Kraft Foods	63
Carol Meyrowitz	TJX	132
Mary Sammons	Rite Aid	142
Anne Mulcahy	Xerox	144
Brenda Barnes	Sara Lee	203
Andrea Jung	Avon Products	265
Susan Ivey	Reynolds American	290
Christina Gold	Western Union	473

There is great room for improvement in removing the *glass ceiling* domestically, especially considering that women make up 47 percent of the U.S. labor force. *Glass ceiling* refers to the invisible barrier in many firms that bars women and minorities from top-level management positions. The United States leads the world in promoting women and minorities into mid- and top-level managerial positions in business.

Boeing's firing of CEO Harry Stonecipher for having an extramarital affair raised public awareness of office romance. However, just 12 percent of 391 companies surveyed by the American Management Association have written guidelines on office dating.[26] The fact of the matter is that most employers in the United States turn a blind eye to marital cheating. Some employers, such as Southwest Airlines, which employs more than 1,000 married couples, explicitly allow consensual office relationships. Research suggests that more men than women engage in extramarital affairs at work, roughly 22 percent to 15 percent; however, the percentage of women having extramarital affairs is increasing steadily, whereas the percentage of men having affairs with co-workers is holding steady.[27] If an affair is disrupting your work, then "the first step is to go to the offending person privately and try to resolve the matter. If that fails, then go to the human-resources manager seeking assistance."[28] Filing a discrimination lawsuit based on the affair is recommended only as a last resort because courts generally rule that co-workers' injuries are not pervasive enough to warrant any damages.

Benefits of a Diverse Workforce

Toyota has committed almost $8 billion over 10 years to diversify its workforce and to use more minority suppliers. Hundreds of other firms, such as Ford Motor Company and Coca-Cola, are also striving to become more diversified in their workforces. TJX Companies, the parent of 1,500 T. J. Maxx and Marshall's stores, has reaped great benefits and is an exemplary company in terms of diversity.

An organization can perhaps be most effective when its workforce mirrors the diversity of its customers. For global companies, this goal can be optimistic, but it is a worthwhile goal.

Corporate Wellness Programs

A recent *BusinessWeek* cover story article details how firms are striving to lower the accelerating costs of employees' health-care insurance premiums.[29] Many firms such as Scotts Miracle-Gro Company (based in Marysville, Ohio), IBM, and Microsoft are implementing wellness programs, requiring employees to get healthier or pay higher insurance premiums. Employees that do get healthier win bonuses, free trips, and pay lower premiums; nonconforming employees pay higher premiums and receive no "healthy" benefits. Wellness of employees has become a strategic issue for many firms. Most firms require a health examination as a part of an employment application, and healthiness is more and more becoming a hiring factor. Michael Porter, coauthor of *Redefining Health Care*, says, "We have this notion that you can gorge on hot dogs, be in a pie-eating contest, and drink every day, and society will take care of you. We can't afford to let individuals drive up company costs because they're not willing to address their own health problems."

Slightly more than 60 percent of companies with 10,000 or more employees had a wellness program in 2008, up from 47 percent in 2005.[30] Among firms with wellness programs, the average cost per employee was $7,173. However, in the weak economy of late, companies are cutting back on their wellness programs. Many employees say they are so stressed about work and finances they have little time to eat right and exercise. PepsiCo in 2008 introduced a $600 surcharge for all its employees that smoke; the company has a smoking-cessation program. PepsiCo's smoking quit rate among employees increased to 34 percent in 2008 versus 20 percent in 2007.

Wellness programs provide counseling to employees and seek lifestyle changes to achieve healthier living. For example, trans fats are a major cause of heart disease. Near elimination of trans fats in one's diet will reduce one's risk for heart attack by as much as 19 percent, according to a recent article. New York City now requires restaurants to inform

TABLE 7-16 **The Key to Staying Healthy, Living to 100, and Being a "Well" Employee**

1. Eat nutritiously—eat a variety of fruits and vegetables daily because they have ingredients that the body uses to repair and strengthen itself.

2. Stay hydrated—drink plenty of water to aid the body in eliminating toxins and to enable body organs to function efficiently; the body is mostly water.

3. Get plenty of rest—the body repairs itself during rest, so get at least seven hours of sleep nightly, preferably eight hours.

4. Get plenty of exercise—exercise vigorously at least 30 minutes daily so the body can release toxins and strengthen vital organs.

5. Reduce stress—the body's immune system is weakened when one is under stress, making the body vulnerable to many ailments, so keep stress to a minimum.

6. Do not smoke—smoking kills, no doubt about it anymore.

7. Take vitamin supplements—consult your physician, but because it is difficult for diet alone to supply all the nutrients and vitamins needed, supplements can be helpful in achieving good health and longevity.

Source: Based on Lauren Etter, "Trans Fats: Will They Get Shelved?" *Wall Street Journal* (December 8, 2006): A6; Joel Fuhrman, MD, *Eat to Live* (Boston: Little, Brown, 2003).

customers about levels of trans fat being served in prepared foods. Chicago is considering a similar ban on trans fats. Denmark in 2003 became the first country to strictly regulate trans fats.

Restaurant chains are only slowly reducing trans fat levels in served foods because (1) trans fat oils make fried foods crispier, (2) trans fats give baked goods a longer shelf life, (3) trans fat oils can be used multiple times compared to other cooking oils, and (4) trans fat oils taste better. Three restaurant chains have switched to oils free of trans fat—Chili's, Ruby Tuesday, and Wendy's—but some chains still may use trans fat oils, including Kentucky Fried Chicken, McDonald's, Dunkin' Donuts, Taco Bell, and Burger King. Marriott International in February 2007 eliminated trans fats from the food it serves at its 2,300 North American hotels, becoming the first big hotel chain to do so, although the 18-hotel Lowes luxury chain is close behind. Marriott's change includes its Renaissance, Courtyard, and Residence Inn brands.

Saturated fats are also bad, so one should avoid eating too much red meat and dairy products, which are high in saturated fats. Seven key lifestyle habits listed in Table 7-16 may significantly improve health and longevity.

Conclusion

Successful strategy formulation does not at all guarantee successful strategy implementation. Although inextricably interdependent, strategy formulation and strategy implementation are characteristically different. In a single word, strategy implementation means *change*. It is widely agreed that "the real work begins after strategies are formulated." Successful strategy implementation requires the support of, as well as discipline and hard work from, motivated managers and employees. It is sometimes frightening to think that a single individual can irreparably sabotage strategy-implementation efforts.

Formulating the right strategies is not enough, because managers and employees must be motivated to implement those strategies. Management issues considered central to strategy implementation include matching organizational structure with strategy, linking performance and pay to strategies, creating an organizational climate conducive to change, managing political relationships, creating a strategy-supportive culture, adapting production/ operations processes, and managing human resources. Establishing annual objectives, devising policies, and allocating resources are central strategy-implementation activities common to all organizations. Depending on the size and type of the organization, other management issues could be equally important to successful strategy implementation.

We invite you to visit the David page on the Prentice Hall Companion Web site at http://www.pearsonhighered.com/david/ for this chapter's review quiz.

Key Terms and Concepts

Annual Objectives (p. 215)
Avoidance (p. 220)
Benchmarking (p. 230)
Bonus System (p. 233)
Conflict (p. 220)
Confrontation (p. 220)
Culture (p. 235)
Decentralized Structure (p. 222)
Defusion (p. 220)
Delayering (p. 229)
Divisional Structure by Geographic Area, Product, Customer, or Process (p. 224)
Downsizing (p. 229)
Educative Change Strategy (p. 234)
Employee Stock Ownership Plans (ESOP) (p. 238)
Establishing Annual Objectives (p. 215)
Force Change Strategy (p. 234)
Functional Structure (p. 222)

Furloughs (p. 237)
Gain Sharing (p. 232)
Glass Ceiling (p. 242)
Horizontal Consistency of Objectives (p. 217)
Just-in-Time (JIT) (p. 237)
Matrix Structure (p. 226)
Policy (p. 217)
Profit Sharing (p. 232)
Rational Change Strategy (p. 234)
Reengineering (p. 230)
Resistance to Change (p. 234)
Resource Allocation (p. 219)
Restructuring (p. 229)
Rightsizing (p. 229)
Self-Interest Change Strategy (p. 234)
Six Sigma (p. 230)
Strategic Business Unit (SBU) Structure (p. 225)
Vertical Consistency of Objectives (p. 217)

Issues for Review and Discussion

1. List the five labor cost-saving activities that you believe would be most effective for (1) Best Buy, (2) your university, and (3) the U.S. Postal Service. Give a rationale for each company.

2. Define and give an example of furloughs as they could apply to your business school.

3. The chapter says strategy formulation focuses on effectiveness, whereas strategy implementation focuses on efficiency. Which is more important, effectiveness or efficiency? Give an example of each concept.

4. In stating objectives, why should terms such as *increase*, *minimize*, *maximize*, *as soon as possible*, *adequate*, and *decrease* be avoided?

5. What are four types of resources that all organizations have? List them in order of importance for your university or business school.

6. Considering avoidance, defusion, confrontation, which method of conflict resolution do you prefer most? Why? Which do you prefer least? Why?

7. Explain why Chandler's strategy-structure relationship commonly exists among firms.

8. If you owned and opened three restaurants after you graduated, would you operate from a functional or divisional structure? Why?

9. Explain how to choose between a divisional-by-product and a divisional-by-region organizational structure.

10. Think of a company that would operate best in your opinion by a division-by-services organizational structure. Explain your reasoning.

11. What are the two major disadvantages of an SBU-type organizational structure? What are the two major advantages? At what point in a firm's growth do you feel the advantages offset the disadvantages? Explain.

12. In order of importance in your opinion, list six advantages of a matrix organizational structure.

13. Why should division head persons have the title president rather than vice president?

14. Is Six Sigma more a restructuring or reengineering management technique? Why?

15. Compare and contrast profit sharing with gain sharing as employee performance incentives.

16. List three resistance to change strategies. Give an example when you would use each method or approach.

17. In order of importance in your opinion, list six techniques or activities widely used to alter an organization's culture.

18. What are the benefits of establishing an ESOP in a company?
19. List reasons why is it important for an organization not to have a "glass ceiling."
20. Allocating resources can be a political and an ad hoc activity in firms that do not use strategic management. Why is this true? Does adopting strategic management ensure easy resource allocation? Why?
21. Compare strategy formulation with strategy implementation in terms of each being an art or a science.
22. Describe the relationship between annual objectives and policies.
23. Identify a long-term objective and two supporting annual objectives for a familiar organization.
24. Identify and discuss three policies that apply to your present strategic-management class.
25. Explain the following statement: Horizontal consistency of goals is as important as vertical consistency.
26. Describe several reasons why conflict may occur during objective-setting activities.
27. In your opinion, what approaches to conflict resolution would be best for resolving a disagreement between a personnel manager and a sales manager over the firing of a particular salesperson? Why?
28. Describe the organizational culture of your college or university.
29. Explain why organizational structure is so important in strategy implementation.
30. In your opinion, how many separate divisions could an organization reasonably have without using an SBU-type organizational structure? Why?
31. Would you recommend a divisional structure by geographic area, product, customer, or process for a medium-sized bank in your local area? Why?
32. What are the advantages and disadvantages of decentralizing the wage and salary functions of an organization? How could this be accomplished?
33. Consider a college organization with which you are familiar. How did management issues affect strategy implementation in that organization?
34. As production manager of a local newspaper, what problems would you anticipate in implementing a strategy to increase the average number of pages in the paper by 40 percent?
35. Do you believe expenditures for child care or fitness facilities are warranted from a cost-benefit perspective? Why or why not?
36. Explain why successful strategy implementation often hinges on whether the strategy-formulation process empowers managers and employees.
37. Discuss the glass ceiling in the United States, giving your ideas and suggestions.
38. Discuss three ways discussed in this book for linking performance and pay to strategies.
39. List the different types of organizational structure. Diagram what you think is the most complex of these structures and label your chart clearly.
40. List the advantages and disadvantages of a functional versus a divisional organizational structure.
41. Discuss recent trends in women and minorities becoming top executives in the United States.
42. Discuss recent trends in firms downsizing family-friendly programs.
43. Research the latest developments in the class-action lawsuit involving women managers versus Wal-Mart Stores and report your findings to the class.
44. List seven guidelines to follow in developing an organizational chart.

Notes

1. Dale McConkey, "Planning in a Changing Environment," *Business Horizons* (September–October 1988): 66.
2. A. G. Bedeian and W. F. Glueck, *Management,* 3rd ed. (Chicago: The Dryden Press, 1983): 212.
3. Boris Yavitz and William Newman, *Strategy in Action: The Execution, Politics, and Payoff of Business Planning* (New York: The Free Press, 1982): 195.
4. E. H. Schein. "Three Cultures of Management: The Key to Organizational Learning," *Sloan Management Review* 38, 1 (1996): 9–20.
5. S. Ghoshal and C. A. Bartlett, "Changing the Role of Management: Beyond Structure to Processes." *Harvard Business Review* 73, 1 (1995): 88.
6. Joann Lublin, "Chairman-CEO Split Gains Allies," *Wall Street Journal* (March 30, 2009): B4.
7. Karen Richardson, "The 'Six Sigma' Factor for Home Depot," *Wall Street Journal* (January 4, 2007): C3.
8. "Want to Be a Manager? Many People Say No, Calling Job Miserable," *Wall Street Journal* (April 4, 1997): 1; Stephanie Armour, "Management Loses Its Allure," *USA Today* (October 10, 1997): 1B.

9. Paul Carroll, "No More Business as Usual, Please. Time to Try Something Different," *Wall Street Journal* (October 23, 2001): A24.

10. Yuka Hayashi and Phred Dvorak, "Japanese Wrestle with CEO Pay as They Go Global," *Wall Street Journal* (November 28, 2008): B1.

11. Kris Maher and Kris Hudson, "Wal-Mart to Sweeten Bonus Plans for Staff," *Wall Street Journal* (March 22, 2007): A11.

12. Richard Brown, "Outsider CEO: Inspiring Change with Force and Grace," *USA Today* (July 19, 1999): 3B.

13. Yavitz and Newman, 58.

14. Phred Dvorak, "Executive Salaries May Fall More Sharply in 2009," *Wall Street Journal* (April 3, 2009): B4.

15. Jack Duncan, *Management* (New York: Random House, 1983): 381–390.

16. E. H. Schein, "The Role of the Founder in Creating Organizational Culture," *Organizational Dynamics* (Summer 1983): 13–28.

17. T. Deal and A. Kennedy, "Culture: A New Look Through Old Lenses," *Journal of Applied Behavioral Science* 19, no. 4 (1983): 498–504.

18. H. Ibsen, "The Wild Duck," in O. G. Brochett and L. Brochett (eds.), *Plays for the Theater* (New York: Holt, Rinehart & Winston, 1967); R. Pascale, "The Paradox of 'Corporate Culture': Reconciling Ourselves to Socialization," *California Management Review* 28, no. 2 (1985): 26, 37–40.

19. T. Deal and A. Kennedy, *Corporate Cultures: The Rites and Rituals of Corporate Life* (Reading, MA: Addison-Wesley, 1982): 256.

20. Robert Stobaugh and Piero Telesio, "Match Manufacturing Policies and Product Strategy," *Harvard Business Review* 61, no. 2 (March–April 1983): 113.

21. Dana Magttioli and Sara Murray, "Employers Hit Salaried Staff with Furloughs," *Wall Street Journal* (February 24, 2009): D1; Laura Petrecca, "More Companies Turn to Furloughs to Save Money, Jobs," *USA Today* (March 5, 2009): B1.

22. R. T. Lenz and Marjorie Lyles, "Managing Human Resource Problems in Strategy Planning Systems," *Journal of Business Strategy* 60, no. 4 (Spring 1986): 58.

23. J. Warren Henry, "ESOPs with Productivity Payoffs," *Journal of Business Strategy* (July–August 1989): 33.

24. Del Jones, "Women Slowly Gain on Corporate America," USA Today (January 2, 2009): 6B.

25. Ibid.

26. Sue Shellenbarger, "Employers Often Ignore Office Affairs, Leaving Co-workers in Difficult Spot," *Wall Street Journal* (March 10, 2005): D1.

27. Ibid.

28. Ibid.

29. Michelle Conlin, "Get Healthy—or Else," *BusinessWeek* (February 26, 2007): 58–69.

30. Laura Petrecca, "Companies Re-Evaluate Wellness Programs," *USA Today* (June 17, 2009): 3B.

Current Readings

Barkema, Harry G., and Mario Schijven. "Toward Unlocking the Full Potential of Acquisitions: The Role of Organizational Restructuring." *Academy of Management Journal* 51, no. 4 (August 2008): 696.

Bennett, Nathan, and Stephen A. Miles. "6 Steps to (Re) Building a Top Management Team." *MIT Sloan Management Review* 50, no. 1 (Fall 2008): 60.

Bergh, Donald D., and Elizabeth Lim. "Learning How to Restructure: Absorptive Capacity and Improvisational Views of Restructuring Actions and Performance." *Strategic Management Journal* 29, no. 6 (June 2008): 593.

Berrone, Pascual, and Luis Gomez-Mejia. "Environmental Performance and Executive Compensation: An Integrated Agency-Institutional Perspective." *Academy of Management Journal* (February 2009): 103–126.

Boeker, Warren, and Frank T. Rothaermel. "Old Technology Meets New Technology: Complementarities, Similarities, and Alliance Formation." *Strategic Management Journal* 29, no. 1 (January 2008): 47.

Brandes, Pamela, Maria Goranova, and Steven Hall. "Navigating Shareholder Influence: Compensation Plans and the Shareholder Approval Process." *Academy of Management Perspectives* 22, no. 1 (February 2008): 41.

Brush, Candida G., and Elizabeth J. Gatewood. "Women Growing Businesses: Clearing the Hurdles." *Business Horizons* 51, no. 3 (May–June 2008): 175.

Canales, J. Ignacio, and Joaquim Vila. "Can Strategic Planning Make Strategy More Relevant and Build Commitment Over Time? The Case of RACC." *Long Range Planning* 41, no. 3 (June 2008): 273.

Conyon, Martin J., Simon I. Peck, and Graham Sadler. "Compensation Consultants and Executive Pay: Evidence from the United States and the United Kingdom." *Academy of Management Perspectives* (February 2009): 43–55.

Crittenden, Victoria L., and William F. Crittenden. "Building a Capable Organization: The Eight Levers of Strategy Implementation." *Business Horizons* 51, no. 4 (July–August 2008): 301.

D'Amelio, Angelo, Jeffrey D. Ford, and Laurie W. Ford. "Resistance to Change: The Rest of the Story." *Academy of Management Review* 33, no. 2 (April 2008): 362.

Ford, Jeffrey D., and Laurie W. Ford. "Decoding Resistance to Change." *Harvard Business Review* (April 2009): 99–104.

Heugens, Pursey, and Michel Lander. "Structure! Agency!: A Meta-Analysis of Institutional Theories of Organization." *Academy of Management Journal* (February 2009): 87–102.

Humphreys, John, and Hal Langford. "Managing a Corporate Culture 'Slide.'" *MIT Sloan Management Review* 49, no. 3 (Spring 2008): 25.

Kaplan, Robert S., and David P. Norton. "Mastering the Management System." *Harvard Business Review* (January 2008): 62.

Kaplan, Steven N. "CEO Compensation: Are U.S. CEOs Overpaid?" *Academy of Management Perspectives* 22, no. 2 (May 2008): 5.

Lam, Kevin, Ji Li, Shirley X.Y. Liu, and James J. M. Sun. "Strategic Human Resource Management, Institutionalization, and Employment Modes: An Empirical Study in China." *Strategic Management Journal* 29, no. 3 (March 2008): 337.

Lawler, Edward E. III. "Why Are We Losing All Our Good People?" *Harvard Business Review* (June 2008): 41.

Love, Geoffrey, and Matthew Kraatz. "Character, Conformity, or the Bottom Line? How and Why Downsizing Affected Corporate Reputation." *Academy of Management Journal* (April 2009): 314–335.

Miller, Susan, David Hickson, and David Wilson. "From Strategy to Action: Involvement and Influence in Top Level Decisions." *Long Range Planning* 41, no. 6 (December 2008): 606–628.

O'Leary-Kelly, Anne, Lynn Bowes-Sperry, Collette, Bates, and Emily Lean. "Sexual Harassment at Work: A Decade (Plus) of Progress." *Journal of Management* (June 2009): 503–538.

Remus, Ilies, Kelly Wilson, and David Wagner. "The Spillover of Daily Job Satisfaction onto Employees Family Lives: The Facilitating Role of Work-Family Integration." *Academy of Management Journal* (February 2009): 87–102

Sutton, Robert. "How to Be a Good Boss in a Bad Economy." *Harvard Business Review* (June 2009): 42–53.

Veloso, Francisco M., and Claudio Wolter. "The Effects of Innovation on Vertical Structure: Perspectives on Transaction Costs and Competences." *Academy of Management Review* (July 2008): 586.

Watkins, Michael. "Picking the Right Transition Strategy." *Harvard Business Review* (January 2009): 46–53.

ASSURANCE OF LEARNING EXERCISES

Assurance of Learning Exercise 7A

Revising McDonald's Organizational Chart

Purpose

Developing and altering organizational charts is an important skill for strategists to possess. This exercise can improve your skill in altering an organization's hierarchical structure in response to new strategies being formulated.

Instructions

Step 1   Turn to the McDonald's Cohesion Case (p. 29) and review the organizational chart. On a separate sheet of paper, answer the following questions:

1. What type of organizational chart is illustrated for McDonald's?
2. What improvements could you recommend for the McDonald's organizational chart? Give your reasoning for each suggestion.
3. What aspects of McDonald's chart do you especially like?
4. What type of organizational chart do you believe would best suit McDonald's? Why?

Assurance of Learning Exercise 7B

Do Organizations Really Establish Objectives?

Purpose

Objectives provide direction, allow synergy, aid in evaluation, establish priorities, reduce uncertainty, minimize conflicts, stimulate exertion, and aid in both the allocation of resources and the design of jobs. This exercise will enhance your understanding of how organizations use or misuse objectives.

Instructions

Step 1   Join with one other person in class to form a two-person team.

Step 2   Contact by telephone the owner or manager of an organization in your city or town. Request a 30-minute personal interview or meeting with that person for the purpose of discussing "business objectives." During your meeting, seek answers to the following questions:

1. Do you believe it is important for a business to establish and clearly communicate long-term and annual objectives? Why or why not?
2. Does your organization establish objectives? If yes, what type and how many? How are the objectives communicated to individuals? Are your firm's objectives in written form or simply communicated orally?
3. To what extent are managers and employees involved in the process of establishing objectives?
4. How often are your business objectives revised and by what process?

Step 3   Take good notes during the interview. Let one person be the note taker and one person do most of the talking. Have your notes typed up and ready to turn in to your professor.

Step 4   Prepare a 5-minute oral presentation for the class, reporting the results of your interview. Turn in your typed report.

Assurance of Learning Exercise 7C

Understanding My University's Culture

Purpose

It is something of an art to uncover the basic values and beliefs that are buried deeply in an organization's rich collection of stories, language, heroes, heroines, and rituals, yet culture can be the most important factor in implementing strategies.

Instructions

Step 1   On a separate sheet of paper, list the following terms: hero/heroine, belief, metaphor, language, value, symbol, story, legend, saga, folktale, myth, ceremony, rite, and ritual.

Step 2   For your college or university, give examples of each term. If necessary, speak with faculty, staff, alumni, administration, or fellow students of the institution to identify examples of each term.

Step 3   Report your findings to the class. Tell the class how you feel regarding cultural products being consciously used to help implement strategies.

CHAPTER 8

Implementing Strategies: Marketing, Finance/Accounting, R&D, and MIS Issues

CHAPTER OBJECTIVES

After studying this chapter, you should be able to do the following:

1. Explain market segmentation and product positioning as strategy-implementation tools.

2. Discuss procedures for determining the worth of a business.

3. Explain why projected financial statement analysis is a central strategy-implementation tool.

4. Explain how to evaluate the attractiveness of debt versus stock as a source of capital to implement strategies.

5. Discuss the nature and role of research and development in strategy implementation.

6. Explain how management information systems can determine the success of strategy-implementation efforts.

Assurance of Learning Exercises

Assurance of Learning Exercise 8A
Developing a Product-Positioning Map for McDonald's

Assurance of Learning Exercise 8B
Performing an EPS/EBIT Analysis for McDonald's

Assurance of Learning Exercise 8C
Preparing Projected Financial Statements for McDonald's

Assurance of Learning Exercise 8D
Determining the Cash Value of McDonald's

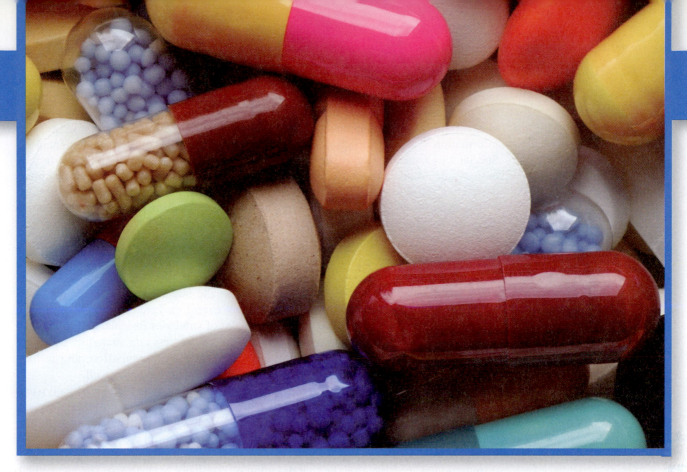

Source: Shutterstock/AJT

"Notable Quotes"

"The greatest strategy is doomed if it's implemented badly."

—Bernard Reimann

"There is no 'perfect' strategic decision. One always has to pay a price. One always has to balance conflicting objectives, conflicting opinions, and conflicting priorities. The best strategic decision is only an approximation—and a risk."

—Peter Drucker

"The real question isn't how well you're doing today against your own history, but how you're doing against your competitors."

—Donald Kress

"As market windows open and close more quickly, it is important that R&D be tied more closely to corporate strategy."

—William Spenser

"Most of the time, strategists should not be formulating strategy at all; they should be getting on with implementing strategies they already have."

—Henry Mintzberg

"It is human nature to make decisions based on emotion, rather than on fact. But nothing could be more illogical."

—Toshiba Corporation

"No business can do everything. Even if it has the money, it will never have enough good people. It has to set priorities. The worst thing to do is a little bit of everything. This makes sure that nothing is being accomplished. It is better to pick the wrong priority than none at all."

—Peter Drucker

Assurance of Learning Exercise 8E
Developing a Product-Positioning Map for My University

Assurance of Learning Exercise 8F
Do Banks Require Projected Financial Statements?

Strategies have no chance of being implemented successfully in organizations that do not market goods and services well, in firms that cannot raise needed working capital, in firms that produce technologically inferior products, or in firms that have a weak information system. This chapter examines marketing, finance/accounting, R&D, and management information systems (MIS) issues that are central to effective strategy implementation. Special topics include market segmentation, market positioning, evaluating the worth of a business, determining to what extent debt and/or stock should be used as a source of capital, developing projected financial statements, contracting R&D outside the firm, and creating an information support system. Manager and employee involvement and participation are essential for success in marketing, finance/accounting, R&D, and MIS activities.

The Nature of Strategy Implementation

The quarterback can call the best play possible in the huddle, but that does not mean the play will go for a touchdown. The team may even lose yardage unless the play is executed (implemented) well. Less than 10 percent of strategies formulated are successfully implemented! There are many reasons for this low success rate, including failing to appropriately segment markets, paying too much for a new acquisition, and falling behind competitors in R&D. Johnson & Johnson implements strategies well.

Strategy implementation directly affects the lives of plant managers, division managers, department managers, sales managers, product managers, project managers, personnel managers, staff managers, supervisors, and all employees. In some situations, individuals may not have participated in the strategy-formulation process at all and may not appreciate, understand, or even accept the work and thought that went into strategy formulation. There may even be foot dragging or resistance on their part. Managers and employees who do not understand the business and are not committed to the business may attempt to sabotage strategy-implementation efforts in hopes that the organization will return to its old ways. The strategy-implementation stage of the strategic-management process is highlighted in Figure 8-1.

Doing Great in a Weak Economy. How?

Johnson & Johnson (J&J)

Founded in 1886 and based in New Brunswick, New Jersey, J&J produces a wide variety of health-care products, ranging from baby powder to Listerine to joint replacement parts to pharmaceutical drugs. J&J is a gigantic well-managed company that pays the fifth highest dividend amount annually of any firm in the world.

Among all the corporations in the world, *Fortune* magazine rated J&J as number 5 on their 2009 "Most Admired Companies" list. J&J's revenues for 2008 increased from $61 billion to $63 billion when most firms endured revenue decreases. Also for calendar 2008, J&J's

net income increased to $12.9 billion from $10.5 billion when most firms experienced dramatic losses.

J&J's CEO, Bill Weldon, says, "Our Credo, laid out by Robert Wood Johnson in 1943, still governs J&J. Our Credo really sets our priorities. And our first priority is to the people who use our products—to make sure we're supplying them with quality products," he says. J&J applicants must read the credo before being hired, and Weldon says that anyone transitioning into a leadership position in the company spends two days with him, J&J's HR boss, and general counsel talking about how the credo "has shaped our organization and decisions" over 66 years.

If you get sick, you likely will begin using J&J products. The diversified giant operates in three segments through more than 250 operating companies located in some 60 countries. The J&J Pharmaceuticals division makes drugs (including schizophrenia medication Risperdal and psoriasis drug Remicade) for an array of ailments, such as neurological conditions, blood disorders, autoimmune diseases, and pain. J&J's Medical Devices and Diagnostics division offers surgical equipment, monitoring devices, orthopedic products, and contact lenses, among other items. The consumer segment makes over-the-counter drugs and products for skin and hair care, oral care, first aid, and women's health.

In mid-2009, J&J agreed to acquire the small cancer drug-developer Cougar Biotechnology for about $894 million in cash. Cougar has an excellent drug for late stage prostate cancer. J&J's purchase price of $43 a share was a 16 percent premium over Cougar's closing stock price.

J&J reported second quarter 2009 net income of $3.21 billion and sales of $15.24 billion. During that quarter, sales of J&J's Remicade treatment for rheumatoid arthritis rose 24 percent to $1.1 billion. In July 2009, the company acquired a minority stake in Elan Corporation, which makes Alzheimer's drugs.

Source: Based on Geoff Colvin, "The World's Most Admired Companies," *Fortune* (March 16, 2009): 76–86; Jessica Shambora, "Most Admired Companies Know Their Values," *CNN Money* (March 5, 2009).

Current Marketing Issues

Countless marketing variables affect the success or failure of strategy implementation, and the scope of this text does not allow us to address all those issues. Some examples of marketing decisions that may require policies are as follows:

1. To use exclusive dealerships or multiple channels of distribution
2. To use heavy, light, or no TV advertising
3. To limit (or not) the share of business done with a single customer
4. To be a price leader or a price follower
5. To offer a complete or limited warranty
6. To reward salespeople based on straight salary, straight commission, or a combination salary/commission
7. To advertise online or not

A marketing issue of increasing concern to consumers today is the extent to which companies can track individuals' movements on the Internet—and even be able to identify an individual by name and e-mail address. Individuals' wanderings on the Internet are no longer anonymous, as many persons still believe. Marketing companies such as DoubleClick, Flycast, AdKnowledge, AdForce, and Real Media have sophisticated methods to identify who you are and your particular interests.[1] If you are especially concerned about being tracked, visit the www.networkadvertising.org Web site, which gives details about how marketers today are identifying you and your buying habits.

Marketing of late has become more about building a two-way relationship with consumers than just informing consumers about a product or service. Marketers today must get their customers involved in their company Web site and solicit suggestions from customers in terms of product development, customer service, and ideas. The online community is much quicker, cheaper, and effective than traditional focus groups and surveys.

Companies and organizations should encourage their employees to create *wikis*—Web sites that allows users to add, delete, and edit content regarding frequently asked questions

FIGURE 8-1

A Comprehensive Strategic-Management Model

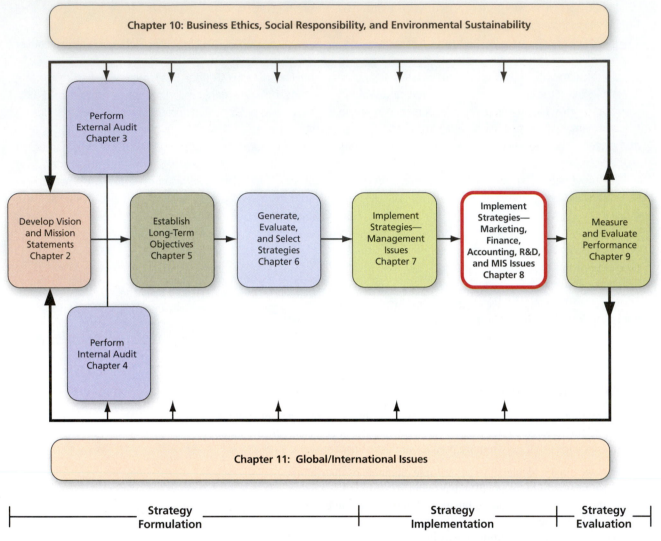

Source: Fred R. David, "How Companies Define Their Mission," *Long Range Planning* 22, no. 3 (June 1988): 40.

and information across the firm's whole value chain of activities. The most common wiki is Wikipedia, but think of wikis as user-generated content. Know that anyone can change the content in a wiki but the group and other editors can change the content or changes that you submit.

Firms should provide incentives to consumers to share their thoughts, opinions, and experiences on the company Web site. Encourage consumers to network among themselves on topics of their choosing on the company Web site. So the company Web site must not be all about the company—it must be all about the customer too. Perhaps offer points or discounts for customers who provide ideas and suggestions. This practice will not only encourage participation but will allow both the company and other customers to interact with "experts."

New Principles of Marketing

Today a business or organization's Web site must provide clear and simple instructions for customers to set up a blog and/or contribute to a wiki. Customers trust each others' opinions more than a company's marketing pitch, and the more they talk freely, the more the firm can learn how to improve its product, service, and marketing. Marketers today monitor blogs daily to determine, evaluate, and influence opinions being formed by customers. Customers must not feel like they are a captive audience for advertising at a firm's Web site. Table 8-1 provides new principles of marketing according to Parise, Guinan, and Weinberg.[2]

Wells Fargo and Bank of America in 2009 began to *tweet* customers, meaning they posted messages of 140 characters or less on Twitter.com to describe features of bank products. Some banks are placing marketing videos on YouTube. Discover Financial, American Express, and Citigroup all now have Facebook or MySpace pages. UMB Financial of Kansas City, Missouri, tweets about everything from the bank's financial stability to the industry's prospects. Steve Furman, Discover's director of e-commerce, says the appeal of social networking is that it provides "pure, instant" communication with customers.[3]

When the big three U.S. automakers were asking lawmakers for bailout funding, all three firms launched extensive Internet marketing campaigns to garner support for their requests and plans for the future. Ford's online marketing campaign was anchored by the Web site www.TheFordStory.com. In addition to a new Web site of its own, Chrysler launched a new marketing YouTube Channel named Grab Democracy and also posted ad information to its blog. GM employed similar marketing tactics to drive visitors to its main Web site. Once any controversial topic arises in a company or industry, millions of people are out there googling, yahooing, aoling, youtubing, facebooking, and myspacing to find out more information in order to form their own opinions and preferences.[4]

Although the exponential increase in social networking and business online has created huge opportunities for marketers, it also has produced some severe threats. Perhaps the greatest threat is that any king of negative publicity travels fast online. For example, Dr Pepper recently suffered immensely when an attorney for the rock band Guns N' Roses accused the company of not following through on giving every American a soft drink if they released their album *Chinese Democracy*. Other examples abound, such as Motrin ads that lightheartedly talked about Mom's back pain from holding babies in slings, and Burger King's Whopper Virgin campaign, which featured a taste test of a Whopper versus a McDonald's Big Mac in remote areas of the world. Even Taco Bell suffered from its ads that featured asking 50 Cent (aka Curtis Jackson) if he would change his name to 79 Cent or 89 Cent for a day in exchange for a $10,000 donation to charity. Seemingly minor ethical and questionable actions can catapult these days into huge public relations problems for companies as a result of the monumental online social and business communications. For example, Domino's, the nation's largest pizza delivery chain, spent a month in 2009 trying to dispel the video on YouTube and Facebook showing two of its employees doing gross things to a Domino's sub sandwich, including passing gas on salami.[5]

In increasing numbers, people living in underdeveloped and poor nations around the world have cell phones but no computers, so the Internet is rapidly moving to cell phone

TABLE 8-1 The New Principles of Marketing

1. Don't just talk at consumers—work with them throughout the marketing process.
2. Give consumers a reason to participate.
3. Listen to—and join—the conversation outside your company's Web site.
4. Resist the temptation to sell, sell, sell. Instead attract, attract, attract.
5. Don't control online conversations; let it flow freely.
6. Find a "marketing technologist," a person who has three excellent skill sets (marketing, technology, and social interaction).
7. Embrace instant messaging and chatting.

Source: Based on Salvatore Parise, Patricia Guinan, and Bruce Weinberg, "The Secrets of Marketing in a Web 2.0 World," *Wall Street Journal* (December 15, 2008): R1.

platforms. This is opening up even larger markets to online marketing. People in remote parts of Indonesia, Egypt, and Russia represent the fastest growing customer base for Opera Software ASA, a Norwegian maker of Internet browsers for mobile devices. Actually, persons who cannot afford computers live everywhere in every country, and many of these persons will soon be on the Internet on their cell phones. Cell phones are rapidly becoming used for data transfer, not just for phone calls. Companies such as Nokia, AT&T, Purple Labs SA of France, Japan's Access, Vodafone Group PLC, Siemens AG, Research in Motion, and Apple are spurring this transition by developing new and improved Web-capable mobile products every day.[6]

Advertising Media

Recent research by Forrester Research reveals that people ages 18 to 27 spend more time weekly on the Internet than watching television, listening to the radio, or watching DVDs or VHS tapes. Table 8-2 reveals why companies are rapidly coming to the realization that social networking sites and video sites are better means of reaching their customers than spending so many marketing dollars on traditional yellow pages or television, magazine, radio, or newspaper ads. Note the time that people spend on the Internet. And it is not just the time. Television viewers are passive viewers of ads, whereas Internet users take an active role in choosing what to look at—so customers on the Internet are tougher for marketers to reach.[7]

New companies such as Autonet Mobile based in San Francisco are selling new technology equipment for cars so the front passenger may conduct an iChat video conference while persons in the back each have a laptop and watch a YouTube video or download music or wirelessly transfer pictures from a digital camera. Everyone in the vehicle can be online except, of course, the driver. This technology is now available for installation in nearly all cars and is accelerating the movement from hard media to Web-based media. With this technology also, when the vehicle drives into a new location, you may instantly download information on shows, museums, hotels, and other attractions around you.

Growth of Internet advertising is expected to decline from a 16 percent increase in 2008 to a 5 percent increase in 2009. With this slowdown, companies are changing the restrictions they previously imposed on the categories and formats of advertising. For example, marketers are more and more allowed to create bigger, more intrusive ads that take up more space on the Web page. And Web sites are allowing lengthier ads to run before short video clips play. And blogs are creating more content that doubles also as an ad. Companies are also waiving minimum ad purchases. Companies are redesigning their Web sites to be much more interactive and are building new sponsorship programs and

TABLE 8-2 **Average Amount of Time That 18- to 27-Year-Olds Spend Weekly on Various Media (in hours)**

Media	Hours
On the Internet	High-13.0
Watching television	
On their cell phone	
Listening to the Radio	Medium-7.0
Watching DVDs or VHSs	
Playing video games	
Reading magazines	Low-1.0

Source: Based on Ellen Byron, "A New Odd Couple: Google, P&G Swap Workers to Spur Innovation," *Wall Street Journal* (November 19, 2008): A1.

other enticements on their sites. Editorial content and advertising content are increasingly being mixed on blogs.

In 2009–2011, consumers will act rationally. JC Penney CEO Mike Ullman says, "Consumers now shop for what they 'need' and less for what they 'want.' And they don't need much." Essentials, such as food, health-care products, and beauty aids are selling, but even in those industries, consumers are shifting to less costly brands and stores. There is a need for marketers to convince consumers that their brand will make life easier or better. Consumers now often wait until prices are slashed 75 percent or more to buy. Consumers today are very cautious about how they spend their money. Gone are the days when retailers could convince consumers to buy something they do not need.

JC Penney is among many firms that today have revamped their marketing to be more digital related. Penney's is segmenting its e-mail databases according to customers' shopping behaviors and then sending out relevant messages. Penney's corporate director of brand communications recently said, "Tailoring the e-mail insures that our customers are receiving timely, relevant information."

Expectations for total U.S. advertising spending in 2009 may decline anywhere from 6.2 percent to 3 percent to about $160 billion as the fallout from global financial crises continues to cut into ad spending.[8] Global ad spending is expected to decline about 0.5 percent. One bright spot, however, is online advertising expenditures that are expected to increase 5 percent in 2009 following a 16 percent increase in 2008. Companies are shifting ad dollars from newspaper, magazine, and radio to online media.

Purpose-Based Marketing

The global marketing chief at Procter & Gamble, Jim Stengel, recently started his own LLC business to try to persuade companies that the best way to sell in a weak economy is to "show customers how they can improve their lives" with your product or service. Stengel calls this "*purpose-based marketing*," and hundreds of firms have now adopted this approach successfully. He says there is need in an ad to build trust and an emotional connection to the customer in order to differentiate your product or service.[9]

In a weak economy when consumers are more interested in buying cheaper brands, Stengel acknowledges that ads must promote price, but he says ads must also show the intrinsic value of the product or service to be cost effective. Stengel contends that ads should do both: promote low price and build emotional equity through "purpose-based appeal."

The Coca-Cola Company is leading the way to another new kind of selling in a weak economy. CEO Muhtar Kent at Coke says marketing today must "employ optimism." That is why Coca-Cola launched a new global ad campaign in 2009 appealing to consumers' longing for comfort and optimism. The new campaign features the new slogan "Open Happiness," which replaced Coke's prior popular slogan of three years, "The Coke Side of Life." The Coke CEO says marketers must use feel-good messages to counter the fallout from the economic crisis. Firms must today project to customers that their products or services offer a beacon of comfort and optimism. Coke's cola volume declined 4.0 percent in the United States in 2008. Coke Classic's U.S. volume fell about 16 percent from 1998 through 2007 as customers switched to bottled water, enhanced teas, and other alternative drinks.[10]

Market Segmentation

Two variables are of central importance to strategy implementation: *market segmentation* and *product positioning*. Market segmentation and product positioning rank as marketing's most important contributions to strategic management.

Market segmentation is widely used in implementing strategies, especially for small and specialized firms. Market segmentation can be defined as the subdividing of a market into distinct subsets of customers according to needs and buying habits.

TABLE 8-3 The Marketing Mix Component Variables

Product	Place	Promotion	Price
Quality	Distribution channels	Advertising	Level
Features and options	Distribution coverage	Personal selling	Discounts and allowances
Style	Outlet location	Sales promotion	Payment terms
Brand name	Sales territories	Publicity	
Packaging	Inventory levels and locations		
Product line	Transportation carriers		
Warranty			
Service level			
Other services			

Source: From E. Jerome McCarthy, *Basic Marketing: A Managerial Approach,* 9th ed. (Homewood, IL: Richard D. Irwin, Inc., 1987): 37–44. Used with permission.

Market segmentation is an important variable in strategy implementation for at least three major reasons. First, strategies such as market development, product development, market penetration, and diversification require increased sales through new markets and products. To implement these strategies successfully, new or improved market-segmentation approaches are required. Second, market segmentation allows a firm to operate with limited resources because mass production, mass distribution, and mass advertising are not required. Market segmentation enables a small firm to compete successfully with a large firm by maximizing per-unit profits and per-segment sales. Finally, market segmentation decisions directly affect *marketing mix variables*: product, place, promotion, and price, as indicated in Table 8-3. For example, SnackWells, a pioneer in reduced-fat snacks, has shifted its advertising emphasis from low-fat to great taste as part of its new market-segmentation strategy.

Perhaps the most dramatic new market-segmentation strategy is the targeting of regional tastes. Firms from McDonald's to General Motors are increasingly modifying their products to meet different regional preferences within the United States. Campbell's has a spicier version of its nacho cheese soup for the Southwest, and Burger King offers breakfast burritos in New Mexico but not in South Carolina. Geographic and demographic bases for segmenting markets are the most commonly employed, as illustrated in Table 8-4.

Evaluating potential market segments requires strategists to determine the characteristics and needs of consumers, to analyze consumer similarities and differences, and to develop consumer group profiles. Segmenting consumer markets is generally much simpler and easier than segmenting industrial markets, because industrial products, such as electronic circuits and forklifts, have multiple applications and appeal to diverse customer groups.

Segmentation is a key to matching supply and demand, which is one of the thorniest problems in customer service. Segmentation often reveals that large, random fluctuations in demand actually consist of several small, predictable, and manageable patterns. Matching supply and demand allows factories to produce desirable levels without extra shifts, overtime, and subcontracting. Matching supply and demand also minimizes the number and severity of stock-outs. The demand for hotel rooms, for example, can be dependent on foreign tourists, businesspersons, and vacationers. Focusing separately on these three market segments, however, can allow hotel firms to more effectively predict overall supply and demand.

Banks now are segmenting markets to increase effectiveness. "You're dead in the water if you aren't segmenting the market," says Anne Moore, president of a bank consulting firm in Atlanta. The Internet makes market segmentation easier today because consumers naturally form "communities" on the Web.

TABLE 8-4 Alternative Bases for Market Segmentation

Variable	Typical Breakdowns
	Geographic
Region	Pacific, Mountain, West North Central, West South Central, East North Central, East South Central, South Atlantic, Middle Atlantic, New England
County Size	A, B, C, D
City Size	Under 5,000; 5,000–20,000; 20,001–50,000; 50,001–100,000; 100,001–250,000; 250,001–500,000; 500,001–1,000,000; 1,000,001–4,000,000; 4,000,001 or over
Density	Urban, suburban, rural
Climate	Northern, southern
	Demographic
Age	Under 6, 6–11, 12–19, 20–34, 35–49, 50–64, 65+
Gender	Male, female
Family Size	1–2, 3–4, 5+
Family Life Cycle	Young, single; young, married, no children; young, married, youngest child under 6; young, married, youngest child 6 or over; older, married, with children; older, married, no children under 18; older, single; other
Income	Under $10,000; $10,001–$15,000; $15,001–$20,000; $20,001–$30,000; $30,001–$50,000; $50,001–$70,000; $70,001–$100,000; over $100,000
Occupation	Professional and technical; managers, officials, and proprietors; clerical and sales; craftspeople; foremen; operatives; farmers; retirees; students; housewives; unemployed
Education	Grade school or less; some high school; high school graduate; some college; college graduate
Religion	Catholic, Protestant, Jewish, Islamic, other
Race	White, Asian, Hispanic, African American
Nationality	American, British, French, German, Scandinavian, Italian, Latin American, Middle Eastern, Japanese
	Psychographic
Social Class	Lower lowers, upper lowers, lower middles, upper middles, lower uppers, upper uppers
Personality	Compulsive, gregarious, authoritarian, ambitious
	Behavioral
Use Occasion	Regular occasion, special occasion
Benefits Sought	Quality, service, economy
User Status	Nonuser, ex-user, potential user, first-time user, regular user
Usage Rate	Light user, medium user, heavy user
Loyalty Status	None, medium, strong, absolute
Readiness Stage	Unaware, aware, informed, interested, desirous, intending to buy
Attitude Toward Product	Enthusiastic, positive, indifferent, negative, hostile

Source: Adapted from Philip Kotler, *Marketing Management: Analysis, Planning and Control,* © 1984: 256. Adapted by permission of Prentice-Hall, Inc., Upper Saddle River, New Jersey.

Does the Internet Make Market Segmentation Easier?

Yes. The segments of people whom marketers want to reach online are much more precisely defined than the segments of people reached through traditional forms of media, such as television, radio, and magazines. For example, Quepasa.com is widely visited by Hispanics. Marketers aiming to reach college students, who are notoriously difficult to reach via traditional media, focus on sites such as collegeclub.com and studentadvantage.com. The gay and lesbian population, which is estimated to comprise about 5 percent of the U.S. population, has always been difficult to reach via traditional media but now can be focused on at sites such as gay.com. Marketers can reach persons interested in specific topics, such as travel or fishing, by placing banners on related Web sites.

People all over the world are congregating into virtual communities on the Web by becoming members/customers/visitors of Web sites that focus on an endless range of topics. People in essence segment themselves by nature of the Web sites that comprise their "favorite places," and many of these Web sites sell information regarding their "visitors." Businesses and groups of individuals all over the world pool their purchasing power in Web sites to get volume discounts.

Product Positioning

After markets have been segmented so that the firm can target particular customer groups, the next step is to find out what customers want and expect. This takes analysis and research. A severe mistake is to assume the firm knows what customers want and expect. Countless research studies reveal large differences between how customers define service and rank the importance of different service activities and how producers view services. Many firms have become successful by filling the gap between what customers and producers see as good service. What the customer believes is good service is paramount, not what the producer believes service should be.

Identifying target customers to focus marketing efforts on sets the stage for deciding how to meet the needs and wants of particular consumer groups. Product positioning is widely used for this purpose. Positioning entails developing schematic representations that reflect how your products or services compare to competitors' on dimensions most important to success in the industry. The following steps are required in product positioning:

1. Select key criteria that effectively differentiate products or services in the industry.
2. Diagram a two-dimensional product-positioning map with specified criteria on each axis.
3. Plot major competitors' products or services in the resultant four-quadrant matrix.
4. Identify areas in the positioning map where the company's products or services could be most competitive in the given target market. Look for vacant areas (niches).
5. Develop a marketing plan to position the company's products or services appropriately.

Because just two criteria can be examined on a single product-positioning map, multiple maps are often developed to assess various approaches to strategy implementation. *Multidimensional scaling* could be used to examine three or more criteria simultaneously, but this technique requires computer assistance and is beyond the scope of this text. Some examples of product-positioning maps are illustrated in Figure 8-2.

Some rules for using product positioning as a strategy-implementation tool are the following:

1. Look for the hole or *vacant niche*. The best strategic opportunity might be an unserved segment.
2. Don't serve two segments with the same strategy. Usually, a strategy successful with one segment cannot be directly transferred to another segment.
3. Don't position yourself in the middle of the map. The middle usually means a strategy that is not clearly perceived to have any distinguishing characteristics. This rule can vary with the number of competitors. For example, when there are only two competitors, as in U.S. presidential elections, the middle becomes the preferred strategic position.[11]

An effective product-positioning strategy meets two criteria: (1) it uniquely distinguishes a company from the competition, and (2) it leads customers to expect slightly less service than a company can deliver. Firms should not create expectations that exceed the service the firm can or will deliver. Network Equipment Technology is an example of a company that keeps customer expectations slightly below perceived performance. This is a constant challenge for marketers. Firms need to inform customers about what to expect and then exceed the promise. Underpromise and then overdeliver is the key!

FIGURE 8-2

Examples of Product-Positioning Maps

A. A PRODUCT-POSITIONING MAP
   FOR BANKS

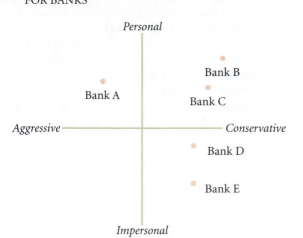

B. A PRODUCT-POSITIONING MAP
   FOR PERSONAL COMPUTERS

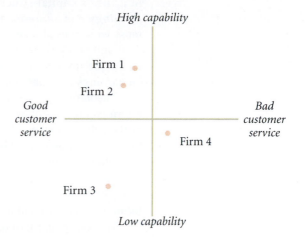

C. A PRODUCT-POSITIONING MAP FOR
   MENSWEAR RETAIL STORES

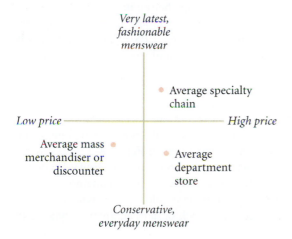

D. A PRODUCT-POSITIONING MAP
   FOR THE RENTAL CAR MARKET

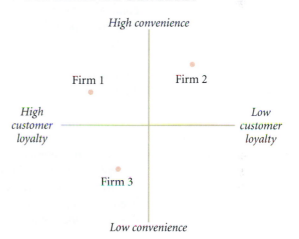

Finance/Accounting Issues

In this section, we examine several finance/accounting concepts considered to be central to strategy implementation: acquiring needed capital, developing projected financial statements, preparing financial budgets, and evaluating the worth of a business. Some examples of decisions that may require finance/accounting policies are these:

1. To raise capital with short-term debt, long-term debt, preferred stock, or common stock
2. To lease or buy fixed assets
3. To determine an appropriate dividend payout ratio
4. To use LIFO (Last-in, First-out), FIFO (First-in, First-out), or a market-value accounting approach
5. To extend the time of accounts receivable
6. To establish a certain percentage discount on accounts within a specified period of time
7. To determine the amount of cash that should be kept on hand

Acquiring Capital to Implement Strategies

Successful strategy implementation often requires additional capital. Besides net profit from operations and the sale of assets, two basic sources of capital for an organization are debt and equity. Determining an appropriate mix of debt and equity in a firm's capital structure can be vital to successful strategy implementation. An *Earnings Per Share/Earnings Before Interest and Taxes (EPS/EBIT) analysis* is the most widely used technique for determining whether debt, stock, or a combination of debt and stock is the best alternative for raising capital to implement strategies. This technique involves an examination of the impact that debt versus stock financing has on earnings per share under various assumptions as to EBIT.

Theoretically, an enterprise should have enough debt in its capital structure to boost its return on investment by applying debt to products and projects earning more than the cost of the debt. In low earning periods, too much debt in the capital structure of an organization can endanger stockholders' returns and jeopardize company survival. Fixed debt obligations generally must be met, regardless of circumstances. This does not mean that stock issuances are always better than debt for raising capital. Some special concerns with stock issuances are dilution of ownership, effect on stock price, and the need to share future earnings with all new shareholders.

Without going into detail on other institutional and legal issues related to the debt versus stock decision, EPS/EBIT may be best explained by working through an example. Let's say the Brown Company needs to raise $1 million to finance implementation of a market-development strategy. The company's common stock currently sells for $50 per share, and 100,000 shares are outstanding. The prime interest rate is 10 percent, and the company's tax rate is 50 percent. The company's earnings before interest and taxes next year are expected to be $2 million if a recession occurs, $4 million if the economy stays as is, and $8 million if the economy significantly improves. EPS/EBIT analysis can be used to determine if all stock, all debt, or some combination of stock and debt is the best capital financing alternative. The EPS/EBIT analysis for this example is provided in Table 8-5.

As indicated by the EPS values of 9.5, 19.50, and 39.50 in Table 8-5, debt is the best financing alternative for the Brown Company if a recession, boom, or normal year is expected. An EPS/EBIT chart can be constructed to determine the break-even point, where one financing alternative becomes more attractive than another. Figure 8-3 indicates that issuing common stock is the least attractive financing alternative for the Brown Company.

EPS/EBIT analysis is a valuable tool for making the capital financing decisions needed to implement strategies, but several considerations should be made whenever using this technique. First, profit levels may be higher for stock or debt alternatives when EPS

TABLE 8-5   EPS/EBIT Analysis for the Brown Company (in millions)

	Common Stock Financing			Debt Financing			Combination Financing		
	Recession	Normal	Boom	Recession	Normal	Boom	Recession	Normal	Boom
EBIT	$2.0	$ 4.0	$ 8.0	$2.0	$ 4.0	$ 8.0	$2.0	$ 4.0	$ 8.0
Interest[a]	0	0	0	.10	.10	.10	.05	.05	.05
EBT	2.0	4.0	8.0	1.9	3.9	7.9	1.95	3.95	7.95
Taxes	1.0	2.0	4.0	.95	1.95	3.95	.975	1.975	3.975
EAT	1.0	2.0	4.0	.95	1.95	3.95	.975	1.975	3.975
#Shares[b]	.12	.12	.12	.10	.10	.10	.11	.11	.11
EPS[c]	8.33	16.66	33.33	9.5	19.50	39.50	8.86	17.95	36.14

[a]The annual interest charge on $1 million at 10% is $100,000 and on $0.5 million is $50,000. **This row is in $, not %.**

[b]To raise all of the needed $1 million with stock, 20,000 new shares must be issued, raising the total to 120,000 shares outstanding. To raise one-half of the needed $1 million with stock, 10,000 new shares must be issued, raising the total to 110,000 shares outstanding.

[c]EPS = Earnings After Taxes (EAT) divided by shares (number of shares outstanding).

FIGURE 8-3

An EPS/EBIT Chart for the Brown Company

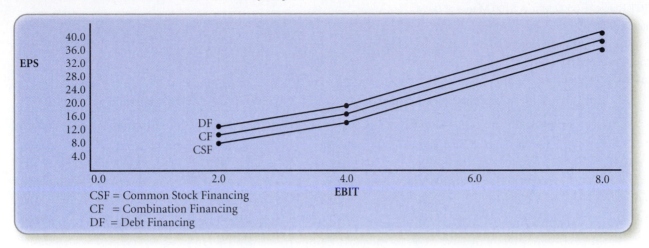

CSF = Common Stock Financing
CF = Combination Financing
DF = Debt Financing

levels are lower. For example, looking only at the earnings after taxes (EAT) values in Table 8-5, you can see that the common stock option is the best alternative, regardless of economic conditions. If the Brown Company's mission includes strict profit maximization, as opposed to the maximization of stockholders' wealth or some other criterion, then stock rather than debt is the best choice of financing.

Another consideration when using EPS/EBIT analysis is flexibility. As an organization's capital structure changes, so does its flexibility for considering future capital needs. Using all debt or all stock to raise capital in the present may impose fixed obligations, restrictive covenants, or other constraints that could severely reduce a firm's ability to raise additional capital in the future. Control is also a concern. When additional stock is issued to finance strategy implementation, ownership and control of the enterprise are diluted. This can be a serious concern in today's business environment of hostile takeovers, mergers, and acquisitions.

Dilution of ownership can be an overriding concern in closely held corporations in which stock issuances affect the decision-making power of majority stockholders. For example, the Smucker family owns 30 percent of the stock in Smucker's, a well-known jam and jelly company. When Smucker's acquired Dickson Family, Inc., the company used mostly debt rather than stock in order not to dilute the family ownership.

When using EPS/EBIT analysis, timing in relation to movements of stock prices, interest rates, and bond prices becomes important. In times of depressed stock prices, debt may prove to be the most suitable alternative from both a cost and a demand standpoint. However, when cost of capital (interest rates) is high, stock issuances become more attractive.

Tables 8-6 and 8-7 provide EPS/EBIT analyses for two companies—Gateway and Boeing. Notice in those analyses that the combination stock/debt options vary from 30/70 to 70/30. Any number of combinations could be explored. However, sometimes in preparing the EPS/EBIT graphs, the lines will intersect, thus revealing break-even points at which one financing alternative becomes more or less attractive than another. The slope of these lines will be determined by a combination of factors including stock price, interest rate, number of shares, and amount of capital needed. Also, it should be noted here that the best financing alternatives are indicated by the highest EPS values. In Tables 8-6 and 8-7, note that the tax rates for the companies vary considerably and should be computed from the respective income statements by dividing taxes paid by income before taxes.

In Table 8-6, the higher EPS values indicate that Gateway should use stock to raise capital in recession or normal economic conditions but should use debt financing under boom conditions. Stock is the best alternative for Gateway under all three conditions if

TABLE 8-6   EPS/EBIT Analysis for Gateway (M = In Millions)

Amount Needed: $1,000 M

EBIT Range: − $500 M to + $100 M to + $500 M

Interest Rate: 5%

Tax Rate: 0% (because the firm has been incurring a loss annually)

Stock Price: $6.00

# of Shares Outstanding: 371 M

	Common Stock Financing			Debt Financing		
	Recession	Normal	Boom	Recession	Normal	Boom
EBIT	(500.00)	100.00	500.00	(500.00)	100.00	500.00
Interest	0.00	0.00	0.00	50.00	50.00	50.00
EBT	(500.00)	100.00	500.00	(550.00)	50.00	450.00
Taxes	0.00	0.00	0.00	0.00	0.00	0.00
EAT	(500.00)	100.00	500.00	(550.00)	50.00	450.00
#Shares	537.67	537.67	537.67	371.00	371.00	371.00
EPS	**(0.93)**	**0.19**	**0.93**	**(1.48)**	**0.13**	**1.21**

	70 Percent Stock—30 Percent Debt			70 Percent Debt—30 Percent Stock		
	Recession	Normal	Boom	Recession	Normal	Boom
EBIT	(500.00)	100.00	500.00	(500.00)	100.00	500.00
Interest	15.00	15.00	15.00	35.00	35.00	35.00
EBT	(515.00)	85.00	485.00	(535.00)	65.00	465.00
Taxes	0.00	0.00	0.00	0.00	0.00	0.00
EAT	(515.00)	85.00	485.00	(535.00)	65.00	465.00
#Shares	487.67	487.67	487.67	421.00	421.00	421.00
EPS	**(1.06)**	**0.17**	**0.99**	**(1.27)**	**0.15**	**1.10**

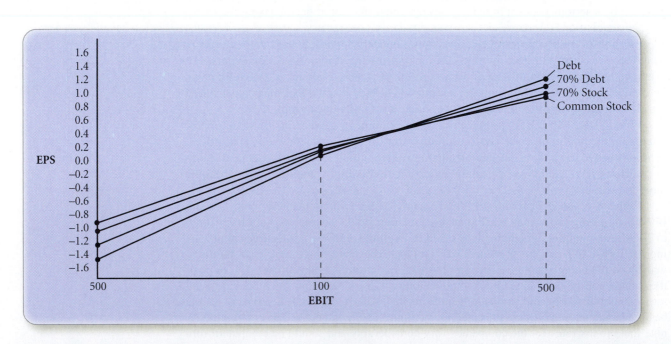

Conclusion: Gateway should use common stock to raise capital in recession or normal economic conditions but should use debt financing under boom conditions. Note that stock is the best alternative under all three conditions according to EAT (profit maximization), but EPS (maximize shareholders' wealth) is the better ratio to make this decision.

TABLE 8-7   EPS/EBIT Analysis for Boeing (M = In Millions)

Amount Needed: $10,000 M

Interest Rate: 5%

Tax Rate: 7%

Stock Price: $53.00

# of Shares Outstanding: 826 M

	Common Stock Financing			Debt Financing		
	Recession	*Normal*	*Boom*	*Recession*	*Normal*	*Boom*
EBIT	1,000.00	2,500.00	5,000.00	1,000.00	2,500.00	5,000.00
Interest	0.00	0.00	0.00	500.00	500.00	500.00
EBT	1,000.00	2,500.00	5,000.00	500.00	2,000.00	4,500.00
Taxes	70.00	175.00	350.00	35.00	140.00	315.00
EAT	930.00	2,325.00	4,650.00	465.00	1,860.00	4,185.00
# Shares	1,014.68	1,014.68	1,014.68	826.00	826.00	826.00
EPS	**0.92**	**2.29**	**4.58**	**0.56**	**2.25**	**5.07**

	70% Stock—30% Debt			70% Debt—30% Stock		
	Recession	*Normal*	*Boom*	*Recession*	*Normal*	*Boom*
EBIT	1,000.00	2,500.00	5,000.00	1,000.00	2,500.00	5,000.00
Interest	150.00	150.00	150.00	350.00	350.00	350.00
EBT	850.00	2,350.00	4,850.00	650.00	2,150.00	4,650.00
Taxes	59.50	164.50	339.50	45.50	150.50	325.50
EAT	790.50	2,185.50	4,510.50	604.50	1,999.50	4,324.50
# Shares	958.08	958.08	958.08	882.60	882.60	882.60
EPS	**0.83**	**2.28**	**4.71**	**0.68**	**2.27**	**4.90**

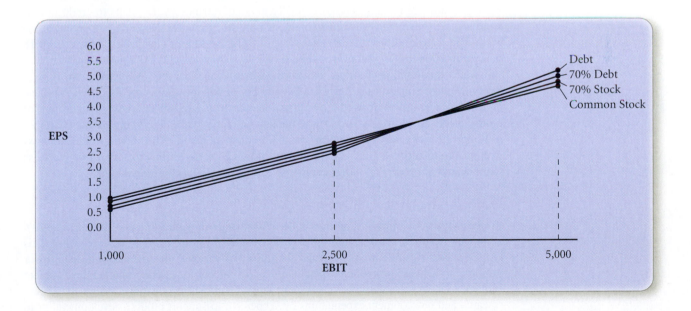

Conclusion: Boeing should use common stock to raise capital in recession (see 0.92) or normal (see 2.29) economic conditions but should use debt financing under boom conditions (see 5.07). Note that a dividends row is absent from this analysis. The more shares outstanding, the more dividends to be paid (if the firm pays dividends), which would lower the common stock EPS values.

EAT (profit maximization) were the decision criteria, but EPS (maximize shareholders' wealth) is the better ratio to make this decision. Firms can do many things in the short run to maximize profits, so investors and creditors consider maximizing shareholders' wealth to be the better criteria for making financing decisions.

In Table 8-7, note that Boeing should use stock to raise capital in recession (see 0.92) or normal (see 2.29) economic conditions but should use debt financing under boom conditions (see 5.07). Let's calculate here the number of shares figure of 1014.68 given under Boeing's stock alternative. Divide $10,000 M funds needed by the stock price of $53 = 188.68 M new shares to be issued + the 826 M shares outstanding already = 1014.68 M shares under the stock scenario. Along the final row, EPS is the number of shares outstanding divided by EAT in all columns.

Note in Table 8-6 and Table 8-7 that a dividends row is absent from both the Gateway and Boeing analyses. The more shares outstanding, the more dividends to be paid (if the firm indeed pays dividends). Paying dividends lowers EAT, which lowers the stock EPS values whenever this aspect is included. To consider dividends in an EPS/EBIT analysis, simply insert another row for "Dividends" right below the "EAT" row and then insert an "Earnings After Taxes and Dividends" row. Considering dividends would make the analysis more robust.

Note in both the Gateway and Boeing graphs, there is a break-even point between the normal and boom range of EBIT where the debt option overtakes the 70% Debt/30% Stock option as the best financing alternative. A break-even point is where two lines cross each other. A break-even point is the EBIT level where various financing alternative represented by lines crossing are equally attractive in terms of EPS. Both the Gateway and Boeing graphs indicate that EPS values are highest for the 100 percent debt option at high EBIT levels. The two graphs also reveal that the EPS values for 100 percent debt increase faster than the other financing options as EBIT levels increase beyond the break-even point. At low levels of EBIT however, both the Gateway and Boeing graphs indicate that 100 percent stock is the best financing alternative because the EPS values are highest.

New Source of Funding

Credit unions were not involved in the subprime-loan market, so many of them are flush with cash and are making loans, especially to small businesses. Deposits to credit unions were also up when many investors abandoned the stock market. Roughly 27 percent of the 8,147 U.S. credit unions offer business loans.[12] The amount of businesses loans was up 18 percent in 2008 to $33 billion, and the average loan size was $215,000.

Many credit unions want to give more business loans, but the 1998 federal law (Credit Union Membership Access Act) caps the amount of business loans credit unions can have at 12.25 percent of their assets. Credit unions are trying to get this law changed, but of course banks are lobbying hard to have the law remain in place. Credit unions are chartered as nonprofit cooperative institutions owned by their members. Thus credit unions are tax-exempt organizations. Bankers argue that allowing credit unions to give more business loans would give them an unfair competitive advantage over traditional banks.

Projected Financial Statements

Projected financial statement analysis is a central strategy-implementation technique because it allows an organization to examine the expected results of various actions and approaches. This type of analysis can be used to forecast the impact of various implementation decisions (for example, to increase promotion expenditures by 50 percent to support a market-development strategy, to increase salaries by 25 percent to support a market-penetration strategy, to increase research and development expenditures by 70 percent to support product development, or to sell $1 million of common stock to raise capital for diversification). Nearly all financial institutions require at least three years of projected financial statements whenever a business seeks capital. A projected income statement and balance sheet allow an organization to compute projected financial ratios under various strategy-implementation scenarios. When compared to prior years and to industry averages, financial ratios provide valuable insights into the feasibility of various strategy-implementation approaches.

Primarily as a result of the Enron collapse and accounting scandal and the ensuing Sarbanes-Oxley Act, companies today are being much more diligent in preparing projected financial statements to "reasonably rather than too optimistically" project future expenses and earnings. There is much more care not to mislead shareholders and other constituencies.[13]

A 2011 projected income statement and a balance sheet for the Litten Company are provided in Table 8-8. The projected statements for Litten are based on five assumptions: (1) The company needs to raise $45 million to finance expansion into foreign markets; (2) $30 million of this total will be raised through increased debt and $15 million through common stock; (3) sales are expected to increase 50 percent; (4) three new facilities, costing a total of $30 million, will be constructed in foreign markets; and (5) land for the new facilities is already owned by the company. Note in Table 8-8 that Litten's

TABLE 8-8 **A Projected Income Statement and Balance Sheet for the Litten Company (in millions)**

	Prior Year 2010	Projected Year 2011	Remarks
PROJECTED INCOME STATEMENT			
Sales	$100	$150.00	50% increase
Cost of Goods Sold	70	105.00	70% of sales
Gross Margin	30	45.00	
Selling Expense	10	15.00	10% of sales
Administrative Expense	5	7.50	5% of sales
Earnings Before Interest and Taxes	15	22.50	
Interest	3	3.00	
Earnings Before Taxes	12	19.50	
Taxes	6	9.75	50% rate
Net Income	**6**	**9.75**	
Dividends	2	5.00	
Retained Earnings	4	4.75	
PROJECTED BALANCE SHEET			
Assets			
Cash	5	7.75	Plug figure
Accounts Receivable	2	4.00	100% increase
Inventory	20	45.00	
Total Current Assets	27	56.75	
Land	15	15.00	
Plant and Equipment	50	80.00	Add three new plants at $10 million each
Less Depreciation	10	20.00	
Net Plant and Equipment	40	60.00	
Total Fixed Assets	55	75.00	
Total Assets	**82**	**131.75**	
Liabilities			
Accounts Payable	10	10.00	
Notes Payable	10	10.00	
Total Current Liabilities	20	20.00	
Long-term Debt	40	70.00	Borrowed $30 million
Additional Paid-in-Capital	20	35.00	Issued 100,000 shares at $150 each
Retained Earnings	2	6.75	$2 + $4.75
Total Liabilities and Net Worth	**82**	**131.75**	

strategies and their implementation are expected to result in a sales increase from $100 million to $150 million and in a net increase in income from $6 million to $9.75 million in the forecasted year.

There are six steps in performing projected financial analysis:

1. Prepare the projected income statement before the balance sheet. Start by forecasting sales as accurately as possible. Be careful not to blindly push historical percentages into the future with regard to revenue (sales) increases. Be mindful of what the firm did to achieve those past sales increases, which may not be appropriate for the future unless the firm takes similar or analogous actions (such as opening a similar number of stores, for example). If dealing with a manufacturing firm, also be mindful that if the firm is operating at 100 percent capacity running three eight-hour shifts per day, then probably new manufacturing facilities (land, plant, and equipment) will be needed to increase sales further.

2. Use the percentage-of-sales method to project cost of goods sold (CGS) and the expense items in the income statement. For example, if CGS is 70 percent of sales in the prior year (as it is in Table 8-8), then use that same percentage to calculate CGS in the future year—unless there is a reason to use a different percentage. Items such as interest, dividends, and taxes must be treated independently and cannot be forecasted using the percentage-of-sales method.

3. Calculate the projected net income.

4. Subtract from the net income any dividends to be paid for that year. This remaining net income is retained earnings (RE). Bring this retained earnings amount for that year (NI − DIV = RE) over to the balance sheet by adding it to the prior year's RE shown on the balance sheet. In other words, every year a firm adds its RE for that particular year (from the income statement) to its historical RE total on the balance sheet. Therefore, the RE amount on the balance sheet is a cumulative number rather than money available for strategy implementation! Note that RE is the first projected balance sheet item to be entered. Due to this accounting procedure in developing projected financial statements, the RE amount on the balance sheet is usually a large number. However, it also can be a low or even negative number if the firm has been incurring losses. The only way for RE to decrease from one year to the next on the balance sheet is (1) if the firm incurred an earnings loss that year or (2) the firm had positive net income for the year but paid out dividends more than the net income. Be mindful that RE is the key link between a projected income statement and balance sheet, so be careful to make this calculation correctly.

5. Project the balance sheet items, beginning with retained earnings and then forecasting stockholders' equity, long-term liabilities, current liabilities, total liabilities, total assets, fixed assets, and current assets (in that order). Use the cash account as the plug figure—that is, use the cash account to make the assets total the liabilities and net worth. Then make appropriate adjustments. For example, if the cash needed to balance the statements is too small (or too large), make appropriate changes to borrow more (or less) money than planned.

6. List comments (remarks) on the projected statements. Any time a significant change is made in an item from a prior year to the projected year, an explanation (remark) should be provided. Remarks are essential because otherwise pro formas are meaningless.

Projected Financial Statement Analysis for Mattel, Inc.

Because so many strategic management students have limited experience developing projected financial statements, let's apply the steps outlined on the previous pages to Mattel, the huge toy company headquartered in El Segundo, California. Mattel designs, manufactures, and markets toy products from fashion dolls to children's books. The company Web site is www.mattel.com. Mattel's recent income statements and balance sheets are provided in Table 8-9 and Table 8-10 respectively.

TABLE 8-9 **Mattel's Actual Income Statements (in thousands)**

	2006	2005	2004
Total Revenue	$5,650,156	5,179,016	5,102,786
Cost of Revenue	3,038,363	2,806,148	2,692,061
Gross Profit	2,611,793	2,372,868	2,410,725
Operating Expenses			
Research Development	-	-	-
Selling General and Administrative	1,882,975	1,708,339	1,679,908
Non-Recurring	-	-	-
Others	-	-	-
Total Operating Expenses	-	-	-
Operating Income or Loss	728,818	664,529	730,817
Income from Continuing Operations			
Total Other Income/Expenses Net	34,791	64,010	43,201
Earnings Before Interest and Taxes	763,609	728,539	774,018
Interest Expense	79,853	76,490	77,764
Income Before Tax	683,756	652,049	696,254
Income Tax Expense	90,829	235,030	123,531
Minority Interest	-	-	-
Net Income from Continuing Ops	592,927	417,019	572,723
Non-Recurring Events			
Discontinued Operations	-	-	-
Extraordinary Items	-	-	-
Effect of Accounting Changes	-	-	-
Other Items	-	-	-
Net Income	592,927	417,019	572,723
Preferred Stock and Other Adjustments	-	-	-
Net Income Applicable to Common Shares	$592,927	$417,019	$572,723

In Tables 8-11 and 8-12, Mattel's projected income statements and balance sheets respectively for 2007, 2008, and 2009 are provided based on the firm pursuing the following strategies:

1. The company desires to build 20 Mattel stores annually at a cost of $1 million each.
2. The company plans to develop new toy products at an annual cost of $10 million.
3. The company plans to increase its advertising/promotion expenditures 30 percent over three years, at a cost of $30 million ($10 million per year).
4. The company plans to buy back $100 million of its own stock (called Treasury stock) annually for the next three years.
5. The company expects revenues to increase 10 percent annually with the above strategies. Mattel can handle this increase with existing production facilities.
6. Dividend payout will be increased from 57 percent of net income to 60 percent.
7. To finance the $380 million total cost for the above strategies, Mattel plans to use long-term debt for $150 million ($50 million per year for three years) and $230 million by issuing stock ($77 million per year for three years).

The Mattel projected financial statements were prepared using the six steps outlined on prior pages and the above seven strategy statements. Note the cash account is used as the plug figure, and it is too high, so Mattel could reduce this number and concurrently reduce a liability and/or equity account the same amount to keep the statement in balance. Rarely is the cash account perfect on the first pass through, so adjustments are needed and made. However, these adjustments are *not* made on the projected statements given in

TABLE 8-10   Mattel's Actual Balance Sheets (in thousands)

	2006	2005	2004
Assets			
Current Assets			
Cash and Cash Equivalents	$1,205,552	997,734	1,156,835
Short-Term Investments	-	-	-
Net Receivables	943,813	760,643	759,033
Inventory	383,149	376,897	418,633
Other Current Assets	317,624	277,226	302,649
Total Current Assets	2,850,138	2,412,500	2,637,150
Long-Term Investments	-	-	-
Property, Plant, and Equipment	536,749	547,104	586,526
Goodwill	845,324	718,069	735,680
Intangible Assets	70,593	20,422	22,926
Accumulated Amortization	-	-	-
Other Assets	149,912	178,304	201,836
Deferred Long-Term Asset Charges	503,168	495,914	572,374
Total Assets	$4,955,884	4,372,313	4,756,492
Liabilities			
Current Liabilities			
Accounts Payable	$1,518,234	1,245,191	1,303,822
Short/Current Long-Term Debt	64,286	217,994	423,349
Other Current Liabilities	-	-	-
Total Current Liabilities	1,582,520	1,463,185	1,727,171
Long-Term Debt	635,714	525,000	400,000
Other Liabilities	304,676	282,395	243,509
Deferred Long-Term Liability Charges	-	-	-
Minority Interest	-	-	-
Negative Goodwill	-	-	-
Total Liabilities	2,522,910	2,270,580	2,370,680
Stockholders' Equity			
Misc. Stocks, Options, Warrants	-	-	-
Redeemable Preferred Stock	-	-	-
Preferred Stock	-	-	-
Common Stock	441,369	441,369	441,369
Retained Earnings	1,652,140	1,314,068	1,093,288
Treasury Stock	(996,981)	(935,711)	(473,349)
Capital Surplus	1,613,307	1,589,281	1,594,332
Other Stockholders' Equity	(276,861)	(307,274)	(269,828)
Total Stockholders' Equity	2,432,974	2,101,733	2,385,812
Total Liabilities and SE	$4,955,884	4,372,313	4,756,492

Tables 8-11 and 8-12, so that the seven strategy statements above can be more readily seen on respective rows. Note the author's comments on Tables 8-11 and 8-12 that help explain changes in the numbers.

The U.S. Securities and Exchange Commission (SEC) conducts fraud investigations if projected numbers are misleading or if they omit information that's important to investors. Projected statements must conform with generally accepted accounting principles (GAAP) and must not be designed to hide poor expected results. The

TABLE 8-11   Mattel's Projected Income Statements (in thousands)

	2009	2008	2007	Author Comment
Total Revenue	$7,520,357	6,836,688	6,215,171	up 10% annually
Cost of Revenue	4,060,992	3,691,811	3,356,192	remains 54%
Gross Profit	3,459,365	3,144,877	2,858,979	subtraction
Operating Expenses				
Research Development	10,000	10,000	10,000	total $30M new
Selling General and Administrative	2,491,717	2,256,107	2,051,006	remains 33% + $10 M annually
Non-Recurring	-	-	-	
Others	-	-	-	
Total Operating Expenses	-	-	-	
Operating Income or Loss	957,648	878,770	797,973	subtraction
Income from Continuing Operations				
Total Other Income/Expenses Net	34,791	34,791	34,791	keep it the same
Earnings Before Interest and Taxes	992,439	913,561	832,764	addition
Interest Expense	97,823	91,423	85,442	up 7%; LTD up 7%
Income Before Tax	894,616	822,138	737,322	
Income Tax Expense	90,829	90,829	90,829	keep it the same
Minority Interest	-	-	-	
Net Income from Continuing Ops	803,787	731,309	646,493	subtraction
Discontinued Operations	-	-	-	
Extraordinary Items	-	-	-	
Effect of Accounting Changes	-	-	-	
Other Items	-	-	-	
Net Income	803,787	731,309	646,493	
Preferred Stock and Other Adjustments	-	-	-	
Net Income Applicable to Common Shares	$803,787	731,309	646,493	

Sarbanes-Oxley Act requires CEOs and CFOs of corporations to personally sign their firms' financial statements attesting to their accuracy. These executives could thus be held personally liable for misleading or inaccurate statements. The collapse of the Arthur Andersen accounting firm, along with its client Enron, fostered a "zero toler-ance" policy among auditors and shareholders with regard to a firm's financial state-ments. But plenty of firms still "inflate" their financial projections and call them "pro formas," so investors, shareholders, and other stakeholders must still be wary of differ-ent companies' financial projections.[14]

On financial statements, different companies use different terms for various items, such as *revenues* or *sales* used for the same item by different companies. For net income, many firms use the term *earnings*, and many others use the term *profits*.

Financial Budgets

A *financial budget* is a document that details how funds will be obtained and spent for a specified period of time. Annual budgets are most common, although the period of time for a budget can range from one day to more than 10 years. Fundamentally, financial budget-ing is a method for specifying what must be done to complete strategy implementation successfully. Financial budgeting should not be thought of as a tool for limiting expendi-tures but rather as a method for obtaining the most productive and profitable use of an organization's resources. Financial budgets can be viewed as the planned allocation of a firm's resources based on forecasts of the future.

There are almost as many different types of financial budgets as there are types of organizations. Some common types of budgets include cash budgets, operating budgets, sales budgets, profit budgets, factory budgets, capital budgets, expense budgets, divisional

TABLE 8-12 Mattel's Projected Balance Sheets (in thousands)

	2009	2008	2007	Author Comment
Assets				
Current Assets				
Cash and Cash Equivalents	$3,232,406	2,972,664	2,570,635	too high, could reduce this and pay off some LTD to keep balance
Short-Term Investments	-	-	-	
Net Receivables	943,813	760,643	759,033	
Inventory	509,969	463,609	421,463	up 10% annually
Other Current Assets	317,624	317,624	317,624	keep it the same
Total Current Assets				
Long-Term Investments	-	-	-	
Property, Plant, and Equipment	596,749	576,749	556,749	up $20M annually
Goodwill	845,324	845,324	845,324	keep it the same
Intangible Assets	70,593	70,593	70,593	keep it the same
Accumulated Amortization	-	-	-	
Other Assets	149,912	149,912	149,912	keep it the same
Deferred Long-Term Asset Charges	503,168	503,168	503,168	keep it the same
Total Assets	7,169,558	6,660,286	6,194,501	
Liabilities				
Current Liabilities				
Accounts Payable	1,518,234	1,518,234	1,518,234	keep it the same
Short/Current Long-Term Debt	64,286	64,286	64,286	keep it the same
Other Current Liabilities	-	-	-	
Total Current Liabilities	1,582,520	1,582,520	1,582,520	
Long-Term Debt	785,714	735,714	685,714	up $50M annually
Other Liabilities	304,676	304,676	304,676	keep it the same
Deferred Long-Term Liability Charges	-	-	-	
Minority Interest	-	-	-	
Negative Goodwill	-	-	-	
Total Liabilities	2,672,910	2,622,910	2,572,910	
Stockholders' Equity				
Misc. Stocks, Options, Warrants	-	-	-	
Redeemable Preferred Stock	-	-	-	
Preferred Stock	-	-	-	
Common Stock	441,369	441,369	441,369	keep it the same
Retained Earnings	2,961,092	2,478,820	2,040,035	60% of NI = div
Treasury Stock	(1,296,981)	(1,196,981)	(1,096,981)	up $100M annually
Capital Surplus	2,114,307	2,037,307	1,960,307	up $77M annually
Other Stockholders' Equity	(276,861)	(276,861)	(276,861)	keep it the same
Total Stockholders' Equity	4,496,648	4,037,376	3,621,591	addition
Total Liabilities and SE	$7,169,558	6,660,286	6,194,501	addition

budgets, variable budgets, flexible budgets, and fixed budgets. When an organization is experiencing financial difficulties, budgets are especially important in guiding strategy implementation.

Perhaps the most common type of financial budget is the *cash budget*. The Financial Accounting Standards Board (FASB) has mandated that every publicly held company in the United States must issue an annual cash-flow statement in addition to the usual financial reports. The statement includes all receipts and disbursements of cash in operations, investments, and financing. It supplements the Statement on Changes in Financial Position formerly included in the annual reports of all publicly held companies. A cash budget for the year 2011 for the Toddler Toy Company is provided in Table 8-13. Note that Toddler is not expecting to have surplus cash until November 2011.

Financial budgets have some limitations. First, budgetary programs can become so detailed that they are cumbersome and overly expensive. Overbudgeting or underbudgeting can cause problems. Second, financial budgets can become a substitute for objectives. A budget is a tool and not an end in itself. Third, budgets can hide inefficiencies if based solely on precedent rather than on periodic evaluation of circumstances and standards. Finally, budgets are sometimes used as instruments of tyranny that result in frustration, resentment, absenteeism, and high turnover. To minimize the effect of this last concern, managers should increase the participation of subordinates in preparing budgets.

Evaluating the Worth of a Business

Evaluating the worth of a business is central to strategy implementation because integrative, intensive, and diversification strategies are often implemented by acquiring other firms. Other strategies, such as retrenchment and divestiture, may result in the sale of a division of an organization or of the firm itself. Thousands of transactions occur each year in which businesses are bought or sold in the United States. In all these cases, it is necessary to establish the financial worth or cash value of a business to successfully implement strategies.

All the various methods for determining a business's worth can be grouped into three main approaches: what a firm owns, what a firm earns, or what a firm will bring in the market. But it is important to realize that valuation is not an exact science. The valuation of a firm's worth is based on financial facts, but common sense and intuitive judgment must enter into the process. It is difficult to assign a monetary value to some factors—such as a loyal customer base, a history of growth, legal suits pending,

TABLE 8-13 **Six-Month Cash Budget for the Toddler Toy Company in 2011**

Cash Budget (in thousands)	July	Aug.	Sept.	Oct.	Nov.	Dec.	Jan.
Receipts							
Collections	$12,000	$21,000	$31,000	$35,000	$22,000	$18,000	$11,000
Payments							
Purchases	14,000	21,000	28,000	14,000	14,000	7,000	
Wages and Salaries	1,500	2,000	2,500	1,500	1,500	1,000	
Rent	500	500	500	500	500	500	
Other Expenses	200	300	400	200	—	100	
Taxes	—	8,000	—	—	—	—	
Payment on Machine	—	—	10,000	—	—	—	
Total Payments	$16,200	$31,800	$41,400	$16,200	$16,000	$8,600	
Net Cash Gain (Loss) During Month	−4,200	−10,800	−10,400	18,800	6,000	9,400	
Cash at Start of Month if No Borrowing Is Done	6,000	1,800	−9,000	−19,400	−600	5,400	
Cumulative Cash (Cash at start plus gains or minus losses)	1,800	−9,000	−19,400	−600	5,400	14,800	
Less Desired Level of Cash	−5,000	−5,000	−5,000	−5,000	−5,000	−5,000	
Total Loans Outstanding to Maintain $5,000 Cash Balance	$3,200	$14,000	$24,400	$5,600	—	—	
Surplus Cash	—	—	—	—	400	9,800	

dedicated employees, a favorable lease, a bad credit rating, or good patents—that may not be reflected in a firm's financial statements. Also, different valuation methods will yield different totals for a firm's worth, and no prescribed approach is best for a certain situation. Evaluating the worth of a business truly requires both qualitative and quantitative skills.

The first approach in evaluating the worth of a business is determining its net worth or stockholders' equity. Net worth represents the sum of common stock, additional paid-in capital, and retained earnings. After calculating net worth, add or subtract an appropriate amount for goodwill, overvalued or undervalued assets, and intangibles. Whereas intangibles include copyrights, patents, and trademarks, goodwill arises only if a firm acquires another firm and pays more than the book value for that firm.

It should be noted that Financial Accounting Standards Board (FASB) Rule 142 requires companies to admit once a year if the premiums they paid for acquisitions, called goodwill, were a waste of money. Goodwill is not a good thing to have on a balance sheet. Note in Table 8-14 that Mattel's goodwill of $815 million as a percent of its total assets ($4,675 million) is 17.4 percent, which is extremely high compared to Nordstrom's goodwill of $53 million as a percentage of its total assets ($5,661 million), 0.94 percent. Pfizer's goodwill to total assets percentage also is high at 19.3 percent.

At year-end 2008, Mattel, Nordstrom, and Pfizer had $815 million, $53 million, and $21,464 billion in goodwill, respectively, on their balance sheets. Most creditors and investors feel that goodwill indeed should be added to the stockholders' equity in calculating worth of a business, but some feel it should be subtracted, and still others feel it should not be included at all. Perhaps whether you are buying or selling the business may determine whether you negotiate to add or subtract goodwill in the analysis. Goodwill is sometimes listed as intangibles on the balance sheet, but technically intangibles refers to patents, trademarks, and copyrights, rather than the value a firm paid over book value for an acquisition, which is goodwill. If a firm paid less than book value for an acquisition, that could be called negative goodwill—which is a line item on Mattel's balance sheets.

The second approach to measuring the value of a firm grows out of the belief that the worth of any business should be based largely on the future benefits its owners may derive through net profits. A conservative rule of thumb is to establish a business's worth as five times the firm's current annual profit. A five-year average profit level could also be used.

TABLE 8-14 Company Worth Analysis for Mattel, Nordstrom, and Pfizer (year-end 2008, in $millions, except stock price and EPS)

Input Data	Mattel	Nordstrom	Pfizer
Shareholders' Equity	$2,117	$1,210	$57,556
Net Income (NI)	379	401	8,104
Stock Price	15	10	15
EPS	1.03	1.83	1.19
# of Shares Outstanding	358	215	6,750
Goodwill + Intangibles	815	53	21,464
Total Assets	235	0	17,721
Company Worth Analyses			
1. Shareholders' Equity + Goodwill + Intangibles	$3,167	$1,263	$ 96,741
2. Net Income × 5	1,895	2,005	40,520
3. (Stock Price/EPS) × NI	5,519	2,191	102,151
4. # of Shares Out × Stock Price	5,340	2,150	101,250
5. Four Method Average	3,988	1,902	76,049
$Goodwill/$Total Assets	17.4%	0.94%	19.3%

When using the approach, remember that firms normally suppress earnings in their financial statements to minimize taxes.

The third approach is called the *price-earnings ratio method*. To use this method, divide the market price of the firm's common stock by the annual earnings per share and multiply this number by the firm's average net income for the past five years.

The fourth method can be called the *outstanding shares method*. To use this method, simply multiply the number of shares outstanding by the market price per share and add a premium. The premium is simply a per-share dollar amount that a person or firm is willing to pay to control (acquire) the other company. A pharmaceutical company based in Tokyo, Astellas Pharma Inc., recently launched an unsolicited takeover of biotechnology company CV Therapeutics Inc., based in Palo Alto, California. Astellas offered $16 a share, or nearly $1 billion, which represented a 41 percent premium over CV's closing stock price of $11.35 on the Nasdaq stock market. The CEO of Astellas said, "We are disappointed that CV's board of directors has rejected outright what we believe is a very compelling all-cash proposal that would deliver stockholders significant immediate value that we believe far exceeds what CV can achieve as a stand-alone company."

Business evaluations are becoming routine in many situations. Businesses have many strategy-implementation reasons for determining their worth in addition to preparing to be sold or to buy other companies. Employee plans, taxes, retirement packages, mergers, acquisitions, expansion plans, banking relationships, death of a principal, divorce, partnership agreements, and IRS audits are other reasons for a periodic valuation. It is just good business to have a reasonable understanding of what your firm is worth. This knowledge protects the interests of all parties involved

Table 8-14 provides the cash value analyses for three companies—Mattel, Nordstrom, and Pfizer—for year-end 2008. Notice that there is significant variation among the four methods used to determine cash value. For example, the worth of the toy company Mattel ranged from $1,895 billion to $5,519 billion. Obviously, if you were selling your company, you would seek the larger values, while if purchasing a company you would seek the lower values. In practice, substantial negotiation takes place in reaching a final compromise (or averaged) amount. Also recognize that if a firm's net income is negative, theoretically the approaches involving that figure would result in a negative number, implying that the firm would pay you to acquire them. Of course, you obtain all of the firm's debt and liabilities in an acquisition, so theoretically this would be possible.

Deciding Whether to Go Public

Going public means selling off a percentage of your company to others in order to raise capital; consequently, it dilutes the owners' control of the firm. Going public is not recommended for companies with less than $10 million in sales because the initial costs can be too high for the firm to generate sufficient cash flow to make going public worthwhile. One dollar in four is the average total cost paid to lawyers, accountants, and underwriters when an initial stock issuance is under $1 million; 1 dollar in 20 will go to cover these costs for issuances over $20 million.

In addition to initial costs involved with a stock offering, there are costs and obligations associated with reporting and management in a publicly held firm. For firms with more than $10 million in sales, going public can provide major advantages: It can allow the firm to raise capital to develop new products, build plants, expand, grow, and market products and services more effectively.

Research and Development (R&D) Issues

Research and development (R&D) personnel can play an integral part in strategy implementation. These individuals are generally charged with developing new products and improving old products in a way that will allow effective strategy implementation.

R&D employees and managers perform tasks that include transferring complex technology, adjusting processes to local raw materials, adapting processes to local markets, and altering products to particular tastes and specifications. Strategies such as product development, market penetration, and related diversification require that new products be successfully developed and that old products be significantly improved. But the level of management support for R&D is often constrained by resource availability.

Technological improvements that affect consumer and industrial products and services shorten product life cycles. Companies in virtually every industry are relying on the development of new products and services to fuel profitability and growth.[15] Surveys suggest that the most successful organizations use an R&D strategy that ties external opportunities to internal strengths and is linked with objectives. Well-formulated R&D policies match market opportunities with internal capabilities. R&D policies can enhance strategy implementation efforts to:

1. Emphasize product or process improvements.
2. Stress basic or applied research.
3. Be leaders or followers in R&D.
4. Develop robotics or manual-type processes.
5. Spend a high, average, or low amount of money on R&D.
6. Perform R&D within the firm or to contract R&D to outside firms.
7. Use university researchers or private-sector researchers.

Pfizer Inc. has only a few new drugs in its pipeline to show for its $7.5 billion R&D budget, so the firm is laying off 5,000 to 8,000 of its researchers and scientists in labs around the world. Cash-strapped consumers are filling fewer prescriptions and are turning more and more to generic drugs. Pfizer is bracing for the 2011 expiration of its patent on cholesterol fighter Lipitor, the world's top-selling drug that alone accounts for a quarter of Pfizer's roughly $48 billion in annual revenue. Pfizer's $7.5 billion R&D budget is the largest of any drug maker. The firm recently scrapped two drugs nearly ready to go to market—insulin spray Exubera and a Lipitor successor drug—after spending billions to develop them. Research areas that Pfizer is exiting include anemia, bone health, gastrointestinal disorders, obesity, liver disease, osteoarthritis, and peripheral artery disease.

There must be effective interactions between R&D departments and other functional departments in implementing different types of generic business strategies. Conflicts between marketing, finance/accounting, R&D, and information systems departments can be minimized with clear policies and objectives. Table 8-15 gives some examples of R&D activities that could be required for successful implementation of various strategies. Many U.S. utility, energy, and automotive companies are employing their research and development departments to determine how the firm can effectively reduce its gas emissions.

TABLE 8-15 Research and Development Involvement in Selected Strategy-Implementation Situations

Type of Organization	Strategy Being Implemented	R&D Activity
Pharmaceutical company	Product development	Test the effects of a new drug on different subgroups.
Boat manufacturer	Related diversification	Test the performance of various keel designs under various conditions.
Plastic container manufacturer	Market penetration	Develop a biodegradable container.
Electronics company	Market development	Develop a telecommunications system in a foreign country.

Many firms wrestle with the decision to acquire R&D expertise from external firms or to develop R&D expertise internally. The following guidelines can be used to help make this decision:

1. If the rate of technical progress is slow, the rate of market growth is moderate, and there are significant barriers to possible new entrants, then in-house R&D is the preferred solution. The reason is that R&D, if successful, will result in a temporary product or process monopoly that the company can exploit.

2. If technology is changing rapidly and the market is growing slowly, then a major effort in R&D may be very risky, because it may lead to the development of an ultimately obsolete technology or one for which there is no market.

3. If technology is changing slowly but the market is growing quickly, there generally is not enough time for in-house development. The prescribed approach is to obtain R&D expertise on an exclusive or nonexclusive basis from an outside firm.

4. If both technical progress and market growth are fast, R&D expertise should be obtained through acquisition of a well-established firm in the industry.[16]

There are at least three major R&D approaches for implementing strategies. The first strategy is to be the first firm to market new technological products. This is a glamorous and exciting strategy but also a dangerous one. Firms such as 3M and General Electric have been successful with this approach, but many other pioneering firms have fallen, with rival firms seizing the initiative.

A second R&D approach is to be an innovative imitator of successful products, thus minimizing the risks and costs of start-up. This approach entails allowing a pioneer firm to develop the first version of the new product and to demonstrate that a market exists. Then, laggard firms develop a similar product. This strategy requires excellent R&D personnel and an excellent marketing department.

A third R&D strategy is to be a low-cost producer by mass-producing products similar to but less expensive than products recently introduced. As a new product is accepted by customers, price becomes increasingly important in the buying decision. Also, mass marketing replaces personal selling as the dominant selling strategy. This R&D strategy requires substantial investment in plant and equipment but fewer expenditures in R&D than the two approaches described previously.

R&D activities among U.S. firms need to be more closely aligned to business objectives. There needs to be expanded communication between R&D managers and strategists. Corporations are experimenting with various methods to achieve this improved communication climate, including different roles and reporting arrangements for managers and new methods to reduce the time it takes research ideas to become reality.

Perhaps the most current trend in R&D management has been lifting the veil of secrecy whereby firms, even major competitors, are joining forces to develop new products. Collaboration is on the rise due to new competitive pressures, rising research costs, increasing regulatory issues, and accelerated product development schedules. Companies not only are working more closely with each other on R&D, but they are also turning to consortia at universities for their R&D needs. More than 600 research consortia are now in operation in the United States. Lifting of R&D secrecy among many firms through collaboration has allowed the marketing of new technologies and products even before they are available for sale. For example, some firms are collaborating on the efficient design of solar panels to power homes and businesses.

Management Information Systems (MIS) Issues

Firms that gather, assimilate, and evaluate external and internal information most effectively are gaining competitive advantages over other firms. Having an effective *management information system (MIS)* may be the most important factor in differentiating successful from unsuccessful firms. The process of strategic management is facilitated immensely in firms that have an effective information system.

Information collection, retrieval, and storage can be used to create competitive advantages in ways such as cross-selling to customers, monitoring suppliers, keeping managers and employees informed, coordinating activities among divisions, and managing funds. Like inventory and human resources, information is now recognized as a valuable organizational asset that can be controlled and managed. Firms that implement strategies using the best information will reap competitive advantages in the twenty-first century.

A good information system can allow a firm to reduce costs. For example, online orders from salespersons to production facilities can shorten materials ordering time and reduce inventory costs. Direct communications between suppliers, manufacturers, marketers, and customers can link together elements of the value chain as though they were one organization. Improved quality and service often result from an improved information system.

Firms must increasingly be concerned about computer hackers and take specific measures to secure and safeguard corporate communications, files, orders, and business conducted over the Internet. Thousands of companies today are plagued by computer hackers who include disgruntled employees, competitors, bored teens, sociopaths, thieves, spies, and hired agents. Computer vulnerability is a giant, expensive headache.

Dun & Bradstreet is an example company that has an excellent information system. Every D&B customer and client in the world has a separate nine-digit number. The database of information associated with each number has become so widely used that it is like a business Social Security number. D&B reaps great competitive advantages from its information system.

In many firms, information technology is doing away with the workplace and allowing employees to work at home or anywhere, anytime. The mobile concept of work allows employees to work the traditional 9-to-5 workday across any of the 24 time zones around the globe. Affordable desktop videoconferencing software allows employees to "beam in" whenever needed. Any manager or employee who travels a lot away from the office is a good candidate for working at home rather than in an office provided by the firm. Salespersons or consultants are good examples, but any person whose job largely involves talking to others or handling information could easily operate at home with the proper computer system and software.

Many people see the officeless office trend as leading to a resurgence of family togetherness in U.S. society. Even the design of homes may change from having large open areas to having more private small areas conducive to getting work done.[17]

Conclusion

Successful strategy implementation depends on cooperation among all functional and divisional managers in an organization. Marketing departments are commonly charged with implementing strategies that require significant increases in sales revenues in new areas and with new or improved products. Finance and accounting managers must devise effective strategy-implementation approaches at low cost and minimum risk to that firm. R&D managers have to transfer complex technologies or develop new technologies to successfully implement strategies. Information systems managers are being called upon more and more to provide leadership and training for all individuals in the firm. The nature and role of marketing, finance/accounting, R&D, and management information systems activities, coupled with the management activities described in Chapter 7, largely determine organizational success.

We invite you to visit the David page on the Prentice Hall Companion Web site at http://www.pearsonhighered.com/david for this chapter's review quiz.

Key Terms and Concepts

Cash Budget (p. 272)
EPS/EBIT Analysis (p. 262)
Financial Budget (p. 271)
Management Information System (MIS) (p. 277)
Market Segmentation (p. 257)
Marketing Mix Variables (p. 258)
Multidimensional Scaling (p. 260)
Outstanding Shares Method (p. 275)

Price-Earnings Ratio Method (p. 275)
Product Positioning (p. 257)
Projected Financial Statement Analysis (p. 266)
Purpose-Based Marketing (p. 257)
Research and Development (R&D) (p. 275)
Tweet (p. 255)
Vacant Niche (p. 260)
Wikis (p. 253)

Issues for Review and Discussion

1. Review a company's Web site that you are familiar with. Discuss the extent to which that organization has instituted the new principles of marketing according to Parise, Guinan, and Weinberg.
2. For companies in general, identify and discuss three opportunities and three threats associated with social networking activities on the Internet.
3. Do you agree or disagree with the following statement? "Television viewers are passive viewers of ads, whereas Internet users take an active role in choosing what to look at— so customers on the Internet are tougher for marketers to reach." Explain your reasoning.
4. How important or relevant do you believe "purpose-based marketing" is for organizations today?
5. Why is it essential for organizations to segment markets and target particular groups of consumers?
6. Explain how and why the Internet makes market segmentation easier.
7. A product-positioning rule given in the chapter is that "When there are only two competitors, the middle becomes the preferred strategic position." Illustrate this for the cruise ship industry, where two firms, Carnival and Royal Caribbean, dominate. Illustrate this for the commercial airliner building industry, where Boeing and Airbus dominate.
8. How could/would dividends affect an EPS/EBIT analysis? Would it be correct to refer to "earnings after taxes, interest, and dividends" as retained earnings for a given year?
9. In performing an EPS/EBIT analysis, where does the first row (EBIT) numbers come from?
10. In performing an EPS/EBIT analysis, where does the tax rate percentage come from?
11. For the Litten Company in Table 8-8, what would the Retained Earnings value have to have been in 2009 on the balance sheet, given that the 2010 NI-DIV value was $4?
12. Show algebraically that the price earnings ratio formula is identical to the number of shares outstanding times stock price formula. Why are the values obtained from these two methods sometimes different?
13. In accounting terms, distinguish between intangibles and goodwill on a balance sheet. Why do these two items generally stay the same on projected financial statements?
14. What are the three major R&D approaches to implementing strategies? Which approach would you prefer as owner of a small software company? Why?
15. Suppose your company has just acquired a firm that produces battery-operated lawn mowers, and strategists want to implement a market-penetration strategy. How would you segment the market for this product? Justify your answer.
16. Explain how you would estimate the total worth of a business.
17. Diagram and label clearly a product-positioning map that includes six fast-food restaurant chains.
18. Explain why EPS/EBIT analysis is a central strategy-implementation technique.
19. How would the R&D role in strategy implementation differ in small versus large organizations?
20. Discuss the limitations of EPS/EBIT analysis.
21. Explain how marketing, finance/accounting, R&D, and management information systems managers' involvement in strategy formulation can enhance strategy implementation.
22. Consider the following statement: "Retained earnings on the balance sheet are not monies available to finance strategy implementation." Is it true or false? Explain.
23. Explain why projected financial statement analysis is considered both a strategy-formulation and a strategy-implementation tool.

24. Describe some marketing, finance/accounting, R&D, and management information systems activities that a small restaurant chain might undertake to expand into a neighboring state.

25. What effect is e-commerce having on firms' efforts to segment markets?

26. How has the Sarbanes-Oxley Act of 2002 changed CEOs' and CFOs' handling of financial statements?

27. To what extent have you been exposed to natural environment issues in your business courses? Which course has provided the most coverage? What percentage of your business courses provided no coverage? Comment.

28. Complete the following EPS/EBIT analysis for a company whose stock price is $20, interest rate on funds is 5 percent, tax rate is 20 percent, number of shares outstanding is 500 million, and EBIT range is $100 million to $300 million. The firm needs to raise $200 million in capital. Use the accompanying table to complete the work.

29. Under what conditions would retained earnings on the balance sheet decrease from one year to the next?

30. In your own words, list all the steps in developing projected financial statements.

31. Based on the financial statements provided for McDonald's (pp. 31–32), how much dividends in dollars did McDonald's pay in 2007? In 2008?

32. Based on the financial statements provided in this chapter for the Litten Company, calculate the value of this company if you know that its stock price is $20 and it has 1 million shares outstanding. Calculate four different ways and average.

33. Why should you be careful not to use historical percentages blindly in developing projected financial statements?

34. In developing projected financial statements, what should you do if the $ amount you must put in the cash account (to make the statement balance) is far more (or less) than desired?

35. Why is it both important and necessary to segment markets and target groups of customers, rather than market to all possible consumers?

36. In full detail, explain the following EPS/EBIT chart.

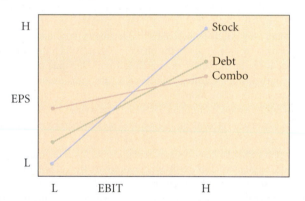

	100% Common Stock	100% Debt Financing	20% Debt-80%Stock
EBIT			
Interest			
EBT			
Taxes			
EAT			
# Shares			
EPS			

Notes

1. Leslie Miller and Elizabeth Weise, "E-Privacy—FTC Studies 'Profiling' by Web Sites," *USA Today* (November 8, 1999): 1A, 2A.

2. Salvatore Parise, Patricia Guinan, and Bruce Weinberg, "The Secrets of Marketing in a Web 2.0 World," *Wall Street Journal* (December 15, 2008): R1.

3. Kathy Chu and Kim Thai, "Banks Jump on Twitter Wagon," *USA Today* (May 12, 2009): B1.

4. Emily Steel, "Car Makers Take Case to the Web," *Wall Street Journal* (December 5, 2006): B7; Salvatore Parise, Patricia Guinan, and Bruce Weinberg, "The Secrets of Marketing in a Web 2.0 World," *Wall Street Journal* (December 15, 2008): R1.

5. Laura Petrecca, "Negative PR Travels Fast Online," *USA Today*, December 8, 2008; Emily Steel, "MySpace Weds the Wider Web," *Wall Street Journal* (December 9, 2008): B5; Bruce Horowitz, "Domino's Nightmare Holds Lessons for Marketers," *Wall Street Journal* (April 16, 2009): 3B.

6. Tom Wright, "Poor Nations Go Online on Cell Phones," *Wall Street Journal* (December 5, 2008): B8.

7. Ellen Byron, "A New Odd Couple: Google, P&G Swap Workers to Spur Innovation," *Wall Street Journal* (November 19, 2008): A1.

8. Emily Steel, "Ad-Spending Forecasts Are Glum," *Wall Street Journal* (December 8, 2008): B5.

9. Susanne Vranica, "Veteran Marketer Promotes a New Kind of Selling," *Wall Street Journal* (October 31, 2008): B4.

10. Betsy McKay and Suzanne Vranica, "Coca-Cola Ads Will Employ Optimism to Sell Coke," *Wall Street Journal* (January 14, 2009): B6.

11. Ralph Biggadike, "The Contributions of Marketing to Strategic Management," *Academy of Management Review* 6, no. 4 (October 1981): 627.

12. Jilian Mincer, "Small Businesses Find a New Source of Funding," *Wall Street Journal* (March 3, 2009): B7.

13. Phyllis Plitch, "Companies in Many Sectors Give Earnings a Pro Forma Makeover, Survey Finds," *Wall Street Journal* (January 22, 2002): A4.

14. Michael Rapoport, "Pro Forma Is a Hard Habit to Break," *Wall Street Journal* (September 18, 2003): B3A.

15. Amy Merrick, "U.S. Research Spending to Rise Only 3.2 Percent," *Wall Street Journal* (December 28, 2001): A2.

16. Pier Abetti, "Technology: A Key Strategic Resource," *Management Review* 78, no. 2 (February 1989): 38.

17. Adapted from Edward Baig, "Welcome to the Officeless Office," *BusinessWeek* (June 26, 1995).

Current Readings

Balmer, John M., Helen Stuart, and Stephen A. Greyser. "Aligning Identity and Strategy: Corporate Branding at British Airways in the Late 20th Century." *California Management Review* (Spring 2009): 6–23.

Bartol, Kathryn M., Dmitry M. Khanin, Michael D. Pfarrer, Ken G. Smith, and Xiaomeng Zhang. "CEOs on the Edge: Earnings Manipulation and Stock-Based Incentive Misalignment." *The Academy of Management Journal* 51, no. 2 (April 2008): 241.

Choi, Jaepil, and Heli Wang. "Stakeholder Relations and the Persistence of Corporate Financial Performance." *Strategic Management Journal* (August 2009): 895–907.

Fernando, Chitru S., and Mark P. Sharfman. "Environmental Risk Management and the Cost of Capital." *Strategic Management Journal* 29, no. 6 (June 2008): 569.

Finkbeiner, Carl, Dominique M. Hanssens, and Daniel Thorpe. "Marketing When Customer Equity Matters." *Harvard Business Review* (May 2008): 117.

Harrington, Richard J., and Anthony K. Tjan. "Transforming Strategy One Customer at a Time." *Harvard Business Review* (March 2008): 62.

Kumar, Minu, and Charles H. Noble. "Using Product Design Strategically to Create Deeper Consumer Connections." *Business Horizons* 51, no. 5 (September–October 2008): 441.

Levitas, Edward, and Ann McFadyen. "Managing Liquidity in Research-Intensive Firms: Signaling and Cash Flow Effects of Patents and Alliance Activities." *Strategic Management Journal* (June 2009): 659–678.

Morgan, Neil, Douglas Vorhies, and Charlotte Mason. "Market Orientation, Marketing Capabilities and Firm Performance." *Strategic Management Journal* (August 2009): 909–920.

Chowdhury, Shamaud, and Eric Wang. "Institutional Activism Types and CEO Compensation: A Time-Series Analysis of Large Canadian Corporations." *Journal of Management* (February 2009): 5–38.

ASSURANCE OF LEARNING EXERCISES

Assurance of Learning Exercise 8A

Developing a Product-Positioning Map for McDonald's

Purpose

Organizations continually monitor how their products and services are positioned relative to competitors. This information is especially useful for marketing managers but is also used by other managers and strategists.

Instructions

Step 1   On a separate sheet of paper, develop a product-positioning map for McDonald's, Wendy's, Burger King, and Hardee's. Include in your diagram.

Step 2   At the chalkboard, diagram your product-positioning map.

Step 3   Compare your product-positioning map with those diagrammed by other students. Discuss any major differences.

Assurance of Learning Exercise 8B

Performing an EPS/EBIT Analysis for McDonald's

Purpose

An EPS/EBIT analysis is one of the most widely used techniques for determining the extent that debt and/or stock should be used to finance strategies to be implemented. This exercise can give you practice performing EPS/EBIT analysis.

Instructions (1-1-10 Data)

Let's say McDonald's needs to raise $1 billion to expand into Africa. Determine whether McDonald's should have used all debt, all stock, or a 50-50 combination of debt and stock to finance this market-development strategy. Assume a 38 percent tax rate, 5 percent interest rate, McDonald's stock price of $50 per share, and an annual dividend of $0.30 per share of common stock. The EBIT range for 2010 is between $6.332 billion and $9 billion. A total of 1 billion shares of common stock are outstanding. Develop an EPS/EBIT chart to reflect your analysis.

Assurance of Learning Exercise 8C

Preparing Projected Financial Statements for McDonald's

Purpose

This exercise is designed to give you experience preparing projected financial statements. Pro forma analysis is a central strategy-implementation technique because it allows managers to anticipate and evaluate the expected results of various strategy-implementation approaches.

Instructions

Step 1   Work with a classmate. Develop a 2008 projected income statement and balance sheet for McDonald's. Assume that McDonald's plans to raise $900 million in 2010 to begin serving Africa and plans to obtain 50 percent financing from a bank and 50 percent financing from a stock issuance. Make other assumptions as needed, and state them clearly in written form.

Step 2   Compute McDonald's current ratio, debt-to-equity ratio, and return-on-investment ratio for 2008 and 2009. How do your 2010 projected ratios compare to the 2008 and 2009 ratios? Why is it important to make this comparison? Use http://finance.yahoo.com to obtain 2009 financial statements.

Step 3   Bring your projected statements to class, and discuss any problems or questions you encountered.

Step 4   Compare your projected statements to the statements of other students. What major differences exist between your analysis and the work of other students?

Assurance of Learning Exercise 8D

Determining the Cash Value of McDonald's

Purpose

It is simply good business practice to periodically determine the financial worth or cash value of your company. This exercise gives you practice determining the total worth of a company using several methods. Use year-end 2008 data as given in the Cohesion Case on pages 31–32.

Instructions

Step 1   Calculate the financial worth of McDonald's based on four methods: (1) the net worth or stockholders' equity, (2) the future value of McDonald's earnings, (3) the price-earnings ratio, and (4) the outstanding shares method.

Step 2   In a dollar amount, how much is McDonald's worth?

Step 3   Compare your analyses and conclusions with those of other students.

Assurance of Learning Exercise 8E

Developing a Product-Positioning Map for My University

Purpose

The purpose of this exercise is to give you practice developing product-positioning maps. Nonprofit organizations, such as universities, are increasingly using product-positioning maps to determine effective ways to implement strategies.

Instructions

Step 1   Join with two other people in class to form a group of three.

Step 2   Jointly prepare a product-positioning map that includes your institution and four other colleges or universities in your state.

Step 3   At the chalkboard, diagram your product-positioning map.

Step 4   Discuss differences among the maps diagrammed on the board.

Assurance of Learning Exercise 8F

Do Banks Require Projected Financial Statements?

Purpose

The purpose of this exercise is to explore the practical importance and use of projected financial statements in the banking business.

Instructions

Contact two local bankers by phone and seek answers to the questions that follow. Record the answers you receive, and report your findings to the class.

1. Does your bank require projected financial statements as part of a business loan application?
2. How does your bank use projected financial statements when they are part of a business loan application?
3. What special advice do you give potential business borrowers in preparing projected financial statements?

CHAPTER 9
Strategy Review, Evaluation, and Control

CHAPTER OBJECTIVES

After studying this chapter, you should be able to do the following:

1. Describe a practical framework for evaluating strategies.

2. Explain why strategy evaluation is complex, sensitive, and yet essential for organizational success.

3. Discuss the importance of contingency planning in strategy evaluation.

4. Discuss the role of auditing in strategy evaluation.

5. Explain how computers can aid in evaluating strategies.

6. Discuss the Balanced Scorecard.

7. Discuss three twenty-first-century challenges in strategic management.

Assurance of Learning Exercises

Assurance of Learning Exercise 9A
Preparing a Strategy-Evaluation Report for McDonald's

Assurance of Learning Exercise 9B
Evaluating My University's Strategies

Source: Shutterstock/Diego Cervo

"Notable Quotes"

"Complicated controls do not work. They confuse. They misdirect attention from what is to be controlled to the mechanics and methodology of the control."

—Seymour Tilles

"Although Plan A may be selected as the most realistic . . . the other major alternatives should not be forgotten. They may well serve as contingency plans."

—Dale McConkey

"Organizations are most vulnerable when they are at the peak of their success."

—R. T. Lenz

"Strategy evaluation must make it as easy as possible for managers to revise their plans and reach quick agreement on the changes."

—Dale McConkey

"While strategy is a word that is usually associated with the future, its link to the past is no less central. Life is lived forward but understood backward. Managers may live strategy in the future, but they understand it through the past."

—Henry Mintzberg

"Unless strategy evaluation is performed seriously and systematically, and unless strategists are willing to act on the results, energy will be used up defending yesterday. No one will have the time, resources, or will to work on exploiting today, let alone to work on making tomorrow."

—Peter Drucker

"Executives, consultants, and B-school professors all agree that strategic planning is now the single most important management issue and will remain so for the next five years. Strategy has become a part of the main agenda at lots of organizations today. Strategic planning is back with a vengeance."

—John Byrne

"Planners should not plan, but serve as facilitators, catalysts, inquirers, educators, and synthesizers to guide the planning process effectively."

—A. Hax and N. Majluf

Doing Great in a Weak Economy. How?

Family Dollar Stores

Founded in 1959 by the father of CEO Howard Levine, Family Dollar Stores (FDO) is doing great in the ongoing recession as cash-strapped consumers hunt for bargains. The company's second-quarter 2009 results exceeded expectations: Sales were up 8.7 percent from last year to $2 billion. Pro-forma earnings are expected to be between 59 and 61 cents per share, safely ahead of the consensus estimate of 50 cents. Family Dollar's same-store sales, a key retail metric, were up 6.4 percent the second quarter of 2009. FDO's fiscal 2009 3rd quarter earnings increased another 36 percent.

Family Dollar's earnings held up well throughout the global recession, beating estimates in each of the last four quarters. The company was one of three S&P 500 companies to have a rising stock price in 2008. For fiscal 2008, FDO's sales increased from $6.8 billion to $6.9 billion. The company's net income for 2008 was $233 million.

The nation's number two dollar store (behind Dollar General), Family Dollar targets women shopping for a family that earns less than $30,000 a year. Family Dollar operates about 6,600 stores in some 45 states and the District of Columbia. Consumables (food, health and beauty aids, and household products) account for about 60 percent of sales; the stores also sell apparel, shoes, and linens. Family Dollar emphasizes neighborhood stores near its low- and middle-income customers in rural and urban areas. Most merchandise is less than $10.

The best formulated and best implemented strategies become obsolete as a firm's external and internal environments change. It is essential, therefore, that strategists systematically review, evaluate, and control the execution of strategies. This chapter presents a framework that can guide managers' efforts to evaluate strategic-management activities, to make sure they are working, and to make timely changes. Management information systems being used to evaluate strategies are discussed. Guidelines are presented for formulating, implementing, and evaluating strategies. Family Dollar Stores evaluates strategies well.

The Nature of Strategy Evaluation

The strategic-management process results in decisions that can have significant, long-lasting consequences. Erroneous strategic decisions can inflict severe penalties and can be exceedingly difficult, if not impossible, to reverse. Most strategists agree, therefore, that strategy evaluation is vital to an organization's well-being; timely evaluations can alert management to problems or potential problems before a situation becomes critical. Strategy evaluation includes three basic activities: (1) examining the underlying bases of a firm's strategy, (2) comparing expected results with actual results, and (3) taking corrective actions to ensure that performance conforms to plans. The strategy-evaluation stage of the strategic-management process is illustrated in Figure 9-1.

FIGURE 9-1

A Comprehensive Strategic-Management Model

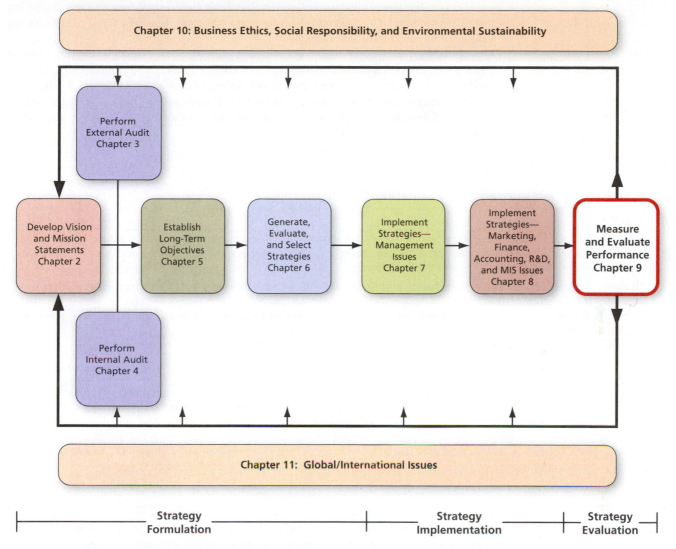

Source: Fred R. David, "How Companies Define Their Mission," *Long Range Planning* 22, no. 3 (June 1988): 40.

Adequate and timely feedback is the cornerstone of effective strategy evaluation. Strategy evaluation can be no better than the information on which it is based. Too much pres sure from top managers may result in lower managers contriving numbers they think will be satisfactory.

Strategy evaluation can be a complex and sensitive undertaking. Too much emphasis on evaluating strategies may be expensive and counterproductive. No one likes to be evaluated too closely! The more managers attempt to evaluate the behavior of others, the less control they have. Yet too little or no evaluation can create even worse problems. Strategy evaluation is essential to ensure that stated objectives are being achieved.

In many organizations, strategy evaluation is simply an appraisal of how well an organization has performed. Have the firm's assets increased? Has there been an increase in profitability? Have sales increased? Have productivity levels increased? Have profit margin, return on investment, and earnings-per-share ratios increased? Some firms argue that their strategy must have been correct if the answers to these types of questions are affirmative. Well, the strategy or strategies may have been correct, but this type of reasoning can be misleading because strategy evaluation must have both a long-run and short-run focus. Strategies often do not affect short-term operating results until it is too late to make needed changes.

It is impossible to demonstrate conclusively that a particular strategy is optimal or even to guarantee that it will work. One can, however, evaluate it for critical flaws. Richard Rumelt offered four criteria that could be used to evaluate a strategy: consistency, consonance, feasibility, and advantage. Described in Table 9-1, *consonance* and *advantage* are mostly based on a firm's external assessment, whereas *consistency* and *feasibility* are largely based on an internal assessment.

Strategy evaluation is important because organizations face dynamic environments in which key external and internal factors often change quickly and dramatically. Success today is no guarantee of success tomorrow! An organization should never be lulled into complacency with success. Countless firms have thrived one year only to struggle for survival the following year. Organizational trouble can come swiftly, as further evidenced by the examples described in Table 9-2.

TABLE 9-1   Rumelt's Criteria for Evaluating Strategies

Consistency

A strategy should not present inconsistent goals and policies. Organizational conflict and interdepartmental bickering are often symptoms of managerial disorder, but these problems may also be a sign of strategic inconsistency. Three guidelines help determine if organizational problems are due to inconsistencies in strategy:

- If managerial problems continue despite changes in personnel and if they tend to be issue-based rather than people-based, then strategies may be inconsistent.
- If success for one organizational department means, or is interpreted to mean, failure for another department, then strategies may be inconsistent.
- If policy problems and issues continue to be brought to the top for resolution, then strategies may be inconsistent.

Consonance

Consonance refers to the need for strategists to examine *sets of trends*, as well as individual trends, in evaluating strategies. A strategy must represent an adaptive response to the external environment and to the critical changes occurring within it. One difficulty in matching a firm's key internal and external factors in the formulation of strategy is that most trends are the result of interactions among other trends. For example, the day-care explosion came about as a combined result of many trends that included a rise in the average level of education, increased inflation, and an increase in women in the workforce. Although single economic or demographic trends might appear steady for many years, there are waves of change going on at the interaction level.

Feasibility

A strategy must neither overtax available resources nor create unsolvable subproblems. The final broad test of strategy is its feasibility; that is, can the strategy be attempted within the physical, human, and financial resources of the enterprise? The financial resources of a business are the easiest to quantify and are normally the first limitation against which strategy is evaluated. It is sometimes forgotten, however, that innovative approaches to financing are often possible. Devices, such as captive subsidiaries, sale-leaseback arrangements, and tying plant mortgages to long-term contracts, have all been used effectively to help win key positions in suddenly expanding industries. A less quantifiable, but actually more rigid, limitation on strategic choice is that imposed by individual and organizational capabilities. In evaluating a strategy, it is important to examine whether an organization has demonstrated in the past that it possesses the abilities, competencies, skills, and talents needed to carry out a given strategy.

Advantage

A strategy must provide for the creation and/or maintenance of a competitive advantage in a selected area of activity. Competitive advantages normally are the result of superiority in one of three areas: (1) resources, (2) skills, or (3) position. The idea that the positioning of one's resources can enhance their combined effectiveness is familiar to military theorists, chess players, and diplomats. Position can also play a crucial role in an organization's strategy. Once gained, a good position is defensible—meaning that it is so costly to capture that rivals are deterred from full-scale attacks. Positional advantage tends to be self-sustaining as long as the key internal and environmental factors that underlie it remain stable. This is why entrenched firms can be almost impossible to unseat, even if their raw skill levels are only average. Although not all positional advantages are associated with size, it is true that larger organizations tend to operate in markets and use procedures that turn their size into advantage, while smaller firms seek product/market positions that exploit other types of advantage. The principal characteristic of good position is that it permits the firm to obtain advantage from policies that would not similarly benefit rivals without the same position. Therefore, in evaluating strategy, organizations should examine the nature of positional advantages associated with a given strategy.

Source: Adapted from Richard Rumelt, "The Evaluation of Business Strategy," in W. F. Glueck (ed.), *Business Policy and Strategic Management* (New York: McGraw-Hill, 1980): 359–367. Used with permission.

TABLE 9-2   **Examples of Organizational Demise**

A. Some Large Companies That Experienced a Large Drop in Revenues in 2008 vs. 2007		B. Some Large Companies That Experienced a Large Drop in Profits in 2008 vs. 2007	
Molson Coors Brewing	−23%	UAL	−1,427%
Citigroup	−29%	Sonic Automotive	−818%
Morgan Stanley	−29%	Citigroup	−865%
Goldman Sachs Group	−39%	CBS	−1,036%
Fannie Mae	−48%	Rite Aid	−4,122%
Freddie Mac	−71%	Pilgrim's Pride	−2,224%
Weyerhaeuser	−32%	Centex	−1,090%
Centex	−41%	Harrah's Entertainment	−939%
Pulte Homes	−32%	American International Group	−1,701%
Massachusetts Mutual Life	−26%	Gannett	−730%
Allstate	−20%	OfficeMax	−899%
American International Group	−90%	Brunswick	−806%
Hartford Financial	−64%	Brightpoint	−822%
Atria Group	−58%	Owens Corning	−974%

Strategy evaluation is becoming increasingly difficult with the passage of time, for many reasons. Domestic and world economies were more stable in years past, product life cycles were longer, product development cycles were longer, technological advancement was slower, change occurred less frequently, there were fewer competitors, foreign companies were weak, and there were more regulated industries. Other reasons why strategy evaluation is more difficult today include the following trends:

1. A dramatic increase in the environment's complexity
2. The increasing difficulty of predicting the future with accuracy
3. The increasing number of variables
4. The rapid rate of obsolescence of even the best plans
5. The increase in the number of both domestic and world events affecting organizations
6. The decreasing time span for which planning can be done with any degree of certainty[1]

A fundamental problem facing managers today is how to control employees effectively in light of modern organizational demands for greater flexibility, innovation, creativity, and initiative from employees.[2] How can managers today ensure that empowered employees acting in an entrepreneurial manner do not put the well-being of the business at risk? Recall that Kidder, Peabody & Company lost $350 million when one of its traders allegedly booked fictitious profits; Sears, Roebuck and Company took a $60 million charge against earnings after admitting that its automobile service businesses were performing unnecessary repairs. The costs to companies such as these in terms of damaged reputations, fines, missed opportunities, and diversion of management's attention are enormous.

When empowered employees are held accountable for and pressured to achieve specific goals and are given wide latitude in their actions to achieve them, there can be dysfunctional behavior. For example, Nordstrom, the upscale fashion retailer known for outstanding customer service, was subjected to lawsuits and fines when employees underreported hours worked in order to increase their sales per hour—the company's primary performance criterion. Nordstrom's customer service and earnings were enhanced until the misconduct was reported, at which time severe penalties were levied against the firm.

The Process of Evaluating Strategies

Strategy evaluation is necessary for all sizes and kinds of organizations. Strategy evaluation should initiate managerial questioning of expectations and assumptions, should trigger a review of objectives and values, and should stimulate creativity in generating alternatives and formulating criteria of evaluation.[3] Regardless of the size of the organization, a certain amount of *management by wandering around* at all levels is essential to effective strategy evaluation. Strategy-evaluation activities should be performed on a continuing basis, rather than at the end of specified periods of time or just after problems occur. Waiting until the end of the year, for example, could result in a firm closing the barn door after the horses have already escaped.

Evaluating strategies on a continuous rather than on a periodic basis allows benchmarks of progress to be established and more effectively monitored. Some strategies take years to implement; consequently, associated results may not become apparent for years. Successful strategies combine patience with a willingness to promptly take corrective actions when necessary. There always comes a time when corrective actions are needed in an organization! Centuries ago, a writer (perhaps Solomon) made the following observations about change:

> There is a time for everything,
> A time to be born and a time to die,
> A time to plant and a time to uproot,
> A time to kill and a time to heal,
> A time to tear down and a time to build,
> A time to weep and a time to laugh,
> A time to mourn and a time to dance,
> A time to scatter stones and a time to gather them,
> A time to embrace and a time to refrain,
> A time to search and a time to give up,
> A time to keep and a time to throw away,
> A time to tear and a time to mend,
> A time to be silent and a time to speak,
> A time to love and a time to hate,
> A time for war and a time for peace.[4]

Managers and employees of the firm should be continually aware of progress being made toward achieving the firm's objectives. As critical success factors change, organizational members should be involved in determining appropriate corrective actions. If assumptions and expectations deviate significantly from forecasts, then the firm should renew strategy-formulation activities, perhaps sooner than planned. In strategy evaluation, like strategy formulation and strategy implementation, people make the difference. Through involvement in the process of evaluating strategies, managers and employees become committed to keeping the firm moving steadily toward achieving objectives.

A Strategy-Evaluation Framework

Table 9-3 summarizes strategy-evaluation activities in terms of key questions that should be addressed, alternative answers to those questions, and appropriate actions for an organization to take. Notice that corrective actions are almost always needed except when (1) external and internal factors have not significantly changed and (2) the firm is progressing satisfactorily toward achieving stated objectives. Relationships among strategy-evaluation activities are illustrated in Figure 9-2.

Reviewing Bases of Strategy

As shown in Figure 9-2, *reviewing the underlying bases of an organization's strategy* could be approached by developing a revised EFE Matrix and IFE Matrix. A *revised IFE Matrix* should focus on changes in the organization's management, marketing, finance/accounting,

TABLE 9-3   A Strategy-Evaluation Assessment Matrix

Have Major Changes Occurred in the Firm Internal Strategic Position?	Have Major Changes Occurred in the Firm External Strategic Position?	Has the Firm Progressed Satisfactorily Toward Achieving Its Stated Objectives?	Result
No	No	No	Take corrective actions
Yes	Yes	Yes	Take corrective actions
Yes	Yes	No	Take corrective actions
Yes	No	Yes	Take corrective actions
Yes	No	No	Take corrective actions
No	Yes	Yes	Take corrective actions
No	Yes	No	Take corrective actions
No	No	Yes	Continue present strategic course

production/operations, R&D, and management information systems strengths and weaknesses. A *revised EFE Matrix* should indicate how effective a firm's strategies have been in response to key opportunities and threats. This analysis could also address such questions as the following:

1. How have competitors reacted to our strategies?
2. How have competitors' strategies changed?
3. Have major competitors' strengths and weaknesses changed?
4. Why are competitors making certain strategic changes?
5. Why are some competitors' strategies more successful than others?
6. How satisfied are our competitors with their present market positions and profitability?
7. How far can our major competitors be pushed before retaliating?
8. How could we more effectively cooperate with our competitors?

Numerous external and internal factors can prevent firms from achieving long-term and annual objectives. Externally, actions by competitors, changes in demand, changes in technology, economic changes, demographic shifts, and governmental actions may prevent objectives from being accomplished. Internally, ineffective strategies may have been chosen or implementation activities may have been poor. Objectives may have been too optimistic. Thus, failure to achieve objectives may not be the result of unsatisfactory work by managers and employees. All organizational members need to know this to encourage their support for strategy-evaluation activities. Organizations desperately need to know as soon as possible when their strategies are not effective. Sometimes managers and employees on the front lines discover this well before strategists.

External opportunities and threats and internal strengths and weaknesses that represent the bases of current strategies should continually be monitored for change. It is not really a question of whether these factors will change but rather when they will change and in what ways. Here are some key questions to address in evaluating strategies:

1. Are our internal strengths still strengths?
2. Have we added other internal strengths? If so, what are they?
3. Are our internal weaknesses still weaknesses?
4. Do we now have other internal weaknesses? If so, what are they?
5. Are our external opportunities still opportunities?
6. Are there now other external opportunities? If so, what are they?
7. Are our external threats still threats?
8. Are there now other external threats? If so, what are they?
9. Are we vulnerable to a hostile takeover?

FIGURE 9-2

A Strategy-Evaluation Framework

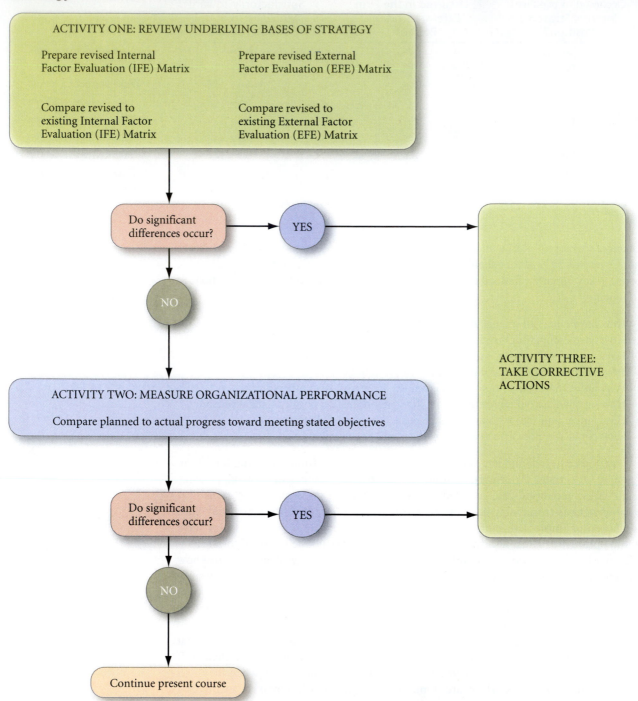

Measuring Organizational Performance

Another important strategy-evaluation activity is *measuring organizational performance.* This activity includes comparing expected results to actual results, investigating deviations from plans, evaluating individual performance, and examining progress being made toward meeting stated objectives. Both long-term and annual objectives are commonly used in this process. Criteria for evaluating strategies should be measurable and easily verifiable. Criteria that predict results may be more important than those that reveal what already has happened. For example, rather than simply being informed that sales in the last quarter were 20 percent under what was expected, strategists need to know that sales in the next quarter may be 20 percent below standard unless some action is taken to counter the trend. Really effective control requires accurate forecasting.

Failure to make satisfactory progress toward accomplishing long-term or annual objectives signals a need for corrective actions. Many factors, such as unreasonable policies, unexpected turns in the economy, unreliable suppliers or distributors, or ineffective strategies, can result in unsatisfactory progress toward meeting objectives. Problems can result from ineffectiveness (not doing the right things) or inefficiency (poorly doing the right things).

Many variables can and should be included in measuring organizational performance. As indicated in Table 9-4, typically a favorable or unfavorable variance is recorded monthly, quarterly, and annually, and resultant actions needed are then determined.

Determining which objectives are most important in the evaluation of strategies can be difficult. Strategy evaluation is based on both quantitative and qualitative criteria. Selecting the exact set of criteria for evaluating strategies depends on a particular organization's size, industry, strategies, and management philosophy. An organization pursuing a retrenchment strategy, for example, could have an entirely different set of evaluative criteria from an organization pursuing a market-development strategy. Quantitative criteria commonly used to evaluate strategies are financial ratios, which strategists use to make three critical comparisons: (1) comparing the firm's performance over different time periods, (2) comparing the firm's performance to competitors', and (3) comparing the firm's performance to industry averages. Some key financial ratios that are particularly useful as criteria for strategy evaluation are as follows:

1. Return on investment (ROI)
2. Return on equity (ROE)
3. Profit margin
4. Market share
5. Debt to equity
6. Earnings per share
7. Sales growth
8. Asset growth

TABLE 9-4 A Sample Framework for Measuring Organizational Performance

Factor	Actual Result	Expected Result	Variance	Action Needed
Corporate Revenues				
Corporate Profits				
Corporate ROI				
Region 1 Revenues				
Region 1 Profits				
Region 1 ROI				
Region 2 Revenues				
Region 2 Profits				
Region 2 ROI				
Product 1 Revenues				
Product 1 Profits				
Product 1 ROI				
Product 2 Revenues				
Product 2 Profits				
Product 2 ROI				

But some potential problems are associated with using quantitative criteria for evaluating strategies. First, most quantitative criteria are geared to annual objectives rather than long-term objectives. Also, different accounting methods can provide different results on many quantitative criteria. Third, intuitive judgments are almost always involved in deriving quantitative criteria. For these and other reasons, qualitative criteria are also important in evaluating strategies. Human factors such as high absenteeism and turnover rates, poor production quality and quantity rates, or low employee satisfaction can be underlying causes of declining performance. Marketing, finance/accounting, R&D, or management information systems factors can also cause financial problems.

Some additional key questions that reveal the need for qualitative or intuitive judgments in strategy evaluation are as follows:

1. How good is the firm's balance of investments between high-risk and low-risk projects?
2. How good is the firm's balance of investments between long-term and short-term projects?
3. How good is the firm's balance of investments between slow-growing markets and fast-growing markets?
4. How good is the firm's balance of investments among different divisions?
5. To what extent are the firm's alternative strategies socially responsible?
6. What are the relationships among the firm's key internal and external strategic factors?
7. How are major competitors likely to respond to particular strategies?

Taking Corrective Actions

The final strategy-evaluation activity, *taking corrective actions,* requires making changes to competitively reposition a firm for the future. As indicated in Table 9-5, examples of changes that may be needed are altering an organization's structure, replacing one or more key individuals, selling a division, or revising a business mission. Other changes could include establishing or revising objectives, devising new policies, issuing stock to raise capital, adding additional salespersons, differently allocating resources, or developing new performance incentives. Taking corrective actions does not necessarily mean that existing strategies will be abandoned or even that new strategies must be formulated.

The probabilities and possibilities for incorrect or inappropriate actions increase geometrically with an arithmetic increase in personnel. Any person directing an overall undertaking must check on the actions of the participants as well as the results that they have achieved. If either the actions or results do not comply with preconceived or planned achievements, then corrective actions are needed.[5]

TABLE 9-5 Corrective Actions Possibly Needed to Correct Unfavorable Variances

1. Alter the firm's structure
2. Replace one or more key individuals
3. Divest a division
4. Alter the firm's vision and/or mission
5. Revise objectives
6. Alter strategies
7. Devise new policies
8. Install new performance incentives
9. Raise capital with stock or debt
10. Add or terminate salespersons, employees, or managers
11. Allocate resources differently
12. Outsource (or rein in) business functions

No organization can survive as an island; no organization can escape change. Taking corrective actions is necessary to keep an organization on track toward achieving stated objectives. In his thought-provoking books *Future Shock* and *The Third Wave,* Alvin Toffler argued that business environments are becoming so dynamic and complex that they threaten people and organizations with *future shock*, which occurs when the nature, types, and speed of changes overpower an individual's or organization's ability and capacity to adapt. Strategy evaluation enhances an organization's ability to adapt successfully to changing circumstances.

Taking corrective actions raises employees' and managers' anxieties. Research suggests that participation in strategy-evaluation activities is one of the best ways to overcome individuals' resistance to change. According to Erez and Kanfer, individuals accept change best when they have a cognitive understanding of the changes, a sense of control over the situation, and an awareness that necessary actions are going to be taken to implement the changes.[6]

Strategy evaluation can lead to strategy-formulation changes, strategy-implementation changes, both formulation and implementation changes, or no changes at all. Strategists cannot escape having to revise strategies and implementation approaches sooner or later. Hussey and Langham offered the following insight on taking corrective actions:

Resistance to change is often emotionally based and not easily overcome by rational argument. Resistance may be based on such feelings as loss of status, implied criticism of present competence, fear of failure in the new situation, annoyance at not being consulted, lack of understanding of the need for change, or insecurity in changing from well-known and fixed methods. It is necessary, therefore, to overcome such resistance by creating situations of participation and full explanation when changes are envisaged.[7]

Corrective actions should place an organization in a better position to capitalize upon internal strengths; to take advantage of key external opportunities; to avoid, reduce, or mitigate external threats; and to improve internal weaknesses. Corrective actions should have a proper time horizon and an appropriate amount of risk. They should be internally consistent and socially responsible. Perhaps most important, corrective actions strengthen an organization's competitive position in its basic industry. Continuous strategy evaluation keeps strategists close to the pulse of an organization and provides information needed for an effective strategic-management system. Carter Bayles described the benefits of strategy evaluation as follows:

Evaluation activities may renew confidence in the current business strategy or point to the need for actions to correct some weaknesses, such as erosion of product superiority or technological edge. In many cases, the benefits of strategy evaluation are much more far-reaching, for the outcome of the process may be a fundamentally new strategy that will lead, even in a business that is already turning a respectable profit, to substantially increased earnings. It is this possibility that justifies strategy evaluation, for the payoff can be very large.[8]

The Balanced Scorecard

Introduced earlier in the Chapter 5 discussion of objectives, the Balanced Scorecard is an important strategy-evaluation tool. It is a process that allows firms to evaluate strategies from four perspectives: financial performance, customer knowledge, internal business processes, and learning and growth. The *Balanced Scorecard* analysis requires that firms seek answers to the following questions and utilize that information, in conjunction with financial measures, to adequately and more effectively evaluate strategies being implemented:

1. How well is the firm continually improving and creating value along measures such as innovation, technological leadership, product quality, operational process efficiencies, and so on?

2.   How well is the firm sustaining and even improving upon its core competencies and competitive advantages?
3.   How satisfied are the firm's customers?

A sample Balanced Scorecard is provided in Table 9-6. Notice that the firm examines six key issues in evaluating its strategies: (1) Customers, (2) Managers/Employees, (3) Operations/Processes, (4) Community/Social Responsibility, (5) Business Ethics/Natural Environment, and (6) Financial. The basic form of a Balanced Scorecard may differ for different organizations. The Balanced Scorecard approach to strategy evaluation aims to balance long-term with short-term concerns, to balance financial with nonfinancial concerns, and to balance internal with external concerns. It can be an excellent management tool, and it is used successfully today by Chemical Bank, Exxon/Mobil Corporation, CIGNA Property and Casualty Insurance, and numerous other firms. The Balanced Scorecard would be constructed differently, that is, adapted, to particular firms in various industries with the underlying theme or thrust being the same, which is to evaluate the firm's strategies based upon both key quantitative and qualitative measures.

TABLE 9-6   An Example Balanced Scorecard

Area of Objectives	Measure or Target	Time Expectation	Primary Responsibility
Customers			
1.			
2.			
3.			
4.			
Managers/Employees			
1.			
2.			
3.			
4.			
Operations/Processes			
1.			
2.			
3.			
4.			
Community/Social Responsibility			
1.			
2.			
3.			
4.			
Business Ethics/Natural Environment			
1.			
2.			
3.			
4.			
Financial			
1.			
2.			
3.			
4.			

Published Sources of Strategy-Evaluation Information

A number of publications are helpful in evaluating a firm's strategies. For example, *Fortune* annually identifies and evaluates the Fortune 1,000 (the largest manufacturers) and the Fortune 50 (the largest retailers, transportation companies, utilities, banks, insurance companies, and diversified financial corporations in the United States). *Fortune* ranks the best and worst performers on various factors, such as return on investment, sales volume, and profitability. In its March issue each year, *Fortune* publishes its strategy-evaluation research in an article entitled "America's Most Admired Companies." Eight key attributes serve as evaluative criteria: people management; innovativeness; quality of products or services; financial soundness; social responsibility; use of corporate assets; long-term investment; and quality of management. In October of each year, *Fortune* publishes additional strategy-evaluation research in an article entitled "The World's Most Admired Companies." *Fortune's* 2009 evaluation in Table 9-7 reveals the firms most admired (best managed) in their industry. The most admired company in the world in 2009 was Nike, followed by Anheuser-Busch, Nestle, and Procter & Gamble.[9]

Another excellent evaluation of corporations in America, "The Annual Report on American Industry," is published annually in the January issue of *Forbes*. It provides a detailed and comprehensive evaluation of hundreds of U.S. companies in many different industries. *BusinessWeek*, *Industry Week*, and *Dun's Business Month* also periodically publish detailed evaluations of U.S. businesses and industries. Although published sources of strategy-evaluation information focus primarily on large, publicly held businesses, the comparative ratios and related information are widely used to evaluate small businesses and privately owned firms as well.

TABLE 9-7   The Most Admired Company in Various Industries (2009)

Industry	The Most Admired Company
Apparel	Nike
Beverages	Anheuser-Busch
Consumer food products	Nestle
Soaps and cosmetics	Procter & Gamble
Credit card services	Visa
Insurance	Berkshire Hathaway
Megabanks	Bank of America
Forest and paper products	International Paper
Pharmaceuticals	Johnson & Johnson
Petroleum refining	Exxon Mobil
Electronics	General Electric
Food services	McDonald's
Railroads	Union Pacific
Motor vehicles	BMW
Industrial and farm equipment	Caterpillar
Airlines	Continental Airlines
Aerospace and defense	United Technologies
Metals	Alcoa

Source: Based on Adam Lashinsky, "The World's Most Admired Companies," *Fortune* (March 16, 2009): 81–91.

Characteristics of an Effective Evaluation System

Strategy evaluation must meet several basic requirements to be effective. First, strategy-evaluation activities must be economical; too much information can be just as bad as too little information; and too many controls can do more harm than good. Strategy-evaluation activities also should be meaningful; they should specifically relate to a firm's objectives. They should provide managers with useful information about tasks over which they have control and influence. Strategy-evaluation activities should provide timely information; on occasion and in some areas, managers may daily need information. For example, when a firm has diversified by acquiring another firm, evaluative information may be needed frequently. However, in an R&D department, daily or even weekly evaluative information could be dysfunctional. Approximate information that is timely is generally more desirable as a basis for strategy evaluation than accurate information that does not depict the present. Frequent measurement and rapid reporting may frustrate control rather than give better control. The time dimension of control must coincide with the time span of the event being measured.

Strategy evaluation should be designed to provide a true picture of what is happening. For example, in a severe economic downturn, productivity and profitability ratios may drop alarmingly, although employees and managers are actually working harder. Strategy evaluations should fairly portray this type of situation. Information derived from the strategy-evaluation process should facilitate action and should be directed to those individuals in the organization who need to take action based on it. Managers commonly ignore evaluative reports that are provided only for informational purposes; not all managers need to receive all reports. Controls need to be action-oriented rather than information-oriented.

The strategy-evaluation process should not dominate decisions; it should foster mutual understanding, trust, and common sense. No department should fail to cooperate with another in evaluating strategies. Strategy evaluations should be simple, not too cumbersome, and not too restrictive. Complex strategy-evaluation systems often confuse people and accomplish little. The test of an effective evaluation system is its usefulness, not its complexity.

Large organizations require a more elaborate and detailed strategy-evaluation system because it is more difficult to coordinate efforts among different divisions and functional areas. Managers in small companies often communicate daily with each other and their employees and do not need extensive evaluative reporting systems. Familiarity with local environments usually makes gathering and evaluating information much easier for small organizations than for large businesses. But the key to an effective strategy-evaluation system may be the ability to convince participants that failure to accomplish certain objectives within a prescribed time is not necessarily a reflection of their performance.

There is no one ideal strategy-evaluation system. The unique characteristics of an organization, including its size, management style, purpose, problems, and strengths, can determine a strategy-evaluation and control system's final design. Robert Waterman offered the following observation about successful organizations' strategy-evaluation and control systems:

> Successful companies treat facts as friends and controls as liberating. Morgan Guaranty and Wells Fargo not only survive but thrive in the troubled waters of bank deregulation, because their strategy evaluation and control systems are sound, their risk is contained, and they know themselves and the competitive situation so well. Successful companies have a voracious hunger for facts. They see information where others see only data. They love comparisons, rankings, anything that removes decision making from the realm of mere opinion. Successful companies maintain tight, accurate financial controls. Their people don't regard controls as an imposition of autocracy but as the benign checks and balances that allow them to be creative and free.[10]

Contingency Planning

A basic premise of good strategic management is that firms plan ways to deal with unfavorable and favorable events before they occur. Too many organizations prepare contingency plans just for unfavorable events; this is a mistake, because both minimizing threats and capitalizing on opportunities can improve a firm's competitive position.

Regardless of how carefully strategies are formulated, implemented, and evaluated, unforeseen events, such as strikes, boycotts, natural disasters, arrival of foreign competitors, and government actions, can make a strategy obsolete. To minimize the impact of potential threats, organizations should develop contingency plans as part of their strategy-evaluation process. *Contingency plans* can be defined as alternative plans that can be put into effect if certain key events do not occur as expected. Only high-priority areas require the insurance of contingency plans. Strategists cannot and should not try to cover all bases by planning for all possible contingencies. But in any case, contingency plans should be as simple as possible.

Some contingency plans commonly established by firms include the following:

1. If a major competitor withdraws from particular markets as intelligence reports indicate, what actions should our firm take?
2. If our sales objectives are not reached, what actions should our firm take to avoid profit losses?
3. If demand for our new product exceeds plans, what actions should our firm take to meet the higher demand?
4. If certain disasters occur—such as loss of computer capabilities; a hostile takeover attempt; loss of patent protection; or destruction of manufacturing facilities because of earthquakes, tornadoes or hurricanes—what actions should our firm take?
5. If a new technological advancement makes our new product obsolete sooner than expected, what actions should our firm take?

Too many organizations discard alternative strategies not selected for implementation although the work devoted to analyzing these options would render valuable information. Alternative strategies not selected for implementation can serve as contingency plans in case the strategy or strategies selected do not work. U.S. companies and governments are increasingly considering nuclear-generated electricity as the most efficient means of power generation. Many contingency plans certainly call for nuclear power rather than for coal- and gas-derived electricity.

When strategy-evaluation activities reveal the need for a major change quickly, an appropriate contingency plan can be executed in a timely way. Contingency plans can promote a strategist's ability to respond quickly to key changes in the internal and external bases of an organization's current strategy. For example, if underlying assumptions about the economy turn out to be wrong and contingency plans are ready, then managers can make appropriate changes promptly.

In some cases, external or internal conditions present unexpected opportunities. When such opportunities occur, contingency plans could allow an organization to quickly capitalize on them. Linneman and Chandran reported that contingency planning gave users, such as DuPont, Dow Chemical, Consolidated Foods, and Emerson Electric, three major benefits: (1) It permitted quick response to change, (2) it prevented panic in crisis situations, and (3) it made managers more adaptable by encouraging them to appreciate just how variable the future can be. They suggested that effective contingency planning involves a seven-step process:

1. Identify both beneficial and unfavorable events that could possibly derail the strategy or strategies.
2. Specify trigger points. Calculate about when contingent events are likely to occur.
3. Assess the impact of each contingent event. Estimate the potential benefit or harm of each contingent event.
4. Develop contingency plans. Be sure that contingency plans are compatible with current strategy and are economically feasible.

5. Assess the counterimpact of each contingency plan. That is, estimate how much each contingency plan will capitalize on or cancel out its associated contingent event. Doing this will quantify the potential value of each contingency plan.

6. Determine early warning signals for key contingent events. Monitor the early warning signals.

7. For contingent events with reliable early warning signals, develop advance action plans to take advantage of the available lead time.[11]

Auditing

A frequently used tool in strategy evaluation is the audit. *Auditing* is defined by the American Accounting Association (AAA) as "a systematic process of objectively obtaining and evaluating evidence regarding assertions about economic actions and events to ascertain the degree of correspondence between these assertions and established criteria, and communicating the results to interested users."[12]

Auditors examine the financial statement of firms to determine whether they have been prepared according to generally accepted accounting principles (GAAP) and whether they fairly represent the activities of the firm. Independent auditors use a set of standards called *generally accepted auditing standards* (GAAS). Public accounting firms often have a consulting arm that provides strategy-evaluation services. The SEC in late 2009 charged General Electric with accounting fraud, specifically for inflating its earnings and revenues in prior years. GE has agreed to pay $50 million to settle the charges. (Students—when preparing projected financial statements as described in Chapter 8, do not inflate the numbers.)

The new era of international financial reporting standards (IFRS) appears unstoppable, and businesses need to go ahead and get ready to use IFRS. Many U.S. companies now report their finances using both the old generally accepted accounting standards (GAAP) and the new IFRS. "If companies don't prepare, if they don't start three years in advance," warns business professor Donna Street at the University of Dayton, "they're going to be in big trouble." GAAP standards comprised 25,000 pages, whereas IFRS comprises only 5,000 pages, so in that sense IFRS is less cumbersome.

This accounting switch from GAAP to IFRS in the United States is going to cost businesses millions of dollars in fees and upgraded software systems and training. U.S. CPAs need to study global accounting principles intensely, and business schools should go ahead and begin teaching students the new accounting standards.

All companies have the option to use the IFRS procedures in 2011, and then all companies are required to use IFRS in 2014, unless that timetable is changed. The U.S. Chamber of Commerce supports the change, saying it will lead to much more cross-border commerce and will help the United States compete in the world economy. Already the European Union and 113 nations have adopted or soon plan to use international rules, including Australia, China, India, Mexico, and Canada. So the United States likely will also adopt IFRS rules on schedule, but this switch could unleash a legal and regulatory nightmare. The United States lags the rest of the world in global accounting. But a few U.S. multinational firms already use IFRS for their foreign subsidiaries, such as United Technologies (UT). UT derives more than 60 percent of its revenues from abroad and is already training its entire staff to use IFRS. UT has redone its 2007 through 2009 financial statements in the IFRS format.

Movement to IFRS from GAAP encompasses a company's entire operations, including auditing, oversight, cash management, taxes, technology, software, investing, acquiring, merging, importing, exporting, pension planning, and partnering. Switching from GAAP to IFRS is also likely to be plagued by gaping differences in business customs, financial regulations, tax laws, politics, and other factors. One critic of the upcoming switch is Charles Niemeier of the Public Company Accounting Oversight Board, who says the switch "has the potential to be a Tower of Babel," costing firms millions when they do not even have thousands to spend.

Others say the switch will help U.S. companies raise capital abroad and do business with firms abroad. Perhaps the biggest upside of the switch is that IFRS rules are more streamlined and less complex than GAAP. Lenovo, the China-based technology firm that bought IBM's personal computer business, is a big advocate of IFRS. Lenovo's view is that they desire to be a world company rather than a U.S. or Chinese company, so the faster the switch to IFRS, the better for them. The bottom line is that IFRS is coming to the United States, sooner than later, so we all need to gear up for this switch as soon as possible.[13]

Twenty-First-Century Challenges in Strategic Management

Three particular challenges or decisions that face all strategists today are (1) deciding whether the process should be more an art or a science, (2) deciding whether strategies should be visible or hidden from stakeholders, and (3) deciding whether the process should be more top-down or bottom-up in their firm.[14]

The Art or Science Issue

This textbook is consistent with most of the strategy literature in advocating that strategic management be viewed more as a science than an art. This perspective contends that firms need to systematically assess their external and internal environments, conduct research, carefully evaluate the pros and cons of various alternatives, perform analyses, and then decide upon a particular course of action. In contrast, Mintzberg's notion of "crafting" strategies embodies the artistic model, which suggests that strategic decision making be based primarily on holistic thinking, intuition, creativity, and imagination.[15] Mintzberg and his followers reject strategies that result from objective analysis, preferring instead subjective imagination. "Strategy scientists" reject strategies that emerge from emotion, hunch, creativity, and politics. Proponents of the artistic view often consider strategic planning exercises to be time poorly spent. The Mintzberg philosophy insists on informality, whereas strategy scientists (and this text) insist on more formality. Mintzberg refers to strategic planning as an "emergent" process whereas strategy scientists use the term "deliberate" process.[16]

The answer to the art versus science question is one that strategists must decide for themselves, and certainly the two approaches are not mutually exclusive. In deciding which approach is more effective, however, consider that the business world today has become increasingly complex and more intensely competitive. There is less room for error in strategic planning. Recall that Chapter 1 discussed the importance of intuition and experience and subjectivity in strategic planning, and even the weights and ratings discussed in Chapters 3, 4, and 6 certainly require good judgment. But the idea of deciding on strategies for any firm without thorough research and analysis, at least in the mind of this writer, is unwise. Certainly, in smaller firms there can be more informality in the process compared to larger firms, but even for smaller firms, a wealth of competitive information is available on the Internet and elsewhere and should be collected, assimilated, and evaluated before deciding on a course of action upon which survival of the firm may hinge. The livelihood of countless employees and shareholders may hinge on the effectiveness of strategies selected. Too much is at stake to be less than thorough in formulating strategies. It is not wise for a strategist to rely too heavily on gut feeling and opinion instead of research data, competitive intelligence, and analysis in formulating strategies.

The Visible or Hidden Issue

An interesting aspect of any competitive analysis discussion is whether strategies themselves should be secret or open within firms. The Chinese warrior Sun Tzu and military leaders today strive to keep strategies secret, as war is based on deception. However, for a business organization, secrecy may not be best. Keeping strategies secret from employees and stakeholders at large could severely inhibit employee and stakeholder communication, understanding, and commitment and also forgo valuable input that these persons could have regarding formulation and/or implementation of that strategy. Thus strategists in a particular firm must decide for themselves whether the risk of rival firms easily knowing and exploiting a firm's strategies is worth the benefit of improved employee and stakeholder motivation and input. Most executives agree that some strategic information should remain confidential to top managers, and that steps should be taken to ensure that such information is not disseminated beyond the inner circle. For a firm that you may own or manage, would you advocate openness or secrecy in regard to strategies being formulated and implemented?

There are certainly good reasons to keep the strategy process and strategies themselves visible and open rather than hidden and secret. There are also good reasons to keep strategies hidden from all but top-level executives. Strategists must decide for themselves what is best for their firms. This text comes down largely on the side of being visible and open, but certainly this may not be best for all strategists and all firms. As pointed out in Chapter 1, Sun Tzu argued that all war is based on deception and that the best maneuvers are those not easily predicted by rivals. Business and war are analogous.

Some reasons to be completely open with the strategy process and resultant decisions are these:

1. Managers, employees, and other stakeholders can readily contribute to the process. They often have excellent ideas. Secrecy would forgo many excellent ideas.
2. Investors, creditors, and other stakeholders have greater basis for supporting a firm when they know what the firm is doing and where the firm is going.
3. Visibility promotes democracy, whereas secrecy promotes autocracy. Domestic firms and most foreign firms prefer democracy over autocracy as a management style.
4. Participation and openness enhance understanding, commitment, and communication within the firm.

Reasons why some firms prefer to conduct strategic planning in secret and keep strategies hidden from all but the highest-level executives are as follows:

1. Free dissemination of a firm's strategies may easily translate into competitive intelligence for rival firms who could exploit the firm given that information.
2. Secrecy limits criticism, second guessing, and hindsight.
3. Participants in a visible strategy process become more attractive to rival firms who may lure them away.
4. Secrecy limits rival firms from imitating or duplicating the firm's strategies and undermining the firm.

The obvious benefits of the visible versus hidden extremes suggest that a working balance must be sought between the apparent contradictions. Parnell says that in a perfect world all key individuals both inside and outside the firm should be involved in strategic planning, but in practice particularly sensitive and confidential information should always remain strictly confidential to top managers.[17] This balancing act is difficult but essential for survival of the firm.

The Top-Down or Bottom-Up Approach

Proponents of the top-down approach contend that top executives are the only persons in the firm with the collective experience, acumen, and fiduciary responsibility to make key strategy decisions. In contrast, bottom-up advocates argue that lower- and middle-level managers and employees who will be implementing the strategies need to be actively involved in the process of formulating the strategies to ensure their support and commitment. Recent strategy research and this textbook emphasize the bottom-up approach, but earlier work by Schendel and Hofer stressed the need for firms to rely on perceptions of their top managers in strategic planning.[18] Strategists must reach a working balance of the two approaches in a manner deemed best for their firms at a particular time, while cognizant of the fact that current research supports the bottom-up approach, at least among U.S. firms. Increased education and diversity of the workforce at all levels are reasons why middle- and lower-level managers—and even nonmanagers—should be invited to participate in the firm's strategic planning process, at least to the extent that they are willing and able to contribute.

Conclusion

This chapter presents a strategy-evaluation framework that can facilitate accomplishment of annual and long-term objectives. Effective strategy evaluation allows an organization to capitalize on internal strengths as they develop, to exploit external opportunities as they emerge, to recognize and defend against threats, and to mitigate internal weaknesses before they become detrimental.

Strategists in successful organizations take the time to formulate, implement, and then evaluate strategies deliberately and systematically. Good strategists move their organization forward with purpose and direction, continually evaluating and improving the firm's external and internal strategic positions. Strategy evaluation allows an organization to shape its own future rather than allowing it to be constantly shaped by remote forces that have little or no vested interest in the well-being of the enterprise.

Although not a guarantee for success, strategic management allows organizations to make effective long-term decisions, to execute those decisions efficiently, and to take corrective actions as needed to ensure success. Computer networks and the Internet help to coordinate strategic-management activities and to ensure that decisions are based on good information. The Checkmate Strategic Planning Software is especially good in this regard (www.checkmateplan.com). A key to effective strategy evaluation and to successful strategic management is an integration of intuition and analysis:

A potentially fatal problem is the tendency for analytical and intuitive issues to polarize. This polarization leads to strategy evaluation that is dominated by either analysis or intuition, or to strategy evaluation that is discontinuous, with a lack of coordination among analytical and intuitive issues.[19]

Strategists in successful organizations realize that strategic management is first and foremost a people process. It is an excellent vehicle for fostering organizational communication. People are what make the difference in organizations.

The real key to effective strategic management is to accept the premise that the planning process is more important than the written plan, that the manager is continuously planning and does not stop planning when the written plan is finished. The written plan is only a snapshot as of the moment it is approved. If the manager is not planning on a continuous basis—planning, measuring, and revising—the written plan can become obsolete the day it is finished. This obsolescence becomes more of a certainty as the increasingly rapid rate of change makes the business environment more uncertain.[20]

We invite you to visit the David page on the Prentice Hall Companion Web site at http://www.pearsonhighered.com/david for this chapter's review quiz.

Key Terms and Concepts

Advantage (p. 288)
Auditing (p. 300)
Balanced Scorecard (p. 295)
Consistency (p. 288)
Consonance (p. 288)
Contingency Plans (p. 299)
Feasibility (p. 288)
Future Shock (p. 295)

GAAS, GAAP, and IFRS (p. 300)
Management by Wandering Around (p. 290)
Measuring Organizational Performance (p. 292)
Reviewing the Underlying Bases of an Organization's Strategy (p. 290)
Revised EFE Matrix (p. 291)
Revised IFE Matrix (p. 290)
Taking Corrective Actions (p. 294)

Issues for Review and Discussion

1. Discuss the nature and implications of the upcoming accounting switch from GAAP to IFRS in the United States.
2. Ask an accounting professor at your college or university the following question and report back to the class: "To what extent would my learning the IFRS standards on my own give me competitive advantage in the job market?"
3. Give an example of "consonance" other than the one provided by Rumelt in the chapter.
4. Evaluating strategies on a continuous rather than a periodic basis is desired. Discuss the pros and cons of this statement.
5. How often should an organization's vision/mission be changed in light of strategy evaluation activities?
6. Compare Mintzberg's notion of "crafting" strategies with this textbook's notion of "gathering and assimilating information" to formulate strategies.
7. Why has strategy evaluation become so important in business today?
8. BellSouth Services is considering putting divisional EFE and IFE matrices online for continual updating. How would this affect strategy evaluation?
9. What types of quantitative and qualitative criteria do you think Ellen Kullman, CEO of DuPont, uses to evaluate the company's strategy?
10. As owner of a local, independent supermarket, explain how you would evaluate the firm's strategy.
11. Under what conditions are corrective actions not required in the strategy-evaluation process?
12. Identify types of organizations that may need to evaluate strategy more frequently than others. Justify your choices.
13. As executive director of the state forestry commission, in what way and how frequently would you evaluate the organization's strategies?
14. Identify some key financial ratios that would be important in evaluating a bank's strategy.
15. As owner of a chain of hardware stores, describe how you would approach contingency planning.
16. Strategy evaluation allows an organization to take a proactive stance toward shaping its own future. Discuss the meaning of this statement.
17. Explain and discuss the Balanced Scorecard.
18. Why is the Balanced Scorecard an important topic both in devising objectives and in evaluating strategies?
19. Develop a Balanced Scorecard for a local fast-food restaurant.
20. Do you believe strategic management should be more visible or hidden as a process in a firm? Explain.
21. Do you feel strategic management should be more a top-down or bottom-up process in a firm? Explain.
22. Do you believe strategic management is more an art or a science? Explain.

Notes

1. Dale McConkey, "Planning in a Changing Environment," *Business Horizons* (September–October 1988): 64.
2. Robert Simons, "Control in an Age of Empowerment," *Harvard Business Review* (March–April 1995): 80.
3. Dale Zand, "Reviewing the Policy Process," *California Management Review* 21, no. 1 (Fall 1978): 37.
4. Eccles. 3: 1–8.
5. Claude George Jr., *The History of Management Thought* (Upper Saddle River, New Jersey: Prentice Hall, 1968): 165–166.
6. M. Erez and F. Kanfer, "The Role of Goal Acceptance in Goal Setting and Task Performance," *Academy of Management Review* 8, no. 3 (July 1983): 457.
7. D. Hussey and M. Langham, *Corporate Planning: The Human Factor* (Oxford, England: Pergamon Press, 1979): 138.
8. Carter Bayles, "Strategic Control: The President's Paradox," *Business Horizons* 20, no. 4 (August 1977): 18.
9. Adam Lashinsky, "The World's Most Admired Companies," *Fortune* (March 16, 2009): 81–91.
10. Robert Waterman, Jr., "How the Best Get Better," *BusinessWeek* (September 14, 1987): 105.
11. Robert Linneman and Rajan Chandran, "Contingency Planning: A Key to Swift Managerial Action in the Uncertain Tomorrow," *Managerial Planning* 29, no. 4 (January–February 1981): 23–27.

12. American Accounting Association, *Report of Committee on Basic Auditing Concepts* (1971): 15–74.

13. Edward Iwata, "Will Going Global Extend to Accounting?" *USA Today* (January 6, 2009): B1.

14. John Parnell, "Five Critical Challenges in Strategy Making," *SAM Advanced Management Journal* 68, no. 2 (Spring 2003): 15–22.

15. Henry Mintzberg, "Crafting Strategy," *Harvard Business Review* (July–August 1987): 66–75.

16. Henry Mintzberg and J. Waters, "Of Strategies, Deliberate and Emergent," *Strategic Management Journal* 6, no. 2: 257–272.

17. Parnell, 15–22.

18. D. E. Schendel and C. W. Hofer (Eds.), *Strategic Management* (Boston: Little, Brown, 1979).

19. Michael McGinnis, "The Key to Strategic Planning: Integrating Analysis and Intuition," *Sloan Management Review* 26, no. 1 (Fall 1984): 49.

20. McConkey, 72.

Current Readings

Franken, Arnoud, Chris Edwards, and Rob Lambert, "Executing Strategic Change: Understanding the Critical Management Elements That Lead to Success." *California Management Review* (Spring 2009): 49–73.

Giraudeau, Martin. "The Drafts of Strategy: Opening Up Plans and Their Uses." *Long Range Planning* 41, no. 3 (June 2008): 291.

Hall, Joseph, and Eric Johnson. "When Should a Process Be Art, Not Science?" *Harvard Business Review* (March 2009): 58–65.

Jarzablowski, Paula. "Shaping Strategy as a Structuration Process." *The Academy of Management Journal* 51, no. 4 (August 2008): 621.

Li, Jing, Changhui Zhou, and Edward Zajac. "Control, Collaboration, and Productivity in International Joint Ventures: Theory and Evidence." *Strategic Management Journal* (August 2009): 865–884.

McFarland, Keith R. "Should You Build Strategy Like You Build Software?" *MIT Sloan Management Review* 49, no. 3 (Spring 2008): 69.

Neilson, Gary L., Karla L. Martin, and Elizabeth Powers. "The Secrets to Successful Strategy Execution." *Harvard Business Review* (June 2008): 60.

Pieter de Man, Ard, and Nadine Roijakkers. "Alliance Governance: Balancing Control and Trust in Dealing with Risk." *Long Range Planning* (February 2009): 75–95.

ASSURANCE OF LEARNING EXERCISES

Assurance of Learning Exercise 9A

Preparing a Strategy-Evaluation Report for McDonald's Corp.

Purpose

This exercise can give you experience locating strategy-evaluation information. Use of the Internet coupled with published sources of information can significantly enhance the strategy-evaluation process. Performance information on competitors, for example, can help put into perspective a firm's own performance.

Instructions

Step 1 Visit http://marketwatch.multexinvestor.com, http://moneycentral.msn.com, http://finance.yahoo.com, www.clearstation.com to locate strategy-evaluation information on competitors. Read some recent articles that discuss the fast-food restaurant business.

Step 2 Summarize your research findings by preparing a strategy-evaluation report for your instructor. Include in your report a summary of McDonald's strategies and performance in 2010 and a summary of your conclusions regarding the effectiveness of McDonald's strategies.

Step 3 Based on your analysis, do you feel that McDonald's is pursuing effective strategies? What recommendations would you offer to McDonald's chief executive officer?

Assurance of Learning Exercise 9B

Evaluating My University's Strategies

Purpose

An important part of evaluating strategies is determining the nature and extent of changes in an organization's external opportunities/threats and internal strengths/weaknesses. Changes in these underlying critical success factors can indicate a need to change or modify the firm's strategies.

Instructions

As a class, discuss positive and negative changes in your university's external and internal factors during your college career. Begin by listing on the board new or emerging opportunities and threats. Then identify strengths and weaknesses that have changed significantly during your college career. In light of the external and internal changes that were identified, discuss whether your university's strategies need modifying. Are there any new strategies that you would recommend? Make a list to recommend to your department chair, dean, president, or chancellor.

CHAPTER 10

Business Ethics/ Social Responsibility/ Environmental Sustainability

CHAPTER OBJECTIVES

After studying this chapter, you should be able to do the following:

1. Explain why good ethics is good business in strategic management.

2. Explain how firms can best ensure that their code of business ethics guides decision making instead of being ignored.

3. Explain why whistle-blowing is important to encourage in a firm.

4. Discuss the nature and role of corporate sustainability reports.

5. Discuss specific ways that firms can be good stewards of the natural environment.

6. Explain ISO 14000 and 14001.

Assurance of Learning Exercises

Assurance of Learning Exercise 10A
Does McDonald's Have a Code of Business Ethics?

Assurance of Learning Exercise 10B
The Ethics of Spying on Competitors

Assurance of Learning Exercise 10C
Who Prepares a Sustainability Report?

Source: Ivan Cholakov Gostock

"Notable Quotes"

"If business is not based on ethical grounds, it is of no benefit to society and will, like all other unethical combinations, pass into oblivion."

—C. Max Killan

"Good ethics is good business."

"Do unto others as you would have them do unto you."

"Be joyful when you do things to conserve, preserve, and enhance the natural environment."

Doing Great in a Weak Economy. How?

Walt Disney

When most firms were struggling in 2008, Walt Disney increased its revenues from $35 billion in 2007 to $37 billion in 2008 with net income of $4.4 billion. *Fortune* magazine in 2009 rated Walt Disney their 13th "Most Admired Company in the World" in terms of management and performance.

Walt Disney is cutting carbon emissions from fuels by half by 2012, and ultimately will emit zero greenhouse gas emissions at its office and retail complexes, theme parks, and cruise lines. Disney's long-term goal is to cut to zero the amount of waste it sends to landfills, which totaled nearly 300,000 tons in 2006, much of it from construction, through diverting some to recycling centers, composting, and buying more postconsumer recycled materials. Beth Stevens, senior vice president of environmental affairs, said Disney has "not put a definite time horizon" on taking emissions to zero and may have to rely in part on technology that is still under development to reach that goal. "We set those (goals) because they were very aspirational," Stevens said. "We thought it was important . . . to communicate a sense of commitment." The environmental plan was released in 2009 in its "corporate responsibility" report.

"Current scientific conclusions indicate that urgent reductions in greenhouse gas emissions are required to avert accelerated climate change," the report said. "A successful response to these challenges demands fundamental changes in the way society, including businesses, use natural resources, and Disney is no exception." Disney works with Conservation International on emissions reduction targets, and it plans to have a third party monitor its progress through annual audits. By 2013, Disney plans to reduce its electricity consumption by 10 percent compared with its 2006 baseline.

The world's number two media conglomerate (behind Time Warner) has extensive assets in movies,

music, publishing, television, and theme parks. Walt Disney's TV holdings include the ABC television network and 10 broadcast stations, as well as cable networks including ABC Family, A&E Television Networks (37 percent owned), and ESPN (80 percent). Walt Disney Studios produces films through such imprints as Walt Disney Pictures, Touchstone, Pixar, and Miramax. Walt Disney Parks and Resorts is one of the top theme park operators in the world, anchored by its popular Walt Disney World and Disneyland resorts. In

May 2009, Disney formed a partnership with Hulu.com to stream ABC's full-episode television programming online as well as many of titles for Disney's television and movie library. In July, Disney announced it would fund a 50/50, $452 million expansion of Disneyland Park in Hong Kong with that city's government.

Source: Geoff Colvin, "The World's Most Admired Companies," *Fortune* (March 16, 2009): 76–86; http://www.reuters.com/article/marketsNews/idAFN0939621220090310?rpc=44.

Although the three sections of this chapter (Business Ethics, Social Responsibility, and Sustainability) are distinct, the topics are quite related. Many people, for example, consider it unethical for a firm to be socially irresponsible. *Social responsibility* refers to actions an organization takes beyond what is legally required to protect or enhance the well-being of living things. *Sustainability* refers to the extent that an organization's operations and actions protect, mend, and preserve rather than harm or destroy the natural environment. Polluting the environment, for example, is unethical, irresponsible, and in many cases illegal. Business ethics, social responsibility, and sustainability issues therefore are interrelated and impact all areas of the comprehensive strategic-management model, as illustrated in Figure 10.1 on page 312.

A sample company that adheres to the highest ethical standards and that has excelled during the recent weak economy is Walt Disney. Disney in March 2009 published an elaborate corporate social responsibility/business ethics/sustainability report that can be found online at http://disney.go.com/crreport/home.html. In that report, the Disney CEO says:

Our Corporate Responsibility team has developed a cohesive strategy for the company with that in mind, incorporating existing outreach, safety, nutrition, environmental and labor programs and working with executives across Disney, ABC and ESPN to coordinate and strengthen our company-wide efforts. They've organized our approach around five broad areas—Children & Family, Content & Products, Environment, Community and Workplaces—with the goal of further embedding corporate responsibility into Disney's business DNA, making sure it continues to be taken into consideration in decisions big and small.[1]

Business Ethics

Good ethics is good business. Bad ethics can derail even the best strategic plans. This chapter provides an overview of the importance of business ethics in strategic management. *Business ethics* can be defined as principles of conduct within organizations that guide decision making and behavior. Good business ethics is a prerequisite for good strategic management; good ethics is just good business!

A rising tide of consciousness about the importance of business ethics is sweeping the United States and the rest of the world. Strategists such as CEOs and business owners are the individuals primarily responsible for ensuring that high ethical principles are espoused and practiced in an organization. All strategy formulation, implementation, and evaluation decisions have ethical ramifications.

Newspapers and business magazines daily report legal and moral breaches of ethical conduct by both public and private organizations. Being unethical can be very expensive. For example, some of the largest payouts for class-action legal fraud suits ever were against Enron ($7.16 billion), WorldCom ($6.16 billion), Cendant ($3.53 billion), Tyco ($2.98 billion), AOL Time Warner ($2.5 billion), Nortel Networks ($2.47 billion), and Royal Ahold ($1.09 billion). A company named Coast IRB LLC in Colorado recently was forced to close after the Food and Drug Administration (FDA) discovered in a sting operation that the firm conducted a fake medical study. Coast is one of many firms paid

FIGURE 10.1

A Comprehensive Strategic-Management Model

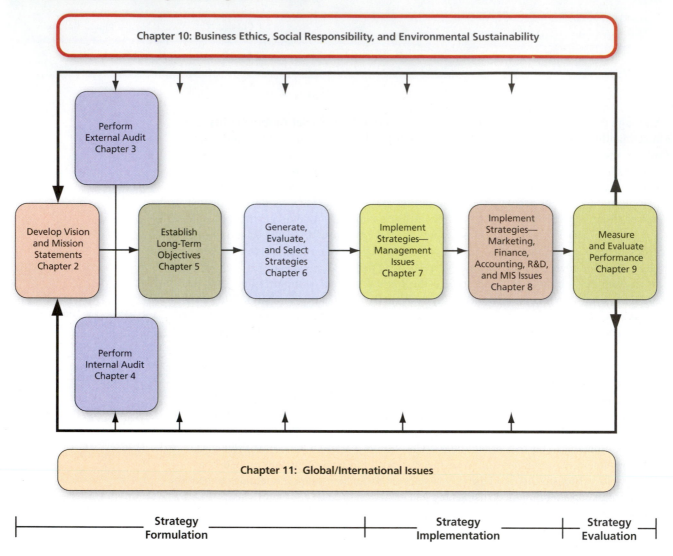

Chapter 10: Business Ethics, Social Responsibility, and Environmental Sustainability

Perform External Audit Chapter 3

Develop Vision and Mission Statements Chapter 2

Establish Long-Term Objectives Chapter 5

Generate, Evaluate, and Select Strategies Chapter 6

Implement Strategies— Management Issues Chapter 7

Implement Strategies— Marketing, Finance, Accounting, R&D, and MIS Issues Chapter 8

Measure and Evaluate Performance Chapter 9

Perform Internal Audit Chapter 4

Chapter 11: Global/International Issues

Strategy Formulation   Strategy Implementation   Strategy Evaluation

Source: Fred R. David, "How Companies Define Their Mission," *Long Range Planning* 22, no. 3 (June 1988): 40.

by pharmaceutical firms to oversee clinical trials and independently ensure that patient safety is protected.

Other business actions considered to be unethical include misleading advertising or labeling, causing environmental harm, poor product or service safety, padding expense accounts, insider trading, dumping banned or flawed products in foreign markets, not providing equal opportunities for women and minorities, overpricing, moving jobs overseas, and sexual harassment.

Code of Business Ethics

A new wave of ethics issues related to product safety, employee health, sexual harassment, AIDS in the workplace, smoking, acid rain, affirmative action, waste disposal, foreign business practices, cover-ups, takeover tactics, conflicts of interest, employee privacy, inappropriate gifts, and security of company records has accentuated the need for strategists to develop a clear code of business ethics. Internet fraud, hacking into company computers, spreading viruses, and identity theft are other unethical activities that plague every sector of online commerce.

United Technologies has a 21-page code of ethics and a vice president of business ethics. Baxter Travenol Laboratories, IBM, Caterpillar Tractor, Chemical Bank, ExxonMobil, Dow Corning, and Celanese are firms that have formal codes of business ethics. A *code of business ethics* is a document that provides behavioral guidelines that cover daily activities and decisions within an organization.

Merely having a code of ethics, however, is not sufficient to ensure ethical business behavior. A code of ethics can be viewed as a public relations gimmick, a set of platitudes, or window dressing. To ensure that the code is read, understood, believed, and remembered, periodic ethics workshops are needed to sensitize people to workplace circumstances in which ethics issues may arise.[2] If employees see examples of punishment for violating the code as well as rewards for upholding the code, this reinforces the importance of a firm's code of ethics. The Web site www.ethicsweb.ca/codes provides guidelines on how to write an effective code of ethics.

An Ethics Culture

An ethics "culture" needs to permeate organizations! To help create an ethics culture, Citicorp developed a business ethics board game that is played by thousands of employees worldwide. Called "The Word Ethic," this game asks players business ethics questions, such as how do you deal with a customer who offers you football tickets in exchange for a new, backdated IRA? Diana Robertson at the Wharton School of Business believes the game is effective because it is interactive. Many organizations have developed a code-of-conduct manual outlining ethical expectations and giving examples of situations that commonly arise in their businesses.

Harris Corporation and other firms warn managers and employees that failing to report an ethical violation by others could bring discharge. The Securities and Exchange Commission (SEC) recently strengthened its whistle-blowing policies, virtually mandating that anyone seeing unethical activity report such behavior. *Whistle-blowing* refers to policies that require employees to report any unethical violations they discover or see in the firm.

An unidentified whistle-blower in 2009 filed a lawsuit against Amgen Inc., accusing the biotechnology company of illegal marketing of its blockbuster drugs Enbrel and Aranesp. The drug company Wyeth co-markets Enbrel with Amgen, and was named as a defendant too, along with wholesale drug distributor AmerisourceBergen Corp., online health-information provider WebMD Health Corp., and others. The federal whistle-blower law protects the identity of the plaintiff. In the drug industry, such suits are often filed by former employees.

One reason strategists' salaries are high is that they must take the moral risks of the firm. Strategists are responsible for developing, communicating, and enforcing the code of business ethics for their organizations. Although primary responsibility for ensuring ethical behavior rests with a firm's strategists, an integral part of the responsibility of all managers is to provide ethics leadership by constant example and demonstration. Managers hold positions that enable them to influence and educate many people. This makes managers responsible for developing and implementing ethical decision making. Gellerman and Drucker, respectively, offer some good advice for managers:

All managers risk giving too much because of what their companies demand from them. But the same superiors, who keep pressing you to do more, or to do it better, or faster, or less expensively, will turn on you should you cross that fuzzy line between right and wrong. They will blame you for exceeding instructions or for ignoring their warnings. The smartest managers already know that the best answer to the question "How far is too far?" is don't try to find out.[3]

A man (or woman) might know too little, perform poorly, lack judgment and ability, and yet not do too much damage as a manager. But if that person lacks character and integrity—no matter how knowledgeable, how brilliant, how successful— he destroys. He destroys people, the most valuable resource of the enterprise. He destroys spirit. And he destroys performance. This is particularly true of the people at the head of an enterprise. For the spirit of an organization is created from the top. If an organization is great in spirit, it is because the spirit of its top people is great. If it decays, it does so because the top rots. As the proverb has it, "Trees die from the top." No one should ever become a strategist unless he or she is willing to have his or her character serve as the model for subordinates.[4]

No society anywhere in the world can compete very long or successfully with people stealing from one another or not trusting one another, with every bit of information requiring notarized confirmation, with every disagreement ending up in litigation, or with government having to regulate businesses to keep them honest. Being unethical is a recipe for headaches, inefficiency, and waste. History has proven that the greater the trust and confidence of people in the ethics of an institution or society, the greater its economic strength. Business relationships are built mostly on mutual trust and reputation. Short-term decisions based on greed and questionable ethics will preclude the necessary self-respect to gain the trust of others. More and more firms believe that ethics training and an ethics culture create strategic advantage.

Ethics training programs should include messages from the CEO or owner of the business emphasizing ethical business practices, the development and discussion of codes of ethics, and procedures for discussing and reporting unethical behavior. Firms can align ethical and strategic decision making by incorporating ethical considerations into long-term planning, by integrating ethical decision making into the performance appraisal process, by encouraging whistle-blowing or the reporting of unethical practices, and by monitoring departmental and corporate performance regarding ethical issues.

Bribes

Bribery is defined by *Black's Law Dictionary* as the offering, giving, receiving, or soliciting of any item of value to influence the actions of an official or other person in discharge of a public or legal duty. A *bribe* is a gift bestowed to influence a recipient's conduct. The gift may be any money, good, right in action, property, preferment, privilege, emolument, object of value, advantage, or merely a promise or undertaking to induce or influence the action, vote, or influence of a person in an official or public capacity. Bribery is a crime in most countries of the world, including the United States.[5]

Siemens AG, the large German engineering firm, recently was fined $800 million for routinely offering bribes to various companies around the world to win overseas contracts. The U.S. Justice Department and the SEC brought suit against Siemens under the U.S. Foreign Corruptions Act. The Siemens fine was 20 times larger than any previous bribery penalty. The SEC claimed that Siemens made at least 4,283 bribe payments totaling $1.4 billion between 2001 and 2007. These bribes allegedly were paid to government officials in 10 countries.

Paying bribes is considered both illegal and unethical in the United States, but in some foreign countries, paying bribes and kickbacks is acceptable. Tipping is even considered bribery in some countries. Important antibribery and extortion initiatives are advocated by many organizations, including the World Bank, the International Monetary Fund, the European Union, the Council of Europe, the Organization of American States, the Pacific Basin Economic Council, the Global Coalition for Africa, and the United Nations.

The U.S. Justice Department in mid-2009 increased its prosecutions of alleged acts of foreign bribery. Businesses have to be much more careful these days. For years, taking business associates to lavish dinners and giving them expensive holiday gifts and even outright cash may be expected in many countries, such as South Korea and China, but there is now stepped-up enforcement of bribery laws. Kellogg Brown and Root (KBR) and Halliburton recently paid $579 million for bribing officials in Nigeria.

Love Affairs at Work

A recent *Wall Street Journal* article recapped current American standards regarding boss-subordinate love affairs at work.[6] Only 5 percent of all firms sampled had no restrictions on such relationships; 80 percent of firms have policies that prohibit relationships between a supervisor and a subordinate. Only 4 percent of firms strictly prohibited such relationships, but 39 percent of firms had policies that required individuals to inform their supervisors whenever a romantic relationship begins with a coworker. Only 24 percent of firms required the two persons to be in different departments.

In Europe, romantic relationships at work are largely viewed as private matters and most firms have no policies on the practice. However, European firms are increasingly adopting explicit, American-style sexual harassment laws. The U.S. military strictly bans officers from dating or having sexual relationships with enlistees. At the World Bank, sexual relations between a supervisor and an employee are considered "a de facto conflict of interest which must be resolved to avoid favoritism." World Bank president Paul Wolfowitz recently was forced to resign due to a relationship he had with a bank staff person.

The United Nations (UN) in mid-2009 was struggling with its own sexual-harassment complaints as many women employees say the organization's current system for handling complaints is arbitrary, unfair, and mired in bureaucracy. Sexual harassment cases at the UN can take years to adjudicate, and accusers have no access to investigative reports. The UN plans to "soon" make changes to its internal justice system for handling harassment complaints; the UN aspires to protect human rights around the world.

Social Responsibility

Some strategists agree with Ralph Nader, who proclaims that organizations have tremendous social obligations. Nader points out, for example, that Exxon/Mobil has more assets than most countries, and because of this such firms have an obligation to help society cure its many ills. Other people, however, agree with the economist Milton Friedman, who asserts that organizations have no obligation to do any more for society than is legally required. Friedman may contend that it is irresponsible for a firm to give monies to charity.

Do you agree more with Nader or Friedman? Surely we can all agree that the first social responsibility of any business must be to make enough profit to cover the costs of the future because if this is not achieved, no other social responsibility can be met. Indeed, no social need can be met by the firm if the firm fails.

Strategists should examine social problems in terms of potential costs and benefits to the firm, and focus on social issues that could benefit the firm most. For example, should a firm avoid laying off employees so as to protect the employees' livelihood, when that decision may force the firm to liquidate?

Social Policy

The term *social policy* embraces managerial philosophy and thinking at the highest level of the firm, which is why the topic is covered in this textbook. Social policy concerns what responsibilities the firm has to employees, consumers, environmentalists, minorities, communities, shareholders, and other groups. After decades of debate, many firms still struggle to determine appropriate social policies.

The impact of society on business and vice versa is becoming more pronounced each year. Corporate social policy should be designed and articulated during strategy formulation, set and administered during strategy implementation, and reaffirmed or changed during strategy evaluation.[7]

In 2009, the most admired companies for social responsibility according to *Fortune* magazine were as follows:

1. Anheuser-Busch
2. Marriott International
3. Integrys Energy Group
4. Walt Disney
5. Herman Miller
6. Edison
7. Starbucks
8. Steelcase

9. Union Pacific
10. Fortune Brands[8]

From a social responsibility perspective, these were the least admired companies in 2009:

1. Circuit City Stores
2. Family Dollar Stores
3. Dillard's
4. Sears Holdings
5. Tribune
6. Hon Hai Precision Industry
7. Fiat
8. PEMEX
9. Surgutneftegas
10. Huawei Technologies[9]

Firms should strive to engage in social activities that have economic benefits. Merck & Co. once developed the drug ivermectin for treating river blindness, a disease caused by a fly-borne parasitic worm endemic in poor tropical areas of Africa, the Middle East, and Latin America. In an unprecedented gesture that reflected its corporate commitment to social responsibility, Merck then made ivermectin available at no cost to medical personnel throughout the world. Merck's action highlights the dilemma of orphan drugs, which offer pharmaceutical companies no economic incentive for profitable development and distribution. Merck did however garner substantial goodwill among its stakeholders for its actions.

Social Policies on Retirement

Some countries around the world are facing severe workforce shortages associated with their aging populations. The percentage of persons age 65 or older exceeds 20 percent in Japan, Italy, and Germany—and will reach 20 percent in 2018 in France. In 2036, the percentage of persons age 65 or older will reach 20 percent in the United States and China. Unlike the United States, Japan is reluctant to rely on large-scale immigration to bolster its workforce. Instead, Japan provides incentives for its elderly to work until ages 65 to 75. Western European countries are doing the opposite, providing incentives for its elderly to retire at ages 55 to 60. The International Labor Organization says 71 percent of Japanese men ages 60 to 64 work, compared to 57 percent of American men and just 17 percent of French men in the same age group.

Sachiko Ichioka, a typical 67-year-old man in Japan, says, "I want to work as long as I'm healthy. The extra money means I can go on trips, and I'm not a burden on my children." Better diet and health care have raised Japan's life expectancy now to 82, the highest in the world. Japanese women are having on average only 1.28 children compared to 2.04 in the United States. Keeping the elderly at work, coupled with reversing the old-fashioned trend of keeping women at home, are Japan's two key remedies for sustaining its workforce in factories and businesses. This prescription for dealing with problems associated with an aging society should be considered by many countries around the world. The Japanese government is phasing in a shift from age 60 to age 65 as the date when a person may begin receiving a pension, and premiums paid by Japanese employees are rising while payouts are falling. Unlike the United States, Japan has no law against discrimination based on age.

Japan's huge national debt, 175 percent of gross domestic product (GDP) compared to 65 percent for the United States, is difficult to lower with a falling population because Japan has fewer taxpaying workers. Worker productivity increases in Japan are not able to offset declines in number of workers, thus resulting in a decline in overall economic production. Like many countries, Japan does not view immigration as a good way to solve this problem.

Japan's shrinking workforce has become such a concern that the government just recently allowed an unspecified number of Indonesian and Filipino nurses and caregivers to work in Japan for two years. The number of working-age Japanese—those between ages 15 and 64—is projected to shrink to 70 million by 2030, from 82 million in 2009. Using foreign workers is known as *gaikokujin roudousha* in Japanese. Many Filipinos have recently been hired now to work in agriculture and factories throughout Japan.

The percentage of foreign workers to the total population is 20 percent in the United States, nearly 10 percent in Germany, 5 percent in the United Kingdom, and less than 1 percent in Japan. But most Japanese now acknowledge that this percentage must move upward, and perhaps quickly, for their nation's economy to prosper.[10]

Environmental Sustainability

The strategies of both companies and countries are increasingly scrutinized and evaluated from a nautral environment perspective. Companies such as Wal-Mart now monitor not only the price its vendors offer for products, but also how those products are made in terms of environmental practices. A growing number of business schools offer separate courses and even a concentration in environmental management.

Businesses must not exploit and decimate the natural environment. Mark Starik at George Washington University says, "Halting and reversing worldwide ecological destruction and deterioration is a strategic issue that needs immediate and substantive attention by all businesses and managers. According to the International Standards Organization (ISO), the word *environment* is defined as "surroundings in which an organization operates, including air, water, land, natural resources, flora, fauna, humans, and their interrelation." This chapter illustrates how many firms are gaining competitive advantage by being good stewards of the natural environment.

Employees, consumers, governments, and society are especially resentful of firms that harm rather than protect the natural environment. Conversely people today are especially appreciative of firms that conduct operations in a way that mends, conserves, and preserves the natural environment. Consumer interest in businesses preserving nature's ecological balance and fostering a clean, healthy environment is high.

No business wants a reputation as being a polluter. A bad sustainability record will hurt the firm in the market, jeopardize its standing in the community, and invite scrutiny by regulators, investors, and environmentalists. Governments increasingly require businesses to behave responsibly and require, for example, that businesses publicly report the pollutants and wastes their facilities produce.

In terms of megawatts of wind power generated by various states in the United States, Iowa's 2,791 recently overtook California's 2,517, but Texas's 7,118 megawatts dwarfs all other states. Minnesota also is making substantial progress in wind power generation. New Jersey recently outfitted 200,000 utility poles with solar panels, which made it the nation's second-largest producer of solar energy behind California. New Jersey is also adding solar panels to corporate rooftops. The state's $514 million solar program will double its solar capacity to 160 megawatts by 2013. The state's goal is to obtain 3 percent of its electricity from the sun and 12 percent from offshore wind by 2020.

What Is a Sustainability Report?

Wal-Mart Stores is one among many companies today that annually provides a sustainability report that reveals how the firm's operations impact the natural environment. This document discloses to shareholders information about Wal-Mart's firm's labor practices, product sourcing, energy efficiency, environmental impact, and business ethics practices.

It is good business for a business to provide a sustainability report annually to the public. With 60,000 suppliers and over $350 billion in annual sales, Wal-Mart works with its suppliers to make sure they provide such reports. Wal-Mart monitors not only prices its vendors' offer for products, but also the vendors' social-responsibility and environmental practices. Many firms use the Wal-Mart sustainability report as a benchmark, guideline, and model to follow in preparing their own report.

The Global Reporting Initiative recently issued a set of detailed reporting guidelines specifying what information should go into sustainability reports. The proxy advisory firm Institutional Shareholder Services reports that an increasing number of shareholder groups are pushing firms to provide sustainability information annually.

Wal-Mart also now encourages and expects its 1.35 million U.S. employees to adopt what it calls Personal Sustainability Projects, which include such measures as organizing weight-loss or smoking-cessation support groups, biking to work, or starting recycling programs. Employee wellness can be a part of sustainability.

Wal-Mart is installing solar panels on its stores in California and Hawaii, providing as much as 30 percent of the power in some stores. Wal-Mart may go national with solar power if this test works well. Also moving to solar energy is department-store chain Kohl's Corp., which is converting 64 of its 80 California stores to using solar power. There are big subsidies for solar installations in some states.

Home Depot, the world's second largest retailer behind Wal-Mart, recently more than doubled its offering of environmentally friendly products such as all-natural insect repellent. Home Depot has made it much easier for consumers to find its organic products by using special labels similar to Timberland's (the outdoor company) Green Index tags. Another huge retailer, Target, now offers more than 500 choices of organic certified food and has 18 buildings in California alone powered only by solar energy. The largest solar power plant in North America is the one in Nevada that powers Nellis Air Force Base outside Las Vegas.[11]

Managers and employees of firms must be careful not to become scapegoats blamed for company environmental wrongdoings. Harming the natural environment can be unethical, illegal, and costly. When organizations today face criminal charges for polluting the environment, they increasingly turn on their managers and employees to win leniency. Employee firings and demotions are becoming common in pollution-related legal suits. Managers were fired at Darling International, Inc., and Niagara Mohawk Power Corporation for being indirectly responsible for their firms polluting water. Managers and employees today must be careful not to ignore, conceal, or disregard a pollution problem, or they may find themselves personally liable.

Lack of Standards Changing

A few years ago, firms could get away with placing "green" terminology on their products and labels using such terms as *organic*, *green*, *safe*, *earth-friendly*, *nontoxic*, and/or *natural* because there were no legal or generally accepted definitions. Today, however, such terms as these carry much more specific connotations and expectations. Uniform standards defining environmentally responsible company actions are rapidly being incorporated into our legal landscape. It has become more and more difficult for firms to make "green" claims when their actions are not substantive, comprehensive, or even true. Lack of standards once made consumers cynical about corporate environmental claims, but those claims today are increasingly being challenged in courts. Joel Makower says, "One of the main reasons to truly become a green firm is for your employees. They're the first group that needs assurance than any claims you make hold water."[12]

Around the world, political and corporate leaders now realize that the "business green" topic will not go away and in fact is gaining ground rapidly. Strategically, companies more than ever must demonstrate to their customers and stakeholders that their green efforts are substantive and set the firm apart from competitors. A firm's performance facts and figures must back up their rhetoric and be consistent with sustainability standards.

Obama Regulations

The Obama administration is imposing strict regulations requiring firms to conserve energy. Federal government buildings are being refitted with energy-efficient improvements. Alternative-energy firms are busy with new customers every day as the federal stimulus package includes adding alternative-energy infrastructure. Venture capitalists and lenders are funding new "clean technology" business start-ups, including solar power, wind power, biofuels, and insulation firms. Such firms are boosting marketing efforts, expanding geographically, and hiring more staff. Venture capital investments in clean technology companies totaled $8.4 billion in 2008, up nearly 40 percent from 2007.

A wide variety of firms are participating in this clean energy growth business, such as Seattle-based Verdiem Corporation. That firm sells software that provides centralized control over power consumption, such as remotely turning off computer monitors left on overnight.[13] General Electric plans to achieve $20 billion in sales by 2011 in eco-friendly technologies that include cleaner coal-fired power plants, a diesel-and-electric hybrid loco-motive, and agricultural silicon that cuts the amount of water and pesticide used in spray-ing fields. This is double GE's sales today in "green" products. GE has a goal to improve its energy efficiency by 30 percent between 2005 and 2012.

The Environmental Protection Agency recently reported that U.S. citizens and organizations annually spend more than about $200 billion on pollution abatement. Environmental concerns touch all aspects of a business's operations, including workplace risk exposures, packaging, waste reduction, energy use, alternative fuels, environmental cost accounting, and recycling practices.

Managing Environmental Affairs in the Firm

The ecological challenge facing all organizations requires managers to formulate strategies that preserve and conserve natural resources and control pollution. Special natural environ-ment issues include ozone depletion, global warming, depletion of rain forests, destruction of animal habitats, protecting endangered species, developing biodegradable products and packages, waste management, clean air, clean water, erosion, destruction of natural resources, and pollution control. Firms increasingly are developing green product lines that are biodegradable and/or are made from recycled products. Green products sell well.

Managing as if "health of the planet" matters requires an understanding of how international trade, competitiveness, and global resources are connected. Managing envi-ronmental affairs can no longer be simply a technical function performed by specialists in a firm; more emphasis must be placed on developing an environmental perspective among all employees and managers of the firm. Many companies are moving environmental affairs from the staff side of the organization to the line side, thus making the corporate environmental group report directly to the chief operating officer. Firms that manage envi-ronmental affairs will enhance relations with consumers, regulators, vendors, and other industry players, substantially improving their prospects of success.

Environmental strategies could include developing or acquiring green businesses, divesting or altering environment-damaging businesses, striving to become a low-cost pro-ducer through waste minimization and energy conservation, and pursuing a differentiation strategy through green-product features. In addition, firms could include an environmental representative on their board of directors, conduct regular envrionmental audits, imple-ment bonuses for favorable environmental results, become involved in environmental issues and programs, incorporate environmental values in mission statements, establish environmentally oriented objectives, acquire environmental skills, and provide environ-mental training programs for company employees and managers.

Should Students Receive Environmental Training?

The *Wall Street Journal* reports that companies actively consider environmental training in employees they hire. A recent study reported that 77 percent of corporate recruiters said "it is important to hire students with an awareness of social and environmental responsibil-ity." According to Ford Motor Company's director of corporate governance, "We want students who will help us find solutions to societal challenges and we have trouble hiring students with such skills."

The Aspen Institute contends that most business schools currently do not, but should, incorporate environmental training in all facets of their core curriculum, not just in special elective courses. The institute reports that the University of Texas, the University of North Carolina, and the University of Michigan, among others, are at the cutting edge in provid-ing environmental coverage at their respective MBA levels. Companies favor hiring graduates from such universities.

Findings from research suggest that business schools at the undergraduate level are doing a poor job of educating students on environmental issues. Business students with limited knowledge on environmental issues may make poor decisions, so business schools should address environmental issues more in their curricula. Failure to do so could result in graduates making inappropriate business decisions in regard to the natural environment. Failing to provide adequate coverage of natural environment issues and decisions in their training could make those students less attractive to employers.[14]

Reasons Why Firms Should "Be Green"

Preserving the environment should be a permanent part of doing business for the following reasons:

1. Consumer demand for environmentally safe products and packages is high.
2. Public opinion demanding that firms conduct business in ways that preserve the natural environment is strong.
3. Environmental advocacy groups now have over 20 million Americans as members.
4. Federal and state environmental regulations are changing rapidly and becoming more complex.
5. More lenders are examining the environmental liabilities of businesses seeking loans.
6. Many consumers, suppliers, distributors, and investors shun doing business with environmentally weak firms.
7. Liability suits and fines against firms having environmental problems are on the rise.

Be Proactive, Not Reactive

More firms are becoming environmentally proactive—doing more than the bare minimum to develop and implement strategies that preserve the environment. The old undesirable alternative of being environmentally reactive—changing practices only when forced to do so by law or consumer pressure more often today leads to high cleanup costs, liability suits, reduced market share, reduced customer loyalty, and higher medical costs. In contrast, a proactive policy views environmental pressures as opportunities and includes such actions as developing green products and packages, conserving energy, reducing waste, recycling, and creating a corporate culture that is environmentally sensitive.

New required diesel technology has reduced emissions by up to 98 percent in all new big trucks, at an average cost increase of $12,000 per truck. "Clean air is not free," says Rich Moskowitz, who handles regulatory affairs for the American Trucking Association, which supports the transition.[15]

ISO 14000/14001 Certification

Based in Geneva, Switzerland, the International Organization for Standardization (ISO) is a network of the national standards institutes of 147 countries, one member per country. ISO is the world's largest developer of sustainability standards. Widely accepted all over the world, ISO standards are voluntary because ISO has no legal authority to enforce their implementation. ISO itself does not regulate or legislate.

Governmental agencies in various countries, such as the Environmental Protection Agency (EPA) in the United States, have adopted ISO standards as part of their regulatory framework, and the standards are the basis of much legislation. Adoptions are sovereign decisions by the regulatory authorities, governments, and/or companies concerned.

ISO 14000 refers to a series of voluntary standards in the environmental field. The ISO 14000 family of standards concerns the extent to which a firm minimizes harmful effects on the environment caused by its activities and continually monitors and improves its own environmental performance. Included in the ISO 14000 series are the ISO 14001 standards in fields such as environmental auditing, environmental performance evaluation, environmental labeling, and life-cycle assessment.

ISO 14001 is a set of standards adopted by thousands of firms worldwide to certify to their constituencies that they are conducting business in an environmentally friendly manner. ISO 14001 standards offer a universal technical standard for environmental compliance that more and more firms are requiring not only of themselves but also of their suppliers and distributors.

The ISO 14001 standard requires that a community or organization put in place and implement a series of practices and procedures that, when taken together, result in an *environmental management system* (EMS). ISO 14001 is not a technical standard and as such does not in any way replace technical requirements embodied in statutes or regulations. It also does not set prescribed standards of performance for organizations. Not being ISO 14001 certified can be a strategic disadvantage for towns, counties, and companies because people today expect organizations to minimize or, even better, to eliminate environmental harm they cause.[16] The major requirements of an EMS under ISO 14001 include the following:

- Show commitments to prevention of pollution, continual improvement in overall environmental performance, and compliance with all applicable statutory and regulatory requirements.
- Identify all aspects of the organization's activities, products, and services that could have a significant impact on the environment, including those that are not regulated.
- Set performance objectives and targets for the management system that link back to three policies: (1) prevention of pollution, (2) continual improvement, and (3) compliance.
- Meet environmental objectives that include training employees, establishing work instructions and practices, and establishing the actual metrics by which the objectives and targets will be measured.
- Conduct an audit operation of the EMS.
- Take corrective actions when deviations from the EMS occur.

Electric Car Networks Are Coming

In August 2009, President Obama announced $2.4 billion in funding for electric car manufacturing. Grants will go to 11 companies in Michigan and 7 in Indiana that are matching the funds.

The company Better Place is building a network of 250,000 electric car recharging stations in the San Francisco/Oakland Bay Area. Each station is about the size of a parking meter. The company has already built such networks in Denmark, Israel, and Australia. City officials in the Bay Area expect that region to lead the United States in electric cars in the near future. The stations are essential because most electric cars need recharging after about 40 miles. Better Place is also building about 200 stations in the Bay Area where electric car batteries can be switched out within 15 minutes, so no waiting is needed for recharging. Even with petroleum prices at low levels, expectations are for the United States and other countries to switch to electric cars quite aggressively over the next 10 years—for pollution minimization reasons and to take advantage of government incentives and eventual mandates.

General Motors and Chrysler are pouring money into developing electric plug-in vehicles. GM is expected to launch its Chevy Volt in late 2010 in the United States. Nissan Motor Co. and Toyota Motor Co. are also quickly developing electric cars.

The Chinese auto maker BYD Co. recently unveiled the country's first all-electric vehicle for mass market. The company's F3DM vehicle runs off batteries that can be charged from a regular electrical outlet. BYD plans to sell this car in the United States in 2010. BYD sold about 10,000 F3DMs in 2009 at a price of 150,000 yuan, or $22,000 each. BYD is headquartered in Shenzhen.

Hawaii is creating an electric car network for the islands that by 2012 is expected to wean the state from near-complete dependence on oil for its energy needs. The firm Better Place is creating 70,000 to 100,000 recharging points throughout the islands to support plug-in electric cars. Under the Hawaii Clean Energy Initiative, the state intends to cut its dependence on oil to 30 percent by 2030. Hawaiians pay very high electricity prices because costly oil is burned to produce power. Electric cars have a driving range of 40 miles between charges, which is suitable for Hawaii.[17]

AT&T Inc. in 2009 committed to spend $565 million over 10 years to replace its 7,100 passenger cars with 8,000 hybrid-electric and natural gas vans to perform its installation and repair activities. The company is paying on average 29 percent more for these vehicles than it would for gasoline-powered models, but this expense will be offset by lower fuel costs, less emissions, and enhanced public image. The AT&T strategy will reduce carbon emissions by 211,000 metric tons over 10 years. AT&T is working with natural gas providers to build up to 40 fueling stations across its operating region. There are only about 110,000 natural gas vehicles in the United States compared to over 10 million such vehicles worldwide. This bold move by AT&T expands on similar initiatives by United Parcel Service and PG&E.[18]

The March 2009 Copenhagen Meeting

More than 2,000 scientists convened together in Copenhagen in March 2009 and warned the world that global warming is worse than expected. They strongly encouraged companies and governments to "vigorously" implement all economic and technological tools available to cut emissions of heat-trapping greenhouse gases. By the end of this century, scientists warn, sea levels will rise at least 20 inches and possibly as much as 39 inches unless companies and governments implement policies to radically reduce greenhouse gas emissions.

The Kyoto Protocol expires in 2012, and the results of this March 2009 Copenhagen Meeting are expected to replace that agreement. Near-coastal areas worldwide will be under water by the end of this century if drastic actions are not implemented soon worldwide to curb greenhouse gas emissions from companies, cars, trucks, power-generating plants, and planes.

Table 10-1 reveals the impact that bad environmental policies have on two of nature's many ecosystems.

TABLE 10-1   Songbirds and Coral Reefs Need Help

Songbirds

Be a good steward of the natural environment to save our songbirds. Bluebirds are one of 76 songbird species in the United States that have dramatically declined in numbers in the last two decades. Not all birds are considered songbirds, and why birds sing is not clear. Some scientists say they sing when calling for mates or warning of danger, but many scientists now contend that birds sing for sheer pleasure. Songbirds include chickadees, orioles, swallows, mockingbirds, warblers, sparrows, vireos, and the wood thrush. "These birds are telling us there's a problem, something's out of balance in our environment," says Jeff Wells, bird conservation director for the National Audubon Society. Songbirds may be telling us that their air or water is too dirty or that we are destroying too much of their habitat. People collect Picasso paintings and save historic buildings. "Songbirds are part of our natural heritage. Why should we be willing to watch songbirds destroyed any more than allowing a great work of art to be destroyed?" asks Wells. Whatever message songbirds are singing to us today about their natural environment, the message is becoming less and less heard nationwide. Listen when you go outside today. Each of us as individuals, companies, states, and countries should do what we reasonably can to help improve the natural environment for songbirds.[19] A recent study concludes that 67 of the 800 bird species in the United States are endangered, and another 184 species are designated of "conservation concern." The birds of Hawaii are in the greatest peril.

Coral Reefs

Be a good steward of the natural environment to save our coral reefs. The ocean covers more than 71 percent of the earth. The destructive effect of commercial fishing on ocean habitats coupled with increasing pollution runoff into the ocean and global warming of the ocean have decimated fisheries, marine life, and coral reefs around the world. The unfortunate consequence of fishing over the last century has been overfishing, with the principal reasons being politics and greed. Trawl fishing with nets destroys coral reefs and has been compared to catching squirrels by cutting down forests because bottom nets scour and destroy vast areas of the ocean. The great proportion of marine life caught in a trawl is "by-catch" juvenile fish and other life that are killed and discarded. Warming of the ocean due to carbon dioxide emissions also kills thousands of acres of coral reefs annually. The total area of fully protected marine habitats in the United States is only about 50 square miles, compared to some 93 million acres of national wildlife refuges and national parks on the nation's land. A healthy ocean is vital to the economic and social future of the nation—and, indeed, all countries of the world. Everything we do on land ends up in the ocean, so we all must become better stewards of this last frontier on earth in order to sustain human survival and the quality of life.[20]

Conclusion

In a final analysis, ethical standards come out of history and heritage. Our predecessors have left us with an ethical foundation to build on. Even the legendary football coach Vince Lombardi knew that some things were worth more than winning, and he required his players to have three kinds of loyalty: to God, to their families, and to the Green Bay Packers, "in that order." Employees, customers, and shareholders have become less and less tolerant of business ethics violations in firms, and more and more appreciative of model ethical firms. Information sharing across the Internet increasingly reveals such model firms versus irresponsible firms.

Consumers across the country and around the world appreciate firms that do more than is legally required to be socially responsible. But staying in business while adhering to all laws and regulations must be a primary objective of any business. One of the best ways to be socially responsible is for the firm to proactively conserve and preserve the natural environment. For example, to develop a corporate sustainability report annually is not legally required, but such a report, based on concrete actions, goes a long way toward assuring stakeholders that the firm is worthy of their support. Business ethics, social responsibility, and environmental sustainability are interrelated and key strategic issues facing all organizations.

Key Terms and Concepts

Bribe (p. 314)	**ISO 14000** (p. 320)
Bribery (p. 314)	**ISO 14001** (p. 320)
Business Ethics (p. 311)	**Social policy** (p. 315)
Code of Business Ethics (p. 313)	**Social responsibility** (p. 311)
Environment (p. 317)	**Sustainability** (p. 311)
EMS (environmental management system) (p. 321)	**Whistle-Blowing** (p. 313)

Issues for Review and Discussion

1. If you owned a small business, would you develop a code of business conduct? If yes, what variables would you include? If no, how would you ensure that ethical business standards were being followed by your employees?
2. What do you feel is the relationship between personal ethics and business ethics? Are they or should they be the same?
3. How can firms best ensure that their code of business ethics ensure is read, understood, believed, remembered, and acted on, rather than ignored?
4. Why is it important *not* to view the concept of "whistle-blowing" as "tattle-telling" or "ratting" on another employee?
5. List six desired results of "ethics training programs" in terms of recommended business ethics policies/procedures in the firm.
6. Discuss bribery. Would actions such as politicians adding earmarks in legislation or pharmaceutical salespersons giving away drugs to physicians constitute bribery? Identify three business activities that would constitute bribery and three actions that would not.
7. How could a strategist's attitude toward social responsibility affect a firm's strategy? On a 1 to 10 scale ranging from Nader's view to Friedman's view, what is your attitude toward social responsibility?
8. How do social policies on retirement differ in various countries around the world?
9. Firms should formulate and implement strategies from an environmental perspective. List eight ways firms can do this.
10. Discuss the major requirements of an EMS under ISO 14001.

Notes

1. http://disney.go.com/crreport/home.html.
2. Joann Greco, "Privacy—Whose Right Is It Anyhow?" *Journal of Business Strategy* (January–February 2001): 32.
3. Saul Gellerman, "Why 'Good' Managers Make Bad Ethical Choices," *Harvard Business Review* 64, no. 4 (July–August 1986): 88.
4. Peter Drucker, *Management: Tasks, Responsibilities, and Practices* (New York: Harper & Row, 1974): 462, 463.
5. www.wikipedia.org.
6. Phred Dvorak, Bob Davis, and Louise Radnofsky, "Firms Confront Boss-Subordinate Love Affairs," *Wall Street Journal* (October 27, 2008): B5.
7. Archie Carroll and Frank Hoy, "Integrating Corporate Social Policy into Strategic Management," *Journal of Business Strategy* 4, no. 3 (Winter 1984): 57.
8. http://money.cnn.com/magazines/fortune/mostadmired/ 2009/best_worst/best4.html.
9. Ibid.
10. Sebastian Moffett, "Fat-Aging Japan Keeps Its Elders on the Job Longer," *Wall Street Journal* (June 15, 2005): A1, A8; Sebastian Moffett, "Japan Seeks More Efficiency as Population Drops," *Wall Street Journal* (December 12, 2006): A2; Yuka Hayashi, "Japan Turns to Foreign Workers Amid Labor Crunch," *Wall Street Journal* (November 30, 2006): A10; Yuka Hayashi and Sebastian Moffett, "Cautiously, an Aging Japan Warms to Foreign Workers," *Wall Street Journal* (May 25, 2007): A1, A12.
11. Antonie Boessenkool, "Activists Push More Firms on Social Responsibility," *Wall Street Journal* (January 31, 2007): B13; Kris Hudson, "Wal-Mart Wants Supplies, Workers to Join Green Effort," *Wall Street Journal* (February 2, 2007): A14; Jayne O'Donnell and Christine Dugas, "More Retailers Go for Green—The Eco Kind," *USA Today* (April 18, 2007): 3B.
12. Kerry Hannon, "Businesses' Green Opportunities Are Wide, But Complex," *USA Today* (January 2, 2009): 5B.
13. Simona Covel, "Alternative-Energy Companies Grow Even as Others Falter," *Wall Street Journal* (January 13, 209): B4.
14. R. Alsop, "Corporations Still Put Profits First, But Social Concerns Gain Ground," *Wall Street Journal* (2001): B14; Jane Kim, "Business Schools Take a Page from Kinder, Gentler Textbook," *Wall Street Journal* (October 22, 2003): B2C; Beth Gardner, "Business Schools Going Green," *Wall Street Journal* (June 6, 2007): B5A.
15. Forest Reinhardt, "Bringing the Environment Down to Earth," *Harvard Business Review* (July–August 1999): 149–158; Christine Rosen, "Environmental Strategy and Competitive Advantage," *California Management Review* 43, no. 3 (Spring 2001): 8–15; Chris Woodyard, "Cleaner Diesel Engine Rules Take Effect," *USA Today* (December 29, 2006): 1B.
16. Adapted from the www.iso14000.com Web site and the www.epa.gov Web site.
17. Jim Carlton, "Electric-Car Network Planned," *Wall Street Journal* (November 21, 2008): B2. Also, "BYD to Introduce China's First Electric Car," *Wall Street Journal* (December 15, 2008): B2. Rebecca Smith, "Hawaii Makes Big Bet on Electric Cars," *Wall Street Journal* (December 3, 2008): A2.
18. Amol Sharma, "AT&T Invests in Green Fleet," *Wall Street Journal* (March 12, 2009): B3.
19. Tom Brook, "Declining Numbers Mute Many Birds' Songs," *USA Today* (September 11, 2001): 4A.
20. John Ogden, "Maintaining Diversity in the Oceans," *Environment* (April 2001): 29–36.

Current Readings

Amram, Martha, and Nalin Kulatilaka. "The Invisible Green Hand: How Individual Decisions and Markets Can Reduce Greenhouse Gas Emissions." *California Management Review* (Winter 2009): 194–218.

Basu, Kunal, and Guido Palazzo. "Corporate Social Responsibility: A Process Model of Sensemaking." *The Academy of Management Review* 33, no. 1 (January 2008): 122.

Berrone, Pascual, and Luis Gomez-Mejia. "Environmental Performance and Executive Compensation: An Integrated Agency-Institutional Perspective." *Academy of Management Journal* 52, no. 1 (February 2009): 103–126.

Cochran, Phillip L., and Robert Neal. "Corporate Social Responsibility, Corporate Governance, and Financial Performance: Lessons from Finance." *Business Horizons* 51, no. 5 (September–October 2008): 535.

Hull, Clyde Eirkur, and Sandra Rothenburg. "Firm Performance: The Interactions of Corporate Social Performance with Innovation and Industry Differentiation." *Strategic Management Journal* 29, no. 7 (July 2008): 781.

Kacmar, Michele. "From the Editors: An Ethical Quiz." *Academy of Management Journal* (June 2009): 432–434.

Kaptein, Muel. "Developing a Measure of Unethical Behavior in the Workplace: A Stakeholder Perspective." *Journal of Management* 34, no.5 (October 2008): 978.

Karniker, Joy, and Margaret Williams. "Organizational Justice and Organizational Citizenship Behavior: A Mediated Multifoci Model." *Journal of Management* (February 2009): 112–135.

Kramer, Roderick. "Rethinking Trust." *Harvard Business Review* (June 2009): 68–78.

Lim, Elizabeth, Shobha Das, and Amit Das. "Diversification Strategy, Capital Structure, and the Asian Financial Crisis (1997–1998): Evidence from Singapore Firms." *Strategic Management Journal* (June 2009): 577–594.

Love, E. Geoffrey, and Matthew Kraatz. "Character, Conformity, or the Bottom Line? How and Why Downsizing Affected Corporate Reputation." *Academy of Management Journal* (April 2009): 314–335.

Peloza, John, and Loren Falkenberg. "The Role of Collaboration in Achieving Corporate Social Responsibility Objectives." *California Management Review* (Spring 2009): 95–113.

Puranam, Phanish, and Bart Vanneste. "Trust and Governance: Untangling a Tangled Web." *Academy of Management Review* (January 2009): 11–31.

Thurston, Ken. "The Green Conversation." *Harvard Business Review* (September 2008): 58.

Urbany, Joel E., Thomas J. Reynolds, and Joan M. Phillips. "How to Make Values Count in Everyday Decisions." *MIT Sloan Management Review* 49, no. 4 (Summer 2008): 75.

Webb, Justin, Laszlo Tihanyi, Duane Ireland, and David Sirmon. "You Say Illegal, I Say Legitimate: Entrepreneurship in the Informal Economy." *Academy of Management Review* (July 2009): 492–510.

ASSURANCE OF LEARNING EXERCISES

Assurance of Learning Exercise 10A

Does McDonald's Have a Code of Business Ethics?

Purpose

This exercise aims to familiarize you with corporate codes of business ethics. Go to Starbucks' Standards of Business Conduct found at their www.starbucks.com Web site and more particularly at the http://www.starbucks.com/aboutus/SoBC_FY09_eng.pdf Web page.

Then see the Code of Business Ethics for McDonald's Corporation or lack of one thereof. (At the time of this writing, the author could only find a social responsibility statement for McDonald's, and it was at the http://www.mcdonalds.com/usa/work/socialresp.html Web page.)

Instructions

Step 1   Go to the two Web sites just listed and print the Standards of Business Conduct information for (1) Starbucks Corp. and (2) McDonald's Corp. Read the two statements.

Step 2   On a separate sheet of paper, list three aspects that you like most and three aspects that you like least about (1) the Starbucks statement and (2) the McDonald's statement. In other words, compare the two statements. Conclude by indicating which statement of conduct you like best. Why do you think it is best?

Step 3   Explain why having a code of business ethics is not sufficient for ensuring ethical behavior in an organization. What other means are necessary to help ensure ethical behavior? Give the class an example of a breach of ethical conduct that you recall in your work experience.

Assurance of Learning Exercise 1B

The Ethics of Spying on Competitors

Purpose

This exercise gives you an opportunity to discuss in class ethical and legal issues related to methods being used by many companies to spy on competing firms. Gathering and using information about competitors is an area of strategic management that Japanese firms do more proficiently than American firms.

Instructions

On a separate sheet of paper, number from 1 to 18. For the 18 spying activities listed as follows, indicate whether or not you believe the activity is ethical or unethical and legal or illegal. Place either an *E* for ethical or *U* for unethical, and either an *L* for legal or an *I* for illegal for each activity. Compare your answers to those of your classmates and discuss any differences.

1. Buying competitors' garbage
2. Dissecting competitors' products
3. Taking competitors' plant tours anonymously
4. Counting tractor-trailer trucks leaving competitors' loading bays
5. Studying aerial photographs of competitors' facilities
6. Analyzing competitors' labor contracts
7. Analyzing competitors' help-wanted ads
8. Quizzing customers and buyers about the sales of competitors' products

9. Infiltrating customers' and competitors' business operations
10. Quizzing suppliers about competitors' level of manufacturing
11. Using customers to buy out phony bids
12. Encouraging key customers to reveal competitive information
13. Quizzing competitors' former employees
14. Interviewing consultants who may have worked with competitors
15. Hiring key managers away from competitors
16. Conducting phony job interviews to get competitors' employees to reveal information
17. Sending engineers to trade meetings to quiz competitors' technical employees
18. Quizzing potential employees who worked for or with competitors

Assurance of Learning Exercise 10C

Who Prepares a Sustainability Report?

Purpose

The purpose of this activity is to determine the nature and prevalence of Sustainability Reports among companies in your state.

Instructions

Contact by phone at least five different plant managers or owners of large businesses in your area. Seek answers to the following questions. Present your findings in a written report to your instructor.

1. Does your company prepare a Sustainability Report? If yes, please describe the nature and scope of the report.
2. Are environmental criteria included in the performance evaluation of managers? If yes, please specify the criteria.
3. Are environmental affairs more a technical function or a management function in your company?
4. Does your firm offer any environmental workshops for employees? If yes, please describe them.

CHAPTER 11
Global/International Issues

CHAPTER OBJECTIVES

After studying this chapter, you should be able to do the following:

1. Explain the advantages and disadvantages of entering global markets.

2. Discuss protectionism as it impacts the world economy.

3. Explain when and why a firm (or industry) may need to become more or less global in nature to compete.

4. Discuss the global challenge facing American firms.

5. Compare and contrast the culture in the United States with Mexico and Japan.

6. Describe how management style varies across Europe.

7. Discuss communication differences across countries.

Assurance of Learning Exercises

Assurance of Learning Exercise 11A
McDonald's Wants to Enter Africa. Help Them.

Assurance of Learning Exercise 11B
Does My University Recruit in Foreign Countries?

Assurance of Learning Exercise 11C
Assessing Differences in Culture Across Countries

Assurance of Learning Exercise 11D
How Well Traveled Are Business Students at Your University?

Source: John Sartin/Shutterstock

"Notable Quotes"

"Sad but true, U.S. businesspeople have the lowest foreign language proficiency of any major trading nation. U.S. business schools do not emphasize foreign languages, and students traditionally avoid them."

—Ronald Dulek

"America's economy has become much less American."

"In God we trust. All others bring data."

—Edward Deming

Doing Great in a Weak Economy. How?

Marriott International

Among all hotels, casinos, and resorts, Marriott International scored the highest on *Fortune's* "Most Admired Companies" both in 2007 and 2008. When most firms were struggling, Marriott made $362 million in net income on $12.88 billion in revenues, quite impressive for a hotel/motel firm in 2008. *Fortune* rated Marriott as their 13th overall "Most Admired Company in the World" in terms of their management and performance. Marriott is looking past the current slump in travel by planning to open 130 new hotels in the next four years. About half of the new hotels are targeted for emerging markets such as China, India, and the United Arab Emirates. The new hotels will add 32,000 rooms to Bethesda, Maryland–based Marriott's capacity of 560,000 rooms at 3,178 properties. Marriott declared a new stock dividend in August 2009.

Marriott is one of the world's leading hoteliers, with some 3,000 properties in more than 65 countries, including Renaissance Hotels and Marriott Hotels & Resorts, as well as Courtyard and Fairfield Inn. It also owns the Ritz-Carlton and time-share properties operated by Marriott Vacation Club International. Marriott additionally provides more than 2,000 rental units for corporate housing and manages 45 golf courses. The Marriott family, including CEO J. W. Marriott Jr., owns about 30 percent of the firm.

Marriott prefers to manage rather than own properties. The firm is planning to purchase some of the Greenbrier Hotel Corporation's assets, including its historic luxury White Sulphur Springs, West Virginia, resort. Then Marriott will sell that property to another hotel owner but maintain management rights to the property. Greenbrier entered Chapter 11 bankruptcy in 2009, which prompted Marriott to offer to acquire some of their assets.

Source: Based On Geoff Colvin, "The World's Most Admired Companies," *Fortune* (March 16, 2009): 76–86; Rachel Feintzeig and Kris Hudson, "Greenbrier Hotel Seeks Chapter 11, Plans to Sell to Marriott," *Wall Street Journal* (March 20, 2009): B3.

As illustrated in Figure 11-1, global considerations impact virtually all strategic decisions. The boundaries of countries no longer can define the limits of our imaginations. To see and appreciate the world from the perspective of others has become a matter of survival for businesses. The underpinnings of strategic management hinge on managers gaining an understanding of competitors, markets, prices, suppliers, distributors, governments, creditors, shareholders, and customers worldwide. The price and quality of a firm's products and services must be competitive on a worldwide basis, not just on a local basis. As indicated above, Marriott International is an example global business that performed outstandingly well during the recent global recession.

The World Trade Organization (WTO) in March 2009 issued the most pessimistic report on global trade in its 62-year history: that global trade would drop by 9 percent or more in 2009.[1] A world market has emerged from what previously was a multitude of

FIGURE 11-1

A Comprehensive Strategic-Management Mode

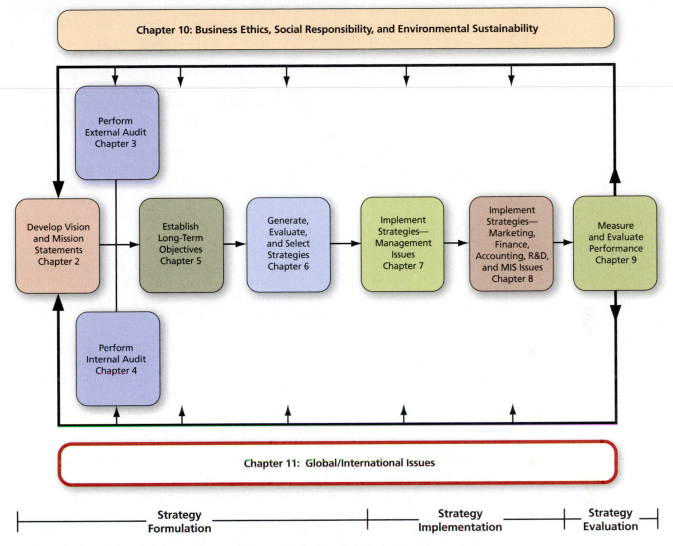

Source: Fred R. David, "How Companies Define Their Mission," *Long Range Planning* 22, no. 3 (June 1988): 40.

distinct national markets, and the climate for international business today is more favorable than in years past. Mass communication and high technology have created similar patterns of consumption in diverse cultures worldwide. This means that many companies may find it difficult to survive by relying solely on domestic markets.

It is not exaggeration that in an industry that is, or is rapidly becoming, global, the riskiest possible posture is to remain a domestic competitor. The domestic competitor will watch as more aggressive companies use this growth to capture economies of scale and learning. The domestic competitor will then be faced with an attack on domestic markets using different (and possibly superior) technology, product design, manufacturing, marketing approaches, and economies of scale.[2]

Multinational Organizations

Organizations that conduct business operations across national borders are called *international firms* or *multinational corporations.* The strategic-management process is conceptually the same for multinational firms as for purely domestic firms; however, the process is more complex for international firms due to more variables and relationships. The social, cultural, demographic, environmental, political, governmental, legal, technological, and competitive opportunities and threats that face a multinational corporation are almost limitless, and the number and complexity of these factors increase dramatically with the number of products produced and the number of geographic areas served.

More time and effort are required to identify and evaluate external trends and events in multinational corporations than in domestic corporations. Geographic distance, cultural and national differences, and variations in business practices often make communication between domestic headquarters and overseas operations difficult. Strategy implementation can be more difficult because different cultures have different norms, values, and work ethics.

Multinational corporations (MNCs) face unique and diverse risks, such as expropriation of assets, currency losses through exchange rate fluctuations, unfavorable foreign court interpretations of contracts and agreements, social/political disturbances, import/export restrictions, tariffs, and trade barriers. Strategists in MNCs are often confronted with the need to be globally competitive and nationally responsive at the same time. With the rise in world commerce, government and regulatory bodies are more closely monitoring foreign business practices. The U.S. Foreign Corrupt Practices Act, for example, monitors business practices in many areas.

Before entering international markets, firms should scan relevant journals and patent reports, seek the advice of academic and research organizations, participate in international trade fairs, form partnerships, and conduct extensive research to broaden their contacts and diminish the risk of doing business in new markets. Firms can also offset some risks of doing business internationally by obtaining insurance from the U.S. government's Overseas Private Investment Corporation (OPIC).

Philips Electronics NV is one of many firms moving into emerging markets. A few of Philips's acquisitions in the year 2008 alone were Medel in Italy, Meditronics in India, Alpha X-Ray Technologies in India, Dixtal Biomedica & Tecnologia in Brazil, Shenzhen Goldway Industrial in China, and VMI-Sistemes Medicos in Brazil.

Advantages and Disadvantages of International Operations

Firms have numerous reasons for formulating and implementing strategies that initiate, continue, or expand involvement in business operations across national borders. Perhaps the greatest advantage is that firms can gain new customers for their products and services, thus increasing revenues. Growth in revenues and profits is a common organizational objective and often an expectation of shareholders because it is a measure of organizational success.

Potential advantages to initiating, continuing, and/or expanding international operations are as follows:

1. Firms can gain new customers for their products.
2. Foreign operations can absorb excess capacity, reduce unit costs, and spread economic risks over a wider number of markets.
3. Foreign operations can allow firms to establish low-cost production facilities in locations close to raw materials and/or cheap labor.
4. Competitors in foreign markets may not exist, or competition may be less intense than in domestic markets.
5. Foreign operations may result in reduced tariffs, lower taxes, and favorable political treatment.
6. Joint ventures can enable firms to learn the technology, culture, and business practices of other people and to make contacts with potential customers, suppliers, creditors, and distributors in foreign countries.
7. Economies of scale can be achieved from operation in global rather than solely domestic markets. Larger-scale production and better efficiencies allow higher sales volumes and lower-price offerings.

8. A firm's power and prestige in domestic markets may be significantly enhanced if the firm competes globally. Enhanced prestige can translate into improved negotiating power among creditors, suppliers, distributors, and other important groups.

The availability, depth, and reliability of economic and marketing information in different countries vary extensively, as do industrial structures, business practices, and the number and nature of regional organizations. There are also numerous potential disadvantages of initiating, continuing, or expanding business across national borders, such as the following:

1. Foreign operations could be seized by nationalistic factions.
2. Firms confront different and often little-understood social, cultural, demographic, environmental, political, governmental, legal, technological, economic, and competitive forces when doing business internationally. These forces can make communication difficult in the firm.
3. Weaknesses of competitors in foreign lands are often overestimated, and strengths are often underestimated. Keeping informed about the number and nature of competitors is more difficult when doing business internationally.
4. Language, culture, and value systems differ among countries, which can create barriers to communication and problems managing people.
5. Gaining an understanding of regional organizations such as the European Economic Community, the Latin American Free Trade Area, the International Bank for Reconstruction and Development, and the International Finance Corporation is difficult but is often required in doing business internationally.
6. Dealing with two or more monetary systems can complicate international business operations.

The Global Challenge

Foreign competitors are battering U.S. firms in many industries. In its simplest sense, the global challenge faced by U.S. business is twofold: (1) how to gain and maintain exports to other nations and (2) how to defend domestic markets against imported goods. Few companies can afford to ignore the presence of international competition. Firms that seem insulated and comfortable today may be vulnerable tomorrow; for example, foreign banks do not yet compete or operate in most of the United States, but this too is changing.

America's economy is becoming much less American. A world economy and monetary system are emerging. Corporations in every corner of the globe are taking advantage of the opportunity to obtain customers globally. Markets are shifting rapidly and in many cases converging in tastes, trends, and prices. Innovative transport systems are accelerating the transfer of technology. Shifts in the nature and location of production systems, especially to China and India, are reducing the response time to changing market conditions.

More and more countries around the world are welcoming foreign investment and capital. As a result, labor markets have steadily become more international. East Asian countries are market leaders in labor-intensive industries, Brazil offers abundant natural resources and rapidly developing markets, and Germany offers skilled labor and technology. The drive to improve the efficiency of global business operations is leading to greater functional specialization. This is not limited to a search for the familiar low-cost labor in Latin America or Asia. Other considerations include the cost of energy, availability of resources, inflation rates, tax rates, and the nature of trade regulations.

Many countries became more protectionist during the recent global economic recession. *Protectionism* refers to countries imposing tariffs, taxes, and regulations on firms outside the country to favor their own companies and people. Most economists argue that protectionism harms the world economy because it inhibits trade among countries and invites retaliation.

When China joined the World Trade Organization in 2001, that country agreed to respect copyright protections and liberalize restrictions on the import and distribution of foreign-made goods. However, Chinese counterfeiters still can be criminally prosecuted for commercial piracy only when caught in possession of at least 500 counterfeit items.[3] In China, pirated goods such as Nike running shoes, new Hollywood movies on DVD, and Microsoft software can be purchased for a fraction of their actual prices on many streets. China still has substantial barriers to sales of authentic U.S.-made copyrighted products. Former U.S. Trade Representative Susan Schwab says, "This is more than a handbag here or a logo item there; it is often theft on a grand scale." China's counterfeit trade practices contribute to an annual bilateral trade deficit of about $250 billion with the United States. Chinese pirating of products is an external threat facing many firms.

Advancements in telecommunications are drawing countries, cultures, and organizations worldwide closer together. Foreign revenue as a percentage of total company revenues already exceeds 50 percent in hundreds of U.S. firms, including Exxon/Mobil, Gillette, Dow Chemical, Citicorp, Colgate-Palmolive, and Texaco.

A primary reason why most domestic firms are engaging in global operations is that growth in demand for goods and services outside the United States is considerably higher than inside. For example, the domestic food industry is growing just 3 percent per year, so Kraft Foods, the second largest food company in the world behind Nestle, is focusing on foreign acquisitions.

Shareholders and investors expect sustained growth in revenues from firms; satisfactory growth for many firms can only be achieved by capitalizing on demand outside the United States. Joint ventures and partnerships between domestic and foreign firms are becoming the rule rather than the exception!

Fully 95 percent of the world's population lives outside the United States, and this group is growing 70 percent faster than the U.S. population. The lineup of competitors in virtually all industries is global. General Motors, Ford, and Chrysler compete with Toyota and Hyundai. General Electric and Westinghouse battle Siemens and Mitsubishi. Caterpillar and John Deere compete with Komatsu. Goodyear battles Michelin, Bridgestone/Firestone, and Pirelli. Boeing competes with Airbus. Only a few U.S. industries—such as furniture, printing, retailing, consumer packaged goods, and retail banking—are not yet greatly challenged by foreign competitors. But many products and components in these industries too are now manufactured in foreign countries. International operations can be as simple as exporting a product to a single foreign country or as complex as operating manufacturing, distribution, and marketing facilities in many countries.

Globalization

Globalization is a process of doing business worldwide, so strategic decisions are made based on global profitability of the firm rather than just domestic considerations. A global strategy seeks to meet the needs of customers worldwide, with the highest value at the lowest cost. This may mean locating production in countries with the lowest labor costs or abundant natural resources, locating research and complex engineering centers where skilled scientists and engineers can be found, and locating marketing activities close to the markets to be served.

A *global strategy* includes designing, producing, and marketing products with global needs in mind, instead of considering individual countries alone. A global strategy integrates actions against competitors into a worldwide plan. Today, there are global buyers and sellers, and the instant transmission of money and information across continents.

It is clear that different industries become global for different reasons. The need to amortize massive R&D investments over many markets is a major reason why the aircraft manufacturing industry became global. Monitoring globalization in one's industry is an important strategic-management activity. Knowing how to use that information for one's competitive advantage is even more important. For example, firms may look around the world for the best technology and select one that has the most promise for the largest number of markets. When firms design a product, they design it to be marketable in as many countries as possible. When firms manufacture a product, they select the lowest-cost source, which may be Japan for semiconductors, Sri Lanka for textiles, Malaysia for simple electronics, and Europe for precision machinery.

A Weak Economy

A weak economy still plagues many countries around the world. The British pound reached a 23-year low against the U.S. dollar in January 2009. Two consecutive quarters of a decline in real gross domestic product is commonly used as a definition of a *recession*, and the last quarter of 2008 marked this occurrence in the United Kingdom. The speed and breadth at which the United Kingdom's economy shrunk makes economists think the UK recession could last through 2012. Like the U.S. government, the UK government has poured hundreds of billions of pounds into stimulus and financial bailout measures. Further interest rate cuts by the Bank of England are expected soon, although the bank's rates are already the lowest in the bank's 315-year history. The pound's fall has done little to boost exports. David Sandall, a businessman in Cheshire, Northern England, says, "It doesn't matter what the price of something is if your customer hasn't got the money." And that is the primary situation in the United Kingdom's two largest trading regions—Europe and the United States.

Unemployment rates are high across the United States and around the world. Consumer spending remains low and cautious while banks continue to be reluctant to loan money. Stock prices have rebounded, but many investors still have an appetite only for government securities. New corporate profit warnings and bankruptcies spell continued recession in many countries.

United States versus Foreign Business Cultures

To compete successfully in world markets, U.S. managers must obtain a better knowledge of historical, cultural, and religious forces that motivate and drive people in other countries. In Japan, for example, business relations operate within the context of *Wa,* which stresses group harmony and social cohesion. In China, business behavior revolves around *guanxi,* or personal relations. In South Korea, activities involve concern for *inhwa,* or harmony based on respect of hierarchical relationships, including obedience to authority.[4]

In Europe, it is generally true that the farther north on the continent, the more participatory the management style. Most European workers are unionized and enjoy more frequent vacations and holidays than U.S. workers. A 90-minute lunch break plus 20-minute morning and afternoon breaks are common in European firms. Guaranteed permanent employment is typically a part of employment contracts in Europe. In socialist countries such as France, Belgium, and the United Kingdom, the only grounds for immediate dismissal from work is a criminal offense. A six-month trial period at the beginning of employment is usually part of the contract with a European firm. Many Europeans resent pay-for-performance, commission salaries, and objective measurement and reward systems. This is true especially of workers in southern Europe. Many Europeans also find the notion of team spirit difficult to grasp because the unionized environment has dichotomized worker–management relations throughout Europe.

A weakness of some U.S. firms in competing with Pacific Rim firms is a lack of understanding of Asian cultures, including how Asians think and behave. Spoken Chinese, for example, has more in common with spoken English than with spoken Japanese or Korean. U.S. managers consistently put more weight on being friendly and liked, whereas Asian and European managers often exercise authority without this concern. Americans tend to use first names instantly in business dealings with foreigners, but foreigners find this presumptuous. In Japan, for example, first names are used only among family members and intimate friends; even longtime business associates and coworkers shy away from the use of first names. Table 11-1 lists other cultural differences or pitfalls that U.S. managers need to know about.

U.S. managers have a low tolerance for silence, whereas Asian managers view extended periods of silence as important for organizing and evaluating one's thoughts. U.S. managers are much more action oriented than their counterparts around the world; they rush to appointments, conferences, and meetings—and then feel the day has been productive. But for many foreign managers, resting, listening, meditating, and thinking is considered productive.

TABLE 11-1 Cultural Pitfalls That May Help You Be a Better Manager

- Waving is a serious insult in Greece and Nigeria, particularly if the hand is near someone's face.
- Making a "good-bye" wave in Europe can mean "No," but it means "Come here" in Peru.
- In China, last names are written first.
- A man named Carlos Lopez-Garcia should be addressed as Mr. Lopez in Latin America but as Mr. Garcia in Brazil.
- Breakfast meetings are considered uncivilized in most foreign countries.
- Latin Americans are on average 20 minutes late to business appointments.
- Direct eye contact is impolite in Japan.
- Don't cross your legs in any Arab or many Asian countries—it's rude to show the sole of your shoe.
- In Brazil, touching your thumb and first finger—an American "Okay" sign—is the equivalent of raising your middle finger.
- Nodding or tossing your head back in southern Italy, Malta, Greece, and Tunisia means "No." In India, this body motion means "Yes."
- Snapping your fingers is vulgar in France and Belgium.
- Folding your arms across your chest is a sign of annoyance in Finland.
- In China, leave some food on your plate to show that your host was so generous that you couldn't finish.
- Do not eat with your left hand when dining with clients from Malaysia or India.
- One form of communication works the same worldwide. It's the smile—so take that along wherever you go.

Sitting through a conference without talking is unproductive in the United States, but it is viewed as positive in Japan if one's silence helps preserve unity.

U.S. managers place greater emphasis on short-term results than foreign managers. In marketing, for example, Japanese managers strive to achieve "everlasting customers," whereas many Americans strive to make a onetime sale. Marketing managers in Japan see making a sale as the beginning, not the end, of the selling process. This is an important distinction. Japanese managers often criticize U.S. managers for worrying more about shareholders, whom they do not know, than employees, whom they do know. Americans refer to "hourly employees," whereas many Japanese companies still refer to "lifetime employees."

Rose Knotts recently summarized some important cultural differences between U.S. and foreign managers:[5]

1. Americans place an exceptionally high priority on time, viewing time as an asset. Many foreigners place more worth on relationships. This difference results in foreign managers often viewing U.S. managers as "more interested in business than people."

2. Personal touching and distance norms differ around the world. Americans generally stand about three feet from each other when carrying on business conversations, but Arabs and Africans stand about one foot apart. Touching another person with the left hand in business dealings is taboo in some countries. American managers need to learn the personal-space rules of foreign managers with whom they interact in business.

3. Family roles and relationships vary in different countries. For example, males are valued more than females in some cultures, and peer pressure, work situations, and business interactions reinforce this phenomenon.

4. Business and daily life in some societies are governed by religious factors. Prayer times, holidays, daily events, and dietary restrictions, for example, need to be respected by American managers not familiar with these practices in some countries.

5. Time spent with the family and the quality of relationships are more important in some cultures than the personal achievement and accomplishments espoused by the traditional U.S. manager.

6. Many cultures around the world value modesty, team spirit, collectivity, and patience much more than the competitiveness and individualism that are so important in the United States.

7. Punctuality is a valued personal trait when conducting business in the United States, but it is not revered in many of the world's societies. Eating habits also differ

dramatically across cultures. For example, belching is acceptable in some countries as evidence of satisfaction with the food that has been prepared. Chinese culture considers it good manners to sample a portion of each food served.

8. To prevent social blunders when meeting with managers from other lands, one must learn and respect the rules of etiquette of others. Sitting on a toilet seat is viewed as unsanitary in most countries, but not in the United States. Leaving food or drink after dining is considered impolite in some countries, but not in China. Bowing instead of shaking hands is customary in many countries. Some cultures view Americans as unsanitary for locating toilet and bathing facilities in the same area, whereas Americans view people of some cultures as unsanitary for not taking a bath or shower every day.

9. Americans often do business with individuals they do not know, unlike businesspersons in many other cultures. In Mexico and Japan, for example, an amicable relationship is often mandatory before conducting business.

In many countries, effective managers are those who are best at negotiating with government bureaucrats rather than those who inspire workers. Many U.S. managers are uncomfortable with nepotism and bribery, which are practiced in some countries. The United States has gained a reputation for defending women from sexual harassment and minorities from discrimination, but not all countries embrace the same values.

American managers in China have to be careful about how they arrange office furniture because Chinese workers believe in *feng shui,* the practice of harnessing natural forces. U.S. managers in Japan have to be careful about *nemaswashio,* whereby Japanese workers expect supervisors to alert them privately of changes rather than informing them in a meeting. Japanese managers have little appreciation for versatility, expecting all managers to be the same. In Japan, "If a nail sticks out, you hit it into the wall," says Brad Lashbrook, an international consultant for Wilson Learning.

Probably the biggest obstacle to the effectiveness of U.S. managers—or managers from any country working in another—is the fact that it is almost impossible to change the attitude of a foreign workforce. "The system drives you; you cannot fight the system or culture," says Bill Parker, president of Phillips Petroleum in Norway.

The Mexican Culture

Mexico is an authoritarian society in terms of schools, churches, businesses, and families. Employers seek workers who are agreeable, respectful, and obedient, rather than innovative, creative, and independent. Mexican workers tend to be activity oriented rather than problem solvers. When visitors walk into a Mexican business, they are impressed by the cordial, friendly atmosphere. This is almost always true because Mexicans desire harmony rather than conflict; desire for harmony is part of the social fabric in worker–manager relations. There is a much lower tolerance for adversarial relations or friction at work in Mexico as compared to the United States.

Mexican employers are paternalistic, providing workers with more than a paycheck, but in return they expect allegiance. Weekly food baskets, free meals, free bus service, and free day care are often part of compensation. The ideal working condition for a Mexican worker is the family model, with people all working together, doing their share, according to their designated roles. Mexican workers do not expect or desire a work environment in which self-expression and initiative are encouraged. Whereas U.S. business embodies individualism, achievement, competition, curiosity, pragmatism, informality, spontaneity, and doing more than expected on the job, Mexican businesses stress collectivism, continuity, cooperation, belongingness, formality, and doing exactly what you're told.

In Mexico, business associates rarely entertain each other at their homes, which are places reserved exclusively for close friends and family. Business meetings and entertaining are nearly always done at a restaurant. Preserving one's honor, saving face, and looking important are also exceptionally important in Mexico. This is why Mexicans do not accept criticism and change easily; many find it humiliating to acknowledge having made a mistake. A meeting among employees and managers in a business located in Mexico is a forum for giving orders and directions rather than for discussing problems or participating in decision making. Mexican workers want to be closely supervised, cared for, and corrected in a civil manner. Opinions expressed by employees are often regarded as back talk in Mexico. Mexican supervisors are viewed as weak if they explain the rationale for their orders to workers.

Mexicans do not feel compelled to follow rules that are not associated with a particular person in authority they work for or know well. Thus signs to wear earplugs or safety glasses, or attendance or seniority policies, and even one-way street signs are often ignored. Whereas Americans follow the rules, Mexicans often do not.

Life is slower in Mexico than in the United States. The first priority is often assigned to the last request, rather than to the first. Telephone systems break down. Banks may suddenly not have pesos. Phone repair can take a month. Electricity for an entire plant or town can be down for hours or even days. Business and government offices may open and close at odd hours. Buses and taxis may be hours off schedule. Meeting times for appointments are not rigid. Tardiness is common everywhere. Effectively doing business in Mexico requires knowledge of the Mexican way of life, culture, beliefs, and customs.

The Japanese Culture

The Japanese place great importance on group loyalty and consensus, a concept called *Wa*. Nearly all corporate activities in Japan encourage *Wa* among managers and employees. *Wa* requires that all members of a group agree and cooperate; this results in constant discussion and compromise. Japanese managers evaluate the potential attractiveness of alternative business decisions in terms of the long-term effect on the group's *Wa*. This is why silence, used for pondering alternatives, can be a plus in a formal Japanese meeting. Discussions potentially disruptive to *Wa* are generally conducted in very informal settings, such as at a bar, so as to minimize harm to the group's *Wa*. Entertaining is an important business activity in Japan because it strengthens *Wa*. Formal meetings are often conducted in informal settings. When confronted with disturbing questions or opinions, Japanese managers tend to remain silent, whereas Americans tend to respond directly, defending themselves through explanation and argument.

Most Japanese managers are reserved, quiet, distant, introspective, and other oriented, whereas most U.S. managers are talkative, insensitive, impulsive, direct, and individual oriented. Americans often perceive Japanese managers as wasting time and carrying on pointless conversations, whereas U.S. managers often use blunt criticism, ask prying questions, and make quick decisions. These kinds of cultural differences have disrupted many potentially productive Japanese–American business endeavors. Viewing the Japanese communication style as a prototype for all Asian cultures is a stereotype that must be avoided.

Communication Differences Across Countries

Americans increasingly interact with managers in other countries, so it is important to understand foreign business cultures. Americans often come across as intrusive, manipulative, and garrulous; this impression may reduce their effectiveness in communication. *Forbes* recently provided the following cultural hints from Charis Intercultural Training:

1. Italians, Germans, and French generally do not soften up executives with praise before they criticize. Americans do soften up folks, and this practice seems manipulative to Europeans.
2. Israelis are accustomed to fast-paced meetings and have little patience for American informality and small talk.
3. British executives often complain that American executives chatter too much. Informality, egalitarianism, and spontaneity from Americans in business settings jolt many foreigners.
4. Europeans feel they are being treated like children when asked to wear name tags by Americans.

5. Executives in India are used to interrupting one another. Thus, when American executives listen without asking for clarification or posing questions, they are viewed by Indians as not paying attention.
6. When negotiating orally with Malaysian or Japanese executives, it is appropriate to allow periodically for a time of silence. However, no pause is needed when negotiating in Israel.
7. Refrain from asking foreign managers questions such as "How was your weekend?" That is intrusive to foreigners, who tend to regard their business and private lives as totally separate.[6]

Americans have more freedom to control their own fates than do the Japanese. Life in the United States and life in Japan are very different; the United States offers more upward mobility to its people. This is a great strength of the United States, as indicated here:

America is not like Japan and can never be. America's strength is the opposite: It opens its doors and brings the world's disorder in. It tolerates social change that would tear most other societies apart. This openness encourages Americans to adapt as individuals rather than as a group. Americans go west to California to get a new start; they move east to Manhattan to try to make the big time; they move to Vermont or to a farm to get close to the soil. They break away from their parents' religions or values or class; they rediscover their ethnicity. They go to night school; they change their names. [7]

Worldwide Tax Rates

The lowest corporate tax rates among developed countries reside in Europe, and European countries are lowering tax rates further to attract investment. The average corporate tax rate among European Union countries is 26 percent, compared with 30 percent in the Asia-Pacific region and 38 percent in the United States and Japan. Ireland and the former Soviet-bloc nations of Eastern Europe recently slashed corporate tax rates to nearly zero, attracting substantial investment. Germany cut its corporate tax rate from 39 percent in 2007 to just under 30 percent in 2008. Great Britain cut its corporate tax rate to 28 percent from 30 percent. France cut its rate from 34 percent to 27 percent in 2008.

Other factors besides the corporate tax rate obviously affect companies' decisions to locate plants and facilities. For example, the large and affluent market and efficient infrastructure in Germany and Britain attract companies, but the high labor costs and strict labor laws keep other companies away.

Ralph Gomory, president of the Alfred P. Sloan Foundation and a former top executive at IBM, warns of a growing divergence between the interests of U.S. corporations and interests of the U.S. government. Specifically, he says U.S. trade liberalization/globalization policies for the last two decades have encouraged corporations to seek the lowest-cost locations for their operations. The new 1,200-worker Intel semiconductor plant in Vietnam is just one example among thousands. Gomory says the United States must use the corporate income tax to *reward* companies that invest in jobs here, especially high-tech jobs, and must *penalize* companies that move facilities overseas. We must make it in the self-interest of companies to invest in America, Gomory says. Otherwise, living standards here will inevitably decline and America will severely weaken economically.[8]

Joint Ventures in India

The government of India is highly in debt, 80 percent of GDP, and is cutting expenses to curtail spending, so the gap between rich and poor is widening further. (The U.S. federal debt is about 65 percent of GDP.) But India's middle class is growing, so foreign firms continue to invest. Nissan Motor is building a factory in Chennai in conjunction with

Mahindra & Mahindra Ltd., India's largest maker of jeeps and tractors. The factory began operating in 2009.

Joint ventures remain mandatory for foreign companies doing business in India. Verizon Business India, a joint venture between Verizon and Videocon Group of Mumbai, is rapidly expanding its phone and Internet services in India to compete more fiercely with AT&T and other telecom companies. Almost 20 million new cell phone customers are added in India every quarter, about the same rate of increase as in China—compared with only about 2.8 million new cell phone customers added in the United States quarterly. India's Reliance Communications Ltd. is in a battle with Britain's Vodafone Group PLC for control of India's fourth-largest cellular service, Hutchison Essar. But Vodafone must find a local partner because Indian law restricts foreign firms to 74 percent ownership of any India-based firm.

Most joint ventures among firms in India and foreign firms fail. Of 25 major joint ventures between foreign and Indian companies between 1993 and 2003, only three survive today. The Indian government has eased the joint-venture restriction in the investment-banking industry, but not in other areas. Even Wal-Mart has an Indian partner, Bharti Enterprises Ltd. Heavy friction exists in virtually all joint-ventures in India. John Band, president of Zoom Cortex in Mumbai, says, "Anyone that gets into a joint venture in India should assume it will fail and should be comfortable with the terms of what happens when it does fail." [9]

Due to tourism growing 12 percent annually, hotel chains are scrambling to get established in India. Hilton Hotels just established a joint venture with New Delhi–based DLF Ltd. to develop 75 hotels in India in 2007–2010. Marriott, Four Seasons, and Carlson Companies are also establishing joint ventures in India and building hotels rapidly.

Conclusion

The population of the world has almost reached 7 billion persons. For centuries before Columbus reached America, and for centuries to come, businesses will search for new opportunities beyond their national boundaries. There has never been a more international-ized and economically competitive society than today's model. Some U.S. industries, such as automobiles, textiles, steel, and consumer electronics, are in complete disarray as a result of the international challenge.

Success in business increasingly depends on offering products and services that are competitive on a world basis, not just on a local basis. If the price and quality of a firm's products and services are not competitive with those available elsewhere in the world, the firm may soon face extinction. Global markets have become a reality in all but the most remote areas of the world. Certainly throughout the United States, even in small towns, firms feel the pressure of world competitors.

This chapter has provided some basic global information that can be essential to consider in developing a strategic plan for any organization. The advantages of engaging in international business may well offset the drawbacks for most firms. It is important in strategic planning to be effective, and the nature of global operations may be the key component in a plan's overall effectiveness.

Key Terms and Concepts

Feng Shui (p. 337)
Global Strategy (p. 334)
Globalization (p. 334)
Guanxi (p. 335)
International Firms (p. 331)
Inhwa (p. 335)

Multinational Corporations (p. 331)
Nemaswashio (p. 337)
Protectionism (p. 333)
Recession (p. 335)
Wa (p. 335)

Issues for Review and Discussion

1. Explain why consumption patterns are becoming similar worldwide. What are the strategic implications of this trend?
2. What are the advantages and disadvantages of beginning export operations in a foreign country?
3. What are the major differences between U.S. and multinational operations that affect strategic management?
4. Why is globalization of industries a common factor today?
5. Compare and contrast U.S. versus foreign cultures in terms of doing business.
6. List six reasons that strategic management is more complex in a multinational firm.
7. Do you feel that protectionism is good or bad for the world economy? Why?
8. Why are some industries more "global" than others? Discuss.
9. *Wa, guanxi,* and *inhwa* are important management terms in Japan, China, and South Korea, respectively. What would be analogous terms to describe American management practices?
10. Why do many Europeans find the notion of "team spirit" in a work environment difficult to grasp?
11. In China, *feng shui* is important in business, whereas in Japan, *nemaswashio* is important. What are analogous American terms and practices?
12. Describe the business culture in Mexico.
13. Describe the business culture in Japan.
14. Compare tax rates in the United States versus other countries. What impact could these differences have on "keeping jobs at home"?
15. Discuss requirements for doing business in India.

Notes

1. John Miller, "WTO Predicts Global Trade Will Slide 9% This Year," *Wall Street Journal* (March 24, 2009): A8.
2. Frederick Gluck, "Global Competition in the 1990s," *Journal of Business Strategy* (Spring 1983): 22–24.
3. David Lynch, "U.S. Complains to WTO on China," *USA Today* (April 10, 2007): B1.
4. Jon Alston, "Wa, Guanxi, and Inhwa: Managerial Principles in Japan, China and Korea," *Business Horizons* 32, no. 2 (March–April 1989): 26.
5. Rose Knotts, "Cross-Cultural Management: Transformations and Adaptations," *Business Horizons* (January–February 1989): 29–33.
6. Lalita Khosla, "You Say Tomato," *Forbes* (May 21, 2001): 36.
7. Stratford Sherman, "How to Beat the Japanese," *Fortune* (April 10, 1989): 145.
8. Marcus Walker, "Europe Competes for Investment with Lower Corporate Tax Rates," *Wall Street Journal* (April 17, 2007): A12.
9. Eric Bellman and P. R. Venkat, "India's Growth Raises Fears Rates May Rise," *Wall Street Journal* (February 8, 2007): A6; Dionne Searcey, "Verizon Targets Business in India," *Wall Street Journal* (February 6, 2007): A7; Peter Wonacott, "India Faces Dark Side of Its Boom," *Wall Street Journal* (February 27, 2007): A10; Amy Chozick, "Nissan Enters Venture to Build Indian Plant," *Wall Street Journal* (February 27, 2007): A4; Cassell Bryan and Eric Bellman, "Vodafone, Reliance Gear Up for Battle in India," *Wall Street Journal* (December 22, 2006): B4; Peter Wonacott and Eric Bellman, "Foreign Firms Find Rough Passage to India," *Wall Street Journal* (February 1, 2007): A6; Binny Sabharwal, "Hilton Expands in India as Market Demand Soars," *Wall Street Journal* (May 10, 2007): D6.

Current Readings

Brouthers, Keith D., Lance Eliot Brouthers, and Steve Werner. "Resource-Based Advantages in an International Context." *Journal of Management* 34, no. 2 (April 2008): 189.

Brown, John Seely, Lang Davison, and John Hagel III. "Shaping Strategy in a World of Constant Disruption." *Harvard Business Review* (October 2008): 80.

Butter, Den, A. G. Frank, and Kees A. Linse. "How Procurement Informs Strategy in the Era of Globalization." *MIT Sloan Management Review* 50, no. 1 (Fall 2008): 76.

Desia, Mihir, A. "The Finance Function in a Global Corporation." *Harvard Business Review* (July–August 2008): 108.

Feinberg, Susan, and Anil Gupta. "MNC Subsidiaries and County Risk: Internalization as a Safeguard Against Weak External Institutions." *Academy of Management Journal* (April 2009): 381–399.

Hitt, Michael A., and Xiaoming He. "Firm Strategies in a Changing Global Competitive Landscape." *Business Horizons* 51, no. 5 (September–October 2008): 363.

Inkpen, Andrew C. "Knowledge Transfer and International Joint Ventures: The Case of NUMMI and General Motors." *Strategic Management Journal* 29, no. 4 (April 2008): 447.

Karra, Neri, Nelson Phillips, and Paul Tracey. "Building the Born Global Firm Developing Entrepreneurial Capabilities for International New Venture Success." *Long Range Planning* 41, no. 4 (August 2008): 420.

Lee, Seung-Hyun, Jiatao Li, and Oded Shenkar. "Cultural Distance, Investment Flow, and Control in Cross-Border Cooperation." *Strategic Management Journal* 29, no. 10 (October 2008): 1117.

Nelson, Phillips, and Paul Tracey. "Institutional Theory and the MNC." *Academy of Management Review* (January 2009): 169–171.

Nill, Alexander, and Clifford Schultz II. "Global Software Piracy: Trends and Strategic Considerations." *Business Horizons* (May–June 2009): 289–298.

Peng, Mike W., Jeffery J. Reuer, and Tony W. Tong. "International Joint Ventures and the Value of Growth Options." *Academy of Management Journal* 51, no. 5 (October 2008): 1014.

Prashantham, Shameen, and Julian Birkinshaw. "Dancing with Gorillas: How Small Companies Can Partner Effectively with MNCs." *California Management Review* 51, no. 1 (Fall 2008): 6–23.

Ren, Hong, Barbara Gray, and Kwangho Kim. "Performance of International Joint Ventures: What Factors Really Make a Difference and How?" *Journal of Management* (June 2009): 805–832.

Strutton, David. "Horseshoes, Global Supply Chains, and an Emerging Chinese Threat: Creating Remedies One Idea at a Time." *Business Horizons* (January–February 2009): 31–43.

ASSURANCE OF LEARNING EXERCISES

Assurance of Learning Exercise 11A

McDonald's Wants to Enter Africa. Help Them.

Purpose

More and more companies every day decide to begin doing business in the forgotten continent—Africa. Research is necessary to determine the best strategy for being the first mover in many African countries (i.e., being the first competitor doing business in various countries).

Instructions

Step 1	Print off a map of Africa.
Step 2	Print off demographic data on 10 African countries.
Step 3	Gather competitive information regarding the presence of fast-food firms doing business in Africa.
Step 4	List in prioritized order eight countries that you would recommend for McDonald's entry. Country 1 is your best, and country 2 is your next best. Based on your research, indicate how many McDonald's restaurants you would recommend building over the next three years in each country. List in prioritized order three cities in each of your eight African countries where you believe McDonald's should build most of its restaurants.

Assurance of Learning Exercise 11B

Does My University Recruit in Foreign Countries?

Purpose

A competitive climate is emerging among colleges and universities around the world. Colleges and universities in Europe and Japan are increasingly recruiting U.S. students to offset declining enrollments. Foreign students already make up more than a third of the student body at many U.S. universities. The purpose of this exercise is to identify particular colleges and universities in foreign countries that recruit U.S. students.

Instructions

Step 1	Select a foreign country. Conduct research to determine the number and nature of colleges and universities in that country. What are the major educational institutions in that country? What programs are those institutions recognized for offering? What percentage of undergraduate and graduate students attending those institutions are U.S. citizens? Do these institutions actively recruit U.S. students? Are any of the schools of business at the various universities AACSB-International accredited?
Step 2	Prepare a report that summarizes your research findings. Present your report to the class.

Assurance of Learning Exercise 11C

Assessing Differences in Culture Across Countries

Purpose

Americans can be more effective in dealing with businesspeople from other countries if they have some awareness and understanding of differences in culture across countries. This is a fun exercise that provides information for your class regarding some of these key differences.

Instructions

Step 1   Identify four individuals who either grew up in a foreign country or who have lived in a foreign country for more than one year. Interview those four persons. Try to have four different countries represented. During each interview, develop a list of eight key differences between American style/custom and that particular country's style/custom in terms of various aspects of speaking, meetings, meals, relationships, friendships, and communication that could impact business dealings.

Step 2   Develop a 15-minute PowerPoint presentation for your class and give a talk summarizing your findings. Identify in your talk the persons you interviewed as well as the length of time those persons lived in the respective countries. Give your professor a hard copy of your PowerPoint presentation.

Assurance of Learning Exercise 11D

How Well Traveled Are Business Students at Your University?

Purpose

It would be interesting to know how traveled are students at your university and also how those students consider their travels to be helpful in becoming an effective businessperson. Generally speaking, the more one has traveled, especially outside the United States, the more tolerant, understanding, and appreciative one is for diversity. Many students even state on their resume the extent to which they have traveled, both across the United States and perhaps around the world.

Instructions

Administer the following survey to at least 30 business students, including your classmates in the strategic management course. Analyze the results. Give a 15-minute presentation to your class regarding your findings. Turn in a written report of your findings to your professor.

The Survey

1. How many states in the United States have you visited?
2. How many states in the United States have you lived for at least three months?
3. How many countries outside the United States have you visited?
4. List the countries outside the United States that you have visited.
5. How many countries outside the United States have you lived for at least three months?
6. List the countries outside the United States that you have lived for at least three months.
7. To what extent do you feel that traveling across the United States can make a person a more effective businessperson? Use a 1 to 10 scale, where 1 is "Cannot Make a Difference" and 10 is "Can Make a Tremendous Difference."
8. To what extent do you feel that visiting countries outside the United States can make a person a more effective business person? Use a 1 to 10 scale, where 1 is "Cannot Make a Difference" and 10 is "Can Make a Tremendous Difference."
9. To what extent do you feel that living in another country can make a person a more effective businessperson? Use a 1 to 10 scale, where 1 is "Cannot Make a Difference" and 10 is "Can Make a Tremendous Difference."
10. What three important ways so you feel that traveling or living outside the United States would be helpful to a person in being a more effective businessperson?

How to Prepare and Present a Case Analysis

CHAPTER OBJECTIVES

After studying this chapter, you should be able to do the following:

1. Describe the case method for learning strategic-management concepts.

2. Identify the steps in preparing a comprehensive written case analysis.

3. Describe how to give an effective oral case analysis presentation.

4. Discuss special tips for doing case analysis.

Assurance of Learning Exercises

Oral Presentation—Step 1
Introduction (2 minutes)

Oral Presentation—Step 2
Mission/Vision (4 minutes)

Oral Presentation—Step 3
Internal Assessment (8 minutes)

Oral Presentation—Step 4
External Assessment (8 minutes)

"Notable Quotes"

"Two heads are better than one."

—Unknown Author

"One reaction frequently heard is 'I don't have enough information.' In reality strategists never have enough information because some information is not available and some is too costly."

—William Glueck

"I keep six honest serving men. They taught me all I know. Their names are What, Why, When, How, Where, and Who."

—Rudyard Kipling

"Don't recommend anything you would not be prepared to do yourself if you were in the decision maker's shoes."

—A. J. Strickland III

"A picture is worth a thousand words."

—Unknown Author

Oral Presentation— Step 5
Strategy Formulation (14 minutes)

Oral Presentation— Step 6
Strategy Implementation (8 minutes)

Oral Presentation— Step 7
Strategy Evaluation (2 minutes)

Oral Presentation— Step 8
Conclusion (4 minutes)

The purpose of this section is to help you analyze strategic-management cases. Guidelines for preparing written and oral case analyses are given, and suggestions for preparing cases for class discussion are presented. Steps to follow in preparing case analyses are provided. Guidelines for making an oral presentation are described.

What Is a Strategic-Management Case?

A *strategic-management case* describes an organization's external and internal conditions and raises issues concerning the firm's mission, strategies, objectives, and policies. Most of the information in a business policy case is established fact, but some information may be opinions, judgments, and beliefs. Strategic-management cases are more comprehensive than those you may have studied in other courses. They generally include a description of related management, marketing, finance/accounting, production/operations, R&D, computer information systems, and natural environment issues. A strategic-management case puts the reader on the scene of the action by describing a firm's situation at some point in time. Strategic-management cases are written to give you practice applying strategic-management concepts. The case method for studying strategic management is often called *learning by doing*.

Guidelines for Preparing Case Analyses

The Need for Practicality

There is no such thing as a complete case, and no case ever gives you all the information you need to conduct analyses and make recommendations. Likewise, in the business world, strategists never have all the information they need to make decisions: information may be unavailable or too costly to obtain, or it may take too much time to obtain. So in preparing strategic-management cases, do what strategists do every day—make reasonable assumptions about unknowns, clearly state assumptions, perform appropriate analyses, and make decisions. *Be practical.* For example, in performing a projected financial analysis, make reasonable assumptions, appropriately state them, and proceed to show what impact your recommendations are expected to have on the organization's financial position. Avoid saying, "I don't have enough information." You can always supplement the information provided in a case with Internet and library research.

The Need for Justification

The most important part of analyzing cases is not what strategies you recommend but rather how you support your decisions and how you propose that they be implemented. There is no single best solution or one right answer to a case, so give ample justification for your recommendations. This is important. In the business world, strategists usually do not know if their decisions are right until resources have been allocated and consumed. Then it is often too late to reverse a decision. This cold fact accents the need for careful integration of intuition and analysis in preparing business policy case analyses.

The Need for Realism

Avoid recommending a course of action beyond an organization's means. *Be realistic.* No organization can possibly pursue all the strategies that could potentially benefit the firm. Estimate how much capital will be required to implement what you recommended. Determine whether debt, stock, or a combination of debt and stock could be used to obtain the capital. Make sure your recommendations are feasible. Do not prepare a case analysis that omits all arguments and information not supportive of your recommendations. Rather, present the major advantages and disadvantages of several feasible alternatives. Try not to exaggerate, stereotype, prejudge, or overdramatize. Strive to demonstrate that your interpretation of the evidence is reasonable and objective.

The Need for Specificity

Do not make broad generalizations such as "The company should pursue a market penetration strategy." Be specific by telling *what, why, when, how, where*, and *who*. Failure to use specifics is the single major shortcoming of most oral and written case analyses. For example, in an internal audit say, "The firm's current ratio fell from 2.2 in 2009 to 1.3 in 2010, and this is considered to be a major weakness," instead of "The firm's financial condition is bad." Rather than concluding from a Strategic Position and Action Evaluation (SPACE) Matrix that a firm should be defensive, be more specific, saying, "The firm should consider closing three plants, laying off 280 employees, and divesting itself of its chemical division, for a net savings of $20.2 million in 2010." Use ratios, percentages, numbers, and dollar estimates. Businesspeople dislike generalities and vagueness.

The Need for Originality

Do not necessarily recommend the course of action that the firm plans to take or actually undertook, even if those actions resulted in improved revenues and earnings. The aim of case analysis is for you to consider all the facts and information relevant to the organization at the time, to generate feasible alternative strategies, to choose among those alternatives, and to defend your recommendations. Put yourself back in time to the point when strategic decisions were being made by the firm's strategists. Based on the information available then, what would you have done? Support your position with charts, graphs, ratios, analyses, and the like—not a revelation from the library. You can become a good strategist by thinking through situations, making management assessments, and proposing plans yourself. *Be original*. Compare and contrast what you recommend versus what the company plans to do or did.

The Need to Contribute

Strategy formulation, implementation, and evaluation decisions are commonly made by a group of individuals rather than by a single person. Therefore, your professor may divide the class into three- or four-person teams and ask you to prepare written or oral case analyses. Members of a strategic-management team, in class or in the business world, differ on their aversion to risk, their concern for short-run versus long-run benefits, their attitudes toward social responsibility, and their views concerning globalization. There are no perfect people, so there are no perfect strategies. Be open-minded to others' views. *Be a good listener and a good contributor*.

Preparing a Case for Class Discussion

Your professor may ask you to prepare a case for class discussion. Preparing a case for class discussion means that you need to read the case before class, make notes regarding the organization's external opportunities/threats and internal strengths/weaknesses, perform appropriate analyses, and come to class prepared to offer and defend some specific recommendations.

The Case Method versus Lecture Approach

The case method of teaching is radically different from the traditional lecture approach, in which little or no preparation is needed by students before class. The *case method* involves a classroom situation in which students do most of the talking; your professor facilitates discussion by asking questions and encouraging student interaction regarding ideas, analyses, and recommendations. Be prepared for a discussion along the lines of "What would you do, why would you do it, when would you do it, and how would you do it?" Prepare answers to the following types of questions:

- What are the firm's most important external opportunities and threats?
- What are the organization's major strengths and weaknesses?
- How would you describe the organization's financial condition?

- What are the firm's existing strategies and objectives?
- Who are the firm's competitors, and what are their strategies?
- What objectives and strategies do you recommend for this organization? Explain your reasoning. How does what you recommend compare to what the company plans?
- How could the organization best implement what you recommend? What implementation problems do you envision? How could the firm avoid or solve those problems?

The Cross-Examination

Do not hesitate to take a stand on the issues and to support your position with objective analyses and outside research. Strive to apply strategic-management concepts and tools in preparing your case for class discussion. Seek defensible arguments and positions. Support opinions and judgments with facts, reasons, and evidence. Crunch the numbers before class! Be willing to describe your recommendations to the class without fear of disapproval. Respect the ideas of others, but be willing to go against the majority opinion when you can justify a better position.

Strategic management case analysis gives you the opportunity to learn more about yourself, your colleagues, strategic management, and the decision-making process in organizations. The rewards of this experience will depend on the effort you put forth, so do a good job. Discussing business policy cases in class is exciting and challenging. Expect views counter to those you present. Different students will place emphasis on different aspects of an organization's situation and submit different recommendations for scrutiny and rebuttal. Cross-examination discussions commonly arise, just as they occur in a real business organization. Avoid being a silent observer.

Preparing a Written Case Analysis

In addition to asking you to prepare a case for class discussion, your professor may ask you to prepare a written case analysis. Preparing a written case analysis is similar to preparing a case for class discussion, except written reports are generally more structured and more detailed. There is no ironclad procedure for preparing a written case analysis because cases differ in focus; the type, size, and complexity of the organizations being analyzed also vary.

When writing a strategic-management report or case analysis, avoid using jargon, vague or redundant words, acronyms, abbreviations, sexist language, and ethnic or racial slurs. And watch your spelling! Use short sentences and paragraphs and simple words and phrases. Use quite a few subheadings. Arrange issues and ideas from the most important to the least important. Arrange recommendations from the least controversial to the most controversial. Use the active voice rather than the passive voice for all verbs; for example, say "Our team recommends that the company diversify" rather than "It is recommended by our team to diversify." Use many examples to add specificity and clarity. Tables, figures, pie charts, bar charts, timelines, and other kinds of exhibits help communicate important points and ideas. Sometimes a picture *is* worth a thousand words.

The Executive Summary

Your professor may ask you to focus the written case analysis on a particular aspect of the strategic-management process, such as (1) to identify and evaluate the organization's existing mission, objectives, and strategies; or (2) to propose and defend specific recommendations for the company; or (3) to develop an industry analysis by describing the competitors, products, selling techniques, and market conditions in a given industry. These types of written reports are sometimes called *executive summaries*. An executive summary usually ranges from three to five pages of text in length, plus exhibits.

The Comprehensive Written Analysis

Your professor may ask you to prepare a *comprehensive written analysis*. This assignment requires you to apply the entire strategic-management process to the particular organization. When preparing a comprehensive written analysis, picture yourself as a consultant who has been asked by a company to conduct a study of its external and internal environment and to make specific recommendations for its future. Prepare exhibits to support your recommendations. Highlight exhibits with some discussion in the paper. Comprehensive written analyses are usually about 10 pages in length, plus exhibits.

Steps in Preparing a Comprehensive Written Analysis

In preparing a **written** case analysis, you could follow the steps outlined here, which correlate to the stages in the strategic-management process and the chapters in this text. (Note—The steps in presenting an **oral** case analysis are given on pages 356–358, are more detailed, and could be used here).

Step 1   Identify the firm's existing vision, mission, objectives, and strategies.

Step 2   Develop vision and mission statements for the organization.

Step 3   Identify the organization's external opportunities and threats.

Step 4   Construct a Competitive Profile Matrix (CPM).

Step 5   Construct an External Factor Evaluation (EFE) Matrix.

Step 6   Identify the organization's internal strengths and weaknesses.

Step 7   Construct an Internal Factor Evaluation (IFE) Matrix.

Step 8   Prepare a Strengths-Weaknesses-Opportunities-Threats (SWOT) Matrix, Strategic Position and Action Evaluation (SPACE) Matrix, Boston Consulting Group (BCG) Matrix, Internal-External (IE) Matrix, Grand Strategy Matrix, and Quantitative Strategic Planning Matrix (QSPM) as appropriate. Give advantages and disadvantages of alternative strategies.

Step 9   Recommend specific strategies and long-term objectives. Show how much your recommendations will cost. Clearly itemize these costs for each projected year. Compare your recommendations to actual strategies planned by the company.

Step 10   Specify how your recommendations can be implemented and what results you can expect. Prepare forecasted ratios and projected financial statements. Present a timetable or agenda for action.

Step 11   Recommend specific annual objectives and policies.

Step 12   Recommend procedures for strategy review and evaluation.

Making an Oral Presentation

Your professor may ask you to prepare a strategic-management case analysis, individually or as a group, and present your analysis to the class. Oral presentations are usually graded on two parts: content and delivery. *Content* refers to the quality, quantity, correctness, and appropriateness of analyses presented, including such dimensions as logical flow through the presentation, coverage of major issues, use of specifics, avoidance of generalities, absence of mistakes, and feasibility of recommendations. *Delivery* includes such dimensions as audience attentiveness, clarity of visual aids, appropriate dress, persuasiveness of arguments, tone of voice, eye contact, and posture. Great ideas are of no value unless others can be convinced of their merit through clear communication. The guidelines presented here can help you make an effective oral presentation.

Organizing the Presentation

Begin your presentation by introducing yourself and giving a clear outline of topics to be covered. If a team is presenting, specify the sequence of speakers and the areas each person will address. At the beginning of an oral presentation, try to capture your audience's interest and attention. You could do this by displaying some products made by the company, telling an interesting short story about the company, or sharing an experience you had that is related to the company, its products, or its services. You could develop or obtain a video to show at the beginning of class; you could visit a local distributor of the firm's products and tape a personal interview with the business owner or manager. A light or humorous introduction can be effective at the beginning of a presentation.

Be sure the setting of your presentation is well organized, with seats for attendees, flip charts, a transparency projector, and whatever else you plan to use. Arrive at the classroom at least 15 minutes early to organize the setting, and be sure your materials are ready to go. Make sure everyone can see your visual aids well.

Controlling Your Voice

An effective rate of speaking ranges from 100 to 125 words per minute. Practice your presentation aloud to determine if you are going too fast. Individuals commonly speak too fast when nervous. Breathe deeply before and during the presentation to help yourself slow down. Have a cup of water available; pausing to take a drink will wet your throat, give you time to collect your thoughts, control your nervousness, slow you down, and signal to the audience a change in topic.

Avoid a monotone by placing emphasis on different words or sentences. Speak loudly and clearly, but don't shout. Silence can be used effectively to break a monotone voice. Stop at the end of each sentence, rather than running sentences together with *and* or *uh*.

Managing Body Language

Be sure not to fold your arms, lean on the podium, put your hands in your pockets, or put your hands behind you. Keep a straight posture, with one foot slightly in front of the other. Do not turn your back to the audience; doing so is not only rude, but it also prevents your voice from projecting well. Avoid using too many hand gestures. On occasion, leave the podium or table and walk toward your audience, but do not walk around too much. Never block the audience's view of your visual aids.

Maintain good eye contact throughout the presentation. This is the best way to persuade your audience. There is nothing more reassuring to a speaker than to see members of the audience nod in agreement or smile. Try to look everyone in the eye at least once during your presentation, but focus more on individuals who look interested than on those who seem bored. To stay in touch with your audience, use humor and smiles as appropriate throughout your presentation. A presentation should never be dull!

Speaking from Notes

Be sure not to read to your audience because reading puts people to sleep. Perhaps worse than reading is merely reciting what you have memorized. Do not try to memorize anything. Rather, practice unobtrusively using notes. Make sure your notes are written clearly so you will not flounder when trying to read your own writing. Include only main ideas on your note cards. Keep note cards on a podium or table if possible so that you won't drop them or get them out of order; walking with note cards tends to be distracting.

Constructing Visual Aids

Make sure your visual aids are legible to individuals in the back of the room. Use color to highlight special items. Avoid putting complete sentences on visual aids; rather, use short phrases and then orally elaborate on issues as you make your presentation. Generally, there should be no more than four to six lines of text on each visual aid. Use clear headings and subheadings. Be careful about spelling and grammar; use a consistent style of lettering. Use masking tape or an easel for posters—do not hold posters in your hand. Transparencies and handouts are excellent aids; however, be careful not to use too many handouts or your audience may concentrate on them instead of you during the presentation.

Answering Questions

It is best to field questions at the end of your presentation, rather than during the presentation itself. Encourage questions, and take your time to respond to each one. Answering questions can be persuasive because it involves you with the audience. If a team is giving the presentation, the audience should direct questions to a specific person. During the question-and-answer period, be polite, confident, and courteous. Avoid verbose responses. Do not get defensive with your answers, even if a hostile or confrontational question is asked. Staying calm during potentially disruptive situations, such as a cross-examination, reflects self-confidence, maturity, poise, and command of the particular company and its industry. Stand up throughout the question-and-answer period.

Tips for Success in Case Analysis

Strategic-management students who have used this text over 12 editions offer you the following tips for success in doing case analysis. The tips are grouped into two basic sections: (1) Content Tips and (2) Process Tips. Content tips relate especially to the content of your case analysis, whereas the Process tips relate mostly to the process that you and your group mates undergo in preparing and delivering your case analysis/presentation.

Content Tips

1. Use the www.strategyclub.com Web site resources. The software described there is especially useful.
2. In preparing your external assessment, use the S&P Industry Survey material in your college library.
3. Go to the http://finance.yahoo.com or http://moneycentral.msn/investor/home.asp and enter your company's stock symbol.
4. View your case analysis and presentation as a product that must have some competitive factor to favorably differentiate it from the case analyses of other students.
5. Develop a mind-set of *why*, continually questioning your own and others' assumptions and assertions.
6. Because strategic management is a capstone course, seek the help of professors in other specialty areas when necessary.
7. Read your case frequently as work progresses so you don't overlook details.
8. At the end of each group session, assign each member of the group a task to be completed for the next meeting.
9. Become friends with the library and the Internet.
10. Be creative and innovative throughout the case analysis process.
11. A goal of case analysis is to improve your ability to think clearly in ambiguous and confusing situations; do not get frustrated that there is no single best answer.
12. Do not confuse symptoms with causes; do not develop conclusions and solutions prematurely; recognize that information may be misleading, conflicting, or wrong.
13. Work hard to develop the ability to formulate reasonable, consistent, and creative plans; put yourself in the strategist's position.
14. Develop confidence in using quantitative tools for analysis. They are not inherently difficult; it is just practice and familiarity you need.
15. Strive for excellence in writing and in the technical preparation of your case. Prepare nice charts, tables, diagrams, and graphs. Use color and unique pictures. No messy exhibits! Use PowerPoint.
16. Do not forget that the objective is to learn; explore areas with which you are not familiar.
17. Pay attention to detail.
18. Think through alternative implications fully and realistically. The consequences of decisions are not always apparent. They often affect many different aspects of a firm's operations.
19. Provide answers to such fundamental questions as *what, when, where, why, who,* and *how.*

20. Do not merely recite ratios or present figures. Rather, develop ideas and conclusions concerning the possible trends. Show the importance of these figures to the corporation.
21. Support reasoning and judgment with factual data whenever possible.
22. Your analysis should be as detailed and specific as possible.
23. A picture speaks a thousand words, and a creative picture gets you an A in many classes.
24. Emphasize the Recommendations and Strategy Implementation sections. A common mistake is to spend too much time on the external or internal analysis parts of your paper. Always remember that the recommendations and implementation sections are the most important part of the paper or presentation.

Process Tips

1. When working as a team, encourage most of the work to be done individually. Use team meetings mostly to assimilate work. This approach is most efficient.
2. If allowed to do so, invite questions throughout your presentation.
3. During the presentation, keep good posture, eye contact, voice tone, and project confidence. Do not get defensive under any conditions or with any questions.
4. Prepare your case analysis in advance of the due date to allow time for reflection and practice. Do not procrastinate.
5. Maintain a positive attitude about the class, working *with* problems rather than against them.
6. Keep in tune with your professor, and understand his or her values and expectations.
7. Other students will have strengths in functional areas that will complement your weaknesses, so develop a cooperative spirit that moderates competitiveness in group work.
8. When preparing a case analysis as a group, divide into separate teams to work on the external analysis and internal analysis.
9. Have a good sense of humor.
10. Capitalize on the strengths of each member of the group; volunteer your services in your areas of strength.
11. Set goals for yourself and your team; budget your time to attain them.
12. Foster attitudes that encourage group participation and interaction. Do not be hasty to judge group members.
13. Be prepared to work. There will be times when you will have to do more than your share. Accept it, and do what you have to do to move the team forward.
14. Think of your case analysis as if it were really happening; do not reduce case analysis to a mechanical process.
15. To uncover flaws in your analysis and to prepare the group for questions during an oral presentation, assign one person in the group to actively play the devil's advocate.
16. Do not schedule excessively long group meetings; two-hour sessions are about right.
17. Push your ideas hard enough to get them listened to, but then let up; listen to others and try to follow their lines of thinking; follow the flow of group discussion, recognizing when you need to get back on track; do not repeat yourself or others unless clarity or progress demands repetition.
18. Develop a case-presentation style that is direct, assertive, and convincing; be concise, precise, fluent, and correct.
19. Have fun when at all possible. Preparing a case is frustrating at times, but enjoy it while you can; it may be several years before you are playing CEO again.
20. In group cases, do not allow personality differences to interfere. When they occur, they must be understood for what they are—and then put aside.
21. Get things written down (drafts) as soon as possible.
22. Read everything that other group members write, and comment on it in writing. This allows group input into all aspects of case preparation.
23. Adaptation and flexibility are keys to success; be creative and innovative.
24. Neatness is a real plus; your case analysis should look professional.

25. Let someone else read and critique your presentation several days before you present it.
26. Make special efforts to get to know your group members. This leads to more openness in the group and allows for more interchange of ideas. Put in the time and effort necessary to develop these relationships.
27. Be constructively critical of your group members' work. Do not dominate group discussions. Be a good listener and contributor.
28. Learn from past mistakes and deficiencies. Improve upon weak aspects of other case presentations.
29. Learn from the positive approaches and accomplishments of classmates.

Sample Case Analysis Outline

There are musicians who play wonderfully without notes and there are chefs who cook wonderfully without recipes, but most of us prefer a more orderly cookbook approach, at least in the first attempt at doing something new. Therefore the following eight steps may serve as a basic outline for you in presenting a strategic plan for your firm's future. This outline is not the only approach used in business and industry for communicating a strategic plan, but this approach is time-tested, it does work, and it does cover all of the basics. You may amend the content, tools, and concepts given to suit your own company, audience, assignment, and circumstances, but it helps to know and understand the rules before you start breaking them.

Depending on whether your class is 50 minutes or 75 minutes and how much time your professor allows for your case presentation, the following outlines what generally needs to be covered. A recommended time (in minutes) as part of the presentation is given for an overall 50-minute event. Of course, all cases are different, some being about for-profit and some about not-for-profit organizations, for example, so the scope and content of your analysis may vary. Even if you do not have time to cover all areas in your oral presentation, you may be asked to prepare these areas and give them to your professor as a "written case analysis." Be sure in an oral presentation to manage time knowing that your recommendations and associated costs are the most important part. You should go to www.strategyclub.com and utilize that information and software in preparing your case analysis. Good luck.

Current Readings

Kearney, Eric, Diether Gebert, and Sven Voelpel. "When Diversity Benefits Teams: The Importance of Team Members' Need for Cognition." *Academy of Management Journal* (June 2009): 581–598.

STEPS IN PRESENTING AN ORAL CASE ANALYSIS

Oral Presentation—Step 1

Introduction (2 minutes)

a. Introduce yourselves by name and major. Establish the time setting of your case and analysis. Prepare your strategic plan for the three years 2010–2012.
b. Introduce your company and its products/services; capture interest.
c. Show the outline of your presentation and tell who is doing what parts.

Oral Presentation—Step 2

Mission/Vision (4 minutes)

a. Show existing mission and vision statements if available from the firm's Web site, or annual report, or elsewhere.
b. Show your "improved" mission and vision and tell why it is improved.
c. Compare your mission and vision to a leading competitor's statements.
d. Comment on your vision and mission in terms of how they support the strategies you envision for your firm.

Oral Presentation—Step 3

Internal Assessment (8 minutes)

a. Give your financial ratio analysis. Highlight especially good and bad ratios. Do not give definitions of the ratios and do not highlight all the ratios.
b. Show the firm's organizational chart found or "created based on executive titles." Identify the type of chart as well as good and bad aspects. Unless all white males comprise the chart, peoples' names are generally not important because positions reveal structure as people come and go.
c. Present your improved/recommended organizational chart. Tell why you feel it is improved over the existing chart.
d. Show a market positioning map with firm and competitors. Discuss the map in light of strategies you envision for firm versus competitors' strategies.
e. Identify the marketing strategy of the firm in terms of good and bad points versus competitors and in light of strategies you envision for the firm.
f. Show a map locating the firm's operations. Discuss in light of strategies you envision. Also, perhaps show a Value Chain Analysis chart.
g. Discuss (and perhaps show) the firm's Web site and e-commerce efforts/abilities in terms of good and bad points.
h. Show your "value of the firm" analysis.
i. List up to 20 of the firm's strengths and weaknesses. Go over each one listed without "reading" them verbatim.
j. Show and explain your Internal Factor Evaluation (IFE) Matrix.

Oral Presentation—Step 4

External Assessment (8 minutes)

a. Identify and discuss major competitors. Use pie charts, maps, tables, and/or figures to show the intensity of competition in the industry.
b. Show your Competitive Profile Matrix. Include at least 12 factors and two competitors.
c. Summarize key industry trends citing Standard & Poor's *Industry Survey* or Chamber of Commerce statistics, etc. Highlight key external trends as they impact the firm, in areas such as the economic, social, cultural, demographic, geographic, technological, political, legal, governmental, and natural environment.
d. List up to 20 of the firm's opportunities and threats. Make sure your opportunities are not stated as strategies. Go over each one listed without "reading" them verbatim.
e. Show and explain your External Factor Evaluation (EFE) Matrix.

Oral Presentation—Step 5

Strategy Formulation (14 minutes)

a. Show and explain your SWOT Matrix, highlighting each of your strategies listed.
b. Show and explain your SPACE Matrix, using half of your "space time" on calculations and the other half on implications of those numbers. Strategy implications must be specific rather than generic. In other words, use of a term such as "market penetration" is not satisfactory alone as a strategy implication.
c. Show your Boston Consulting Group (BCG) Matrix. Again focus on both the numbers and the strategy implications. Do multiple BCG Matrices if possible, including domestic versus global, or another geographic breakdown. Develop a product BCG if at all possible. Comment on changes to this matrix as per strategies you envision. Develop this matrix even if you do not know the profits per division and even if you have to estimate the axes information. However, make no wild guesses on axes or revenue/profit information.
d. Show your Internal-External (IE) Matrix. Because this analysis is similar to the BCG, see the preceding comments.
e. Show your Grand Strategy Matrix. Again focus on implications after giving the quadrant selection. Reminder: Use of a term such as "market penetration" is not satisfactory alone as a strategy implication. Be more specific. Elaborate.
f. Show your Quantitative Strategic Planning Matrix (QSPM). Be sure to explain your strategies to start with here. Do not go back over the internal and external factors. Avoid having more than one 4, 3, 2, or 1 in a row. If you rate one strategy, you need to rate the other because, that particular factor is affecting the choice. Work row by row rather than column by column on preparing the QSPM.
g. Present your Recommendations Page. This is the most important page in your presentation. Be specific in terms of both strategies and estimated costs of those strategies. *Total your estimated costs.* You should have ten or more strategies. Divide your strategies into two groups: (1) Existing Strategies to Be Continued, and (2) New Strategies to Be Started.

Oral Presentation—Step 6

Strategy Implementation (8 minutes)

a. Show and explain your EPS/EBIT analysis to reveal whether stock, debt, or a combination is best to finance your recommendations. Graph the analysis. Decide which approach to use if there are any given limitations of the analysis.
b. Show your projected income statement. Relate changes in the items to your recommendations rather than blindly going with historical percentage changes.

c. Show your projected balance sheet. Relate changes in your items to your recommendations. Be sure to show the retained earnings calculation and the results of your EPS/EBIT decision.

d. Show your projected financial ratios and highlight several key ratios to show the benefits of your strategic plan.

Oral Presentation—Step 7

Strategy Evaluation (2 minutes)

a. Prepare a Balanced Scorecard to show your expected financial and nonfinancial objectives recommended for the firm.

Oral Presentation—Step 8

Conclusion (4 minutes)

a. Compare and contrast your strategic plan versus the company's own plans for the future.

b. Thank audience members for their attention. Seek and answer questions.

INDEX

Strategic Management
CASES

Walt Disney Company — 2009

Mernoush Banton
Adjunct Faculty/Consultant

DIS

www.disney.com

High unemployment, lingering recession, slow economic growth, and reduced consumer spending all contributed to a 7 percent drop in revenue and a 46 percent drop in Walt Disney's profitability for the first quarter of 2009. For eight decades, the Walt Disney Company has captured the attention of millions of people, offering family entertainment products and services such as theme parks, resorts, recreations, movies, TV shows, radio programming, and memorabilia. Walt Disney brought Mickey Mouse and Donald Duck to the world. Walt Disney offers a variety of family entertainment all around the world.

History

Mr. Walt Disney and his brother Roy arrived in California in the summer of 1923 to sell his cartoon called *Alice's Wonderland.* A distributor named M. J. Winkler contracted to distribute the Alice Comedies on October 16, 1923, and the Disney Brothers Cartoon Studio was founded. Over the years, the company produced many cartoons, from *Oswald the Lucky Rabbit* (1927) to *Silly Symphonies* (1932), *Snow White and the Seven Dwarfs* (1937), and *Pinocchio* and *Fantasia* (1940). The name of the company was changed to Walt Disney Studio in 1925. Mickey Mouse emerged in 1928 with the first cartoon in sound.

In 1950, Disney completed its first live action film, *Treasure Island,* and in 1954, the company began television with Disneyland anthology series. In 1955, Disney's most successful series, *The Mickey Mouse Club,* began. Also in 1955, the new Disneyland Park in California was opened. Disney created a series of releases from 1950s through 1970s, including *The Shaggy Dog, Zorro, Mary Poppins,* and *The Love Bug.* Mr. Walt Disney died in 1966. In 1969, the Disney started its educational films and materials. Another important time of Disney's history was opening the Walt Disney World project in Orlando, Florida, on October 1, 1971. In 1982, the Epcot Center was opened as part of Walt Disney World. And, on April 15, 1983, Tokyo Disneyland opened.

After leaving the network television in 1983, the company was ready to get into its cable network, The Disney Channel. In 1985, Disney's Touchstone division began the successful *Golden Girls* and *Disney Sunday Movie.* In 1988, Disney opened Grand Floridian Beach and Caribbean Beach Resorts at Walt Disney World along with three new gated attractions: the Disney/MGM Studios Theme Park, Pleasure Island, and Typhoon Lagoon. At the same time, filmmaking hit new heights as Disney for the first time led Hollywood studios in box-office gross. Some of the successful films were: *Who Framed Roger Rabbit, Good Morning Vietnam, Three Men and a Baby,* and later, *Honey, I Shrunk the Kids, Dick Tracy, Pretty Woman,* and *Sister Act.* Disney moved into new areas by starting Hollywood Pictures and acquiring the Wrather Corp. (owner of the Disneyland Hotel) and television station KHJ (Los Angeles), which was renamed KCAL. In merchandising, Disney purchased Childcraft and opened numerous highly successful and profitable Disney Stores.

By 1992, Disney's animation began reaching even greater audiences with *The Little Mermaid, The Beauty and the Beast,* and *Aladdin.* Hollywood Records was formed to offer a wide selection of recordings ranging from rap to movie soundtracks. New television shows, such as *Live with Regis and Kathy Lee, Empty Nest, Dinosaurs,* and *Home*

Improvement, expanded Disney's television base. For the first time, Disney moved into publishing, forming Hyperion Books, Hyperion Books for Children, and Disney Press, which released books on Disney and non-Disney subjects. In 1991, Disney purchased *Discover* magazine, the leading consumer science monthly. As a totally new venture, Disney was awarded, in 1993, the franchise for a National Hockey League team, the Mighty Ducks of Anaheim.

In 1992, Disneyland Paris opened in France. Disney successfully completed many projects throughout the 1990s by venturing into Broadway shows, opening up to 725 Disney Stores, acquiring the California Angels baseball team to add to its hockey team, opening Disney's Wide World of Sports in Walt Disney World, and acquiring Capital Cities/ABC. From 2000 to 2007, Disney created new attractions in its theme parks, produced many successful films, opened new hotels, and built Hong Kong Disneyland.

Internal Issues

Organizational Structure and Mission

As indicated in Exhibit 1, Disney operates using a strategic business unit (SBU) type organizational structure. Note that Disney's four SBUs consist of (1) Disney Consumer Products, (2) Studio Entertainment, (3) Parks and Resorts, and (4) Media Networks and Broadcasting.

Disney's mission statement is "To be one of the world's leading producers and providers of entertainment and information. Using our portfolio of brands to differentiate our content, services and consumer products, we seek to develop the most creative, innovative and profitable entertainment experiences and related products in the world." Disney does not have a vision statement.

EXHIBIT 1   Disney's Corporate Structure

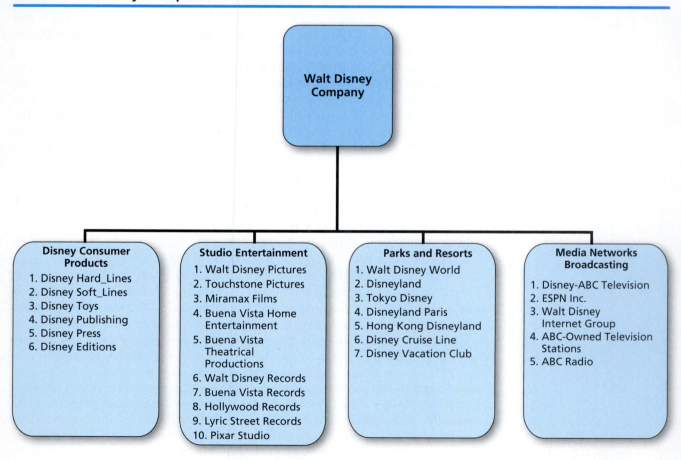

EXHIBIT 2   Consolidated Income Statement (in millions, except per share data)

	2008	2007	2006
Revenues	$ 37,843	$ 35,510	$ 33,747
Costs and expenses	(30,439)	(28,681)	(28,392)
Other (expense)/income	(59)	1,004	88
Net interest expense	(524)	(593)	(592)
Equity in the income of investees	581	485	473
Income from continuing operations before income taxes and minority interests	7,402	7,725	5,324
Income taxes	(2,673)	(2,874)	(1,837)
Minority interests	(302)	(177)	(183)
Income from continuing operations	4,427	4,674	3,304
Discontinued operations, net of tax	—	13	70
Net income	$ 4,427	$ 4,687	$ 3,374
Diluted Earnings per share:			
Earnings per share, continuing operations	$ 2.28	$ 2.24	$ 1.60
Earnings per share, discontinued operations	—	0.01	0.03
Earnings per share	$ 2.28	$ 2.25	$ 1.64
Basic Earnings per share:			
Earnings per share, continuing operations	$ 2.34	$ 2.33	$ 1.65
Earnings per share, discontinued operations	—	0.01	0.03
Earnings per share	$ 2.34	$ 2.34	$ 1.68
Weighted average number of common and common equivalent shares outstanding:			
Diluted	1,948	2,092	2,076
Basic	1,890	2,004	2,005

Source: Walt Disney Company, *Annual Report* (2008).

Consolidated Financial Statements

Disney's recent income statements and balance sheets are provided in Exhibits 2 and 3, respectively. Note the increase in profit from 2006 to 2007, and the decline from 2007 to 2008.

The most recent Disney's Consolidated Balance Sheet, shown in Exhibit 3, reveals over $22 billion in Goodwill and nearly $11.1 billion in Long Term Debt.

Financials by Segment

Exhibit 4 demonstrates the company's revenue and operating income by each business segment. Note that Disney's Media Networks brings in the most revenues and operating income for the company. This division, as well as the Parks and Resorts segment, is growing. However, the company's Studio Entertainment business segment and their Consumer Products businesses have experienced declining revenues in the last three years.

As shown in Exhibit 5, Disney derives 76 percent of its revenue and 77 percent of its operating income from businesses in the United States and Canada. The company's revenues and income are growing in all regions of the world, with Europe being second behind the United States/Canada in both revenues and income.

Disney Business Segments

In percentage terms, Disney revenues in 2008 were derived from Media Networks (43 percent), Parks and Resorts (31 percent), Studio Entertainment (20 percent), and

EXHIBIT 3 Consolidated Balance Sheets (in millions, except per share data)

	September 27, 2008	September 29, 2007
ASSETS		
Current assets		
Cash and cash equivalents	$ 3,001	$ 3,670
Receivables	5,373	5,032
Inventories	1,124	641
Television costs	541	559
Deferred income taxes	1,024	862
Other current assets	603	550
Total current assets	11,666	11,314
Film and television costs	5,394	5,123
Investments	1,563	995
Parks, resorts and other property, at cost		
Attractions, buildings and equipment	31,493	30,260
Accumulated depreciation	(16,310)	(15,145)
	15,183	15,115
Projects in progress	1,169	1,147
Land	1,180	1,171
	17,532	17,433
Intangible assets, net	2,428	2,494
Goodwill	22,151	22,085
Other assets	1,763	1,484
Total Assets	$ 62,497	$ 60,928
LIABILITIES AND SHAREHOLDERS' EQUITY		
Current liabilities		
Accounts payable and other accrued liabilities	$ 5,980	$ 5,949
Current portion of borrowings	3,529	3,280
Unearned royalties and other advances	2,082	2,162
Total current liabilities	11,591	11,391
Borrowings	11,110	11,892
Deferred income taxes	2,350	2,573
Other long-term liabilities	3,779	3,024
Minority interests	1,344	1,295
Commitments and contingencies		
Shareholder's equity		
Preferred stock, $.01 par value Authorized–100 million shares, Issued–none	—	—
Common stock, $.01 par value Authorized–3.6 billion shares, Issued–2.6 billion shares	26,546	24,207
Retained earnings	28,413	24,805
Accumulated other comprehensive loss	(81)	(157)
	54,878	48,855
Treasury stock, at cost, 777.1 million shares at September 27, 2008, and 637.8 million shares at September 29, 2007	(22,555)	(18,102)
	32,323	30,753
Total Liabilities and SE	$ 62,497	$ 60,928

Source: Walt Disney Company, *Annual Report* (2008).

EXHIBIT 4   Revenue and Operating Income by Segment (2008 vs. 2007)

(in millions)	2008	2007	2006	Percentage of change 2008 vs. 2007	2007 vs. 2006
Revenues:					
Media Networks	$ 16,116	$ 15,104	$ 14,186	7	6
Parks and Resorts	11,504	10,626	9,925	8	7
Studio Entertainment	7,348	7,491	7,529	(2)	(1)
Consumer Products	2,875	2,289	2,107	26	9
Total Consolidated Revenues	$ 37,843	$ 35,510	$ 33,747	7	5
Segment operating income					
Media Networks	$ 4,755	$ 4,275	$ 3,481	11	23
Parks and Resorts	1,897	1,710	1,534	11	11
Studio Entertainment	1,086	1,195	728	(9)	64
Consumer Products	718	631	607	14	4
Total segment operating income	$ 8,456	7,811	$ 6,350	8	23

Source: Walt Disney Company, *Annual Report* (2008).

Consumer Products (8 percent). Operating income was derived from Media Networks (57 percent), Parks and Resorts (23 percent), Studio Entertainment (13 percent), and Consumer Products (9 percent). These percentages reveal a bit of a weakness in Studio Entertainment because this segment creates 20 percent of revenues but only 13 percent of operating income.

Media Networks/Broadcasting

Disney owns ABC Television Network, which includes ABC Entertainment, ABC Daytime, ABC News, ABC Sports, ABC Kids, Touchstone Television, and ABC Radio. Also included in this segment, Disney owns ESPN, Disney Channel, ABC Family, Toon Disney, SOAPnet, and Buena Vista Television. Disney has equity interest in Lifetime

EXHIBIT 5   Revenue and Operating Income by Region

(in millions)	2008	2007	2006
Revenue			
United States and Canada	$ 28,506	$ 27,286	$ 26,027
Europe	6,805	5,898	5,266
Asia Pacific	1,811	1,732	1,917
Latin America and Other	721	594	537
	$ 37,843	$ 35,510	$ 33,747
Segment operating income			
United States and Canada	$ 6,472	$ 6,026	$ 4,797
Europe	1,423	1,192	918
Asia Pacific	386	437	542
Latin America and Other	175	156	93
	$ 8,456	$ 7,811	$ 6,350

Source: Walt Disney Company, *Annual Report* (2008).

Entertainment Services, A&E Television Networks, E! Entertainment, ESPN, History Channel, The Biography Channel, Hyperion Books, and Disney Mobile.

The increase in revenue in this segment was primarily due to growth from cable and satellite operators, which are generally derived from fees charged on a per subscriber basis, contractual rate increases, and higher adverting rates at ESPN. The increase in broadcasting revenue was due to growth at the ABC Television Network and increased sales of Touchstone Television series as well as an increase in prime-time advertising revenues. Increase in sales from Touchstone Television series was as a result of higher international syndication and DVD sales of hit dramas such as *Lost, Grey's Anatomy,* and *Desperate Housewives,* as well as higher third-party license fees led by *Scrubs,* which completed its fifth season of network television.

Two major TV networks of Disney (ABC and ESPN) recently struck a deal with cable operator Cox Communication whereby these companies now offer hit shows and football games on demand. Although advertising in the network is a source of additional revenue for the broadcasters, it requires selectivity for charging for each episode. Video-on-demand is a major industry and is expected to grow to $3.9 billion by 2010.

Disney recently unveiled Disney Xtreme Digital, a networking site aimed at children younger than 14 years of age. This service will be competing against MySpace (owned by News Corporation). Disney has reported an increase in fiscal 2009 second-quarter net income mostly as a result of strong gains at cable network ESPN. Higher advertising revenues are reflected due to NASCAR programming at ESPN, an increase at ABC Family primarily due to higher rates, higher other revenues by DVD sales primarily from *High School Musical*, and a favorable settlement of a claim with an international distributor.

Exhibit 6 provides specific segment information for the Media Networks division. Disney's domestic broadcast television stations are listed in Exhibit 7. Disney's international media network operations are described in Exhibit 8. In prime time, higher advertising rates and sold inventory were partially offset by lower rating from some of the problems. Increased sales of ABC Studios productions reflected higher international and DVD sales of hit drams such as *Desperate Housewives, Grey's Anatomy,* and *Ugly Betty.*

Parks and Resorts

Disney owns and operates Walt Disney World Resort & Cruise Lines in Florida, Disneyland Resort in California, ESPN Zone facilities in many states, 17 hotels at the Walt Disney World Resort, Disney's Fort Wilderness Camping and Recreation, Downtown Disney, Disney's Wide World of Sports, Disney Cruise Line, 7 Disney Vacation Club Resorts, Adventures by Disney, and 5 resort locations with 11 theme parks on three continents. With theme parks, Disney has 51 percent ownership in Disneyland Resort Paris,

EXHIBIT 6   Media Network Segment: Revenue and Operating Income

(in millions)	2008	2007	2006	Change 2008 vs. 2007	Change 2007 vs. 2006
Revenues:					
Cable Networks	$ 10,041	$ 9,167	$ 8,159	10%	12%
Broadcasting	6,075	5,937	6,027	2%	(1)%
	$ 16,116	$ 15,104	$ 14,186	7%	6%
Segment operating income:					
Cable Networks	$ 4,100	$ 3,577	$ 3,001	15%	19%
Broadcasting	655	698	480	(6)%	45%
	$ 4,755	$ 4,275	$ 3,481	11%	23%

Source: Walt Disney Company, *Annual Report* (2008).

EXHIBIT 7   Disney's Domestic Broadcast Television Stations

Market	TV Station	Analog Channel	Television Market Ranking
New York, NY	WABC-TV	7	1
Los Angeles, CA	KABC-TV	7	2
Chicago, IL	WLS-TV	7	3
Philadelphia, PA	WPVI-TV	6	4
San Francisco, CA	KGO-TV	7	6
Houston, TX	KTRK-TV	13	10
Raleigh-Durham, NC	WTVD-TV	11	28
Fresno, CA	KFSN-TV	30	55
Flint, MI	WJRT-TV	12	66
Toledo, OH	WTVG-TV	13	72

Source: Walt Disney Company, *Form 10K* (2008).

EXHIBIT 8   Disney's International Cable Satellite Networks and Broadcast Operations

Property	Estimated Domestic Subscribers (in millions)[1]	Estimated International Subscribers (in millions)[2]	Number of Channels	Ownership %
ESPN				
ESPN[1]	98	—		80.0
ESPN2	97	—		80.0
ESPN Classic	63	—		80.0
ESPNEWS	67	—		80.0
ESPN Deportes	4	—		80.0
ESPNU	20	—		80.0
Disney Channels Worldwide				
Disney Channel	97	78	30	100.0
Playhouse Disney	—	32	19	100.0
Toon Disney	71	19	9	100.0
Jetix Europe	—	52	25	73.3
Jetix Latin America	—	20	4	100.0
Hungama	—	7	1	100.0
ABC Family	97	—	1	100.0
SOAPnet	70	—	1	100.0
A&E				
A&E	97	—	1	37.5
The History Channel	97	—	1	37.5
The Biography Channel	52	—	1	37.5
History International	52	—	1	37.5
Lifetime				
Lifetime Television	97	—	1	50.0
Lifetime Movie Network	66	—	1	50.0
Lifetime Real Women[2]	11	—	1	50.0

(1) Estimated U.S. subscriber counts according to Nielsen Media Research as of September 2008.

Source: Walt Disney Company, *Form 10K* (2008).

EXHIBIT 9   Disney's Offerings Under Parks and Resorts

Walt Disney World Resorts	Disneyland Resort	Disneyland Resort Paris	Hong Kong Disneyland Resort	Tokyo Disney Resort	Disney Cruise Line	ESPN Zone	Walt Disney Imagineering
Epcot	Disneyland	Disneyland Park	Hong Kong Disneyland	Tokyo Disneyland			
Disney-MGM Studios	Disneyland's California Adventure	Walt Disney Studios Park	Resort Facilities	Tokyo DisneySea			
Magic Kingdom	Resort Facilities						
Disney's Animal Kingdom							
Resort Facilities							

Source: Walt Disney Company, *Form 10K* (2008).

43 percent ownership in Hong Kong Disneyland, 100 percent ownership in Tokyo Disney Resort as well as Disneyland in both California and Florida. Exhibit 9 summarizes Disney's key parks and resort holdings.

Disney revenues at its Parks and Resorts division increased 7 percent in 2008, or $701 million, to $10.6 billion due to increases of $483 million and $218 million at its domestic and international resorts, respectively. Domestic Parks and Resorts revenues increased due to increased guest spending, theme park attendance, and hotel occupancy, as well as higher sales at Disney Vacation Club. Higher guest spending was due to a higher average daily hotel room rate, higher average ticket prices, and greater merchandise spending at both resorts.

Disneyland Resort Paris experienced increased revenues, offset by a decrease at Hong Kong Disneyland Resort due to lower theme park attendance. Some of the increase in revenue was due to favorable impact of foreign currency translation (weakening of the U.S. dollar against the euro). Operating income from the Parks and Resorts segment increased 11 percent, or by $524 million, to $1.897 billion. Exhibit 10 presents Disney's attendance, per capita theme park guest spending, and hotel statistics for its domestic properties:

EXHIBIT 10   Disney Parks and Resorts Data (2008 vs. 2007)

	East Coast Resorts		West Coast Resorts		Total Domestic Resorts	
	FY 2008	FY 2007	FY 2008	FY 2007	FY 2008	FY 2007
Increase in Attendance	6%	5%	(1)%	6%	3%	5%
Increase in Per Capita Guest Spending	3%	1%	2%	8%	3%	3%
Occupancy	89%	86%	92%	93%	89%	87%
Available Room Nights (in thousands)	8,614	8,834	810	810	9,424	9,644
Per Room Guest Spending	$217	$211	$309	$287	$225	$218

Source: Walt Disney Company, *Annual Report* (2008).

The company also has been hosting VIP tours (additional fees applies), offering added-value services such as number of attractions being covered along with personal guide tours, preferred seating, and front-of-line access to rides. The company also offers package deals for major corporations and schools.

Disney has plans to change its concept of the theme parks from the masses to a more concentrated perspective. This move allows Disney to offer more stand-alone theme parks and resorts in cities and beach resorts, as well as Disney-branded retail and dining districts, and smaller and more sophisticated parks. This permits the company in using the Disney brand name to expand in other areas of the travel business. The company has built time-share vacation homes in popular places in the United States. Some of the challenges in this marketing strategy have been tailoring the niche attractions to the local markets while keeping the Disney brand reputation. However, there is a challenge of avoiding cannibalization of existing parks and attractions. The goal would be entering into new markets without harming or cannibalizing Disney's brand.

Studio Entertainment

Disney produces live-action and animated motion pictures, direct-to-video programming, musical recordings, and live-stage plays. Disney motion pictures are distributed under the names Walt Disney Pictures and Television, Touchstone Pictures, Hollywood Pictures, Miramax Films, and Buena Vista Home Entertainment International, which includes Walt Disney Records, Buena Vista Records, Hollywood Records, Lyric Street Records, and Disney Music Publishing. Disney owns Pixar, a computer animation leader, and produces feature animation films under both the Disney and Pixar banners. The company also produces stage plays, musical recordings, and live entertainment events. As of September 2008, Disney had released 928 full-length movies, 80 full-length animated features, and 546 cartoon shorts. Product offerings include Pay-Per-View, Pay Television, Free Television, Pay Television 2, and International Television.

Consumer Products

The Consumer Products segment includes partners with licenses, manufacturers, publishers, and retailers worldwide who design, promote, and sell a wide variety of products based on new and existing Disney characters. The product offerings are Character Merchandise and Publications Licensing, Books and Magazines, Buena Vista Games, DisneyShopping.com, and The Disney Store. Products include books, interactive games, food and beverages, fine art, apparel, toys, and even home decor.

In 2008, the revenues from this segment increased 26 percent to $2.9 billion. Sales growth at the Disney Stores was due to the acquisition of the Disney Stores North America. Sales growth at Merchandise Licensing was driven by higher earned royalties across multiple product categories.

Operating income of this segment increased 14 percent to $718 million, mostly due to growth at Merchandise Licensing partially offset by a decrease at the Disney Stores due to the acquisition of the Disney Stores North America. In April 2008, Disney acquired inventory, leasehold improvements, and certain fixed assets of the Disney Stores North America for approximately $64 million. The acquisition included the assumption of the leases of 229 stores.

Competition

Disney's competitors differ in each segment of business. Time Warner is a major competitor to Disney and is composed of five divisions: AOL, Cable, Filmed Entertainment, Networks, and Publishing. Time Warner owns Time Inc., AOL, Warner Brothers, and TBS Networks. Walt Disney generally is classified as Entertainment-Diversified, which directly competes with Time Warner, Inc. (as shown in Exhibit 11).

CBS Corporation and News Corporation directly compete with the Walt Disney Company in the Media Network segment, but they are not rivals in the Consumer Products and Parks and Resorts segments. CBS Corporation was a part of Viacom, Inc., but now operates independently under CBS Corp. News Corporation is a diversified international media and entertainment company that operates in eight segments: Filmed Entertainment,

EXHIBIT 11   Disney vs. the Industry: Comparative Data

	DIS	CBS	TWX	Industry
Market Cap	39.00B	4.31B	26.28B	499.59M
# of Employees	150,000	25,920	87,000	7.51K
Qtrly Rev Growth	−8.20%	−6.20%	−2.70%	5.10%
Revenue	$ 36.99B	13.95B	46.98B	930.87M
Gross Margin	17.81%	37.99%	41.92%	41.92%
EBITDA	$ 8.18B	2.69B	13.34B	166.44M
Oper Margins	17.81%	15.48%	18.62%	10.39%
Net Income	$ 4.02B	−11.67B	−13.40B	N/A
EPS	$ 2.100	−17.428	−11.224	N/A

DIS = Walt Disney Company
CBS = CBS Corporation
TWX = Time Warner Inc.

Source: Based on finance.yahoo.com (April 2009).

Television, Cable Network Programming, Direct Broadcast Satellite Television, Magazines and Inserts, Newspapers, Book Publishing, and Other. Due to recent corporate restructuring for both CBS Corporation and News Corp., there are no industry data available for comparison purposes. Next we discuss the competition for each segment of Walt Disney.

Competition: Media Networks/Broadcasting

The global media industry is a $1 trillion business that includes advertising, cable firms, newspapers, radio, and television. This industry is dominated by conglomerates Walt Disney, Time Warner, Inc., New York Times, News Corp., and CBS Corporation. Typically, these companies prosper during election years due to heavy advertising revenue invested by the politicians. Special events such as the Olympics also generate additional advertising revenue for such companies.

Disney competes for viewers primarily with other television networks, independent television stations, and other video media such as cable and satellite television programming services, DVD, video games, and the Internet. Radio networks likewise compete with other radio network stations and programming services. Disney also competes with other advertising media such as newspapers, magazines, billboards, and the Internet.

Exhibit 12 reveals some major competitors to Disney in this segment of business, as well as percentages that indicate attractiveness of that venue to consumers ages 18 to 24.

CBS Corp. is composed of five segments: Television, Radio, Outdoor, Interactive, and Publishing. CBS Television is composed of CBS Network and its own television stations,

EXHIBIT 12   Disney Rival Firms in Media Networks/Broadcasting

Major Competitors	% Attractiveness*
Discovery Networks	72%
Disney/ESPN Media Networks	68%
MTV Networks	52%
Turner Entertainment Networks	48%
Scripps Networks	43%
NBC Universal Cable	39%
Comcast Cable Networks	34%
Fox Cable Networks	31%

*To consumers ages 18 to 24.

Source: Based on *Multichannel News* 28, no. 10 (2007): 30; ISSN: 0276-8593.

television production, and syndication, Showtime, and CSTV Networks. In 2008, the Television segment of CBS contributed 64 percent of company's total revenue (approximately $8.99 billion). The Radio segment derives revenue primarily from advertising sales. In 2008, the Radio segment generated 11 percent of CBS's total revenue (approximately $1.5 billion).

News Corp., with $33 billion in revenue, operates in eight industry segments: Filmed Entertainment, Television, Cable Network Programming, Direct Broadcast Satellite Television, Magazines and Inserts, Newspapers, Book Publishing, and Other. For the fiscal year 2008, the Filmed Entertainment, Television, Cable Network Programming, and Direct Broadcast Satellite Television contributed approximately 65 percent or $21.2 billion to the company's total revenue. The company has been moving aggressively toward digital technologies such as broadband, mobility, storage, and wireless. News Corp. owns MySpace.com, one of the Internet's most popular social networking site, and IGN.com (a gaming and entertainment site). Fox TV, owned by News Corp., ranks as one of the most popular networks on television with an average audience of 7.6 million every night, followed by CBS with 6.7 million viewers during each prime time, Walt Disney Company's ABC with 5.4 million viewers per night, and finally NBC (owned by General Electric Company) with 4.8 million viewers during each prime-time period. News Corp. recently acquired Dow Jones & Company and Liberty Media Corporation, which included approximately 41 percent interest in the DIRECTV Group, Inc.

Time Warner's media and entertainment segments include AOL, Cable, Filmed Entertainment, Networks, and Publishing. The Cable segment services primarily analog and digital video services, and advanced services such as VOD and HDTV with set-top boxed equipped with digital video recorders. The Filmed Entertainment segment produces and distributes theatrical motion pictures and television shows. The Network segment consists of HBO and Cinemax pay television programming services. The Publishing segment publishes magazines and Web sites in a variety of areas and has a strategic alliance with Google, Inc. Exhibit 13 demonstrates Time Warner's revenue by segment.

Competition: Parks and Resorts

Disney's theme parks and resorts compete with all other forms of entertainment, lodging, tourism, and recreational activities. Many uncontrollable factors may influence the profitability of the leisure-time industry such as economic conditions, including business cycle and exchange rate fluctuations; travel industry trends; amount of available leisure time; oil and transportation prices; and weather patterns. Seasonality is another concern for this segment because all of the theme parks and the associated resort facilities are operated year-round. Peak attendance and resort occupancy generally occur during the summer months when school vacations take place and during early winter and spring holiday periods.

According to a survey conducted by the International Association of Amusement Parks and Attractions (IAAPA), there are more than 400 amusement parks in the United States, generating approximately $11.5 billion in revenues. The Magic Kingdom at Walt Disney World in Florida was the most visited amusement park in the world. The amusement parks in the United States employ approximately 500,000 year-round and seasonal employees.

EXHIBIT 13   Time Warner, Inc., Revenue (in millions) by Segment (2007)

Segment	Revenue	Percentage of Total Sales	Operating Income
Cable	$ 17,200	35.44	$ (11,782)
AOL	4,165	8.58	(1,147)
Filmed Entertainment	11,398	23.49	823
Networks	11,154	23.00	3,118
Publishing	4,608	9.49	(6,624)
Total	48,525		

Source: Time Warner Inc., *Form 10K* (2008).

The second largest amusement park company after Disney is Six Flags, Inc., based in Oklahoma City, Oklahoma, with 20 parks across the United States, Mexico, and Canada and soon in Dubai and Qatar with more than $1 billion in revenue (2008). Six Flags recently acquired Dick Clark Productions, which owns television hits such as the *American Music Awards, The Golden Globe Awards, the Academy of Country Music Awards, Dick Clark's New Year's Rockin' Eve,* and *So You Think You Can Dance.*

Ocean Park in Hong Kong has been aggressively competing with Disney. Ocean Park is a theme park that covers over 870,000 square meters and receives more than 5 million tourists each year. In March 2009, Ocean Park launched two new sightseeing locations in Shanghai to attract tourists from regions such as the Yangtze River Delta. Ocean Park has the advantage of understanding the local market because they have been in business for more than 30 years. They offer a range of transportation facilities to link Hong Kong with major cities in the Pearl River Delta. In 2008, Ocean Park established an office in Shanghai. Ocean Park plans to complete construction of four new themed travel attractions between 2010 and 2013. It also seems that the residents in Hong Kong are not very impressed with the small version of Disney built there because many have visited Disneyland in Tokyo or Anaheim, California. Disney in mid-2009 reached an agreement with the Hong Kong government to enlarge Hong Kong Disneyland. That city government owns 57 percent of that Disney theme park.

Competition: Studio Entertainment

The success of Studio Entertainment operations depends heavily on public taste and preferences. Operating results fluctuate due to the timing and performance of releases in the theatrical, home entertainment, and television markets. Release dates are determined by competition and the timing of vacation and holiday periods. Many companies produce and/or distribute theatrical and television films, exploit products in the home entertainment market, provide pay television programming services, and sponsor live theater. Disney also competes to obtain creative and performing talents, story properties, advertiser support, broadcast rights, and market share.

Movies have historically been a reasonable priced entertainment for families, and comprise more than $150 billion in revenues annually. The most important regions contributing to this industry are the United States (49.8 percent), Europe (33 percent), and Asia and developing countries (14 percent). Consolidation has been very common in the movie and entertainment industry. As such, a few companies dominate the industry and control the production and distribution of most movies, including: Warner Brothers (17.10 percent), Walt Disney (11.70 percent), Twentieth Century Fox (10.3 percent), Viacom (6.3 percent), and other (54.6 percent).

Competition: Consumer Products

Leading competitors to Disney in this segment are Warner Brothers, Fox, Sony, Marvel, and Nickelodeon. Disney competes in its character merchandising and other licensing, publishing, interactive, and retail activities with other licensors, publishers, and retailers of character, brand, and celebrity names. Disney is perhaps the largest worldwide licensor of character-based merchandise and producer/distributor of children's film-related products based on retail sales. Operating results for the licensing and retail distribution business are influenced by seasonal consumer purchasing behavior and by the timing and performance of animated theatrical releases.

Risk

A wide range of factors could materially affect the future and the performance of the Disney, such as:

1. A prolonged recession in the United States and other regions of the world could have an adverse affect on the company's business.
2. The success of the business depends on the ability to consistently create and distribute programs/products (movies, films, programs, theme park attractions, resort services, and consumer products) that consumers want. As such, heavy

investment is required in such product/service offerings in order to earn consumer acceptance and attention.

3. Changes in technology and in consumer consumption.
4. Technologies such as peer-to-peer, high-speed digital transmission, illegal digital video recorders, and so on are vulnerable to piracy. Disney must devote substantial resources to protect its intellectual property.
5. Changes in travel and tourism could impact the company's business, such as adverse weather conditions, natural disasters, terrorist attacks, health concerns, international concerns, political or military developments, and war.
6. High unemployment rates.

Source: The Walt Disney Company, *Form 10K* (2008).

Conclusion

Walt Disney's net income fell 26 percent for the third quarter (2009) with no division or segment of the company reporting an increase. The worst performing division for the quarter was Movie Studio, which reported an operating loss of $12 million on a revenue drop of 12 percent. Disney's DVD sales slowed dramatically.

As the economic recession lingers and consumers still spend money on what the need rather than what they want, Disney needs a clear strategic plan for the future. Shareholders do not want to see a repeat of the firm's third-quarter type results. Let's say Disney asks your assistance in developing a strategic plan. Help Disney reverse its slipping revenues.

References

Datamonitor Industry Market Research
finance.yahoo.com
Investor's Business Daily
Multichannel News, available from www.multichannel.com
News Corporation, available from www.newscorp.com
The *Wall Street Journal*, available from www.wsj.com
The Walt Disney Company, available from www.disney.com
TheStreet.com, available from www.thestreet.com
Time Warner, Inc., available from www.timewarner.com
Standard & Poor's, available from www.standardandpoors.com
USAToday.com, available from www.usatoday.com

2 Merryland Amusement Park — 2009

Gregory Stone
Regent University

In September 2009, the "Support Merryland" advocacy group was started to draw public interest in the historic Merryland Amusement Park. Anthony (Tony) Kenworthy is currently aligned with this Kansas historical preservation group for the purpose of gaining federal government influence toward a "historical site" designation, which would help to secure the property and its assets for potential investors for the purpose of site restoration. There is also a growing grassroots level interest throughout Kansas in seeing Merryland restored to its previous days of carnival-like splendor. Tony is fully aware of this state sentiment and intends to use it to move a state-based initiative forward for just that purpose.

Tony has to make a decision! The owners of Merryland Amusement Park, a derelict "50 acres of fun!" amusement park located in Kansas City, have again put the attraction up for sale after several failed attempts to reopen the park. Merryland officially closed its entrance gates to the public in 2009. If Tony waits too long, his colossal theme park dream will vaporize. If he acts too quickly, he might get the keys to the *Titanic*.

Poor financial management and other factors contributed to the owners' decision to close and sell the park. Tony has three investment options, and investors associated with each are ready to move, even in the face of poor park performance—or, in this case, nonexistent performance. Tony's entrepreneurial magic is just what the amusement park needs, if not more of an entrepreneurial miracle. The park is the perfect fit for providing fun activities for disabled children—Tony's personal passion.

Tony's first option is to buy the park, make the renovations, and reopen it under his management. Altria, a major corporation, has offered all the cash he needs to make the purchase representing Tony's second option. Finally a local consortium of entrepreneurs gives him more control, but far less cash. Choosing the right option could make or break Tony's career, his finances, his life, his reputation, and even his personal relationships.

Background

Merryland is a local theme/fun park that originally opened in 1955. The park was started and managed for 33 years by Stanley Merry, a nephew of the man the park was named after. In 1988, Stanley Merry died and left the park to his only heir, his widowed daughter-in-law, Samantha Steinberg.

Samantha had little interest in owning, and much less in operating, an amusement park. Her second husband, Alan, took up the responsibility for most of the day-to-day operations. Although the couple operated the park from 1988 to 2008, Samantha's heart was never in the business. Maintenance budgets and the total number of employees were annually reduced to the detriment of the park's operations. They simultaneously, however, kept annually increasing park entrance fees, "to suck every last dime we can get out of the park," according to Samantha.

Falling revenues and a noticeable degrading of the park's facilities prompted long-time owners Samantha and Alan Steinberg to put the park up for sale in the fall of 2006, with an asking price of $5.8 million for the 50-acre facility. Twenty of those acres were still in woods and fields behind the 30-acre theme park area.

Two other groups tried unsuccessfully to take over the operations and keep Merryland going prior to the amusement park officially closing in 2009, but both found refurbishing costs and operating costs were far more than anticipated. Rising liability insurance costs were equally challenging. In late 2007, Alan Steinberg, now 85, and Samantha Steinberg, herself 87 years old, again had full control of the park and desire a minimum of $2 million this time around.

"It has to be cash," Samantha stated adamantly. "This time there is no leasing or holding the note." She did quickly add that she and her husband, however, would consider proposals to do something else with the undeveloped land, such as building a corporate headquarters, expanding the park, or some other kind of development opportunity.

Although Merryland only closed its doors in 2009, it has since become a target for vandals, with more than 20 break-ins recently reported. Police arrested two men a month ago after they found spray-painted swastikas and other graffiti on buildings. "They were really reckless," Alan Steinberg lamented. "They turned over ticket booths, broke into the office, and threw furniture out the windows."

Tony, Just Another Hard-Working Entrepreneurial Guy

Born in Chesapeake, Virginia, Tony graduated from the University of Richmond with a double major in economics and accounting. He served as president of his fraternity and improved the overall quality of the food, house services, negotiated better utility rates, and achieved all of it without having to increase monthly member rent rates.

Tony's Love for the Summer Camp Kids

Between his freshman and sophomore years, one of Tony's fraternity brothers hired him to work during the summer at an eastern Virginia youth camp. It didn't take long for Tony to work his entrepreneurial magic again. He was instrumental in helping the camp managers get a grip on cash flow and a better system of managing camp expenses. As he implemented his new marketing initiatives, they quickly measured increases in both new campers and the subsequent revenue generated from the steady increase in the number of camp attendees.

He was the leader, the hero, and garnished the attention once again. The campers loved the camp programs, the parents loved the camp, the camp managers loved Tony, and Tony discovered that he really, truly loved working with the kids. The camp finally had a brand identity in the marketplace, a focus, and was gaining a positive reputation throughout the community and state. Although Tony enjoyed working with the camp managers, he soon found that his one true camp love was working with the actual campers. He especially thrived from seeing kids with disabilities tackle their obstacles and discover their unique talents. The corporate sponsorship opportunity he created significantly increased the number of kids who could finally attend the camp. Working with "his kids" would often cause him to tear up as he watched them learn about their special abilities and skills.

His love for the kids and his ability to make them happy made this the perfect summer job throughout his college career. Sure, the pay wasn't the best, but he got to work with his fraternity brothers. Tony was able to maintain as much fun off the clock as he had during the day with the kids. His "panty raid" attempts occasionally sparked the ire and disdain of the women counselors who felt he should have long outgrown such childish pranks.

Graduation from the university landed Tony the position of business manager for the camp. The work was fun but didn't allow the level of daily involvement with the kids, and he sorely missed that. His position did, however, bring him into increased contact with Jennifer, and she actually seemed to be "warming" up to him. Managing a not-for-profit organization put a cap on his entrepreneurial drive and prevented him from deriving financial dividends from the increased profits he brought to the operation. He was far more the capitalist, with the desire to be rewarded for a job well done. Without the creativity and opportunity to innovate, he quickly lost motivation—especially in light of the lack of financial gain.

Tony as a Showbiz Pizza Business Manager

The job as a business manager for a Showbiz Pizza franchise in nearby Camden, Virginia, got Tony's entrepreneurial DNA quickly engaged again. The franchise was a combination pizza parlor, game room, and bar. A local favorite for children's birthday parties and a place for area families to have their family night out, Tony was able to interact more frequently with kids again. During his three years as business manager, he implemented numerous small operational changes that increased corporate profitability (see Exhibit 1).

He entered into a lease agreement with a local vendor to develop the business model to lease the gaming equipment to all the Virginia Showbiz franchises. This enabled Showbiz to offer its owner/operators the most current games all while reducing operating and repair costs. He also shut the restaurant down at 10 PM to families and children, and then reopened the bar operation an hour later until 2 AM for locals to drink, dance, carouse, play pool, play video games, and have good clean adult fun. Then Tony heard from one of his fraternity brothers that Merryland Amusement Park was up for sale, and he knew his dream job had arrived!

The Sale of Merryland

During the unsuccessful sale attempt and subcontracted operation of Merryland, general park maintenance was neglected. Falling revenues were also attributed to the growing interest in nontraditional theme park attractions fueled by the cost of gasoline and increasingly tight economic conditions (see Exhibit 1). Local real estate values, the lack of maintenance, and no new investment into the park resulted in steadily declining values from 2004 to 2008 (see Exhibit 2).

Other local patrons were more willing to make the longer drives to stay for several days or a week to the larger "mega" theme parks such as Six Flags St. Louis as a family vacation. Although there were no directly competing amusement parks in Kansas, the Steinbergs never seemed to fully grasp the significance of that opportunity (see Exhibit 3). Consequently, small niche amusement centers based in malls had begun to spring up. The bigger, more lavish

EXHIBIT 1   Merryland Income Statements for 2004–2008

	2004	2005	2006	2007	2008
Sales Revenues	1,245,000	1,450,000	1,253,000	1,020,000	890,000
Cost of Goods Sold	310,000	465,000	403,000	323,000	301,000
Gross Margin	935,000	985,000	850,000	697,000	589,000
Operating Expense	736,000	796,000	780,000	595,000	502,000
Operating Income	199,000	189,000	70,000	102,000	87,000
Interest Expense	15,000	18,000	15,000	12,000	9,500
Net Income Before Taxes	184,000	171,000	55,000	90,000	77,500
Taxes	73,600	68,400	22,000	36,000	31,000
Net Income	**110,400**	**102,600**	**33,000**	**54,000**	**46,500**

Key Financial Ratios					
	2004	2005	2006	2007	2008
Current Ratio	2.3	2.4	1.9	1.6	1.4
Total Asset Turnover Ratio	1.5	1.7	1.3	1.1	0.9
Net Profit Margin	0.089	0.071	0.026	0.053	0.052

Other Data					
	2004	2005	2006	2007	2008
Employees	10 full, 32 part	10 full, 35 part	8 full, 30 part	7 full, 25 part	5 full, 30 part
Maintenance Expenditures	54,000	44,000	45,000	36,000	29,000
Average Number of Rides Operating per Day	22	22	20	19	15

EXHIBIT 2 Merryland Amusement Park Balance Sheets 2005–2009

ASSETS	FY 2005	FY 2006	FY 2007	FY 2008	FY 2009
Current Assets					
Cash	$102,600	$33,000	$54,000	$46,500	$0
Other Current Assets	$ 0	$ 0	$ 0	$ 0	$0
Total Current Assets =	**$102,600**	**33,000**	**$54,000**	**$46,500**	**$0**

PROPERTY, PLANT, & EQUIPMENT	FY 2005	FY 2006	FY 2007	FY 2008	FY 2009
Land	$4,225,675	$3,877,925	$2,722,583	$2,077,748	$1,893,932
Land Improvements	$ 37,500	$ 32,250	$ 25,500	$ 5,000	$ 0
Buildings	$ 202,600	$ 183,000	$ 172,000	$ 156,500	$ 125.000
Equipment (Rides)	$ 425,000	$ 375,000	$ 325,000	$ 225,000	$ 175,000
Total Prop Plnt & Eqmt =	**$4,890,775**	**$4,468,175**	**$3,245,083**	**$2,464,248**	**$2,193,932**
Total Assets =	**$4,993,375**	**$4,501,175**	**$3,299,083**	**$2,510,748**	**$2,193,932**

LIABILITIES & CAPITAL	FY 2005	FY 2006	FY 2007	FY 2008	FY 2009
Current Liabilities					
Accounts Payable	$ 75,702	$ 80,950	$ 68,064	$ 89,325	$ 98,783
Current Borrowing	$ 72,146	$ 75,388	$ 72,466	$ 74,539	$ 107,414
Other Current Liabilities	$ 26,723	$ 28,943	$ 24,889	$ 29,385	$ 31,845
Subtotal Current Liabilities	**$ 174,571**	**$ 185,281**	**$ 165,419**	**$ 193,249**	**$ 238,042**
Short-term Liabilities	$ 54,723	$ 50,630	$ 46,598	$ 42,554	$ 39,784
Total Liabilities =	**$ 229,294**	**$ 235,911**	**$ 212,017**	**$ 235,803**	**$ 277,826**
Net Worth =	**$4,764,081**	**$4,265,264**	**$3,087,066**	**$2,274,945**	**$1,916,106**

EXHIBIT 3 Kansas Entertainment Attractions

Name	Address	Facility Type	Attraction Description
All Star Adventures (East)	1010 N. Webb Road Wichita, KS 67206	Amusement Park	Wichita's only amusement park with rides for kids and go karts.
Wild West World	7300 North Wild West Drive Valley Center, KS 67147	Theme Park	Featuring cowboys and Indians, Wild West World is the first major theme park in Kansas and the world's only one sporting an all-Western theme. The park opened in May 2007 and closed in July 2007. Its owners declared bankruptcy and were hoping to sell the park so that it could reopen. Those plans failed, however. The rides were sold to other parks.
Zonkers	20070 W. 151st Street Olathe, KS 66061	Theme Park	Zonkers (previously Jeepers!) is an indoor theme park serving families with children of all ages. The park provides a diverse mix of arcade games and amusement rides built to scale for indoor use. Rides include the popular Python Pit (roller coaster), Yak Attack (mini-Himalaya), Venetian Carousel, Train, and Banana Squadron (airplane ride).

EXHIBIT 4 Missouri Entertainment Attractions

Name	Address	Facility Type	Attraction Description
Carousel Park	3834 W. 7th Street Joplin, MO 64801	Amusement Park	This is a family fun park for young and old. Park features dozens of amusement rides, two 18-hole miniature golf courses, multispeed batting cages, the fastest go karts in the area, water-spraying bumper boats, an exciting indoor arcade, indoor and outdoor birthday party areas.
Silver Dollar City	399 Indian Point Road Branson, MO 65616	Theme Park	Park for all ages combines the wholesome family fun of a major theme park with the timeless appeal of crafts and a dedication to preserving 1880s Ozarks culture.
Six Flags St. Louis	P.O. Box 60 Eureka, MO 63025	Theme Park	Six Flags St. Louis is a major amusement park featuring eight themed lands of adventure. The six flags that fly over the park represent the countries and states that have influenced St. Louis history—France, Spain, Great Britain (which at one time had jurisdiction over the area), Illinois, Missouri, and the U.S.A. The park features more than 40 attractions and game areas, more than 25 food outlets and gift shops, live shows, and a tropical paradise water park called Hurricane Harbor.
Worlds of Fun	4545 NE Worlds of Fun Drive Kansas City, MO 64161	Theme Park	The park is themed around the Jules Verne book, *Around the World in Eighty Days*, and is divided into five major sections—Scandinavia, Africa, Europa, the Orient, and Americana. Rides, attractions, shops, shows, and restaurants are named according to the area theme. The park also has an attached water park called Oceans of Fun.

theme parks, however, offered highly attractive water parks, modern steel coasters, entertainers, and an endless array of promotions, discounts, and family fun "packages" that made it worth the several-hundred-mile drive to be thrilled and entertained (see Exhibit 4).

Merryland's lack of marketing and promotion in lieu of higher ticket prices further contributed to its own declining backyard patron interest. Alan and Samantha, unlike the previous owners, were far removed from the changing needs, wants, and desires of a new generation of amusement park children, teens, and adults that began to take shape in the early 1990s. Customer demographics had shifted, and Merryland didn't shift with them.

The Steinbergs initiated a lawsuit against the interim operators. In the lawsuit, they listed Louie the Clown as one of the items damaged or taken from the park. The interim operators all said they knew nothing about the missing clown's whereabouts. The Steinbergs were also attempting to collect $450,000 in back rent and damages, but the former operators have said that they don't owe anyone any rent for anything.

Merryland's "Screamer" Roller Coaster

For residents of Kansas City, there was only one reason to go to Merryland—the roller coaster! Some people nicknamed it the "scream machine" and with good reason. The history of the "Screamer" reflected a constant search for greater and more death-defying thrills.

Merryland Park's Screamer roller coaster was a product of the Philadelphia Toboggan Company and one of the last surviving original wooden coasters designed by Herbert Paul Schmeck. Along with the Screamer, another of the trademark attractions was the park's Wurlitzer organ with Louie the Clown in front of it.

Patrons always loved the wooden coaster and would swear they noticed a big difference in the ride of Merryland's over others. Although it wasn't all that tall and not as fast as those in other parks, Merryland's made up for all those shortcomings with its sway— the back-and-forth motion that created the "out-of-control" sense of pending disaster, especially on the curves. That was due primarily to the Screamer's state-of-the-art wheel technology.

The Screamer was one of the first coasters to have some of the newly developed coaster wheel technology of its day. Once underway, the different types of wheels on the coaster work together to keep the ride smooth. The running wheels guide the coaster on the track. The friction wheels control the lateral sway (movement to either side of the track) motion. The final set of wheels keeps the coaster on the track. Those would have kept it firmly glued to the rails even if it had been inverted. Improved compressed air brakes stopped the train as the ride ended, adding a somewhat last moment of unintentionally designed thrill. The Screamer provided a distinctively rough, noisy, and out-of-control feeling for its riders, and its reputation was known throughout Kansas.

Tony's Interest in Merryland

Tony's believes that operating a theme park would enable him to directly serve disabled kids and their families of Kansas and surrounding states. Additionally, he would have his own business where he could put his creativity and innovative marketing skills to work. And, he could derive compensation commensurate with the work and profits. He could achieve the independent financial success he had not yet accomplished but still very much desired.

During his investigation into purchasing the park, Tony discovered that many of the rides were old and their deterioration was reflected on the company's balance sheets (see Exhibit 2). Although antique rides are considered to be an attractive and uniquely distinguishing characteristic for a theme park, it also requires the rides to be in a high-quality refurbished condition. That was not the case for those at Merryland. Maintenance alone would not help their survival; a major renovation of all the rides along with the park's infrastructure would have to be undertaken.

New machinery along with several new primary attraction park rides would need to be purchased and installed. A major renovation of several classic rides also had to occur, and those were expensive to stay true to the original engineering designs, paint schemes, and operational format. Many of the replacement ride parts would have to be custom manufactured.

Rotational Motion Consultants

Tony needed an amusement park ride expert, preferably a contractor who knew the industry and could visit Merryland with him. That's when he found Rotational Motion, a company based in Maryville, Tennessee, that sells all types of new and used amusement rides for theme parks, carnivals, family centers, and equipment for location-based entertainment venues. They also have a large inventory of rides available for short- or long-term lease and are willing to install/lease for a week, month, or even up to a year.

James Millner, account representative with Rotational Motion. arranged to meet Tony at Merryland on a crisp fall day. "The park is over 50 years old, but they have those old carousels and that big old roller coaster," explained Tony, pointing at the permanently parked coaster train. "Obviously some people lack the appreciation for roller-coaster history. Sure, the roller coaster looks as if it could fall apart at any given moment, but the locals say it's still one of the best roller coasters they've ever ridden. This was one of those places you could go with your friends and family on weekends—and have fun!"

James spent two full days with Tony evaluating the rides, and his early estimates indicated the necessary renovations could not be done for anything less than $5 million. Rotational Motion is a full service equipment rebuilder. They specialize in working with the best engineers in the industry to ensure all restoration work is done to current safety standards. Their modern company has the machine shops and fabrication facilities capable of working with rides in any state of deterioration. All their refurbishing work is conducted under the direction of structural and electrical professional engineers. Their electrical system work always meets or exceeds current American Society for Testing and Materials (ASTM) standards.

"This place should have closed 10 years ago based on the equipment condition," lamented James. He continued, "Simple and old-fashioned are appealing qualities, but ragged, rusty, and scary aren't. Merryland is proof this region must be highly resistant to change."

Tony explored options for the 20 acres of land behind the park. He reasoned that it could be sold to an expanding industrial park for about $1 million or perhaps leased for a long-term income option. On discussing the possibility of using the acreage for other purposes with the contractor, he noted that the land could also be used to expand the park by adding more rides or even a water park.

James explains that more rides, such as a scenic train ride, can be added for about $1 million. He notes, however, that a water park will be considerably more expensive, costing upward of $10 million. Tony soon realizes the land parcel is not large enough to add both a water park and expand the park with new rides.

The Steinbergs sent Tony a market psychographics report that had been prepared for them two years earlier by a local university marketing class. Tony believes the most important information in it is that kids under seven like simple rides while kids over seven (including adults) want a variety of rides including water-based attractions.

The Purchase Options Available to Tony

Several organizations with ties to Kansas City have strong interest, albeit different motivations, for seeing Merryland continue. Each group, however, lacks amusement park management experience to adequately tackle the obstacles facing the operation. The Steinbergs did keep them informed of Tony's interest, and they subsequently contacted him to discuss their various levels of interest. As Tony met with each, he soon found that three funding options are potentially good matches for the talents he can bring to Merryland.

Option 1: Altria's Cash Offer to Purchase

An executive for Altria had become aware of Tony's growth performance with Showbiz Pizza and was genuinely impressed with his ability to build business, profits, and market share. They originally wanted Tony to work for them but soon realized that he would fit best in an entrepreneurial setting. Their expansive U.S. market interests had them aware of Merryland, and it wasn't long before they learned of Tony's interest in the amusement park. Such a venture would help diversify their corporate holdings while providing market penetration.

Altria meets with Tony and offers to carry the entire cost of the renovation and add a water park, something Altria deems necessary for the park to reopen as a profitable operation. Altria's finance executives place a call to Tony and offer to invest $25 million in the existing park. That amount will include the purchase price, all the required renovations, and the new water park. Additionally, many of the park's attractions will be included in a new climate-controlled energy-efficient "green dome" for year-round operation.

Tony is genuinely interested but wants to know more about the company that is making such a lucrative offer. His research discovers that on January 27, 2003, Philip Morris Companies, Inc. changed its name to Altria Group, Inc. Philip Morris USA was a wholly owned subsidiary of Altria Group. Even under this new name, Altria continued to own 100 percent of Philip Morris USA. In the fall of 2003, Philip Morris moved its headquarters from New York City to Richmond, Virginia.

Philip Morris USA had split from Philip Morris International in 2008. The resulting drop in cigarette exports motivated Philip Morris to plan a shutdown of its Concord, North Carolina, manufacturing facility and move all domestic production to Richmond. The shutdown is planned to be completed by 2010.

Some view the name change as an effort by Altria to deemphasize its historical association with tobacco products. Altria also formerly owned Kraft Foods but spun the company off in March 2007 to focus on its tobacco business and products. Despite the problems that Altria faces, its sales continue to grow as evidenced by its third quarter 2009 revenue increase of 5 percent to $5.2 billion, primarily from higher sales of its Phillip Morris USA cigarette brands.

Altria Group has a 28.7 percent economic and voting interest in SABMiller, the world's second-largest brewer. Several consumer groups, however, have called for boycotting all Miller Beer products to put pressure on Altria/Philip Morris to really end smoking by children and underaged teens.

Altria's specific funding conditions are fourfold:

1. The park must promote only the Altria product line. This will include displaying the Altria name prominently around the park, having all of the rides and game kiosks offer prizes that emphasize the Altria product line, and banning the sale of all other competitors' products.
2. As manager, Tony must offer/honor free tickets and/or discounts to customers who mail in a certain number of points from Altria product cartons and packages.
3. The name of the park must be changed to Altria Gardens and Water Park.
4. Altria wants 10 percent of the gross profit. They agree to give Tony total control of operations but insist that he consult with them before he makes any single expenditure over $50,000. Altria will promote the theme park on its product packages and cartons during pre- and early-season promotions in March and April, and again during July for a fall push.

Option 2: A Consortium of Local Business Entrepreneurs

A consortium of local Kansas City business entrepreneurs also contact Tony with an offer to purchase the park. Having grown up with Merryland as a part of their community life, strong feelings of nostalgia have motivated them to consider the investment to preserve Merryland as a historical site. Several of them are actively involved with the Kansas City Historical Preservation Society. They laid out the following offer to Tony:

1. They will allow Tony to make the renovations to the existing park and let Tony completely manage and control the daily operations.
2. These "venture capitalists" want 40 percent of the park's net income but will give Tony total autonomy in running the park's day-to-day operations.
3. They also want the additional 20 acres of land signed over to their control for additional purposes they will not disclose. They state their primary interest in rebuilding the park is to offer the people of Kansas and surrounding states the same experience as they had while growing up.
4. Each of the investors currently runs at least one other business and guarantees park promotion and publicity through those existing enterprises.

Option 3: Getting a Loan

The final option Tony considers is getting a conventional business loan himself. One of his former fraternity brothers is an investment banker in Norfolk, Virginia.

1. This friend believes Tony could get a loan for the purchase of the park without any difficulty, but he does not believe he can get the full amount needed to renovate Merryland and build the water park. An initial inquiry reveals that Tony could get $9.2 million for the purchase and renovations.
2. His friend believes that if the park is profitable for the first two years, then he can obtain another $10 million to build the water park. His friend, however, did not specify what is considered "profitable."

The Things to Consider

Those who leave the Kansas City area say other theme parks just aren't the same. One of Tony's fraternity brothers, Franklin, grew up in Kansas City and was a Merryland Park regular. He explained to Tony, "Just last year I moved back to Virginia near the DC area, and I've been to parks around the United States—from California to Texas, Maryland to Virginia, Florida, and places in between. I still prefer, and horribly miss, my Merryland experience!"

Merryland Park was an integral part of Kansas City's history, and it's been a fine part of it (see Exhibits 5, 6, and 7). Where else could you ride a 50-plus-year-old coaster? The "old" part of that is the thrill. Merryland Park was dirt cheap and a nice place to take children. It may have been considered a beginner's theme park, but at those prices, how could you resist going without kids? It was a great place for first dates and senior citizens as well.

EXHIBIT 5   2008 General Kansas City, Kansas, Population Demographics

Subject	Number	%	Subject	Number	%
Total population =	**146,866**	**100.0**	**HISPANIC OR LATINO AND RACE**		
BY SEX AND AGE			**Total population =**	**146,866**	**100.0**
Male	71,769	48.9	Hispanic or Latino (of any race)	24,639	16.8
Female	75,097	51.1	Mexican	20,597	14.0
Under 5 years	11,953	8.1	Puerto Rican	253	0.2
5 to 9 years	11,868	8.1	Cuban	178	0.1
10 to 14 years	11,388	7.8	Other Hispanic or Latino	3,611	2.5
15 to 19 years	11,314	7.7	Not Hispanic or Latino	122,227	83.2
20 to 24 years	10,975	7.5	White alone	71,870	48.9
25 to 34 years	21,341	14.5			
35 to 44 years	21,946	14.9	**HOUSEHOLD BY TYPE**		
45 to 54 years	17,717	12.1	**Total households =**	**55,500**	**100.0**
55 to 59 years	6,253	4.3	Family households (families)	36,226	65.3
60 to 64 years	5,072	3.5	With own children under 18 yrs	18,032	32.5
65 to 74 years	8,973	6.1	Married-couple family	22,878	41.2
75 to 84 years	6,056	4.1	With own children under 18 yrs	10,246	18.5
85 years and over	2,010	1.4	Female householder, no husband present	10,108	18.2
Median age (years)	32.3	(X)	With own children under 18 yrs	6,176	11.1
18 years and over	104,917	71.4	Nonfamily households	19,274	34.7
Male	50,196	34.2	Householder living alone	16,180	29.2
Female	54,721	37.3	Householder 65 years and over	5,512	9.9
21 years and over	98,122	66.8	Households with individuals under 18 years	20,826	37.5
62 years and over	19,964	13.6	Households with individuals 65 years & over	12,720	22.9
65 years and over	17,039	11.6	Average household size	2.62	(X)
Male	6,830	4.7	Average family size	3.25	(X)
Female	10,209	7.0			
RACE			**SCHOOL ENROLLMENT**		
One race	142,481	97.0	Population 3 years and over enrolled in school	39,564	100.0
White	81,910	55.8	Nursery school, preschool	2,812	7.1
Black or African American	44,240	30.1	Kindergarten	2,286	5.8
American Indian & Alaska Native	1,103	0.8	Elementary school (grades 1–8)	19,158	48.4
Asian	2,527	1.7			
Asian Indian	219	0.1			
Chinese	250	0.2			
Filipino	107	0.1			
Japanese	35	—			
Korean	134	0.1			
Vietnamese	206	0.1			
Other Asian	1,576	1.1			

continued

EXHIBIT 5   2008 General Kansas City, Kansas, Population Demographics—continued

Subject	Number	%	Subject	Number	%
Native Hawaiian & Other Pacific Islander	56	—	High school (grades 9–12)	8,804	22.3
Native Hawaiian	16	—	College or graduate school	6,504	16.4
Guamanian or Chamorro	11	—	**EDUCATIONAL ATTAINMENT**		
Samoan	21	—	Population 25 years and over	89,540	100.0
Other Pacific Islander	8	—	Less than 9th grade	8,132	9.1
Some other race	12,645	8.6	9th to 12th grade, no diploma	15,671	17.5
Two or more races	4,385	3.0	High school graduate (includes equivalency)	30,780	34.4
			Some college, no degree	19,580	21.9
			Associate degree	4,922	5.5
			Bachelor's degree	6,566	7.3
			Graduate or professional degree	3,889	4.3
			% high school graduate or higher	73.4	(X)
			% bachelor's degree or higher	11.7	(X)

— Represents zero or rounds to zero.

EXHIBIT 6   2008 Kansas City, Kansas, Marriage Status, Income, and Employment Data

Subject	Number	%	Subject	Number	%
MARITAL STATUS			**DISABILITY STATUS OF THE CIVILIAN NONINSTITUTIONALIZED POPULATION**		
Population 15 years and over	111,531	100.0			
Never married	33,889	30.4			
Now married, except separated	51,863	46.5	Population 5 to 20 years	36,723	100.0
Separated	3,049	2.7	With a disability	3,569	9.7
Widowed	8,166	7.3	Population 21 to 64 years	81,013	100.0
Female	6,653	6.0	With a disability	21,334	26.3
Divorced	14,564	13.1	Percent employed	54.7	(X)
Female	8,243	7.4	No disability	59,679	73.7
			Percent employed	74.4	(X)
GRANDPARENTS AS CAREGIVERS			Population 65 years and over	16,381	100.0
			With a disability	8,289	50.6
Grandparent living in household with one or more own grandchildren under 18 years	4,643	100.0	**EMPLOYMENT STATUS**		
			Population 16 years and over	**109,206**	**100.0**
Grandparent responsible for grandchildren	2,210	47.6	In labor force	68,858	63.1
			Civilian labor force	68,791	63.0

continued

EXHIBIT 6   **2008 Kansas City, Kansas, Marriage Status, Income, and Employment Data—continued**

Subject	Number	%	Subject	Number	%
VETERAN STATUS			Employed	62,940	57.6
Civilian population			Unemployed	5,851	5.4
18 years & over	104,921	100.0	Percent of civilian labor force	8.5	(X)
Civilian veterans	13,780	13.1	Armed Forces	67	0.1
			Not in labor force	40,348	36.9
INCOME			**Females 16 years**		
Households	**55,533**	**100.0**	**and over**	**56,961**	**100.0**
Less than $10,000	7,289	13.1	In labor force	32,977	57.9
$10,000 to $14,999	4,310	7.8	Civilian labor force	32,968	57.9
$15,000 to $24,999	8,784	15.8	Employed	30,301	53.2
$25,000 to $34,999	8,694	15.7	**Own children under**		
$35,000 to $49,999	9,962	17.9	**6 years**	**13,044**	**100.0**
$50,000 to $74,999	9,683	17.4	All parents in family		
$75,000 to $99,999	4,222	7.6	in labor force	7,737	59.3
$100,000 to $149,999	2,005	3.6			
$150,000 to $199,999	280	0.5	**INCOME**		
$200,000 or more	304	0.5	**Families**	**36,581**	**100.0**
Median household income			Less than $10,000	3,064	8.4
(dollars)	33,011	(X)	$10,000 to $14,999	1,903	5.2
With earnings	43,921	79.1	$15,000 to $24,999	5,208	14.2
Mean earnings (dollars)[1]	41,825	(X)	$25,000 to $34,999	5,718	15.6
With Social Security income	14,879	26.8	$35,000 to $49,999	7,257	19.8
Mean Social Security income			$50,000 to $74,999	7,773	21.2
(dollars)[1]	10,923	(X)	$75,000 to $99,999	3,561	9.7
With Supplemental			$100,000 to $149,999	1,649	4.5
Security Income	3,063	5.5	$150,000 to $199,999	225	0.6
Mean Supplemental Security			$200,000 or more	223	0.6
Income (dollars)[1]	5,774	(X)	Median family income		
With public assistance income	2,545	4.6	(dollars)	39,491	(X)
Mean public assistance			Per capita income (dollars)[1]	15,737	(X)
income (dollars)[1]	2,492	(X)			
With retirement income	8,804	15.9			
Mean retirement					
income (dollars)[1]	14,900	(X)			
Median earnings (dollars):					
Male full-time, year-round					
workers	30,992	(X)			
Female full-time, year					
round workers	24,543	(X)			

[1]If the denominator of a mean value or per capita value is less than 30, then that value is calculated using a rounded aggregate in the numerator.

— Represents zero or rounds to zero.

(X) Not applicable.

EXHIBIT 7   Kansas Employment Summary by Industry

	2008	2009	Level Change	Percent Change
Total Nonfarm	**1,384,042**	**1,387,871**	**3,829**	**0.3%**
Production Sectors	**260,502**	**260,838**	**336**	**0.1%**
Natural Resources, Mining, & Construction	74,329	75,006	677	0.9%
Manufacturing	186,073	185,333	−740	−0.4%
Durable Goods	120,175	120,431	256	0.2%
Nondurable Goods	65,898	64,901	−997	−1.5%
Trade, Transportation, & Utilities	**261,824**	**258,253**	**−3,571**	**−1.4%**
Wholesale Trade	60,476	60,895	419	0.7%
Retail Trade	147,394	144,713	−2,681	−1.8%
Transportation & Utilities	53,954	52,645	−1,309	−2.4%
Service Sectors	**601,921**	**607,922**	**6,001**	**1.0%**
Information	40,614	39,179	−1,435	−3.5%
Financial Activities	74,139	74,963	824	1.1%
Professional & Business Services	147,037	149,603	2,566	1.7%
Educational & Health Services	172,545	175,496	2,951	1.7%
Leisure & Hospitality	115,457	116,230	773	0.7%
Other Services	52,129	52,451	322	0.6%
Government	**259,795**	**260,858**	**1,063**	**0.4%**

*Annual values are derived from average quarterly observations and projections. Detail may not sum to total due to rounding.

Conclusion

Tony ponders the following questions as well as his three options:

- Who exactly are Merryland's customers?
- What are their needs, wants, and desires?
- What is the best way to market/advertise/promote the park to its consumers/customers?
- Is control of the operations really important for Tony as an entrepreneur?
- What is the right balance of control/risk for each of the purchase options?
- How will Tony's core values impact his ability to make important decisions?
- Is Tony's passion to help disabled kids overshadowing his ability to bring corporate life back to Merryland?

The Steinbergs have just notified Tony that by next Friday they intend to put Merryland up for sale on eBay—lock, stock, and barrel—at a starting bid of $1.6 million, unless they hear from him definitively within a week. Prepare a strategic analysis for Tony.

3 JetBlue Airways Corporation — 2009

Mernoush Banton
Adjunct Faculty/Consultant

JBLU

www.jetblue.com

In April 2009, the fear of a swine flu outbreak shocked the airline industry and airline stocks dropped by almost 16 percent. JetBlue's stock slipped by 7 percent to $4.91. A bad outbreak could be disastrous for this industry because most airlines already are suffering from high unemployment, slow economic growth, and significant drops in business and leisure travel. The stake is particularly high for JetBlue, which is on track to generate free cash flow this year for the first time in its nine years of flying. A low-fare, low-cost passenger airline headquartered in Forest Hills, New York, JetBlue expects its 2009 full year revenue and profit to rise slightly. It is ranked as the number-ten U.S. airline by traffic. Southwest Airlines, based in Dallas, Texas, is 1.

JetBlue employs over 11,000 crew members and recently achieved the number-one customer service ranking among low-cost carriers, according to J. D. Power and Associates. The company offers passengers new aircraft, roomy leather seats with lots of leg room, 36 channels of free DirecTV, 100 channels of free XM satellite radio, and for purchase, premium movie channel offerings from multiple major movie studios. JetBlue's onboard offerings include free and unlimited brand-name snacks and beverages, and for purchase, premium beverages and specially designed products for overnight flights.

As of mid-August 2009, JetBlue operates 650 flights per day, serving 56 cities in 19 states, Puerto Rico, Mexico, and five countries in the Caribbean and Latin America. JetBlue in mid-2009 began international flights to Montego Bay (Jamaica), Cancun (Mexico), Barbados, Saint Lucia, Kingston (Jamaica), and Santa Domingo (Dominican Republic).

History

JetBlue was incorporated in Delaware in 1998 and commenced service in 2000 with primary base of operations at New York's John F. Kennedy International Airport. The company's goal has been to establish itself as a leading low-fare, low-cost passenger airline by offering its customers high-quality customer service and a differentiated product. The airline focused on serving "underserved markets" and large metropolitan areas that have high average fares with a diversified geographic flight schedules that includes both short- and long-haul routes.

From its first day of operation, JetBlue differentiated itself from other airlines by:

- Starting the business with a lot of money—the only carrier with over $100 million startup capital
- Flying new planes that are more reliable and certainly more efficient. Seats are covered in leather with individual monitors for viewing programs from DirecTV.
- Hiring the best people by screening the employees rigorously, offering exceptional training, and equipping them with best tools. The employees are highly motivated and are trained to be service oriented.
- Focusing on service by listening to customers and ensuring their flight is joyful and friendly.

Much of JetBlue's business model of low faces came right out of Southwest Airlines' playbook. This is no surprise since JetBlue founder, David Neeleman, was fired by Southwest in 1999.

In 2006, JetBlue published its first corporate sustainability report, the "1st Annual Environmental and Social Report 2006," addressing its environmental efforts concerning greenhouse gas emissions, conservation efforts, and social responsibility initiatives. In regard to community services, the company also is committed and has aligned itself with not-for-profit organizations that focus on children, education, communities, and the environment. The company also encourages its crew members to help make a difference by enriching the lives of the individuals and communities they serve.

Like Southwest, JetBlue prides itself on providing superior customer service. In 2007, JetBlue introduced the JetBlue Airways Customer Bill of Rights, which provides compensation to customers who experience avoidable inconveniences (and some unavoidable circumstances). The Bill of Rights commits JetBlue to perform at high service standards by holding it accountable if it does not. The company is the first and currently the only major airline to provide such a fundamental benefit for its customers.

In 2008, JetBlue introduced refundable fares and new payment options for customers, and it also launched jetblue.com en español, a Spanish version of their Web site, http://hola.jetblue.com/enes/. JetBlue was also able to maintain cost per available seat mile, excluding fuel, of 5.94 cents, which is among the lowest reported by all other major U.S. airlines. By scheduling and operating aircraft efficiently, JetBlue has high aircraft utilization as it spreads fixed costs over many flights and available seat miles. For the year ended December 31, 2008, their aircraft operated an average of 12.1 hours per day, which is the highest among all major U.S. airlines. Exhibit 1 shows the JetBlue organizational chart.

For years, JetBlue and Southwest avoided head-to-head competition, but in 2009 the companies began battling each other in the same airports, such as New York, Baltimore, Washington, D.C., and most recently Boston. These two lost-cost carriers use to cross each other only in a few cities.

Marketing

JetBlue offers a variety of in-flight entertainment such as DirecTV with 36 channels of free programming. Thus far, no other airline offers such live satellite TV option for free. The company is planning to increase the number of channels from 36 to 100+ channels. The aircraft are equipped with an in-seat digital entertainment system. Each individual seat has a monitor with armrest remote with channel and volume controls.

JetBlue is well positioned in the New York metropolitan areas, which is one of the largest travel markets. In 2008, JetBlue completed a state-of-the-art terminal in its main

EXHIBIT 1   Organizational Chart (2008)

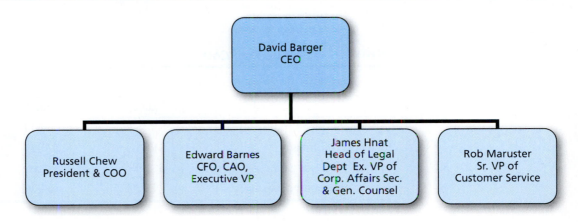

hub (Terminal 5 in John F. Kennedy Airport in New York). The new terminal offers many modern amenities and concession offerings. Southwest now flies out of New York's LaGuard: an airport eight miles from Kennedy.

JetBlue continuously markets itself through advertising and promotions in newspapers, magazines, television, radio, and on billboards. The firm relies on word of mouth because it believes this is the most effective advertising for the company. The primary distribution channel is through the company's Web site (www.jetblue.com), promoting its low-fare partnership with American Express Rewards, discounts, and customer loyalty program (TrueBlue Flight Gratitude). TrueBlue Flight Gratitude is an online program designed to reward and to recognize the company's customer. This program offers many incentives; the members earn points for each one-way trip flown based on the length of the trip. Points accumulate for each member in an account and then expires after 12 months. The member receives a free round-trip award to any JetBlue destination after attaining 100 points within a consecutive 12-month period.

Through American Express, JetBlue offers the JetBlue Business Card, which provides small business owners with a 5 percent discount on JetBlue travel and automatic enrollment in the American Express OPEN Savings program. In addition, small business owners with any American Express OPEN small business card receive a 3 percent discount on JetBlue travel. Every time card members make a purchase, either by their JetBlue Card or a JetBlue Business Card from American Express, they earn points. The company also has an agreement with American Express allowing its cardholders to convert their Membership Reward points into JetBlue TrueBlue points.

E-Commerce

The percentage of JetBlue's total sales booked on their Web site averaged 77 percent for the year ended December 31, 2008. In 2008, their bookings through global distribution systems, or GDSs, and online travel agencies, or OTAs, became their second largest distribution channel, accounting for 13 percent of our sales. They booked the remaining 10 percent of their 2008 sales through the 800-JETBLUE channel.

The number of estimated travel awards outstanding at year-end 2008 was approximately 196,000 awards and includes an estimate for partially earned awards. The number of travel awards used on JetBlue during 2008 was approximately 297,000, which represented 4 percent of the total revenue passenger miles. Due to the structure of the program and low level of redemptions as a percentage of total travel, the displacement of revenue passengers by passengers using TrueBlue awards has been minimal to date.

Financial Conditions

Behind labor, the second largest operating expense for airlines is fuel. JetBlue enters into crude oil option contracts and swap agreements to partially protect itself against significant increases in fuel prices. Exhibit 2 provides JetBlue fuel costs.

Exhibits 3 and 4 provide a historical data on company's finances since 2006.

EXHIBIT 2   JetBlue Fuel Cost

	Year Ended December 31		
	2008	2007	2006
Gallons consumed (millions)	453	444	377
Total cost (millions)	$1,352	$ 929	$ 752
Average price per gallon	$ 2.98	$ 2.09	$ 1.99
Percent of operating expenses	41.2%	34.8%	33.6%

Source: JetBlue, *Form 10K* (2008).

EXHIBIT 3 **JetBlue Airways Corporation: Consolidated Balance Sheets (in millions, except share data)**

	December 31,	
	2008	2007
ASSETS		
CURRENT ASSETS		
Cash and cash equivalents	$ 561	$ 190
Investment securities	10	644
Receivables, less allowance (2008-$5; 2007-$2)	86	92
Inventories, less allowance (2008-$4; 2007-$2)	80	26
Restricted cash	78	—
Prepaid expenses and other	91	111
Deferred income taxes	106	53
Total current assets	962	1,116
PROPERTY AND EQUIPMENT		
Flight equipment	3,832	3,547
Predelivery deposits for flight equipment	163	238
	3,995	3,785
Less accumulated deprecjation	406	336
Other property and equipment	487	475
	3,589	3,449
Less accumulated depreciation	134	130
	353	345
Assets constructed for others	533	452
Less accumulated depreciation	5	—
	528	452
Total property and equipment	4,470	4,246
OTHER ASSETS		
Investment securities	244	—
Purchased technology, less accumulated amortization (2008-$61; 2007-$48)	8	21
Restricted cash	69	53
Other	270	162
Total other assets	591	236
TOTAL ASSETS	$ 6,023	$ 5,598

	December 31,	
	2008	2007
LIABILITIES AND STOCKHOLDERS' EQUITY		
CURRENT LIABILITIES		
Accounts payable	$ 144	$ 140
Air traffic liability	445	426
Accrued salaries, wages and benefits	107	110

continued

EXHIBIT 3   JetBlue Airways Corporation: Consolidated Balance Sheets
(in millions, except share data)—continued

	December 31,	
	2008	2007
Other accrued liabilities	113	120
Short-term borrowings	120	43
Current maturities of long-term debt and capital leases	152	417
Total current liabilities	1,081	1,256
LONG-TERM DEBT AND CAPITAL LEASE OBLIGATIONS	2,883	2,588
CONSTRUCTION OBLIGATION	512	438
DEFERRED TAXES AND OTHER LIABILITIES		
Deferred income taxes	194	192
Other	92	88
	286	280
COMMITMENTS AND CONTINGENCIES		
STOCKHOLDERS' EQUITY		
Preferred stock, $.01 par value; 25,000,000 shares authorized, none issued	—	—
Common stock, $ 01 par value; 500,000,000 shares authorized, 288,633,882 issued and 271, 763,139 outstanding in 2008 and 181,593,440 shares issued and outstanding in 2007	3	2
Treasury stock, at cost; 16,878,876 shares	—	—
Additional paid-in capital	1,256	853
Retained earnings	86	162
Accumulated other comprehensive income (loss), net of taxes	(84)	19
Total stockholders' equity	1,261	1,036
TOTAL LIABILITIES AND STOCKHOLDERS' EQUITY	$ 6,023	$ 5,598

Source: JetBlue, *Form 10K* (2008).

EXHIBIT 4   JetBlue Corporation: Consolidated Statements of
Operations (in millions, except per share amounts)

	Year Ended December 31,		
	2008	2007	2006
OPERATING REVENUES			
Passenger	$ 3,056	$ 2,636	$ 2,223
Other	332	206	140
Total operating revenues	3,388	2,842	2,363
OPERATING EXPENSES			
Aircraft fuel	1,352	929	752
Salaries, wages and benefits	694	648	553
Landing fees and other rents	199	180	158

continued

EXHIBIT 4   JetBlue Corporation: Consolidated Statements of Operations (in millions, except per share amounts)—continued

	Year Ended December 31,		
	2008	2007	2006
Depreciation and amortization	205	176	151
Aircraft rent	129	124	103
Sales and marketing	151	121	104
Maintenance materials and repairs	127	106	87
Other operating expenses	422	389	328
Total operating expenses	3,279	2,673	2,236
OPERATING INCOME	109	169	127
OTHER INCOME (EXPENSE)			
Interest expense	(232)	(225)	(173)
Capitalized interest	48	43	27
Interest income and other	(1)	54	28
Total other income (expense)	(185)	(128)	(118)
INCOME (LOSS) BEFORE INCOME TAXES	(76)	41	9
Income tax expense	—	23	10
NET INCOME (LOSS)	$ (76)	$18	$ (1)
EARNINGS (LOSS) PER COMMON SHARE:			
Basic	$ (0.34)	$ 0.10	$ —
Diluted	$ (0.34)	$ 0.10	$ —

Source: JetBlue, *Form 10K* (2008).

Industry Overview

Airline profitability is influenced by the state of the economy, international events, industry capacity, and offerings by other airlines in the forms of bundling and packaging (with hotels, cruise lines, etc.). The airlines also compete through flight scheduling, availability, fares, routes served, safety records, on-time arrival, and customer service reputation.

Passengers are increasingly interested low price as well as comfort and amenities of the aircraft. Therefore, airlines are designing more living space into new planes and retrofitting old ones. For example, Delta Air Lines and American Airlines are rewiring their planes to provide Wi-Fi access and enhanced in-flight entertainment options, including live TV.

According to the Air Transport Association, in 2008, the operating expenses in the industry increased 4.1 percent to $163.9 billion. Flying operations, the industry's largest functional cost center at 37.9 percent, climbed 3.9 percent to $62.1 billion. Fuel drove the major share of this category as crude oil prices averaged $72.34 per barrel in 2007, up $6.29 from 2006, and the average jet fuel crack spread—the additional amount charged for refining—rose from $16.69 to $18.59. Consequently, even after factoring in the airlines' fuel hedging programs, the average price paid for jet fuel, excluding pipeline tariffs, tank fees, and state and federal taxes, rose 7.0 percent, from $1.97 per gallon in 2006 to $2.10 per gallon in 2007.

Transport-related expenses, principally payments from mainline carriers to their regional airline partners, constituted the industry's second-largest cost at 16.9 percent, up 4.3 percent to a total of $27.6 billion. Demand for regional airline capacity remained strong as mainline carriers continued to align capacity more closely with demand across their respective networks. Aircraft and traffic servicing, and maintenance were the industry's third and fourth largest functional costs, respectively. Notably, general and administrative expenses rose 8.1 percent. At U.S. passenger airlines, a 2.7 percent increase in average salary and wage was more than offset by an 11.9 percent reduction in average benefits and pension expenses and a 3.4 percent reduction in payroll taxes, pulling the average cost of a full-time equivalent (FTE) employee down 0.9 percent to $74,786. Salaries and wages composed 75 percent of total compensation.

A major problem that airlines face is union labor contracts. Typically, labor contract negotiations in the airline industry take as long as 1.3 years. Once negotiation is finalized, then it goes through several months of federal mediation. In most cases, the duration of negotiation is to be attributed to which airline and unions are bargaining and not necessarily to the economic conditions. Unions such as the International Association of Machinists and the Aircraft Mechanics Fraternal Association worked hard to negotiate contracts on behalf of ramp workers and customer-service agents with United Airlines in order to avoid a U.S. bankruptcy ruling. Such a ruling could void the current labor contracts and allow United Airlines to impose new terms. The pitfall is that such unions can plan to strike if no agreements are reached.

The Bureau of Transportation Statistics reports in Exhibit 5 that airline fuel cost and consumption has been increasing annually.

The U.S. Federal Aviation Administration (FAA) says that an increase in fuel costs is not just from more flights or high oil prices but also due to the level of obesity in the United States. One study reported that in 2000, obese passengers cost airlines an extra $275 million in fuel costs by forcing aircraft to burn 350 more gallons of fuel due to extra weight. The fuel cost could increase further as passengers may have additional or heavier carryon or luggage weights. The additional fuel also is a problem for environment as it releases additional 3.5 million tons of carbon dioxide into the air.

Congress placed a security reform after the terrorist attacks of September 11, 2001. In November 2001, the Congress decided to take responsibility for airline security. By November 2002, the Transportation Security Administration (TSA) was to assume operational control of security at the nation's 429 commercial airports. TSA also hired 429 federal security directors (FSDs) with a salary range of $105,000 to $150,000; most of them are former military and law-enforcement officers. TSA was responsible for installing over 1,600 explosives detection systems (EDS) machines and 4,500 explosives detection trace (ETS) at airports, with an estimated cost of $2 billion. In February 2009, President Obama outlined his administration's 2010 budget plan, which proposes to increase passenger fees to $2.50 per-segment Aviation Passenger Security Fee for airport security and additional investment in subsidies for small community air service and further to fund next-generation air traffic control projects.

Rising break-even load factor is also threatening airline finances. Since 2000, most passenger airlines have been suffering in a sharp increase in their break-even load factor,

EXHIBIT 5 **Airline Fuel Cost and Consumption (U.S. Carriers Scheduled): 2000–2009**

Year	Domestic			International			Total		
	Consumption (million gallons)	Cost (million dollars)	Cost per Gallon (dollars)	Consumption (million gallons)	Cost (million dollars)	Cost per Gallon (dollars)	Consumption (million gallons)	Cost (million dollars)	Cost per Gallon (dollars)
2003	12,417.0	10,315.4	0.83	4,451.0	3,838.2	0.86	16,868.0	14,153.7	0.84
2004	13,380.0	15,141.2	1.13	4,764.7	5,690.7	1.19	18,144.7	20,831.9	1.15
2005	13,284.2	21,682.9	1.63	5,040.3	8,600.8	1.71	18,324.5	30,283.7	1.65
2006	13,019.4	25,105.4	1.93	5,220.3	10,535.2	2.02	18,239.7	35,640.6	1.95
2007	12,998.8	26,899.9	2.07	5,428.0	11,685.0	2.15	18,426.8	38,584.9	2.09
2008	12,451.3	37,158.2	2.98	5,508.9	17,773.5	3.23	17,960.2	54,931.7	3.06

Source: Bureau of Transportation Statistics.

EXHIBIT 6   Airline Bookings 2008

Airline	Book Ticket by Phone ($)	Preferred Seat ($)	Ticket Change Fee ($)[1]
AirTran	15	6–20	75
American	20	NA	150
Continental	15	NA	150
Delta	25	NA	100
Frontier	25	NA	150
JetBlue	15	10–30	100
Northwest	20	5–35	150
Southwest	0	15–20	0
Spirit	0	Up to several hundred dollars	80–90
United	25	14–149	150[2]
US Airways	25	5–25	150

[1]Ticket bought from a travel agent may have different fee.
[2]Some routes may have a smaller fee.

Source: USA Today, August 8, 2008.

measured by the number of seats they have to sell to cover operating expenses. The break-even load factor is determined by passenger yield, which has been fallen due to recently bankrupt carriers and unit costs that have been rising due to many factors such as labor wages and fuel costs. Available seats per mile (ASM) is another indicator that measures the total number of seats in the active fleet, multiplied by the number of miles flown.

An additional source of revenue for airlines has been fees they charge for cancelation, premium seats, flight changes, and so on. Airlines charge from $20 to $150 for curbside baggage checks depending on the distance, weight, and other restrictions. Other fees are for premium seat selection, food and beverage charges, processing fees for frequent-miles traveling, itinerary changes, booking fees via calling the airline directly instead of using their Web site, and many others. Per *USA Today*, higher fee revenue will help pay companies to offset the increase cost of jet fuel and other operating expenses. In August 2008, US Airways announced it expects $400 million to $500 million annually from its à la carte pricing strategy, which includes charging for a first checked bag, nonalcoholic beverages, and processing frequent-flier-award tickets (see Exhibit 6).

Airlines also are compared against each other for mishandling of luggage. Carriers posted a mishandled baggage rate of 3.6 reports per 1,000 passengers in February 2009, an improvement over both February 2008's rate of 6.4 and January 2009's 5.2 rate.

On-Time Statistics and Causes of Delays

An important part of airline selection for a passenger is the reliability and on-time arrival of the carrier. The delay or cancelation of a flight could vary from bad weather conditions, unsafe environment, emergencies on the tarmac, airport congestion, to late arrival of the crew from another flight, maintenance, and so on. For example, Northwest reported the most number of flights—10—that had tarmac delays of more than three hours. US Airways flight 1165 from Philadelphia to Charlotte on February 3 was delayed on the tarmac for 4 hours 19 minutes before being canceled (Exhibit 7).

Taxes and Fees

Along with other expenses that airlines have, such as payroll, operations, and maintenance, there are also taxes and fees that may not be visible to a passenger. U.S. and foreign taxes have grown in number, amount, and scope since the advent of air transport. Exhibit 8 shows the breakdown of taxes and fees.

EXHIBIT 7 Airline On-Time Statistics—Year 2008

Airline	On-Time Arrival (Percentage)
Hawaiian	90.0%
Southwest	80.5%
US Airways	80.1%
Frontier	79.0%
Alaska	78.3%
Northwest	76.8%
AirTran	76.7%
Delta	76.4%
Atlantic Southeast	74.2%
Continental	74.0%
JetBlue	72.9%
American Eagle	72.9%
United	71.6%
Comair	69.9%
American	69.8%

Source: Bureau of Transportation Statistics, February 2009.

Competition

Competition is stronger than ever in many medium- to long-haul connecting markets, where major carriers compete for passengers over their respective hub-and-spoke networks. The domestic airline industry generally is characterized as having low profit margins, high fixed costs, and significant price competition. Exhibits 9, 10, 11, and 12 compare some direct competitors.

EXHIBIT 8 Sample Round-Trip Itinerary: Peoria, IL (PIA) to Raleigh/Durham, NC (RDU) via Chicago O'Hare (ORD)

Base Airline Fare	$300.00
Federal Ticket (Excise) Tax (7.5%)	22.50
Passenger Facility Charge (PIA)	4.50
Federal Flight Segment Tax (PIA-ORD)	3.60
Federal Security Surcharge (PIA-ORD)	2.50
Passenger Facility Charge (ORD)	4.50
Federal Flight Segment Tax (ORD-RDU)	3.60
Federal Security Surcharge (ORD-RDU)	2.50
Passenger Facility Charge (RDU)	4.50
Federal Flight Segment Tax (RDU-ORD)	3.60
Federal Security Surcharge (RDU-ORD)	2.50
Passenger Facility Charge (ORD)	4.50
Federal Flight Segment Tax (ORD-PIA)	3.60
Federal Security Surcharge (ORD-PIA)	2.50
Total Taxes and Fees	$ 64.90
Taxes as % of Fare	21.6%
Taxes as % of Ticket	17.8%

Source: http://www.airlines.org.

EXHIBIT 9 **Direct Competitor Comparison (April 2009)**

	JBLU	AMR	LUV	UAUA	Industry
Market Cap	1.35B	1.31B	5.09B	791.37M	646.77M
Employees	8,902	84,100	35,499	50,000	4.52K
Qtrly Rev Growth	9.70%	−3.80%	9.70%	−9.60%	13.10%
Revenue	3.39B	23.77B	11.02B	20.19B	1.48B
Gross Margin	26.18%	19.15%	22.07%	4.88%	22.07%
EBITDA	304.00M	531.00M	1.05B	−813.00M	90.07M
Oper Margins (ttm)	2.77%	−2.84%	4.07%	−8.47%	8.37%
Net Income	−76.00M	−2.07B	178.00M	−5.35B	N/A
EPS	−0.336	−7.996	0.241	−42.200	N/A
P/E	N/A	N/A	28.55	N/A	9.45

AMR = AMR Corp
LUV = Southwest Airlines Inc
UAUA = UAL Corp
Industry = Regional Airlines

Source: http://finance.yahoo.com.

EXHIBIT 10 **Airlines Ranked by Revenue Passenger Miles (April 2009)**

Company	Symbol	Price	Change	Market Cap
AMR Corporation	AMR	4.70	−13.28%	1.31B
UAL Corporation	UAUA	5.50	−14.33%	791.37M
Delta Air Lines Inc.	DAL	6.75	−14.34%	4.71B
Northwest Airlines Corporation	Private -BAIRY.PK	21.99	−7.33%	N/A
Southwest Airlines Co.	LUV	6.88	−9.35%	5.09B
Continental Airlines, Inc.	CAL	11.08	−16.38%	1.37B

M = Millions
B = Billions

*Source:*http://finance.yahoo.com.

EXHIBIT 11 **JetBlue vs. Industry Leaders (April 2009)**

Statistic	Industry Leader		JBLU	JBLU's Rank
Market Capitalization	LUV	5.09B	1.35B	3/17
P/E Ratio	LUV	28.55	N/A	N/A
PEG Ratio	LUV	1.50	0.82	3/17
Revenue Growth	CPA	21.60%	9.70%	7/17
EPS Growth	ALGT	288.10%	N/A	N/A
Long-Term Growth Rate (5 yr)	AAI	30%	13%	10/17
Return on Equity	BLTA.OB	54.41%	−6.62%	11/17
Long-Term Debt/Equity				N/A
Dividend Yield	LFL	13.20%	N/A	N/A

Source: http://finance.yahoo.com.

EXHIBIT 12   Airline Industry: Leaders in Total Revenue (April 2009)

Company (Symbol)	Total Revenue (ttm)
Southwest Airlines [LUV]	$ 11.0 B
LAN Airlines SA ADS [LFL]	$ 4.5 B
JetBlue Airways Corporation [JBLU]	$ 3.4 B
AirTran Holdings, Inc. [AAI]	$ 2.6 B

Source: http://finance.yahoo.com.

American Airlines, Inc., provides services to approximately 150 destinations throughout North America, the Caribbean, Latin America, Europe, and Asia. They also offer a range of freight and mail services to shippers. AMR Eagle Holding Corporation, another subsidiary of AMR, and under the name of American Eagle, owns and operates two regional airlines and provides connecting service from nine of American's high traffic cities to smaller markets throughout the United States, Canada, Mexico, and the Caribbean.

On May 2009, American Airlines announced that its traffic fell 4.7 percent during April. They flew 10.28 billion revenue passenger miles (revenue passenger miles equal one passenger flown 1 mile) during April, down from 10.79 billion a year ago. The company reported a profit of $504 million in 2006 versus a loss of $2,071 million in 2008.

Southwest sells frequent flyer credits to those who participate in their Rapid Reward frequent flyer program. Southwest remains the nation's leading low-fare carrier and continues to distinguish itself from other airlines by offering reliable and exemplary customer service. The company also differentiates itself by not charging the customers for their first two bags (size and weight limits apply), no additional fees for window or aisle seat, and continues offering complementary snacks, sodas, and coffee.

What Is Next for JetBlue?

Southwest in mid-2009 announced it would begin offering flights from Boston to Baltimore for $49.00. A week later, JetBlue began offering the same flight for $39.00. The rivalry between Southwest and JetBlue has reached an all-time high.

Develop a clear strategic plan for JetBlue.

References

JetBlue Inc., *Annual Report,* 2008.
http://www.jetblue.com
http://www.airlines.org
http://www.airliners.net
http://finance.yahoo.com
http://www.bts.gov
http:///wsj.com
http://www7.nationalacademies.org
http://www.usatoday.com/money/industries/travel/2008-08-11-rising-airline-fees_N.htm

4 AirTran Airways, Inc. — 2009

Charles M. Byles
Virginia Commonwealth University

AAI

www.airtran.com

In July 2009, AirTran became the first airline to offer Wi-Fi on all flights—all 136 of its Boeing 737 and 717 jets. Based in Orlando, Florida, the low-fare carrier now lets all customers access the Web from a handheld device or laptop for $7.95 to $12.95 per flight, depending on the device and length of the flight. Rival firms are more slowly equipping their planes with wireless, including Virgin America, Delta, United Airlines, Air Canada, and American.

The *Airline Quality Report* released April 6, 2009, had good news for AirTran. The airline was ranked second in overall quality following its number-one ranking the prior year, and had been ranked in the top three for the last five years. However, the airline industry overall is not doing well. Earlier, on March 24, Giovanni Bisignani, the director general and CEO of the International Air Transportation Association, summed up the industry situation as follows:

> The state of the airline industry today is grim. Demand has deteriorated much more rapidly with the economic slowdown than could have been anticipated even a few months ago. Our loss forecast for 2009 is now US$4.7 billion. Combined with an industry debt of US$170 billion, the pressure on the industry balance sheet is extreme.

AirTran's profit loss in 2008 was the airline's only loss in the last nine years. The company's first quarter of 2009 was grim with passenger unit revenue down 7 to 8.5 percent, total unit revenue down 2 to 3.5 percent, and nonfuel costs up 8 to 9.5 percent. But AirTran seemed upbeat in its view about the outlook for all of 2009. It expects profits in all quarters of 2009, assuming fuel remains at current prices. The company views its low-cost strategy as a strength in the current economic downturn.

History

The 1978 deregulation of the U.S. airline industry resulted in the entry of several low-cost airlines such as AirTran Airways (then known as ValuJet Airlines). Although it came close to failure in 1996, AirTran was able to recover, and today it is one of the most successful low-cost carriers. In 1992, the predecessor of AirTran, ValuJet Airlines, Inc., was founded by an executive group from the former Southern Airways, and pilots, mechanics, and flight attendants from the recently bankrupt Eastern Airlines. ValuJet's first commercial flight was between Atlanta and Tampa on October 26, 1993. Although profitable, ValuJet was plagued with several safety incidents, the worst being the May 1996 crash of flight 592 in the Florida Everglades killing 110 people. ValuJet was held partially liable and grounded for four months by the Federal Aviation Administration. Although it resumed flying, the ValuJet name was so tarnished that the airline needed to reinvent itself.

On July 10, 1997, ValuJet Inc. (the holding company for ValuJet Airlines) announced the acquisition of Airways Corporation Inc. (the holding company for AirTran Airways, Inc.) of Orlando, Florida. Later, ValuJet Airlines and AirTran Airways merged, the resulting airline retaining the name of AirTran Airways. Since then, AirTran has gained a reputation as a safe airline through its commitment to safety and the use of new state-of-the-art aircraft. In the last nine years (with the exception of 2008), AirTran has been profitable and recognized for a number of achievements, most recently the good service quality ratings mentioned earlier.

Internal Factors

AirTran Airways, Inc., is a subsidiary of AirTran Holdings Inc. and operates scheduled airline service in the United States (and one destination in Mexico—Cancun), primarily in short-haul markets in the eastern United States. Although the company has its headquarters in Orlando, its main hub of flight operations is Atlanta, where it is the second-largest carrier. As of March 2009, AirTran operates 86 Boeing 717-200 aircraft (117 seats) and 50 Boeing 737-700 aircraft (137 seats) offering 700 daily flights to 57 destinations in the United States (including San Juan, Puerto Rico) and Cancun, Mexico. The airline is classified by the U.S. Department of Transportation as a "major airline" because of its $1 billion or more annual revenue.

Mission, Guiding Principles, and Values

AirTran's mission statement is: "Innovative people dedicated to delivering the best flying experience to smart travelers. Every day." AirTran also has some guiding principles. The first and most important is *safety,* which appears as the first guiding principle ("Taking personal responsibility for the safety of each traveler and every crew member) and the first value ("A Total Commitment to Safety—in every decision and every action, every time, every day). The second important aspect of air travel addressed in these statements is *service*. The mission of AirTran is "Innovative people dedicated to delivering the best flying experience to smart travelers. Every day." Other guiding principles are courtesy, pride, teamwork, and innovation. A full statement of the company's mission, guiding principles, and values is given on its Web site.

Management and Human Resources

AirTran's leadership team consists of Robert L. Fornaro, chairman, president, and CEO; Stephen Kolski, executive vice president, operations and corporate affairs; Steven A. Rossum, executive vice president of corporate development; as well as senior vice presidents, vice presidents, and other managers. The board of directors consists of 10 members including Fornaro.

Robert L. Fornaro joined AirTran Airways in March 1999 as president and chief financial officer. He became chief operating officer and was elected to the board in 2001 and was appointed chief executive officer on November 1, 2007. Fornaro had prior airline experience at Braniff International Airways, Trans World Airlines, Northwest Airlines, and most recently at US Airways, where he directed the airline's route planning, pricing and revenue management, and overall corporate strategy. Fornaro's total compensation for 2008 was $1.5 million (including a bonus of $375,000), a 69 percent drop from his 2007 total compensation, which was $4.9 million. During 2008, AirTran's stock price fell nearly 36 percent. Exhibit 1 contains a list of AirTran's leadership team as identified on the company's Web site (which also gives a detailed biography of each executive). AirTran operates from a functional (centralized) organizational structure with no profit centers or divisions. Note there is only one female among the top 17 executives.

AirTran employs over 9,000 crew members in a variety of job positions as follows:

- Administrative/Professional/Technical (e.g., finance, accounting, information technology, human resources, and marketing)
- Customer Service—Airport Operations (e.g., ticketing, baggage operations, managing arrival and departure gates)
- Customer Service—Reservations/Call Center (e.g., providing flight information, making reservations)
- Ground Operations (e.g., loading and unloading baggage, mail, and cargo, catering and cleaning aircraft)
- Flight Operations—flight attendants, pilots, flight operations, management
- Maintenance/Engineering (e.g., aircraft maintenance and repairs)

EXHIBIT 1   **AirTran's Leadership Team**

Robert Fornaro	Chairman, President, and Chief Executive Officer
Stephen Kolski	Executive Vice President, Operations and Corporate Affairs
Steven Rossum	Executive Vice President of Corporate Development
Loral Blinde	Senior Vice President, Human Resources and Administration
Klaus Goersch	Senior Vice President, Operations
Arne Haak	Senior Vice President of Finance, Treasurer and Chief Financial Officer
Kevin Healey	Senior Vice President, Marketing and Planning
Richard Magurno	Senior Vice President, General Counsel and Secretary
Jack Smith	Senior Vice President, Customer Service
Rocky Wiggins	Senior Vice President and Chief Information Officer
Tad Hutcheson	Vice President, Marketing and Sales
Mark Osterberg	Vice President, Chief Accounting Officer
Peggy Sauer-Clark	Vice President, Inflight Service
Jim Tabor	Vice President, Operations
Kirk Thornberg	Vice President, Maintenance and Engineering
Jean-Pierre Dagon	Director, Corporate Safety
Jeff Miller	General Manager, Flight Operations

Source: "AirTran Airways—Investor Relations." Retrieved March 12, 2009, from http://investor.airtran.com/phoenix.zhtml?c=64267 &p=irol-IRHome.

Aircraft Fleet and Maintenance

According to its *2008 Annual Report*, the average fleet age of AirTran's 86 Boeing 717 and 50 Boeing 737 aircraft is 5.6 years (as of February 2009). How does this average fleet age compare to AirTran's competitors? The most recent comparison data of fleet age is available from AirSafe.com and is based on 2007 data. That comparison placed AirTran at an average fleet age of 4.5 years, JetBlue at 3.2 years, Southwest at 9.8, and Delta at 13.8 years. Although not current, the comparison suggests that AirTran has a relatively young fleet compared to its direct competitors, which should contribute to lower operating and maintenance costs.

Aircraft maintenance is completed by both AirTran and outside contractors at the cities served by the airline. AirTran's maintenance, materials, and rent costs per Available Seat Mile (ASM) only increased 1.5 percent between 2007 and 2008 (see Exhibit 4, which appears later in this case). In its *2008 Annual Report*, AirTran notes that its long-term aircraft maintenance costs will be within industry norms.

Strategy

AirTran's strategy is one of low cost within a narrow geographic area (the eastern United States) with a target market of both business and leisure travelers. AirTran attributes its low-cost advantage to a company-wide emphasis on cost controls, an emphasis on higher labor productivity, and higher asset utilization. In addition, the use of only two aircraft types and a fairly young Boeing 737 fleet contributes to overall efficiencies. Many of AirTran's competitors, however, have similar advantages, especially JetBlue and Southwest Airlines. JetBlue operates only two aircraft types (Southwest operates only one) and has a younger fleet; Southwest has a slightly older fleet. Both JetBlue and Southwest have cost advantages over AirTran (as discussed in the later section on operating performance). As such, AirTran does not appear to have a low-cost advantage when compared to JetBlue and Southwest. It does, however, have a low-cost advantage over Delta and most likely other legacy carriers with which it competes.

The Atlanta-Hartsfield Airport is the major hub for AirTran (62 percent of system daily flights) and is where it has its major competition with Delta. Although AirTran's leading strategy is focused low cost, it differentiates itself from other low-cost carriers in a number of ways. First, AirTran has business class seating on all aircraft and operates a hub-and-spoke system (as opposed to point-to-point). Second, it offers free digital XM Radio, a student travel program, and requires no roundtrip purchase or minimum overnight stays. Finally, AirTran has food for sale on flights. In early 2009, AirTran began offering Sky Bites on all flights, which are à la carte food items ranging in price from $1 to $4 (Kraft Foods snacks such as Oreo Cakesters or Chips Ahoy! cookies) or combination packages ranging from $4 to $6 (Kraft Foods snacks and drinks).

One new dimension of AirTran's business strategy is the increasing use of ancillary revenues as a means to generate profits. These are optional fees for advance seat assignments or call center services, in addition to fees for pets, alcoholic drinks, excess baggage, and fees related to the transportation of unaccompanied minors.

In its *2008 Annual Report*, AirTran noted significant increases in its ancillary revenues, especially fees for the second bag ($25) and a fee for the first checked bag ($15). According to a recent *Wall Street Journal* article (February 9, 2009), AirTran collected $77 million in ancillary revenues in 2005. That amount increased to $233 million in 2008 and is expected to grow to $300 million in 2009. A comparison of fees among AirTran and its main competitors Delta, JetBlue, and Southwest can be seen in Exhibit 3, which appears later in the chapter. The exhibit reveals that AirTran is more similar in its fees to the legacy carrier Delta than to its low-cost competitors. Of these competitors, Delta clearly charges the highest ancillary fees, followed by AirTran, JetBlue, and Southwest (which has the lowest fees charged).

The rationale behind the use of ancillary fees is that they do not appear in most reservation systems when consumers are shopping for fares because airlines are not required to advertise fees that only some travelers will pay (such as fees for checked bags). If the fees were included in the fares, customers may make different choices in booking tickets and would shop around for airlines with lower fees. A recent *Wall Street Journal* article (March 10, 2009) says by the end of 2009, consumers will be able to comparison shop for airfares with the ancillary fees included in the price quote. Web sites such as TripAdvisor.com and Flying.fees.com already offer a way of calculating ancillary fees. Later in 2009, advanced technology will include fees in fare quotes from travel agents, online vendors, and airline Web sites.

Two major airline booking companies, Sabre Holdings Corp. and Amadeus IT Group SA, are expected to have tools available to travel agents, Web sites, and airlines later in 2009 that will add fees into ticket prices. TripAdvisor (a company owned by Expedia) has added to its differentiation by providing its users with a "fee estimator" based on the services that the traveler is intending to use. As such, it provides the traveler with a more realistic price of the price offering. The somewhat similar Flyingfees.com does not provide ticket prices but instead has data on ancillary fees for 27 airlines including some international carriers. When the traveler enters the airline name, a list of all ancillary fees is presented.

Service Quality

The nationally recognized *2009 Airline Quality Rating* (AQR) (for the year 2008) ranked AirTran second in overall quality ahead of its competitors Delta (number 12), JetBlue (number 3) and Southwest (number 6) (see Exhibit 2). The specific comments given in the report are as follows:

> **AirTran Airways (FL)** On-time performance remained the same in 2008 (76.8% in 2007 compared to 76.7% in 2008). AirTran's denied boardings performance (0.15 per 10,000 passengers in 2007 compared to 0.34 in 2008) was worse. An increase in customer complaint rate to 1.10 complaints per 100,000 passengers in 2008 was higher than the 2007 rate of 0.83. The mishandled baggage rate of 4.06 per 1,000 passengers in 2007 was improved to 2.87 for 2008. This was the best mishandled baggage rate of all airlines rated for 2008. (http://aqr.aero/aqrreports/2009aqr.pdf)

EXHIBIT 2 Airline Quality Rating Ranks for 2007 and 2008

	2008 Rank	2007 Rank
AirTran	2	1
American	9	9
American Eagle	16	15
Atlantic Southeast	17	16
Continental	8	6
Delta	12	10
JetBlue	3	2
Northwest	4	4
Southwest	6	3
United	11	8
US Airways	10	11

Rankings for 2008 reflect the addition of Hawaiian to the airlines tracked.

Source: Based on *2009 Airline Quality Rating*, by Brent D. Bowen, St. Louis University, and Dean Headley, Wichita State University, April 2009, http://aqr.aero/aqrreports/2009aqr.pdf.

EXHIBIT 3 Airline Bag Fees

Airline	First Checked Bag	Second Checked Bag	Additional Bags
AirTran	$15	$25	$50 per bag, after first two
Delta	$15	$25	$125 for 3rd (domestic), $200 (international), $200 (bags 4–10 US), $350 (bags 4–5 international)
JetBlue	Free (less than 50 lbs.)	$20	$75
Southwest	Free	Free	$25 (bag 3) $50 (bags 4–9)

Source: Based on "Airline Fees: A Snapshot of Carrier Policies," *Wall Street Journal*, February 23, 2009; http://blogs.wsj.com/middleseat/2009/02/23/airline-fees-a-snapshot-of-carrier-policies/tab/print/.

Operating Performance

Operating costs per available seat mile (CASM) increased 15.5 percent from 2007 to 2008 (see Exhibit 4). Aircraft fuel had the greatest increase in CASM of 41.8 percent from 2007 to 2008. AirTran's fuel price per gallon (including taxes and into-plane fees) increased 45.7 percent from $2.23 in 2007 to $3.25 in 2008. In 2008, however, AirTran realized a $15.7 million gain from fuel-related derivative financial instruments that reduced fuel expenses. Other costs that increased are distribution expenses (7.7 percent), landing fees and other expenses (7.4 percent), and depreciation and amortization costs (19.0 percent).

The cost per available seat mile is operating costs divided by ASM and is frequently used to compare operating efficiencies of airlines. How does AirTran compare to its competitors? *Yahoo! Finance* identifies Delta, JetBlue, and Southwest as AirTran's main competitors. The 2008 CASM data in Exhibit 5 shows AirTran (11.02¢) to be more efficient than Delta (18.72¢) but less efficient than JetBlue (9.87¢) and Southwest (10.24¢). AirTran's operating expenses for 2008 rose by 15.5 percent (see Exhibit 4) compared to JetBlue's increase of 20.6 percent and Southwest's increase of 12.5 percent. The greatest increase in operating expenses for all three airlines was fuel (AirTran, 41.8 percent; JetBlue, 43.1 percent; and Southwest, 33.3 percent, respectively).

EXHIBIT 4   AirTran's Operating Costs per ASM* (CASM)**

	Year Ended December 31		
	2008	2007	Percent Change
Aircraft fuel	5.02¢	3.54¢	41.8%
Salaries, wages, and benefits	1.99	1.99	—
Aircraft rent	1.02	1.07	(4.7)
Maintenance, materials, and rent	0.68	0.67	1.5
Distribution	0.42	0.39	7.7
Landing fees and other rents	0.58	0.54	7.4
Aircraft insurance and security services	0.09	0.10	(10.0)
Marketing and advertising	0.17	0.18	(5.6)
Depreciation and amortization	0.25	0.21	19.0
Gain on sale of assets	(0.10)	(0.03)	233.3
Impairment of goodwill	0.04	—	—
Other operating	0.86	0.88	(2.3)
Total CASM**	11.02¢	9.54¢	15.5%

*ASM = Available Seat Mile and is a measure of an airline's carrying capacity. ASM is the number of seats available multiplied by the number of miles flown.
**CASM = Cost per Available Seat Mile and is operating costs divided by ASM. CASM is frequently used to compare the operating efficiency of airlines.

Source: Reproduced from "Securities and Exchange Commission *Form 10K* for AirTran Holdings, Inc., 13 February 2009, Item 7—Management's Discussion and Analysis of Financial Condition and Results of Operations," p. 42; http://yahoo.brand.edgar-online.com/displayfilinginfo.aspx?FilingID=6412237-160691-264193&type=sect&dcn=0000948846-09-000005.

AirTran's load factor (the percentage of seats occupied by revenue-paying passengers) increased slightly in 2008 to 79.6 percent (see Exhibit 5), but is well below the break-even load factor of 89.3 percent. In 2006 and 2007, the load factors were above the break-even point. Exhibit 5 shows that AirTran's load factor is higher than Southwest's but slightly below Delta and JetBlue. Finally, the average yield per RPM (the average amount one passenger pays to fly one mile, or a measure of the airline's efficiency in generating revenues) is the highest for Delta (14.52¢) followed by Southwest (14.35¢) AirTran (12.73¢), and JetBlue (11.72¢).

Financial Performance

Exhibit 5 shows that AirTran had an operating loss of $72 million, a net income loss of $273.8 million for 2008, and an earnings loss per share of $2.51. In its *2008 Annual Report*, AirTran attributed this loss to a deteriorated economic environment, increases in jet fuel prices (see Exhibits 4 and 5 for data on fuel cost increases), and tightened credit markets. Exhibit 8 shows a direct competitor comparison showing the strongest financial performance coming from Southwest Airlines. Of the direct competitors, Delta Air Lines had the worst financial performance with an $8.82 billion net income loss and a $19.064 EPS loss in 2008.

External Factors

Fuel Prices

Aircraft fuel is the highest operating cost for AirTran. In Exhibit 4, fuel cost per Available Seat Mile (ASM) is 5.02¢ out of a total cost per available seat mile (CASM) of 11.02¢, or about 45.6 percent of its CASM. Of all its expenses, fuel prices have increased the most (41.8 percent). AirTran's *2008 Annual Report* notes that fuel price increases are a major risk for the airline because its main source of fuel (80 percent of supplies) is concentrated in the Gulf Coast. This fuel source concentration is attributed to AirTran's concentration of

EXHIBIT 5   AirTran's Selected Financial and Operating Data

In 000s except per share data	2008	2007	2006
Operating revenues	$2,552,478	$2,309,983	$1,892,083
Operating income (loss)	$ (72,010)	$ 144,160	$ 40,861
Net income (loss)	$ (273,829)	$ 52,683	$ 14,714
Earnings (Loss) per Common Share			
Basic	$ (2.51)	$ 0.58	$ 0.16
Diluted	$ (2.51)	$ 0.56	$ 0.16
Total assets at year-end	$2,062,860	$2,058,466	$1,603,582
Long-term debt and capital lease obligations including current maturities at year-end	$1,117,300	$1,057,889	$ 811,110
Operating Data			
Revenue passengers	24,619,120	23,780,058	20,051,219
Revenue passenger miles (RPM)* (000)	18,955,843	17,297,724	13,836,378
Available seat miles (ASM)** (000)	23,809,190	22,692,355	19,007,416
Passenger load factor	79.6%	76.2%	72.8%
Break-even load factor	89.3%	73.2%	71.8%
Average fare (excl. transportation taxes)	$ 98.04	$ 92.47	$ 90.51
Average yield per RPM***	12.73¢	12.71¢	13.12¢
Passenger revenue per ASM	10.14¢	9.69¢	9.55¢
Operating cost per ASM	11.02¢	9.54¢	9.74¢
Gallons of fuel consumed (000)	367,169	359,759	310,926
Average stage length (miles)	728	695	652
Average cost of fuel per gallon including taxes and fees	3.25	2.23	2.17
Average daily utilization (hours: minutes)	11:00	11:00	11:06
Number of operating aircraft in fleet at end of year	136	137	127
Comparison Data			
Delta passenger load factor	81.1%		
JetBlue passenger load factor	80.4%		
Southwest passenger load factor	71.2%		
Delta average yield per RPM	14.52¢		
JetBlue average yield per RPM	11.72¢		
Southwest average yield per RPM	14.35¢		
Delta operating cost per ASM	18.72¢		
JetBlue operating cost per ASM	9.87¢		
Southwest operating cost per ASM	10.24¢		

Notes:

*The number of scheduled revenue miles flown by passengers.

**The number of seats available for passengers multiplied by the number of miles the seats are flown.

***The average amount one passenger pays to fly one mile.

operations in the southeast United States and Atlanta in particular. Any disruption of those supplies because of weather or other reasons could severely affect the operations of the company.

Labor Costs

In its *2008 Annual Report*, AirTran notes that increased labor costs, union disputes, employee strikes, and other labor-related disruptions are risks facing the airline and the industry because labor costs are a significant percentage of total operating costs. Exhibit 4

EXHIBIT 6   **Balance Sheet (all numbers in thousands)**

Period Ending	31 Dec 08	31 Dec 07	31 Dec 06
Assets			
Current Assets			
Cash and Cash Equivalents	$ 401,204	$ 236,491	$ 183,915
Short Term Investments	23,357	124,154	151,100
Net Receivables	94,571	52,548	47,467
Inventory	15,428	14,488	17,236
Other Current Assets	49,847	52,256	17,239
Total Current Assets	**584,407**	**79,937**	**416,957**
Long Term Investments	5,497	8,230	—
Property, Plant and Equipment	1,282,972	1,365,912	1,015,229
Goodwill	—	8,350	8,350
Intangible Assets	21,587	21,567	21,567
Accumulated Amortization	—	—	—
Other Assets	168,417	164,470	133,707
Deferred Long Term Asset Charges	—	—	7,772
Total Assets	**2,062,860**	**2,048,466**	**1,603,582**
Liabilities			
Current Liabilities			
Accounts Payable	437,648	376,014	311,242
Short/Current Long Term Debt	230,346	99,671	86,845
Other Current Liabilities	43,853	32,449	—
Total Current Liabilities	**711,847**	**508,134**	**398,087**
Long Term Debt	977,216	962,973	724,265
Other Liabilities	120,342	99,575	101,947
Deferred L T Liability Charges	7450	31,434	—
Minority Interest	—	—	—
Negative Goodwill	—	—	—
Total Liabilities	**1,816,855**	**1,602,116**	**1,224,299**
Stockholders' Equity			
Misc Stocks Options Warrants	—	—	—
Redeemable Preferred Stock	—	—	—
Preferred Stock	—	—	—
Common Stock	120	92	91
Retained Earnings	(225,745)	48,084	(4,599)
Treasury Stock	—	—	—
Capital Surplus	497,390	396,824	389,043
Other Stockholders' Equity	(25,760)	1,350	(5,252)
Total Stockholders' Equity	**246,005**	**446,350**	**379,283**
Total Liabilities and SE	**$2,062,860**	**$2,048,466**	**$1,603,582**

Source: Reproduced from "Balance Sheet for AirTran Holdings," *Yahoo! Finance*, http://finance.yahoo.com/q/bs?s=AAI&annual.

EXHIBIT 7   Income Statement (all numbers in thousands)

Period Ending	31 Dec 08	31 Dec 07	31 Dec 06
Total Revenue	**$2,552,478**	**$2,309,983**	**$1,892,083**
Cost of Revenue	2,234,935	1,796,048	1,572,270
Gross Profit	**317,543**	**513,935**	**319,813**
Operating Expenses	—	—	—
Research and Development	—	—	—
Selling and General and Admin	345,770	327,524	248,874
Non Recurring	(14,835)	—	—
Others	58,618	48,485	30,078
Total Operating Expenses	—	—	—
Operating Income or Loss	**(72,010)**	**137,926**	**40,861**
Income from Continuing Ops			
Total Other Income/Expenses Net	(147,157)	15,730	21,714
Earnings Before Income and Taxes	(219,167)	153,656	62,575
Interest Expense	72,725	66,304	37,918
Income Before Tax	(291,892)	87,352	24,657
Income Tax Expense	(18,063)	34,669	9,943
Minority Interest	—	—	—
Net Income from Continuing Ops	(273,829)	52,683	14,714
Non-recurring Events	—	—	—
Discontinued Operations	—	—	—
Extraordinary Items	—	—	—
Effect of Accounting Changes	—	—	—
Other Items	—	—	—
Net Income	**(273,829)**	**52,683**	**14,714**
Preferred Stock and Other Adjustments	—	—	—
Net Inc Applic to Common Shares	**($ 273,829)**	**$ 52,683**	**$ 14,714**

Source: Reproduced from "Income Statement for AirTran Holdings," *Yahoo! Finance,* http://finance.yahoo.com/q/is?s=AAI&annual/.

EXHIBIT 8   Direct Competitor Comparison (2008)

	AirTran	Delta	JetBlue	Southwest	Industry
Market Capitalization	603.43M	4.64B	1.20B	5.08B	608.35M
Employees	7,600	84,306	8,902	35,499	5.4K
Qtr. Rev. Growth	1.00%	43.30%	9.70%	9.70%	13.10%
Revenue	2.55B	22.70B	3.39B	11.02B	1.48B
Gross Margin	13.29%	13.33%	26.18%	22.07%	22.07%
EBITDA	−21.86M	1.28B	304.00M	1.05B	90.07B
Oper. Margins	−3.40%	0.50%	2.77%	4.07%	7.45%
Net Income	−273.83M	−8.82B	−76.00M	178.00M	N/A
EPS	−2.509	−19.064	−0.336	0.241	N/A
P/E	N/A	N/A	N/A	28.46	8.44

Source: Reproduced from *Yahoo! Finance,* April 5, 2009, http://finance.yahoo.com/q/co?s=AAI.

shows that labor costs are AirTran's second-highest cost category. Much of the workforce is represented by labor unions with different unions for flight attendants, pilots, dispatchers, and maintenance technicians and inspectors. Each group is covered by collective bargaining agreements that provide for annual pay rate increases. AirTran has reduced its labor costs in 2008 through voluntary leaves of absence and early exits.

Exhibit 4 indicates that the labor costs (salaries, wages, and benefits) per ASM were the same for 2007 and 2008. AirTran stated in its *2008 Annual Report* that it may reduce workforce levels and/or seek new wage concessions in response to significant fuel price increases. A recent article in the Associated Press (April 10, 2009) noted that AirTran pilots recently voted to become part of the Air Line Pilots Association (ALPA), the largest pilot union in the world.

The Airline Industry and Competition

Several of which compete using the low-cost model (such as AirTran and JetBlue). The intensity of competition and high fuel prices contributed to many airlines declaring Chapter 11 bankruptcy, including many legacy carriers such as Delta, Continental, Northwest, United, and US Airways. Within the last year, at least six airlines declared bankruptcy (and some have ceased operations): Aloha Airlines, ATA Airlines, Skybus Airlines, Frontier Airlines, Eos Airlines, and Sun Country Airlines. Of these six, only Aloha Airlines and Eos Airlines are not low-cost carriers. As such, within the industry, AirTran, JetBlue, and Southwest would be considered examples of airlines that have successfully implemented the low-cost model of competition.

More recently, several airlines have cut back on flights in response to the economic recession. For example, Delta announced plans to cut overall flight capacity by 8 percent in 2009. AirTran in its *2008 Annual Report* stated that it reduced capacity in the last four months of 2008 and plans additional capacity cuts in 2009.

AirTran, Delta, JetBlue, and Southwest all have the U.S. Department of Transportation "major airline" classification because of their $1.00 billion or greater revenues (Exhibit 8). Exhibit 9 shows that in this competitor group, Southwest has the highest domestic market share (13.0 percent), followed by Delta (10.8 percent), JetBlue (4.3 percent), and AirTran (3.3 percent). Exhibit 8 shows that for 2008, Delta has the most employees (84,306) and highest revenues ($22.7 billion) compared to AirTran, which has the fewest employees (7,600) and smallest revenues ($2.55 billion). The most profitable competitor was Southwest

EXHIBIT 9   Airline Domestic Market Share February 2008– January 2009

Airline	Share
American	14.3%
Southwest	13.0%
United	11.0%
Delta	10.8%
US Airways	8.3%
Continental	7.6%
Northwest	6.4%
JetBlue	4.3%
AirTran	3.3%
Alaska	2.9%
Other	18.1%

Market share is based on Revenue Passenger Miles for February 2008 to January 2009.
Revenue Passenger Miles (RPMs) is a measure of passenger traffic calculated by multiplying the total number of revenue-paying passengers aboard by the distance traveled in miles.

Source: Adapted from Research and Innovative Technology Administration (RITA), Bureau of Transportation Statistics, April 29, 2009, http://www.transtats.bts.gov/.

EXHIBIT 10   AirTran's Top Domestic Markets*
(February 2008–January 2009)

Market	Volume	Share**
Atlanta, GA	8,178,000	20.98%
Orlando, FL	2,030,260	12.85%
Baltimore, MD	1,422,490	14.35%
Tampa, FL	749,370	8.75%
Boston, MA	641,050	5.87%
Other	11,576,050	2.07%

*Based on the total enplaned passengers at all airports in a city.
**The table shows the airline's share in each of the markets.

Source: Reproduced from RITA BTS Airline Data, 2009 Carrier Fact Sheets, April 29, 2009; http://www.transtats.bts.gov/printcarriers.asp?Carrier=FL.

EXHIBIT 11   Delta's Top Domestic Markets*
(February 2008–January 2009)

Market	Volume	Share**
Atlanta, GA	20,750,000	53.22%
New York, NY	3,920,000	16.81%
Salt Lake City, UT	3,810,000	40.03%
Cincinnati, OH	2,030,000	33.85%
Los Angeles, CA	1,980,000	9.73%
Other	26,680,000	4.89%

*Based on the total enplaned passengers at all airports in a city.
**The table shows the airline's share in each of the markets.

Source: Reproduced from RITA BTS Airline Data, 2009 Carrier Fact Sheets, April 29, 2009; http://www.transtats.bts.gov/printcarriers.asp?Carrier=DL.

with $178 million in net income, and the least profitable was Delta with a net income loss of $8.82 billion.

Dependence of AirTran on the Atlanta market brings it into intense competition with the much bigger Delta Air Lines. When looking at key markets for AirTran and its main competitors (see Exhibits 10 through 13), most market overlap occurs between AirTran and Delta in the Atlanta market. Both airlines have most of their total enplaned passengers in this city, and for both it represents the market for which each airline has its largest market share, although Delta has a significantly larger share (53.22 percent) than AirTran (20.98 percent). AirTran does, however, have a cost advantage over Delta as shown earlier and has not sustained as large financial losses as Delta.

The Future

The airline industry continues to be a turbulent one in which some airlines are able to operate profitably while others are near bankruptcy. Prepare a strategic plan for AirTran considering challenges such as the following:

1. How should AirTran improve its low-cost position given the cost advantages of JetBlue and Southwest Airlines?
2. Should AirTran continue to focus on the eastern United States (and the Atlanta market in particular) or should it expand to other regions? If so, which regions provide the most opportunities?

EXHIBIT 12   JetBlue's Top Domestic Markets*
(February 2008–January 2009)

Market	Volume	Share**
New York, NY	5,800,000	24.86%
Boston, MA	1,820,000	16.68%
Orlando, FL	1,570,000	9.95%
Fort Lauderdale, FL	1,380,000	14.78%
Long Beach, CA	1,100,000	77.47%
Other	8,680,000	1.49%

*Based on the total enplaned passengers at all airports in a city.
**The table shows the airline's share in each of the markets.

Source: Reproduced from RITA BTS Airline Data, 2009 Carrier Fact Sheets,
April 29, 2009; http://www.transtats.bts.gov/printcarriers.asp?Carrier=B6.

EXHIBIT 13   Southwest's Top Domestic Markets*
(February 2008–January 2009)

Market	Volume	Share**
Las Vegas, NV	7,600,000	39.20%
Chicago, IL	6,690,000	18.73%
Phoenix, AZ	5,640,000	30.39%
Baltimore, MD	5,280,000	53.28%
Dallas, TX	3,800,000	95.39%
Other	72,240,000	12.98%

*Based on the total enplaned passengers at all airports in a city.
**The table shows the airline's share in each of the markets.

Source: Reproduced from RITA BTS Airline Data, 2009 Carrier Fact Sheets,
April 29, 2009; http://www.transtats.bts.gov/printcarriers.asp?Carrier=WN.

3. How sustainable is the practice of having separate ancillary fees as a means of generating additional revenues? Should AirTran make any changes?
4. What are the main external opportunities and threats facing AirTran? List these in order of priority.
5. How important are fuel prices (compared to other costs) as a determinant of profitability? Is AirTran taking appropriate action to manage these costs now and in the future?

References

"A unique airline philosophy—one that works," AirTran Web site, March 12, 2009,
    http://www.airtranairways.com/about-us/corporate_info.aspx.

"Airline Classification," U.S. Department of Transportation, March 22, 2009,
    http://ostpxweb.dot.gov/aviation/airlineclassifications.htm.

"Airlines Look to Fees for a Financial Edge," *Wall Street Journal*, February 9, 2009,
    http://blogs.wsj.com/middleseat/2009/02/09/airlines-charging-more-baggage-fees-refreshment/.

"AirTran," *Raymond James Institutional Investors Conference*, March 2009,
    http://www.sec.gov/Archives/edgar/data/948846/000094884609000006/ex99-1.htm.

"AirTran Airways History," AirTran Web site, March 21, 2009, http://www.
    airtranairways.com/about-us/history.aspx?print=true.

"AirTran Airways Launches Buy-On-Board Food with Sky Bites (SM)," *AirTran Press Release*, February 11, 2009, http://pressroom.airtran.com/phoenix.zhtml?c=201565&p=irol-newsArticle_print&ID=1255586&highlight.

AirTran Airways 2008 Annual Report, http://investor.airtran.com/phoenix.zhtml?c=64267&p=irol-reportsAnnual.

"AirTran CEO received $1.5M in 2008 compensation," *Yahoo! Finance (AP)*, April 3, 2009, http://finance.yahoo.com/news/AirTran-CEO-received-15M-in-apf-14843920.html.

"AirTran pilots vote to join largest union," *Yahoo! Finance (AP)*, April 10, 2009, http://finance.yahoo.com/news/AirTran-pilots-vote-to-join-apf-14902119.html?.v=1.

"Average Fleet Age for Selected Carriers," *AirSafe.com*, April 26, 2009, http://www.airsafe.com/events/airlines/fleetage.htm.

"Awards and recognition," AirTran Web site, April 11, 2009, http://www.airtranairways.com/about-us/awards.aspx

Bowen, Brent D., and Dean E. Headley. *2009 Airline Quality Rating,* April 2009, http://www.aqr.aero/aqrreports/2009aqr.pdf.

Gardner, Amy, and Spencer S. Hsu. "Airline Apologizes for Booting 9 Muslims," *Washington Post*, January 3, 2009, http://www.washingtonpost.com/wp-dyn/content/story/2009/01/02/ST2009010201697.html.

"Grim Prospects—Deep Recession, Bigger Losses," *IATA Press Releases*, March 24, 2009, http://www.iata.org/pressroom/pr/2009-03-24-01.htm.

McCartney, Scott. "Airfare Quotes That Lay Bare Hidden Fees," *Wall Street Journal*, March 10, 2009, http://online.wsj.com/article/SB123664662318478683.html.

McCartney, Scott. "The Next Airline Fee: Buying Tickets," *Wall Street Journal,* March 3, 2008, http://online.wsj.com/article/SB123604492886515417.html.

Mission statement," AirTran Web site, March 12, 2009, http://www.airtran.com/Jobs/mission_statement.aspx/

Prada, Paulo, and Susan Carey. "Airlines Plan Further Reductions in Flights, Staff," *Wall Street Journal*, http://online.wsj.com/article/SB123672652139988491.html.

Family Dollar Stores, Inc. — 2009

Joseph W. Leonard
Miami University

FDO

www.familydollar.com

As the economy limps along in mid-2009 and pushes more households into lower incomes, Family Dollar Store's CEO Howard R. Levine is overseeing continued expansion and growth. His father, Leon Levine, founded the company when he was in his early 20s in 1959, and the elder Levine now sports the title chairman emeritus. Family Dollar offers customers a variety of high-quality, good-value merchandise. The company caters to the low- to low-middle income group (defined as households under $30,000 or $35,000 of annual income) with offerings of competitively priced merchandise in convenient neighborhood stores. Family Dollar Stores has 31 percent of its items priced at a dollar or less.

For 2008, the Dow Jones Average was down 34 percent, the worst year since 1931. Of the S&P 500 stocks index, only 24 stocks were up in 2008. Family Dollar Stores led the way with an increase of 35 percent. Will this solid performance continue?

History

In 1959, when Family Dollar opened its first store in Charlotte, North Carolina, Leon Levine offered customers a varied of good-valued merchandise for under $2. The concept was simple, "The customers are the boss, and you need to keep them happy." Family Dollar went public in 1970, achieved annual sales of $100 million with just under 300 stores by 1977, opened its 1,500th store in 1989 and its 2,500th store in 1996, and grew to nearly 5,000 stores and sales approaching $5 billion when he retired as chairman in 2003. In his high school and college years, his son Howard Levine worked for Family Dollar. Howard was named CEO in 1998, and when his father retired in January 2003, he became chairman and CEO. At age 49, he continues today as chairman and CEO.

Today's Facts and Financials

Family Dollar operates more than 6,600 stores in 44 states plus the District of Columbia. The company does have a small role in international business because about 51 percent of its merchandise is procured from international manufacturers often through agents but also from direct importing from the manufacturers. No single supplier accounts for more than 8 percent of the merchandise purchases. Family Dollar Stores is ranked number 359 on the *Fortune* 500.

Family Dollar continues its strategy of geographic expansion and new store openings. Headquartered near Charlotte, North Carolina, Family Dollar employs 44,000 people, about 25,000 full time and the others as part-timers. Family Dollar's revenues of $6.984 billion in FY2008—the 12 months ended August 2008—showed an increase of 2.2 percent over the year ending August 2007. As indicated in Exhibit 1, the operating profits during FY2008 were $365 million, a decrease of 6 percent from FY2007. The net profit in FY2008 was $233 million, a 4 percent decrease from FY2007.

Divisions of the Company

For FY2008, Family Dollar Stores broke revenues into four broad product categories: consumables, home products, apparel and accessories, and seasonal and electronics. Making comparisons from FY2007 to FY2008, three of the broad product categories had increased sales, but apparel and accessories decreased. Consumables increased by 6.1 percent and represent 61.1 percent of FY2008's total revenues of $6.984 billion. Home products increased by 3.2 percent and make up 14.3 percent of revenues. Apparel and accessories decreased by 6.9 percent and make up 13.1 percent of revenues. Seasonal and electronics increased by 0.8 percent and make up 11.5 percent of revenues. Exhibits 1 and 2 reveal Family Dollar's recent balance sheets.

Since May 1998, the company has provided quarterly cash dividends to its shareholders. The amount per share of these dividends has increased each year (from 4.5 cents per share on July 15, 1998, to 13.5 cents per share on July 15, 2009). This latest dividend yield is about a 1.7 percent return per year, well ahead of the industry average.

Family Dollar continues to seek good locations and contractors to build and maintain stores. The company is involved in real estate management, construction, and store maintenance. Family Dollar has about 15 to 20 percent of its stores up for lease renewal each year. On February 28, 2009, Howard Levine said that the company would definitely try to "leverage the current market to negotiate better rents."

In 2008, Family Dollar opened 205 new stores, closed 64 stores, relocated 17 stores within the same shopping area or market area, and expanded 80 stores. In 2007, the company opened 301 new stores and closed 43 stores.

EXHIBIT 1   Income Statements for Family Dollar

Income Statements for Years Ending August 2008, 2007, 2006
(in millions, except for EPS & Dividends)

	Aug 08	Aug 07	Aug 06
Revenue	$6,983.6	6,834.3	6,394.8
Cost of Goods Sold	4,637.8	4,512.2	4,276.5
Gross Profit	2,345.8	2,322.1	2,118.3
Gross Profit Margin	33.6%	34.0%	33.1%
SG&A Expense	1,980.5	1,933.4	1,756.0
Depreciation & Amortization	149.6	144.1	134.6
Operating Income	376.3	399.3	324.2
Operating Margin	5.4%	5.8%	5.1%
Nonoperating Income	0.0	0.0	0.0
Nonoperating Expenses	(3.5)	–	–
Income Before Taxes	361.8	381.9	311.1
Income Taxes	128.7	139.0	116.0
Net Income After Taxes	233.1	242.9	195.1
Continuing Operations	233.1	242.9	195.1
Discontinued Operations	–	–	–
Total Operations	233.1	242.9	195.1
Total Net Income	$ **233.1**	**242.9**	**195.1**
Net Profit Margin	3.3%	3.6%	3.1%
Diluted EPS from Total Net Income ($)	1.66	1.62	1.26
Dividends per Share	0.49	0.45	0.41

Source: www.familydollar.com

EXHIBIT 2   Family Dollar's Balance Sheets for Years Ending August 2008, 2007, 2006 (in millions)

Assets	Aug 08	Aug 07	Aug 06
Current Assets			
Cash	$ 158.5	87.2	79.7
Net Receivables	7.0	44.4	2.4
Inventories	1,032.7	1,065.9	1,037.9
Other Current Assets	145.9	339.8	298.9
Total Current Assets	1,344.1	1,537.3	1,418.8
Net Fixed Assets	1,071.9	1,060.7	1,077.6
Other Noncurrent Assets	245.8	26.2	26.6
Total Assets	**2,661.8**	**2,624.2**	**2,523.0**

Liabilities and Shareholders' Equity	Aug 08	Aug 07	Aug 06
Current Liabilities			
Accounts Payable	$ 570.7	644.1	556.5
Short-Term Debt	–	–	–
Other Current Liabilities	498.3	486.2	429.6
Total Current Liabilities	1,069.0	1,130.3	986.1
Long-Term Debt	250.0	250.0	250.0
Other Noncurrent Liabilities	88.7	69.2	78.5
Total Liabilities	1,407.7	1,449.5	1,314.6
Shareholders' Equity			
Preferred Stock Equity	–	0.0	0.0
Common Stock Equity	1,254.1	1,174.6	1,208.4
Total Equity	**1,254.1**	**1,174.6**	**1,208.4**
Shares Outstanding (mil.)	140.2	140.2	140.2

Source: www.familydollar.com

Competition and Industry

The small-box discount retailers industry reported strong performance in the last half of 2008 and the first half of 2009.

The three largest small-box discount retailers are Dollar General, Family Dollar, and Dollar Tree. These three dollar stores realize that they are different from the giant Wal-Mart in many ways, including offering lower prices.

All three of these small-box companies have to deal with many rivals, including Fred's, 99 Cents Only, Wal-Mart, Big Lots, CVS, J.C. Penney, Kmart, Meijer, Sears, Target, Walgreen, Costco, Kroger, and many other small regional chains and one-of-a-kind retailers. Exhibit 3 compares the three largest small-box discount retailers.

Dollar General

Headquartered in Tennessee, Dollar General's stores are typically located in small towns, but big-city stores (usually situated in lower-income neighborhoods) account for 30 percent of its total. About 35 percent of its products are priced at $1 or less. Dollar General was taken private by affiliates of KKR and Goldman Sachs in 2007.

Dollar Tree

Headquartered in Virginia, Dollar Tree stresses the $1 price points and offers a range of merchandise including housewares, seasonal goods, food, toys, personal accessories, health

EXHIBIT 3   **The Three Largest Small-Box Discount Retailers**

	Dollar General	Family Dollar	Dollar Tree
2008 Annual Sales	$9,454 Million	$6,984 Million	$4,645 Million
Sales Growth	2.9%	2.2%	9.5%
2008 Net Income	($13 Million)	$233 Million	$230 Million
Long-Term Debt	$4,130 Million	$250 Million	$268 Million
# of Stores	8,400	6,600	3,600
Store Size (sq ft)	7,000	7,500 to 9,000	5,000 to 10,000
# of States	35	44	48
# of Employees	71,500	44,000	46,000
# of Distribution Centers	9	9	9
Year Started	1939	1959	1953
Fortune 500 Rank	359	499	

Source: Company *Form 10K* Reports.

and beauty care products, party goods, greeting cards, and books, mostly for $1 even. Dollar Tree operates stores called Dollar Tree, Dollar Bill, Dollar Express, Only 1.00, and Only One. About 40 percent of the company's merchandise is imported, mostly from China. Dollar Tree does offer online sales. Dollar Tree Inc. recently sneaked into the latest *Fortune* 500, now at number 499.

Mission

Family Dollar's mission statement is provided in Exhibit 4.

Operations

Even compared to Wal-Mart, Family Dollar is considered to be a leader in keeping costs low. The company continues to review and improve each step in the supply chain, from vendor selection to stocking store shelves. Family Dollar has undertaken initiatives to improve supply chain effectiveness.

Nearly all Family Dollar stores range in size from 7,500 to 9,000 square feet and are operated in leased facilities. The company pursues this strategy of relatively small stores as a way to open new stores in rural areas, small towns, and large urban neighborhoods. Whenever feasible, Family Dollar likes to have a parking lot located immediately near the store's entrance, and nearly all stores have only one entrance. The size of the stores (about 1/22 the square footage of a typical Wal-Mart Supercenter) has appeal to customers who like the convenience and short walk, which cannot be matched by some of the large store chains.

Over the past few years, Family Dollar has improved its logistics network and is moving toward a world-class distribution system. CEO Howard Levine said. "It's a Wal-Mart formula. We have to deliver goods efficiently to the stores, and we've been able to do that."

EXHIBIT 4   **Mission Statement and CEO's Comment**

Family Dollar's mission states the three most important relationships critical to making our business successful: our customers, our associates, and our investors.

For our customers, we offer a compelling place to shop by providing convenience and low prices;

For our associates, we offer a compelling place to work by providing exceptional opportunities and rewards for achievement;

For our investors, we offer a compelling place to invest by providing outstanding returns.

To support its retail operations, Family Dollar operates nine automated full-service distribution centers (each ranging in size from 850,000 square feet to 907,000 square feet) that ship directly to company stores. The company uses a Web-based transportation management system, voice-recognition software, radio-frequency technology and high-speed sorting systems for better distribution process efficiency. Family Dollar has a strong presence in the southern United States. Seven of its nine distribution centers are located in the South (northern Virginia, western North Carolina, panhandle of Florida, eastern Kentucky, eastern Arkansas, southwestern Oklahoma, and western Texas); the other two are in upstate New York and eastern Iowa. The company operates few stores in the Rocky Mountain region and only the Nevada stores in the Pacific time zone. Exhibit 5 shows the store locations.

EXHIBIT 5 Family Dollar, by State and Number of Stores

Number of Stores per 100,000 population	
# of Stores	# of Stores per 100,000 Population
NORTHEAST	
Maine 46	3.49
New Hampshire 22	1.67
Vermont 12	1.93
Massachusetts 99	1.53
Rhode Island 20	1.90
Connecticut 51	1.46
New York 290	1.49
Pennsylvania 264	2.11
New Jersey 80	0.92
Delaware 21	2.41
Maryland 92	1.64
District of Columbia 3	0.50
SOUTH	
Virginia 214	2.75
West Virginia 115	6.34
North Carolina 364	3.95
South Carolina 198	4.42
Georgia 303	3.07
Florida 363	1.98
Kentucky 186	4.36
Tennessee 204	3.28
Alabama 145	3.13
Mississippi 118	4.02
Arkansas 98	3.43
Louisiana 229	5.19
MIDWEST	
Ohio 411	3.58
Indiana 195	3.04
Michigan 348	3.48
Wisconsin 140	2.49
Illinois 238	1.84

continued

EXHIBIT 5   **Family Dollar, by State and Number of Stores—continued**

# of Stores	# of Stores per 100,000 Population
Minnesota 71	1.36
Iowa 32	1.07
Missouri 96	1.62
North Dakota 11	1.71
South Dakota 22	2.73
Nebraska 31	1.74
Kansas 35	1.25
SOUTHWEST & MOUNTAIN	
Oklahoma 128	3.51
Texas 817	3.36
Wyoming 20	3.75
Colorado 104	2.14
New Mexico 90	4.54
Arizona 130	2.00
Utah 60	2.19
Idaho 31	2.03
Nevada 24	0.92

Aggregate Information

44 + DC 6,572 2.61 one store per 38,380 population

There are no stores in Montana, Washington, Oregon, California, Alaska, and Hawaii.

Source: Family Dollar Stores, *Annual Report* (2008); www.infoplease.com/ipa/A004986.html.

Family Dollar's transportation technologies include a Web-based Transportation Management System (TMS) that allows vendors to release purchase orders electronically. Family Dollar Trucking, Inc. (FDTI) provides a private fleet of trucks that have received safety rewards. More recently, Family Dollar is beginning to use some of these same systems in international transportation.

Family Dollar is now using POS (point of service) systems that provide access to both centralized and decentralized store applications, enabling higher employee productivity, improved customer service, and some new revenue streams. Family Dollar is working with Toshiba TEC American on this. According to Howard Levine, the company is "accelerating the completion of the POS rollout by January or February of 2010, which we're well on track of doing." In these endeavors, Family Dollar continues to partner with Toshiba TEC America and Microsoft.

Family Dollar recently hired Sylvania Lighting Services (SLS) to install new lighting to save energy, reduce maintenance, drive down operation costs, and improve store light (brightness) levels in all its stores. "The new lighting program is a huge win for Family Dollar, which yields a reduction in overall lighting maintenance costs, budget future lighting expenses over four years at fixed costs and allows them to achieve tremendous energy savings while integrating environmental sustainability," said Scott Agnew, SLS executive account manager. The lighting upgrades also gave Family Dollar some tax breaks.

Marketing

While other retailers have courted a more upscale clientele by adding designer clothes and fine jewelry, Family Dollar has stayed true to its roots. A typical shopper earns just $35,000 per year. According to Howard Levine, "We want our customers to know they can afford anything in our store."

Beyond the four broad product categories, Family Dollar's merchandise assortment are divided into 11 product classifications that include apparel, food, cleaning and paper products, home decor, beauty and health aids, toys, pet products, automotive products, domestics, seasonal goods, and electronics.

Family Dollar's merchandise includes national brands, Family Dollar private labels, and unbranded items that sell for less than $10. Whereas some other discount retailers focus on factory closeouts, these make up only about 2 percent of Family Dollar's sales. The company carries many name-brand items found in supermarkets, such as Tide, Colgate, and Clorox. Some analysts estimate that Family Dollar's prices are 20 to 40 percent cheaper than those found in traditional supermarkets and are roughly on par with big-box discounters such as Wal-Mart and Target or lower.

Family Dollar emphasizes convenience for its customers. It sees the typical scenario as based on easy-to-shop neighborhood locations that allow "Mom to get what she needs, close to home to take care of her family." In 2008, the company introduced a new logo to facilitate achieving this emphasis. Along with the new logo, Family Dollar has developed a new tag line: "My family. My family dollar." These recent updates assist the company toward conveying its commitment to providing value and convenience with a family focus.

Family Dollar does not make use of Web site sales. The company has lagged behind many other retailers in accepting food stamps and other payment forms. Family Dollar and its dollar-store direct competitors still face an image problem of a perception of an old, cluttered, and dirty store. One customer complained that one week the store might carry Green Giant canned corn and then Libby's the next. From the management of Family Dollar's perspective, this would be termed "opportunistic buying." By late 2009, Family Dollar plans to introduce 250 new edible items, including Triscuits and Double Stuf Oreos as a way to attract more customers. Some would categorize the company's increased emphasis on food and slightly increased plan to put more stores in urban areas as a differentiation strategy.

Human Resources

About 15 percent of Family Dollar's top 41 executives are women. Family Dollars' corporate board of directors has 10 members ranging in age from 47 to 78 (with a mean and median age in the mid-60s), which includes three women but only one insider (Howard R. Levine) with the other nine being nonemployees of the company.

In July 2006, Family Dollar lost a federal court case in Tuscaloosa, Alabama, that amounted to $35.6 million. This decision was upheld on December 16, 2008, by the U.S. 11th Circuit Court. The case involved store managers not being paid for overtime. The class action judgment was on behalf of 1,424 managers. The affected managers were awarded back pay. The managers had argued that Family Dollar owed them overtime wages under the Fair Labor Standards Act (FLSA). Family Dollar's corporate management contended that the managers held executive authority and were thus exempt from the FLSA requirements. Partly because the store managers had no power to hire and fire staff, they reportedly often worked 60 to 70 hours per week doing a variety of nonmanagerial work activities such as operating cash registers and manual labor such as stocking shelves, unloading trucks, and cleaning floors.

Conclusions and the Future

Family Dollar believes it can prosper in a limping U.S. economy and perform even better in a strong economy. But with issues such as litigation, competition, increasing labor costs, and efficiency issues in supply chain management and elsewhere, Family Dollar faces challenges as it continues to grow toward 10,000 stores.

In April 2009 as the economic recession continued, Family Dollar's Public Relations Manager Josh Braverman said, "Thrift is in. Saving money is in. And it still will be even after the economy recovers." Although penny-pinching moms are important to Family Dollar, the future is not a sure thing. Can Family Dollar perform well both in good economic times and in bad economic times? To many business experts, it seems unreasonable to be able to have it both ways.

As indicated in Exhibits 6 and 7, Family Dollar's third-quarter (ending May 30, 2009) results were excellent. Compared to one year earlier (May 31, 2008), net sales

EXHIBIT 6   Family Dollar's Consolidated Statements of Income (unaudited)

(in thousands, except except per share amounts)	For the Third Quarter Ended			
	May 30, 2009	% of Net Sales	May 31, 2008	% of Net Sales
Net sales	$1,843,089	100.0%	$1,702,197	100.0%
Cost of sales	1,175,897	63.8%	1,112,755	65.4%
Gross profit	667,192	36.2%	589,442	34.6%
Selling, general and administrative expenses	528,158	28.7%	487,835	28.7%
Operating profit	139,034	7.5%	101,607	5.9%
Interest income	879	0.0%	2,973	0.2%
Interest expense	3,216	0.2%	3,361	0.2%
Income before income taxes	136,697	7.3%	101,219	5.9%
Income taxes	48,976	2.7%	36,546	2.1%
Net income	$ 87,721	4.6%	$ 64,673	3.8%

Source: Family Dollar Stores, Inc.

increased by 8.3 percent, net income increased by 35.6 percent, net income per common share increased from 46 cents to 63 cents. Net sales increased by 12.6 percent for consumables, dropped by 5.0 percent for apparel and accessories, rose by 3.5 percent for home products, and increased by 5.8 percent for seasonal and electronics. The number of "stores in operation" was 6,654 on May 30, 2009, up from 6,545 on May 31, 2008. Sales in comparable stores reported to increase by 6.2 percent. During the quarter, Family Dollar repurchased approximately 1.2 million shares of its common stock at a total cost of $38.5 million. Exhibit 8 reveals the company's recent store opening/closing activity.

EXHIBIT 7   Family Dollar Stores, Inc., and Subsidiaries Selected Additional Information

Net Sales by Category

(in thousands)	For the Third Quarter Ended		
	May 30, 2009	May 31, 2008	% Change
Consumables	$1,201,033	$1,066,649	12.6%
Home products	237,384	229,528	3.4%
Apparel and accessories	219,193	230,784	−5.0%
Seasonal and electronics	185,479	175,236	5.8%
TOTAL	$1,843,089	$1,702,197	8.3%

(in thousands)	For the Three Quarters Ended		
	May 30, 2009	May 31, 2008	% Change
Consumables	$3,565,542	$3,139,544	13.6%
Home products	771,577	774,518	−0.4%
Apparel and accessories	620,175	686,341	−9.6%
Seasonal and electronics	631,888	617,448	2.3%
TOTAL	$5,589,182	$5,217,851	7.1%

Source: Family Dollar Stores, Inc.

EXHIBIT 8 Family Dollar's Stores in Operation

Stores in Operation	For the Three Quarters Ended	
	May 30, 2009	May 31, 2008
Beginning Store Count	6,571	6,430
New Store Openings	148	165
Store Closings	(65)	(50)
Ending Store Count	6,654	6,545
Total Square Footage (000s)	56,527	55,575
Total Selling Square Footage (000s)	47,060	46,194

Source: Family Dollar Stores, Inc.

References

www.familydollar.com
www.hoovers.com
www.marketlineinfo.com
www.datamonitor.com
www.finance.yahoo.com
www.biz.yahoo.com
www.wsjonline.com
www.reuters.com
www.fortune.com
www.forbes.com
www.usatoday.com
www.cnn.com
www.marketwatch.com
www.moneycentral.msn.com
www.mergentonline.com
www.dollargeneral.com
www.dollartree.com

6 Wal-Mart Stores, Inc. — 2009

Amit J. Shah and Michael L. Monahanat
Frostburg State University

WMT

www.walmart.com

In May 2009, Wal-Mart began revamping the electronics departments in its 3,500 U.S. stores to make them much more interactive and roomier. The company wants all the business that Circuit City's failure left and also wants Best Buy and Amazon's business. Wal-Mart now carries more sophisticated electronics products such as Research in Motion Ltd.'s Blackberry smart phones, Palm Inc.'s Pre smart phone, and Blu-ray disc players. In June 2009, Wal-Mart began selling Dell Inc.'s new Studio One 19 touch-screen computers.

In July 2009, Wal-Mart broke ranks with most other large corporations by announcing support for legislation that would require employers to provide health insurance to employees, a centerpiece of President Obama's effort to provide near-universal coverage to Americans. As the largest private employer in the United States, Wal-Mart desires to level the playing field with its rival firms because it already provides health insurance to all its employees. The U.S. Chamber of Commerce has actively fought against such legislation for several years.

During the recession of 2008–2009, Wal-Mart was the Dow's top performer. Headquartered in Bentonville, Arkansas, Wal-Mart's sales rose from $374.3 billion in fiscal year 2008 to $401.2 billion in 2009 while net income rose from $12.7 billion to $13.4 billion. For more than a decade, Wal-Mart has been growing by leaps and bounds and rolling over large competitors such as Kmart as well as thousands of small businesses. Financial statements are shown in Exhibit 1 and Exhibit 2. (Note: Wal-Mart's fiscal year ends January 31.)

In 1995, Wal-Mart ended a five-year battle with local leaders of Bennington, Vermont, and opened its first store in that state, thereby laying claim to having stores in all 50 states (see Exhibit 3). The Bennington store was Wal-Mart's 2,158th store. To get approval for this store, Wal-Mart abandoned its usual 200,000-square-foot store near a major highway exit and instead located in a downtown building containing just 50,000 square feet. Environmentalists in Vermont say the rural character of the state is endangered by "sprawl-mart development." Other chains, such as Kmart, have operated in Vermont for years, so some residents are mystified by the current controversy. As of the end of fiscal 2009, there only four Wal-Mart stores in Vermont.

Wal-Mart does not have a formal mission statement. When asked about Wal-Mart's lack of a mission, Public Relations Coordinator Kim Ellis recently replied, "We believe that our customers are most interested in other aspects of our business, and we are focused on meeting their basic consumer needs. If, in fact, we did have a formal mission statement, it would be something like this: 'To provide quality products at an everyday low price and with extended customer service . . . always.' "

Found on the company's Website is a statement pertaining to the culture of Wal-Mart. "As Wal-Mart continues to grow into new areas and new mediums, our success will always be attributed to our culture. Whether you walk into a Wal-Mart store in your hometown or one across the country while you're on vacation, you can always be assured you're getting low prices and genuine customer service that you've come to expect from us. You'll feel at home in any department of any store . . . that's our culture." The Wal-Mart culture is based on three basic beliefs of Sam Walton: 1) respect for the individual, 2) service to our customers, and 3) strive for excellence.

EXHIBIT 1 Consolidated Statements of Income (amounts in millions except per share data)

	Fiscal Year Ended January 31		
	2009	2008	2007
Revenues:			
Net sales	$401,244	$374,307	$344,759
Membership and other income	4,363	4,169	3,609
	$405,607	$378,476	$348,368
Costs and Expenses:			
Cost of sales	306,158	286,350	263,979
Operating, selling, general and administrative expenses	76,651	70,174	63,892
Operating income	22,798	21,952	20,497
Interest:			
Debt	1,896	1,863	1,549
Capital leases	288	240	260
Interest income	(284.00)	(309.00)	(280.00)
Interest, net	1,900	1,794	1,529
Income from continuing operations before income taxes and minority interest	20,898	20,159	18,968
Provision for Income Taxes:			
Current	6,564	6,897	6,265
Deferred	581	(8)	89
	7,145	6,889	6,354
Income from continuing operations before minority interest	13,753	13,269	12,614
Minority interest	(499)	(406)	(425)
Income from continuing operations	13,254	12,863	12,189
Income (loss) from discontinued operations, net of tax	146	(132)	(905)
Net income	13,400	12,731	11,284
Net Income per Common Share:			
Basic income per common share from continuing operations	$ 3.36	$ 3.16	$ 2.93
Basic income (loss) per common share from discontinued operations	0.04	(0.03)	(0.22)
Basic net income per common share	$ 3.40	$ 3.13	$ 2.71
Diluted income per common share from continuing operations	$ 3.35	$ 3.16	$ 2.92
Diluted income (loss) per common share from discontinued operations	0.04	(0.03)	(0.21)
Diluted net income per common share	$ 3.39	$ 3.13	$ 2.71
Weighted Average Number of Common Shares:			
Basic	3,939	4,066	4,164
Diluted	3,951	4,072	4,168
Dividends declared per common share	$ 0.95	$ 0.88	$ 0.67

Source: Wal-Mart, *Annual Report* (2009).

EXHIBIT 2   Consolidated Balance Sheets (amounts in millions except per share data)

	January 31 2009	2008
ASSETS		
Current Assets:		
Cash and cash equivalents	$ 7,275	$ 5,492
Receivables	3,905	3,642
Inventories	34,511	35,159
Prepaid expenses and other	3,063	2,760
Current assets of discontinued operations	195	967
Total Current Assets	$ 48,949	$ 48,020
Property and Equipment, at Cost:		
Land	19,852	19,879
Buildings and improvements	73,810	72,141
Fixtures and equipment	29,851	28,026
Transportation equipment	2,307	2,210
Property and equipment, at cost	125,820	122,256
Less accumulated depreciation	(32,964)	(28,531)
Property and equipment, net	92,856	93,725
Property under Capital Lease:		
Property under capital lease:	5,341	5,736
Less accumulated depreciation	(2,544)	(2,594)
Property under capital lease	2,797	3,142
Goodwill	15,260	15,879
Other assets and deferred charges	3,567	2,748
Total Assets	$ 163,429	$ 163,514
LIABILITIES AND STOCKHOLDERS' EQUITY		
Current Liabilities:		
Commercial paper	$ 1,506	$ 5,040
Accounts payable	28,849	30,344
Accrued liabilities	18,112	15,725
Accrued income taxes	677	1,000
Long-term debt due within one year	5,848	5,913
Obligations under capital leases due within one year	315	316
Current liabilities of discontinued operations	83	140
Total current liabilities	$ 55,390	$ 58,478
Long-term debt	31,349	29,799
Long-term obligations under capital leases	3,200	3,603
Deferred income taxes and other	6,014	5,087
Minority interest	2,191	1,939
Commitments and contingencies		

continued

EXHIBIT 2 Consolidated Balance Sheets—continued

	January 31	
	2009	2008
Shareholders' Equity:		
Preferred stock($0.10 par value; 100 shares authorized, none issued	—	—
Common stock ($0.10; 11,000 shares authorized, 3,925 and 3973 issued and outstanding at January 31, 2009, and January 31, 2008, respectively)	393	397
Capital in excess of par value	3,920	3,028
Retained earnings	3,660	57,319
Accumulated other comprehensive (loss) income	(2,688)	3,864
Total Shareholders' Equity	65,285	64,608
Total Liabilities and Shareholders' Equity	**$163,429**	**$163,514**

Source: Wal-Mart, Annual Report (2009).

EXHIBIT 3 End-of-Year Store Count Wal-Mart Stores, Inc.

State	Discount Stores	Supercenters	Neighborhood	Sam's Clubs	Grand Total Markets
Alabama	6	90	5	13	114
Alaska	4	4	—	3	11
Arizona	9	62	22	16	109
Arkansas	15	66	8	6	95
California	140	35	—	37	212
Colorado	9	56	—	16	81
Connecticut	29	5	—	3	37
Delaware	4	5	—	1	10
Florida	39	161	25	42	267
Georgia	7	126	—	22	155
Hawaii	8	—	—	2	10
Idaho	3	16	—	2	21
Illinois	57	90	—	29	176
Indiana	15	84	3	16	118
Iowa	11	47	—	8	66
Kansas	9	48	3	7	67
Kentucky	11	73	7	8	99
Louisiana	6	77	5	12	100
Maine	10	12	—	3	25
Maryland	31	13	—	12	56
Massachusetts	39	7	—	3	49
Michigan	19	65	—	26	110
Minnesota	19	42	—	13	74
Mississippi	5	59	1	6	71
Missouri	27	91	—	15	133
Montana	3	10	—	1	14
Nebraska	—	30	—	3	33
Nevada	4	26	11	7	48

continued

EXHIBIT 3   End-of-Year Store Count Wal-Mart Stores, Inc.—continued

State	Discount Stores	Supercenters	Neighborhood	Sam's Clubs	Grand Total Markets
New Hampshire	16	11	—	4	31
New Jersey	46	3	—	10	59
New Mexico	3	31	2	7	43
New York	40	52	—	17	109
North Carolina	23	107	—	22	152
North Dakota	1	10	—	3	14
Ohio	24	119	—	30	173
Oklahoma	14	71	16	8	109
Oregon	14	16	—	—	30
Pennsylvania	42	83	—	23	148
Rhode Island	7	2	—	1	10
South Carolina	8	63	—	9	80
South Dakota	—	12	—	2	14
Tennessee	4	103	6	16	129
Texas	40	297	33	72	442
Utah	2	30	5	8	45
Vermont	4	—	—	—	4
Virginia	18	71	1	16	106
Washington	19	28	—	3	50
West Virginia	2	35	—	5	42
Wisconsin	25	58	—	12	95
Wyoming	—	10	—	2	12
United States Totals	**891**	**2,612**	**153**	**602**	**4,258**

International

International unit counts and operating formats as of January 31, 2009:

Country	Supermarkets	Discount Store	Supercenters	Hypermarkets	Other	Total
Argentina	—	—	22	—	6	28
Brazil (1)	155	—	34	71	85	345
Canada (2)	—	256	56	—	6	318
Chile	46	76	—	75	—	197
China	—	—	132	103	8	243
Costa Rica	25	122	—	6	11	164
El Salvador	30	45	—	2	—	77
Guatemala	29	109	—	6	16	160
Honduras	7	36	—	1	6	50
Japan	264	—	—	106	1	371
Mexico (3)	163	67	154	—	813	1,197
Nicaragua	7	44	—	—	—	51
Puerto Rico	31	7	8	—	10	56
United Kingdom	307	—	30	—	21	358
Grand Total	**1,064**	**762**	**436**	**370**	**983**	**3,615**

1. "Other" format includes 22 Sam's Clubs, 23 cash-n-carry stores, 39 combination discount and grocery stores, and 1 general merchandise store.
2. "Other" format includes 6 Sam's Clubs that were closed in March of fiscal 2010.
3. "Other" format includes 91 Sam's Clubs, 279 combination discount and grocery stores, 83 department stores, and 360 restaurants.

Source: Wal-Mart, *Annual Report* (2009).

History

No word better describes Wal-Mart than *growth*. In 1945, Sam Walton opened his first Ben Franklin franchise in Newport, Arkansas. Living in rural Bentonville, Arkansas, at the time, Walton, his wife Helen, and his brother Bud operated the nation's most successful Ben Franklin franchises. "We were a small chain," said Walton of his 16-store operation. "Things were running so smoothly [that] we even had time for our families." What more could a man want? A great deal, as it turned out.

Sam and Bud Walton could see that the variety store was gradually dying because supermarkets and discounters were developing. Far from being secure, Walton knew that he was under siege and decided to counterattack. He first tried to convince the people in top management of Ben Franklin to enter discounting. After their refusal, Sam Walton made a quick trip around the country in search of ideas. He then began opening his own discount stores in small Arkansas towns like Bentonville and Rogers.

The company opened its first discount department store (Wal-Mart) in November 1962. The early stores had bare tile floors and pipe racks. Wal-Mart did not begin to revamp its image significantly until the mid-1970s, and growth in the early years was slow. However, once the company went public in 1970, sales began to increase rapidly. When it initially went public, 100 shares of Wal-Mart stock would have cost $1,650. Now, those 100 shares are worth over $6 million.

Such retailers as Target, Venture, and Kmart provided the examples that Wal-Mart sought to emulate in its growth. The old Wal-Mart store colors, dark blue and white (too harsh), were dumped in favor of a three-tone combination of light beige, soft blue, and burnt orange. Carpeting, which had long been discarded on apparel sales floors, was put back. New racks were put into use that displayed the entire garment instead of only an outer edge.

Sam Walton died in 1992. Bud Walton died in 1995. Wal-Mart's 1995 *Annual Report* was dedicated to Bud. Sam Walton once said about Bud, "Of course, my number-one retail partner has been my brother, Bud. Bud's wise counsel and guidance kept us from many a mistake. Often, Bud would advise taking a different direction or maybe changing the timing. I soon learned to listen to him because he has exceptional judgment and a great deal of common sense."

In 2000, H. Lee Scott was named president and CEO of Wal-Mart. In February 2009, Mike Duke became the new president and CEO when Scott retired from the position. According to Duke, "Our Company is so well positioned for today's difficult economy and tomorrow's changing world. We have an exceptionally strong management team, able to execute our strategy, perform every single day, and deliver results." Exhibit 4 shows Wal-Mart's organizational chart.

Divisions

Wal-Mart Stores

Most Wal-Mart stores are located in towns of 5,000 to 25,000. On occasion, smaller stores are built in communities of less than 5,000. As indicated in Exhibit 3 for fiscal 2009, Wal-Mart, Inc. currently operates domestically 891 Wal-Mart discount stores, 2,612 Supercenters, 602 Sam's Clubs, and 153 Neighborhood Markets. Most of Wal-Mart's $405.6 billion in fiscal 2009 sales came from Wal-Mart stores and Supercenters. Exhibit 5 provides a breakdown of net sales per division, and Exhibit 6 provides other pertinent financial data per division. International sales accounted for approximately 24.6 percent of total company sales in fiscal 2009. This is up from 9.13 percent in fiscal 2008. For fiscal 2009, Wal-Mart operated internationally in 13 countries and Puerto Rico, with 762 discount stores and 436 Supercenters.

In 2003, Wal-Mart grouped its smaller discount stores, such as the one in Bennington, Vermont, into a new Hometown USA program. This strategy allows the company to give special attention to customers in smaller markets in rural America. Hometown USA consists of the stores are less than 50,000 square feet and are under one regional manager. The idea is to enable these stores to develop locally and with a different mix from the large prototypes. Although these stores represent Wal-Mart's heritage, they had become lost in the shuffle as the company opened 120,000- to 150,000-square-foot stores.

EXHIBIT 4   Wal-Mart's Organizational Chart

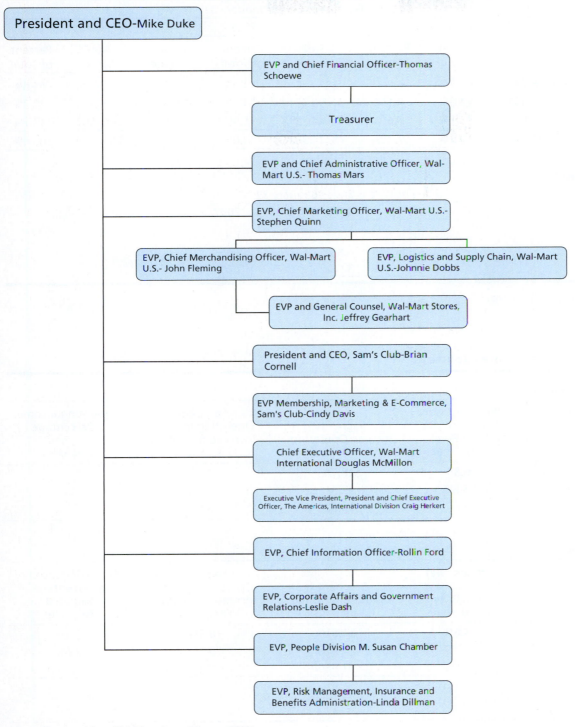

Source: Developed from Wal-Mart, *Annual Report* (2009).

Wal-Mart stores generally have 36 departments and offer a wide variety of merchandise, including apparel for women, girls, men, boys, and infants. Each store also carries curtains, fabrics and notions, shoes, housewares, hardware, electronics, home supplies, sporting goods, toys, cameras and supplies, health and beauty aids, pharmaceuticals, and jewelry. Nationally advertised merchandise accounts for a majority of sales of the stores. Wal-Mart has begun marketing limited lines of merchandise under the brand name Sam's Choice. The merchandise is carefully selected to ensure quality and must be made in the United States. Wal-Mart has also developed new apparel lines, such as the Kathie Lee career sportswear and dress collection, Basic Equipment sportswear, and McKids children's clothing.

EXHIBIT 5   Net Sales by Operating Segment (amounts in millions)

| | Fiscal Year Ended January 31 | | | | | | | |
| | 2009 | | | 2008 | | | 2007 | |
	Net Sales	Percent of Total	Percent Increase	Net Sales	Percent of Total	Percent Increase	Net Sales	Percent of Total
Wal-Mart U.S.	$255,745	63.7%	6.8%	$239,529	64.0%	5.8%	$226,294	65.6%
International	98,645	24.6%	9.1%	90,421	24.1%	17.6%	76,883	22.3%
Sam's Club	46,854	11.7%	5.6%	44,357	11.9%	6.7%	41,582	12.1%
Total net sales	$401,244	100.0%	7.2%	$374,307	100.0%	8.6%	$344,759	100.0%

Comparable Store Sales

| | Fiscal Year Ended January 31 | | |
	2009	2008	2007
Wal-Mart U.S.	3.2%	1.0%	1.9%
Sam's Club	4.8%	4.9%	2.5%
Total U.S.	3.5%	1.6%	2.0%

Source: Wal-Mart, *Annual Report* (2009).

EXHIBIT 6   Wal-Mart Stores Segment

Wal-Mart U.S. Segment

Fiscal Year	Segment Net Sales Increase from Prior Fiscal Year	Segment Income Operating (in millions)	Segment Operating Income Increase from Prior Fiscal Year	Operating Income as a Percentage of Segment Net Sales
2009	**6.8%**	**$18,763**	**7.1%**	**7.3%**
2008	5.8%	17,516	5.4%	7.3%
2007	7.8%	16,620	8.9%	7.3%

Sam's Club Segment

Fiscal Year	Segment Net Sales Increase from Prior Fiscal Year	Segment Operating Income (in millions)	Segment Operating Income Increase from Prior Fiscal Year	Operating Income as a Percentage of Segment Net Sales
2009	**5.6%**	**$1,610**	**−0.5%**	**3.4%**
2008	6.7%	1,618	9.3%	3.6%
2007	4.5%	1,480	5.2%	3.6%

International Segment

Fiscal Year	Segment Net Sales Increase from Prior Fiscal Year	Segment Operating Income (in millions)	Segment Operating Income Increase from Prior Fiscal Year	Operating Income as a Percentage of Segment Net Sales
2009	**9.1%**	**$4,940**	**4.6%**	**5.0%**
2008	17.6%	4,725	10.8%	5.2%
2007	29.8%	4,265	24.8%	5.5%

Sam's Clubs

Sam's Clubs are membership only, cash-and-carry operations. A financial service credit-card program (Discover Card) is available in all clubs. In addition to Discover Card, Sam's have also recently started accepting MasterCards for payments. As of February 2009, business members paid an annual membership fee of $35 for the primary membership card, with a spouse card available at no additional cost. The annual membership fee for an individual member is $40 for the primary membership card, with a spouse card available at no additional cost. The Advantage Plus Program offers additional benefits and services such as automotive extended service contracts, roadside assistance, home improvement, auto brokering, and pharmacy discounts. The annual membership fee for an Advantage Plus Member is $100.

Sam's offers bulk displays of name-brand merchandise, some soft goods, and institutional-size grocery items. Sam's Clubs usually offer over 3,500 items, which are used most often by the consumers they serve. Each Sam's also carries jewelry, sporting goods, toys, tires, stationery, and books. Most clubs have fresh-food departments, such as bakery, meat, and produce sections.

Sam's is a $46.8 billion business that is starting to grow again. The clubs were never designed to sell merchandise categories, but rather items. Furthermore, because the number of items is limited to around 2,000 for the wholesale part of the business and between 1,000 and 1,500 for personal and individual use, it is very important for the items to be appropriate for the location. Also, the items have to come and go seasonally, so continuity by category is not appropriate. Thus, there is a problem for buyers who are item merchants and compete for space in the clubs.

At the end of fiscal 2009, Wal-Mart had a total of 602 domestic Sam's Clubs in operation. Sales for the Wal-Mart's Sam's Clubs segment increased by 5.6 percent in fiscal 2009, compared to fiscal 2008.

Supercenters

Wal-Mart's Supercenters combine groceries with general merchandise, giving customers one-stop shopping. As shown in Exhibit 3, Wal-Mart operated 2,612 domestic and 436 international Supercenters in fiscal 2009.

Supercenters constitute the company's fastest growing division, and management is extremely pleased with them. Currently, the limitation is distribution, and Wal-Mart is working hard to expand its food distribution capabilities. Most of the Supercenters replace Wal-Mart stores, so they have a jump-start on the general merchandise side of the store, whereas food has tended to build slowly. However, the company has gained market share more quickly than planned. Wal-Mart likes to locate Supercenters near the strongest food retailers so their facilities will "either get better or be run out of town."

The Wal-Mart Supercenter is one of the most important retail concepts on the landscape at this time. As with the discount stores, their real competitive impact comes not in the year they open but in the third year because they have a maturation curve that's more like a Wal-Mart store than a food store. Also, the one-stop convenience aspect of the stores has such broad appeal that it is drawing a larger customer audience on a regular basis. Supercenters are continuing to get better in many categories and are attracting a higher-income audience, in addition to their traditional customers. Supercenters provide mart carts and are all one-story buildings, making the stores handicapped accessible. Wal-Mart's Supercenters average 186,000 square feet of retail space. They usually employ between 200 and 550 associates, contingent on store size and consumer needs. The company's broad assortments and everyday low prices are very compelling; extensive advertising is not needed. This represents an enormous saving over the competition. Furthermore, as Supercenters move more into food distribution, they gain a major cost advantage over Super Kmart and Super Target.

The Supercenters are designed with wider aisles, directory signs, departmental directories, and 24-hour service. They are usually equipped with a customer service desk and scanning registers to provide more efficient checkout procedures.

Neighborhood Markets

Wal-Mart's Neighborhood Markets first began operations in 1998 and are generally located in markets with Wal-Mart Supercenters. The Neighborhood Markets offer customers groceries, pharmaceuticals, and general merchandise. These Markets are 42,000 square feet and usually employ 80 to 100 associates. They provide about 28,000 items to customers, including fresh produce, meats, and dairy items; one-hour photo processing; drive-through pharmacies; pet supplies; and household chemicals. For fiscal 2009, Wal-Mart operated 153 Neighborhood Markets.

International

As indicated in Exhibit 3, for fiscal 2009, the company had 318 Wal-Mart brands in Canada, 1,197 in Mexico, and 56 in Puerto Rico. The company operated over 3,600 Wal-Mart brand stores internationally. Mexico is home to Wal-Mart's oldest and most extensive international operations. Wal-Mart de Mexico is strengthened by strong customer support, and the opening of several new stores in the near future is planned.

Wal-Mart maintains a strategic competitive focus on global positioning. Wal-Mart expanded into the international markets so that customers everywhere will associate their name with low cost, best value, greatest selection of quality merchandise and highest standards of customer service. The fact that the International segment has grown to nearly $100 billion in sales shows the potential of this market.

In December 2008, although known for its megastores, Wal-Mart launched a pilot program in China and entered the convenience store market under the name "Smart Choice" or Hui Xuan in Chinese. These are only 300 square meters in size and meant to serve the needs of the local community. In May 2009, company indicated it will observe the performance of these pilot stores and determine whether to expand this idea. Wal-Mart currently employs 70,000 employees in China.

Nationally and internationally, Wal-Mart has been faced with the United Food and Commercial Workers Union, trying to persuade employees to become part of the union. Wal-Mart has strongly opposed unions in its stores. They argue that the company is structured so that employees derive the most benefit and best conditions by working directly with Wal-Mart, as opposed to through a union. Recently, employees in Canada rejected the union. China is now seeing the same pressures from the union as were seen in Canada.

Community involvement, responding to local needs, merchandise preferences, and buying locally are all hallmarks of the International Wal-Marts, just as they are in the United States.

Internal Issues

Distribution Centers

Wal-Mart has distribution centers nationwide. Some of them are grocery distribution centers and also a small number are import distribution centers. Wal-Mart's distribution operations are highly automated. A typical Wal-Mart Discount Store has more than 70,000 standard items in stock. Supercenters carry more than 20,000 additional grocery items, including perishables. As a result, such items have to be ordered frequently. Associates use handheld computers that are linked by radio-frequency network to area stores. To place orders, each store wires merchandise requests to warehouses, which in turn either ship immediately or reorder. Wal-Mart computers are linked directly to over 200 vendors, making deliveries quicker. Wal-Mart has one of the world's largest private satellite communication systems, which enables it to control distribution. In addition, Wal-Mart has installed point-of-sale bar code scanning in all of its stores.

Wal-Mart owns a fleet of truck-tractors that can deliver goods to any store in 38 to 48 hours from the time the order is placed. After trucks drop off merchandise, they frequently pick up merchandise from manufacturers on the way back to the distribution center. This back-haul rate averages over 60 percent and is yet another way Wal-Mart cuts costs.

With an information systems staff of 1,200 and system links with about 5,000 manufacturers, Wal-Mart leads the industry in information technology. This means Wal-Mart is dedicated to providing its associates with the technological tools they need to work smarter everyday. With this technology, Wal-Mart is getting better, quicker, and more accurate information to manage and control every aspect of their business.

Walmart.com

Wal-Mart is in the retail business, which also includes Internet e-tailing. The Internet has interesting aspects and will definitely serve a growing market throughout the 21st century. Profits are not easily made over the Internet, and issues of cost of delivery, merchandise returns, and data security are top concerns prior to building business over the Internet. Wal-Mart moved into the Internet arena in 1996 with the introduction of Wal-Mart On-line, and then it relaunched the site on January 1, 2000, as Walmart.com. Wal-Mart looks at Internet retailing as another store with possibility, but without walls.

Walmart.com, with its headquarters located in the San Francisco Bay Area, is a wholly owned subsidiary of Wal-Mart Stores, Inc. This location choice affords Walmart.com access to the best pool of Internet executive and technical talent. The company was able to attract a top retail management talent in Jeanne Jackson as the CEO of Walmart.com. This venture combines the better of two worlds, technology and retailing, in order to provide customers easy access to more things at Wal-Mart 24 hours a day and 7 days a week. Its distinct purpose is to provide consumers with a convenient and rewarding online shopping experience. Walmart.com will have a separate management team and board of directors. Ultimately, it might choose to go public; however, Wal-Mart Stores will retain a majority ownership of the new venture. Walmart.com provides easy access 24/7/365 to more than a million products. Items ordered online can be shipped to the customer's homes for a modest fee or free shipping to the customer's nearest Wal-Mart store. In addition Wal-Mart is developing new services such as music downloads and 1-hour photos.

Operations

Wal-Mart's expense structure, measured as a percentage of sales, continues to be among the lowest in the industry. Although Walton watched expenses, he rewarded sales managers handsomely. Sales figures are available to every employee at Wal-Mart. Monthly figures for each department are ranked and made available throughout the organization. Employees who do better than average get rewarded with raises, bonuses, and personal recognition. Poor performers are only rarely fired, although demotions are possible.

All employees (referred to as "associates") have a stake in the financial performance of the company. Store managers earn as much as $100,000 to $150,000 per year. Even part-time clerks qualify for profit sharing and stock-purchase plans. Millionaires among Wal-Mart's middle managers are not uncommon. Executives frequently solicit ideas for improving the organization from employees and often put them to use. The Walton family and management (as insiders) own nearly 44 percent of Wal-Mart stock. These holdings are worth nearly $28 billion today. Continuing a Walton tradition, Wal-Mart invites over 100 analysts and institutional investors to the field house at the University of Arkansas for its annual meeting in mid-June. During the day-and-a-half session, investors meet top executives as well as Wal-Mart district managers, buyers, and 200,000 hourly salespeople. Investors see a give-and-take meeting between buyers and district managers.

Employee Benefits

Wal-Mart management takes pride in the ongoing development of its people. Training is seen as critical to outstanding performance, and new programs are often implemented in all areas of the company. The combination of grassroots meetings, the open-door policy, videos, printed material, classroom and home study, year-end management meetings, and on-the-job training has enabled employees to prepare themselves for advancement and added responsibilities.

Wal-Mart managers stay current with new developments and needed changes. Executives spend one week each year in hourly jobs in various stores. Walton himself used to travel at least three days per week, visiting competitors' stores and attending the opening of new stores, leading the Wal-Mart cheer, "Give me a W, give me an A . . ."

Wal-Mart encourages employee stock purchases. During fiscal 2008, participants could contribute up to 50 percent of their pretax earnings, but not more than statutory limits. Associates may choose from among 13 different investment options for the 401(k) component of the plan and 14 investment options for the profit-sharing component of the plan. For associates who did not make an election, their 401(k) balance in the plan was placed in a balanced fund. Associates' 401(k) funds immediately vest, and associates may change their investment options at any time. Associates with three years of service have full diversification rights with the 14 investment options for the profit-sharing component of the plan. Prior to January 31, 2008, associates were fully vested in the profit-sharing component of the plan after seven years of service, with vesting starting at 20 percent at three years of service and increasing 20 percent each year until year 7. Effective January 31, 2008, associates are fully vested in the profit-sharing component of the plan after six years of service, with vesting starting at 20 percent at two years of service and increasing 20 percent each year until year six. Annual contributions made by the company to the United States and Puerto Rico Profit Sharing and 401(k) Plans are made at the sole discretion of the company. Expense associated with these plans was $945 million, $890 million, and $827 million in fiscal 2008, 2007, and 2006, respectively.

Company contributions can be withdrawn only on termination. If employment with the company is terminated because of retirement, death, or permanent disability, the company contribution is fully vested (meaning the entire amount is nonforfeitable). If termination of employment occurs for any other reason, the amount that is nonforfeitable depends on the number of years of service with the company. After completion of the third year of service with the company, 20 percent of each participant's account is nonforfeitable for each subsequent year of service. After seven years of service, a participant's account is 100 percent vested.

Predatory Pricing

Does Wal-Mart engage in predatory pricing? Three independent pharmacies in Conway, Arkansas, filed a suit, claiming Wal-Mart was deliberately pricing products below cost to kill competition. Wal-Mart argued that it priced products below cost not to harm competitors but to meet or beat rivals' prices. Chancery Court Judge David L. Reynolds on October 11, 1996, found Wal-Mart guilty of predatory pricing and ordered the company to pay the pharmacies $286,407 in damages. The judge also forbade Wal-Mart from selling products below cost in Conway in the future.

Wal-Mart appealed the ruling to the Arkansas Supreme Court, which reversed and dismissed the case. It is Wal-Mart's policy that its store managers monitor the retail prices charged by competitors in their respective market areas and lower prices for highly competitive merchandise without regard to the cost of individual items. This price is frequently below Wal-Mart's cost of acquiring some of these products in highly competitive markets. The stated purpose of Wal-Mart's pricing policy is to "meet or beat" the retail prices contemporaneously charged by competitors for highly competitive, price-sensitive merchandise; to maintain "low-price leadership" in the local marketplace; and to "attract a disproportionate number of customers into a store to increase traffic."

The store's pricing practices with regard to specific articles did not violate the Arkansas Unfair Practices Act section prohibiting vendors from selling at or below their cost. The mere proof of below-cost sales was not sufficient to prove a violation of the act absent intent to destroy competition. There was no evidence showing exactly which individual items were sold below cost, the frequency of those sales, the duration of the sales, and to what extent the sales existed.

Diversity Among Employees

Sam Walton was admittedly old-fashioned in many respects and Wal-Mart store policies reflected many of his values. For example, store policies forbid employees from dating other employees without the prior approval of the executive committee. Also, women are rarely found in management positions. However, promotions have recently been made so there are now women in senior officer positions. Walton also resisted placing women on the board of directors; however, there are three women on the board at this time. Wal-Mart is an Equal Employment Opportunity/Affirmative

Action (EEO/AA) employer, but it has managed to get away with certain past discriminatory policies.

Wal-Mart has instituted several initiatives to increase the recruitment and promotion of women and minorities, including the following:

- A mentoring program encompassing more than 750 women and minority managers
- A women's leadership group, in partnership with Herman Miller and ServiceMaster, to develop opportunities for high-potential female managers
- Store internships during the summer for college students between their junior and senior years, with 70 percent of them for women or minorities.
- Expansion of its business with minority- and women-owned companies by more than 25 percent in 2008
- Creation of a Hispanic scholarship fund for Hispanic high school students
- Recognition in 2008, as one of the "Best Companies for Asian Pacific Americans"

Sustainability

According to CEO Mike Duke, "Sustainability is an important part of our culture. It helps us to remove waste, lower costs and provide savings to our customers." Its initiative, "Sustainability 360°," is a companywide effort to take sustainability beyond Wal-Mart's direct footprint to encompass Wal-Mart's associates, suppliers, communities and customers.

"Wal-Mart's environmental goals are to be supplied 100 percent by renewable energy; to create zero waste; and to sell products that sustain our resources and the environment." In 2009, Wal-Mart pledged to double its use of solar energy in California. In addition, in February 2009, Wal-Mart Foundation annouced it will donate $5.7 million for the creation of green jobs in the United States. Also, in its stores, home efficiency products to conserve and reduce electricity and water are prominently featured.

Philanthropy and Community Involvement

Wal-Mart's community involvement year after year is phenomenal. According to the *Chronicle of Philanthropy*, the Wal-Mart Foundation is the largest corporate cash contributor in America. In 2009, Wal-Mart and its foundations gave $423 million in the communities it serves, an increase of 25.5 percent over 2008. In 2006, through its foundation, charitable partners, and donations from customers and associates, Wal-Mart provided more than $415 million in cash and in-kind merchandise to more than 100,000 organizations around the world. More importantly 90 percent of donations were at the local level where they can have the greatest impact. Education is a primary beneficiary of Wal-Mart charitable giving. Some examples follow:

- 2009, $1 million grant from the Wal-Mart Foundation for education, job-training, and entrepreneurial support programs for women and girls
- 2009, $5 million to help 128 Red Cross chapters prepare for disasters
- 2008, a $12.5 million letter of credit from Wal-Mart Foundation to expedite construction of Martin Luther King, Jr. National Memorial
- 2008, Wal-Mart stores provided 70 million meals to families in need
- 2008, Wal-Mart Foundation donates $5 million to YouthBuild USA to re-engage out-of-school youth nationwide
- 2007, Wal-Mart Stores, Sam's Clubs and the Wal-Mart Foundation gave more than $296 million to 4,000-plus communities in the United States
- 2007, donated $4 million in cash and products to those affected by natural disasters
- 2007, Wal-Mart gave $5 million in cash and $35 million in products to America's Second Harvest food banks to help feed the nation's hungry.

Wal-Mart's previous efforts were recognized in May 2002 when President George W. Bush honored Wal-Mart with the prestigious Ron Brown Corporate Leadership Award. This award is presented to the best corporate citizens in America. It recognizes companies that have demonstrated a deep level of commitment to empower employees and communites while also advancing in business interests. Wal-Mart's corporate citizenship extends well beyond U.S. borders and into every country in which the company operates.

Marketing

The discount retailing business is seasonal to a certain extent. Generally, the highest volume of sales and net income occurs in the fourth fiscal quarter, and the lowest volume occurs during the first fiscal quarter. Wal-Mart draws customers into the store by radio and television advertising, monthly circulars, and weekly newspaper ads. Television advertising is used to convey an image of everyday low prices and quality merchandise. Radio is used to a lesser degree to promote specific products that are usually in high demand. Newspaper advertisements and monthly circulars are major contributors to the program, emphasizing deeply discounted items, and they are effective at luring customers into the stores.

Efforts are also made to discount corporate overhead. Visitors often mistake corporate headquarters for a warehouse because of its limited decor and "show." Wal-Mart executives share hotel rooms when traveling to reduce expenses. The company avoids spending money on consultants and marketing experts. Instead, decisions are made based on the intuitive judgments of managers and employees and on the assessment of strategies of other retail chains.

Wal-Mart censors some products. The company has banned recordings and removed magazines based on lyrics and graphics; it has also stopped marketing teen rock magazines. Wal-Mart advertises a "Buy American" policy in an effort to keep production at home. Consequently, Wal-Mart buyers are constantly seeking vendors in grass roots America. In Tulsa, Oklahoma, Zebco, the fishing equipment company, responded to Wal-Mart's challenge by bucking the trend toward overseas fishing tackle manufacturing. Zebco created more than 200 U.S. jobs to assemble rods and to manufacture bait-and-cast reels. The company's bait-and-cast reels are the first to be manufactured in the United States in thirty years.

Competitors

Target has now become a fierce competitor of Wal-Mart and is ranked second among discount retailers with sales of nearly $65 billion with 366,000 employees. As of February 2, 2009, Target had 1,681 domestic Target stores including 239 Super Targets and ranks 28th on the Fortune 500 list. Target has created a niche for itself by offering more upscale, fashionable merchandise than that of Wal-Mart and has earned a reputation for inexpensive, chic merchandise.

Kmart used to be the main competitor for Wal-Mart, but in 2001 it declared bankruptcy. During 2002 Kmart shut down 600 stores in the United States, Guam, Puerto Rico, and the U.S. Virgin Islands. However, under new management, Kmart's stock increased dramatically in 2004, which allowed it to buy Sears for $11 billion. Now Kmart operates as a subsidiary of Sears Holding and follows Target in third place among discount retailers with sales of $17 billion.

Costco Wholesale Corporation is also a competitor of Wal-Mart. Costco competes with the Sam's Club segment. They are the largest wholesale club operator in the United States, just ahead of Sam's. Costco currently has 550 warehouses, 403 in the United States and the rest dispersed from Canada to Japan. Most recent comparisons show that while the Sam's Club division of Wal-Mart brought in over $44 billion in net sales. Costco finished the year at just over $72 billion.

Future

What strategies would you recommend to current CEO Mike Duke? How can Wal-Mart benefit from Internet retailing? How aggressively should Wal-Mart expand internationally and where? Should Wal-Mart expand the convenient store concept in China and other markets? Should Wal-Mart get a foothold in Europe before competitors seize the initiative? Should Wal-Mart expand further in Mexico, the United States, or Canada? Should Wal-Mart make further acquisitions, like its Woolco acquisition in Canada? Is Wal-Mart's rate of growth of Supercenters too fast? What private-label products should Wal-Mart consider developing? What can Wal-Mart do to improve its Sam's Clubs operations? Develop a three-year strategic plan for CEO Mike Duke.

Whole Foods Market, Inc. — 2009

James L. Harbin and Patricia Humphrey
Texas A&M University-Texarkana

WFMI

www.wholefoods.com

On August 27, 2009, two more labor unions joined thousands of voices already calling for a boycott of Whole Foods stores nationwide. Why? In retaliation for CEO John Mackey voicing strong opposition to President Obama's health care policy in an article in the *Wall Street Journal*. Whole Foods' customer base is very liberal and is attracted to the company's liberal actions as much as to their high-quality food. For example, Whole Foods employees are paid well above market averages, enjoy free gym memberships, same-sex partner benefits, and a strict nondiscrimination policy. However, Mackey is a self-proclaimed libertarian who strongly advocates a small role for government programs. Mackey is firmly anti-union, although his corporation is unionized. This public drama is hurting Whole Foods' image and business.

Whole Foods Market is the world's leading natural and organic foods supermarket. As of September 2008, Whole Foods had 264 stores in the United States, 6 in Canada, and 5 in the United Kingdom. Few companies attract the kind of following Whole Foods and its CEO/founder have both among customers and the national media. Type *Whole Foods* on Google and you would get over 3 million hits. Type *John Mackey* and you would get some 100,000+. Their corporate Web site averages more than 50,000 visitors a day.

The Whole Foods impressive new headquarters building is located above its 80,000-square-foot flagship store in Austin, Texas. Through a long series of acquisitions, CEO John Mackey has created a niche retailer that enjoys lofty profits in a very price-competitive industry that is typically characterized by low profit margins. With projected 2009 sales of more than $8 billion, and a goal of $12 billion by 2010, Whole Foods currently has 50,000 plus team members (employees) working.

For the first six months of their fiscal year 2009, Whole Foods sales were $4.3 billion. If second half of the year sales are consistent with its year to date results, total sales should be just under $8.0 billion. This would be identical to 2008 sales. Mackey was quoted as saying, "despite flat sales year over year, we exhibited strong expense control leading to a 10% increase in income." While first-half 2009 sales were flat and income up slightly, comparable store sales decreased 4.4% versus an 8.2% increase in the prior year.

Despite stricter federal requirements, Whole Foods Market remained committed to organic certification. In November of 2008, the USDA's National Organic Program declared there could no longer be "group" certified stores and that each store had to be certified individually. This was a change from a sampling model that had been used previously. Joe Dickson, quality standards coordinator for Whole Foods, remarked, "While some certified retailers may have just a few departments certified, and focus on shrink-wrapped organic produce, we've opted to go all out, in our stores, every department that handles organic food is certified—produce, meat, bulk, cheese, even stores with organic salad bars are certified."

At the end of the second quarter 2009, the company had 280 stores totaling 10.3 million square feet. Only seven new stores were opened in the first half of the year, three of which were relocations. Over the years, Whole Foods business model has been centered on rapid expansion driving revenue growth. In their effort to contain costs rather than raise prices, this rapid expansion plan has been cut in half, maybe more. As of the summer of 2009, the company only had plans to open a total of 60 stores in the next four and a half years. Furthermore, they had intentions of only entering eight new markets with these 60 new stores.

It may be hard to justify the building of even bigger stores (the average size for their newer stores is 56,000 square feet) given that traffic is down and their customers are buying less each trip. Some of their newer stores were also built in lower income areas, bringing them into direct competition with more established and lower cost competitors.

As the recession drags on and unemployment continues to grow, many economists fear an even deeper retrenchment shopping pattern for the consumer. All of this increases the company's struggle to maintain their higher margins and pricey image.

While the company continues to earn accolades (they were only 1 of 3 companies to receive the 2009 Socially Responsible Retailer Award for the Whole Planet Foundation), their future outlook remains murky. If yearly earnings continue to fall in 2009, it would be the third year in a row for lower net income. Like many other businesses, analysts' sentiments are mixed. One says that Whole Foods Market stringent cost controls and reduced capital expenditures will serve them well; another believes that shoppers will likely continue to scale back their trips to Whole Foods because of its "high-end" reputation.

History

Two years after opening his SaferWay store in 1978, John Mackey merged with Clarksville Natural Grocery in Austin, Texas. This resulted in the opening of the original Whole Foods Market in 1980. In 1984, Whole Foods expanded out of Austin into Houston, Dallas, New Orleans, and one store in California. This expansion was accomplished in significant part through acquisitions of other natural food chains throughout its three-decade history.

In 2004, Whole Foods entered the United Kingdom by acquiring an existing chain of seven natural food stores. In 2007, they opened an 80,000-square-foot, three-level store in West London. Initially the firm planned for up to 40 more stores in that country. During 2007 and 2008, the firm opened five more stores but later closed one of them. Fiscal year 2008 sales in the United Kingdom accounted for approximately 3 percent of total sales. The company's goal is to approach break even in fiscal year 2011 for the UK market.

In early 2007, Whole Foods announced its proposal for acquiring Wild Oats Market, Inc., for approximately $565 million and assumption of almost $106 million debt. This represented Whole Foods' biggest acquisition to date. Wild Oats Market was their largest, closest competitor with a little over a billion a year in sales, slightly over 100 stores, and 8,500-plus employees.

Whole Foods Market is one of only 13 companies to be included in *Fortune* magazine's annual list of the "100 Best Companies to Work For" every year since the list's inception in 1996. In 2009, it was rated at number 16 out of 100. John Mackey has a long list of awards, ranging from making the top-30 corporate leaders named by *Barron's* to being named the 2003 Overall National Ernst & Young Entrepreneur of the Year. Whole Foods' employee-friendly touches include capping executives' pay at 19 times the average workers' annual wages, up from 14 times a few years earlier.

The company is heavily involved in environmental issues and community involvement. They donate at least 5 percent of their net profits yearly to charitable causes. Whole Foods made the U.S. Environmental Protection Agency's list of the "Top 25 Green Power Partners" with such efforts as eliminating plastic, working to ensure the humane treatment of animals, protection of the fishing industry, and offsetting its energy costs through wind power credits.

Mission, Culture, and Strategy

Whole Foods Market's mission is "to promote the vitality and well-being of all individuals by supplying the highest quality, most wholesome foods available." Their aspiration is to become an international brand synonymous with not just natural and organic goods, but also to be the best food retailer in every community in which they locate. Perishable product sales accounted for approximately 67 percent of their total retail sales in fiscal year 2008. Prepared meals (which allow for rich premium prices) represent almost 20 percent of total sales.

Whole Foods is more than a "fancy grocery store." With its culture and cult following, one might more aptly describe it as a lifestyle store. Some customers say they are making a statement by shopping there. Their motto "Whole Foods, Whole People, Whole Planet" emphasizes the company's vision as more than just a food retailer. In the Harris Interactive/The *Wall Street Journal* ranking of the world's best and worst corporate reputations, Whole Foods Recently placed 12th overall and received the best score of any company for social responsibility. The firm was recently rated as the number-one "green brand" with Generation Y.

Customers come from a 20-mile radius to shop at Whole Foods as compared to just 2 miles for the typical supermarket shopper. Yet only 25 percent of Whole Foods shoppers provide 75 percent of total sales. Whole Foods caters to local tastes by giving their managers discretion to stock 10 percent of each store with whatever might sell best in that area. Managers are allowed to set prices on locally competitive products.

"We're selling the highest quality foods in the world," says John Mackey. He goes on to reject any comparison with Wal-Mart: "It's like comparing a Hyundai to a Lexus: their focus is on getting the cheapest stuff in; we're focused on getting the best stuff."

Whole Foods has several competitive advantages due to their differentiation strategies. Generally speaking, their associates are much more knowledgeable and willing to help than in the average grocery store. Another competitive edge lies in the depth and breath of their item selection. Fifty different brands of olive oil is but one example. Such excess, combined with, in some cases, obscenely high prices, might be a turnoff for some customers.

What might be considered both a plus and a minus is the fact that the store shuns most major brands in favor of specialty ones. Because their niche is so narrow, and there are so few of their stores in each area, they can skim the market. This is a major factor contributing to their higher profits.

Whole Foods is also somewhat different from competitors in the area of prepared foods. There's a wealth of selection for lunch, dinner, and dessert. You can eat in or take out. About 28 percent of shoppers do not know what they are having just two hours before the meal, according to the Food Marketing Institute, so preparing a meal is a great opportunity for grocers. Although premade food carries a higher price tag than buying ingredients for meals, it is still less expensive than dining out, and has become more popular as high-end consumers look for ways to curb spending in a weak U.S. economy.

The company relies primarily on word-of-mouth advertising. They only spend about 0.5 percent of their total sales on advertising and marketing, much less than the industry. They also contribute at least 5 percent of after-tax profits to not-for-profit organizations. Ninety-two percent of their 53,000-plus employees are full-time team members. Those who work 30 or more hours per week and have worked a minimum of 800 service hours qualify as full time. Whole Foods Market provides healthcare insurance at no cost to its approximately 47,000 full-time members.

Wild Oats Markets, Inc.

Whole Foods has a long history of acquisitions. Approximately a third of its existing square footage was derived from acquisitions. The Wild Oats acquisition represented the company's largest, both by square footage and dollars ($565 million). Wild Oats Markets, Inc. was started in Boulder, Colorado in 1987. By 2006, it had grown into the nation's second largest natural and organic foods supermarket chain, with more than 110 stores in 24 states and British Columbia, and annual sales of more than $1 billion.

One of the arguments for the merger-acquisition was so Whole Foods could compete against much larger rivals like Kroger, Safeway, and Wal-Mart, all of which are starting to offer organic and natural products. It further gained Whole Foods entry into 15 new markets and 5 new states. As with most mergers, the company anticipated significant synergies; however, some industry experts remain skeptical. One grocery consultant commented, "They get some additional store locations at probably a reasonable price versus building them, but I'm not convinced that this is a marriage made in heaven." Their postacquisition plans included selling some 35 non–Wild Oats stores (Henry's & Sun Harvest), closing 10 to 30 Wild Oats stores, relocating 7, and remodeling/enlarging many more.

The Federal Trade Commission initially raised antitrust concerns over the acquisition as early as May-June 2007. They contended that the two chains would compete directly against one another in 21 geographic areas and that this combination would limit competition, and therefore increase prices in the marketplace for natural and organic foods. Whole Foods countered that it already faced plenty of competition from Kroger, Safeway, and other big supermarket chains as well as local producers selling directly to customers in that segment.

In August 2007, a U.S. District Court ruled that the two companies could proceed after finding that the "marginal" customers (those more likely to seek out better prices), rather than core customers (those more loyal), could easily find the products in other stores. The judge based his decision in part on the fact that about 60 percent of natural and organic foods are sold by conventional grocery stores. The FTC still was not convinced, and the U.S. Court of Appeals in mid-2008, by a 2–1 vote, sent the case back to the lower court to consider the evidence more fully, suggesting that the judge there had rushed the decision. Following the ruling, one antitrust lawyer commented, "What are you going to do—the eggs have already been scrambled." Another critic of the FTC's action commented, "We've got bigger problems than organic grocery monopolies." While all this was being sorted out, Whole Foods was proceeding with their plans for the Wild Oats acquisition.

In early March 2009, a final settlement was announced. Whole Foods agreed to divest itself of 31 Wild Oats stores in 12 states, including 19 that had already been closed, and 1 Whole Foods store. They also agreed to relinquish the rights to the Wild Oats brand, which could be sold to a potential competitor. In exchange, the FTC agreed to drop its legal bid to undo the merger. Neither side could claim a victory. In that Whole Foods paid roughly $565 million for 110 stores under the Wild Oats name, and suffered another $19 million in settlement issues, one analyst likened it to an exercise in killing the competition rather than gaining a major brand.

The Organic Food Industry

The global market for organic food and beverages was worth $22.75 billion in 2007, after more than doubling in five years, according to market research firm Euromonitor International. The United States accounted for about 45 percent of that total. Typical growth rates of 20 to 30 percent for organic food sales in the United States eased in the second half of 2008 as middle- and upper-income families felt the effects of layoffs and declining portfolios. Although it may be safe to assume that organic food is past the stage of being a fad and there is a hard core of customers, the future for this industry is cloudy at best.

It is still debatable exactly what organic food is or how to define it. The issue of whether it is healthier or more "green" is still open to question by some. There is, however, according to some estimates, a core group of organic consumers that consists of approximately 15 percent of the overall American population. This core is willing to spend the price premium that organic foods carry (which typically ranges from 20 to 200 percent over regular foods).

One health and wellness marketing research group postulates that the past years' double-digit growth of organic foods has started to level off. Supervalu (the number four or five grocer) closed down their five-store Sunflower market, which focused on organic items in 2008, after opening it in 2006, because it failed to meet the company's expectations.

In contrast, since food companies have been increasing prices to offset the rising commodity prices and currency-related effects, the pricing gap between regular food products and organic products has narrowed. This narrowing of prices could make organic products more appealing to a greater number of customers.

Industry Trends

Grocery stores are ranked among the largest industries in the United States. Cashiers, stock, and order fillers make up 50 percent of all grocery store workers. At one time the retail grocery store sector of retail was, in relative terms, a higher paid industry; however, over the past 25 years the grocery industry has become one of low wages and part-time employees.

At retail, the industry makes less than a penny of profit on every dollar spent. Safeway and Kroger have spent millions, if not billions, sprucing up their stores in an effort to confront Wal-Mart.

Recent trends in the industry of grocery stores consist of expanding their offerings, trying to draw in customers with Web sites, recipes, loyalty cards, cooking classes, ready-to-eat meals, sit-down spaces to eat, salad bars, and coffee (Starbucks in some cases) areas. Higher gas prices, mortgage failures, job losses, stock market fears, and food inflation have taken their toll. Many grocery shoppers have begun looking for bargains. In this recent downturn, even the affluent are showing signs of pulling back. A 2008 survey found that many adults are preparing more meals at home (43 percent), using more coupons (40 percent), or going out of their way to look for lower-cost items (37 percent) as a result of higher food costs.

The Food Marketing Institute found that in 2008 some 64 percent of shoppers said they often or always buy a store brand rather than a national one. That was up from 59 percent the prior year. These cost-conscious shoppers are turning away from premium priced goods produced by name-brand labels such as General Mills and Kraft to individual store brands. Kroger has led the movement by capitalizing on their Private Label brand, which is the most extensive line in the industry. Their brand is expected to generate over a billion dollars in 2008 sales and represented some 27 percent of their total sales.

Competitors

With over 100,000 grocery stores in the United States, the landscape is filled with a vast variety. Stores range from the mom-and-pop operations to the super-huge (a Woodman's in Wisconsin with over 240,000 square feet, and a Wegman's 130,000-square-footer in Virginia with projected sales of over $125 million, which will make it America's highest volume grocery store).

Currently, Trader Joe's may represent the supermarket closest in appeal to Whole Foods. In 2008, they had 300 stores in 25 states and were growing. Their stores are concentrated in California and along the mid-to-upper East Coast, with some single stores spread throughout the United States. Trader Joe's products are usually priced lower in comparison to Whole Foods. Sunflower Farmers Market represents the discounter of organic and natural foods. In 2008, they had some 14 to 15 stores concentrated in the southwestern United States.

Wegman's is a growing force to be dealt with in the industry with their European open-air market concept. With $4.8 billion in 2008 sales, they placed 30th on the list of top-25 supermarkets based on sales. They have 70+ stores with most in New York and the rest in neighboring states. Many consider them to be the best of breed in the industry. They are consistently rated in the very top tier of *Fortune*'s annual list of the 100 best companies to work for.

There is a lengthy list of other firms both large and small that aggressively compete for the consumer's food dollar. Some examples would include the Fresh Market chain of 86 stores in 17 states, and the Central Markets of 7 or 8 stores in Texas. Then there are the individual stores like Stu Leonard's two New England stores, which have been called the "Disneyland of dairy stores," and Jungle Jim's 6 acres of food in Fairfield, Ohio, which attracts over 50,000 people a week with food from more than 70 countries.

In addition to the more unique grocery companies, there are the more traditional. Companies like Wal-Mart (the number-one seller of groceries—over $100 billion in 2008), Kroger (over $76 billion in 2,500 stores), Safeway (over $44 billion in 1,750 stores), Albertson's, and Winn-Dixie all compete for some of the same dollars that Whole Foods seeks. In early 2009, Wal-Mart announced plans to completely overhaul its oldest and biggest store brand. Their Great Value store brand is not only the biggest brand Wal-Mart carries, it is the biggest store grocery brand in the entire country.

Whole Foods, in late summer of 2008, began emphasizing value, offering greater discounts, and lower-priced goods in an attempt to recast at least somewhat their premium price image due to the economic downturn.

Kroger is the number-one pure grocer in sales and has, with some degree of success, taken on Wal-Mart the discounter and Whole Foods the natural/organic retailer. Kroger is still in the experimental stages of expanding its Marketplace store concept, where it sells not only groceries, but also furniture, appliances, and home furnishings, with some locations featuring some of its own Fred Meyer's jewelry stores, Starbucks, and even pizzerias.

The Future

"In all my profound wisdom, I decreed a maximum of 100 stores, and thought that would saturate the United States," recalls John Mackey of the time when his company went public in 1992. Although the company has a store in 40 different states, almost 50 percent of Whole Foods Market stores are in just 6 states. Currently, CEO Mackey is thinking in the neighborhood of 500 stores for the future.

Although Whole Foods Market's past success can hardly be contested, its future is somewhat cloudy. One of Mackey's immediate goals is to convince more of his customers to do all their shopping at his chain, rather than cherry-picking the items they can't find at the big-name chains. Companies like Wal-Mart, Safeway, and Kroger are all increasing their offerings of organic goods. Many smaller competitors, like Trader Joe's, offer a similar product mix on the cheap (e.g., its "Two-Buck Chuck" wines).

Digesting the Wild Oats Market has taken its toll on the company, both legally and financially. Entering fiscal year 2008 Whole Foods had $736 million in long-term debt, and over $14 million in legal fees alone. Combined with a third-quarter 2008 slowdown in store growth, revenue growth, and profit growth, this has Mackey and his investors nervous. In a late 2008 earnings conference call, Mackey said of the Wild Oats purchase, "If I could get my money back, I'd take it back." At that time only 55 of the 109 Wild Oats stores that Whole foods originally purchased remained open.

All of these negative happenings have put a damper on Whole Foods Market stock. In late 2006, one financial analyst rated its stock as a buy stating, "History shows little to no relationship between the company's sales and data for economic growth, employment, or even consumer spending." However, after peaking at almost $80 in January 2006, its stock has continued a downward slide from then. In the spring of 2009, it fluctuated between lows of around $9 and highs around $19.

In January 2009, Mackey was quoted as saying, "We have to manage the business differently; economic growth used to be the tailwind that the company built into its business plan. The new era requires a different mindset—we have to be more frugal, to think about every expense, every capital investment—because we won't be bailed out by growth." During the fiscal years of 2008 and 2009, Whole Foods implemented several strategies to deal with the tough economic times. These included the following:

- cutting in half the planned new store openings (30 to 15)
- cutting discretionary spending by 50 percent
- suspending its cash dividend
- increasing the range of lower-priced items
- strengthening its value image
- launched its Whole Trade product line

The company faces multiple strategic issues in its efforts to continue its growth and success. For one, its distribution effectiveness isn't nearly the equivalent of its national competitors. A second issue would be how they maintain its differentiation competitive advantage. This is always a problem for a niche or focused player. Their differentiation advantage has narrowed due to the competition's encroachment on that niche. A third issue would be these questions: How does the economy's downturn affect even those "core" customers who have been willing to pay a premium for natural and organic? Will Whole Foods overexpand and go the Starbucks/Gap route? Just how big is the market for Whole Foods? How many more stores are viable in the United States? Additionally, will the Wild Oats acquisition pay off in the long run or has the company ended up with egg on its face as well as a huge debt? And last, but not least, who might succeed John Mackey in the event of his leaving, dying, or being relieved by the board? Whole Foods Market clearly needs a clear strategic plan going forward.

EXHIBIT 1 Whole Foods Market, Inc., Summary Financial Information

	(in thousands)		
	2008	2007	2006
Consolidated Statements of Operations Data			
Sales	$ 7,953,912	$ 6,591,773	$ 5,607,376
Cost of goods sold and occupancy costs	5,247,207	4,295,170	3,547,734
Gross profit	2,706,705	2,296,642	1,959,642
Direct store expenses	2,107,940	1,711,229	1,421,968
General and administrative expenses	270,428	217,743	181,244
Pre-opening expenses	55,554	59,319	32,058
Relocation, store closure and lease termination costs	36,545	10,861	5,363
Operating income	236,238	297,451	319,009
Interest expense	(36,416)	(4,208)	(32)
Investment and other income	6,697	11,324	20,736
Income before income taxes	206,519	304,567	339,713
Provision for income taxes	91,995	121,827	135,885
Net income	$ 114,524	$ 182,740	$ 203,828
Basic earnings per share	$ 0.82	$ 1.30	$ 1.46
Weighted average shares outstanding	140,011	141,836	145,082
Diluted earnings per share	$ 0.82	$ 1.29	$ 1.41
Weighted average shares outstanding, diluted basis	140,011	141,836	145,082
Dividends declared per share	$ 0.60	$ 0.87	$ 2.45
Consolidated Balance Sheets Data			
Net working capital	$ (43,571)	$ (104,364)	$ 114,211
Total assets	3,380,736	3,213,128	2,042,996
Long-term debt (including current maturities)	929,170	760,868	8,655
Shareholders' equity	1,506,024	1,458,804	1,404,143
Operating Data			
Number of stores at end of fiscal year	275	276	186
Average store size (gross square footage)	36,000	34,000	34,000

Source: WFMI, *Annual Report* (2008).

EXHIBIT 2 Whole Foods Market, Inc., Consolidated Balance Sheets

	(in thousands)	
Assets	2008	2007
Current assets:		
Cash and cash equivalents	$ 30,534	$ —
Restricted cash	617	2,310
Accounts receivable	115,424	105,209
Proceeds receivable for divestiture	—	165,054
Merchandise inventories	327,452	288,112
Prepaid expenses and other current assets	68,150	40,402
Deferred income taxes	80,429	66,899
Total current assets	622,606	667,986

continued

EXHIBIT 2 Whole Foods Market, Inc., Consolidated Balance Sheets—continued

	(in thousands)	
Assets	2008	2007
Property and equipment, net of accumulated depreciation and amortization	1,900,117	1,666,559
Goodwill	659,559	668,850
Intangible assets, net of accumulated depreciation	78,499	97,683
Deferred income taxes	109,002	104,877
Other assets	10,953	7,173
Total assets	**$ 3,380,736**	**$ 3,213,128**

Liabilities and Shareholders' Equity	2008	2007
Current liabilities:		
Current installments of long-term debt and capital lease obligations	$ 308	$ 24,781
Accounts payable	181,134	225,728
Accrued payroll, bonus and other benefits due team members	196,233	181,290
Dividends payable	−25,060	
Other current liabilities	286,430	315,491
Total current liabilities	666,177	772,350
Long-term debt and capital lease obligations, less current installments	928,790	736,087
Deferred lease liabilities	199,635	152,552
Other long-term liabilities	80,110	93,335
Total liabilities	1,874,712	1,754,324
Shareholders' equity:		
Common stock, no par value, 300,000 shares authorized; 140,286 and 143,787 shares issued, 140,286 and 139,240 shares outstanding in 2008 and 2007, respectively	1,066,180	1,232,845
Common stock in treasury, at cost	—	(199,961)
Accumulated other comprehensive income	422	15,722
Retained earnings	439,422	410,198
Total shareholders' equity	1,506,024	1,458,804
Commitments and contingencies		
Total liabilities and shareholders' equity	**$ 3,380,736**	**$ 3,213,128**

Source: WFMI, *Annual Report* (2008).

EXHIBIT 3 Whole Foods Market, Inc., Percentage Revenues by Product Category

	2008	2007	2006
Grocery	33.2%	32.9%	31.5%
Prepared foods	19.3%	19.8%	19.6%
Other perishables	47.5%	48.3%	48.8%
Total sales	**100.0%**	**100.0%**	**100.0%**

Source: WFMI, *Annual Report* (2008).

EXHIBIT 4 Whole Foods Properties (as of September 28, 2008)

Location	#Stores	Location	#Stores	Location	#Stores
Alabama	1	Louisiana	3	Oregon	6
Arkansas	1	Maine	2	Pennsylvania	7
Arizona	7	Maryland	7	Rhode Island	3
California	51	Massachusetts	19	South Carolina	2
Colorado	18	Michigan	5	Tennessee	3
Canada	6	Minnesota	2	Texas	14
Connecticut	5	Missouri	3	United Kingdom	5
District of Columbia	3	Nebraska	1	Utah	4
Florida	14	Nevada	4	Virginia	9
Georgia	7	New Jersey	9	Washington	5
Hawaii	1	New Mexico	5	Wisconsin	2
Illinois	16	New York	8		
Indiana	2	North Carolina	5		
Kansas	2	Ohio	6		
Kentucky	2	Oklahoma	1		

Source: WFMI, *Annual Report* (2007): 21.

EXHIBIT 5 Whole Foods Management (as of November 20, 2007)

Regional Presidents

Name	Age	Tenure	Position
Scott Allshouse	45	7	South Region
Michael Besancon	61	13	Southern Pacific Region
Patrick Bradley	47	21	Midwest Region
Mark Dixon	45	24	Southwest Region
David Lannon	41	14	Northern California Region
Ron Megahan	37	18	Pacific Northwest Region
Kenneth Meyer	39	12	Mid-Atlantic Region
Christina Minardi	41	12	Northeast Region
Juan Nunez	49	25	Florida Region
William Paradise	47	17	Rocky Mountain Region
Jeff Turnas	35	12	North Atlantic Region

Executive Officers of the Registrant

Name	Age	Tenure	Position
John P. Mackey	54	29	Chairman of the Board & CEO
Albert Gallo	54	14	Co-President & COO
Walter Robb	54	16	Co-President & COO
Glenda Chamberlain	54	19	Exec. VP & CFO
James Sud	55	10	Exec. VP of Growth & Bus. Dev.
Lee Valkenaar	51	20	Exec. VP of Global Support

Source: WFMI, *Annual Report* (2007): 16.

EXHIBIT 6 **Drop In Average Consumer Spending per Visit (January 2008—October 2008)**

Whole Foods	19%
SuperValue	16%
Trader Joe	12%
Food Lion	12%
Publix	8%
Albertson's	6%
Safeway	5%
Stop & Shop	1%

Average Spent per Visit at Popular Supermarket Chains (October 2008)

Safeway	$45
Publix	42
Stop & Shop	42
SuperValue	38
Trader Joe	38
Food Lion	32
Albertson's	30
Whole Foods	28

Source: Geezeo, "Whole Foods in a Whole Lot of Trouble," http://www.seekingalpha.com/article/105807-whole-fodds-in-a-lot-of-trouble?source=yah.

Macy's, Inc. — 2009

Rochelle R. Brunson and Marlene M. Reed
Baylor University

M

http://www.macysinc.com

Macy's sales for the first quarter of 2009 total $5.199 billion, down 9.5 percent from sales of $5.747 billion in the first 13 weeks of 2008. On a same store basis, Macy's, Inc.'s first quarter sales were down 9.0 percent. Online sales (macys.com and bloomingdales.com combined) were up 16.2 percent.

Macy's operating loss totaled $114 million or 2.2 percent of sales for the quarter ended May 2, 2009, compared with operating income of $30 million or 0.5 percent of sales for the same period last year. On May 15, 2009, the board of directors of Macy's, Inc. declared a regular quarterly dividend of 5 cents per share on Macy's common stock.

Terry J. Lundgren, Macy's chairman, president and chief executive officer, suggested, "We continue to successfully navigate the very difficult economic environment. Our first quarter sales were consistent with our initial expectations, while earnings and cash flow performance were better than expected. By the end of the first quarter, we completed rollout of our My Macy's localization initiative. We have entered the second quarter with our new organizational structure in place and expect to benefit from approximately $400 million of annual expense savings beginning in 2010 (and $250 million in the partial year of 2009). Meanwhile, we expect to see an improvement in sales trend from My Macy's beginning in the fourth quarter of 2009 and especially in spring 2010."

On June 11, 2009, Macy's announced it would open two new Macy's stores in the Central Valley of California in the fall of 2009. Both are former Gottschalks locations for which Macy's submitted successful bids in the Gottschalks bankruptcy process.

Macy's second quarter 2009 ended August 1 and showed an earnings drop of 90 percent to $7 million and a sales drop of 9.7 percent to $5.16 billion. For that quarter, Macy's said their sales of mattresses, furniture, and handbags remained very weak, while their sales of apparel, cosmetics, and children's clothing were up slightly. Due to reduced orders from Macy's, other retailers too are suffering. For example, Liz Claiborne considers Macy's to be its biggest customer. Liz Claiborne for the second quarter of 2009 showed a sales drop of 29 percent to $683.8 million and an earnings loss of $82.1 million. Macy's needs a clear strategic plan for the future.

History

In 1851, Rowland Hussey Macy established a dry goods store in Haverhill, Massachusetts, to serve the whaling community. Then in 1858, he moved to New York City and established a new store named "R.H. Macy & Company" on the corner of 14th Street and 6th Avenue. Later he expanded his store to 18th Street and Broadway, which was the elite shopping district of that century.

After Rowland Macy's death, Nathan Straus and his brother, Isidor Straus, bought the store in 1893. Before purchasing the store, Nathan had held a license to sell china to the Macy's store. In 1902, the flagship store moved uptown to Herald Square at 34th Street and Broadway.

Macy's went public in 1922 and opened additional stores around New York and Long Island. In 1924, Macy's began acquiring stores outside of the New York City region in such cities as Toledo, San Francisco, and Kansas City. Then in 1983, the company began opening its own stores outside of New York.

In 1986, Macy's chairman Edward Finkelstein led a $3.5 billion buyout of Macy's and took it private. The company's debt load increased into the early 1990s, and Macy's filed for bankruptcy in 1992. Three years later, Federated Stores bought the 82 Broadway Stores and renamed 52 of them Macy's in 1996.

In 2001, Federated Stores decided to convert 19 of its Stern's locations in New Jersey and New York to its two strongest department store brands: Macy's and Bloomingdale's. In the first half of 2006, five underperforming Lord & Taylor stores were closed and a sixth was converted to a Macy's store.

In June 2007, Federated Stores changed its corporate name to that of its most famous brand, Macy's. Along with its name, the department store operator changed its ticker symbol to "M" on the New York Stock Exchange. In September 2007, the Martha Stewart Collection of merchandise for the home (including bed and bath textiles, housewares, casual dinnerware, flatware and glassware, and cookware) debuted in all Macy's full-line stores. In 2007, Macy's opened 10 stores and a single furniture gallery. Then in 2008, Macy's celebrated its 150th birthday by opening four new Macy's stores and one furniture gallery.

On August 30, 2005, Federated completed its $11 billion acquisition of rival May Department Stores. Then in October 2006, Federated completed the sale of its 48-store Lord & Taylor department store chain to NRDC Equity Partners LLC for nearly $1.1 billion. Lord & Taylor operated stores in a dozen states and the District of Columbia.

In early 2007, the department store operator completed the divestment of its bridal division with the January sale of David's Bridal to buyout firm Leonard Geen & Partners for about $750 million. In April of that year, Macy's sold After Hours Formalwear to The Men's Wearhouse for about $100 million.

Internal Factors

Basic Values

Macy's has some well-published values intended to guide the behavior of all their employees, as follows:

- We subscribe to ethical business practices in every facet of our business.
- We will protect the interests of our shareholders.
- We will provide quality and value to our customers in all dealings.
- We will obey all laws.
- We will treat others as we want them to treat us.
- We will respect the rights and property of others.
- We will be good corporate citizens.

Macy's believes that the timeless values that made our nation strong are the same values that make the company strong. These values are:

- A belief in the promise of the future with the energy and determination to get us there.
- A belief that our heritage mirrors the optimism, inclusion and integrity that provide for both stability and growth.
- A belief that taking advantage of the right opportunities will continue to lead us to success in all that we do.

Organization

Macy's has developed a new organizational strategy named "My Macy's" based on customer research and input from Macy's store managers, senior division executives, merchandise vendors, and industry experts. Exhibit 1 shows Macy's divisional organization chart, and Exhibit 2 provides Macy's division review.

Merchandising

Macy's strives to bring to customers niche brands and categories as indicated in Exhibit 3. The company has recently rolled out fresh, handmade cosmetics, soaps, and bath products

EXHIBIT 1 Macy's Divisional Organization Chart

from Lush. The recent use of robotic machines to sell iPods, iPod accessories, and other electronic products has been a very successful action plan. By 2008, private brands and labels represented about 19 percent of Macy's sales.

Macy's has always been known as an innovator. They pioneered such revolutionary business practices as the one-price system (the same item was sold to every customer at one price), quoting specific prices for goods in newspaper advertising, introducing such items as the tea bag, the Idaho baked potato, and colored bath towels. The company was also the first retailer to hold a New York City liquor license. Macy's also piloted new food concepts in selected stores, many of which were developed from the Macy's Culinary Council. Several stores have recently launched quick-service concepts such as La Brea Baker shops and newly developed Taste Bars.

Technology

Macy's direct-to-consumer businesses, including Macys.com, continues to be the fastest-growing part of the company. Two new 600,000-square-foot distributions centers in Portland,

EXHIBIT 2 Macy's Division Review

	Number of Division Stores	Total Store Square Footage	Number of Employees
Macy's Central	239	42,543 million	39,200
Macy's East	253	52,896 million	57,700
Macy's Florida	62	10,277 million	10,200
Macy's West	259	40,507 million	46,700

EXHIBIT 3 **2008 Macy's, Inc., Sales by Merchandise Categories (as a percentage of sales)**

	2008	2007	2006
Furniture, Accessories, Intimate Apparel, Shoes, & Cosmetics	36%	36%	35%
Feminine Apparel	27%	27%	28%
Men's & Children's	22%	22%	22%
Home/Miscellaneous	15%	15%	15%
Total	100%	100%	100%

Tennessee, and Goodyear, Arizona, are part of a $300 million investment in direct-to-consumer technology and operations. Macy's recently began installing a network of 50,000 new registers and point-of-sale systems that will be fully in place by the end of 2010. New "smart registers" are allowing sales associates to handle complex tasks more simply. The supporting software for this system will enable multichannel retailing in the future.

Sustainability Issues

Macy's has made a commitment to making a meaningful difference in improving the natural environment. The company has been able to reduce its total energy consumption by nearly 10 percent over the past five years. They have begun hosting solar panels on 28 Macy's stores in California. In addition, their customer-oriented fund-raising programs in the spring of 2008 benefited such organizations as the National Park Foundation and the National Resources Defense Council.

Through Macy's Rwanda Path to Peace Project, the company offers a collection of colorful baskets hand made by Rwandan widows who are survivors of that country's civil war and genocide. The baskets provide a lifeline of sustainable income to these exceptional artisans while offering to their customers high-quality, unique baskets that are not available anywhere else.

Many of Macy's new products are eco-friendly, such as Haven by Hotel Collection. These include products for the bed and bath such as organic cotton sheets and towels.

Macy's has a stringent Vendor/Supplier Code of Conduct. This code sets out specific standards and requirements for any vendor doing business with the company. All of the company's vendors are required to sign written affirmations in which they agree to comply with the company's Code of Conduct. In addition to other requirements, the code requires Macy's vendors allow unannounced factory inspections for contractual compliance as well as compliance with child labor laws and regulations.

Macy's has also adopted welfare-to-work programs with government and service organization partners in cities from coast to coast. The purpose of such programs is to provide training that will help welfare recipients gain employable skills and move into gainful employment. Macy's provides employment for many of the participants in these programs.

Macy's encourages charitable giving and employee volunteerism at both the national and local levels. Contributions from the company and its charitable foundations totaled $35.7 million in fiscal 2007. The company matched more than $4 million in employee gifts to nonprofit organizations across the country. In addition, Macy's efforts resulted in an additional $42.7 million in contributions from employees and customer through United Way drives, their Thanks for Sharing holiday campaign, Shop for a Cause charity shopping days, Passport and Glamorama fashion events, and other programs.

Advertising

Macy's uses network and cable television, fashion magazines, and an increasing amount of digital and online media to provide for national brand advertising. They use a balanced level of promotional advertising and direct marketing. The Macy's Thanksgiving Day Parade has had a worldwide impact. The most recent parade had 3.5 million live spectators and a television audience of 50 million.

Macy's recently launched a series of breakthrough brand ads featuring more than a dozen design celebrities behind unique merchandise sold in their stores and online. These celebrities ranged from Martha Stewart and Donald Trump to Usher, Jessica Simpson, Tyler Florence, Sean Combs, and Kenneth Cole. The campaign ads, which depict the celebrities interacting inside Macy's, are planned to continue into the future with new faces and themes.

Financial Performance

Macy's has adopted the following financial objectives:

- To accelerate comparable store sales growth.
- To continue to increase the company's profitability levels (earnings before interest, taxes, depreciation, and amortization) as a percentage of sales to a level of 14 percent to 15 percent.
- To effectively use excess cash flow through a combination of strategic growth opportunities and stock buybacks.
- To grow earnings per share while increasing return on gross investment.

Macy's financial performance in 2008 is provided in Exhibits 4 and 5.

Competitors

Macy's considers Dillard's, Inc., J.C. Penney Corporation, Inc., and Saks, Inc., to be its closest competitors (see Exhibit 6). As compared with its closest competitors in 2008, Macy's 167,000 employees were considerably more than Dillard's (33,433) and Saks'

EXHIBIT 4   Consolidated Statements of Income (millions, except per share data)

	Jan. 31, 2009	Jan. 31, 2008
Net sales	$24,892	$26,313
Cost of goods sold	15,009	15,677
Gross margin	9,883	10,636
Selling, general and administrative expenses	(8481)	(8,554)
Division consolidation costs and store closing related costs	(187)	-0-
Asset impairment charges	(211)	-0-
May integration costs	-0-	(219)
Operating income	1,004	1,863
Interest expense (net)	560	(543)
Income from continuing operations before Income taxes	444	1,320
Federal, state and local income tax expense	(164)	(411)
Income from continuing operations	280	909
Discontinued operations, net of income taxes	-0-	(16)
Net income	$280	$893
Basic earnings (loss) per share:		
Income from continuing operations	$.67	$2.04
Loss from discontinued operations	-0-	(.04)
Net income	$.67	$2.00
Diluted earnings (loss) per share:		
Income from continuing operations	$.66	$2.01
Loss from discontinued operations	-0-	(.04)
Net income	$.66	$1.97

EXHIBIT 5 Consolidated Balance Sheets (millions as of January 31)

	2009	2008
Assets		
Current Assets:		
Cash and cash equivalents	$ 1,306	$ 583
Accounts receivable	439	463
Merchandise inventories	4,769	5,060
Supplies and prepaid expenses	226	218
Total current assets	6,740	6,324
Property and Equipment–net	10,442	10,991
Goodwill	9,125	9,133
Other Intangible Assets–net	719	831
Other Assets	501	510
Total Assets	**$27,527**	**$27,789**
Liabilities and Shareholders' Equity		
Current Liabilities:		
Short-term debt	$ 966	$ 666
Merchandise accounts payable	1,282	1,398
Accounts payable and accrued liabilities	2,628	2,729
Income taxes	28	344
Deferred income taxes	224	233
Total Current Liabilities	5,360	6,095
Long-Term Debt	8,733	9,087
Deferred Income Taxes	1,416	1,446
Other Liabilities	2,521	1,989
Shareholders' Equity: stock		
Total Shareholders' Equity	9,729	9,907
Total Liabilities and Shareholders' Equity	**$27,527**	**$27,789**

EXHIBIT 6 Macy's Closest Competitors

	Macy's	Dillard's	J.C. Penney	Saks
Market Cap	4.85 B	532 M	N/A	5.19 B
Employees	167 T	33 T	155 T	10 T
Qtrly. Rev. Growth	−7.70%	−5.70%	N/A	N/A
Revenue	24.69 B	6.99 B	19.86 B	3.03 B
Gross Margin	39.70%	30.92%	N/A	32.14%
EBITDA	2.68 B	166.17 M	N/A	17.07 M
Operating Margins	5.63%	−1.69%	N/A	−3.88%
Net Income	−$4.08 B	−$241.07 M	$1.11 B	−$122.76 M
EPS	−$11.403	−$3.245	N/A	−$1.120

T = thousand
M = million
B = billion

(10,860) and 12,000 more than J.C. Penney's. Macy's also leads in the area of total revenues with $24.89 billion as compared with Dillard's ($6.99 billion), J.C. Penney ($19.86 billion), and Saks ($3.03 billion).

In terms of gross margin, Macy's also leads with 39.70 percent as compared with Dillard's 30.92 percent, and Saks's 32.14 percent. Penney's gross margin percentage is not available for comparison. A review of the net income of Macy's indicates that it had a loss of $4.80 billion in 2008, Dillard's lost $241.07 million, J.C. Penney had a positive net income of $1.18 billion, and Saks lost $122.76 million.

U.S. Retail Clothing Industry in 2009

In an economic recession such as the 2007–2009 period of time, a comparison of same-store year-to-year sales numbers becomes more important than in other economic periods. The January 2009 sales changes for same stores as compared to January 2008 revenues for selected retail clothing stores are as follows:

Store Name	Change in Jan. 2008 to Jan. 2009 Revenues
The Buckle, Inc.	+14.7%
Aeropostale	+11.0%
Gottschalk's	+8.8%
Macy's, Inc.	−4.5%
Limited	−9.0%
Chico's FAS	−10.9%
Nordstrom's	−11.4%
Dillard's	−12.0%
Kohl's	−13.4%
J.C. Penney	−16.4%
Neiman Marcus	−18.3%
Abercrombie & Fitch	−20.0%
Saks, Inc.	−24.0%

Source: Barbara Farfan, "January 2009 Same Store Sales Figures: Complete U.S. Retail Industry Report." About.com—Retail Industry. Available at http://retailindustry.about.com.

Because of the lack of sales growth among many retail clothing stores in 2008, the following companies announced employee layoffs in January of 2009:

Store Name	Number of Employee Layoffs
Saks, Inc.	1,100
Macy's, Inc.	960
Neiman Marcus	375
New York & Company	310
Stein Mart	209
Chico's FAS	180
Gottschalk's	"dozens"

Source: Barbara Farfan, 2009 Retail Industry Job Cuts: Top U.S. Retail Employee Layoffs and Unemployment. About.com—Retail Industry. Available at http://retailindustry.about.com.

Conclusion

Macy's press release of January 8, 2009, says the company was going to close 11 under-performing stores as indicated in Exhibit 7. Chairman Terry J. Lundgren commented on that revelation by suggesting, "These closings are part of our normal-course process to prune underperforming locations each year in order to maintain a healthy portfolio of

EXHIBIT 7 Macy's, Inc., Store Closings, 2008–2009

Facility Location	City	Square Footage	No. of Employees
Ernst & Young Plaza	Los Angeles, CA	135,000	136
The Citadel	Colorado Springs, CO	195,000	105
Westminster Mall	Westminster, CO	190,000	71
Mauna Lani Bay Hotel	Island of Hawaii, HI	3,000	3
Lafayette Square	Indianapolis, IN	160,000	84
Brookdale Center	Brooklyn Center, MN	195,000	72
Crestwood Mall	St. Louis, MO	166,000	76
Natrona Heights Plaza	Natrona Heights, PA	73,000	124
Century III Furniture & Clearance	West Miffin, PA	83,000	3
Bellevue Center	Nashville, TN	211,000	76

stores. While new store growth has slowed in the current economy, our long-term strategy is to continue to selectively add new stores while closing those that are underperforming."

A month later, a *Wall Street Journal* article on dated February 3, 2009, stated that Macy's intends to shed 7,000 jobs or 4 percent of its workforce. Macy's also is cutting its dividends by 62 percent, ending merit pay increases for executives, and slashing its 2009 capital-spending budget by another $100 million to $150 million. The original budget was $1 billion (Dodes, 2009).

Retail consultant Howard Davidowitz suggests that "Chief executives of retailers with high debt levels are especially vulnerable." He pointed to Terry J. Lundren of Macy's as "someone who needs to make significant progress after poor 2008 results and the ill-timed acquisition of May Company" (Bymes and McConnon, 2009).

On a more positive level, Macy's corporate vision contains the following statements:

"A belief in the promise of the future with the energy and determination to get us there;

A belief that our heritage mirrors the optimism, inclusion and integrity that provide for both stability and growth; and

A belief that taking advantage of the right opportunities will continue to lead us to success in all that we do."

In lieu of the company's optimistic vision statement and the serious economic downturn in the economy of the United States, which resulted in the closing of 11 Macy's stores, Lundgren and the rest of the company leadership were faced with determining an appropriate strategy to avoid more layoffs and store closings.

References Cited

Bymes, Nanette, and Aili McConnon. "Executives on a Tightrope." *BusinessWeek* (January 19, 2009): 43.

Dodes, Rachel. "Macy's to Shed 7,000 jobs, Cut Payout by 62%." *Wall Street Journal* (Februrary 3, 2009): B1.

Farfun, Barbara. "Retail Recession News: Consumer Belief Makes It So." October 29, 2008. http://www.retailindustry.about.com

Farfun, Barbara. "January 2009 Same Store Sales Figures: Complete U.S. Retail Industry Report." January 29, 2009. http://www.retailindustry.about.com

Farfun, Barbara. "2009. Retail Industry Job Cuts: Top U.S. Retail Employee Layoffs and Unemployment." January 2009. http://www.retailindustry.about.com

"Macy's, Inc. to Close 11 Stores." Macy's Press Release, January 8, 2009.

Macy's, Inc. *Annual Report for 2008* (April 2009)

Macy's, Inc. Web site, http://www.macys.com

9 Yahoo! Inc. — 2009

Hamid Kazeroony
William Penn University

YHOO

www.yahoo.com

In January 2009, Carol Bartz replaced Jerry Yang as Yahoo!'s CEO. Yahoo! has resumed discussions with Microsoft about search and advertising partnerships as both firms struggle to compete with Google. Yahoo! in 2008 had rejected Microsoft's unsolicited $44.6 billion offer and then rejected that firm's attempt to acquire just Yahoo!'s Internet-search business, which is second behind Google in market share.

Headquartered in Sunnyvale, California, Yahoo! has offices in more than 25 countries, provinces, or territories. Yahoo!'s revenues from 2007 to 2008 increased by 3.4 percent to $7.2 billion. However, net income decreased by 35.7 percent to $424 million. Yahoo! is the second leading global Internet brand and one of the most trafficked Internet destinations worldwide. Together with its owned and operated online properties and services, it also provides its advertising offerings and access to Internet users beyond Yahoo! through its distribution network of third-party entities, who have integrated its advertising offerings into their Web sites. Yahoo! generates revenues by providing marketing services to advertisers across hundreds of Web sites. Although many of the services Yahoo! provides to users are free, it does charge fees for a range of premium services.

The core of Yahoo!'s strategy and operations is to become the starting point for Internet users; to provide must-buy marketing solutions for the world's largest advertisers; and to deliver industry-leading open platforms that attract developers and publishers.

Yahoo! posted a 78 percent first quarter 2009 profit decline and reacted by eliminating another 675 jobs, or 5 percent of its workforce on top of 2,500 jobs cut in 2008. For that quarter, Yahoo!'s revenues dropped 13 percent to $1.58 billion. Yahoo!'s online advertising business is also deteriorating rapidly as the firm's overall revenue fell 13 percent in the second quarter of 2009 compared to the prior year. For that second quarter, aggressive cost cutting allowed Yahoo! to post a 7 percent increase in profit up to $141.4 million, but the firm laid off another 700 employees to end with 13,000 employees.

In July 2009, Yahoo! closed its third video property, Maven Networks, based in Cambridge, Massachusetts. Yahoo! plans to close twenty video services, including its social network site Yahoo! 360 and its Web hosting service GeoCities. The company needs an excellent strategic plan to negotiate a deal with Microsoft or to continue alone.

History

Yahoo! began as a student hobby and evolved into a global brand that has changed the way people communicate with each other, find and access information, and purchase things. The two founders of Yahoo!, David Filo and Jerry Yang, were PhD candidates in electrical engineering at Stanford University when they started this company in a campus trailer in 1994 as a way to keep track of their personal interests on the Internet. Soon these two men were spending more time on their home-brewed lists of favorite links than on their doctoral dissertations. Eventually, Jerry and David's lists became too long and unwieldy, and they broke them out into categories. When the categories became too full, they developed subcategories and the core concept behind Yahoo! was born.

The Web site started out as "Jerry and David's Guide to the World Wide Web" but eventually received a new moniker with the help of a dictionary. The name Yahoo! is an acronym for "Yet Another Hierarchical Officious Oracle," but Filo and Yang insist they selected the name because they liked the general definition of a yahoo: "rude, unsophisticated, uncouth." Yahoo! itself first resided on Yang's student workstation, "Akebono," while the software was lodged on Filo's computer, "Konishiki"—both named after legendary sumo wrestlers.

Yahoo! was incorporated in 1995 in Delaware and launched a highly successful initial public offering IPO in April 1996 with a total of 49 employees. Its stock rose to the high of $120 in 2000 but for most of 2009 has been trading under $14.

Yahoo! Segments

Yahoo! offerings include Yahoo! Groups, Yahoo! Answers, and Flickr and are generally provided to users free of charge. Revenue in Communities' offerings is primarily generated through display advertising. Yahoo! search offerings include Yahoo! Search, Yahoo! Local, Yahoo! Yellow Pages and Yahoo! Maps and are available free to users and are often the starting point for users navigating the Internet and searching for information. Yahoo! generates revenues through its Search offerings from search and display advertising.

The Yahoo! Communications segment include Yahoo! Mail, Zimbra Mail, and Yahoo! Messenger and provides a wide range of communication services to users. Yahoo! generates display advertising revenues from these offerings.

Yahoo!'s vision and/or mission statement is "Yahoo! powers and delights our communities of users, advertisers, and publishers—all of us united in creating indispensable experiences, and fueled by trust." Yahoo!'s code of ethics is embedded in its six values: Excellence, Innovation, Customer Fixation, Teamwork, Community, and Fun.

Yahoo! lost 1 percent in rich media revenue, 1 percent in sponsorship, and 2 percent in classified ads in 2008 as compared to 2007. Although the revenue from search increased by 3 percent in 2008 compared to 2007, the increase was due to growth in the entire Internet business rather than a shift to Yahoo!

External Issues

According to technology research firm IDC, there were 1.1 billion Internet users around the world and 211 million in the United States as of the end of 2006 (latest data available). To offer some perspective, the size of the worldwide population of Internet users is comparable to the population of India (estimated at 1.1 billion as of mid-2008, according to the U.S. Central Intelligence Agency), and the size of the U.S. population of Internet users is comparable to the population of Brazil (191 million).

Economic growth in the United States and around the world has slowed amid crisis in the housing and credit markets. The prices of consumables, from fuel to food commodities, are near all-time highs, yet the values of personal assets, like homes and property, have fallen dramatically. Add rising unemployment and problematic geopolitics to the mix, and we have a difficult economic backdrop, to say the least. Although Internet-related businesses have perhaps held up better than their non digital counterparts, they have still suffered from macroeconomic malaise. In 2009, a number of Internet content and advertising companies (including Bankrate Inc., Knot Inc., ValueClick Inc., WebMD Health Corp., and Yahoo! Inc.) reported disappointing financial results and lowered their forward financial outlooks. Even Google Inc. expressed economic-related caution in conjunction with its second quarter results, and Internet media and market research firm comScore Inc. expressed concerns about deceleration in online spending growth.

Internet advertising revenues in the United States remain strong, topping $23 billion, according to the 2008 Internet Advertising Revenue Report, released by the Interactive Advertising Bureau and PricewaterhouseCoopers LLP (PwC). Despite a difficult U.S. economy, as illustrated in Exhibit 1 to 5, Internet advertising continues to grow, albeit at a slower pace. This trend confirms marketers' increased recognition that consumers spend more and more of their time online.

EXHIBIT 1   **Consolidated Statements of Income**

	Years Ended December 31		
	2006	2007	2008
	(in thousands, except per share amounts)		
Revenues	**$ 6,425,679**	**$ 6,969,274**	**$ 7,208,502**
Cost of revenues	2,675,723	2,838,758	3,023,362
Gross profit	3,749,956	4,130,516	4,185,140
Operating expenses:			
Sales and marketing	1,322,259	1,610,357	1,563,313
Product development	833,147	1,084,238	1,221,787
General and administrative	528,798	633,431	705,136
Amortization of intangibles	124,786	107,077	87,550
Restructuring charges, net	—	—	106,854
Goodwill impairment charge	—	—	487,537
Total operating expenses	2,808,990	3,435,103	4,172,177
Income from operations	940,966	695,413	12,963
Other income, net	157,034	154,011	82,838
Income before provision for income taxes, earnings in equity interests, and minority interests	1,098,000	849,424	95,801
Provision for income taxes	(458,011)	(337,263)	(262,717)
Earnings in equity interests	112,114	150,689	596,979
Minority interests in operations of consolidated subsidiaries	(712)	(2,850)	(5,765)
Net income	**$ 751,391**	**$ 660,000**	**$ 424,298**
Net income per share-basic	$ 0.54	$ 0.49	$ 0.31
Net income per share-diluted	$ 0.52	$ 0.47	$ 0.29
Shares used in per share calculation-basic	1,388,741	1,338,987	1,369,476
Shares used in per share calculation-diluted	1,457,686	1,405,486	1,400,101
Stock-based compensation expense by function:			
Cost of revenues	$ 6,621	$ 10,628	$ 13,813
Sales and marketing	155,084	246,472	182,826
Product development	144,807	218,207	178,091
General and administrative	118,418	97,120	63,113
Restructuring expense reversals	—	—	(30,236)
Total stock-based compensation expense	$ 424,930	$ 572,427	$ 407,607

Source: http://yhoo.client.shareholder.com/sec.cfm?DocType=Annual

EXHIBIT 2   **Consolidated Balance Sheets**

	2006	2007	2008
ASSETS			
Current assets:			
Cash and cash equivalents	$ 1,569,871	$ 1,513,930	$ 2,292,296
Short-term marketable debt securities	1,031,528	487,544	1,159,691
Accounts receivable, net of allowance of $46,521 and $51,600, respectively	930,964	1,055,532	1,060,450

continued

EXHIBIT 2   **Consolidated Balance Sheets—continued**

	2006	2007	2008
Prepaid expenses and other current assets	217,779	180,716	233,061
Total current assets	3,750,142	3,237,722	4,745,498
Long-term marketable debt securities	935,886	361,998	69,986
Property and equipment, net	1,101,379	1,331,632	1,536,181
Goodwill	2,968,557	4,002,030	3,440,889
Intangible assets, net	405,882	611,497	485,860
Other long-term assets	459,988	503,945	233,989
Investments in equity interests	1,891,834	2,180,917	3,177,445
Total assets	**$ 11, 513,608**	**$ 12,229,741**	**$ 13,689,848**
LIABILITIES AND STOCKHOLDERS' EQUITY			
Current liabilities:			
Accounts payable	$ 109,130	$ 176,162	$ 151,897
Accrued expenses and other current liabilities	1,046,882	1,006,188	1,139,894
Deferred revenue	317,982	368,470	413,224
Short-term debt		749,628	—
Total current liabilities	$ 1,473,994	2,300,448	1,705,015
Long-term deferred revenue	64,939	95,129	218,438
Capital lease and other long-term liabilities	806,009	28,086	77,062
Deferred and other long-term tax liabilities, net		260,993	420,372
Commitments and contingencies		—	—
Minority interests in consolidated subsidiaries	8,056	12,254	18,019
Stockholders' equity:			
Preferred stock, $0.001 par value; 10,000 shares	—	—	
authorized; none issued or outstanding Common stock, $0.001 par value; 5,000,000 shares			
authorized; 1,534,893 and 1,600,220 shares issued, respectively, and 1,330,828 and 1,391,560 shares outstanding, respectively	1,493	1,527	1,595
Additional paid-in capital	8,615,915	9,937,010	11,548,393
Treasury stock at cost, 204,065 and 208,660 shares, respectively	(3,324,863)	(5,160,772)	(5,267,484)
Retained earnings	3,717,560	4,423,864	4,848,162
Accumulated other comprehensive income	150,505	331,202	120,276
Total stockholders' equity	9,160,610	9,532,831	11,250,942
Total liabilities and stockholders' equity	**$ 11,513,608**	**$ 12,229,741**	**$ 13,689,848**

Source: http://yhoo.client.shareholder.com/sec.cfm?DocType=Annual

- Yahoo!'s full-year 2008 revenues totaled a record $23.4 billion, exceeding 2007's performance, itself the former record of $21.2 billion, by $2.2 billion or 10.6 percent. By comparison, a variety of sources indicate weakness in overall advertising spending. The Nielsen Company, for example, reported that U.S. advertising for the full year 2008 was down 2.6 percent compared to the full year 2007.
- Fourth-quarter revenues of $6.1 billion mark the first time the interactive (Internet) advertising industry achieved, and surpassed, $6 billion in a single quarter. The figures represent a $154 million or 2.6 percent increase from 2007's fourth quarter, which had revenues of $5.9 billion.
- This is the fifth consecutive year of record results.

EXHIBIT 3   Yahoo! Revenues by Groups of Similar Services (dollars in thousands)

	2006*		2007*		2008*		%change	
							06–07	07–08
Owned and Operated sites	$3,074,803	48%	3,669,816	52%	$4,045,996	56%	19%	10%
Affiliate sites	2,552,404	40%	2,418,423	35%	2,270,210	32%	(5)%	(6)%
Marketing services	5,627,207	88%	6,088,239	87%	6,316,206	88%	8%	4%
Fees	798,472	12%	881,035	13%	892,296	12%	10%	1%
Total revenues	$6,425,679	100%	6,969,274	100%	$7,208,502	100%	8%	3%

*Percentage of total revenue.

Source: http://yhoo.client.shareholder.com/sec.cfm?DocType=Annual

EXHIBIT 4   Yahoo! Organizational Chart

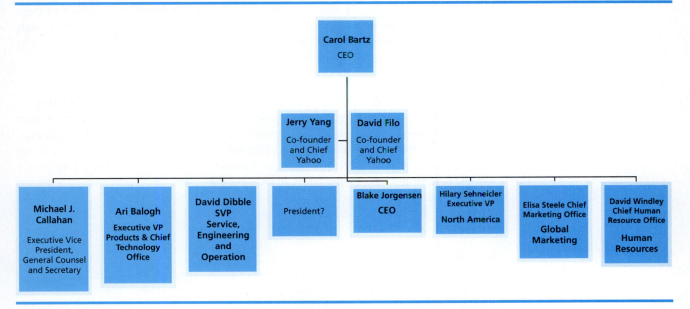

Source: Based on Yahoo!'s 2008 *Form 10K.*

EXHIBIT 5   Yahoo! Segment Revenues

	FY 2008 Share of revenue $'s (000)	FY 2007 Share of revenue $'s (000)
Search	45% ($10,546)	42% ($8,805)
Display Related	33% ($7,640)	33% ($7,072)
Banner Ads	21% ($4,877)	21% ($4,456)
Rich Media	7% ($1,642)	8% ($1,656)
Digital Video	3% ($734)	2% ($324)
Sponsorship	2% ($387)	3% ($636)
Classifieds	14% ($3,174)	16% ($3,321)
Referrals/Lead Generation	7% ($1,683)	7% ($1,584)
E-mail	2% ($405)	2% ($424)

Source: http://eon.businesswire.com

EXHIBIT 6   **Search Engine Use Compared**

Search Engine Utilization	Percent of total
Google	49.2
Yahoo!	23.8
MSN	9.6
AOL	6.3
Ask	2.6
Others	8.5

Source: NetRating for SearchEngineWatch.com

Competition

Yahoo! operates in the Internet products, services, and content markets, which are characterized by rapid change, converging technologies, and increasing competition. Yahoo!'s most significant competition, as demonstrated in Exhibit 6, is from Google Inc., Microsoft Corporation, and Time Warner Inc.'s America Online business. Each of these firms offer an integrated variety of Internet products and services. During 2008, Google had 72 percent of Internet traffic while Yahoo! only possessed 17 percent followed by MSN at 6 percent and IACI at 4 percent.

Microsoft

Both a friend and foe of Yahoo! in many ways, Microsoft's $6 billion acquisition of Quantive Inc., an advertising solutions company, in August 2007 marked an important change. Microsoft lost out in a bidding war for privately held DoubleClick Inc., a digital marketing technology and services company, Microsoft recommitted itself to the category, offering to acquire aQuantive at a massive premium and valuation to ensure that the deal would be consummated. In October 2007, Microsoft purchased a 2 percent stake in social networking firm Facebook Inc., valuing the private company at an astounding $15 billion. Microsoft has an obvious and strong desire to increase its Internet presence.

Google

In early 2009, Google is in talks with the popular micro-blogging site, Twitter, about a possible partnership. Google has expanded well beyond search-related functions into areas such as e-mail (Gmail), mapping (Google Earth and Google Maps), Web-based productivity applications (Google Apps), video (Google Video and YouTube Inc., which Google acquired in November 2006), a finance offering (Google Finance), a payment service (Google Checkout), a personalized portal offering (iGoogle), a mobile Internet software platform (Android), and browser software (Google Chrome).

Google's pursuit of mobile Internet opportunities has made it one of the main application providers for Apple Inc.'s iPhone. Perhaps more importantly, Google has successfully pushed for more open standards in the mobile space, which will eventually allow users to choose more easily the carriers and handsets they want. As a result of Google's efforts, the Federal Communications Commission (FCC) adopted flexible access rules for users and wireless resellers in conjunction with the agency's early 2008 wireless spectrum auction. As illustrated in Exhibit 7, Google commands a good portion of the revenue in the industry and is a formidable competitor to Yahoo! in particular. From its first year of operation as a public company (2004), Google has increased its operating profit to $6.7 billion from a modest $852 million.

Industry Trends

As broadband prices fall, ISPs are pursuing new business strategies, such as bundling Internet access with voice and video services. AOL LLC, a division of Time Warner Inc., shifted its business model from paid subscriptions to a free, advertiser-based portal that is

EXHIBIT 7   Yahoo! versus Google Comparison

	YHOO	GOOG	Industry
Market Cap	18.29B	100.13B	43.26M
Employees	N/A	20,222	75
Qtrly Rev Growth	−1.40%	18.10%	15.40%
Revenue	7.21B	21.80B	71.90M
Gross Margin	58.06%	60.44%	65.60%
EBITDA	1.32B	8.13B	6.65M
Oper Margins	8.43%	30.43%	−3.21%
Net Income	424.30M	4.23B	N/A
EPS	0.295	13.312	N/A
P/E	44.47	23.86	18.87
PEG (5 yr expected)	2.48	0.81	0.71
P/S	2.59	4.60	1.13

Source: http://finance.yahoo.co?s=yhoo

similar to those offered by Yahoo! Inc. and Google Inc. In early 2008, Time Warner indicated that it might look to sell its AOL access business. EarthLink Inc. has indicated that it wants to be a segment consolidator. Each company is committed to attract as many visitors (as Exhibit 8 demonstrates) as possible. The industry, due to its low barrier entry—technical and regulatory—makes the projection of its business viability for existing companies difficult. Due to changes in legislative requirements concerning technology sharing, patent rights, and information security, future expenses and profitability of the companies operating within this industry are harder to predict. Future innovations and shifts in technology also make long-term strategies regarding the Internet and software services industry difficult.

EXHIBIT 8   Top 25 Internet Properties

Top 25 Internet Properties[†]	Unique Visitors (000)	% Reach[*]
1. Google sites	140,163	73.8
2. Yahoo! sites	140,080	73.8
3. Microsoft sites	119,677	63.0
4. AOL	110,841	58.4
5. Fox Interactive Media	85,998	45.3
6. eBay	72,972	38.4
7. Amazon sites	57,002	30.0
8. Wikipedia sites	53,337	28.1
9. Ask.com network	51,646	27.2
10. Apple Inc.	45,396	23.9
11. Viacom Digital	45,053	23.7
12. Turner Network	43,515	22.9
13. New York Times Digital	42,373	22.3
14. Glam Media	40,775	N/A
15. Facebook.com	37,375	19.7
16. The Weather Channel	34,963	18.4
17. CNET Networks	32,822	17.3

continued

EXHIBIT 8   **Top 25 Internet Properties—continued**

Top 25 Internet Properties[†]	Unique Visitors (000)	% Reach[*]
18. Craigslist Inc.	31,870	16.8
19. Wal-Mart	30,398	16.0
20. Superpages.com network	30,155	15.9
21. Disney Online	30,012	15.8
22. Adobe sites	29,378	15.5
23. Time Warner (excluding AOL)	29,250	15.4
24. Gorilla Nation	29,216	15.4
25. Verizon Communications Corp.	28,266	14.9

Data for June 2008: United States only

[†]Home, work, and university usage.

[*]The percentage of Web-active individuals who visited a site at least once during the month (per comScore).

Source: S & P Market Insight, 2008.

References

http://yhoo.client.shareholder.com/press

http://world.yahoo.com/ca

http://yhoo.client.shareholder.com/secfiling.cfm?filingID=1193125-09-41172

http://online.wsj.com/article/BT-CO-20090310-712818.html?mod=crnews

http://docs.yahoo.com/info/misc/history.html

http://www.thestreet.com

http://eon.businesswire.com

http://searchenginewatch.com

Yahoo! 10-K filing with SEC

Google 10-K filing with SEC

S & P: Industry Surveys, Computers: Consumer Services & the Internet, Internet Software & Services Analyst Scott H. Kessler, Internet Software & Services Analyst September 25, 2008

10 eBay Inc. — 2009

Lori Radulovich
Baldwin-Wallace College

EBAY

eBay.com

In August 2009, eBay Inc. formed a partnership with General Motors enabling hundreds of GM dealers in California to help consumers negotiate purchase of new GM cars and trucks through the eBay online marketplace. Nearly all of California's 250 GM dealers took part in the program so consumers could visit Web pages like gm.ebay.com and chevy.ebay.com to browse new 2008 and 2009 GM vehicles, ask dealers questions, and figure out financing. This program marked a shift for San Jose, California-based eBay, since most of the vehicles sold on eBay Motors—a site that sells various types of vehicles and auto parts—had historically been used.

For the second quarter of 2009, eBay's profit fell 29 percent and revenue declined 4 percent as the company continued its turnaround strategy in a harsh climate for consumer spending. These weak results were, however, better than analysts expected. For that quarter, eBay reported nice growth in both their PayPal and Skype business segments, which offset decline in their Marketplaces business segment. EBay also that quarter announced they would spin off and make an initial public offering of their Skype business segment in the beginning of year 2010.

History

How did the idea of selling practically anything to anyone, anytime, anywhere start? Surprisingly, it all began with Pez candy! One evening in September 1995, Pierre Omidyar, the founder of eBay, and his wife were discussing their desire to contact other Pez collectors. To solve the problem, Omidyar created an online auction in the form of a sole proprietorship business. As a result, eBay was created over the Labor Day weekend by Pierre, a computer programmer, who devised a code that enabled and ran the eBay auction Web site from his home computer. Later in May 1996, eBay was incorporated in California and became public on September 24, 1998. The first eBay auction was also conducted on Labor Day. As of 2008, eBay has a 14 percent share of global e-commerce with 86.3 million active users.

EBay, the first virtual online business community, empowers entrepreneurial individuals to become e-commerce business owners. EBay.com offers a sense of community to buyers and sellers that is sustained by communication and high transaction rates on a wide selection of goods/services (eBay.com, 2006). EBay's popularity is due to the value offered to its users. EBay provides a "faster, easier, safer online commerce experience" (eBay, 2006, p. 7). EBay's global networked community of buyers and sellers interact 24/7 in a secure and trusted global marketplace. E-commerce is supported by eBay's proprietary Skype VoIP technology, which allows free telephone calls using a broadband Internet connection to any telephone number. Skype is available in 28 languages in over 225 countries (eBay, 2006). EBay's e-commerce platform also provides full support for the buying process (registration, bidding, management of outbids, item listing, and transaction close), community bulletins, chat, a proprietary product search engine, purchase protection programs, customer support, value added services for auction users, a personal home page that includes tailored information, and fully automated merchant services. EBay's success is sustained through communication and trust (eBay 2006).

EBay Inc. encompasses eBay.com, the online marketplace, PayPal, which refers to the online payments platform, and Skype, the Voice over Internet Protocol (VoIP) offered by eBay's subsidiary Skype Technologies S.A. Corporate revenues are earned primarily from three business segments: (1) Marketplaces, (2) Payments, and (3) Communications. The Marketplaces segment generates revenues from listings and fees paid by sellers; the Payments segment revenues are generated from fees paid by merchants for payment processing services through PayPal and Bill Me Later. The Communications segment generates usage revenues from Skype VoIP for connection to traditional fixed and mobile telephones under eBay's subsidiary Skype Technologies S.A. Communications fees are assessed either on a subscription basis or per minute charge for "SkypeOut minutes." Additional revenues are also earned from advertising and revenue-sharing contracts with third parties that provide transaction services to eBay and PayPal account users.

In 2008, eBay.com generated approximately $59.7 billion in gross merchandise revenues with consumer electronics accounting for the largest percentage of trade at $6.0 billion or 17 percent, as indicated in Exhibit 1. PayPal earned approximately $30.4 billion of net total payment revenues directly from eBay.com transactions, which represented approximately 51 percent of PayPal's net Total Payment Volume during 2008 and 9 percent of global e-commerce transactions revenue (eBay.com 2009a). Why is eBay so popular?

The eBay Marketplace

EBay transformed the Internet and the way many of us shop and do business worldwide. EBay's marketplace, or "marketspace," is an online virtual trading platform for the sale of goods and services by a community of users that comprises individual buyers and sellers, as well as small business owners. EBay provides the virtual marketplace auction where the market determines the price of items sold. EBay offers millions of items for trade through auction-style and fixed-price trading in 39 markets and boasts 86.3 million active global users as of 2008. In 2007, eBay sold nearly $60 billion goods, which equates to worldwide eBay users trading more than $1,900 worth in goods every second. As of December 31, 2008, eBay Inc. employed approximately 16,200 people.

EXHIBIT 1 eBay Gross Merchandise Volume by Category

	eBay	
	Annualized 4th Quarter 2008 Gross Merchandise Volume by Category *(in billions)*	
Consumer Electronics	$6.90	17.51%
Computers	$3.60	9.14%
Clothing & Accessories	$5.00	12.69%
Home & Garden	$3.80	9.64%
Collectibles	$2.40	6.09%
Books/Music/Movies	$2.60	6.60%
Sports	$2.60	6.60%
Business & Industrial	$2.10	5.33%
Toys	$2.40	6.09%
Jewelry & Watches	$2.20	5.58%
Camera & Photo	$1.60	4.06%
Antiques & Art	$1.20	3.05%
Coins & Stamps	$1.20	3.05%
Tickets & Travel	$1.80	4.57%
Total		100.00%

Source: Adapted from eBay.com 2009 Marketplaces Fact Sheet.

By 2009, eBay has attained customized local sites across four major areas of the world in the following regional markets:

World Market	Regional Markets
Asia Pacific	Australia, China, Hong Kong, India, Malaysia, New Zealand, Philippines, Singapore, South Korea, Taiwan
Europe	Austria, Belgium, France, Germany, Ireland, Italy, Netherlands, Poland, Spain, Sweden, Switzerland, United Kingdom
North America	Canada, United States
Latin America	Argentina, Brazil, Chile, Colombia, Ecuador, Mexico, Peru, Uruguay and Venezuela, Costa Rica, the Dominican Republic, and Panama

Vision and Mission

What is eBay's plan? Although eBay Inc. does not have a formal mission or vision statement, the following statements can be found in eBay's yearly annual reports.

> We intend to achieve our mission of creating the world's online marketplace by improving and expanding across three main areas: categories, formats, and geographies *(2005 Annual Report)*
>
> We intend to achieve our mission of creating the world's leading e-commerce franchise by building upon our core Marketplaces business and building our adjacent businesses. *(2006 Annual Report)*
>
> We intend to continue to work toward our mission of creating the world's leading ecommerce franchise by investing in our core Marketplaces segment and continuing to build our adjacent Marketplaces businesses. *(2007 Annual Report)*

eBay Inc. (EBAY)

EBay common stock is traded on the Nasdaq Global Select Market exchange under the ticker symbol EBAY. As of February 11, 2009, there were approximately 4,800 common stock owners. To date, eBay has never paid a cash dividend on stock and specifically states that there are no anticipated cash dividends forthcoming in the future. The stock price for 2005 through 2009 ranged from a high around $60 per share to a low near $10. Year-end stock price values were $58.17 at 2004, $43.22 as of 2005, $30.07 by 2006, $33.19 in 2007, and 13.96 at the end of the calendar year 2008.

Business Segment I: Marketplaces, Platforms, and Services

EBay Inc.'s Marketplaces platforms and services segment includes eBay.com, StubHub, Online Classifieds, Online Advertising, Shopping.com, and Rent.com.

eBay.com Platform

Buyers and sellers enjoy trading among a wide selection of goods and services in a secure, trusted, and efficient commerce environment. Listings of items for sale have exceeded 140.0 million per day. The key to success is eBay's user support, such as announcements, bulletin boards, customer support, personal pages, and more. EBay's Marketplaces platform brings buyers and sellers together through fully automated online Web sites 24/7. As of December 2008, approximately 516,000 online storefronts were listed in locations across the globe. The Marketplaces platform is the core online commerce platform eBay.com. Other marketplaces platforms consist of classified Web sites, StubHub, Shopping.com, Half.com, and Rent.com.

In the Marketplaces platform, eBay.com, traditional auction-style or fixed-price options are offered in 39 markets. Auction-style listing allows a seller to select a minimum price for opening bids that stay open for a period of time. Alternatively, the fixed-price format allows sellers to name a sale price upon listing instead of waiting for the auction period to expire.

A Trusted Online Community

To facilitate trading with unknown partners on the Internet, eBay Inc. provides a trusted and safe trading environment by offering the following services: Feedback Forum, Safe Harbor Program, Verified Rights Owner Program, Customer Support, Value-Added Tools and Services, and Loyalty Programs.

Feedback Forum provides feedback, comments, and ratings on other users that can be viewed by potential users when considering a purchase. Information is recorded up to 12 months and provides color-coded star ratings. EBay recently adopted a policy that no longer permits sellers to leave negative feedback. The *SafeHarbor Program* provides guidelines for resolving disputes among parties. Complaints are investigated and offenders may receive warnings that are posted to users. Violators may be suspended from either bidding on or listing items for sale. The *Verified Rights Owner Program* enforces intellectual property owners' rights by allowing owners to request the removal of listings that contain infringements. This program protects intellectual property and reduces counterfeit trade. EBay has also expanded specific *Customer Support* efforts, such as online self-help features to increase efficiency of trades. EBay offers both "pre-trade" and "post-trade" *Value-Added Tools and Services* to facilitate faster and safe trading and collections. Examples of value added service tools include a calculator, shipping and UPS labels, PayPal, and so on. Lastly, *Loyalty Programs* that provide cash back buyer rewards coupons were selectively distributed to recognize large buyers to sustain customer loyalty.

StubHub is a leading U.S. ticket marketplace that allows users to buy and sell tickets to sporting, events, theater, and other entertainment events.

EBay Inc. also offers online classified advertisements to members in hundreds of cities and regions of the world, such as the Netherlands, Germany, and so on. Online classifieds help people meet, share ideas, and offer goods/services at a local city or regional level.

Online advertising, mailing, and other services are offered to eBay's strategic partners and members. In 2008, eBay launched an advertising service that enables third parties to advertise their eBay listings and eBay stores on eBay Web sites.

Acquired by eBay Inc. in 2005, Shopping.com is an online comparison shopping site that offers comparisons on millions of products and product reviews. Shopping.com is available in the United States, the United Kingdom, France, Germany, and Australia. Revenue is earned from advertisers and retailers who pay a fee for directing shoppers to their own sites.

Rent.com, acquired by eBay in 2005, is the most visited online apartment listing service with over 20,000 listings in the United States. Rent.com lists apartment availability, rental costs, virtual tours, roommate searches, and more. Revenue is earned from landlords who pay a fee for renters who find apartments through Rent.com.

EBay plans to expand the Marketplaces segment by focusing on customers to improve the buyer's experience and reduce seller costs by enhancing products and services, improving online trust and safety, enhancing customer support, extending product offerings geographically and into new categories, and developing retention strategies.

Business Segment II: Payments

EBay's Payments segment is composed of PayPal and Bill Me Later transaction services. *PayPal* was founded in December 1998 and acquired by eBay Inc. in 2002. PayPal is a recognized global leader in online payment solutions with 70 million active accounts. PayPal generated $60 billion in net total payment volume in 2008, an increase of 27 percent over 2007. PayPal has captured 15 percent of U.S. e-commerce and 9 percent of global e-commerce trade. International business processing accounted for 45 percent of PayPal's total revenues for 2008. Higher fees earned on international transactions have provided eBay with higher revenues and gross margins in comparison to revenues from domestic transactions.

PayPal is available to any online or offline individual or business with an e-mail address and allows members to securely send and receive payments online securely without sharing sensitive financial information. PayPal is accepted both online and offline in 190 markets worldwide and processes payments in 19 currencies. PayPal also reports a very low percentage of 0.33 percent loss from fraud.

Bill Me Later, acquired by eBay Inc. in 2008, offers consumers instant credit at the point of sale through over 1000 online U.S. merchants. Retailers that offer the Bill Me Later service include: Borders, Continental Airlines, Fujitsu, JetBlue, Overstock, QVC, Toshiba, Toys "R" Us, and Walmart.com. Because Bill Me Later is not a chartered financial institution, an arrangement with CIT Bank allows Bill Me Later to extend credit to customers. When a consumer makes a purchase on credit, CIT Bank initiates a consumer loan at the point of sale. Bill Me Later then purchases the consumer's loan from CIT Bank. Bill Me Later earns revenues from interest on the outstanding balances, late fees, and transaction fees.

EBay's management seeks to become the number-one online payment solution. EBay plans to focus on improving the customer experience, enhancing security, expanding product offerings, enhancing buyer and seller protection programs, adding innovative features, and expanding its sales channels. Global expansion and increased revenues are to be gained by integrating PayPal with eBay.com listings and other Marketplaces businesses. Expansion into international markets and more currencies is expected to improve the ease and efficiency of cross-border transactions and grow both the Marketplaces and Payments segments.

Business Segment III: Communications

Skype

The Communications segment is composed of Skype, which was founded in 2003 and acquired by eBay in 2005. Skype is the world's fastest-growing Internet communication software platform. As of 2008, Skype had approximately 405.3 million registered users worldwide. Skype headquarters are located in Luxembourg, with global offices in Europe, the United States, and Asia. EBay's proprietary Skype technology has been downloaded more than a billion times. Why? Skype allows buyer/seller communications 24/7 in a secure and trusted community that is supported by free unlimited Internet voice and video communication to over 225 countries in 28 languages. Interestingly, nearly 11 million Skype downloads are to mobile devices.

Skype revenue is earned through premium services such as making/receiving domestic or international calls to and from landline and mobile phones, voicemail, call forwarding, and personalization, such as ringtones. As of December 2008, Skype had acquired 370 million users, a 51 percent growth over the same time a year ago. Registered subscribers are expected to reach 500 million by 2012 and revenues are anticipated to double by 2011. In 2008, Skype users logged approximately 16 billion minutes in a single quarter, an increase of 54 percent from the prior year. Large volumes are also easily supported by Skype software. At any given point in time there may be 300,000 simultaneous calls and over 100,000 information queries per second. Overall, Skype accounted for 6 percent of international worldwide calling minutes in 2007. Business calls represent 30 percent of current Skype usage and 25 percent of calls also use video technology.

EBay Inc. plans to implement a customer management program that emphasizes acquiring new users and upgrading current Skype users to premium products. Future plans include expanding Skype's desktop product to mobile user devices and other Web-based devices. Plans include also offering solutions to a more diverse business user and enhancing the Skype's current platform for greater revenues because the worldwide communications market is expected to grow by 5.5 percent annually with U.S. Web conferencing expected to grow 14.1 percent from 2008 through 2011 (eBay.com 2009). EBay's prior expenditures were focused on traditional wired routes; however, 50 percent of expenditures are now in the wireless telecommunications sector.

Competition

E-Bay competitors include: online and offline retailers, distributors, liquidators, import and export companies, online and offline auctioneers, catalog and mail-order companies, classifieds, directories, search engines, products of search engines, virtually all online and offline commerce participants (consumer-to-consumer, business-to-consumer and business-to-business), and online and offline shopping channels and networks. However, Amazon's strong growth and satisfied customer base pose the greatest threat to eBay.

The success of eBay and Amazon are built on similar customer-centric entrepreneurial business models that focus on customer-driven value creation. Examination of the strategies, business models, and customer benefits of eBay and Amazon reveals a common emphasis on relationship value and customer-focused solutions. The focus of eBay's business strategy is to compete on price, product selection, and services. However, growth of eBay has slowed and market share has declined in some segments. The Payments segment competes against other online payment services and offline payment methods, such as cash, check, money order, and established credit card merchants. The Communications segment faces competition from local telephone or cable companies and other VoIP providers. Furthermore, eBay anticipates the need for substantial resource investments in technology and marketing in order to remain competitive.

Highlight: Marketplaces Competition

Competition is expected to increase in the future because barriers to entry in this segment are low and new online sites can be launched at a nominal cost. Competitors include traditional department, warehouse, discount, and general merchandise stores, emerging online retailers, online classified services, and other offline and online home shopping networks such as Wal-Mart, Target, Sears, Macy's, J.C. Penney, Costco, Office Depot, Staples, OfficeMax, Sam's Club, Amazon.com, Buy.com, AOL.com, Yahoo! Shopping, MSN, QVC, and Home Shopping Network. Companies such as Google Base and Microsoft Live Expo also offer similar online services and classified ads.

Highlight: Skype Competition

Competition is intense in communications services and subject to rapid technological change. Traditional communications companies offer bundled services, such as cable or satellite television, along with internet and voice communications services. The potential also exists for Skype technology to become obsolete. Lastly, the resources of existing competitor firms are larger and as a result, competitors could weather an economic downturn.

Amazon.com (AMZN)

Amazon, a leading online retailer, reported net revenues of $19.2 billion as of year end 2008. From 2007 to 2008, sales grew at a rate of 29 percent (as indicated in Exhibit 2), even in a declining economic environment. Amazon has initiated alliances with partners

EXHIBIT 2   Amazon Gross Profit by Region

	Year Ended December 31		
Gross Profit by Region:	2006	2007	2008
		(in millions)	
Gross Profit:			
North America	$ 1,525	$ 2,031	$ 2,495
International	931	1,322	1,775
Consolidated	$ 2,456	$ 3,353	$ 4,270
Gross Profit Growth Rate:			
North America	20%	33%	23%
International	21	42	34
Consolidated	20	37	27
Gross Margin:			
North America	26.0%	25.1%	24.4%
International	19.2	19.6	19.9
Consolidated	22.9	22.6	22.3

Source: Amazon *10K* SEC Filing; Amazon.com.

to gains sales by referring customers to Amazon.com through several other online marketing channels such as: (1) syndicated store programs, (2) sponsored searches, (3) portal advertising, and (4) e-mail campaigns (Amazon.com, 2006, p. 37). Amazon also generates fees from online auctions and web hosting for business e-commerce. Amazon states their success is based on: the ability to attract buyers and sellers; the volume of transactions, price, and selection of goods; customer service; brand recognition, community cohesion, interaction, and size; system reliability; delivery and payment reliability; Web site convenience and accessibility; level of service fees; and quality of search tools (eBay, 2006).

Economic Climate

Weak global economic conditions, in addition to the mortgage and worldwide credit-related financial crisis, are expected to limit revenue growth, particularly in the Marketplaces segment, which is closely tied to consumer purchase patterns.

Given that eBay conducts approximately 45 percent of its business outside the United States, profitability is also affected by currency exchange rates. Specifically, PayPal uses fixed exchange rate conversions and holds assets in foreign currency denominations. If the U.S. dollar weakens against foreign currencies, transactions conducted in foreign currency denominations will increase and inflate revenues, operating expenses, and net income. Alternatively, financial measures will be negatively impacted by a rise in the value of the U.S. dollar.

In response to the weak economy, eBay undertook a 10 percent reduction in its workforce with the elimination of 1,000 jobs in 2008 and incurred $49,000 in restructuring costs. In the same year, eBay acquired Bill Me Later and announced an anticipated second acquisition of a vehicle classified ad site, eBay Motors.

Bill Me Later Risk

Although Bill Me Later accounts are funded by CIT Bank, Bill Me Later is responsible for all functions related to the account. Bill Me Later initially funds consumers' loans using cash from business activities and a line of credit. As a result of the global financial crisis, eBay's available line of credit was reduced. If credit availability is further reduced, Bill Me Later may not be able to extend credit to customers. Future profitability depends on the ability to manage credit while attracting new profitable consumers. EBay's Bill Me Later has significant exposure to consumers' potential default on loans.

Political and Legal Environment

Sales Tax and Other Taxes

EBay Inc. does not collect taxes on the sale of goods or services. However, legislation is in effect which requires collection of taxes beginning after December 31, 2010. This new legislation may cause a reduction in trading activity that would negatively affect several business segments. In addition, tax compliance will increase costs.

Long-term Contractual Obligations

EBay is involved in long-term contractual agreements with firms that provide marketing, customer support, and technology. If revenue significantly declines, eBay may not be able to meet contractual obligations. EBay recently increased its fee structure for its Marketplaces business, which may negatively impact the number of new customers and revenue from existing users. Any reduction in trading would also spillover to a reduction in PayPal revenues.

Pirated or Counterfeit Items

EBay has recently been involved in litigation with Tiffany & Co., Rolex, Louis Vuitton, Christian Dior, L'Oréal, and Lancôme for a lack of policing trade and infringement on trademarks and copyrights for the sale of "not for resale" and counterfeit items on eBay's Web sites. In June 2008, eBay Inc. was found liable for damages in the amount of €38.6 million Euro payable to the Louis Vuitton and Christian Dior firms. Pending lawsuits may adversely affect future profitability if eBay is found liable. The German Federal Supreme Court has also ruled that eBay may owe penalties from illegal listings of counterfeit and stolen goods. These events may also negatively affect eBay's reputation. In order to halt illegal activity, eBay has indicated that it may need to invest a substantial amount of resources.

Legislation has also been proposed to prohibit sharing of certain information over the Internet, such as comments provided by customers in eBay's Feedback Forum. This limitation would adversely affect eBay's ability to provide a reliable and secure community that shares purchase information and aspects of trades with other members of eBay's Marketplaces segment. Furthermore, as of October 2008 certain transactions on eBay.com purchased using PayPal are protected for the full purchase price in the event that the buyer does not receive the goods. This may result in greater losses and write-offs incurred by eBay Inc.

Security Breach and Identity Theft

Breaches in data security are on the rise. EBay's Korean subsidiary experienced a data breach that affected the majority of its 20 million users. Approximately 141,000 users have filed litigation. In Korea, courts have granted "consolation money" to plaintiffs. Significant resources are needed to upgrade security and insurance policies may not be adequate enough to cover potential losses.

Internal Challenges

Expansion of eBay both in the United States and internationally has placed a significant strain on management, operations, and financial resources. Particular areas that are strained include the following:

- *Web Site Usability.* Growth in the number of products and Web site features has caused the site to become less user-friendly.
- *Web Site Stability.* Increased volume and greater complexity requires additional expensive investments in hardware, software, and personnel.
- *Customer Account Billing.* Transaction-processing and revenue collection becomes more difficult as the number of transactions increase and consumers default on loans.
- *Customer Support.* Customer support is challenged from greater trade activity and an increased number of users.

Financial Overview

EBay's challenges include realizing the anticipated synergistic benefits of recent acquisitions and recouping goodwill costs that have inflated the purchase price of acquired businesses. For example, the $1.4 billion goodwill associated with the purchase of Skype must be recouped.

EBay experienced a downward trend in revenues, ending the 2008 year with an unimpressive performance. Total net revenue for the 2008 year increased 11 percent to $8.5 billion; however, this is a decrease in prior revenue growth of 29 percent experienced from 2006 to 2007. On a positive note, eBay's operating margin of 24 percent showed a return to the 24 percent to 32 percent range experienced over the years 2004 to 2008 after a dip to 8 percent in 2007. EBay claims that increased costs are due to greater customer support and Web site operations costs (28 percent increase), payment processing (24 percent increase) and Skype telecommunication costs (28 percent increase). Exhibit 3 shows eBay's consolidated income statement.

With regard to segment revenues, the Marketplaces segment reported only a 4 percent increase in revenue growth from 2007 to 2008, as opposed to the 24 percent growth from 2006 to 2007. Overall profitability was supported by other segments. The Payments segment earned a 25 percent increase in revenue over 2007, although this is a decrease in the 34 percent growth rate experienced from 2006 to 2007. The third business segment, Communications, reported strong growth of 44 percent from 2007 to 2008, albeit lower than the 96 percent growth reported from 2006 to 2007. Revenue growth details for each eBay segment are provided in Exhibit 4.

Revenue contributions by segment are provided in Exhibit 5. EBay's organizational structure is depicted in Exhibit 6.

EXHIBIT 3   eBay Consolidated Income Statement

5 Year Consolidated Statement of Income:	Year Ended December 31		
	2006	2007	2008
	(in thousands, except per share amounts)		
Net revenues	**$ 5,969,741**	**$ 7,672,329**	**$ 8,541,261**
Cost of net revenues	1,256,792	1,762,972	2,228,069
Gross profit	4,712,949	5,909,357	6,313,192
Operating expenses:			
Sales and marketing	1,587,133	1,882,810	1,881,551
Product development	494,695	619,727	725,600
General and administrative	744,363	904,681	998,871
Provision for transaction and loan losses	266,724	293,917	347,453
Amortization of acquired intangible assets	197,078	204,104	234,916
Restructuring	—	—	49,119
Impairment of goodwill	—	1,390,938	—
Total operating expenses	3,289,993	5,296,177	4,237,510
Income from operations	1,422,956	613,180	2,075,682
Interest and other income, net	130,017	154,271	115,919
Interest expense	(5,916)	(16,600)	(8,037)
Income before income taxes	1,547,057	750,851	2,183,564
Provision for income taxes	(421,418)	(402,600)	(404,090)
Net income	**$ 1,125,639**	**$ 348,251**	**$ 1,779,474**
Net income per share:			
Basic	$ 0.80	$ 0.26	$ 1.37
Diluted	$ 0.79	$ 0.25	$ 1.36
Weighted average shares:			
Basic	1,399,251	1,358,797	1,303,454
Diluted	1,425,472	1,376,174	1,312,608

Source: eBay *10K* SEC Filing; *Annual Report* (2009), eBay.com.

EXHIBIT 4   eBay Net Revenues by Segment and Geography (in thousands, except percent changes)

Net transaction revenues					
Marketplaces	$ 3,864,502	21%	$ 4,680,835	1%	$ 4,711,057
Payments	1,401,824	31%	1,838,539	26%	2,320,495
Communications	189,110	93%	364,564	44%	525,803
Total net transaction revenues	5,455,436	26%	6,883,938	10%	7,557,355
Marketing services and other revenues					
Marketplaces	469,788	45%	683,056	28%	875,694
Payments	38,706	128%	88,077	(6)%	83,174
Communications	5,811	197%	17,258	45%	25,038

continued

EXHIBIT 4 eBay Net Revenues by Segment and Geography (in thousands, except percent changes)—continued

Net transaction revenues

Total marketing services and other revenues	514,305	53%	788,391	25%	983,906
Total net revenues	$ 5,969,741	29%	$ 7,672,329	11%	$ 8,541,261
Net Revenues by Segment:					
Marketplaces	$ 4,334,290	24%	$ 5,363,891	4%	$ 5,586,751
Payments	1,440,530	34%	1,926,616	25%	2,403,669
Communications	194,921	96%	381,822	44%	550,841
Total net revenues	$ 5,969,741	29%	$ 7,672,329	11%	$ 8,541,261
Net Revenues by Geography:					
U.S.	$ 3,108,986	20%	$ 3,742,670	6%	$ 3,969,482
International	2,860,755	37%	3,929,659	16%	4,571,779
Total net revenues	$ 5,969,741	29%	$ 7,672,329	11%	$ 8,541,261

Source: eBay *10K* SEC Filing; *Annual Report* (2009), eBay.com.

EXHIBIT 5 eBay Percentage Change in Expenses for Years 2006–2008

% Change in Expenses 2006 - 2008	Year Ended December 31			Change from 2006 to 2007		Change from 2007 to 2008	
	2006	2007	2008	in Dollars	in %	in Dollars	in %
			(in thousands, except percentages)				
Cost of net revenues	$1,256,792	$1,762,972	$2,228,069	$506,180	**40%**	$465,097	**26%**
Sales and marketing	1,587,133	1,882,810	1,881,551	295,677	**19%**	(1,259)	**(0)%**
Product development	494,695	619,727	725,600	125,032	**25%**	105,873	**17%**
General and administrative	744,363	904,681	998,871	160,318	**22%**	94,190	**10%**
Provision for transaction and loan losses	266,724	293,917	347,453	27,193	**10%**	53,536	**18%**
Amortization of acquired intangible assets	197,078	204,104	234,916	7,026	**4%**	30,812	**15%**
Restructuring	—	—	49,119	—	—	49,119	**100%**
Impairment of goodwill	—	1,390,938	—	1,390,938	**100%**	(1,390,938)	**(100)%**
Interest and other income, net	130,017	154,271	115,919	24,254	**19%**	(38,352)	**(25)%**
Interest expense	5,916	16,600	8,037	10,684	**181%**	(8,563)	**(52)%**
Provision for income taxes	421,418	402,600	404,090	(18,818)	**(4)%**	1,490	**0%**

Source: eBay *10K* SEC Filing; *Annual Report* (2009), eBay.com.

EXHIBIT 6   eBay Supplemental Operating Data on Business Segments

	Year Ended December 31		
	2006	2007	2008
	(in millions)		
Supplemental Operating Data:			
Marketplaces Segment:			
Gross merchandise volume	$52,474	$59,353	$59,650
Payments Segment:			
Net total payment volume	$35,800	$47,470	$60,146
Communications Segment:			
Registered Users	171.2	276.3	405.3
SkypeOut Minutes	4,095	5,650	8,374

Source: eBay *10K* SEC Filing; *Annual Report* (2009), eBay.com.

EXHIBIT 7   eBay Consolidated Balance Sheet

CONSOLIDATED BALANCE SHEET	December 31, 2007	December 31, 2008
	(in thousands, except par value amounts)	
ASSETS		
Current assets:		
Cash and cash equivalents	$4,221,191	$3,188,928
Short-term investments	676,264	163,734
Accounts receivable, net	480,557	435,197
Loans receivable, net	—	570,071
Funds receivable and customer accounts	1,513,578	1,467,962
Other current assets	230,915	460,698
Total current assets	7,122,505	6,286,590
Long-term investments	138,237	106,178
Property and equipment, net	1,120,452	1,198,714
Goodwill	6,257,153	7,025,398
Intangible assets, net	596,038	736,134
Other assets	131,652	239,425
Total assets	**$15,366,037**	**$15,592,439**
LIABILITIES AND STOCKHOLDERS' EQUITY		
Current liabilities:		
Accounts payable	$156,613	$170,332
Funds payable and amounts due to customers	1,513,578	1,467,962
Accrued expenses and other current liabilities	951,139	784,774
Deferred revenue and customer advances	166,495	181,596
Income taxes payable	111,754	100,423
Borrowings under credit agreement	200,000	1,000,000
Total current liabilities	3,099,579	3,705,087
Deferred and other tax liabilities, net	510,557	753,965
Other liabilities	51,299	49,529
Total liabilities	3,661,435	4,508,581

continued

EXHIBIT 7 eBay Consolidated Balance Sheet—continued

CONSOLIDATED BALANCE SHEET	December 31, 2007	December 31, 2008
	(in thousands, except par value amounts)	
Stockholders' equity:		
Common stock, $0.001 par value; 3,580,000 shares authorized; 1,350,219 and 1,282,025 shares outstanding	1,458	1,470
Additional paid-in capital	8,996,303	9,585,853
Treasury stock at cost, 107,522 and 188,200 shares	(3,184,981)	(5,376,970)
Retained earnings	4,190,546	5,970,020
Accumulated other comprehensive income	1,701,276	903,485
Total stockholders' equity	11,704,602	11,083,858
Total liabilities and stockholders' equity	**$15,366,037**	**$15,592,439**

Source: eBay *10K* SEC Filing; *Annual Report* (2009), eBay.com.

EXHIBIT 8 Organizational Chart

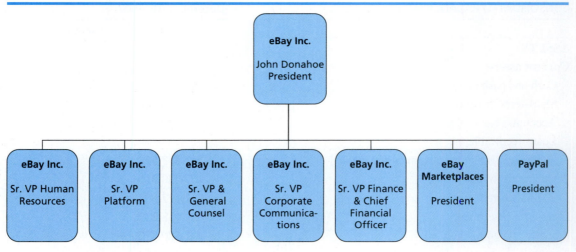

Source: eBay.com.

eBay's Future

For the quarter ending July 30, 2009, eBay's Payments division reported $669.3 million in revenue, an increase of 11 percent year over year. The growth was driven by continued momentum in PayPal Merchant Services and the contribution made by Bill Me Later. EBay's Marketplaces division reported $1.26 billion in revenue, a 14 percent year-over-year decline. The revenue drop was attributable to the impact of the stronger dollar and the lingering weak economy with high unemployment. Approximately 57 percent of Marketplaces revenue, however, came from markets outside of the United States. In eBay's Communications segment, Skype contributed $170.0 million in revenue for the quarter, representing 25 percent year-over-year growth. Skype added 37.3 million registered users during the quarter and ended the period with more than 480.5 million registered users.

The future for eBay is anything but certain. The company needs a clear strategic plan.

Wells Fargo Corporation — 2009

Donald L. Crooks
Wagner College

Robert S. Goodman
Wagner College

John Burbridge
Elon University[1]

WFC

www.wellsfargo.com

The year of 2009 witnessed continued deterioration in the housing and credit markets, high unemployment rates, and tight credit. Many banks are stuggling and many have recently failed, including Colonial National and Guaranty Financial Group. Like many banks today, Guaranty had more than $3 billion of securities backed by adjustable-rate mortgages. Delinquency rates on their holdings soared as high as 40 percent before federal officials seized the bank in August 2009. Many homeowners today cannot make mortgage payments. The value of houses has dropped below the amount borrowed, causing great problems for all.

This is the environment that Wells Fargo Bank and its competitors in the financial services industries face as they look to the future.

History

Wells Fargo is a storied name in American Old West folklore going back to the days of the stagecoach. Wells Fargo is the result of over 200 mergers including, most recently, Wachovia. The vast majority of these acquisitions, except for Wachovia, involved financial institutions in the far western part of the United States. An important acquisition came in 1998 when San Francisco–based Wells Fargo acquired Norwest Corporation in a stock swap that valued Wells Fargo at $34 billion. The result was a San Francisco–based bank with branches in 21 states in the West and Midwest, $191 billion in combined assets, and almost 6,000 service outlets worldwide. Because Norwest was the country's largest mortgage underwriter, the new bank became a major force in that market. It also had a presence in Canada, the Caribbean, Latin America, and other countries.

By the end of 2008, Wells Fargo had built a very creditable reputation and was widely recognized as an industry leader. The following statistics based on industry sources and government statistics clearly show its size and strength:

- 41st in revenue among all U.S. companies as ranked by *Fortune*
- 17th most profitable company in the United States
- 33rd largest employer in the United States
- 18th most respected company in the world as ranked by *Barron's*
- "Aaa" credit-rated by Moody's

EXHIBIT 1   **Wells Fargo Organizational Chart**

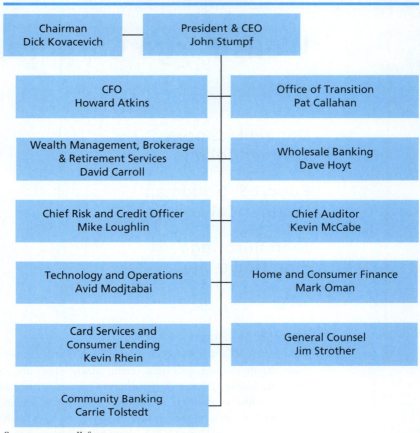

Source: www.wellsfargo.com.

- The only Standard & Poor's "AAA" bank in the United States.
- Among the top 50 companies as ranked by Diversity, Inc.
- Retail Banker of the Year according to *U.S. Banker*
- Number-one commercial real estate lender [number of transactions]
- 18th among the world's most valuable brands according to the *Financial Times*

Internal Issues

Vision and Ethics

> "Our product: SERVICE. Our Value-added: FINANCIAL ADVICE. Our competitive advantage: OUR PEOPLE."

Wells Fargo provides banking, insurance, investments, mortgage, and consumer finance services for more than 25 million customers through over 6,000 stores, the Internet, and other distribution channels across North America and elsewhere internationally. The company's statement says, "We're headquartered in San Francisco, but we are decentralized so every local Wells Fargo store is a headquarters for satisfying all our customers' financial needs and helping them succeed financially."

Wells Fargo strives to be the number-one financial services provider in each of their markets. As can be seen below, it has made great strides in that direction in the United States:

- Number-one small business lender
- Number-one agricultural lender
- Number-two debit card issuer
- Number-two prime home-equity lender
- Number-three mutual fund provider among U.S. banks

EXHIBIT 2   Wells Fargo/Wachovia U.S. Locations

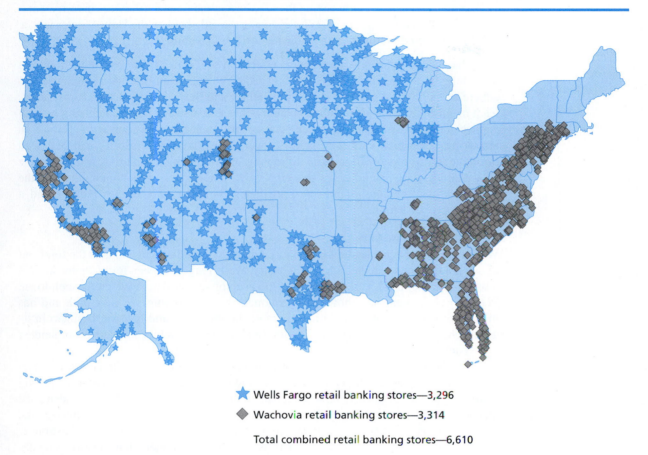

★ Wells Fargo retail banking stores—3,296

◆ Wachovia retail banking stores—3,314

Total combined retail banking stores—6,610

Source: Wells Fargo 4Q2008 financial results presentation.

Wells Fargo's chairman and CEO, Richard M. Kovacevich, discusses the bank's vision at length. He says, "This is not a task. This is a journey. Every journey has a destination. To get to that destination, you need a vision. Ours is an ambitious one."

Kovacevich further states, "We are a big company. We will continue to grow—not to become bigger but as a result of getting better. . . . Regardless of how big we are and how much territory we cover our team shares certain values that hold us together wherever we are and whatever we do."

Wells Fargo puts considerable emphasis on its culture and image as seen by the following values:

- Known by Our Own Team Members. "We'll be known as a company that believes in people as a competitive advantage, a great place to work, an employer of choice, a company that really cares about people, knows the value that a diverse work force can bring, that encourages innovation: new and better ways of serving customers."
- Known by Our Customers. "We want to be known by our customers as a financial partner, for outstanding service and sound financial advice, satisfying all of their financial needs and helping them to succeed financially. Our customers, external and internal, are our friends. They're the center of everything we do."
- Known by Our Communities. "We'll be regarded as the premier financial services company in each of our markets. We'll promote the economic advancement of everyone in our communities including those not yet able to be economically self-sufficient, who have yet to share fully in the prosperity of our extraordinary country. We'll be known as an active community leader in economic development, in services that promote economic self-sufficiency, education, social services and the arts."

- Known by Our Shareholders. "We'll be known as a great investment. We'll have financial results, not only among the very best in the financial services industry, but among the entire Fortune 500. Today, we're the only bank in the United States with a Moody's credit rating of "Aaa" [the highest possible rating].

Wells Fargo also believes that competing effectively and ethically are both at the forefront of its long-term objectives. Wells Fargo expects all of its team members (employees) to adhere to the highest possible standard of ethics and business conduct with customers, team members, stockholders, and the communities that it serves while complying with all applicable laws, rules, and regulations that govern its business. Its aim is to promote an atmosphere in which ethical behavior is well recognized as a priority and practiced throughout the organization. The following statement by Richard Kovacevich, the chairman and CEO, summarizes this emphasis: "Integrity is not a commodity. It's the most rare and precious of personal attributes. It is the core of a person's—and a company's—reputation."

Recent Performance

Wells Fargo has been a leading innovator in the use of the Internet and is in the forefront of using e-commerce in the financial industry. Wells Fargo has been fortunate to sidestep most of the subprime market mess and the accompanying derivative credit meltdown. Senior management has shown keen acumen in not pursuing the easy path and has moved forward to capture more and more of the mortgage and banking business in its geographic area. Wells Fargo has a vision (noted earlier), and its strategies complement that vision.

At the end of 2008, Wells Fargo was in an enviable position as the largest financial institution headquartered in the western United States. It has an unbroken record of paying increasing dividends since 1995, when it paid $0.0525 per share. In 2008, the dividend had increased to $0.34 per share. A strong balance sheet and the ability to steer through the pitfalls that plagued many of its larger competitors have allowed Wells Fargo a stronger force in the banking industry in 2009. This is an important moment in its history as it considers its future. The following information provides additional information concerning the present:

The Wachovia Acquisition

In the fall of 2008, Wells Fargo considered acquiring Wachovia Bank. Wachovia, headquartered in Charlotte, North Carolina, had been a rising East Coast bank growing by leaps and bounds over the previous decade. Since Wachovia's merger with First Union Bank a few years before, Wachovia seemed to be very well positioned to take the next step in order to compete with the likes of Bank of America, Citigroup, Merrill Lynch, and even Morgan Stanley. However, all was not well with Wachovia, which had its own subprime mortgage problems. It was also overcommitted in credit default swaps, the same issue that brought down Bear Stearns, Merrill Lynch, and Lehman Brothers.

Wells Fargo agreed to acquire all of Wachovia's almost 2.2 billion shares of stock for $7 per share. It also announced it would issue $20 billion in new shares to pay for the transaction. Wells Fargo was purchasing an extensive banking system, especially strong in the East but saddled with a large portfolio of subprime mortgages. So although there would be continued downward pressure on housing prices, the value of Wachovia could drop. Wells Fargo management could only make an educated guess of potential loss.

Wells Fargo and Wachovia saw this outwardly as a tremendous marriage of convenience presenting opportunities for one and survival for the other. Robert Steele, CEO of Wachovia, stated that the deal would enable Wachovia to remain intact and preserve the value of the integrated company without government support. Wells Fargo CEO Richard Kovacevich was quick to add that "the agreement provides superior value compared to the previous [Citigroup] offer to acquire only the banking operations of the company and because Wachovia shareholders will have a meaningful opportunity to participate in the growth and success of a combined Wachovia-Wells Fargo that will be one of the world's

EXHIBIT 3   Wells Fargo's Income Statements (all numbers in thousands)

PERIOD ENDING	31-Dec-08	31-Dec-07	31-Dec-06
Total Revenue	**$52,389,000**	**$53,593,000**	**$47,998,000**
Cost of Revenue	4,521,000	8,152,000	7,174,000
Gross Profit	**47,868,000**	**45,441,000**	**40,824,000**
Operating Expenses			
Research Development	—	—	—
Selling General and Administrative	22,661,000	22,824,000	20,742,000
Non Recurring	—	—	—
Others	16,716,000	4,939,000	2,223,000
Total Operating Expenses	—	—	—
Operating Income or Loss	**8,491,000**	**17,678,000**	**17,859,000**
Income from Continuing Operations			
Total Other Income/Expenses Net	—	—	—
Earnings Before Interest and Taxes	8,491,000	17,678,000	17,859,000
Interest Expense	5,234,000	6,051,000	5,114,000
Income Before Tax	3,257,000	11,627,000	12,745,000
Income Tax Expense	602,000	3,570,000	4,263,000
Minority Interest	—	—	—
Net Income from Continuing Ops	2,655,000	8,057,000	8,482,000
Non-recurring Events			
Discontinued Operations	—	—	—
Extraordinary Items	—	—	—
Effect of Accounting Changes	—	—	—
Other Items	—	—	—
Net Income	**2,655,000**	**8,057,000**	**8,482,000**
Preferred Stock and Other Adjustments	(286,000)	—	—
Net Income Applicable To Common Shares	**$ 2,369,000**	**$ 8,057,000**	**$ 8,482,000**

Source: www.wellsfargo.com.

EXHIBIT 4   Wells Fargo's Balance Sheets (all numbers in thousands)

PERIOD ENDING	31-Dec-08	31-Dec-07	31-Dec-06
Assets			
Current Assets			
Cash and Cash Equivalents	$ 23,763,000	$ 22,484,000	$ 20,635,000
Short Term Investments	49,433,000	2,754,000	6,078,000
Net Receivables	28,854,000	13,890,000	10,195,000
Inventory	—	—	—
Other Current Assets	—	—	—
Total Current Assets	—	—	—
Long Term Investments	1,110,195,000	502,358,000	415,326,000
Property Plant and Equipment	13,520,000	5,771,000	8,212,000
Goodwill	22,627,000	13,106,000	11,275,000
Intangible Assets	15,515,000	435,000	383,000
Accumulated Amortization	—	—	—
Other Assets	45,732,000	14,644,000	9,892,000
Deferred Long Term Asset Charges	—	—	—
Total Assets	**$1,309,639,000**	**$575,442,000**	**$481,996,000**

continued

EXHIBIT 4 Wells Fargo's Balance Sheets
(all numbers in thousands)—continued

PERIOD ENDING	31-Dec-08	31-Dec-07	31-Dec-06
Liabilities			
Current Liabilities			
Accounts Payable	53,921,000	30,706,000	25,903,000
Short/Current Long Term Debt	108,074,000	53,255,000	12,829,000
Other Current Liabilities	781,402,000	344,460,000	310,243,000
Total Current Liabilities	—	—	—
Long Term Debt	267,158,000	99,393,000	87,145,000
Other Liabilities	—	—	—
Deferred Long Term Liability Charges	—	—	—
Minority Interest	—	—	—
Negative Goodwill	—	—	—
Total Liabilities	**$1,210,555,000**	**$527,814,000**	**$436,120,000**
Stockholders' Equity			
Misc Stocks Options Warrants	—	—	—
Redeemable Preferred Stock	—	—	—
Preferred Stock	31,332,000	450,000	384,000
Common Stock	7,273,000	5,788,000	5,788,000
Retained Earnings	36,543,000	38,970,000	35,277,000
Treasury Stock	(4,666,000)	(6,035,000)	(3,203,000)
Capital Surplus	36,026,000	8,212,000	7,739,000
Other Stockholders' Equity	(7,424,000)	243,000	(109,000)
Total Stockholders' Equity	**99,084,000**	**47,628,000**	**45,876,000**
Total Liabilities and SE	**$1,309,639,000**	**$575,442,000**	**$481,996,000**

Source: www.wellsfargo.com.

EXHIBIT 5 Wells Fargo—Business Segment Results

(Income/Expense in $ millions, average balances in $ billions)

	2009	2008				
	Q1	FY	Q4	Q3	Q2	Q1
COMMUNITY BANKING						
Net interest income	8,497	20,542	5,296	5,293	5,235	4,718
Provision for credit losses	4,004	13,622	6,789	2,202	2,766	1,865
Noninterest income	5,456	12,424	2,096	3,209	3,637	3,482
Noninterest expense	7,158	16,507	4,320	3,982	4,300	3,905
Income (loss) before income tax exp. (benefit)	2,791	2,837	(3,717)	2,318	1,806	2,430
Income tax expense (benefit)	890	659	(1,606)	764	604	897
Net income (loss) b/ non-controlling interests	1,901	2,178	(2,111)	1,554	1,202	1,533
Less net income from non-controlling interests	62	32	(11)	14	18	11
Net income (loss)	1,839	2,146	(2,100)	1,540	1,184	1,522

continued

EXHIBIT 5   **Wells Fargo—Business Segment Results—continued**

(Income/Expense in $ millions, average balances in $ billions)

	2009		2008			
	Q1	FY	Q4	Q3	Q2	Q1
Average loans	552.8	n/a	288.9	287.1	283.2	282.7
Average assets	801.3	n/a	466.0	452.3	439.9	431.8
Average core deposits	538.0	n/a	260.6	252.8	251.1	246.6
WHOLESALE BANKING						
Net interest income	2,367	4,516	1,400	1,065	1,025	1,026
Provision for credit losses	545	1,115	414	294	246	161
Noninterest income	2,540	3,685	515	631	1,388	1,151
Noninterest expense	2,531	5,282	1,251	1,329	1,358	1,344
Income before income tax expense	1,831	1,804	250	73	809	672
Income tax expense	647	416	31	(30)	235	180
Net income (loss) b/ non-controlling interests	1,184	1,388	219	103	574	492
Less net income from non-controlling interests	4	11	4	—	(2)	9
Net income	1,180	1,377	215	103	576	483
Average loans	271.9	n/a	124.2	116.3	107.7	100.8
Average assets	400.4	n/a	163.2	158.1	151.4	140.0
Average core deposits	138.5	n/a	81	64.4	64.8	68.2
WEALTH, BROKERAGE & RETIREMENT SERVICES						
Net interest income	737	827	251	223	199	154
Provision for credit losses	25	302	293	3	4	2
Noninterest income	1,902	1,839	417	458	481	483
Noninterest expense	2,219	1,992	512	498	497	485
Income before income tax expense	395	372	(137)	180	179	150
Income tax expense	158	141	(52)	68	68	57
Net income (loss) b/ non-controlling interests	237	231	(85)	112	111	93
Less net income from non-controlling interests	(22)	—	—	—	—	—
Net income	259	231	(85)	112	111	93
Average loans	46.7	n/a	16.5	15.9	14.8	13.7
Average assets	104.0	n/a	20.0	19.1	17.8	16.7
Average core deposits	102.6	n/a	25.6	23.5	22.5	21.0
OTHER						
Net interest income	(225)	(742)	(223)	(200)	(181)	(138)
Provision for credit losses	(16)	940	948	(4)	(4)	—
Noninterest income	(257)	(1,214)	(275)	(302)	(324)	(313)
Noninterest expense	(90)	(1,183)	(273)	(308)	(310)	(292)
Income before income tax expense	(376)	(1,713)	(1,173)	(190)	(191)	(159)
Income tax expense (benefit)	(143)	(614)	(409)	(72)	(73)	(60)
Net income (loss) b/ non-controlling interests	(233)	(1,099)	(764)	(118)	(118)	(99)

continued

EXHIBIT 5 **Wells Fargo—Business Segment Results—continued**

(Income/Expense in $ millions, average balances in $ billions)

	2009	2008				
	Q1	FY	Q4	Q3	Q2	Q1
Less net income from non-controlling interests	—	—	—	—	—	—
Net income (loss)	(233)	(1,099)	(764)	(118)	(118)	(99)
Average loans	(15.8)	n/a	(15.7)	(15.1)	(14.2)	(13.3)
Average assets	(16.0)	n/a	(16.0)	(15.3)	(14.4)	(13.5)
Average core deposits	(25.2)	n/a	(22.2)	(20.6)	(20.0)	(18.5)

Source: www.wellsfargo.com.

great financial services companies." On the surface, the fourth and fifth largest banks in assets appear extremely similar. Both were oversized super-regional's that had never seemed to have national aspirations. Both emphasized consumer banking over lending to big institutional clients. Both were built on a platform of strong sales culture and attention to detail in operations.

The resultant combined company had total deposits of $787 billion and assets of $1.42 trillion, more than doubling Wells Fargo's totals on both counts. The bank will operate more than 10,000 locations and currently employs 280,000 people, although there will be anticipated downsizing because of duplication of labor and functions.

On December 31, 2008, the deal was completed, creating according to Wells Fargo's press release "The Most Extensive Financial Services Company, Coast-to-Coast in Community Banking." The new entity was traded on the New York Stock Exchange under the symbol WFC; the Wachovia symbol WB was retired.

The Future

The first half of 2009 was not kind to the banking industry or Wells Fargo. Moody's Investor Service reduced Wells Fargo's debt rating two levels during January, citing a "significantly weakened" capital position and the likelihood that Wachovia assets would hurt earnings. The shares lost half their value in January, falling to the lowest level since 1997. On March 6, 2009, Wells Fargo cut its dividend 85 percent to a nickel per share in a move to attempt to solidify its balance sheet.

As we enter the second half of 2009, the question facing Wells Fargo management is how to move this large national bank with an international presence forward. The banking industry has undergone an amazing transition in the past six months. Investment

EXHIBIT 6 **Selected Banks' Key Financial Data 2006–2008 ($ billions)**

	Wells Fargo			Citi			Bank of America		
	2008	2007	2006	2008	2007	2006	2008	2007	2006
Revenue	42.2	39.4	35.7	52.8	81.7	81.6	72.8	68.1	73.8
Net Income	2.8	8	8.4	(27.7)	3.6	21.5	3.6	14.9	21.1
P/E (%)	14.6	12.7	14.3	—	40.8	13.1	10.7	12.5	11.6
RoA (%)	0.44	1.55	1.73	(1.28)	0.17	1.28	0.22	0.94	1.44
RoE (%)	4.79	17.12	19.52	(28.8)	2.9	18.8	1.80	11.08	16.27

Source: Companies' 2007–2008 *Annual Reports*, except for P/E ratio where the source is Morningstar.

EXHIBIT 7 Wells Fargo versus Rivals

	Weels Fargo	Bank of America	Citigroup	US Bancorp	Industry Average
Market Cap	130.52B	151.06B	25.89B	42.60B	19.63B
Employees	269,900	283,000	279,000	57,904	42.31K
Qtrly Rev Growth	106.20%	33.10%	68.00%	−14.40%	11.70%
Revenue	42.84B	62.09B	34.69B	10.15B	7.98B
Oper Margins	21.64%	15.44%	−57.85%	26.57%	23.69%
Net Income	3.58B	3.47B	−23.79B	1.46B	n/a
EPS	0.912	0.597	−3.651	0.820	0.91

Source: Company *Form 10k* Reports and www.france.yahoo.com.

banks have all but disappeared. The large national banks have become bigger while community banks still exist to satisfy local communities. All of the larger banks world-wide are attempting to grow globally. The lack of regulation today has blurred the products and services banks offer. Given the lingering economic recession and changes in the banking industry, how should Wells Fargo Bank proceed from a strategic and operational standpoint during the next few years? This is the question facing the Wells Fargo board and its chairman and CEO.

In July 2009, Wells Fargo announced that the firm is significantly expanding its securities business that it largely inherited from Wachovia. Prior to the December 31, 2008, Wachovia acquisition, Wells Fargo basically did no securities business. The new business at Wells Fargo is to be called Wells Fargo Secuities and will begin offering merger advice, stock and bond underwriting, loan syndications, and fixed-income trading.

Wells Fargo today has approximately 6,700 bank branches in some 40 states. It also has more than 4,000 mortgage and consumer finance offices nationwide and is one of the largest residential mortgage lenders in the United States.

How should Wells Fargo position itself in the future? Should it strengthen its retail presence, grow internationally, or move into the void created by the disappearance of investment banks? This case provides the opportunity to analyze the future of the financial services industry and develop a plan to position Wells Fargo to better compete in this industry over the next several years.

Endnotes

1. The authors would like to thank Alex Profis, Dr. Donald Crooks's graduate assistant at Wagner College, who helped tremendously with research for this case study.

12   Krispy Kreme Doughnuts (KKD) — 2009

John Burbridge

Coleman Rich
Elon University

KKD

www.krispykreme.com

In early 2009, Yahoo Finance published a list of 15 firms that have a high probability of going bankrupt during the year. Krispy Kreme was on the list. KKD's fiscal 2009 year ended on February 1, 2009. On June 5, 2009, KKD reported a 53 percent drop in its first-quarter 2010 earnings to $1.9 million, down from $4 million the prior year. KKD's revenue decreased 9.9 percent to $93.4 million. KKD's sales for that first quarter, however, were up 2.1 percent at KKD company-owned stores as opposed to franchised stores. Krispy Kreme needs a clear strategic plan to survive through 2011 and beyond while competing against Dunkin' Donuts, Starbucks, and even McDonald's.

History

Although Krispy Kreme (KKD) is perceived as a North Carolina institution, its origins are in Louisiana and Kentucky. The founder of Krispy Kreme, Vernon Randolph, worked at his uncle's shop in Paducah, Kentucky, when the uncle purchased a secret recipe for making doughnuts from someone in Lake Charles, Louisiana. After working for his uncle, Vernon took the recipe to Nashville, Tennessee, to be part of a startup operation. After a relatively short time, Vernon sold his interest in the Nashville store and opened the first Krispy Kreme operation in Winston-Salem, North Carolina, in 1937. Initially, the company sold its doughnuts to local grocery stores. However, Vernon quickly realized that a direct market existed and began selling his hot glazed doughnuts to customers coming to the Winston-Salem location.

As a result of the initial success in North Carolina, Krispy Kreme began expanding throughout the Southeast. With expansion in the 1950s, the process of making doughnuts was transformed to an entirely mechanized process with the introduction of an automatic dough cutter. A further change was introduced in 1962 when an extrusion process replacing cutting.

In 1976, KKD became a wholly owned subsidiary of Beatrice Foods. However, in 1982, a group of franchisees dissatisfied with Krispy Kreme being part of a large organization purchased the business back from Beatrice. Krispy Kreme spent the rest of the 1980s expanding and strengthening its position in the southeastern United States.

As the stock market soared in the late 1990s, the idea of going public intrigued the Krispy Kreme management. In 2000, Krispy Kreme was very successful in raising significant capital with its initial public offering. At first, the shares of stock were traded on the NASDAQ using the ticker symbol KREM. Since May 17, 2001, Krispy Kreme has been listed on the New York Stock exchange under the current symbol, KKD.

After going public, Krispy Kreme went through a period of rapid expansion both domestically and, to some degree, internationally. The stock price quadrupled and opportunities appeared to prove endless. The hot sugar-glazed Krispy Kreme doughnut had a mystique associated with it. Krispy Kreme became a hot brand. Investors pursued exclusive franchising rights to open stores in various parts of the country. A franchise producing high-quality southern-style doughnuts freshly baked in an observable oven was a concept that generated great interest. Opportunities for this hot brand seemed endless. KKD opened its first store in Canada in 2001. By 2004 Krispy Kreme was also operating stores in Australia and South Korea.

The year 2004 began a period of steep decline for Krispy Kreme. Early that year, Krispy Kreme announced that it had missed its quarterly earnings forecast and posted its first loss ever. The company blamed a diet-conscious public pursuing the low-carbohydrate Atkins diet for its problems. The stock price plunged from $40 per share to under $10.

Since 2005, Krispy Kreme has gone through a period of contraction. In Arizona and New Mexico, the main franchisee filed for bankruptcy closing all the Krispy Kreme stores. In 2008, another franchisee opened some stores in those states. In 2006, Krispy Kreme terminated the franchise license of Great Circle Family Foods that operated 28 stores in California. While the dispute was settled, Great Circle filed for Chapter 11 bank-ruptcy in 2007. Sheetz, a large convenience store chain on the East Coast and one of Krispy Kreme's largest customers, quit buying doughnuts in 2008 because it decided to open its own kitchen. Finally, international outlets shrunk with stores in Canada and Hong Kong shut down.

These trends have impacted the profitability of the company. For the last three fiscal years, KKD has posted an operating loss. Quarterly earnings while mainly negative have been quite erratic. The year 2008 has seen more bad news with all quarterly earnings negative.

Exhibits 1 and 2 show both the income statements and balance sheets for the past three fiscal years.

In 2006, turnaround artist Stephen Cooper left Krispy Kreme, and Darryl Brewster became CEO. Brewster left the company in early 2008. The CEO position was filled by Jim Morgan, who continues to serve as chairman today. Krispy Kreme, however, continues to experience declining sales in the United States. A more health-conscious public has tended to shy away from glazed doughnuts, which have the perception of too many calories and carbohydrates.

EXHIBIT 1   Krispy Kreme Doughnuts Income Statement

	Period Ended February 1, 2009 (in thousands)		
	1-Feb-09	3-Feb-08	28-Jan-07
Revenues	**$ 383,984**	**429,319**	**461,195**
Operating expenses:	—	—	—
Direct operating expenses (exclusive of depreciation and amortization shown below)	345,007	380,014	389,379
General and administrative expenses	23,458	26,303	48,860
Depreciation and amortization expense	8,709	18,433	21,046
Impairment charges and lease termination costs	548	62,073	12,519
Settlement of litigation	—	(14,930)	15,972
Other operating (income) and expense, net	1,501	13	1,916
Operating income (loss)	$ 4,761	$(42,587)	$(28,497)
Interest income	331	1,422	1,627
Interest expense	(10,679)	(9,796)	(20,334)
Loss on extinguishment of debt	—	(9,622)	—
Equity in losses of equity method franchisees	(786)	(933)	(842)
Other non-operating income and (expense), net	2,815	(3,211)	7,021
Loss before income taxes	$(3,558)	$(64,727)	$(41,025)
Provision for income taxes	503	2,324	1,211
Net loss	**$(4,061)**	**$(67,051)**	**$(42,236)**

Source: www.krispykreme.com.

EXHIBIT 2 **Krispy Kreme's Balance Sheets (all numbers in thousands)**

PERIOD ENDING	1-Feb-09	3-Feb-08	28-Jan-07
Assets			
Current Assets			
Cash and Cash Equivalents	35,538	24,735	36,242
Short Term Investments	—	—	—
Net Receivables	20,770	26,764	64,227
Inventory	15,587	19,987	26,162
Other Current Assets	3,911	4,594	5,187
Total Current Assets	**75,806**	**76,080**	**131,818**
Long Term Investments	1,365	2,024	4,261
Property Plant and Equipment	85,075	90,996	168,654
Goodwill	23,496	23,496	28,094
Intangible Assets	1,036	1,531	1,900
Accumulated Amortization	—	—	—
Other Assets	6,144	5,855	9,226
Deferred Long Term Asset Charges	2,004	2,369	5,539
Total Assets	**194,926**	**202,351**	**349,492**
Libilities			
Current Liabilities			
Accounts Payable	27,816	30,630	133,140
Short/Current Long Term Debt	3,761	3,788	1,730
Other Current Liabilities	8,039	8,800	—
Total Current Liabilities	**39,616**	**43,218**	**134,870**
Long Term Dept	97,449	75,156	105,966
Other Liabilities	—	23,865	25,656
Deferred Long Term Liability Charges	106	3,488	4,038
Minority Interest	—	—	—
Negative Goodwill	—	—	—
Total Liabilities	**137,171**	**145,727**	**270,530**
Stockholders' Equity			
Misc Stocks Options Warrants	—	—	—
Redeemable Preferred Stock	—	—	—
Preferred Stock	—	—	—
Common Stock	361,801	355,615	310,942
Retained Earnings	(303,133)	(299,072)	(233,246)
Treasury Stock	—	—	—
Capital Surplus	—	—	—
Other Stockholders' Equity	(913)	81	1,266
Total Stockholders' Equity	**57,755**	**56,624**	**78,962**
Total Liabilities and SE	**194,926**	**202,351**	**349,492**

Source: www.krispykreme.com.

KKD Divisions and Operations

As of February 1, 2009, the end of the last fiscal year, Krispy Kreme was operating 523 stores in the United States, Australia, Bahrain, Canada, Hong Kong, Indonesia, Japan, Kuwait, Lebanon, Mexico, the Philippines, Puerto Rico, Qatar, Saudi Arabia, South Korea, the United Arab Emirates, and the United Kingdom.

There are two types of Krispy Kreme stores. Again, as of February 1, 2009, there are 281 factory stores with 185 of these stores located in the United States. Factory stores usually contain a doughnut-making production line in addition to a retail establishment. They can produce from 4,000 to 10,000 dozen doughnuts daily. Factory stores support other sales channels, including other stores, so as to better penetrate the market. These other sales channels include sales to convenience stores, grocery stores, mass merchants, and other food service and institutional accounts. Some factory stores are termed commissaries, which are mainly focused on serving the other sales channels. To do so, they have higher production capacities. There were 19 commissaries worldwide with six operated by Krispy Kreme as of February 1, 2009.

The second type of KKD store is the satellite store, which sells doughnuts and beverages. Some satellite stores contain what is termed a hot shop, tunnel oven doughnut heating equipment, which allows the consumer to have a hot doughnut experience. Even with a hot shop, satellite stores are much smaller than a factory store. Another form of satellite store is the kiosk format.

Exhibit 3 shows the numbers of each store at the end of the last four fiscal years.

KKD revenue is generated from three main sources:

1. Company stores, meaning stores owned by Krispy Kreme (Company Stores). Revenue is generated through on-premises sales meaning customers coming to either the factory or satellite store or through promotions with community organizations. Both doughnuts and beverages are sold. The majority of the sales outside the United States are on-premises. Off-premises sales are also a source of revenue. Krispy Kreme branded doughnuts are sold through a variety of outlets such as convenience and supermarkets. In these outlets, the doughnuts are placed on shelves or on specifically designed display units or cases.

EXHIBIT 3   Number of Each Type of Store at the End of FYs 2009, 2008, 2007, and 2006

	At February 1, 2009	At February 3, 2008	At January 28, 2007	At January 29, 2006
By Owner				
Company Stores	93	105	113	133
Franchise Stores	430	344	282	269
Total Systemwide	523	449	395	402
By Type				
Factory Stores				
Company	83	97	108	128
Franchise	198	198	188	195
Total Factory Stores	281	295	296	323
Satellites				
Company	10	8	5	5
Franchise	232	146	94	74
Total Satellites	242	154	99	79
Total Systemwide	523	449	395	402
By Location				
Domestic Stores				
Company	93	100	107	127
Franchise	132	145	165	207
Total Domestic Stores	225	245	272	334
International Stores				
Company	5	6	6	
Franchise	298	199	117	62
Total International Stores	298	204	123	68
Total Systemwide	523	449	395	402

Source: Krispy Kreme's 2009 *Form 10K.*

2. Franchise fees and royalties from franchisees (Franchise). Revenues are generated through the collection of franchise fees and royalties resulting from sales of the Krispy Kreme products by the franchisees.
3. Vertically integrated supply chain (KK Supply Chain). The KK Supply Chain produces doughnut mixes and also manufactures the doughnut-making equipment, which all factory stores are required to purchase. KK Supply Chain also operates two distribution centers that provide stores with supplies. The Supply Chain also is responsible for the purchasing of the necessary raw materials, which are primarily flour, sugar, and shortening. Other ingredients are purchased through various commodity markets.

There are four business units within KK Supply:

- Mix manufacturing. All proprietary doughnut mixes are produced in Winston-Salem, North Carolina. All franchisees are required to use these proprietary mixes. For international operations, a concentrate is produced in Winston-Salem, shipped internationally, and mixed with local sources of supply.
- Equipment. Krispy Kreme manufactures its doughnut-making equipment, which all franchisees are required to use. The line of machines can produce from 65 to 1,000 dozen doughnuts per hour. Smaller machines such as the tunnel ovens used in hot shops are sold by Krispy Kreme but manufactured by others.
- Beverage program. Many of the beverages purchased from third parties are provided by Krispy Kreme.
- Distribution centers. The distribution centers are located in Winston-Salem and the greater Los Angeles area. These centers supply the domestic stores and some international operations with supplies.

Exhibit 4 shows Krispy Kreme revenues and expenses by business segment for the last three fiscal years.

EXHIBIT 4   **Krispy Kreme Doughnuts Segmented Revenues and Expenses**

| | (in thousands) | | |
YEAR ENDED	Feb. 1, 2009	Feb. 3, 2008	Jan. 28, 2007
REVENUES BY BUSINESS SEGMENT:			
Company Stores	$ 265,890	$ 304,444	$326,199
Franchise	25,537	22,958	21,075
KK Supply Chain	92,557	101,917	113,921
Total Revenues	$ 388,984	$ 429,319	$ 461,195
OPERATING EXPENSES BY BUSINESS MANAGEMENT :			
Company Stores	$ 268,098	$ 299,806	$ 307,635
Franchise	8,936	8,746	4,602
KK Supply Chain	67,973	71,462	77,142
Total Operating Expenses	$ 345,007	$ 380,014	$ 389,379
DEPRECIATION AND AMORTIZATION EXPENSES :			
Company Stores	$ 6,402	$ 11,558	$ 15,979
Franchise	86	92	119
KK Supply Chain	1,019	5,586	3,469
Corporate administration	1,202	1,197	1,479
Total depreciation and amortization expenses	$ 8,709	$ 18,433	$ 21,046

Source: Krispy Kreme Doughnuts Inc. *2009 Annual Report*, p. 34, 92.

Mission and Vision

The current company philosophy is geared to continuing making the Krispy Kreme doughnut the centerpiece of the business and to grow that business internationally. It is strongly believed that Krispy Kreme has a unique product, a heated fresh doughnut with a distinctive taste. The mission and values statements are as follows:

Vision
- To be the global leader in doughnuts and complementary products while creating magic moments worldwide.

Values (with acknowledgment to our Founder, Vernon Rudolph)

We Believe . . .

- Consumers are our lifeblood, the center of the doughnut
- There is no substitute for quality in our service to consumers
- Impeccable presentation is critical wherever Krispy Kreme is sold
- We must produce a collaborative team effort that is unexcelled
- We must cast the best possible image in all that we do
- We must never settle for "second best"; we deliver on our commitments
- We must coach our team to ever-better results

Competition

Dunkin' Donuts

The most formidable KKD competitor is Dunkin' Donuts. Another doughnut competitor is Tim Hortons, a Canadian firm that has over 3,400 stores mainly in Canada but more than 500 stores in the United States. Dunkin' Donuts, which is part of Dunkin' Brands and is privately owned, has the largest number of stores in the retail doughnut industry. As of 2008, Dunkin' Donuts has a total of 6,395 domestic franchisees and 2,440 international locations in 31 countries. Dunkin' Donuts is a baked goods coffee shop using the original coffee blend created by its founder. Sales can be classified in two categories: beverages or coffee make up 60 percent of sales and baked goods or doughnuts, muffins, and bagels make up the remaining 40 percent of sales.

Dunkin' continue to grow sales by expanding their baked goods menu offerings and through other retail channels for their coffee outside their franchises. Their customer base is fiercely loyal to the Dunkin' Donuts brand. They are working people who just want a cup of coffee and quick bite to eat so they can move on to their work day. Dunkin' Donuts originated in Massachusetts and seeks to grow in the southern and western states of the United States and expand into China. In addition to Dunkin' Donuts and Tim Hortons as competitors, there are many regional and locally owned doughnut shops and distributors.

Starbucks

Recently, there has been a growth in coffeehouses such as Starbucks, Caribou Coffee, and Java City and ice cream shops that all sell doughnuts and other baked items. The most formidable of these is Starbucks. This specialty coffee retailer has over 176,000 employees in 9,217 company-operated stores and 7,463 licensed retails stores worldwide. The company is not only known for its coffee but also branded products sold through multiple retail channels worldwide. Some of these products include ice cream, coffee liqueur, teas, and instant coffee. Like Dunkin' Donuts, Starbucks has strong brand loyalty toward its quality products. Starbucks, which has less food offerings than Dunkin' Donuts, looks to capitalize on creating a "Starbucks Experience," which not only provides a comfortable atmosphere to enjoy a cup of coffee but also rewards customers for their loyalty through their Starbucks Rewards program.

Krispy Kreme also sells its doughnuts in major retail outlets. Therefore, it is also competing with any company selling baked goods in supermarkets, convenience

EXHIBIT 5   Doughnut Sales for Calendar Year 2007

Doughnuts 2007		
Top 10 Brands of Doughnuts (for the 52 weeks ending November 4, 2007)		
Brand Name	Dollar Sales	Unit Sales
Krispy Kreme	$130,409,808	42,774,572
Private Label	$ 88,304,008	38,358,984
Entenmann's	$ 85,233,104	25,656,796
Hostess Donettes	$ 83,839,496	36,445,068
Entenmann's Softees	$ 33,668,032	10,643,769
Little Debbie	$ 30,860,856	24,837,084
Entenmann's Extreme Pop'ems	$ 17,163,728	5,244,544
Hostess	$ 17,089,810	5,745,155
Merita	$ 13,363,270	6,303,118
Blue Bird	$ 11,534,341	8,092,483

Source: Baking Management (January 2008): 10.

stores, mass merchants, and other retail establishments. Dolly Madison, Entenmann's, Hostess, and regional brands are competitors of Krispy Kreme in this marketing channel.

Exhibit 5 shows doughnut sales for calendar year 2007 for Krispy Kreme and competitors.

Although Krispy Kreme has 20 different doughnut products, the signature offering is the hot glazed doughnut. From its origins, Krispy Kreme has marketed not only the doughnut but that eating such a doughnut is a unique experience. Krispy Kreme also enhanced the experience by providing its customers with the ability of seeing the doughnuts produced in many stores.

Exhibit 6 shows the organization chart for Krispy Kreme.

Operations

The main operations associated with Krispy Kreme are its stores. For each store, whether owned by Krispy Kreme or a franchisee, there are uniform specifications and designs. These specifications and designs include products, appropriate sales channels, packaging, signage, use of logos and trademarks, marketing and advertising, and the furniture and fixtures. As can be seen, Krispy Kreme controls the image projected in all stores.

EXHIBIT 6   Krispy Kreme Organizational Chart

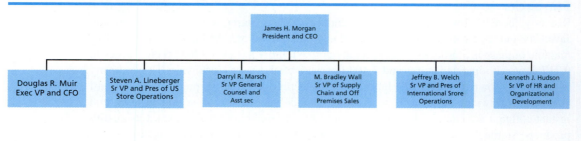

Source: Based on information in Krispy Kreme's 2009 *Form 10K.*

All stores are required to have a specific point of sale (POS) system. In addition to providing the ability to manage on-premises sales, the POS system provides headquarters and permits stores to communicate with each other. The headquarters site in Winston-Salem retrieves sales information from the POS system and price changes can be downloaded to the POS system within a store.

Krispy Kreme also has an enterprise resource planning (ERP) system that supports both the financial and operating needs of the organization. Embedded within the ERP system is a data warehouse that also supports the Company Stores and KK Supply Chain. The mix manufacturing facility is in Winston-Salem. Krispy Kreme had opened a plant in Effingham, Illinois, but closed it in January 2008. The result was a total consolidation of all mix manufacturing at Winston-Salem.

Mix manufacturing is critical in supporting the high quality of Krispy Kreme doughnuts. To ensure high quality, the following has been instituted:

1. To ensure freshness, truckloads of the main ingredients are received on a regular basis,
2. Each incoming shipment of ingredients is tested, and
3. Each batch of mix is tested.

In addition to mix manufacturing, Krispy Kreme also produces the primary doughnut-making equipment. Franchisees are required to use such equipment.

The two main distribution centers are located in Winston-Salem and the greater Los Angeles area. The various types of stores are serviced through these centers.

Global Issues

Markets outside the United States are a great source of growth for KKD. In the last fiscal year, Krispy Kreme saw a net increase of 94 new international stores while experiencing a net loss of 20 stores in the United States. Much of this expansion is in the Middle East and Asia. The rationale for expanding in these areas is their favorable demographics, relatively high levels of sweet goods consumption, and the acceptability of Western brands. As of February 3, 2008, KKD planned to open an additional 170 stores in fiscal year 2009 and beyond.

Future Risks

Krispy Kreme recently reported that its franchisees have grown stronger and it may open 160 more new stores internationally in 2010 and beyond while acknowledging its domestic franchisees still face financial strain. This international strategy is consistent with prior announcements. However, the key questions still remain. Can Krispy Kreme survive? What should its turnaround strategy be?

References

Anderson, J. Richard. "Lessons from Krispy Kreme." *Journal of Business Case Studies* 4, no. 4 (2008).

Duff, Cynthia. "Krispy Kreme Doughnuts Inc.—2004." In *Strategic Management,* ed. Fred David (New York: McGraw-Hill, 2005).

"Dunkin' Brands, Company Profile." *Datamonitor.* Reproduced in Business Source Premier EBSCOhost, Belk Library. Elon, NC: Elon University, 2008.

Gutierrez, B. M. "Krispy Kreme's Struggles Have It Looking Overseas for Growth Opportunities." *The Business Journal of the Greater Triad Area* (September 5, 2008).

http://banker.thomsonib.com

http://en.wikipedia.org/wiki/Krispy_Kreme

http://finance.yahoo.com/news/15-Companies-That-Might-Not-usnews-14279875.html

http://www.krispykreme.com

"Krispy Kreme CEO Resigns; New Chief Executive Named." *The Business Journal of the Greater Triad Area* (January 7, 2008).

Krispy Kreme *Form 10-K* for the fiscal year ended February 3, 2008. Winston-Salem, NC: Krispy Kreme.

Krispy Kreme *Form 10-K* for the fiscal year ended February 1, 2009. Winston-Salem, NC: Krispy Kreme.

"Krispy Kreme to Open Stores in China." *The Business Journal of the Greater Triad Area* (October 9, 2008).

O'Daniel, A. "Big Holes to Fill: A Q&A with Krispy Kreme's Jim Morgan." *The Business Journal of the Greater Triad Area* (January 30–February 5, 2009): 9.

O'Sullivan, K. "Kremed! The Rise and Fall of Krispy Kreme Is a Cautionary Tale of Ambition, Greed, and Inexperience." *CFO Magazine* (June 1, 2005).

Reuters. "UPDATE 1—"Krispy Kreme May Open 160 Int'l Stores in 2010, Beyond." (April 17, 2009).

Shepherd, L. "Krispy Kreme Hopes to Heat Up Sales with Ice Cream." *USA Today* (September 21, 2008).

Starbucks Corporation, Company Profile. *Datamonitor*. Reproduced in Business Source Premier EBSCOhost, Belk Library. Elon, NC: Elon University, 2009.

13 Starbucks Corporation — 2009

Sharynn Tomlin
Angelo State University

SBUX

www.starbucks.com

You can now wake up to smell the $4.00 per cup coffee at Starbucks. But McDonald's is now running an ad saying, "$4.00 coffee is dumb" as the firm attacks Starbucks around the world with its $1.00 (and less) coffee. Starbucks needs a clear strategic to offset the new attacks of McDonald's that are trying to attract all Starbucks' customers.

In July 2009, Starbucks began grinding coffee each time a new pot is brewed, instead of grinding coffee only in the morning. Starbucks wants customers to smell coffee aroma all day long. This change is part of the company's effort to reinvigorate the "Starbucks experience" in the face of heavy competition from McDonald's, 7-Eleven, and Dunkin' Donuts. On June 15, 2009, 7-Eleven began rolling out iced coffee at its 5,000 self-service beverage counters across the United States. Iced coffee has become a very popular drink in the United States, especially among women and teenage girls. Iced coffee is clearly a female drink according to many analysts, perhaps because it is low calorie and high caffeine. To capitalize on this trend, Starbucks sold a 16-ounce iced coffee for $1.95 for the first half of 2009.

For the third quarter of 2009, Starbucks reported earnings of $151.5 million compared to a loss of $6.7 million the prior year. Howard Schultz, Starbucks's CEO, says the media exposure concerning McDonald's versus Starbucks coffee products actually helped his firm by creating "unprecedented awareness for the coffee category overall."

History

Starbucks was founded in 1971 by Gordon Bowker, Jerry Baldwin, and Zev Siegl, who joined forces to open a coffee shop in Seattle, Washington. By 1972, with the success of the first store, they opened a second store in University Village, Washington. Its wholesale business, which sold coffee primarily to local restaurants, changed its name to Caravali out of concern that the Starbucks' name would become tarnished by retailers who sold the coffee after its shelf life has expired. In the next 10 years, the business expanded to five stores and hired Howard Schultz to manage retail sales and marketing.

By 1993 the company ventured into the East Coast market in Washington, D.C., and entered into a venture with Barnes & Noble to sell its coffee at the bookseller's stores. At this point, the company had licensed 12 stores and was operating 260 company-owned facilities with revenues reaching $176.5 million and net earnings at $8.3 million.

Starbucks opened 200 new stores outside of the United States during 2000, 150 of which were in the Asia-Pacific region, and opened its first stores in Dubai and Hong Kong, and its 100th stores in both Japan and the United Kingdom. The following year, Starbucks opened a store in Zurich, Switzerland, marking its first venture into continental Europe.

Starbucks experienced its first setback in 2002 when its Japanese operation posted a $3.9 million loss, despite a 15 percent increase in revenues and 108 new store openings, and the first low performance locations were closed. But not discouraged by this, international expansion continued as Starbucks opened its first store in Turkey and acquired 129 Seattle's Best Coffee coffeehouses, as well as certain wholesale distribution rights. In the following two years, its long-term U.S. expansion goal was set at 50 percent and Starbucks announced it will eventually open 15,000 domestic outlets, and

30,000 worldwide. However, then the worldwide economic recession hit in 2007 and simultaneously McDonald's entered the coffee business big time. Starbucks closed 600 underperforming stores in the United States in 2008 and plans to open only about 200 new stores in 2009.

Structure, Mission, Vision

Starbucks' organizational chart is provided in Exhibit 1.

In a short, succinct statement, vision is "To inspire and nurture the human spirit—one person, one cup, and one neighborhood at a time." The company further elaborates by stating the following guiding principles:

EXHIBIT 1   Starbucks' Organizational Chart

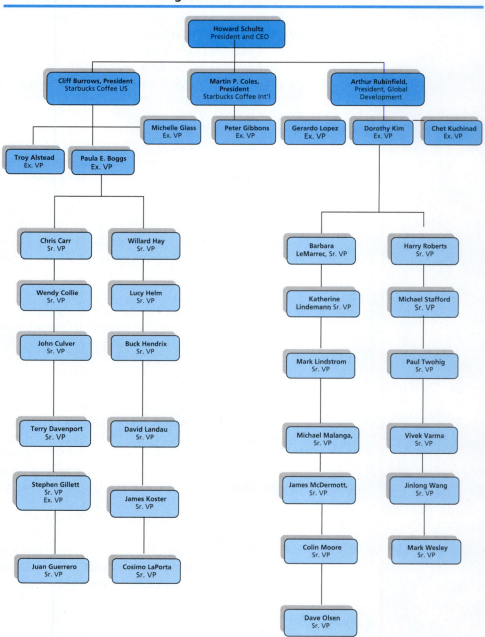

Source: www.starbucks.com.

Our Coffee

It has always been, and will always be, about quality. We're passionate about ethically sourcing the finest coffee beans, roasting them with great care, and improving the lives of people who grow them. We care deeply about all of this; our work is never done.

Our Partners

We're called partners, because it's not just a job, it's our passion. Together, we embrace diversity to create a place where each of us can be ourselves. We always treat each other with respect and dignity. And we hold each other to that standard.

Our Customers

When we are fully engaged, we connect with, laugh with, and uplift the lives of our customers—even if just for a few moments. Sure, it starts with the promise of a perfectly made beverage, but our work goes far beyond that. It's really about human connection.

Our Stores

When our customers feel this sense of belonging, our stores become a haven, a break from the worries outside, a place where you can meet with friends. It's about enjoyment at the speed of life—sometimes slow and savored, sometimes faster. Always full of humanity.

Our Neighborhood

Every store is part of a community, and we take our responsibility to be good neighbors seriously. We want to be invited in wherever we do business. We can be a force for positive action—bringing together our partners, customers, and the community to contribute every day. Now we see that our responsibility—and our potential for good—is even larger. The world is looking to Starbucks to set the new standard, yet again. We will lead.

Our Shareholders

We know that as we deliver in each of these areas, we enjoy the kind of success that rewards our shareholders. We are fully accountable to get each of these elements right so that Starbucks—and everyone it touches—can endure and thrive.[1]

Company Facilities

Marketing

Starbucks strives to elevate the simple task of drinking coffee to a new level with its retail outlets seen as a place for socialization, relaxation, and reflection. Its stores are designed to make customers comfortable. Starbucks also provides electrical outlets and, in some stores, wireless access, for customers who might need to use their MP3 players or laptop computers. Additionally, they have introduced the Starbucks' card with the hope of strengthening customer loyalty by improving service.

Research and development is constantly in pursuit of the new products and service that are both trendy and stable. Starbucks' products can be found in convenience stores, grocery stores, department stores, movie theaters, businesses, schools, and even airports. In response to recent economic times, the company has also adjusted prices on certain of its more popular products in an effort to show responsiveness to the more budget-conscious consumer. Starbucks relies more on its image advertising than traditional advertising. Part of that image is how the customer not only views the retail outlet but how responsible the company is to their communities and employees. Starbucks is rated by ten *Fortune* as one of the best top 10 places to work.[2] Starbucks also encourages the use of its Web site where customers are able to register their Starbucks' cards, receive nutritional information about Starbucks' products, shop online, search for careers, and much more.

Financial Position

Starbucks' income statements and balance sheets shown in Exhibits 2 and 3 reveal continuous growth in revenues, but a 47 percent drop in earnings in one year. For the 26 weeks ending March 2009, Starbucks' revenues decreased 7 percent to $4.95 billion and net income decreased 72 percent to $89.3 million. Moody's Investors Service recently downgraded Starbucks' credit ratings.

Fiscal 2009 Targets

Starbucks expects to add approximately 20 net new stores to its global store base in fiscal 2009. This plan includes closing approximately 425 company-operated stores in the United States and adding of approximately 60 company-operated stores internationally. The company plans to open approximately 65 net new licensed stores in the United States and approximately 320 net new licensed stores internationally. Capital expenditures for fiscal 2009 are expected to remain unchanged, at approximately $600 million.

Segments

Starbucks has three reportable operating segments: United States, International, and Global Consumer Products (CPG).

UNITED STATES The U.S. operations represent 80 percent of total company-operated retail revenues, 55 percent of total specialty revenues, and 76 percent of total net revenues

EXHIBIT 2 Starbucks' Income Statement (values in 000's)

PERIOD ENDING	28-Sep-08	30-Sep-07	1-Oct-06
Total Revenue	$10,383,000	9,411,497	7,786,942
Cost of Revenue	4,645,300	3,999,124	3,178,791
Gross Profit	**5,737,700**	**5,412,373**	**4,608,151**
Operating Expenses			
Research Development	—	—	—
Selling General and Administrative	4,531,200	3,999,274	3,420,925
Non Recurring	153,300	-	(93,937)
Other	549,300	467,160	387,211
Total Operating Expenses	—	—	—
Operating Income or Loss	**503,900**	**945,939**	**893,952**
Income from Continuing Operations			
Total Other Income/Expenses Net	9,000	2,419	12,291
Earnings Before Interest And Taxes	512,900	1,056,364	906,243
Interest Expense	53,400	—	—
Income Before Tax	459,500	1,056,364	906,243
Income Tax Expense	144,000	383,726	324,770
Minority Interest	—	—	—
Net Income from Continuing Ops	315,500	672,638	581,473
Non-recurring Events			
Discontinued Operations	—	—	—
Extraordinary Items	—	—	—
Effect of Accounting Changes	—	—	(17,214)
Other Items	—	—	—
Net Income	**$ 315,500**	**$ 672,638**	**$ 564,259**

Source: www.starbucks.com

EXHIBIT 3   Starbucks' Balance Sheet (values in 000's)

PERIOD ENDING	28-Sep-08	30-Sep-07	1-Oct-06
Current Assets			
Cash and Cash Equivalents	$269,800	$281,261	$312,606
Short Term Investments	$52,500	$157,433	$141,038
Net Receivables	$563,700	$417,378	$313,048
Inventory	$692,800	$691,658	$636,222
Other Current Assets	$169,200	$148,757	$126,874
Total Current Assets	**$1,748,000**	**$1,696,487**	**$1,529,788**
Long Term Assets			
Long Term Investments	$374,000	$279,868	$224,904
Fixed Assets	$2,956,400	$2,890,433	$2,287,899
Goodwill	$266,500	$215,625	$161,478
Intangible Assets	$66,600	$42,043	$37,955
Other Assets	$261,100	$219,422	$186,917
Total Assets	**$5,672,600**	**$5,343,878**	**$4,428,941**
Current Liabilities			
Accounts Payable	$955,100	$1,147,643	$1,002,932
Short Term Debt/Current Portion of Long Term Debt	$713,700	S711,023	$700,762
Other Current Liabilities	$520,900	S296,900	$231,926
Total Current Liabilities	**$2,189,700**	**$2,155,566**	**$1,935,620**
Long Term Debt	$549,600	S550,121	$1,958
Other Liabilities	$120,200	$65,086	$48,215
Deferred Liability Charges	$303,900	S271,736	$203,903
Minority Interest	$18,300	$17,252	$10,739
Total Liabilities	**$3,181,700**	**$3,059,761**	**$2,200,435**
Stockholders' Equity			
Common Stocks	$700	$738	$756
Capital Surplus	$39,400	$39,393	$39,393
Retained Earnings	$2,402,400	$2,189,366	$2,151,084
Other Equity	$48,400	$54,620	$37,273
Total Equity	**$2,490,900**	**$2,284,117**	**$2,228,506**
Total Liabilities & Equity	**$5,672,600**	**$5,343,878**	**$4,428,941**

Source: www.starbucks.com.

for fiscal year 2008. U.S. operations sell coffee and other beverages, complementary food, whole bean coffees, and coffee brewing equipment and merchandise primarily through company-operated retail stores. Specialty operations within the United States include licensed retail stores and foodservice accounts. At the end of the fiscal 2008, the U.S. segment reported total revenues of $7,877 million with an operating income of $528.1 million. Company-operated retail revenues increased primarily due to the opening of 445 new company-operated retail stores in the 2008 fiscal year but was partially offset by a 5 percent decrease in comparable store sales for the same period. The U.S. company-operated retail business continued deteriorating trends. Licensing revenues increased primarily due to higher product sales and royalty revenues as a result of opening 438 new licensed retail stores in the last 12 months.

For the second quarter of fiscal 2009, U.S. total net revenues were $1.8 billion, a decline of $131.5 million, or 6.8 percent, due to decreased revenues from company-operated retail stores. U.S. comparable store sales declined 8 percent, due to a 5 percent decline in the number of transactions and a 3 percent decrease in the average value per transaction. Specialty revenues declined 3.9 percent to $202.6 million, driven by softer foodservice revenues. The U.S. segment produced operating income of $90.6 million, compared with $193.9 million for the same period a year ago. Operating margin was 5.0 percent of related revenues for the second quarter fiscal 2009 compared with 10.0 percent in the corresponding period of fiscal 2008. This decrease was driven by restructuring charges of $106.8 million recorded in the period.[3]

INTERNATIONAL   Starbucks' International operations represent the remaining 20 percent of company-operated retail revenues and 21 percent of total specialty revenues as well as 20 percent of total net revenues for fiscal year 2008. International operations sell coffee and other beverages, complementary food, whole bean coffees, and coffee brewing equipment and merchandise through company-operated retail stores in the United Kingdom, Canada, and nine other markets. Specialty operations in International primarily include retail store licensing operations in nearly 40 countries and foodservice accounts, primarily in Canada and Japan. Many of Starbucks' International operations are in early stages of development that require a more extensive support organization relative to the current levels of revenue and operating income in the United States.[4]

Company-operated retail revenues increased due to the opening of 236 new company-operated retail stores in the last 12 months, favorable foreign currency exchange rates, primarily on the Canadian dollar, and comparable store sales growth of 2 percent for fiscal 2008. In the fourth quarter of fiscal 2008, company-operated retail revenues grew at a slower rate year-over-year of 12 percent, and comparable store sales were flat compared to the same quarter in fiscal 2007, both driven by slowdowns in the United Kingdom and Canada, due to the weakening global economy. Specialty revenues increased primarily due to higher product sales and royalty revenues from opening 550 new licensed retail stores in the last 12 months.[5]

International total net revenues were $433.7 million for the 13 weeks ended March 29, 2009, down $59.7 million, or 12.1 percent, compared with the same period last year, primarily due to the impact of a stronger U.S. dollar relative to the British pound and Canadian dollar. Also contributing to the decrease in International revenues was a 3 percent decline in comparable store sales, due to a 2 percent decline in the number of transactions and a 1 percent decrease in the average value per transaction. The UK and Canadian markets reported negative comparable store sales for the quarter. International operating income decreased to $6.0 million for the second quarter of fiscal 2009 versus $17.8 million for the same period a year ago.[6]

GLOBAL CONSUMER PRODUCTS (CPG)   As indicated in Exhibit 4, Starbucks' CPG segment represents 24 percent of total specialty revenues and 4 percent of total net revenues for fiscal year 2008. CPG operations sell a selection of whole bean and ground coffees as well as a selection of premium Tazo teas through licensing arrangements in U.S. and international markets. CPG operations also produce and sell ready-to-drink beverages that include, among others, bottled Frappuccino beverages, Starbucks' DoubleShot espresso drinks, and Discoveries chilled cup coffee, as well as Starbucks' super-premium ice creams and Starbucks' Coffee and Cream Liqueurs, through its joint ventures and marketing and distribution agreements.[7]

Global Consumer Products Group total net revenues decreased by 2 percent to $94.8 million for the second quarter of fiscal 2009, due primarily to lower margin on sales of packaged coffee as a result of discounting, as well as lower volume to the trade.[8]

EXHIBIT 4 Segment Financial Data

Segment Financial Data by Product Category—2008 (millions)

	US	International	CPG
Net Revenues			
Company operated retail	$6997.7	$1774.2	
Specialty:			
Licensing	504.2	274.8	392.6
Food Service	385.1	54.4	
Total Net Revenues	7887.0	2103.4	392.6
Operating Income	528.1	110.0	205.3

Source: Starbucks, *Annual Report* (2008).

Competition

Dunkin' Donuts

Primarily known for fresh donuts, Dunkin' Donuts competes directly with Starbucks through the addition of branded coffee both in their stores and in grocery stories. Dunkin' is a privately owned, multiconcept quick-service franchisor, with more than 13,000 locations in more than 40 countries, including its popular Dunkin' Donuts and Baskin-Robbins chains. Having more than 7,900 shops in 30 countries (5,800 of which are in North America), Dunkin' is the world's leading chain of donut shops. Baskin-Robbins is a leading seller of ice cream and frozen snacks with its nearly 6,000 outlets, half of which are located in the United States. About 1,100 locations offer a combination of the company's brands. Recently the company began competing aggressively for Starbucks' market share by offering their unique blend of coffees in grocery stores nationwide. Dunkin' Brands has released estimated net sales of $517 million for the 2008 fiscal year.[9]

Caribou Coffee

Caribou Coffee is a gourmet coffeehouse operator in the United States with 464 coffeehouses, including 24 franchised locations reported in 2006. The company operates coffeehouses located in 18 states and the District of Columbia, including 193 coffeehouses in Minnesota and 62 coffeehouses in Illinois. Additionally, Caribou has been expanding internationally, but at a more measured pace than Starbucks, their competitor. Caribou provides gourmet coffee, espresso-based beverages, and specialty teas, baked goods, whole bean coffee, branded merchandise, and related products. Caribou also sells its products to grocery stores and mass merchandisers, office coffee providers, airlines, hotels, sports and entertainment venues, college campuses, and other commercial customers. Caribou, smaller, is the closest competitor to Starbucks in terms of product offerings and concept. However, their financial results reported at the end of 2008, although generating $253,899,000 in total revenues, posted a net income loss of $16,342,000.[10]

Peet's Coffee and Tea

Peet's Coffee and Tea is a specialty coffee roaster and marketer of roasted whole bean coffee, hand-selected tea, and related merchandise. Peet's sells its products in grocery stores, home delivery, office, restaurant and foodservice accounts, through both company-owned and operated stores in six states in the United States. Peet's roasts to order and ships coffee directly from its roasting facility to its home delivery customers. Peet's operation is divided into two business segments: retail and specialty sales. The company operates 166 retail stores in California, Colorado, Illinois, Oregon, Massachusetts, and Washington. In addition to sales through its retail stores, Peet's sells products in Safeway Inc.,

Albertson's, Ralph's, and Whole Foods Market. Peet's reported total revenues of $284,822,000 with a resulting operating income of $17,001,000 for the 2008 fiscal year.[11]

McDonald's (MCD)

MCD remains the world's number-one fast-food company by sales, with about 32,000 restaurants serving burgers and fries in about 120 countries, with nearly 14,000 locations in the United States alone. Well known for its Big Macs, Quarter Pounders, and Chicken McNuggets, McDonald's also offers coffee and the traditional breakfast items of Egg McMuffins and pancakes. Although most of its outlets are free-standing units, MCD also has many units located in airports and retail areas. Each eatery gets its food and packaging from approved suppliers to ensure product quality. About 80 percent of the restaurants are run by franchisees or affiliates. MCD reported staggering total revenue of $23.5 billion in 2008, generating a net income of $4.3 billion.[12]

Krispy Kreme Doughnuts (KKD)

Although coffee is not the mainstay of KKD's sweet treats, the two products do complement each other perfectly. KKD operates a chain of almost 300 doughnut shops and more than 200 smaller format locations throughout the United Kingdom and in more than a dozen other countries. The shops are popular for their glazed doughnuts that are served fresh and hot out of the fryer. In addition to its original glazed variety, KKD serves cake and filled doughnuts, crullers, and fritters, as well as hot coffee and other beverages. Nearly 100 locations are company-owned: the rest are franchised. KKD also markets its doughnuts through grocery stores and supermarkets. Like other competitors, their profits have been impacted by the economy of 2009, posting a loss of net income of $4,061,000 (2008) from their net sales of $383,984,000.[13]

Industry Analysis

The 2007–2009 global recession negatively affected the specialty coffee industry.

The 1990s noted above-average coffee consumption in the Pacific, Middle Atlantic, and New England states and found gourmet coffee drinkers tended to be slightly more affluent than average and lived or worked in large cities. Gourmet coffee consumption also rose with the drinker's educational level. Those who finished college bought 49 percent more gourmet coffee on average, and those with some postgraduate education bought 71 percent more. They also found that households with children and two working parents bought 28 percent more gourmet coffee. The Specialty Coffee Association of America (SCAA) described its typical customer as "an educated urban resident with the disposable income to spend on fine coffee." However, recent trends have shown that some of the consuming public is concerned about the nutritional value of such products as those offered by the specialty coffee sector and have even challenged the correctness of the labeling and calorie information posted on the products available at retail outlets.[14]

Despite its size, Starbucks alone purchases only 2 percent of the coffee produced worldwide. The SCAA, in its "Retail in the USA 2006" report, showed that at the end of 2006, specialty coffee sales had reached $12.27 billion, up from $11.05 billion in 2005 and $8.3 billion in 2001. Sales were divided into several subgroups: 15,500 coffee cafés (retailers with seating) had sales of $8.53 billion; 3,600 coffee kiosks (retailers without seating), $1.08 billion; 2,900 coffee carts (mobile retailers) $400 million; and 1,900 coffee bean roasters/retailers (roasting on the premises), $1.76 billion. Sixteen percent of the U.S. adult population consumed specialty coffee on a daily basis, whereas 63 percent indulged occasionally. These figures illustrate the growth in popularity of specialty coffees, as only 13 percent and 59 percent of people reported daily and occasional consumption, respectively, in 2002.[15]

Another trend that has surfaced in the past decade has been consumer requests for organic coffees, and more emphasis was placed by retailers on the growing environment of the beans. Starbucks was addressing the concern proactively, going directly to the source to ensure better quality coffee by opening a Costa Rican support office for coffee farmers and rewarding environmentally responsible farms through its CAFE Practices program.

Conclusion

Starbucks continues to be the "coffeehouse of choice" for many domestic and international consumers. Their strategy remains one of progressive expansion, but perhaps with more measured caution given the economic times. Recent closures of less than profitable locations combined with worldwide economic conditions presents challenges for the company. Firms such as McDonald's and Dunkin' Brands desire to lure all Starbucks' customers away to cheaper cups of coffee. Develop a clear strategic plan for Starbucks.

References

http://starbucks.com
http://coffeebean.com/index.aspx

Endnotes

1. www.starbucks.com.
2. "America's Best Companies to Work For, 2008." *Fortune,* 100 Best Companies to Work For (annual), February 4, 2008, p. 75. Business Rankings Annual 2009. Online Edition. Gale, 2008.
3. http://www.mergentonline.com.
4. Starbucks, *Annual Report* (2008).
5. Starbucks, *Annual Report* (2008).
6. http://www.mergentonline.com.
7. Starbucks, *Annual Report* (2008).
8. http://www.mergentonline.com.
9. http://www.mergentonline.com; Hoover's Company Records—In-Depth Records, May 28, 2009.
10. Hoover's Company Records—In-Depth Records, May 28, 2009.
11. http://www.mergentonline.com.
12. Hoover's Company Records—In-Depth Records, May 28, 2009.
13. Hoover's Company Records—In-Depth Records, May 28, 2009.
14. http://invreports.galegroup.
15. http://invreports.galegroup.

14 The United States Postal Service (USPS) — 2009

Fred and Forest David
Francis Marion University

www.usps.com

Postal prices went up in January 2009 for Express Mail, Priority Mail, Parcel Select, Parcel Return Service, and some international shipping products. Express Mail prices now start at $13.05. That was the first time the United States Postal Service (USPS) had separate price adjustment and implementation dates for their shipping and packaging business versus their mailing services and products business. For the latter, which includes first class mailings, postal prices increased in May 2009. A first class stamp is now 44 cents. More and more consumers are bypassing the USPS by using e-mail. This fact, coupled with the global recession, has placed the Postal Service in a precarious position going forward. USPS needs a clear strategic plan.

USPS is an independent federal agency that makes deliveries to more than 140 million addresses every day. USPS is the only service provider to deliver to every address in the nation. USPS is the world's leading provider of mail and delivery services, offering some of the most affordable postage rates in the world. However, the USPS completed fiscal year 2008 ending September 30 with a net loss of $2.8 billion as indicated in Exhibit 1. The loss occurred despite more than $2 billion in cost-cutting measures that included the use of 50 million fewer work hours than fiscal 2007. On a positive note, on-time delivery of first class mail reached record levels in 2008. Mail volume in 2008 totaled 202.7 billion pieces, a decline of 9.5 billion pieces, or 4.5 percent, from 2007.

USPS's total revenue in 2008 was $75 billion, unchanged from 2007. Expenses totaled $77.8 billion, including the $5.6 billion payment required by the Postal Act of 2006 to prefund retiree health benefits.[1]

Mission and Vision

The Postal Reorganization Act of 1970 defines the mission of the Postal Service as follows:

> The Postal Service is to bind the nation together through the correspondence of the people, to provide access in all communities, and to offer prompt, reliable postal services at uniform prices.

In the early 1990s, the USPS management reviewed the mission and developed a Statement of Purpose:

> To provide every household and business across the United States with the ability to communicate and conduct business with each other and the world through prompt, reliable, secure and economical services for the collection, transmission, and delivery of messages and merchandise.

The Postal Service receives no taxpayer dollars for routine operations but derives its operating revenues solely from the sale of postage, products, and services. *Vision 2013* is a term that refers to the Postal Service's five-year strategic plan. The organization's vision as stated in that document is as follows:

> Our vision of the future begins with a strong foundation. We will continue to strengthen our core operations and services, balancing an immediate and urgent

EXHIBIT 1 **USPS Summary Financial Data**

Years Ended September 30—Percent Change from Preceding Year

	2008	2007	2006	2008	2007	2006
(Dollars in millions)						
Operating revenue	$ 74,932	$ 74,778	$ 72,650	0.2%	2.9%	3.9%
Operating expenses	$ 77,738	$ 80,105	$ 71,681	(3.0%)	11.8%	5.0%
Income from Operations	$ (2,806)	$ (5,327)	$ 969			
Operating margin	(3.7%)	(7.1%)	1.3%			
Net (loss) income	$ (2,806)	$ (5,142)	$ 900			
Purchase of capital property and equipment	$ 1,995	$ 2,715	$ 2,630	(26.5%)	3.2%	13.5%
Debt	$ 7,200	$ 4,200	$ 2,100			
Interest expense	$ 36	$ 10	$ 5			
Capital contributions of U.S. government	$ 3,034	$ 3,034	$ 3,034			
Retained (deficit) earnings since reorganization	$ (4,706)	$ (1,900)	$ 3,242			
Total Net Capital	$ (1,672)	$ 1,134	$ 6,276			
Number of employees	663,238	684,762	696,138	(3.1%)	(1.6%)	(1.2%)
Actual Mail volume (in millions of pieces)	202,703	212,234	213,138	(4.5%)	(0.4%)	0.7%
New delivery points served	1,199,764	1,818,326	1,847,831			

Source: www.usps.com.

need to reduce costs with a continued commitment to strategies such as Intelligent Mail®, which are essential to our future. We will be guided by one principle: we exist to serve our customers. This vision is our commitment to ensuring a vital Postal Service for future generations. Our vision rests on three major strategies: (1) Focus on what matters most to customers. (2) Leverage our strengths to create customer value and profits to invest in continued improvement. (3) Embrace change in the way we respond to emerging customer needs and a rapidly evolving business environment.

History

Communication between colonists, colonies, and England depended primarily on friends, merchants, and the Native Americans. In 1639, the first official notice of a postal service appeared in the colonies. It was the responsibility of local authorities to operate postal routes. A Continental Congress was organized in Philadelphia in May 1775 to establish an independent government. One of its first questions was how to deliver the mail. Benjamin Franklin led the Committee of Investigation to establish a postal system. On July 26, 1775, over 225 years ago, the Continental Congress appointed Franklin as postmaster general. Following the adoption of the Constitution in May 1789, the Act of September 22, 1789, temporarily established a post office and created the Office of the Postmaster General. At that time there were 75 post offices and about 2,000 miles of post roads, although as late as 1780 the postal staff consisted only of a postmaster general, a secretary/comptroller, three surveyors, one inspector of dead letters, and 26 post riders.

The Post Office Department was not specifically established as an executive department by Congress until June 8, 1872 (17 Stat. 284–4). As mail delivery evolved from foot to horseback, stagecoach, steamboat, railroad, automobile, and airplane, with intermediate and overlapping use of balloons, helicopters, and pneumatic tubes, mail contracts ensured the income necessary to build the great highways, rail lines, and airways that eventually spanned the continent. By the turn of the nineteenth century, the Post Office Department had purchased a number of stagecoaches for operation on the nation's better post roads—a post road was any road on which the mail traveled—and continued to encourage new designs to improve passenger comfort and carry mail more safely.

The Postal Service Act of 1969 transformed the Post Office Department into the United States Postal Service, an independent establishment of the executive branch of the government of the United States. The Postal Reorganization Act of 1970 stated:

> The United States Postal Service shall be operated as a basic and fundamental service provided by the government of the United States, authorized by the Constitution, created by an Act of Congress, and supported by the people. The Postal Service shall have as its basic function the obligation to provide postal services to bind the nation together through the personal, educational, literary, and business correspondence of the people. It shall provide prompt, reliable, and efficient services to patrons in all areas and shall render postal services to all communities.   (*Source:* USPS Annual Report, 2002 p. 3.)

The Postal Reorganization Act required that the government agency be self-supporting. This was achieved in 1982, and the postal services have been free from taxpayer support since then. This achievement was one of the first and most important results sought by the Postal Reorganization Act. Financial self-sufficiency is a major goal in strategic planning for the postal service.

In April 2003, the Postal Service delivered its Transformation Plan to Congress defining the short- and long-term strategies that will enable the Postal Service to successfully carry out its long-standing mission of providing affordable, universal service. In August 2003, Public Law 107–210 was signed by the president and allows the Customs Service to open outbound international mail weighing more than 16 ounces.

The Postal Reorganization Act, as specified by Congress, was to ensure that residents of both urban and rural communities have access to an effective postal service. The Postal Service has established a nationwide network of facilities, centralized delivery units, and rural and highway contract delivery routes. A change in community postal needs or the loss of suitable facilities may lead to the closing of a post office, but customers who may lose a postal service are still provided benefits.

Internal Issues

Business Structure

Public Law 109–435 (P.L.109–435), signed by President Bush in December 2006, divided postal services into two broad categories or divisions: market-dominant services and competitive services. Market-dominant services include, but are not limited to, First Class Mail, Standard Mail, Periodicals, and Package Services. Price increases for these services are subject to a price cap based on the Consumer Price Index—All Urban Consumers (CPI-U). Competitive Services, such as Priority Mail, Express Mail, Bulk Parcel Post, and Bulk International Mail, have greater pricing flexibility.

The USPS board of governors is similar to a corporate board of directors. The board of nine governors are appointed by the president and approved by the Senate. The governors are chosen to represent the public interest, and no more than five can come from the same political party. The nine governors select the postmaster general, who becomes a member of the board. The postmaster general serves for an indefinite term as well as the deputy postmaster, who is also selected by the board. The postmaster general and the deputy postmaster general participate with the governors on all matters except for voting on rate or classification adjustments, adjustments to the budget of the Postal Rate Commission, or election of the chairman of the board. They work together on approval of rate and class changes.

Employees

The USPS has nine collective bargaining agreements with seven unions covering approximately 726,000 employees. As of September 30, 2008, there were 663,238 career USPS

EXHIBIT 2 USPS Operating Expenses (dollars in millions)

	2008	2007	2006
Compensation and Benefits	$ 53,585	$ 54,186	$ 54,665
Retiree Health Benefits	7,407	10,084	1,637
Transportation	6,961	6,502	6,045
Other Expenses	9,785	9,333	9,334
Total Operating Expenses	$ 77,738	$ 80,105	$ 71,681

Source: www.usps.com.

employees, substantially all of whom reside in the United States. USPS had 101,850 non-career employees. As indicated in Exhibit 2, these employees reaped $53.585 billion in compensation and benefits in 2008. The USPS labor force is primarily represented by the American Postal Workers Union (APWU), National Association of Letter Carriers (NALC), National Postal Mail Handlers Union (NPMHU), and National Rural Letter Carriers Association (NRLCA). More than 85 percent of USPS career employees are covered by collective bargaining agreements.

Postal Service unions cover a full range of topics involving wages, benefits, and conditions of employment. The Postal Service wants to ensure leadership continuity and build talent from within the organization. The objectives are to develop people for corporate needs, to identify individuals who can move into executive positions, and to foster diversity among leadership ranks. Individuals are identified as potential successors based on their leadership skills, functional and management expertise, and performance results. After completing the eighth full year of succession planning, less than 1 percent of executive vacancies are filled by outside hires.

Work hours are a major driver of USPS compensation and benefits expense. As indicated in Exhibit 3, mail processing, customer service, city delivery, and other work hours decreased by 50 million in 2008 compared to 2007, offsetting the higher labor rates. The reduction in work hours was in part an outcome of lower mail volumes, which reduced workload. As mail volume fell throughout the year, management initiated a number of efforts to reduce work hours, especially overtime.

Transportation

As indicated in Exhibit 4, USPS's total transportation expenses in 2008 were $6.961 billion. Highway transportation expenses for 2008 were $3,499 million, an increase of 11.1 percent over 2007. The increases were attributed to higher fuel prices, contract labor rates, and contract Consumer Price Index (CPI) rates. Also, some mail that was previously transported via air was moved to surface transportation during the year. In 2008, the average price of gasoline increased approximately 30.4 percent compared to 2007. Diesel fuel, which makes up 93 percent of the fuel purchased for highway contracts, was an

EXHIBIT 3 USPS Work Hours by Function (in thousands)

	2008	2007	2006
City Delivery	452,288	462,040	468,918
Mail Processing	293,108	315,825	332,269
Customer Services & Retail	217,236	233,791	246,538
Rural Delivery	189,950	189,709	186,164
Other, including Plant, Operational Support, and Administrative	220,772	221,636	224,840
Total Work Hours	1,373,354	1,423,001	1,458,729

Source: www.usps.com.

EXHIBIT 4 USPS Income Statement (dollars in millions)

	2008	2007	2006
Operating revenue	**$ 74,932**	**$ 74,778**	**$ 72,650**
Operating expenses:			
Compensation and benefits	53,585	54,186	54,665
Retiree health benefits	7,407	10,084	1,637
Transportation	6,961	6,502	6,045
Other	9,785	9,333	9,334
Total operating expenses	77,738	80,105	71,681
(Loss) Income from operations	(2,806)	(5,327)	969
Interest and investment income	36	195	167
Interest expense on deferred retirement obligations	—	—	(231)
Other interest expense	(36)	(10)	(5)
Net (Loss) Income	**$ (2,806)**	**$ (5,142)**	**$ 900**

Source: www.usps.com.

average of $3.87 per gallon in 2008, compared to $2.70 per gallon in 2007, an increase of 43.3 percent.

Air transportation expenses at USPS for 2008 were $3,047 million, a 1.9 percent increase over 2007. Domestic air transportation expenses for 2008 were $2,336 million, a decrease of $57 million or 2.4 percent, compared to 2007. International air expenses increased $114 million primarily due to the shift from surface to air delivery, resulting from the elimination of the Global Economy service offering.

First Class Mail

The First Class Mail category includes First Class Mail International. As indicated in Exhibits 5, 6, and 7, First Class Mail revenue decreased $226 million, or 0.6 percent, while volume decreased by 4.6 billion pieces, or 4.8 percent, in 2008. The revenue decrease occurred in spite of two price increases. Only nonautomation presort and First Class International letters experienced increases in volume. The most significant decline was in single-piece First Class letters, with a decrease of over 3 billion pieces of mail. The long-term continued decline in single-piece volume reflects the impact of electronic diversion as businesses, nonprofit organizations, governments, and households continue to move their correspondence and transactions to electronic alternatives, such as Internet bill payment, automatic deduction, and direct deposit. The rate of decline accelerated significantly in 2008 as the economy weakened.

EXHIBIT 5 USPS Operating Revenue

Operating Revenue	2008	2007	2006
(Dollars in millions)			
First Class Mail	$ 38,179	$ 38,405	$ 37,605
Standard Mail	20,586	20,779	19,876
Periodicals	2,295	2,188	2,215
Package Services	1,845	1,812	1,751
Other Mailing Services	3,645	3,720	3,715
Total Mailing Services	66,550	66,904	65,162
Total Shipping Services	8,382	7,874	7,488
Total Operating Revenue	$ 74,932	$ 74,778	$ 72,650

Source: www.usps.com.

EXHIBIT 6   USPS 2008 Mail Revenue Percent Breakdown

First Class Mail	52%
Shipping Services	11%
Standard Mail	27%
Other Mailing Services	10%
Other Mailing Services	5%

Source: www.usps.com.

EXHIBIT 7   USPS Mail Volume by Type (pieces in millions)

	2008	2007	2006
First Class Mail	91,697	96,297	98,016
Standard Mail	99,084	103,516	102,460
Periodicals	8,605	8,796	9,023
Package Services	846	914	919
Other Mailing Services	896	1,081	1,084
Total Mailing Services	201,128	210,604	211,502
Total Shipping Services	1,575	1,630	1,636
Total Mail Volume by Type	202,703	212,234	213,138

Source: www.usps.com.

Strategic Planning

The Government Performance and Results Act (GPRA) requires all federal agencies to develop and publish a five-year strategic plan. The Postal Service updates its plan annually to accommodate ongoing business environment changes. This annual planning process incorporates an assessment of recent performance, refinement of strategies, and prioritization of objectives, programs, and budgets to optimize results. In October 2008, USPS published Vision 2013, a five-year strategic plan, covering the period 2009 to 2013. Vision 2013 was designed to build on the successes of the Postal Service's Strategic Transformation Plan, which helped guide multiple improvements in service, efficiency, and workplace conditions.

Competitors

FedEx

Headquartered in Memphis, Tennessee, and founded in 1971, FedEx is a major competitor to USPS. This company has over $37 billion in annual revenues and more than 220,000 employees. FedEx Express unit is the world's number-one express transportation provider, delivering about 3.5 million packages daily to more than 220 countries and territories. It maintains a fleet of about 675 aircraft and more than 44,000 motor vehicles. In addition to its express delivery business, FedEx Ground provides small-package ground delivery in North America, and less-than-truckload (LTL) carrier FedEx Freight hauls larger shipments. FedEx Office stores offer a variety of document-related and other business services and serve as retail hubs for other FedEx units. For 2008, FedEx made over $1.1 billion in net income representing a 3 percent profit margin.

United Parcel Service

Headquartered in Atlanta, Georgia, UPS was founded in 1907 as a messenger company in the United States and has grown into a gigantic corporation. UPS is a global company with one of the most recognized and admired brands in the world. It is the world's largest package delivery company and services more than 200 countries. UPS had $51.4 billion in revenues in 2008 and a net income of over $3 billion. UPS is most known for its chocolate-colored trucks. UPS transports some 16 million packages and documents per business day throughout the United States and to more than 200 countries and territories. Its delivery operations use a fleet of about 107,000 motor vehicles and about 570 aircraft. In addition to package delivery, the company offers services such as logistics and freight forwarding, through UPS Supply Chain Solutions, and less-than-truckload (LTL) freight transportation through UPS Ground Freight.

E-mail

E-commerce companies offer products and services that substitute for traditional postal services. E-mail has indeed become one of the most common means of communication for people across the country and around the world. E-mail saves people time, money, and use-less effort. The well-known phrase "You've got mail" has become a significant part of the English language. People have become extremely reliant on the instantaneous delivery and short response time provided by e-mail and the Internet, and this has made it a significant competitor of the USPS.

Future Outlook

The outlook for the USPS is somewhat gloomy. A weak economy, advertising decreases, e-mail, FedEx, and UPS all hurt the USPS, which is having to downsize. Some analysts argue that the USPS should convert to a centralized mailbox delivery system rather than home delivery to all. This change would save millions. Note in Exhibits 8, 9, and 10 respectively, there were 27,232 post offices in 2008, 269 processing centers, and 197,898 delivery and collection vehicles. Other analysts suggest that the USPS should cease to continue with cooperative agreements with FedEx and UPS. It has been said that these companies gain more from the USPS than they give, so therefore the deals are not in the best interest of the USPS. Exhibits 11, 12, 13, and 14 provide more operating data for USPS. Help this organization manage better strategically in the future.

Note: Much of this case is based on the USPS 2008 *Annual Report.*

EXHIBIT 8   USPS Real Estate Inventory

	2008	2007
(Actual numbers)		
Leased Facilities	25,272	25,450
Owned Facilities	8,546	8,487
GSA/Other Government Facilities	357	381
Total Real Estate Inventory	34,175	34,318
Annual Rent Paid to Lessors (Dollars in millions)	$ 1,011	$ 973
Retail and Delivery Facilities		
(Actual numbers)		
Post Offices	27,232	27,276
Classified Branches	1,493	1,508
Classified Stations	3,358	3,379
Carrier Annexes	658	532
Contract Postal Units	3,148	3,131
Community Post Offices	834	895
Total Retail and Delivery Facilities	36,723	36,721

Source: www.usps.com.

EXHIBIT 9   USPS Processing Facilities (actual numbers)

Processing and Distribution Centers	269	269
Customer Service Facilities	195	195
Bulk Mail Centers	21	21
Logistics and Distribution Centers	14	14
Annexes	64	66
Surface Transfer Centers	20	14
Airmail Processing Centers	20	29
Remote Encoding Centers	6	10
International Service Centers	5	5
Total Processing Facilities	614	623

Source: www.usps.com.

EXHIBIT 10   USPS Vehicle Inventory (actual numbers)

Delivery and Collection Vehicles (1/2 – 2 1/2 ton)	197,898	195,211
Mail Transport Vehicles (Tractors and Trailers)	6,455	6,824
Administrative Vehicles and Other Vehicles	5,906	6,169
Service Vehicles (Maintenance)	5,272	5,539
Inspection Service and Law Enforcement Vehicles	3,288	3,482
Mail Transport Vehicles (3–9 ton)	2,228	2,297
Total Vehicles	221,047	219,522

Source: www.usps.com.

EXHIBIT 11   Other USPS Operating Expenses (dollars in millions)

	2008	2007	2006
Supplies and Services	$ 2,597	$ 2,594	$ 2,643
Depreciation and Amortization	2,319	2,152	2,149
Rent and Utilities	1,779	1,700	1,721
Vehicle Maintenance Service	926	760	709
Information Technology and Communications	658	630	649
Rural Carrier Equipment Maint. Allowance	545	495	485
Other	961	1,002	978
Total	$ 9,785	$ 9,333	$ 9,334

Source: www.usps.com.

EXHIBIT 12   USPS Balance Sheet (dollars in millions)

	2008	2007
Assets		
Current Assets:		
Cash and cash equivalents	$ 1,432	$ 899
Receivables:		
Foreign countries	450	425
U.S. government	133	155

continued

EXHIBIT 12 **USPS Balance Sheet (dollars in millions)—continued**

	2008	2007
Other	187	223
Receivables before allowances	770	803
Less allowances	41	44
Total receivables, net	729	759
Supplies, advances and prepayments	193	201
Total Current Assets	2,354	1,859
Property and Equipment, at Cost: Buildings	22,269	21,591
Equipment	21,544	21,060
Land	2,971	2,914
Leasehold improvements	914	842
	47,698	46,407
Less allowances for depreciation and amortization	25,886	24,688
	21,812	21,719
Construction in progress	1,381	1,877
Total Property and Equipment, Net	23,193	23,596
Other Assets—Principally Revenue Forgone Receivable	439	392
Total Assets	**$ 25,986**	**$ 25,847**
Liabilities and Net (Deficiency) Capital		
Current Liabilities:		
Compensation and benefits	$ 3,466	$ 3,571
Payables and accrued expenses:		
Trade payables and accrued expenses	1,246	1,503
Foreign countries	413	452
U.S. government	85	111
Total payables and accrued expenses	1,744	2,066
Customer deposit accounts	1,449	1,499
Deferred revenue-prepaid postage	1,689	1,142
Outstanding postal money orders	720	847
Prepaid box rent and other deferred revenue	461	479
Debt	7,200	4,200
Total Current Liabilities	16,729	13,804
Noncurrent Liabilities:		
Workers' compensation costs	7,003	6,800
Employees' accumulated leave	2,208	2,129
Deferred appropriation and other revenue	525	591
Long-term portion capital lease obligations	587	618
Deferred gains on sales of property	312	310
Contingent liabilities and other	294	461
Total Noncurrent Liabilities	10,929	10,909
Total Liabilities	27,658	24,713
Net Capital		
Capital contributions of the U.S. government	3,034	3,034
Deficit since 1971 reorganization	(4,706)	(1,900)
Total Net (Deficiency) Capital	(1,672)	1,134
Total Liabilities and Net (Deficiency) Capital	**$ 25,986**	**$ 25,847**

Source: www.usps.com.

EXHIBIT 13   USPS Operating Statistics (in millions of units)

Category of Service	2008	2007	2006
MAILING SERVICES			
First Class Mail			
Revenue	$ 38,179.3	$ 38,404.5	$ 37,604.9
Pieces, Number	91,696.7	96,297.3	98,016.2
Weight, Pounds	4,165.1	4,401.4	4,418.1
Standard Mail			
Revenue	$ 20,586.3	S 20,778.6	$ 19,876.5
Pieces, Number	99,084.2	103,516.1	102,459.6
Weight, Pounds	11,017.2	11,820.7	11,771.2
Periodicals			
Revenue	$ 2,294.9	$ 2,187.9	$ 2,215.2
Pieces, Number	8,605.2	8,795.8	9,022.5
Weight, Pounds	3,676.9	3,895.6	4,040.7
Package Services			
Revenue	$ 1,845.5	$ 1,812.3	$ 1,751.1
Pieces, Number	846.2	914.5	918.8
Weight, Pounds	2,155.3	2,297.5	2,323.2
U.S. Postal Service			
Pieces, Number	823.7	1,008.4	1,010.1
Weight, Pounds	148.9	140.6	128.1
Free Matter for the Blind			
Pieces, Number	72.0	72.0	74.2
Weight, Pounds	33.3	33.6	35.4
Total Mailing Services Mail			
Revenue	$ 62,906.0	$ 63,183.3	$ 61,447.7
Pieces, Number	201,128.0	210,604.1	211,501.4
Weight, Pounds	21,196.7	22,589.4	22,716.7
ANCILLARY & SPECIAL SERVICES			
Registered Mail			
Revenue	$ 56.9	$ 53.3	$ 72.8
Number of articles	3.9	4.3	7.1
Certified Mail			
Revenue	$ 717.8	$ 698.2	$ 631.6
Number of articles	268.9	280.2	265.7
Insurance			
Revenue	$ 144.6	$ 156.7	$ 136.7
Number of articles	51.6	57.0	52.8
Delivery Receipt Services			
Revenue	$ 704.6	$ 639.7	$ 619.9
Number of articles	1,192.2	1,098.3	1,020.3
Money Orders			
Revenue	$ 204.8	$ 210.5	$ 191.2
Face value of issues (non-add)	$ 25,709.3	$ 27,194.0	$ 28,277.4
Number of articles	149.1	162.9	176.2

continued

EXHIBIT 13 USPS Operating Statistics (in millions of units)—continued

Category of Service	2008	2007	2006
Box rent revenue	$ 896.7	$ 836.9	$ 813.7
Stamped envelope and card revenue	$ 24.4	$ 16.9	$ 25.2
Other Mailing Services Revenue	$ 894.5	$ 1,108.2	$ 1,224.0
Total Ancillary & Special Services Revenue	$ 3,644.3	$ 3,720.4	$ 3,715.1
Total Mailing Services Revenue	$ 66,550.3	$ 66,903.7	$ 65,162.8
Category of Service (in millions of units)	2008	2007	2006
SHIPPING SERVICES			
Revenue	$ 8,355.0	$ 7,851.6	$ 7,461.1
Pieces, Number	1,574.9	1,629.9	1,636.3
Weight, Pounds	3,040.6	3,053.8	3,215.1
Shipping Services Ancillary & Special Services Revenue	$ 26.7	$ 22.8	$ 26.5
Total Shipping Services Revenue	$ 8,381.7	$ 7,874.4	$ 7,487.6
Postal Service Totals			
Revenue	$ 71,261.0	$ 71,034.9	$ 68,908.8
Pieces, Number	202,702.9	212,234.0	213,137.7
Weight, Pounds	24,237.3	25,643.2	25,931.8
Total Ancillary & Special Services Revenue	$ 3,671.0	$ 3,743.2	$ 3,741.6
Total Operating Revenue	$ 74,932.0	$ 74,778.1	$ 72,650.4
(Actual numbers)			
Career Employees			
Headquarters and HQ Related Employees			
Headquarters	2,892	2,856	2,761
Headquarters—Field Support Units	4,429	4,527	4,402
Inspection Service—Field	2,890	2,991	3,130
Inspector General	1,159	1,147	1,071
Total HQ and HQ Related Employees	11,370	11,521	11,364
Field Employees			
Area Offices	1,316	1,281	1,395
Postmasters / Installation Heads	25,250	25,285	25,429
Supervisors / Managers	31,787	32,635	33,201
Professional Administration and Technical Personnel	8,010	8,058	8,539
Clerks	194,773	204,145	213,920
Nurses	134	160	166
Mail Handlers	55,812	57,882	57,158
City Delivery Carriers	211,661	222,132	224,400
Motor Vehicle Operators	8,558	8,726	8,715
Rural Delivery Carriers—Full Time	68,900	67,584	66,344
Building and Equipment			
Building and Equipment Maintenance Personnel	40,248	39,948	39,986

continued

EXHIBIT 13   USPS Operating Statistics (in millions of units)—continued

Category of Service	2008	2007	2006
Vehicle Maintenance Employees	5,419	5,405	5,521
Total Field Employees	651,868	673,241	684,774
Total Career Employees	663,238	684,762	696,138
Noncareer Employees			
Casuals	12,000	22,078	22,518
Nonbargaining Temporary	1,119	1,244	1,135
Rural Part Time: Subs / RCA / RCR / AUX	58,072	60,444	59,087
Postmaster Relief and Leave Replacements	12,327	12,169	12,188
Transitional Employees	18,332	5,232	5,133
Total Noncareer Employees	101,850	101,167	100,061
Total Employees	765,088	785,929	796,199

Source: www.usps.com.

EXHIBIT 14   Post Offices, Stations, and Branches (in actual units)

	2008	2007	2006
Post Offices	27,232	27,276	27,318
Classified Stations, Branches, and Carrier			
Annexes	5,509	5,419	5,557
Contract Postal Units	3,148	3,131	3,014
Community Post Offices	834	895	937
Total Offices, Stations, and Branches	36,723	36,721	36,826
Residential Delivery Points			
City Delivery	79,848,415	79,470,894	78,949,153
Rural	37,684,158	37,022,488	36,068,838
PO Box	15,639,031	15,635,480	15,615,744
Highway Contract	2,516,783	2,473,323	2,345,255
Total Residential Delivery	135,688,387	134,602,185	132,978,990
Business Delivery Points			
City Delivery	7,436,965	7,411,582	7,343,020
Rural	1,407,942	1,360,478	1,297,022
PO Box	4,587,454	4,548,973	4,490,102
Highway Contract	71,538	69,304	65,062
Total Business Delivery	13,503,899	13,390,337	13,195,206
Total Delivery Points	149,192,286	147,992,522	146,174,196
Change in Delivery Points	1,199,764	1,818,326	1,847,831

Source: www.usps.com.

15 National Railroad Passenger Corporation (AMTRAK) — 2009

Kristopher J. Blanchard
Crown College

www.amtrak.com

Amtrak's longtime inspector general, Fred Weiderhold, abruptly resigned on June 18, 2009, saying "the independence and effectiveness of the inspector general's office is being substantially impaired by Amtrak managers." That month, Amtrak managers were cited for interfering with the railroad's $1.3 billion in economic stimulus funding. Senator Chuck Grassley from Iowa said, "Amtrak managers are interfering with the system of checks and balances." Vice President Joe Biden's son, Hunter Biden, was a member of Amtrak's board of directors from July 2006 through February 2009.

On August 19, 2009, Amtrak extended through the end of the year its fare promotion in the Northeast. For example, you can ride Amtrak from New York to Washington, D.C., for $49 or New York to Philadelphia for $34 or Boston to New York for $49, etc. There are no additional fares or fees to these low prices.

In 2009, Amtrak provides services across 21,000 miles of track in 46 states, the District of Columbia, and three Canadian provinces. Amtrak is the sole nationwide passenger rail carrier in the United States. The National Railroad Passenger Corporation (Amtrak) was organized under the Rail Passenger Service Act in 1970 and operations began in May 1971.

Exhibit 1 provides a map of Amtrak service routes. It is a large and complex passenger rail system, operating corridor and long-distance passenger rail service in and through 46 states of the contiguous United States. Amtrak's best known service may be its Northeast Corridor (NEC) service between Boston and Washington, D.C., but the company operates more than 315 trains per day over 43 routes, carrying an average of 78,500 passengers per day.

Amtrak has approximately 19,000 employees, and revenue for the 2008 fiscal year was $2.4 billion. This included intercity passenger rail service revenues and revenues from related businesses and state capital payments. In fiscal 2008, Amtrak carried nearly 29 million passengers to more than 500 destinations. In addition to Amtrak riders, an average of 850,000 people traveled over Amtrak infrastructure or on commuter trains operated under contract every weekday.[1] Amtrak has contracts to provide passenger rail service to 14 states; this represents nearly half of Amtrak's departures. Additionally there are seven state transportation, or commuter, agencies that contract with Amtrak for the use of various facilities and assets or for delivery of commuter service. These agencies include Caltrain, Maryland Area Regional Commuter, Connecticut's Shore Line East, and Virginia Railway Express. Amtrak also conducts maintenance for the Sounder Commuter Rail System in Seattle, dispatching and maintenance-of-way service for Massachusetts Bay Transportation Authority, and dispatching for the South Florida Regional Transportation Authority Tri-Rail service.

Amtrak owns 363 miles of the 456-mile Northeast Corridor from Washington to Boston, where *Acela Express* trains operate at speeds of up to 150 mph; a 62-mile track segment from New Haven, Connecticut, to Springfield, Massachusetts; 104 miles between Philadelphia and Harrisburg over which trains travel up to 110 mph; and 97 miles of track in Michigan over which trains travel at 95 mph. About 70 percent of the miles traveled by Amtrak trains are on tracks owned by freight and commuter railroads. This has resulted in Amtrak paying host railroads $101.5 million for reimbursed costs and incentives to travel

EXHIBIT 1   Amtrak Route Map

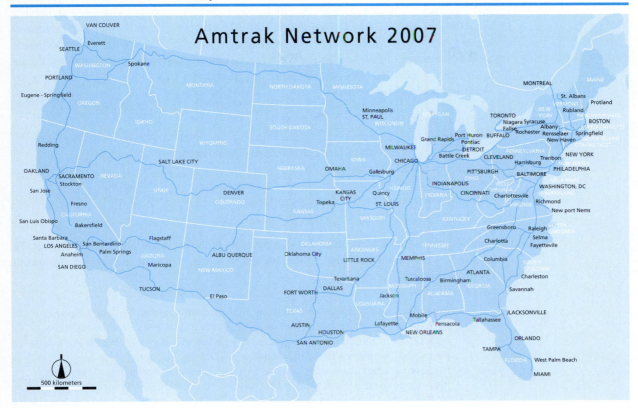

26 million train-miles. Amtrak also depends on host railroads for the dispatching and timely movement of its trains. The seven largest host railroads are BNSF Railway, Union Pacific Railroad, CSX Transportation, Norfolk Southern Railway, CN Railway, Canadian Pacific Railway, and Metro-North Railroad.

Internal Information

Organizational Structure

Amtrak is a government-owned corporation that was organized to provide intercity passenger train service in the United States. All of Amtrak's preferred stock is owned by the U.S. federal government. The members of the board of directors are appointed by the president of the United States and are subject to confirmation by the U.S. Senate. Common stock was issued in 1971 to railroads that contributed capital and equipment. Even though these shares convey almost no benefits, the holders declined a 2002 buyout offer by Amtrak.

Leadership

In 2006, Alexander Kummant was named president and CEO of Amtrak, but he was asked to resign in November 2008 because of a dispute about debt restructuring. According to statements from Amtrak, both revenue and ridership reached record highs during Kummant's tenure. "He also successfully oversaw the completion of labor agreements with all of the unions representing Amtrak's employees," said Donna McLean, Amtrak chairwoman.[2] On November 25, 2008, the board of directors for Amtrak announced they had appointed Joseph Boardman to a one-year term as president and CEO of the railway to replace Kummant.

Company Mission and Ethics Statement

The mission of Amtrak is to "provide efficient and effective intercity passenger rail mobility consisting of high quality service that is trip-time competitive with other intercity travel options, and provide additional or complementary intercity transportation service to ensure mobility in times of national disaster or other instances where other travel options are not adequately available."[3] As Amtrak works to implement this vision, it has adopted the following goals and objectives:

- Increase ridership
- Increase revenue through increased ridership and improved revenue management
- Contain cost growth through productivity and efficiency improvements
- Improve financial transparency
- Provide a safe and secure environment for passengers and employees
- Improve management of human capital
- Improve environmental stewardship

Amtrak is committed to pursuing these goals and objectives in a highly ethical manner. To ensure that all employees conduct themselves in a highly ethical manner, the following code of ethics have been adopted:

- You are personally responsible for your own conduct in complying with all provisions of the Code of Ethics and for promptly reporting known or suspected violations of this Code of Ethics or Amtrak policies to your supervisor, manager or the Amtrak Ethics and Compliance Hotline (1-866-908-7231);
- If you are a supervisor or manager, you are responsible and accountable for ensuring that your employees understand and comply with this Ethics Policy;
- No one in this Company has the authority or right to order, request or even influence you to violate this Code of Ethics or the law;
- You will not be excused for violating the Code of Ethics for any reason, even at the request of another person, including your supervisors, managers or Company officers;
- Any attempt by any person to have another violate the Code of Ethics, whether successful or not, is itself a violation and may be a violation of the law;
- Any retaliation or threat of retaliation against any person for refusing to violate the Code of Ethics or for reporting in good faith a violation or suspected violation of the Code of Ethics is itself a violation and may be a violation of the law;
- Every reported violation of the Code of Ethics will be investigated, and every actual violation will constitute a basis for disciplinary action involving the person violating the Code of Ethics and may result in civil or criminal action against that person; and
- Any employee who acts contrary to the Code of Ethics, or who knowingly gives a false report regarding a violation of the Code of Ethics, may be subject to disciplinary action, up to and including termination of employment.

Operations

Amtrak earns revenues from the following business activities:

Ticket and Food & Beverage Revenue—Amtrak's FY2009 ridership (29.9 million trips), ticket, and food and beverage revenue targets were projected to continue to benefit from the trends that propelled the ridership and revenue growth of FY2008. This budget, first reviewed by Amtrak's board of directors in July 2008, did not predict the uncertainty of the near-term outlook for travel due to the country's current economic crisis or the extreme volatility of gasoline prices.

State-Supported Revenue—The State-Supported Train business segment includes funding by the states to Amtrak for providing rail passenger services through contractual agreements. It includes intrastate and interstate train services with service origination in the contracted state. Amtrak is planning to partner with several states for launching train services in high-density state corridors to ease congestion.

Commuter—The Commuter business segment includes the results from the operating activities Amtrak provides to commuter agencies through contractual arrangements. Additional opportunities exist for Amtrak to perform work above the level specified in the existing commuter contracts. A number of commuter agencies also make operating and capital payments to Amtrak for the use of Amtrak-owned assets. These payments are accounted for under the Reimbursable Activity and Engineering Infrastructure section.

Reimbursable Activity—The Reimbursable business segment reports financial results from various activities Amtrak performs for other entities. These include maintenance-of-way services for the benefit of other railroads or agencies that do not fall under the Commuter umbrella and limited maintenance of equipment activities. As the title implies, this revenue is projected to offset the costs of activities that are budgeted in operating expenses in equal amounts.

Commercial Business—The Commercial business segment includes real estate/real property leases/easements/sales, parking, advertising, telecommunications, pipe and wire occupancy rights, retail leases at Amtrak stations, filming, and other commercial development.

Other Transportation Revenue—Items in this revenue area include items that are not consistent in nature and would include things like the sale of capital equipment.

Marketing

Advertising for Amtrak is regional. Amtrak primarily uses its Web site, www.amtrak.com, for booking reservations, and tickets can also be purchased at the station. Amtrak is also using the Web site www.orbitz.com as a partner. Amtrak has launched a new area on their Web site called the Whistle Stop, in which passengers can log in and share stories of the experience of riding an Amtrak train.

Financials

Exhibits 2 and 3 show the financial statements for Amtrak. Note in Exhibit 2 that Amtrak's revenues increased annually from 2005 through 2008. However, the organization experienced a net loss every year of more than $1.1 billion. Note in Exhibit 3 that Amtrak has more than $3.0 billion in long term debt.

Strategy

A review of the Amtrak Strategic Reform Proposal, dated 2006, highlighted that intercity passenger rail can make a valuable contribution in the meeting of several key transportation policy objectives, including the following:

- An alternative consumer travel choice to the automobile, bus, and air
- Additional capacity with opportunity for growth and intermodal connection
- An important link in rural areas where transportation alternatives are limited
- A stimulus to economic development and commercial activity
- An environmentally sound, energy-efficient, and disability-friendly alternative to other transportation modes

Although there is evidence to support these claims, the reality is that Amtrak will need to make substantial changes in operations prior to seeing these results. In the Independent Auditor's Report, KPMG stated, "The company has a history of substantial operating losses and is highly dependent upon substantial Federal government subsidies to sustain its operations. Without such subsidies, Amtrak will not be able to continue to operate in its current form and significant operating changes, restructuring or bankruptcy may occur. Such changes or restructuring would likely result in asset impairments."[4]

EXHIBIT 2   **National Railroad Passenger Corporation and Subsidiaries (Amtrak)**

Consolidated Statements of Operations (in thousands)

	2008	2007	2006	2005
Revenues:				
Passenger Related	$1,955,422.00	$1,730,926.00	$1,565,540.00	$1,435,884.00
Commuter	$ 129,545.00	$ 117,424.00	$ 115,394.00	$ 119,354.00
Other	$ 340,504.00	$ 302,254.00	$ 328,598.00	$ 302,322.00
State Capital Payments	$ 27,309.00	$ 2,011.00	$ 33,045.00	$ 28,692.00
Total Revenues	**$2,452,780.00**	**$2,152,615.00**	**$2,042,577.00**	**$1,886,252.00**
Salaries, Wages, and Benefits	$1,625,186.00	$1,661,838.00	$1,557,929.00	$1,511,656.00
Train Operations	$ 220,368.00	$ 209,881.00	$ 203,201.00	$ 193,277.00
Fuel, Power, and Utilities	$ 370,032.00	$ 284,184.00	$ 275,677.00	$ 228,511.00
Materials	$ 201,676.00	$ 179,044.00	$ 144,240.00	$ 132,544.00
Facility, Communications, and Office Related	$ 151,919.00	$ 141,154.00	$ 136,299.00	$ 130,390.00
Advertising and Sales	$ 98,056.00	$ 83,160.00	$ 75,389.00	$ 71,093.00
Casualty and Other Claims	$ 62,936.00	$ 25,708.00	$ 59,215.00	$ 25,771.00
Depreciation—net of amortization	$ 498,563.00	$ 454,085.00	$ 446,252.00	$ 557,901.00
Other	$ 294,189.00	$ 247,091.00	$ 218,457.00	$ 194,992.00
Indirect costs capitalized to property and equipment	−$ 113,304.00	-$ 106,537.00	−$ 111,183.00	−$ 105,839.00
Total Expenses	$3,409,621.00	$3,179,608.00	$3,005,476.00	$2,940,296.00
Net loss from continuing operations before other (income) and expense	$ 956,841.00	$1,026,993.00	$ 962,899.00	$1,054,044.00
Other (Income) and Expense:				
Interest income	−$ 90,593.00	-$ 99,349.00	−$ 94,967.00	−$ 82,062.00
Interest expense	$ 266,530.00	$ 193,265.00	$ 200,058.00	$ 206,783.00
Other expense—net	$ 175,937.00	$ 93,916.00	$ 105,091.00	$ 124,721.00
Net loss	$1,132,778.00	$1,120,909.00	$1,067,990.00	$1,178,765.00
Net (income) loss from discontinued operations	$ 0.00	$ 0.00	$ 0.00	$ 13,580.00
Net loss	**$1,132,778.00**	**$1,120,909.00**	**$1,067,990.00**	**$1,192,345.00**

EXHIBIT 3   **National Railroad Passenger Corporation and Subsidiaries (Amtrak)**

Consolidated Balance Sheets

	2008	2007	2006	2005
Assets				
Current Assets				
Cash and cash equivalents	$329,813.00	$223,949.00	$ 37,988.00	$ 75,261.00
Restricted cash	$ 10,012.00	$ 10,393.00	$ 3,081.00	
Short-term investments	$ 0.00	$ 9,950.00	$174,000.00	$ 63,164.00
Accounts receivable	$100,892.00	$141,645.00	$ 88,248.00	$ 96,810.00
Materials and supplies—net	$155,583.00	$174,897.00	$152,939.00	$147,202.00
Other current assets	$ 40,927.00	$ 44,026.00	$ 37,997.00	$ 72,786.00

continued

EXHIBIT 3   **National Railroad Passenger Corporation and Subsidiaries (Amtrak)—continued**

Consolidated Balance Sheets

	2008	2007	2006	2005
Total Current Assets	$ 637,227.00	$604,860.00	$ 494,253.00	$ 455,223.00
Property and Equipment				
Locomotives	$ 1,365,541.00	$ 1,405,200.00	$ 1,517,231.00	$ 1,500,447.00
Passenger cars and other rolling stock	$ 2,642,830.00	$ 2,650,963.00	$ 2,796,359.00	$ 2,851,008.00
Right-of-way and other properties	$ 8,693,663.00	$ 8,363,818.00	$ 8,080,656.00	$ 8,302,136.00
Leasehold improvements	$ 331,314.00	$ 310,503.00	$ 301,277.00	$ 229,574.00
Property and equipment—gross	$13,033,348.00	$12,730,484.00	$12,695,523.00	$12,883,165.00
Less—Accumulated depreciation and amortization	−$ 4,592,516.00	−$ 4,424,569.00	−$ 4,495,937.00	−$ 4,808,414.00
Total Property and Equipment, Net	$ 8,440,832.00	$ 8,305,915.00	$ 8,199,586.00	$ 8,074,751.00
Other Assets, Deposits, and Deferred Charges				
Escrowed proceeds on sale-leasebacks	$ 894,752.00	$ 874,744.00	$ 862,940.00	$ 853,631.00
Deferred charges, deposits, and other	$ 327,057.00	$ 379,942.00	$ 359,508.00	$ 363,846.00
Total other assets, deposits, and deferred charges	$ 1,221,809.00	$ 1,254,686.00	S 1,222,448.00	$ 1,217,477.00
Total assets	**$10,299,868.00**	**$10,165,461.00**	**$ 9,916,287.00**	**$ 9,747,451.00**
Liabilities and Capitalization				
Current Liabilities				
Accounts Payable	$ 217,681.00	$ 207,776.00	$ 199,430.00	$ 213,114.00
Accrued expenses and other current liabilities	$ 647,523.00	$ 537,054.00	$ 481,678.00	$ 481,072.00
Deferred ticket revenue	$ 111,758.00	$ 82,167.00	$ 73,402.00	$ 68,750.00
Current maturities of long-term debt and capital lease obligations	$ 146,864.00	$ 132,852.00	$ 143,577.00	$ 138,434.00
Total Current Liabilities	$ 1,123,826.00	$ 959,849.00	$ 898,087.00	$ 901,370.00
Long-Term Debt and Capital Lease Obligations				
Capital lease obligations	$ 2,782,771.00	$ 2,851,761.00	$ 2,994,144.00	$ 3,118,170.00
Mortgages	$ 212,955.00	$ 227,510.00	$ 240,805.00	$ 252,950.00
Equipment and other debt	$ 56,690.00	$ 92,657.00	$ 114,576.00	$ 154,331.00
Total long-term debt and capital lease obligations	$ 3,052,416.00	$ 3,171,928.00	$ 3,349,525.00	$ 3,525,451.00
Other Liabilities and Deferred Credits				
Deferred federal and state capital payments	$ 752,279.00	$ 701,357.00	$ 591,782.00	$ 509,441.00
Casualty reserves	$ 195,186.00	$ 212,469.00	$ 223,319.00	$ 185,603.00
Deferred gain on sale-leasebacks net	$ 262,222.00	$ 305,462.00	$ 400,116.00	$ 439,762.00
Postretirement employee benefits obligation	$ 566,760.00	$ 620,152.00	$ 325,989.00	$ 281,562.00
Environmental reserve	$ 62,342.00	$ 63,500.00	$ 67,014.00	$ 56,102.00
Other	$ 67,508.00	S 177,996.00	S 17,858.00	$ 18,100.00
Total Other Liabilities and Deferred Credits	$ 1,906,297.00	S 2,080,936.00	S 1,626,078.00	$ 1,490,570.00
Total Liabilities	$6,082,539.00	$6,212,713.00	$5,873,690.00	$5,917,391.00

continued

EXHIBIT 3 **National Railroad Passenger Corporation and Subsidiaries (Amtrak)—continued**

Consolidated Balance Sheets

	2008	2007	2006	2005
Commitments and Contingencies Capitalization				
Preferred stock	$10,939,699.00	$10,939,699.00	$10,939,699.00	$10,939,699.00
Common stock	$ 93,857.00	$ 93,857.00	$ 93,857.00	$ 93,857.00
Debt and other paid-in capital	$17,415,041.00	$16,100,513.00	$14,829,886.00	$13,559,085.00
Accumulated deficit	−$24,094,909.00	−$22,962,131.00	−$21,819,117.00	−$20,751,127.00
Accumulated other comprehensive income (loss)	−$ 136,359.00	−$ 219,190.00	−$ 1,728.00	−$ 11,454.00
Total Capitalization	$ 4,217,329.00	$ 3,952,748.00	$ 4,042,597.00	$ 3,830,060.00
Total Liabilities and Capitalization	**$10,299,868.00**	**$10,165,461.00**	**$ 9,916,287.00**	**$ 9,747,451.00**

The key to Amtrak's future, in the words from the 2006 Strategic Initiative document, "hinges first on a defined mission, including adequate and predictable capital funding, and over the longer term on the emergence of competition and private sector alternatives to Amtrak." Specifically, the vision of management is to develop an intercity passenger rail system. To do this, the following objectives will need to be accomplished:

- Development of passenger rail corridors based on a federal-state capital matching program, with states serving as the developers and purchasers of competitively bid corridor services
- Return of the Northeast Corridor infrastructure to a state of good repair and operational reliability, with all users gradually assuming financial responsibility for their proportionate share of operating and capital needs
- Continuation and possible addition/elimination of certain national long-distance routes based on established performance thresholds, with a phase-in period to allow for performance improvements and state participation where needed to meet thresholds
- Emergence of markets for competition and private commercial participation in all passenger rail functions and services, including outsourcing of selected functions and competition among operators for corridor routes

Amtrak's vision for the coming years is to:

- Deliver superior service—including continued excellence in operational safety and security and infrastructure/asset management—while becoming more market and customer oriented
- Serve as a catalyst for change—helping the nation's intercity passenger rail system achieve the long-term objectives from above
- Evolve into one of a number of competitors for passenger rail services and routes, all positioned on equal competitive footing

Competitors

Amtrak has many competitors because they are in the business of transportation. A primary competition that Amtrak faces is the automobile. Automobiles provide consumers with more flexibility and generally are a faster form of transportation. The main difference is that consumers must own a car and provide their own transportation. Beyond the automobile, the main competition comes from Greyhound Bus Lines and airlines.

GREYHOUND Although the time required to travel using Greyhound is very similar to that of Amtrak, passengers are likely to spend less when traveling by bus. The difference is that the accommodations on the train tend to be more comfortable than those on the bus.

Founded in 1914, Greyhound Lines, Inc. is the largest provider of intercity bus transportation, serving more than 2,300 destinations with 13,000 daily departures across North America. It has become an American icon, providing safe, enjoyable, and affordable travel to nearly 25 million passengers each year. The Greyhound running dog is one of the most recognized brands in the world.

Although Greyhound is well known for its regularly scheduled passenger service, the company also provides a number of other services for its customers. Greyhound PackageXpress service offers value-priced same-day and early-next-day package delivery to thousands of destinations. And the company's Greyhound Travel Services unit offers charter packages for businesses, conventions, schools, and other groups at competitive rates.

It is also important to note that Greyhound is not only a competitor to Amtrak; it is also a partner. Amtrak passengers use Greyhound to make connections to cities not served by rail on Amtrak Thruway service, by purchasing a ticket for the bus connection from Amtrak in conjunction with the purchase of their rail ticket. Passengers can also purchase tickets directly from Greyhound.

AIRLINES   In mid-to-late 2009, airline ticket prices have dropped dramatically, eroding substantially Amtrak's business. The major drawback to traveling by train of course is the amount of time that it takes to go from the origination point to the destination. Because time tends to be a major consideration for travelers, airlines provide an alternative to travel by car, bus, and train; the drawback, of course, is that they are more expensive. Airlines provide passengers with a faster travel alternative.

Southwest Airlines, for example, flies over 100 million passengers a year to 65 great cities all across the country. Southwest consistently leads the entire airline industry with the lowest ratio of complaints per passengers boarded. Many airlines have tried to copy Southwest's business model, and the culture of Southwest is admired and emulated by corporations and organizations in all walks of life. Always the innovator, Southwest pioneered Senior Fares, a same-day air freight delivery service, and Ticketless Travel. Southwest led the way with the first airline Web page, southwest.com; DING! the first-ever direct link to customers' computer desktops that delivers live updates on the hottest deals; and the first airline corporate blog, Nuts About Southwest.

Conclusion

Amtrak today faces obstacles that include uncertainty of government funding, competition, fuel prices, the regulatory environment in which they operate, and creating a leadership development program. Only time will tell if Amtrak's CEO, Joseph Boardman, will be able to deliver on his promise to help the company "work through its challenges and capitalize on the opportunities we have to build a safer, greener, healthier Amtrak that connects America coast-to-coast and border-to-border."[5] Amtrak needs a clear strategic plan for the future.

Endnotes

1. Adapted from Amtrak, *Annual Report* (2008).
2. T. Ramstack, "Amtrak CEO Kummant Resigns," *Washington Times* (November 15, 2008). Accessed at http://www.washingtontimes.com/news/2008/nov/15/amtrak-ceo-kummant-resigns/.
3. From the Passenger Rail Investment and Improvement Act of 2008.
4. Amtrak, *Annual Report* (2008).
5. Amtrak, *Annual Report* (2008), p. 5.

Goodwill of San Francisco, San Mateo and Marin Counties — 2009

16

Mary E. Vradelis, Consultant
Berkeley, California

www.sfgoodwill.org

In February 2009, the CEO and president of Goodwill of San Francisco, San Mateo and Marin Counties (Goodwill), Deborah Alvarez-Rodriguez, prepares for the launch of a challenging fund-raising campaign that will determine how the organization weathers the next few years. Only a few months into the new fiscal year (which started in July 2008), Alvarez-Rodriguez realized that the organization was facing a projected deficit of $3 million that threatened its ability to provide many services that are the core of its mission. The nonprofit organization, with a budget of over $32 million, was deeply affected by the national economic downturn. Goodwill operates independently as a member of Goodwill Industries International Inc. Goodwill International has 184 autonomous chapters in the United States, Canada, and 14 other countries.

The first major blow to Goodwill's cash flow resulted from the failed sale of its headquarters in July 2008, which was in final contract status when the buyer defaulted. This resulted in a loss of $6 million in investment capital and nearly $1 million in operating capital. Since then, Goodwill's revenues from the sale of salvage materials, such as metal and wood, have plummeted with the drop in world commodity prices. Like many nonprofit organizations across the country, Goodwill's grant income is threatened by a significant drop in foundation portfolio values. Demand for Goodwill's free job-training and placement services, however, is skyrocketing—with monthly attendance already at five times the contract projections.

Alvarez-Rodriguez is proud of the work that Goodwill accomplishes with its commitment to give hope to people in need. Of those who receive job training and development, 46 percent have been incarcerated or detained by the criminal justice system, 25 percent have been homeless in the last three months, 20 percent have a severe disability, and some participants deal with all of these barriers. Alvarez-Rodriguez believes that despite the financial crisis (and because of it), "eliminating services is not an option."

Between October 2008 and January 2009, Alvarez-Rodriguez and her senior team tapped their combined business acumen and passion for Goodwill's mission to reduce a $3 million deficit to $1 million, without impacting services. However, to maintain high standards for quality service and meet the demand created by the nation's highest monthly unemployment growth rate in 60 years, Goodwill is poised to launch the first fund-raising campaign in its 93-year history. Alvarez-Rodriguez has two options: raise $1 million from individual donors to fill the budget gap or reduce the critical services that the organization provides. An individual donor campaign is an ambitious project in a recession. However, the Obama administration's American Recovery and Reinvestment Act offers opportunities for new funding.

History

Goodwill International was founded in 1902 in Boston by Dr. Edgar Helms. As a Methodist minister, he gathered household goods and clothing for parishioners, of whom a majority were poor immigrants. Rather than just give away the used goods, he trained the unemployed to repair the donated goods. He then sold the goods in the community or gave them to the people who repaired them. This evolved into a core program philosophy to give people a "hand up, not a hand out," which became the impetus for a national "Goodwill

Movement." In 1916, Helms worked with a Bay Area religious leader, Reverend Samuel Quickmire. Together they opened the third Goodwill in the nation, Goodwill of San Francisco, to help local citizens who were still recovering from the 1906 earthquake. Over the next 20 years, Goodwill opened seven more operations in Northern California.

Deborah Alvarez-Rodriguez joined Goodwill in 2004 when she inherited an organization that was struggling operationally and financially. Prior to this she had been the director of San Francisco City and County's Department of Children, Youth and their Families. In 2008, the *San Francisco Business Times* named her the Most Admired Nonprofit CEO. In 2009, she was named one of the Bay Area's most influential women in business for the fourth year in a row.

Immediately after her appointment, Alvarez-Rodriguez began a planning process in collaboration with the Goodwill board of directors and a newly developed internal, cross-functional Change Management Team. The intensive process began with a revision of Goodwill's mission and vision. This interdisciplinary team, which involved staff from all levels of the organization, not only reviewed the organization's mission, goals, and values; it also researched the external forces (social, governmental, and economic) that challenge Goodwill's ability to offer successful programs for the population it was designed to serve. Their work resulted in the following new Vision and Mission statements, which were unanimously adopted by the Board of Directors in 2006:

> *Vision:* Our Goodwill envisions a world free of poverty where people have the power to support themselves and their families, live in safe and thriving communities, and actively care for the environment.
> *Mission:* We create solutions to poverty through the businesses we operate.

To implement this new mission, Alvarez-Rodriguez, the management team, and the board of directors committed to change the way it operated—integrating job training and service providing into the core of its revenue-generating business model. Alvarez-Rodriguez worked to eliminate what she calls "silos within silos" that had developed within the organization and prevented it from infusing its primary mission—helping poor and disadvantaged people attain skills and find work—in all departments. In a 2007 interview in the *Chronicle of Philanthropy,* Alvarez-Rodriguez stated, "There was a split between the mission side and the retail side. We needed to put the organization in a position where it could thrive." The Change Management Team worked to create a transformational model that would embed training and professional development into all of the revenue-generating departments of the organization. In addition, this transformational model required social services programs to be self-sustaining, keeping a keen focus on their "profitability." By the end of the planning process, Alvarez-Rodriguez put the organization on a path of reflection, development, and change that was comparable to the work that Goodwill expected of its participants.

Operations

Based on its new mission, in November 2006 Goodwill's board of directors adopted a new strategy of workforce creation through an environmental value recovery business platform. The board adopted the following three-part definition of *workforce creation*:

- *We operate businesses* that recruit and employ people who are overcoming barriers to employment, we provide them with training, experience and support so they can achieve long-term sustainable employment and the capacity to advance in careers.
- *We form strategic partnerships* by partnering to invest in and strengthen the economic infrastructure of neighborhoods with special emphasis on employing and developing people who are overcoming some of the greatest barriers to employment.
- *We support neighborhood businesses* that are owned or co-owned by our participants and others overcoming barriers to employment.

Goodwill of San Francisco, San Mateo and Marin Counties, Inc. has almost 500 employees, and operates 17 retail stores in the three counties. To support the retail operations, it has over 30 collection sites across the diverse region that it serves. Goodwill's central administrative offices and flagship retail store are located at 1500 Mission Street, San Francisco (http://www.sfgoodwill.org/StoreLocations2.aspx).

Because Goodwill has seen a decline in the profit margin of its brick-and-mortar stores, it has developed an e-commerce business as well. Through collaboration with eBay, it lists over 10,000 items (http://stores.shop.ebay.com/Goodwill-San-Francisco_W0QQ_armrsZ1). In addition, Goodwill has launched a range of new marketing strategies, including direct marketing based on psychographics and demographic targeting; e-blasts; social networking on Facebook, MySpace, and Linkedin; and SeamSoGood.com, a blog dedicated to fashion and style.

Goodwill offers job training in all three counties of its jurisdiction. In addition to gaining hands-on retail experience, participants can get a class A (big truck) license, train extensively in computer skills, improve basic skills in English as a second language, polish interview and resume skills, improve financial literacy, support asset building, and complete GED coursework. In FY 2007–2008, the program provided job training and career counseling to 1,728 Bay Area residents—up 42 percent from the previous fiscal year. Through the institution of One-Stop Career Link Centers (formed in collaboration with other local work development programs), Goodwill expects this number to triple in FY 2008–2009. For the participants with the highest level of need, Goodwill is able to offer paid training for up to six months. Although shown to be highly successful, this program is the most costly.

GOODWILL NOT LANDFILL   As part of its triple-bottom line, Goodwill's vision encompasses environmental stewardship. One of the programs that Alvarez-Rodriguez is proudest of is the electronic donations program. This was a logical outgrowth of the reuse retail business that had been a core of Goodwill since the beginning. The electronics salvage/reuse program focuses on providing free computer recovery and recycling for Bay Area residents.

In fact, the organization likes to think of itself as the "original recycler." In 2007–2008, Goodwill launched a major six-month advertising campaign to increase public awareness of their overall recycling and reuse businesses, and to encourage responsible recycling. The campaign included radio and newspaper ads, as well as signs on bus shelters and buses. In addition, there were contests sponsored by two local radio stations. The culmination of the campaign was an Earth Day event that resulted in the collection of 40,000 pounds of electronic waste. As indicated in Exhibit 1, by the end of that fiscal year, Goodwill had saved the following:

- Over 7.3 million pounds of clothing and other textiles saved from going to landfill
- 49,528 computers from going to landfill
- A total of 18.4 million pounds of material diverted from landfill

In support of increasing the reuse program, the San Francisco Department of the Environment awarded Goodwill a $200,000 grant to support a two-year pilot program to reuse and recycle donated furniture And the California Emerging Technology Fund granted Goodwill a three-year $600,000 grant to embed training in its ReCompute

EXHIBIT 1   **Selected Success Metrics**

	FY 2007–2008	FY 2006–2007
Pounds of material goods diverted from landfill	18,402,438	17,178,916
Employers who hired Goodwill participants	217	235
Computers saved from gong to landfill by recycling and refurbishing	49,528	59,863
Bay Area residents who received job training and career counseling	1,214	1,728
Pairs of shoes saved from going to landfill	896,905	844,478

Source: Company documents.

electronics recycling/repurpose program. In December 2008, Goodwill began training classes encompassing everything from basic computer literacy to advanced information technology (IT) skills.

To strengthen its infrastructure and reach, Goodwill collaborates with several strategic corporate partners: SalesForce, Dell, Levis, Microsoft, McCall's Design group, and BBDO West (part of Omnicom, a worldwide advertising agency). Alvarez-Rodriguez's philosophy emphasizes the importance of nonprofits to look for corporate partners by identifying where there is a synergy of perspectives and approach, and an alignment of values. She continually asks herself, "How can we create value for ourselves and for the company?" In November 2007, it launched a pilot of repurposed clothing and accessories, William Good, which was created under the creative direction of Nick Graham (the founder of Joe Boxer). Given the economic downturn and lack of startup capital, this pilot is not currently being developed.

When the 2008–2009 budget was approved in April 2008, Goodwill anticipated a 17 percent increase in revenues. Revenue drivers included operational, fund development, extraordinary revenue items, and interest income. As Exhibit 2 shows Goodwill's business operations generate a significant amount of its projected revenue ($32.3 million). Value Recovery Enterprises, generating 85 percent of its revenue, consist primarily of the Retail Stores (projected to be $21 million alone) and the E-Store ($950,000). The Environmental Businesses (As-Is, Transportation, Salvage, ReCompute, and pilot projects) comprise the remaining $4.5 million of Goodwill's Value Recovery revenue. Goodwill's balance sheets are provided in Exhibit 3.

Ethics Code of Business

Goodwill's values are in alignment with the values of Goodwill Industries International, Inc.:

- Respect—We treat all people with dignity and respect.
- Stewardship—We honor our heritage by being socially, financially, and environmentally responsible.
- Ethics—We strive to meet the highest ethical standards.
- Learning—We challenge each other to strive for excellence and to continually learn.
- Innovation—We embrace continuous improvement, bold creativity and change.

EXHIBIT 2 Goodwill Proposed Budget for FY 2008–2009

	Revenues		
	2008–2009 Projected	2007–2008* Actual	Variance %
Value Recovery Enterprises	26,219,346	24,467,661	7%
Career Services	2,926,063	1,738,387	68%
Organizational Advancement	1,349,700	288,788	367%
Corporate Services	767,944	1,066,394	−28%
Executive Office	1,000,000	39,598	2425%
Total Agency Revenues	**32,263,053**	**27,600,828**	**17%**

	Expenses		
	2008–2009 Projected	2007–2008* Actual	Variance %
Total Wages & Benefits	21,376,712	18,154,042	18%
Other Operating Expenses	10,975,193	9,272,938	18%
Depreciation	1,239,635	1,102,181	12%
Total Agency Expenses	**33,591,540**	**28,529,161**	**18%**
Profit (Loss)	**(1,328,487)**	**(928,333)**	**43%**

*Actual amounts for FY 2007–2008 are estimates derived from year-to-date results through April 2008.

Source: Company documents.

EXHIBIT 3   **Goodwill Industries of San Francisco, San Mateo and Marin Counties, Inc.**

Statement of Financial Position, June 30, 2008
(with comparative totals for 2007)

	2008	(Restated) 2007
ASSETS		
Current assets		
Cash and cash equivalents	$ 4,136,260	$ 1,124,389
Accounts receivable, net	623,000	665,683
Contributions receivable, current portion	225,000	600,000
Note receivable, net	68,191	—
Merchandise Inventories	1,878,513	1,854,514
Prepaid Expenses	575,749	582,446
Total current assets	7,506,713	4,827,032
Property and equipment, net	15,108,862	15,413,230
Contributions receivable, net of current portion	75,000	—
Deposits and other assets	289,219	287,240
Total assets	**$ 22,979,794**	**$ 20,527,502**
LIABILITIES AND NET ASSETS		
Current liabilities		
Accounts payable and accrued expenses	$ 2,158,617	$ 1,488,677
Deferred revenue	326,574	434,806
Building deposit	3,000,000	0
Current Maturities of note payable	105,394	97,398
Total current liabilities	**5,590,585**	**2,020,881**
Deferred rent	69,718	29,002
Note payable, less current maturities	855,042	968,430
Total liabilities	6,515,345	3,018,313
Net assets		
Unrestricted	15,808,634	16,709,503
Temporarily restricted	655,815	799,686
Total net assets	16,464,449	17,509,189
Total liabilities and net assets	**$ 22,979,794**	**$ 20,527,502**

Source: Company documents.

Goodwill of San Francisco, San Mateo and Marin Counties is also the first Goodwill in the nation to develop a triple bottom line mission: "An enterprising organization, Goodwill operates a robust business measured against a triple bottom line of people, planet and performance. There is transparency and accountability as Goodwill unlocks the value in both people and material donations."

Organizational Chart

Goodwill is one of 184 autonomous not-for-profit nonsectarian Goodwill organizations affiliated with Goodwill Industries International, Inc. The Bay Area organization is overseen by a board of directors. As a nonprofit, it is required to have the oversight of this volunteer body because its primary focus is to protect the public interest and because it

EXHIBIT 4   CEO Direct Reports Organization Chart 2009

Source: Company documents.

receives preferential tax treatment. Governing responsibilities include financial oversight; legal compliance; mission, vision, and overall strategic planning; fund-raising; and oversight of the executive director.

As indicated in Exhibit 4, Alvarez-Rodriguez guides the organization in collaboration with an executive team that consists of the chief operating officer; the chief of organizational advancement (in charge of marketing, PR, communications, branding, and fund-raising); the chief of value recovery (which encompasses all commercial businesses); and the chief of people services. In addition, she has three direct reports: two executive assistants; a business development and strategy specialist. In turn, the executive team oversees several senior managers including directors of finance, IT, retail operations, donations, e-commerce, marketing, human resources, training, Workforce Investment Act, and criminal justice and reentry. This management team draws from a diversity of life and work experiences, including government, retail, environmental businesses, real estate, as well as "graduates" of Goodwill's training program.

Industry and Competitors

Nonprofit

Goodwill is one of thousands of nonprofits operating in California. In 2006, there were 102,677 nonprofit organizations in California. This was a 59.4 percent increase since 1996. In 2006, 862 nonprofits were in the employment/job-related field, with a total revenue of $1,330,679, 056. (Goodwill's budget of $32 million comprised 2 percent of the entire revenue for the field in California.) As a nonprofit organization, Goodwill competes with other charitable organizations for donations from individuals, foundations, and corporations, as well as for government contracts. Because of the national financial crisis, the majority of the top 100 U.S. foundations say that they will be likely to reduce funding in 2009.[1] Only one foundation, the Bill & Melinda Gates Foundation, recently committed to increase its giving.

Retail

According to Rachael Grossman, chief of organizational advancement, many people assume that other nonprofit reuse retailers are Goodwill's only competition, such as the Salvation Army and St. Vincent de Paul. Instead, the organization discovered that key competitors also include major discount retailers such as Ross and Target. Studies that Goodwill conducted in October 2007 projected that retail would be the fastest growing industry in San Francisco, adding 7,800 jobs from 2002 to 2012. Goodwill is well positioned to capitalize on this growing market and prepare its participants for jobs. In fact, history has proven that Goodwill's largest revenue stream has been anticyclical. The impact of the other anticipated revenue drops are cushioned by the relatively recession-proof retail operations that Goodwill runs. As indicated in Exhibit 5, Goodwill's brick-and-mortar stores have maintained a 4 percent comp store increase over last year, and its e-commerce business has grown in excess of 93 percent.

EXHIBIT 5 Financial Overview

	FY 2007–2008	FY 2006–2007
Goodwill Revenues		
Retail Stores	$20,920,001	$20,048,814
Education, Training & Employment	$ 211,796	$ 174,597
Salvage/Recycling	$ 3,012,885	$ 2,579,886
Corporate Services	$ 1,069,851	$ 472,864
Public Support	$ 2,843,483	$ 3,094,790
Total Revenue	**$28,058,016**	**$26,370,951**
Goodwill Expenses		
Education, Training & Employment (includes collecting, processing, selling donated goods)	$18,853,894	$17,415,497
Fundraising	$ 26,419	$ 189,646
Operating Expenses	$ 5,090,583	$ 3,439,955
Occupancy	$ 3,909,105	$ 3,691,013
Investment in Plant & Facilities	$ 1,078,884	$ 1,020,244
Total Expenses	**$28,958,885***	**$25,756,355**
Surplus (Deficit)	**($900,869)**	**$ 614,596**

*87% of this figure equals direct services and 13% equals overhead.

Source: Company documents.

Job Development and Placement Services

The normal competitors for Goodwill programs were nonprofit and government-run workforce development programs. Goodwill has adopted a "coopetition" strategy, however, in which it has reached out to former competitors to develop collaborations that can provide mutual and community benefits. Goodwill now partners with former competitors, such as Jewish Vocational Services and Rubicon, in the new city-sponsored One-Stop System to increase job training services and placements for San Francisco residents. The greatest threat to the job placement industry is a national economy in crisis. It is likely that many of the hotels, retail stores, and transport companies will be forced to reduce staffing levels during the recession. According to the *Wall Street Journal* (March 6, 2009), "U.S. nonfarm payrolls dropped 651,000 in February, almost right on expectations of a 652,000 loss. The unemployment rate rose to 8.1%, from 7.6% in January. The jobless rate is the highest since 1983. The economy has now shed 4.4 million jobs since the recession began in December 2007, with almost half of those losses occurring in the last three months alone." That high rate of increase has not been seen since World War II.

Conclusion

The recession has threatened Goodwill's ability to raise money from individuals, private and corporate foundations, and city and state governments. Without new funding, the necessary investments in innovation, scale, and impact may need to be delayed. And as a nonprofit, the organization doesn't have access to equity markets. It has done what streamlining it can to protect its core delivery of services. Deeper cuts could impact the technology, marketing, fund-raising, and retail functions that are essential to its revenue stream. Exhibit 6 reveals Goodwill's historical revenue growth.

Alvarez-Rodriguez needs to act fast to close the projected budget gap. Her goal is to raise $1 million in new donations. If Goodwill is not able to meet this goal soon, what steps would she need to keep the organization solvent?

EXHIBIT 6   Goodwill Revenue Growth

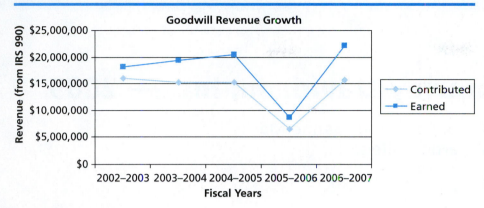

Source: Company documents.

A clear three-year strategic plan needs to be developed in order to raise the new funds needed. Potential donors want to see how their funds would be used and what the expected impact over three years will be. Prepare this 2009–2011 strategic plan for the CEO.

References

www.sfgoodwill.org

National Center for Charitable Statistics: http://nccs.urban.org

Interviews with Rachael Grossman, Chief of Organizational Advancement, on March 11, 2009, and April 8, 2009.

2008–2009 Goodwill Proposed Plan and Budget, June 11, 2008 board meeting

Goodwill Industries International, Inc., http://www.goodwill.org

Katherine Weinstein Miller, "From Remediation to Transformation: Goodwill's New Human Capital Development Model," October 2007.

Endnotes

1. Lawrence T. McGill, senior vice president, and Steven Lawrence, senior director of research, "Grantmakers Describe the Impact of the Economic Crisis on Their Giving," Foundation Center, March 2009.

17 Harley-Davidson, Inc. — 2009

Carol Pope and Joanne Mack
Alverno College

HOG

www.harley-davidson.com

In the first half of 2010, Harley-Davidson opened its first five dealerships in India. High import tariffs of 90 percent on motorcycles historically kept Harley out, but the growing upper class in India now warrants Harley opening dealerships there.

Harley-Davidson announced in April 2009 that it will shed an additional 300 to 400 hourly jobs in the 2009–2010 timeframe, on top of the 1,100 jobs it previously planned to eliminate during that period. Its stock declined from 48.05 per share to 9.78 per share in the time period March 8, 2008 to March 7, 2009, although a recent surge put the stock price at 19.45 as of April 27, 2009. Harley is closing several facilities and has indicated its motorcycle sales decreased 13 percent during the first two months of 2009. However, Harley has continued to remain profitable throughout the economic crisis, although its second quarter 2009 profits declined 91 percent. For that quarter, Harley's U.S. sales fell 35 percent while non-U.S. sales dropped 18 percent.

Any serious discussion about Harley-Davidson includes the power of its brand. Mention of Harley creates a vision of rugged individualism, American iron, and passion. The passion runs so deep that many customers and admirers sport a Harley tattoo to express that passion. There aren't too many corporations that inspire that kind of following. How many Honda or Kawasaki tattoos have you seen on riders' arms? What is it about Harley that sets it apart from its competitors, and even from mega-successful companies that aren't its competitors? The mystique is magical.

Harley's heritage is symbolic of the American dream. Harley's workers and customers relate to and find motivation in this American dream that became a reality. An extension of this concept of "family" is also a key to Harley's success. The HOG (Harley Owner's Group) is a worldwide family of Harley owners that is a million strong. When one purchases a Harley, one becomes part of a family of owners that rides together and parties together, in locations on nearly every continent. Indeed, the Harley Web site beckons riders to "share the adventure." Aside from the shared experience, many Harley riders treasure taking in the back roads and the beauty of scenery unique to each locale. This is especially true in Harley's hometown of Milwaukee, where riders wait impatiently for the snow to melt so that they can experience the year's solo inaugural ride. Nostalgia is also badge of Harley's success. Its unique "potato-potato-potato" sound created by its famous V-twin engine is still heard in the rumblings of its motorcycles on the road today, and its legendary styling, overseen by "Willie G" Davidson, himself an icon, has created continuity over the decades. For these reasons and more, Harley remains an American icon more than 100 years after its formation.

Harley's History: The Building of a Legend

Harley's Web site announces to online visitors that this is "Where Dreams Come True" and beckons readers to "Join the Family You've Always Wanted." The mystique of Harley begins with two families, the Harleys and the Davidsons, who had big dreams back at the turn of the twentieth century in Milwaukee, Wisconsin.

In 1903, what was to become a legendary motorcycle company was formed in the Davidson family's backyard. The "factory" in which they worked was a 10- by 15-foot wooden shed with the words "Harley-Davidson Motor Company" scrawled on the door. The Davidson brothers, William D., Walter, Arthur, and William S. Harley, made their first motorcycle there.

During World War I, Harley-Davidson supplied the military with 20,000 motorcycles. During this time, there were major advancements in the design of motorcycles, and Harley was the leader. However, a decade after the war ended, the Great Depression devastated the motorcycle industry. Only Harley-Davidson and Indian survived through the 1930s. Harley also contributed to the successful U.S. efforts in World War II, during which it supplied more than 90,000 motorcycles to the military. After the war, demand for motorcycles exploded, and Harley-Davidson added facilities in Milwaukee in 1947. After competitor Indian closed in 1953, Harley-Davidson was the sole American motorcycle manufacturer for decades. Harley ended family ownership in 1965 with a public offering. Only four years later, the company merged with the American Machine and Foundry Company (AMF), a longtime producer of leisure products.

By the early 1970s, the Japanese were importing huge numbers of lower-priced motorcycles into the United States. Japanese firms were able to capture a large portion of Harley's market share. Because it had expanded production so quickly, Harley was also having quality problems. In 1981, 13 of Harley's senior executives purchased the business from AMF. In 1986, Harley-Davidson, Inc. became publicly held for the first time since 1969. That same year, Harley regained its place at the top of the U.S. super-heavyweight market, beating out Honda. Harley was listed on the New York Stock Exchange in 1987, and its market share continued to grow.

Notable events in the first decade of the twenty-first century for Harley include celebration of its 100th year anniversary in 2003, and 105th in 2008, and the opening of the Harley-Davidson Museum in Milwaukee in 2008. According to Harley, its museum project was designed to deliver a unique experience that builds and strengthens bonds between riders and Harley-Davidson, and enhances the brand among the public at large. The facility also includes a restaurant and café, a retail store, and special event place. Also taking place in 2008 was Harley-Davidson's acquisition of MV Agusta. Throughout this first decade of the twenty-first century, Harley-Davidson continues to be highly regarded in the philanthropy area. Harley might be best known for its association with the Muscular Dystrophy Association, raising upward of $50 million for the charity. The Harley-Davidson Foundation focuses its giving on education and community revitalization, and it also supports arts and culture, health initiatives, and the environment.

Mission Statement, Vision Statement, and Values

Harley's mission statement is:

> We fulfill dreams through the experiences of motorcycling, by providing to motorcyclists and to the general public an expanding line of motorcycles, branded products and services in selected market segments.

This philosophy is what helps set Harley apart from its competitors. According to Harley, it takes more than just building and selling motorcycles to fulfill the dreams of its customers. It takes unforgettable experiences, and Harley is dedicated to creating experiences and developing relationships with all of its stakeholders. Harley believes that is what sets it apart from the crowd, and why its brand strength is legendary.

Harley's vision statement is:

> Harley-Davidson is an action-oriented, international company, a leader in its commitment to continuously improve its mutually beneficial relationships with stakeholders (customers, suppliers, employees, shareholders, government, and society). Harley-Davidson believes the key to success is to balance stakeholders' interests through the empowerment of all employees to focus on value-added activities.

Harley also emphasizes the importance of its five stated Values: (1) Tell the Truth; (2) Be Fair; (3) Keep Your Promises; (4) Respect the Individual; and (5) Encourage

EXHIBIT 1   Harley-Davidson, Inc. Organizational Structure: Executive Officers

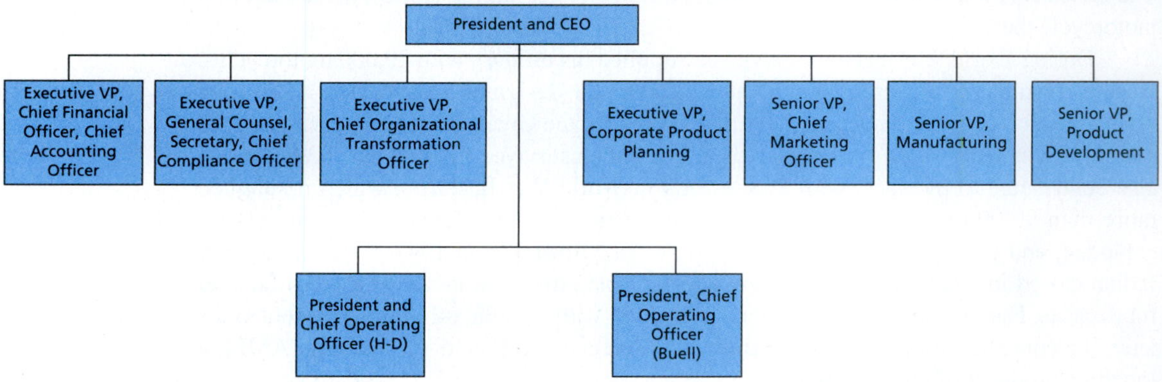

Source: www.harley-davidson.com and their 2008 *Form 10-K.*

Intellectual Curiosity. According to Harley, it Values represent the heart of how it runs its business. The Values guide their actions and serve as the framework for the decisions and contributions its employees make at every level of the Company. Harley-Davidson states that the Values are more than just a list of "feel good" buzzwords; they reflect how Harley employees relate to each other and to all of their stakeholders, including customers, dealers, and suppliers.

Organizational Structure

As indicated in Exhibit 1, Harley's organizational structure consists of executive vice presidents and senior vice presidents, who oversee key functional areas. These vice presidents are members of a group of leaders known as the Senior Leadership Group. The Senior Leadership Group consists of a broad group of leaders representing key functions and individuals in the Motor Company, Buell, MV, HDFS, and Harley-Davidson. The group meets several times each year to have a dialogue with the chief executive officer (CEO) and to share business information. Although this group is not a decision-making body, it evaluates and discusses critical, enterprise-wide business challenges throughout the year. The CEO of Harley determines membership in the Senior Leadership Group.

Certain members of the Senior Leadership Group are also members of the Leadership and Strategy Council, which consists of the CEO of Harley-Davidson and the presidents of the Motor Company, Buell and HDFS, certain senior officers of the Motor Company (senior vice president, manufacturing; senior vice president, product development; and senior vice president and chief marketing officer) and certain other Harley-Davidson executives (executive vice president and chief financial officer; executive vice president, chief organizational transformation officer; and executive vice president, general counsel and secretary).

Harley's Business Segments

Harley-Davidson operates in two segments: (1) financial services and (2) motorcycles and related products.

Financial Services

The financial services segment includes the group of companies doing business as Harley-Davidson Financial Services (HDFS), which provides wholesale and retail financing and, as an agent, provides insurance and insurance-related programs primarily to Harley-Davidson and Buell dealers and their retail customers. HDFS conducts business principally in the United States and Canada. HDFS's 2008 operating income decreased 61.0 percent. In February 2009, billionaire Warren Buffet's Berkshire Hathaway invested $300 million in Harley-Davidson. Harley says Berkshire and Harley's biggest shareholder, Davis Selected Advisers, L.P., are each committed to buying $300 million in senior unsecured notes, due in 2014. The money will be used to support Harley's finance company and its ongoing motorcycle lending activities.

Motorcycles and Related Products

The motorcycle and related products segment of Harley-Davidson includes (1) Parts & Accessories (P&A); (2) General Merchandise; (3) Licensing; and (4) Motorcycles. The major P&A products are replacement parts and mechanical and cosmetic accessories. Worldwide P&A net revenue comprised 15.4 percent, 15.2 percent, and 14.9 percent of net revenue in the Motorcycles segment in 2008, 2007, and 2006, respectively. Worldwide General Merchandise net revenue, which includes apparel and collectibles, comprised 5.6 percent, 5.3 percent, and 4.8 percent of net revenue in the Motorcycles segment in 2008, 2007, and 2006, respectively. With regarding to licensing, the company creates an awareness of its most significant brand, Harley-Davidson, among its customers and the nonriding public through a wide range of products by licensing the name "Harley-Davidson" and other trademarks owned by the company. Licensed products include T-shirts, jewelry, small leather goods, and toys. Although the majority of licensing activity occurs in the United States, Harley continues to expand these activities in international markets, such as into India in 2010. Royalty revenues from licensing, included in Motorcycles segment net revenue, were $45.4 million, $46.0 million, and $45.5 million in 2008, 2007, and 2006, respectively.

Harleys are sold under the brands of Harley-Davidson Motor Company, Buell Motorcycle Company, Cagiva, and MV Agusta (which was acquired by Harley-Davidson in 2008). The Motorcycle segment designs, manufactures, and sells at wholesale primarily heavyweight (engine displacement of 651+cc) touring, custom, and performance motorcycles. Harley-Davidson, which is the only major American motorcycle manufacturer, conducts business globally, with sales primarily in North America, Europe, Asia/Pacific, and Latin America. (See Exhibits 2 and 3 for a summary of Harley's motorcycle shipments by product line and by region.)

Harley's worldwide motorcycles sales generated approximately 80 percent of the total net revenue in the Motorcycles segment during each of the years 2008, 2007, and 2006.

The company manufactures five families of motorcycles: (1) Touring, (2) Dyna, (3) Softail, (4) Sportster, and (5) VRSC. The engines range in size from 883cc's to 1803cc's. Harley's heavyweight class of motorcycles is divided into four segments: standard,

EXHIBIT 2 Harley-Davidson Motorcycle Shipments by Product Line*

Motorcycle Unit Shipments and Net Revenue

Motorcycle Unit Shipments	2008		2007		(Decrease) Increase	% Change
United States	206,309	68.0%	241,539	73.1%	(35,230)	(14.6)%
International	97,170	32.0%	89,080	26.9%	8,090	9.1
Harley-Davidson Motorcycle units	303,479	100.0%	330,619	100.0%	(27,140)	(8.2)
Touring motorcycle units	101,887	33.6%	114,076	34.5%	(12,189)	(10.7)
Custom motorcycle units (Dyna, Softail, VRSC, and CVO)	140,908	46.4%	144,507	43.7%	(3,599)	(2.5)
Sportster motorcycle units	60,684	20.0%	72,036	21.8%	(11,352)	(15.8)
Harley-Davidson Motorcycle units	303,479	100.0%	330,619	100.0%	(27,140)	(8.2)
Buell motorcycle units	13,119		11,513		1,606	13.9%

* The table includes wholesale motorcycle unit shipments for the Motorcycles segment.

During 2008, the company shipped 303,479 Harley-Davidson motorcycles, a decrease of 27,140 motorcycles, or 8.2 percent, from last year. The company's shipments in the U.S. in 2008 continued to be negatively impacted by the challenging economic environment, but were consistent with the company's expectations to ship 23,000 to 27,000 fewer Harley-Davidson motorcycles in 2008 than were shipped in 2007. The company's shipments in international markets grew during 2008, and the percentage of units shipped to international customers increased, consistent with the company's strategic focus on global markets.

Source: www.harley-davidson.com and their 2008 *Form 10-K.*

EXHIBIT 3 Harley-Davidson Motorcycle Shipments by Region

Harley-Davidson Motorcycle Retail Sales [a]
Heavyweight (651+cc)

	2008	2007	(Decrease) Increase	%Change
North America Region				
United States	218,939	251,772	(32,833)	(13.0)%
Canada	16,502	14,779	1,723	11.7
Total North American Region	235,441	266,551	(31,110)	(11.7)
Europe Region (Includes Middle East and Africa)				
Europe[b]	40,725	38,866	1,859	4.8
Other	4,317	3,436	881	25.6
Total Europe Region	45,042	42,302	2,740	6.5
Asia Pacific Region				
Japan	14,654	13,765	889	6.5
Other	10,595	9,689	906	9.4
Total Asia Pacific Region	25,249	23,454	1,795	7.7
Latin America Region	8,037	5,467	2,570	47.0
Total Worldwide Retail Sales	313,769	337,774	(24,005)	(7.1)%

(a) Data source for retail sales figures shown above is sales warranty and registration information provided by Harley-Davidson dealers and compiled by the company. The company must rely on information that its dealers supply concerning retail sales and this information is subject to revision. Only Harley-Davidson motorcycles are included in the Harley-Davidson Motorcycle Retail Sales data.
(b) Data for Europe include Austria, Belgium, Denmark, Finland, France, Germany, Greece, Italy, Netherlands, Norway, Portugal, Spain, Sweden, Switzerland, and the United Kingdom.

Source: www.harley-davidson.com and their 2008 *Form 10-K.*

performance, touring, and custom. The standard segment emphasizes simplicity and cost, and the performance segment emphasizes handling and acceleration. The touring segment for the company focuses on comfort for long-distance travel. Harley-Davidson pioneered this segment of the heavyweight market. Harley's custom segment gives owners the opportunity to customize their bikes. Limited-edition, factory-custom motorcycles are sold through its Custom Vehicle Operation (CVO) program. Motorcycles sold through the CVO program are available in limited quantities and offer unique features, paint schemes, and accessories.

Buell motorcycle products emphasize innovative design, responsive handling, and overall performance. Buell manufactures four families of motorcycles: (1) Sportbike, (2) Street, (3) Adventure, and (4) Blast. The Blast features a smaller 492cc single-cylinder engine, ideal for many new riders. MV motorcycle products emphasize exquisite design and high performance. Buell is active in the racing community and gains publicity from those efforts.

The heavyweight (651+cc) motorcycle market is highly competitive. Harley-Davidson's major competitors are based outside the United States and generally have financial and marketing resources that are substantially greater than those of Harley-Davidson. They also have larger worldwide revenue and are more diversified than Harley-Davidson. In addition to these larger, established competitors, Harley-Davidson has competitors headquartered in the United States. These competitors generally offer heavyweight motorcycles with traditional styling that compete directly with many of Harley-Davidson's products. These competitors currently have production and sales volumes that are lower than Harley-Davidson's and have considerably lower U.S. market share than Harley-Davidson.

Harley actively promotes the motorcycling lifestyle in the form of events, rides, rallies, and Harley Owners Group (HOG). Harley considers the availability of financing through HDFS as a competitive advantage.

In the United States, Harley-Davidson competes most heavily in the touring and custom segments of the heavyweight motorcycle market, which accounted for approximately

84 percent, 80 percent, and 79 percent of total heavyweight retail unit registrations in the United States during 2008, 2007, and 2006, respectively. The larger-displacement custom and touring motorcycles are generally the most profitable for Harley-Davidson. During 2008, the heavyweight portion of the market represented approximately 55 percent of the total U.S. motorcycle market in terms of new units registered. For the last 21 years, Harley-Davidson motorcycles have led the industry in the United States for retail unit registrations of new heavyweight motorcycles. The Harley-Davidson motorcycle share of the heavyweight market was 45.5 percent and 48.7 percent in 2008 and 2007, respectively.

Marketing and Distribution

Harley-Davidson has approximately 686 independently owned full-service dealerships in the United States. The marketing efforts are divided between dealer promotions, customer events, and advertising through national television, print, radio and direct mailings, as well as electronic advertising. Harley-Davidson also sponsors racing activities and special promotional events, and it participates in all major motorcycle consumer shows and rallies. On an ongoing basis, Harley-Davidson promotes its products and lifestyle through The Harley Owners Group (HOG), which was founded in 1983 and currently has approximately1.1 million members worldwide. HOG is the industry's largest company-sponsored motorcycle enthusiast organization (www.hog.com). The Buell Riders' Adventure Group (BRAG) formed in recent years has grown to approximately 10,000 members. Both HOG and BRAG sponsor events, including national rallies and rides, across the United States and around the world for motorcycle enthusiasts. Harley faces the competitive forces from companies such as Honda, Suzuki, Kawasaki, and Yamaha to maintain its dominant overall market share in the U.S. Heavyweight Motorcycle market.

To reach out to current nonriders as well as expert riders, Harley-Davidson created its Academy of Motorcycling in 2000. The Academy's Rider's Edge program offers a series of rider education experiences that provide both new and experienced riders with deeper engagement in the sport of motorcycling by teaching basic and advanced motorcycling skills and knowledge in a way that is fun and engaging. The courses are conducted by a network of select Harley-Davidson dealerships nationwide enabling students to experience the Harley-Davidson lifestyle, environment, people, and products as they learn. The company Web site, www.harley-davidson.com, is also used to market its products and services. The Web site features an online catalog that allows retail customers to create and share product wish lists, use a dealer locator, and place catalog orders.

The average U.S. retail purchaser of a new Harley-Davidson motorcycle is a married man in his mid to late forties (nearly two thirds of U.S. retail purchasers on new Harley-Davidson motorcycles are between the ages of 35 and 54) with a median household income of approximately $87,000. Nearly three quarters of the U.S. retail sales of new Harley-Davidson motorcycles are to buyers with at least one year of education beyond high school, and 32 percent of the buyers have college/graduate degrees. Approximately 12 percent of U.S. retail motorcycle sales of new Harley-Davidson motorcycles are to female buyers.

International Sales

The European heavyweight motorcycle market is roughly 80 percent of the size of the U.S. market. Traditional U.S.-style touring motorcycles represent less than 5 percent of the European heavyweight motorcycle market. Harley-Davidson continues to expand its product offerings to compete in the standard and performance segments with motorcycles such as Harley-Davidson's XR1200 and Nightster, the Buell 1125R, and MV models. Harley-Davidson's traditional Harley-Davidson products compete primarily in the custom and touring segments.

In addition to Europe and the United States, Harley-Davidson also competes in Canada, Japan, and Australia. In Canada, the company's market share based on registrations was 41.9 percent, 39.0 percent, and 38.2 percent during 2008, 2007, and 2006, respectively.

In terms of non-U.S. distribution, Harley-Davidson has 71 full service dealerships in Canada, 383 in Europe, 201 in Asia Pacific, and 32 in Latin America. The MV brand, which was added in 2008, distributes its motorcycles and prints and advertising (P&A) to independent dealers primarily through subsidiaries located in Germany, Switzerland, and the United States. In Italy and France, MV distributes its products to independent dealers directly. MV's network of approximately 500 independent dealers is primarily located in Europe with approximately 40 independent dealers in the United States.

Competitors

Harley-Davidson's revenue for the full year 2008 was $5.59 billion compared to $5.73 billion in 2007, a 2.3 percent decrease. The 2008 full-year net income was $654.7 million, compared to $933.8 million in 2007. Diluted earnings per share were $2.79, a decrease of 25.4 percent compared to $3.74 in 2007. For 2008, wholesale shipments of Harley-Davidson motorcycles were 303,479 units, an 8.2 percent decrease compared to 330,619 units in 2007. For the full year 2009, Harley-Davidson plans to ship between 264,000 and 273,000 new Harley-Davidson motorcycles, a 10 to 13 percent reduction from 2008. Most Harley competitors are diversified in the automotive market. Harley's suggested retail price for its motorcycles is generally higher than its competitors'. Harley's financial services operations face competition from various banks, insurance companies, and other financial institutions that may have access to additional sources of capital at more competitive rates and terms.

Harley's competitors include Honda, Yamaha, Suzuki, Kawasaki, Polaris, BMW, and Triumph. Honda is the world's largest motorcycle producer, ahead of Yamaha and Suzuki, which are the second and third largest. Honda's sales are favorable, particularly in Asia, and it is looking to increase production in India. Honda is planning for growth in Asia, continued recovery in Europe, and for a probable downturn in the United States. Honda produces a number of products other than motorcycles, most notably the Honda and Acura brand automobiles. All-terrain vehicles (ATVs), generators, personal watercraft, snowblowers, and scooters are also sold under the Honda brand.

Like Honda, Yamaha and Suzuki are also more diversified than Harley in terms of product offerings. Both focus on ATVs, scooters, and marine and watercraft in addition to various motorcycle product lines. Currently, Yamaha has seen decreasing motorcycle sales in Japan, the United States, and Europe, but is faring better in Southeast Asia and Latin America. Yamaha recently has undertaken temporary factory shutdowns in Japan and bonus pay reductions at least through 2009. Suzuki, which also sells automobiles, operates in more than 190 countries. Suzuki's motorcycle product line includes cruisers, motocross, off-road, scooter, street, and touring models. Kawasaki's motorcycle production is a part of its consumer products and machinery division. Polaris, based in Minnesota, is one of the world's top makers of snowmobiles and off-road vehicles, and it is also known for its Victory cruiser and touring motorcycles. Polaris's plan is to achieve $3 billion in overall sales by 2009. It is focusing on developing new products, including its first luxury touring motorcycle models.

BMW and Triumph are also competitors of Harley-Davidson, and both have a cachet attached to their brands. BMW (Bayerische Motoren Werke), a top German automaker, also includes motorcycles as part of its product offerings. The 2007 figures indicate that BMW motorcycle sales broke the 100,000 unit mark for the second year in a row. BMW also offers leather suits, gloves, boots, and other motorcycling apparel. Triumph Motorcycles, a private company in the United Kingdom, finds its roots in the original Triumph organization, which built cars that had quite a following. The automaker went bankrupt in the early 1980s, and the Triumph Motorcycle Company emerged in 1983 when John S. Bloor bought the Triumph name and manufacturing rights. Triumph's sales in 2007 reached $398,600,000. Triumph is known for its liquid-cooled three-cylinder engines, and, like Harley-Davidson, sells trademarked motorcycling apparel. Triumph's motorcycles are sold in over 20 major national markets.

Finance

Harley's income statements and balance sheets are provided in Exhibits 4 and 5. In its *Form 10-K (Annual Report)* filed on February 17, 2009, Harley-Davidson's 2008 net revenue and

EXHIBIT 4   Income Statements (2006–2008)

HARLEY-DAVIDSON, INC.
ANNUAL INCOME STATEMENTS
Unaudited
YEAR ENDED DECEMBER 31
(in thousands, except per share amounts)

	2008	2007	2006
NET REVENUE:			
H-D Motorcycle	$4,278,241	$4,446,637	$4,553,561
Parts & Accessories	858,748	868,297	862,251
General Merchandise	313,835	305,435	277,490
Buell Motorcycle	123,086	100,534	102,227
Defense and Other	20,397	5,945	5,157
TOTAL	**5,594,307**	**5,726,848**	**5,800,686**
Gross Profit	1,930,819	2,114,100	2,232,847
HDMC Operating Exp	964,429	883,457	823,857
HDMC Operating Income	966,390	1,230,643	1,408,990
HDFS Operating Income	82,765	212,169	210,724
Corporate Operating Exp	20,131	17,251	22,561
Total Operating Income	1,029,024	1,425,561	1,597,153
Investment Income	9,495	22,258	27,087
Interest Expense	4,542	—	—
Income Before Provision for Taxes	1,033,977	1,447,819	1,624,240
Provision for Income Taxes	379,259	513,976	581,087
Net Income from Continuing Ops	654,718	933,843	1,043,153
Net Income (Loss) from Disc Ops	—	—	—
Extraordinary Items	—	—	—
Net Income	**$654,718**	**$933,843**	**$1,043,153**
Basic/Primary Earnings per Common Share:	$2.80	$3.75	$3.94
Diluted Earnings per Common Share:	$2.79	$3.74	$3.93
Weighted Ave Shares:			
Basic	234,225	249,205	264,453
Diluted	234,477	249,882	265,273
Dividends Paid	$1.290	$1.060	$0.810
Domestic Revenue	3,853,242	4,206,427	4,629,895
International Revenue	1,741,065	1,520,421	1,170,791
	5,594,307	5,726,848	5,800,686

Source: www.harley-davidson.com and their 2008 *Form 10-K.*

Note: Per FASB's Emerging Issues Task Force on "Accounting for Shipping and Handling Fee and Costs" and "Accounting for Certain Sales Incentive," certain 2000 and 2001 year balances have been reclassified.

EXHIBIT 5 Harley-Davidson's Balance Sheets

	(all numbers in thousands)		
Period Ending	31-Dec-08	31-Dec-07	31-Dec-06
Assets			
Current Assets			
Cash and Cash Equivalents	$593,558	$402,854	$238,397
Short Term Investments	3,822,426	2,475	658,133
Net Receivables	419,585	2,641,058	2,317,804
Inventory	400,908	349,697	287,798
Other Current Assets	141,404	71,230	48,501
Total Current Assets	**5,377,881**	**3,467,314**	**3,550,633**
Long Term Investments	817,102	845,044	725,957
Property Plant and Equipment	1,094,487	1,060,590	1,024,469
Goodwill	138,579	61,401	58,800
Intangible Assets	—	—	—
Accumulated Amortization	—	—	—
Other Assets	112,336	167,881	129,305
Deferred Long Term Asset Charges	288,240	54,376	42,986
Total Assets	**7,828,625**	**5,656,606**	**5,532,150**
Liabilities			
Current Liabilities			
Accounts Payable	525,727	450,361	763,186
Short/Current Long Term Debt	1,762,152	1,154,369	832,491
Other Current Liabilities	315,878	300,349	—
Total Current Liabilities	**2,603,757**	**1,905,079**	**1,595,677**
Long Term Debt	2,176,238	980,000	870,000
Other Liabilities	933,027	396,036	309,736
Deferred Long Term Liability Charges	—	—	—
Minority Interest	—	—	—
Negative Goodwill	—	—	—
Total Liabilities	**5,713,022**	**3,281,115**	**2,775,413**
Stockholders' Equity			
Misc. Stocks Options Warrants	—	—	—
Redeemable Preferred Stock	—	—	—
Preferred Stock	—	—	—
Common Stock	3,357	3,352	3,343
Retained Earnings	6,458,778	6,117,567	5,481,126
Treasury Stock	(4,670,802)	(4,420,394)	(3,266,955)
Capital Surplus	846,796	812,224	766,382
Other Stockholders' Equity	(522,526)	(137,258)	(227,159)
Total Stockholders' Equity	**2,115,603**	**2,375,491**	**2,756,737**
Net Tangible Assets	**$1,977,024**	**$2,314,090**	**$2,697,937**

Source: www.harley-davidson.com and their 2008 *Form 10-K.*

net income were down 2.3 percent and 29.9 percent, respectively, compared to 2007. Operating income for the Motorcycles segment was down 21.5 percent, and operating income for the Financial Services segment decreased 61.0 percent. Diluted earnings per share were $2.79 in 2008, a 25.4 percent decrease compared to last year's $3.74. Worldwide retail sales of Harley-Davidson motorcycles were down 7.1 percent in 2008 as compared to 2007. In the United States, retail sales of Harley-Davidson motorcycles in 2008 were down 13.0 percent; international retail sales were up 10.3 percent as compared to 2007. However, international retail sales growth slowed to 0.7 percent during the fourth quarter of 2008 as a result of deteriorating economic conditions outside the United States.

Harley CEO James Ziemer just retired and with that came the installation of Keith Wandell as president and chief executive officer of the company on May 1, 2009. CEO Wandell says Harley's credit losses have risen to 3.41 percent, from 2.71 percent the prior year, creating havoc for the company as hundreds of buyers and dealers cannot obtain financing and hundreds more default on loans. Many Harley owners who have put their heart and soul into their bikes now are having to sell them, which is a windfall benefit for other folks who have always wanted a Harley at a deal/steal. Basic consumer and commercial financing problems continue to plague Harley as 2009 nears an end. Discretionary spending on high-end consumer goods such as motorcycles has declined drastically.

Prepare a clear three-year strategic plan for CEO Wandell and Harley-Davidson.

18 Ford Motor Company — 2009

Alen Badal
The Union Institute

F

www.ford.com

Ford recently received $5.9 billion in Energy Department loans to help retool its plants in Illinois, Kentucky, Michigan, Missouri, and Ohio to produce 13 fuel-efficient models, including 5,000 to 10,000 electric cars per year starting in 2011. In mid-2009, Nissan Motor was granted $1.6 billion in loans also from the U.S. Department of Energy to build as many as 100,000 electric cars a year at its plant in Smyrna, Tennessee, by 2013.

Ford's newest competitor may be the U.S. government because GM and Chrysler LLC are in line to get $62 billion in investments from the U.S. Treasury. GM and Chrysler have cut their debt and closed hundreds of dealers with that money, while Ford still has $33 billion in debt including its obligations to retirees. Since CEO Alan Mulally's arrival at Ford in 2006, the company has cut 40,000 jobs and closed 17 plants, reducing costs by more than $5 billion. Ford has a $10 billion note that comes due in 2011.

Ford increased its production 16 percent in the third quarter of 2009 versus the third quarter of 2008. This was good news for Ford shareholders and customers. In May 2009, Toyota posted a $4.4 billion loss for its fiscal year, the first time Toyota posted an annual loss since 1963. Virtually all automobile companies are suffering in the bad economy. Ford is on track, however, to break even or perhaps make a profit in 2011.

Ford is also trying to sell its Volvo division but has decided to wait until GM completes the sale of its Opel division in efforts to get a higher price for Volvo. Three firms as of August 2009 were bidding on Volvo: Geely Holding Group, Beijing Automotive Industry Holding, and a Europe-based group of investors. Sales of Volvo in the United States fell 36 percent in the first six months of 2009 as compared to 2008.

An American icon for over a century, Ford's revenue decreased from $172.5 billion in 2007 to $146.3 billion in 2008. Born in 1863, Henry Ford founded Ford Motor Company in 1903 and launched the Model T in 1908. Henry died in 1947. The great-grandson of Henry, William Ford, is today chairman of the board of Ford. Exhibit 1 features the leadership of the Ford Motor Company. Ford's icon vehicles, such as the Mustang and the F-150 truck, can be spotted on the roadways worldwide.

Headquartered in Dearborn, Michigan, Ford has a 13.8 percent market share of the auto industry as of February 2009, as compared to 17.5 percent in 2007. Ford Motor operates two service businesses: Ford Motor Credit Company and Genuine Parts and Motorcraft.

Ford manufactures and distributes automobiles across six continents with a team of about 246,000 employees. The company operates about 108 plants globally and produces such models as Ford, Lincoln, Mazda, Mercury, and Volvo. The company has sold its Jaguar, Land Rover, and Aston Martin businesses.

The subsidiary, Ford Motor Credit Company, offers auto financing to both dealers and customers globally. The company also assists dealerships with funding for such

EXHIBIT 1   Ford Motor Company Corporate Officers

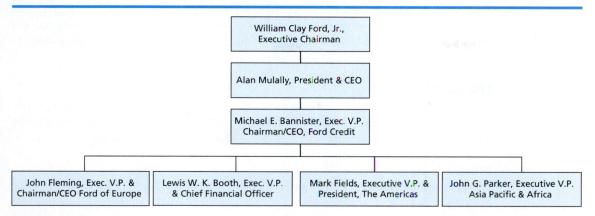

Source: www.ford.com.

EXHIBIT 2   Ford versus Toyota and the Industry

	Ford	Toyota	Industry
Market Capitalization	$24.9B	135.3B	24.9B
# Employees	213,000	324,222	33,200
Revenue	113.8B	193.9B	14.5B
Gross Margin	7.69%	7.25%	17.83%
Earnings Before Interest and Taxes	2.95B	4.36B	176.2M
Net Income	−5.22B	−9.28B	—
EPS	−2.072	−5.92	−0.14

Note: M = million; B = billion

Source: Based on info at www.financeyahoo.com.

EXHIBIT 3   The U.S. Market Share of Top 11 Auto Firms (February 2009)

Company	% of Market Share
General Motors Corp.	18.8
Toyota Motor Sales USA Inc.	16.9
Ford Motor Company	13.8
Chrysler LLC	10.9
American Honda Motor Co. Inc.	10.6
Nissan North America Inc.	8.0
Hyundai Motor America	4.1
Kia Motors America Inc.	3.3
Mazda Motor of America Inc.	2.4
Subaru of America Inc.	1.9
Mitsubishi Motors N A, Inc.	0.7

Source: Based on http://online.wsj.com/mdc/public/page/2_3022-autosales.html#autosalesD.

purposes as improving sites and acquiring real estate. Ford's Motorcraft division offers parts for its vehicles through the company's Web site (www.ford.com).

Ford's major competitors are General Motors, Toyota, and Chrysler. Ford and rival General Motors are losing market share to Toyota and other foreign automakers. Exhibit 2 and 3 provide comparative information on Ford versus its rival firms. Note that Ford is number three in market share in the United States. The 2009 Motor Trend truck of the year was the Ford F-150.

Company Brands

Ford consists of five brands and is generally perceived as being an affordable brand name catering to a variety of consumer needs and wants. The vehicles span cars, trucks, and super utility vehicles (SUVs). Ford also produces the Mondeo found in Europe and the EcoSport in South America and some parts of Asia.

Lincoln/Mercury

Ford's Lincoln (www.lincoln.com) vehicles are perceived as a luxury line and include five models such as the popular Navigator and Town Car. Ford's Mercury (www.mercuryvehicles.com) line also offers five different models, such as the Mountaineer and the Milan.

Mazda

A Japanese line named after the ancient god of wisdom is Mazda (www.mazda.com). Mazda evolved in 1931 representing a three-wheeled truck combining a motorcycle and automobile. Mazda today offers 11 different models along with its Mazda Verisa. The company posted sales in the first nine months of fiscal 2008 of 2.1 million yen (¥). The company's Web site contains information about Mazda in some 54 different countries. Mazda's revenues dropped from 2.5 million yen in the first nine months of 2007 to 2.0 million yen during that period in 2008.

Volvo

Volvo (www.volvocars.com), a brand name that created the first three-point seat belt, has built strong brand recognition as a safe vehicle. Volvo in 1955 began exporting cars to the United States. Ford acquired Volvo in 1999, but the division is now up for sale. Volvo markets in some 58 countries. This Sweden-headquartered division sells the line in more than 185 markets. This division sold 374,297 units worldwide in 2008, an 18 percent decrease in sales from 2007. The stronger demand was in the United Kingdom while the U.S. and Sweden markets weakened. Volvo achieved net sales of $14.7 billion in 2008, compared to $17.9 billion in 2007, as described in Exhibit 4.

Ford Motor Credit

Founded in 1923, Ford Motor Credit Company (www.fordcredit.com) offers financing to consumers and dealerships nationwide and is the world's largest finance company. Ford Credit offers innovative products and competitive financing rates with flexible terms applied toward leasing and/or financing purchases.

Genuine Parts & Service

Genuine Parts & Service (www.genuineflmservice.com) offers the know-how about parts, repairs, and maintenance to owners of Ford, Lincoln, and Mercury vehicles. First introduced in 1991, the concept was to help provide better owner satisfaction, which has provided better vehicle brand success for Ford.

EXHIBIT 4 Ford Motor Company Sector Revenues (2007 vs. 2008)

Sector	2007	2008
North America	$71.5 billion	$53.4 billion
South America	$ 7.6 billion	$ 8.6 billion
Europe	$36.5 billion	$39 billion
Volvo	$17.9 billion	$14.7 billion
Asia Pacific/Africa	$ 7 billion	$ 6.5 billion
Mazda	$ 0	$ 0
JLR & Aston Martin	$15 billion	$ 0
Financial Services	$18 billion	$17 billion

Source: Adapted from www.ford.com.

Motorcraft

Ford purchased Electric Autolite Company in 1961 and later changed the name to Motorcraft (www.motorcraft.com), which makes parts for Mercury, Lincoln, and Ford vehicles. The division is a subsidiary business offering premium parts/services ranging from motor oil to transmission assemblies. This business emerged for Ford as a result of the lack of replacement vehicle parts available by the manufacturers.

Global Operations

Ford markets vehicles in over 200 markets across 6 continents. Ford's recent One Ford strategy focuses on standardizing the production of vehicles, technologically tracing production throughout the life cycle, cross-shipping of components to ensure speedier time to markets, and finding the Ford-ingredients to meet the automotive needs of the global market. One such example is Ford's Fiesta, which is available in Europe and expected in 2010 in the United States. Ford's truck lines are still strong with the award-winning F-150.

The Euro (€), British pound (£), and the Japanese yen (¥) currencies have been valued more than the U.S. dollar ($). Ford's North America sales have dropped substantially; however, South America and Europe achieved sales increases in 2008 for Ford, as shown in Exhibit 4.

Ford's income statements are provided in Exhibit 5. Note Ford's massive losses in both 2006 and 2008. Ford's balance sheets are provided in Exhibit 6. Note that Ford is

EXHIBIT 5 Ford Motor Company Income Statement

Period Ending	(all numbers in thousands)		
	31-Dec-08	31-Dec-07	31-Dec-06
Total Revenue	146,277,000	172,455,000	160,123,000
Cost of Revenue	127,103,000	142,587,000	148,869,000
Gross Profit	19,174,000	29,868,000	11,254,000
Operating Expense	—	—	—
Research Development	—	—	—
Selling Gen & Admin	21,430,000	21,169,000	19,180,000
Non Recurring	—	2,400,000	—
Others	1,874,000	668,000	241,000
Total Operating Expenses			
Operating Income or Loss	**(4,130,000)**	**(5,631,000)**	**(8,167,000)**
Income from Continuing Oper	—	—	—
Total Other Income/Exp. Net	(755,000)	(1,550,000)	(1,899,000)
EBIT	(4,722,000)	(7,181,000)	(6,268,000)
Interest Expense	9,682,000	10,927,000	8,783,000
Income Before Tax	(14,404,000)	(3,746,000)	(15,051,000)
Income Tax Expense	63,000	(1,294,000)	(2,646,000)
Minority Interest	(214,000)	(312,000)	(210,000)
Net Income from Cont. Ops	(14,681,000)	(2,764,000)	(12,615,000)
Non-recurring Events	—	—	—
Discontinued Operations	9,000	41,000	2,000
Extraordinary Items	—	—	—
Effect of Acct. Changes	—	—	—
Other Items	—	—	—
Net Income	**(14,672,000)**	**(2,723,000)**	**(12,613,000)**

Source: www.ford.com.

EXHIBIT 6 Ford's Balance Sheets

	(all numbers in thousands)		
PERIOD ENDING	31-Dec-08	31-Dec-07	31-Dec-06
Assets			
Current Assets			
Cash and Cash Equivalents	$22,049,000	$35,283,000	$28,894,000
Short Term Investments	—	—	—
Not Receivables	6,165,000	8,863,000	8,772,000
Inventory	8,618,000	10,121,000	11,578,000
Other Current Assets	—	—	—
Total Current Assets	**36,832,000**	**54,267,000**	**49,244,000**
Long Term Investments	112,487,000	160,676,000	136,378,000
Property Plant and Equipment	54,303,000	36,239,000	38,505,000
Goodwill	1,190,000	1,504,000	5,839,000
Intangible Assets	403,000	565,000	30,932,000
Accumulated Amortization	—	—	—
Other Assets	10,005,000	22,513,000	12,706,000
Deferred Long Term Charges	3,108,000	3,500,000	4,950,000
Total Assets	**218,328,000**	**279,264,000**	**278,554,000**
Liabilities			
Current Liabilities			
Accounts Payable	78,158,000	44,411,000	24,416,000
Short/Current Long Term Debt	—	—	—
Other Current Liabilities	—	4,093,000	28,128,000
Total Current Liabilities	**78,158,000**	**48,504,000**	**52,544,000**
Long Term Debt	154,196,000	168,530,000	172,049,000
Other Liabilities	55,000	50,158,000	51,477,000
Deferred Long Term Liability Charges	2,035,000	5,023,000	4,790,000
Minority Interest	1,195,000	1,421,000	1,159,000
Negative Goodwill	—	—	—
Total Liabilities	**235,639,000**	**273,636,000**	**282,019,000**
Stockholders' Equity			
Misc Stocks Options Warrants	—	—	—
Redeemable Preferred Stock	—	—	—
Preferred Stock	—	—	—
Common Stock	24,000	22,000	19,000
Retained Earnings	(16,145,000)	(1,485,000)	(17,000)
Treasury Stock	(181,000)	(185,000)	(183,000)
Capital Surplus	9,076,000	7,834,000	4,562,000
Other Stockholders' Equity	(10,085,000)	(558,000)	(7,846,000)
Total Stockholders' Equity	**(17,311,000)**	**5,628,000**	**(3,465,000)**
Total Liabilities and SE	**218,328,000**	**279,264,000**	**278,554,000**

Source: www.ford.com.

carrying over $1 billion in goodwill, which is not good. Nor is its $154 billion in long-term debt a good thing. The company may be doing better than some of its rival firms, but make no mistake, Ford is in financial trouble.

Ford produces energy hybrid vehicles and has joined forces with British Petroleum (BP) to develop hydrogen power. Ford's Rouge Center in Dearborn, Michigan, represents the world's largest living roof and covers the Dearborn Truck Plant's final assembly building.

Competitors

Chrysler LLC

Founded in 1883, Chrysler LLC (www.chryslerllc.com) currently holds 10.9 percent of the U.S. market share as of February 2009. At the conclusion of fiscal 2008, Chrysler employed approximately 54,007 employees. A privately owned company, Cerberus Capital Management, currently owns 80.1 percent of Chrysler, with the remainder owned by Daimler, the former parent company of Chrysler. The company manufactures seven different models, including Jeep and Dodge. Chrysler LLC also owns Global Electric Motorcars (GEM), low-speed vehicles often used in parks and industrial campuses. The company sells parts and vehicle accessories under a MOPAR brand name and has a Chrysler Financial division, which offers financing opportunities for buyers in North America, Puerto Rico, and Venezuela.

Chrysler received $9 billion in bailout monies from the United States, with a possibility of needing an extra $3 billion. It reportedly used up $3 billion in cash in the last quarter of 2008. Headed by previous CEO of Home Depot, Robert Nardelli, Chrysler had requested $7 billion in "bridge funding" to save the company.

Chrysler has contracted with Nissan and Volkswagen to manufacture cars. This cost-saving strategy, coupled with speculations of Envi, an electric car, and smaller cars built by Nissan, are expected to improve the firm's financial position. Chrysler's sales in February 2009 as compared to February 2008 were down 44 percent.

General Motors Corporation (GM)

Headquartered in Detroit, Michigan, GM (www.gm.com) employs approximately 244,500 and reported annual revenues of $149 billion in 2008 as compared to $181 billion in 2007. GM manufactures cars and trucks in 34 countries. GM also operates a Financing and Insurance Operation. Saab, Pontiac, and Cadillac are among the many GM models. GM holds an industry leading 18.8 percent of the U.S. market share as of February 2009. GM's sales in February 2009 when compared to the prior year were down by 53 percent.

GM experienced a steady decline in sales and received an $18 billion (with more requested) government bailout from the United States. GM's Saab division in Sweden is attempting to isolate itself from GM to avoid the country losing a carmaker. Saab's units-sold in 2008 were down 34.7 percent compared to 2007. GM has plans to phase out its Saturn and Hummer brands. The plans also call for reducing Pontiac production.

GM has been criticized for not adapting its cars and production system to address the needs of consumers. The future of GM is reliant on hybrid electric Chevy Volt along with models such as the Malibu. GM's cars have produced negative sales figures, such as a 50.9 percent reduction in Hummer units sold in 2008 as compared to 2007. Chevrolet, Cadillac, GMC, and Buick have ranged from 20.4 percent to 26.2 percent reduction in units sold in 2008 compared to the previous year. GM's goal is to have a production-ready fuel-cell vehicle by 2010.

Toyota Motor Corporation

Headquartered in Toyota City, Japan, Toyota Motor Corporation (www.toyota.co.jp) reported annual revenues of $249.5 billion in 2008. Toyota currently holds 16.9 percent of the U.S. market share as of February 2009. The company has 316,212 employees and was founded in 1933. It was ranked by J.D. Power and Associates as number one in customer loyalty, with 68.9 percent of new purchases whose previous new vehicle was from Toyota. Not all of Toyota's makes and models are manufactured in America; the company has production plants across the globe.

Toyota operates in two segments: Automotive and Non-Automotive Operations. Toyota models include the Corolla and RAV4. Its financial service helps consumers subsidize vehicles and mortgage loans. Toyota provides financing to dealers. Other operations include designing and manufacturing of prefabricated housing and information technology related businesses. The company operates an e-commerce marketplace known as Gazoo.com and sells vehicles in Japan, North America, Europe, and Asia. However, Toyota experienced a 40 percent decrease in revenues in February 2009 compared to 2008. Honda and Nissan experienced similar figures with a decrease of 38 percent and 37 percent, respectively.

Toyota is focusing on its all-new Prius, which promises fuel economy to exceed the current model's 48 mpg. Also, Toyota will become the first automaker of a hybrid-only luxury car: the Lexus HS250h, with fuel economy of 40 mpg.

Industry Analysis

The auto manufacturing industry has been crushed of late by the global economic recession as consumer demand for new autos has plummeted. Consumer confidence is the lowest in 40 years, and unemployment rates exceed 10 percent in many areas. Unavailability of credit and high unemployment have pushed automakers to rethink methods of producing and selling cars. Automakers have faced rising costs of health care and pensions. The Big Three hope to gain further concessions from the United Auto Workers regarding labor costs, among others, in times of hardship. The Big three also suffer from an oversupply for dealers.

The few consumers purchasing vehicles are doing so for practical reasons, with a focus on fuel efficiency, durability, and carmaker's sustainability. Consumers are concerned over the Big Three's possibility of going out of business in terms of voided warranties. According to CSM Worldwide, an automotive research firm, light vehicle production exceeded the production of cars and trucks in North America and Europe by an estimated 16 percent and 14 percent, respectively.

Many banks are just not making car loans. This situation has been detrimental to auto firms. In 2008, the Big Three began offering lowered interest rates or zero percent financing to lure buyers. Ford, Chrysler, and even Toyota are offering employee prices to consumers.

The auto industry has experienced a shift from trucks and SUVs to hybrid and small fuel-efficient vehicles. The government bailout money is diminishing, and Ford has exhausted its credit lines.

Emerging Automotive Markets

While the economy in the United States slowed and new car sales drastically declined, Russia's grew 15.1 percent, Brazil's 15.5 percent, China's 12 percent, and India's 5 percent, respectively, in the third quarter of 2008. GM and Ford have had some success in markets outside the United States. GM achieved 61 percent of total revenues in the third quarter of 2008 outside of North America. Ford is counting on China for sales as is Volkswagen, AG.

The Future

Ford's midsize 2010 Fusion in August 2009 set a monthly sales record for the model for the fifth consecutive month. A sedan redesigned for the 2010 model year, the Fusion competes with the high-volume Toyota Camry and Honda Accord in one of the biggest segments of the U.S. auto market. "It's a very tough segment to be in. It's been dominated by the imports over the last several years," Chantel Lenard, Ford's global small and medium car group marketing manager, said in an interview. "We are starting to break through and break that grip the imports have had on that segment."

The Fusion has a long way to go to meet the U.S. sales volumes generated by the Toyota Camry and Honda Accord. Through July, sales of Ford's Fusion totaled 102,756 in 2009, while Camry sales totaled 184,216 and Accord totaled 160,817. Both the Camry and Accord cracked the top 10 in cars bought under the U.S. government Cash for Clunkers incentive program that ended in August 2009. Ford reported strong Fusion sales in the program, but it did not crack the top 10 list.

In late 2009, Ford added shifts at its truck plants in Michigan and Missouri due to increased demand for its F-150 pickup trucks and Escape SUVs. The company's Dearborn, Michigan, truck plant and the Kansas City, Missouri, plant returned to a three-shift operation. The action increased production of F-150 pickup trucks by about 10,000 units and boosted production of Ford's Escape and Mercury Mariner SUVs together by 2,400 units.

Ford's increased production for the third and fourth quarters of 2009 were somewhat driven by strong sales in the Cash for Clunkers program. The program, launched by the U.S. government in July 2009, enabled qualifying consumers to trade in their old gas-guzzling cars and trucks with a mileage of 18 miles per gallon (mpg) or less for a value of up to $3,500–$4,500. Ford had two models in the top-10 buy list of the Cash for Clunkers program. The company's Ford Focus (30 mpg) ranked fourth and Ford Escape SUV (24 mpg) ranked tenth. Ford boosted third quarter 2009 production in North America to 495,000 vehicles and then produced 570,000 vehicles for the fourth quarter, a 33 percent rise from the year-ago period.

For July 2009, Ford reported an astounding 2 percent year-over-year sales gain when other major automakers reported declines. The sales gain was the company's first since November 2007. Ford still, however, is in financial trouble.

Develop a strategic plan of action for Ford. Provide a detailed strategic analysis for CEO Alan Mulally. Include the methodology and costs associated with implementation of your recommended strategies for the next three years.

19 Kraft Foods Inc. — 2009

Kristopher J. Blanchard
Crown College

KFT

www.kraftfoodscompany.com

The board of directors of Kraft Foods Inc. declared a regular quarterly dividend of $0.29 per common share of Class A stock payable on July 14, 2009. According to their advertising, Kraft Foods makes today delicious in 150 countries around the globe. Their 100,000 employees work to make delicious foods consumers can feel good about. Kraft's American brand icons include Kraft cheeses, dinners, and dressings, Maxwell House coffees and Oscar Mayer meats, to global powerhouse brands like Oreo and LU biscuits, Philadelphia cream cheeses, Jacobs and Carte Noire coffees, Tang powdered beverages, and Milka, Cote d'Or, Lacta, and Toblerone chocolates.

The largest food company in the United States, Kraft's first quarter 2009 profit increased 10 percent and its organic revenues increased 2.3 percent. The company's North American sales rose 2.9 percent, helped by much higher demand for its cereals. Kraft's second quarter 2009 earnings increased 11 percent to $827 million but sales dropped 5.9 percent to $10.16 billion. The weakest performing segment of the company was North American Foodservice, which reported a 10 percent drop in sales. Kraft's European segment reported a doubling of profit of the quarter.

History

James Kraft founded what is now known as the Kraft Food Company in 1903 when he sold a few standard varieties of cheese wholesale in Chicago. The company grew and was soon distributing some 30 varieties of cheese packaged under the brand names of Kraft and Elkhorn. By 1914, the cheeses were available in most towns across the United States. In 1916, Kraft was granted a patent for what came to be known as processed cheese. Kraft began to mass-produce a number of specialty cheeses like Gouda and blue cheese and began to export products to Canada and Europe in 1920; plants would later be established in both England and Germany.

A key to the success of Kraft Food was James Kraft's commitment to developing new products and using innovative advertising methods. Kraft was an early user of all communications media and, as early as 1911, was advertising on Chicago elevated trains, using outdoor billboards and mailing circulars to retail grocers. He was among the first to advertise in consumer journals and was also the first to use colored advertisements in national magazines. In 1933, the company started to use radio on an extensive scale. It sponsored the one-hour weekly musical and variety show *Kraft Musical Review* which headlined notable show business personalities. Kraft's commitment to innovation was demonstrated through the variety of products that were introduced. These products include items like Velveeta (1928), Miracle Whip salad dressing (1933), Kraft macaroni and cheese dinner (1937), Parkay margarine (1940), sliced processed cheese (1951), and Cheez Whiz (1952).

Even though Kraft Foods has a fairly well-documented company history, it has primarily operated as a subsidiary to other larger corporations. The first of these was the National Dairy Company in 1930; Kraft would later be purchased by Philip Morris in 1988 for $12.9 billion. In March 1989, Philip Morris merged Kraft and its General Foods unit into one entity called Kraft General Foods, Inc. As a result of the merger, the company became the largest food company in the United States and the second largest in the world. Initially the merger created a competitive advantage for the newly formed subsidiary; the company was able to save $400 million through consolidations and increased purchasing power.

Philip Morris acquired Nabisco for $14.9 in cash plus the assumption of $4 billion in debt. Philip Morris completed its acquisition of Nabisco in December 2000 and immediately began integrating the Nabisco operations into those of Kraft Foods and Kraft Foods International. In 2001, Philip Morris created a new holding company for the combined operations known as Kraft Foods Inc. (lacking the comma of the previous Kraft Foods, Inc.). The previous Kraft Foods was renamed Kraft Foods North America, giving the new Kraft Foods two main units: Kraft Foods North America and Kraft Foods International. The two CEOs of these units, Betsy D. Holden and Roger K. Deromedi, respectively, were named co-CEOs of Kraft Foods Inc. In June 2001, Philip Morris sold a 16.1 percent stake in Kraft Foods to the public, retaining the remaining shares. The second largest initial public offering (IPO) in U.S. history, the offering raised $8.68 billion, which Philip Morris earmarked to reduce debt it had incurred in acquiring Nabisco. The result of this IPO is that Kraft Foods Inc. is a company that is less than 10 years old.

Internal Information

Organizational Structure

It took several years to complete the spin-off of Kraft Foods Inc. from the Philip Morris Company. During that process, Kraft Foods Inc. saw a number of changes in its leadership team. The most significant was that Irene Rosenfeld was appointed CEO in June 2006; she assumed the position of chairman of the board in March 2007. The organizational structure of the management team is provided in Exhibit 1. Note the chart is divisional by geographic region. Some analysts feel that a by-product divisional structure would be more effective for Kraft.

Company Mission and Ethics Statement

The Kraft Foods Inc. mission statement was presented to the general public during the CAGNY Conference in February 2009. According to the Kraft Foods Inc. Web site (http://www.kraftfoodscompany.com/About/who-we-are/), the mission statement consists of three words and reads as follows:

> **Make Today Delicious.**
> In order to fulfill this mission Kraft Foods Inc. focuses on consumers in everything that they do. The company also understands that actions speak louder than words, so at Kraft Foods:
>
> * We inspire trust.
> * We act like owners.
> * We keep it simple.
> * We are open and inclusive.
> * We tell it like it is.
> * We lead from the head and the heart.
> * We discuss. We decide. We deliver.[1]

EXHIBIT 1   Structure of Management Team at Kraft Foods Inc.

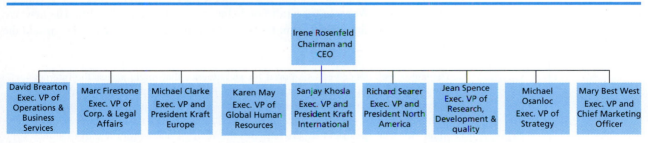

Source: www.kraftfoodscompany.com and Company *Form 10K.*

EXHIBIT 2 Kraft's Sales by Segment/Percent

	For the Years Ended December 31		
	2008	2007	2006
		(2007 & 2006 restated)	
Kraft North America:			
U.S. Beverages	8.50%	7.60%	4.70%
U.S. Cheese	14.30%	9.60%	15.20%
U.S. Convenient Meals	9.10%	9.30%	9.50%
U.S. Grocery	23.00%	24.30%	28.80%
U.S. Snacks	12.20%	14.50%	10.20%
Canada & N.A. Foodservice	10.00%	9.70%	9.80%
Kraft International:			
European Union	9.50%	13.60%	12.60%
Developing Markets	13.40%	11.40%	9.20%
Total Kraft Segment Operating	100.00%	100.00%	100.00%

Source: www.kraftfoodscompany.com. and Company *Form 10K.*

Operating Segments

Kraft Foods Inc. manages over 100 different brand-name food products and tracks operating income to five specific consumer segments. Exhibit 2 provides a summary of the Kraft Brands and operating segments.

- Snacks—primarily biscuits (cookies and crackers), salted snacks, and chocolate confectionery
- Beverages—primarily coffee, packaged juice drinks, and powdered beverages
- Cheese—primarily natural, process, and cream cheeses
- Grocery—primarily spoonable and pourable dressings, condiments, and desserts
- Convenient Meals—primarily frozen pizza, packaged dinners, lunch combinations, and processed meats

Exhibit 2 provides a percentage breakdown of the segment sales for the U.S. and international operations. Note that U.S. Grocery comprises the largest segment followed by U.S. Cheese.

According to the Neilson Company, Kraft Foods only lost 0.3 percent market share during 2008 despite a 9.8 percent increase in pricing.

Marketing

The reintroduction of Kraft Foods Inc. in February 2009 was accompanied by the launch of a new corporate Web site: http://www.newkraft.com. Visitors at the site can view commercials from around the world while learning about new product innovations. Kraft Foods Inc. has also launched several Web sites that would be considered viral in nature. One of these is the Oreo Double Stuf Racing League (DSRL) site: http://www.dsrl.com; visitors can watch videos, play games, and of course they can join the league.

Even the main Web site for Kraft Foods Inc. has undergone a facelift. The new site address is http://www.kraftfoods.com. In its review of the site, brandchannel.com said the following:

> The site is well conceived as a portal for an audience that might access the Internet through a dial-up modem. Staying away from roll-over images, the HTML-based home page is efficient, using fairly compact pictures—except for a promotional 180 × 150 banner that flirts with a surprisingly high 30K. Surfing through the site, the visitor will enjoy the same consistent experience. Besides recipes, noteworthy features include Product Info and a Recipe Box. If the former is self-explanatory, the latter is a smart

way of creating some interactivity with the visitor. The Recipe Box allows one to store and retrieve favorite recipes, whether personal ones (up to 100) or from Kraft. The registration process is in line with the overall browsing experience: painless and respectful. To illustrate this point, it is worth mentioning that the visitor is not asked to provide a last name and the newsletter(s) options are off by default.

Financials

Kraft' recent income statements are provided in Exhibit 3. Note the company's revenues increased to $42.2 billion 2008, while earnings increased to $2.9 billion. Kraft weathered the 2008 global recession really well from a revenue/earnings perspective.

Kraft's recent balance sheets are provided in Exhibit 4. Note the company has over $27.5 billion in goodwill, which is not good, and also has over $18.5 billion in long-term debt, which is also not good. Kraft's long-term debt increased about 50 percent in 2008 from 2007.

Current Strategy

CEO Rosenfeld has been leading the Kraft through a turn-around process designed to return the company to sustainable growth.

EXHIBIT 3   Kraft Foods Inc. and Subsidiaries Consolidated Statements of Earnings

	For the Years Ended December 31 (in millions of dollars, except per share data)		
	2008	2007	2006
Net revenues	$ 42,201	$ 36,134	$ 33,256
Cost of sales	28,186	24,057	21,344
Gross profit	14,015	12,077	11,912
Marketing, administration and research costs	9,059	7,673	7,120
Asset impairment and exit costs	1,024	440	999
Gain on redemption of United Biscuits investment	—	—	(251)
Losses/(gains) on divestitures, net	92	(15)	(117)
Amortization of intangibles	23	13	7
Operating income	3,817	3,966	4,154
Interest and other expense, net	1,240	604	510
Earnings from continuing operations before income taxes	2,577	3,362	3,644
Provision for income taxes	728	1,002	816
Earnings from continuing operations	1,849	2,360	2,828
Earnings and gain from discontinued operations, net of	1,052	230	232
Net earnings	$ 2,901	S 2,590	$ 3,060
Per share data:			
Basic earnings per share:			
Continuing operations	$ 1.24	$ 1.50	$ 1.72
Discontinued operations	0.71	0.14	0.14
Net earnings	$ 1.95	$ 1.64	$ 1.86
Diluted earnings per share:			
Continuing operations	$ 1.22	$ 1.48	$ 1.71
Discontinued operations	0.70	0.14	0.14
Net earnings	$ 1.92	$ 1.62	$ 1.85
Dividends declared	$ 1.12	$ 1.04	$ 0.96

Source: www.kraftfoodscompany.com. and Company *Form 10K.*

EXHIBIT 4   Kraft Foods Inc. and Subsidiaries Consolidated Balance Sheets

	at December 31 (in millions of dollars)		
	2008	2007	2006
ASSETS			
Cash and cash equivalents	$ 1,244	$ 567	$ 239
Receivables (net of allowances of $129 in 2008 and $94 in 2007)	4,704	5,197	3,869
Inventories, net	3,729	4,096	35065
Deferred income taxes	861	575	387
Other current assets	828	302	253
Total current assets	11,366	10,737	8,254
Property, plant and equipment	9,917	10,778	9,693
Goodwill	27,581	31,193	25,553
Intangible assets, net	12,926	12,200	10,177
Prepaid pension assets	56	1,648	1,168
Other assets	1,232	1,437	729
TOTAL ASSETS	**$ 63,078**	**$ 67,993**	**$ 55,574**
LIABILITIES			
Short-term borrowings	$ 897	$ 7,385	$ 1,715
Current portion of long-term debt	765	722	1,418
Accounts payable	3,373	4,065	2602
Due to Altria Group, Inc. and affiliates			607
Accrued marketing	1,803	1,833	1,626
Accrued employment costs	951	913	750
Other current liabilities	3,255	2,168	1755
Total current liabilities	11,044	17,086	10473
Long-term debt	18,589	12,902	7,081
Deferred income taxes	4,064	4,876	3,930
Accrued pension costs	2,367	810	1,022
Accrued postretirement health care costs	2,678	2,846	3,014
Other liabilities	2,136	2,178	1,499
TOTAL LIABILITIES	40,878	40,698	27,019
Contingencies			
SHAREHOLDERS' EQUITY			
Common Stock, no par value (1,735,000,000 shares issued in 2008 and 2007)	—	—	—
Additional paid-in capital	23,563	23,445	23,626
Retained earnings	13,345	12,209	11,128
Accumulated other comprehensive losses	(5,994)	(1,835)	(3,069)
Treasury stock, at cost	(8,714)	(6,524)	(3,130)
TOTAL SHAREHOLDERS' EQUITY	22,200	27,295	28,555
TOTAL LIABILITIES AND SHAREHOLDERS' EQUITY	**$ 63,078**	**$ 67,993**	**$ 55,574**

Source: www.kraftfoodscompany.com. and Company *Form 10K.*

At year-end 2009, the company had saved a total of $1.1 billion through streamlined manufacturing and a simplified organizational structure. These savings were realized, in part, to the closing of 36 plants and the elimination of 19,000 positions. The company plans to see an additional savings of $200 million in 2009.

External Information

Industry Trends and Information

More people are dining out, and food producers are devoting more attention to products designed for restaurants, vending machines, and other foodservice providers. Thus, companies are spending more money researching consumers' eating habits and preferences at home and at restaurants. This is bad news for grocery retailers, but food makers realize food eaten away from home is still food they can provide, many times at higher margins.

Another trend in the industry has been the development of health foods, such as those containing less trans fat or fewer calories, or those containing only organic ingredients. Bottled water has become well established in the market and enhanced waters containing vitamins or supplements are gaining popularity.

Related to the development of health foods is the concern of childhood obesity, which has reached epidemic proportions in the twenty first century with rising rates in both the developed and developing world. Rates of obesity in Canadian boys increased from 11 percent in the 1980s to over 30 percent in the 1990s; during this same time period rates increased from 4 to 14 percent in Brazilian children. As with obesity in adults, many different factors contribute to the rising rates. Changing diet and decreasing physical activity are believed to be the two most important in causing the recent increase in the rate of obesity. Activities from self-propelled transport, to school physical education, and organized sports has been declining in many countries. Treatments used in children are primarily lifestyle interventions and behavioral techniques.

Rising costs of petroleum cause a twofold increase in cost for companies in the food industry: Costs have increased at the agriculture end, which increases raw materials costs for food processors who also deal with increased production and transportation costs at their end. Because the industry is so competitive, it is difficult for these companies to raise their prices accordingly, and profit margins have suffered as a result. At the same time, consumer prices for baked goods increased 10.7 percent in January 2009 compared to January 2008, despite lower costs for bakeries. Input costs for bakers, included commodities such as wheat, eggs, and natural gas, have declined recently. Some bakeries may be passing along the cost of supplies purchased on contracts signed before commodity prices began to fall in mid-2008. As contracts expire and are renegotiated, some food manufacturing companies may discover that they have slight advantage for a short time.

The U.S. market for packaged and processed foods has seen large profits in retail sales, and this number is expected to see steady growth. Worldwide, demand is also on the rise for this type of food as more people adopt a lifestyle that includes less time for the preparation of food. The greatest asset of any retail and consumer product company is its reputation and perceived value among consumers. For this reason, corporate and brand reputations are expected to become increasingly important as consumers are trying to stretch their dollar further and competition is increasing. Food safety programs have been adopted recently as issues of chemical and bacterial contamination and new food-borne pathogens remain a public health concern.

Workers at one of Kraft's manufacturers in Illinois turned up a batch of fruits and nuts that were contaminated with salmonella in December 2007. Another positive sample appeared again in September 2008. It was only after the company conducted thousands of tests that it was able to pinpoint the source for the second positive test. This test showed that the tainted nuts came from a California-based supplier; more specifically from Setton Pistachio of Terra Bella, Inc. Even though there have not been any reports of pistachio-related illnesses, the company voluntarily recalled more than 2 million pounds of nuts and temporarily shut down its manufacturing plants.

Customers today view food as an expression of their cultural and social identity and are therefore asking a lot more from producers than just good quality. Environmental concern, social responsibility, and economic viability are commonly identified as the three pillars of sustainability. With global inequalities becoming more pronounced, food costs climbing, and global warming becoming a major political issue, food producers are simultaneously cast as perpetrator and potential healer. Meeting the needs of the present without compromising the future has to be taken into account by the food industry without undermining bottom line balance sheets.

Competitors

Kraft Foods Inc. is the second largest food processing company in the world, second only to Nestle. Nestle is more than just a food company; it also produces health and beauty and pet care products. The majority of Nestle's revenues are from international sales, whereas Kraft Foods Inc. is primarily a North American company. Domestically Kraft Foods Inc. competes with a number of companies, a few of which include ConAgra Foods, Heinz Company, and Sara Lee. Beyond other packaged food companies, Kraft also finds itself competing with generic products and retailer brands, wholesalers, and cooperatives. These products are most likely going to be the largest competitive threat to Kraft Foods Inc. Many consumers are cutting back on their spending by switching to store-brand products. Additionally, as the U.S. dollar gains strength overseas, this will make Kraft Foods products more expensive.

ConAgra Foods

ConAgra Foods, ticker symbol CAG, is the largest publicly held firm that Kraft Foods competes with in the U.S. market. As indicated in Exhibit 5, ConAgra Foods is a leading branded foods company and is the trusted name behind many leading brands, including Healthy Choice, Chef Boyardee, Egg Beaters, Hebrew National, Hunt's, Orville Redenbacher's, PAM, and Banquet, among others. Their consumer brands are found in 97 percent of U.S. households, and 26 are ranked first or second in their category. ConAgra Foods also has a very significant presence in commercial food products and is one of the nation's leading specialty potato providers to restaurants and other foodservice establishments. With a vision statement: "One company growing by nourishing lives and finding a better way today one bite at a time," the company is dedicated to providing customers and consumers with food they can count on to taste great and provide good nutrition at a fair value.

Like Kraft Foods, ConAgra Foods has undergone a number of changes since 2005. Many of these changes are the result of Gary Rodkin being named CEO in 2005. While addressing industry leaders at the 2009 CAGNY conference, Rodkin stated:

EXHIBIT 5 **Kraft versus ConAgra**

	Kraft	ConAgra	Food Industry
Market Cap:	37.50B	8.25B	1.21B
Employees:	98,000	25,000	3.50K
Revenue	41.55B	12.54B	1.03B
Gross Margin	33.70%	21.28%	33.70%
EBITDA	6.14B	1.39B	127.92M
Oper Margins	12.54%	8.57%	13.68%
Net Income	1.96B	555.60M	N/A
EPS	1.981	2.159	1.98

CAG = ConAgra Foods, Inc.
Source: Based on information at www.finance.yahoo.com.

Prior to 2006, ConAgra was a holding company. It was built over several decades by dozens of acquisitions. But unlike most major competitors, there was no strategy to integrate. The company grew much bigger, but developed no scale leverage. It was characterized by independent operating companies and functional silos. In large part, its success or failure was deal driven. And there was a mandate that all businesses, all brands must grow and were handed resources without much segmentation or prioritization.

The most visible change that has occurred at ConAgra Foods was the sale of the commodity trading group; the result of this action is that ConAgra now has a total focus on food rather than food, fertilizer, and ethanol. Other changes include integrating the supply chain infrastructure, upgrading food safety, investing $25 million into training initiatives, focusing on research and development, and investing $170 million into manufacturing automation and modernization.

Conclusion

After reviewing Kraft Foods' *Form 14A,* which details executives' compensation for 2008, a number of analysts have increased their criticism of Rosenfeld because her compensation grew by more than 50 percent in 2008. But this woman is one of the top, if not the top (most effective), female managers in the United States.

Kraft just reported strong second quarter 2009 result although revenues declined 5.9 percent year-over-year to $10.2 billion, primarily due to the unfavourable negative 8.1 percent impact of foreign currency and a negative 0.7 percent impact from divestitures. Kraft's organic revenues increased 2.9 percent. For that quarter, Kraft's North American segment (KNAC) sales were flat year-over-year as gains in U.S. Convenient Meals (7.1 percent), U.S. Grocery (6.7 percent), U.S. Beverages (6.0 percent), and U.S. Snacks (1.3 percent) were offset by the declines in U.S. Cheese (8.7 percent) and Canada & North American Foodservice (10.0 percent). In the International segment, net revenues in the European Union decreased 17.4 percent. Based on the strong year-to-date performance, CEO Rosenfeld has raised guidance for 2009. She now expects earnings of at least $1.93 per share compared to $1.88 guided earlier.

Endnotes

1. www.kraftfoodscompany.com

20 Hershey Company — 2009

Anne Walsh and Ellen Mansfield
La Salle University

HSY

www.hersheys.com

The largest producer of chocolate in North America, Hershey Company reported second quarter 2009 sales up 5.9 percent to $1.17 billion and profit of $71.3 million on July 23, the fourth strong quarter in a row for the company. Advertising expenses for the quarter increased by 46 percent as the company continued to promote iconic brands such as the Hershey Kiss and Reese's products.

Some of Hershey's premium products of have faltered lately as customers switched to lower price products. So, the company plans to discontinue their Cacao Reserve brand as well as their Starbucks chocolate partnership. The company also plans to close their online gift business, which featured seasonal products and gifts that could be personalized by the consumer.

Due to lower commodity prices, total charges to Hershey's Global Supply Transformation Program have been forecasted downward from $665 million to $640 million. Hershey now expects year-end 2009 profits of 6 to 8 percent. Thus, the company overall has weathered the economic recession quite well as their recent news releases have been pretty sweet.

History

Although most visitors think of "Chocolate World" in Hershey, Pennsylvania, as a theme park designed for the true chocolate lover, the facility was designed to include housing, parks, and schools for employees of Hershey Foods. On August 31, 2009, the theme park eclipsed having its 75th million visitor. By 1909, Milton Hershey and his wife had established the Milton Hershey School for orphan boys and subsequently donated their entire personal fortune to the Hershey Trust Company to administer the school. The school continues to operate in Hershey, and provides free education and residential services including meals and health care to almost 17,000 children in need, and still is be administered via The Hershey Trust Company. More than 77 percent of the students who attend the school are from Pennsylvania, and the enrollment is ethnically diverse with both boys and girls attending the school.

Ethics/Sustainability

Hershey's commitment to social responsibility extends beyond their school to both their products and supplier relationships. The company is actively involved in the International Cocoa Initiative Foundation, designed to eliminate child labor or forced labor in cocoa-producing regions. Hershey is also actively involved in organizations such as the World Cocoa Foundation, which supports environmental projects that include nonchemical pest management practices, and which encourage sustainable farming practices to support ecosystems in the region. Hershey also closely monitors its supply relationships and purchases palm oil from suppliers with membership in the Roundtable on Sustainable Oil.

Hershey's role as an environmental steward is also evident that its plants use recycled water that is later purified for various landscaping projects. Changes in product packaging have resulted in lighter materials and less waste during the manufacturing process, and Hershey extensively recycles materials from their East Coast factories. Hershey monitors greenhouse gas emissions from operations and has installed energy-efficient lighting in all of their plants.

With revenues in excess of $5 billion, Hershey continues to produce chocolate and confectionery products in Hershey, Pennsylvania, and has recently expanded its global presence via joint ventures in China and India.

Internal Issues

Mission Statement

The mission of the Hershey Company is "**Bringing sweet moments of Hershey happiness to the world every day.**"

To our stakeholders, this means:

Consumers: Delivering quality consumer driven confectionery experiences for all occasions.

Employees: Winning with an aligned and empowered organization while having fun.

Business Partners: Building collaborative relationships for profitable growth with our customers, suppliers, and partners.

Shareholders: Creating sustainable value.

Communities: Honoring our heritage through continued commitment to making a positive difference.

Marketing and Sales

Hershey's iconic brands such as Hershey Bar, Hershey Kisses, and Reese's are instantly recognized within the domestic market. Hershey concentrates advertising revenues on these brands while also promotes the health benefits of flavonols in its dark chocolate products. The company offers a line of natural and organic chocolates under the Dagoba brand that are sold in natural food and gourmet stores. Other snack products of the company include Hershey Snacksters, Hershey and Reese's granola bass, and Mauna Loa macadamia nuts. Hershey plans to increase its advertising from $30 million to $35 million in 2009 in order to promote its iconic brands.

Seasonal sales such as Halloween and Valentine's Day account for 10 percent of the annual sales in the industry. Hershey sales are higher during the third and fourth quarter of the year, reflecting these industry trends. The company relies on special promotions to increase holiday sales, and it also uses advertising programs to supplement seasonal sales. Hershey also has special editions products that are themed with events, such as their Dark Knight Collection (milk chocolate peanut butter bats) created for the release of the movie *Dark Knight*. The company also encourages customers to personalize messages and gifts via its interactive home page (www.hersheygifts.com).

Hershey was one of the first companies to engage in experiential marketing with the launch of the Hershey Chocolate World in 1973 in Hershey, Pennsylvania, which encouraged consumers to visit the theme park replete with Hershey products. Hershey opened their first flagship store at New York City's Time Square and recently opened Hershey Chocolate World in Shangahi prior to the 2008 Olympics.

Hershey products are sold to more than 2 million retail outlets, including wholesale distributors, chain grocery stores, convenience stores, and wholesale clubs as well as natural food stores. The McLean Company is the largest wholesale distributor of Hershey products and accounts for 26 percent of the total net sales for the company.

Research and Development

Hershey uses cross-functional product development to produce new products and expand product lines for their iconic brands such as Hershey's and Reese's products. Direct research on consumer preferences as well as process innovations are supported via the Hershey Center of Health and Nutrition developed in 2007. This center is involved in scientific research and also collaborates with external organizations to develop products to support both weight management and heart health. Due to increased consumer preferences for healthy and organic products, the company portfolio of healthy snacks has expanded to include Payday Pro energy bars and sugar-free products such as Twizzlers (www.marketline.com).

Human Resources

Hershey employs about 12,800 full-time and 1,600 part-time employees, and approximately 47 percent of the workforce is covered via collective bargaining agreements. Due to global supply initiatives, the company projects a reduction of 1,500 positions over the next three-year period. Hershey recently closed their Reading, Pennsylvania, plant in 2009, eliminating 300 jobs, and provided a severance package of two weeks of pay for each year of service up to 65 weeks for plant workers.

David West, named chief executive officer in 2007, received a 40 percent increase in his compensation in 2008. Company officials believe that West's renewed emphasis on marketing is responsible for the increase in Hershey sales during the past year. His predecessor, Richard H. Lenny, had a more contentious relationship with the board of directors and resigned in 2007 over frustration with the trust that controls Hershey. Exhibit 1 describes key company executives and their various functional roles within The Hershey Company.

Finance

As illustrated in Exhibit 2, Hershey's sales increased by 3.8 percent from $4,946,716,000 in 2007 to $5,132,768,000 in 2008. The company's net income in 2008 was $311,405,000, or $1.36 per share diluted, compared with $214,154,000, or $0.93 per share diluted for 2007. Higher energy and input costs were associated with increased costs along with the full cost of operation for Godrej Hershey in 2008. Selling, marketing, and administrative costs were attributed to higher incentive compensation expenses for employees, expansion of international markets, and increased retail coverage in the United States (*Form 10K* 2008). Hershey projects a net sales growth of 2 to 3 percent in 2009 due to a decline in core brand sales as well as unfavorable currency exchange rates.

Exhibit 3 shows that Hershey has more long-term debt than key competitors such as Cadbury and Nestle. The company's long-term debt increased from $1,279,965 in 2007 to $1,505,954 in 2008. Hershey's other assets declined to $151,561 in 2008 from $540,249 in 2007, and this decline was primarily associated with a change in the funded status of Hershey pension plans, which resulted in a significant reduction in the fair value of the pension plan assets (*Form 10K* 2008).

EXHIBIT 1 **Key Hershey Executives**

David J. West	President and Chief Executive Officer
Humberto P. Alfonso	Senior Vice President, Chief Financial Officer
C. Daniel Azzara	Vice President, Global Research and Development
John P. Bilbrey	Senior Vice President, President Hershey North America
Charlene H. Binder	Senior Vice President, Chief People Officer
Michele G. Buck	Senior Vice President, Global Chief Marketing Officer
George F. Davis	Senior Vice President, Chief Information Officer
Javier H. Idrovo	Senior Vice President, Strategy and Business Development
Thaddeus J. Jastrzebski	Senior Vice President, President Hershey International
Terence L. O'Day	Senior Vice President, Global Operations
Burton H. Snyder	Senior Vice President, General Counsel and Secretary

Source: Hershey Company's 2008 *Form 10K*.

EXHIBIT 2 The Hershey Company Consolidated Statements of Income

For the years ended December 31	2008	2007	2006
In thousands of dollars except per share amounts			
Net Sales	**$ 5,132,768**	**$ 4,946,716**	**$ 4,944,230**
Costs and Expenses:			
Cost of sales	3,375,050	3,315,147	3,076,718
Selling, marketing and administrative	1,073,019	895,874	860,378
Business realignment and impairment charges, net	94,801	276,868	14,576
Total costs and expenses	4,542,870	4,487,889	3,951,672
Income before Interest and Income Taxes	589,898	458,827	992,558
Interest expense, net	97,876	118,585	116,056
Income before Income Taxes	492,022	340,242	876,502
Provision for income taxes	180,617	126,088	317,441
Net Income	**$ 311,405**	**$ 214,154**	**$ 559,061**
Net Income Per Share—Basic—Class B Common Stock	$ 1.27	$ .87	$ 2.19
Net Income Per Share—Diluted—Class B Common Stock	$ 1.27	$ .87	$ 2.17
Net Income Per Share—Basic—Common Stock	$ 1.41	$ .96	$ 2.44
Net Income Per Share—Diluted—Common Stock	$ 1.36	$ .93	$ 2.34

Source: Hershey Company's 2008 *Form 10K.*

EXHIBIT 3 Hershey Company's Balance Sheets

PERIOD ENDING	(all numbers in thousands)		
	31-Dec-08	31-Dec-07	31-Dec-06
Assets			
Current Assets			
Cash and Cash Equivalents	37,103	129,198	97,141
Short Term Investments	—	—	—
Net Receivables	526,056	570,953	584,033
Inventory	592,530	600,185	648,820
Other Current Assets	189,256	126,238	87,818
Total Current Assets	**1,344,945**	**1,426,574**	**1,417,812**
Long Term Investments	—	—	—
Property Plant and Equipment	1,458,949	1,539,715	1,651,300
Goodwill	554,677	584,713	501,955
Intangible Assets	110,772	155,862	140,314
Accumulated Amortization	—	—	—
Other Assets	151,561	540,249	446,184
Deferred Long Term Asset Charges	13,815	—	—
Total Assets	**3,634,719**	**4,247,113**	**4,157,565**
Liabilities			
Current Liabilities			
Accounts Payable	768,708	574,773	609,540
Short/Current Long Term Debt	501,504	856,392	843,998
Other Current Liabilities	—	187,605	—
Total Current Liabilities	**1,270,212**	**1,618,770**	**1,453,538**

continued

EXHIBIT 3   **Hershey Company's Balance Sheets—continued**

	(all numbers in thousands)		
PERIOD ENDING	31-Dec-08	31-Dec-07	31-Dec-06
Long Term Debt	1,505,945	1,279,965	1,248,128
Other Liabilities	504,963	544,016	486,473
Deferred Long Term Liability Charges	3,646	180,842	286,003
Minority Interest	31,745	30,598	—
Negative Goodwill	—	—	—
Total Liabilities	**3,316,520**	**3,654,191**	**3,474,142**
Stockholders' Equity			
Misc Stocks Options Warrants	—	—	—
Redeemable Preferred Stock	—	—	—
Preferred Stock	—	—	—
Common Stock	359,901	359,901	359,901
Retained Earnings	3,975,762	3,927,306	3,965,415
Treasury Stock	(4,009,931)	(4,001,562)	(3,801,947)
Capital Surplus	352,375	335,256	298,243
Other Stockholders' Equity	(359,908)	(27,979)	(138,189)
Total Stockholders' Equity	**318,199**	**592,922**	**683,423**
Total Liabilities and SE	**3,634,719**	**4,247,113**	**4,157,565**

Source: Hershey Company 2008 *Form 10K.*

Production

Many of the ingredients which are used for Hershey products are grown in West Africa, South America, and the Far East. Cacao beans are a primary ingredient in Hershey chocolates, and this commodity is traded on commodity exchanges via brokers. Cocoa future contract prices in 2008 ranged from $0.86 to $1.50 per pound, which represented a significant increase from 2007 prices. Sugar, another commodity found in confectionery products, is controlled via government regulations which often result in prices that are often double those found in the world sugar market. Due to their forward purchasing contracts, however, price fluctuations may not impact Hershey to the same degree as smaller firms in the industry (Hershey, *Form 10K*, 2008).

Global Segments

Hershey has five operating segments by geographic regions: (1) United States, (2) Canada, (3) Mexico, (4) Brazil, and (5) other international locations (India, the Philippines, Korea, Japan, and China). For segment reporting purposes, Hershey aggregates operations in the Americas (United States, Canada, Mexico and Brazil). The company aggregates their other international operations with the Americas to form one reportable segment" (Hershey, *Form 10K*, 2008).

Hershey's sales outside of the United States accounted for 14.4 percent of sales in 2008, 13.8 percent of sales in 2007, and 10.9 percent of sales in 2006. Core brands of the company such as Hershey's and Reese's drove increased sales in the United States, and the company has recently launched joint ventures in India and China to expand their international presence (Hershey, *Form 10K*, 2008).

Hershey remains heavily dependent on its domestic markets with about 86 percent of revenues derived from operations in the United States. In contrast, competitors such as Cadbury generate about 71 percent of their sales from outside the United States. During the past several years, the company has expanded its global presence through a variety of acquisitions and joint ventures with established firms in the international market (www.marketline.com).

In 2007, Hershey announced a joint venture with Lotte Confectionery Company, a leading confectionary company in Korea, to produce products for China. The manufacturing facility, that is located in Jinshan, China, is designed to produce Hershey and Lotte products that are tailored to the needs of the Chinese market. The joint venture is also designed to expand Hershey's presence in other Asian markets such as Korea and Japan. Hershey will also distribute and promote Lotte's refreshment products in the United States.

Hershey also announced a joint venture with Godrej Beverages, a leading consumer goods, confectionery, and food company in India in 2007. The Hershey and Godrej venture will distribute Hershey products via Godrej's distribution network to over 1.6 million outlets in India. Hershey will have a 51 percent ownership stake in the joint venture, which is designed to capitalize on Hershey's strong brands in the confectionery industry with projected annual sales of $70 million for the company.

Hershey acquired Grupo Lorena, a leading confectionary company in Mexico, with sales in excess of $30 million. This acquisition allowed Hershey to leverage these acquired brands both within Mexico and within the emerging Hispanic markets in the United States (www.lexis-nexis.com).

Governance

All of the outstanding shares of the Hershey Trust Company are owned by the Milton Hershey School Trust, which is the controlling stockholder for The Hershey Company. As the controlling stockholder, the "trust has the right to cast 79.9% of all the votes entitled to be cast on matters requiring the vote of the Common Stock and Class B Common Stock voting together." (Hershey, *10K,* 2008). There are 10 directors on the Milton Hershey Trust Company, and three members—James Nevels, LeRoy Zimmerman, and Robert Cavanaugh—are members of the board of directors of the Hershey Trust Company, members of the board of managers of the Milton Hershey School, and board directors of The Hershey Company.

According to the 2008 *Annual Report,* there are nine directors on the board of The Hershey Company, and the board meets six times per year in addition to meetings scheduled by various committees of the board. Board members are required to own at least 200 shares of common stock, and they are compensated annually. The Hershey board has several standing committees, including an Audit, Governance, Compensation, and Executive Organization, and an Executive committee that meet periodically in accordance with governance guidelines. A complete list of committee charters is available at www.thehersheycompany.com/about committees.

In February of 2008, the company announced that James E. Nevels, a board member of the Hershey Trust Company, would replace Kenneth Wolf as chairman of the board of directors of The Hershey Company. This resignation was requested by the Hershey Trust Company, trustee of the Milton Hershey School, and The Hershey Company's controlling stockholders. The trust did consider a sale of The Hershey Company in 2002, but the sale was appealed by the attorney general of Pennsylvania due to public opposition from various stakeholders in the community. Existing legislation requires that the Milton Hershey Trust give notice to the attorney general of Pennsylvania prior to a sale of the company.

Industry Analysis

Confectionery products include chocolate, gum, cereal bars, and sugar confectionery products with a projected global market value of $107.4 billion by 2010. Chocolate currently accounts for 55.8 percent of the market's overall global value. Mergers and acquisitions in the past few years have influenced both the market share and product portfolio of global firms in the confectionery industry. Mars, a privately owned company, acquired William Wrigley, one of the largest chewing gum firms in America, for $23 billion in May 2008. Nestle, one of the global leaders in the industry, expanded its nutritional product with the acquisition of Jenny Craig, a company with an established brand of nutritional weight-management products.

EXHIBIT 4 Hershey versus Cadbury (January 2009)

	Hershey	Cadbury	Confectioners Industry Average
Market Cap	8.91B	51.24B	1.32B
Employees	12,800	45,000	2.20K
Qtrly Rev Growth	5.90%	13.40%	0.10%
Revenue	5.27B	9.29B	505.67M
Gross Margin	36.73%	45.61%	33.89%
EBITDA	1.03B	1.38B	88.79M
Oper Margins	15.46%	11.71%	10.91%
Net Income	353.89M	466.89M	N/A
EPS	1.549	0.679	0.68

Source: Based on information at www.finance.yahoo.com.
Note: B = Billion; M = Million

Many of these acquisitions appear to reflect increased health consciousness among consumers as well as preferences for healthy products in both established and emerging markets. Consumers are increasingly aware of the nutritional value of various product ingredients with purchase decisions reflecting a preference for organic and nonadulterated products. Consequently, organic foods products are one of the fastest growing sectors in the United States with a projected value of $26.3 billion by 2011. Hershey's organic line includes Dagoba Organic, a company with a strong product line of high-quality organic chocolates and baking products that are sold via natural food and gourmet stores. Hershey also continues to appeal to consumers with its premium line of dark chocolates that promote the antioxidant benefits of flavonoids found in these products. Despite the dominance of major companies such as Cadbury, Mars, and Nestle, the major 50 firms in the industry control less than 40 percent of the market. The confectionery industry is fragmented with consumer tastes that drive the diverse demand for products in the industry which range from gums and jelly beans to chocolate products. Exhibit 4 provides some key comparative information on Hershey versus Cadbury and the candy industry overall.

Key Competitors in the Industry

Nestle

Nestle, one of the largest food and beverage companies in the world, is headquartered in Vevey, Switzerland. It has operations in the Americas, Europe, Asia, and Africa. The company has six business divisions that are organized along product groups including the beverage division (Nescafe coffee, Libby fruit juices, and Nestle waters), prepared dishes, and cooking aids division (Stouffer's, Lean Cuisine, breakfast cereals), milk products, nutrition and ice cream division (Nido, Everyday, Haagen Dazs, Dryers, Power Bar, and Jenny Craig products), pet care division (Purina Dow Chow and Purina One), a pharmaceutical products division (ophthalmic drugs and surgical equipment, contact lens solutions), and their confectionary division (Kit Kat, Butterfinger). Nestle brands enjoy worldwide recognition, and the company has the 63rd position in the Top Global Brands ranking by *BusinessWeek*. Nestle recently entered the organic products segment with projected sales of $24 billion by 2010. Company acquisitions include the medical nutritional business of Novartis, Gerber baby foods, and Jenny Craig, a company with an established brand of nutritional weight-management products. Nestle's image, however, has suffered within the global community due to allegations about sourcing of cocoa from farms that employed children in Africa, as well as its marketing tactics used to promote its infant milk substitutes in developing nations. Consolidated sales of the Nestle Group for 2008 were CHF 109.9 billion, an increase of 2.2 percent increase from the previous year (www.marketline.com).

Cadbury

Cadbury, formerly known as Cadbury Schweppes, is a confectionery and nonalcoholic beverage company headquartered in London. In May 2008, the board of Cadbury Schweppes made the decision to split the company into two separately listed companies. The company was split into Cadbury plc (currently the worldwide confectionery operations listed on the London Stock Exchange) and The DPS (Dr Pepper Snapple) Group, formerly Cadbury Schweppes American Beverages (CSAB) now listed as DPS in on the New York Stock Exchange. Key brands include Dr Pepper, Canada Dry, Snapple, and Sunkist products with DPS brands ranked as the third largest refreshment beverage business in North America.

Some of the leading chocolate brands of the company include the Cadbury Chocolate Cream Egg and Mr. Big Bar, as well as confectionary brands such as Trident gum and Dentyne Ice, which complement the gum brands of the company. The company also makes Hall's cough drops, and controls over 22 percent of the medicated confectionery market. Due to increased consumer concerns about artificial ingredients, the company also manufactures a line of products with no artificial colors or artificial flavorings under the Natural Confectionery Company. The company is a market leader in the global confectionery industry with a market share of 10.1 percent. Within the chocolate category, Cadbury has a 71 percent market share in India, and enjoys a 53 percent market share in the chocolate category in Australia. Cadbury reported revenues of $5,384 million and operating profit of $388 million in 2008. Revenue growth was particularly strong in emerging markets such as India, South Africa, and South America (www.marketline.com).

Mars

Mars is a privately held company headquartered in McLean, Virginia. The company was formed by Frank Mars in 1922 and currently operates in over 66 countries. Mars has several business units, including snack food (42 percent), pet care (49.5 percent), food (6.5 percent), and drinks (1.8 percent), which contribute to their diverse product portfolio. Some of the leading brands of the company include M & M's and Snickers, Pedigree and Whiskas pet food, as well as Flavia drinks, and Uncle Ben's rice. Due to increased consumer preference for low-fat and organic products, Mars Nutrition and Health Well Being has also developed a line of low-fat products and healthy snacks.

In 2008, Mars purchased the William Wrigley Company, which includes such brands as Orbit and Doublemint gum. Under the terms of the $23 billion acquisition, the Wrigley Company will become a subsidiary of Mars and will operate along with Mars's other business units of Chocolate, Pet Care, Food, Drinks, and Symbioscience. Mars nonchocolate confectionery brands such as Skittles and Starburst will also be transferred to the Wrigley unit. Wrigley sells products in over 180 countries, and the acquisition extends the brand portofolio of the company and increased worldwide distribution channels for Mars. Mars products are sold worldwide, and the company has locations in North America, Latin America, Europe, and the Middle East (www.marketline.com).

Future Direction

Hershey, as well as other competitors in the industry, is acquiring nonchocolate products as well as nutritional products to complement its existing products.

Hershey uses tons of sugar. However, poor harvests in two of the world's largest producers of sugar, Brazil and India, sent sugar prices soaring in the second half of 2009. Wholesale sugar prices in the U.S. were up more than 70 percent in the first eight months of 2009, reaching a near 30-year high of 22.21 cents a pound. Some research analysts expect that international wholesale sugar prices may reach 40 cents a pound. "I think U.S. consumers should expect elevated prices for a while," said Jack Roney, an economist with the American Sugar Alliance, an organization that represents U.S. sugar growers and their interests. India, which up until two years ago was a net exporter of sugar, has become a net importer of sugar after two straight poor harvests and resilient demand. Brazil's sugarcane harvest is suffering from too much rain. And Brazil, which produces nearly half of the world's sugar, has been converting up to half of its supplies into ethanol instead of refined sugar.

Prepare a three-year strategic plan for Hershey Company.

References

www.thehersheycompany.com
www.lexis-nexis.com
www.globalbusinessinsight.com/marketline
www.netadvantage.standardandpoors.com
www.reuters.com
www.finance.yahoo.com

21 Johnson & Johnson — 2009

Sharynn Tomlin, Matt Milhauser, Bernhard Gierke,
Thibault Lefebvre, and Mario Martinez
Angelo State University

JNJ

www.jnj.com

When we hear the name Johnson & Johnson (J&J), we think of infants and the clean, fresh smell of baby powder. The company has certainly worked to maintain that image, but J&J sells a much wider scope of products and operations. Based in New Brunswick, New Jersey, J&J is one of the world's leading providers of health-care products and services encompassing the globe with 147 facilities in over 50 countries. J&J grossed over $63.7 billion in total revenue in 2008.

J&J offers a wide variety of products and services to hospitals, retailers, and families and continues to hold some of the most well-known titles in medicine and medical technologies such as K.Y., LifeScan, Band-Aid, Tylenol, Listerine, Zyrtec, Acuvue, Ortho birth control options, and a host of medical device and diagnostic applications. In the realm of pharmaceuticals, J&J offers prescription drugs for some of the world's most serious illnesses. These drugs range from cardiovascular treatment to advancements in reproductive health, with ongoing developments into drugs geared toward the treatment of HIV and continued advancement in the field of cancer treatment.

In July 2009, J&J purchased an 18.4 percent stake in Irish biotech company Elan Corp. in order to gain access to the $3 billion market for Alzheimer's disease treatments. The Elan purchase gives J&J access to Bapineuzumab, a late-stage in development potential Alzheimer drug. In the United States alone, more than 4.5 million people suffer from Alzheimer's, which slowly destroys a person's memory. If Bapineuzumab could actually halt progression of Alzheimer's, some analysts say the drug would be worth $25 billion in annual sales worldwide.

J&J also just in mid-2009 acquired the small cancer drug-developer Cougar Biotechnology for about $894 million in cash. Cougar has an excellent drug for late stage prostate cancer. J&J's purchase price of $43 a share was a 16 percent premium over Cougar's closing stock price.

J&J reported second quarter 2009 net income of $3.21 billion and sales of $15.24 billion. During that quarter, sales of J&J's Remicade treatment for rheumatoid arthritis rose 24 percent to $1.1 billion.

History

J&J started with a simple idea to create clean and sterile dressings. Robert Johnson and his two brothers, James and Edward, created J&J in 1886 with the production of sterile dressings and medical plaster. In 1887, just one year after being founded, Johnson & Johnson was incorporated. Through the end of the nineteenth century, J&J continued its rise in the health-care sector with the introduction of baby powder. In 1921, Band-Aid was created by Earle Dickson, an employee of J&J. After having to bandage his wife numerous times, Earle lined the company's medical gauze with an adhesive tape and Band-Aid was born; this simple preparation allowed for self-application. With continuing success, J&J looked abroad and in 1924 established J&J Limited in the United Kingdom; this was the beginning of what was to become one of the largest multinational companies in the world.

With the onset of World War II, Robert Johnson II took the helm of J&J. Items needed in the war led to the development of duct tape by the Permcel division of J&J. Military officials found that duct tape was essential in protecting munitions during the war. Even today duct tape remains a staple of the everyman's toolbox and sometimes is even elevated to art. The war also helped to cement the Band-Aid brand by shipping millions of the self-adhesive bandages in combat first aid kits. In 1943, J&J created the company credo; this document outlines the company's responsibilities to doctors, patients, customers, and employees. J&J went public in 1944. With brands like Tylenol, AccuView, LifeScan, Neutrogena, and Band-Aid, J&J brands have become a part of American culture, so much so that many of their product brand names have become generic household words, such as Band-Aid.

Vision/Mission/Ethics

J&J has translated its strong company philosophy and values to their vision stated as follows:

> To maximize the global power of diversity and inclusion to drive superior business results and sustainable competitive advantage.[1]

Furthermore, they have incorporated that vision into their mission statement:

We will achieve our vision by:

— Fostering Credo-based inclusive cultures that embrace our differences and drive innovation to accelerate growth (workplace)
— Achieving a skilled, high performance workforce that is reflective of the diverse global marketplace (workforce)
— Working with business leaders to identify and establish targeted market opportunities for consumers across diverse demographic segments (marketplace)
— Cultivating external relationships with professional, patient and civic groups to support business priorities (external stakeholders)

Demanding the highest of standards in their products and services, the company demands the same of their employees, including their top officers and board of directors. J&J's top executives are shown in Exhibit 1. J&J's mission statement is given in Exhibit 2.

On July 23, 2009, J&J announced availability of its 2008 Sustainability Report at http://www.jnj.com/connect/caring/environment-protection/. It is J&J's sixth annual Sustainability Report and the twelfth year of reporting on environmental progress. "We see corporate citizenship, or sustainability, not as a set of 'add-ons' to our business but rather as intrinsic to everything we do," says William C. Weldon, chairman, board of directors, and chief executive officer. "Our mission is reflected in the way we run our business around the world, every day."

EXHIBIT 1   J&J's Organizational Chart

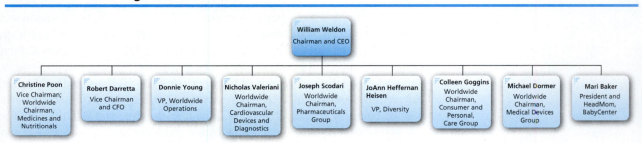

Source: http://www.cogmap.com/chart/johnson-johnson.

EXHIBIT 2   J&J's Mission Statement

We believe our first responsibility is to the doctors, nurses and patients, to mothers and fathers and all others who use our products and services. In meeting their needs, everything we do must be of high quality. We must constantly strive to reduce our costs in order to maintain reasonable prices. Customers' orders must be serviced promptly and accurately. Our suppliers and distributors must have an opportunity to make a fair profit.

We are responsible to our employees, the men and women who work with us throughout the world. Everyone must be considered as an individual. We must respect their dignity and recognize their merit. They must have a sense of security in their jobs. Compensation must be fair and adequate, and working conditions clean, orderly and safe. We must be mindful of ways to help our employees fulfill their family responsibilities. Employees must feel free to make suggestions and complaints. There must be equal opportunity for employment, development and advancement for those qualified. We must provide competent management, and their actions must be just and ethical.

We are responsible to the communities in which we live and work and to the world community as well. We must be good citizens—support good works and charities and bear our fair share of taxes. We must encourage civic improvements and better health and education. We must maintain in good order the property we are privileged to use, protecting the environment and natural resources.

Our final responsibility is to our stockholders. Business must make a sound profit. We must experiment with new ideas. Research must be carried on, innovative programs developed and mistakes paid for. New equipment must be purchased, new facilities provided and new products launched. Reserves must be created to provide for adverse times. When we operate according to these principles, the stockholders should realize a fair return.

Source: J&J's 2008 *Annual Report.*

Marketing

J&J has a diverse brand portfolio with products ranging from simple bandages to complex antiviral drugs for the treatment of HIV, each requiring different marketing strategies for each individual brand. J&J has also embraced diverse, nontraditional advertising that includes both online and outdoors while scaling back on prescription drug advertising. This section highlights some of J&J's most prominent consumer brands.

LifeScan

Headquartered in Milpitas, California, J&J's LifeScan offers diabetics a sense of freedom that before was unobtainable. The company offers state-of-the-art blood glucose meters such as the One Touch Ultra used in both homes and hospitals alike. These are offered in both the domestic market (which accounts for 98 percent of users) as well as foreign markets. LifeScan products are targeted at those who have difficulty with the pain involved in alternative meters and are more compact and advanced than the competition and can provide the user with results in five seconds. Also, if users are uncomfortable using their finger as the test site, this device offers the capability to test in alternative sites.

The One Touch also boasts amenities that include before- and after-meal flags, 7-, 14-, and 30-day averages as well as the ability to average before and after meal results for the chosen time period.

Tylenol

Tylenol was added to the J&J portfolio with the acquisition of McNeil Laboratories in 1959. In 1960, Tylenol became available without a prescription, just one year after its acquisition. Tylenol is no longer a single product, but it is a product family that extends from a children's formula to Tylenol PM. Currently J&J supports 16 different varieties of Tylenol with each new type requiring a different approach.

Tylenol's online advertising campaign uses subtle ads strategically placed with large online advertisers like Yahoo, Google, and MSN. Tylenol recently increased its online advertising budget and also reduced its print media budget in response to consumer changes. Tylenol.com is not used as an advertising platform; rather it has been positioned to be used as a repository for information, not just selling the products. Tylenol looks to control its image and continue to add value to the brand.

Research and Development

Research and development (R&D) is the lifeblood of health-care companies. The industry experiences above average R&D expenses required in the development of new pharmaceuticals and medical equipment. At the end of 2008, J&J reported $7.6 billion in research and developments expenditures, which was a slight decrease from 2007. These expenditures relate to the development of new products, improvement of existing products, technical support of products, and compliance with governmental regulations for the protection of consumers and patients. The reduction in the pharmaceutical research and development spending was primarily due to increased efficiencies in pharmaceutical research and development activities.[2]

Business Segments

J&J has three segments representing the operations of the company: Consumer Products, Medical Devices and Equipment, and Pharmaceuticals. J&J's 2008 performance by product category is provided in Exhibit 3. The location of J&J's facilities by product category is provided in Exhibit 4.

EXHIBIT 3   J&J's 2008 Performance by Product Category

	2008 Sales	% Change from 2007
Consumer Health Care	**$ 16.0B**	**up 10.8**
Skin Care	3.4	up 11.0
Baby Care	2.2	up 12.0
Women's Health	1.9	up 6.0
Wound Care/Other	1.0	up 1.0
Oral Care	1.6	up 9.0
Over-the-Counter Drugs and Vitamins	5.9	up 15.0
Medical Devices and Diagnostics	**23.1B**	**up 6.4**
Ethicon 1	4.3	up 12.0
Depuy	5.0	up 9.0
Ethicon 2	3.9	up 7.0
Cordis	3.1	up 9.0
Vision Care	2.5	up 13.0
Ortho-Clinical	1.8	up 8.0
Diabetes	2.5	up 7.0
Pharmaceuticals	**24.6B**	**down 1.2**
Aciphex	1.2	up 15.0
Duragesic	1.0	up 11.0
Levaquin	1.6	up 3.0
Topamax	2.7	up 11.0
Remicade	3.7	up 13.0
Procrit	2.5	up 15.0
Risperdal 1	2.1	up 38.0
Risperdal 2	1.3	up 16.0
Concerta	1.2	up 21.0
Other	7.3	up 11.0

Source: J&J's 2008 *Annual Report.*

EXHIBIT 4   J&J Facilities

Pharmaceuticals Sector

Consumer Sector

Medical Devices & Diagnostics

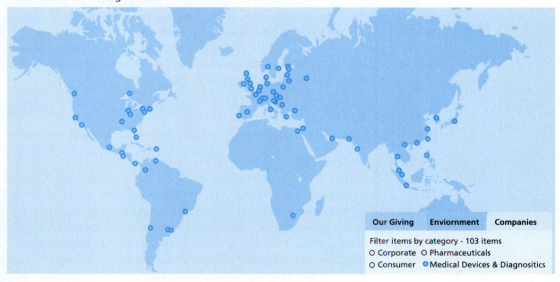

Source: http://www.jnj.com/connect/about-jnj/diversity/?flash=true.

Consumer Products

The Consumer segment includes a broad range of products used in the baby care, skin care, oral care, wound care, and women's health-care fields, as well as nutritional and over-the-counter pharmaceutical products. Segment sales in 2008 were $16.0 billion, an increase of 10.8 percent over 2007, with 8.3 percent of this change due to operational growth and the remaining 2.5 percent due to positive currency fluctuations. The segment's operating profit increased 17.4 percent from 2007 to $2,674 million in 2008. As a percent to sales, 2008 operating profit increased to 16.7 percent. Cost synergies and lower integration costs in 2008 related to the acquisition of the Consumer Healthcare business of Pfizer Inc., and other cost containment initiatives contributed to the increased operating profit.[3]

Pharmaceuticals

The Pharmaceutical segment includes products in the following therapeutic areas: anti-infective, antipsychotic, cardiovascular, contraceptive, dermatology, gastrointestinal, hematology, immunology, neurology, oncology, pain management, urology, and virology. These products are distributed directly to retailers, wholesalers, and health-care professionals for prescription use. Segment sales in 2008 were $24.9 billion, a decrease of 1.2 percent over 2007, with an operational decline of 3.1 percent and 1.9 percent increase due to the positive impact of currency fluctuations. Segment sales were $14.9 billion, a decrease of 4.9 percent. International Pharmaceutical segment sales were $9.7 billion, an increase of 5.1 percent, which included 0.1 percent of operational growth and 5.0 percent related to the positive impact of currency fluctuations. The Pharmaceutical segment operating profit increased 16.3 percent from 2007, and operating profit increased 31.0 percent to a total of $7,605 million in 2008.[4]

Medical Devices and Diagnostics

The Medical Devices and Diagnostics segment includes a broad range of products used principally in the professional fields by physicians, nurses, therapists, hospitals, diagnostic laboratories, and clinics. These products include Cordis's circulatory disease management products; DePuy's orthopedic joint reconstruction, spinal care, and sports medicine products; Ethicon's surgical care and women's health products; Ethicon Endo-Surgery's minimally invasive surgical products; LifeScan's blood glucose monitoring and insulin delivery products; Ortho-Clinical Diagnostics' professional diagnostic products; and Vistakon's disposable contact lenses. The segment achieved sales of $23.1 billion in 2008, representing an increase of 6.4 percent over the prior year, with operational growth of 3.5 percent and 2.9 percent, respectively, due to a positive impact from currency fluctuations. U.S. sales were $10.5 billion, an increase of 1.0 percent. International sales were $12.6 billion, an increase of 11.3 percent, with 5.8 percent from operations and a positive currency impact of 5.5 percent. Operating profit in the segment increased 49.1 percent from 2007 to a total of $7,223 million in 2008. As a percent to sales, 2008 operating profit increased to 31.2 percent. The improved operating profit was the result of the $429 million gain from net litigation settlements, favorable product mix, manufacturing efficiencies, and lower research and development charges of $174 million in 2008 versus $807 million in 2007.[5]

Competitors

Exhibit 5 provides a list of companies that J&J considers to be major competitors.

Abbott Laboratories

Abbott Laboratories is engaged in the discovery, development, manufacture, and sale of a variety of health-care products through four business segments: Pharmaceutical Products, Diagnostic Products, Nutritional Products, and Vascular Products. The company's primary products are prescription pharmaceuticals, nutritional products, vascular products, and diagnostic testing products. In addition, the company has a 50.0 percent-owned joint venture, TAP Pharmaceutical Products Inc., with Takeda Pharmaceutical Company Ltd. of Japan, through which the company develops, markets, and sells pharmaceutical products such as Lupron, Lupron Depot, and Prevacid (lansoprazole) within the Untied States,

EXHIBIT 5   **Large Competitors to J&J**

Company	Stock Symbol
Amgen Inc.	AMGN
Genentech, Inc.	Private
Biogen Idec Inc.	BHB
Genzyme Corp.	GENZ
Merck Serono S.A.	Private
Sandoz International GmbH	Private
Watson Pharmaceuticals Inc.	WPI
Barr Pharmaceuticals Inc.	Private
King Pharmaceuticals Inc.	KG
Ranbaxy Laboratories Limited	Private
Mylan, Inc.	MYL
Pfizer Inc.	PFE
Chiron Corporation	Private
Gilead Sciences Inc.	GILD
Medimmune, Inc.	Private
Life Technologies Corporation	LIFE
Teva Pharmaceutical Industries Limited	TEVA
GlaxoSmithKline plc	GSK
Sanofi-Aventis	SNY
AstraZeneca plc	AZN
Abbott Laboratories	ABT
Merck & Co. Inc.	MRK
Bristol-Myers Squibb Co.	BMY
Novartis AG	MVS
Eli Lilly	LLY
Procter & Gamble	PG

Puerto Rico, and Canada. Abbott reported 2008 total revenues of $29,525.5 million with a net income of $4,880.7 million.[6]

Merck & Co. Inc.

A top competitor of J&J is Merck & Co. Inc., which offers treatments and medications for adults and children over a wide range of applications. Merck has a strong position in the world of pharmaceuticals with such advancements as Gardasil, the world's first anticancer vaccine; diabetes medications; eye disease treatments; and multiple cardiovascular drugs such as Cozaar and Hyzaar. Merck has a keen understanding of the industry as shown by its continuous growth and improvement. Recently, Merck and Insmed Inc. reached an agreement in which Merck will acquire Insmed for $130 million to access their follow-on biologics platform and all assets associated with follow-on biologics. In 2008, Merck reported total revenues of $23,850.3 million with a net income of $7,808.4 million.[7]

Novartis

Exhibit 6 provides a comparison of J&J with Novartis.

Novartis offers over 60 pharmaceutical products including one of the most well-known drugs, Ritalin, and has received more approvals than any other pharmaceutical company in the industry since 2000. In addition to its wide range of pharmaceuticals, Novartis also sells generic drugs through their division Sandoz, making Novartis the only company to have obtained a leadership position in both pharmaceutical and generic drugs. The company supports an employee-centered philosophy in that every employee will be heard and is given the

EXHIBIT 6 **J&J versus Three Major Rivals (2009)**

	J&J	Eli Lilly	Novartis	Procter & Gamble
Market Cap	166.23B	37.92B	104.84B	154.29B
Employees	118,700	40,500	99,000	135,000
Qtrly Rev Growth	−7.40%	2.80%	−2.30%	−10.60%
Revenue	61.37B	20.76B	42.05B	79.03B
Gross Margin	70.92%	81.53%	73.15%	50.78%
EBITDA	18.97B	7.48B	11.19B	19.20B
Oper Margins	26.29%	30.37%	21.44%	20.40%
Net Income	12.74B	−1.62B	7.57B	11.10B
EPS	4.551	−1.481	3.34	4.260

Source: Company *Form 10K* Reports.

power to voice their opinion regarding the company's ventures. The expansive portfolio of Novartis is accompanied by a division devoted to animal health. The global animal health division provides care to both domesticated animals as well as farm animals with applications designed to cure or treat ailments such as internal/external parasites, pain control, arthritic pain control, heart, allergenic, renal, and illnesses related to insecticides used in agriculture. With a growth in revenue in 2008 of over $3.6 billion in comparison to the previous fiscal year, Novartis has shown firm financial strength and outstanding growth. In 2008, Novartis reported total revenues of $38,947 million with a net income of $11,946 million.[8]

Pfizer

Pfizer has two segments: Pharmaceutical, which develops and produces products that treat cardiovascular and metabolic diseases, central nervous system disorders, arthritis and pain, infectious and respiratory diseases, urogenital conditions, cancer, eye disease, endocrine disorders, and allergies; and Animal Health, which discovers, develops, and sells products for the prevention and treatment of diseases in livestock and companion animals. Pfizer also operates several other businesses, such as the manufacture of empty soft-gelatin capsules, contract manufacturing, and bulk pharmaceutical chemicals. Total revenues reported at the end of 2008 were $48,296 million, with a net income of $8,104 million.[9]

Procter & Gamble

Note in Exhibit 6 the comparison between J&J and P&G. Procter & Gamble (P&G)'s extensive product offering includes applications for personal, home, family/baby, pet nutrition and care, and online expert advice solutions regarding each product. Family branding includes Tide detergent products, Charmin, Bounty, Crest dental products, Pampers baby products, CoverGirl beauty products, Lacoste fragrances, IAMS pet nutrition and care, Vicks, and prescription drugs such as Actonel and Didronel. P&G has also shown that it is an environmentally friendly company. In 2008 alone, P&G reduced energy consumption by 6 percent, carbon dioxide usage by 6 percent, and water consumption by 7 percent. This year P&G was recognized among the "100 most-sustainable corporations" and reported that in 2008 the company reached 60 million children through their corporate cause, Live, Learn and Thrive. P&G reported total revenues of $83,503 million with a net income of $12,075 million in 2008.[10]

Industry Issues

J&J has strived to maintain its profit margins through cost reduction programs, productivity improvements, and periodic price increases. The company faces various worldwide health-care changes that may continue to result in pricing pressures that include health-care cost containment and government legislation relating to sales, promotions, and reimbursement.[11] In turn, the currency rate fluctuations brought about by the economic uncertainty are proving to be a challenge for the most stable companies.

Even the largest pharmaceutical companies are being forced to cut thousands of jobs. For example, Pfizer and AstraZeneca cut 19,500 and 15,000 jobs, respectively, over the first three months of 2009. The economic crisis also is directly affecting the R&D budgets of many drug companies, instilling fear into both prospective and established investors of pharmaceutical companies. The cost of R&D has been increasing at an astounding rate, rising currently at a rate of eightfold per year. With R&D the lifeblood of major drug companies, further reductions could severely affect the advancement and development of new drugs. However, the economic threat to drug production is only one of many threats looming on the horizon.

Additionally, changes in the behavior and spending patterns of purchasers of health-care products and services, including delaying medical procedures, rationing prescription medications, reducing the frequency of physician visits, and forgoing health-care insurance coverage, as a result of the current global economic downturn, will continue to impact the major drug industry.[12]

Patent Expiration

Generic drug firms have filed Abbreviated New Drug Applications (ANDAs) seeking to market generic forms of most of the key pharmaceutical products, prior to expiration of the applicable patents covering those products. In the event companies are not successful in defending the patent claims challenged in ANDA filings, the generic firms will then introduce generic versions of the product at issue, resulting in the potential for substantial market share and revenue losses. By 2012, many major patents, often referred to as Patent Cliffs, will expire, clearing the way for companies involved in the production of generics to begin manufacturing the most effective and high-grossing drugs on the market. For example, Pfizer's Lipitor, which accounts for roughly 25 percent of the company's revenue (over $12 billion), will lose patent protection in late 2011. This poses both a threat for the major drug companies that rely on these drugs as their cash cows and an opportunity for generic drug companies to increase profits significantly.

The Future

J&J had sales of $15.2 billion for the second quarter of 2009, a decrease of 7.4 percent as compared to the second quarter of 2008. Domestic sales declined 6.7 percent, while international sales declined 8.0 percent, reflecting operational growth of 3.9 percent and a negative currency impact of 11.9 percent. Net earnings and diluted earnings per share for the second quarter of 2009 were $3.2 billion and $1.15, respectively.

Regarding J&J's divisions, Worldwide Consumer sales of $3.9 billion for the second quarter represented a decrease of 4.5 percent versus the prior year. Domestic sales in this division increased 0.8 percent; while international sales decreased 8.4 percent, which reflected an operational increase of 4.7 percent and a negative currency impact of 13.1 percent. Listerine, Neutrogena, and Aveeno did exceptionally well during the quarter. Other growth drivers were sales from the recently completed acquisition of a French company, Vania Expansion SNC.

J&J's Worldwide Pharmaceutical division's sales of $5.5 billion for the second quarter represented a decrease versus the prior year of 13.3 percent with an operational decline of 8.5 percent and a negative impact from currency of 4.8 percent. Domestic sales decreased 16.4 percent; while international sales decreased 8.7 percent, Remicade, Prezista, Velcade, and Concerta did especially well. Related to this division in this quarter, J&J's new acquisitions were Cougar Biotechnology and Elan Corporation.

J&J's Worldwide Medical Devices and Diagnostics sales of $5.9 billion for the second quarter represented a decrease of 3.1 percent versus the prior year with an operational increase of 2.9 percent and a negative currency impact of 6.0 percent. Domestic sales increased 1.9 percent; while international sales decreased 7.2 percent, which reflected an operational increase of 3.7 percent and a negative currency impact of 10.9 percent.

As indicated in Exhibit 5, J&J has many competitors. Develop a three year strategic plan for J&J that will allow the company to continue progress—as showcased in Exhibit 7 and Exhibit 8.

EXHIBIT 7   J&J Income Statements, 2006–2008

	2008	2007	2006
Sales to costumers	$63,747	61,095	53,324
Cost of products sold (with Depreciation)	18,511	17,751	15,324
Gross Profit	45,236	43,344	38,267
Selling, marketing and administrative expenses	21,490	20,451	17,433
Research expense	7,577	7,680	7,125
Purchased in-process R&D	0	807	599
Restructuring	0	745	0
Interest income	−361	−452	−829
Interest expense	435	296	63
Other (income) expense	3,666	534	−671
	28,307	30,061	23,680
Earnings before provision for taxes on income	16,929	13,283	14,587
Provision for taxes on income	3,980	2,707	3,534
Net earnings	**$12,949**	**10,576**	**11,053**
Basic net earnings per share	4.62	3.67	3.76
Diluted net earnings per share	4.57	3.63	3.73

Source: Johnson & Johnson, *Annual Report;* marketwatch.com.

EXHIBIT 8   J&J Balance Sheets 2006–2008

Assets	2008	2007	2006
Current assets			
Cash and cash equivalents	$107,680	7,770	4,083
Marketable securities	N/A	1,545	1
Accounts receivable trade, less allowances for doubtful accounts	9,719	9,444	8,712
Inventories	5,052	5,110	4,889
Deferred taxes on income	3,430	2,609	2,094
Prepaid expenses and other receivables	3,430	3,467	3,196
Total current assets	34,377	29,945	22,975
Marketable securities, non-current	N/A	2	16
Property, plant and equipment, net	14,365	14,185	13,044
Intangible assets, net	13,976	15,348	15,348
Goodwill, net	13,719	14,123	13,340
Deferred taxes on income	5,841	4,889	3,210
Other assets	2,634	3,170	2,623
Total assets	**$ 84,912**	**80,954**	**70,556**
Liabilities and Shareholders' Equity			
Current liabilities			
Loans and notes payable	3,732	2,463	4,579
Accounts payable	7,503	6,909	5,691
Accrued liabilities	N/A	6,412	4,587

continued

EXHIBIT 8   J&J Balance Sheets 2006–2008—continued

Assets	2008	2007	2006
Accrued rebates, returns and promotions	N/A	2,318	2,189
Accrued salaries, wages and commissions	1,430	1,512	1,391
Accrued taxes on income	N/A	223	724
Total current liabilities	20,852	19,837	19,161
Long-term debt	8,120	7,074	2,014
Deferred taxes on income	1,432	1,493	1,319
Employee related obligations	7,790	5,402	5,584
Other liabilities	4,210	3,829	3,160
Total liabilities	**42,401**	**37,635**	**31,238**
Shareholders' equity			
Preferred stock—without par value (authorized and unissued 2,000,000 shares)	—	—	—
Common stock—par value $1.00 per share (authorized 4,320,000,000 shares; issued 3,119,843,000 shares)	3,120	3,120	3,120
Accumulated other comprehensive income	N/A	−693	−2,118
Retained earnings	63,379	55,280	49,290
	N/A	57,707	50,292
Less: common stock held in treasury, at cost (279,620,000 shares and 226,612,000 shares)	−19,033	−14,388	−10,974
Total shareholders' equity	**42,511**	**43,319**	**39,318**
Total liabilities and shareholders' equity	**$ 84,912**	**80,954**	**70,556**

Source: Johnson & Johnson, *Annual Report;* Marketwatch.com; aol.finance.com.

Endnotes

1. http://www.jnj.com/wps/wcm/connect/7bb2d7004ae70eb9bc5cfc0f0a50cff8/global-diversity-and-inclusion.pdf?MOD=AJPERES.
2. Johnson & Johnson, *Annual Report* (2008).
3. Johnson & Johnson, *Annual Report* (2008).
4. Johnson & Johnson, *Annual Report* (2008).
5. Johnson & Johnson, *Annual Report* (2008).
6. www.mergentonline.com.
7. http://www.hoovers.com/merck/—ID__10986—/free-co-factsheet.xhtml.
8. http://www.hoovers.com/novartis/—ID__52941—/free-co-factsheet.xhtml.
9. www.mergentonline.com.
10. http://www.hoovers.com/procter-&-gamble/—ID__11211—/free-co-factsheet.xhtml.
11. Johnson & Johnson, *Annual Report* (2008).
12. Johnson & Johnson, *Annual Report* (2008).

## 22

Avon Products Inc. — 2009

Rochelle R. Brunson and Marlene M. Reed
Baylor University

AVP

http://www.avoncompany.com

The January 20, 2009, issue of the *Wall Street Journal* under the headline "Consumers Scrimp on Beauty Items" reported the following: "Elizabeth Arden Inc. and Estée Lauder Co. cut their sales and earnings forecast Friday and watched their stocks take a beating, as consumers—already buying fewer sweaters and handbags—began to sacrifice their beauty regimens to the recession."

History

In 1886, David H. McConnell founded a company named The California Perfume Company (CPC) when he was only 28 years old. The first company office was in New York, and the manufacturing and shipping office operated from a room that was 20 feet by 25 feet.

The great San Francisco earthquake of 1906 destroyed CPC's California office; however, before long the company was able to reopen. By this time, CPC had 10,000 representatives and Depot Managers selling 117 different articles in 600 styles and package sizes. In October of that year, the company produced its first color brochure.

In 1914, CPC opened its first office outside the United States in Montreal, Canada. When World War I broke out across the Atlantic, 5 million units a year of CPC's products were sold in North America.

As the Roaring Twenties reached its peak, CPC had more than doubled its sales to $2 million in the years since the end of the war. By this time, there were 25,000 representatives in the United States. The company's home office was now moved to Fifth Avenue in New York City. The first products were now offered under the brand name Avon. These products were a toothbrush, talcum, and a vanity set.

In 1937, David McConnell died, and his son, David Jr., became the president of the company. By this time, their products were guaranteed, and many of them bore the Good Housekeeping Seal of Approval. In September 1938, the company's name was changed to Avon Products Inc. after the British town Stratford-upon-Avon.

Over half of Avon's Suffern, New York, plant was relinquished to military support in 1944. However, their product sales continued to rise to nearly $16 million. With the death of McConnell Jr., J. A. Ewald became the president; and he introduced mechanized billing and took the company public in 1946.

In 1954, Avon launched its very successful television advertising campaign entitled "Avon Calling." Avon for the first time moved overseas to Puerto Rico and Caracas, Venezuela. Then in 1956 they entered Cuba. The company became a household name in the United States in the 1960s with its famous television advertisements with the catch phrase, "Ding dong, Avon calling."

With U.S. sales topping $750 million in 1970 and an overseas business that was growing at an average of 25 percent annually, Avon was one of Wall Street's "Nifty Fifty" stocks. That year, the first Asian Avon business opened in Japan and throughout Western Europe. To close out this decade, Avon purchased the jeweler Tiffany's in 1979.

James Preston, the CEO of Avon, fought in 1990 to preserve Avon's independence from a series of takeover attempts (including Amway and Mary Kay). This year, Avon also announced a permanent end to animal testing—becoming the first major U.S. cosmetic manufacturer to do so.

By 1997, there were 2.6 million independent representatives worldwide earning $2 billion in commissions for themselves and their families. Avon had now moved into the countries of the former Soviet Union bloc with its products. In addition, in only five years the Avon Worldwide Fund for Women's Health had raised $50 million.

Internal Operations

Mission and Values

Avon has adopted the following mission statement:

- **The Global Beauty Leader**—We will build a unique portfolio of Beauty and related brands, striving to surpass our competitors in quality, innovation and value, and elevating our image to become the Beauty company most women turn to worldwide.
- **The Women's Choice for Buying**—We will become the destination store for women, offering the convenience of multiple brands and channels, and providing a personal high touch shopping experience that helps create lifelong customer relationships.
- **The Premier Direct Seller**—We will expand our presence in direct selling and lead the reinvention of the channel, offering an entrepreneurial opportunity that delivers superior earnings, recognition, service and support, making it easy and rewarding to be affiliated with Avon and elevating the image of our industry.
- **The Best Place to Work**—We will be known for our leadership edge, through our passion for high standards, our respect for diversity and our commitment to create exceptional opportunities for professional growth so that associates can fulfill their highest potential.
- **The Largest Women's Foundation**—We will be a committed global champion for the health and well-being of women through philanthropic efforts that eliminate breast cancer from the face of the earth, and that empower women to achieve economic independence.
- **The Most Admired Company**—We will deliver superior returns to our shareholders by tirelessly pursuing new growth opportunities while continually improving our profitability, a socially responsible, ethical company that is watched and emulated as a model of success.

The five values of Avon are: Trust, respect, belief, humility, and integrity.

The *Business Ethics Magazine* has rated Avon for six consecutive years as one of the "100 Best Corporate Citizens."

Channel of Distribution

Avon believes its success has always rested on its channel of distribution—direct selling. The company is the world's largest direct seller with 5.4 million Avon representatives in over 100 countries. Avon's business model provides for the company to sell products to its representatives on credit, so that for the most part, the representatives do not pay the company until they get paid by their customers. This makes the company the largest microlender to women. In addition, there are minimal startup costs for an Avon business. The brand has been found to have 90 percent recognition worldwide and is listed as one of the world's top global brands.

Since 2006, Avon has expended a great deal of time and money improving its representatives' earnings and selling experiences. In 2007, the company increased its investment in representatives by over $120 million. This amount funded a number of initiatives including the rollout of a new sales leadership opportunity, improved training, and changes in the commission structure. The company also funded new Web-based and mobile-technology tools.

Marketing

Avon distributes three product categories—beauty, fashion, and home. Each of these product categories accounts for 10 percent or more of consolidated net sales as indicated in Exhibit 1. Exhibit 2 provides a revenue breakdown by product category. Note that Avon's Home segment had a 3.2 percent decline in revenues in 2008 whereas the Beauty division had a 9.6 percent increase in revenues. Exhibit 3 provides a revenue breakdown by geographic area. Note that Latin America contributes more revenue and profit for Auon than any other area.

During 2008, Avon made a monumental change in the marketing of its beauty products. Since its inception, the company had always concentrated on a homey image that catered more to suburban housewives than urban trendsetters.

Avon's president, Geralyn R. Breig, suggests that one of the company's global challenges is generating buzz. "In market after market, we found that we were meeting women's needs in quality, variety, and innovation. Where we fell short was in the image of the brand."[1]

EXHIBIT 1　Net Sales by Product Categories

	(for the years ended December 31)		
	2008	2007	2006
Beauty	72%	70%	69%
Fashion	18%	18%	18%
Home	10%	12%	13%

Source: Avon's 2008 *Form 10K.*

EXHIBIT 2　Avon's Revenue by Product Segment (in millions)

	2008	%	2007	2006
Beauty	7,603.7	+9.6	6,932.5	6,019.6
Fashion	1,863.3	+6.2	1,753.4	1,562.7
Home	1,121.9	−3.2	1,159.5	1,095.0
Total	**$ 10,588.9**	**7.5**	**9,845.2**	**8,677.3**

EXHIBIT 3　Avon's by Geographic Segment Revenues and Operating Profit (in millions)

	2008		2007	
	Revenue	Operating Profit	Revenue	Operating Profit
Latin America	3,884.1	690.3	3,298.9	483.1
North America	2,492.7	213.9	2,622.1	213.1
Central and Eastern Europe	1,719.5	346.2	1,577.8	296.1
Western Europe, Middle East, and Africa	1,351.7	121.0	1,308.6	33.9
Asia Pacific	891.2	102.4	850.8	64.3
China	350.9	17.7	280.5	2.0
Total	**$ 10,690.1**	**1,491.5**	**9,938.7**	**1,092.5**

In their new promotions, the Avon lady is being played by actress Reese Witherspoon, MTV star Lauren Conrad, and James Bond girl Gemma Arterton and represented by Patrick Dempsey of the hit TV drama *Grey's Anatomy*. Creating a new glamorous image for Avon does not come cheap. The company's ad spending went from $136 million in 2005 to $249 million in 2006 and $368 million in 2007. Avon's ad budget for 2008 was 14 percent higher than the year before. Reese Witherspoon is now appearing in ads for Avon makeup, skin care products, and fragrances. In addition, she is also traveling worldwide as the Avon Foundation's first global ambassador and honorary chairwoman.

In December 2008, as a part of the company's strategy to continue growing its universe of celebrity and designer beauty alliances, Avon announced a celebrity deal with Courteney Cox to be the face of the brand's new women's fragrance, Spotlight, launched in April 2009. The April introduction was followed by a global launch in summer via Avon's 600,000 sales representatives in the United States and avon.com. Spotlight was described as a "fresh, oriental scent" by the company (Edgar, Michelle, December 5, 2008).

The new campaigns may be coming at a good time. In a study of mass-market cosmetic brands, the research firm Brand Keys found that Avon lagged behind seven of their cosmetic companies in customer loyalty. Mary Kay Cosmetics (another direct marketer) was at the top of the list. Robert Passikoff, CEO of Brand Keys, suggested, "Avon's problem is that it isn't associated with anything in particular. It's almost like a commodity."[2]

Manufacturing and Logistics

As of 2008, Avon's largest manufacturing plants—in Brazil, China, and Poland—received ISO 14001 certification. This designate is the international standard for environmental management practices. The company's plant in the Philippines has also received ISO 14001 certification.

Avon's manufacturing plant in Mexico received the Clean Industry Certificate from the federal Environmental Protection Agency in 2008. By the end of 2008, 60 percent of Avon's production volume was being produced at sites where ISO 14001 certification has been achieved.

Avon Brazil received an environmental award in 2008 from the Brazilian Benchmarking Environmental Program. Since 2003, this award has recognized environmental best practices among Brazilian businesses. The winning project involved a reduction of greenhouse gas (GHG) emissions in the company's logistics operations. By optimizing the truck routes within the region, Avon was able to cut costs, reduce the distance traveled, and lower GHG emissions. The project will be fully implemented by July 2009, will save 4.1 million kilometers traveled, and cut GHG emissions by 12,707 tons annually.

By 2008, Avon owned the following properties outside the United States measuring 50,000 square feet or more which were used for manufacturing and logistics purposes:

- Two distribution centers for primary use in North American operations (other than in the United States).
- Five manufacturing facilities, ten distribution centers in Latin America.
- Four manufacturing facilities in Europe, primarily serving Western Europe, the Middle East and Africa, and Central and Eastern Europe.

Financials

Avon's income statements and balance sheets are provided in Exhibits 4 and 5 respectively. Note that for 2008, Avon's revenues increased 7.5 percent and their net income increased 65 percent. Avon does have, however, $224 million in goodwill, which is not good; nor is their $1.4 billion in long-term debt.

EXHIBIT 4 **Avon's Income Statements (all numbers in thousands)**

PERIOD ENDING	31-Dec-08	31-Dec-07	31-Dec-06
Total Revenue	$ 10,690,100	$ 9,938,700	$ 8,763,900
Cost of Revenue	3,949,100	3,941,200	3,434,600
Gross Profit	**6,741,000**	**5,997,500**	**5,329,300**
Operating Expenses			
Research Development	—	—	—
Selling General and Administrative	5,401,700	5,124,800	4,567,900
Non Recurring	—	—	—
Others	—	—	—
Total Operating Expenses	—	—	—
Operating Income or Loss	**1,339,300**	**872,700**	**761,400**
Income from Continuing Operations			
Total Other Income/Expenses Net	(600)	35,600	41,700
Earnings Before Interest and Taxes	1,338,700	908,300	803,100
Interest Expense	100,400	112,200	99,600
Income Before Tax	1,238,300	796,100	703,500
Income Tax Expense	362,700	262,800	223,400
Minority Interest	(300)	(2,600)	(2,500)
Net Income From Continuing Ops	875,300	530,700	477,600
Non-recurring Events			
Discontinued Operations	—	—	—
Extraordinary Items	—	—	—
Effect of Accounting Changes	—	—	—
Other Items	—	—	—
Net Income	**875,300**	**530,700**	**477,600**

EXHIBIT 5 **Avon's Balance Sheets (all numbers in thousands)**

PERIOD ENDING	31-Dec-08	31-Dec-07	31-Dec-06
Assets			
Current Assets			
Cash and Cash Equivalents	$ 1,104,700	$ 963,400	$ 1,198,900
Short Term Investments	40,100	—	—
Net Receivables	1,166,000	840,400	700,400
Inventory	1,007,900	1,041,800	900,300
Other Current Assets	238,200	669,800	534,800
Total Current Assets	**3,556,900**	**3,515,400**	**3,334,400**
Long-Term Investments	212,600	127,300	—
Property, Plant and Equipment	1,343,900	1,278,200	1,100,200
Goodwill	224,500	222,200	—
Intangible Assets	28,600	43,600	—
Accumulated Amortization	—	—	—
Other Assets	106,700	160,700	803,600
Deferred Long Term Asset Charges	600,800	368,800	—
Total Assets	**6,074,000**	**5,716,200**	**5,238,200**

continued

EXHIBIT 5   Avon's Balance Sheets (all numbers in thousands)—continued

PERIOD ENDING	31-Dec-08	31-Dec-07	31-Dec-06
Liabilities			
Current Liabilities			
Accounts Payable	1,880,800	1,901,600	1,524,300
Short/Current Long Term Debt	1,031,400	929,500	615,600
Other Current Liabilities	—	222,300	410,200
Total Current Liabilities	**2,912,200**	**3,053,400**	**2,550,100**
Long Term Debt	1,456,200	1,167,900	1,170,700
Deferred Long Term Liability Charges	—	—	30,100
Minority Interest	—	38,200	37,000
Negative Goodwill	—	—	—
Total Liabilities	**5,399,100**	**5,004,600**	**4,447,800**
Stockholders' Equity			
Misc Stocks Options Warrants	—	—	—
Redeemable Preferred Stock	—	—	—
Preferred Stock	—	—	—
Common Stock	185,600	184,700	183,500
Retained Earnings	4,118,900	3,586,500	3,397,100
Treasury Stock	(4,537,800)	(4,367,200)	(3,683,400)
Capital Surplus	1,874,100	1,724,600	1,549,800
Other Stockholders' Equity	(965,900)	(417,000)	(656,600)
Total Stockholders' Equity	**674,900**	**711,600**	**790,400**
Total Liabilities and SE	**$ 6,074,000**	**$ 5,716,200**	**$ 5,238,200**

Avon, to meet the 2008 downturn in the economy, began cutting jobs, closing unprofitable operations, simplifying its product line, and moving work to countries with low labor costs. The company also raised prices to help offset rising costs for commodities such as oil ("Sales Abroad Lift Profit for Avon," *New York Times,* October 31, 2008).

The Cosmetic Industry

The cosmetics industry is one in which products tend to be countercyclical. Demand for such products normally remains constant and unaffected by economic distress.

In terms of color cosmetics, Euromonitor International, Inc. predicts that many of these markets will see a slowdown in volume demand. However, they also believe that the compound annual growth rate for eye makeup will be 1.31 percent compared to −0.26 percent for overall color cosmetics for the period 2009 to 2113.

A growing trend in the cosmetics industry is the introduction of "green" products. In fact, more than one in seven (16 percent) of global beauty products launched in 2008 were certified organic, ethical, or all natural. There are concerns, however, that the global economic climate will stifle new product development, innovation, and sustainability programs in 2009. An economic slowdown usually curbs companies from investing in research and development, and it is that research that has brought forth a wealth of green cosmetics. However, retailers such as Wal-Mart are increasingly requiring more eco-friendly supply chains. In addition, Amarjit Sahota of *Organic Monitor* forecasts that consumers are unlikely to give up their commitments to organic products just to save a

EXHIBIT 6 **Avon's Closest Competitors**

	Avon	Revlon
Market Cap	$9.71 Bill.	242.84 Mill.
Employees	42,000	5,600
Qtrly Rev. Growth	−12.90%	−2.70%
Revenue	10.37 Bill.	1.34 Bill.
Gross Margin	63.03%	63.48%
EBITDA	1.44 Bill.	171.40 Mill.
Operating Margins	12.07%	11.42%
Net Income	807.90 Mill.	28.50 Mill.
EPS	1.884	1.422

few pennies. Aveda Cosmetics found that 68 percent of consumers will remain loyal to a company that has a social and environmental commitment. Many consumers are now "voting with dollars" for organic products and supporting brands that support values similar to their own.

Competitors

Avon Products Inc. considers its two closest competitors to be Mary Kay, Inc. and Revlon, Inc. Exhibit 6 provides a financial comparison of Avon versus Revlon. Note that Avon is nearly eight times larger than Revlon. In terms of channel of distribution, Mary Kay, Inc. most closely resembles Avon because both use a direct marketing approach. Revlon, in contrast, sells its products through cosmetic counters in department stores and pharmacies.

Avon has 42,000 employees worldwide, and Mary Kay has 5,000 and Revlon has 5,600. The large difference in company representatives is attributable to the necessity of employing more people to sell directly to customers than selling products through a storefront. The revenues of Avon also far exceed those of its closest competitors, with Mary Kay selling $2.40 billion and Revlon selling $1.35 billion in 2008 as compared to Avon's $10.37 billion.

Conclusion

On May 5, 2009, Avon Products Inc. reported first quarter 2009 total revenue of $2.2 billion, which was 13 percent lower than that of 2008's first quarter. However, this was up 3 percent on a local currency basis as foreign exchange pressured growth. Beauty sales in the first quarter 2009 were 12 percent lower versus the prior year period but increased 5 percent on a local currency basis. Beauty units increased 2 percent. On May 7, 2009, Avon declared a regular quarterly dividend on its common stock of $.21 per share.

For the second quarter of 2009, Avon's revenues increased 5 percent in local currency, after the 3 percent increase in the first quarter. Beauty revenues in local currencies were up 5 percent. Pressuring these strong performances, however, was the continuing negative impact from currency exchange. Overall revenues and beauty revenues both declined 10 percent.

Avon is implementing a 2009 restructuring program that includes closure of two manufacturing facilities. The company continues to invest heavily in online search engines and Internet carrier sites. For that second quarter, Avon's revenues were up 13 percent in Latin America, 4 percent in North America, 8 percent in Western Europe,

EXHIBIT 7   Avon's Executive Team

Andrea Jung, Chairman and Chief Executive Officer

Elizabeth A. Smith, President

Charles Cramb, Vice Chairman, Chief Finance & Strategy Officer

Lucien Alziari, Senior Vice President, Human Resources

Geralyn R. Breig, Senior Vice President and President, North America

Jeri B. Finard, Senior Vice President, Global Brand President

Bennett R. Gallina, Senior Vice President, Asia Pacific, China, Western Europe, the Middle East and Africa

Nancy Glaser, Senior Vice President, Global Communications

Donagh Herlihy, Senior Vice President, Chief Information Officer

Charles M. Herington, Executive Vice President, Latin America

John Higson, Senior Vice President, Central and Eastern Europe

Srdjan Mijuskovic, Senior Vice President, Global Sales

John F. Owen, Senior Vice President, Global Supply Chain

Kim Rucker, Senior Vice President and General Counsel

James Wei, Senior Vice President, Special Projects

6 percent in Central and Eastern Europe, 10 percent in Asia Pacific and 52 percent in China.

Avon's executive team, as provided in Exhibit 7, needs a clear strategic plan for the future. Help the executives out in this regard.

References

Byron, Ellen. "Avon Investigates Its Operations in China." *Wall Street Journal* 252, no. 95 (2008): B10.

Edgar, Michelle. "Courteney Cox in the Spotlight for Avon." *Women's Wear Daily* 196, no. 118 (2008): 10.

"In Brief." *Soap, Perfumery & Cosmetics* 81, no. 11 (2008): 7–7.

"The Rap on Overwrapping." Available at www.ConsumerReports.org (November 2008).

Endnotes

1. Gogoi & Pallavi, 2008.
2. Gogoi & Pallavi, 2008.

## 23

Molson Coors — 2009

Amit J. Shah
Frostburg State University

TAP

www.molsoncoors.com

When you hear the word "Coors," what images comes to your mind? If you have watched any of the company's television commercials (Frost-Brewed Coors Light, the world's most refreshing beer), the name brings up the images of cool mountain streams, clear blue skies, and all that is inspiring about the Rocky Mountain West. It is a name associated with an uncompromising commitment to quality—a reputation that began over a century ago and continues to thrive to this day.

How about Molson? It's a name that extends back over 200 years in Canadian brewing history. The names Molson and Coors are held dear in the hearts of beer lovers both across the continent and, increasingly, around the globe. This is the story behind the merger of two great companies with a new name yet maintaining the brand loyalty of each original firm: Molson Coors.

Molson Coors Brewing Company, formerly Adolph Coors Company, is one of the largest brewers by volume in the world, producing more than 42 million barrels of beer. Founded in 1872 in the foothills of the Rocky Mountains, Coors was the third-largest brewer in the United States. Coors' corporate headquarters and primary brewery is located in Golden, Colorado, which is the world's largest brewery on a single site. Coors also has other major brewing facilities in Memphis, Tennessee, and packaging facilities in Virginia's Shenandoah Valley, near the town of Elkton. In addition, Coors owns major aluminum can and end manufacturing facilities near Golden.

History

Adolph Coors was born in Barmen, Prussia, in 1847. As a prelude to founding the Coors Brewing Company, the young German immigrant began an apprenticeship at age 14 at the Henry Wenker Brewery in Dortmund, Germany. Soon after he became an apprentice at the brewing company, both of Adolph's parents died, leaving him to take care of his younger brother and sister. As an apprentice, he received clothing, food, and a place to live. It is also believed that Adolph was the brewery's nighttime bookkeeper, which enabled him to earn extra money.

Adolph continued to work at the Henry Wenker Brewery until the war in Germany caused him to stow away on a United States bound ship at age 21. He arrived penniless in Baltimore with no job, but like most immigrants he had a dream. His was to own his own brewery. Adolph traveled west through to Naperville, Illinois, where he was hired as a foreman at the Stenger Brewery. Apparently, the owner of the brewery, who had three daughters, saw son-in-law potential in his new foreman. So, to avoid being pushed into marriage, after two and half years, Adolph continued his journey westward. Adolph arrived in Denver, Colorado, in 1872 and within a month, he had purchased a partnership in a Denver bottling company. Less than a year later, Adolph was sole owner of the company.

In 1873, Adolph and Jacob Schueler, one of Adolph's bottling customers, opened "The Golden Brewery" with $18,000 from Schueler and Adolph's life savings of $2,000. The venture was a huge success. Adolph not only proved he knew how to brew good beer, but he also proved he knew how to market it. The brewing company began shipping beer by train to early settlers of other Western territories and in less than a year, the brewery was making a profit. Coors beer was distributed into Colorado, California, New Mexico, and Wyoming. In 1880, Adolph had earned enough money to buy his partner's share of the business and become sole owner.

Even though Prohibition became a reality in 1916, Adolph and his three sons found ways to keep the brewery open and profitable during the 18 dry years by producing beverages such as malted milk and a near-beer called Mannah.

Adolph died in 1929 before Prohibition ended, but one of his sons, Adolph Jr., assumed control of the brewery. In the year after the end of Prohibition, the brewery produced more than 136,000 barrels of beer. Coors had only distributed their beer in a few isolated markets before Prohibition, but they began to expand their market to include 11 western states.

World War II presented Coors with yet another hurdle to cross. It was customary that resources were diverted from business to support the war. However, because beer was viewed as important for the morale of the troops, the government enabled breweries to purchase enough barley and other materials to continue brewing beer. However, the beer produced was different than it was before the war. The alcohol content was reduced from 4.6 percent to only 3.2 percent. Coors set aside half of all the beer they produced for sale to the military. When the war finally ended, demand continued to grow, allowing Coors to double the amount of barrels of beer that had been produced before the war. By 1955, Coors was producing over 1 million barrels of beer.

Coors

Coors produces, markets, and sells high-quality malt-based beverages. Their portfolio of brands is designed to appeal to a wide range of consumer tastes, style, and price preferences. Coors' brand portfolio is composed of Coors Light, the third-largest-selling beer in the country, Coors (previously called Original Coors), and more than a dozen other malt-based beverages, including primarily premium and super-premium beers. Coors' beverages are sold throughout the United States and in select international markets. Coors Light has captured 13 percent of the market share and is the largest-selling light beer and the second-best selling beer brand overall in Canada (Molson Coors, *Annual Report*, 2008).

Under the direction of fourth-generation Peter Coors, Coors began the 1990s by having the fastest volume growth rate in the industry and by reaching their long-sought goal of becoming the nation's third-largest brewer. In addition, the company started expanding internationally, making its products available to consumers in Japan, Canada, Ireland, the United Kingdom, and other countries. Coors products are now sold in about 30 international markets in North America, Latin America, the Caribbean, Europe, and Asia.

Coors adds nothing artificial to its beers. In fact, in 2000, Coors developed special strains of barley from its own malts. Coors methodically and deliberately takes approximately 55 days to brew, age, finish, and package its lagers—about twice as long as its major competitors. The result is a naturally aged, stable, and smooth product. Coors beers are packaged in dark amber bottles and protective cartons to guard against light damage. Most of its beer products are kept cold throughout the brewing, packaging, and distribution process. In addition, they are shipped cold in insulated or refrigerated railcars and trucks. Coors gives free brewery tours in both Golden (daily except Sundays and holidays) and Memphis (Thursday through Saturday). More than 250,000 visitors tour Coors' breweries each year.

Molson

Canada's "preeminent brewer," Molson was founded in 1786 by John Molson, who opened his first brewery on the banks of the St. Lawrence River in Montreal. With over 3,000 employees and six breweries across the country, Molson is one of Canada's premier consumer brand names and North America's oldest beer brand.

Molson's vision is to become and remain one of the top-performing beer companies in the world. It has a specific structure for achieving that vision within the company.

According to Molson, "The realization of this vision entails delivering profitable growth and sustainable long-term shareholder value. This vision is being aligned with the corporate direction of Molson Coors, the company resulting from the merger of equals between two breweries both with rich family and social heritage in North America."

Molson Coors

Coors, along with other breweries, began to experiment with beer production with regard to packaging, sizes, and even types of beer produced. Before 1959, kegs and bottles were the primary means of selling beer. Then, Coors introduced the first all-aluminum two-piece beverage can along with a recycling campaign that offered one penny for every can returned to the brewery. Because the introduction of the can helped increase demand for Coors' beer, the third-generation owner, Bill Coors, decided to develop additional new technologies to use in the brewing industry as well as to serve international markets in the 1970s.

Coors introduced the Coors Light brand, also known as the Silver Bullet, in 1978. Today, Coors' products are available in about 30 international markets (Molson Coors, *Annual Report,* 2008).

The merger between Adolph Coors Brewing Co. and Molson Brewing was completed February 9, 2005. The A and B shares of stock for the firm are available on the New York Stock Exchange and Toronto Stock Exchange under the ticker symbol TAP.

Molson Coors Brewing Company's offers some of the world's most popular beers with a well-diversified product portfolio that includes nearly 40 distinct beer brands. Its strategic brands include the following:

Coors Light—#7, Global	Carling C2—United Kingdom	Molson Dry—Canada
Blue Moon—United States	Molson Canadian—Canada	Rickard's Red—Canada
Keystone Lt.—United States	Molson Ex—Canada	Creemore Springs—Canada
Carling—United Kingdom		

MillerCoors

The merger between Molson and Adolph Coors was just the beginning of strategic alliances for this brewing giant. Molson Coors and SABMiller plc combined the U.S. and Puerto Rico operations of their respective subsidiaries, Coors Brewing Company and Miller Brewing Company, in the MillerCoors joint venture, effective July 1, 2008 (Molson Coors, *Annual Report,* 2009). The two companies expect that the enhanced brand portfolio, scale, and combined management strength of the joint venture will allow their businesses to compete more forcefully in the aggressive and rapidly changing U.S. marketplace.

For the first quarter of 2009, Molson Coors reported that profits rose to $75.7 million, but sales fell 59 percent to $559 million. The weakest product for the company continued to be Miller Lite, but Miller Genuine Draft recorded its first volume growth in ten years.

MillerCoors' volume of beer sold worldwide slipped 3.2 percent in the three-month period ending in June 2009, including a drop of more than 12 percent in Britain, where Molson Coors sells market-leading Carling. But price increases helped buffer the drop, as revenue came in ahead of analyst expectations. Profits for the joint venture rose 75 percent to $304.9 million in the quarter, which also helped Molson Coors' bottom line.

Consumers are limiting their spending at bars and restaurants and trading down to less expensive drinks in stores, reported MillerCoors, the joint venture Molson Coors started last summer with SABMiller's U.S. unit. For the second quarter of 2009, the joint company saw double-digit growth in Keystone Light and low single-digit growth in Miller High Life, both less expensive brands.

Molson and Grupo Modelo established a 50/50 joint venture, Modelo Molson Imports, L.P., to import, distribute, and market the Modelo beer brand portfolio across all Canadian provinces and territories. Also, on January 13, 2006, Molson Coors sold its 68 percent of equity interest in Kaiser Brasil to FEMSA Cerveza (Molson Coors, *Annual Report,* 2008).

Internal Factors

Business Structure

Molson Coors Brewing Company is the principal holding company, and its operating subsidiaries include Molson Canada, Coors Brewing Company, and Coors Brewers Limited.

Molson Canada brews and is responsible for all the "Canadian" brands previously and once again held entirely by Molson. Coors Brewing Company operated in the United States prior to the formation of MillerCoors LLC. Coors Brewing Company also has the distribution and bottling facilities in parts of the United States. Coors Brewers Limited is responsible for operations in the United Kingdom and Ireland, where it has a highly successful beer, Carling, number one among its segment in the United Kingdom.

Nine of the members of the Molson Coors Board are independent of management and the controlling shareholders—that is, they are not a part of either family. Exhibit 1 shows the organizational chart of Molson Coors.

Goals and Values

The accountability for corporate responsibility rests with our corporate and division leaders who are committed to work ethically (http://molsoncoors.com/responsibility/great-brands-the-right-way/shared-values, 2009). Molson Coors also has numerous shared values as provided on the same Web page (http://molsoncoors.com/responsibility/great-brands-the-right-way/shared-values).

U.S. and International Operations

Molson Coors Brewing Company is the fifth-largest brewer in the world and sells its products in more than 30 markets internationally, including North America, Europe, Latin America, and Asia. Molson Coors is the third-largest brewer in the United States, the second largest in the United Kingdom, and the leading brewer in Canada by sales volume. The Molson Coors corporate headquarters and primary brewery is in Golden, Colorado, previously headquarters of Adolph Coors, as well as CBL brewing, packaging, and malting facilities in the United Kingdom. In addition, Coors owns major facilities in Colorado to manufacture aluminum cans and ends, as well as bottles, and is a partner in ventures that operate these plants (www.coors.com 2009).

EXHIBIT 1 **Molson Coors Organizational Chart**

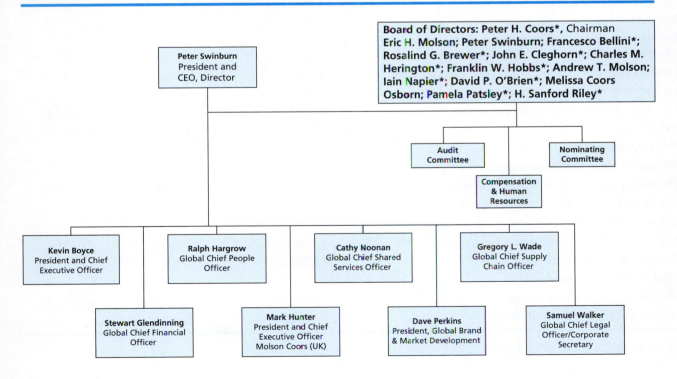

The executive offices and headquarters of Molson Coors are located in the metropolitan areas of Denver, Colorado, and Montreal, Quebec. The Canadian operational headquarters will be in Toronto, Ontario, and the UK headquarters are in Burton-on-Trent, Staffordshire.

Financial Issues

Exhibits 2 and 3 present Molson Coors' annual financial statements. Note in Exhibit 2 the dramatic revenue and profit decline in 2008 versus 2007. On the 2008 balance sheet in Exhibit 3, note the company still carries over $1.8 billion in long-term debt.

EXHIBIT 2 Molson Coors Income Statement (in millions, except for share data)

	For the Years Ended		
	December 28, 2008	December 30, 2007	December 31, 2006
Sales	$ 6,651.8	$ 8,319.7	$ 7,901.6
Excise taxes	(1,877.5)	(2,129.1)	(2,056.6)
Net sales	4,774.3	6,190.6	5,845.0
Cost of goods sold	(2,840.8)	(3,702.9)	(3,481.1)
Gross profit	1,933.5	2,487.7	2,363.9
Marketing, general and administrative expenses	(1,333.2)	(1,734.4)	(1,705.4)
Special items, net	(133.9)	(112.2)	(77.4)
Equity income in MillerCoors	155.6	—	—
Operating income	622.0	641.1	581.1
Other (expense) income, net			
Interest expense	(103.3)	(126.5)	(143.0)
Interest income	17.3	26.6	16.3
Debt extinguishment costs	(12.4)	(24.5)	—
Other (expense) income, net	(8.4)	17.7	17.7
Total other expense	(106.8)	(106.7)	(109.0)
Income from continuing operations before income taxes and minority interests	515.2	534.4	472.1
Income tax expense	(102.9)	(4.2)	(82.4)
Income from continuing operations before minority interests	412.3	530.2	389.7
Minority interests in net income of consolidated entities	(12.2)	(15.3)	(16.1)
Income from continuing operations	400.1	514.9	373.6
Loss from discontinued operations, net of tax	(12.1)	(17.7)	(12.6)
Net income	$ 388.0	$ 497.2	$ 361.0
Other comprehensive (loss) income, net of tax:			
Foreign currency translation adjustments	(1,281.0)	795.0	157.2
Unrealized gain (loss) on derivative instruments	49.0	(3.4)	18.4
Realized gain (loss) reclassified to net income	3.9	2.9	(4.6)
Ownership share of MillerCoors other comprehensive loss	(211.2)	—	—
Pension and other postretirement benefit adjustments	(196.9)	(6.6)	131.1
Comprehensive (loss) income	$ (1,248.2)	$ 1,285.1	$ 63.1
Diluted net income per share	$ 2.09	$ 2.74	$ 2.08
Weighted average shares—basic	182.6	178.7	172.2
Weighted average shares—diluted	185.5	181.4	173.3

Source: Molson Coors, *Annual Report* (2009).

EXHIBIT 3   Molson Coors Consolidated Balance Sheet (in millions)

	As of	
	December 28, 2008	December 30, 2007
Assets		
Current assets:		
Cash and cash equivalents	$ 216.2	$ 377.0
Accounts and notes receivable:		
Trade, less allowance for doubtful accounts of $7.9 and $8.8, respectively	432.9	758.5
Affiliates	39.6	—
Current notes receivable and other receivables, less allowance for doubtful accounts of $3.3 and $3.2, respectively	162.9	112.6
Inventories:		
Finished, less allowance for obsolete inventories	89.1	164.0
In process	13.4	40.7
Raw materials	43.3	82.3
Packaging materials, less allowance for obsolete inventories	46.3	82.6
Total inventories	192.1	369.6
Maintenance and operating supplies, less allowance for obsolete supplies of $4.6 and $10.6, respectively	14.8	34.8
Other current assets, less allowance for advertising supplies	47.1	100.9
Deferred tax assets	—	17.9
Discontinued operations	1.5	5.5
Total current assets	1,107.1	1,776.8
Properties, less accumulated depreciation of $673.5 and $2,715.1, respectively	1,301.9	2,696.2
Goodwill	1,298.0	3,346.5
Other intangibles, less accumulated amortization of $274.9 and $312.1, respectively	3,923.4	5,039.4
Investment in MillerCoors	2,418.7	—
Deferred tax assets	105.3	336.9
Notes receivable, less allowance for doubtful accounts of $8.1 and $7.9, respectively	51.8	71.2
Other assets	203.4	179.5
Discontinued operations	7.0	5.1
Total assets	$ 10,416.6	$ 13,451.6
Liabilities and stockholders' equity		
Current liabilities:		
Accounts payable:		
Trade	$ 152.8	$ 351.6
Affiliates	17.7	29.1
Accrued expenses and other liabilities	690.8	1,189.1
Deferred tax liabilities	107.8	120.6
Short-term borrowings	—	0.1
Current portion of long-term debt	0.1	4.2

continued

EXHIBIT 3 Molson Coors Consolidated Balance Sheet (in millions)—continued

	As of	
	December 28, 2008	December 30, 2007
Discontinued operations	16.9	40.8
Total current liabilities	986.1	1,735.5
Long-term debt	1,831.7	2,260.6
Pension and post-retirement benefits	581.0	677.8
Derivative hedging instruments	225.9	477.4
Deferred tax liabilities	399.4	605.4
Unrecognized tax benefits	230.4	285.9
Other liabilities	47.6	90.9
Discontinued operations	124.8	124.8
Total liabilities	4,426.9	6,258.3
Commitments and contingencies (Note 20)		
Minority interests	9.4	43.8
Stockholders' equity		
Capital stock:		
Preferred stock, non-voting, no par value (authorized: 25.0 shares; none issued)	—	—
Class A common stock, voting, $0.01 par value (authorized: 500.0 shares; issued and outstanding: 2.7 shares at December 28, 2008, and December 30, 2007, respectively)	—	—
Class B common stock, non-voting, $0.01 par value (authorized: 500.0 shares; issued and outstanding: 157.1 shares and 149.6 shares at December 28, 2008, and December 30, 2007, respectively)	1.6	1.5
Class A exchangeable shares (issued and outstanding: 3.2 shares and 3.3 shares at December 28, 2008, and December 30, 2007, respectively)	119.4	124.8
Class B exchangeable shares (issued and outstanding: 20.9 shares and 25.1 shares at December 28, 2008, and December 30, 2007, respectively)	786.3	945.3
Total capital stock	907.3	1,071.6
Paid-in capital	3,270.4	3,022.5
Retained earnings	2,199.4	1,950.5
Accumulated other comprehensive (loss) income	(396.8)	1,104.9
Total stockholders' equity	**5,980.3**	**7,149.5**
Total liabilities and stockholders' equity	**$ 10,416.6**	**13,451.6**

Source: Molson Coors, *Annual Report* (2009).

Marketing

According to market data, beer consumers skew toward the following demographic profile:

- Male
- Younger
- Moderately educated
- Blue collar
- Moderate- to high-income households

The market for the target customer is increasingly competitive, especially on product differentiation by price. Another important product differentiation is the import and premium categories. Growth is anticipated in these categories. Coors has posted a decline in market share compared to other brewers, including the market leader Anheuser-Busch, which has posted steady growth. Micro and regional brewers are picking up momentum, as are imports, whereas Coors and Molson (separate but combined volume) have leveled off right above 10 percent of market share. The joint venture with SABMiller has now placed Molson Coors in second to Anheuser-Busch in the United States. Anheuser-Busch has 48.2 percent of the domestic market share (*Beer Industry Overview,* 2008).

Molson and Coors each have a strong presence in Canada with the National Hockey League. Molson Coors is the second-largest brewer in Canada with 41 percent market share. As of December 2008, Molson Coors advertising and promotions include marketing at sports arenas, stadiums, and other venues and events, totaling approximately $281 million over the next five years and afterward.

C2, one of the most recent new products marketed under the Coors name, is a lower-alcohol version of Carling, the United Kingdom's biggest selling lager, owned by Coors. The brew is only 2 percent alcohol by volume, thereby offering a good alternative for those drinkers who want to enjoy the taste and experience of beer but do not want the alcohol buzz. It is also for those who want to drink moderately but do not want to turn to soft drinks. Coors says the new lager "is naturally brewed and is different than a low-alcohol or non-alcoholic beer, which has its alcohol removed after brewing" (www.realbeer.com, December 2004). Carling lager represented more than 78 percent of its European segment's sales volume in fiscal 2007 (*Drinks MarketWatch,* 2009).

Coors is continuing its low carbohydrate and low-calorie craze. With the SABMiller joint venture, Coors now brews or distributes Miller Lite, MGD 64 (only 64 calories), Milwaukee's Best Light, Amstel Light, and other health-conscious beer to its portfolio of beers (Molson Coors Brewing Co., 2009). Competition is extensive for low-carb brews to appeal to the Atkins diet crowd.

Coors has also indicated plans of targeting female drinkers as UK beer sales continue to decline. Currently, women account for 14 percent of beer sales in the United Kingdom and 25 percent in North America. Brewers have introduced a variety of fruity flavors and low-calorie options to appeal to women (*Drinks MarketWatch,* 2009).

Molson Coors has also introduced new packaging with some of its products, including a Coors Light quick-cool 8-ounce can. It has also introduced an 18-pack plastic bottle cooler box. These are great summer items targeted at anyone who wants to take their beer on the go—camping, to the beach, to a barbecue, and so on. The quick-cool idea is new to the U.S. market but has been tested extensively with product market research, and Molson Coors anticipates it will have great success. In addition, David Wiggins and his team were able to produce a bottle called Containerlite that reduced overall packaging weight by 4,500 tons or a full 13 percent of annual shipped product weight since its debut in the summer of 2006 (www.molsoncoors.com, 2009).

Responsibility in Advertising

"21 means 21." Pete Coors has been quoted as saying, "If you're under the legal drinking age, we'll wait for your business at Coors." Coors has established its own guidelines to promote responsible decisions about drinking. In fact, Coors was the first brewer to incorporate alcohol awareness messages into national product advertising. Coors places advertising only where the clear majority of the audience is 21 years old or over. Coors regularly monitors all advertising placements for compliance with industry and company standards, and it publicly discloses independent audits of television placements. To ensure compliance, television commercials are targeted to programs that had at least 60 percent of viewers age 21 or over in the prior reporting period. Strict internal reviews are also conducted on all advertising and marketing materials to avoid any advertising that may be misconstrued as targeted to those under 21 years old.

Coors has also developed, with the help of Bill Young, an initiative called MVParents. The initiative was created to promote responsible alcohol consumption and aims to help parents address underage drinking by nurturing strong, healthy kids and by being the "most valuable players" in their children's lives. The program was created with a partnership between the Search Institute, a leading nonprofit organization that studies and recommends strategies for raising healthy children and adolescents, and with PLAYERS INC, a subsidiary of the NFL Players Association, which aims to "take the helmets off" players and present them as community and civic champions. Addressing underage drinking is a top priority not only for Bill, but also for Coors in general. "Our message to kids is 'we'll wait for your business,'" says Bill (www.molsoncoors.com, 2009).

The company's Coors and Molson Web sites each prompt users to enter their date of birth to verify they are of legal drinking age if they want access to promotions within the site. Any advertising content is also screened and steered to the parts of the Web site that are behind this prompt. Financial and investor-related corporate data is available without such a prompt at any of the sites.

External Factors

Exhibit 4 compares Molson Coors to the beverage industry. Note how much better the company is doing on EPS than the industry average.

The Alcohol Beverage Industry

The alcohol beverage market is truly a behemoth in the U.S. economy, contributing more than $189 billion. The industry employs over 1.7 million people paying almost $55 billion in wages. The beer industry also contributes more than $36 billion in federal, state, and local excise, business, and consumption (www.beerinstitute.org). The U.S. brewery industry is composed of approximately 1,400 breweries with annual revenue of about $18 billion. Major companies are Anheuser-Busch InBev and MillerCoors. These top two companies account for 90 percent of revenue. The majority of breweries are small with fewer than five employees. The majority of brewery products are malt beverages, primarily beer and ale, packaged in cans, bottles, barrels, or kegs (Hoover's Industry Overview, 2009).

Another factor is the approximately 3 million children of the baby boomers (baby-boomlets) who began hitting their prime drinking years in 1996. These customers are not content to stay with the status quo and may bring profound changes to the industry (Chura, 2002). An array of choices to cater to more niche markets may include sweeter brews and concoctions that taste different from what their parents drink. However as more products emerge, the fickleness of customers increases, which detracts from brand loyalty. In addition, Morgan Stanley found spirits were the most popular drink choice among 21- to 27-year-olds, the key marketing segment that brewers target. Spirits are perceived to have a stronger image among twenty somethings, and consistently beat beer on taste, quality, and sophistication (Arndofer, 2005).

EXHIBIT 4 Molson Coors versus the Beverage Industry (2009)

	Molson Coors	Beverage Industry
Market Cap	$ 8.90B	548.44M
Employees	14,000	775
Qtrly Rev Growth	−54.50%	16.10%
Revenue	3.02B	1.46B
Gross Margin	41.99%	45.96%
EBITDA	616.30M	325.90M
Oper Margins	13.96%	14.09%
Net Income	531.90M	N/A
EPS	$ 2.895	0.13

Note:
B = billion $
M = million $

Another factor has been the current economic conditions. Many people view the alcohol industry as recession-proof. Although it may be true that consumers won't stop drinking altogether, they will drink less and convert to cheaper products during an economic downturn (Chong, 2009). Due to a renewal of mainstream brands, as well as growth in the craft segment, domestic beer continued its recovery in 2008. According to the Beer Institute, in Washington, D.C., estimated domestic brewer volumes were up 1.1 percent in 2008, and exports of U.S. beers to other countries increased 12.4 percent compared to 2007. Import volumes fell 3.4 percent for the year (Theodore, 2009).

Advertising may be a way for beer producers to gain market share. Molson Coors plans to spend approximately $281 million over the next five years and thereafter on advertising and promotions, including marketing at sports arenas, stadiums, and other venues and events.

According to a beer industry overview, beer is a $98 billion category among beverages including wine and spirits. Beer accounts for more than half of beverage alcohol dollar sales, and up to 85 percent of total consumption by (sales) volume. Although there has been a leveling off in the industry sales of cans, sales of bottles and beer in general have generally increased over the last four years.

About 4 of every 10 adults of legal drinking age (age 20 and older) is a regular beer consumer, defined as drinking within the past week (27 percent) or the past month (12 percent), according to data compiled by this market research. Furthermore, beer drinkers buy beer frequently, and over a third of beer drinkers are "frequent beer shoppers," shipping for beer either one to two times (26 percent) or even up to three times a week or more (5 percent). The occasional shoppers (between once every two weeks and once every three to four weeks) account for the next 50 percent of beer shoppers. Greater category sales are expected as we progress further into this decade. There was a bottoming out in the late 1990s, but "a core beer consumer demographic" is expected to grow through 2010. Overall beer industry shipments increased slightly over one year ago, by 1.4 percent. Lastly, the tactical (price) segment is expected to lose share to the high end and premium segments over the next three years, from 2003 to 2006. By 2006, premium and high-end beers are expected to account for over 75 percent of the market for beer. Beer consumers skew toward male, younger, moderately educated, and higher income households (Anheuser-Busch, 2008).

Competitors

Anheuser-Busch Companies, Inc.

In November 2008, InBev acquired Anheuser-Busch (A-B). InBev paid $52 billion for A-B and became the world's largest brewer. The new company Anheuser-Busch InBev has a product list of over 200 beers. In addition, the company owns 50 percent of Mexico's largest brewer, Grupo Modelo, maker of Corona. A-B InBev now has operations in more than 30 countries around the globe (Hoover's Anheuser-Busch InBev, 2009).

Anheuser-Busch accounts for approximately 50 percent of domestic market share. Bud Light is the industry's largest brand and it maintained its leadership position during the past year. It achieved a slight 0.05 percent increase in its total share of market through IRI's grocery, drug, and mass merchandise outlets (excluding Wal-Mart) for the year ending February 22, 2009 (Theodore, 2009).

A-B has also entered into an agreement with Asahi Breweries. According to this agreement, Asahi will acquire 19.9 percent of Tsingtao Brewery from A-B InBev for $667. A-B InBev has started a deleveraging program and the divestiture of this stake in Tsingtao as part of it. It allows the company to unlock shareholder value, generating proceeds that will be used to repay debt incurred as a result of the acquisition of A-B (*Drinks MarketWatch*).

A-B has recognized the increasingly competitive beverage alcohol market. Its annual report highlights the need to compete aggressively for the contemporary 21-plus crowd with increasingly sophisticated tastes. Hard liquor is once again experiencing growth in the industry, after a long, slow, steady decline to wine and beer. Flavored liquors can take some of the credit for this improvement as well. A-B is now emphasizing its on-premise marketing to develop the beer brand image, especially among "contemporary adults," and they are also introducing new brands and packaging, much like Molson Coors.

Boston Beer Company

The Boston Beer Company, Inc. is the largest craft brewer and the fourth largest brewer overall in the United States. The company sold over 20 beers under the Samuel Adams or the Sam Adams brand names, 7 flavored malt beverage products under the Twisted Tea brand name, and 1 hard cider product under the HardCore brand name during 2008. Boston Beer produces malt beverages and hard cider products at company-owned breweries and under contract arrangements at other brewery locations. The company-owned breweries are located in Cincinnati, Ohio; Lehigh Valley, Pennsylvania; and Boston, Massachusetts. During 2008, the company brewed certain products under contract at breweries located in Eden, North Carolina; Rochester, New York; Latrobe, Pennsylvania; and LaCrosse, Wisconsin (Boston Beer Company, *Annual Report,* 2009).

Boston Beer products are also distributed through a network of some 400 distributors and are available at pubs, restaurants, stadiums, grocery chains, package stores, and other retail outlets. Boston Beer offers Extreme Beers, those with 25 percent alcohol, and seasonal brews to keep adventurous drinkers brand-loyal (Hoover's Boston Beer Company, 2009).

Challenges

The biggest challenge facing Molson Coors is the problem faced by every brewer: declining sales, changing tastes, and increased competition. So far, A-B is winning the competition and marketing battle over Molson Coors, but Coors is also doing very well in its share of the market, given its past sales volume and new potential for growth with the combined strengths and geographic diversification of Molson Coors.

The current economic conditions pose a challenge for Molson Coors because it is directly affected by the fluctuations in the foreign exchange rate. In addition to the economic turmoil, Molson Coors may not realize the cost savings and other benefits from MillerCoors. The integration of the two operations is a complex undertaking and may result in operational problems, expenses and liabilities, and diversion of management's attention.

Other challenges include A-B and Bud Light being able to outspend Molson Coors on advertising for the highly competitive summer season. The combined company will likely not be able to out-discount its top competitors either. Anheuser-Busch can afford to deeply discount across the board, whereas Molson Coors will rely on its marketing to bring home sales without competing primarily through discounting.

The Future

For the three-month period ending in June, 2009, Molson Coors Brewing Co. earned $187.3 million, or $1.01 a share, up from earnings of $91.8 million or 49 cents a share in the same period last year, before Molson Coors and SABMiller PLC formed their joint venture MillerCoors.

Net sales fell 55 percent to $798.9 million in the quarter, down from $1.76 billion in the same period last year, before the MillerCoors joint venture started. The results beat the estimates of analysts, who predicted revenue of $750.66 million.

Molson Coors said the current quarter's results were hurt by unfavorable foreign exchange rates. A strong U.S. dollar weighs down international sales once they are converted back into dollars. The company has sizable business in Canada and Britain.

Net sales for the MillerCoors joint venture rose about 1 percent to $2.14 billion in the quarter. The venture in the U.S. and Puerto Rico, which began last summer, aims to cut $500 million in costs in three years and better compete against industry leader Anheuser-Busch.

As the recession lingers, economy beers are selling much better nationwide than premium beers. For example, Busch Light and MillerCoors's Keystone Light generally cost about $14 a case, or $5 less than a case of Bud Light or Coors Light. Whereas drinkers a few years ago were "trading up" to imports and small-batch "craft" beers, the trend now is towards economy beers. For thousands of consumers today, drinking less beer is not the best option, so finding the cheapest way to drink is preferred. For example, at 7-Eleven's 6,000 USA stores, sales of economy beers are up 9 percent in 2009.

Competitor Anheuser-Busch InBev NV announced in mid-2009 that they desire to own all their distributors, rather than have 600 un-owned distributors. Currently Anheuser distributes only 7 percent of its products but would like to see that number increase to 50 percent soon.

For the 13 weeks ending July 12, 2009, the top beer selling brands in the United States were Bud Light ($1.3 billion), Budweiser ($570 million), Coors Light ($491 million), Miller Lite ($453 million), Natural Light ($286 million), Corona Extra ($285 million), Busch Light ($178 million), Busch ($163 million), Heineken ($156 million), and Miller High Life ($126 million). Clearly Molson Coors needs a clear strategic plan to compete with its rival breweries, especially gigantic Anheuser-Busch.

References

Adolph Coors, 2004 Annual Statements.

"After Prices Rise, Profit Narrows at Molson Coors." *New York Times* (2009). Available at: www.lexisnexis.com.

Arndofer, James. "The Death of Beer." *Advertising Age* 76 (2005):18.

Beer Industry Overview: 1st Quarter 2008. Available at: http://www.supermarketbusiness.com/progressivegrocer/profitguides/beer/images/pdf/IndustryOverview.pdf.

"Beer Sales." Retrieved May 19, 2009, from www.bevindustry.com.

"Beer Statistics." Retrieved May 19, 2009, from www.beerinstitute.org.

"Big Shoes, Little Feet." Retrieved April 28, 2009, from www.molsoncoors.com.

Chura, Hillary. "Boom Drinkers Complicate Drinks." *Advertising Age* 73 (2002): 25.

Chong, Pooi Koon. "Alcohol Business Feels the Pinch Too." 2009. Available at: www.lexisnexis.com.

"Containerlite: Less is More." Retrieved April 28, 2009, from www.molsoncoors.com.

"Coors to Close Memphis Brewery." Retrieved February 14, 2005, from www.realbeer.com.

Drinks MarketWatch. "Company Spotlight: Molson Coors." (2009). Datamonitor.

Drinks MarketWatch. "Industry Update." (2009). Datamonitor.

Hoover's Company Records. "Molson Coors Brewing Company." Retrieved February 17, 2009, from www.hoovers.com.

Hoover's Company Records. "Anheuser-Busch InBev." Retrieved February 17, 2009, from www.hoovers.com.

Hoover's Company Records. "The Boston Beer Company." Retrieved February 17, 2009, from www.hoovers.com.

Hoover's Industry Overview. "Breweries." Retrieved April 28, 2009, from www.hoovers.com.

"Molson and Coors Complete Merger to Form Molson Coors Brewing Company." Press Release, February 9, 2005. Retrieved June 5, 2005, from www.molsoncoors.com.

"Molson Information" (n.d.) Retrieved June 5, 2005, from www.molsoncoors.com.

Molson Coors, *Annual Report* (2009).

"Molson Coors Brewing Company Announces Management Changes." Canada: *PRNewswire* (March 18, 2005).

Theodore, Sarah. "2009 Beer Report: Beer defies the odds." 2009. Available at: http://www.bevindustry.com/CDA/Articles/Cover_Story/BNP_GUID_9-5-2006_A_10000000000000572434.

The Boston Beer Company, *Annual Report* (2009).

## 24

PepsiCo — 2009

John and Sherry Ross
Texas State University–San Marcos

PEP

http://www.pepsico.com

The "cola wars" refers to the all-out battle between Coke and Pepsi for world cola domination. Stop now and think of the PepsiCo brand products you might consume in a typical day. For breakfast you might have a bowl of Quaker Oats, or perhaps Cap'N Crunch cereal, or perhaps pancakes with Aunt Jemima syrup and a Tropicana juice. As you left for class you might have grabbed an Aquarian bottled water, or a bottle of Gatorade, or Propel fitness water. For lunch, a sandwich with a bag of Fritos or some baked Doritos chips makes a fast and enjoyable choice. Later in the afternoon a SunChips multigrain snack with an AMP energy drink will hold you over until dinner, when a Rice-A-Roni product accompanies your main course. You may be much more familiar with PepsiCo than you think.

First quarter 2009 PepsiCo's net revenues of $8,263 million were down $70 million from the same quarter in 2008. However, PepsiCo controlled costs by decreasing cost of goods sold by $90 million. This resulted in a net profit of $1,141 million, which is $90 million less than last year's first quarter. PepsiCo may need to further adjust costs to reflect continuing economic troubles as consumers shift to less costly drinks and snacks. There is also a shift away from bottled water and back to the tap. Second quarter PepsiCo results continued the downward trend with beverage volume down 6 percent, Frito-Lay down 3 percent and Quaker down 4 percent. However, international volume was up 1 percent snacks and 6 percent in beverages.

PepsiCo opened a new factory in Shanghai in June 2009 and plans to open another five plants in China over the next two year. PepsiCo's total investment over the 2009–2012 period is $1 billion to bolster manufacturing and its sales force throughout China. Some of PepsiCo's potato chip brands in China are Beijing Duck, Cool Lemon, and Lychee. The new plant will manufacture Pepsi-Cola, Mountain Dew, Gatorade, Tropicana juices, and bottled water. The new PepsiCo plant uses 22 percent less water and 23 percent less energy than the average Pepsi plant in China.

PepsiCo's strategy in China is to overtake Coke, which has a 47.3 percent market share in the country's cola market versus Pepsi' 44.5 percent, according to Euromonitor International. In overall beverage sales, Coke has a 15.3 percent market share in China versus Pepsi's 6.2 percent. PepsiCo has pledged to invest $1 billion in Russia over the next three years, bringing its total investment to $4 billion over a ten-year time span. PepsiCo will also invest over $1 billion in China over the next 4 years. This is in addition to continued investments in Japan, India, Europe, Mexico, and Latin America.

PepsiCo recently offered $6 billion to retake ownership of its two largest bottlers, Pepsi Bottling Group (PBG) and PepsiAmericas (PAS). Non-carbonated products are today about 40 percent of Pepsi-Cola volume, versus less than 15 percent 10 years ago. Pepsi's desire to own its own bottlers is to spur its non-carbonated health and wellness products, which are often smaller-volume, slower-moving products. PBG and PAS distribute nearly 75 percent of Pepsi drinks in the United States, excluding Gatorade.

History

Pepsi-Cola was invented by Caleb Bradham in New Bern, North Carolina, in 1898 and quickly became a popular drink with some 300 bottlers by the start of World War I.

Bradham followed the example of Coca-Cola and used the bottling franchise system in which he produced the syrup and others bottled and distributed. This business model allowed for quick expansion and market penetration. However, Bradham went bankrupt after World War I when the price of sugar plummeted and his stockpiles became worthless.

Pepsi floundered under various owners until 1932 when, in the midst of the Depression, it was purchased by Loft Candy. In 1933, to improve sales and gain market, Loft doubled the size of its bottle to 12 ounces, charging one nickel, when the standard was 6 ounces. This low-cost differentiation strategy proved very successful and allowed the renamed Pepsi-Cola company to expand and become a major player in the cola industry.

Since that time, Pepsi and Coke have battled to become the largest worldwide producer of nonalcoholic beverages. However, where as Coca-Cola has kept a fairly narrow focus, Pepsi has ventured into conglomerate diversification from van moving lines to sporting goods to fast foods. PepsiCo of late has a more focused strategy in the snack, breakfast food, and nonalcoholic beverage markets. After all, what goes better with a cola than a salty or sweet snack? Pepsi seems to be developing synergy between product categories with breakfast foods and juices, colas and salty snacks, and at the same time moving into the water and sport beverage market. This strategy has developed over an extended period of time and seems to be working successfully, as shown by revenue growth and profitability. However, consumer taste continues to change, and Pepsi must also continue to change.

Today

Although you might have thought of Pepsi as a bottler of soft drinks, the company produces Mountain Dew, Mug Root Beer, Sierra Mist, Slice, Aquafina, Dole juices, and SoBe. But these are just under the Pepsi-Cola brands. You also need to add Lay's potato chips, Doritos, Tostitos, Fritos, and Cheetos under the Frito-Lay brand. In addition, PepsiCo includes the brands of Quaker (the oats company), Tropicana, and Gatorade. And this is just a partial list of the branded products sold by Pepsi.

PepsiCo, Inc. is indeed a large company and is defined in the *10K* as "a leading global beverage, snack and food company." Additionally it "manufacture(s) or use(s) contract manufacturers, (to) market and sell a variety of salty, convenient, sweet and grain-based snacks, carbonated and non-carbonated beverages and foods in approximately 200 countries, with our largest operations in North America (United States and Canada), Mexico and the United Kingdom" (*10K,* 2008). Globally, PepsiCo operates in Canada, Latin America, Europe, Middle East, Asia, Northern Asia, Australia, and the Asian Pacific.

With total revenues over $43 billion (up from $39 billion in 2007) and net profits over $5 billion in 2008, Pepsi continues to expand its markets in both the beverage and snack food industries through market penetration, mergers, and acquisitions.

Organizational Structure

PepsiCo is organized using three strategic business units of PepsiCo Americas Foods, PepsiCo Americas Beverages, and PepsiCo International as indicated in Exhibit 1. This structure shows divisions along both product categories and geographical locations. PepsiCo Americas Beverages is a separate division that reflects its importance to the organization. At a time when many companies give only lip service to inclusion and diversity, PepsiCo has promoted to the position of CEO (October 1, 2006) and chairman (May 2, 2007) Indra K. Nooyi. Beginning her career in India, Nooyi has held many positions including vice president (VP) corporate strategy for Motorola, senior VP of strategy and strategic marketing for Asea Brown Boveri, and senior VP and CFO of PepsiCo, and president and CFO of PepsiCo. She holds a BS from Madras Christian College, an MBA from the Indian Institute of Management in Calcutta, and a master's of public and private management from Yale University.

Marketing

Nooyi is leading a worldwide consumer goods manufacturing company that primarily uses differentiation to attract and hold customers. Although its major customers are large retailers

EXHIBIT 1 PepsiCo's Organizational Structure

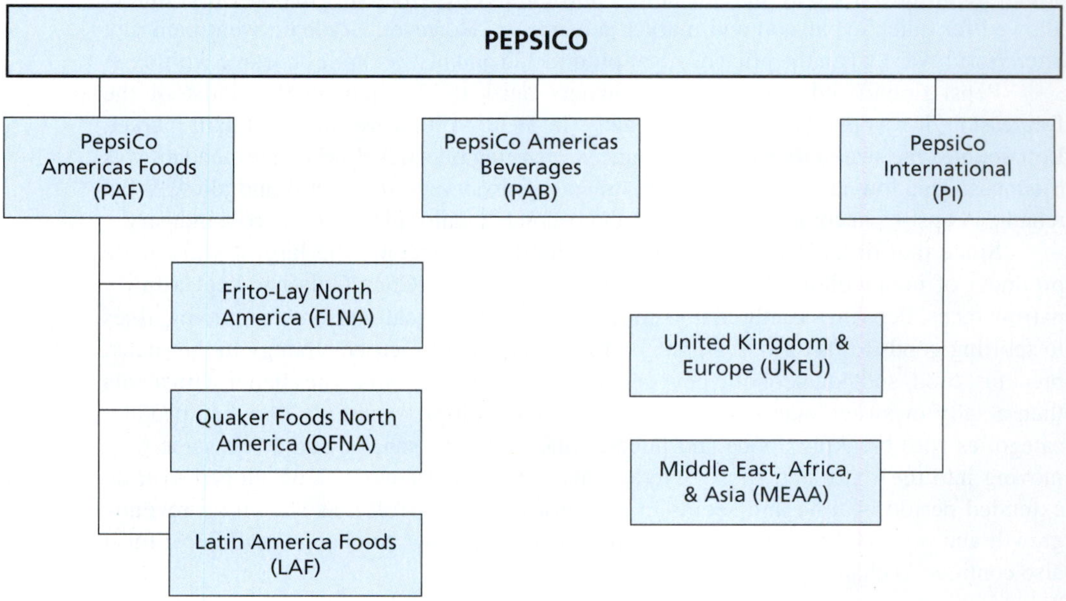

Source: PepsiCo, 2009 *Form 10K* (2009).

(Wal-Mart accounts for approximately 12 percent of total revenues and 18 percent of North American revenues), PepsiCo must appeal to the ultimate consumer through extensive advertising and promotional activities. This pull marketing strategy is highly dependent on creative marketing and the development of catchy slogans, along with the continued development of new and reinvented brands (Pepsi-Cola Brands). As consumer tastes have changed, PepsiCo has developed liquid refreshment products that are light, calorie free, sugar free, caffeine free, sports and energy directed, and flavored (Pepsi, Voltage, Aquafina). Snacks now have less salt and less fat and are baked, kettled, and made with vegetables (Frito-Lay TrueNorth). This strategy continues into the juice segment (Tropicana) and the Quaker product line as well as the Gatorade products.

PepsiCo works closely with its bottlers and retailers in promoting and advertising its entire range of products around the world. In 2006, PepsiCo spent approximately $10.1 billion on sales incentives and discounts; in 2007, it spent $11.3 billion, and in 2008, $12.5 billion was spent. This does not include advertising expenses, which were $1.8 billion in 2008 and 2007, and $1.6 billion in 2006. Although these numbers may seem excessive, the level of worldwide competition (particularly Coca-Cola, which spent some $2.9 billion on advertising alone in 2008) requires extensive advertising and promotion to remain in the minds of the ultimate consumer. PepsiCo uses all available media to promote its products and attempts to attract younger consumers through Web-related media such as YouTube, and having appealing Web pages with the latest ads and product-related games.

Advertising for both Pepsi and Coca-Cola has generally been built around short, memorable slogans to attract and hold the attention of consumers. Of the more than 40 slogans and songs created since 1939, some of the more successful slogans for Pepsi have included: "Twice as Much for a Nickel" (1939–1950), which allowed Pepsi to grow during the depression; "Have a Pepsi Day" (1961–1963); "Pepsi Now! Take the Challenge" (1983–1984) was one of the most successful; "Drink Pepsi. Get Stuff" (1995–1996); "For Those Who Think Young" (1999–2000); "Pepsi Stuff" (2008) Super Bowl commercial; and today's "Refresh Everything" and "Every Generation Refreshes the World" (2009).

Financials

Recent consolidated financial data obtained from the 2009 *10K* are presented in Exhibits 2 through 6. Although the financials appear very good with revenues increasing from just

EXHIBIT 2 PepsiCo 2008 Income Statement

(in millions)	2008	2007	2006
Net Revenue	**$ 43,251**	**$ 39,474**	**$ 35,137**
Cost of sales	20,351	18,038	15,762
Selling, general and administrative expenses	15,901	14,208	12,711
Amortization of intangible assets	64	58	162
Operating Profit	6,935	7,170	6,502
Bottling equity income	374	560	553
Interest expense	(329)	(224)	(239)
Interest income	41	125	173
Income before Income Taxes	7,021	7,631	6,989
Provision for Income Taxes	1,879	1,973	1,347
Net Income	**$ 5,142**	**$ 5,658**	**$ 5,642**
Net Income per Common Share			
Basic	$ 3.26	$ 3.48	$ 3.42
Diluted	$ 3.21	$ 3.41	$ 3.34

Source: Form 10K (2009).

EXHIBIT 3 Balance Sheet Assets

(in millions except share amounts)	2008	2007	2006
ASSETS			
Current Assets			
Cash and cash equivalents	$ 2,064	$ 910	$ 1,651
Short-term investments	213	1,571	1,171
Accounts and notes receivable, net	4,683	4,389	3,725
Inventories	2,522	2,290	1,926
Prepaid expenses and other current assets	1,324	991	657
Total Current Assets	10,806	10,151	9,130
Property, Plant and Equipment, net	11,663	11,228	9,687
Amortizable Intangible Assets, net	732	796	637
Goodwill	5,124	5,169	4,594
Other nonamortizable intangible assets	1,128	1,248	1,212
Nonamortizable Intangible Assets	6,252	6,417	5,806
Investments in Noncontrolled Affiliates	3,883	4,354	3,690
Other Assets	2,658	1,682	980
Total Assets	$ 35,994	$ 34,628	S 29,930
Balance Sheet Liabilities			
LIABILITIES AND SHAREHOLDERS' EQUITY			
Current Liabilities			
Short-term obligations	$ 369	$ 0	$ 274
Accounts payable and other current liabilities	8,273	7,602	6,496
Income taxes payable	145	151	90
Total Current Liabilities	8,787	7,753	6,860

continued

EXHIBIT 3 **Balance Sheet Assets—continued**

(in millions except share amounts)	2008	2007	2006
Long-Term Debt Obligations	7,858	4,203	2,550
Other Liabilities	7,017	4,792	4,624
Deferred Income Taxes	226	646	528
Total Liabilities	23,888	17,394	14,562
Commitments and Contingencies			41
Preferred Stock, no par value	41	41	(120)
Repurchased Preferred Stock	−138	−132	
Common Shareholders' Equity			
Common stock, par value 1 2/3 per share (authorized 3,600 shares, issued 1,782 shares)	30	30	30
Capital in excess of par value	351	450	584
Retained earnings	30,638	28,184	24,837
Accumulated other comprehensive loss	−4,694	−952	(2,246)
Repurchased common stock, at cost (229 and 177 shares, respectively)	−14,122	−10,387	(7,758)
Total Common Shareholders' Equity	12,203	17,325	15,447
Total Liabilities and Shareholders' Equity	$ 35,994	$ 34,628	$ 29,930

Source: Form 10K (2009).

EXHIBIT 4 **Net Revenues and Percentages of Net Revenues by Division**

Net Revenue and Percent	2008	Percent	2007	Percent	2006	Percent
PepsiCo total	$ 43,251	100%	$ 39,474	100%	$ 35137	100%
Division						
Frito-Lay North America (FLNA)	$ 12,507	28.9	$ 11,586	29.3	$ 10,844	30.8
Quaker Foods North America (QFNA)	$ 1,902	4.3	$ 1,860	4.7	$ 1,769	5.0
Latin American Foods (LAF)	$ 5,895	13.6	$ 4,872	12.3	$ 3,972	11.3
PepsiCo Americas Beverages (PAB)	$ 10,937	25.2	$ 11,090	28.0	$ 10,362	29.9
United Kingdom & Europe (UKEU)	$ 6,435	14.8	$ 5,492	13.9	$ 4,750	13.5
Middle East, Africa, & Asia (MEAA)	$ 5,575	12.8	$ 4,574	11.5	$ 3,440	9.7

Source: Form 10K (2009).

EXHIBIT 5 **Operating Profit by Division**

	2008	2007	2006
Total Net Revenue	$ 43,251	$ 39,474	$ 35,137
Operating Profit by Division			
FLNA	$ 2,959	$ 2,845	$ 2,615
QFNA	582	568	554
LAF	897	714	655
PAB	2,026	2,487	2,315
UKEU	811	774	700
MEAA	667	535	401

Source: Form 10K (2009).

EXHIBIT 6   **World Demand for the Nonalcoholic Beverage Market**

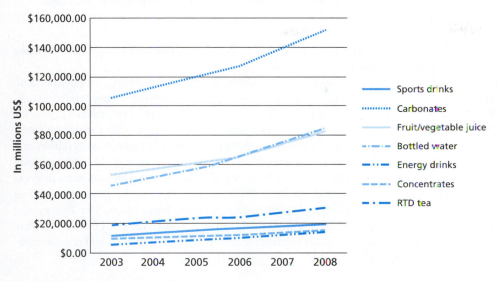

Source: *Euromonitor International* (2008).

over $35 billion in 2006 to over $43 billion in 2008, a closer look reveals some negative trends. On the income statement, cost of sales has increased as would be expected. However, these costs have increased from 41.32 percent of sales to 43.43 percent of sales and net income has decreased from $5.6 billion to $5.1 billion. Also during this time return on assets has dropped from 18.81 percent to 15.17 percent, inventory turnover has decreased from 8.02 times to 7.81 times, and long term debt has increased from $4.203 billion (24.45 percent of common equity) in 2007 to $7.858 in 2008 (65.13 percent of common equity). None of the changes necessarily indicate a company in trouble. However, the trends might indicate future problem areas. It should also be noted that in 2008 some $543 million was charged to net income in conjunction with the "Productivity for Growth" program, which included closing six plants, upgrading the product portfolio, and creating a more streamlined organization structure.

Divisional financial results for the years 2006–2008 show the importance of snack and breakfast foods as well as the decline in carbonated beverages. Also shown is the increase in international revenues.

Mission

The following is PepsiCo's mission and vision as taken directly from their Web site (PepsiCo Mission and Vision, March 2009):

Our Mission
Our mission is to be the world's premier consumer products company focused on convenient foods and beverages. We seek to produce financial rewards to investors as we provide opportunities for growth and enrichment to our employees, our business partners and the communities in which we operate. And in everything we do, we strive for honesty, fairness and integrity.

Our Vision
PepsiCo's responsibility is to continually improve all aspects of the world in which we operate–environment, social, economic–creating a better tomorrow than today.
Our vision is put into action through programs and a focus on environmental stewardship, activities to benefit society, and a commitment to build shareholder value by making PepsiCo a truly sustainable company.

Performance with Purpose
At PepsiCo, we're committed to achieving business and financial success while leaving a positive imprint on society–delivering what we call Performance with Purpose.

Our approach to superior financial performance is straightforward–drive shareholder value. By addressing social and environmental issues, we also deliver on our purpose agenda, which consists of human, environmental, and talent sustainability.

The final "Performance with Purpose" is part of PepsiCo's 2008 restructuring plan to make the company more efficient and profitable.

Additionally, PepsiCo has extensive statements on sustainability, the environment, health and wellness, and diversity (see Web site, PepsiCo—Purpose). These topics are critical to the long-term success of PepsiCo. The principal ingredient of its primary product is water. Both nationally and globally, an adequate supply of fresh, clean water becomes paramount, particularly in lesser developed countries. News of contamination (either real or perceived) can quickly destroy consumers' confidence in a company's ability to provide a safe, healthy product.[1] To help in this effort, PepsiCo has undertaken numerous projects and alliances around the world, working with such groups as the Earth Institute at Columbia University, the Chinese Woman's Development Foundation, The Energy and Resources Institute, Keep America Beautiful, Exnora, and UNICEF. Divisions within PepsiCo have also initiated projects to increase use of recycled materials and reduce materials used in packaging.

Industries

PepsiCo is a global company operating in the non-alcoholic beverage industry, the salty or savory snack food industry, and the breakfast food industry. Although these industries may be seen as concentrically related, they are analyzed separately.

Industry: Nonalcoholic Beverage

The global nonalcoholic beverage industry is composed of carbonated soft drinks, fruit and vegetable juices, bottled water, sports and energy drinks, concentrates, and ready-to-drink coffee and teas. These drinks make up a $395 billion world market with carbonated drinks the largest share of the market at $150 billion (see Exhibit 6). World demand has continued a slow but steady overall growth for the last five years of around 9 percent with sports drinks, bottled water, and energy drinks showing the largest growth. However, in the United States, the carbonated soft drink market has shown a decline of 0.4 percent in 2007 as consumers shifted from soft drinks to bottled water and sports drinks. In the United States, the carbonated soft drink market shrank to $63.4 billion in 2007 and is projected to continue to diminish to a value of $61.5 billion by 2012, a decrease of 2.7 percent. Growth in the carbonated drink market was largest in Asia and Europe.

Although there are many producers of nonalcoholic beverages, the industry is highly concentrated, with Coca-Cola and PepsiCo holding the largest share of the U.S. market at 23 percent and 25 percent, respectively. Coca-Cola, however, holds the largest share of the U.S. cola market at 41 percent with Pepsi second at 36.7 percent.

This industry continues to operate in the same general manor as it has for over 100 years. Both Pepsi and Coke manufacture the concentrates and syrups, which are then sold to bottlers. Bottlers then distribute the finished product to grocery stores, convenience stores, restaurants, vending machines, and so on. Pepsi and Coke spend heavily on national advertising as well as provide large promotional incentives to the bottlers. The market for these products depends on the changing taste of consumers and requires manufactures to constantly develop new products to meet those changing demands. In recent years we have seen the introduction of diet, free, and zero colas as well as flavored water sports and energy drinks. These companies are also highly dependent on supplies of clean water. The downturn in the economy has also affected the sale of colas and water as some consumers have switched to store brands and tap water as cheaper alternatives to the national brands. Additionally, a recent environmental campaign against plastic containers has impacted the sale of bottled water and forced manufactures to develop more environmentally friendly containers.

EXHIBIT 7   World Chip Market

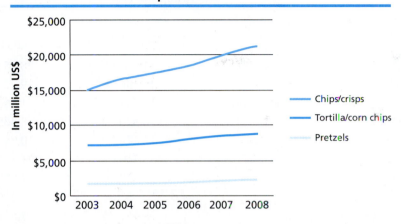

Source: Euromonitor International (2008).

Industry: Savory Snack

The U.S. savory snack market is composed of over 400 companies with combined annual revenues of $23 billion. This industry is also highly concentrated with the top 50 companies controlling 75 percent of the market. The largest competitors in this industry include PepsiCo's Frito-Lay (with 39 percent), Kraft's Nabisco (with 11 percent), and Kellogg's Retail Snacks division. By itself, the global chip market is over $32 billion, with an annual growth rate of approximately 6.35 percent (see Exhibit 7). This market is also driven by consumer taste and health considerations.

The largest product segment of this market is potato chips (30 percent of industry revenues) followed by tortilla chips (20 percent) and bulk nuts (10 percent). The remainder of the market is composed of canned nuts, corn chips, peanut butter, popcorn, and hard pretzels. It is estimated that 99 percent of all American households have salty snacks and the average household spends approximately $80 yearly on 32 pounds of these products.

Companies in this industry must compete against each other through extensive advertising, product promotions, and product innovation. As consumer tastes have changed, we have seen the introduction of products with less salt, sea salt, baked, zero trans fat, made of vegetables, low carb, organic, hot, sweet, black, green, and with chili or cheese added. Some of the new products are designed to compete on taste; others are designed to reflect a particular consumer concern such as obesity or hypertension.

Industry: Breakfast Cereals

The global breakfast foods market is composed of more than just cereals: it also includes bread, pastries, breakfast bars, and spreads. Bread is by far the largest segment of this market followed by pastries and then cereals. However, growth for bread is low at 1.6 percent, with pastries at 3.5 percent and cereals at 2.6 percent. The greatest growth for breakfast food appears to be in breakfast bars, and the fastest regional growth is the Asian-Pacific market. The largest markets continue to be Europe and America, but both are mature with low growth rates.

PepsiCo is primarily in the U.S. breakfast cereal market with the Quaker division generating approximately 4 percent of total revenues, down from 5 percent in 2007 and 2006. This market is a highly concentrated $9 billion market with the top four companies accounting for 80 percent of the market. The major competitors in this market are Kellogg and General Mills. Demand is driven by consumer demographics (age and lifestyle) and health considerations because a fast-paced life and health concerns shape our perceptions of the first meal of the day. Ready-to-eat cereals comprise about 90 percent of total industry revenue.

EXHIBIT 8 Coca-Cola

Two-Year Annual Income Statement

(all numbers in millions)	12/31/08	12/31/07
Sales	31,944.00	28,857.00
Cost of Goods Sold	10,146.00	9,229.00
Depreciation, Depletion & Amortization	1,228.00	1,163.00
Gross Income	20,570.00	18,465.00
Selling, General & Admin Expenses	11,774.00	10,945.00
Total Operating Expenses	23,266.00	21,337.00
Operating Income	8,678.00	7,520.00
Non-Operating Interest Income	333.00	236.00
Earnings Before Interest & Taxes	8,751.00	7,661.00
Interest Expense on Debt	438.00	456.00
Pretax Income	8,313.00	7,205.00
Income Taxes	1,632.00	1,892.00
Equity Interest Earnings	−874.00	668.00
Net Income Available to Common	5,807.00	5,981.00

Source: Thompson Banker (2008).

Competition

Coca-Cola

Coca-Cola, the brand known around the world, is the largest producer and distributor of dark colas in the world and as such is PepsiCo's major competitor. With net revenues of $31.944 billion and net profits of $5.807 billion in 2008 as seen in Exhibit 8, the Coca-Cola Company continues to expand even in the current monetary crises. The financials for Coca-Cola show a strong cash position of $4.979 billion and long-term debt of only $2.781 billion. Coca-Cola has also invested in purchasing bottlers and streamlining its operations.

"Rather, our entire Coca-Cola system is focused on what critically matters to our business: investing in our brands enhancing our communications to the customers who sell our beverages and the consumers who invite us into their lives each day; and streamlining our operations" (President's letter, 2008 *Annual Report*). Coca-Cola seems to be following a very concentrated strategy by focusing almost exclusively on nonalcoholic beverages with little, if any, tendency to diversify. This strategy is enhanced by extensive advertising ($3 billion expense in 2008) through the bottling and distribution network and toward the ultimate consumer. Additionally, as the demand for dark colas has diminished, Coca-Cola has continued to strengthen their juice, ready-to-drink tea and coffee products, water and sport drinks along with the introduction of Truvia as a sweetener.

Coke generates most of its operating revenue outside the United States with international concentrate sales accounting for 77 percent and U.S. sales 23 percent. Coke is a strong, well-known competitor and spent, in addition to advertising, $4.4 billion in promotion to bottlers and resellers in 2008. This amount of spending on promotion and advertising has led to volume growth in Eurasia of 7 percent, Europe of 3 percent, Latin America of 8 percent, and the Pacific of 8 percent. However, in the North America market volume growth was down 1 percent. This follows the global trends of a mature and declining market in North America with growth in other parts of the world.

Advertising for Coca-Cola is similar to Pepsi in that they also rely heavily on short catchy slogans, songs, and celebrity endorsements. Since 1886 Coke has been successful with such slogans as "Delicious and Refreshing" (1904), "The Pause That Refreshes" (1929), "Things Go Better With Coke" (1963), "It's the Real Thing" (one of the most successful: 1969), "Have a Coke and a Smile" (1979), "Life Tastes Good" (2001), and currently "Open Happiness" (2009).

Coca-Cola will continue to concentrate on its cola business but expand its water and juice sales and continue growth in international markets. However, the North American market generates 25.7 percent of revenue, and Coke will continue to spend heavily on promotion and advertising in this market. Interestingly, Coke's recent purchases of bottling facilities account for 27 percent of revenues. Europe is the second largest market; it contributes 15 percent to revenues and it should also see continued promotional activity.

Kraft

Kraft Foods is currently in the process of reinventing itself by restructuring the organization into two major divisions, North America and International. The North American division is composed of Beverages, Cheese & Foodservice, Convenient Meats, Grocery, and Snacks & Cereals. The International division consists of European Union and Developing Markets. Additionally they have brought in new top management and six new independent board directors. These changes are designed to strengthen the position of Kraft in the highly competitive and dynamic markets in which it currently operates.

The Kraft financials in Exhibit 9 for 2008 show a 13.32 percent increase in net revenues over 2007 to $42.201 billion. This growth is a continuation of increasing growth from 2007. Growth from 2004 to 2006 was relatively stagnant with growth rates of 3.76 percent, 6.02 percent, and 0.71 percent, respectively. Kraft's new strategies seem to be paying off in increased revenue and possible future growth.

The North American Snacks and Cereals division produced $5.025 billion in revenues in 2008, an increase of 3 percent over 2007 revenue of $4.879 billion. This division's products include Oreo, Chips Ahoy!, Newtons, Nilla, Nutter Butter and SnackWell's

EXHIBIT 9   Kraft

Two-Year Annual Income Statement

(all numbers in millions)	12/31/08	12/31/07
Sales	**$ 42,201.00**	**$ 37,241.00**
Cost of Goods Sold	27,185.00	23,711.00
Depreciation, Depletion & Amortization	986.00	886.00
Gross Income	14,030.00	12,644.00
Selling, General & Admin Expenses	8,992.00	7,749.00
Total Operating Expenses	37,163.00	32,346.00
Operating Income	5,038.00	4,895.00
Non-Operating Interest Income	0.00	20.00
Earnings Before Interest & Taxes	3,849.00	4,351.00
Interest Expense on Debt	1,272.00	624.00
Pretax Income	2,577.00	3,727.00
Income Taxes	728.00	1,137.00
Minority Interest	0.00	0.00
Equity Interest Earnings	0.00	0.00
Net Income Before Extraordinary Items & Disc Ops	1,849.00	2,590.00
Extraordinary Items & Gain(Loss) Sale of Assets	1,052.00	0.00
Net Income Before Preferred Dividends	2,901.00	2,590.00
Preferred Dividend Requirements	0.00	0.00
Net Income Available to Common	1,849.00	2,590.00

Source: Thompson Banker (2008).

cookies; Ritz, Premium, Triscuit, Wheat Thins, Cheese Nips, Honey Maid Grahams, Teddy Grahams and Kraft macaroni and cheese crackers; Nabisco 100 Calorie Packs; South Beach Living (under license) crackers, cookies, and snack bars; Planters nuts and trail mixes; Handi-Snacks two-compartment snacks; Back to Nature granola, cookies, crackers, nuts, and fruit and nut mixes; and Balance nutrition and energy bars.

As Kraft continues to improve in the coming years, it should become a stronger competitor in all divisions. However, with long-term debt of $18.5 billion (LTD to common equity of 83.73 percent), debt coverage could slow its progress.

Future Direction

Pepsi and Coke have fought the cola wars for decades, and Coke has generally beaten out Pepsi for market share. However, today we see that PepsiCo is a larger and more diversified company than Coca-Cola with numerous opportunities and directions for growth. Although the market for colas nationally may be somewhat stagnant, the international markets for colas and snacks continue to grow. In some countries, these have increased in double-digit figures.

Additionally, PepsiCo has continued to expand in noncola foods that seem to enhance the opportunities for synergy between colas and salty snacks, water and sports drinks, and breakfast and juices. These combinations and promotions allow PepsiCo's bottlers enhanced ability to gain retail shelf space. However, the proliferation of products for specific market segments (light, sugar free, caffeine free, etc.) and the increasing use of house brands by retailers will continue to force PepsiCo to innovate new products and at the same time reevaluate current product offerings.

PepsiCo spent $650,000 in the second quarter of 2009 to lobby on sugar, food safety, food labeling, patent reform, energy, taxes, and other issues. Besides Congress, PepsiCo lobbied the Agriculture Department, Executive Office of the President, and other entities, according to a report filed July 20, 2009, with the House of Representatives clerk's office in Washington, D.C.

In late 2009, PepsiCo acquired Amacoco Nordeste Ltda and Amacoco Sudeste Ltda, Brazil's largest makers of packaged coconut water drinks. PepsiCo is expanding its presence in South America's largest nation. These Brazilian companies make the Kero Coco and Trop Coco drinks.

Also in late 2009, PepsiCo acquired and combined its two largest independent bottlers for $7.8 billion–PepsiAmericas and the Pepsi Bottling Group. This forward integration strategy has been a major initiative of PepsiCo for many months.

Develop a clear three-year strategic plan for PepsiCo.

Endnotes

1. J. Slater, "Coke, Pepsi Fight Product Contamination Charges in India" *Wall Street Journal* (August 15, 2003): B1.

## 25

Pfizer, Inc. — 2009

Vijaya Narapareddy
University of Denver

PFE

www.pfizer.com

On May 9, 2009, Japanese pharmaceutical manufacturer Eisai threatened Pfizer to terminate its long-standing partnership on the news of Pfizer's proposed acquisition of Wyeth. Eisai's venture with Pfizer dates back to the mid-1990s when Pfizer entered into an alliance to sell Eisai's Aricept, the world's leading medicine for the treatment of Alzheimer's disease. Headquartered in New York City, Pfizer generated about $482 million in 2008 from the sale of Aricept, an increase of 20 percent from 2007, as shown in Exhibit 1. Pfizer vows to fight back, claiming that Eisai lacks any legal basis for termination of their alliance.

Pfizer engages in the discovery, development, manufacture, and marketing of prescription medicines for humans and animals worldwide. Some of its well-known drugs are Lipitor, Viagra, Lyrica, Zeldox, and Aricept used for people, as well as Draxxin used for cattle.

The Wyeth Acquisition

The proposed Pfizer acquisition of Wyeth, a company based in Madison, New Jersey, for a cash and stock purchase of $68 billion would enable Pfizer to diversify its product offerings and make further inroads into emerging markets. Exhibit 2 provides details of the benefits of the proposed Wyeth acquisition.

Pfizer's Business Segments

Pfizer operates from three business segments, Pharmaceuticals, Animal Health, and a third one that contains "Corporate & Other." The Pharmaceuticals business offers human health products for the treatment of cardiovascular diseases, central nervous system disorders, arthritis and pain, infectious and respiratory diseases, urogenital conditions, cancer, eye disease, endocrine disorders, and allergies, among others. Pfizer is well known for its prescription medicines and the many over-the-counter medical products it offers. The over-the-counter self-medications range from oral care, upper respiratory health to tobacco dependence, skin and eye care, and hair growth. The Animal Health division offers medicines for livestock and pets. The company also manufactures empty gelatin capsules and engages in producing contract and bulk pharmaceuticals/chemicals, which it classifies under "Corporate/other" business.

The company's revenues by segment are provided in Exhibit 3 and reveal that the Pharmaceuticals business dominates the portfolio with over 90 percent of the revenues generated each year, whereas the Animal Health division accounts for only 5 percent each year. The "Corporate/other" segment is the smallest of all, with less than 3 percent of total sales.

Global Operations

Pfizer's international operations contributed $27.9 billion in revenues in 2008 as opposed to the $20.4 billion generated in the United States. Exhibit 4 provides detailed statistics of revenues by business segment and geographic region. This exhibit indicates that the double-digit declines in U.S. sales of Pharmaceuticals have been offset by double-digit growth in international sales.

EXHIBIT 1 Revenues by Key Products ($ in millions)

PRODUCT	PRIMARY INDICATIONS	YEAR ENDED DECEMBER 31			% CHANGE	
		2008	2007	2006	08/07	07/06
Cardiovascular & metabolic diseases:						
Lipitor	Reduction of LDL cholesterol	$ 12,401	$ 12,675	$ 12,886	(2)	(2)
Norvasc	Hypertension	2,244	3,001	4,866	(25)	(38)
Chantix/Champix	An aid to smoking cessation	846	883	101	(4)	773
Caduet	Reduction of LDL cholesterol and hypertension	589	568	370	4	54
Cardura	Hypertension/Benign prostatic hyperplasia	499	506	538	(1)	(6)
Central nervous system disorders:						
Lyrica	Epilepsy, post-herpetic neuralgia and diabetic peripheral neuropathy fibromyalgia	2,573	1,829	1,156	41	58
Geodon/Zeldox	Schizophrenia and acute manic or mixed episodes associated with bipolar disorder	1,007	854	758	18	13
Zoloft	Depression and certain anxiety disorders	539	531	2,110	2	(75)
Aricept(a)	Alzheimer's disease	482	401	358	20	12
Neurontin	Epilepsy and post-herpetic neuralgia	387	431	496	(10)	(13)
Xanax/Xanax XR	Anxiety/Panic disorders	350	325	316	8	3
Relpax	Migraine headaches	321	315	286	2	10
Arthritis and pain:						
Celebrex	Arthritis pain and inflammation, acute pain	2,489	2,290	2,039	9	12
Infectious & respiratory diseases:						
Zyvox	Bacterial infections	1,115	944	782	18	21
Vfend	Fungal infections	743	632	515	18	23
Zithromax/Zmax	Bacterial infections	429	438	638	(2)	(31)
Diflucan	Fungal infections	373	415	435	(10)	(5)
Urology:						
Viagra	Erectile dysfunction	1,934	1,764	1,657	10	6
Detrol/Detrol LA	Overactive bladder	1,214	1,190	1,100	2	8
Oncology:						
Sutent	Advanced and/or metastatic renal cell carcinoma (mRCC) and refractory gastrointestinal stromal tumors (GIST)	847	581	219	46	166
Camptosar	Metastatic colorectal cancer	563	969	903	(42)	7
Aromasin	Breast cancer	465	401	320	16	25
Ophthalmology:						
Xalatan	Glaucoma and ocular hypertension	1,745	1,604	1,453	9	10
Endocrine disorders:						
Genotropin	Replacement of human growth hormone	898	843	795	6	6

continued

EXHIBIT 1   Revenues by Key Products ($ in millions)—continued

PRODUCT	PRIMARY INDICATIONS	YEAR ENDED DECEMBER 31			% CHANGE	
		2008	2007	2006	08/07	07/06
All other:						
Zyrtec/Zyrtec D	Allergies	**129**	1,541	1,569	(92)	(2)
Alliance revenues	Alzheimer's disease (Aricept), neovascular (wet) age-related macular degeneration (Macugen), Parkinson's disease (Mirapex), hypertension (Exforge and Olmetec), multiple sclerosis (Rebif) and chronic obstructive pulmonary disease (Spiriva)	**2,251**	1,789	1,374	26	30

(a) Represents direct sales under license agreement with Eisai Co., Ltd. Certain amounts and percentages may reflect rounding adjustments.

Source: Pfizer's 2008 *Form 10k.*

EXHIBIT 2   The Proposed Wyeth Merger Benefits to Pfizer

Wyeth **diversifies offering** and **expands presen**ce in EMS

Pfizer inc

Pharmaceuticals
• Primary care
• Specialty Care
• Oncology
• Established Products

Research
• Pfizer Global R&D

Market presence
• Significant in Emerging Markets

Pfizer inc + Wyeth

Biopharmaceuticals
• Primary care
• Specialty Care
  – Vaccines
  – Biologics
• Oncology
• Established Products

Diversified businesses
• Animal Health
• Capsugel
• Consumer Health
• Nutritional Health

Research
• Pharma Therapeutics Research Group
• Bio Therapeutics Research Group

Market presence
• Enhanced in Emerging Markets

Source: www.pfizer.com.

EXHIBIT 3   Total Revenues by Business Segment

	2008	2007	2006
Pharmaceuticals	91.5%	91.8%	93.2%
Animal Health	5.8%	5.4%	4.8%
Corporate Other	2.7%	2.8%	2.0%
TOTAL REVENUES	100.0%	100.0%	100.0%

Source: Pfizer *Annual Report* (2008).

Operating a global business is associated with complex challenges. In addition to multiple and diverse regulatory environments to contend with, global companies like Pfizer are subject to unexpected changes in revenues and profits resulting from unpredictable currency fluctuations. Pfizer's income statement is provided in Exhibit 5. Note that Pfizer's sales in 2006, 2007, and 2008 were approximately $48.37 billion, $48.42 billion, and $48.3 billion, respectively. During the same time period, Pfizer's net income was $19.34 billion, $8.14 billion, and $8.10 billion, respectively. Note that Pfizer's Research & Development expenditures rose $7.6 billion in 2006 to $7.9 billion in 2008, whereas Selling, General, and Administrative (SG&A) expenses declined from $15.59 billion in 2006 to $14.54 billion in 2008.

EXHIBIT 4 Revenues by Business and Geographical Segment

(In millions of $)		U.S.			INTERNATIONAL	
Year ended Dec. 31,	2008	2007	2006	2008	2007	2006
Pharmaceuticals	$ 18,851	$ 21,548	$ 24,503	$ 25,323	$ 22,876	$ 20,580
Animal Health	1,168	1,132	1,032	1,657	1,507	1,279
Corporate/Other	416	473	287	881	882	690
TOTAL	$ 20,435	$ 23,153	$ 25,822	$ 27,861	$ 25,265	$ 22,549

ANNUAL PERCENTAGE CHANGES

	WORLDWIDE TOTALS		US		INTERNATIONAL	
% CHANGE	2008/07	2007/06	2008/07	2007/06	2008/07	2007/06
Pharmaceuticals	(1)	(1)	(13)	(12)	11	11
Animal Health	7	14	3	10	10	18
Corporate/Other	—	—	(12)	(10)	10	12

Source: Pfizer *Annual Report* (2008).

EXHIBIT 5 Pfizer's Income Statement (in thousands)

PERIOD ENDING	31-Dec-08	31-Dec-07	31-Dec-06
Total Revenue	**$48,296,000**	**48,418,000**	**48,371,000**
Cost of Revenue	8,112,000	11,239,000	7,640,000
Gross Profit	**40,184,000**	**37,179,000**	**40,731,000**
Operating Expenses			
Research Development	7,945,000	8,089,000	7,599,000
Selling General and Administrative	14,537,000	15,626,000	15,589,000
Non Recurring	3,308,000	2,817,000	2,158,000
Others	2,668,000	3,128,000	3,261,000
Total Operating Expenses	28,458,000	29,660,000	28,607,000
Operating Income or Loss	**11,726,000**	**7,519,000**	**12,124,000**
Income from Continuing Operations			
Total Other Income/Expenses Net	(1,516,000)	2,156,000	1,392,000
Earnings Before Interest and Taxes	10,210,000	9,675,000	13,516,000
Interest Expense	516,000	397,000	488,000
Income Before Tax	9,694,000	9,278,000	13,028,000
Income Tax Expense	1,645,000	1,023,000	1,992,000
Minority Interest	(23,000)	(42,000)	(12,000)
Net Income from Continuing Ops	8,026,000	8,213,000	11,024,000
Non-recurring Events			
Discontinued Operations	78,000	(69,000)	8,313,000
Extraordinary Items	—	—	—
Effect of Accounting Changes	—	—	—
Other Items	—	—	—
Net Income	**8,104,000**	**8,144,000**	**19,337,000**
Preferred Stock and Other Adjustments	—	—	—
Net Income Applicable to Common Shares	**$ 8,104,000**	**$ 8,144,000**	**$ 19,337,000**

Source: Pfizer's 2008 *Form 10k.*

Pfizer's consolidated Balance Sheet in Exhibit 6 reveals that total assets shrunk from $114.84 billion in 2006 to $111.15 billion in 2008, and total liabilities increased from $43.48 billion in 2006 to $53.59 billion in 2008. Note that total stockholders' equity fell 19.34 percent, from $71.36 billion in 2006 to $57.56 billion in 2008.

Competition

Pfizer faces high competition in all its business segments due to the presence of many players, large and small, in the industry. Bayer AG, Merck & Co., and Novartis AG are Pfizer's direct competitors in the pharmaceutical industry. Of the four major players in the pharmaceutical industry, Pfizer and Merck are American companies Bayer is German, and Novartis is Swiss. A comparison of key indicators included in Exhibit 7 shows that Pfizer leads the pack, with Novartis trailing closely behind.

With $97.13 billion in market capitalization, Pfizer is the largest company in this strategic group. It has 80,250 employees, second to Novartis, but it is the leader in revenues ($47.32 billion), gross margins (85.86 percent), operating margins (36.13 percent), and net income of $7.96 billion. However, note that Pfizer has the lowest earnings per share ($1.23) and price-earnings (P/E) ratio among its direct competitors.

Potential Risks

The Wyeth acquisition is fraught with potential risks. First and foremost, there are several regulatory hurdles to overcome not only from regulators in the United States, but also overseas. Some of these approvals include the expiration or termination of the waiting period under the Hart-Scott-Rodino Act, a decision to be issued by the European Commission under the EC Merger Regulation declaring that the proposed merger is compatible with the Common Market, and the approval of the proposed acquisition under the China Anti-Monopoly Law and by regulators in Canada and Australia as well.

The acquisition would also increase Pfizer's debt because it is set to take on about $22.5 billion of debt in addition to assuming Wyeth's debt. Servicing this much additional debt is a risky move for Pfizer, which experienced a decline of revenues from $48.42 billion in 2007 to $48.3 billion in 2008.

Assuming the merger agreement moves forward unencumbered, Pfizer will assume all responsibilities for pending litigation facing Wyeth. Like other companies in the industry, Wyeth is currently facing various lawsuits and litigation claims related to patents, product liability, consumers, commercial, securities, environmental and tax laws, and government investigations. Outcomes of these pending claims can overburden Pfizer and mitigate potential benefits from the Wyeth acquisition.

Pfizer also faces litigation in several courts around the world. For example, Pfizer is in a contentious battle in a Jamaican court to protect its patented medication amlodipine (Norvasc) used for treating high blood pressure to avoid complications of severe congestive heart failure, stroke, renal failure, and other vascular complications due to hypertension. The company is fighting the Jamaican court's decision that Pfizer's patent on its drug expired in Jamaica as it had expired in other countries.

At home, Pfizer spent about $900 million in June 2008 to settle pending U.S. consumer fraud-related class action lawsuits and personal injury claims involving Celebrex and Bextra. Several of Pfizer's key products are slated to expire in the near future, as indicated in Exhibit 8.

Pfizer's Focus on Emerging Markets

As shown in Exhibit 9, Pfizer is determined to become the leading biopharmaceutical company in emerging markets through bold and innovative partnerships.

In addition to traditional partnerships, alliances, mergers and acquisitions, Pfizer recently partnered with world-class foundations and nonprofit organizations like the Grameen Foundation in Bangladesh, whose founder is Mohammad Yunus, the recipient of the Nobel Peace Prize in 2006 for his efforts in alleviating poverty through microfinancing. Pfizer recently entered into a partnership with Grameen Health, an affiliate of Grameen Foundation, to bring sustainable health-care delivery models that address

EXHIBIT 6   Pfizer's Balance Sheet

	(all numbers in thousands)		
PERIOD ENDING	31-Dec-08	31-Dec-07	31-Dec-06
Assets			
Current Assets			
Cash and Cash Equivalents	$ 2,122,000	3,406,000	1,827,000
Short Term Investments	22,433,000	22,686,000	26,400,000
Net Receivables	13,992,000	9,843,000	9,392,000
Inventory	4,529,000	5,416,000	6,111,000
Other Current Assets	—	5,498,000	3,219,000
Total Current Assets	**43,076,000**	**46,849,000**	**46,949,000**
Long Term Investments	11,478,000	4,856,000	3,892,000
Property Plant and Equipment	13,287,000	15,734,000	16,632,000
Goodwill	21,464,000	21,382,000	20,876,000
Intangible Assets	17,721,000	20,498,000	24,350,000
Accumulated Amortization	—	—	—
Other Assets	4,122,000	1,844,000	2,138,000
Deferred Long Term Asset Charges	—	4,105,000	—
Total Assets	**$ 111,148,000**	**115,268,000**	**114,837,000**
Liabilities			
Current Liabilities			
Accounts Payable	6,233,000	7,787,000	12,443,000
Short/Current Long Term Debt	9,320,000	5,825,000	2,434,000
Other Current Liabilities	11,456,000	8,223,000	6,512,000
Total Current Liabilities	**27,009,000**	**21,835,000**	**21,389,000**
Long Term Debt	14,531,000	7,314,000	5,546,000
Other Liabilities	8,909,000	13,299,000	8,529,000
Deferred Long Term Liability Charges	2,959,000	7,696,000	8,015,000
Minority Interest	184,000	114,000	—
Negative Goodwill	—	—	—
Total Liabilities	**53,592,000**	**50,258,000**	**43,479,000**
Stockholders' Equity			
Misc. Stocks Options Warrants	—	—	—
Redeemable Preferred Stock	—	—	—
Preferred Stock	73,000	93,000	141,000
Common Stock	443,000	442,000	441,000
Retained Earnings	49,142,000	49,660,000	49,669,000
Treasury Stock	(57,391,000)	(56,847,000)	(46,740,000)
Capital Surplus	70,283,000	69,913,000	69,104,000
Other Stockholders' Equity	(4,994,000)	1,749,000	(1,257,000)
Total Stockholders' Equity	**57,556,000**	**65,010,000**	**71,358,000**
Total Liabilities and SE	**$ 111,148,000**	**115,268,000**	**114,837,000**

EXHIBIT 7   Overview of Direct Competitors

	Pfizer	Merck	Novartis	Industry
Market Cap	97.13B	52.31B	86.79B	73.99M
Employees	80,250	54,100	98,000	335
Revenue	47.32B	23.41B	42.29B	253.49M
Gross Margin	85.86%	76.03%	73.10%	71.00%
Operat. Margins	36.13%	25.53%	21.60%	5.89%
Net Income	7.96B	5.93B	7.79B	N/A
EPS	1.193	2.785	3.43	N/A

Source: Company *Form 10k* Reports.

EXHIBIT 8   Pfizer's Product Patent Expiration Information

Drug	U.S. Basic Product Patent Expiration Year
Aricept	2010
Lipitor	2010
Xalatan	2011
Geodon	2012
Viagra	2012
Detrol	2012
Celebrex	2014
Zyvox	2015
Lyrica	2018
Chantix	2020
Selzentry	2021
Sutent	2021

Source: SEC *Form 10K,* February 27, 2009.

EXHIBIT 9   Pfizer's Mission and Vision in Emerging Markets

Our Vision and Mission

Vision

We will be recognized for meeting the **diverse medical needs** of patients in Emerging Markets **around the world** in an **innovative, socially responsible** and **commercially viable** manner.

Mission

We will...

develop **bold** and **innovative** partnerships

reach patients we have **never reached before**

provide medicines and services in an **affordable** manner

be recognized for having the **best talent** in healthcare

become a **leading biopharmaceutical company** in Emerging Markets

Source: www.pfizer.com.

the needs of 4 billion people worldwide with incomes of less than $3,000 a year. Another innovative partnership involves Pfizer and PlaNet Finance, which is examining ways in which health-care access may be expanded in China.

Good News

In May 2009, Pfizer announced it was giving away more than 70 of its most widely prescribed drugs, including Lipitor and Viagra, for up to a year to people who have lost jobs in calendar 2009 and had been taking the drug for three months or more. "Everybody knows now a neighbor, a relative who has lost their job and is losing their insurance. People are definitely hurting out there," Dr. Jorge Puente, Pfizer's head of pharmaceuticals outside the United States and Europe, told the Associated Press in an exclusive interview. "Our aim is to help people bridge this point."

The 70-plus drugs covered in the new Pfizer program include several diabetes drugs as well as some of Pfizer's top money makers, from cholesterol fighter Lipitor to painkiller Celebrex. Also included are fibromyalgia treatment Lyrica and also Viagra, used for male erectile dysfunction. The new Pfizer program includes some antibiotics, antidepressants, heart medications, contraceptives, and smoking cessation products. Cheaper generic versions are available for most of the drugs. The new program will likely help prevent patients from switching to cheaper brands or generics through the worst of the recession and could help retain those taking top-seller Lipitor, which will begin competing with generic versions in 2010. Many analysts contend that the giveaway is a brilliant marketing move that will generate low-cost publicity, build consumer loyalty, and keep inventory from piling up.

Bad News

In September 2009, Pfizer agreed to pay a record $2.3 billion to settle civil and criminal charges over marketing of its recalled Bextra arthritis drug and three other medicines. The charges involved representatives of Pfizer promoting drugs for conditions that they had not been approved for and giving doctors kickbacks to encourage them to prescribe the medications. This is the largest such settlement in the United States for claims of off-label drug promotion, topping the $1.42 billion Eli Lilly (LLY) agreed to pay earlier in 2009 for off-lable sales of its Zyprexa schizophrenia drug. Moreover, the $1.3 billion criminal penalty related only to Bextra is "the largest criminal fine ever imposed in the United States for any matter," according to the U.S. Department of Justice. The settlement also involves pain management pill Lyrica, the schizophrenia treatment Geodon, and the anti-infection drug Zyvox, as well as nine other medicines.

The world's biggest drugmaker, Pfizer spent nearly $5.6 million lobbying the U.S. government in the second quarter of 2009 on health-care reform, government spending on medication, and patent and trade issues, according to a recent disclosure report. Pfizer nearly doubled its lobbying spending from the $3.1 million in the year-ago period. The company lobbied on legislation on numerous health reform provisions, including health insurance, information technology, electronic prescriptions, drug pricing, allowing generic versions of expensive biologic drugs, and requiring research comparing the effectiveness of medications and other types of treatment as well as on U.S. patent reform and on international patent, market access, and regulatory issues involving at least 20 countries.

Conclusion

Drug firms are reducing, not adding, to their sales forces. By the end of 2008, the number of pharmaceutical sales representatives in the United States had decreased to 90,000 from a high of about 106,000 in 2006. In early 2009, Amylin Pharmaceuticals cut 35 percent of its sales force, or 200 representatives.

For the first time in fifty years, sales of prescription drugs in the United States declined in 2009 for a variety of reasons. The United States has historically been the industry's largest and most profitable area, but now drug companies are looking more and more to developing countries such as Venezuela. Sales of prescription drugs in developing or emerging markets increased to $152.7 billion in 2008, up from $67.2 billion in 2003. This number should reach $265 billion in 2013, according to IMS Health, which monitors such issues. In addition to Venezuela, Pfizer is expanding rapidly into China, India, Brazil, Russia, and Turkey. During the first quarter of 2009, Pfizer's revenues from emerging markets were $1.4 billion, out of $10.8 billion total Pfizer revenues that quarter. Rather than focusing on middle- and upper-class people, Pfizer and its rival firms are now also focusing on lower-class people in emerging countries.

Prepare a clear three-year strategic plan for Pfizer.

## 26

Merck & Company Inc. — 2009

Mernoush Banton
Adjunct Faculty/Consultant

MRK

www.merck.com

The eighth-largest pharmaceutical firm in the world, Merck, is acquiring the eighteenth-largest pharmaceutical firm, Schering-Plough, for $41 billion. Merck plans to reorganize once its acquisition of Schering-Plough goes through in the fourth quarter of 2009. Merck says it then will name the heads of five main divisions: (1) global human health, (2) animal health, (3) consumer health care, (4) manufacturing, and (5) Merck Research Laboratories. The leaders of each division will answer to Merck CEO Richard Clark. The newly formed structure will aid Merck in penetrating the vaccine and biologics markets, as well as emerging markets. About 40 percent of Schering-Plough's (NYSEP:SGP) senior leaders will be part of the newly combined company and a "substantial majority of Schering-Plough employees will remain with the combined company."

Acquiring Schering-Plough allows Merck to leapfrog to number two worldwide, just behind Pfizer. The new Merck will have about $42.4 billion in annual sales. Merck and Schering-Plough are already partners on the blockbuster cholesterol drugs Vytorin and Zetia. The marriage will unite Merck's asthma and allergy treatment Singulair and cervical cancer vaccine Gardasil with Schering-Plough's allergy spray Nasonex and well-known consumer products including the Coppertone sun care line and Dr. Scholl's foot care items.

Buying Schering-Plough also boosts Merck's sagging pipeline of drugs in development, gives it a sizable biotech unit, and creates a dominant player in vaccines as well as cholesterol, respiratory, and women's drugs. The merger will also allow the new Merck to slash costs—including roughly 15,000 jobs—to deal with increasing generic competition and the unknown impact of health care reform.

Merck's mission statement is as follows:

> The mission of Merck is to provide society with superior products and services by developing innovations and solutions that improve the quality of life and satisfy customer needs, and to provide employees with meaningful work and advancement opportunities, and investors with a superior rate of return.

History

Merck was established in 1891 to engage in the discovery, development, manufacture, and marketing of a variety of products, mostly to improve human and animal health. Merck sells products through drug wholesalers and retailers, hospitals, clinics, government, and managed health service providers. Over the years, Merck has devoted itself to increase access and to deliver donated medicines through far-reaching programs to those people who need them. Merck further publishes unbiased health reports as a not-for-profit service. Through the 1980s, the company proved to be successful by being research driven and keeping the pipeline filled with new and innovative products. During this time, Merck was the pioneer in introducing 10 major new drugs, including Mevacor (for high cholesterol) and Vasotec (for high blood pressure).

Throughout the years, Merck has entered into many joint-venture agreements with companies such as Sanofi Pasteur S.A., Rhone-Poulenc S.A., Johnson & Johnson, Astra

EXHIBIT 1   Merck's Recent Acquisitions and Divestitures

Year	Event
2000	Provantage Health Services Inc. for $12.25 per share.
2001	Acquired Rosetta Inpharmatics, Inc. for $635.0 million.
2003	Completed the spinoff of Medco Health Solutions Inc. Co. Distributed 270,000,000 shares to its shareholders.
2004	(1) Acquired all the remaining interest in Banyu Pharmaceutical Company, Ltd. that it did not already own.
	(2) Acquired Aton Pharma, Inc.
	(3) Sold its 50% equity stake in Johnson & Johnson MSD Europe to Johnson & Johnson.
2006	(1) Launched the mercksource Doctor's Bag, a new online search tool available only on mercksource.com.
	(2) Acquired Sirna Therapeutics, Inc. for $954,100,000 in cash.
2007	Completed the acquisition of Novacardia, Inc. for $366.4 million.
2009	Acquired Insmed Inc.'s INS-19 and INS-20 products and related intellectual property for $130,000,000 in cash. Schering-Plough acquisition pending.

Source: Based on information at www.merck.com.

AB, Schering-Plough, and many more. Exhibit 1 provides a summary of Merck's recent acquisitions and spinoffs.

In 2004, Merck withdrew their well-known drug Vioxx after a company-sponsored test found there could be an increased risk of heart attack and stroke for those who took the medication after 18 months of daily usage. From 2004 to 2007, as a result of a class-action lawsuit, the company appeared in several courts and hearings. Finally, in late 2007, Merck entered into a settlement agreement with the plaintiff's Steering Committee and paid the claimants $500 million in August 2008 and an additional $250 million in October 2008.

A primary measure for the success of a drug manufacturing company is the number of new products introduced and approved by the U.S. Food and Drug Administration (FDA). Exhibit 2 reveals Merck's organizational structure before the Schering-Plough

EXHIBIT 2   Merck & Company: Organizational Structure

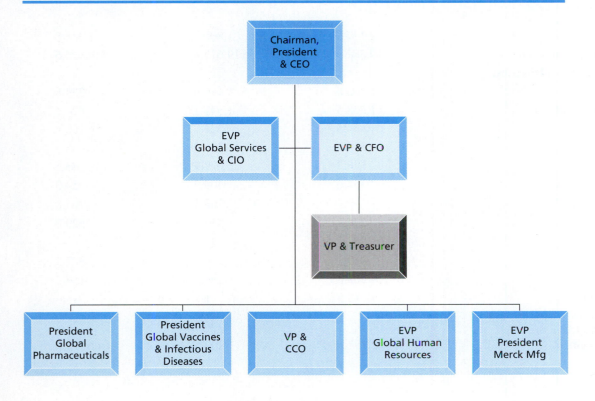

acquisition. Note the two divisions: (1) Pharmaceutical Products, and (2) Vaccines and Infectious Diseases. Exhibit 3 gives details on some of Merck's products.

Distribution

Merck sells its human health pharmaceutical products to drug wholesalers, distributors, retailers, hospitals, government agencies, and managed health-care providers such as health maintenance organizations, pharmacy benefit managers, and other institutions. The company's professional representatives communicate the effectiveness, safety, and value of the products to health-care professionals in private practices, group practices, and managed care organizations through samples, pamphlets, brochures, coupons, and rebates.

EXHIBIT 3   Merck's Sales by Product Categories

($ in millions)	2008	2007	2006
Pharmaceutical:			
Singulair	$ 4,336.9	$ 4,266.3	$ 3,579.0
Cozaar/Hyzaar	3,557.7	3,350.1	3,163.1
Fosamax	1,552.7	3,049.0	3,134.4
Januvia	1,397.1	667.5	42.9
Cosopt/Trusopt	781.2	786.8	697.1
Zocor	660.1	876.5	2,802.7
Maxalt	529.2	467.3	406.4
Propecia	429.1	405.4	351.8
Arcoxia	377.3	329.1	265.4
Vasotec/Vaseretic	356.7	494.6	547.2
Janumet	351.1	86.4	—
Proscar	323.5	411.0	618.5
Emend	263.8	204.2	130.8
Other pharmaceutical	2,278.9	2,422.9	2,780.5
Vaccine and infectious disease product sales included in the Pharmaceutical segment	2,187.6	1,800.5	1,315.8
Pharmaceutical segment revenues	$19,382.9	$19,617.6	$19,835.6
Vaccines and Infectious Diseases:			
Gardasil	$ 1,402.8	$ 1,480.6	$ 234.8
ProQuad/M-M-R II/Varivax	1,268.5	1,347.1	820.1
RotaTeq	664.5	524.7	163.4
Zostavax	312.4	236.0	38.6
Hepatitis vaccines	148.3	279.9	248.5
Other vaccines	354.6	409.9	354.0
Primaxin	760.4	763.5	704.8
Cancidas	596.4	536.9	529.8
Isentress	361.1	41.3	—
Crixivan/Stocrin	275.1	310.2	327.3
Invanz	265.0	190.2	139.2
Other infectious disease	15.5	1.7	—
Vaccine and infectious disease product sales included in the Pharmaceutical segment	(2,187.6)	(1,800.5)	(1,315.8)

continued

EXHIBIT 3   Merck's Sales by Product Categories—continued

($ in millions)	2008	2007	2006
Vaccines and Infectious Diseases segment revenues	$ 4,237.0	$ 4,321.5	$ 2,244.7
Other segment revenues	81.8	162.0	162.1
Total segment revenues	23,701.7	24,101.1	22,242.4
Other	148.6	96.6	393.6
	$23,850.3	$24,197.7	$22,636.0

Source: Merck & Co. Inc., *Form 10K* (2008).

Financials

Merck's revenue dropped by approximately $347 million from 2007 to 2008, although it increased from 2006 to 2007 by $1.56 billion (Exhibit 4). As shown in Exhibit 4, Merck's net income more than doubled in 2008. As shown in Exhibit 5, Merck carries more than $1.4 billion in goodwill on its balance sheet and close to $4 billion long-term debt. It is alarming to notice that this increase is mostly attributed from net receivable and inventory (Exhibit 5).

EXHIBIT 4   Merck & Company Income Statement

Annual Data	(all numbers in thousands)		
PERIOD ENDING	31-Dec-08	31-Dec-07	31-Dec-06
Total Revenue	**$23,850,300**	**24,197,700**	**22,636,000**
Cost of Revenue	5,582,500	6,140,700	6,001,100
Gross Profit	**18,267,800**	**18,057,000**	**16,634,900**
Operating Expenses:			
Research Development	4,805,300	4,882,800	4,782,900
Selling General and Administrative	7,377,000	7,556,700	8,165,400
Non Recurring	1,032,500	5,177,100	142,300
Others	—	—	—
Total Operating Expenses	—	—	—
Operating Income or Loss	**5,053,000**	**440,400**	**3,544,300**
Income from Continuing Operations			
Total Other Income/Expenses Net	2,445,500	459,500	878,300
Earnings Before Interest And Taxes	10,059,100	3,755,000	6,596,500
Interest Expense	251,300	384,300	375,100
Income Before Tax	9,807,800	3,370,700	6,221,400
Income Tax Expense	1,999,400	95,300	1,787,600
Minority Interest	—	(121,400)	(120,500)
Net Income from Continuing Ops	7,808,400	3,275,400	4,433,800
Non-recurring Events			
Discontinued Operations	—	—	—
Extraordinary Items	—	—	—
Effect of Accounting Changes	—	—	—
Other Items	—	—	—
Net Income	**$7,808,400**	**3,275,400**	**4,433,800**
Preferred Stock and Other Adjustments	—	—	—
Net Income Applicable to Common Shares	**$7,808,400**	**$3,275,400**	**$4,433,800**

Source: http://finance.yahoo.com.

EXHIBIT 5   **Merck & Company Balance Sheet**

Annual Data	(all numbers in thousands)		
PERIOD ENDING	31-Dec-08	31-Dec-07	31-Dec-06
Assets			
Current Assets			
Cash and Cash Equivalents	$4,368,300	5,336,100	5,914,700
Short Term Investments	1,118,100	2,894,700	2,798,300
Net Receivables	11,535,200	3,636,200	3,314,800
Inventory	2,283,300	1,881,000	1,769,400
Other Current Assets	—	1,297,400	1,433,000
Total Current Assets	**19,304,900**	**15,045,400**	**15,230,200**
Long Term Investments	6,491,300	7,159,200	7,788,200
Property Plant and Equipment	11,999,600	12,346,000	13,194,100
Goodwill	1,438,700	1,454,800	1,431,600
Intangible Assets	525,400	713,200	943,900
Accumulated Amortization	—	—	—
Other Assets	7,435,800	11,632,100	5,981,800
Deferred Long Term Asset Charges	—	—	—
Total Assets	**47,195,700**	**48,350,700**	**44,569,800**
Liabilities			
Current Liabilities			
Accounts Payable	12,021,600	10,434,600	11,437,600
Short/Current Long Term Debt	2,297,100	1,823,600	1,285,100
Other Current Liabilities	—	—	—
Total Current Liabilities	**14,318,700**	**12,258,200**	**12,722,700**
Long Term Debt	3,943,300	3,915,800	5,551,000
Other Liabilities	—	—	—
Deferred Long Term Liability Charges	7,766,600	11,585,300	6,330,300
Minority Interest	2,408,800	2,406,700	2,406,100
Negative Goodwill	—	—	—
Total Liabilities	**$28,437,400**	**30,166,000**	**27,010,100**
Stockholders' Equity			
Misc Stocks Options Warrants	—	—	—
Redeemable Preferred Stock	—	—	—
Preferred Stock	—	—	—
Common Stock	29,800	29,800	29,800
Retained Earnings	43,698,800	39,140,800	39,095,100
Treasury Stock	(30,735,500)	(28,174,700)	(27,567,400)
Capital Surplus	8,319,100	8,014,900	7,166,500
Other Stockholders' Equity	(2,553,900)	(826,100)	(1,164,300)
Total Stockholders' Equity	**18,758,300**	**18,184,700**	**17,559,700**
Total Liabilities and SE	**$47,195,700**	**48,350,700**	**44,569,800**

Source: Merck's 2008 *Form 10K*.

Industry Issues, Facts, and Figures

The industry is marked by rapid advances and is heavily based on research and development. About 1,500 companies in the U.S. manufacture and market medicinal drugs. Over $200 billion in U.S. revenue is driven from the sales of prescription drugs (brand name and generic) and over-the-counter (OTC) medicines. The United States leads the world with the highest market share and is the home of five of the ten largest drug manufacturers (Bristol-Myers Squibb, Johnson & Johnson, Merck & Co., Pfizer, and Abbott Laboratories). Europe, ranked second, is the home of the other five of the world's top pharmaceutical companies (AstaZeneca, Sanofi-Aventis, Novartis, Roche Group, and GlaxoSmithKline). Japan takes third place with companies such Sankyo Co., Takeda Chemical Industries, and Yamanouchi Pharmaceutical.

The industry is highly concentrated: The 50 largest companies control more than 80 percent of the market. The pharmaceutical industry accounts for 27.3 percent of the healthcare sector and is capital intensive with exorbitant research and development costs. The industry also has been growing at over 10 percent annually and is under pressure from Wall Street to keep up such growth.

Regulations and Patents

Drug discovery and development is a highly sophisticated process that can take several years to complete and may cost more than $500 million. The cost has escalated 10-fold every 20 years since the late 1950s when research and development could cost only $1.5 million. Once the drug is registered and has received a patent, it is protected by competition from similar or generic drugs for 5 to 15 years. As such, loss of patent protection could harm the company's sales and earnings. In some cases, there could be legal attacks against the validity of a patent. Such problem could be problematic by incurring additional costs in a legal battle.

Industry Structure

Generic drugs rapidly enter the market when a patent expires by the original brand-named drug manufacturer. Also, because large research budgets do not guarantee new products, many large drug companies supplement their own efforts by buying or licensing products from other companies. As a result, the industry has seen a vast number of mergers and acquisitions in recent years. Although the merger and acquisition could cost the company millions or billions of dollars, in some ways, it guarantees future income to the new owner. In recent months, Merck acquired Schering-Plough for $41 billion, and Pfizer acquired rival drug maker Wyeth for $68 billion.

Advertising

Drug manufacturers spend billions of dollars in advertising and promotions through front-end standard media such as television, radio, newspapers, and magazines. The back-end promotion is accomplished by offering samples and other incentives to doctors and retailers for prescribing their drugs. Aggressive advertising has been questioned by many government agencies and organizations. Congress has been considering changing advertising laws, which will impact the drug companies considerably. Most drug companies have already reconsidered how to market their drugs by explaining their risks. One strategy of the drug companies has been to push for more conversations with doctors and by better explaining the risks. For patients, most companies now offer toll-free hotlines and useful information through the company's Web site. Lack of exposing the risks could harm the company's reputation and brand.

The Pharmaceutical Research and Manufacturers of America (PhRMA), the drug industry's lobbyist, announced a voluntary guiding principle for advertising drugs to all parties. This working document is requesting that drug companies discuss new drugs with doctors before launching any advertising to prospective consumers. The organization also argues that direct-to-consumer (DTC) advertising can be a powerful tool in educating millions of consumers and improving their health if they are aware of the drugs, and their side effects and potential benefits.

Merck & Co. Inc. spent more than $1.5 million in the second quarter of 2009 alone lobbying on health-care reforms, vaccine funding, and government drug pricing. That was up 30 percent from the $1.17 million that Merck spent lobbying in the year-ago period. Merck lobbied on several health care reform issues, including supporting increasing coverage for uninsured people and requiring research comparing the effectiveness of different medical treatments. Merck also lobbied against allowing cheaper prescription drugs to be imported back into the United States from countries that impose price controls and to require that any such re-imported drugs, if allowed, be certified as safe. Merck also lobbies against increasing the rebates drug companies pay the government under the Medicaid drug program and against changing Medicare rules to impose government price controls on prescription drugs. Merck also lobbies for ensuring that the Medicare program gives "appropriate access to vaccines," and for a boost to funding for the Centers for Disease Control and Prevention's immunization program for low-income children.

In 1997, the FDA relaxed its rules, allowing drug manufacturers to advertise on television. The FDA Amendments Act of 2007 went into effect on March 25, 2008, mandating that published DTC advertisements for prescription drugs must include this printed message: "You are encouraged to report negative side effects of prescription drugs to the FDA. Visit www.fda.gov/medwatch, or call 1-800-FDA-1088."

Most often, drug companies have direct promotional expenses such as contractually agreed expenses related to market research, detailing aids, agency fees, DTC advertising, meetings and symposia, trade programs, launch meetings, special sales force incentive programs, and product samples. A research study released by two York University researchers estimates that the U.S. pharmaceutical industry spends almost twice as much on promotion as it does on research and development. The research estimates that from data collected directly from the industry and doctors during 2004, the U.S. pharmaceutical industry spent 24.4 percent of its sales dollar on promotion versus 13.4 percent for research and development, as a percentage of U.S. domestic sales of $235.4 billion.

Research and Development

In 2008, R&D spending in the drug industry reached a record level of $65.2 billion. R&D investment per employee in the sector is eight times higher than other manufacturing industries. The entire drug development may take many years, with only a small percentage of candidate drugs surviving the testing and the FDA approval process. On average, companies could be working on 100 to 150 new drugs, with the probability of 1 to 3 percent getting approved and reaching the market. The life span from discovering, developing, clinical testing, and FDA approval for a new drug could take approximately between 10 to 15 years, with a cost of $500 million to $750 million.

Drug companies face constant challenges as their competitors pioneer in getting patent approval from the FDA. As stated earlier, drug discovery and development is a very sophisticated process that can take many years. Because the success of a company is based on the number of drugs in the market and the years of patent protection, the cost of R&D plays a major role in the company's financial position and analysis.

Companies in the pharmaceutical industry spend heavily on R&D to ensure they have a number of patents in the pipeline. With R&D costs rising, drug makers mostly focus on products for chronic rather than acute diseases, on the large patient population with cancer, arthritis, and cardiovascular problems. The top drug categories are medications for cancer, and ulcer, and treatments for high cholesterol and depression. According to PhRMA, member companies invested a record $50.2 billion in 2009 in research and development for new medicines.

Trend

Another factor impacting the industry is the world's increasing elderly population. The over-65 age group consumer uses three times more drugs than the younger population and is expected to reach 690 million by 2025. In the 1990s, more than 150 products were brought into the market for age-related conditions, and approximately 600 more are in the development stage. The aging population also has increased the demand for low-cost prescriptions. Because the price of prescription drugs is climbing, many states are reducing their Medicaid drug benefits.

Due to the high cost of prescription drugs in the United States, many consumers are finding alternative ways of getting the prescription filled. The common trend is filling and importing medicines from Canada at a lower price. The Canadian government is taking a proactive position by trying to block or to reduce the exportation of the drugs to the United States. In a recent press release, the Canadian health minister stated the intention to introduce legislation under Canada's Food and Drug Act that would prohibit companies from exporting bulk prescription drugs to the United States.

Competitors

Pharmaceutical companies are marked by rapid advances in scientific knowledge by producing more effective medicines. Profitability is determined mainly by the ability to discover new drugs while keeping their cost low. The industry is dominated by large manufacturers that manufacture drugs, have large research operations, and have resources for conducting clinical testing along with more than adequate funds for marketing and distribution.

As indicated in Exhibit 6, Merck competes directly with large drug manufacturers that offer similar products, especially if a patent has expired. The company also competes indirectly with smaller drug manufacturers because many may be more innovative or are able to produce generic brands at a lower cost.

GlaxoSmithKline is a global health-care group engaged in the creation and discovery, development, manufacture, and marketing of pharmaceutical products, including vaccines, OTC medicines, and health-related consumer products. The company operates in two segments: Pharmaceuticals, which produce pharmaceutical products for therapeutic areas; and Consumer Health Care, which focuses on OTC medicines, oral care, and nutritional health care. The company had reportedly been in talks early in 2009 to be acquired by Johnson & Johnson and Novartis AG.

Pfizer discovers, develops, produces, and markets prescription medicines for humans and animals. The company has two segments: Pharmaceutical, which develops and produces products that treat cardiovascular and metabolic diseases, central nervous system disorders, arthritis and pain, infectious and respiratory diseases, urogenital conditions, cancer, eye disease, endocrine disorders and allergies; and Animal Health, which discovers, develops, and sells products for the prevention and treatment of diseases in livestock and companion animals. Pfizer also operates several other businesses such as the manufacture of empty soft-gelatin capsules, contract manufacturing, and bulk pharmaceutical chemicals. Their popular drugs are Lipitor (commonly used to reduce high cholesterol), Celebrex (for treating arthritis), and Viagra (prescribed to treat erectile dysfunction). The company recently acquired Wyeth pharmaceuticals, giving Pfizer the ability to complete in nine diverse heath-care businesses.

EXHIBIT 6   Merck versus Competitors (April 2009)

	Merck	GlaxoSmithKline	Pfizer	Sanofi-Aventis	Drug Industry
Market Cap	$48.84B	77.47B	90.32B	70.84B	78.72M
Employees	54,100	99,003	81,800	98,213	335
Revenue	23.41B	35.73B	48.30B	N/A	253.49M
Gross Margin	76.03%	77.14%	85.08%	74.54%	73.14%
Oper Margins	25.53%	36.57%	34.77%	N/A	5.89%
Net Income	5.93B	6.75B	8.02B	N/A	N/A
EPS	2.785	2.58	1.201	N/A	N/A

Source: Based on information at http://finance.yahoo.com.

The Future

Companies that do business in this industry face many risks and uncertainties due to litigations against the company, regulations, competition, demographic changes, patent protection, a slow economy, and the high cost of manufacturing due to an increase in R&D and selling and general administration expenses. Merck needs a clear strategic plan to define its future business in the drug manufacturing business. Merck's shareholders and stakeholders in general expect continual growth and a better than average return on the investment.

27 Nike, Inc. — 2010[1]

Randy Harris
California State University, Stanislaus

NKE

www.nike.com

In September 2009, Michael Jordan was inducted into the NBA Hall of Fame. Ironically, that was the same time that Jordan became the first athlete to be worth over $1 billion; and it was the same time that his Nike brand, Jordan, topped $1 billion in annual revenue. That event came 23 years after the company Nike reached $1 billion in revenue for the first time.

Nike is all about marketing. Nike's other men, Tiger Woods and LeBron James, are expected to be the next athletes to be worth $1 billion. Tiger should reach this milestone in 2010. The rise of Jordan as a marketing icon is an amazing story. The kid from the University of North Carolina, who had never worn Nikes before he signed his contract, made buying Air Jordans an annual ritual. And now, years after he played his last game, the business continues to grow. At more than $1 billion in sales, the Jordan brand now makes up roughly 5 percent of Nike's overall revenues.

Regarding Jordan's importance to Nike, consider the following two facts provided by SportsOneSource, a sports market retail tracking firm:

1. The Jordan brand has a 10.8 percent share of the overall U.S. shoe market, which makes it the second biggest brand in the country and more than twice the size of Adidas' share.
2. Three out of every four pairs of basketball shoes sold in this country are Jordan, while 86.5 percent of all basketball shoes sold over $100 are Jordan.

The Nike's fiscal 2009 year ended May 31, 2009. As indicated in the company's income statement provided in Exhibit 1, Nike's 2009 revenues increased 2.9 percent to $19.1 billion; their net income decreased 21 percent to $1.48 billion.

History

Based in Beaverton, Oregon, Nike is the world's largest designer, marketer, and distributor of athletic footwear and athletic apparel. The company also designs, markets, and distributes sports-related apparel, equipment, and accessories. Led by the company's flagship Nike brand footwear, as well as Nike Golf, the company also owns a number of subsidiaries, such as Cole Haan, Converse, Hurley International, and Umbro Ltd.

Nike was founded in 1964 as Blue Ribbon Sports by Bill Bowerman, a University of Oregon track and field coach, and Phil Knight, a talented middle-distance runner. Knight, who had recently completed an MBA at Stanford University, had written a paper where he proposed that quality running shoes could be manufactured in Japan that would compete with the more established German brands. Knight originally sold their shoes out of the trunk of his green Plymouth Valiant at track meets, and the company opened its first store in Santa Monica, California, in 1966.

The company introduced its Nike brand of shoes in 1972, just in time for the U.S. Track & Field trials, which were held in Eugene, Oregon, that year. The Nike name, which took its name from the Greek goddess of victory, had its famous "swoosh" logo designed by Carolyn Davidson, a graphic design student at Portland State University. The company

EXHIBIT 1 Nike's Recent Income Statements

PERIOD ENDING	(all numbers in thousands)		
	31-May-09	31-May-08	31-May-07
Total Revenue	**$19,176,100**	**$18,627,000**	**$16,325,900**
Cost of Revenue	10,571,700	10,239,600	9,165,400
Gross Profit	**8,604,400**	**8,387,400**	**7,160,500**
Operating Expenses			
Research Development	—	—	—
Selling General and Administrative	6,149,600	5,953,700	5,028,700
Non Recurring	596,300	—	—
Others	—	—	—
Total Operating Expenses	—	—	—
Operating Income or Loss	**1,858,500**	**2,433,700**	**2,131,800**
Income from Continuing Operations			
Total Other Income/Expenses Net	98,000	69,200	68,100
Earnings Before Interest and Taxes	1,956,500	2,502,900	2,199,900
Interest Expense	—	—	—
Income Before Tax	1,956,500	2,502,900	2,199,900
Income Tax Expense	469,800	619,500	708,400
Minority Interest	—	—	—
Net Income from Continuing Ops	1,486,700	1,883,400	1,491,500
Non-recurring Events			
Discontinued Operations	—	—	—
Extraordinary Items	—	—	—
Effect of Accounting Changes	—	—	—
Other Items	—	—	—
Net Income	**$1,486,700**	**$1,883,400**	**$1,491,500**

Source: Nike's 2009 *Form 10 K.*

officially renamed itself Nike in 1978. By 1980, the company had reached a 50 percent market share in the U.S. athletic shoe market and had become a publicly traded company.

Missteps in the 1980s, particularly miscalculating the aerobics boom of that time period, found Nike trailing the rest of the athletic footwear industry. Changes at the company by Phil Knight, particularly the introduction of a Michael Jordan–endorsed basketball shoe in 1985, propelled Nike back to the top of the industry by 1988. The company also began to diversify at that time with the purchase of Cole Haan shoes, a casual and dress shoe company. From this point, Nike would go on to acquire other brands, such as Bauer (acquired 1995), Hurley (acquired 2002), Converse (acquired 2003), Starter (acquired 2004, divested 2007), and eventually Umbro Ltd. in 2008.

Internal Issues

Vision, Mission, and Strategic Goals

The vision of Nike is to "bring inspiration and innovation to every athlete in the world." Bill Bowerman, the co-founder, defined an athlete by saying, "If you have a body, you are an athlete." Bowerman saw endless possibilities for human potential in sports. Nike's mission is to carry on Bowerman's legacy of innovative thinking, develop products that help athletes of every level of ability reach their full potential, and to create business opportunities that set Nike apart from the competition and provide value for their shareholders.

The company has set a strategic goal of $23 billion in revenues by the end of fiscal 2011. Commenting on this ambitious target, Parker states, "When I stepped into the CEO role . . . the leadership team reaffirmed a simple concept that I knew was true from my nearly 30 years of experience here—Nike is a growth company." Parker saw the company's strategy as based on three principles: pursuing the greatest growth opportunities, leveraging Nike resources and capabilities, and serving customers with premium products and experiences.

Company Operations

Nike's Beaverton, Oregon, world headquarters is a 176-acre facility that encompasses 17 buildings, and houses almost 6,000 employees. Nike has a smaller facility in Hilversum, the Netherlands, that serves as the headquarters for the company's Europe, Middle East, and Africa (EMEA) region.

Inside the United States, Nike has three significant distribution and customer service facilities. Two are located in Memphis, Tennessee, one of which is leased, and one facility located in Wilsonville, Oregon, which is also leased. Nike subsidiary Cole Haan also operates a distribution facility in Greenland, New Hampshire. Outside the United States, Nike owns and operates two main distribution facilities, one located in Tomisatomachi, Japan, and the other in Laakdal, Belgium.

Almost all of Nike's footwear is manufactured outside the United States by independent contractors. In fiscal 2008, contract manufacturers in China, Vietnam, Indonesia, and Thailand manufactured 99 percent of Nike's footwear worldwide. No individual manufacturer accounted for more than 6 percent of total Nike footwear production. Nike brand apparel is produced in a similar manner, through independent contractors located outside the United States, in countries such as China, Thailand, Indonesia, and Malaysia, among others. The largest apparel factory accounted for approximately 8 percent of total Nike apparel production. Raw materials for Nike products are typically sourced in the countries where production takes place, purchased in bulk, and are typically not difficult to obtain.

Nike estimates that they sell products to more than 25,000 retail accounts in the United States. Nike products are found in a wide variety of retail locations, including footwear stores, sporting goods stores, athletic specialty stores, department stores, and skate, tennis, and golf shops. The company also uses independent sales representatives to sell specialty products for golf, skating, and outdoors. The company's Internet Web site, www.nikebiz.com, allows customers to design and purchase Nike products directly from the company. As indicated in Exhibit 2, the company also operates 338 retail

EXHIBIT 2   Nike's U.S. Retail Stores

U.S. Retail Stores	Number
Nike factory stores (which carry primarily overstock and close-out merchandise)	140
Nike stores (including one Nike Women store)	16
Niketowns (designed to showcase Nike products)	11
Nike employee-only stores	3
Cole Haan stores (including factory stores)	111
Converse factory stores	43
Hurley stores (including factory and employee stores)	14
Total	338

Note: Nike's apparel and equipment products are shipped from our Memphis, Tennessee, and Foothill Ranch, California, distribution centers. Cole Haan products are distributed primarily from Greenland, New Hampshire. Converse products are shipped primarily from Ontario, California, and Hurley products are distributed from Irvine, California.

Source: Nike's 2009 *Form 10K.*

outlets in the United States, including 140 Nike factory stores that sell overstock and closeout merchandise. Nike's U.S. sales accounted for 43 percent of total company revenues in fiscal 2008.

Outside the United States, Nike sells to more than 27,000 retail accounts, including Nike-owned stores and a mix of independent distributors and licensees around the world. The company has international branch offices and subsidiaries in 52 countries around the world and operates 336 retail outlets outside the United States. These Nike-owned retail facilities outside the United States include 184 Nike factory stores, 61 Nike stores, 4 Niketowns, 12 Nike employee-only stores, 74 Cole Haan stores, and 1 Hurley store, as indicated in Exhibit 3. Nike's non-U.S. sales accounted for 66 percent of total company revenues in fiscal 2008, up from 62 percent in 2007, as indicated in Exhibit 4. Exhibit 5 reveals Nike's income before taxes by region.

Nike has five wholly owned subsidiaries: Cole Haan, Converse, Hurley International, Nike Golf, and Umbro Ltd. Cole Haan, headquartered in Yarmouth, Maine, designs and distributes dress and casual footwear under the Cole Haan and Bragano brand names. Converse, headquartered in Yarmouth, Massachusetts, designs and distributes athletic and casual footwear under the Converse, Chuck Taylor, and All Star brand names, among others. Hurley International, based in Costa Mesa, California, designs and distributes a line of sports apparel for surfing, skating, and snowboarding under the Hurley trademark. Finally, Umbro Ltd., based in Manchester, England, designs and distributes athletic and casual footwear, apparel, and equipment for soccer under the Umbro trademark. Sales from these five subsidiaries was $2.4 billion in fiscal 2008, as indicated in Exhibit 6.

EXHIBIT 3   **Nike's Retail Outlets Outside the U.S.**

International Markets

Non-U.S. Retail Stores	Number
Nike factory stores	184
Nike stores	61
Niketowns	4
Nike employee-only stores	12
Cole Haan stores	74
Hurley stores	1
Total	336

Source: Nike's 2009 *Form 10K.*

EXHIBIT 4   **Nike's Revenues by Region**

	Fiscal 2009	Fiscal 2008	FY09 vs. FY08	Fiscal 2007	FY08 vs. FY07
			(in millions)		
U.S. Region	$ 6,542.9	$ 6,414.5	2%	$ 6,131.7	5%
EMEA Region	5,512.2	5,629.2	−2%	4,764.1	18%
Asia Pacific Region	3,322.0	2,887.6	15%	2,295.7	26%
Americas Region	1,284.7	1,164.7	10%	966.7	20%
Total Nike Brand Revenues	16,661.8	16,096.0	4%	14,158.2	14%
Other	2,514.3	2,531.0	−1%	2,167.7	17%
Total Nike, Inc. Revenues	$ 19,176.1	$ 18,627.0	3%	$ 16,325.9	14%

Source: Nike's 2009 *Form 10K.*

EXHIBIT 5   Nike's Income Before Taxes by Region

	Fiscal 2009	Fiscal 2008	FY09 vs. FY08	Fiscal 2007	FY08 vs. FY07
			(in millions)		
U.S. Region	$ 1,337.0	$ 1,402.0	−5%	$ 1,386.0	1%
EMEA Region	1,316.0	1,281.0	3%	1,050.0	22%
Asia Pacific Region	853.4	694.2	23%	515.4	35%
Americas Region	274.1	242.3	13%	199.3	22%
Other	(196.7)	364.9	−154%	299.7	22%
Corporate Expense	(1,629.)	(1,482.)	−10%	(1,250.)	−19%
Total Pre-tax Income	$ 1,956.	$ 2,502.	−22%	$ 2,199.	14%

Source: Nike's 2009 *Form 10K.*

EXHIBIT 6   Nike's Revenues from Subsidiaries

	Fiscal 2009	Fiscal 2008	FY09 vs. FY08	Fiscal 2007	FY08 vs. FY07
			(in millions)		
Revenues					
Converse	$ 915.3	$ 729.0	26%	$ 563.8	29%
Nike Golf	648.3	725.2	−11%	646.3	12%
Cole Haan	471.6	496.2	−5%	468.6	6%
Hurley	202.9	171.1	19%	150.6	14%
Umbro	174.0	53.9	223%	—	—
Bauer	—	201.9	−100%	166.1	22%
Exeter	—	35.1	−100%	67.7	−48%
Other					
Total	$2,412.10	$2,412.4		$2,063.10	

Nike Products

Nike designs, markets, and sells products in three main categories: footwear, apparel, and equipment. In footwear, Nike sells products that are designed primarily for athletic usage, although a significant percentage of Nike customers wear them for leisure or as a fashion accessory. Nike places a great deal of emphasis on the design of the footwear as well as high-quality construction. Footwear designed for running, training, basketball, soccer, and urban wear are among the top-selling categories for the company. In fiscal 2009, footwear accounted for 69.5 percent of Nike's total U.S. sales, as indicated in Exhibit 7.

Nike's sports-related apparel is designed to complement the company's athletic footwear products, and it is often sold through the same location and/or distribution channel. Typical apparel products include shirts with licensed college or professional team logos, athletic bags and accessories, running shorts, and baseball caps, all emblazoned with the ubiquitous Nike "swoosh." Apparel accounted for 25.4 percent of Nike U.S. sales in fiscal 2009, as indicated in Exhibit 7.

Sports equipment rounds out the Nike portfolio at 24.5 percent of U.S. sales. Sports equipment, typically sold under the Nike brand name, includes items such as bags, socks, sports balls, eyewear, golf clubs, and bats and gloves.

EXHIBIT 7 Nike's Revenues and Pre-Tax Income by Product within Regions

U.S. Region

	Fiscal 2009	Fiscal 2008	FY09 vs. FY08	Fiscal 2007	FY08 vs. FY07
			(in millions)		
Revenues					
Footwear	$ 4,550.1	$ 4,326.2	5%	$ 4,067.0	6%
Apparel	1,664.2	1,745.2	−5%	1,716.0	2%
Equipment	327.7	342.6	−4%	348.4	−2%
Total Revenues	$ 6,542.0	$ 6,414.0	2%	$ 6,131.4	5%
Pre-tax Income	$ 1,337.0	$ 1,402.0	−5%	$ 1,386.4	1%

EMEA Region

	Fiscal 2009	Fiscal 2008	FY09 vs. FY08	Fiscal 2007	FY08 vs. FY07
			(in millions)		
Revenues					
Footwear	$ 3,136.4	$ 3,112.0	1%	$ 2,608.0	19%
Apparel	1,970.3	2,083.9	−5%	1,757.1	19%
Equipment	405.3	433.1	−6%	398.9	9%
Total Revenues	$ 5,512.0	$ 5,629.0	−2%	$ 4,764.0	18%
Pre-tax Income	$ 1,316.0	$ 1,281.0	3%	$ 1,050.0	22%

Asia Pacific Region

	Fiscal 2009	Fiscal 2008	FY09 vs. FY08	Fiscal 2007	FY08 vs. FY07
			(in millions)		
Revenues					
Footwear	$ 1,727.4	$ 1,499.0	15%	$ 1,159.0	29%
Apparel	1,322.0	1,140.0	16%	909.3	25%
Equipment	272.6	248.1	10%	227.2	9%
Total Revenues	$ 3,322.0	$ 2,887.1	15%	$ 2,295.5	26%
Pre-tax Income	$ 853.4	$ 694.2	23%	$ 515.4	35%

Americas Region

	Fiscal 2009	Fiscal 2008	FY09 vs. FY08	Fiscal 2007	FY08 vs. FY07
			(in millions)		
Revenues					
Footwear	$ 892.1	$ 792.7	13%	$ 679.0	17%
Apparel	287.8	265.4	8%	193.8	37%
Equipment	104.8	106.6	−2%	93.2	14%
Total Revenues	$ 1,284.7	$ 1,164.7	10%	$ 966.0	20%
Pre-tax Income	$ 274.1	$ 242.3	13%	$ 199.0	22%

Source: Nike's 2009 *Form 10K.*

Nike Customers and Price Points

Because Nike competes primarily in athletic footwear, apparel, and related sporting equipment, its sales are heavily concentrated in the youth and young adult market. In particular, Nike sales are heavily skewed toward the 12- to 24-year-old age bracket.

Younger consumers are also less price sensitive in this age bracket and generally spend more on casual and athletic footwear than older consumers. After the age of 40, the typical consumer is not willing to pay more than $35 to $40 per pair for athletic footwear. Nike is the dominant competitor for athletic footwear priced above $60 per pair, holding better than a 50 percent market share for athletic footwear priced $85 per pair or higher.

Key Executives

The chairman of the board for Nike is Phil H. Knight, age 70, one of the cofounders of the company. Knight has been with the company since its beginning in the 1960s. He holds an MBA from Stanford University and has been a certified public accountant as well an assistant professor of business administration at Portland State University.

As indicated in Exhibit 8, the chief executive officer (CEO) of Nike is Mark G. Parker, age 52. Parker has been with the company since 1979 and was appointed CEO in January 2006. Prior to being named CEO, Parker had been president of the Nike brand from 2001 to 2006.

The president of the Nike brand is Charles D. Denson, age 52. Denson has also been employed by the company since 1979 and had been an assistant manager of Nike's first retail store in Portland, Oregon. Denson was credited with pioneering Nike's expansion into China, India, and Brazil.

The chief financial officer (CFO) for Nike is Donald W. Blair, age 50. Blair arrived at Nike in November 1999. Prior to joining Nike, he held several positions at Pepsico, Inc., and had been a certified public accountant with Deloitte, Haskins and Sells.

Nike characterizes its organization as a collaborative matrix organization. Executives often report in several areas, such as by region of the world, by product or by global function. Exhibit 8 presents an organizational chart for the company and the key executive officers.

Exhibit 9 presents Nike's balance sheets from fiscal 2006 to 2009. Note the company has very little long-term debt.

EXHIBIT 8   **Nike Organizational Chart, 2009**

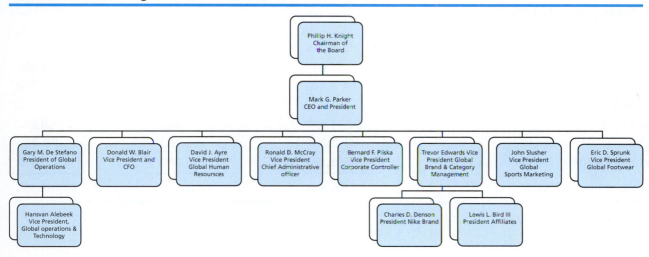

Source: Nikebiz.com.

EXHIBIT 9   Nike's Recent Balance Sheets

	(all numbers in thousands)		
Period Ending	31-May-09	31-May-08	31-May-07
Assets			
Current Assets			
Cash and Cash Equivalents	$ 2,291,100	2,133,900	1,856,700
Short Term Investments	1,164,000	642,200	990,300
Net Receivables	3,156,300	3,022,500	2,714,400
Inventory	2,357,000	2,438,400	2,121,900
Other Current Assets	765,600	602,300	393,200
Total Current Assets	**9,734,000**	**8,839,300**	**8,076,500**
Long Term Investments	—	—	—
Property Plant and Equipment	1,957,700	1,891,100	1,678,300
Goodwill	193,500	448,800	130,800
Intangible Assets	467,400	743,100	409,900
Accumulated Amortization	—	—	—
Other Assets	—	—	—
Deferred Long Term Asset Charges	897,000	520,400	392,800
Total Assets	**$ 13,249,600**	**12,442,700**	**10,688,300**
Liabilities			
Current Liabilities			
Accounts Payable	3,245,000	2,200,200	2,553,500
Short/Current Long Term Debt	32,000	179,600	30,500
Other Current Liabilities	—	941,700	—
Total Current Liabilities	**3,277,000**	**3,321,500**	**2,584,000**
Long Term Debt	437,200	441,100	409,900
Other Liabilities	—	—	—
Deferred Long Term Liability Charges	842,000	854,500	668,700
Minority Interest	—	—	—
Negative Goodwill	—	—	—
Total Liabilities	**4,556,200**	**4,617,100**	**3,662,600**
Stockholders' Equity			
Misc Stocks Options Warrants	—	—	—
Redeemable Preferred Stock	300	300	300
Preferred Stock	—	—	—
Common Stock	2,800	2,800	2,800
Retained Earnings	5,451,400	5,073,300	4,885,200
Treasury Stock	—	—	—
Capital Surplus	2,871,400	2,497,800	1,960,000
Other Stockholders' Equity	367,500	251,400	177,400
Total Stockholders' Equity	**8,693,100**	**7,825,300**	**7,025,400**
Total Liabilities and SE	**$ 13,249,600**	**12,442,700**	**10,688,300**

Source: Nike's 2009 *Form 10K.*

Competition

Competition in the athletic footwear and apparel industry is extremely fierce. Exhibit 10 provides comparative information of Nike versus all athletic footwear firms. Numerous brands compete worldwide for athlete endorsements, customer loyalty, and sales. Worldwide, Nike is the leader in athletic footwear, with an estimated 37 percent of worldwide sales.

Adidas

The number-two competitor in athletic footwear is Adidas, with an estimated 22 percent of worldwide sales. Adidas, based in Herzogenaurach, Germany, was founded in 1924 by the brothers Adolf and Rudolf Dassler. The company took its name from "Adi," a nickname for Adolf, and "Das" from Dassler. The foundation of what would become the Adidas group began with the equipping of several athletes for the 1928 Olympics, and it was cemented with Jesse Owen's quadruple gold medal performance at the 1936 Summer Olympics wearing Adidas footwear.

Today, the Adidas group is a world-class provider of athletic footwear, apparel, and sporting equipment. Their mission is "to be the leading sports brand in the world." Led by their flagship Adidas brand, the company posted 2008 revenues of 10.8 billion euros, a 4.9 percent improvement over its 2007 results. Worldwide, the company employs over 23,000 employees and tallied a record operating profit of 3.8 billion euros with a gross margin of 48.7 percent. Adidas was the Official Sportswear Partner for the Beijing 2008 Olympic Games, supplying more than 3 million products to participants and organizers of the Games. The company also contracts with Chinese basketball superstar Yao Ming to endorse a line of Reebok basketball shoes, contributing to Adidas's position as a market leader in both Europe and China.

The company is organized into three main divisions: Adidas, Reebok, and TaylorMade Golf. Its core Adidas division sells athletic footwear, apparel, and equipment under the brand name Adidas. Net sales in this division were 7.8 billion euros, a 10 percent improvement over 2007 performance. Reebok was acquired by Adidas in 2006. With roots in women's fitness, this division sells athletic footwear, apparel, and equipment under the Reebok, Rockport, and Reebok-CCM Hockey brand names. Net sales for the Reebok division were 2.1 billion euros, a net decline of 8 percent over 2007 results. Commenting on the Reebok division's results, Herbert Hainer, CEO of Adidas, said, "2008 was a challenging year and I am disappointed not to be able to show the financial improvements we anticipated at the beginning of the year." The TaylorMade Golf division was acquired by Adidas in 1997. This division sells golf clubs, balls, footwear, and apparel under the TaylorMade, Adidas Golf, and Ashworth brand names. Net sales for this division were 812 million euros in 2008, a 1 percent improvement over its 2007 results.

EXHIBIT 10   **Nike versus All Firms in the Athletic Footwear Industry**

	Nike	Athletic Footwear Industry
Market Capitalization	26.74B	308.96M
# Employees	34,300	740
Qtrly Rev Growth	−7.40%	4.50%
Revenue	19.18B	303.83M
Gross Margin	44.87%	38.93%
EBIT	2.80B	11.21M
Oper Margins	12.80%	0.93%
Net Income	1.49B	N/A
EPS	3.030	0.52

Note: M = millions
    B = billions

Source: Based on information at www.finance.yahoo.com.

Recently, the company has issued a profit warning, announcing that net profits for the first quarter of 2009 would plunge 97 percent, and it blamed the global recession for these results. Hainer, CEO of Adidas, also cited rising raw materials prices, falling sales in Europe and the United States, and a weaker dollar against the euro for the sudden downturn in Adidas profits. Hainer also warned that business for the rest of 2009 would be difficult, with margins and earnings expected to decline further.

Puma

Puma is the distant number-three competitor in the global market for athletic footwear. Puma develops and markets a broad range of athletic and lifestyle articles, including footwear, apparel, and accessories. Its 2008 sales were 2.5 billion euros. Selling products under the Puma and Tretorn brands, the company employs more than 10,000 employees and distributes its products in over 130 countries around the world. The company was founded in 1948 when Rudolf "Rudi" Dassler split his business from his brother Adolf. Rudi moved his business to the other side of the Aurach River from the Adidas company in Herzogenaurach, Germany.

Puma has the long-term mission of becoming the most desirable sport lifestyle company. Not one to be outdone by its larger competitors, Puma made a splash in 2008 at the Beijing Olympics. Before a stunned Olympic crowd, and wearing gold Puma Theseus II spikes, Usain Bolt broke world records in the men's 100-meter dash, 200-meter dash, and the 4×100 meter relay.

Other Competitors

The athletic footwear industry contains numerous smaller competitors worldwide, such as K-Swiss, Inc. in the United States and Li Ling Shoes in China. Athletic footwear companies also compete with other footwear companies for sales because consumers often wear athletic footwear for leisure and fashion. Companies that competed in leisure and fashion footwear included Crocs, Inc., Deckers Outdoor Group, Skechers USA Inc., and Timberland Company.

Global Issues

The footwear industry is global in scale and scope, with several large, well-capitalized firms competing worldwide for customers and market share, including firms like Nike, Adidas, and Puma. These companies have been conducting business worldwide on the basis of global competitive advantage, rather than local, by sourcing production to countries that provided a cost advantage, conducting research and development (R&D) from their home location, and then marketing and selling their products in numerous countries over sometimes as many as four different continents.

These multinational strategies allow the largest competitors to cope with slowing demand in their core markets, such as the United States, by shifting their emphasis to countries and regions that have higher rates of sales growth, such as Brazil, Eastern Europe, India, and China. Companies like Adidas and Nike have moved aggressively into these areas to capitalize on the rapid pace of expansion in these emerging markets. In addition, companies have diversified their holdings into sports apparel and equipment in order to complement their core footwear offerings, expand revenues, and "deepen" their relationships with customers.

Footwear Production Is Outsourced

U.S. footwear imports totaled 2.36 billion pairs in 2007, or roughly 7.9 pairs per capita. This number was up 0.4 percent from 2006. Domestic shoe production now accounts for less than 5 percent of all shoe purchases in the United States. The remaining U.S. production of footwear is primarily focused on protective or safety footwear, typically steel-toed boots.

The drive for domestic manufacturers of footwear to offshore their production has been part of an ongoing industry effort to cut expenses. This trend had been aided by the implementation of the North American Free Trade Agreement (NAFTA) in 1995 and the entry of China into the World Trade Organization (WTO) in 2001, both of which helped eliminate quotas and tariff barriers for foreign footwear manufacturers to ship their goods into the United States. China alone accounts for 86.4 percent (by volume) of all U.S. imports of footwear into the United States.

Virtually all of Nike's footwear is produced outside of the United States. In fiscal 2009, contract suppliers in China, Vietnam, Indonesia, and Thailand manufactured 36 percent, 36 percent, 22 percent, and 6 percent of total Nike brand footwear, respectively. The company also has manufacturing agreements with independent factories in Argentina, Brazil, India, and Mexico to manufacture footwear for sale primarily within those countries. Nike's largest single footwear factory accounted for approximately 5 percent of total fiscal 2009 footwear production.

Almost all of Nike brand apparel is manufactured outside of the United States by independent contract manufacturers located in 34 countries. Most of this apparel production occurred in China, Thailand, Indonesia, Malaysia, Vietnam, Turkey, Sri Lanka, Cambodia, Taiwan, El Salvador, Mexico, India, and Israel. Nike's largest single apparel factory accounted for approximately 5 percent of total fiscal 2009 apparel production.

Technological Changes

The Internet allows footwear companies to pursue a direct to consumer sales channel. Sales of apparel, accessories, and footwear on the Internet has been growing at a double-digit pace, considerably faster than more traditional sales models such as retail stores. Forrester Research predicts that Internet sales of apparel, accessories, and footwear could reach 18 percent of category sales by 2012, up from 6.5 percent of all sales in 2006. Companies that added a Web-based sales strategy are able to customize footwear and other merchandise directly to the customer's needs and taste, which enables companies to achieve considerably better pricing as well as "deepening" the emotional bond consumers have with the brand.

The Future

Nike needs a clear three-year strategic plan to succeed in the future. Provide this for Nike's top management team.

Endnotes

1. This case study was prepared as a basis for class discussion rather than to illustrate either effective or ineffective handling of an administrative situation. Not for reproduction or distribution without permission of the author. Contact info: Randall Harris. Dept. of Management. CSU. Stanislaus. 801 W. Monte Vista Avenue. Turlock. CA 95382. raharris@csustan.edu (209) 667–3723. Review copy for *Strategic Management, 13th Edition*. © 2009 by Randall Harris. Draft dated May 8, 2009.

28 Callaway Golf Company — 2009

Amit J. Shah
Frostburg State University

ELY

www.callawaygolf.com

Who was the most dominant player in women's golf in the world through 2008–2009, and what clubs does she use? The answers are Annika Sorenstam and Callaway clubs. Callaway makes premium-priced golf clubs that are popular with both amateurs and professionals, as well as high-tech golf balls including the HX, CTU 30, and CB1. Callaway's drivers include the ERC II, Hawk Eye VFT, Steelhead, Big Bertha Titanium 454, FT-9, and the latest FT-iQ.

Callaway recently developed Fusion Technology, which has led to the world's smartest, most advanced driver: the new FT-iQ Driver. Through robot testing measuring hits across multiple face locations, the FT-iQ Driver is the longest driver Callaway Golf Company has ever made. It also licenses its corporate name for apparel, shoes, and other golf accessories.

In June 2009, Callaway slashed its dividend. Since 1997, it had paid a constant $.28 per share annually, but, in order to conserve cash, it lowered the payout to just $.04. Also that month, the company used the proceeds of a $140 million convertible preferred stock sale to pay off its entire short-term debt. This move was quite embarassing to management, as Callaway had been acquiring shares from the time current CEO Fellows arrived in 2005 (with no debt on the balance sheet) through 2007.

Callaway will report a loss for calendar 2009, with the cost of the preferred equity ($.09 per share) as well as weak business trends contributing. Analysts do, however, forecast a strong recovery in 2010 and 2011. The bulk of Callaway's sales come from golf clubs, but even sales of golf balls declined more than 20 percent in 2009. Callaway historically has spent 5 percent of revenues on R&D but now spends only 3 percent.

Callaway's management surprisingly does not own that much of the company's stock. CEO Fellows owns just 1.2 percent and the entire top management team and the board hold just under 3 percent of the company's outstanding stock.

History

In 1982, Ely Callaway founded Callaway Hickory Stick USA, Inc., which later became Callaway Golf Company (CGC). Although the company was incorporated in California in 1982, it was reincorporated in Delaware in 1999. CGC's products are designed and built on an eight-building campus in Carlsbad, California, where the majority of its 2,700 employees work (as of December 2008).

In its early years, Callaway revolutionized the industry with golf clubs that were "very forgiving" and therefore very welcome to the average golfer. New technologies and production methods turned the smallest golf club manufacturer into the world's largest maker of premium golf clubs and a dominant force in the industry. During the years of growth, Callaway acquired well-known brands like Odyssey, a manufacturer of putters, in 1997; Strata, a manufacturer of golf balls; and Ben Hogan, a competitor in golf clubs.

In 2000, Callaway entered the golf ball business with the release of its first golf ball. In 2004, the company acquired all of the issued and outstanding shares of stock of FrogTrader, Inc. (which subsequently changed its name to Callaway Golf Interactive, Inc.).

The company acquired FrogTrader to stimulate purchases of new clubs by growing its Trade In! Trade Up! program and to enable the company to better manage the distribution of preowned golf clubs. In 2008, the company acquired certain assets and liabilities of uPlay, LLC, a developer and marketer of global positioning system (GPS) devices. The company acquired uPlay to expand its accessories business by adding satellite-based range finders and for the potential application for other products as well.

Callaway won the bidding war in 2003 for Top-Flite Golf, with a $174 million offer that ended a struggle with rival Adidas-Salomon, owner of Taylor Made Golf. Top-Flite is a leading manufacturer of golf balls and has a high reputation among professionals and recreational players. Top-Flite, the nation's second-largest golf ball maker behind industry leader Titleist, had $250 million in 2002 golf ball sales. The company's $530 million in debt and the highly competitive market forced it into bankruptcy. Under the deal, Callaway assumed Top-Flite's debt.

Vision and Mission

CGC does not have a vision statement published on its Web site, but it does have a mission statement, as follows:

> Callaway Golf Company is driven to be a world class organization that designs, develop, makes and delivers demonstrably superior and pleasing different golf products that incorporate breakthrough technologies, backs those products with noticeably superior customer service, and generates a return to the shareholders in excess of the cost of capital. We share every golfer's passion for the game, and commit our talents and our technology to increasing the satisfaction and enjoyment all golfers derive from pursuing that passion.

Current Operations

CGC boosted its net income to $66 million in 2008 as indicated in Exhibit 1.

Despite the challenging and unfavorable global economic conditions, CGC posted 2008 net sales of $1.117 billion, which was the second highest sales level in the company's history and only slightly less than the record sales of $1.125 billion in 2007. Callaway has also delivered a proforma earnings per share of $1.04, an increase of approximately 6 percent.

EXHIBIT 1 Callaway Golf Company Five-Year Statement of Operations

	Year Ended December 31				
	2008	2007	2006	2005	2004
	(in thousands, except per share data)				
Net sales	$1,117,204	$1,124,591	$1,017,907	$998,093	$934,564
Cost of sales	630,371	631,368	619,832	583,679	575,742
Gross profit	486,833	493,223	398,075	414,414	358,822
Selling, general and administrative expenses	373,275	371,020	334,235	370,219	352,967
Research and development expenses	29,370	32,020	26,785	26,989	30,557
Income (loss) from operations	84,188	90,183	37,055	17,206	(24,702)
Interest and other income, net	1,863	3,455	3,364	(390)	1,934
Interest expense	(4,666)	(5,363)	(5,421)	(2,279)	(945)
Unrealized energy derivative losses	19,922	—	—	—	—
Income (loss) before income taxes	101,307	88,275	34,998	14,537	(23,713)
Income tax provision (benefit)	35,131	33,688	11,708	1,253	(13,610)
Net income	**66,176**	**54,587**	**23,290**	**13,284**	**(10,103)**

Source: Callaway Golf Company, *Annual Report/Form 10K* (2008).

During the second half of 2008, the deteriorating economic conditions in the United States spread to most of the Callaway's international markets and resulted in an overall decrease in net sales for 2008 from 2007. In spite of the economic struggles, CGC's financial position remains strong because the company has little long-term debt and high liquidity. Exhibit 2 presents the consolidated balance sheet of Callaway.

EXHIBIT 2   **Callaway Golf Company Consolidated Balance Sheets (in thousands, except share and per share data)**

	December 31	
	2008	2007
ASSETS		
Current assets:		
Cash and cash equivalents	$ 38,337	$ 49,875
Accounts receivable, net	120,067	163,515
Inventories, net	257,191	253,001
Deferred taxes	27,046	42,219
Income taxes receivable	15,549	9,232
Other current assets	31,813	30,190
Total current assets	490,003	496,581
Property, plant and equipment, net	142,145	128,036
Intangible assets, net	146,945	140,985
Goodwill	29,744	32,060
Deferred taxes	6,299	—
Other assets	40,202	40,416
TOTAL	**$ 855,338**	**$ 838,078**
LIABILITIES AND SHAREHOLDERS' EQUITY		
Current liabilities:		
Accounts payable and accrued expenses	$ 126,167	$ 130,410
Accrued employee compensation and benefits	25,630	44,245
Accrued warranty expense	11,614	12,386
Credit Facilities	90,000	36,507
Total current liabilities	253,411	223,548
Long-term liabilities:		
Deferred taxes, net	—	2,367
Deferred compensation	6,566	8,200
Energy derivative valuation account	—	19,922
Income taxes payable	14,993	13,833
Commitments and contingencies (Note 15)		
Shareholders' equity:		
Preferred Stock, $.01 par value, 3,000,000 shares authorized, none issued and outstanding at December 31, 2008 and 2007	—	—
Common Stock, $.01 par value, 240,000,000 shares authorized, 66,276,236 shares and 66,281,693 shares issued at December 31, 2008 and 2007, respectively	663	663
Additional paid-in capital	102,329	111,953

continued

EXHIBIT 2 Callaway Golf Company Consolidated Balance Sheets (in thousands, except share and per share data)—continued

	December 31	
	2008	2007
Unearned compensation	(279)	(2,158)
Retained earnings	518,851	470,469
Accumulated other comprehensive income	(6,376)	18,904
Less: Grantor Stock Trust held at market value, 1,440,570 shares and 1,813,010 shares at December 31, 2008 and 2007, respectively	(13,383)	(31,601)
Less: Common Stock held in treasury, at cost, 1,768,695 shares and 0 shares at December 31, 2008 and 2007, respectively	(23,650)	—
Total shareholders' equity	578,155	568,230
	$ 855,338	**$ 838,078**

Source: Callaway Golf Company, *Annual Report/Form 10K* (2008).

CGC has also licensed its trademarks to IZZO Golf, TRG Accessories, LLC, Fossil, Inc., Nikon Vision Co., Ltd., and Global Wireless Entertainment, Inc. Prior to April 2006, the company had a licensing arrangement with Tour Golf Group, Inc. (TGG) for a line of Callaway Golf footwear. In April 2006, the company terminated the licensing arrangement and acquired certain assets of TGG. CGC recognized royalty income under its various licensing agreements of $8,847,000, $8,672,000, and $8,292,000 during 2008, 2007, and 2006, respectively.

Callaway Products

Exhibit 3 portrays Callaway's contribution of net sales by principal product group. CGC's sales of drivers and woods increased in 2007, due to a more extensive line of drivers in 2007 relative to 2008. The decrease in new driver introductions contributed to a reduction in over-all average selling prices within the woods category because drivers, particularly premium Fusion Technology drivers, carry a higher sales price than fairway woods and hybrids. Sales of putters and irons in 2008 have also declined from 2007. However, sales of golf balls and accessories have made significant increases from 2007. In 2007, overall sales increased from the previous year by more than $106 million; however, in 2008, sales decreased from the previous year by $7.4 million. The company's drivers, fairway woods, irons, and golf balls are sold under the Callaway Golf, Top-Flite, and Ben Hogan brands. The putters are sold under the Odyssey, Callaway Golf, Ben Hogan, and Top-Flite brands.

Golf Datatech reports that the number of golf rounds played in the United States declined by 4 percent between February 2008 and 2009. According to Golf Datatech, the

EXHIBIT 3 Contribution of Net Sales Attributable to Principal Product Groups

	Year Ended December 31					
	2008		2007		2006	
	(in thousands)					
Drivers and fairway woods	$ 268,286	24%	$ 305,880	27%	$ 266,478	26%
Irons	308,556	28%	309,594	28%	287,960	29%
Putters	101,676	9%	109,068	10%	102,714	10%
Golf balls	223,075	20%	213,064	19%	214,783	21%
Accessories and other	215,611	19%	186,985	16%	145,972	14%
Net sales	1,117,204	100%	1,124,591	100%	1,017,907	100%

Source: Callaway Golf Company, *Form 10K* (2008).

EXHIBIT 4 Sales Information by Region

Net sales:	2008	2007	Percent change	2006	Percent change
			Year Ended December 31		
			(in thousands)		
United States	$ 554,029	$ 597,569	−7%	$ 566,600	5%
Europe	191,089	193,336	−1%	159,886	21%
Japan	166,476	120,148	39%	105,705	14%
Rest of Asia	80,011	86,133	−7%	75,569	14%
Other foreign countries	125,599	127,405	−1%	110,147	16%
Total	1,117,204	1,124,591	−1%	1,017,907	10%

Source: Callaway Golf Company, *Form 10K* (2008).

regions with the strongest growth in number of rounds played include the West North Central, East North Central, and New England.

In 2008, approximately 50 percent of the CGC's net sales were generated within the United States, and 50 percent were generated elsewhere. The company does business in more than 100 countries around the world. The majority of the company's international sales are made through its wholly owned subsidiaries located in Europe, Japan, Canada, Korea, and Australia. Exhibit 4 provides sales information for CGC based on international regions. From 2006 to 2007, no region incurred a loss in sales; however, between 2007 and 2008, three regions incurred losses, which were Europe (1 percent loss), the rest of Asia (7 percent loss), and other foreign countries (1 percent loss).

Business Ethics and Environmental Matters

CGC adopted a corporate Code of Conduct and Ethics Policy in 1997 applicable to all employees and directors, including senior financial officers. CGC previously permitted loans to employees, including executive officers, in restricted amounts (up to $150,000) and for limited purposes (purchase of a primary residence). There are currently no outstanding loans to executive officers under this program and only two loans outstanding to nonexecutive officers.

CEO/CFO certification procedures pursuant to Section 302 of Sarbanes-Oxley, established in November 2002, have been implemented at CGC. The company also has an insider trading policy that is written, distributed to all employees, and accompanied by training. Officers and key employees are subject to "gatekeeper" review and approval by the CGC's legal department.

CGC operations are subject to federal, state, and local environmental laws. During the ordinary course of its manufacturing process, CGC creates toxic waste through the use of special materials and production processes. The waste is regularly transported off site by registered waste haulers. As a standard procedure, a comprehensive audit of the treatment, storage, and disposal facilities with which the company contracts for the disposal of hazardous waste are performed annually by CGC. The company employs two full-time environmental engineers at its Carlsbad, California, facility and a director of environmental, health, and safety matters at its Chicopee, Massachusetts, facility to manage the program. It is also a charter member of the U.S. Environmental Protection Agency's National Performance Track program, which recognizes facilities that have demonstrated a commitment to superior environmental performance and compliance.

Business Operations

CGC has subsidiaries all over the world; those wholly owned by CGC include Callaway Golf Sales Company, Callaway Golf Ball Operations, Inc. (formerly known as The Top-Flite Golf Company), Callaway Golf Interactive, Inc., Callaway Golf Europe Ltd., Callaway Golf K.K., Callaway Golf Korea Ltd., Callaway Golf Canada Ltd., Callaway Golf South

Pacific PTY Ltd., Callaway Golf (Shanghai) Trading Company, Ltd., Callaway Golf Malaysia Sdn. Bhd. (formerly known as Titanium Winners Sdn. Bhd.), and Callaway Golf (Thailand) Ltd. CGC distributes directly to the retailers or to the wholly owned subsidiaries and third-party distributors. The company also licenses its trademarks and service marks to third parties in exchange for royalty fees. Exhibit 5 presents CGC's organizational chart.

Manufacturing golf clubs is primarily done at CGC's facilities in Carlsbad, California. Some of the products are assembled outside the United States. Assembly of the clubs is done using components from suppliers from both within and outside the United States. The golf club assembly process is "very labor intensive."

Prior to the Top-Flite acquisition, CGC manufactured its golf balls in its Carlsbad, California, facility, and Top-Flite manufactured their golf balls primarily in its Chicopee, Massachusetts, and Gloversville, New York, facilities. Since the acquisition, however, the company has moved the majority of its golf ball manufacturing to the Chicopee and Gloversville facilities and is in the process of moving the remainder to those facilities over the course of this year. The golf ball manufacturing process is "much more automated" than the golf club assembly process, although, the company points out, much labor is still used in the golf ball manufacturing process.

The golf business is highly seasonal. In the busy summer season, CGC employees are required to work many hours of overtime, whereas in the winter, production capacity is only about 68 percent. These special conditions require a special employment contract based on a working-hours account, which allows employees to use overtime work hours, gathered during high production, to make up the unused work time in the off season. As of year-end 2008, CGC and its subsidiaries employed 2,700 employees full time and part time. CGC employees "historically have not been represented by unions," according to the company's annual report. The manufacturing employees at the Top-Flite plant are represented by a union. CGC had approximately 480 employees covered under a collective bargaining agreement, as of December 31, 2008. Callaway has renegotiated a new collective bargaining agreement with the union in Chicopee, which is scheduled to expire on September 30, 2011. The production employees in Canada and Australia are also unionized. According to CGC, the company "considers its employee relations to be good."

EXHIBIT 5   Calloway Organizational Chart

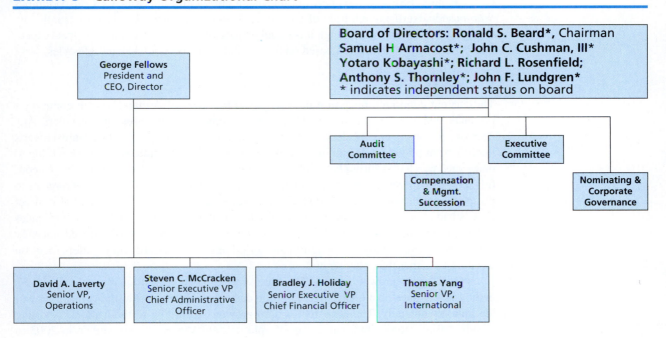

Marketing

Rapid introduction of new golf clubs or golf balls could result in closeouts of existing inventories at both wholesale and retail levels. Closeouts result in reduced margins on the sale of older products as well as reduced sales of new products.

CGC announced a contract renewal with the number-two golfer in the world, Phil Mickelson, in early 2009. Callaway also uses point-of-purchase displays for its products in golf shops and retail stores worldwide.

Callaway has seen tremendous success under the Trade In! Trade Up! Program (www.tradeintradeup.com). Under this agreement, Callaway consumers can receive trade-in allowances on their previously owned Callaway golf clubs toward the purchase of new Callaway clubs. This option has become popular for consumers looking to upgrade their equipment. It also provides a convenient avenue for consumers looking to purchase cheaper used clubs. This program certainly helps Callaway build and strengthen customer loyalty.

Callaway has long been known for its commitment to innovation in its technology. CGC's tradition is built on product leadership and "the proof is in the more than 1,100 United States patents—more than any other golf manufacturer." CGC has recently launched the Callaway Golf FT Irons. According to CGC's Web site, FT Irons are "the evolution of Fusion Technology, delivering the utmost in performance and playability in Callaway Golf irons for mid to low handicap players who demand the latest innovation with proven results." Since the introduction of the FT Irons, Callaway has introduced the FT i-brid irons. These irons are CGC's most technologically advanced game-improvement set. The FT i-brid irons provide the ultimate in forgiveness and playability by incorporating three hybrid-like clubs designed to replace hard-to-hit long irons and game-improvement short irons.

Callaway has introduced a men's and women's version of the FT-iQ—the smartest, straightest driver the company has ever marketed and sold. The club is available with features that are accommodating to all golfers, with available lofts of 9, 10, and 11 degrees, as well as a High Trajectory [HT] model that offers 13 degrees. These higher degrees of loft make getting the ball airborne easier on the player. The advanced head shape has a sleek look and increases the moment of inertia (MOI) for extraordinary accuracy off the tee. For feel and performance, the FT-iQ driver has an exclusive Fubuki shaft from Mitsubishi Rayon.

In advertising, CGC relies mainly on a combination of printed and television advertisements. Advertisements in print include national magazines, such as *Golf Magazine*, *Sports Illustrated,* and *Golf Digest,* and television commercials included primarily on The Golf Channel, ESPN, and on network television during golf telecasts. CGC also employs Web-based advertising. Outside of the United States, advertising is generally handled by CGC's subsidiaries, and although it is based on its global brand principles, the local execution is tailored by each region based on their unique consumer market and lifestyles.

External Factors

The current economic recession has decreased the level of demand for the company's products, which are recreational and therefore discretionary purchases for consumers. Any decrease in consumer confidence, adverse economic conditions, or political unrest diverts interest from playing golf and hurts Callaway's business. Individuals are more willing to make such purchases during favorable economic conditions and when they are feeling confident and prosperous. Adverse economic conditions have caused consumers to forgo or to postpone purchasing new golf products. The severe economic downturn may also affect CGC's bad debt, which has been historically low. Natural disasters, such as the hurricanes in Florida and along the East Coast, can negatively affect golf rounds played not only during the storms but also for a significant period of time afterward while golfers focus on cleaning up rather than playing golf.

Golf is not a growth industry. There are approximately 26 million recreational players in the United States, but on average 3 million customers enter and 3 million customers exit the industry annually. The net effect is zero growth. According to the National Sporting Goods Association's 2008 survey, golf's player pool shrank 7.3 percent from 2003 to 2007. The latest report from the National Golf Foundation shows rounds played are down

3.5 percent for the first quarter of 2008. Also, it takes a lot of time to play golf. People today have so many other ways to spend their time. A positive trend for CGC, however, is that the world's population is aging, and many older people both play golf and have discretionary income to purchase golf equipment. Golf courses are overbuilt in the United States; the number of rounds played was down 4 percent in the United States in 2008 from 2007. More and more companies are chasing the same customers, which means that a gain in market share for one is a loss for another.

For CGC to grow its sales of golf clubs or golf balls significantly, the company must either increase its share of the market for golf clubs or balls, or the market for these items itself must grow. Because CGC already possesses a substantial share of the market in sales of clubs and balls, additional market share may be limited. In addition, the company does not believe there will be any material increase in the number of golfers worldwide in the next four years.

Competitors

The business of golf has grown to become a billion-dollar industry worldwide, but due to the economic downturn, small companies may fall and big companies need to right-size and reset their business to survive. Industry leaders spend millions on endorsement contracts for the game's best players to entice recreational players. For example, Nike pays Tiger Woods to use and endorse its products. A popular but expensive way to gain market share is using PGA Tour players to promote your product. "The PGA Tour is the one bright spot in the whole industry," says Drapeau. "The TV ratings are up; the attendance is up. A large part of that is due to Tiger Woods." Woods is so popular that Nike signed him to an endorsement contract and then over time built an entire golf division around him. Woods once played Titleist equipment, but he shifted to Nike. Each time he changed, he said he would not have changed unless Nike made the best product for him to play.

Titleist is one of CGC's biggest competitors. A subsidiary of Fortune Brands, Inc., Acushnet Company, owns the brand Titleist, among other brands. Titleist manufactures various types of golf clubs, as well as balls, equipment, and accessories. Other golf-related Acushnet brand names include FootJoy, Cobra, and Pinnacle. Acushnet primarily sells its products to on-course golf pro shops and select off-course golf specialty and sporting goods stores throughout the United States. International distributors and agents sell the products throughout the global market, including the United Kingdom, Canada, Germany, Austria, Denmark, Ireland, France, Sweden, the Netherlands, South Africa, Thailand, Singapore, Malaysia, Australia, New Zealand, Korea, and Japan. Acushnet attributes about 42 percent of its sales to its international markets. The company is very strong in the golf shoe and golf glove markets (FootJoy) and is the leading producer in golf balls (Titleist). Between 2007 and 2008, net sales for golf-related operations at Fortune decreased from $1,405.4 million to $1,368.9 million. This is attributed to the unfavorable global economic conditions. Callaway competes with Acushnet in all three of its main markets: shoes and gloves, clubs, and balls.

More and more well-known athletic goods manufacturers such as Nike, Wilson, and Adidas, just to mention a few, are diversifying and expanding into the market. These companies have very good reputations, which helps them enter the golf equipment and accessories market. Several companies that produce high-quality tennis racquets, such as Prince, Fila, Head, and Wilson, are becoming a big threat to Callaway Golf. Wilson already does a substantial golf business.

CGC's biggest domestic competition with respect to metal woods and irons are TaylorMade, Titleist, Cobra, Cleveland (Srixon), Ping, Mizuno, Bridgestone, and Nike. For putters, Callaway's major competitors are Ping, Titleist, and TaylorMade. CGC competes with Dunlop and Yamaha among others in Japan and throughout Asia. Mizuno is Japan's largest sporting goods maker and has made strides in the golf equipment industry. In the golf ball business, CGC faces competition from Titleist, Nike, Spalding, Sumitomo Rubber Industry, and Bridgestone (Precept). Titleist has an estimated market share in excess of 50 percent and is therefore leading in the golf ball industry. In 2008, CGC was number two on the PGA tour for golf ball usage. The company also achieved the number-two retail market share, second to Titleist, for the same year.

TaylorMade-Adidas Golf (TAG), one of the largest golf club manufacturers in the world, is a subsidiary of Adidas-Salomon A.G. TAG enjoys a 28 percent market share in the United States and hopes to have achieve the same market share worldwide that it has in the United States in 2010. In February 2008, TAG divested the Maxfli brand, which accounted for 1 percent of its 2007 sales. TaylorMade has also launched a $35 million advertising push for its golf equipment in 2008. This advertising campaign is the most expensive one in TaylorMade's history.

Nike went into the golf business with Tiger Woods, and the company has been steadily growing in the golf industry with Tiger Wood's success. In 2007, Nike Golf grew 12 percent to nearly $650 million. Nike Golf accounted for approximately 43 percent of total revenues for the athletic footwear and apparel manufacturer.

Global Issues

The global golf market is uniform in the sense that firms do not have to develop different products for different markets. But different economic and competitive situations in global markets make it sometimes difficult to place products in the right way with the right price, and at the same time generate profit. Rules vary for different professional tours, like the PGA Tour, the European Tour, the Canadian Tour, and the Asian-Pacific Tour. It is difficult to introduce and market a new product that conflicts with rules for the professional players. An innovation is difficult to market if professional players are not allowed to play with the new equipment and the recreational players will never see new equipment developed for their game.

A negative factor CGC has to face is the mass amount of imitation of its products, especially in the Asian-Pacific area. It is very difficult for the company to track the imitations, which results in high administration costs and loss of revenues. Interruptions and high fuel costs in air carrier or shipping services, anti-American sentiments, and social, economic, and political instability all negatively affect the performance of CGC. On March 24, 2009, according to a CGC press release, the Beijing Chaoyang Administration for Industry and Commerce (AIC) and the Chaoyang Public Security Bureau (PSB) jointly conducted raids against an assembly and warehouse facility of the Sunshine Golf Store located at Shangxinpu, Huanggang Village, Chaoyang District, Beijing. The raids resulted in the seizure of nearly 10,000 pieces of counterfeit golf equipment, including more than 740 assembled golf clubs, 1,500 club heads, 4,700 golf grips, 2,300 shafts, 280 head covers, and assorted golf towels, golf bags, and apparel.

Patent infringements are another large risk for Callaway. According to a CGC press release, on March 3, 2009, it filed a new patent infringement lawsuit against Acushnet. The lawsuit alleges that the new 2009 Titleist Pro V1 and Pro V1x golf balls, available in spring 2009, breach golf ball patents owned by Callaway Golf. This new lawsuit follows the successful patent infringement action filed by CGC against Acushnet in February 2006 that resulted in a permanent ruling halting sales of earlier versions of the Pro V1 family of golf balls.

The Chinese government continues to raid counterfeiters responding to the complaints of U.S. golf manufacturers including CGC, Acushnet, Cleveland Golf, Ping, Nike, and TaylorMade-Adidas. These raids are attempts to track down and stop counterfeiting efforts to make knock-off golf clubs and equipment. Rob Duncanson, an attorney advising the companies, made this statement after one of the raid: "The manufacture and sale of counterfeit golf equipment by these modern pirates not only cost US companies millions in lost revenues, but affects the brand integrity and reputations of companies who invest substantial resources in R&D and marketing, ultimately undermining the trust of the unsuspecting consumer."

Conclusion

For many golfers, the current business climate means bargains. The National Golf Foundation, an industry group, reports that the number of golfers has ranged between 26 million and 37 million, but the recession has scared many people away from the courses. Americans are not playing as much golf this year as they did last year. Many public and private golf clubs are experiencing weak demand and have been lowering prices to attract customers. According to Golf Datatech, golf equipment is selling but at lower prices. A few golf companies have declared bankruptcy, including San Diego–based Carbite Inc., a wedge and putter maker. Some equipment manufacturers, including Plano-based Adams Golf Inc., are struggling as well, and CGC itself laid off 370 employees in 2008 to improve its manufacturing efficiencies and effectiveness as well as reduce operating costs.

The global economic recession hurts Callaway. Golf products are discretionary rather than essential items. Other factors that also harm the golf business include high unemployment, increased consumer debt levels, and declining consumer confidence and spending. Other threats to Callaway include imitation clubs, limited growth opportunity in golf clubs and golf balls, intense competition, international exchange rate fluctuations, international political instability and terrorist attacks, natural disasters and pandemic diseases, and the seasonality nature of the sport.

Chevron Corporation — 2009

Linda Herkenhoff
Saint Mary's College

CVX

www.chevron.com

Wonder whether the price per gallon of gas soon will be over $4.00 like it was in May 2008 or will it be below $2.00 per gallon as in the first quarter of 2009? Gasoline is what keeps America moving. Joe Petrowski, Gulf Oil LP CEO, recently said that the price of oil could sink to $20 per barrel, meaning that gasoline prices could drop as low as $1 per gallon by early 2010. But like many oil companies, Chevron had an outstanding 2008, earning $23.9 billion, a new record.

The tumultuous world of energy continues to make headlines in 2009, with Chevron announcing a 71 percent drop in their second quarter profits to the lowest level in five years. In the first quarter, Chevron generated $1.75 billion, but during the same three months in 2008, Chevron's profits hit $5.98 billion. The critical difference is that oil prices soared to $145 per barrel in July of 2008 and in July 2009 are hovering around $69 per barrel.

But Chevron in not alone in their state of reduced profits. ExxonMobil Corp. announced a drop of 66 percent in their second quarter profits, while Royal Dutch Shell announced a 67 percent reduction and BP announced a 53 percent reduction. Conoco Phillips had the most significant reduction in profits out of the Big Five, recording a drop in profit of 76 percent for their second quarter.

Chevron's total revenue fell 51 percent to $40 billion from $81 billion a year ago. The company boosted capital and exploratory operations, spending $11.4 billion in the first half of the year, compared with $10.3 billion in the first six months of 2008. As we look to the future, a real concern is that if companies eventually decide to reduce exploration and production, there could be supply shortages and that could certainly mean higher prices down the road for all of us. Specifically within Chevron, their refining and marketing operations actually lost $95 million in the second quarter despite the fact that gas rose to $3 per gallon in some states. On the West Coast, their refining profits dropped 45 percent from this same time last year.

Chevron's strategies to compensate for these losses includes stopping drilling new gas wells in the continental U.S. and stopping buying back its own stock. The executive vice president of exploration and production, George Kirkland, explained that with current gas prices it does not makes sense to be drilling gas wells.

On the global scene, Chevron continues to look to its high profile projects to increase their oil production. New wells in Angola and Brazil contributed to an increase of 5 percent in Chevron's net oil equivalent production in the second quarter. These production numbers are impressive when compared with some of the other major oil companies. Royal Dutch Shell's production dipped 6 percent while ExxonMobil's production fell 3 percent.

History

Chevron began with an oil discovery north of Los Angeles in 1879 followed by the formation of the Pacific Coast Oil Company, the oldest predecessor of Chevron Corporation. Standard Oil Company (owned by John D. Rockefeller) subsequently bought Pacific Coast Oil in 1900, and six years later the merged name became Standard Oil Company (California). But in 1911, the Sherman Antitrust Act resulted in the breakup of the parent

Standard Oil and created Standard of California as an independent company. After the war ended, the company merged with Pacific Oil Company, becoming Standard Oil Company of California (Socal). Socal formed a joint venture with Texaco in 1936, Caltex, to develop and market oil in the Middle East and Indonesia. By the end of the 1930s, the Aramco partnership was formed in the Middle East, composed of Socal, Texaco, Exxon, and Mobil. Following World War II, the additives and petroleum-based chemicals invented for the war were quickly turned to peacetime uses. The age of petrochemicals had arrived, and with it came Chevron Chemical Company. By 1980, Aramco was entirely owned by the Saudis, and in 1988 the name was changed to Saudi Arabian Oil Corporation. In 1984, the merger between Standard Oil of California and Gulf Oil was the largest merger in history at that time, nearly doubling the company's worldwide proved oil and gas reserves. As part of the merger, Socal changed its name to Chevron Corporation. Through the purchase of Tenneco Inc.'s U.S. Gulf of Mexico crude oil and natural gas properties in 1988, Chevron became one of the largest gas producers in the United States. Chevron merged with NGC Corporation in the area of natural gas to form Dynegy in 1998. In 1993, Chevron formed Tengizchevroil, a joint venture with the Republic of Kazakhstan, becoming the first major Western oil company to enter newly independent Kazakhstan.

In 2001, Chevron acquired Texaco for $37.5 billion and changed its name yet again to ChevronTexaco Corporation. But after spending sizable amounts on changing the name/logo on everything from letterhead to the credit union's legal name, on May 9, 2005, the name returned to Chevron. In 2005, Chevron had another name change opportunity through its acquisition of Unocal Corporation. But this time it opted to leave the brand unchanged and reduce confusion. The Unocal acquisition made Chevron the world's largest producer of geothermal energy in the world.

Present Conditions

Chevron is the second-largest integrated energy company in the United States and among the largest corporations in the world, based on market capitalization as of December 31, 2008. Headquartered in San Ramon, California, with the stock ticker symbol CVX, it conducts business in more than 100 countries. Exhibit 1 provides a list of those countries where Chevron has extensive business involvement.

Chevron engages in every aspect of the crude oil and natural gas industry, including exploration and production, manufacturing, marketing and transportation, chemicals manufacturing and sales, geothermal, power generation, and renewables. Its global workforce consisted of approximately 66,000 employees at year-end 2008. The firm's executive positions with reporting relationships are provided in Exhibit 2.

In 2008, Chevron produced 2.53 million barrels of net oil-equivalent per day. About 75 percent of that volume occurred outside the United States in more than 20 different countries. Chevron had a global refining capacity of more than 2 MM barrels of oil per day at the end of 2008 and invested $22.8 billion in capital projects last year.

The marketing network supports more than 25,000 retail outlets (including affiliate operations) on six continents, with investments in 13 power-generating facilities in the

EXHIBIT 1 **Main Countries of Chevron Global Operations**

Angola	Chad	New Zealand	Thailand & Cambodia
Argentina	China	Nigeria	Trinidad & Tobago
Australia	Columbia	Philippines	United Kingdom
Azerbaijan	India	Russia	United States
Bangladesh	Indonesia	Saudi Arabia	Venezuela
Belgium	Kazakhstan	Singapore	
Brazil	Kuwait	South Africa	
Canada	Netherlands	South Korea	

Source: Adapted from www.chevron.com (2009).

EXHIBIT 2   Board of Directors

Chairman and Chief Executive Officer: David J. O'Reilly

Vice Chairman of the Board: Peter J. Robertson

Board of Directors: Samuel H. Armacost, Linnet F. Deily, Robert E. Denham, Robert J. Eaton, Sam Ginn, Enrique Hernandez Jr, Franklyn G. Jenifer, Sam Nunn, Donald B. Rice, Kevin W. Sharer, Charles R. Shoemate, Ronald D. Sugar, Carl Ware Laymon, Zygocki and Director of Global Security report to Vice Chair Robertson; all other officers and General Manager of Global Diversity report to Chairman O'Reilly unless indicated otherwise

Executive VP Technology and Service: John Bethancourt

Reporting to this position—Corporate Aviation Services, Energy Solutions, Oronite, Mining Inc.

Executive VP Global Upstream and Gas: George Kirkland

Reporting to this position—E&P: Asia Pacific, Eurasia

Executive VP of Strategy and Development: John Watson

Reporting to this position: Project Resources, Procurement

Executive VP Global Downstream: Michael Wirth

Reporting to this position—Global: Lubricants, Marketing, Manufacturing, Supply & Trading

Source: Adapted from www.chevron.com (2009).

United States and Asia. Of the 10,000 retail outlets in the United States, Chevron only owned a few hundred by year-end 2008. Chevron has had 21 consecutive annual increases in dividends, with dividends growing at an average annual rate of 12 percent over the past 5 years. The growth rate is 7 percent for the last 21 years. At the end of March 2009, the dividend yield was about 4 percent. Over the last five years, cash returned to stockholders has totaled more than $46 billion, $25 billion in share buybacks and over $21 MM in dividends. The return on average stockholders' equity is 29.2 percent for 2008.

Chevron's balance sheet had a debt ratio at year-end 2008 of just over 9 percent. Last year's return on capital employed (ROCE) for the corporation was 26.6 percent, and has been over 20 percent for each of the last 5 years. In 2008, Chevron's ROCE was the second highest in its five-company peer group (ExxonMobil, Royal Dutch Shell, BP, and ConocoPhillips). Sales and other operating revenues totaled $265 billion with an overall net income of $23.9 billion for 2008. The net income results were the highest annual earnings in the company's history. The income statements and balance sheets are provided in Exhibits 3 and 4.

In 2008, Chevron's Exploration added 1.7 billion barrels of oil-equivalent resources, resulting in a drilling success rate of 49 percent. The company produced 2.53 MM net-oil equivalents barrels per day; about 75 percent of those barrels came from outside the United States in more than 20 countries. The company achieved a reserve replacement in 2008 of 146 percent.

In March 2009, Chevron was presented with the HART Energy Publishing Refiner of the Year Award, which is based on achievements in the following categories: cleaner environment, investment and corporate growth, and lastly vision.

Vision

The Chevron vision is to be the global energy company most admired for its people, partnership and performance. That vision means Chevron will strive to: provide energy products vital to sustainable economic progress and human development throughout the world; have superior capabilities and commitment both at the individual employee level as well as at the organizational level; deliver world-class performance; and earn the admiration of all our stakeholders—investors, customers, host governments, local communities and Chevron employees—not only for the goals but how they are achieved.

EXHIBIT 3 Statement of Income

(millions of dollars)	2008	2007	2006
Revenues and Other Income			
Sales and Other Operating Revenues			
Gasolines	$ 53,254	47,074	42,639
Jet fuel	23,056	16,333	15,577
Gas oils and kerosene	40,940	32,170	31,647
Residual fuel oils	9,937	7,348	7,086
Other refined products	6,407	5,886	5,723
Total Refined Products	133,594	108,811	102,672
Crude oil and condensate	78,600	61,542	61,842
Natural gas	31,814	24,437	22,515
Natural gas liquids	5,517	4,483	3,488
Other petroleum revenues	3,116	2,460	2,862
Excise taxes	9,700	9,959	9,486
Total Upstream and Downstream	262,341	211,692	202,865
Chemicals	1,750	1,582	1,395
All Other	867	817	632
Less: Revenues from discontinued operations	—	—	—
Total Sales and Other Operating Revenues	264,958	214,091	204,892
Income from equity affiliates	5,366	4,144	4,255
Other income	2,681	2,669	971
Total Revenues and Other Income	273,005	220,904	210,118
Costs and Other Deductions			
Purchased crude oil products	171,397	133,309	128,151
Operating expenses	20,795	16,932	14,624
Selling, general and administrative expenses	5,756	5,926	5,093
Exploration expenses	1,169	1,323	1,364
Depreciation, depletion and amortization	9,528	8,708	7,506
Taxes other than on income	21,303	22,266	20,883
Interest and debt expense	—	166	451
Minority interests	100	107	70
Total Costs and Other Deductions	230,048	188,737	178,142
Income from Continuing Operations Before			
Income Tax Expense	42,957	32,167	31,976
Income Tax Expense	19,026	13,479	14,838
Income from Continuing Operations	23,931	18,688	17,138
Income from Discontinued Operations	—	—	—
Net Income	$ 23,931	$ 18,688	17,138

Source: Adapted from Chevron, *Annual Report Supplement* (2008).

EXHIBIT 4   Consolidated Balance Sheet

(millions of dollars)	2008	2007	2006
Assets			
Cash and cash equivalents	$ 9,347	$ 7,362	$ 10,493
Marketable securities	213	732	953
Accounts and notes receivable, net inventories	15,856	22,446	17,628
Crude oil and petroleum products	5,175	4,003	3,586
Chemicals	459	290	258
Materials, supplies and other	1,220	1,017	812
Total inventories	6,854	5,310	4,656
Prepaid expenses and other current assets	2,200	3,527	2,574
Total Current Assets	36,470	39,377	36,304
Long-term receivables, net	2,431	2,194	2,203
Investments and advances	20,920	20,447	18,552
Properties, plant and equipment at cost	173,299	154,084	137,747
Less: Accumulated depreciation, depletion and amortization	81,519	75,474	68,889
Net properties, plant and equipment	91,780	78,610	68,858
Deferred charges and other assets	4,711	3,491	2,088
Goodwill	4,619	4,637	4,623
Assets held for sale	252	—	—
Total Assets	$ 161,165	$ 148,786	$ 132,628
Liabilities and Stockholder's Equity			
Short-term debt	$ 2,818	$ 1,162	$ 2,159
Accounts payable	16,580	21,756	16,675
Accrued liabilities	8,077	5,275	4,546
Federal and other taxes on income	3,079	3,972	3,626
Other taxes payable	1,469	1,633	1,403
Total Current Liabilities	32,023	33,789	28,409
Long-term debt and capital lease obligations	6,083	6,070	7,679
Deferred credits and other noncurrent obligations	17,678	15,007	11,000
Noncurrent deferred income taxes	11,539	12,170	11,647
Reserves for employee benefit plans	6,725	4,449	4,749
Minority interests	469	204	209
Total Liabilities	74,517	71,698	63,693
Stockholders' Equity	86,648	77,088	68,935
Total Liabilities and Stockholders' Equity	$ 161,165	$ 148,786	$ 132,628

Source: Adapted from Chevron, *Annual Report Supplement* (2008).

Marketing

Marketing in an energy company is more complex than just selling more gas at the pump. Chevron focused in large part in its 2008 television campaign on the environmentally friendly and human side of its world-class operations. This type of reputation marketing is particularly important in an industry with an image problem.

Chevron's marketing organization is responsible for the marketing, advertising, sale, and delivery of products and services to retail, commercial, and industrial customers worldwide. This includes the 25,000 retail outlets (including affiliate operations), which are located primarily on the West Coast of North America, the U.S. Gulf Coast, Latin America, the Caribbean, Asia, South Africa, and the United Kingdom. The three key marketing strategies include provide clean, safe and reliable operations through operational excellence; align the marketing portfolio to capture integration value with the refining system; and leverage brands to grow value in key markets.

The marketing portfolio has become more closely aligned with the company's refining system through market exits and divestitures of retail sites in an attempt to focus in areas of market strength. During 2008, the company sold its heating-oil business in the United Kingdom and announced the sale of its marketing and other businesses in Nigeria, Kenya, Uganda, Benin, Cameroon, Republic of the Congo, Côte d'Ivoire, and Togo, and its fuels-marketing business in Brazil. Following the close of these sales, the company will have exited the fuels-marketing business in 22 countries since 2004.

Chevron markets under three main brands: Chevron, Texaco, and Caltex. In 2008, an independent source ranked Chevron as the most powerful gasoline brand in the United States for the fifth consecutive year. By the end of 2008, more than 5,000 Chevron retail sites had been updated as part of a multiyear marketing program to refresh the Chevron brand image. The company's convenience store brand, ExtraMile, was ranked as the number-one convenience store by an independent survey for the second year in a row. Chevron continues its market thrust in clean premium fuels through the expanded incorporation of patented additives such as Techron. In 2008, Chevron sold gasoline with Techron in 27 countries, comprising 90 percent of the branded gasoline sold worldwide.

Industry

Despite OPEC restrictions, civil wars, and hurricanes, the oil industry is alive and well in 2009. This is indeed a volatile industry, as indicated by the 2008 oil price that fell from a peak of $144 per barrel in early July to as low as $34 per barrel in December. This industry faces some unique business challenges, including managing a negative image as consumers correlate high prices at the pump with oil company greed. And of course carbon dioxide emissions from the continuing use of fossil fuels does not improve the image. This industry is composed of three categories of players: investor-owned oil companies, national oil companies that operate as corporate entities, and national oil companies that operate as government agencies.

Investor-owned oil companies, such as Chevron, are primarily concerned with maximizing shareholder return. These companies, often referred to as multinationals or international oil companies (IOCs), typically move quickly to develop and produce the oil resources to which they have obtained access and sell their output in competitive markets. Within the IOCs, Chevron is identified as a supermajor along with ExxonMobil, Royal Dutch Shell, BP, and, to some degree, ConocoPhillips.

National oil companies (NOCs) with strategic and operational autonomy that function as corporate entities, such as Petrobras (Brazil), often balance profit-oriented concerns and the objectives of their country with their corporate strategy. Although these companies may support their country's goals, they are primarily commercially driven entities.

National oil companies that operate as an extension of the government or as a government agency, such as Pemex (Mexico), support their government's programs either financially or strategically. They provide fuels to domestic consumers at prices lower than world customers pay. These companies often develop their proven reserves at a slower pace than commercial companies. These national oil companies pursue a diversity of objectives that are not necessarily market oriented, such as employing their citizens, generating long-term revenue, and supplying inexpensive domestic energy.

The American Petroleum Institute (www.api.com) divides the petroleum industry into five sectors: Upstream (exploration, development and production of crude oil or natural gas), Downstream (oil tankers, refiners, retailers, and consumers), Pipeline, Marine, and Service and Supply.

During the 1960s, multinationals had access to more than 80 percent of global oil and natural gas reserves. In 2007, Western multinationals controlled just over 10 percent of the world's oil, and NOCs exercised exclusive control over roughly 78 percent, according to a November 2007 paper by Doug Young at Rice University's James Baker Institute. According to *Petroleum Intelligence Weekly* (vol. 47, no. 48), in 2007, roughly 78 percent of total world oil was produced by 50 companies, and of that production, 70 percent was produced by national oil companies.

The oil industry experienced a hiring surge in the late 1970s and early 1980s followed by an extended period of decline. The recent hiring activity has not remedied the issue that over half of today's workforce will be eligible for retirement within the next 10 years. This workplace shortage is affectionately referred to in the industry as "the big crew change."

Competition

Chevron is considered as one of the Big Five along with ExxonMobil (XOM), BP (BP), Shell (RDS), and ConocoPhillips (COP). The Big Five are big in many ways, one of which happens to be their sheer size in terms of number of employees. This may seem like a good comparative statistic, but in actuality the head count statistic is a bit tricky. Some companies count contractors in different ways, and the head count at the best of times is a moving target. But Chevron came in as somewhere between 58,000 and 66,000 employees in the first quarter of 2009. ExxonMobil has approximately 80,700 employees; Royal Dutch Shell checks in at over 100,000 employees. BP has close to 98,000 employees, and ConocoPhillips has only about 30,000 employees. All of the Big Five have extensive overseas operations. ConocoPhillips operates in more than 30 countries, and the rest of the Big Five companies each operate in over 100 countries.

ExxonMobil (www.exxonmobil.com), the largest publicly traded energy company in the world, earned a record net income in 2008 of $45.2 billion ($8.69 per share). The Exxon Mobil Corporation global headquarters are located in Irving, Texas. ExxonMobil markets products around the world under the brands of Exxon, Mobil, and Esso. It also owns hundreds of smaller subsidiaries such as Imperial Oil (69.6 percent ownership) in Canada. ExxonMobil accounts for only approximately 3 percent of world production. The 2008 ROCE was 34 percent with a cash flow from operations and asset sales about $66 billion. The upstream division dominates the company's cash flow, accounting for approximately 70 percent of revenue with more than 50 percent return on average capital employed.

British Petroleum (www.bp.com) is the third largest global energy company, with headquarters in London. In 2008, BP retained 50 percent ownership in its Russian joint venture. BP's replacement cost profit for the year was a record $25.6 billion, with a return on average capital employed greater than 20 percent. BP spent $50 billion on share buybacks in 2008. It was also a good year in 2008 for BP exploration with major new discoveries in Algeria, Angola, Egypt, and the Gulf of Mexico. BP gained new access to oil sands in Canada and shale gas in the United States, as well as gaining licenses to explore in the Canadian Arctic. BP reports a resource replacement of 283 percent and a reserve replacement of 121 percent. About 50 percent of BP's capacity is in the United States, compared with about 33 percent for the rest of the Big Five. BP has between $5 billion and $6 billion of bond maturities to refinance in 2009. BP's 2008 solar sales were up by 41 percent. BP has the third largest wind portfolio in the United States.

Royal Dutch Shell (www.shell.com) has Dutch and British origins. It is the second largest private sector energy corporation in the world. The company's headquarters are in The Hague, Netherlands, with its registered office in London. The company's main business is in the exploration and production, processing, transportation, and marketing of oil and gas. Oil and gas, accounted for just over 90 percent of Shell's revenue in 2008. Shell markets oil products in more countries than any other oil company. Shell also has a significant petrochemicals business. Forbes Global 2000 ranked Shell the eighth largest company in the world in 2007. The 2008 earnings were $31.4 billion compared with $27.6 billion for 2007 with earnings per share increasing by 16 percent. Exploration & Production earnings were over $20 billion compared to about $14.7 billion in 2007. Sakhalin II, one of the world's largest integrated oil and gas projects, began year-round oil shipments in 2008 and is preparing to start exports of liquefied natural gas (LNG) in 2009. Shell made 11 notable discoveries of potential resources and secured rights to some 40,000 km of new exploration acreage in 2008. In mid-2009, there will be a major change in leadership when the former chief financial officer will step up into the role of CEO.

The ConocoPhillips Company (www.cop.com) headquarters are located in Houston, Texas. It is the fifth largest private sector energy corporation in the world. Its fuel stations are known under the Phillips 66, Conoco, and 76 brand names. It was created through the merger of Conoco Inc. and the Phillips Petroleum Company in 2002. ConocoPhillips maintains a balance in their portfolio of about 70 to 75 percent in Exploration & Production, and about 20 to 25 percent in refining, marketing, and transportation. The capital program has $12.5 billion slated for 2009. The debt ratio is above 30 percent, but the company plans to put more cash toward debt reduction to get their debt ratio back to 20 to 25 percent. ConocoPhillips is the smallest of the four, but the company spent $10 billion to repurchase stock in 2008 and had earnings per share of $3.39 with 2008 revenues of $241 billion.

There is a contrast in dividends between ExxonMobil and Chevron. Chevron pays 2.60 percent annually, whereas ExxonMobil pays only 1.60 percent. Exxon paid out dividends that totaled $1.55 per share in 2008. Chevron's trailing 12-month dividend on the stock was $2.53 at the end of 2008. BP had a trailing dividend totaling $3.30. The BP dividend per share has grown on average 15 percent per year from 2001 to 2008. ConocoPhillips had a trailing dividend totaling $1.88, which is high compared to its stock price of $49.52. Shell announced an interim dividend in respect of the fourth quarter of 2008 of US $0.40 per A and B ordinary share, an increase of 11 percent over the U.S. dollar dividend for the same quarter last year.

ExxonMobil is so strong financially that it is in a negative debt position, ending its last quarter in 2008 with $38.43 billion in cash and debt of only $10.96 billion. The company made its last significant acquisition when it bought Mobil Oil during the energy downturn in 1998. Although not quite as strong as Exxon Mobil, BP also holds $6.1 billion cash. British Petroleum acquired Amoco Corp. for $48 billion in 1998, which at the time was the biggest foreign takeover of an American company. In 2008, Shell completed the acquisition of Duvernay Oil Corp., providing the company with acreage containing significant gas resources in western Canada. Royal Dutch Shell reported over $15 billion of cash on hand as of year-end 2008. In March 2006, ConocoPhillips Corporation bought Wilhelmshaven Raffiniegesellschaft and Burlington Resources. Although its market cap is near $75 billion, ConocoPhillips held more than $1 billion in cash at the end of the third quarter of 2008. Chevron was also in a negative net debt position with $11 billion in cash and a debt of $7 billion in 2008. Many analysts are expecting a wave of acquisitions by the Big Five as they eye some of the smaller companies such as Devon Energy Corporation (DVD), Anadarko Petroleum Corporation (APC), or Apache Corporation (APA).

Membership in the Big Five does not protect these giants against political controversy. BP faced spills in Alaska in both 2006 (oil) and 2007 (methanol). ExxonMobil is still dealing with litigation surrounding the 1989 *Valdez* oil spill in Alaska. A court ruling in June 2008 reduced the damages accessed against ExxonMobil from $2.5 billion to $507.5 MM. In the same month Royal Dutch Shell was forced to shut down its largest oil production unit in Nigeria when Nigerian separatists attacked the offshore facility. In 2007, Friends of the Earth alleged that the damage caused by Shell's oil activities to local communities and the wider environment could be assessed at $20 billion. In 2006, ConocoPhillips agreed to pay $2.2 MM to the federal government to cover costs of cleaning up of a Puget Sound oil spill. In October 2007, Polar Tankers, a subsidiary of ConocoPhillips, was fined $2.5 MM for an oil spill in the Pacific that occurred in 2004.

When comparing Chevron with its competitors from 2003 to 2007, Chevron had a 106 percent resource replacement through exploration ratio. This is approximately 40 percent higher than the nearest competitor, BP. This ratio is often difficult to compare across the Big Five because each company defines it slightly differently. Not only has

Chevron replaced, through exploration, more resources than any other of the Big Five, but it has done so with the lowest exploration cost in the industry. Being able to find new resources at a comparatively low cost is an important skill, especially when commodity prices are falling.

Chevron's upstream earnings of $21.7 billion translate to earnings per barrel of $22.85. Chevron's competitive position moved up to second in both 2007 and 2008 relative to the Big Five. The 2008 ROCE results of 36.6 percent look promising for Chevron to maintain this competitive position in 2009.

Competitive data for 2008 indicates that Royal Dutch Shell achieved the highest average capital employed; ExxonMobil had the highest return on average capital employed. Although Chevron had impressive reported earnings figures, it was not the top contender. ExxonMobil had the highest reported net income, followed by Royal Dutch Shell and then BP.

The Obama administration wants to increase renewable energy supplies and reduce carbon emissions. But the Big Five have mixed responses to Washington. Shell announced it would freeze investments in wind, solar, and hydrogen power and instead is focusing on biofuels. BP is cutting back on its renewable program. ExxonMobil announced in the last quarter of 2008 that it will invest more than $1 billion in three refineries in the United States and Europe to increase the supply of cleaner burning diesel by about 6 million gallons per day. Chevron spent about $3.2 billion on renewables since 2002 and plans to spend another $2.7 billion over the next three years. In total, the Big Five spent about $5 billion in the last 15 years to develop renewable energy. This represents about 10 percent of the approximate $50 billion contributed by other investors. Although the Big Five consider renewables an important investment for the future, renewable energy is not a mainstream business for them.

Conclusion

Forty-five percent of Chevron's planned 2009 spending will be in OECD (Organization for Economic Co-operation and Development) countries. In 2008, Chevron exited 20 markets and will continue with planned market exits in 2009. These future exits will result in a projected workforce reduction of 1,500 employees, a reduction in operating expense by $300 MM per year, and a reduction in capital employed by nearly $1 billion. The announced 2009 projected capital and exploratory expenditures will total $22.8 billion, including $1.8 billion of affiliate expenditures. The production from new capital projects is anticipated to increase from 153,000 barrels per day in 2008 to 650,000 barrels per day in 2010.

Nine new projects greater than $200 MM (net Chevron share) are planned to come online in 2009, followed by another eight in 2010. LNG accounts for about 35 percent volume of the 2008 portfolio and should be considered as an important player in Chevron's future. In downstream the continuing focus will be on improving refinery reliability. Downstream will account for approximately $4.3 billion of the capital and exploratory program in 2009.

Chevron hopes to take advantage of opportunities in Iraq beginning with a review of the Iraqis' bidding guidelines for upcoming oil leases, to be released in the second quarter of 2009. Note that Iraq does not have an OPEC quota and thus is allowed to produce oil at will as it struggles to rebuild its oil industry. However, the four focus areas for exploration capital dollars in 2009 will include the Gulf of Mexico, Northwest Australia, West Africa deepwater, and the Gulf of Thailand. But the bottom line is that Chevron will continue to face increasing geopolitical risk as it expands its dependence on non–North American properties for its reserves. To date it seems that Chevron has proved to be good at managing these risks to retain commercial opportunities.

Chevron plans continued investments in renewable energy technologies, with an objective of capturing profitable positions in important renewable sources of energy. Chevron will continue to invest in the next generation of energy sources and support the transition to a low-carbon economy. Alternative energy production is growing but currently represents just 2 percent of global energy production, so the world will need fossil fuels for years to come, even if demand slows. In fact, the U.S. Energy Information Administration and the International Energy Agency (a cooperation grouping of most of the OECD members) suggest that by 2030 the world could be consuming about 57,000 gallons of oil per second.